> Choose your format

Print or eBook? Softcover, spiral-bound, or loose-leaf? Black-and-white or color? Perforated, three-hole punched, or regular paper? No matter the format, Create has the best fit for you—and for your students.

> Customize your cover

Pick your own cover image and include your name and course information right on the cover. Students will know they're purchasing the right book—and using everything they purchase!

Introducing McGraw-Hill Create *ExpressBooks*!

ExpressBooks contain a combination of pre-selected chapters, articles, cases, or readings that serve as a starting point to help you quickly and easily build your own text through McGraw-Hill's self-service custom publishing website, Create. These helpful templates are built using content available on Create and organized in ways that match various course outlines across all disciplines. We understand that you have a unique perspective. Use McGraw-Hill Create ExpressBooks to build the book you've only imagined!

The American
DEMOCRACY
Texas Edition

The American
DEMOCRACY

Eleventh Edition

Texas Edition

Thomas E. Patterson

Bradlee Professor of Government and the Press
John F. Kennedy School of Government
Harvard University

Gary M. Halter

Professor of Political Science
Texas A&M University

THE AMERICAN DEMOCRACY: TEXAS EDITION, ELEVENTH EDITION

Published by McGraw-Hill, a business unit of The McGraw-Hill Companies, Inc., 1221 Avenue of the Americas, New York, NY 10020. Copyright © 2013 by The McGraw-Hill Companies, Inc. All rights reserved. Printed in the United States of America. Previous editions © 2011, 1009, and 2008. No part of this publication may be reproduced or distributed in any form or by any means, or stored in a database or retrieval system, without the prior written consent of The McGraw-Hill Companies, Inc., including, but not limited to, in any network or other electronic storage or transmission, or broadcast for distance learning.

Some ancillaries, including electronic and print components, may not be available to customers outside the United States.

This book is printed on acid-free paper.

1 2 3 4 5 6 7 8 9 0 RJE/RJE 1 0 9 8 7 6 5 4 3 2

ISBN 978—0—07—742418—3
MHID 0—07—742418—2

Senior Vice President, Products & Markets: *Kurt L. Strand*
Vice President, General Manager, Products & Markets: *Michael Ryan*
Vice President, Content Production & Technology Services: *Kimberly Meriwether David*
Managing Director: *Gina Boedeker*
Director: *Matthew Busbridge*
Brand Manager: *Meredith Grant*
Brand Coordinator: *Ryan Viviani*
Development Manager: *Barbara A. Heinssen*
Development Editor: *Naomi Friedman and Elisa Adams*
Senior Director of Development: *Dawn Groundwater*
Marketing Manager: *Josh Zlatkus*
Project Manager: *Kelly A. Heinrichs/April R. Southwood*
Buyer: *Nicole Baumgartner*
Designer: *Tara McDermott*
Cover Design: *Maureen McCutcheon*
Cover Image: *"Stars and Stripes, opus 500," folded by Robert J. Lang from a single uncut square of Elephant Hide paper. Photograph by Dwight Eschliman*
Content Licensing Specialist: *Shawntel Schmitt*
Photo Research: *Toni Michaels*
Compositor: *Aptara®, Inc.*
Typeface: *10/12 Palatino*
Printer: *R. R. Donnelley*

All credits appearing on page or at the end of the book are considered to be an extension of the copyright page.

Library of Congress Cataloging-in-Publication Data

Patterson, Thomas E.
  The American democracy / Thomas E. Patterson. – Eleventh edition, Texas edition.
     pages cm
  Includes index.
  ISBN 978–0–07–742418–3 — ISBN 0–07–742418–2 (hard copy : alk. paper) 1. United States–Politics and government–Textbooks. 2. Texas–Politics and government–Textbooks. I. Halter, Gary M. II. Title.
  JK276.P37 2012
  320.473–dc23   2012038361

The Internet addresses listed in the text were accurate at the time of publication. The inclusion of a website does not indicate an endorsement by the authors or McGraw-Hill, and McGraw-Hill does not guarantee the accuracy of the information presented at these sites.

www.mhhe.com

TO MY CHILDREN ■ **Alex and Leigh**

About the Authors

THOMAS E. PATTERSON is Bradlee Professor of Government and the Press in the John F. Kennedy School of Government at Harvard University. He was previously Distinguished Professor of Political Science in the Maxwell School of Citizenship at Syracuse University. Raised in a small Minnesota town near the Iowa and South Dakota borders, he attended South Dakota State University as an undergraduate and served in the U.S. Army Special Forces in Vietnam before enrolling at the University of Minnesota, where he received his Ph.D. in 1971.

He is the author of numerous books and articles, which focus mainly on elections and the media. His book *The Vanishing Voter* (2002) describes and explains the long-term decline in Americans' electoral participation. An earlier book, *Out of Order* (1994), received national attention when President Clinton said every politician and journalist should be required to read it. In 2002, *Out of Order* received the American Political Science Association's Graber Award for the best book of the past decade in political communication. Another of Patterson's books, *The Mass Media Election* (1980), received a *Choice* award as Outstanding Academic Book, 1980–1981. Patterson's first book, *The Unseeing Eye* (1976), was selected by the American Association for Public Opinion Research as one of the fifty most influential books of the past half-century in the field of public opinion. His most recent book, *Corruption of Information*, is scheduled for publication in 2013. It examines the causes and consequences of the misinformation that has recently become a prominent feature of the American media system.

His research has been funded by major grants from the National Science Foundation, the Markle Foundation, the Smith-Richardson Foundation, the Ford Foundation, the Knight Foundation, The Carnegie Corporation, and the Pew Charitable Trusts.

GARY HALTER is a native of Amarillo and Wichita Falls, Texas, and is a Professor of Political Science at Texas A&M University in College Station, Texas. He earned his B.A. from Midwestern University and his Ph.D. from the University of Maryland. He served as the Mayor of College Station, Texas for six years and as a council member for five years. He has worked as a consultant to many city councils in Texas and in other states on goal setting and policy making. He is the author of *Government & Politics of Texas: A Comparative Approach*, published by McGraw-Hill, currently in its eighth edition, and with Harvey Tucker, he is a co-author of the *Texas Legislative Almanac*, published by Texas A&M Press.

Contents in Brief

PART 5 Texas Government and Politics

Contents

Preface xxii | Acknowledgments xxvii

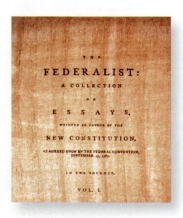

3 Federalism: Forging a Nation 54

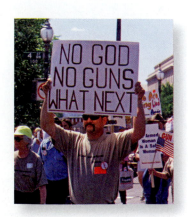

4 Civil Liberties: Protecting Individual Rights 82

5 Equal Rights: Struggling toward Fairness   114

PART 2 Mass Politics

6 Public Opinion and Political Socialization: Shaping the People's Voice   142

7 Political Participation: Activating the Popular Will 166

8 Political Parties, Candidates, and Campaigns: Defining the Voter's Choice 188

9 Interest Groups: Organizing for Influence   218

10 The News Media: Communicating Political Images   244

PART 3 Governing Institutions

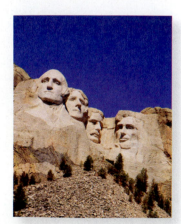

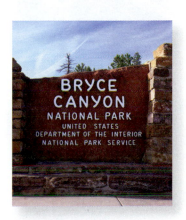

PART 4 Public Policy

PART 5 Texas Government and Politics

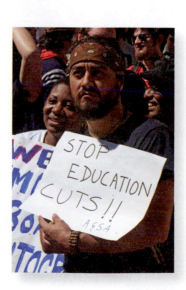

22 The Texas Legislature 544

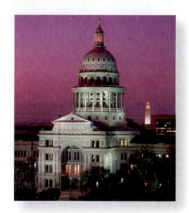

23 The Office of Governor and State Agencies in Texas 574

24 The Court System in Texas 602

25 Public Policy in Texas 622

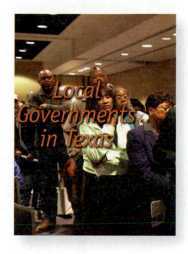

Preface

A Letter from the Authors

Anyone who writes an introductory American government text faces the challenge of explaining a wide range of subjects. One way is to pile fact upon fact and list upon list. It's a common approach to textbook writing but it turns politics into a pretty dry subject. Politics doesn't have to be dry, and it certainly doesn't have to be dull. Politics has all the elements of drama, and the added feature of affecting the everyday lives of real people.

Our goals have been to make this text the most readable one available. Rather than piling fact upon fact, the text relies on narrative. A narrative text weaves together theory, information, and examples in order to bring out key facts and ideas. The response to this approach has been gratifying. Earlier this year, we received the following note from a long-time instructor:

> I read this book in about three days, cover to cover. . . . I have never seen a better basic government/politics textbook. I think reading standard textbooks is "boring" (to use a favorite student word), but this one overcomes that.

When writing the text, we regularly reminded ourselves that the readers were citizens as well as students. For this reason, the text highlights "political thinking," by which we mean critical thinking in the context of both the study of politics and the exercise of citizenship. Each chapter has a set of boxes that ask you to "think politically." It is a skill that can be developed and that can help you to become a more responsible citizen, whether in casting a vote, forming an opinion about a public policy, or contributing to a political cause.

Finally, we have attempted in this book to present American government through the analytical lens of political science but in a way that captures the vivid world of real-life politics. Only a tiny fraction of students in the introductory course are taking it because they intend to pursue an academic career in political science. Most students take it because they are required to do so or because they have in interest in politics. We have sought to write a book that will deepen political interest in the second type of student and kindle it in the first type.

The American Democracy has now been in use in college classrooms for two decades. During that time, the three versions of this title, including this *Texas Edition*, which provides a thorough introduction to Texas government and politics, have been adopted at more than a thousand colleges and universities. We are extremely grateful to all who have used it. We are particularly indebted to the many instructors and students who have sent suggestions for making it better. The University of Northern Colorado's Steve Mazurana and Crowder College's Ron Cole were among the instructors who sent comments that helped inform this edition's revisions. If you have ideas you would like to share, please contact us at the John F. Kennedy School, Harvard University, Cambridge, MA 02138, or by e-mail: thomas_patterson@harvard.edu.

Thomas E. Patterson
Gary M. Halter
November 2012

Learning to Think Politically

Political thinking enables us, as citizens, to gather and weigh evidence, to apply foundational principles to current events, and to consider historical context when evaluating contemporary issues. In short, it allows us to have informed judgment. This text aims to help you learn how to think about politics by introducing you to the perspectives and tools of political science.

Tools for Political Thinking: What Political Science Can Contribute

This text will not tell you *what* to think politically. Instead, it will help you learn *how* to think politically by providing you with analytical tools that can sharpen and deepen your understanding of American politics:

- Reliable information about how the U.S. political system operates;
- Systematic generalizations about major tendencies in American politics;
- Terms and concepts that precisely describe key aspects of politics.

Pedagogical Elements for Political Thinking

Each chapter in *The American Democracy* includes a set of boxed inserts that are designed to sharpen your ability to think politically.

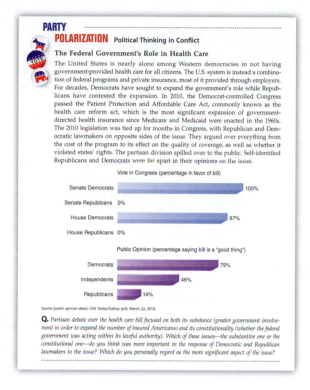

NEW! PARTY POLARIZATION POLITICAL THINKING IN CONFLICT

These boxes show the widening gap in the views and actions of Republicans and Democrats and ask you to think about the political implications. The box in Chapter 3, for example, considers the federal government's role in health care.

Political Thinking

These boxes ask you to think critically about enduring and topical political issues. For instance, Chapter 13 has a Political Thinking box about whether a balanced federal budget is a good or bad idea.

HOW THE 50 STATES DIFFER POLITICAL THINKING THROUGH COMPARISONS

These boxes use color-coded maps to reveal differences in the politics of our 50 states and ask you to assess the differences. The box in Chapter 4, for example, compares incarceration rates across the 50 states.

HOW THE U.S. DIFFERS POLITICAL THINKING THROUGH COMPARISONS

These boxes ask you to reflect on how aspects of our political system compare with those of other democracies. Chapter 5, for instance, has a box comparing women's representation in the U.S. Congress with their representation in the national legislatures of other democracies.

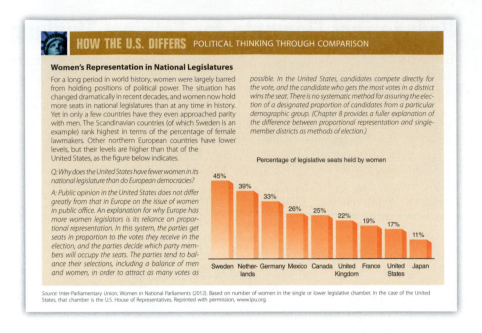

Government in Action

Students can apply what they're learning in American Government by competing against a computer or each other in a first-of-its-kind virtual world in which students learn by doing. In *Government in Action*, students run for re-election and pass legislation, touching on every aspect of the course in their attempt to gain Political Capital. Be sure to ask your sales representative for details.

DEBATING THE ISSUES POLITICAL THINKING IN ACTION

These boxes present opposing positions on some of great issues of our time and ask you to adopt and defend one of the positions. The box in Chapter 1 debates whether corporations should be allowed to spend unlimited amounts on federal election campaigns.

New to this Edition

This revision of *The American Democracy, Texas Edition* includes the many remarkable political developments of the past two years, ranging from the 2012 presidential election to the withdrawal of U.S. forces from Iraq to the rise of the Occupy Wall Street movement. Nearly every chapter also has significant updates based on the most recent scholarly research on American politics.

Each chapter has a new feature: a box on **Party Polarization.** The widening gap between Republicans and Democrats has become a defining feature of the nation's politics, encompassing an ever larger swath of political thought and action. The **Party Polarization** boxes describe aspects of this development, explain the implications, and ask for the reader's assessment.

We have listed below the chapters that have been most substantially revised. The list understates the extent of the changes. Nearly every chapter has important modifications from the previous edition.

Chapter 1: Political Thinking and Political Culture: Becoming a Responsible Citizen Additions include a full section on the American political culture. The section examines the origins and power of the nation's traditional ideals: liberty, individualism, equality, and self-government. The chapter now also includes a discussion of the major stages of the policy process.

Chapter 3: Federalism: Forging a Nation Additions include the Supreme Court's important 2012 rulings on the constitutionality of the health care reform bill (the 2010 Patient Protection and Affordable Care Act) and the state of Arizona's immigration control law.

Chapter 7: Political Participation: Activating the Popular Will This chapter has a new section on the Tea Party and Occupy Wall Street movements and a new section on the relationship between participation and political interest.

Chapter 8: Political Parties, Candidates, and Campaigns: Defining the Voter's Choice The new version more fully examines the scope and implications of party polarization. The section on minor parties has been reorganized. The sudden emergence of Super PACs as a force in U.S. elections is discussed and explained. (Super PACs are also a newly featured subject in Chapter 9: Interest Groups and Chapter 11: Congress.)

Chapter 10: The News Media: Communicating Political Images The chapter includes additional material on Internet-based communication and has a new section that is entitled "The News Audience" that examines two emergent "divides" that have resulted from Americans' media choices: the partisan divide that is contributing to partisan polarization and the generational divide that is creating a widening information gap between younger and older citizens.

Chapter 11: Congress: Balancing National Goals and Local Interests This chapter has a number of major revisions including how party polarization has both empowered and challenged congressional party leaders and how the 2010 midterm election, the Tea Party, and the federal government's fiscal problems have altered the legislative process. The outcome of the 2012 congressional elections is included in the revised version.

Chapter 12: The Presidency: Leading the Nation The 2012 Republican presidential nominating race and the 2012 presidential general election are prominently featured in the new version.

Chapter 15: Economic and Environmental Policy: Contributing to Prosperity The section on monetary policy has been reorganized and lengthened to reflect the increasingly central role of the Federal Reserve System (the Fed) in managing the U.S. economy. Changes include a fuller description of the Fed's organization and policy tools, the role of the Open Markets Committee, and the controversies surrounding Fed policies, including the use of Quantitative Easing (QE).

Chapter 17: Foreign Policy: Protecting the American Way This chapter's revisions include the many important foreign policy developments of the past two years, including the Iraq withdrawal, the continuing struggle in Afghanistan, the growing importance of Pakistan, the threat of nuclear weapons in Iran, the recent free trade agreements, the instability of global markets, the increasingly assertive foreign policies of China, and the Defense Department's plan for restructuring America's armed forces.

Teaching and Learning with *The American Democracy, Texas Edition*

Online Learning Center

www.mhhe.com/pattersontadtx11e
The book's website includes separate instructor and student areas. The instructor area contains the instructor's manual, test bank, and PowerPoints, while the student area hosts a wealth of study materials such as chapter outlines, chapter objectives, multiple-choice and essay quizzes, and Web links. All chapter-by-chapter material has been updated for the new edition.

Study Materials

Through the book's Online Learning Center, students have free access to the following materials: chapter outlines, chapter objectives, multiple-choice and essay quizzes, and weblinks. In addition, the site offers a Presidential Timeline, a Spanish-English Glossary, and guidelines for avoiding plagiarism.

Instructor's Manual/Test Bank

Available online, the instructor's manual includes the following for each chapter: learning objectives, focus points and main points, a chapter summary, a list of major concepts, and suggestions for complementary lecture topics. The test bank consists of approximately fifty multiple-choice questions and five suggested essay topics per chapter, with page references given alongside the answers.

PowerPoints and CPS questions are also available to instructors.

Create

Craft your teaching resources to match the way you teach! With McGraw-Hill Create™, you can personalize your book's appearance by selecting the cover and adding your name, school, and course information. Order a Create book and you'll receive a complimentary print review copy in three to five business days or a complimentary electronic review copy (eComp) via e-mail in about one hour. To get started, go to **www.mcgrawhillcreate.com** and register today.

Introducing McGraw-Hill Create™ ExpressBooks!

ExpressBooks contain a combination of pre-selected chapters, articles, cases, or readings that serve as a starting point to help you quickly and easily build your own text through McGraw-Hill's self-service custom publishing website, Create. These helpful templates are built using content available on Create and organized in ways that match various course outlines across all disciplines. We understand that you have a unique perspective. Use McGraw-Hill Create ExpressBooks to build the book you've only imagined! **www.mcgrawhillcreate.com**

CourseSmart eTextbooks

This text is available as an eTextbook at **www.CourseSmart.com**. At CourseSmart your students can take advantage of significant savings off the cost of a print textbook, reduce their impact on the environment, and gain access to powerful Web tools for learning. CourseSmart eTextbooks can be viewed online or downloaded to a computer. The eTextbooks allow students to do full text searches, add highlighting and notes, and share notes with classmates. CourseSmart has the largest selection of eTextbooks available anywhere. Visit **www.CourseSmart.com** to learn more and to examine a sample chapter.

Acknowledgments

Nearly two decades ago, when planning the first edition of *The American Democracy*, my editor and I concluded that it would be enormously helpful if a way could be found to bring into each chapter the judgment of those political scientists who teach the introductory course year in and year out. Thus, in addition to soliciting general reviews from a select number of expert scholars, we sent each chapter to a dozen or so faculty members at U.S. colleges and universities of all types—public and private, large and small, two-year and four-year. These political scientists, 213 in all, had well over a thousand years of combined experience in teaching the introductory course, and they provided countless good ideas.

Since then, several hundred other political scientists have reviewed subsequent editions. These many reviewers will go unnamed here, but my debt to all of them remains undiminished by time. For the eleventh edition, I have benefitted yet again from the thoughtful advice of conscientious reviewers. Their sound advice has helped shape nearly every page of the book. These scholars are:

Jodi Balma, *Fullerton College*

Amy Brandon, *El Paso Community College, Valle Verde*

Daniel Bunye, *South Plains College—Reese Center*

Jenna Duke, *Lehigh Carbon Community College*

Ethan Fishman, *University of South Alabama*

Jeremiah Hindman, *Northeast Texas Community College*

Ray Sandoval, *Richland College*

Costas Spirou, *National Louis University—Chicago*

Cheryl Walniuk, *University of Maryland University College*

I also want to thank those at McGraw-Hill who contributed to the eleventh edition. At McGraw-Hill, I'd like to thank Elisa Adams, Dawn Groundwater, Barbara Heinssen, Meredith Grant, Kelly Heinrichs, Matt Busbridge, Nikki Weissman, Ryan Viviani, Patrick Brown, Josh Zlatkus. At Harvard, I had the painstaking and cheerful support of Kristina Mastropasqua. I owe her a deep thanks.

Thomas Patterson

CHAPTER **1**

Political Thinking and Political Culture: Becoming a Responsible Citizen

The worth of the state, in the long run, is the worth of the individuals composing it. John Stuart Mill[1]

As U.S. troops moved into position along the Iraq border, pollsters were busy asking Americans what they thought about the prospect of war with Iraq. A narrow majority expressed support for an attack on Iraq without United Nations approval if President George W. Bush deemed it necessary. But Americans' level of support for war varied with their knowledge of the enemy.

Contrary to fact, about half of the American public believed that Iraq was aligned with al Qaeda, the terrorist group that had attacked the United States on September 11, 2001. Some of these Americans mistakenly thought that Iraq helped plan the attacks; others erroneously believed that Iraq was equipping al Qaeda.[2] Some Americans even claimed that Iraqi pilots were flying the passenger jets that slammed into the World Trade Center towers and the Pentagon on that tragic September day.[3]

Compared with Americans who knew that Iraqi leader Saddam Hussein and al Qaeda were avowed enemies, those who falsely believed they were allies were more than twice as likely to support an American attack on Iraq.[4] Some of these individuals undoubtedly had other reasons for backing the invasion. Hussein was a tyrant who had brutalized his own people and thwarted United Nations resolutions calling for inspection of his weapons systems. But their belief that Iraq was in league with al Qaeda terrorists was pure fiction and hardly a reasonable basis for supporting an invasion.

The journalist Walter Lippmann worried that most citizens are unprepared to play the role democracy assigns them. They live in the real world but think in an imagined one. "While men are willing to admit that there are two sides to a question," Lippmann noted, "they do not believe that there are two sides to what they regard as fact."[5] In a self-governing society, citizens are expected to act on behalf of themselves and others. But how can they govern themselves if they are out of touch with reality?

Lippmann's concern has been confirmed by dozens of scholarly studies. Political scientists Bruce Ackerman and James Fishkin put it

Although most Americans say they have a duty to vote, they do not necessarily take the time to cast an informed vote.

Source: Dave Granlund, politicalcartoons.com

bluntly: "If six decades of modern public opinion research establish anything, it is that the general public's political ignorance is appalling by any standard."[6] *Newsweek* recently gave one thousand Americans who were already citizens the test that immigrants must pass as a condition of citizenship. Four of every ten that took the test failed it.[7] In a survey conducted shortly after Americans went to the polls in the 2010 midterm election, respondents were asked multiple-choice factual questions about eleven issues, ranging from health care to the Afghanistan War, that had been raised during the campaign. The question on Afghanistan, for example, asked whether troop levels had increased, decreased, or stayed the same during the two years that Barack Obama had been president. On every issue, a third or more of the respondents picked a wrong answer and, on most issues, half or more did so.[8]

A lack of information obviously does not keep citizens from voting, nor are uninformed citizens lacking in opinions. Some of them speak out more often and more loudly than people who are informed. But their sense of the world is wildly at odds with the reality of it. They are like the ancient mariners who, thinking the world was flat, stayed close to shore, fearing they might sail off the edge.

Learning to Think Politically

political thinking

Reflective thinking focused on deciding what can reasonably be believed and then using this information to make political judgments.

This text aims to help students, as citizens, learn how to think about politics. Political thinking is not the mere act of voicing an opinion. **Political thinking** is reflective thinking focused on deciding what can reasonably be believed and then using this information to make political judgments. It enables citizens to act responsibly, whether in casting a vote, forming an opinion on a political issue, or contributing to a political cause. It is not defined by the conclusions that a person reaches. Individuals differ in their values and interests and can reasonably have opposing opinions. Political thinking is defined instead by the process through which conclusions are reached. It involves the careful evaluation of information in the process of forming a judgment about the issue at hand. Opinions not reached in this way are likely to be incomplete at best, perhaps even wildly off base. "Ignorance of the [facts]," Mark Bauerlein notes, "is a fair gauge of deeper deficiencies."[9]

Responsible citizenship was what English philosopher John Stuart Mill had in mind when he said that democracy is the best form of government. Any form of government, Mill asserted, should be judged on its ability to promote the individual "as a progressive being."[10] It was on this basis that Mill rejected authoritarianism and embraced democracy. Authoritarian governments suppress individuality, forcing people to think and act in prescribed ways or risk punishment. Democracy liberates the individual. Although democracy provides the *opportunity* for personal development, the individual bears responsibility for using this opportunity. In this sense, democracy is double edged. By liberating individuals, democracy frees them to make choices. They can develop the habit of political thinking, or they can devise cockeyed visions of reality. There is nothing to stop them from thinking the world is flat rather than round.

Obstacles to Political Thinking

The major barrier to political thinking is the unwillingness of citizens to make the effort. Political thinking requires close attention to politics, a responsibility that many people refuse to accept. They are, as James David Barber said, "dangerously unready when the time comes for choice."[11]

Others pay close attention, but they do so in counterproductive ways. A paradox of modern communication is that, although political information is more widely available than ever before, it is also less trustworthy than ever before. Two decades ago, the "knowledge gap" was defined largely by the amount of attention that people paid to the news. Citizens who followed the news closely were much better informed on average than those who did not.[12] That's less true today because of where people get their information. Nearly half of adult Americans now get most of their news from cable television, talk shows, or Internet blogs.[13] Most of these outlets—whether on the left or right—have dropped all but the pretense of accuracy. They rarely tell flat-out lies, but they routinely slant information to fit their purpose while burying contradictory facts. Once in a while, they expose a truth that mainstream news outlets have missed or were too timid to tackle. For the most part, however, they are in the business of concocting versions of reality that will lure an audience and promote a cause. "The talk show culture," media analyst Ellen Hume notes, "is a blur of rumor, fact, propaganda, and infotainment."[14] A recent University of Maryland study concluded that "false or misleading information is widespread in [today's] information environment."[15]

Political leaders also "spin" their messages. Although this has always been true, the scale of the effort today is unlike anything that has gone before.[16] The White House press office, for example, was once run by a single individual. It is now a communication machine that reaches deep into the federal agencies and involves scores of operatives, each of whom is intent on putting a presidential slant on the day's news.[17] In the period before the Iraq war, the Bush administration, through its hold on the intelligence agencies, tightly controlled the messages coming from the U.S. government. Iraq and al Qaeda were lumped together as targets of the war on terror, leading some Americans—most of them Republicans—to conclude that Iraq and al Qaeda were indistinguishable. During the recent economic downturn, the Obama administration put a favorable slant on the impact of its economic stimulus program, leading some Americans—most of

Stephen Colbert (in cape) and Jon Stewart are part of the "new media" but, unlike many of the others, do not pretend that all of the information they provide is reliable. Says Stewart, "It's style over substance."

them Democrats—to conclude that the administration had saved or created many more jobs than it actually had.

Research suggests that faulty perceptions are becoming more prevalent, and that changes in communication are largely to blame.[18] During the buildup to the Iraq invasion, for example, the worst-informed Americans were those that obtained their news from cable television shows. Their misinformation level exceeded even that of citizens who paid infrequent attention to news.

The audience appeal of the "new news" is understandable.[19] Many people prefer messages that conform to what they already believe. It is not surprising that liberal bloggers and talk show hosts have an audience made up mostly of liberals, whereas conservative bloggers and talk show hosts have a largely conservative audience. Studies indicate that misinformation spreads easily when those in touch with the like-minded are not also in contact with other information sources.[20] Rather than expanding people's thinking, such exposure tends to narrow and distort it.[21]

Citizens cannot know whether their ideas are sound until they have heard alternative views and weighed them against their own. The test of an opinion is not whether it sounds good by itself but whether it makes sense when held up against opposing views. "He who knows only his one side of the case knows little of that," Mill wrote. "His reasons may be good, and no one may have been able to refute them. But if he is equally unable to refute the reasons of the opposite side, if he does not so much as know what they are, he has no ground for preferring either opinion."[22]

Beyond its contribution to sound opinions, political knowledge fosters an interest in politics. The more citizens know about politics, the more likely they are to want to play an active part in it. For more than fifty years, the Intercollegiate Studies Association (ISA) has surveyed college students to determine their political information and participation levels. The ISA has found that the best predicator of students' later participation in the nation's civic and political life is not whether they finished college but whether they have a solid understanding of public affairs. "Greater civic knowledge," the ISA says, is "positively correlated with all . . . facets of active engagement . . . [everything from] the private functions of writing a letter to the editor and contacting a public official . . . [to] the more public role of a campaign worker or attendee at a political meeting or rally."[23]

Reporters gather in the cramped space of the White House press room, where they receive daily briefings on the president's activities. Like other political leaders, presidents have become increasingly adept at putting a favorable "spin" on their messages.

What Political Science Can Contribute to Political Thinking

This text will not try to tell you *what* to think politically. There is no correct way of thinking when it comes to the "what" of politics. People differ in their political values and interests and, thus, also differ in their political opinions.

Instead, this text will help you learn *how* to think politically by providing you with analytical tools that can sharpen your understanding of American politics. The tools are derived from **political science**—the systematic study of government and politics. Political science has developed largely through the work of scholars, but political practitioners and writers have also contributed. One of America's foremost political scientists was the chief architect of the U.S. Constitution and later a president. Even today, James Madison's essays on constitutional design (two of which can be found in this book's appendixes) are masterpieces of political science.

As a discipline, political science is descriptive and analytical—that is, it attempts to depict and explain politics. This effort takes place through various frameworks, including rational choice theory, institutional analysis, historical reasoning, behavioral studies, legal reasoning, and cultural analysis. Political science offers a set of analytical tools that can increase one's ability to think politically:

■ Reliable information about how the U.S. political system operates

■ Systematic generalizations about major tendencies in American politics

■ Terms and concepts that precisely describe key aspects of politics

These tools will broaden your understanding of American politics and help you to think more clearly about it.

Like any skill, political thinking needs to be developed through practice. For this reason, each of the text's chapters includes boxes that ask you to think politically. Some political thinking boxes deal with current issues, such as immigration and health care reform. Other boxes deal with perennial questions, such as the president's war powers and the proper relation between the nation and the states. Still other boxes ask you to think politically by comparing how politics in the United States and in your state differs from that of other nations and states. Finally, each chapter includes two boxes—"Debating the Issues" and "Party Polarization"—that ask you to evaluate opposing political views. These boxes reflect John Stuart Mill's test of a sound opinion—whether you can refute opposing views as effectively as you can defend your own.

political science
The systematic study of government and politics.

Political Culture: Americans' Enduring Beliefs

An understanding of U.S. politics properly begins with an assessment of the nation's political culture. Every country has its **political culture**—the widely shared and deep-seated beliefs of its people about politics.[24] These beliefs derive from the country's traditions and help to define the relationship of citizens to their government and to each other.

Although every country has a distinctive political culture, the United States, as the British writer James Bryce observed, is a special case.[25] Americans' beliefs are the foundation of their national identity. Other people take their identity from the common ancestry that led them gradually to gather under one flag. Thus, long before there was a France or a Japan, there were French and Japanese people, each a kinship group united through ancestry. Even today, it is kinship that links them. There is no way to become fully Japanese except to be born of Japanese parents. Not so for Americans. They are a multitude of people from different lands—England, Germany, Ireland, Africa, Italy, Sweden, Poland, Mexico, and

political culture
The widely shared and deep-seated political beliefs of a particular people.

FIGURE 1-1
Country of Origin of U.S. Immigrants, 1820-2010
As a nation of immigrants, Americans are bound together, not by a common ancestry as is the case with the people of most nations, but by a common set of beliefs. Shown here are the ten countries that have contributed the largest number of immigrants.

Source: U.S. Office of Immigration Statistics, 2012.

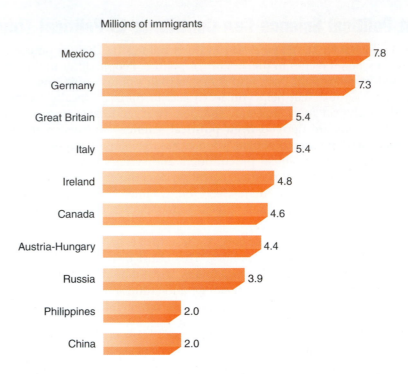

Millions of immigrants

Mexico	7.8
Germany	7.3
Great Britain	5.4
Italy	5.4
Ireland	4.8
Canada	4.6
Austria-Hungary	4.4
Russia	3.9
Philippines	2.0
China	2.0

China, to name just a few (see Figure 1-1). Americans are linked not by a shared ancestry but by allegiance to a common set of ideals. The French writer Alexis de Tocqueville was among the first to recognize how thoroughly certain beliefs were embedded in the American mind. "Habits of the heart" was how he described them.

America's core ideals are rooted in the European heritage of the first white settlers. They arrived during the Enlightenment period, when people were awakening to the idea of individual choice, a possibility that was much larger in the New World than in the Old World.

Ultimately, the colonists overturned the European way of governing. The American Revolution was the first successful large-scale rebellion in human history driven largely by the desire to create a radically different form of society.[26] In the words of the Declaration of Independence:

> We hold these truths to be self-evident, that all men are created equal; that they are endowed by their Creator with certain unalienable rights; that among these, are life, liberty, and the pursuit of happiness. That, to secure these rights, governments are instituted among men, deriving their just powers from the consent of the governed; that, whenever any form of government becomes destructive of these ends, it is the right of the people to alter or to abolish it, and to institute a new government, laying its foundation on such principles, and organizing its powers in such form, as to them shall seem most likely to effect their safety and happiness.

A decade later, in the drafting of the Constitution of the United States, many of these ideas were put into writing: leaders would be required to govern within a set of rules designed to protect people's rights and interests.

Core Values: Liberty, Individualism, Equality, and Self-Government

An understanding of America's cultural ideals begins with recognition that the individual is paramount. Government is secondary. Its role is to serve the people, as opposed to a system where people are required to serve it. No clearer statement

This is a portion of Thomas Jefferson's handwritten draft of the Declaration of Independence, a formal expression of America's governing ideals.

of this principle exists than the Declaration of Independence's reference to "unalienable rights"—freedoms that belong to each and every citizen and that cannot lawfully be taken away by government.

Liberty, individualism, equality, and self-government are widely regarded as America's core political ideals. **Liberty** is the principle that individuals should be free to act and think as they choose, provided they do not infringe unreasonably on the freedom and well-being of others. The United States, as political scientist Louis Hartz said, was "born free."[27] Political liberty was nearly a birthright for early Americans. They did not have to accept the European system of absolute government when greater personal liberty was as close as the next area of unsettled land. Religious sentiments also entered into the thinking of the early Americans. Many of them had fled Europe to escape religious persecution and came to look upon religious freedom as part of a broader set of rights, including freedom of speech. Unsurprisingly, these early Americans were determined, when forming their own government, to protect their liberty. The Declaration of Independence rings with the proclamation that people are entitled to "life, liberty, and the pursuit of happiness." The preamble to the Constitution declares that the U.S. government was founded to secure "the Blessings of Liberty to ourselves and our Posterity."

liberty
The principle that individuals should be free to act and think as they choose, provided they do not infringe unreasonably on the freedom and well-being of others.

POLITICAL THINKING   How Important is Religion?

America, said the British writer G. K. Chesterton, is "a nation with the soul of a church" and "the only country founded on a creed."[28] He was referring to the high ideals—liberty, individualism, equality, and self-government—that defined the Declaration of Independence. Chesterton could have extended the argument to include the Constitution. The first colonists formed religious communities governed by written covenant, a model for the written Constitution drafted and ratified by Americans more than a century later. Can you think of ways today that religious beliefs affect American politics?

---

individualism

The idea that people should take the initiative, be self-sufficient, and accumulate the material advantages necessary for their well-being.

equality

The notion that individuals are equal in their moral worth and are thereby entitled to equal treatment under the law.

self-government

The principle that the people are the ultimate source and proper beneficiary of governing authority; in practice, a government based on majority rule.

Early Americans also enjoyed unprecedented economic opportunities. Unlike Europe, America had no hereditary nobility that owned virtually all the land. The New World's great distance from Europe and its vast stretches of open territory gave ordinary people the chance to own property, provided they were willing to work hard enough to make it a success. Out of this experience grew a sense of self-reliance and a culture of "rugged individualism." **Individualism** is a commitment to personal initiative and self-sufficiency. Observers from Tocqueville onward have seen fit to note that liberty in America, as in no other country, is tied to a desire for economic independence. Americans' chief aim, wrote Tocqueville, "is to remain their own masters."[29]

A third American political ideal is **equality**—the notion that all individuals are equal in their moral worth and thereby entitled to equal treatment under the law. Europe's rigid system of aristocratic privilege was unenforceable in frontier America. It was this natural sense of personal equality that Thomas Jefferson expressed so forcefully in the Declaration of Independence: "We hold these truths to be self-evident, that all men are created equal." However, equality has always been America's most perplexing ideal. Even Jefferson professed not to know its exact meaning. A slave owner, Jefferson distinguished between free citizens, who were entitled to equal rights, and slaves, who were not. After slavery was abolished, Americans continued to argue over the meaning of equality, and the debate continues today. Does equality require that wealth and opportunity be widely shared? Or does it merely require that artificial barriers to advancement be removed? Despite differing opinions about such questions, an insistence on equality is a distinctive feature of the American experience. Americans, said Bryce, reject "the very notion" that some people might be "better" than others merely because of birth or position.[31]

America's fourth great political ideal is **self-government**—the principle that the people are the ultimate source of governing authority and should have a voice in their governing. Americans' belief in self-government formed in colonial America. The Old World was an ocean away, and European governments had no option but to give the American colonies a substantial degree of self-determination. Out of this experience came the vision of a self-governing nation that led tens of thousands of ordinary farmers, merchants, and tradesmen to risk their lives during the American Revolution. "Governments," the Declaration of Independence proclaims, "deriv[e] their just powers from the consent of the governed." The Constitution of the United States opens with the words "We the People." Etched in a corridor of the Capitol in Washington, D. C., are the words Alexander Hamilton spoke when asked about the foundation of the nation's government: "Here, sir, the people govern."

HOW THE U.S. DIFFERS   POLITICAL THINKING THROUGH COMPARISONS

Individualism and Tax Policy

The United States was labeled "the country of individualism par excellence" by William Watts and Lloyd Free in their book *State of the Nation.*[30] They were referring to the emphasis that Americans place on economic self-reliance and free markets. In European democracies, such views also prevail but are moderated by a greater acceptance of tax and social policies that redistribute wealth. The differences between American and European culture reflect their differing political cultures. Colonial America was an open country ruled by a foreign power, and its revolution was fought largely over the issue of personal liberty. In the European revolutions, economic and social equality was also at issue, because wealth was held by hereditary aristocracies. Europeans' concern with equality was gradually translated into a willingness to use government as a means of economic redistribution.

These cultural differences affect tax rates, as the figure here indicates. As measured by the total amount of individual taxes relative to a country's gross domestic product (GDP), the tax rate is relatively high in Canada and Europe, reflecting the greater extent to which these governments seek through taxes to provide economic security to those that are temporary or permanently at an economic disadvantage. Most European countries, for example, grant working women paid leave from their jobs for several months after childbirth. In the United States, working women by law must

be given leave in this situation but employers do not have to pay them wages while they are on leave.

Q: Government spending includes programs other than economic assistance for the less-well-off. In which policy area do you think the United States spends significantly more than do European democracies?

A: Military spending by the United States far exceeds that of European nations. The United States spends more than 6 percent of its annual GDP on defense, compared with less than 3 percent for the average European country.

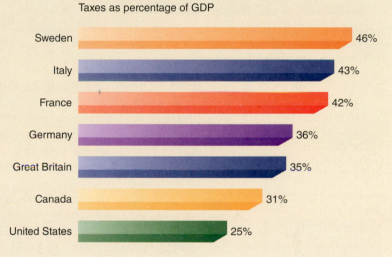

Taxes as percentage of GDP

Country	Percentage
Sweden	46%
Italy	43%
France	42%
Germany	36%
Great Britain	35%
Canada	31%
United States	25%

Source: Organization for Economic Cooperation and Development, 2012.

The Limits and Power of Americans' Ideals

America's cultural beliefs are idealistic. They hold out the promise of a government of high purpose, in which power is widely shared and used for the common good, and where individuals are free, independent, and equal under the law.

Yet high ideals do not come with a guarantee that people will live up to them. The clearest proof in the American case is the human tragedy that began nearly four centuries ago and continues today. In 1619 the first black slaves were brought in chains to America. Slavery lasted 250 years. Slaves worked in the fields from dawn to dark (from "can see, 'til can't"), in both the heat of summer and the cold of winter. The Civil War brought an end to slavery but not to racial oppression. Slavery was followed by the Jim Crow era of legal segregation: black people in the South were forbidden by law to use the same schools, hospitals, restaurants, and restrooms as white people. Those who spoke out against this system were subjected to beatings, firebombings, rapes, and murder—hundreds of African Americans were lynched in the early 1900s by white vigilantes. Today, African Americans have equal rights under the law, but in fact they are far from equal. Compared with white children, black children are twice as likely to live in poverty and to die in infancy.[32] There have always been two Americas, one for whites and one for blacks.

During the Jim Crow era of racial segregation in the South, black citizens were prohibited from using the same public facilities as whites. Included in the ban were schools, transportation facilities, and parks.

Despite the lofty claim that "all men are created equal," equality has never been an American birthright. In 1882, Congress suspended Chinese immigration on the assumption that the Chinese were an inferior people. Calvin Coolidge in 1923 asked Congress for a permanent ban on Chinese immigration, saying that people "who do not want to be partakers of the American spirit ought not to settle in America."[33] Not to be outdone, California enacted legislation prohibiting individuals of Japanese descent from purchasing property in the state. Not until 1965 was discrimination against the Chinese, Japanese, and other Asians eliminated from U.S. immigration laws.

America's callous treatment of some groups is not among the stories that the American people like to tell about themselves. A University of Virginia survey found that American adults are far more likely to want children to be taught about the nation's achievements than its shortcomings (see Table 1-1). Selective memory can be found among all peoples, but the tendency to recast history is perhaps exaggerated in the American case because Americans' beliefs are so idealistic. How could a nation that claims to uphold the principle of equality have barred the Chinese, enslaved the blacks, declared wives to be the "property" of their husbands,[34] and stolen Indian lands?

Although America's ideals obviously do not determine exactly what people will do, they are hardly empty promises. If racial, gender, ethnic, and other forms of intolerance constitute the nation's sorriest chapter, the centuries-old struggle of Americans to build a more equal society is among its finest. Few nations have battled so relentlessly against the insidious discrimination that

TABLE 1-1 | Americans' Preferences in Teaching Children about the Nation's History

In teaching the American story to children, how important is the following theme?	Essential/very important	Somewhat important	Somewhat unimportant/very unimportant/leave it out of the story
With hard work and perseverance, anyone can succeed in America.	83%	14%	4%
Our founders limited the power of government so government would not intrude too much into the lives of its citizens.	74%	19%	8%
America is the world's greatest melting pot in which people from different countries are united into one nation.	73%	21%	5%
America's contribution is one of expanding freedom for more and more people.	71%	22%	6%
Our nation betrayed its founding principles by cruel mistreatment of blacks and American Indians.	59%	24%	17%
Our founders were part of a male-dominated culture that gave important roles to men while keeping women in the background.	38%	28%	35%

Source: Used by permission of the Survey of American Political Culture, James Davison Hunter and Carol Bowman, directors, Institute for Advanced Studies in Culture, University of Virginia. Reprinted by permission.

stems from superficial human differences such as the color of one's skin. The abolition and suffrage movements of the 1800s and the more recent civil rights movements of black Americans, women, Hispanics, and gays testify to Americans' persistent effort to build a more equal society. In 1848, at the first-ever national convention on women's rights, the delegates issued the Declaration of Sentiments, which read in part: "We hold these truths to be self-evident: that all men and women are created equal." At the height of the Civil War, which was the bloodiest conflict to date in the whole of world history, Abraham Lincoln emancipated the slaves, saying "I never, in my life, felt more certain that I was doing right." [35] A century later, speaking at the Lincoln Memorial at the peak of the black civil rights movement, Martin Luther King Jr. said: "'We hold these truths to be self-evident, that all men are created equal.'"[36]

Americans' determination to build a more equal society can also be seen in its public education system. In the early 1800s, the United States pioneered the idea of a free public education for children—this at a time when education in Europe was reserved for children of the wealthy. Even today, the United States spends more heavily on public education than do European countries (see Figure 1-2). The United States also has the world's most elaborate system of higher education, which now includes more than three thousand two-year and four-year institutions. Although some of America's youth do not have a realistic chance of attending college, the nation's college system is relatively open. Roughly a fourth of America's adult citizens have a college degree, which ranks second only to Canada worldwide. Even West Virginia—the American state with the lowest proportion of college graduates—has a higher percentage of residents with a bachelor's degree than does the typical European country (see "How the 50 States Differ").

The principles of liberty and self-government have also shaped American society. No country holds as many elections or has as many publicly elected officials as does the United States, which is also nearly the only country to have instituted primary elections in order to give voters the power to choose party nominees. And few people have pursued their individual rights—ranging from free-expression rights to fair-trial protections—as relentlessly as Americans have. In the end, the power of America's ideals is nowhere more evident than in their continuing influence. Every new generation of Americans has embraced the nation's founding principles and sought ways to update and strengthen them. The writer Theodore H. White aptly described America as a nation doggedly "in search of itself"—a country striving to realize its founding principles. Said White: "Americans are a nation born of an idea; not the place, but the idea, created the United States Government."[37]

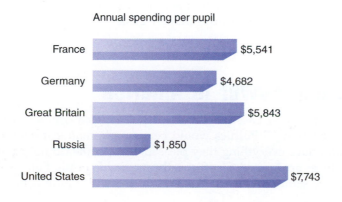

Annual spending per pupil

France	$5,541
Germany	$4,682
Great Britain	$5,843
Russia	$1,850
United States	$7,743

FIGURE 1-2

Government Spending on Primary and Secondary Schools in Selected Countries
Americans' belief in equality has contributed to a higher level of spending on public schools in the United States than is the case in Europe.

Source: MAT (Masters of Arts in Teaching) Program, University of Southern California, 2011.

HOW THE 50 STATES DIFFER POLITICAL THINKING THROUGH COMPARISONS

A COLLEGE EDUCATION

Reflecting their cultural beliefs of individualism and equality, Americans have developed the world's largest college system. Every state has at least eight colleges within its boundaries. No European democracy has as many colleges as either California or New York—each of which has more than three hundred institutions of higher education. The extensive U.S. college system has enabled large numbers of Americans to earn a college degree. Among adults aged twenty-five years or older, roughly one in four is a college graduate. Even the states that rank low on this indicator have a higher percentage of college graduates than do most European countries.

Q: Why do the northeastern and western coastal states have a higher percentage of adults with college degrees?

A: The northeastern and western coastal states are wealthier and more urbanized than most states. Accordingly, young people in these states can better afford the costs of college and are more likely to pursue careers that require a college degree.

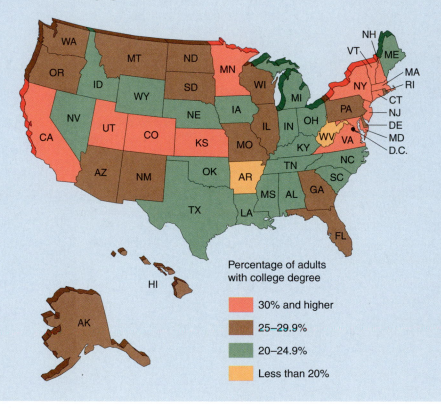

Percentage of adults with college degree

- 🟥 30% and higher
- 🟫 25–29.9%
- 🟩 20–24.9%
- 🟧 Less than 20%

Source: U.S. Bureau of the Census, 2010. Based on percentage of adults twenty-five years of age or older with a college degree.

America's distinctive cultural beliefs are only one of the elements that affect the nation's politics, as subsequent chapters will show. The rest of this chapter introduces concepts and distinctions that are basic to an informed understanding of politics.

Politics and Power in America

politics

The process through which a society settles its conflicts.

Political scientist Harold Lasswell described politics as a conflict over "who gets what, when, and how."[38] **Politics** would be a simple matter if everyone thought alike and could have everything they pleased. But people do not think alike, and society's resources are limited. Conflict is the inevitable result. Politics is the means by which society settles its conflicts and allocates the resulting benefits and costs.

Iranians took to the streets to protest their authoritarian regime's rigging of the country's 2009 election. Authorities responded with mass beatings and arrests. Many of those arrested were tortured and some were executed.

Those who prevail in political conflicts are said to have **power,** a term that refers to the ability of persons, groups, or institutions to influence political developments.[39] Power is basic to politics. Actors who have enough power can provide or refuse health benefits, block or impose gun control, raise or cut taxes, permit or prohibit abortions, protect or take away private property, impose or relax trade barriers, and make war or declare peace. With so much at stake, it is not surprising that Americans, like people elsewhere, seek political power.

French philosopher Michel Foucault called politics "war by other means,"[40] a phrase that literally describes politics in some countries. *Authoritarian governments* openly repress their political opponents as a means of staying in power. The most extreme form of authoritarian government, *totalitarianism,* admits to no limits on its power: the state controls the media, directs the economy, dictates what can and cannot be taught in schools, defines family relations, and decides which religions—if any—can be practiced openly. Authoritarian governments are characterized by one-party rule, although some of them allow a semblance of party competition. Iran's ruling party, for example, conducted a sham election in 2009, stuffing the ballot boxes to assure its victory and then brutally attacking those who took to the streets in protest.

The United States has "rules" designed to keep politics within peaceful bounds. These rules—democracy, constitutionalism, and a free market—determine which side will prevail when conflict occurs, as well as what is off limits to the winning side (see Table 1-2).

power
The ability of persons, groups, or institutions to influence political developments.

TABLE 1-2 | Governing Systems and Political Power

System	Description and implications
Democratic	A system of majority rule through elections; empowers majorities (majoritarianism), groups (pluralism), and officials (authority)
Constitutional	A system based on rule of law, including legal protections for individuals; empowers individuals by enabling them to claim their rights in court (legal action)
Free market	An economic system that centers on the transactions between private parties; empowers business firms (corporate power) and the wealthy (elitism)

A Democratic System

The word *democracy* comes from the Greek words *demos,* meaning "the people," and *kratis,* meaning "to rule." In simple terms, **democracy** is a form of government in which the people govern, either directly or through elected representatives. A democracy is thus different from an *oligarchy* (in which control rests with a small group, such as top-ranking military officers or a few wealthy families) and from an *autocracy* (in which control rests with a single individual, such as a king or dictator).

In practice, democracy has come to mean majority rule through the free and open election of representatives. More direct forms of democracy exist, such as town meetings in which citizens vote directly on issues affecting them, but the impracticality of such an arrangement in a large society has made majority rule through elections the operative form of democratic government, including that of the United States (see Chapter 2).

POLITICAL

THINKING Just Like Kansas City?

In 1940, Senator Kenneth Wherry exclaimed soberly, "With God's help, we will lift Shanghai up and up, ever up, until it is just like Kansas City."[41] Like many Americans before and since, Wherry assumed that the American system of government could be transplanted anywhere in the world. The United States has recently helped to create governments in Afghanistan and Iraq that are based on democratic principles, such as free and open elections. Can true democracy take root in these countries, or in other such countries that have a tradition of authoritarian rule or where the population is bitterly divided along religious, ethnic, or tribal lines?

When political leaders respond to the policy desires of the majority, the result is **majoritarianism**.[42] In the American case, majoritarianism occurs primarily through the competition between the Republican and Democratic parties. When the economy went into a tailspin in 2008, it helped the Democrats win control of the presidency and both houses of Congress. The Democrat-controlled Congress in 2009 enacted a $787 billion economic stimulus bill, responding to majority demand for economic assistance. Unemployment was rising, and a CNN poll showed that 54 percent of Americans backed the legislation. A year later, with the economy still reeling, a CNN poll showed that 56 percent of Americans viewed the stimulus bill as a mistake. With majority opinion now having turned against the spending bill, Republicans had a powerful campaign issue that helped them take control of the House of Representatives in the 2010 midterm elections.

Although competition between the political parties has intensified in the past few decades (see "Party Polarization"), majoritarianism has its limits. The public as a whole takes an interest in only a few of the hundreds of policy decisions that officials make each year (see Chapter 6). Even if they wanted to, party leaders would have difficulty getting the majority to pay attention to most issues. Accordingly, most policies are formulated in response to the groups that have an immediate interest in the issue. Farmers, for example, have more influence over agricultural price supports than do other groups, even though farm subsidies have far-reaching effects, including the price that shoppers pay for food. Some political scientists, like Yale's Robert Dahl, argue that democracies more often operate as pluralistic (multi-interest) systems than as majoritarian systems.[43] **Pluralism** holds that, on most issues, the preference of the special interest largely determines what government does (see Chapter 9).

democracy

A form of government in which the people govern, either directly or through elected representatives.

majoritarianism

The idea that the majority prevails not only in elections but also in policy determination.

pluralism

A theory of American politics that holds that society's interests are substantially represented through power exercised by groups.

PARTY POLARIZATION   Political Thinking in Conflict

Conflict Between the Political Parties Has Risen Sharply in Recent Years.

Conflict between America's two major parties—the Republicans and the Democrats—has intensified in the past few decades. Partisan divisions have surfaced on nearly every major issue, and the fights have been bitter and prolonged, so much so that the term **party polarization** is used to characterize today's party politics. Subsequent chapters will examine the roots and manifestations of this polarization, but two things should be noted at the outset: the situation is much different than it was a few decades ago but is not very different from what it was during most of the nation's history.

A high level of bipartisanship—cooperation between the parties—marked the period from the end of World War II in 1945 until the late 1960s, particularly in the area of foreign affairs. Leaders and voters of both parties were in agreement on the need to contain Soviet communism and to spread U.S. influence in the world. In addition, Republican leaders had largely abandoned their effort to turn back the New Deal policies of President Franklin Roosevelt, which had given the federal government a larger role in economic security (for example, the social security program) and economic regulation (for example, oversight of the stock market). During much of their earlier history, however, America's major political parties had fought intensely and, in the case of the Civil War, took the fight even to the battlefield. In fact, periods of bipartisanship are the exception rather than the rule. President George Washington's first years in office, the so-called Era of Good Feeling in the early 1800s, and the World War I and World War II periods are among the few times Americans have put partisan differences largely aside.

Q. *How do you reconcile the fact that Americans share a common set of ideals and yet often find themselves on opposite sides when it comes to party politics?*

party polarization (or partisan polarization)
The condition in which opinions and actions in response to political issues and situations divides substantially along political party lines.

A democratic system also bestows another form of power. Although officials are empowered by the majority, they also exercise power in their own right as a result of the positions they hold. When President Obama decided in 2009 to increase troop levels in Afghanistan, he did so despite polls that showed most Americans would have preferred a reduction in U.S. forces there.[44] In making the decision, Obama was exercising his constitutional authority as commander-in-chief of the armed forces. Such grants are a special kind of power. **Authority** is the recognized right of officials to exercise power. Members of Congress, judges, and bureaucrats, as well as the president, routinely make authoritative decisions, only some of which are a response to power asserted by the majority or special interests.

authority
The recognized right of officials to exercise power as a result of the positions they hold.

A Constitutional System

In a democracy, the votes of the majority prevail over those of the minority. If this principle were unlimited, the majority could treat the minority with impunity, depriving it even of its liberty or property. As fanciful as this prospect might seem, it preoccupied the writers of the U.S. Constitution. The history of democracies was filled with examples of majority tyranny, and the nation's early experience was no exception. In 1786, debtors had gained control of Rhode Island's legislature and made paper money a legal means of paying debts, even though contracts called for payment in gold. Creditors were then hunted down and held captive in public places so that debtors could come and pay them in full with worthless paper money. A Boston newspaper wrote that Rhode Island ought to be renamed Rogue Island.

DEBATING THE ISSUES POLITICAL THINKING IN ACTION

Should Corporations Be Allowed to Spend Unlimited Amounts on Federal Election Campaigns?

Just as voting majorities and groups exercise power in the American political system, so do business firms. Corporate power is likely to increase as a result of a recent Supreme Court decision *Citizens United v. Federal Election Commission* (2010). Before the Court's ruling, corporations and unions had been banned from spending money to influence the outcome of U.S. federal elections. Individuals within corporations or unions, just as any other American, could contribute money to political candidates, but corporations and unions were barred by law from spending organizational funds on elections. In *Citizens United*, the Supreme Court ruled that corporations and unions have the same First Amendment free speech rights as individuals when it comes to spending money on campaigns. The ruling was widely regarded as having special significance for corporations. Unlike unions, which depend on membership dues and have somewhat limited funds, U.S. corporations reap billions in profits each year. The Supreme Court's decision has been praised by many—most of whom are Republicans—and criticized by many—most of whom are Democrats. Here are two responses to the Supreme Court's decision, one by Senator Mitch McConnell, a Republican, and the other by President Barack Obama, a Democrat.

YES Contrary to what the President, and some of his surrogates in Congress say, foreign persons, corporations, partnerships, associations, organizations or other combination of persons are strictly prohibited from any participation in U.S. elections, just as they were prohibited before the Supreme Court's *Citizens United* decision. I've explained what the ruling didn't do. Now let me explain what the ruling did do. The Court ruled unconstitutional sections of federal law that barred corporations and unions from spending their own money to express their views about issues and candidates. This was the right decision because democracy depends upon free speech, not just for some but for all. As Justice Kennedy, writing for the majority, concluded: "Under our law and our tradition it seems stranger than fiction for our Government to make political speech a crime." In *Citizens United*, the Court ended the suppression of corporate and union speech. Many have predicted this would have dire consequences. What they fail to mention is that 26 states already allow corporate and union speech, something that has had no discernable adverse impact. Any proponent of free speech should applaud this decision. *Citizens United* is and will be a First Amendment triumph of enduring significance.

—*Mitch McConnell, U.S. senator (R-Ky.)*

NO The United States Supreme Court handed a huge victory to the special interests and their lobbyists—and a powerful blow to our efforts to rein in corporate influence. This ruling strikes at our democracy itself. By a 5-4 vote, the Court overturned more than a century of law—including a bipartisan campaign finance law written by Senators John McCain and Russ Feingold that had barred corporations from using their financial clout to directly interfere with elections by running advertisements for or against candidates in the crucial closing weeks. This ruling opens the floodgates for an unlimited amount of special interest money into our democracy. It gives the special interest lobbyists new leverage to spend millions on advertising to persuade elected officials to vote their way—or to punish those who don't. That means that any public servant who has the courage to stand up to the special interests and stand up for the American people can find himself or herself under assault come election time. Even foreign corporations may now get into the act. I can't think of anything more devastating to the public interest. The last thing we need to do is hand more influence to the lobbyists in Washington, or more power to the special interests to tip the outcome of elections.

—*Barack Obama, president of the United States*

Q: Do you think corporations should be allowed to use their profits to influence the outcome of election campaigns? A larger question is whether corporations should have the same legal status as individuals when it comes to constitutional protections. Do you think corporations are entitled to the same free speech rights that citizens possess?

constitutionalism

The idea that there are lawful limits on the power of government.

To guard against oppressive majorities, the writers of the Constitution devised an elaborate system of checks and balances, dividing authority among the legislative, executive, and judicial branches so that each branch could check the power of the others (see Chapter 2). The Bill of Rights was added to the Constitution a few years later as a further check on the majority. For example, Congress would be prohibited from enacting laws that abridge freedom of speech, press, or religion. These limits reflect the principle of **constitutionalism**—the idea that there are lawful restrictions on government's power. Officials are obliged to act within the limits of the law, which include protections of individual rights.

The Bill of Rights in combination with an independent judiciary and a firm attachment to private property have made **legal action**—the use of the courts as a means of asserting rights and interests—a channel through which ordinary citizens exercise power. Americans have an expansive view of their rights and turn more readily to the courts to make their claims than do people elsewhere (see Chapters 4 and 5).[45] A handwritten note by a penniless convict, for example, triggered the U.S. Supreme Court's landmark *Gideon v. Wainwright* ruling.[46] Clarence Gideon had been made to stand trial in Florida without the aid of a lawyer for breaking into a pool hall. When he appealed his conviction, the Supreme Court concluded that his Sixth Amendment right to counsel had been violated. The ruling established a new policy: if the accused is too poor to hire a lawyer, the government must provide one.

The significance of legal action in the United States can be seen from the size of its legal profession.[47] On a per-capita basis, there are roughly twice as many lawyers in the United States as in Britain, Italy, and Germany, and five times as many as in France (see Figure 1-3). The United States, as political scientist James Q. Wilson noted, is "not more litigious because we have more lawyers; we have more lawyers because we are so litigious."[48]

Rhode Island was nicknamed "Rogue Island" for its disregard of property rights. Shown here is the Rhode Island three-dollar bank note, which came to be worth no more than the paper on which it was printed and yet was used to pay off gold debts.

legal action

The use of courts of law as a means by which individuals protect their rights and settle their conflicts.

A Free-Market System

Politics is not confined to the halls of government. Many of society's costs and benefits are allocated through the private sector, although economic systems differ in the degree of government intervention. Under *communism*, which characterized the former Soviet Union and is practiced most fully today in North Korea, the

The handwritten letter that Clarence Gideon (insert) sent to the Supreme Court in 1962. The letter led eventually to the *Gideon* decision, in which the Court held that states must provide poor defendants with legal counsel (see Chapter 4).

Gideon's Letter to the Supreme Court
John F. Davis, Clerk, Supreme Court of the United States

FIGURE 1-3
Legal Action and Lawyers
Reflecting the country's emphasis on legal action as a means of pursuing individual rights and interests, the United States has more lawyers than do other Western democracies.

Source: American Bar Association and Council of European Lawyers data, as of 2007.

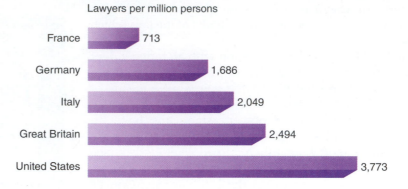

Lawyers per million persons

France	713
Germany	1,686
Italy	2,049
Great Britain	2,494
United States	3,773

free-market system

An economic system based on the idea that government should interfere with economic transactions as little as possible. Free enterprise and self-reliance are the collective and individual principles that underpin free markets.

corporate power

The power that corporations exercise in their effort to influence government and maintain control of the workplace.

elitism

The notion that wealthy and well-connected individuals exercise power over certain areas of public policy.

Lobbying offers groups and corporations a chance to make their views known to public officials and thus to influence public policy.

government owns most or all major industries and also takes responsibility for overall management of the economy, including production quotas, supply points, and pricing. Under *socialism*, as it is practiced today in Sweden and other countries, government does not attempt to manage the overall economy, but owns a number of major industries and guarantees every individual a minimal standard of living. In contrast, a **free-market system** operates mainly on private transactions. Firms are largely free to make their own production, distribution, and pricing decisions, and individuals depend largely on themselves for economic security.

The U.S. economy is chiefly a free-market system, although government intervenes through regulatory, taxing, and spending policies. The nation's economy is similar in this respect to that of most European democracies, but is nonetheless distinctive in the extent to which private transactions determine the allocation of economic costs and benefits. The tax rate, as we saw earlier in the chapter, is lower in the United States than in European countries because they make greater use of taxation to redistribute income to the less advantaged in the form of economic assistance, such as government-provided health care for all.

Enormous concentrations of wealth and power exist in the U.S. private sector, primarily in the hands of large corporations, like Google, Ford, and Bank of America. **Corporate power** operates in part through the influence that firms have with policymakers. Roughly two-thirds of all lobbyists in the nation's capital represent business firms, which also contribute heavily to political candidates. Corporate power can also be seen in the workplace, where U.S. firms have greater control over wages and working conditions than do firms in other Western democracies. The annual income of a minimum-wage worker, for instance, is roughly $15,000 in the United States, compared with roughly $18,000 in France and $22,000 in Great Britain.[49]

Wealth is also the foundation of **elitism,** which refers to the power exercised by well-positioned and highly influential individuals.[50] Sociologist C. Wright Mills concluded that corporate elites, operating behind the scenes, have more control over economic policy than do "the politicians in the visible government."[51] Some scholars dispute Mills' claim, while others contend that a sizeable portion of the corporate elite is motivated to serve society's interests as well as its own.[52] Few scholars, however, would dispute the claim that the corporate elite has more political power in America than it does in most Western democracies.

Who Governs?

This text's perspective is that a full explanation of American politics requires an accounting of all these forms of power—as exercised by the majority, interest groups, elites, corporations, individuals through legal action, and those in positions of governing authority. In fact, a defining characteristic of American politics is the widespread sharing of power. Few nations have as many competing interests and institutions as does the United States.

The Text's Organization

American politics operates within a constitutional system that defines how power is to be obtained and exercised. This system is the focus of the next few chapters, which examine how, in theory and practice, the Constitution defines the institutions of governments and the rights of individuals. The discussion then shifts to the political role of citizens and of the intermediaries that enable citizens to act together and connect them to government. These subjects are explored in chapters on public opinion, political participation, political parties, interest groups, and the news media. The functioning of governing officials is then addressed in chapters on the nation's elective institutions—the Congress and the presidency—and its appointive institutions—the federal bureaucracy and the federal courts. These chapters describe how these institutions are structured but aim chiefly to explain how their actions are affected by internal and external factors, as well as by the constitutional system in which they operate.

Throughout the text, but particularly in the concluding chapters, attention is given to **public policies,** which are the decisions of government to pursue particular courses of action. No aspect of a nation's politics is more revealing of how it is governed than are its policies—everything from how it chooses to educate its children to how it chooses to use its military power.

Policies are the result of political interactions that political scientists call the **public policy process** (see Figure 1-4). The process has three stages. The first stage—*problem recognition*—refers to the emergence of an issue. Problems sometimes develop gradually, as in the case of the slow loss of American jobs to countries with inexpensive labor. The job losses were barely noticeable at first, but, as they accumulated, policymakers came to recognize them as a problem. In other cases, problem recognition happens suddenly, even shockingly, as in the case of Hurricane Katrina, which devastated New Orleans and the Gulf Coast in 2005. After a policy problem is recognized, the second stage of the policy process—*policy formulation*—commences. This stage is marked by efforts to develop a course of action for dealing with the problem. In the case of Katrina, the response included the decision to construct a new levee system that could better protect New Orleans from flooding. After a policy is adopted, it has to be put into effect—the *policy implementation* stage. This stage can be a difficult one, particularly when lawmakers misjudge a policy's consequences. When the United States invaded Iraq in 2003, for example, many analysts thought the war would be over within months. As it happened, U.S. combat units did not leave Iraq until 2011—more than eight years after the fighting began.

public policies

Decisions by government to pursue particular courses of action.

public policy process

The political interactions that lead to the recognition of a policy problem, the development of a response to it, and the implementation of the response.

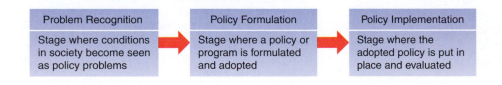

FIGURE 1-4
The Public Policy Process
The public policy process refers to the political interactions that lead to the emergence and resolution of public policy issues. The process includes three stages, although each stage can involve elements of the other two stages.

Underlying the text's discussion of American politics and policy is the recognition of how difficult it is to govern effectively and how important it is to try. It cannot be said too often that the issue of governing is the most difficult issue facing a democratic society. It also cannot be said too often that governing is a quest rather than a resolved issue. Political scientist E. E. Schattschneider said it clearly: "In the course of centuries, there has come a great deal of agreement about what democracy is, but nobody has a monopoly on it and the last word has not been spoken."[53]

Summary
Self-Test www.mhhe.com/pattersontadtx11e

Political thinking is the careful gathering and sifting of information in the process of forming knowledgeable views of political developments. Political thinking is a key to responsible citizenship, but many citizens avoid it by virtue of paying scant attention to politics. The tools of political science can contribute to effective political thinking.

The United States is a nation that was formed on a set of ideals. Liberty, individualism, equality, and self-government are foremost among these ideals. These ideals became Americans' common bond and today are the basis of their political culture. Although imperfect in practice, these ideals have guided what generations of Americans have tried to achieve politically.

Politics is the process by which it is determined whose values will prevail in society. The basis of politics is conflict over scarce resources and competing values. Those who have

power win out in this conflict and are able to control governing authority and policy choices. In the United States, no one faction controls all power and policy. Majorities govern on some issues, while other issues are dominated by groups, elites, corporations, individuals through legal action, or officials who hold public office.

Politics in the United States plays out through rules of the game that include democracy, constitutionalism, and free markets. Democracy is rule by the people, which in practice refers to a representative system of government in which the people rule through their elected officials. Constitutionalism refers to rules that limit the rightful power of government over citizens. A free-market system assigns private parties the dominant role in determining how economic costs and benefits are allocated.

CHAPTER 1

Study Corner

Key Terms

authority (*p. 17*)
constitutionalism (*p. 18*)
corporate power (*p. 20*)
democracy (*p. 16*)
elitism (*p. 20*)
equality (*p. 10*)
free-market system (*p. 20*)
individualism (*p. 10*)
legal action (*p. 19*)
liberty (*p. 9*)
majoritarianism (*p. 16*)

party (partisan) polarization (*p. 17*)
pluralism (*p. 16*)
political culture (*p. 7*)
political science (*p. 7*)
political thinking (*p. 4*)
politics (*p. 14*)
power (*p. 15*)
public policies (*p. 21*)
public policy process (*p. 21*)
self-government (*p. 10*)

Self-Test: Multiple Choice

1. Barriers to political thinking include which of the following?
   a. People's inattentiveness to politics
   b. People's reliance on sources that slant information to fit their agendas
   c. The tendency of politicians to "spin" information
   d. All of the above

2. America's political culture includes all except which of the following ideals?
   a. Elitism
   b. Liberty
   c. Equality
   d. Self-government

3. When people are able to control policy decisions and prevail in political conflicts, they are said to have
   a. Political culture.
   c. Pluralism.
   b. Political power.
   d. Diversity.

4. America's commitment to the principle of constitutionalism means
   a. The majority can decide all policy issues.
   b. There are limits on the rightful power of government over citizens.
   c. Direct democracy will be favored over representative democracy.
   d. A "mixed economy" must be upheld at all costs.

5. The text mentions each of the following theories of power concerning who governs America, *except*
   a. Majoritarianism.
   c. Factionalism.
   b. Pluralism.
   d. Elitism.

6. In a free-market system, the allocation of benefits and costs is determined primarily by
   a. Interaction between a private party and another private party.
   b. Interaction between a government entity and another government entity.
   c. Interaction between a private party and government.
   d. None of the above.

7. An obstacle to majoritarianism is the fact that the general public pays little attention to most policy issues. (T/F)

8. In the United States, as compared with most other democracies, corporations are relatively weak in terms of their political influence and control over what happens in the workplace. (T/F)

9. Authority can be defined as the recognized right of officials to make binding decisions. (T/F)

10. Cultural beliefs are based on wishful thinking and serve no useful purpose for society. (T/F)

Self-Test: Essay

Explain the types of power that result from each of America's major systems of governing: democracy, constitutionalism, and free market.

Suggested Readings

Bellamy, Richard. *Political Constitutionalism*. Cambridge, England: Cambridge University Press, 2007. An assessment of constitutionalism that goes beyond a narrowly legalistic perspective.

Domhoff, G. William. *Who Rules America? Challenges to Corporate and Class Dominance*, 6th ed. New York: McGraw-Hill, 2009. A critical assessment of American government by a contemporary proponent of elite theory.

Foley, Michael. *American Credo: The Place of Ideas in American Politics*. New York: Oxford University Press, 2007. An analysis of the political influence of Americans' core beliefs.

Friedman, Milton. *Capitalism and Freedom*. Chicago: University of Chicago Press, 2002. A treatise (originally published in 1962) on free markets by one of the twentieth century's leading economists.

Galston, William A. *The Practice of Liberal Pluralism*. New York: Cambridge University Press, 2004. A careful look at how pluralism works in practice.

Mill, John Stuart. *On Liberty*. White Plains, N.Y.: Longman Publishers, 2006. A classic theory (originally published in 1859) of personal liberty and democracy.

Stout, Jeffrey. *Democracy and Tradition*. Princeton, N.J.: Princeton University Press, 2004. An analysis of the moral claims associated with democracy.

Wood, Gordon S. *The Idea of America: Reflections on the Birth of the United States*. New York: Penguin Press, 2011. A study of America's persistent ideals by one of America's preeminent historians.

List of Websites

www.conginst.org
A site that provides up-to-date survey data on the American public

www.loc.gov
The Library of Congress website; provides access to over 70 million historical and contemporary U.S. documents

www.realclearpolitics.com
A site filled with information about current issues and developments in American politics

www.stateline.org
A University of Richmond/Pew Charitable Trusts site dedicated to providing citizens with information on major policy issues

Participate!

Political thinking is a key to responsible citizenship. As a prelude to preparing yourself for effective political thinking, reflect on your current habits. From what sources do you get most of your political information? Are they reliable sources (that is, do they place a premium on accuracy)? How frequently do you encounter opposing arguments or opinions? How carefully do you listen to them? When forming political opinions, do you tend to reflect upon your choices or do you tend to make quick judgments?

Extra Credit

For up-to-the-minute *New York Times* articles, interactive simulations, graphics, study tools, and more links and quizzes, visit the text's Online Learning Center at **www.mhhe.com/pattersontad11e**.

Self-Test Answers

1. d, 2. a, 3. b, 4. b, 5. c, 6. a, 7. T, 8. F, 9. T, 10. F

CHAPTER 2

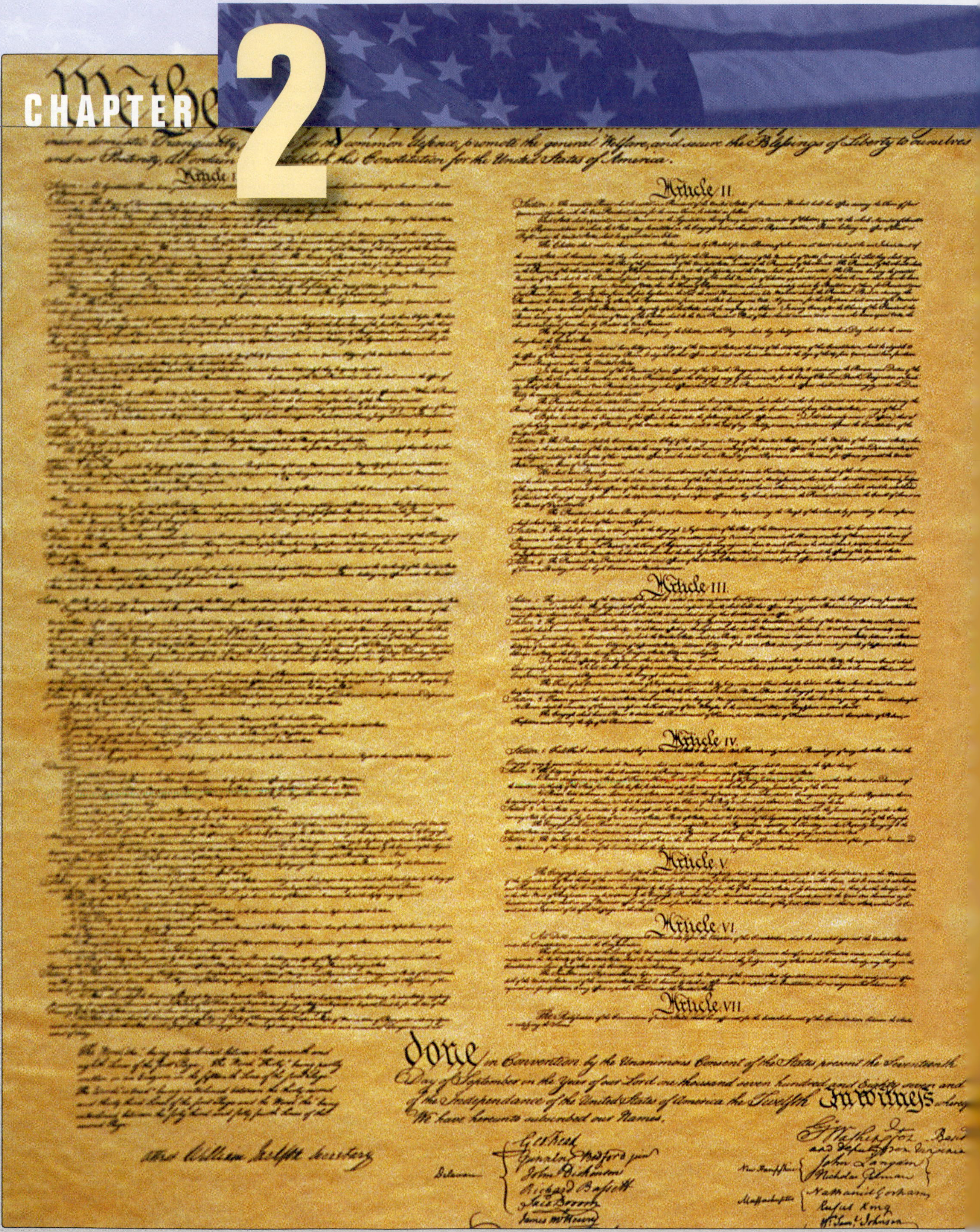
Article II.
Article III.
Article IV.
Article V.
Article VI.
Article VII.

Constitutional Democracy: Promoting Liberty and Self-Government

limited government

A government that is subject to strict limits on its lawful uses of power and, hence, on its ability to deprive people of their liberty.

> Why has government been instituted at all? Because the passions of man will not conform to the dictates of reason and justice, without constraint. Alexander Hamilton[1]

Late on the night of November 6, 2012, Barack Obama stepped to the podium to accept his reelection as president of the United States. Earlier that day, more than 100 million Americans had cast their ballots, choosing Obama over his Republican challenger, Mitt Romney. In his victory speech, Obama spoke of renewing the American dream. He called upon Americans to move forward in common purpose and to put aside the differences that were dividing them. He pledged to use his second term to strengthen the nation's values and to restore Americans' confidence in their government. "America's never been about what can be done for us," said President Obama. "It's about what can be done by us together through the hard . . . but necessary work of self-government."

The ideas that guided Obama's speech would have been familiar to any generation of Americans. The same ideas have been invoked when Americans have gone to war, declared peace, celebrated national holidays, launched major policy initiatives, and asserted new rights.[2] The ideas expressed in Obama's speech were the same ones that shaped the speeches of George Washington and Abraham Lincoln, Susan B. Anthony and Franklin D. Roosevelt, Martin Luther King Jr., and Ronald Reagan.

The ideas were there at the nation's beginning, when Thomas Jefferson put them into words in the Declaration of Independence. They had been nurtured by the colonial experience in the New World, which offered the settlers a degree of liberty, equality, and self-government unimaginable in Europe. When the Revolutionary War settled the issue of American independence in the colonists' favor, they faced the question of how to turn their ideals into a system of government. The Constitution of the United States became the instrument for that effort. The framers of the Constitution sought to create a **limited government**—one that is subject to strict legal limits on the uses of power, so that it would not threaten the people's liberty. They

Barack Obama and Mitt Romney debating at the University of Denver in the first of their three 2012 presidential debates.

representative government

A government in which the people govern through the selection of their representatives.

also sought to establish a system of **representative government**—one in which the people would govern through the selection of their representatives.

The challenge facing the framers was that, although limited government and representative government can be reinforcing, they can also conflict. Representative government requires that the majority through its elected representatives has the power to rule. However, limited government requires that majority rule stop at the point where it infringes on the legitimate rights and interests of the minority. This consideration led the framers to forge a constitution that provides for majority rule but has built-in restrictions on the power of the majority and its elected representatives.

This chapter describes how the principles of representative government and limited government are embodied in the Constitution and explains the tension between them. The chapter also indicates how these principles have been modified in practice in the course of American history. The main points presented in this chapter are:

- *America during the colonial period developed traditions of limited government and representative government.* These traditions were rooted in governing practices, political theory, and cultural values.

- *The Constitution provides for limited government mainly by defining lawful powers and by dividing those powers among competing institutions.* The Constitution, with its Bill of Rights, also prohibits government from infringing on individual rights. Judicial review is an additional safeguard.

- *The Constitution in its original form provided for representative government mainly through indirect methods of electing representatives.* The framers' theory of representative government was based on the notion that political power must be separated from immediate popular influences if sound policies are to result.

- *The idea of popular government—in which the majority's desires have a more direct and immediate impact on governing officials—has gained strength since the nation's beginning.* Originally, the House of Representatives was the only institution subject to direct vote of the people. This mechanism has been extended to other institutions and, through primary elections, even to the nomination of candidates for public office.

Before the Constitution: The Colonial and Revolutionary Experiences

Early Americans' admiration for limited government stemmed from their British heritage. Unlike other European governments of the time, Britain did not have an absolute monarchy. Parliament was an independent body with lawmaking power and local representation. Many of the colonial charters conferred upon Americans "the rights of Englishmen," which included, for example, the right to trial by jury.

The colonies also had experience in self-government. Each colony had an elected representative assembly, which was subject to British oversight but nevertheless had important legislative powers. Moreover, most colonists were Protestants, and many of them belonged to sects that had self-governing congregations.

The American Revolution was partly a rebellion against Britain's failure to uphold the colonies' established traditions. After the French and Indian War (1754–1763), during which colonists fought alongside British soldiers to drive the French out of the western territories, the British government for the first time imposed heavy taxes on the colonies. The war with France, which was also waged in Europe, had created a budget crisis in Britain. Taxing the colonies was a way to reduce the debt, so Parliament levied a stamp tax on colonial newspapers and business documents. The colonists were not represented in Parliament, and they objected. "No taxation without representation" was their rallying cry.

Although Parliament backed down and repealed the Stamp Act, it then passed the Townshend Act, which imposed taxes on all glass, paper, tea, and lead sold in the colonies. The colonists again objected, and Parliament again backed down, except for the tax on tea, which Britain retained to show that it

THE DESTRUCTION OF TEA AT BOSTON HARBOR.

The Boston Tea Party was a response to a tax on tea imposed by the British to demonstrate their control over the colonies. The destruction of a shipload of tea in Boston Harbor by a band of patriots contributed to the start of the Revolutionary War.

was still in charge of colonial affairs. The tea tax sparked an act of defiance that became known as the Boston Tea Party. In December 1773, under the cover of darkness, a small band of patriots disguised as Native Americans boarded an English ship in Boston Harbor and dumped its cargo of tea overboard. When the British demanded that the city pay for the tea, and Boston refused, the British navy blockaded its port.

In 1774, the colonists met in Philadelphia at the First Continental Congress to formulate their demands on Britain. They asked for their own councils for the imposition of taxes, an end to the British military occupation, and a guarantee of trial by local juries. (British authorities had resorted to shipping "troublemakers" to London for trial.) King George III rejected their demands, and British troops and Massachusetts minutemen clashed at Lexington and Concord on April 19, 1775. Eight colonists died on the Lexington green in what became known as "the shot heard 'round the world." The American Revolution had begun.

The Declaration of Independence

Although grievances against Britain were the immediate cause of the American Revolution, ideas about the proper form of government also fueled the rebellion.[3] Building on the writings of Thomas Hobbes,[4] John Locke claimed that government is founded on a **social contract.** Locke asserted that people living in a state of nature enjoy certain **inalienable rights** (or **natural rights**), including those of life, liberty, and property, which are threatened by individuals who steal, kill, and otherwise act without regard for others. To protect against such individuals, people agree among themselves to form a government (the social contract). They submit to the government's authority in return for the protection it can provide, but, in doing so, they retain their natural rights, which the government is obliged to respect. If it fails to do so, Locke contended, people can rightfully rebel against it.[5]

Thomas Jefferson declared that Locke "was one of the three greatest men that ever lived, without exception." Jefferson paraphrased Locke's ideas in passages of the Declaration of Independence, including those asserting that "all men are created equal," that they are entitled to "life, liberty, and the pursuit of happiness," that governments derive "their just powers from the consent of the governed," and that "it is the right of the people to alter or abolish" a tyrannical government. The Declaration was a call to revolution rather than a framework for a new form of government, but the ideas it contained—liberty, equality, individual rights, self-government, lawful powers—became the basis, eleven years later, for the Constitution of the United States. (The Declaration of Independence and the Constitution are reprinted in their entirety in this book's appendixes.)

The Articles of Confederation

A **constitution** is the fundamental law that defines how a government will legitimately operate—the method for choosing its leaders, the institutions through which these leaders will work, the procedures they must follow in making policy, and the powers they can lawfully exercise. The U.S. Constitution is exactly such a law; it is the highest law of the land. Its provisions define how power is to be acquired and how it can be used.

The first government of the United States, however, was based not on the Constitution but on the Articles of Confederation. The Articles, which were

---

social contract

A voluntary agreement by individuals to form a government that is then obliged to act within the confines of the agreement.

---

inalienable (natural) rights

Those rights that persons theoretically possessed in the state of nature, prior to the formation of governments. These rights, including those of life, liberty, and property, are considered inherent and, as such, are inalienable. Since government is established by people, government has the responsibility to preserve these rights.

---

constitution

The fundamental law that defines how a government will legitimately operate.

adopted during the Revolutionary War, created a very weak national government that was subordinate to the states. Under the Articles, each state retained its full "sovereignty, freedom, and independence." The colonies had always been governed separately, and their people considered themselves Virginians, New Yorkers, Pennsylvanians, and so on, as much as they thought of themselves as Americans. Moreover, they were wary of a powerful central government. The American Revolution was sparked by grievances against the arbitrary policies of King George III, and Americans were in no mood to replace him with a strong national authority of their own making.

Under the Articles of Confederation, the national government had no judiciary and no independent executive. All authority was vested in the Congress, but it was largely a creature of the states. Each of the thirteen states had one vote in Congress, and each state appointed its congressional representatives and paid their salary. Legislation could be enacted only if nine of the thirteen agreed to it. The rule for constitutional amendments was even more imposing. The Articles of Confederation could be amended only if each state agreed.

The Articles prohibited Congress from levying taxes, so it had to ask the states for money. It was slow to arrive, if it arrived at all. During one period, Congress requested $12 million from the states but received only $3 million. By 1786, the national government was so desperate for funds that it sold the navy's ships and reduced the army to fewer than a thousand soldiers—this at a time when Britain had an army in Canada and Spain had one in Florida. Congress was also prohibited from interfering with the states' trade policies, so it was powerless to forge a national economy. States, free to do what they wanted, tried to cripple their competitors. Connecticut, for example, placed a higher tariff on goods manufactured in neighboring Massachusetts than it did on the same goods shipped from England.

The American states had stayed together out of necessity during the Revolutionary War. They would have lost to the British if each state had tried to fend for itself. Once the war ended, however, the states felt free to go their separate ways. Several states sent representatives to Europe to negotiate their own trade agreements. New Hampshire, with its eighteen-mile coastline, established a separate navy. In a melancholy letter to Thomas Jefferson, George Washington wondered whether the United States deserved to be called "a nation."

A Nation Dissolving

In late 1785 at his Mount Vernon home, Washington met with leaders of Virginia and Maryland to secure an agreement between the two states on commercial use of the Potomac River. During the meeting, they decided on the desirability of a commerce policy binding on all the states, which would require an amendment to the Articles of Confederation.

A revolt in western Massachusetts added urgency to the situation. A ragtag army of two thousand farmers armed with pitchforks marched on county courthouses to prevent foreclosures on their land. Many of the farmers were veterans of the Revolutionary War; their leader, Daniel Shays, had been a captain in the American army. They had been given assurances during the Revolution that their land, which sat unploughed because they were away at war, would not be confiscated for unpaid debts and taxes. They were also promised the back pay owed to them for their military service. (Congress had run out of money during the Revolution.) Instead, they received no back pay, and heavy new taxes were levied on their farms. Many farmers faced not only losing their property but being sent to prison for unpaid debts.

County courthouses in Massachusetts in 1786 were the scenes of brawls between angry farmers and citizens who supported the state's attempts to foreclose on farmers' property because of unpaid debts. The violence of Shays' Rebellion convinced many political leaders that anarchy was spreading and that a more powerful national government was required to stop it.

Shays' Rebellion frightened wealthy interests, who called on the governor of Massachusetts to put down the revolt. He in turn asked Congress for help, but it had no army to send. Although Shays' Rebellion was quashed by a private militia hired and funded by wealthy merchants, the rebellion exposed the weaknesses of the national government. Virginia and Maryland invited the other eleven states to join them at Annapolis to work out amendments to the Articles of Confederation. Only five states sent delegates to the Annapolis Convention, which meant no change could be made in the Articles. However, James Madison and Alexander Hamilton convinced the delegates to adopt a resolution calling for a convention "to render the Constitution of the Federal government adequate to the exigencies of Union." Congress concurred and scheduled a constitutional convention of all the states in Philadelphia. Congress placed a restriction on the delegates: they were to meet for "the sole and express purpose of revising the Articles of Confederation."

POLITICAL THINKING How Powerful Should Government Be?

The American political tradition includes a suspicion of government power, expressed in the adage "That government is best which governs least." Government sometimes tries to do too much. But can government also do too little? What is the lesson of the government under the Articles of Confederation? Is the issue of government's power a question, not of how much or how little power, but whether its power is equal to its responsibilities?

Negotiating toward a Constitution

The delegates to the Philadelphia constitutional convention ignored the instructions of Congress, instead drafting a plan for an entirely new form of government. Prominent delegates (among them George Washington, Benjamin Franklin, and James Madison) were determined from the outset to establish an American nation built on a stronger central government.

The Great Compromise: A Two-Chamber Congress

Debate at the constitutional convention of 1787 began over a plan put forward by the Virginia delegation, which was dominated by strong nationalists. The **Virginia Plan** (also called the **large-state plan**) included separate judicial and executive branches as well as a two-chamber Congress that would have supreme authority in all areas "in which the separate states are incompetent," particularly defense and interstate trade. Members of the lower chamber would be chosen by the voters, while members of the upper chamber would be selected by members of the lower chamber from lists of nominees provided by their respective state legislatures. In both chambers, the heavily populated states would have a greater number of representatives than would the lightly populated ones. Small states such as Delaware and Rhode Island would be allowed only one representative in the lower chamber, while large states such as Massachusetts and Virginia would have more than a dozen.

The Virginia Plan was sharply attacked by delegates from the smaller states. They rallied around a counterproposal made by New Jersey's William Paterson. The **New Jersey Plan** (also called the **small-state plan**) called for a stronger national government than that provided for by the Articles of Confederation. It would have the power to tax and to regulate commerce among the states. In most other respects, however, the Articles would remain in effect. Congress would have a single chamber in which each state, large or small, would have a single vote.

The debate over the two plans dragged on for weeks before the delegates reached what is now known as the **Great Compromise**. It provided for a bicameral (two-chamber) Congress. One chamber, the House of Representatives, would be apportioned on the basis of population. States with larger populations would have more House members than states with smaller populations, although each state would have at least one representative. The other chamber, the Senate, would be apportioned on the basis of an equal number of senators (two) for each state. This compromise was critical. The small states would not have agreed to join a union in which their vote was always weaker than that of large states, a fact reflected in Article V of the Constitution: "No state, without its consent, shall be deprived of its equal suffrage in the Senate."

Virginia (large-state) Plan
A constitutional proposal for a strong Congress with two chambers, both of which would be based on numerical representation, thus granting more power to the larger states.

New Jersey (small-state) Plan
A constitutional proposal for a strengthened Congress but one in which each state would have a single vote, thus granting a small state the same legislative power as a large state.

Great Compromise
The agreement at the constitutional convention to create a two-chamber Congress with the House apportioned by population and the Senate apportioned equally by state.

The Three-Fifths Compromise: Issues of Slavery and Trade

Differences between the interests of northern states and southern states forced a second major compromise, this time over the issues of slavery and trade. The South's delegates were concerned that northern representatives in Congress would tax or even bar the importation of slaves. A decade earlier, at the insistence of southern states, a statement critical of slavery had been deleted from Jefferson's initial draft of the Declaration of Independence, and southern delegates to the Philadelphia convention were determined to block any attempts to end slavery through a new constitution.

The southern delegates were also concerned that the North, which included more states and had a larger population, would use its numerical majority in the House and Senate to enact tax policies injurious to the South. Most of the nation's manufacturing was based in the North, and if Congress sought to protect it by placing a heavy tax (tariff) on manufactured products imported from Europe, the higher cost of these imports would be borne by the South, which was more dependent on them. If Congress also imposed a heavy tariff on the export of agricultural goods, which would make them more expensive and therefore less attractive to foreign buyers, the South would again bear most of the tax burden because it provided most of the agricultural goods shipped abroad, such as cotton and tobacco.

After extended debate, a compromise was reached. Congress would have the authority to tax imports but would be prohibited from taxing exports. Congress also would be prohibited until 1808 from passing laws to end the slave trade. However, the most controversial trade-off was the so-called **Three-Fifths Compromise.** For purposes of apportionment of taxes and seats in the U.S. House of Representatives, each slave was to count as less than a full person. Northern delegates had argued against the counting of slaves because they did not have legal rights. Southern delegates wanted to count them as full persons for purposes of apportioning House seats (which would have the effect of increasing the number of southern representatives) and to count them as non-persons for purposes of apportioning taxes (which would have the effect of decreasing the amount of federal taxes levied on the southern states). The delegates finally settled on a compromise that included both taxation and apportionment but counted each slave as three-fifths of a person, which was the ratio necessary to give the southern states nearly half of the seats in the House of Representatives. If slaves had not been counted at all, the southern states would have had only about a third of the House seats. If they had been counted as full persons, southern states would have had a majority of House members, even though slaves would have had no say in their selection.

These compromises have led critics to claim that the framers of the Constitution had no objections to slavery. In fact, most of the delegates were deeply troubled by it, recognizing the stark inconsistency between the practice of slavery and the nation's professed commitment to liberty and equality. "It is inconsistent with the principles of the Revolution," Maryland's Luther Martin stated. George Mason, a Virginian and a slaveholder, said: "[Slaveholders] bring the judgment of heaven on a country."[6] Benjamin Franklin and Alexander Hamilton were among the delegates who were involved in antislavery organizations.

Yet the southern states' dependence on slavery was a reality that had to be confronted if there was to be a union of the states. The northern states had few slaves, whereas the southern economies were based on slavery (see Figure 2-1). John Rutledge of South Carolina asked during the convention debate whether the North regarded southerners as "fools." Southern delegates insisted that their states would form a separate union rather than join one that banned slavery.

Three-Fifths Compromise

A compromise worked out at the 1787 convention between northern states and southern states. Each slave was to be counted as three-fifths of a person for purposes of federal taxation and congressional apportionment (number of seats in the House of Representative).

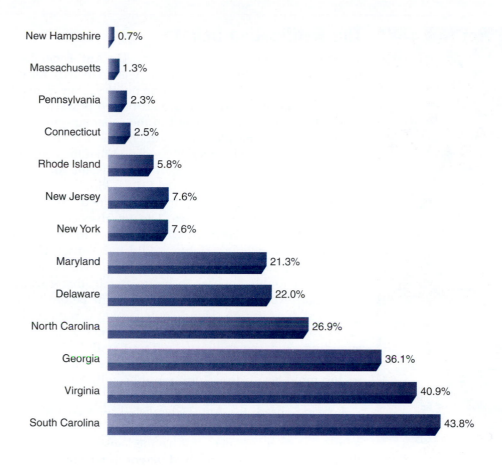

FIGURE 2-1

African Americans as a Percentage of State Population, 1790
At the time of the writing of the Constitution, African Americans (most of whom were slaves) were concentrated in the southern states.
Source: U.S. Bureau of the Census.

A Strategy for Ratification

The compromises over slavery and the structure of the Congress took up most of the four months that the convention was in session. Some of the other issues were the subject of remarkably little debate. Decisions on the structure of the federal judiciary and bureaucracy, for example, were largely delegated to Congress.

The last issue that had to be decided was a process for ratifying the proposed constitution. The delegates realized that all their work would amount to nothing if the states could not be persuaded to adopt the new constitution. They also recognized that ratification would be difficult; many state leaders would oppose giving strong powers to the national government. Moreover, Congress had not authorized a complete restructuring of the federal government. In fact, in authorizing the Philadelphia convention, Congress had stated that any proposed change in the Articles of Confederation would have to be "agreed to in Congress" and then "confirmed by [all] the states."

In a bold move, the delegates ignored Congress's instructions and established their own ratification process. The document was to be submitted to the states, where it would become law if approved by at least nine states in special ratifying conventions of popularly elected delegates. It was a masterful strategy. There was little hope that all thirteen state legislatures would approve the Constitution, but nine states through conventions might be persuaded to ratify it. Indeed, North Carolina and Rhode Island were steadfastly opposed to the new union and did not ratify the Constitution until the other eleven states had ratified it and begun the process of establishing the new government.

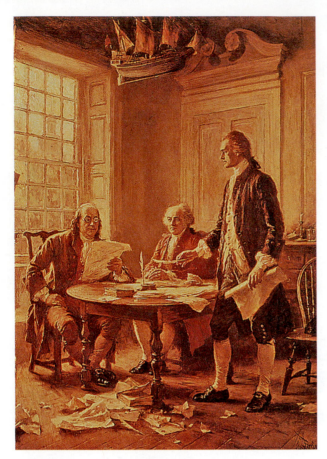

Drafting the Declaration of Independence, a painting by J. L. Ferris. Benjamin Franklin, John Adams (seated, center), and Thomas Jefferson (standing) drafted the historic document. Jefferson was the principal author; he inserted the inspirational words about liberty, equality, and self-government. The initial draft included criticism of slavery but it was removed out of fear that it would lead southern states to reject the call for independence.

Anti-Federalists

A term used to describe opponents of the Constitution during the debate over ratification.

The Ratification Debate

The debate over ratification was historic. The **Anti-Federalists** (as opponents of the Constitution were labeled) raised arguments that still echo in American politics. They claimed that the national government would be too powerful and would threaten self-government in the separate states and the liberty of the people. Many Americans had an innate distrust of centralized power and worried that the people's liberty could be eclipsed as easily by a distant American government as it had been by the British king.

The fact that the Constitution contained no bill of rights heightened this concern. Did its absence indicate that the central government would be free to define for itself what the people's rights would be? Patrick Henry expressed outrage at the omission, saying: "The necessity of a Bill of Rights appears to be greater in this government than ever it was in any government before." The proposed constitution, Henry noted, would require the states to surrender to Congress the powers of taxation, spending, and the military "without a Bill of Rights, without check, limitation, or control." The consequences in his mind were dire: "our republic will be lost, and tyranny must and will arise."

Looking ahead, the Anti-Federalists saw a central government controlled by political elites. The Anti-Federalists admired state governments for having legislatures in which the members were not greatly different in wealth from the voters who elected them. New York's Melancton Smith, a powerful public speaker, argued that such representatives are "more competent" than "those of a superior class" whose concerns were far removed from the realities of most people's lives. The election districts in the new Congress would be so large that ordinary people would not have much contact with their representatives, or they with the people they represented. "I am convinced," Smith said, that members of Congress will become "the natural aristocracy of the country. . . . The government will fall into the hands of the few and the great. This will be a government of repression."

The presidency was another source of contention. The office of chief executive did not exist under the Articles of Confederation, and some worried that it would degenerate into an American monarchy. The fact that the president would be chosen by electors appointed by the states (the Electoral College) lessened but did not eliminate this concern.

Even the motives of the men who wrote the Constitution came under attack. They were men of wealth and education who had acted in response to debtors' riots. Would the Constitution become a tool by which the wealthy ruled over those with little or no money? And who would bear the burden of additional taxation? For Americans struggling with local and state tax payments, the thought of also paying national taxes was not appealing.

The Anti-Federalists acknowledged the need for more economic cooperation between the states and for a stronger common defense, but they opposed the creation of a strong national government as the mechanism, arguing that a revision of the Articles of Confederation could accomplish these goals without the risk of establishing an overly powerful central government. (The Anti-Federalist argument is discussed further in Chapter 3.)

The **Federalists** (as the Constitution's supporters called themselves) responded with a persuasive case of their own. Their strongest arguments were set forth by James Madison and Alexander Hamilton, who along with John Jay wrote a series of essays (*The Federalist Papers*) that were published in a New York City newspaper under the pen name Publius. Madison and Hamilton argued that the government of the Constitution would correct the defects of the Articles; it would have the power necessary to forge a secure and prosperous union. At the same time, because of restrictions on its powers, the new government would endanger neither the states nor personal liberty. In *Federalist* Nos. 47, 48, 49, 50, and 51, for example, Madison explained how the separation of national institutions was designed both to empower and to restrict the federal government. (The Federalist argument is discussed further in Chapter 3.)

Whether the ratification debate changed many minds is unclear. Historical evidence suggests, however, that a majority of ordinary Americans opposed the Constitution's ratification. But their voice in the state ratifying conventions was smaller than that of wealthier interests, which in the main supported the change. The pro-ratification forces were also bolstered by the assumption that George Washington, the country's most trusted and popular leader, would become the first president. In the view of historians, this assumption, and the fact that Washington had presided over the Philadelphia convention, tipped the balance in favor of ratification.

Delaware was the first state to ratify the Constitution, and Connecticut, Georgia, and New Jersey soon followed, an indication that the Great Compromise had satisfied some of the small states. In the early summer of 1788, New Hampshire became the ninth state to ratify. The Constitution was law. But neither Virginia nor New York had ratified it, and a stable union without these two large states was almost unthinkable. As large in area as many European countries, they conceivably could have survived as independent nations. In fact, they nearly did choose a separate course. In both states, the Constitution passed only after Federalists said they would support changing it to include a bill of rights.

Federalists

A term used to describe supporters of the Constitution during the debate over ratification.

"Join, or Die" is one of America's most famous political cartoons. Created in 1754 by Benjamin Franklin, it became a symbol of freedom two decades later at the onset of the Revolutionary War. It was resurrected again during the debate over ratification of the Constitution.

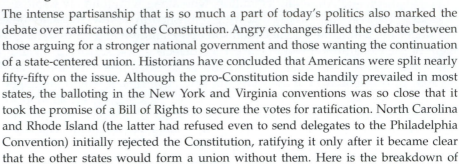

PARTY
POLARIZATION Political Thinking in Conflict

The Fight over Ratification of the Constitution

The intense partisanship that is so much a part of today's politics also marked the debate over ratification of the Constitution. Angry exchanges filled the debate between those arguing for a stronger national government and those wanting the continuation of a state-centered union. Historians have concluded that Americans were split nearly fifty-fifty on the issue. Although the pro-Constitution side handily prevailed in most states, the balloting in the New York and Virginia conventions was so close that it took the promise of a Bill of Rights to secure the votes for ratification. North Carolina and Rhode Island (the latter had refused even to send delegates to the Philadelphia Convention) initially rejected the Constitution, ratifying it only after it became clear that the other states would form a union without them. Here is the breakdown of the ratifying vote in each state:

State	Date of ratification	Vote totals
Delaware	December 12, 1787	46 for, 23 against
Pennsylvania	December 17, 1787	30 for, 0 against
New Jersey	December 18, 1787	38 for, 0 against
Georgia	January 2, 1788	26 for, 0 against
Connecticut	January 9, 1788	128 for, 40 against
Massachusetts	February 6, 1788	187 for, 168 against
Maryland	April 28, 1788	63 for, 11 against
South Carolina	May 23, 1788	149 for, 73 against
New Hampshire	June 21, 1788	57 for, 47 against
Virginia	June 25, 1788	89 for, 79 against
New York	July 26, 1788	30 for, 27 against
North Carolina	November 21, 1789	194 for, 77 against
Rhode Island	May 29, 1790	34 for, 32 against

Q. *If historians are correct in concluding that Americans were evenly split over ratification of the Constitution, why might the pro-Constitution side have prevailed in so many states and so easily in some states?*

A. *State and local governments were in charge of selecting the delegates to the state ratifying conventions. For the most part, they choose prominent individuals to serve as delegates, with the result that merchants, city dwellers, large landholders, and leading public officials were overrepresented at the conventions. These groups were more supportive of the Constitution than were the underrepresented groups, which included small farmers, craftsmen, and storeowners.*

The Framers' Goals

The Englishman James Bryce ranked America's Constitution as its greatest contribution to the practice of government. The Constitution offered the world a new model of government in which a written document defining the government's lawful powers would represent a higher authority than the dictates of any political leader or institution.

The Constitution embodied the framers' vision of a proper government for the American people (see Table 2-1). One of the framers' goals was the creation of a national government strong enough to meet the nation's needs, particularly in the areas of defense and commerce. Another goal was to preserve the states

TABLE 2-1 | Major Goals of the Framers of the Constitution

1. To establish a government strong enough to meet the nation's needs—an objective sought through substantial grants of power to the federal government in areas such as defense and commerce (see Chapter 3)
2. To establish a government that would not threaten the existence of the separate states—an objective sought through federalism (see Chapter 3) and through a Congress connected to the states through elections
3. To establish a government that would not threaten liberty—an objective sought through an elaborate system of checks and balances
4. To establish a government based on popular consent—an objective sought through provisions for the direct and indirect election of public officials

as governing entities. Accordingly, the framers established a system of government (federalism) in which power is divided between the national government and the states. Federalism is discussed at length in Chapter 3, which also explains how the Constitution laid the foundation for a strong national government.

The framers' other goals were to establish a national government that was restricted in its lawful uses of power (limited government) and that gave the people a voice in their governance (representative government). These two goals and the story of how they were written into the Constitution are the focus of the rest of this chapter.

Protecting Liberty: Limited Government

The framers of the Constitution sought a national government that could act decisively but not one that would act irresponsibly. History had taught them to mistrust unrestricted majority rule. In times of stress or danger, popular majorities had often acted recklessly, trampling on the liberty of others. In fact, **liberty**—the principle that individuals should be free to act and think as they choose, provided they do not infringe unreasonably on the freedom and well-being of others—was the governing ideal that the framers sought most to uphold. Americans enjoyed an unparalleled level of personal freedom as a result of their open society, and the framers were determined that it not be sacrificed to either European-style monarchy or mob-driven democracy.

The threat to liberty was inherent in government because of its coercive power. Government's unique characteristic is that it alone can legally arrest, imprison, or even kill people who violate its directives. Force is not the only basis by which government maintains order, but without it, lawless individuals would prey on innocent people. The dilemma is that government itself can use force to intimidate or brutalize its opponents. "It is a melancholy reflection," James Madison wrote to Thomas Jefferson shortly after the Constitution's ratification, "that liberty should be equally exposed to danger whether the government has too much or too little power."[7]

Grants and Denials of Power

The framers chose to limit the national government in part by confining its scope to constitutional **grants of power** (see Table 2-2). Congress's lawmaking powers are specifically listed in Article I, Section 8 of the Constitution. Seventeen in number, these listed powers include, for example, the powers to tax, establish an army and navy, declare war, regulate commerce among the states, create a

grants of power
The method of limiting the U.S. government by confining its scope of authority to those powers expressly granted in the Constitution.

TABLE 2-2 | Constitutional Provisions for Limited Government

Mechanism	Purpose
Grants of power	Powers granted to the national government; accordingly, powers not granted it are denied it unless they are necessary and proper to the carrying out of the granted powers.
Separated institutions	The division of the national government's power among three power-sharing branches, each of which is to act as a check on the powers of the other two.
Federalism	The division of political authority between the national government and the states, enabling the people to appeal to one authority if their rights and interests are not respected by the other authority.
Denials of power	Powers expressly denied to the national and state governments by the Constitution.
Bill of Rights	The first ten amendments to the Constitution, which specify rights of citizens that the national government must respect.
Judicial review	The power of the courts to declare governmental action null and void when it is found to violate the Constitution.
Elections	The power of the voters to remove officials from office.

denials of power

A constitutional means of limiting government by listing those powers that government is expressly prohibited from using.

national currency, and borrow money. Powers *not* granted to the government by the Constitution are in theory denied to it. In a period when other governments had unrestricted powers, this limitation was remarkable.

The framers also used **denials of power** as a means to limit government, prohibiting certain practices that European rulers had routinely used to oppress political opponents. The French king, for example, could imprison a subject indefinitely without charge. The U.S. Constitution prohibits such action: citizens have the right to be brought before a court under a writ of habeas corpus for a judgment as to the legality of their confinement. The Constitution also forbids Congress and the states from passing ex post facto laws, under which citizens can be prosecuted for acts that were legal at the time they were committed.

Although not strictly a further denial of power, the framers made the Constitution difficult to amend, thereby making it hard for those in office to increase their power by changing the rules. An amendment could be proposed only by a two-thirds majority in both chambers of Congress or by a national constitutional convention called by two-thirds of the state legislatures. Such a proposal would then become law only if ratified by three-fourths of state legislatures or state conventions. (Over the course of the nation's history, all amendments have been proposed by Congress and only one amendment—the Twenty-First, which repealed the prohibition on alcohol—was ratified by state conventions. The others were ratified by state legislatures.)

Using Power to Offset Power

Although the framers believed that grants and denials of power could act as controls on government, they had no illusion that written words alone would suffice. As a consequence, they sought to limit government by dividing its powers among separate branches.[8]

Decades earlier, the French theorist Montesquieu had argued that the power of government could be controlled by dividing it among separate branches rather than investing it entirely in a single individual or institution. His concept of a

separation of powers was widely admired in America, and when the states drafted new constitutions after the start of the Revolutionary War, they built their governments around the ideal. Pennsylvania was an exception, and its experience only seemed to prove the necessity of separated powers. Unrestrained by an independent judiciary or executive, Pennsylvania's all-powerful legislature ignored basic rights and freedoms: Quakers were disenfranchised for their religious beliefs, conscientious objectors to the Revolutionary War were prosecuted, and the right of trial by jury was eliminated.

In *Federalist* No. 10, Madison asked why governments often act according to the interests of overbearing majorities rather than according to principles of justice. He attributed the problem to "the mischiefs of faction." People, he argued, are divided into opposing religious, geographical, ethnic, economic, and other factions. These divisions are natural and desirable in that free people have a right to their personal opinions and interests. Yet if a faction gains full power, it will seek to use government to advance itself at the expense of all others. (*Federalist* No. 10 is widely regarded as the finest political essay ever written by an American. It is reprinted in this book's appendixes.)

Out of this concern came the framers' special contribution to the doctrine of the separation of powers. They did not believe that it would be enough, as Montesquieu had proposed, to divide the government's authority strictly along institutional lines, granting all legislative power to the legislature, all judicial power to the courts, and all executive power to the presidency. This total separation would make it too easy for a single faction to exploit a particular type of political power. A faction that controlled the legislature, for example, could enact laws ruinous to other interests. A safer system would be one in which each branch had the capacity to check the power of the others. This system would require separate but overlapping powers. Because no one faction could easily gain control over all institutions, factions would have to work together, a process that would result in compromise and moderation.[9]

Separated Institutions Sharing Power: Checks and Balances

Political scientist Richard Neustadt devised the term **separated institutions sharing power** to describe the framers' governing system.[10] The separate branches are interlocked in such a way that an elaborate system of **checks and balances** is created (see Figure 2-2). No institution can act decisively without the support or acquiescence of the other institutions. Legislative, executive, and judicial powers in the American system are divided in such a way that they overlap: each of the three branches of government checks the others' powers and balances those powers with powers of its own.

As natural as this system now might seem to Americans, most democracies are of the parliamentary type, with executive and legislative power combined in a single institution rather than vested in separate ones. In a parliamentary system, the majority in the legislature selects the prime minister, who then serves as both the legislative leader and the chief executive (see "How the U.S. Differs" on p. 41).

Shared Legislative Powers

Under the Constitution, Congress has legislative authority, but that power is partly shared with the other branches and thus is checked by them. The president can veto acts of Congress, recommend legislation, and call special sessions of Congress.

---

separation of powers

The division of the powers of government among separate institutions or branches.

separated institutions sharing power

The principle that, as a way to limit government, its powers should be divided among separate branches, each of which also shares in the power of the others as a means of checking and balancing them. The result is that no one branch can exercise power decisively without the support or acquiescence of the others.

checks and balances

The elaborate system of divided spheres of authority provided by the U.S. Constitution as a means of controlling the power of government. The separation of powers among the branches of the national government, federalism, and the different methods of selecting national officers are all part of this system.

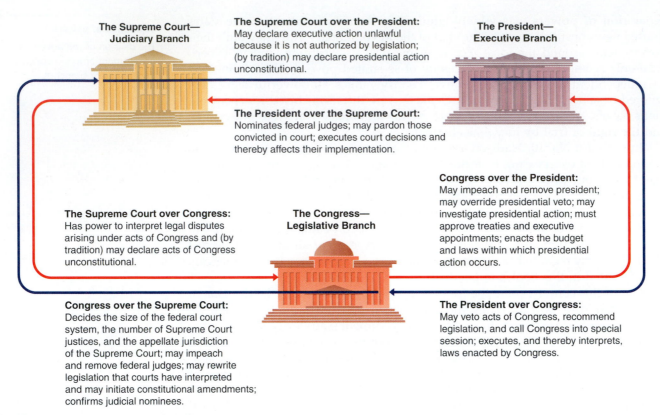

The Supreme Court—Judiciary Branch

The Supreme Court over the President: May declare executive action unlawful because it is not authorized by legislation; (by tradition) may declare presidential action unconstitutional.

The President—Executive Branch

The President over the Supreme Court: Nominates federal judges; may pardon those convicted in court; executes court decisions and thereby affects their implementation.

Congress over the President: May impeach and remove president; may override presidential veto; may investigate presidential action; must approve treaties and executive appointments; enacts the budget and laws within which presidential action occurs.

The Supreme Court over Congress: Has power to interpret legal disputes arising under acts of Congress and (by tradition) may declare acts of Congress unconstitutional.

The Congress—Legislative Branch

Congress over the Supreme Court: Decides the size of the federal court system, the number of Supreme Court justices, and the appellate jurisdiction of the Supreme Court; may impeach and remove federal judges; may rewrite legislation that courts have interpreted and may initiate constitutional amendments; confirms judicial nominees.

The President over Congress: May veto acts of Congress, recommend legislation, and call Congress into special session; executes, and thereby interprets, laws enacted by Congress.

FIGURE 2-2 **The System of Checks and Balances** This elaborate system of divided spheres of authority was provided by the U.S. Constitution as a means of controlling the power of government. The separation of powers among the branches of the national government; federalism, and the different methods of selecting national officers are all part of this system.

The president also has the power to execute—and thereby interpret—the laws Congress makes.

The Supreme Court has the power to interpret acts of Congress that are disputed in legal cases. The Court also has the power of judicial review: it can declare laws of Congress void when it finds that they are not in accord with the Constitution.

Within Congress, there is a further check on legislative power: for legislation to be passed, a majority in each chamber of Congress is required. Thus, the Senate and the House of Representatives can block each other from acting.

Shared Executive Powers

Executive power is vested in the president but is constrained by legislative and judicial checks. The president's power to make treaties and appoint high-ranking officials, for example, is subject to Senate approval. Congress also has the power to impeach and remove the president from office. In practical terms, Congress's greatest checks on executive action are its lawmaking and appropriations powers. The executive branch cannot act without laws that authorize its activities or without the money that pays for these activities.

The judiciary's major check on the presidency is its power to declare an action unlawful because it is not authorized by the laws that the executive claims to be implementing.

Checks and Balances

All democracies place constitutional limits on the power of government. The concept of rule by law, for example, is characteristic of democratic governments but not of authoritarian regimes. Democracies differ, however, in the extent to which political power is restrained through constitutional mechanisms. The United States is an extreme case in that its government rests on an elaborate system of constitutional checks and balances. The system employs a separation of powers among the executive, legislative, and judicial branches. It also includes judicial review, the power of the courts to invalidate actions of the legislative or executive branch. These constitutional restrictions on power are not part of the governing structure of all democracies. The courts in France and Great Britain, for example, do not have the power of judicial review. Most democracies have parliamentary systems, which invest both executive and legislative leadership in the office of prime minister. Britain is an example of this type of system. Parliament under the leadership of the prime minister is the supreme authority in Britain. Its laws are not subject to override by Britain's high court, which has no power to review the constitutionality of parliamentary acts. Moreover, in parliamentary systems there is typically only one legislative chamber or, if two, the second has much less

power. The British House of Lords, for example, has only a limited ability to check the actions of the British House of Commons, which the prime minister heads. In the United States, the two legislative chambers—the House and the Senate—are coequal bodies. Because legislation can be enacted only with the approval of both houses, each serves as a check on the other.

Q: The framers of the Constitution saw checks and balances as a means of fostering political moderation. Is there a relationship between the number of checks and balances Western democracies have and their tendency toward political moderation?

A: There is no clear relationship. Great Britain, for example, is often cited as an example of political moderation although it lacks an elaborate system of checks and balances. By contrast, Mexico, which has such a system, is often held up as an example of political extremes. This fragmentary evidence does not mean that checks and balances are ineffective in controlling power, but the evidence does suggest that other factors, such as a country's political culture, must also be taken into account in any full explanation of political moderation.

Shared Judicial Powers

Judicial power rests with the Supreme Court and with lower federal courts, which are subject to checks by the other branches of the federal government. Congress is empowered to establish the size of the federal court system, to restrict the Supreme Court's appellate jurisdiction in some circumstances, and to impeach and remove federal judges from office. More important, Congress can rewrite legislation that the courts have misinterpreted and can initiate amendments when it disagrees with court rulings on constitutional issues.

The president has the power to appoint federal judges with the consent of the Senate and to pardon persons convicted in the courts. The president also is responsible for executing court decisions, a function that provides opportunities to influence the way rulings are carried out.

The Bill of Rights

Although the delegates to the Philadelphia convention discussed the possibility of placing a list of individual rights (such as freedom of speech and the right to a fair trial) in the Constitution, they ultimately decided that such a list was unnecessary because of the doctrine of expressed powers: government could not lawfully engage in actions, such as the suppression of speech, that were not authorized by the Constitution. Moreover, the delegates argued that a bill of rights was undesirable because government might feel free to disregard any right that was inadvertently left off the list or that might emerge in the future.

The Constitution was written in Philadelphia during the summer of 1787 in the East Room of the Old Pennsylvania State House, where the Declaration of Independence had been signed a decade earlier. George Washington (standing on the right) presided over the constitutional convention. As presiding officer, Washington remained neutral during the deliberations, allowing the other delegates to debate and decide upon the Constitution's provisions.

Bill of Rights

The first ten amendments to the Constitution. They include rights such as freedom of speech and religion.

These arguments did not persuade leading Americans who believed that no possible safeguard of liberty should be omitted. Of particular concern was the fact that the Constitution, unlike the Articles of Confederation, granted the federal government direct authority over individual citizens and yet did not contain a list of their rights. "A bill of rights," Jefferson argued, "is what the people are entitled to against every government on earth, general or particular, and what no just government should refuse or rest on inference." Jefferson had included a bill of rights in the constitution he wrote for Virginia at the outbreak of the Revolutionary War, and all but four states had followed Virginia's example.

Ultimately, the demand for a bill of rights led to its addition to the Constitution. Madison himself introduced a series of amendments during the First Congress, ten of which were soon ratified by the states. These amendments, traditionally called the **Bill of Rights,** include rights such as freedom of speech and religion and due process protections (such as the right to a jury trial) for persons accused of crimes. (These rights, termed *civil liberties*, are discussed in Chapter 4.)

The Bill of Rights is a precise expression of the concept of limited government. In consenting to be governed, the people agree to accept the authority of government in certain areas but not in others; the people's constitutional rights cannot lawfully be denied by government officials.

Judicial Review

The writers of the Constitution both empowered and limited government. But who was to decide whether officials were operating within the limits of their constitutionally authorized powers? The framers did not specifically entrust this power to a particular branch of government, although they did grant the Supreme Court the authority to decide on "all cases arising under this Constitution." Moreover, at the ratifying conventions of at least eight of the thirteen states, it was claimed that the judiciary would have the power to nullify actions that violated the Constitution.[11]

Nevertheless, because the Constitution did not explicitly grant the judiciary this authority, the principle had to be established in practice. The opportunity arose with an incident that occurred after the election of 1800, in which John Adams lost his bid for a second presidential term after a bitter campaign against

DEBATING THE ISSUES   POLITICAL THINKING IN ACTION

Should the President Have the Power to Send the Nation to War?

In dividing the powers of government, but overlapping them, the framers of the Constitution sought to control the uses of power. Few aspects of this system have provoked more controversy than the question of whether the president has the unilateral authority to wage war. The Constitution assigns to Congress the power "to declare war," while granting to the president the authority as "commander in chief of the Army and Navy of the United States." It was understood from the beginning that the president could act unilaterally in the case of an invasion of the United States because an immediate military response would be required. But what if the United States is not under immediate and direct threat? Does the president have the authority to act unilaterally in this situation? In practice, presidents have assumed the authority to do so. American involvement in the Korean, Vietnam, Iraq, and Afghanistan wars was initiated by presidential order rather than by a congressional declaration of war. When President Barack Obama in 2011 ordered U.S. military aircraft to bomb the Libyan forces of the dictator Moammar Gadhafi, he did so based on his authority as commander in chief and without seeking approval from Congress. Such actions have provoked debate about whether modern presidents have assumed authority beyond what the Constitution provides. Here are two different views on the issue. The first is the opinion of John Yoo, who was deputy legal counsel to President George W. Bush. The opposing position is argued by Louis Fisher, a constitutional law scholar at the Library of Congress.

YES The power of the President is at its zenith under the Constitution when the President is directing military operations of the armed forces, because the power of Commander in Chief is assigned solely to the President. It has long been the view of this Office that the Commander-in-Chief Clause is a substantive grant of authority to the President and that the scope of the President's authority to commit the armed forces to combat is very broad. . . . If the Framers had wanted to require congressional consent before the initiation of military hostilities, they knew how to write such provisions. . . . [I]t is clear that Congress's power to declare war does not constrain the President's independent and plenary constitutional authority over the use of military force. . . . There can be little doubt that the decision to deploy military force is "executive" in nature, and was traditionally so regarded. It calls for action and energy in execution, rather than the deliberate formulation of rules to govern the conduct of private individuals. Moreover, the Framers understood it to be an attribute of the executive. "The direction of war implies the direction of the common strength," wrote Alexander Hamilton [*Federalist* No. 74], "and the power of directing and employing the common strength forms a usual and essential part in the definition of the executive authority." As a result, to the extent that the constitutional text does not explicitly allocate the power to initiate military hostilities to a particular branch . . . it remain[s] among the President's unenumerated powers.

—*John Yoo, former deputy counsel to the president*

NO Referring to the title "commander in chief" does not explain what powers go with it. The powers do not include starting wars. Identifying only the war-declaring clause of Congress ignores seven other clauses in the U.S. Constitution that vest in the legislative branch military and national security powers (raise and support armies, make rules for the military, grant letters of marque and reprisal, call forth the militia, provide for organizing, arming, and disciplining the militia . . .). For 160 years, there was no ambiguity. Until President Harry S Truman went to war on his own in 1950 against North Korea, no one recognized a conflict or tension between the war-declaring power of Congress and the commander-in-chief responsibilities of the president. No one argued that the president could initiate war. The president was only commander in chief *after* Congress declared or authorized war. He had certain limited defensive powers ("to repel sudden attacks"). There was nothing ambiguous about the constitutional requirement that Congress is the branch of government authorized to decide to take the country from a state of peace to a state of war. . . . James Madison . . . wrote to Thomas Jefferson that the Constitution "supposes, what the History of all Governments demonstrates, that the Executive is the branch of power most interested in war, and most prone to it. It has accordingly with studied care vested the question of war in the Legislature."

—*Louis Fisher, constitutional scholar, Library of Congress*

Q. Which interpretation of the Constitution do you find more persuasive? If you believe the president's power to wage war is far reaching, how do you reconcile that with the principle of checks and balances on the uses of power? If you believe that Congress should have the power to decide whether war will be waged, would that power extend also to the scale of the war or would the president have the power to determine the level of military involvement?

Jefferson. Between November 1800, when Jefferson was elected, and March 1801, when he was inaugurated, the Federalist-controlled Congress created fifty-nine additional lower-court judgeships, enabling Adams to appoint loyal Federalists to the positions before he left office. However, Adams' term expired before his secretary of state could deliver the judicial commissions to all the appointees. Without this authorization, an appointee could not take office. Knowing this, Jefferson told his secretary of state, James Madison, not to deliver the commissions. William Marbury was one of those who did not receive his commission, and he asked the Supreme Court to issue a writ of mandamus (a court order directing an official to perform a specific act) that would force Madison to deliver it.

Marbury v. Madison (1803) became the foundation for judicial review by the federal courts. Chief Justice John Marshall wrote the *Marbury* opinion, which declared that Marbury had a legal right to his commission. The opinion also said, however, that the Supreme Court could not issue him a writ of mandamus because it lacked the constitutional authority to do so. Congress had passed legislation in 1789 that gave the Court this power, but Marshall noted that the Constitution prohibits Congress from expanding the Supreme Court's authority except through a constitutional amendment. That being the case, Marshall argued, the legislation that provided the authorization was constitutionally invalid.[12] In striking down this act of Congress on constitutional grounds, the Court asserted its power of **judicial review**—that is, the power of the judiciary to decide whether a government official or institution has acted within the limits of the Constitution and, if not, to declare its action null and void.

Marshall's decision was ingenious because it asserted the power of judicial review without creating the possibility of its rejection by either the executive or the legislative branch. In declaring that Marbury had a right to his commission, the Court in effect said that President Jefferson had failed in his constitutional duty to execute the laws faithfully. However, because it did not order Jefferson to deliver the commission, he was deprived of the opportunity to disregard the Court's ruling. At the same time, the Court reprimanded Congress for passing legislation that exceeded its constitutional authority. But Congress also had no way to retaliate. It could not force the Court to accept the power to issue writs of mandamus if the Court itself refused to do so.

Providing for Representative Government

"We the People" is the opening phrase of the Constitution. It expresses the idea that in the United States the people will have the power to govern themselves. In a sense, there is no contradiction between this idea and the Constitution's provisions for limited government, because individual *liberty* is an essential element of *representative government*. If people cannot express themselves freely, they cannot be truly self-governing. In another sense, however, the contradiction is clear: restrictions on the power of the majority are a denial of its right to govern society as it sees fit.

The framers believed that the people deserved and required a voice in their government, but they worried that the people would become inflamed by a passionate issue or fiery demagogue and act rashly. To the framers, the great risk of popular government was **tyranny of the majority**: the people acting as an irrational mob that tramples on the rights of the minority. The history of unfettered democracies was not encouraging, leading James Madison to say in *Federalist* No. 10 that they "have ever been spectacles of turbulence and

judicial review

The power of courts to decide whether a governmental institution has acted within its constitutional powers and, if not, to declare its action null and void.

tyranny of the majority

The potential of a majority to monopolize power for its own gain to the detriment of minority rights and interests.

contention; have ever been found incompatible with personal security or the rights of property; and have in general been as short in their lives as they have been violent in their deaths."

Democracy versus Republic

No form of representative government could eliminate completely the threat to liberty of majority tyranny, but the framers believed that the danger would be greatly diminished by creating a republican government as opposed to a democratic government.[13] Today, the terms *democracy, republic,* and *representative government* are often used interchangeably to refer to a system of government in which political power rests with the people through their ability to choose representatives in free and fair elections. To the writers of the Constitution, however, a democracy and a republic were different forms of government.

By the term **democracy,** the framers meant a government in which the power of the majority is unlimited, whether exercised directly (as in the case of town meetings open to all citizens) or through a representative body. The majority's will is absolute. Should it decide to act tyrannically—to run roughshod over the minority—there is nothing in the law to stop it. By the term **republic,** the framers meant a government that consists of carefully designed institutions that are responsive to the majority but not captive to it. It is representative democracy in a true sense, but the people's representatives decide policy through institutions that are structured in ways that foster deliberation, slow the decision process, and operate within constraints that protect individual rights. A republic is designed, not to prevent the people from having a say in their governing, but to filter popular sentiment in ways that reduce the likelihood of hasty, ill-conceived, and reckless policies. To the framers, the Constitution's separation of powers and other limits on power were features of the republican form of government, as opposed to the democratic form, which places no limits on the majority.[14]

The framers believed that a republic, to work well in practice, requires virtuous representatives—lawmakers who have an enlightened sense of the public interest. Their outlook mirrored that of the English theorist Edmund Burke. In his *Letter to the Sheriffs of Bristol* in 1777, Burke argued that representatives should act as the public's **trustees;** representatives are obliged to serve the interest of those who elect them, but the nature of this interest is for the representatives, not the voters, to decide. Burke was concerned with the ease with which a majority can behave like a mob, and he argued that representatives should not surrender their judgment to irrational majorities.

Limited Popular Rule

The Constitution provided that all power would be exercised through representative institutions. There was no provision for any form of direct popular participation in the making of policy decisions. In view of the fact that the United States was much too large to be governed directly by the people in popular assemblies, a representative system was a necessity. However, the framers went beyond this point, creating a system of representation that placed most federal officials a step removed from the people they represented (see Table 2-3).

The House of Representatives was the only institution that would be based on direct popular election—its members would be elected to serve for two years by a vote of the people. Frequent and direct election of House members was intended to make government responsive to the concerns of popular majorities.

James Madison has been called "the father of the Constitution." Madison himself rejected that label, but he was the framer who saw most clearly how the new government should be structured. Through his *Federalist* essays, Madison was also instrumental in securing ratification of the Constitution. Madison would go on to serve as the nation's fourth president.

democracy (according to the framers)

A form of government in which the power of the majority is unlimited, whether exercised directly or through a representative body.

republic

A form of government in which the people's representatives decide policy through institutions structured in ways that foster deliberation, slow the progress of decision making, and operate within restraints that protect individual liberty. To the framers, the Constitution's separation of powers and other limits on power were defining features of a republican form of government, as opposed to a democratic form, which places no limits on the majority.

trustees

Elected representatives whose obligation is to act in accordance with their own consciences as to what policies are in the best interests of the public.

TABLE 2-3 | Original Methods of Choosing National Leaders

Office	Method of selection	Term of service
President	Electoral College	4 years
U.S. senator	State legislature	6 years (one-third of senators' terms expire every 2 years)
U.S. representative	Popular election	2 years
Federal judge	Nominated by president, approved by Senate	Indefinite (subject to "good behavior")

Electoral College

An unofficial term that refers to the electors who cast the states' electoral votes.

electoral votes

The method of voting used to choose the U.S. president. Each state has the same number of electoral votes as it has members in Congress (House and Senate combined). By tradition, electoral voting is tied to a state's popular voting. The candidate with the most popular votes in a state (or, in a few states, the most votes in a congressional district) receives its electoral votes.

U.S. senators would be appointed by the legislatures of the states they represented. Because state legislators were popularly elected, the people would be choosing their senators indirectly. Every two years, a third of the senators would be appointed to six-year terms. The Senate was expected to check and balance the House. The Senate, by virtue of the less frequent and indirect election of its members, was expected to be less responsive to popular pressure.

Presidential selection was an issue of considerable debate at the Philadelphia convention. Direct election of the president was twice proposed and twice rejected because it would link executive power directly to popular majorities. The framers finally chose to have the president selected by the votes of electors (the so-called **Electoral College**). Each state would have the same number of **electoral votes** as it had members in Congress and could select its electors by a method of its choosing. The president would serve four years and be eligible for reelection.

The framers decided that federal judges and justices would be appointed rather than elected. They would be nominated by the president and confirmed through approval by the Senate. Once confirmed, they would "hold their offices during good behavior." In effect, they would be allowed to hold office for life unless they committed a crime. The judiciary was an unelected institution that would uphold the rule of law and serve as a check on the elected branches of government.[15]

These differing methods of selecting national officeholders would not prevent a determined majority from achieving unchecked power, but control could not be attained quickly. Unlike the House of Representatives, institutions such as the Senate, presidency, and judiciary would not yield to an impassioned majority in a single election. The delay would reduce the chance that government would degenerate into mob rule driven by momentary passions.

Altering the Constitution: More Power to the People

The framers' conception of representative government was at odds with what the average American in 1787 would have expected.[16] Self-government was an ideal that had led tens of thousands of ordinary farmers, merchants, and tradesmen to risk their lives in the American Revolution. The ensuing state constitutions had put the ideal into practice. Every state but South Carolina held annual legislative elections, and several states also chose their governors through direct annual election.

Not long after ratification of the Constitution, Americans began to challenge the Constitution's restrictions on majority rule (see Table 2-4).

Jeffersonian Democracy: A Revolution of the Spirit

Thomas Jefferson was among the prominent Americans who questioned the Constitution's limited provisions for self-government. In a letter to Madison, he objected to its system of representation, voicing the Anti-Federalist's fear that

TABLE 2-4 | Measures Taken to Make Government More Responsive to Popular Majorities

Earlier situation	Subsequent development
Separation of powers, as a means of dividing authority and blunting passionate majorities	Political parties, as a means of uniting authorities and linking them with popular majorities
Indirect election of all national officials except House members, as a means of buffering officials from popular influence	Direct election of U.S. senators and popular voting for president (linked to electoral votes), as a means of increasing popular control of officials
Nomination of candidates for public office through political party organizations	Primary elections, as a direct means of selecting party nominees

federal officials would lose touch with the people and discount their interests. His concern intensified when John Adams became president after Washington's retirement. Under Adams, the national government increasingly favored the nation's wealthy interests. Adams publicly indicated that the Constitution was designed for a governing elite and hinted that he might use force to suppress dissent.[17] Jefferson asked whether Adams, with the aid of a strong army, intended to deprive ordinary people of their rights. Jefferson challenged Adams in the next presidential election and, upon defeating him, hailed his victory as the "Revolution of 1800."

Although Jefferson was a champion of the common people, he had no clear vision of how a popular government might work in practice. He saw Congress, not the presidency, as the institution better suited to representing majority opinion.[18] He also had no illusions about the ability of a largely uneducated population to play a substantial governing role and feared the consequences of inciting the masses to rise against the rich. Jeffersonian democracy was mostly a revolution of

The framers' mistrust of popular majorities has been stood on its head. During the past century, the public has been mistrustful of politicians. The Progressive movement was an early manifestation of this attitude. A more recent one is the term-limit movement, which seeks to restrict the length of time that elected officials can hold office.

the spirit. Jefferson taught Americans to look on national government institutions as belonging to all, not just to the privileged few.[19]

Jacksonian Democracy: Linking the People and the Presidency

Not until the election of Andrew Jackson in 1828 did the nation have a powerful president who was willing and able to involve the public more fully in government. Jackson carried out the constitutional revolution that Jeffersonian democracy had foreshadowed.

Jackson recognized that the president was the only official who could legitimately claim to represent the people as a whole. Unlike the president, members of Congress were elected from separate states and districts rather than from the entire country. Yet the president's claim to popular leadership was weakened by the fact that the president was chosen by electors rather than by the voters. To connect the presidency more closely to the people, Jackson urged the states to award their electoral votes to the candidate who wins the state's popular vote. Soon thereafter, nearly all states adopted this method. This arrangement, still in effect, places the selection of the president in the voters' hands in most elections. The candidate who gets the most popular votes nationally is also likely to finish first in enough states to win a majority of the electoral votes. Since Jackson's time, only three candidates—Rutherford B. Hayes in 1876, Benjamin Harrison in 1888, and George W. Bush in 2000—have won the presidency after losing the popular vote. (The Electoral College is discussed further in Chapter 12.)

The Progressives: Senate and Primary Elections

The Progressive Era of the early 1900s brought another wave of democratic reforms. The Progressives rejected the Burkean idea of representatives as trustees, instead embracing the idea of representatives as **delegates**—officeholders who are obligated to carry out the expressed opinions of the people they represent.

The Progressives sought to place power more directly in the hands of the people.[20] They succeeded in changing the way some state and local governments operate. Progressive reforms at state and local levels include the initiative and the referendum, which enable citizens to vote directly on legislative issues (see "How the 50 States Differ"). Another Progressive reform is the recall election, which enables citizens through petition to force an officeholder to submit to reelection before the regular expiration of his or her term. (In 2003, a recall election enabled actor Arnold Schwarzenegger to become California's governor.)

The Progressives also instigated two changes in federal elections. One was the **primary election,** which gives rank-and-file voters the power to select party nominees. In the early 1900s, nearly all states adopted the primary election as a means of choosing nominees for at least some federal and state offices. Prior to this change, nominees were selected by party leaders. The second change was the direct election of U.S. senators, who before the ratification of the Seventeenth Amendment in 1913 were chosen by state legislatures and were widely perceived as agents of big business (the Senate was nicknamed the "Millionaires' Club"). Senators who stood to lose their seats in a direct popular vote had blocked earlier attempts to change the Constitution. However, as a result of several developments, including revelations that a number of senators owed their seats to corporate bribes, the Senate was finally persuaded to support the amendment.

The Progressive Era even spawned attacks on the framers. A prominent criticism was laid out in historian Charles S. Beard's *An Economic Interpretation*

---

delegates

Elected representatives whose obligation is to act in accordance with the expressed wishes of the people they represent.

---

primary election

A form of election in which voters choose a party's nominees for public office. In most states, eligibility to vote in a party's primary election is limited to voters who are registered members of the party.

HOW THE 50 STATES DIFFER POLITICAL THINKING THROUGH COMPARISONS

Direct Democracy: The Initiative and Popular Referendum

In some states, by gathering enough signatures on a petition, citizens can directly enact or defeat legislation through their votes in an election. This action can occur through either an initiative (in which citizens place a legislative proposal of their own choosing on the ballot) or a popular referendum (in which citizens place an act of the state legislature on the ballot, which the voters can then accept or reject). A popular referendum is different from a legislative referendum, in which the state legislature itself places a proposal on the ballot for the voters to accept or reject. All states have a form of the legislative referendum, but only some states, as indicated in the map below, have the initiative and the popular referendum.

Q: Why are the northeastern and southern states less likely than states in other regions to have the initiative and popular referendum?

A: The initiative and popular referendum were introduced in the early 1900s by the Progressives, who sought to weaken the power of political bosses and give voters a larger voice in their governance. In the Northeast, party machines had enough strength in state legislatures to block their enactment. In the South, these devices were blocked by the white establishment, which feared that blacks and poor whites might use them to gain power.

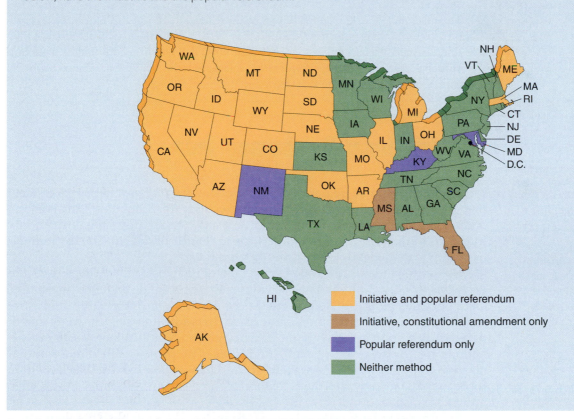

Source: From Initiative and Referendum Institute, University of Southern California. Reprinted with permission.

of the Constitution.[21] Arguing that the Constitution grew out of wealthy Americans' fears of the debtor rebellions, Beard claimed that the Constitution's elaborate systems of power and representation were devices for keeping power in the hands of the rich. As evidence, Beard cited the Constitution's protections of property and referred to Madison's notes on the Philadelphia convention, which showed that property concerns were high on the framers' agenda. Beard further noted that not one of the delegates was a workingman or farmer. Most of the framers had large landholdings and controlled substantial interests, or were major credit holders.

Beard's thesis was challenged by other historians, and he later acknowledged that he had not taken the framers' full array of motives into account. Their conception of separation of powers, for example, was a governing principle that had earlier been incorporated into state constitutions. Nevertheless, Beard held onto his claim that the Constitution was designed to protect the interests of the wealthy rather than to promote self-government.

Beard's claim has some validity, but to say that the framers were foes of democracy is inaccurate. Although they did not have great trust in popular rule, they were determined to balance the need to create a system of self-government with the need to create a system of limited government. Convinced that unchecked majority rule was likely to devolve into tyranny, the framers devised institutions that were responsive to majority opinion but not beholden to it.

POLITICAL THINKING   Trustees or Delegates?

Theorists and practitioners have long argued over the proper role of elected representatives. What is your view? Should they behave as trustees, who act in what they think is society's best interest, even if their judgment conflicts with that of their constituents? Or should they perform as delegates, who act in accordance with the expressed desires of those they represent?

Constitutional Democracy Today

constitutional democratic republic

A government that is constitutional in its provisions for minority rights and rule by law; democratic in its provisions for majority influence through elections; and a republic in its mix of deliberative institutions, which check and balance each other.

The type of government created in the United States in 1787 could accurately be called a **constitutional democratic republic.** It is *constitutional* in its requirement that power gained through elections be exercised in accordance with law and with due respect for individual rights; *democratic* in its provisions for majority influence through elections; and a *republic* in its mix of deliberative institutions, each of which moderates the power of the others.[22]

By some standards, the American system of today is a model of *representative government*.[23] The United States schedules the election of its larger legislative chamber (the House of Representatives) and its chief executive more frequently than does any other democracy. In addition, it is the only major democracy to rely extensively on primary elections rather than party organizations for the selection of party nominees. The principle of direct popular election to office, which the writers of the Constitution regarded as a method to be used sparingly, has been extended further in the United States than anywhere else.

By other standards, however, the U.S. system is less democratic than some. Popular majorities must work against the barriers to power devised by the framers—divided branches, staggered terms of office, and separate constituencies. In fact, the link between an electoral majority and a governing majority is less direct in the American system than in nearly all other democratic systems. In the European parliamentary democracies, for example, legislative and executive power is not divided, is not subject to close check by the judiciary, and is acquired through the winning of a legislative majority in a single national election. The framers' vision was a different one, dominated by a concern with liberty and therefore with controls on political power. It was a response to the experiences they brought with them to Philadelphia in the summer of 1787.

Summary
Self-Test www.mhhe.com/ pattersontadtx11e

The Constitution of the United States is a reflection of the colonial and revolutionary experiences of the early Americans. Freedom from abusive government was a reason for the colonies' revolt against British rule, but the English tradition also provided ideas about government, power, and freedom that were expressed in the Constitution and, earlier, in the Declaration of Independence.

The Constitution was designed in part to provide for a limited government in which political power would be confined to proper uses. The framers wanted to ensure that the government they were creating would not itself be a threat to freedom. To this end, they confined the national government to expressly granted powers and also denied it certain specific powers. Other prohibitions on government were later added to the Constitution in the form of stated guarantees of individual liberties in the Bill of Rights. The most significant constitutional provision for limited government, however, was a separation of powers among the three branches. The powers given to each branch enable it to act as a check on the exercise of power by the other two, an arrangement that during the nation's history has in fact served as a barrier to abuses of power.

The Constitution, however, made no mention of how the powers and limits of government were to be judged in practice.

In its historic ruling in *Marbury v. Madison*, the Supreme Court assumed the authority to review the constitutionality of legislative and executive actions and to declare them unconstitutional and thus invalid.

The framers of the Constitution, respecting the idea of self-government but distrusting popular majorities, devised a system of government that they felt would temper popular opinion and slow its momentum so that the public's "true interest" (which includes a regard for the rights and interests of the minority) would guide public policy. Different methods were advanced for selecting the president, the members of the House and the Senate, and federal judges as a means of insulating political power against momentary majorities.

Since the adoption of the Constitution, the public gradually has assumed more direct control of its representatives, particularly through measures that affect the way officeholders are chosen. Presidential popular voting (linked to the Electoral College), direct election of senators, and primary elections are among the devices aimed at strengthening the majority's influence. These developments are rooted in the idea, deeply held by ordinary Americans, that the people must have substantial direct influence over their representatives if government is to serve their interests.

CHAPTER 2

Study Corner

Key Terms

Anti-Federalists (*p. 34*)
Bill of Rights (*p. 42*)
checks and balances (*p. 39*)
constitution (*p. 28*)
constitutional democratic republic (*p. 50*)
delegates (*p. 48*)
democracy (according to the framers) (*p. 45*)
denials of power (*p. 38*)
Electoral College (*p. 46*)
electoral votes (*p. 46*)
Federalists (*p. 35*)
grants of power (*p. 37*)

Great Compromise (*p. 31*)
inalienable (natural) rights (*p. 28*)
judicial review (*p. 44*)
limited government (*p. 25*)
New Jersey (small-state) Plan (*p. 31*)
primary election (*p. 48*)
representative government (*p. 26*)
republic (*p. 45*)
separated institutions sharing power (*p. 39*)
separation of powers (*p. 39*)

social contract (*p. 28*)
Three-Fifths Compromise (*p. 32*)
trustees (*p. 45*)
tyranny of the majority (*p. 44*)
Virginia (large-state) Plan (*p. 31*)

Self-Test: Multiple Choice

1. The principle of checks and balances in the U.S. system of government
   a. requires the federal budget to be a balanced budget.
   b. provides that checks cashed at U.S. banks will be honored as legal tender.
   c. was a principle invented by the Progressives.
   d. allows the majority's will to work through representative institutions but places checks on the power of those institutions.

2. The U.S. Constitution provides for limited government mainly
   a. through direct election of representatives.
   b. through indirect systems of popular election of representatives.
   c. by defining lawful powers and by dividing those powers among competing institutions.
   d. by making state law superior to national law when the two conflict.

3. The U.S. Constitution provides for representative government mainly
   a. through direct and indirect systems of popular election of representatives.
   b. by defining the lawful powers of government.
   c. by dividing governing powers among competing institutions.
   d. by giving the majority absolute power to govern as it pleases.

4. The Articles of Confederation
   a. established a weak central government that was subordinate to the states.
   b. defined the legal relationship between the colonies and Great Britain.
   c. were proposed by the Progressives as a means of strengthening the power of the voters.
   d. were the constitutional articles proposed by the southern states at the 1787 Philadelphia convention.

5. The addition of the Bill of Rights to the U.S. Constitution meant that
   a. a list of individual rights would be protected by law.
   b. the Anti-Federalists no longer had any reason to oppose the adoption of the Constitution.
   c. the national government could infringe on the rights of the states.
   d. the state governments could infringe on the rights of the national government.

6. Of the issues taken up during the constitutional convention, which one consumed the most time and attention?
   a. structure of the presidency
   b. structure of Congress
   c. structure and powers of the federal judiciary
   d. ratification of the new Constitution

7. The framers of the Constitution feared political apathy more than tyranny of the majority. (T/F)

8. The idea of popular government—in which the majority's desires have a more direct and immediate impact on public policy—has gained strength since the nation's beginning. (T/F)

9. The Supreme Court decision in *Marbury v. Madison* gave courts the power to declare governmental action null and void when it is found to violate the Constitution. (T/F)

10. The Virginia Plan (also known as the large-state plan) called for a Congress with equal representation of each state but with greatly strengthened powers. (T/F)

Self-Test: Essay

How does the division of power in the U.S. political system contribute to limited government? How do the provisions for representative government (the various methods of choosing national officials) contribute to limited government?

Suggested Readings

Beard, Charles S. *An Economic Interpretation of the Constitution.* New York: Macmillan, 1941. Argues that the framers had selfish economic interests uppermost in their minds when they wrote the Constitution.

Ellis, Joseph J. *Founding Brothers: The Revolutionary Generation.* New York: Vintage, 2002. A riveting account of the lives of America's leading founders.

Federalist Papers. Many editions, including a one-volume paperback version edited by Isaac Kramnick (New York: Penguin, 1987). A series of essays written by Alexander Hamilton, James Madison, and John Jay under the pseudonym Publius; the essays, published in a New York newspaper in 1787–1788, explain the Constitution and support its ratification.

Ostrom, Vincent. *The Political Theory of a Compound Republic: Designing the American Experiment.* Lanham, Md.: Lexington Books, 2007. An analysis of the logic of the Constitution as its writers envisioned it.

Pottinger, John R. *Reaping the Whirlwind: Liberal Democracy and the Religious Axis.* Washington, D.C.: Georgetown University Press, 2007. A thoughtful examination of the historical and contemporary relationship between religious expression and liberal democracy.

Sheehan, Collean A. *James Madison and the Spirit of Republican Self-Government.* New York: Cambridge University Press, 2009. An account of Madison's analysis of the conditions under which self-government would thrive in America.

Tocqueville, Alexis de. *Democracy in America,* vols. 1 and 2, ed. J. P. Mayer. New York: Doubleday/Anchor, 1969. A classic analysis (originally published 1835–1840) of American democracy by an insightful French observer.

List of Websites

www.nara.gov
The National Archives site; includes an in-depth look at the history of the Declaration of Independence

http://odur.let.rug.nl/~usa/P/aj7/about/bio/jackxx.htm
The focus is on Andrew Jackson and his role in shaping U.S. politics.

http://avalon.law.yale.edu/subject_menus/constpap.asp
Find documents here relating to the writing of the Constitution.

http://avalon.law.yale.edu/subject_menus/jeffpap.asp
This site includes the papers of Thomas Jefferson, as well
as his autobiography.

Participate!

The classroom provides an everyday opportunity to develop a
skill that is basic to effective citizenship—the ability to speak
clearly and persuasively. To the Greek philosopher Aristotle,
rhetoric was the defining skill of citizenship. Aristotle did not
define rhetoric as it is often used today, as a derisive term for
speech that is long on wind and short on reason. Rather, he
saw rhetoric as a tool in the search for truth, a form of persuasion that flourishes when people exchange ideas. The college
classroom is a good place to develop rhetorical skills. Speak up

in the classroom when you have a point to make and can support it. Rhetorical skills are honed only through practice, and
few settings offer more opportunities for practice than the
classroom.

Extra Credit

For up-to-the-minute *New York Times* articles, interactive
simulations, graphics, study tools, and more links and quizzes, visit the text's Online Learning Center at **www.mhhe.
com/ pattersontad11e**.

Self-Test Answers

1. d, 2. c, 3. a, 4. a, 5. a, 6. b, 7. F, 8. T, 9. T, 10. F

THE FEDERALIST:

A COLLECTION

OF

ESSAYS,

WRITTEN IN FAVOUR OF THE

NEW CONSTITUTION,

AS AGREED UPON BY THE FEDERAL CONVENTION,
SEPTEMBER 17, 1787.

IN TWO VOLUMES.

VOL. I.

Federalism: Forging a Nation

The question of the relation of the states to the federal government is the cardinal question of our Constitutional system. It cannot be settled by the opinion of one generation, because it is a question of growth, and each successive stage of our political and economic development gives it a new aspect, makes it a new question. Woodrow Wilson[1]

It was one of the most anxiously awaited Supreme Court decisions in years. At issue was the constitutionality of provisions of the 2010 health care reform act that required individuals to purchase health insurance or face a tax penalty. Enacted by the Democratic-controlled Congress at the urging of President Barack Obama, the legislation had been opposed from the start by Republicans. Every Senate and House Republican voted against the bill, and Republican state attorneys general quickly filed suit to have the bill declared unconstitutional on grounds that it usurped the authority of the states to decide whether their residents will be required to have health insurance. Democrats saw the issue differently, claiming that Congress has the lawful power to require individuals to have personal health insurance or face a penalty.

Challenges to the law in federal district courts produced mixed verdicts, with some judges upholding the law and others striking it down. In late 2011, the Supreme Court announced that it would take up the issue by hearing a case in which the state of Florida was challenging the law on grounds that it was an improper exercise of federal authority. Joining Florida's challenge were twenty-five other states: Alabama, Alaska, Arizona, Colorado, Georgia, Idaho, Indiana, Iowa, Kansas, Louisiana, Maine, Michigan, Mississippi, Nebraska, Nevada, North Dakota, Ohio, Pennsylvania, South Carolina, South Dakota, Texas, Utah, Washington, Wisconsin, and Wyoming.

In June of 2012, the Supreme Court issued its ruling, upholding the health care act in a 5-4 decision that hinged on the power of Congress to levy taxes. Writing for the majority, Chief Justice John Roberts said: "It is reasonable to construe what Congress has done

The 2010 health care reform act raised the question of the limits of federal authority. Although the legislation had determined backers, it also faced intense opposition on grounds it infringed on state authority. Conflicts over the boundaries between federal and state authority have occurred countless times in American history.

as increasing taxes on those who have a certain amount of income, but choose to go without health insurance. Such legislation is within Congress's power to tax." Roberts went on to say: "The federal government does not have the power to order people to buy health insurance. . . . The federal government does have the power to impose a tax on those without health insurance." The four justices in the minority issued a sharp dissent, saying: "Whether federal spending legislation crosses the line from enticement to coercion is often difficult to determine . . . . In this case, however, there can be no doubt."[2]

The controversy surrounding the health care reform act is one of thousands of disagreements over the course of American history that have hinged on whether national or state authority should prevail. Americans possess what amounts to dual citizenship: they are citizens both of the United States and of the state where they reside. The American political system is a *federal system*, in which constitutional authority is divided between a national government and state governments. Each government is assumed to derive its powers directly from the people and therefore to have sovereignty (final authority) over the policy responsibilities assigned to it. The federal system consists of nation *and* states, indivisible yet separate.[3]

The relationship between the nation and the states was the most pressing issue when the Constitution was written and has been a divisive issue ever since. In one case, the Civil War, it nearly caused the dissolution of the United States. Throughout the nation's history, federalism has been a source of contention between the Republican and Democratic parties, although they have shifted sides when it served their political goals. This chapter examines federalism—its creation through the Constitution, its evolution during the nation's history, and its current status. The main points presented in the chapter are:

■ *The power of government must be equal to its responsibilities.* The Constitution was needed because the nation's preceding system (under the Articles of Confederation) was too weak to accomplish its expected goals, particularly those of a strong defense and an integrated economy.

■ *Federalism—the Constitution's division of governing authority between two levels, nation and states—was the result of political bargaining.* Federalism was not a theoretical principle, but rather a compromise made necessary in 1787 by the prior existence of the states.

■ *Federalism is not a fixed principle for allocating power between the national and state governments, but rather a principle that has changed over time in response to political needs and partisan ideology.* Federalism has passed through several distinct stages in the course of the nation's history.

■ *Contemporary federalism tilts toward national authority, reflecting the increased interdependence of American society.*

PARTY POLARIZATION Political Thinking in Conflict

The Federal Government's Role in Health Care

The United States is nearly alone among Western democracies in not having government-provided health care for all citizens. The U.S. system is instead a combination of federal programs and private insurance, most of it provided through employers. For decades, Democrats have sought to expand the government's role while Republicans have contested the expansion. In 2010, the Democrat-controlled Congress passed the Patient Protection and Affordable Care Act, commonly known as the health care reform act, which is the most significant expansion of government-directed health insurance since Medicare and Medicaid were enacted in the 1960s. The 2010 legislation was tied up for months in Congress, with Republican and Democratic lawmakers on opposite sides of the issue. They argued over everything from the cost of the program to its effect on the quality of coverage, as well as whether it violated states' rights. The partisan division spilled over to the public. Self-identified Republicans and Democrats were far apart in their opinions on the issue.

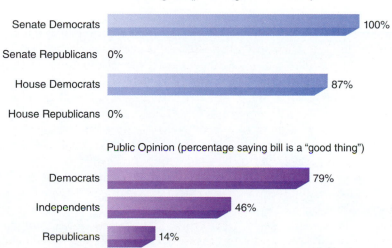

Vote in Congress (percentage in favor of bill)

Senate Democrats — 100%
Senate Republicans — 0%
House Democrats — 87%
House Republicans — 0%

Public Opinion (percentage saying bill is a "good thing")

Democrats — 79%
Independents — 46%
Republicans — 14%

Source (public opinion data): USA Today/Gallup poll, March 22, 2010.

Q. *Partisan debate over the health care bill focused on both its substance (greater government involvement in order to expand the number of insured Americans) and its constitutionality (whether the federal government was acting within its lawful authority). Which of these issues—the substantive one or the constitutional one—do you think was more important in the response of Democratic and Republican lawmakers to the issue? Which do you personally regard as the more significant aspect of the issue?*

Federalism: National and State Sovereignty

At the time of the writing of the Constitution, some of America's top leaders were dead set against the creation of a stronger national government. When rumors began to circulate that the Philadelphia convention was devising just such a government, Virginia's Patrick Henry said that he "smelt a rat." His fears were confirmed when he obtained a copy of the draft constitution. "Who authorized them," he asked, "to speak the language of 'We, the People,' instead of 'We, the States'?"

The question of "people versus states" was precipitated by the failure of the Articles of Confederation. It had created a union of the states, and they alone had authority over the people (see Chapter 2). The national government could not tax or conscript citizens, nor could it regulate their economic activities. Its directives applied only to the states, and they often ignored them. Georgia and North Carolina, for example, contributed no money at all to the national treasury between 1781 and 1786, and the federal government had no way to force them to pay. The only feasible solution to this problem was to give the federal government direct authority over the people. If individuals are ordered to pay taxes, most of them will do so rather than accept the alternative—imprisonment or confiscation of their property.

At the same time, the writers of the Constitution wanted to preserve the states. The states had their own constitutions and a governing history extending back to the colonial era. Although their residents thought of themselves as Americans, many of them identified more strongly with their states. When Virginia's George Mason said that he would never agree to a constitution that abolished the states, he was speaking for nearly all the delegates.

These two realities—the need to preserve the states and the need for a national government with direct authority over the people—led the framers to invent an entirely new system of government. Before this point in history, **sovereignty** (supreme and final governing authority) had been regarded as indivisible. By

sovereignty

The supreme (or ultimate) authority to govern within a certain geographical area.

Patrick Henry was a leading figure in the American Revolution ("Give me liberty or give me death!"). He later opposed ratification of the Constitution on grounds that the national government should be a union of states and not also of people.

definition, a government cannot be sovereign if it can be overruled by another government. Nevertheless, the framers divided sovereignty between the national government and the states, a system now know as **federalism.** Each level—the national government and the state governments—directly governs the residents within its assigned territory. Each level has authority that is not subject to the other's approval. And each level is constitutionally protected. The national government cannot abolish a state, and the states cannot abolish the national government.

In 1787, other nations in the world were governed by a **unitary system,** in which sovereignty is vested solely in the national government. Local or regional governments in a unitary system do not have sovereignty. They have authority only to the degree that it is granted by the national government, which can also withdraw any such grant. (This situation applies to America's local governments. They are not sovereign, but instead derive their authority from their respective state governments, which can, though it occurs rarely, even choose to abolish a local unit of government.)

Federalism is also different from a **confederacy,** which was the type of government that existed under the Articles of Confederation. In a confederacy, the states alone are sovereign. They decide the authority, even the continuing existence, of the central government. Confederacies have been rare in human history, but the government of the Articles was not the first. The ancient Greek city-states and medieval Europe's Hanseatic League were of this type. (Despite its name, the Confederate States of America—the South's Civil War government—had a federal constitution rather than a confederate one. Sovereignty was divided between the central and state governments.)

The federal system established in 1787 divides the responsibilities of government between the nation and the states (see Figure 3-1). The system gives states the power to address local issues in ways of their choosing; they have primary responsibility, for example, for public education and police protection. The national government, on the other hand, is responsible for matters of national scope, such as military defense and the currency. The national and state governments also have some concurrent powers (that is, powers exercised over the same policy areas). Each of them has, for example, the power to raise taxes and borrow money.

federalism
A governmental system in which authority is divided between two sovereign levels of government: national and regional.

unitary system
A governmental system in which the national government alone has sovereign (ultimate) authority.

confederacy
A governmental system in which sovereignty is vested entirely in subnational (state) governments.

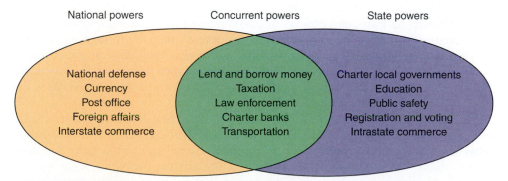

FIGURE 3-1
Federalism as a Governing System: Examples of National, State, and Concurrent Powers
The American federal system divides sovereignty between a national government and the state governments. Each is constitutionally protected in its existence and authority, although their powers overlap somewhat even in areas granted to one level (for example, the federal government has a role in education policy).

Federal Versus Unitary Governments

Federalism involves the division of sovereignty between a national government and subnational (state) governments. It was invented in the United States in 1787 to maintain the preexisting American states while establishing an effective central government. Since then, other countries have established a *federal* government, but most countries continue to have a *unitary* government, in which all sovereignty is vested in the national government.

Even within these alternative political systems, differences exist. In Germany's federal system, for example, the states have limited lawmaking powers but exercise broad authority in determining how national laws will be implemented. By comparison, the U.S. federal system grants substantial lawmaking powers to the states except in specified areas such as national defense and currency. Unitary systems also differ. In Britain, the national government has delegated substantial authority to regions; Scotland, for example, has its own parliament, which exercises lawmaking powers. In France's unitary government, on the other hand, political authority is highly centralized.

In nearly all federal systems, the national legislature has two chambers—one apportioned by population (as in the case of the U.S. House of Representatives) and one apportioned by geographical area (as in the case of the U.S. Senate). The U.S. Senate is a pure federal institution in the sense that each state has the same number of senators. In some federal systems, such as Germany's, the states are not equally represented even in the legislative chamber that is apportioned on the basis of geography rather than population.

Q: Federal systems typically have a two-chamber legislature. Unitary systems, on the other hand, typically have a single legislative chamber. Why?

A: In a unitary system, there is no constitutional need for a second legislative chamber based on geographical subdivisions (states), as is the case with a federal system.

Country	Form of government
Canada	Federal
France	Unitary
Germany	Federal
Great Britain	Modified unitary
Italy	Modified unitary
Japan	Unitary
Mexico	Modified federal
Sweden	Unitary
United States	Federal

The Argument for Federalism

The strongest argument for federalism in 1787 was that it would correct the defects in the Articles. Two of the defects were particularly troublesome: the national government had neither the power to tax nor the power to regulate commerce among the states. Without money from taxes, the national government lacked the financial means to maintain an army strong enough to prevent encroachment by European powers or to maintain a navy strong enough to protect America's merchant ships from harassment and attack by foreign navies and pirates. And without the ability to regulate commerce, the national government could neither promote the general economy nor prevent trade wars between the states. New York and New Jersey were among the states that imposed taxes on goods shipped into their state from other states.

Although it is sometimes claimed that "the government which governs least is the government that governs best," the Articles proved otherwise. The problems with the too-weak national government were severe: public disorder, economic chaos, and an inadequate defense. Although the problems were widely recognized, many Americans in 1787 feared that a strong central government would eventually swallow up the states. An outspoken Anti-Federalist (as opponents of the Constitution were called) proclaimed: "[The states] will eventually be absorbed by our grand continental vortex, or dwindle into petty corporations, and have power over little else than yoking hogs or determining the width of cart wheels."[4]

The challenge of providing a response fell to James Madison and Alexander Hamilton. During the ratification debate, they argued in a series of essays (the so-called *Federalist Papers*) that a federal system would protect liberty and moderate the power of government.

Protecting Liberty

Although theorists such as John Locke and Montesquieu had not proposed a division of power between national and local authorities as a means of protecting liberty, the framers argued that federalism was a part of the system of checks and balances.[5] Alexander Hamilton wrote in *Federalist* No. 28 that the American people could shift their loyalties back and forth between the national and state governments in order to keep each under control. "If [the people's] rights are invaded by either," Hamilton wrote, "they can make use of the other as the instrument of redress." In *Federalist* No. 46, Madison argued that the national government would not be a threat to liberty because people had a stronger allegiance to their state, which would serve as a barrier to federal encroachment. If a state should somehow fail to respect people's rights and interests, they could appeal to the national government. "The people ought not surely to be precluded," Madison wrote, "from giving most of their confidence where they may discover it to be the most due."

Moderating the Power of Government

To the Anti-Federalists, the sacrifice of the states' power to the nation was as unwise as it was unnecessary. They claimed that a distant national government could never serve the people's interests as well as the states could. Liberty *and* self-government, the Anti-Federalists argued, were enhanced by state-centered government. In support of their contention, they turned to Montesquieu, who had concluded that a small republic is more likely than a large one to serve people's interests. When government encompasses a large area, he argued, its leaders lose touch with the people and disregard their welfare.

In *Federalist* No. 10, James Madison took issue with this claim. He argued that whether a government serves the common good is a function not of its size but of the range of interests that share political power. The problem with a small republic, Madison claimed, is that it can have a dominant faction—whether it be landholders, financiers, an impoverished majority, or some other group—that is strong enough to control government and use it for selfish purposes. A large republic is less likely to have an all-powerful faction. If financiers are strong in one area of a large republic, they are likely to be weaker elsewhere. The same will be true of farmers, merchants, laborers, and other groups. A large republic, Madison argued, would make it difficult for a single group to gain full control, which would force groups to share in the exercise of power. In making this claim, Madison was arguing not for central authority but for limited government, which he believed would result if power were shared widely. "Extend the sphere," said Madison, "and you take in a greater variety of parties and interests; you make it less probable that a majority of the whole will have a common motive to invade the rights of other citizens."

The Powers of the Nation and the States

The U.S. Constitution addresses the lawful authority of the national government, which is provided through *enumerated and implied powers*. Authority that is not granted to the national government is left—or "reserved"—to the states. Thus, the states have *reserved powers*.

Enumerated Powers and the Supremacy Clause

Article I of the Constitution grants to Congress seventeen **enumerated (expressed) powers.** The framers expected these powers to establish a government strong enough to forge a union that was secure in its defense and stable in its economy. Congress's powers, for example, to regulate commerce among the states, to create a national currency, and to borrow money would provide a foundation for a sound national economy. Its power to tax, combined with its authority to establish an army and navy and to declare war, would enable it to provide for the common defense.

In addition, the Constitution prohibits the states from actions that would encroach on national powers. Article I, Section 10, prohibits the states from making treaties with other nations, raising armies, waging war, printing money, or entering into commercial agreements with other states without the approval of Congress.

The writers of the Constitution recognized that the lawful exercise of national authority would at times conflict with the laws of the states. In such instances, national law was intended to prevail. Article VI of the Constitution grants this dominance in the so-called **supremacy clause,** which provides that "the laws of the United States . . . shall be the supreme law of the land."

Implied Powers: The Necessary and Proper Clause

The writers of the Constitution recognized that government, if it was to be effective, had to be capable of adjusting to change. A weaknesses of the Articles was that the national government was prohibited from exercising powers not expressly granted it, which limited its ability to meet the country's changing needs after the end of the Revolutionary War. To avoid this problem with the new government, the framers included in Article I of the Constitution the **"necessary and proper" clause** or, as it later came to be known, the **elastic clause.** It gives Congress the power "to make all laws which shall be necessary and proper for carrying into execution the foregoing [enumerated] powers." This clause gives the national government **implied powers:** powers that are not listed in the Constitution but are related to the exercise of the powers that are listed.

Reserved Powers: The States' Authority

The supremacy and "necessary and proper" clauses were worrisome to the Anti-Federalists. The two clauses stoked their fear of an overly powerful national government because they provided a constitutional basis for expanding the government's authority. Such concerns led them to demand a constitutional amendment that would protect states' rights and interests. Ratified in 1791 as the Tenth Amendment to the Constitution, it reads: "The powers not delegated to the United States by the Constitution, nor prohibited by it to the States, are reserved to the States." The states' powers under the U.S. Constitution are thus called **reserved powers.**

Federalism in Historical Perspective

Since ratification of the Constitution over two centuries ago, no aspect of it has provoked more frequent or bitter conflict than federalism. By establishing two levels of sovereign authority, the Constitution created two centers of power and ambition, each of which was sure to claim disputed areas as belonging to it. Ambiguities in the Constitution have also contributed to conflict between the

---

enumerated (expressed) powers

The seventeen powers granted to the national government under Article I, Section 8, of the Constitution. These powers include taxation and the regulation of commerce as well as the authority to provide for the national defense.

supremacy clause

Article VI of the Constitution, which makes national law supreme over state law when the national government is acting within its constitutional limits.

"necessary and proper" (elastic) clause

The authority granted Congress in Article I, Section 8, of the Constitution "to make all laws which shall be necessary and proper" for the implementation of its enumerated powers.

implied powers

The federal government's constitutional authority (through the "necessary and proper" clause) to take action that is not expressly authorized by the Constitution but that supports actions that are so authorized.

reserved powers

The powers granted to the states under the Tenth Amendment to the Constitution.

nation and the states. The document does not delineate, for example, the dividing line between *interstate* commerce (which the national government is empowered to regulate) and *intrastate* commerce (which is reserved for regulation by the states).

Not surprisingly, federalism has been a contentious and dynamic system, its development determined less by constitutional language than by the strength of partisan interests and by the country's changing needs. Federalism can be viewed as having progressed through three historical eras, each of which has involved a different relationship between the nation and the states. At the same time, each era has ended with a national government that was stronger than at the start of the era. Over the long term, the United States has undergone a process of **nationalization**—an increase in national authority. The shift is due primarily to economic growth and political action.

An Indestructible Union (1789–1865)

The issue during the first era—which lasted from the time the Constitution went into effect (1789) until the end of the Civil War (1865)—was the Union's survival. Given America's state-centered history before the Constitution, it was inevitable that the states would dispute national policies that threatened their interests.

The Nationalist View: *McCulloch v. Maryland*

An early dispute over federalism arose when President George Washington's secretary of the treasury, Alexander Hamilton, proposed that Congress establish a national bank. Hamilton and his supporters claimed that because the federal government had constitutional authority to regulate currency, it had the "implied power" to establish a national bank. Thomas Jefferson, Washington's secretary of state, opposed the bank on the grounds that its activities would enrich the wealthy at the expense of ordinary people. Jefferson claimed the bank was unlawful because the Constitution did not expressly authorize it. Jefferson said: "I consider the foundation of the Constitution as laid on this ground that 'all powers not delegated to the United States by the Constitution, nor prohibited by it to the states, are preserved to the states or to the people.' . . . To take a single step beyond the boundaries thus drawn . . . is to take possession of a boundless field of power, no longer susceptible of any definition."

Jefferson's argument failed to sway Congress. In 1791, it established the First Bank of the United States, granting it a twenty-year charter. Although Congress did not renew the bank's charter when it expired in 1811, Congress decided in 1816 to establish the Second Bank of the United States. State and local banks did not want competition from a national bank and sought help from their state legislatures. Several states, including Maryland, levied taxes on the national bank's operations within their borders, hoping to drive it out of existence by making it unprofitable. James McCulloch, who was in charge of the Maryland branch of the national bank, refused to pay the Maryland tax and the resulting dispute was heard by the Supreme Court.

The chief justice of the Supreme Court, John Marshall, was a fervent nationalist, and in *McCulloch v. Maryland* (1819) the Court ruled decisively in favor of national authority. It was reasonable to infer, Marshall concluded, that a government with powers to tax, borrow money, and regulate commerce could establish a bank in order to exercise those powers effectively. Marshall's argument was a clear statement of *implied powers*—the idea that through the "necessary and proper" clause, the national government's powers extend beyond a narrow reading of its enumerated powers.

nationalization

The process by which national authority has increased over the course of U.S. history as a result primarily of economic change but also of political action.

Of the framers, Alexander Hamilton had the clearest vision of what was needed to create a strong national government. As secretary of the treasury under President Washington, Hamilton succeeded in getting Congress to establish a national bank and to consolidate state debts at the federal level. Thereafter, creditors at home and abroad put their trust in the federal government rather than the state governments.

Marshall's ruling also addressed the meaning of the Constitution's supremacy clause. The state of Maryland had argued that, even if the national government had the authority to establish a bank, a state had the authority to tax it. The Supreme Court rejected Maryland's position, concluding that valid national law overrides conflicting state law. Because the national government had the power to create the bank, it also could protect the bank from state actions, such as taxation, that might destroy it.[6]

The *McCulloch* decision served as precedent for later rulings in support of national power. In *Gibbons v. Ogden* (1824), for example, the Marshall-led Court rejected a New York law granting one of its residents a monopoly on a ferry that operated between New York and New Jersey, concluding that New York had encroached on Congress's power to regulate commerce among the states. The Court asserted that Congress's commerce power was not limited to trade between the states, but to all aspects of that trade, including the transportation of goods. Accordingly, congressional action on interstate commerce overrides any and all conflicting state law. "The power over commerce, the Court said, "is vested in Congress as absolutely as it would be in a single government."[7]

Marshall's opinions asserted that legitimate uses of national power took precedence over state authority and that the "necessary and proper" clause and the commerce clause were broad grants of national power. As a nationalist, Marshall provided the U.S. government with the legal justification for expanding its power in ways that fostered the development of the United States as a nation rather than as a collection of states. This constitutional vision was of utmost significance. As Justice Oliver Wendell Holmes Jr. noted a century later, the Union would not have survived if each state had been allowed to decide for itself which national laws it would obey.[8]

The States' Rights View: The Dred Scott Decision

Although John Marshall's rulings strengthened national authority, the issue of slavery posed a growing threat to the Union's survival. Westward expansion and immigration into the northern states were tilting power in Congress toward the free states, which increasingly signaled their determination to outlaw slavery at some future time. Fearing the possibility, southern leaders did what others have done throughout American history: they developed a constitutional interpretation fitted to their political purpose. John C. Calhoun declared that the United States was founded upon a "compact" between the states. The national government, he said, was "a government of states . . . not a government of individuals."[9] This line of reasoning led Calhoun to his famed "doctrine of nullification," which declared that a state has the constitutional right to nullify a national law.

In 1832, South Carolina invoked the doctrine, declaring "null and void" a national tariff law that favored northern interests. President Andrew Jackson called South Carolina's action "incompatible with the existence of the Union," a position that gained force when Congress gave Jackson the authority to take military action against South Carolina. The state backed down when Congress amended the tariff act to soften its impact on the South. The dispute foreshadowed the Civil War, a confrontation of far greater consequence. Although war would not break out for another three decades, the dispute over states' rights was intensifying.

'The Supreme Court's infamous *Dred Scott* decision (1857), written by Chief Justice Roger Taney, an ardent states'-rights advocate, inflamed the dispute. Dred Scott, a slave who had lived in the North for four years, applied for his

The American Civil War was the bloodiest conflict the world had yet known. Ten percent of fighting-age males died in the four-year war, and uncounted others were wounded. The death toll—618,000 (360,000 from the North, 258,000 from the South)—exceeded that of the American war dead in World War I, World War II, the Korean War, and the Vietnam War combined. This death toll was in a nation with a population only one-tenth the size it is today. Shown here, in one of the earliest war photos ever taken, are the bodies of soldiers killed at the battle of Antietam.

freedom when his master died, citing a federal law—the Missouri Compromise of 1820—that made slavery illegal in a free state or territory. The Supreme Court ruled against Scott, claiming that slaves were not citizens and therefore had no right to have their case heard in federal court. The Court also invalidated the Missouri Compromise by holding that slaves were property, not people. Accordingly, since the Constitution prohibited Congress from interfering with owners' property rights, Congress did not have the power to outlaw slavery in any part of the United States.[10]

The Taney Court's decision provoked outrage in the North and contributed to a sectional split in the nation's majority party, the Democrats. In 1860, the Democratic Party's northern and southern wings nominated separate candidates for the presidency, which split the Democratic vote, enabling the Republican candidate, Abraham Lincoln, to win the presidency with only 40 percent of the popular vote. Lincoln had campaigned on a platform that called, not for an immediate end to slavery, but for its gradual abolition through payments to slaveholders. Nevertheless, southern states saw Lincoln's election as a grave threat to their way of life. By the time Lincoln assumed office, seven southern states, led by South Carolina, had left the Union. Four more states were to follow. In justifying his decision to wage war on the secessionists, Lincoln said, "The Union is older than the states." In 1865, the superior strength of the Union army settled by force the question of whether national authority is binding on the states.

Dual Federalism and Laissez-Faire Capitalism (1865–1937)

Although the North's victory in the Civil War preserved the Union, new challenges to federalism were surfacing. Constitutional doctrine held that certain policy areas, such as interstate commerce and defense, belonged exclusively to the national government, whereas other policy areas, such as public health and intrastate commerce, belonged exclusively to the states. This doctrine, known as **dual federalism,** was based on the idea that a precise separation of national and state authority was both possible and desirable. "The power which one possesses," said the Supreme Court, "the other does not."[11]

American society, however, was in the midst of changes that raised questions about the suitability of dual federalism as a governing concept. The Industrial

dual federalism

A doctrine based on the idea that a precise separation of national power and state power is both possible and desirable.

Revolution had given rise to large business firms, which were using their economic power to dominate markets and exploit workers. Government was the logical counterforce to this economic power. Which level of government—state or national—would regulate business?

There was also the issue of the former slaves. The white South had lost the war but was hardly of a mind to share power with the newly freed slaves. Would the federal government be allowed to intervene in state affairs to ensure the fair treatment of African Americans?

Dual federalism became a barrier to an effective response to these issues. From the 1860s through the 1930s, the Supreme Court held firm to the idea that there was a sharp line between national and state authority and, in both areas, a high wall of separation between government and the economy. The era of dual federalism was characterized by state supremacy in racial policy and business supremacy in commerce policy.

The Fourteenth Amendment and State Discretion

Ratified after the Civil War, the Fourteenth Amendment was intended to protect the newly freed slaves from discriminatory action by state governments. A state was prohibited from depriving "any person of life, liberty, or property without due process of law," from denying "any person within its jurisdiction the equal protection of the laws," and from abridging "the privileges or immunities of citizens of the United States."

Supreme Court rulings in subsequent decades, however, undermined the Fourteenth Amendment's promise of liberty and equality for all. In 1873, for example, the Court held that the Fourteenth Amendment did not substantially limit the power of the states to determine the rights to which their residents were entitled.[12] Then, in *Plessy v. Ferguson* (1896), the Court issued its infamous "separate but equal" ruling. A black man, Homer Adolph Plessy, had been convicted of violating a Louisiana law that required white and black citizens to ride in separate railroad cars. The Supreme Court upheld his conviction, concluding that state governments could force blacks to use separate facilities as long as the facilities were "equal" in quality to those reserved for use by whites. "If one race be inferior to the other socially," the Court concluded, "the Constitution of the United States cannot put them on the same plane." The lone dissenting justice in the case, John Marshall Harlan, had harsh words for his colleagues: "Our Constitution is color-blind and neither knows nor tolerates classes among citizens. . . . The thin disguise of 'equal' accommodations . . . will not mislead anyone nor atone for the wrong this day done."[13]

With its *Plessy* decision, the Supreme Court sanctioned government-based racial segregation in the South. Black children were forced into separate public schools that seldom had libraries and usually had few teachers. Public hospitals for blacks had few doctors and nurses and almost no medical supplies and equipment. The *Plessy* ruling had become a justification for the separate and *unequal* treatment of black Americans.[14]

Judicial Protection of Business

After the Civil War, the Supreme Court also gave nearly free rein to business. A majority of the Court's justices favored laissez-faire capitalism (which holds that business should be "allowed to act" without interference) and interpreted the Constitution in ways that restricted government's attempts to regulate business activity. In 1886, for example, the Court decided that corporations were "persons" within the meaning of the Fourteenth Amendment, and thereby were protected

POLITICAL THINKING

Protector of Rights, Nation or States?

During the debate over ratification of the Constitution, Americans argued over whether individual liberty and equality would be better protected by the states or by the nation. The Anti-Federalists argued that a small republic was closer to the people and therefore would do more to uphold individual rights. Arguing for the Federalist side, James Madison countered by saying that a large republic was preferable because its wide diversity of interests would prevent a dominant group from taking control and using government's power to suppress weaker groups. Historically, which level of government do you think has been the more protective of liberty and equality? What historical issues or examples would you use to support your argument? Can you think of contemporary issues or examples that would suggest one level of government or the other is more protective today of liberty and equality?

from substantial regulation by the states.[15] In other words, a constitutional amendment that had been enacted to protect newly freed slaves from being treated as second-class persons was ignored for that purpose but used instead to protect fictitious persons—business corporations.

The Court also weakened the national government's regulatory power by narrowly interpreting its commerce power. The Constitution's **commerce clause** says that Congress shall have the power "to regulate commerce" among the states. However, the clause does not spell out the economic activities included in the grant of power. When the federal government invoked the Sherman Antitrust Act (1890) in an attempt to break up the monopoly on the manufacture of sugar (a single company controlled 98 percent of it), the Supreme Court blocked the action, claiming that interstate commerce covered only the "transportation" of goods, not their "manufacture."[16] Manufacturing was deemed part of intrastate commerce and thus, according to the dual federalism doctrine, subject to state regulation only. However, because the Court had previously decided that the states' regulatory powers were limited by the Fourteenth Amendment, the states were not allowed to regulate manufacturing activity in a significant way.

Although some business regulation was subsequently allowed, the Supreme Court remained an obstacle to efforts to curb abusive business practices. An example is the case of *Hammer v. Dagenhart* (1918), which arose from a 1916 federal act that prohibited the interstate shipment of goods produced by child labor. The act had public support in that factory owners were exploiting children, working them for long hours at low pay. Nevertheless, the Court invalidated the law, ruling that the Tenth Amendment gave the states, and not the federal government, the power to regulate factory practices.[17] However, in an earlier case, *Lochner v. New York* (1905), the Court had prevented states from regulating labor practices, concluding that such action violated owners' property rights.[18]

In effect, the Court had negated the principle of self-government. Neither the people's representatives in Congress nor their representatives in the state legislatures were allowed to regulate business activity. America's corporations, with the Supreme Court as their protector, were in control.[19]

commerce clause
The authority granted Congress in Article I, Section 8, of the Constitution "to regulate commerce" among the states.

Source: Bartholomew, Minneapolis Journal (1904)

Between 1865 and 1937, the Supreme Court's rulings severely restricted national power. Narrowly interpreting Congress's regulatory power under the commerce clause, the Court allowed business monopolies to act largely as they pleased in establishing prices, wages, and working conditions.

National Authority Prevails

The Democratic Party with its working-class base attacked the Court's position, and its candidates increasingly called for greater regulation of business and more rights for labor. Progressive Republicans like Theodore Roosevelt also fought against uncontrolled business power, but the Republican Party as a whole was ideologically committed to unregulated markets and to a small role for the federal government. Accordingly, when the Great Depression began in 1929, Republican president Herbert Hoover refused to use federal authority to put people back to work. Adhering to his party's free-market philosophy, Hoover argued that the economy would soon rebound on its own and that government intervention would only delay the recovery.

In the 1932 election, voters elected as president the Democratic candidate, Franklin D. Roosevelt, who recognized that the economy had become a national one. More than 10 million workers (compared to one million in 1860) were employed by industry, whose products were marketed throughout the nation. Urban workers typically were dependent on landlords for their housing, on farmers and grocers for their food, and on corporations for their jobs. Farmers were more independent, but they too were increasingly a part of a larger economic network. Farmers' income depended on market prices and shipping and equipment costs.[20] Economic interdependence meant that, when the depression hit in 1929, its effects could not be contained. At the depths of the Great Depression, one-fourth of the nation's workforce was unemployed and another fourth could find only part-time work.

The states by tradition had responsibility for helping the unemployed, but they were nearly penniless because of declining tax revenues and the huge demand for welfare assistance. Franklin Roosevelt's New Deal programs were designed to ease the hardship. The 1933 National Industry Recovery Act (NIRA), for example, established a federal jobs program and enabled major industries to coordinate their production decisions. Economic conservatives strenuously opposed such programs, accusing Roosevelt of leading the country into socialism. They found an ally in the Supreme Court. In *Schecter Poultry Corp. v. United States* (1935), just as it had done in previous New Deal cases, the Supreme Court in a 5-4 ruling declared the NIRA to be unconstitutional.[21]

Frustrated by the Court's rulings, Roosevelt in 1937 sought to exploit the fact that the Constitution gives Congress the power to determine the number of Supreme Court justices. Although the number had stayed at nine justices for seven decades, there was no constitutional barrier to enlarging the number, which, in fact, had been altered several times in the nation's early years. Roosevelt asked Congress to pass legislation that would allow a president to nominate a new justice whenever a seated member passed the age of seventy and a half. Since some of the justices had already reached that age, the legislation would enable Roosevelt to appoint enough new justices to swing the Court to his side. Congress hesitated to do so, but the attempt ended with the "switch in time that saved nine." For reasons that have never been fully clear, Justice Owen Roberts switched sides on New Deal cases, giving the president a 5-4 majority on the Court.

Within months, the Court upheld the 1935 National Labor Relations Act, which gave employees the right to organize and bargain collectively.[22] In passing the legislation, Congress claimed that disputes between labor and management disrupted the nation's economy and therefore could be regulated through the commerce clause. In upholding the act, the Supreme Court endorsed Congress's reasoning.[23] In a subsequent ruling, the Court declared that Congress's commerce power is "as broad as the needs of the nation."[24] Congress would be allowed to regulate *all* aspects of commerce. During this same period, the Court also loosened its restrictions on Congress's power to tax and spend.[25]

The Supreme Court had finally acknowledged the obvious: that an industrial economy is not confined by state boundaries and must be subject to national regulation. It was a principle that business also increasingly accepted. The nation's banking industry, for example, was saved from almost complete collapse in the 1930s by the creation of a federal regulatory agency, the Federal Deposit Insurance Corporation (FDIC). By insuring depositors' savings against loss, the FDIC stopped the panic withdrawals that had already ruined thousands of the nation's banks.

Subsequent Supreme Court decisions altered the constitutional doctrine of federalism in other policy areas, including civil rights. In *Brown v. Board of Education* (1954), for example, the Supreme Court held that states could not force black children to attend public schools separate from those for white children (see Chapter 5).[26] National citizenship—the notion that Americans should be equal in their rights and opportunities regardless of the state in which they reside—became a more encompassing idea than it had previously been.

Contemporary Federalism (since 1937)

Since the 1930s, the relation of the nation to the states has changed so fundamentally that dual federalism is no longer even a roughly accurate description of the American situation. An understanding of today's federalism requires the recognition of two countervailing developments. The larger trend is a long-term *expansion* of national authority that began in the 1930s and continues to this day. The national government now operates in many policy areas that were once almost exclusively within the control of states and localities. The national government does not dominate in these policy areas, but it does play a significant role.

Many of the national initiatives trace to the 1960s as part of President Lyndon Johnson's Great Society program. A Democrat in the mold of Franklin Roosevelt, Johnson believed that federal power should be used to assist the economically disadvantaged. Traditional divisions of responsibility between the nation and the states were of less concern to Johnson than the policy goals that could be met though federal action. However, unlike Roosevelt's New Deal, which dealt mostly with the economy, Johnson's Great Society dealt mostly with social welfare issues, which have an indirect constitutional basis. The Constitution does not grant Congress the power to regulate "social welfare." However, Congress may tax and spend for that purpose, which was the basis of the Great Society. Johnson's presidency was marked by dozens of new federal assistance grants to states for programs in health care, public housing, nutrition, public assistance, urban development, education, and other social welfare issues traditionally reserved to state and localities. Johnson's initiatives were both creative and coercive: creative in the large number of new federal programs and coercive in the restrictions placed on states and localities as a condition of their receipt of federal funds.

A smaller and more recent development is the attempt to "pass down" authority from the national level to the state and local levels in selected areas. Known as *devolution*, this development peaked in the 1990s. Although it has since receded, devolution remains a component of contemporary federalism, as is discussed later in the chapter.

Shown here is a pelican covered with oil from the oil spill that occurred in the Gulf of Mexico on 2010. The federal, state, and local governments worked together in the relief effort. *Cooperative federalism* is a term used to describe these joint efforts, although they are also a source of tension. Some local and state officials criticized the federal government's response to the oil spill, saying it acted too slowly.

cooperative federalism

The situation in which the national, state, and local levels work together to solve problems.

Interdependency and Intergovernmental Relations

Interdependency is a reason why national authority has increased dramatically. Modern systems of transportation, commerce, and communication transcend local and state boundaries. These systems are national—and even international—in scope, which means that problems affecting Americans living in one part of the country are likely to affect Americans living elsewhere. This situation has required Washington to assume a larger policy role. National problems typically require national solutions.

Interdependency has also encouraged national, state, and local policymakers to work together to solve policy problems. This collaborative effort has been described as **cooperative federalism**.[27] The difference between the older dual federalism and cooperative federalism has been likened to the difference between a layer cake, whose levels are separate and a marble cake, whose levels flow together.[28]

Cooperative federalism is based on shared policy responsibilities rather than sharply divided ones. An example is the Medicaid program, which was created in 1965 as part of President Johnson's Great Society initiative and provides health care for the poor. The Medicaid program is jointly funded by the national and state governments, operates within eligibility standards set by the national government, and gives states some latitude in determining recipients' benefits. The Medicaid program is not an isolated example. Literally hundreds of policy programs today are run jointly by the national and state governments. In many cases, local governments are also involved. These programs have the following characteristics:

- Jointly funded by the national and state governments (and sometimes by local governments)
- Jointly administered, with the states and localities providing most of the direct service to recipients and a national agency providing general administration
- Jointly determined, with both the state and national governments (and sometimes the local governments) having a say in eligibility and benefit levels and with federal regulations, such as those prohibiting discrimination, imposing a degree of uniformity on state and local efforts

Cooperative federalism should not be interpreted to mean that the states are powerless and dependent.[29] States have retained most of their traditional authority in areas such as education, health, public safety, and roadways. Nevertheless, the federal government's involvement in policy areas traditionally reserved for the states has increased its policy influence and diminished state-to-state policy differences. Before the enactment of the federal Medicaid program in 1965, for example, poor people in many states were not entitled to government-paid health care. Afterward, most poor people were eligible for health benefits regardless of where they resided.

Government Revenues and Intergovernmental Relations

The interdependency of American society—the fact that developments in one area affect what happens elsewhere—is one of three major reasons the federal government's policy role has expanded greatly since the early twentieth century. A second reason is that Americans want government services. Whenever an area of the country is hit by a natural disaster, for example, its residents seek relief from Washington. Moreover, whenever a federal program, such as student loans or farm supports, has been established, its recipients will fight to keep it. As a consequence, federal programs rarely end while new ones get added each year. A third reason is the federal government's superior taxing capacity. States and localities are in a competitive situation with regard to taxation. A state with high corporate and personal income taxes will lose firms and people to states with lower taxes. Firms and people are less likely to move to another country in search of lower taxes. The result is that the federal government raises as much in tax revenue as do all fifty states and the thousands of local governments combined (see Figure 3-2).

Fiscal Federalism

The federal government's revenue-raising advantage has made money a basis for relations between the national government and the states and localities. **Fiscal federalism** refers to the expenditure of federal funds on programs run in part through state and local governments.[30] The federal government provides some or all of the money through **grants-in-aid** (cash payments) to states and localities, which then administer the programs. The pattern of federal assistance to states and localities is shown in Figure 3-3. Federal grants-in-aid have increased dramatically since the mid-1950s. Roughly one in every five dollars spent by local and state governments in recent decades has been raised not by them, but by the federal government in Washington (see "How the 50 States Differ").

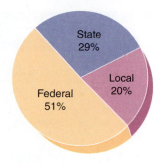

FIGURE 3-2

Federal, State, and Local Shares of Government Tax Revenue
The federal government raises as much revenue as do all state and local governments combined.

Source: Office of Management and Budget (OMB), 2012.

fiscal federalism

A term that refers to the expenditure of federal funds on programs run in part through states and localities.

grants-in-aid

Federal cash payments to states and localities for programs they administer.

FIGURE 3-3

Federal Grants to State and Local Governments
Federal aid to states and localities has increased dramatically since the 1950s. Figure is based on constant (2000) dollars in order to control for the effect of inflation.

Source: Office of Management and Budget, 2012.

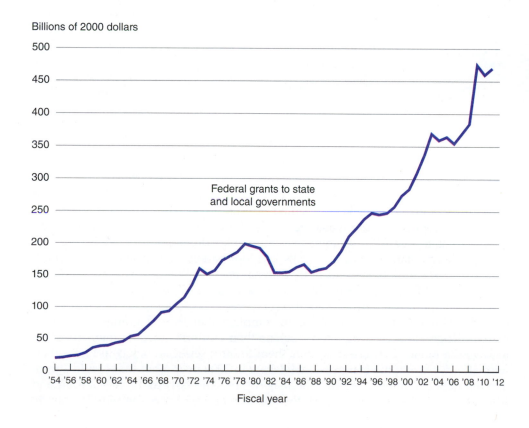

Billions of 2000 dollars

Federal grants to state and local governments

Fiscal year

HOW THE 50 STATES DIFFER POLITICAL THINKING THROUGH COMPARISONS

Federal Grants-in-Aid to the States

Federal assistance accounts for a significant share of state revenue, but the variation is considerable. New Mexico (with a third of its total revenue coming from federal grants-in-aid) is at one extreme. Nevada (a seventh of its revenue) is at the other.

Q: Why do states in the South, where anti-Washington sentiment is relatively high, get more of their revenue from the federal government than do most other states?

A: Many federal grant programs are designed to assist low-income people, and poverty is more widespread in the South. Moreover, southern states traditionally have provided fewer government services, and federal grants accordingly constitute a larger proportion of their budgets.

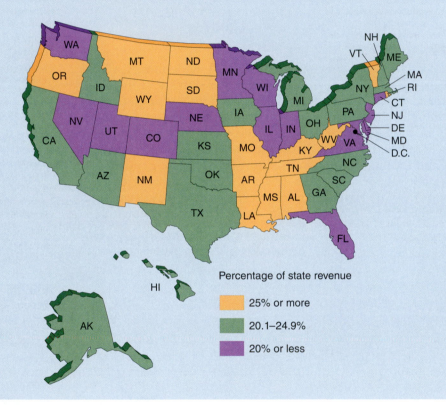

Percentage of state revenue

- 25% or more
- 20.1–24.9%
- 20% or less

Source: U.S. Census Bureau, 2010.

Cash grants to states and localities have increased Washington's policy influence. State and local governments can reject a grant-in-aid, but if they accept it they must spend it in the way specified by Congress. Also, because most grants require states to contribute matching funds, the federal programs in effect determine how states will allocate some of their own tax dollars. Further, federal grants have pressured state and local officials to adopt national goals, such as the elimination of racial and other forms of discrimination. A building constructed with the help of federal funds, for example, must be accessible to persons with disabilities. Nevertheless, federal grants-in-aid also serve the policy interests of state and local officials. Although these officials often complain that federal grants contain too many restrictions and infringe too much on their authority, most of them are eager to have the money because it permits them to offer services they could not otherwise afford. During the congressional debate in 2009 over a bill that would stimulate the nation's ailing economy, the majority of state governors, Republican and Democratic alike, urged passage of the bill. It contained more than $100 billion to help states cover their widening budget and program deficits. Said one observer: "For governors, it's free money—they get the benefits and they don't have to pay the costs of raising the revenues."[31]

Categorical and Block Grants

State and local governments receive two major types of assistance—categorical grants and block grants—which differ in the extent to which Washington defines the conditions of their use. **Categorical grants,** the more restrictive type, can be used only for a designated activity. An example is funds directed for use in school lunch programs. These funds cannot be diverted to other school purposes, such as the purchase of textbooks or the hiring of teachers. **Block grants** are less restrictive. The federal government specifies the general area in which the funds must be used, but state and local officials select the specific projects. A block grant targeted for the health area, for example, might give state and local officials the authority to decide whether to use the money for hospital construction, medical equipment, the training of nurses, or some other health care activity.

State and local officials prefer federal money that comes with fewer strings attached and thus favor block grants. In contrast, members of Congress have typically preferred categorical grants, because this type of assistance gives them more control over how state and local officials spend federal funds. Most grants are of the categorical type, but block grants have increased in frequency since the 1980s as a result of a movement known as devolution.

This familiar sign illustrates the power of fiscal federalism. Three decades ago, persons younger than twenty-one could legally buy alcohol in half the states. The policies changed when Congress enacted legislation requiring states to set the drinking age at twenty-one in order to receive federal highway funds. Although they complained, the financial stakes were too high for them to keep their existing policies.

Devolution

Devolution embodies the idea that American federalism can be strengthened by a partial shift in power from the federal government to the state and local governments.[32] Devolution rests on a belief—held more strongly by Republicans than Democrats—that federal authority has extended too far into areas traditionally governed through state and local governments.

The expansion of the federal government's domestic policy role from the 1930s onward was largely initiated by Democratic lawmakers, with strong backing from the public. The New Deal and Great Society programs had broad public support at the outset. After the 1960s, however, public support for federal domestic spending declined. Some of the programs, particularly those providing welfare benefits to the poor, were widely seen as too costly, too bureaucratic, and too lax—there was a widespread perception that many welfare recipients were getting benefits they neither needed nor deserved. Republican leaders increasingly questioned the effectiveness of the programs, a position that meshed with the party's ideology of lower taxes and local control.

Republican presidents Richard Nixon and Ronald Reagan proposed versions of a "new federalism" that would give more control to states and localities. "After a third of a century of power flowing from the people and the states to Washington," Nixon said in 1969, "it is time for a new federalism in which power, funds and responsibility flow from Washington and the states back to the people." Nixon's approach centered on the policy of *revenue sharing*, whereby the federal government would simply give money to the states for them to use as they saw fit. Unlike block or categorical grants,

categorical grants

Federal grants-in-aid to states and localities that can be used only for designated projects.

block grants

Federal grants-in-aid that permit state and local officials to decide how the money will be spent within a general area, such as education or health.

devolution

The passing down of authority from the national government to the state and local governments.

revenue sharing placed almost no restrictions on how the money would be spent. Congress, which was controlled by a Democratic majority, provided some funding for revenue sharing, though less than Nixon proposed. State and local governments used most of the money to fund their normal operations, which is not what Congress had in mind, and the program was eventually terminated.

In issuing an executive order to implement his idea of a new federalism, Reagan said: "Federalism is rooted in the knowledge that our political liberties are best assured by limiting the size and scope of national government." Reagan promoted the use of block grants as opposed to categorical grants and placed strict limits on federal agencies' activities. They were prohibited from submitting to Congress any legislative proposal that would "regulate the states in ways that would interfere" with their "traditional governmental functions." Reagan also ordered that any new federal regulation affecting the states was to be kept "to the minimum level."

The Republican Revolution

When the Republican Party scored a decisive victory in the 1994 congressional elections, Speaker of the House Newt Gingrich declared that "1960s-style federalism is dead." Republican lawmakers proposed to cut some federal programs, but, even more, they sought to devolve power to the state and local levels. The GOP-controlled Congress grouped a number of categorical grants into block grants in order to give states more control over how the federal money would be spent. Congressional Republicans also passed legislation to reduce *unfunded mandates*—federal programs that require action by states or localities but provide no or insufficient funds to pay for it. For example, states and localities are required by federal law to make their buildings accessible to the physically handicapped, but Washington pays only part of the cost of these accommodations. In the Unfunded Mandates Reform Act of 1995, Congress eliminated some of these mandates, although under threat of a veto by Democratic president Bill Clinton, kept those relating to civil rights and civil liberties (see Chapters 4 and 5).

The most significant change occurred in 1996, when Congress enacted the sweeping Welfare Reform Act. Opinion polls at the time indicated that a majority of Americans felt that government was spending too much on welfare and that too many welfare recipients were exploiting the system. The Welfare Reform Act tightened spending and eligibility. The legislation's key element, the Temporary Assistance for Needy Families (TANF) block grant, ended the decades-old federal program that granted cash assistance to every poor family with children. TANF restricts a family's eligibility for federal assistance to five years, and after two years, a family head normally has to go to work for the benefits to continue. Moreover, TANF gives states wide latitude in setting benefit levels, eligibility criteria, and other regulations affecting aid to poor families. TANF also places states in charge of developing training and education programs that will move people off of welfare and into jobs. (TANF and other aspects of the 1996 welfare reform legislation are discussed further in later chapters.)

The 1996 Welfare Reform Act was informed partly by state efforts to find new approaches to welfare. Wisconsin's program, which had job training and placement at its core, was instrumental in shaping provisions of the 1996 federal law. This type of influence was not new. Proponents of federalism have long held that states are "laboratories" for trying new policy approaches, which, if successful, can be adapted for use by other states or the federal government.

The Supreme Court's Contribution to Devolution

After the 1930s, the Supreme Court held that the line between "traditional and "nontraditional" state functions was legally vague and that states should rely on the political process rather than the courts for protection against what they regarded as unwarranted federal encroachment. Reasoning that members of Congress are elected from states and districts within states, the Court said that the states should look to these elected officials for protection from national actions that "unduly burden the states."[33]

The Court's position began to change as a result of the appointment of more conservative justices to the Court by Reagan and his Republican successor, George H. W. Bush. In the view of these justices, Congress had overstepped its constitutional authority in some areas.[34] In *United States v. Lopez* (1995), the Court cited the Tenth Amendment in striking down a federal law that prohibited the possession of guns within one thousand feet of a school. Congress had invoked the commerce power in passing the bill, but the Republican-dominated Supreme Court ruled that the ban had "nothing to do with commerce, or any sort of economic activity."[35] Two years later, in *Printz v. United States* (1997), the Court struck down a provision of the federal Handgun Violence Prevention Act (the so-called Brady bill) that required local law enforcement officers to conduct background checks on prospective handgun buyers. The Court said the provision violated the Tenth Amendment because it required state employees—in this case, police officers—to "enforce a federal regulatory program."[36] Congress can require federal employees to take such action, but it cannot order state employees to do so. They work for the state, not the federal government. (In 2012, the Supreme Court turned the tables, citing the supremacy of federal authority in striking down most of an Arizona law that gave state officials broad authority over immigration[37]—see "Debating the Issues.")

The Court has also used the Eleventh Amendment to limit Congress's authority over state governments. The Eleventh Amendment—sometimes called the "sovereign immunity amendment"—protects a state from being sued in federal court by a private citizen, unless the state agrees to the suit. The amendment has limits; it does not protect a state from suit in federal court when the state is alleged to have violated a right guaranteed by the U.S. Constitution, such as the right of the accused to have legal counsel. But the Supreme Court recently has used the Eleventh Amendment to restrict the scope of a few federal laws. In *Kimel v. Board of Regents* (2000), for example, the Supreme Court held that age discrimination, unlike racial and sexual discrimination, is not among the rights guaranteed under the Constitution and that Florida was not bound by federal law in deciding the age policies that apply to state employees.[38] (It should be noted that this ruling applies only to *state* government *employees*. Employees working for private firms in a state are protected by federal laws banning age discrimination.)

Nationalization, the More Powerful Force

Along with the 1996 Welfare Reform Act and other legislation, these Supreme Court rulings contributed to a shift in policy and power to the states. However, these actions did not constitute a wholesale change in American federalism. Federal grants-in-aid continued to flow from Washington to the states, shaping and funding many of their activities. In its 2012 decision that upheld the individual health insurance mandate, the Supreme Court reaffirmed the principle established during the 1930s that Congress's taxing and spending powers are broad and substantial.

Moreover, the devolution movement slowed dramatically after passage of the 1996 Welfare Reform Act. One of Republican president George W. Bush's first domestic policy initiatives was the No Child Left Behind Act (NCLB), which thrust federal authority more deeply than ever into local and state education

DEBATING THE ISSUES   POLITICAL THINKING IN ACTION

Should States Also Have Control over Immigration Policy?

Federalism has led to countless disputes between states and the national government. A recent dispute is whether the states have authority to pass laws regulating immigration. The issue arose when Arizona enacted a law that made illegal immigration a state crime and instructed police to check the citizenship of individuals they encountered in the course of their duties. Individuals without proof of citizenship were to be detained until the legality of their presence in the country could be determined. Illegal immigrants were then to be turned over to federal authorities for deportation. Several other states—including Alabama, Georgia, Indiana, South Carolina, and Utah—subsequently enacted similar laws. The U.S. Justice Department

filed suit to block implementation of the laws, arguing that the U.S. Constitution gives authority over immigration policy to the federal government. The Justice Department was also concerned that the state laws would lead to "racial profiling"—heightened scrutiny of individuals from particular groups, such as Hispanics and Asians. In *Arizona v. United States* (2012), the Supreme Court in a 5-3 ruling sided for the most part with federal authority, saying that Arizona "may not pursue policies that undermine federal law." However, the Court upheld the provision of the Arizona law that requires law enforcement officials to check the immigration status of those they stop or arrest for other reasons.

YES [The Arizona law will enable us] to solve a crisis we did not create and the federal government has refused to fix—the crisis caused by illegal immigration and Arizona's porous border. . . . This bill strengthens the laws of our state, protects all of us, every Arizona citizen. It does so while ensuring that the constitutional rights of all remain solid, stable. . . . We cannot sacrifice our safety to the murderous greed of drug cartels. We cannot stand idly by as drophouses, kidnappings and violence compromise our quality of life. . . . The truth is the Arizona law is both reasonable and constitutional. It mirrors substantially what has been federal law in the United States for many decades. . . . The best thing government can do is to create a stable, predictable environment, governed by an easily understood set of rules or laws. We do not need to make this more complicated than it already is. We must first and foremost create a secure border.

—Jan Brewer, governor of Arizona

NO [The] Justice Department will not hesitate to challenge a state's immigration law . . . if we find that the law interferes with the federal government's enforcement of immigration. It is understandable that communities remain frustrated with the broken immigration system, but a patchwork of state laws is not the solution and will only create problems. We will continue to monitor the impact these laws might have on our communities and will evaluate each law to determine whether it conflicts with the federal government's enforcement responsibilities . . . I think we have to understand that the immigration problem that we have, illegal immigration problem that we have, is a national one, and a state-by-state solution to it is not the way in which we ought to go. . . . I don't think [the state laws are] racist in motivation. But I think we could potentially get on a slippery slope where people will be picked on because of how they look as opposed to what they have done.

—Eric Holder, attorney general of the United States

Q: Do you think the states should have authority to devise their own immigration laws? If you think so, would you place restrictions on these laws, such as a prohibition on racial profiling?

policy. Bush argued that the United States needed a *national* education standard if it was to meet the challenge of the global economy. NCLB requires the states to test their public school students annually as a condition of receiving federal aid. A commission of the National Conference of State Legislatures had scathing words for NCLB, saying it was based on "questionable constitutional underpinnings," "coerced" states by tying the receipt of federal education funds to participation in the program, and forced schools to "teach to the test."[39] Utah was among the states that refused to comply with NCLB provisions that were not adequately funded. The terrorist attacks of September 11, 2001, also led to an expansion of federal authority, including the creation in 2002 of the Department of Homeland Security, a cabinet-level federal agency with policing and emergency responsibilities traditionally belonging to states and localities.

POLITICAL THINKING National Testing, Good Idea or Bad?

The No Child Left Behind Act (NCLB) requires states to administer nationally standardized tests to their public school students as a condition for receiving federal education funds. Do you think these tests improve public education, or do you think they weaken it by reducing teachers' flexibility? Do you think the national government through NCLB is intruding on a policy area that properly belongs to states and localities?

The economic crisis triggered by the near-collapse of the financial markets in 2008 contributed to a further increase in national power. As the crisis worsened, President Bush provided federal funds to bail out the troubled banks and other financial institutions. When President Barack Obama took office in 2009, he and the Democrat-controlled Congress bailed out the U.S. automobile industry and then enacted a nearly $800 billion economic stimulus bill. A significant portion of the stimulus money went to states and localities; their budgets were in the red because the economic downturn had produced a drop in their tax revenues. The Republican governors of Alaska, Mississippi, Louisiana, and South Carolina—over the objections of some Republicans in their states—said they would refuse to take federal stimulus funds. Other Republican governors urged passage of the stimulus bill and some, like Florida's Charlie Crist, actively lobbied for it. In the end, all states accepted federal money, although they did so in varying degrees, which is their option under federalism. The key point, however, is that the states faced a stark choice: if they did not take the federal money, they would have to cut programs, lay off state and local employees, and forego the new jobs that would be created by the federally funded stimulus projects, such as new roadways and schools. The realities of the economic downturn were far stronger than partisan ideology or federalism theory in determining how states responded to the stimulus legislation.

Federal spending for the economic recovery, combined with the continuing high cost of military intervention in the Middle East, resulted in a ballooning of the federal debt. In 2011, Congress made significant cuts in federal spending and passed legislation that will result in even deeper cuts in future years. However, the cuts are unlikely to dramatically alter the balance of federal and state power. The fact is, American federalism is today a vastly different system than what it was before the 1930s. The demands of contemporary life—an economy that is complex and integrated, a public that is insistent on its rights and accustomed to government services, a global environment that is filled with challenges and opportunities—have combined to give the federal government a bigger role in federal-state relations. The change can be seen even in the structure of the federal government. Five cabinet departments—Health and Human Services, Housing and Urban Development, Transportation, Education, and Homeland Security—were created after the 1930s to administer federal programs in policy areas traditionally reserved to the states.

In the 1990s, some policy responsibilities were shifted from the federal government to the states, a process called *devolution*. This trend stalled after 2000 for several reasons, including the terrorist attacks of September 11, 2001, which required a national response. Part of that response was a larger role for the federal government in the area of public safety. Shown here is a scene familiar to air travelers. The screening of airline passengers is the responsibility of federal officers rather than state or local police.

The Public's Influence: Setting the Boundaries of Federal-State Power

Public opinion has had a decisive influence on the ebb and flow of federal power during the past century. As Americans' attitudes toward the federal government and the states changed, the balance of power between these two levels of government also shifted. Every major change in federalism has been driven by a major shift in public support toward one level of government or the other.

During the Great Depression, when it was clear that the states would be unable to help, Americans turned to Washington for relief. For people without jobs, the fine points of the Constitution were of little consequence. They needed assistance, and would take it from whichever level of government could provide it. President Roosevelt's New Deal programs, which offered both jobs and income security, were a radical departure from the past, but quickly gained public favor. A 1936 Gallup poll indicated, for example, that 61 percent of Americans supported Roosevelt's social security program, whereas only 27 percent opposed it. This support reflected a new public attitude: the federal government, not the states, was expected to take the lead in protecting Americans from economic hardship.[40] The second great wave of federal social programs—Lyndon Johnson's Great Society—was also driven by public demands. Income and education levels had risen dramatically after the Second World War, and Americans wanted more and better services from government.[41] When the states were slow to respond, Americans pressured federal officials to act. The Medicare and Medicaid programs, which provide health care for the elderly and the poor, respectively, are examples of the Johnson administration's response. A 1965 Gallup poll indicated that two-thirds of Americans approved of federal involvement in the provision of medical care, despite the fact that health was traditionally the states' responsibility.

Public opinion was also behind the rollback of federal authority in the 1990s. In a 1994 *Times Mirror* survey, 66 percent of respondents expressed the view that most officials in Washington did not care what people like them were thinking. An even larger proportion felt that the federal government had become too large and intrusive. Americans' dissatisfaction with federal programs and spending provided the springboard for the Republican takeover of Congress in the 1994 midterm election, which led to policies aimed at devolving power to the states, including the widely popular 1996 Welfare Reform Act.[42]

In similar fashion, Americans backed the economic stimulus bill that Barack Obama and the Democratic Congress enacted in early 2009. According to a Gallup poll, 70 percent of Americans believed that the stimulus bill was "critically important" or "important" to the nation's economic recovery. The public had reservations about the scale of the spending but this worry was secondary at the time. A year later, as the federal deficit continued to mount, polls indicated that a majority of Americans believed the government in Washington was spending too freely. This sentiment gave birth to the Tea Party movement (see Chapter 7) and set the stage for the Republican surge in the 2010 midterm elections. Campaigning on the theme of cutting the federal budget, Republicans gained six Senate seats and a whopping sixty-three House seats, the largest midterm election gain by either party since 1938.

The public's role in determining the boundaries between federal and state power would come as no surprise to the framers of the Constitution. For them, federalism was a pragmatic issue, one to be decided by the nation's needs rather than by inflexible rules. Alexander Hamilton suggested that Americans would shift their loyalties between the nation and the states according to whichever level seemed more likely to serve their immediate purpose. James Madison said much the same thing in predicting that Americans would look to whichever level of government was more responsive to their interests. Indeed, each succeeding generation of Americans has seen fit to devise a balance of federal and state power suited to its needs.

Summary

Self-Test www.mhhe.com/
pattersontadtx11e

A foremost characteristic of the American political system is its division of authority between a national government and state governments. The first U.S. government, established by the Articles of Confederation, was essentially a union of the states.

In establishing the basis for a stronger national government, the U.S. Constitution also made provision for safeguarding state interests. The result was the creation of a federal system in which sovereignty was vested in both national and state governments. The Constitution enumerates the general powers of the national government and grants it implied powers through the "necessary and proper" clause. Other powers are reserved to the states by the Tenth Amendment.

From 1789 to 1865, the nation's survival was at issue. The states found it convenient at times to argue that their sovereignty took precedence over national authority. In the end, it took the Civil War to cement the idea that the United States was a union of people, not of states. From 1865 to 1937, federalism reflected the doctrine that certain policy areas were the exclusive responsibility of the national government, whereas responsibility in other policy areas belonged exclusively to the states. This constitutional position validated the laissez-faire doctrine that big business was largely beyond governmental control. It also allowed the states to discriminate against African Americans in their public policies. Federalism in a form recognizable today began to emerge in the 1930s.

In the areas of commerce, taxation, spending, civil rights, and civil liberties, among others, the federal government now plays an important role, one that is the inevitable consequence of the increasing complexity of American society and the interdependence of its people. National, state, and local officials now work closely together to solve the nation's problems, a situation known as cooperative federalism. Grants-in-aid from Washington to the states and localities have been the chief instrument of national influence. States and localities have received billions in federal assistance; in accepting federal money, they also have accepted both federal restrictions on its use and the national policy priorities that underlie the granting of the money.

Throughout the nation's history, the public through its demands on government has influenced the boundaries between federal and state power. The devolutionary trend of the 1990s, for example, was sparked by Americans' sense that a rollback in federal power was desirable, whereas the subsequent expansion of federal power has been a response to Americans' concerns about terrorism and economic recovery.

CHAPTER 3

Study Corner

Key Terms

block grants (*p. 73*)
categorical grants (*p. 73*)
commerce clause (*p. 67*)
confederacy (*p. 59*)
cooperative federalism (*p. 70*)
devolution (*p. 73*)
dual federalism (*p. 65*)
enumerated (expressed)
  powers (*p. 62*)
federalism (*p. 59*)

fiscal federalism (*p. 71*)
grants-in-aid (*p. 71*)
implied powers (*p. 62*)
nationalization (*p. 63*)
"necessary and proper"
  (elastic) clause (*p. 62*)
reserved powers (*p. 62*)
sovereignty (*p. 58*)
supremacy clause (*p. 62*)
unitary system (*p. 59*)

Self-Test: Multiple Choice

1. Describing the United States as having a federal system of government means that
   a. the states are not included in the power arrangement.
   b. constitutional authority for governing is divided between a national government on the one hand and the state governments on the other.
   c. the states are not bound by the rules and regulations of the national government.
   d. America set up the same type of governing structure as Britain except for its monarchy.

2. The significance of the Preamble to the Constitution's reading "We the People" rather than "We the States" is that
   a. there was to be no change in the power relationship between the states and the nation in the new Constitution.
   b. the new Constitution symbolically recognized the people for winning the Revolutionary War.
   c. the states would not have to pay their war debts.
   d. the national government under the Constitution would have direct power over the people, which it did not have under the Articles of Confederation.

3. Which type of power was given to the states under the Constitution?
   a. the power to declare war
   b. supremacy over the national government
   c. reserved power
   d. necessary and proper power

4. The Supreme Court in *McCulloch v. Maryland*
   a. ruled in favor of state-centered federalism.
   b. affirmed that national law is supreme over conflicting state law.
   c. established the principle of judicial review.
   d. declared the "necessary and proper" clause unconstitutional.

5. Which one of the following does *not* describe trends in government revenues and intergovernmental relations in the United States?
   a. The federal government raises roughly as much revenue as do all state and local governments combined.
   b. Unlike states and localities, the federal government controls the American dollar and has a nearly unlimited ability to borrow money to cover its deficits.
   c. The states possess the organizational resources to make fiscal federalism a workable arrangement.
   d. Financial assistance from the federal government to the states is gradually being eliminated.

6. The concept of devolution is used to explain
   a. a shift in authority from the federal government to state and local governments.
   b. the necessity for keeping federal and state spheres of responsibility absolutely separate from each other.
   c. Supreme Court rulings in the period between the Civil War and the New Deal.
   d. increased recognition that the industrial economy is not confined by state boundaries and must be subject to national regulation.

7. Categorical grants allow the states more flexibility and discretion in the expenditure of funds than do block grants. (T/F)

8. The primary goal of the writers of the Constitution was to establish a national government strong enough to forge a union secure in its defense and open in its commerce. (T/F)

9. Dual federalism is the idea that the national and state governments should not interfere in each other's activities. (T/F)

10. Fiscal federalism involves the states raising money for programs and the federal government administering the programs. (T/F)

Self-Test: Essay

How have interdependency and the federal government's superior taxing power contributed to a larger policy role for the national government? Where do block grants and categorical grants fit into the trend?

Suggested Readings

Broadway, Robin, and Anwar Shah. *Fiscal Federalism*. New York: Cambridge University Press, 2009. A comparative analysis of the role of money in federal-state relations.

Cornell, Saul. *The Other Founders: Anti-Federalism and the Dissenting Tradition in America*. Chapel Hill: University of North Carolina Press, 1999. An analysis of Anti-Federalist thought, its origins, and its legacy.

Elkins, Stanley, and Eric McKitrick. *The Age of Federalism: The Early American Republic, 1788–1800*. New York: Oxford University Press, 1993. An award-winning book on the earliest period of American federalism.

LaCroix, Alison L. *The Ideological Origins of American Federalism*. Cambridge, Mass.: Harvard University Press, 2011. An examination of the normative ideas, as opposed to the pragmatic ones, that contributed to federalism's adoption.

Nugent, John D. *Safeguarding Federalism: How States Protect Their Interests in National Policymaking*. Norman: University of Oklahoma Press, 2009. An assessment of how states promote their interest in the context of federal initiatives.

Ross, William G. *A Muted Fury: Populists, Progressives, and Labor Unions Confront the Courts, 1890–1937*. Princeton, N.J.: Princeton University Press, 1993. A valuable study of the politics surrounding the judiciary's laissez-faire doctrine in the period 1890–1937.

List of Websites

http://lcweb2.loc.gov/ammem/amlaw/lawhome.html
A site containing congressional documents and debates from 1774 to 1873.

www.csg.org
The site of the Council of State Governments; includes current news from each of the states and basic information about their governments.

http://avalon.law.yale.edu/subject_menus/fed.asp
A documentary record of the *Federalist Papers*, the Annapolis convention, the Articles of Confederation, the Madison debates, and the U.S. Constitution.

www.civilwarhome.com/csconstitution.htm
The constitution of the confederate South during the Civil War. Its provisions are more like those of the U.S. Constitution than those of the Articles of Confederation.

Participate!

The U.S. federal system of government offers an array of channels for political participation. Vital governing decisions are made at the national, state, and local levels, all of which provide opportunities for citizens to make a difference and also to build skills—such as public speaking and working with others—that will prove valuable in other areas of life. You have a participatory arena close at hand: your college campus. Most colleges and universities support a variety of activities in which students can engage. Student government is one such opportunity; another is the student newspaper. Most colleges and universities offer a wide range of groups and sponsored programs, from debate clubs to fraternal organizations. If you are not now active in campus groups, consider joining one. If you join—or if you already belong to such a group—take full advantage of the participatory opportunities it provides.

Extra Credit

For up-to-the-minute *New York Times* articles, interactive simulations, graphics, study tools, and more links and quizzes, visit the text's Online Learning Center at **www.mhhe.com/pattersontad11e**.

Self-Test Answers

1. b, 2. d, 3. c, 4. b, 5. d, 6. a, 7. F, 8. T, 9. T, 10. F

Civil Liberties: Protecting Individual Rights

A bill of rights is what the people are entitled to against every government on earth, general or particular, and what no just government should refuse, or rest on inference. —Thomas Jefferson[1]

Without a warrant from a judge, the police and FBI were tracking Antoine Jones's car wherever it went. They had secretly attached a GPS tracking device to its undercarriage and knew exactly where it was at any time of the day or night. For a month, they monitored the car's every turn. They subsequently arrested Jones on charges of conspiracy to sell drugs. The evidence obtained through the tracking device helped prosecutors to get a conviction, and Jones was sentenced to life in prison.

Jones appealed his conviction and won a temporary victory when a federal appellate court—noting that individuals are protected by the Fourth Amendment from "unreasonable searches and seizures"—concluded that the officers should have sought a warrant from a judge, who would have decided whether they had sufficient cause to justify a search of Jones's possessions, much less the placing of a tracking device on his car.

In a unanimous 9-0 vote, the Supreme Court in *United States v. Jones* (2012) upheld the lower court's judgment. The Court rejected the government's argument that attaching a small device to a car's undercarriage was too trivial an act to constitute an "unreasonable search." The government had also claimed that anyone driving a car on public streets can expected to be monitored, even continuously in some circumstances—after all, police had legally been "tailing" suspects for decades. The Court rejected those arguments, though the justices disagreed on exactly why the Constitution prohibits what the officers had done. Five of the justices said that the Fourth Amendment's protection of "persons, houses, papers, and effects" reasonably extends to private property such as an automobile. For them, the fact that the officers had placed a tracking device on the suspect's property without a warrant invalidated the evidence. Four of the justices went further, saying that the officers' actions intruded not only on the suspect's property rights but also on his "reasonable expectation of privacy." At its core, said the four justices, the Fourth Amendment "protects people, not places."[2]

Thomas Jefferson was critical of the framers of the Constitution for their failure to include a listing of individual rights. At the urging of Jefferson and other leading Americans, the first Congress passed a set of amendments (the Bill of Rights) aimed at protecting these rights. Earlier, Jefferson had drafted a bill of rights for the state of Virginia's constitution.

civil liberties

The fundamental individual rights of a free society, such as freedom of speech and the right to a jury trial, which in the United States are protected by the Bill of Rights.

As the case illustrates, issues of individual rights are complex. The Fourth Amendment protects Americans not from *all* searches but from *unreasonable* searches. The public would be unsafe if law officials could never track a suspect. Yet citizens would forfeit their privacy if police could track at will anyone they choose. The challenge for a civil society is to establish a level of police authority that meets the demands of public safety without infringing unduly on personal freedom. The balance point, however, is always subject to dispute. In this particular case, the Supreme Court sided with the accused. In other cases, it has sided with law enforcement officials.

This chapter examines issues of **civil liberties**—specific individual rights, such as freedom of speech, that are constitutionally protected against infringement by government. Although the term *civil liberties* is sometimes used synonymously with the term *civil rights*, they can be distinguished. Civil liberties refer to specific *individual* rights, such as protection against self-incrimination, whereas civil rights have to do with whether members of differing groups—racial, sexual, religious, and the like—are treated equally by government and, in some cases, by private parties. Issues of civil rights are addressed in the next chapter.

Civil liberties issues have become increasingly complex. The framers of the Constitution could not possibly have foreseen the United States of the early twenty-first century, with its huge national government, enormous corporations, pervasive mass media, urban crowding, vulnerability to terrorist acts, and technology that can track people's locations and eavesdrop on their conversations. These developments are potential threats to personal liberty, and the judiciary in the past century has seen fit to expand the rights to which individuals are entitled. However, these rights are constantly being weighed against competing rights and society's collective interests. The Bill of Rights operates in an untidy world where people's highest aspirations collide with their worst passions, and it is at this juncture that issues of civil liberties arise. Should a murder suspect be entitled to recant a confession? Should the press be allowed to print military secrets whose publication might jeopardize national security? Should extremist groups be allowed to publicize their messages of prejudice and hate? Such questions are among the subjects of this chapter, which focuses on these points:

- *Freedom of expression is the most basic of democratic rights, but like all rights, it is not unlimited.*
- *"Due process of law" refers to legal protections (primarily procedural safeguards) designed to ensure that individual rights are respected by government.*
- *Over the course of the nation's history, Americans' civil liberties have been broadened in law and more fully protected by the courts.* Of special significance has been the Supreme Court's use of the Fourteenth Amendment to protect individual rights from action by state and local governments.
- *Individual rights are constantly being weighed against the demands of majorities and the collective needs of society.* All political institutions are involved in this process, as is public opinion, but the judiciary plays a central role and is the institution that is typically most protective of civil liberties.

The Constitution: The Bill of Rights and the Fourteenth Amendment

Bill of Rights [Q1]

The first ten amendments to the Constitution. They include rights such as freedom of speech and religion and due process protections (such as the right to a jury trial) for persons accused of crimes.

The Constitution's failure to enumerate individual freedoms led to demands for the **Bill of Rights** (see Chapter 2). Enacted in 1791, these first ten amendments to the Constitution specify certain rights of life, liberty, and property that the federal government is obliged to protect (see Table 4-1). Among these rights are

TABLE 4-1 | The Bill of Rights: A Selected List of Constitutional Protections

First Amendment

Speech: You are free to say almost anything except that which is obscene, slanders another person, or has a high probability of inciting others to take imminent lawless action.

Assembly: You are free to assemble, although government may regulate the time and place for reasons of public convenience and safety, provided such regulations are applied evenhandedly to all groups.

Religion: You are protected from having the religious beliefs of others imposed on you, and you are free to believe what you like.

Fourth Amendment

Search and seizure: You are protected from unreasonable searches and seizures, although you forfeit that right if you knowingly waive it.

Arrest: You are protected from arrest unless authorities have probable cause to believe that you have committed a crime.

Fifth Amendment

Self-incrimination: You are protected against self-incrimination, which means that you have the right to remain silent and to be protected against coercion by law enforcement officials.

Double jeopardy: You cannot be tried twice for the same crime if the first trial results in a verdict of innocence.

Due process: You cannot be deprived of life, liberty, or property without proper legal proceedings.

Sixth Amendment

Counsel: You have a right to be represented by an attorney and can demand to speak first with an attorney before responding to questions from law enforcement officials.

Prompt and reasonable proceedings: You have a right to be arraigned promptly, to be informed of the charges, to confront witnesses, and to have a speedy and open trial by an impartial jury.

Eighth Amendment

Bail: You are protected against excessive bail or fines.

Cruel and unusual punishment: You are protected from cruel and unusual punishment, although this provision does not protect you from the death penalty or from a long prison term for a minor offense.

freedoms of speech, press, assembly, and religion (First Amendment); the right to bear arms (Second Amendment); protection against unreasonable search and seizure (Fourth Amendment); protection against self-incrimination and double jeopardy (Fifth Amendment); right to a jury trial, to an attorney, and to confront witnesses (Sixth Amendment); and protection against cruel and unusual punishment (Eight Amendment).

The Supreme Court has assumed responsibility for defining what the Bill of Rights guarantees will mean in practice. In some areas, the Court has devised specific tests to determine whether authorities have acted properly. A test applied in the area of free speech, for example, is whether general rules (such as restrictions on the time and place of a political rally) are reasonable and are applied fairly. Government officials would fail to meet this standard if they allowed rallies only on a particular day of the week or if they were more accommodating to groups they like than to those they dislike.

Originally, the guarantees in the Bill of Rights applied only to the actions of the national government. When this limitation on the Bill of Rights was challenged in *Barron v. Baltimore* (1833), the Supreme Court upheld it, saying that the first ten "amendments contain no expression indicating an intention to apply them to the state governments."[3] As a result, the Bill of Rights originally had little meaning in the daily lives of ordinary Americans because state governments have authority over most of the activities, such as law enforcement, in which individual rights are at issue.

Selective Incorporation of Free Expression Rights

Today, most of the rights contained in the Bill of Rights *are* protected from action by the state governments. This development occurred slowly and in stages.

Immediately after the Civil War, several southern states enacted laws denying newly freed slaves the rights held by whites, such as the right to own property and to travel freely. Congress responded by proposing a constitutional amendment designed to protect the rights of former slaves. The former Confederate states with the exception of Tennessee refused to ratify it. Congress then passed the Reconstruction Act, which placed the southern states under military rule until they ratified the amendment and adopted state constitutions that conformed with the U.S. Constitution. In 1868, the Fourteenth Amendment was ratified. It includes a **due process clause** that says "no state shall . . . deprive any person of life, liberty, or property, without due process of law." In the ensuing decades, with the tacit consent of the Supreme Court (see Chapter 3), the southern states ignored the clause.

Then, in 1925, the Supreme Court invoked the Fourteenth Amendment's due process clause in a free speech case. In *Gitlow v. New York* (1925), the Supreme Court upheld a New York law that made it illegal to advocate the violent overthrow of the U.S. government. In doing so, however, the Court held that states do *not* have complete authority over what their residents can say and write. The Court said: "For present purposes we may and do assume that freedom of speech and of the press—which are protected by the First Amendment from abridgement by Congress—are among the fundamental personal rights and 'liberties' protected by the due process clause of the Fourteenth Amendment from impairment by the states."[4]

By interpreting the Fourteenth Amendment's due process clause to protect a First Amendment right, the Court positioned itself to broaden the protection to include all First Amendment rights. Within a dozen years, the Court heard a set of free-expression cases that allowed it to do just that. The Court invalidated state laws restricting expression in the areas of speech (*Fiske v. Kansas*), press (*Near v. Minnesota*), religion (*Hamilton v. Regents, University of California*), and assembly and petition (*DeJonge v. Oregon*).[5] The *Near* decision is the best known of these rulings. Jay Near was the publisher of a Minneapolis weekly newspaper that regularly made defamatory statements about blacks, Jews, Catholics, and labor union leaders. His paper was closed down on the basis of a Minnesota law banning "malicious, scandalous, or defamatory" publications. Near appealed the shutdown on the grounds that it infringed on freedom of the press, and the Supreme Court ruled in his favor, saying that the Minnesota law was "the essence of censorship."[6]

In these cases, the Supreme Court engaged in what came to be known as **selective incorporation**—the process by which certain of the rights contained in the Bill of Rights become applicable through the Fourteenth Amendment to actions by the state governments. In *Gitlow,* for example, the Court selectively incorporated the First Amendment guarantee of free expression into the Fourteenth Amendment, enabling citizens who believe their free expression rights were violated by a state to sue it in federal court. (The incorporation process is called *selective* because the Supreme Court has chosen to protect some Bill of Rights guarantees from state action but not others. Even today, for example, the Seventh Amendment right to a jury trial in civil cases is not binding on the states.)

Selective Incorporation of Fair Trial Rights

As the Supreme Court was moving to protect free-expression rights from state action in the 1920s and 1930s, it held back on doing the same for the rights of the accused. The Court claimed that free-expression rights were more deserving

due process clause (of the Fourteenth Amendment)
The clause of the Constitution that has been used by the judiciary to apply Bill of Rights protections to the actions of state governments.

selective incorporation
The process by which certain of the rights (for example, freedom of speech) contained in the Bill of Rights become applicable through the Fourteenth Amendment to actions by the state governments.

of federal protection because they are "the indispensable condition of nearly every other form of freedom."[7] The Court did make an exception, however, in capital punishment cases, holding that states had to provide legal counsel to defendants who were too poor to hire one. The ruling came in *Powell v. Alabama* (1932), a case involving eight African American men who were sentenced to death without benefit of counsel on trumped-up rape charges.[8]

The Supreme Court's position on the rights of the accused in state courts changed abruptly in the 1960s. Advances in public education and communication had made Americans more aware of their rights, and the civil rights movement dramatized the fact that the poor and minorities had fewer rights in practice than did other Americans. In response, the Supreme Court in the 1960s began to protect the rights of the accused from action by the states.

The selective incorporation process began with *Mapp v. Ohio* (1961). Police forcibly entered the home of Dollree Mapp, a black woman, saying they had a tip she was harboring a fugitive. After discovering that the fugitive was not there, they handcuffed her and began rummaging through her closets. In the basement, they found a chest that contained obscene photographs. Mapp was arrested and convicted of violating an Ohio law that prohibited the possession of such material. The Supreme Court overturned her conviction, ruling that police had acted unconstitutionally, citing the Fourth Amendment, which reads in part: "The right of the people to be secure in their persons, houses, papers, and effects, against unreasonable searches and seizures, shall not be violated." The Court concluded that evidence acquired through an unconstitutional search cannot be used to obtain a conviction in state courts.[9]

During the 1960s, the Court also ruled that defendants in state criminal proceedings must be provided a lawyer in felony cases if they cannot afford to hire one,[10] cannot be compelled to testify against themselves,[11] have the right to remain silent and to have legal counsel at the time of arrest,[12] have the right to confront witnesses who testify against them,[13] must be granted a speedy trial,[14] have the right to a jury trial in criminal proceedings,[15] and cannot be subjected to double jeopardy.[16]

Through these decisions, and the earlier ones involving free expression, the Supreme Court has broadly protected Bill of Rights guarantees from action by the states. The following sections examine more closely the law and practice of Americans' civil liberties.

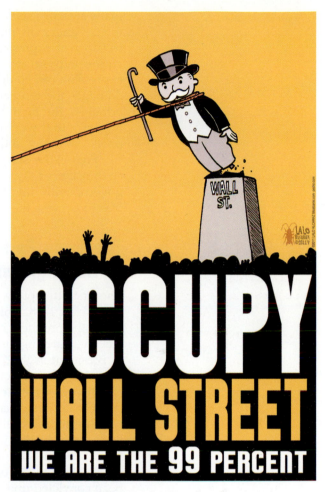

Exercising their constitutional right to free speech and assembly, Occupy Wall Street protesters camped out in cities across the country in 2011. Their rallying cry was "We are the 99 percent." This slogan was meant to distinguish them from America's richest one percent, which they saw as the undeserving beneficiaries of favorable government policies.
© 2011 Lalo Alcaraz. Reprinted with permission.

Freedom of Expression

Freedom of expression is widely regarded as the most basic of individual rights. As Justice Harlan Fisk Stone argued in 1938, a government that can silence those who speak out against it has the power to control elections and to abridge other rights.[17]

The First Amendment provides for **freedom of expression**—the right of individual Americans to hold and communicate thoughts of their choosing. For

freedom of expression

Americans' freedom to communicate their views, the foundation of which is the First Amendment rights of freedom of conscience, speech, press, assembly, and petition.

many reasons, such as a desire to conform to social pressure or a fear of harassment, Americans do not always choose to express themselves freely. Moreover, freedom of expression, like other rights, is not absolute in practice. It does not entitle individuals to say whatever they want to whomever they want. Free expression can be denied, for example, if it endangers national security, wrongly damages the reputation of others, or deprives others of their basic rights. Nevertheless, the First Amendment provides for freedom of expression by prohibiting laws that would unreasonably abridge the freedoms of conscience, speech, press, assembly, and petition.

Free expression is vigorously protected by the courts. Today, under most circumstances, Americans can freely express their political views without fear of governmental interference or retribution. In earlier times, Americans were less free to express their opinions.

The Early Period: The Uncertain Status of the Right of Free Expression

The first attempt by the U.S. government to restrict free expression was the Sedition Act of 1798, which made it a crime to print harshly critical newspaper stories about the president or other national officials. Thomas Jefferson called the Sedition Act an "alarming infraction" of the Constitution and, upon replacing John Adams as president in 1801, pardoned those who had been convicted under it. Nevertheless, the Sedition Act was not tested in a Supreme Court case, which left open the question of whether Congress had the power to regulate free expression and, if so, how far its power extended. The Supreme Court also did not rule on the question during the Civil War era, when the government substantially restricted free expression. In this instance, Congress passed legislation barring the Court from hearing appeals of free expression cases, and the Court accepted the limitation.[18]

In 1919, the Court finally ruled on a free-expression case. The defendant had been convicted under the 1917 Espionage Act, which prohibited forms of dissent, including the distribution of antiwar leaflets that could harm the nation's effort in World War I. In *Schenck v. United States* (1919), the Court unanimously upheld the constitutionality of the Espionage Act. In the opinion written by Justice Oliver Wendell Holmes, the Court said that Congress could restrict speech that was "of such a nature as to create a clear and present danger" to the nation's security. In a famous passage, Holmes argued that not even the First Amendment would permit a person to falsely yell "Fire!" in a crowded theater and create a panic that could kill or injure innocent people.[19]

Although the *Schenck* decision upheld a law that limited free expression, it also established a constitutional standard—the **clear-and-present-danger test**—for determining when government could legally do so. According to the test, the government has to clearly demonstrate that spoken or written expression presents a clear and present danger before it can prohibit the expression.

The Modern Period: Protecting Free Expression

Until the twentieth century, the tension between national security interests and free expression was not a pressing issue in the United States. The country's great size and ocean barriers provided protection from potential enemies, minimizing concerns about internal subversion. World War I, however, intruded on America's isolation, and World War II brought it to an abrupt end. Since then, Americans' rights of free expression have been defined largely in the context of national security concerns.

clear-and-present-danger test

A test devised by the Supreme Court in 1919 to define the limits of free speech in the context of national security. According to the test, government cannot abridge political expression unless it presents a clear and present danger to the nation's security.

Free Speech

In the period after World War II, many Americans believed that the Soviet Union was bent on destroying the United States, and the Supreme Court allowed government to limit subversive expression. In 1951, for example, the Court upheld the convictions of eleven members of the U.S. Communist Party who had been prosecuted under a federal law that made it illegal to advocate the forceful overthrow of the U.S. government.[20]

By the late 1950s, however, fear of internal communist subversion was subsiding, and the Supreme Court changed its stance.[21] Ever since, it has held that national security must be endangered before government can lawfully prohibit citizens from speaking out. During this period, which includes the Vietnam and Iraq wars, not a single individual has been convicted solely for criticizing the government's war policies. (Some dissenters have been found guilty on other grounds, such as inciting a riot or assaulting a police officer.)

As was noted previously, the Supreme Court in the 1920s moved to protect speech from actions by the states. It has continued to do so. A defining free speech case is *Brandenburg v. Ohio* (1969). In a speech delivered at a Ku Klux Klan rally, Clarence Brandenburg said that "revenge" might have to be taken if the national government "continues to suppress the white Caucasian race." He was convicted under an Ohio law, but the Supreme Court reversed the conviction, saying a state cannot prohibit speech that advocates the unlawful use of force unless it meets a two-part test: first, the speech must be "directed at inciting or producing imminent lawless action" and, second, it must be "likely to produce such action."[22] This test—the likelihood of **imminent lawless action**—is a refinement of the clear-and-present-danger test that allows individuals more latitude in what they say. It is extremely rare for words alone to lead others to engage in rioting or other forms of lawless action.

The imminent lawless action test effectively gives Americans the freedom to voice nearly any political opinion they desire. This freedom extends to hate speech. In a unanimous 1992 opinion, the Court struck down a St. Paul, Minnesota, ordinance making it a crime to engage in speech likely to arouse "anger or alarm" on the basis of "race, color, creed, religion or gender." The Court said that the First Amendment prohibits government from "silencing speech on the basis of its content."[23] This protection of hate *speech* does not, however, extend to hate *crimes,* such as assault, motivated by racial or other prejudice. A Wisconsin law that provided for increased sentences for hate crimes was challenged as a violation of the First Amendment. In a unanimous 1993 opinion, the Court said that the law was aimed, not at free speech, but at "conduct unprotected by the First Amendment."[24]

Few cases illustrate more clearly the extent to which Americans are free to express themselves than does *Snyder v. Phelps* (2011). Pastor Fred Phelps of the Westboro Baptist Church (WBC) led a protest demonstration at the funeral of Matthew Snyder, a U.S. Marine killed in Iraq. Like their protests at other military funerals, WBC's protest at Snyder's funeral service was directed at what WBC claims is America's tolerance of gays and lesbians. Displaying signs such as "Fag

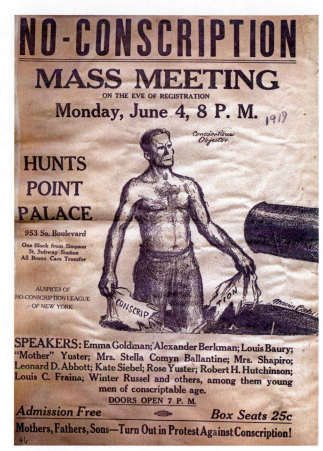

The 1917 Espionage Act made it a crime to distribute antiwar material that could harm the nation's efforts in World War I. The Supreme Court upheld the law but used it as the basis for establishing a constitutional test—the clear and present danger test—for judging how far the government can lawfully go in restricting free expression.

imminent lawless action test

A legal test that says government cannot lawfully suppress advocacy that promotes lawless action unless such advocacy is aimed at producing, and is likely to produce, imminent lawless action.

troops" and "Thank God for dead soldiers," the protestors were otherwise orderly, holding down their voices and staying three blocks away from the memorial service. Snyder's father sued WBC for "emotional distress" and was awarded $5 million in a federal jury trial. In an 8-1 decision, the Supreme Court overturned the award, concluding that the WBC's protest, although "hurtful," was protected by the First Amendment."[25]

symbolic speech

Action (for example, the waving or burning of a flag) for the purpose of expressing a political opinion.

The Supreme Court's protection of **symbolic speech** has been less substantial than its protection of verbal speech. For example, the Court in 1968 upheld the conviction of a Vietnam War protester who had burned his draft registration card. The Court concluded that the federal law prohibiting the destruction of draft cards was intended to protect the military's manpower needs and not to prevent people from criticizing government policy.[26] Nevertheless, the Supreme Court has generally protected symbolic speech. In 1989, for example, the Court ruled that the symbolic burning of the American flag is a lawful form of expression. The ruling came in the case of Gregory Lee Johnson, who had set fire to a flag outside the hall in Dallas where the 1984 Republican National Convention was being held. The Supreme Court rejected the state of Texas's argument that flag burning is, in every instance, an imminent danger to public safety. "If there is a bedrock principle underlying the First Amendment," the Court ruled in the *Johnson* case, "it is that the Government may not prohibit the expression of an idea simply because society finds the idea itself offensive or disagreeable."[27]

In general, the Supreme Court has held that government attempt to regulate the *content* of a message is suspect. In the flag-burning case, for example, Texas was regulating the content of the message—contempt for the flag and the principles it represents. Texas could not have been regulating the act itself, for the Texas government's own method of disposing of worn-out flags is to burn them.

Free Assembly

In a key case involving freedom of assembly, the U.S. Supreme Court in 1977 upheld a lower-court ruling against local ordinances of Skokie, Illinois, that had been invoked to prevent a parade there by the American Nazi Party.[28] Skokie had a large Jewish population, including survivors of Nazi Germany's concentration camps. The Supreme Court held that the right of free expression takes

Members of the Westboro Baptist Church picket the funeral of an American killed in the Middle East. Despite the horrific nature of their signs and slogans, which they have displayed at numerous military funerals, the Supreme Court has ruled that their actions are protected by the First Amendment.

DEBATING THE ISSUES POLITICAL THINKING IN ACTION

Should Flag Burning Be a Crime?

Few Americans believe that the burning of the American flag is an acceptable form of protest. Even fewer would choose to burn the flag as a symbol of their disagreement with U.S. policy. Yet flag burning has been a leading political issue since the Supreme Court in 1989 held that it is a constitutionally protected form of expression. Since then, Congress has tried several times to initiate a constitutional amendment that would ban flag burning. If such an amendment were ratified, courts would be obliged to uphold it. In 2006, Congress came within one vote in the Senate of obtaining the two-thirds majority in each chamber that is necessary to send a flag-burning amendment to the states for ratification. The congressional debate was heated as proponents of reverence for the flag faced off against proponents of free expression. Below are the statements of two of the senators who took opposite sides on the issue.

YES We enjoy a greater measure of liberty and justice and equality than any other country in human history. . . . There is one symbol that above all others encapsulates that hope, that freedom, our history and our values, and that is the American flag. From the time we are schoolchildren, we honor our flag and all it stands for. . . . In times of crisis, raising those Stars and Stripes has symbolized our unity, our perseverance as a nation, as a people. Whether it is the marines struggling to plant the flag on Iwo Jima or firefighters lifting the flag above the ruins of the World Trade Center, it is that flag which inspires us to great acts of heroism, of courage, of strength. Unfortunately, however, there are no laws on the books to stop anyone from destroying this cherished symbol. Today, we have a new opportunity to change that and to honor the wishes of the American people. We are a Nation founded on principles. Our flag is what binds us to those principles, to one another; it is that physical symbol of our values, liberty, justice, freedom, and independence. It commands our loyalty. To countless people around the world, the red, white, and blue represents the highest of human ideals—freedom. I know we have heard again and again through the media the whole issue about flag burning being protected as an exercise of free speech. But is defacing a Government building free speech? Do we let our monuments be vandalized? Clearly, the answer is no. I believe that our American flag deserves the same respect.

—*Bill Frist, U.S. senator (R-Tenn.)*

NO Let me make one thing clear at the outset. Not a single Senator who opposes the proposed constitutional amendment, as I do, supports burning or otherwise showing disrespect to the flag. Not a single one. None of us think it is "OK" to burn the flag. None of us view the flag as "just a piece of cloth." On those rare occasions when some malcontent defiles or burns our flag, I join everyone in this Chamber in condemning that action. But we must also defend the right of all Americans to express their views about their Government, however hateful or spiteful or disrespectful those views may be, without fear of their Government putting them in jail for those views. America is not simply a Nation of symbols, it is a Nation of principles. And the most important principle of all, the principle that has made this country a beacon of hope and inspiration for oppressed peoples throughout the world, is the right of free expression. This amendment threatens that right, so I must oppose it. We have heard at various times over the years that this amendment has been debated that permitting protestors to burn the American flag sends the wrong message to our children about patriotism and respect for our country. I couldn't disagree more with that argument. We can send no better, no stronger, no more meaningful message to our children about the principles and the values of this country than if we oppose efforts to undermine freedom of expression, even expression that is undeniably offensive.

—*Russell Feingold, U.S. senator (D-Wisc.)*

Q: Where do you stand on the issue? Is flag burning so disrespectful of a revered national symbol that it should be made a federal crime? Or does the First Amendment's guarantee of free expression take precedence?

precedence over the mere *possibility* that the exercise of that right might have undesirable consequences. Before government can lawfully prevent a speech or rally, it must demonstrate that the event will likely cause harm and also must demonstrate that it lacks an alternative way (such as assigning police officers to control the crowd) to prevent the harm from happening.

The Supreme Court has recognized that freedoms of speech and assembly may conflict with the routines of daily life. Accordingly, individuals do not have the right to hold a public rally at a busy intersection during rush hour, nor do they have the right to immediate access to a public auditorium or the right to turn up the volume on loudspeakers to the point where they can be heard miles away. The Occupy Wall Street protesters that recently set up camp sites in public spaces in cities throughout the country were within their right to peacefully assemble. However, the right did not extend to an indefinite occupation of public spaces or one that could result in a safety, sanitation, or fire hazard. The Court allows public officials to regulate the time, place, and conditions of public assembly, provided the regulations are reasonable and are applied fairly to all groups, whatever their issue.[29]

Press Freedom and Prior Restraint

Freedom of the press also receives strong judicial protection. In *New York Times Co. v. United States* (1971), the Court ruled that the *Times*'s publication of the "Pentagon Papers" (secret government documents revealing that officials had deceived the public about aspects of the Vietnam War) could not be blocked by the government, which claimed that publication would harm the war effort. The documents had been obtained illegally by antiwar activists, who then gave them to the *Times*. The Court ruled that "any system of prior restraints" on the press is unconstitutional unless the government can clearly justify the restriction.[30]

prior restraint

Government prohibition of speech or publication before the fact, which is presumed by the courts to be unconstitutional unless the justification for it is overwhelming.

The unacceptability of **prior restraint**—government prohibition of speech or publication before it occurs—is basic to the current doctrine of free expression. The Supreme Court has said that any attempt by government to prevent expression carries "a 'heavy presumption' against its constitutionality."[31] News organizations are legally responsible after the fact for what they report or say (for example, they can be sued by an individual whose reputation is wrongly damaged by their words), but government ordinarily cannot prevent a news organization from reporting whatever it wants to report. One of the few exceptions is wartime reporting; in some circumstances, the government can censor news reports that contain information that might compromise a military operation or endanger the lives of American troops.

Libel and Slander

libel

Publication of false material that damages a person's reputation.

The constitutional right of free expression is not a legal license to avoid responsibility for the consequences of what is said or written. If false information harmful to a person's reputation is published (**libel**) or spoken (**slander**), the injured party can sue for damages. If it were easy for public officials to claim defamation and win large amounts of money, individuals and news organizations would be reluctant to criticize those in power. As it happens, slander and libel laws in the United States are based on the assumption that society has an interest in encouraging citizens and news organizations to express themselves freely. Accordingly, public officials can be criticized nearly at will without fear that the writer or speaker will have to pay them damages for slander or libel. (The courts are less protective of the writer or speaker when allegations are made about a private citizen. What is said about private individuals is considered to be less basic to the democratic process than what is said about public officials.)

slander

Spoken falsehoods that damage a person's reputation.

The Supreme Court has held that true statements disseminated by the media have "full constitutional protection."[32] In other words, factually accurate statements, no matter how damaging they might be to a public official's career or reputation, are a protected form of expression. Even false or conjectural statements enjoy considerable legal protection. In *New York Times Co. v. Sullivan* (1964), the Supreme Court overruled an Alabama state court that had found the *New York Times* guilty of libel for publishing an advertisement that claimed Alabama officials had mistreated student civil rights activists. Although only some of the allegations were true, the Supreme Court backed the *Times*, saying that libel of a public official requires proof of actual malice, which was defined as a knowing or reckless disregard for the truth.[33] It is very difficult to prove that a publication recklessly or deliberately disregarded the truth. In fact, no federal official has won a libel judgment against a news organization in the four decades since the *Sullivan* ruling.

Obscenity

Obscenity is a form of expression that is not protected by the First Amendment and thus can legally be prohibited. However, the Supreme Court has found it difficult to develop a legal test for distinguishing obscene material from sexually oriented material that adults have a right to see or possess. No test had the support of a majority on the Court until *Miller v. California* (1973). In this ruling, the Court held that for material to be judged obscene, it had to meet a three-part test: first, the material must depict sexual conduct in a "patently offensive" way; second, the material must be precisely described in law as obscene; and three, the material "taken as a whole" must appeal to "prurient interest" and have "no redeeming social value." In determining whether material is patently offensive, the standard should be "contemporary community standards," based on the locale. The Court said that what might offend residents of "Mississippi might be found tolerable in Las Vegas."[34] The Court subsequently ruled that material cannot be judged obscene simply because the "average" local resident might object to it. "Community standards" were to be judged in the context of a "reasonable person"—someone with a broad enough outlook to evaluate the material on its overall merit rather than its most objectionable feature. The Court later also modified its content standard, saying that the material must be of a "particularly offensive type."[35]

These efforts illustrate the Court's difficulty in developing a tight legal standard that can be applied consistently so that the outcome of an obscenity trial does not rest on the personal opinions of a judge or jury members. Even the justices of the Supreme Court, when examining allegedly obscene material in the case before them, have disagreed on whether it appealed to prurient interest and was without redeeming social value.

The Supreme Court has distinguished between obscene materials in public places and those in the home. A unanimous ruling in 1969 held that what adults read and watch in the privacy of their homes cannot be made a crime.[36] The Court created an exception to this rule in 1990 by upholding an Ohio law making it a crime to possess pornographic photographs of children.[37] The Court reasoned that the purchase of such material encourages producers to use children in the making of pornographic materials, which is a crime. In a 2008 decision, the Court extended the ban by upholding a 2003 federal statute that makes it a crime to offer or solicit child pornography, even if the material is based on computer-generated or digitally altered images that merely appear to be those of children. Writing for the majority in the Court's 7-2 decision, Justice Antonin Scalia said: "Offers to provide or requests to obtain child pornography are categorically excluded from the First Amendment."[38]

Children have also been a consideration in court cases involving material transmitted on cable television or over the Internet. On several occasions, Congress has enacted legislation that would restrict the transmission of sexually explicit material that children might see. The Supreme Court has struck down some of these restrictions on grounds that they would ban material that adults have a constitutional right to see if they so choose.[39] The Court has required officials to devise targeted ways to keep such material from being seen by children. An example is the federal requirement that a cable operator, if requested to do so by a subscriber, must scramble the signal of any channel coming into the subscriber's home that conveys sexually explicit material.

Freedom of Religion

Free religious expression is the precursor of free political expression, at least within the English tradition of limited government. England's Glorious, or Bloodless, Revolution of 1689 centered on the issue of religion and resulted in the Act of Toleration, which gave members of Protestant sects the right to worship freely and publicly. The First Amendment reflects this tradition; it protects religious freedom, as well as freedom of speech, press, assembly, and petition.

In regard to religion, the First Amendment reads: "Congress shall make no law respecting an establishment of religion, or prohibiting the free exercise thereof." It will be noted that this statement contains two clauses, one referring to the "establishment of religion" (the establishment clause) and one referring to the "free exercise" of religion (the free-exercise clause). Each clause has been the subject of Supreme Court rulings.

The Establishment Clause

establishment clause

The First Amendment provision stating that government may not favor one religion over another or favor religion over no religion, and prohibiting Congress from passing laws respecting the establishment of religion.

The **establishment clause** has been interpreted by the courts to mean that government may not favor one religion over another or support religion over no religion. (This position contrasts with that of a country such as England, where Anglicanism is the official, or "established," state religion, though no religion is prohibited.)

To this end, the Court in recent decades has prohibited religious teachings and observances in public schools. A leading case was *Engel v. Vitale* (1962), which held that the establishment clause prohibits the reciting of prayers in public schools.[40] A year later, the Court struck down Bible readings in public schools.[41] Efforts to bring religion into the schools in less direct ways have also been invalidated. For example, an Alabama law attempted to circumvent the prayer ruling by permitting public schools to set aside one minute each day for silent prayer or meditation. In 1985, the Court declared the law unconstitutional, ruling that "government must pursue a course of complete neutrality toward religion."[42] The Court in 2000 reaffirmed the ban by extending it to include organized student-led prayer at public school football games.[43]

The Supreme Court has also banned religious displays on public property when the purpose of such a display is overtly religious and lacks a historical context. Because of the prominence of religion in American life, many public buildings display religious symbols. For instance, a statue of Moses holding the Ten Commandments stands in the rotunda of the Library of Congress building, which opened in 1897. Legal challenges to such displays have rarely succeeded.

The First Amendment's protection of free expression includes religious freedom, which has led the courts to hold that government cannot in most instances promote or interfere with religious practices.

In *Van Orden v. Perry* (2005), for example, the Supreme Court rejected a suit asking for the dismantling of a display of the Ten Commandments on a monument at the Texas State Capitol. The Court noted that the display had been installed nearly a half-century earlier, had been paid for by a nonreligious group, and had not previously been the subject of dispute.[44] On the other hand, in *McCreary County v. American Civil Liberties Union* (2005), the Supreme Court struck down displays of the Ten Commandments on the walls of two Kentucky courthouses. The displays were recent and had initially hung by themselves on the courtroom walls. Only after county officials were sued did they mount a few historical displays alongside the religious ones. The Supreme Court concluded that the officials had religious purposes in mind when they erected the displays and had to remove them.[45]

Although the Court can be said to have applied the *wall of separation doctrine* (a strict separation of church and state) in these rulings, it has also relied upon what is called the *accommodation doctrine.* This doctrine allows government to aid religious activity if no preference is shown toward a particular religion and if the assistance is of a secular nature. For example, the Court has allowed states to provide busing for children who attend religious schools. In deciding whether government assistance for such activities is lawful, the Court at times has applied a test articulated in *Lemon v. Kurtzman* (1971), a case involving state funding of the salaries of religious school instructors who teach secular subjects, such as math and English. In its ruling, the Court articulated a three-point test that has come to be known as the **Lemon test.** Government action must meet all three conditions for it to be acceptable: first, the statute must have a secular legislative purpose; second, its principal or primary effect must be one that neither advances nor inhibits religion; finally, the statute must not foster "an excessive government entanglement with religion."[46]

In the *Lemon* case, the Court held that state funding of religious school teachers failed the test. The Court concluded that such payments involve "excessive government entanglement with religion" because an instructor, even though teaching a subject such as math or science, might use the classroom as an opportunity to promote religious teachings. In contrast, the Court in another case allowed states to pay for math, science, and other secular textbooks used in church-affiliated schools, concluding that the textbooks had little if any religious content in them.[47]

Nevertheless, in a key 2002 decision (*Zelman v. Simmons-Harris*), the Supreme Court upheld an Ohio law that allows students in Cleveland's failing public schools to receive a tax-supported voucher to attend a private or religious school. Even though 90 percent of the vouchers were being used to attend religious schools, the Court's majority concluded that the program did not violate the establishment clause because students had a choice between secular and religious education. Four members of the Court dissented with the majority's reasoning. Justice John Paul Stevens said the ruling went beyond accommodation and had in effect removed a "brick from the wall that was once designed to separate religion from government."[48]

The Free-Exercise Clause

The First and Fourteenth Amendments also prohibit government interference with the free exercise of religion. The **free-exercise clause** has been interpreted to mean that Americans are free to hold any religious belief of their choosing. Americans are not always free, however, to act on their belief. The Supreme Court has allowed government interference when the exercise of religious belief conflicts with otherwise valid law. Examples include the prohibition on the practice

Lemon test
A three-part test to determine whether a law relating to religion is valid under the religious establishment clause. To be valid, a law must have a secure purpose, serve neither to advance nor inhibit religion, and avoid excessive government entanglement with religion.

free-exercise clause
A First Amendment provision that prohibits the government from interfering with the practice of religion.

of polygamy by those of the Mormon faith and court-ordered medical care for children with life-threatening illnesses whose parents have denied them treatment on religious grounds. A more recent example is *Employment Division v. Smith* (1990), in which the Supreme Court upheld Oregon's refusal to grant unemployment benefits to a person fired for using peyote, even though its use was a ritual of the person's religion.[49]

In some instances, the free exercise of religion clashes with the prohibition on the establishment of religion, and the Supreme Court is forced to choose between them. In 1987, for example, the Court overturned a Louisiana law that required creationism (the Bible's account of how God created the world in seven days) to be taught along with the theory of evolution in public school science courses. The Court concluded that creationism is a religious doctrine, not a scientific theory, and that its inclusion in public school curricula violates the establishment clause by promoting a religious belief.[50] In 2005, a federal judge blocked a Pennsylvania public school district from requiring intelligent design (the belief that God has guided evolution) to be taught in science classes. The judge ruled that intelligent design is a disguised version of creationism, that it has no basis in science, and that the teaching of it would violate the establishment clause.[51] Certain religious groups claim that such decisions violate the free-exercise clause because some children are required to study a version of creation—evolution—that contradicts their religious belief about the origin of life.

POLITICAL

THINKING Establishment, or Free Exercise?

The Supreme Court in 1987 ruled that creationism (the biblical account of how the world was created) cannot be taught in public school science courses. The Court holds that creationism is a religious doctrine and that the teaching of it as an alternative to evolutionary theory is a violation of the First Amendment's *establishment clause*. Opponents of the ruling claim that it violates the First Amendment's *free-exercise clause* because some students are forced to study a version of creation—the theory of evolution—that conflicts with their religious beliefs. How would you have ruled in this case? What arguments would you make in support of your decision?

The Right to Bear Arms

The Second Amendment to the Constitution says: "A well regulated Militia, being necessary to the security of a free State, the right of the people to keep and bear Arms, shall not be infringed." The amendment is widely understood to prevent the federal government from abolishing state militias (such as National Guard units), but there has been disagreement over whether the amendment also gives individuals the right to possess weapons outside their use in military service.

Remarkably, more than two centuries passed before the Supreme Court squarely addressed the issue of how the Second Amendment is to be interpreted. The decision came in *District of Columbia v. Heller* (2008). In its ruling, the Court said that "the Second Amendment protects an individual right to possess a firearm unconnected with service in a militia, and to use that arm for traditionally lawful purposes, such as self-defense within the home." The ruling struck down a District of Columbia law that had banned the possession of handguns but not rifles or shotguns within the district's boundaries. Writing for the 5-4 majority, Justice Antonin Scalia said that the justices were "aware of the problem of handgun violence in this country." But Scalia concluded: "The enshrinement of constitutional rights necessarily takes certain policy choices off the table. These include the absolute prohibition of handguns held and used for self-defense in the home."[52] In a sharply worded dissent, Justice John Paul Stevens said the majority had devised a ruling that fit its partisan agenda rather than what the framers intended. Stevens declared: "When each word in the text is given full effect, the Amendment is most naturally read to secure to the people a right to use and possess arms in conjunction with service in a well-regulated militia. So far as it appears, no more than that was contemplated by its drafters or is encompassed within its terms."

The scope of the *Heller* decision was not immediately clear. The District of Columbia is federal territory, and there was the question of whether the Supreme Court through selective incorporation would apply the same principle to state and local gun laws. In *McDonald v. Chicago* (2010), the Court by a 5-4 majority answered the question. The Court struck down a Chicago ordinance that banned handgun possession, saying that the right to "keep and bear arms" is constitutionally protected from infringement by state and local officials.[53] In its *Heller* and *McDonald* decisions, the Court did not rule out all gun restrictions, such as the ban on gun ownership by former felons. However, the Court did not explicitly list the set of allowable restrictions, leaving the issue to be decided in future cases.

The Right of Privacy

Until the 1960s, Americans' constitutional rights were confined largely to those listed in the Bill of Rights. This situation prevailed despite the Ninth Amendment, which reads, "The enumeration in the Constitution, of certain rights, shall not be construed to deny or disparage others retained by the people." In 1965, however, the Supreme Court added to the list of individual rights, declaring that Americans have "a right of privacy." This judgment arose from the case of *Griswold v. Connecticut*, which challenged a state law prohibiting the use of condoms and other birth control devices, even by married couples. The Supreme Court struck down the statute, concluding that a state had no business interfering with a married couple's decision regarding contraception. Rather than invoking the

Gay rights proponents won a right-to-privacy lawsuit when the Supreme Court in 2003 overturned a state ban on sexual relations among consenting adults of the same sex.

right of privacy

A right implied by the freedoms in the Bill of Rights that grants individuals a degree of personal privacy upon which government cannot lawfully intrude. The right gives individuals a level of free choice in areas such as reproduction and intimate relations.

Ninth Amendment, the Court's majority reasoned that the freedoms in the Bill of Rights imply an underlying **right of privacy.** The Court held that individuals have a "zone of [personal] privacy" that government cannot lawfully invade.[54]

Although the right of privacy has not been applied broadly by the Supreme Court, it has been invoked in two major areas—a woman's right to choose an abortion and consensual relations among same-sex adults.

Abortion

The right of privacy was the basis for the Supreme Court's ruling in *Roe v. Wade* (1973), which gave women full freedom to choose abortion during the first three months of pregnancy. In overturning a Texas law banning abortion except to save the life of the mother, the Court said that the right of privacy is "broad enough to encompass a woman's decision whether or not to terminate her pregnancy."[55]

The *Roe* decision was met with praise by some Americans and condemnation by others, provoking a still-continuing debate. Americans are sharply divided over the abortion issue and have been throughout the nearly four decades since *Roe* (see the "Party Polarization" box). The dispute has included violent confrontations at abortion clinics. In 1994, Congress passed a law that makes it illegal to block the entrance to abortion clinics or otherwise prevent people from entering. (The Supreme Court upheld the law, concluding that it regulated actions as opposed to words and thus did not violate free speech rights.[56])

After the *Roe* ruling, antiabortion activists sought a constitutional amendment that would ban abortion, but failed in that effort, prompting them to pursue alternatives. They persuaded the Missouri legislature to pass a law that prohibited abortions from being performed in the state's publicly funded medical facilities, a policy that the Supreme Court upheld in *Webster v. Reproductive Health Services* (1989).[57] The *Webster* decision was followed by a Pennsylvania abortion case, *Planned Parenthood v. Casey* (1992), which anti-abortion advocates had hoped would reverse the *Roe* precedent. Instead, by a 5-4 margin, the Supreme Court upheld a constitutional right to abortion, concluding that "the essential holding of *Roe v. Wade* should be retained and once again reaffirmed."[58] At the same time, the Court upheld the part of the Pennsylvania law that requires a minor to have parental or judicial consent before obtaining an abortion. Any such restriction, the Court said, is constitutional as long as it does not impose an "undue burden" on the woman. A decade later, the Court struck down a New Hampshire parental-consent law because it had no exception in the case of a medical emergency. The omission, the Court ruled, could place an "undue burden" on a pregnant minor who faced a life-threatening emergency.[59]

In *Gonzales v. Carhart* (2007), the Supreme Court for the first time upheld a ban on the use of a particular type of abortion. At issue was the federal Partial-Birth Abortion Ban Act, passed by Congress in 2003. The law provides for a fine and prison term for physicians who perform an abortion during the birth process even if the mother's life or health is endangered. In any earlier case, *Stenberg v. Carhart* (2000), the Supreme Court had invalidated a nearly identical Nebraska law.[60] However, the Nebraska case was decided by a narrow 5-4 margin, with Justice Sandra Day O'Connor providing the swing vote. By the time the 2007 case reached the Supreme Court, O'Connor had retired, and her replacement, the more conservative Samuel Alito, voted the opposite way, resulting in a 5-4 vote upholding the congressional ban. Writing for the majority, Justice Anthony Kennedy said that the federal act did not place an "undue burden" on women. In her dissenting opinion, Justice Ruth Bader Ginsburg, the lone woman on the Court, called the decision "alarming," arguing that it ignored established legal precedent and put women's lives and health at risk.[61]

PARTY POLARIZATION   Political Thinking in Conflict

Pro-Life vs. Pro-Choice

Although party polarization in the United States has risen dramatically since the 1980s, some issues predate this development and have contributed to it. Abortion is such an issue. It has divided Americans from the day that the Supreme Court said in *Roe v. Wade* (1973) that a woman has a constitutional right to choose abortion. At first, Republicans and Democrats differed only slightly in how they saw the issue but the gap has widened to the point where they are far apart. Some Republican voters and Republican-aligned groups (such as the Christian Coalition of America) regard opposition to abortion as a "litmus test" for political candidates and judicial nominees. They refuse to support anyone that upholds a woman's right to choose. Some Democratic voters and Democrat-aligned groups (such as Emily's List) apply the opposite test in determining whom they will support. Since *Roe*, every Republican national party platform has expressed opposition to abortion. In the same period, every Democratic national party platform has had a pro-choice plank. The partisan divide can also be seen in where self-identified Democratic and Republican voters stand on the issue, as the following graph shows:

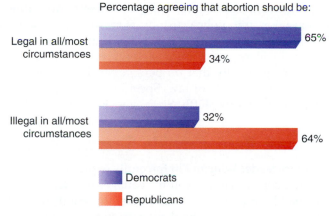

Percentage agreeing that abortion should be:

Legal in all/most circumstances — Democrats 65%, Republicans 34%

Illegal in all/most circumstances — Democrats 32%, Republicans 64%

Democrats
Republicans

Source: Pew Research Center for the People and the Press. 2011.

Q. *Do you think there is a "middle ground" that could bring Republicans and Democrats together on the abortion issue? Or is the moral and political divide over the issue so great that no compromise is possible? And if that's so, do you foresee anything but continuing partisan conflict over the issue?*

Consensual Sexual Relations among Same-Sex Adults

Although the Supreme Court's 1965 *Griswold* ruling on contraceptive use was widely said to have taken "government out of people's bedrooms," a clear exception remained. All states prohibited sexual relations between consenting adults of the same sex. A number of states eliminated this prohibition over the next two decades, and others stopped enforcing it. Nevertheless, in a 1986 Georgia case, *Bowers v. Hardwick,* the Supreme Court held that the right of privacy did not extend to consensual sexual relations among adults of the same sex.[62]

In 2003, the Court reversed itself and in the process struck down the sodomy laws of the thirteen states that still had them. In *Lawrence v. Texas,* the Court in a 6-3 vote concluded that Texas's sodomy law violated "the right of privacy" implied by the grant of liberty in the Fourteenth Amendment's due process clause. The Court said: "The petitioners are entitled to respect for their private lives. The State cannot demean their existence or control their destiny by making their private sexual conduct a crime."[63] The decision was hailed by gay and lesbian rights groups but condemned by some religious groups, who said it opened the door to same-sex marriage (see Chapter 5).

Rights of Persons Accused of Crimes

procedural due process

The constitutional requirement that government must follow proper legal procedures before a person can be legitimately punished for an alleged offense.

Due process refers to legal protections that have been established to preserve the rights of individuals. The most significant of these protections is **procedural due process;** the term refers primarily to procedures that authorities must follow before a person can lawfully be punished for an offense. No system of justice is foolproof. Even in the most careful systems, innocent people have been wrongly accused, convicted, and punished with imprisonment or death. But the scrupulous application of procedural safeguards, such as a defendant's right to legal counsel, greatly increases the likelihood of a fair trial. "The history of liberty has largely been the history of the observance of procedural guarantees," said Justice Felix Frankfurter in *McNabb v. United States* (1943).[64]

The U.S. Constitution offers procedural safeguards designed to protect a person from wrongful arrest, conviction, and punishment. According to Article I, Section 9, a person taken into police custody is entitled to seek a writ of habeas corpus, which requires law enforcement officials to bring the suspect into court and to specify the legal reason for the detention. The Fifth and Fourteenth Amendments provide generally that no person can be deprived of life, liberty, or property without due process of law. Specific procedural protections for the accused are listed in the Fourth, Fifth, Sixth, and Eighth Amendments.[65]

Suspicion Phase: Unreasonable Search and Seizure

In 1766, Parliamentary leader William Pitt forcefully expressed a principle of English common law: "The poorest man may, in his cottage, bid defiance to all the forces of the Crown. It may be frail; its roof may shake; the wind may blow through it; the rain may enter; but the King of England may not enter; all his force dares not cross the threshold."[66] In the period immediately preceding the American Revolution, few things provoked more anger among the colonists than Britain's disregard for the sanctity of the home. British soldiers regularly forced their way into colonists' houses, looking for documents or other evidence of anti-British activity.

The Fourth Amendment was included in the Bill of Rights to prohibit such actions by the U.S. government. The Fourth Amendment reads: "The right of the people to be secure in their persons, houses, papers, and effects, against unreasonable searches and seizures, shall not be violated, and no Warrants shall issue, but upon probable cause, supported by Oath of Affirmation, and particularly describing the place to be searched, and the persons or things to be seized."

The Fourth Amendment does not provide blanket protection against search and seizure. A person caught in the act of a crime can be arrested (seized) on the spot and can be searched for weapons and incriminating evidence. The Fourth Amendment does, however, provide protection against speculative or arbitrary police action. If someone is suspected of a crime, the police ordinarily cannot act until they can convince a judge that they have sufficient evidence to be granted a search warrant. The failure of police and FBI agents to obtain a warrant contributed to the Supreme Court's 2012 decision to overturn a conviction that had been obtained by placing a tracking device on the suspect's car.[67]

The 2012 case notwithstanding, the Supreme Court has generally lowered the standard police must meet to lawfully search a person. In the 1960s, the Court ruled that police must have a substantial basis ("probable cause") for believing that an individual had committed a crime before they could stop, apprehend, and search the person. In *Whren v. United States* (1996), however, the Court upheld the conviction of an individual who had been found with drugs sitting in plain view in the front seat of his car. The police had no evidence (no "probable cause") indicating that drugs were in the car, but they had a hunch that the driver was a drug dealer and used a minor traffic infraction as a pretext to stop his car. The Supreme Court accepted the defense's arguments that the police had no concrete evidence to back their suspicion, that the traffic infraction was not the real reason he was stopped, and that police usually

Most of the issues surrounding procedural due process involve the conduct of police officers when they detain, search, and question suspects. In exceptional cases, the evidence they collect is not admissible in court if obtained in violation of a suspect's constitutional rights.

do not stop a person for the infraction in question (turning a corner without signaling). However, the Court concluded that the officers' motive was irrelevant as long as an officer in some situations might reasonably stop a car for the infraction in question.[68] The ruling gave police more latitude in stopping suspected individuals. It also reaffirmed an earlier decision upholding the admissibility of evidence found in plain sight (*the plain view doctrine*) even when the evidence relates to an infraction other than the one for which the individual was stopped.[69]

The Supreme Court also allows warrantless searches in some circumstances. It has held, for example, that police roadblocks to check drivers for signs of intoxication are legal as long as the action is systematic and not arbitrary (for example, stopping only young drivers would be unconstitutional, whereas stopping all drivers is acceptable). The Court justified this decision by saying that roadblocks serve an important highway safety objective.[70] However, the Court does not allow police roadblocks to check for drugs. In *Indianapolis v. Edmund* (2001), the Court held that narcotics roadblocks serve a general law enforcement purpose rather than one specific to highway safety and therefore violate the Fourth Amendment's requirement that police have suspicion of wrongdoing before they can search an individual's auto.[71] The Court has also held that police cannot use thermal-imaging devices to scan homes to detect the presence of heat sources that might reveal the production of illegal drugs. Ordinarily, police cannot physically enter a home without a search warrant, and the Court reasoned that the same procedure should apply to searches based on modern technology.[72]

The Fourth Amendment protects individuals in their persons as well as in their homes and vehicles. In *Ferguson v. Charleston* (2001), for example, the Court held that patients in public hospitals cannot be forced to take a test for illegal drugs if the purpose is to report to police those patients who test positive. Such action, said the Court, constitutes an illegal search of the person.[73] Authorities have more leeway when it comes to students in public schools. For example, in *Board of Education of Independent School District No. 92 of Pottawatomie County v. Earls* (2002), the Court held that random drug testing of high school students involved in extracurricular activities does not violate the ban on unreasonable searches.[74] In general, the Court has usually deferred to school administrators on grounds that they are responsible for student safety, which can be endangered if drugs, weapons, and other dangerous items make their way into schools.

In a controversial 2012 decision (*Florence v. Board of Chosen Freeholders*), the Supreme Court in a 5-4 ruling held that law enforcement officials can strip search anyone arrested of a crime, even if it's a minor infraction and even if they do not have reason to believe the individual is hiding a weapon or contraband. The case arose when Albert Florence's wife was pulled over for a traffic violation. Florence was sitting in the passenger seat and the police ran a routine check on him as well as on his wife. They discovered an outstanding warrant for his arrest for failure to pay a fine. (In fact, he had paid the fine but the warrant hadn't been removed from the computerized records). Police held him in jail for six days and twice subjected him to a strip search. He sued the police on grounds they had violated his constitutional right to be free of unreasonable search. A federal appellate court ruled in his favor but the Supreme Court's majority reversed the decision, holding that even when the chances are remote than an individual poses a threat, police have the authority to conduct a thorough search.[75]

Arrest Phase: Protection against Self-Incrimination

The Fifth Amendment says, in part, that an individual cannot "be compelled in any criminal case to be a witness against himself." This provision is designed to protect individuals from the age-old practice of coerced confession. Trickery, torture, and the threat of an extra-long prison sentence can lead people to confess to acts they did not commit.

At the time of arrest, police cannot legally begin their interrogation until the suspect has been warned that his or her words can be used as evidence. This warning requirement emerged from *Miranda v. Arizona* (1966), which centered on Ernesto Miranda's confession to kidnapping and rape during police questioning. The Supreme Court overturned his conviction on the grounds that police had not informed him of his right to remain silent and to have legal assistance. The Court reasoned that suspects have a right to know their rights. The Court's ruling led to the formulation of the "Miranda warning" that police are now required to read to suspects: "You have the right to remain silent. . . . Anything you say can and will be used against you in a court of law. . . . You have the right to an attorney." (Miranda was subsequently retried and convicted on the basis of evidence other than his confession.) The Miranda warning has helped protect the rights of the accused. The benefit has accrued mainly to the poor and uneducated; they are less likely than the well-to-do or the highly educated to be aware of their rights. In a 2000 case, *Dickerson v. United States*, the Supreme Court reaffirmed the *Miranda* decision, saying that it was an established "constitutional rule" that Congress could not abolish by ordinary legislation.[76] The Court further strengthened the Miranda precedent in *Missouri v. Siebert* (2004). This ruling came in response to a police strategy of questioning suspects before informing them of their Miranda rights and then questioning them a second time in a more formal way, often with the use of a tape or video recorder. In such instances, suspects who admitted wrongdoing in the first round of questioning often did so also in the second round. The Court concluded that the police strategy was intended "to undermine the Miranda warnings" and was a violation of suspects' rights.[77] In 2010, however, the Supreme Court weakened the Miranda warning to some extent. In one ruling, the Court held that suspects who invoke their rights can be questioned at a later time if they have been released from custody and are read their rights again before the questioning begins.[78] In another case, the Court ruled that police, after reading suspects their Miranda rights, can question them if they fail to ask for an attorney or fail to express their intent to remain silent.[79] Previously, the Court had held that suspects must "knowingly and intelligently waive" their rights before they can be questioned.

Trial Phase: The Right to a Fair Trial

The right to a fair trial is basic to any reasonable notion of justice. If the trial process is arbitrary or biased against the defendant, justice is denied. It is sometimes said the American justice system is based on the principle that it is better to let one hundred guilty parties go free than to convict one innocent person. The system does not actually work that way. Once a person has been arrested and charged with a crime, prosecutors are determined to get a conviction. Defendants in such instances have fair-trial guarantees that are designed to protect them from wrongful conviction.

Legal Counsel and Impartial Jury

Under the Fifth Amendment, suspects charged with a *federal* crime cannot be tried unless indicted by a grand jury. The grand jury hears the prosecution's evidence and decides whether it is strong enough to allow the government to try the suspect. This protection has not been incorporated into the Fourteenth Amendment. As a result, states are not required to use grand juries, although roughly half of them do so. In the rest of the states, the prosecutor usually decides whether to proceed with a trial.

The Sixth Amendment provides a right to legal counsel before and during trial. But what if a person cannot afford a lawyer? For most of the nation's history, poor people had no choice but to act as their own attorneys. In *Johnson v. Zerbst* (1938), the Supreme Court held that criminal defendants in federal cases must be provided a lawyer at government expense if they cannot afford legal counsel.[80] The Court extended this requirement to include state felony cases with its ruling in *Gideon v. Wainwright* (1963). This case centered on Clarence Gideon, who had been convicted in a Florida court of breaking into a pool hall. He had asked for a lawyer, but the trial judge denied the request, forcing Gideon to act as his own attorney. He appealed his conviction, and the Supreme Court overturned it on grounds that he did not have adequate legal counsel.[81]

Criminal defendants also have the right to a speedy trial and to confront witnesses against them. At the federal level and sometimes at the state level, they have a right to jury trial, which is to be heard by an "impartial jury." The Court has ruled that a jury's impartiality can be compromised if the prosecution stacks a jury by race or ethnicity.[82] There was a period in the South when blacks accused of crimes against whites were tried by all-white juries, which invariably returned a guilty verdict. The jury's makeup can be an issue for other reasons as well. In *Witherspoon v. Illinois* (1968), for example, the Supreme Court invalidated Illinois's policy of allowing the prosecution an unlimited number of challenges in capital cases. The prosecution used the challenges to remove from the jury anyone who expressed even the slightest qualms about sentencing the defendant to death if found guilty. To allow that practice, the Court ruled, is to virtually guarantee "a verdict of death." "Whatever else might be said of capital punishment," the Court said, "it is at least clear that its imposition by a hanging jury cannot be squared with the Constitution."[83]

exclusionary rule

The legal principle that government is prohibited from using in trials evidence that was obtained by unconstitutional means (for example, illegal search and seizure).

The Exclusionary Rule

An issue in some trials is the admissibility of evidence obtained in violation of the defendant's rights. The **exclusionary rule** bars the use of such evidence in some circumstances. The rule was formulated on a limited basis in a 1914 Supreme Court decision and was devised to deter police from violating people's rights. If police know that illegally obtained evidence will be inadmissible in court, they presumably will be less inclined to obtain it. As the Court wrote in *Weeks v. United States* (1914): "The tendency of those who execute the criminal laws of the country to obtain convictions by means of unlawful searches and enforced confessions . . . should find no sanction in the judgment of the courts."[84]

In the 1960s, the liberal-dominated Supreme Court expanded the exclusionary rule to the point where almost any illegally obtained evidence was inadmissible in federal or state court. Opponents accused the Court of "coddling criminals," and the appointment of more conservative justices to the Court led to a weakening of the exclusionary rule in the 1980s. In *United States v. Leon* (1984), the Court ruled that evidence discovered under a faulty warrant was admissible because the police had acted in "good faith."[85] This position was reaffirmed in *Herring v. United States* (2008), a case in which police, acting on an arrest warrant issued by another jurisdiction, found firearms and drugs in the individual's truck, only to later discover that the warrant was invalid because it had expired.[86] The *good faith exception* holds that otherwise excludable evidence can be admitted in trial if police believed they were following proper procedures.

A second principle by which tainted evidence can be admitted is the *inevitable discovery exception*. It was developed in the case of *Nix v. Williams* (1984). An eyewitness account had led police to believe that Williams had kidnapped a young girl. Police obtained a warrant and arrested him at a distant location. While being transported by police, despite verbal assurances to his lawyer that he would not be questioned en route, Williams was interrogated and told police where the girl's body could be found. When Williams appealed his conviction, the Court acknowledged that his rights had been violated but concluded that police had other evidence that would have enabled them to find the girl's body. "Exclusion of physical evidence that would have inevitably been discovered adds nothing to either the integrity or fairness of a criminal trial," the Court said.[87]

As some observers see it, the Court has sought to weaken the exclusionary rule without going so far as to allow police to do whatever they please. Other observers believe the Court has narrowed the exclusionary rule nearly to the point where it applies only to extreme forms of police misconduct, although the Court's 2012 ruling on tracking devices suggests it is worried that modern technology could give police too much discretionary authority.

POLITICAL THINKING What Constitutes "Unreasonable Search and Seizure"?

Now that you've had the opportunity to read about the fair trial guarantees provided by the U.S. Constitution, think back to the chapter's opening example—the case of Antoine Jones. Police and FBI officers, acting without a warrant and using a GPS device, tracked his car 24 hours a day for nearly a month. The information they gathered contributed to his arrest and conviction on drug charges. If you had been on the Supreme Court, how would you have voted in this case? Would you have allowed the evidence to be used? What arguments would you have made to support your position?

HOW THE 50 STATES DIFFER POLITICAL THINKING THROUGH COMPARISONS

INCARCERATION RATES

The U.S. Constitution imposes some uniform requirements on state justice systems. All states are required, for example, to provide legal counsel to defendants who cannot afford to hire an attorney. Otherwise, the states are free to go their own way, with the result that the state justice systems differ markedly in some areas. Some states, for example, prohibit the death penalty, while other states apply it liberally. Roughly a third of all executions in the past quarter-century have taken place in Texas alone. States also differ substantially in the size of their prison populations. Louisiana has the highest incarceration rate, with 865 inmates for every 100,000 residents. Mississippi, Texas, Oklahoma, and Alabama are the other states in the top five. Maine has the lowest incarceration rate—159 inmates per 100,000 residents. On a per-capita

basis, Louisiana imprisons more than five times as many of its residents as does Maine. The four other states in the lowest five in terms of prison population are Minnesota, North Dakota, Rhode Island, and Utah.

Q: What do many of the states with low incarceration rates have in common?

A: Most of these states are relatively affluent and rank high on indicators of educational attainment, which are correlated with lower crime rates. Most of these states also have relatively small minority-group populations. Studies have found that the poor and minority-group defendants are more likely than affluent and white defendants to be convicted and, when convicted, to receive a lengthier sentence.

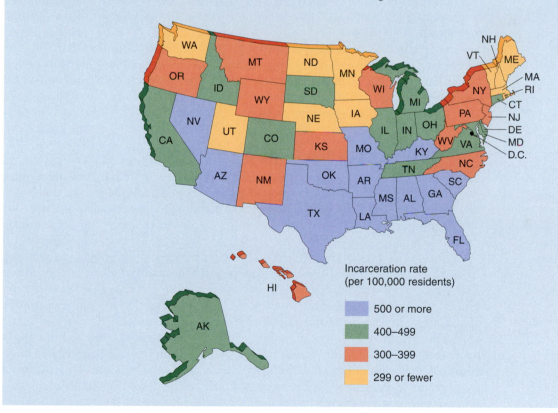

Incarceration rate (per 100,000 residents)

- 500 or more
- 400–499
- 300–399
- 299 or fewer

Source: U.S. Department of Justice, 2010

Sentencing Phase: Cruel and Unusual Punishment

Most issues of criminal justice involve *procedural* due process. However, adherence to proper procedures does not necessarily produce reasonable outcomes. The Eighth Amendment was designed to address this issue. It prohibits "cruel and unusual punishment" of those convicted of crime. The Supreme Court has applied several tests in determining whether punishment is cruel and unusual, including whether it is "disproportionate to the offence," violates "fundamental standards of good conscience and fairness," and is "unnecessarily cruel."

However, the Supreme Court has typically let Congress and the state legislatures determine the appropriate penalties for crime. Thus, the Supreme Court in 1991 upheld a conviction under a Michigan law that mandated life imprisonment without parole for a nonviolent first offense involving 1.5 pounds of cocaine.[88] The Court also upheld a conviction under California's "three strikes and you're out" law that sent a twice previously convicted felon to prison for life without parole for shoplifting videotapes worth $100.[89]

On the other hand, the Supreme Court has recently employed the Eighth Amendment to narrow the use of the death penalty. In *Atkins v. Virginia* (2002) and again in *Panetti v. Quarterman* (2007), the Court outlawed the death penalty for the mentally retarded on grounds that it constitutes "cruel and unusual punishment."[90] The Court also recently invoked the Eighth Amendment to ban the death penalty in cases involving juveniles and for crimes other than murder.[91] In 2010, the Supreme Court broadened the ban on extreme punishment of juveniles to include life without parole in nonhomicide cases. The ruling grew out of a Florida case in which a teenager, who had previously been convicted of robbery, was sentenced to life without parole for participating in a home invasion.[92]

In some instances, courts have applied the Eighth Amendment to officials to relieve inmate overcrowding and improve prison facilities, although the Supreme Court has said that such action is warranted only if prison conditions are truly appalling.[93] In 2011, the U.S. Supreme Court gave California two years to release 33,000 prisoners to relieve overcrowding in its prisons.[94]

Appeal: One Chance, Usually

The Constitution does not guarantee an appeal after conviction, but the federal government and all states permit at least one appeal. The Supreme Court has ruled that the appeal process cannot discriminate against poor defendants. At a minimum, government must provide indigent convicts with the legal resources to file a first appeal.

Prisoners who believe their constitutional rights have been violated by state officials can appeal their conviction to a federal court. A 1960s Supreme Court case gave prisoners the right to have their appeal heard in federal court unless they had "deliberately bypassed" the opportunity to first make their appeal in state courts.[95] This precedent was overturned in 1992 when the Court held that inmates can lose the right to a federal hearing even if a lawyer's mistake is the reason they failed to first present their appeal properly in state courts.[96] In *Bowles v. Russell* (2007), the Court in a 5-4 decision went so far as to deny an appeal in a case in which the deadline for filing the appeal was missed because a federal judge had given the inmate's lawyer the wrong date.[97] Yet in *Maples v. Thomas* (2012), the Court in a 7-2 decision ruled that a death-row defendant whose court-appointed lawyers had dropped his case without informing him was entitled to file an appeal even though the filing deadline had been missed.[98]

The greatest restriction on appeals is a federal law that bars in most instances a second federal appeal by a state prison inmate.[99] Upheld by the Supreme Court in *Felker v. Turpin* (1996), this law is designed to prevent frivolous and multiple federal court appeals. State prisoners had used appeals to contest even small issues, and some inmates—particularly those on death row—had filed appeal after appeal. An effect was the clogging of the federal courts and a delay in hearing other cases. The Supreme Court has ruled that, except in unusual cases,[100] it is fair to ask inmates to first pursue their options in state courts and then to confine themselves to a single federal appeal.

Crime, Punishment, and Police Practices

Although the exclusionary rule and the appeals process have been weakened, there has not been a return to the lower procedural standards that prevailed prior to the 1960s. Most of the key precedents established in that decade remain in effect, including the most important one of all: the principle that procedural protections guaranteed to the accused by the Bill of Rights must be observed by the states as well as by the federal government.

Supreme Court rulings have changed police practices. Most police departments, for example, require their officers to read suspects the Miranda warning before questioning them. Nevertheless, research indicates that constitutional rights are applied unevenly. An example is the use of *racial profiling,* which is the assumption that individuals from particular groups are more likely to commit crimes and therefore require closer scrutiny.[101] A study conducted in 1999 found, for example, that 80 percent of the motorists stopped and searched by Maryland State Police on Interstate 95 were minorities and only 20 percent were white, despite the fact that white motorists constituted 75 percent of all drivers and were just as likely as minority motorists to violate the traffic laws.[102] Such findings have led federal, state, and local law enforcement agencies to create training programs aimed at reducing the practice. Although racial profiling continues to be a problem in some localities, recent studies indicate that its frequency has declined.[103]

Sentencing policies are also an issue. Being "tough on crime" is popular with some voters, and most state legislatures during the past two decades have enacted stiffer penalties for crime while also limiting the ability of judges to reduce sentences, even for nonviolent crime when the perpetrator has no prior criminal record. As a result, the number of federal and state prisoners has more than doubled since 1990. In fact, on a per-capita basis, the United States has the largest prison population in the world (see "How the U.S. Differs"). Russia is the only country that is even close to the United States in terms of the percentage of its citizens who are behind bars.

As the human and financial costs of keeping so many people in prison have risen, debate over America's criminal justice system has intensified. The incarceration of nonviolent drug offenders is one such issue. U.S. drug policy is at odds with that of other Western countries, which relies more heavily on treatment programs than on prisons in dealing with drug offenders. Critics also cite studies showing that minorities and the poor receive harsher sentences than do middle-class white persons convicted of comparable crimes. An example is the disparity in sentences for those convicted of powder-cocaine and crack-cocaine offenses. African Americans make up roughly three-fourths of crack-cocaine defendants whereas whites make up about three-fourths of powder-cocaine defendants. Federal law calls for nearly twice as much prison time for a crack-cocaine conviction as for a powder-cocaine conviction involving comparable amounts of cocaine.[104] In 2007, the Supreme Court gave judges the authority to reduce crack-cocaine sentences below the federal guidelines to bring them closer into line with powder-cocaine sentences.[105]

Law and Order

Individual rights are a cornerstone of the American governing system and are protected by the courts. The government's ability to restrict free expression is limited, and the individual's right to a fair trial is protected through significant due process guarantees, such as the right to legal counsel. According to Freedom House, an independent organization that tracks civil liberties, the United States ranks in the upper tier (the "free" nations) for its protection of civil liberties. However, Freedom House gives the United States a low mark on its sentencing and incarceration policies. Of all the nations in the world, the United States on a per capita basis has the largest number of people in prison. Defenders of this situation say that, although overall crime rates are about the same here as elsewhere, there is more violent crime in America. Critics reply that, although the murder rate is high in the United States, it is also true that more than half of the people in prison were convicted of a nonviolent offense, such as drug use or a crime against property. In any case, the United States is rivaled only by Russia in the proportion of its people who are in prison.

Q: Does it surprise you that the United States leads the world in the percentage of its inhabitants who are behind bars? What do you think accounts for this fact? If you believe that the United States should lower its incarceration rate, what steps would you take to accomplish your goal, keeping in mind that public safety is also a policy priority?

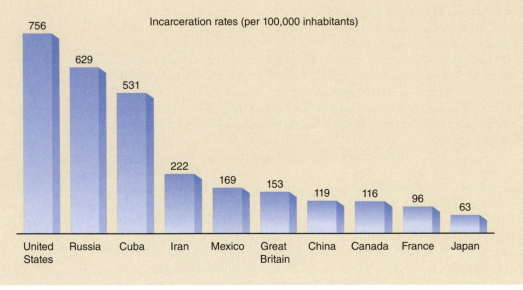

Incarceration rates (per 100,000 inhabitants)

United States	756
Russia	629
Cuba	531
Iran	222
Mexico	169
Great Britain	153
China	119
Canada	116
France	96
Japan	63

Source: World Prison Brief, King's College, London, 2012.

Rights and the War on Terrorism

In time of war, the courts have upheld government policies that would not be permitted in peacetime. After the Japanese attack on Pearl Harbor in 1941, for example, President Franklin D. Roosevelt ordered the forced relocation of tens of thousands of Japanese Americans living on the West Coast to detention camps in Arizona, Utah, and other inland locations. Congress endorsed the policy, and the Supreme Court upheld it in *Korematsu v. United States* (1944).[106] Another Supreme Court ruling during World War II denied a U.S. citizen arrested as a Nazi collaborator a court trial after the government decided to try him before a military tribunal.[107] After the terrorist attacks of September 11, 2001, the Bush administration invoked precedents such as these in declaring that customary legal protections would not be afforded to individuals it deemed to have engaged in terrorist activity.

Detention of Enemy Combatants

The Bush administration soon announced its policy for handling captured "enemy combatants"—individuals judged to be engaged in, or in support of, hostile military actions against U.S. military forces. Some of these prisoners were sent to a detention facility created at the U.S. naval base at Guantanamo Bay on the tip of Cuba. Others were imprisoned in Afghanistan, Iraq, and elsewhere. Requests by lawyers and international agencies like the Red Cross to see the detainees were denied or strictly limited. Some prisoners were subject to abusive treatment, although the practice was denied by U.S. officials until photographic and other evidence surfaced.

In 2004, the Supreme Court issued its first ruling on these practices, holding that the Guantanamo Bay detainees had the right to challenge their detention in court. The Court reasoned that the naval base, though in Cuba, is on land leased to the United States and therefore under the jurisdiction of U.S. courts.[108] In a second 2004 case (*Hamdi v. Rumsfeld*), the Court ruled that one of the Guantanamo Bay detainees, who was a U.S. citizen by virtue of having been born in the United States though he was raised in Saudi Arabia, had the right to be heard in U.S. courts. The Court said: "As critical as the government's interest may be in detaining those who actually pose an immediate threat to the national security of the United States during ongoing international conflict, history and common sense teach us that an unchecked system of detention carries the potential to become a means of oppression and abuse of others who do not present that sort of threat."[109]

Two years later, the Supreme Court issued its sharpest rebuke of the Bush administration's detention policies. In a ruling nearly unprecedented in its challenge to a president's wartime authority, the Court held that the detainees were protected both by the U.S. Uniform Code of Military Justice and by the Geneva Conventions. At issue was the Bush administration's use of secret military tribunals to try detainees. In *Hamdan v. Rumsfeld* (2006), the Court ruled that the tribunals were unlawful because they did not provide even minimal protections of detainees' rights, including the right to see the evidence against them.[110] Then, in a 2008 ruling, the Court struck down a provision of an act of Congress that had been passed two years earlier at the Bush administration's insistence. The provision had denied federal courts the authority to hear appeals from prisoners who sought to challenge their detentions. Writing for the majority in a 5-4 decision, Justice Anthony Kennedy said: "The laws and Constitution are designed to survive, and remain in force, in extraordinary times."[111]

Surveillance of Suspected Terrorists

After the September 11 terrorist attacks and in response to the Bush administration's request for expanded surveillance powers, Congress passed the USA Patriot Act, which lowered the standard for judicial approval of wiretapping when terrorist activity was at issue. The law also allowed information from intelligence surveillance to be shared with criminal investigators when evidence was found of criminal activity unrelated to terrorism. Previously, such information could be shared only when obtained by the stricter standards that apply to criminal investigations. The new law also gave government increased authority to examine medical, financial, and student records and allowed the government in some situations to secretly search homes and offices (so-called "sneak and peek" searches).

The Bush administration promised to act with restraint in its exercise of the new powers, and congressional oversight committees were generally satisfied with its actions until the *New York Times* revealed in late 2005 that President Bush without judicial approval had secretly authorized the National Security Agency (NSA)

Shown here is the detention center at the U.S. naval base at Guantanamo Bay, where enemy detainees from the Afghanistan and Iraq conflicts are held. In *Hamdan v. Rumsfeld* (2006), the Supreme Court ruled that the Bush administration's trial procedures for detainees were in violation of U.S. and international law. The ruling led Congress to change the procedures.

"As you know, the police and FBI agents always inform suspects of their constitutional right to remain silent and to have a lawyer present during any questioning. Do you think law enforcement officials should or should not follow this practice for people who are suspected of attempting to commit an act of terrorism?"

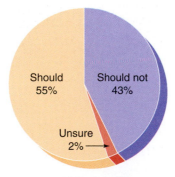

Should 55%

Should not 43%

Unsure 2%

FIGURE 4-1

Opinions on the Rights of Individuals Suspected of Terrorist Acts

More than two-fifths of Americans would deny information about constitutional rights to individuals apprehended on suspicion of terrorism.

Source: CNN/Opinion Research Corporation poll, Feb. 12–15, 2010.

to wiretap international phone calls and e-mail messages originating in the United States. Such wiretaps are expressly prohibited by the Foreign Intelligence Surveillance Act (FISA) of 1978. Bush rejected allegations that he had broken the law, saying that he had acted legally under his wartime powers as commander-in-chief and under authority implicitly granted him by the Patriot Act. When Barack Obama became president, some observers expected him to disclose the NSA's warrantless wiretap activities. Instead, the Obama administration declared that release of the information "would cause exceptionally grave harm to national security."

The Courts and a Free Society

The United States was founded on the idea that individuals have an innate right to liberty—to speak their minds, to worship freely, to be secure in their homes and persons, to be assured of a fair trial. Americans embrace these freedoms in the abstract. In particular situations, however, many Americans think otherwise. A 2010 CNN survey found, for example, that more than two in five Americans think that individuals arrested by police on suspicion of terrorism should not be read their Miranda rights (see Figure 4-1).

The judiciary is not isolated from the public mood. Judges inevitably must balance society's need for security and public order against the rights of the individual. Nevertheless, relative to elected officials, police officers, or the general public, judges are typically more protective of individual rights. How far the courts will go in protecting a person's rights depends on the facts of the case, the existing status of the law, prevailing social needs, and the personal views of the judges (see Chapter 14). Nevertheless, most judges and justices regard the protection of individual rights as a constitutional imperative, which is the way the framers saw it. The Bill of Rights was created to transform the abstract idea that individuals have inalienable rights to life, liberty, and happiness into a set of specified constitutional rights, thereby bringing them under the protection of courts of law.[112]

Summary

Self-Test www.mhhe.com/pattersontadtx11e

The Bill of Rights was added to the Constitution shortly after its ratification. These amendments guarantee certain political, procedural, and property rights against infringement by the national government.

The guarantees embodied in the Bill of Rights originally applied only to the national government. Under the principle of selective incorporation of these guarantees into the Fourteenth Amendment, the courts extended them to state governments, though the process was slow and uneven. In the 1920s and 1930s, First Amendment guarantees of freedom of expression were given protection from infringement by the states. The states continued to have wide discretion in criminal proceedings until the early 1960s, when most of the fair-trial rights in the Bill of Rights were given federal protection.

Freedom of expression is the most basic of democratic rights. People are not free unless they can freely express their views. Nevertheless, free expression may conflict with the nation's security needs during times of war and insurrection. The courts at times have allowed government to limit expression substantially for purposes of national security. In recent decades, however, the courts have protected a wide range of free expression in the areas of speech, press, and religion. They have also established a right of privacy, which in some areas, such as abortion, remains a source of controversy and judicial action.

Due process of law refers to legal protections that have been established to preserve individual rights. The most significant form of these protections consists of procedures designed to ensure that an individual's rights are upheld (for example, the right of an accused person to have an attorney present during police interrogation). A major controversy in this area is the breadth of the exclusionary rule, which bars the use in trials of illegally obtained evidence.

The war on terrorism that began after the attacks on September 11, 2001, has raised new issues of civil liberties, including the detention of enemy combatants, the use of harsh interrogation techniques, and warrantless surveillance. The Supreme Court has not ruled on all such issues but has generally held that the president's war-making power does not include the authority to disregard provisions of statutory law, treaties (the Geneva Conventions), and the Constitution.

Civil liberties are not absolute but must be judged in the context of other considerations (such as national security or public safety) and against one another when different rights conflict. The judicial branch of government, particularly the Supreme Court, has taken on much of the responsibility for protecting and interpreting individual rights. The Court's positions have changed with time and conditions, but the Court is usually more protective of civil liberties than are elected officials or popular majorities.

CHAPTER 4

Study Corner

Key Terms

Bill of Rights (p. 84)
civil liberties (p. 84)
clear-and-present-danger test (p. 88)
due process clause (of the Fourteenth Amendment) (p. 86)
establishment clause (p. 94)
exclusionary rule (p. 104)
free-exercise clause (p. 95)
freedom of expression (p. 87)

imminent lawless action test (p. 89)
Lemon test (p. 95)
libel (p. 92)
prior restraint (p. 92)
procedural due process (p. 100)
right of privacy (p. 98)
selective incorporation (p. 86)
slander (p. 92)
symbolic speech (p. 90)

Self-Test: Multiple Choice

1. Which constitutional amendment, as interpreted by the Supreme Court after 1925, provides protection of individual rights against the actions of state and local governments?
   a. Fourteenth
   b. Tenth
   c. Fifth
   d. Fourth
   e. First

2. The exclusionary rule holds that
   a. people who are biased against the defendant may be excluded from serving on a jury.
   b. a court can order or constrain an action by an individual.
   c. evidence obtained by unconstitutional methods ordinarily cannot be used in a trial.
   d. "fighting words" can be excluded from constitutional protection.

3. The U.S. Bill of Rights as originally approved and interpreted protected individual liberties from violation by
   a. state governments only.
   b. the national government only.
   c. both national and state governments.
   d. all levels of government in the United States.

4. The establishment clause prohibits government from
   a. establishing exceptions to the Bill of Rights.
   b. interfering in any matters where the church and the state conflict.
   c. favoring one religion over another or supporting religion over no religion.
   d. interfering with a person's practice of religion.

5. The right of privacy was the basis for the Supreme Court ruling in
   a. *Roe v. Wade.*
   b. *Mapp v. Ohio.*
   c. *Miranda v. Arizona.*
   d. *Schenck v. United States.*

6. The term that refers to the methods that authorities must use before a person can legitimately be punished for an offense is
   a. the three-point test.
   b. the right of privacy.
   c. procedural due process.
   d. substantive due process.

7. Sexual material that is offensive to any one individual in society is automatically deemed obscene and is not protected under the First Amendment. (T/F)

8. Selective incorporation refers to the process by which the Supreme Court through the Fourteenth Amendment's due process clause has applied many of the Bill of Rights guarantees to actions by state governments. (T/F)

9. To win a libel suit, public officials must prove that a news organization or journalist acted with knowing or reckless disregard for the truth. (T/F)

10. The Supreme Court supported the effort of the state of Texas to outlaw the burning of the American flag. (T/F)

Self-Test: Essay

What is the process of selective incorporation, and why is it important to the rights you have today?

Suggested Readings

Abraham, Henry J. *Freedom and the Court.* New York: Oxford University Press, 2003. A comprehensive analysis of the Supreme Court's work on civil rights and civil liberties.

Ackerman, Bruce. *Before the Next Attack: Preserving Civil Liberties in an Age of Terrorism.* New Haven, Conn.: Yale University Press, 2007. A thoughtful analysis of how Western democracies should treat civil liberties in the era of global terrorism.

Hull, N. E. H., and Peter Charles Hoffer. *Roe v. Wade: The Abortion Rights Controversy in American History.* Lawrence: University Press of Kansas, 2001. A thorough assessment of both sides of the abortion conflict, beginning with the *Roe v. Wade* decision.

Perry, Michael J. *Religion in Politics: Constitutional and Moral Perspectives.* New York: Oxford University Press, 1997. A legal and philosophical analysis of the role of religion in politics.

Schwarz, John E. *Freedom Reclaimed: Rediscovering the American Vision.* Baltimore, Md.: Johns Hopkins University Press, 2005. An impassioned argument for an expansive view of liberty, both from and through government action.

Stone, Geoffrey. *War and Liberty: An American Dilemma: 1790 to the Present.* New York: Norton, 2007. A historical assessment of the tension between civil liberties and national security.

List of Websites

www.fepproject.org
The site of the Free Expression Policy Project; includes information and opinions on a wide range of free-expression policy issues.

www.aclu.org
The American Civil Liberties Union site; provides information on current civil liberties and civil rights issues, including information on recent and pending Supreme Court cases.

www.findlaw.com/casecode/supreme.html
An excellent source of information on Supreme Court and lower-court rulings.

www.ncjrs.gov
The site of the National Criminal Justice Reference Service, a federally funded organization that compiles information on a wide range of criminal-justice issues.

Participate!

Although their right of free expression is protected by law, Americans often choose not to exercise this right for fear of social pressure or official reprisal. Yet constitutional rights tend to wither when people fail to exercise them. The failure of citizens to speak their minds, Alexis de Tocqueville said, reduces them "to being nothing more than a herd of timid and industrious animals of which government is the shepherd." Think of an issue that you care about but that is unpopular on your campus or in your community. Consider writing a letter expressing your opinion to the editor of your college or local newspaper. (Practical advice: keep the letter short and to the point; write a lead sentence that will get readers' attention; provide a convincing and courteous argument for your position; and be sure to sign the letter and provide a return address so that the editor can contact you if there are questions.)

Extra Credit

For up-to-the-minute *New York Times* articles, interactive simulations, graphics, study tools, and more links and quizzes, visit the text's Online Learning Center at **www.mhhe. com/pattersontad11e**.

Self-Test Answers

1. a, 2. c, 3. b, 4. c, 5. a, 6. c, 7. F, 8. T, 9. T, 10. F

CHAPTER

5

Equal Rights: Struggling toward Fairness

"The assertion that '"all men are created 'equal' was of no practical use in effecting our separation from Great Britain, and it was placed in the Declaration not for that, but for future use." Abraham Lincoln[1]

The producers of ABC television's *Primetime Live* put hidden cameras on two young men, equally well dressed and groomed, and then sent them on different routes to do the same things—search for an apartment, shop for a car, look at albums in a record store. The cameras recorded people's reactions to the two men. One was more often greeted with smiles and quick service, while the other was more often greeted with suspicious looks and was sometimes made to wait. Why the difference? The explanation was straightforward: the young man who was routinely well received was white; the young man who was sometimes treated poorly was black.

The Urban Institute conducted a more substantial experiment. It included pairs of specially trained white and black male college students who were comparable in key aspects—education, work experience, speech patterns, physical builds—except for their race. The students responded individually to nearly five hundred classified job advertisements in Chicago and Washington, D.C. The black applicants got fewer interviews and received fewer job offers than did the white applicants. An Urban Institute spokesperson said, "The level of reverse discrimination [favoring blacks over whites] that we found was limited, was certainly far lower than many might have been led to fear, and was swamped by the extent of discrimination against black job applicants."[2]

The two studies suggest why some Americans still struggle for equality. Although Americans in theory have equal rights, they are not now equal, nor have they ever been. African Americans, women, Hispanic Americans, the disabled, Jews, Native Americans, Catholics, Mormons, Asian Americans, gays and lesbians, and members of other minority groups have been victims of discrimination in fact and in law. The nation's creed—"all men are created equal"—has encouraged disadvantaged groups to demand equal treatment, but there is considerable disagreement over how far government should go in helping them attain it. Should government's responsibility extend only to efforts aimed at ensuring Americans are treated equally under the law? Or should its responsibility extend also to efforts aimed at reducing Americans' unequal access to opportunities, such as employment and college admission?

This chapter focuses on **equal rights,** or **civil rights**—terms that refer to the right of every person to equal protection under the laws and equal access to society's opportunities and public facilities. As Chapter 4 explained, civil liberties refer to specific *individual* rights, such as freedom of speech, that are protected from infringement by government. Equal rights, or civil rights, are a question of whether individual members of differing *groups,* such as racial, gender, and ethnic groups, are treated equally by government and, in some instances, by private parties.

Although the law refers to the rights of individuals first and to those of groups in a secondary and derivative way, this chapter concentrates on groups because the history of civil rights has been largely one of group claims to equality. The catchphrase of nearly every group's claim to a more equal standing in American society has been "equality under the law." When secure in their legal rights, people are positioned to pursue equality in other arenas, such as the economic sector. This chapter examines the major laws relating to equality and the conditions that led to their adoption. The chapter concludes with a brief look at some of the continuing challenges facing America's historically disadvantaged groups. The chapter emphasizes these points:

- *Americans have attained substantial equality under the law.* In purely legal terms, although not always in practice, they have equal protection under the laws, equal access to accommodations and housing, and an equal right to vote.

- *Legal equality for all Americans has not resulted in de facto equality.* African Americans, women, Hispanic Americans, and other traditionally disadvantaged groups have a disproportionately small share of America's opportunities and benefits. However, the issue of what, if anything, government should do to deal with this problem is a major source of contention.

- *Disadvantaged groups have had to struggle for equal rights.* African Americans, women, Native Americans, Hispanic Americans, Asian Americans, and a number of other groups have had to fight for their rights in order to achieve a fuller measure of equality.

Equality through Law

Equality has always been the least developed of America's founding concepts. Not even Thomas Jefferson, who had a deep admiration for the "common man," believed that a precise meaning could be given to the claim of the Declaration of Independence that "all men are created equal."[3] Nevertheless, the promise contained in that phrase has placed history on the side of those seeking greater equality. Every civil rights movement, from suffrage for males without property in the 1830s to gay rights today, has derived moral strength from the nation's pledge of equality for all.

Nevertheless, America's history reveals that disadvantaged groups have rarely achieved a greater measure of equality without a struggle.[4] The policies that protect these groups today are the result of intense and sustained political action that forced entrenched interests to relinquish or share their privileged status.

equal rights, or **civil rights**
The right of every person to equal protection under the laws and to equal access to society's opportunities and public facilities.

POLITICAL THINKING   What Does Equality Mean?

From the nation's beginning, Americans have debated the meaning of equality. Although the term is enshrined in the Declaration of Independence—"all men are created equal"—it has been the source of endless dispute. How would you define equality? Do you see it purely as a question of equal treatment under the law, or do you think equality should extend to other things, such as access to jobs, health care, and college admission?

The Fourteenth Amendment: Equal Protection

The Fourteenth Amendment, which was ratified in 1868 after the Civil War, declares in part that no state shall "deny to any person within its jurisdiction the equal protection of the laws." The **equal-protection clause** is a basis for equal treatment under the law, but nearly a century lapsed before the courts applied the clause in a substantial way. After federal troops withdrew from the South in 1877, the region's white majority took control, enacting laws that prohibited blacks from using the same public facilities as whites. In *Plessy v. Ferguson* (1896), the Supreme Court endorsed these laws, ruling that "separate" public facilities for the two races did not violate the Constitution as long as the facilities were "equal."[5] The *Plessy* decision became a justification for the separate and *unequal* treatment of African Americans (see Chapter 3). Black children were forced, for example, to attend separate schools that rarely had libraries or enough teachers.

These practices were challenged through legal action, but not until the late 1930s did the Supreme Court begin to respond. In a first ruling, the Court held that blacks must be allowed to use public facilities reserved for whites in cases where they did not have separate facilities. When Oklahoma, which had no law school for blacks, was ordered to admit Ada Sipuel as a law student in 1949, it created a separate law school for her—she sat alone in a roped-off corridor of

equal-protection clause
A clause of the Fourteenth Amendment that forbids any state to deny equal protection of the laws to any individual within its jurisdiction.

Two police dogs attack a black civil rights activist (center left) during the 1963 Birmingham demonstrations. Such images of hatred and violence shook many white Americans out of the complacency about the plight of African Americans.

the state capitol building. The white students, meanwhile, continued to meet at the University of Oklahoma's law school in Norman, twenty miles away. The Supreme Court then ordered the law school to admit her to regular classes. The law school did so but roped off her seat from the rest of the class and stenciled the word *colored* on it. She was also forced to eat alone in a roped-off area of the law school's cafeteria. In her memoir, Sipuel wrote that, although the law school itself was less than welcoming, some law students helped out, including those who gave her notes from classes she had missed while studying alone at the capitol building.[6]

Segregation in the Schools

Substantial judicial intervention on behalf of African Americans finally occurred in 1954 with *Brown v. Board of Education of Topeka.* The case began when Linda Carol Brown, a black child in Topeka, Kansas, was denied admission to an all-white elementary school that she passed every day on her way to her all-black school, which was twelve blocks farther away. In a unanimous decision, the Court invoked the Fourteenth Amendment's equal protection clause, declaring that racial segregation of public schools "generates [among black children] a feeling of inferiority as to their status in the community that may affect their hearts and minds in a way unlikely ever to be undone. . . . Separate educational facilities are inherently unequal."[7]

A 1954 Gallup poll indicated that a sizable majority of southern whites opposed the *Brown* decision, and billboards were erected along southern roadways that called for the impeachment of Chief Justice Earl Warren. In the so-called Southern Manifesto, southern congressmen urged their state governments to "resist forced integration by any lawful means." Rioting broke out in 1957 when Arkansas's governor called out the state's National Guard to prevent black students from entering Little Rock's high school. They achieved entry only after President Dwight D. Eisenhower used his power as commander in chief to place the Arkansas National Guard under federal control.

Although the *Brown* decision banned forced segregation in the public schools, it did not require states to take active steps to integrate their schools. Most children attended neighborhood schools, and because most residential neighborhoods were racially segregated, so too were the schools. Even as late as fifteen years after *Brown,* 95 percent of black children were attending schools that were mostly or entirely black.

In 1971, the Supreme Court endorsed the busing of children as a remedy for segregated schools. The Court held in *Swann v. Charlotte-Mecklenburg County Board of Education* (1971) that the busing of children out of their neighborhoods for the purpose of achieving racially integrated schools was constitutionally permissible in cases where previous acts of racial discrimination contributed to school segregation. "The basis of our decision," the Court said, "[is] the prohibition of the Fourteenth Amendment that no state shall deny to any person within its jurisdiction the equal protection of the laws."[8] Few Court decisions have provoked the outcry that followed *Swann.* A 1972 University of Michigan survey indicated that more than 80 percent of white Americans disapproved of forced busing. Angry demonstrations lasting weeks took place in Charlotte. When busing was ordered in Detroit and Boston, the protests turned violent as white demonstrators burned buses and beat black residents. Unlike *Brown,* which affected mainly the South, *Swann* also applied to northern communities where blacks and whites lived separately because of discriminatory real estate practices.

Racial busing had mixed results. Studies found that busing improved school children's racial attitudes and improved minority children's performance on standardized tests without diminishing the performance of white classmates.[9]

On the other hand, the policy forced many children to spend long hours each day riding buses to and from school. Busing also contributed to white flight to the suburbs, which were protected by a 1974 Supreme Court decision that prohibited busing across school districts except where district boundaries had been deliberately drawn to keep the races apart.[10] The declining number of white students in city schools made it harder, even with the use of busing, to create racially balanced classrooms.

In the 1990s, the Supreme Court ordered cutbacks in busing, saying that it was meant to be a temporary solution.[11] Then, in 2007, the Supreme Court essentially declared an end to forced busing. At issue were voluntary (as opposed to court-ordered) busing programs in Seattle and Louisville that took race, neighborhood, and student preference into account in assigning students to particular schools. The large majority of students were placed in their school of choice, but some were forced to go elsewhere, which led to lawsuits on their behalf. In a 5-4 decision, the Supreme Court ruled they had been denied equal protection under the Fourteenth Amendment. Writing for the majority, Chief Justice John Roberts said, "Before *Brown*, schoolchildren were told where they could and could not go to school based on the color of their skin. The school districts in [Seattle and Louisville] have not carried the heavy burden of demonstrating that we should allow this once again—even for very different reasons." In the dissenting opinion, Justice Stephen Breyer said, "It is a cruel distortion of history to compare Topeka, Kansas in the 1950s to Louisville and Seattle in the modern day."[12]

As a result of the end of racial busing and white flight to private and suburban schools, America's schools have become less racially diverse. Compared with 40 percent at the peak of the busing era, only 30 percent of Hispanic and black children now attend a school that is predominately white, In fact, America's schools are now more ethnically and racially segregated than they were when busing began.[13]

Judicial Tests of Equal Protection

The Fourteenth Amendment's equal-protection clause does not require government to treat all groups or classes of people equally in all circumstances. The judiciary allows inequalities that are "reasonably" related to a legitimate government interest. In applying this **reasonable-basis test,** the courts require government only to show that a particular law is reasonable. For example, twenty-one-year-olds can legally drink alcohol but twenty-year-olds cannot. The courts have held that the goal of reducing fatalities from alcohol-related accidents involving young drivers is a valid reason for imposing an age limit on the purchase and consumption of alcohol.

The reasonable-basis test does not apply to racial or ethnic classifications (see Table 5-1). Any law that treats people differently because of race or ethnicity is

reasonable-basis test

A test applied by courts to laws that treat individuals unequally. Such a law may be deemed constitutional if its purpose is held to be "reasonably" related to a legitimate government interest.

TABLE 5-1 | Levels of Court Review for Laws That Treat Americans Differently

Test	Application	Standard Used
Strict scrutiny	Race, ethnicity	Suspect category—assumed unconstitutional in the absence of an overwhelming justification
Intermediate scrutiny	Gender	Almost suspect category—assumed unconstitutional unless the law serves a clearly compelling and justified purpose
Reasonable basis	Other categories (such as age and income)	Not suspect category—assumed constitutional unless no sound rationale for the law can be provided

strict-scrutiny test

A test applied by courts to laws that attempt a racial or an ethnic classification. In effect, the strict-scrutiny test eliminates race or ethnicity as a legal classification when it places minority-group members at a disadvantage.

suspect classifications

Legal classifications, such as race and national origin, that have invidious discrimination as their purpose and therefore are unconstitutional.

subject to the **strict-scrutiny test,** which presumes that the law is unconstitutional unless government can provide a compelling basis for it. The strict-scrutiny test has virtually eliminated race and ethnicity as permissible classifications when the effect is to place a hardship on a racial or ethnic minority. The Supreme Court's position is that race and national origin are **suspect classifications**—in other words, laws that classify people differently on the basis of their race or ethnicity are presumed to have discrimination as their purpose.

Although the notion of suspect classifications was implicit in earlier cases, including *Brown,* the Court did not use those words until *Loving v. Virginia* (1967). The state of Virginia had a law that prohibited white residents from marrying a person of a different race. When Richard Loving, a white man, and Mildred Jeter, a woman of African American and Native American descent, went to Washington, D.C., to get married and then returned home to Virginia, police invaded their home and arrested them. The state of Virginia claimed that its ban on interracial marriage did not violate the equal protection clause because the penalty for the offense—a prison sentence of one to five years—was the same for both the white and the non-white spouse. The Supreme Court ruled otherwise, saying the Virginia law was "subversive of the principle of equality at the heart of the Fourteenth Amendment." The Court concluded that the law was based solely on "invidious racial discrimination" and that any such "classification" was unconstitutional.[14]

When women began to assert their rights more forcefully in the 1970s, some observers thought the Supreme Court would expand the scope of strict scrutiny to include gender. Instead, the Court held that men and women can be treated differently if the policy in question is "substantially related" to the achievement of "important governmental objectives."[15] The Court thus placed gender classifications in an intermediate (or almost suspect) category. Gender classifications were to be scrutinized more closely than some others (for example, income or age) but were constitutionally valid if government could clearly show why men and women should be treated differently. In *Rostker v. Goldberg* (1980), the Court upheld such a classification, ruling that the male-only draft registration law served the important objective of excluding women from *involuntary* combat duty.[16]

Although women are excluded by law from having to register for the draft, they are eligible to enlist voluntarily in the U.S. military. Shown here is a woman on military duty in the Middle East. Roughly 2 percent of American military casualties in the Iraq and Afghanistan conflicts have been women.

Since then, however, the Supreme Court has struck down nearly all the gender-based laws it has reviewed. A leading case is *United States v. Virginia* (1996), in which the Court invalidated the male-only admissions policy of Virginia Military Institute (VMI), a 157-year-old state-supported college. The state had created an alternative program for women at another college, but the Court said it was no substitute for VMI's unique education. In its ruling, the Court said that Virginia had failed to provide an "exceedingly persuasive" argument for its policy. This standard would appear to be a stricter one than the "important governmental objectives" standard applied earlier. However, the Court did not explicitly say it was toughening the standard for gender classifications. (The VMI decision had the effect of also ending the all-male admissions policy of the Citadel, a state-supported military college in South Carolina.)[17]

The Civil Rights Act of 1964

The Fourteenth Amendment prohibits discrimination by government but not by private parties. As a result, for a long period in American history, private employers could freely discriminate in their hiring practices, and owners of restaurants, hotels, theaters, and other public accommodations could legally bar black people from entering. That changed with passage of the 1964 Civil Rights Act. Based on Congress's power to regulate commerce, the legislation entitles all persons to equal access to public accommodations. The legislation also bars discrimination on the basis of race, color, religion, sex, or national origin in the hiring, promotion, and wages of employees of medium-size and large firms. A few forms of job discrimination are still lawful under the Civil Rights Act. For example, an owner-operator of a small business can discriminate in hiring his or her coworkers, and a church-related school can take the religion of a prospective teacher into account.

The Black Civil Rights Movement

The impetus behind the 1964 Civil Rights Act was the black civil rights movement. Without it, the legislation would undoubtedly have come later, and possibly have been less sweeping.

During World War II, African American soldiers fought against Nazi racism only to return to an America where racial discrimination was legal, widespread, and oppressive.[18] The contradiction was stark and led to growing demands for change, which intensified after an incident in Montgomery, Alabama, on December 1, 1955. Upon leaving work that day, Rosa Parks boarded a bus for home, taking her seat as required by law in the section reserved for blacks. When all the seats for white passengers were occupied, the bus driver ordered Parks to give her seat to a white passenger. She refused, whereupon she was arrested and fined. The incident provoked outrage in Montgomery's black community, which organized a boycott of the city's bus system. A young pastor at a local Baptist church, Dr. Martin Luther King Jr., led the boycott, which spread quickly to other cities. African Americans also conducted sit-ins at lunch counters that served only whites. The black civil rights movement was now fully under way and would persist for more than a decade. A peak moment occurred in 1963 with the March on Washington for Jobs and Freedom, which attracted 250,000 marchers, one of the largest gatherings in the Capital's history. In his speech to the crowd, King said: "I have a dream that my four little children will one day live in a nation where they will not be judged by the color of their skin but by the content of their character."[19]

The momentum of the March on Washington carried over into Congress, where major civil rights legislation was languishing in House committee. Although opponents employed every possible legislative maneuver in an effort to block it, it finally cleared the House the following February. Senate maneuvering and debate—including a fifty-five-day filibuster—took another four months. Finally, in early July, President Lyndon Johnson signed into law the Civil Rights Act of 1964.

Resistance to the Civil Rights Act was widespread. Many restaurants, hotels, and other establishments refused to serve black customers. An Atlanta restaurant owner, Lester Maddox, responded to the legislation by standing outside his restaurant brandishing a handgun, threatening to shoot any African American who entered. Maddox was elected governor of Georgia three years later, but lawsuits against Maddox and other defiant proprietors slowly ended resistance to the new law, with the effect that overt forms of discrimination in the area of public accommodations gradually ceased. Even today, some restaurants and hotels may provide better service to white customers, but outright refusal to serve African Americans or other minority-group members is rare. Any such refusal violates

Martin Luther King Jr. is the only American of the twentieth century to be honored with a national holiday. The civil rights leader was the pivotal figure in the movement to gain legal and political rights for black Americans. The high point was a triumphal gathering of a quarter million supporters on the Washington Mall. The recipient of the Nobel Peace Prize in 1964 (the youngest person ever to receive that honor), King was assassinated in Memphis in 1968 as he was preparing to lead a march on behalf of the city's sanitation workers.

PARTY
POLARIZATION — Political Thinking in Conflict

The Politics of Civil Rights

Before the 1960s, neither political party stepped forward to take up the issue of civil rights out of fear of the long-term electoral consequences. The Democratic Party finally took the lead in enacting the 1964 Civil Rights Act and 1965 Voting Rights Act. Backed by large Democratic majorities in the House and Senate, President Lyndon Johnson pressed for passage of the legislation but said Democrats were "signing away the South" for a generation or more. It was more than a prophecy. Enough white southern Democrats switched sides to quickly turn the South into a Republican stronghold in presidential elections and later into a Republican stronghold in congressional elections as well. The civil rights issue has broadly affected partisan alignments. The groups that have benefited most directly from civil rights policies—particularly African Americans and Hispanics—are far more Democratic than those that have not—white males particularly. The figures below show some of the differences. They are based on a recent Pew survey that asked Americans about their party identification. Independents have been excluded from the calculations; the percentages are based only on the respondents that said they identified with either the Republican or the Democratic Party.

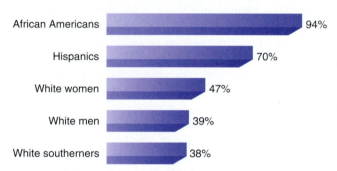

Percentage Democratic identifiers (of those identifying with a party)

- African Americans 94%
- Hispanics 70%
- White women 47%
- White men 39%
- White southerners 38%

Source: Pew Research Center for the People & the Press, July 22, 2011. Used with permission.

Q. *Factors such as race and ethnicity are only part of the explanation for the partisan differences among the groups shown in the graph. What other factors do you think need to be taken into account in a fuller explanation?*

A. *There are several other important factors, but income is likely the main one. Disadvantaged groups have substantially lower incomes on average than do advantaged groups. The Republican and Democratic parties have differed in their income and tax policies and therefore in their appeal to different income groups (see Chapter 8).*

federal law and can be proven in many instances. Discrimination in job decisions is harder to prove, and the Civil Rights Act has been less effective in stopping it, as is discussed in a later section.

The Movement for Women's Rights

The black civil rights movement inspired other disadvantaged groups to become more demanding of their rights. Women were the most vocal and successful of these groups.

The United States carried over from English common law a political disregard for women, forbidding them to vote, hold public office, or serve on juries.[20]

Upon marriage, a woman essentially lost her identity as an individual and could not own and dispose of property without her husband's consent. Even a wife's body was not fully hers. A wife's adultery was declared by the Supreme Court in 1904 to be a violation of the husband's property rights.[21]

The first large and well-organized attempt to promote women's rights came in 1848 in Seneca Falls, New York. Lucretia Mott and Elizabeth Cady Stanton had been barred from the main floor of an antislavery convention and decided to organize a women's rights convention. Thereafter, the struggle for women's rights became closely aligned with the abolitionist movement. However, when Congress wrote the Fifteenth Amendment after the Civil War, women were not included in its provisions despite promises to the contrary. The Fifteenth Amendment declared only that the right to vote could not be abridged on account of race or color. Not until passage of the Nineteenth Amendment in 1920 did women acquire the right to vote.

The Nineteenth Amendment's ratification encouraged women's leaders in 1923 to propose a constitutional amendment granting equal rights to women. Congress rejected the proposal but fifty years later approved the Equal Rights Amendment (ERA) and submitted it to the states for ratification. The ERA failed by three states to receive the required three-fourths majority.[22] Women did succeed in other efforts, however. Among the congressional measures were the Equal Pay Act of 1963, which prohibits sex discrimination in salary and wages by some categories of employers; Title IX of the Education Amendment of 1972, which prohibits sex discrimination in education; and the Equal Credit Act of 1974, which prohibits sex discrimination in the granting of financial credit. Women are also protected by Title VII of the Civil Rights Act of 1964, which bans gender discrimination in employment, a topic that is discussed in a later section.

Hispanic Americans and the Farm Workers' Strikes

Although the Civil Rights Act of 1964 was largely a response to the black civil rights movement, Hispanics also had their political movement. Its centerpiece was the farm workers' strikes of the late 1960s and the 1970s, which sought labor rights for migrant workers. Migrants were working long hours for low pay, were living in shacks without electricity or plumbing, and were unwelcome in many local schools as well as in some local hospitals. Farm owners at first refused to bargain with the workers, but a well-organized national boycott of California grapes and lettuce forced the state to pass a law giving migrant workers the right to bargain collectively. The strikes were led in California by Cesar Chavez, who himself grew up in a Mexican American migrant family. Chavez's tactics were copied with less success in other states, including Texas.[23]

The Hispanic civil rights movement lacked the scope of the black civil rights movement but brought about some policy changes, including a congressional act that requires states to provide bilingual ballots in local areas with large numbers of non-English-speaking minorities.

Native Americans and Their Long-Delayed Rights

When white settlers first arrived, an estimated five to ten million Native American lived in what is now the United States. By 1900, they numbered only about a quarter of a million. In the whole of recorded history, no people had suffered such a huge population decline in such a short period. Smallpox and other diseases brought by white settlers took the heaviest toll, but wars and massacres also contributed. As part of a policy of westward expansion, settlers and U.S. troops mercilessly drove the eastern Indians from their ancestral lands to the Great Plains and then seized most of the territory there as well. Until Congress changed the

Cesar Chavez led the first successful farm workers' strike in the nation's history. A migrant worker as a child, Chavez was called "one of the heroic figures of our time" by Robert F. Kennedy and is widely regarded as the most influential Latino leader of the twentieth century.

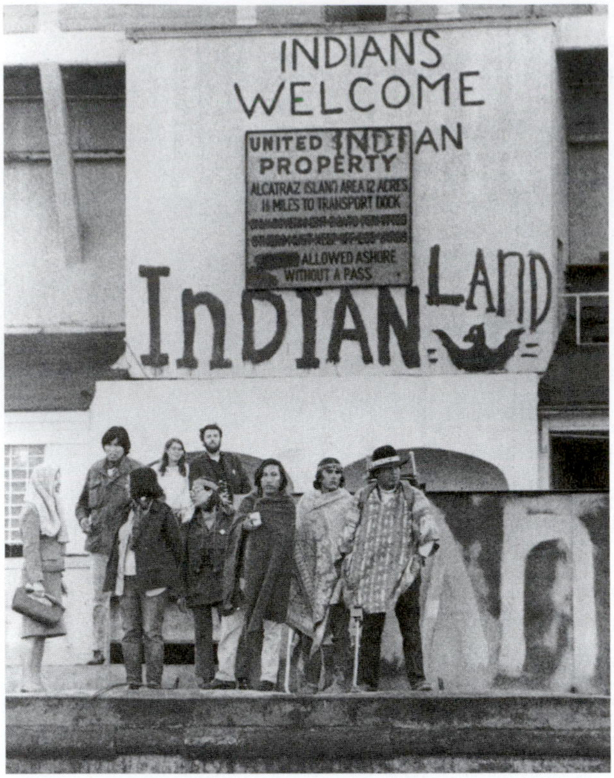

During the 1960s civil rights era, Native Americans voiced long-standing grievances. Their first major protest was held at the abandoned federal prison on Alcatraz Island in San Francisco Bay. For nineteen months beginning in late 1969, Native Americans from tribes across the country occupied the prison. From there, the protest spread to other locations, including Washington, D.C., and Wounded Knee, South Dakota.

policy in 1924, Native Americans by law were denied citizenship, which meant they lacked even the power to vote.

At first, Native Americans were not part of the 1960s civil rights movement. That changed in 1972 when Native American leaders organized the "Trail of Broken Treaties," a caravan that journeyed from California to Washington, D.C., to protest federal policy. Upon arriving in Washington, they occupied the Bureau of Indian Affairs, renaming it the Native American Embassy. The occupation ended when the government agreed to establish a committee to investigate their grievances. The next year, armed Native Americans took control of the village of Wounded Knee on a Sioux reservation in South Dakota; over the next two months they exchanged sporadic gunfire with U.S. marshals that left two Native Americans dead and one marshal paralyzed. Eight decades earlier at Wounded Knee, U.S. cavalry had shot to death three hundred disarmed Sioux men, women, and children.

In 1974, Congress passed legislation that granted Native Americans living on reservations greater control over federal programs that affect them. Six years earlier, Congress had enacted the Indian Bill of Rights, which gives Native Americans on reservations constitutional guarantees similar to those held by other Americans.

Asian Americans and Immigration

Chinese and Japanese laborers were brought to the western states during the late 1800s to work in mines and to build railroads. When the need for this labor declined, Congress in 1892 suspended Asian immigration on grounds that Asians were inferior. Over the next seven decades, laws and informal arrangements blocked residents of most Asian countries, including China and Japan, from coming to the United States. In 1965, as part of its broader civil rights agenda, Congress lifted restrictions on Asian immigration. Tight limits on Hispanic immigration were also lifted at this time, and since then, most immigrants have come from Latin America and Asia (see Figure 5-1).

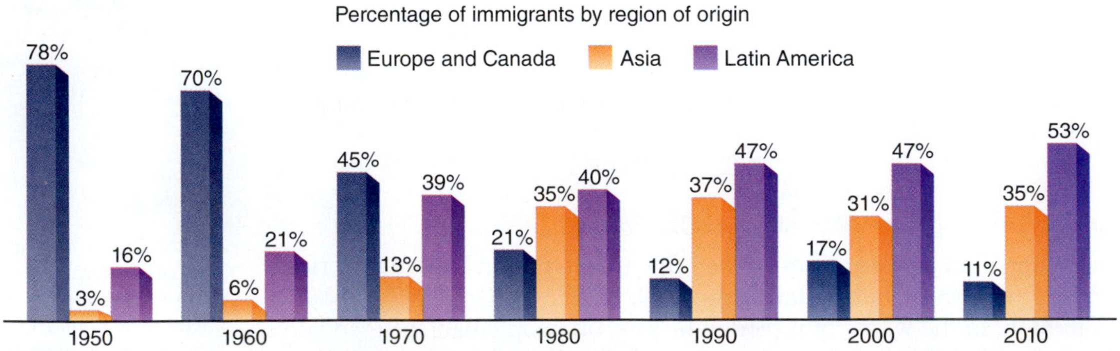

FIGURE 5-1 **The Changing Face of Immigration** Until 1965, immigration laws were biased in favor of European immigrants. The laws enacted in 1965 increased the proportion of immigrants from Asia and Latin America. Percentages are totals for each decade, for example, the 2010 figures are for the 2001-2010 period.

Source: U.S. Immigration and Naturalization Service, 2012.

Asian Americans were not politically active to any great extent during the 1960s, but their rights were expanded by the 1964 Civil Rights Act and other policies adopted in response to action by other minority groups. However, in *Lau v. Nichols* (1974), a case initiated by a Chinese American family, the Supreme Court ruled unanimously that placing public school children for whom English is a second language in regular classrooms without special assistance violates the Civil Rights Act because it denies them the opportunity to obtain a proper education.[24] The Court did not mandate bilingual instruction, but the *Lau* decision prompted many schools to offer it. Since then, however, some states have restricted its use. For example, California's Proposition 227, enacted in 1998, requires most children for whom English is a second language to take courses taught in English after a single year in school.

POLITICAL THINKING   Should Private Discrimination Be Allowed?

The Fifth and Fourteenth Amendments prohibit discrimination by government, but not by private organizations. The courts have ruled that social clubs and other private organizations are sometimes within their rights in discriminating against individuals because of color, sexual orientation, creed, national origin, and other characteristics. For example, the Supreme Court in *Boy Scouts of America v. Dale* (2000) ruled that the Boy Scouts, as a private organization with a right to free association, can ban gays because the Scout creed prohibits homosexuality. How far would you go in permitting discrimination by private organizations?

The Voting Rights Act of 1965

Free elections are the bedrock of American democracy, but the right to vote has only recently become a reality for many Americans, particularly African Americans. Although the 1870 Fifteenth Amendment granted blacks the right to vote, southern whites invented an array of devices, from whites-only primaries to rigged literacy tests, to keep blacks from registering and voting. In the mid-1940s, for example, there were only 2,500 registered black voters in the entire state of Mississippi, even though its black population numbered half a million.[25]

Racial barriers to voting began to crumble in the mid-1940s when the Supreme Court declared that whites-only primary elections were unconstitutional.[26] Two decades later, the Twenty-fourth Amendment outlawed the poll tax, which was a fee that an individual had to pay in order to register to vote. However, the major step toward electoral participation by African Americans was passage of the Voting Rights Act of 1965, which forbids discrimination in voting and registration. The legislation empowers federal agents to register voters and, as interpreted by the courts, prohibits the use of literacy tests as a registration requirement. The Voting Rights Act had an immediate impact on black participation. In the ensuing presidential election, black turnout in the South increased by twenty percentage points and has continued to rise, affecting state and local elections in addition to federal elections.

Congress has renewed the Voting Rights Act several times. The most recent renewal will keep the law in effect until 2030. The act includes a provision that requires states and localities to clear with federal officials any electoral change that has the effect, intended or not, of reducing the voting power of a minority group. This requirement, for example, has prevented states from creating election districts that deliberately dilute the minority vote. A recent example is

League of United Latin American Voters v. Perry (2006), a case involving Texas's twenty-third congressional district, the boundaries of which were drawn in a way designed to make Hispanics a minority of the voters within the district. In ordering the state of Texas to redraw the district, the Supreme Court said, "The troubling blend of politics and race—and the resulting vote dilution of a group that was beginning to [overcome] prior electoral discrimination—cannot be sustained."[27] However, the court also does not allow election districts to be created for the sole purpose of giving control to a minority group. In some areas, a district will naturally have a minority group as the voting majority, which is acceptable. States are not permitted, however, to draw district lines in a way deliberately intended to create a district that has a minority group as its majority. Any such districting, the Court has ruled, violates the equal-protection rights of white voters.[28]

The Civil Rights Act of 1968

In 1968, Congress passed civil rights legislation designed to prohibit discrimination in housing. A building owner cannot refuse to sell or rent housing because of a person's race, religion, ethnicity, or sex. An exception is allowed for owners of small multifamily dwellings who reside on the premises.

Despite legal prohibitions on discrimination, housing in America remains highly segregated. Only a third of African Americans live in a neighborhood that is mostly white. One reason is that the annual income of most black families is substantially below that of most white families. Another reason is banking practices. At one time, banks contributed to housing segregation by *redlining*—refusing to grant mortgage loans in certain neighborhoods, typically those with large black populations. Since buyers could not get a mortgage, homeowners had to lower the price of their houses to sell them. As home values plummeted, white families increasingly left these neighborhoods, which had the effect of increasing the percentage of black families. The 1968 Civil Rights Act prohibits redlining, but many of the segregated neighborhoods it helped to create still exist. Moreover, minority status continues to be a factor in the lending practices of some banks. Studies indicate that Hispanics and African Americans have more difficulty obtaining mortgages than do white applicants of comparable income.[29]

Affirmative Action

Changes in the law seldom have large or immediate effects on how people behave. For example, although the 1964 Civil Rights Act prohibited discrimination in employment on the basis of race, color, religion, sex, or national origin, disadvantaged group members did not suddenly obtain jobs for which they were qualified. Many employers continued to prefer white male employees. Other employers adhered to established employment procedures that kept women and minorities at a disadvantage. Membership in many union locals, for example, was handed down from father to son. Moreover, the Civil Rights Act did not require employers to prove that their employment practices were not discriminatory. Instead, the burden of proof was on the woman or minority-group member who was denied a job. It was costly and usually difficult for an individual to prove in court that gender or race was the reason for not being hired or promoted. Moreover, a victory in court applied only to the individual in question; it did not help other women and minorities faced with job discrimination.

Affirmative action programs were devised as a remedy for such problems. **Affirmative action** refers to deliberate efforts to provide full and equal opportunities in employment, education, and other areas for members of traditionally disadvantaged groups. Affirmative action applies only to organizations—such as universities, agencies, and construction firms—that receive federal funding or contracts. These organizations are required to establish programs designed to ensure that all applicants are treated fairly. They also bear a burden of proof. If an organization grants a disproportionate share of opportunities to white males, it must show that the pattern is the result of necessity (such as the nature of the job or the locally available labor pool) and not the result of systematic discrimination.

Although most equality-oriented policies have been established through congressional or judicial action, affirmative action is an exception. It was established by presidential action. The term *affirmative action* first appeared in an executive order issued in 1961 by President John F. Kennedy, who directed federal contractors to "take affirmative action to ensure that applicants are employed . . . without regard to their race, creed, color, or national origin." In 1967, President Lyndon Johnson extended affirmative action to include women and summarized the policy's goal: "We seek . . . not just equality as a right and a theory, but equality as a fact and a result." *Equality of result* was a new concept. Other major civil rights policies had sought to eliminate **de jure discrimination,** which is discrimination based on law, as in the case of the state laws requiring black and white children to attend separate schools during the pre-*Brown* period. Affirmative action policy sought to alleviate **de facto discrimination**—the condition whereby historically disadvantaged groups have fewer opportunities and benefits because of prejudice and economic circumstances, such as their inability to pay for a college education.

Few issues have sparked more controversy than has affirmative action, and even today the public has a mixed response to it, as Figure 5-2 indicates. Most Americans support programs designed to ensure that historically disadvantaged groups receive equal treatment, but oppose programs that would give them preferential treatment. Preference programs are deeply divisive. Whereas nearly 60 percent of African Americans and more than 50 percent of Hispanics support them, only slightly more than 20 percent of whites do so.[30]

affirmative action

Refers to programs designed to ensure that women, minorities, and other traditionally disadvantaged groups have full and equal opportunities in employment, education, and other areas of life.

de jure discrimination

Discrimination on the basis of race, sex, religion, ethnicity, and the like that results from a law.

de facto discrimination

Discrimination on the basis of race, sex, religion, ethnicity, and the like that results from social, economic, and cultural biases and conditions.

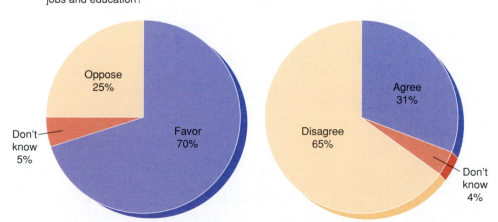

"In order to overcome past discrimination, do you favor or oppose affirmative action programs designed to help blacks, women, and other minorities get better jobs and education?"

Oppose 25%
Don't know 5%
Favor 70%

"We should make every possible effort to improve the position of blacks and other minorities, even if it means giving them preferential treatment."

Agree 31%
Disagree 65%
Don't know 4%

FIGURE 5-2

Opinions on Affirmative Action Most Americans support affirmative action when it comes to programs that will give women and minorities an equal chance at opportunities but oppose it when it comes to programs that will give them preferential treatment.

Source: From Pew Research Center for the People and the Press, June 2, 2009. Reprinted with permission.

The University of Michigan was the focus of national attention in 2003 as a result of its affirmative action admissions programs. Shown here are demonstrators from both sides of the issue. In its 2003 ruling, the Supreme Court upheld the use of race as a factor in admissions but rejected the use of a "point system" as the method of applying it.

Policies that pit individuals against each other typically end up in the Supreme Court, and affirmative action is no exception. In *University of California Regents v. Bakke* (1978), the Court issued its first affirmative action ruling. A white male, Alan Bakke, had been rejected by a medical school that admitted minority applicants with significantly lower test scores. The Court ruled that the medical school, because it had reserved a fixed number ("a quota") of admissions for minority applicants, had violated Bakke's right to equal protection. However, the Court did not strike down affirmative-action admissions per se, saying instead that race could be among the factors take into account by schools in their effort to create a diverse student body.[31]

The scope of affirmative action has narrowed considerably since the *Bakke* decision. Subsequent appointees to the Supreme Court have taken the policy in a conservative direction. In *Adarand v. Pena* (1995), for example, the Court overturned an earlier ruling that had upheld a federal policy that "set aside" a certain percentage of federally funded construction projects for minority-owned firms.[32] In its *Adarand* decision, the Court said that "past discrimination in a particular industry cannot justify" granting an advantage to minority-owned construction firms that have not been the direct victims of this discrimination.[33] Another example is *Ricci v. DeStefano*, in which the Supreme Court held that an organization, after establishing an equal opportunity program, has to abide by it even if minorities are adversely affected. At issue was a promotion test that the city of New Haven administered to firefighters. None of the city's black firefighters scored high enough to be considered for promotion and, after an exhaustive assessment of the exam's contents, the city concluded it had been biased and rescinded the results. The white firefighters who passed the exam then sued, and the Supreme Court ruled in their favor, concluding that New Haven had violated the 1964 Civil Rights Act's prohibition on discrimination by employers.[34]

Opponents of affirmative action have argued that the Supreme Court should end the policy entirely. They thought the Court might do so when it reviewed two University of Michigan admission policies in 2003. By a 6-3 vote in *Gratz v. Bollinger*, the Court did strike down Michigan's undergraduate admission policy, which had a point system that granted 20 points (out of 150 possible points) to minority applicants. The Court said the policy was unconstitutional because it assigned a specific weight to race.[35] However, by a 5-4 vote in *Grutter v. Bollinger*, the Court upheld Michigan's law school admission policy, which took race (along with other factors such as work experience and extracurricular activities) into account in admission decisions. The Court concluded that Michigan's program was being applied sensibly and that it fostered Michigan's "compelling interest in obtaining the educational benefits that flow from a diverse student body."[36]

(In 2012, the Supreme Court agreed to hear a Texas case—*Fisher v. University of Texas*—that some analysts believe could end race preferences in higher education. The case involves a white woman who was denied admission to the University of Texas, which took race and ethnicity into account in its admissions decisions. She sued on grounds that she was denied admission because she is white. The reason some analysts believe her case could be precedent setting is that the Court now has four members who were not on it at the time of the Michigan decision. One of these justices is Samuel Alito, who is substantially more conservative than the justice he succeeded, Sandra Day O'Connor. She cast the deciding vote in the Court's 5-4 Michigan decision and wrote the majority's opinion. The Texas case is scheduled to be decided sometime in 2013.)

The Continuing Struggle for Equality

Although progress has been made toward a more equal America, civil rights problems involve deeply rooted conditions, habits, and prejudices. As a consequence, America's traditionally disadvantaged groups are still substantially unequal in their daily lives. The following discussion describes some, though hardly all, of the problems these groups confront.

African Americans

Martin Luther King Jr.'s dream of an equal society for black Americans remains elusive.[37] Poverty is a persistent problem in the black community, affecting everyone from the very old to the very young. The median net worth of households headed by retired black people is less than $20,000, compared with roughly $200,000 for retired white people. Among adults of employment age, the jobless rate of African Americans is twice that of white Americans. As for black children, roughly 40 percent live below the government-defined poverty line, compared with about 10 percent of white children. Nearly a third of black children, compared with a twentieth of white children, live in extremely poor families—those with incomes that are 50 percent or more below the poverty line. Such families live on less than $10,000 a year. The mortality rate of black infants is two-and-a-half times higher than that of white babies.[38]

Even the legal rights of African Americans do not, in practice, match the promise of the civil rights movement. Studies have found that African Americans accused of crime are more likely than white Americans to be convicted, and they are more likely to receive stiffer sentences for comparable offenses. The U.S. Department of Justice found, for example, that among persons convicted of drug felonies in state courts, half of black defendants received prison sentences, compared with a third of white defendants.[39] Crime rates are also substantially higher in the black community, a situation that is attributable in part to higher unemployment and lower education rates. An effect is that Africans Americans make up more than a third of all prison inmates, even though they account for only one-eighth of the U.S. population (see Figure 5-3). Based on current incarceration rates, roughly one in four black males will spend time in prison, which is higher than the number projected to finish college. By comparison, Hispanic males have about a one in six chance of going to prison, and non-Hispanic white males have a one in twenty-three chance.[40]

A distinguishing characteristic of the black community, and a source of controversy within it, is the status of the family. Compared with other children, many fewer black children grow up in a household with both parents. More than half of black children grow up in a single-parent family, and 8 percent grow up in a home where neither parent is present. The African American entertainer Bill Cosby was widely criticized within the black community when he suggested that many of its problems trace to the unwillingness of many black fathers to meet their family responsibilities. When Barack Obama made the same point during the 2008 presidential campaign, he was attacked by black leader Jesse Jackson, who said that the problem of absentee fathers is largely the result of job and criminal-justice discrimination. Nearly everyone within the black community agrees, however, that black children are harmed by the disintegration of the black family—the proportion of black

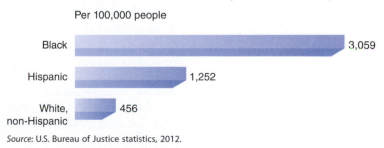

FIGURE 5-3 **Prison Incarceration Rates, by Race and Ethnicity**

Per 100,000 people

Black — 3,059
Hispanic — 1,252
White, non-Hispanic — 456

Source: U.S. Bureau of Justice statistics, 2012.

HOW THE U.S. DIFFERS POLITICAL THINKING THROUGH COMPARISON

Women's Representation in National Legislatures

For a long period in world history, women were largely barred from holding positions of political power. The situation has changed dramatically in recent decades, and women now hold more seats in national legislatures than at any time in history. Yet in only a few countries have they even approached parity with men. The Scandinavian countries (of which Sweden is an example) rank highest in terms of the percentage of female lawmakers. Other northern European countries have lower levels, but their levels are higher than that of the United States, as the figure below indicates.

Q: Why does the United States have fewer women in its national legislature than do European democracies?

A: Public opinion in the United States does not differ greatly from that in Europe on the issue of women in public office. An explanation for why Europe has more women legislators is its reliance on proportional representation. In this system, the parties get seats in proportion to the votes they receive in the election, and the parties decide which party members will occupy the seats. The parties tend to balance their selections, including a balance of men and women, in order to attract as many votes as

possible. In the United States, candidates compete directly for the vote, and the candidate who gets the most votes in a district wins the seat. There is no systematic method for assuring the election of a designated proportion of candidates from a particular demographic group. (Chapter 8 provides a fuller explanation of the difference between proportional representation and single-member districts as methods of election.)

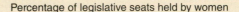

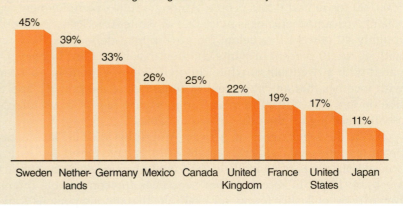

Percentage of legislative seats held by women

Sweden	Netherlands	Germany	Mexico	Canada	United Kingdom	France	United States	Japan
45%	39%	33%	26%	25%	22%	19%	17%	11%

Source: Inter-Parliamentary Union, Women in National Parliaments (2012). Based on number of women in the single or lower legislative chamber. In the case of the United States, that chamber is the U.S. House of Representatives. Reprinted with permission, www.ipu.org.

children living with a single parent or no parent has nearly doubled since the 1960s. Those who grow up in a single-parent household are substantially more likely to have inadequate nutrition, not finish high school, not attend college, end up in prison, and be unemployed.

One area in which African Americans have made substantial progress since the 1960s is elective office. Although the percentage of black elected officials is still far below the proportion of African Americans in the population, it has risen sharply in recent decades.[41] There are now roughly five hundred black mayors and forty black members of Congress. The most stunning advance, of course, was the election of Barack Obama in 2008 as the first African American president.

Women

Women, too, have made substantial gains in the area of appointive and elective offices. In 1981, President Ronald Reagan appointed the first woman to serve on the Supreme Court, Sandra Day O'Connor. When the Democratic Party in 1984 chose Geraldine Ferraro as its vice presidential nominee, she became the first woman to run on the national ticket of a major political party. Sarah Palin became the second when she ran as the 2008 Republican vice presidential nominee. Hillary Clinton nearly won the 2008 Democratic presidential nomination, which would have been the first time that a woman headed a major party's national ticket. After the 2008 election, President Obama chose Clinton to head the State Department. Each of the last three presidents has appointed a woman as secretary of

In 2009, Hillary Clinton became the third woman to serve as U.S. secretary of state. Earlier she served as a U.S. senator from New York. The Gallup poll annually asks Americans which woman they "most admire." Clinton has topped the list more than a dozen times—the most of any woman in Gallup's eighty-year history.

state—Madeleine Albright and Condoleezza Rice are the other two women to serve in that position, which is regarded as the top Cabinet post. Nevertheless, women are still a long way from attaining political parity.[42] Women hold only one in six congressional seats and one in five statewide and city council offices (see "How the U.S. Differs").

In recent decades, increasing numbers of women have entered the job market. They are six times more likely today than a half century ago to work outside the home and have made inroads in male-dominated occupations. Women now compose, for example, nearly half of graduating lawyers and physicians. The change in women's work status is also reflected in general education statistics. A few decades ago, more men than women were enrolled in college. Today, the reverse is true. A recent U.S. Education Department report showed that women are ahead of men in more than just college enrollment; they are also more likely to complete their degree, to do it in a shorter period, and to get better grades.[43]

Nevertheless, women have not achieved job equality. Women increasingly hold managerial positions, but, as they rise through the ranks, they can encounter the so-called glass ceiling, which refers to the invisible but nonetheless real barrier that some women face when firms choose their top executives. Of the five hundred largest U.S. corporations, less than 5 percent are headed by women. Women also earn less than men: the average pay for full-time female employees is about 80 percent of that for full-time male employees. One reason is that women are more likely than men to interrupt their careers to raise a family. Another reason is that many of the jobs traditionally held by women, such as office assistant, pay less than many of the jobs traditionally held by men, such as truck driver. Women's groups have had only limited success in persuading courts and employers to institute *comparable worth policies* that would give women and men equal pay for jobs that require a similar level of training and education.[44] In 2011, the Supreme Court dismissed a class-action suit by Wal-Mart's female employees. They were seeking back pay for receiving lower wages than the firm's male employees. Some members of the Court suggested that a subsequent suit

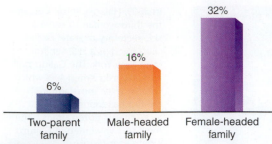

FIGURE 5-4 **Percentage of Families Living in Poverty, by Family Composition** Poverty is five times higher among female-headed households than among two-parent households.

Source: U.S. Census Bureau, 2012.

might succeed if limited to women employees who had been clearly and substantially underpaid.[45]

Women have had more success in getting courts and employers to address the problem of sexual harassment—lewd comments and unwelcome advances—in the workplace. In 2004, the Supreme Court ruled that companies and government agencies can be sued for failing to create a work environment in which sexual harassment is discouraged and punished.[46] The Court has also held that employees can sue an organization if it retaliates against them for filing a sexual harassment complaint. The case involved a woman who, after filing such a complaint, was removed from her position as a forklift operator and assigned a lower-level job in the company.[47]

Women gained a major victory in the workplace in 1993 when Congress passed the Family and Medical Leave Act. It provides for up to twelve weeks of unpaid leave for employees to care for a new baby or a seriously ill family member. Upon return from leave, the employee ordinarily must be given the original or an equivalent job position with equivalent pay and benefits. These provisions apply to men as well as women, but women were the instigating force behind the legislation and are the primary beneficiaries in that they usually bear the larger share of responsibility for newborn or sick family members.

Most single-parent families are headed by women, and about one in three of these families live below the poverty line, which is five times the level of two-parent families (see Figure 5-4). The situation has been described as "the feminization of poverty." Especially vulnerable are single-parent families headed by women who work in a nonprofessional field. Women without a college education or special skills often cannot find jobs that pay significantly more than the child-care expenses they incur if they work outside the home. Adding to their burden is the fact that some of them receive no or only token child-support payments from the father.

Native Americans

Full-blooded Native Americans, including Alaska Natives, currently number more than two million, about half of whom live on or close to reservations set aside for them by the federal government. State governments have no direct authority over federal reservations, and the federal government's authority is defined by the terms of its treaty with the particular tribe. U.S. policy toward the reservations has varied over time, but the current policy is aimed at fostering self-government and economic self-sufficiency.[48] Preservation of Native American culture is another policy goal.[49] For example, children in schools run by the Bureau of Indian Affairs can now be taught in their native language. At an earlier time, English was required. Nevertheless, tribal languages have declined sharply in use. Of the larger tribes, the Navajo and Pueblo are the only ones in which a majority of the people still speak their native language at home. Ninety percent or more of the Cherokee, Chippewa, Creek, Iroquois, and Lumbee speak only English (see Figure 5-5).

Native Americans have filed suit to reclaim lost ancestral or treaty lands and have won a few settlements. In 2006, for example, land that had once belonged to the Seneca tribe in New York was returned to it after property owners agreed to vacate their property in return for cash settlements from New York State. However, such settlements are infrequent, cover relatively small areas, and offer no promise of substantial future grants of land.

In recent years, some tribes have erected gaming casinos on reservation land. The world's largest casino, Foxwoods, is operated by the Mashantuket Pequots in Connecticut. Casinos have brought economic opportunities to the Native Americans living on or near the reservations where they are located. The employment level of these Native Americans has increased by a fourth and their income has increased substantially.[50] However, the casinos have also brought controversy—traditionalists argue that the casinos are creating a gaming culture that, whatever its economic benefits, is eroding tribal traditions. Political scientist W. Dale Mason notes that the gaming issue has also created conflict between tribal governments and the state governments. The tribes claim the legal right to conduct their own affairs while the states claim the power to regulate gambling within their borders. Revenue is also an issue. Tribal gaming is largely beyond the states' taxing power. Congress has taken measures to give states a degree of control over tribal gaming, but tensions remain. "What remains to be seen," Mason writes, "is whether the historic tribal-state conflict can be alleviated and replaced by a new era of trust and cooperation."[51]

Although casino gambling has raised Native Americans' average income level, it is still far below the national average. Native Americans are a disadvantaged group by other indicators as well. For example, they are less than half as likely as other Americans to have completed college, and their infant mortality rate far exceeds the national average.[52]

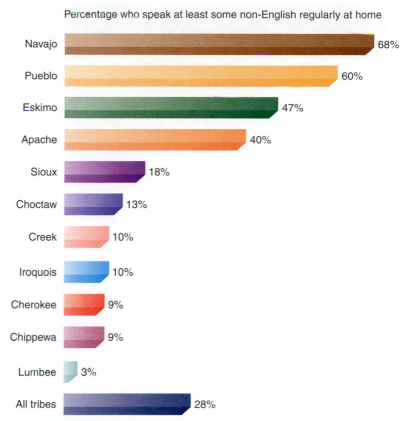

FIGURE 5-5   Native American Language Use in the Home   The original languages of Native Americans are disappearing from use in their homes. English is now the only language in use by many Native Americans, although there is considerable variation by tribe.
Source: U.S. Census Bureau, 2008.

Hispanic Americans

Hispanic Americans—that is, people of Spanish-speaking background—are one of the nation's oldest ethnic groups. Hispanics helped colonize California, Texas, Florida, New Mexico, and Arizona before those areas were annexed by the United States. Most Hispanics, however, are immigrants or the children or grandchildren of immigrants.

Hispanics are the fastest-growing minority in the United States and recently surpassed African Americans as the nation's largest racial or ethnic minority group. More than 50 million Hispanics live in the United States—twice the number of two decades ago. They have emigrated to the United States primarily from Mexico and the Caribbean islands, mainly Cuba and Puerto Rico. About half of all Hispanics in the United States were born in Mexico or claim a Mexican ancestry. Hispanics are concentrated in their states of entry. Florida, New York, and New Jersey have large numbers of Caribbean Hispanics, whereas California, Texas, Arizona, and New Mexico have many Mexican immigrants. Hispanics, mostly of Mexican descent, constitute more than half of the population of Los Angeles.

HOW THE 50 STATES DIFFER POLITICAL THINKING THROUGH COMPARISONS

HISPANIC POPULATION IN THE STATES

Since the 1960s, Hispanics have constituted the largest percentage of new immigrants. There are now roughly 50 million Hispanics in the United States, which is twice that of two decades ago. During this period, Hispanics surpassed blacks as America's largest minority group. They now account for roughly one in six Americans. As their numbers have risen, Hispanics have acquired political influence. More than four thousand Hispanics now hold public office in the United States. Nevertheless, Hispanics' political influence varies considerably from one state to the next, depending largely on their proportion of the state population. The map shows the percentage of each state's population that is Hispanic.

Q: What accounts for differences between the states in the percentage of Hispanic population?

A: The Hispanic population is concentrated in states on or near the border with Mexico, as in the case of California and Texas, or in states that are major ports of entry into the United States, as in the case of Florida and New York. Most Hispanics that hold public office have been elected in states with large Hispanic populations, particularly California, New Mexico, Texas, and Florida.

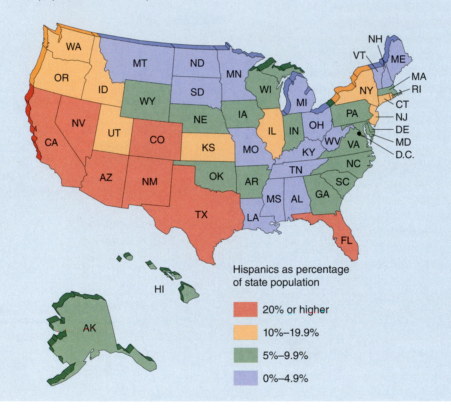

Hispanics as percentage of state population

- 20% or higher
- 10%–19.9%
- 5%–9.9%
- 0%–4.9%

A significant number of Hispanics—ten million or more by some estimates—are in the United States illegally. Most of them crossed into the United States from Mexico in search of jobs. U.S. authorities have had only limited success in stopping the influx, and illegal immigration has become a leading political issue. It is also a divisive issue, so much so that those in Congress who favor a softer line in dealing with illegal aliens have been unable to reach agreement with those who favor a harder line on a comprehensive approach to the problem.

Illegal immigration exploded into the headlines in 2010 when the state of Arizona enacted legislation that called for police to check for evidence of legal status whenever in the course of duty they stopped a person for another reason. If the person was an illegal alien, he or she would be detained, charged with a state crime, and turned over to federal authorities for deportation. In response, Hispanics organized protest rallies in communities throughout Arizona and elsewhere, claiming that the law was a thinly disguised assault on the Latino community. Most Americans, however, supported the Arizona law. A Pew Research Center poll found that Americans, by a margin of two to one, believed local police should be required to ascertain the citizenship of individuals they encounter in the course of duty. In 2012, the Supreme Court invalidated part of the Arizona law, concluding that it interfered with the federal government's constitutional authority over immigration policy (see Chapter 3).

On the other hand, Americans have divided opinions on the question of the long-term answer to illegal immigration. Polls indicate that most Americans favor a path to citizenship for illegal aliens who have been in the country for a relatively long period if they meet certain conditions, including holding a job, paying back taxes, and having no criminal record. However, most Americans also believe that border security should be tightened greatly, that new illegal entrants should be deported immediately, and that employers who hire undocumented aliens should face stiff penalties.

Hispanics' average annual income is substantially below the national average, but the consequences are buffered somewhat by the fact that the family is the foundation of the Hispanic culture (see Figure 5-6). As compared with black Americans, Hispanics are nearly twice as likely to live in a two-parent family, often a two-income family. As a result, fewer Hispanic families live below the poverty line. Health researchers have concluded that family structure also helps to account for the fact that Hispanics are healthier and have a longer life expectancy than would be expected based on their education and income levels.

More than four thousand Hispanic Americans hold public office. Hispanics have been elected to statewide office in several states, including New Mexico and Arizona, and roughly two-dozen Hispanic Americans currently serve in the House of Representatives. In 2009, Sonia Sotomayor was appointed to serve on the U.S. Supreme Court, becoming the first Hispanic to do so. The political influence of Hispanic Americans continues to increase. At present, only about half of all Hispanics are registered to vote, limiting the group's political power. Nevertheless, the sheer size of the Hispanic population in states such as Texas and California will make the group a potent political force in the years to come.

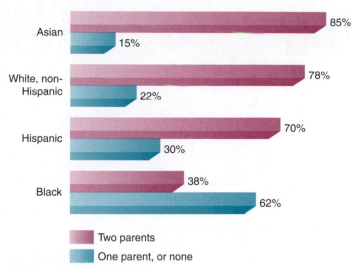

FIGURE 5-6   Family Structure, by Race and Ethnicity   Most American children live in two-parent households. The exception is black children, who are more likely to be raised in a single-parent family.

Source: U.S. Census Bureau, 2012.

Asian Americans

Asian Americans now number about twelve million, or roughly 4 percent of the total U.S. population. Most Asian Americans live on the West Coast, particularly in California. China, Japan, Korea, India, Vietnam, and the Philippines are the ancestral homes of most Asian Americans.

Asian Americans are an upwardly mobile group.[53] Most Asian cultures emphasize family-based self-reliance, which, in the American context, includes an emphasis on academic achievement. For example, Asians make up a disproportionate share of the students at California's leading public universities, which base admission primarily on high school grades and standardized test scores. Asian Americans have the highest percentage of two-parent families of any racial

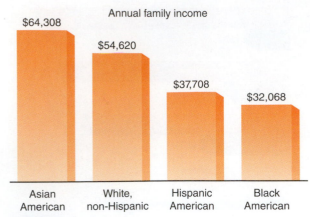

Annual family income

$64,308 — Asian American
$54,620 — White, non-Hispanic
$37,708 — Hispanic American
$32,068 — Black American

FIGURE 5-7 **U.S. Family Income, by Race and Ethnicity** The median family incomes of Asian Americans and non-Hispanic whites are substantially higher than those of Hispanics and blacks.

Source: U.S. Census Bureau, 2012.

group, which, in combination with educational attainment, has led to their emergence in the past two decades as the group with the highest median family income (see Figure 5-7). The median Asian American family's income exceeds $60,000, which is about $10,000 more than that of the median non-Hispanic white family and almost double that of the median black or Hispanic family.

Nevertheless, Asian Americans are still underrepresented in certain areas of the workplace. According to U.S. government figures, Asian Americans account for about 5 percent of professionals and technicians, which is slightly more than their percentage of the population. Yet they have not attained a proportionate share of top business positions; they hold less than 2 percent of managerial jobs.

Asian Americans are also underrepresented politically, even by comparison with Hispanics and blacks.[54] Fewer than ten Asian Americans currently serve in the Congress. Not until 1996 was an Asian American elected governor of a state other than Hawaii, and not until 2000 did an Asian American hold a presidential cabinet position. A prominent Asian American politician today is Bobby Jindal, who became a leading figure in Republican politics upon winning Louisiana's 2007 race for governor. In 2011 he was reelected to a second term by a landslide.

Gays and Lesbians

The Civil Rights Act of 1964 classified women and minorities as legally protected groups, which has made it easier for them to pursue their claims in federal court. Other disadvantaged groups do not have the same high level of legal protection, but they have increasingly resorted to judicial action, none more so than gays and lesbians.[55]

They gained a significant legal victory when the Supreme Court in *Romer v. Evans* (1996) struck down a Colorado constitutional amendment that nullified all existing and any new legal protections for homosexuals. In a 6-3 ruling, the Court said that the Colorado law violated the Fourteenth Amendment's equal-protection clause by subjecting individuals to employment and other forms of discrimination simply because of their sexual orientation. The Court concluded that the law had no reasonable purpose and was motivated entirely by hostility toward homosexuals.[56] In *Lawrence v. Texas* (2003), the Court handed gays and lesbians another victory by invalidating state laws that prohibited sexual relations between consenting adults of the same sex (see Chapter 4).[57]

Until Congress passed the Don't Ask, Don't Tell Repeal Act in 2010, gay and lesbian service members had to adhere to the military's "don't ask, don't tell" (or, "don't harass, don't pursue") policy. As long as they did not by word or action reveal their sexual preference, they could enlist and stay in the service. In turn, other service members were prohibited from trying to entrap them. Nevertheless, roughly a thousand gays and lesbians were dismissed from service each year because of their sexual orientation.[58] Gays and lesbians can now serve openly in the armed services, and some of those forced out earlier have returned to duty.

Gay and lesbian couples have had some success in acquiring the rights and privileges afforded opposite-sex couples. Some states, cities, and firms have extended employee benefits, such as health insurance, to their employees' same-sex partners. In 2009, President Obama signed an executive order requiring

DEBATING THE ISSUES   POLITICAL THINKING IN ACTION

Should Same-Sex Marriage Be Legal?

In 2004, Massachusetts became the first state to authorize same-sex marriage. Polls at the time indicated that Americans by a wide margin opposed the policy. Today, a handful of states permit same-sex marriage, and polls indicate that Americans are about evenly split on the question of whether same-sex couples should be allowed to marry, thereby entitling them to many of the same legal rights of inheritance, spousal benefits, and so on that married opposite-sex couples enjoy. On the other hand, about half the states have enacted laws prohibiting same-sex marriage within their boundaries. The following are opposing statements on the issue of same-sex marriage. The first is a portion of a legal brief filed by the American Psychological Association, the American Psychiatric Association, and the National Association of Social Workers when same-sex marriage was being reviewed by the California Supreme Court. The other is a statement by the U.S. Conference of Catholic Bishops.

YES The institution of marriage affords individuals a variety of benefits that have a favorable impact on their physical and psychological well-being. A large number of children are currently being raised by lesbians and gay men, both in same-sex couples and as single parents. Empirical research has consistently shown that lesbian and gay parents do not differ from heterosexuals in their parenting skills, and their children do not show any deficits compared to children raised by heterosexual parents. State policies that bar same-sex couples from marrying are based solely on sexual orientation. As such, they are both a consequence of the stigma historically attached to homosexuality, and a structural manifestation of that stigma. . . . [A]llowing same-sex couples to marry would give them access to the social support that already facilitates and strengthens heterosexual marriages, with all of the psychological and physical health benefits associated with that support. In addition, if their parents are allowed to marry, the children of same-sex couples will benefit not only from the legal stability and other familial benefits that marriage provides, but also from elimination of state-sponsored stigmatization of their families. There is no scientific basis for distinguishing between same-sex couples and heterosexual couples with respect to the legal rights, obligations, benefits, and burdens conferred by civil marriage.

—Legal brief of the American Psychological Association, the American Psychiatric Association, and the National Association of Social Workers

Q: What is your view on same-sex marriage?

NO Across times, cultures, and very different religious beliefs, marriage is the foundation of the family. The family, in turn, is the basic unit of society. Thus, marriage is a personal relationship with public significance. Marriage is the fundamental pattern for male-female relationships. It contributes to society because it models the way in which women and men live interdependently and commit, for the whole of life, to seek the good of each other. The marital union also provides the best conditions for raising children: namely, the stable, loving relationship of a mother and father present only in marriage. The state rightly recognizes this relationship as a public institution in its laws because the relationship makes a unique and essential contribution to the common good. Laws play an education role insofar as they shape patterns of thought and behavior, particularly about what is socially permissible and acceptable. . . . When marriage is redefined so as to make other relationships equivalent to it, the institution of marriage is devalued and further weakened. The weakening of this basic institution at all levels and by various forces has already exacted too high a social cost.

—U.S. Conference of Catholic Bishops

hospitals that receive Medicare funding to grant visitation rights to same-sex partners. Other benefits, such as inheritance rights, are reserved by law in many states to opposite-sex couples and their families.

In 2000, Vermont became the first state to legalize the civil union of same-sex couples, thereby granting them the same rights under Vermont law as opposite-sex couples have. Four years later, upon order of the state's high court, Massachusetts gave same-sex couples the right to marry, becoming the first state to do so. A handful of states now permit same-sex marriage, and a few additional ones have granted legal recognition to same-sex marriages performed in other states.

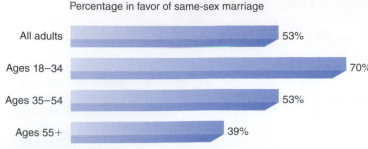

Percentage in favor of same-sex marriage

All adults	53%
Ages 18–34	70%
Ages 35–54	53%
Ages 55+	39%

FIGURE 5-8 **Opinions on Same-Sex Marriage, by Age** A majority of Americans now say they support same-sex marriage, though opinions vary considerably by age group.
Source: Gallup poll, 2011.

On the other hand, more than two dozen states, by either statute or constitutional provision, have recently enacted laws that limit marriage to opposite-sex couples.

In 1996, Congress passed the Defense of Marriage Act (DOMA), which defines marriage as "a legal union of one man and one woman as husband and wife." The law authorizes states to deny marital rights to a same-sex couple that has been granted these rights by another state. Under the U.S. Constitution's "full faith and credit clause," states are required to recognize the laws and contracts of other states, although Congress can create exceptions, as it did with DOMA. (DOMA also contains a provision that denies federal benefits, such as the opportunity to file a joint income tax return, to same-sex couples that were married in a state that allows such marriages. In 2012, a U.S. court of appeals ruled that the provision is unconstitutional because it interferes with a state's ability under the Tenth Amendment to define marriage. The case is expected to be heard by the U.S. Supreme Court, which could decide the issue as early as 2013.)

The American public has become more accepting of gay and lesbian relationships. A Gallup Poll in 2011 found, for the first time, that a narrow majority of Americans believe same-sex marriage should have the same standing in law as traditional marriages. Support for same-sex marriage is particularly high among younger adults (see Figure 5-8). In any case, the issue has been a divisive one, as well as a partisan one. During the 2012 presidential campaign, Barack Obama announced he had changed his mind about same-sex marriage. Citing discussions with gay staff members, friends, and service members. Obama said "I think same-sex couples should be able to get married."[59] Mitt Romney took the opposite position. "I have the same view on marriage that I had when I was governor and I've stated many times," Romney said. "I believe marriage is a relationship between a man and a woman."[60]

Other Disadvantaged Groups

The Age Discrimination Act of 1975 and the Age Discrimination in Employment Act of 1967 prohibit discrimination against older workers in hiring for jobs in which age is not a critical factor in job performance. More recently, mandatory retirement ages for most jobs have been eliminated by law. However, age discrimination is not among the forms of discrimination prohibited by the U.S. Constitution, and the courts have given government and employers leeway in establishing age-based policies.[61] Forced retirement for reasons of age is permissible if justified by the nature of a particular job or the performance of a particular employee. Commercial airline pilots, for example, are required by law to retire at sixty-five years of age and must pass a rigorous physical examination to continue flying after they reach the age of sixty.

The disabled are also not protected by the Constitution from discrimination, but they are protected through statutes. In 1990, for example, Congress passed the Americans with Disabilities Act, which grants employment and other protections to the disabled. Government entities are required, for instance, to take reasonable steps, such as installing access ramps, to make public buildings and services available to the disabled.[62] Earlier, through the Education for All Handicapped Children Act of 1975, Congress required that schools provide all children, however severe their disability, with a free and appropriate education. Before the legislation, four million children with disabilities were getting either no education or an inappropriate one (as in the case of a blind child who is not taught Braille).

Other groups could be described in this section. The United States has, for example, a long history of religious discrimination, targeted at various times and places against Catholics, Jews, Mormons, Muslims, various Protestant sects, and others. Numerous ethnic groups, including the Irish, the Italians, and the Poles, have likewise faced severe discrimination. Space precludes the discussion of the various forms of discrimination in America, but the point of any such discussion would be the same: equality has been America's most elusive ideal.

Discrimination: Superficial Differences, Deep Divisions

In 1944, Swedish sociologist Gunnar Myrdal gained fame for his book *An American Dilemma,* whose title referred to deep-rooted racism in a country that idealized equality.[63] Equality is a difficult idea in practice because it requires people to shed preconceived notions about how other people think, behave, and feel. People have difficulty looking beyond superficial differences—whether those differences relate to skin color, national origin, religious preference, gender, age, disability, or lifestyle.[64] Myrdal called discrimination "America's curse." He could have broadened the generalization. Discrimination is civilization's curse, as is clear from the thousands of ethnic, national, and religious conflicts that have marred human history. But America carries a special responsibility because of its high ideals. In the words of Abraham Lincoln, the United States is a nation "dedicated to the proposition that all men are created equal."

Summary

Self-Test www.mhhe.com/ pattersontadtx11e

During the past half-century, the United States has undergone a revolution in the legal status of its traditionally disadvantaged groups, including African Americans, women, Native Americans, Hispanic Americans, and Asian Americans. Such groups are now provided equal protection under the law in areas such as education, employment, and voting. Discrimination by race, sex, and ethnicity has not been eliminated from American life, but it is no longer substantially backed by the force of law. This advance was achieved against strong resistance from established interests, which only begrudgingly and slowly responded to demands for equality in law.

Traditionally disadvantaged Americans have achieved fuller equality primarily as a result of their struggle for greater rights. The Supreme Court has been an instrument of change for disadvantaged groups. Its ruling in *Brown v. Board of Education* (1954), in which racial segregation in public schools was declared a violation of the Fourteenth Amendment's equal-protection clause, was a major breakthrough in equal rights. Through its affirmative action and other rulings, such as those providing equal access to the vote, the Court has also mandated the active promotion of social, political, and economic equality. However, because

civil rights policy involves large issues concerned with social values and the distribution of society's opportunities and benefits, questions of civil rights are inherently contentious. For this reason, legislatures and executives have been deeply involved in such issues. The history of civil rights includes landmark legislation, such as the 1964 Civil Rights Act and 1965 Voting Rights Act.

In more recent decades, civil rights issues have receded from the prominence they enjoyed during the 1960s. The scope of affirmative action programs has narrowed, and the use of forced busing to achieve racial integration in America's public schools has been nearly eliminated. At the same time, new issues have emerged, including the question of whether same-sex couples will have the same rights as opposite-sex couples.

The legal gains of disadvantaged groups over the past half-century have not been matched by material gains. Although progress in areas such as education, income, and health care have been made, it has been slow. Tradition, prejudice, and the sheer difficulty of social, economic, and political progress stand as formidable obstacles to achieving a more equal America.

Study Corner

Key Terms

affirmative action (*p. 127*)
civil rights (*p. 116*)
de facto discrimination
 (*p. 127*)
de jure discrimination
 (*p. 127*)

equal-protection clause
 (*p. 117*)
equal rights (*p. 116*)
reasonable-basis test (*p. 119*)
strict-scrutiny test (*p. 120*)
suspect classifications (*p. 120*)

Self-Test: Multiple Choice

1. The term *civil rights* refers to
   a. treating groups equally under the law.
   b. protecting an individual's right to religious belief.
   c. protecting public safety.
   d. permitting marriage by justices of the peace.

2. The Supreme Court of the United States
   a. has never tolerated discriminating against people on the basis of their race.
   b. outlawed discrimination based on race in the *Plessy* case.
   c. refused to hear the legal case involving school segregation in Topeka, Kansas, because Kansas was not considered part of the South.
   d. in *Brown v. Board of Education* prohibited the practice of separate public schools for the purposes of racial segregation.

3. The legal test that in some cases (such as the legal consumption of alcohol) allows government to treat people differently based on their characteristics (such as age) is called the
   a. reasonable-basis test.
   b. strict-scrutiny test.
   c. suspect classification standard.
   d. none of the above.

4. Government policies that have been implemented to eliminate discrimination with the goal of achieving "equality of result" include
   a. food stamps.
   b. affirmative action.
   c. unemployment benefits.
   d. all of the above.

5. Regarding job-related issues, women
   a. have made gains in many traditionally male-dominated fields.
   b. have achieved gains in the workplace through programs such as day care and parental leave.
   c. hold a disproportionate number of the lower-wage jobs and are less likely to hold top-level management positions.
   d. all of the above.

6. Regarding affirmative action, Supreme Court decisions in the 1980s and 1990s have
   a. moved to outlaw it entirely.
   b. moved to narrow its application to specific past acts of discrimination.
   c. asked Congress to clarify the policy.
   d. asked the president to clarify the policy.

7. De facto discrimination is much harder to overcome than de jure discrimination. (T/F)

8. The history of discrimination against Hispanics is virtually the same as the history of discrimination against African Americans, which helps account for the similarity of their political and economic situations. (T/F)

9. In recent years, the equal-protection clause of the Fourteenth Amendment has been extended to include the elderly but not the disabled. (T/F)

10. Asian Americans have made such great progress in overcoming discrimination that the percentage of Asian Americans in top managerial positions and elected political offices is greater than the percentage of Asian Americans in the U.S. population. (T/F)

Self-Test: Essay

What role have political movements played in securing the legal rights of disadvantaged groups? How has the resulting legislation contributed to a furtherance of these groups' rights?

Suggested Readings

Arnold, Kathleen R. *American Immigration after 1996: The Shifting Ground of Political Inclusion*. University Park: Pennsylvania State University Press, 2011. An insightful analysis of how the immigration issue has changed in recent years.

Blackmon, Douglas A. *Slavery by Another Name: The Re-Enslavement of Black Americans from the Civil War to World War II*. New York: Doubleday, 2008. A historical analysis of the Jim Crow era.

Fong, Timothy P. *Contemporary Asian American Experience: Beyond the Model Minority*. Upper Saddle River, N.J.: Prentice-Hall, 2009. A comprehensive look at today's Asian Americans, including their political empowerment.

Garcia, F. Chris, and Gabriel Sanchez. *Hispanics and the U.S. Political System: Moving Into the Mainstream*. Upper Saddle River, N.J.: Prentice-Hall, 2007. A broad examination of Hispanics' growing influence on American politics.

Hanson, Kenneth, and Tracy Skopek. *The New Politics of Indian Gaming: The Rise of Reservation Interest Groups.* Reno: University of Nevada Press, 2011. A careful look at how Indian gaming has increased tribal political activity.

Lawless, Jennifer L., and Richard L. Fox. *It Still Takes a Candidate: Why Women Don't Run for Office.* New York: Cambridge University Press, 2010. An assessment of why fewer women than men seek public office.

Reeves, Keith. *Voting Hopes or Fears? White Voters, Black Candidates, and Racial Politics in America.* New York: Oxford University Press, 1997. A critical assessment of race and politics in American society.

Rimmerman, Craig A., and Clyde Wilcox. *The Politics of Same-Sex Marriage.* Chicago: University of Chicago Press, 2007. A careful assessment of the political forces surrounding the same-sex marriage issue.

List of Websites

www.airpi.org
The website of the American Indian Policy Center, which was established by Native Americans in 1992; includes a political and legal history of Native Americans and examines current issues affecting them.

www.naacp.org
The website of the National Association for the Advancement of Colored People (NAACP); includes historical and current information on the struggle of African Americans for equal rights.

www.nclr.org
The website of the National Council of La Raza, an organization dedicated to improving the lives of Hispanics; contains information on public policy, immigration, citizenship, and other subjects.

www.cawp.rutgers.edu
The website of the Center for the American Woman and Politics at Rutgers University's Eagleton Institute of Politics.

Participate!

Think of a disadvantaged group that you would like to assist. It could be one of the federal government's designated groups (such as Native Americans), one of the other groups mentioned in the chapter (such as the disabled), or some other group (such as the homeless). Contact a college, community, national, or international organization that seeks to help this group, and volunteer your assistance. (The Internet provides the names of thousands of organizations, such as Habitat for Humanity, that are involved in helping the disadvantaged.)

Extra Credit
For up-to-the-minute *New York Times* articles, interactive simulations, graphics, study tools, and more links and quizzes, visit the text's Online Learning Center at **www.mhhe.com/pattersontad11e**.

Self-Test Answers

1. a, 2. d, 3. a, 4. b, 5. d, 6. b, 7. T, 8. F, 9. F, 10. F

Public Opinion and Political Socialization: Shaping the People's Voice

Towering over Presidents and [Congress] . . . public opinion stands out, in the United States, as the great source of power, the master of servants who tremble before it. James Bryce[1]

As President Barack Obama weighed the recommendation of his military advisors to increase the number of troops in Afghanistan, Americans were divided on the best course of action. Polls indicated that they were nearly evenly split in their opinion as to whether the Afghan war was worth fighting. Those loyal to the president's party were the least supportive of a troop buildup. By a 58 percent to 31 percent margin, Democrats were against expanding the U.S. military mission in Afghanistan.[2]

In a nationally televised address on December 1, 2009, President Obama announced his decision on Afghanistan, saying he would send an additional 30,000 troops to what he called the "epicenter of the violent extremism practiced by al Qaeda." The surge would raise the number of American forces in Afghanistan to nearly 100,000. Obama promised a quick deployment of the troops, so that they would be in position to mount combat operations the following spring. At the same time, Obama announced that America's commitment to Afghanistan was not open ended. "After 18 months," he said, "our troops will begin to come home." During the eighteen-month period, U.S. forces would train and equip Afghan police and military units, so that the Afghans themselves could take responsibility for the war effort.

Polls taken soon after Obama's speech indicated that most Americans had liked what they heard. By a margin of 58 percent to 37 percent, they expressed approval of his decision to send more troops to Afghanistan. Support for his policy was strongest among Republicans—71 percent expressed approval. But Democrats, too, were swayed by his announcement. They were now evenly split on the issue of a troop increase.[3]

Obama's Afghanistan buildup is a telling example of the influence of public opinion on government: public opinion rarely forces officials to take a particular course of action. If President Obama had decided against deploying additional troops in Afghanistan, public opinion likely would have shifted toward support for that policy, just as it moved in the opposite direction when he announced the troop buildup. As long as a policy seems reasonable, political leaders usually have leeway in deciding a course of action.

This chapter discusses public opinion and its influence on U.S. politics. In this text, **public opinion** is viewed as the politically relevant opinions held by ordinary citizens that they express openly.[4] Their expression could be verbal, as when a citizen voices an opinion to a neighbor or responds to a question asked over the phone in an opinion poll. But the expression need not be verbal. It can also take the form, for example, of participation in a protest demonstration or casting a vote in an election. The key point is that people's private thoughts become public opinion when they are revealed to others.

A major theme of the chapter is that public opinion is a powerful yet inexact force.[5] The policies of the U.S. government cannot be understood apart from public opinion; at the same time, public opinion is not a precise determinant of public policies. The main points made in this chapter are:

■ *Public opinion consists of those views held by ordinary citizens that are openly expressed.* Public officials have various means of gauging public opinion but increasingly use public opinion polls for this purpose.

■ *The process by which individuals acquire their political opinions is called political socialization.* This process begins during childhood, when, through family and school, people acquire many of their basic political values and beliefs. Socialization continues into adulthood, during which time the news media, peers, and political leaders are among the major influences.

■ *Americans' political opinions are shaped by several frames of reference, including partisanship, ideology, and group attachments.*

■ *Public opinion has an important influence on government but ordinarily does not determine exactly what officials will do.*

Political Socialization: The Origins of Americans' Opinions

People's opinions form in response to events, issues, and problems that catch their attention or are enduring enough to retain their interest. But opinions also reflect people's interests and values. Developments invariably provoke different responses, depending on people's prior beliefs. A particularly striking example is the differing opinions of Republicans and Democrats toward U.S. military intervention in Kosovo in 1999 and in Iraq in 2003. Democrats were more supportive of the first war, whereas Republicans were more supportive of the second war. Although differences in the nature and purpose of these wars might partially explain this split, partisanship clearly does. The first of these conflicts was initiated by a Democratic president, Bill Clinton. The second was begun by a Republican president, George W. Bush.

Partisanship is a learned response. People are not born as Democrats or as Republicans, but instead they acquire these attachments. This learning is called **political socialization.** Just as a language, a religion, or an athletic skill is acquired through a learning process, so too are people's political orientations. Opinions

public opinion

The politically relevant opinions held by ordinary citizens that they express openly.

political socialization

The learning process by which people acquire their political opinions, beliefs, and values.

originate in the attitudes and information that people have acquired. When Congress in 2010 addressed the question of regulating the nation's financial institutions, most Americans had an opinion on the issue. Their views owed partly to what Congress was planning to do, but owed mainly to longstanding attitudes toward business regulation.

Broadly speaking, the process of political socialization has two distinguishing characteristics. First, although socialization continues throughout life, most people's political outlooks are influenced by childhood learning. Basic ideas about which political party is better, for example, are often formed uncritically in childhood, in much the same way that belief in the superiority of a particular religion—typically, the religion of one's parents—is acquired. A second characteristic of political socialization is that its effect is cumulative. Political orientations usually grow firmer with age. Early learning affects later learning because people's beliefs affect how new information is interpreted. Prior attitudes serve as a psychological screen through which new information is filtered, as in the case of the contrasting responses of Republicans and Democrats to the wars in Kosovo and Iraq.

The political socialization process takes place through **agents of socialization.** They can be divided between primary and secondary agents. *Primary agents* interact closely and regularly with the individual, usually early in life, as in the case of the family. *Secondary agents* have a less intimate connection with the individual and are usually more important later in life, as in the case of work associates. It is helpful to consider briefly how various primary and secondary agents affect political learning.

agents of socialization
Those agents, such as the family and the media, that have a significant impact on citizens' political socialization.

Primary Socializing Agents: Family, School, and Church

The family is a powerful primary agent because it has a near-monopoly on the attention of the young child, who places great trust in what a parent says. By the time children reach adulthood, many of the beliefs and values that will stay with them throughout life are firmly in place. Indeed, as sociologist Herbert Hyman concluded from his research: "Foremost among agencies of socialization into politics is the family."[6] Many adults are Republicans or Democrats today almost solely because their parents backed that party. They can give all sorts of reasons for preferring their party to the other, but the reasons came later in life. The family also contributes to basic orientations that, while not directly political, have political significance. American children, for example, often have a voice in family decisions, contributing to a sense of social equality.[7]

The school, like the family, affects children's basic political beliefs. Teachers at the elementary level praise the country's political institutions and extol the exploits of national heroes such as George Washington, Abraham Lincoln, and Martin Luther King.[8] Although teachers in the middle and high school grades present a more nuanced version of American history, they tend to emphasize the nation's great moments—for example, its decisive role in the two world wars. U.S. schools are more instrumental in building support for the nation and its cultural beliefs than are the schools in most other democracies. The Pledge of Allegiance, which is recited daily in many U.S. schools, has no equivalent in Europe. Schools there do not open the day by asking students to take a pledge of national loyalty.

Religious organizations are a powerful socializing agent for some children. Although many American children do not experience religion or do so only fleetingly, others attend church regularly. Scholars have not studied the influence of religion on childhood political socialization as closely as they have studied

Students in an elementary school recite the Pledge of Allegiance. Such childhood socialization experiences can have a profound impact on an individual's basic political beliefs.

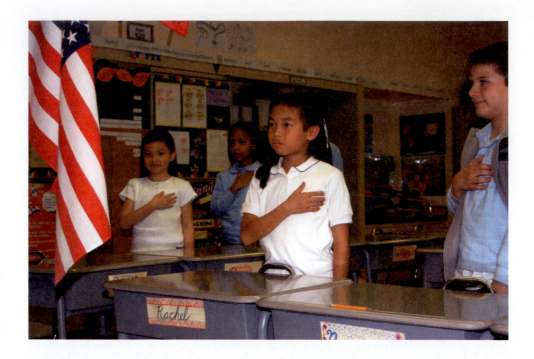

the influence of families or schools.[9] Nevertheless, religion can have a formative influence on children's attitudes, including beliefs about society's obligations to the poor and the unborn.

Secondary Socializing Agents: Peers, Media, Leaders, and Events

With age, additional socializing agents come into play. An individual's peers—friends, neighbors, coworkers, and the like—become sources of opinion. Research indicates that many individuals are unwilling to deviate too far politically from what their peers think. In *The Spiral of Silence*, Elisabeth Noelle-Neumann shows that individuals tend to withhold opinions that are at odds with those of the people around them. If nearly everyone in a group favors legalizing same-sex marriage, for example, a person who believes otherwise is likely to remain silent. As a result, the group's dominant opinion will appear to be more widely held than it actually is, which can persuade those with lightly held opinions to adopt the group opinion as their own.[10]

The mass media are also a powerful socializing agent. Politics for the average citizen is a second-hand affair, observed mainly through the media rather than directly. In the words of journalist Walter Lippmann, "the pictures in our heads of the world outside" owe substantially to how that world is portrayed for us by the media.[11] For example, heavy exposure to crime on television, whether through news or entertainment, can lead people to believe that society itself is more dangerous than it actually is.[12] The example illustrates the media's *agenda-setting effect*—the ability of the media to influence what is on people's minds. (This media effect and others are discussed more fully in Chapter 10.)

Individuals in positions of authority are also sources of opinion.[13] In the American case, no authority figure has more influence on public opinion than does the president. After the terrorist attacks of September 11, 2001, for example, many Americans were confused about who the enemy was and how America

HOW THE U.S. DIFFERS POLITICAL THINKING THROUGH COMPARISONS

National Pride

Americans are justifiably proud of their nation. It is the oldest continuous democracy in the world, an economic powerhouse, and a diverse yet harmonious society. What Americans may not recognize, because it is so much a part of everyday life in America, is the degree to which they are bombarded with messages and symbols of their nation's greatness. Political socialization in the United States is not the rigid program of indoctrination that some societies impose on their people. Nevertheless, Americans receive a thorough political education. Their country's values are impressed on them by every medium of communication: newspapers, daily conversations, television, movies, books, magazines, and so on.

The words and symbols that regularly tell Americans of their country's greatness are important to its unity. In the absence of a common ancestral heritage to bind them, Americans need other methods to instill and reinforce the idea that they are one people. America's political ideals have this effect, as do everyday reminders such as the flying of the flag on homes and private buildings, a practice that is almost uniquely American. (Elsewhere, flags are typically displayed only on public buildings.)

One indicator of Americans' political socialization is the pride they express in their nationality. Americans rank high on this indicator, as shown by the following chart, which is based on polls conducted by the World Values Survey. The percentages are the proportion of respondents in each country who said they were "very proud" or "proud" of their nationality.

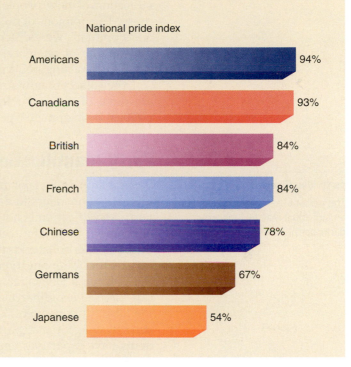

should respond. Their opinions became firmer a few days later when President George W. Bush in a nationally televised speech identified al Qaeda members as the perpetrators and declared that America would attack Afghanistan if it continued to provide them sanctuary. Polls indicated that nine of every ten Americans supported Bush's stance on Afghanistan. On the other hand, political leaders' ability to influence public opinion depends on their standing. After President Bush led America into a costly war in Iraq on the erroneous claim that it had weapons of mass destruction, his political support weakened, as did his ability to persuade Americans that the war in Iraq was worth fighting.

Finally, no accounting of the political socialization process would be complete without considering the impact of major events. The Great Depression, World War II. the Vietnam War, and the 2001 terrorist attacks are examples of events that had a lasting influence on Americans' opinions. America's costly and inconclusive war in Vietnam, for example, changed how many citizens thought about military force. Opinion polls in the war's aftermath revealed a sharp decline in public support for military intervention and spending. As with other such events, the Vietnam War affected the views of adults of all ages, but particularly those of a young age. Major developments make a greater impression on younger citizens because their political beliefs are usually less fully developed. Scholars use the term *generational effect* to describe the influence of watershed events on the political outlook of younger citizens.

Frames of Reference: How Americans Think Politically

Through the socialization process, citizens acquire frames of reference (or schemas) that serve as reference points by which they evaluate issues and developments. These frames of reference are important for two reasons. First, they provide an indication of how people think politically. Second, they are a basis for common cause. The opinions of millions of Americans would mean almost nothing if everyone's opinions were different from those of all others. If enough people share the same frame of reference, however, they have strength in numbers and have a chance of exerting political influence.

The subject of how Americans think politically fills entire books. Outlined here are three of the major frames of reference through which Americans evaluate political developments: partisanship, ideological leanings, and group attachments.

Party Identification

Partisanship is a major frame of political reference for many Americans. **Party identification** refers to a person's ingrained sense of loyalty to a political party. Party identification is not formal membership in a party but rather an emotional attachment to it—the feeling that "I am a Democrat" or "I am a Republican." Scholars and pollsters typically have measured party identification with a question of the following type: "Generally speaking, do you think of yourself as a Republican, a Democrat, an Independent, or what?" About two-thirds of adults call themselves either Democrats or Republicans. Of the one-third who prefer the label "Independent," most say they lean toward one party or the other and usually vote for that party's candidates. In short, most self-described independents have a partisan tendency.

Early studies of party identification concluded that it was highly stable and seldom changed over the course of adult life.[14] Subsequent studies have shown that party loyalty is more fluid than originally believed; it can be influenced by

party identification

The personal sense of loyalty that an individual may feel toward a particular political party.

Although the traditional images of America's two parties—the Democratic donkey and the Republican elephant—have lost much of their symbolic power, the party labels have not. Millions of Americans identify with one of the two parties and are loyal to it, consistently backing its policies and candidates.

the issues and candidates of the moment.[15] Nevertheless, many adults remain lifelong Republicans or Democrats even if their personal lives change in ways that might reasonably lead them to identify with the other party. Historically, major shifts in the party attachments of large numbers of Americans have occurred only in the context of a momentous upheaval. Even then, the shift has usually been concentrated among younger adults because their partisanship tends to be less firmly rooted. During the Great Depression, for example, Franklin Roosevelt's New Deal prompted many younger Republicans, but relatively few older ones, to change their loyalty to the Democratic Party.

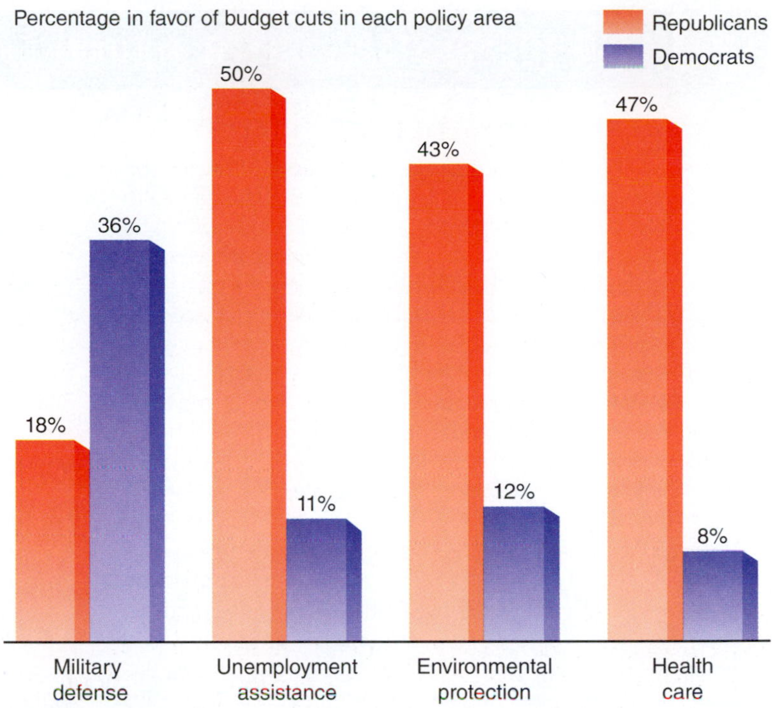

Once acquired, partisanship affects what people "see." *Selective perception* is the process whereby people selectively choose from incoming information those aspects that support what they already believe. Studies of presidential debates have found, for example, that Republicans and Democrats are watching the same candidates but "seeing" different ones. When their party's candidate is speaking, they tend to see sincerity and strength. When the other party's candidate is speaking, they tend to see evasiveness and weakness.[16]

In the everyday world of politics, no source of opinion divides Americans more clearly than does their partisanship. On nearly every major issue, Republicans and Democrats have contrasting opinions. As budget cuts were being deliberated in Congress in 2011, for example, a Pew Research Center poll asked Americans about their preferences. Republicans and Democrats had differing opinions, with Republicans favoring cuts in domestic programs and Democrats favoring cuts in military spending (see Figure 6-1). Even developments that have little to do with policy can provoke a partisan response. When the news broke that President Obama had been awarded the 2009 Nobel Peace Prize, Republicans were twice as likely as Democrats to say he did not deserve it. Three-fourths of Republicans said "politics" rather than merit was behind the award.[17]

For most people, partisanship is not blind faith in their party. Although Republican and Democratic identifiers vote predominately for their party's candidates, their votes in most cases have roots in party traditions and policies. The Democratic Party, for example, has promoted the nation's social welfare and workers' rights policies, whereas the Republican Party has spearheaded the nation's pro-business and tax reduction policies. The fact that most union workers are Democrats and most people in business are Republicans is hardly a coincidence.[18] (Partisanship is examined in additional detail at various points later in this book, particularly in Chapters 7, 8, 11, and 12.)

Percentage in favor of budget cuts in each policy area

FIGURE 6-1   **Partisanship and Opinions on Federal Budget Cuts**
Opinions on which areas of the federal budget should be cut are an example of the differing policy preferences of Republicans and Democrats.
Source: Pew Research Center for the People and the Press, 2011.

Political Ideology

Karl Marx's collaborator, Friedrich Engels, said that he saw no real chance of communism taking root in the United States. Writing in 1893, Engels said America's workers lacked sufficient class consciousness, being concerned instead about

HOW THE 50 STATES DIFFER POLITICAL THINKING THROUGH COMPARISONS

PARTY LOYALTIES IN THE STATES

The strength of the major parties varies substantially among the states. One indicator of party dominance is the degree to which the party identification of state residents favors one party or the other. In opinion polls, party identification is measured by a question of the following type: "Generally speaking, do you think of yourself as a Republican, a Democrat, an Independent, or what?" In 2011, the Gallup Organization aggregated the results of its daily tracking polls to estimate the state-by-state distribution of Republican and Democratic identifiers. Nationwide, more Americans identify with the Democratic Party than the Republican Party, but the variation across the states is considerable. For the map below, the fifty states (plus the District of Columbia) have been divided into three groups, using the categorization method employed by Gallup. States are considered Democratic or Republican if one party's identifiers exceed those of the other party by more than five percentage points. Competitive states are those where the difference is less than five percentage points. By this indicator, Republican strength is concentrated in the Plains and the Rocky Mountains, whereas Democratic strength is concentrated in the coastal states and the northern Midwest. According to the Gallup indicator, Hawaii, Maryland, Connecticut, New York, Massachusetts, and Vermont (in that order) are the six most heavily Democratic states, whereas Utah, Idaho, Wyoming, Alaska, North Dakota, and Kansas (in that order) are the most heavily Republican states. It should be noted that most of the southern states are categorized as competitive by the Gallup indicator, even though Republicans have dominated most elections in the region. Studies show that southern Democrats have lower turnout rates in elections than southern Republicans, partly because they have lower average income (see Chapter 7 for a discussion of the relationship between income and voter turnout).

Q: Why is the concentration of Republicans particularly high in the Great Plains and the Rocky Mountains?

A: The Great Plains and Rocky Mountain areas have traditionally been Republican, a reflection in part of the rugged individualism that defined their early settlement and contributed to a preference for small government.

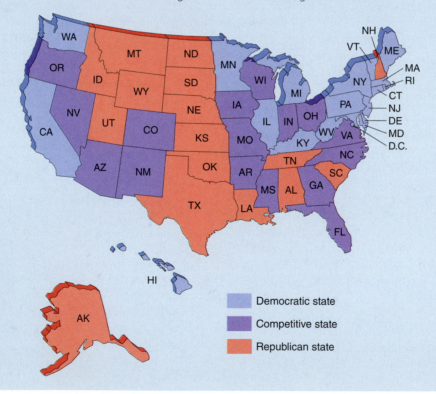

Democratic state
Competitive state
Republican state

getting ahead on their own.[19] In broader historical terms, Americans did not embrace any of the large twentieth-century ideologies—communism, fascism, or socialism—that captured the imagination of many Europeans. Historian Daniel Boorstin argued that Americans are pragmatists at heart, driven less by allegiance to ideology than by a desire to find workable solutions to problems.[20]

Congressman Ron Paul is shown here speaking at a college campus during his 2012 campaign for the Republican presidential nomination. Paul ran on a platform of small government in all areas and was frequently described as a libertarian rather than as a conservative or liberal.

Of course, political ideology does not have to take extreme forms, as it did in the case of Soviet communism and German fascism. In simplified form, an **ideology** can be defined as a general belief about the role and purpose of government.* Some Americans believe, for instance, that government should use its power to help the economically disadvantaged. Such individuals can be labeled **economic liberals.** Other Americans believe that the government should leave the distribution of economic benefits largely to the workings of the free market. They can be described as **economic conservatives.** Americans differ also in their views on government's role in regard to social and cultural issues, such as same-sex marriage and abortion. **Cultural (social) liberals** would leave lifestyle choices to the individual. In contrast, **cultural (social) conservatives** would use government to promote traditional values—for example, by passing laws that would limit marriage to opposite-sex couples.

Although it is sometimes said that liberals believe in big government while conservatives believe in small government, this claim is inaccurate, as the foregoing discussion would indicate. Conservatives prefer a smaller role for government on economic issues but want to use government power to uphold cultural traditions. The reverse is true of liberals. Each group wants government to be active or inactive, depending on which approach serves its policy goals.

There is no logical reason, of course, why an economic liberal also has to be a cultural liberal. Although most economic liberals are also cultural liberals, some are not. The term **populist** (although some analysts prefer the term *communitarian*) is used to describe an individual who is an economic liberal and a cultural conservative. Similarly, some economic conservatives are cultural liberals. They believe government should refrain from undue intervention in the economic marketplace *and* in people's private lives. The term **libertarian** is used to characterize someone with this set of beliefs.

ideology
A general belief about the role and purpose of government.

economic liberals
Those who believe government should do more to assist people who have difficulty meeting their economic needs on their own.

economic conservatives
Those who believe government tries to do too many things that should be left to private interests and economic markets.

cultural (social) liberals
Those who believe it is not government's role to buttress traditional values at the expense of unconventional or new values.

cultural (social) conservatives
Those who believe government power should be used to uphold traditional values.

populists
Those who believe government should do more to assist people who have difficulty meeting their economic needs and who look to government to uphold traditional values.

libertarians
Those who believe government tries to do too many things that should be left to firms and markets, and who oppose government as an instrument for upholding traditional values.

*Some scholars define ideology in a stricter way, arguing that it can be said to exist only when an individual has a consistent pattern of opinions across a broad range of specific issues. By this definition, most Americans don't have an ideology. This conception is analytically useful in some situations, but it blunts the discussion of general belief tendencies in the public as a whole, which is the purpose here.

Because most citizens are liberal or conservative in both their economic and their cultural beliefs, most politicians also think this way. They were elected in part because their ideology aligned with that of most of their party's voters. (Most economic and cultural conservatives vote Republican while most economic and cultural liberals vote Democratic.) But not every politician fits the conventional mold. An example is Congressman Ron Paul of Texas, who unsuccessfully sought the Republican presidential nomination in 2008 and 2012. Although Paul's economic stands were conservative, he also campaigned on legalizing marijuana and ending U.S. military involvement abroad—positions more often associated with liberals than with conservatives. Paul once ran for Congress as a Libertarian Party candidate and was frequently described by the media as a libertarian. In any case, his political platform appealed especially to younger Republican voters. In the Iowa caucuses that kicked off the 2012 Republican presidential nominating race, he finished third but received nearly half the votes of those under 30 years of age.[21] He was backed by endorsements from several student newspapers, including *The Daily Iowan,* the student newspaper at the University of Iowa.

POLITICAL

THINKING   What Is Your Ideology?

The Gallup poll measures Americans' ideology by posing two sets of alternatives: (1) Some people think the government should make greater use of its taxing and spending power to help the less-well-off while other people think government should do less in this realm, leaving economic benefits to be distributed largely through the marketplace. (2) Some people think the government should make greater use of its power to promote traditional values in our society while other people think government should do less in this realm, leaving decisions about lifestyle to each individual. According to Gallup, a *conservative* thinks government should do less in the economic realm but do more to promote traditional values; a *liberal* thinks government should do more to help the less-well-off but do less in promoting traditional values; a *libertarian* would like government to do less in both areas; and a *populist* would like government to do more in both realms. Do you ever use one of these labels to describe yourself? Is it the same one that would be assigned to you by the Gallup method? If not, how would you explain the difference?

Group Orientations

Many Americans see politics through the lens of a group affinity. Their identity or self-interest is tied to the group, and they respond accordingly when a policy issue arises that affects it. Issues surrounding social security, for example, usually evoke a stronger response from senior citizens than from younger adults. Later chapters examine group tendencies more fully, but it is useful here to describe briefly a few groupings—religion, economic class, region, race and ethnicity, gender, and age.

Religion

Religious beliefs have long been a source of solidarity among group members and a source of conflict with outsiders. As Catholics and Jews came to America in large numbers in the nineteenth and early twentieth centuries, they encountered intense hostility from some Protestants. Today, Catholics, Protestants, and Jews hold similar opinions on many policy issues. Nevertheless, important religious differences remain, although the alignment shifts as the issue shifts.[22]

Fundamentalist Protestants and Roman Catholics are more likely than mainline Protestants and Jews to oppose legalized abortion, a split that partly reflects differing religious beliefs about whether human life begins at conception or later in the development of the fetus. Religious beliefs also affect opinions on poverty programs. Support for such programs is higher among Catholics and Jews than among Protestants. An obligation to help the poor is a central theme of Catholic and Jewish teachings, whereas self-reliance is a central theme in the teachings of some Protestant denominations.

The most powerful religious force in today's politics is the so-called religious right, which consists mostly of individuals who see themselves as born-again Christians and who view the Bible as infallible truth (see "Party Polarization"). Their opinions on issues such as gay rights, abortion, and school prayer differ significantly from those of the population as a whole. A *Time*/CNN survey found that born-again Christians are substantially more likely than other Americans to agree that "the Supreme Court and the Congress have gone too far in keeping religious and moral values like prayer out of our laws, schools, and many areas of our lives."[23]

PARTY
POLARIZATION   Political Thinking In Conflict

Religion and Politics

Between the 1930s Great Depression and the early 1970s, religion was a small part of American politics, except in 1960 when John F. Kennedy became the first Catholic to win the presidency. In the 1972 presidential election, however, a gap opened in the voting pattern of those who went to church frequently and those that did not. Ever since, religious values have been a part of the so-called culture war that has been waged between the Republican and Democratic parties over issues such as abortion, school prayer, same-sex marriage, and stem-cell research. The Republican Party has made major gains among white fundamentalist Christians, who now regularly cast about 75 percent of their votes for GOP presidential and congressional candidates. Catholics were once reliable Democratic voters but are now split, with tradition-oriented Catholics voting mostly Republican and modern-oriented Catholics voting mostly Democratic. The level of formal religious commitment also matters in how Americans vote. According to the University of Akron's National Survey of Religion and Politics, for example, over 60 percent of those who went to church at least once a week voted Republican in the 2000 presidential race compared with less than 40 percent of those who seldom or never went to church. Americans of the Jewish faith have been less affected politically by the increased salience of religion in politics. They vote strongly Democratic and have done so for decades.

Q. *What's your sense of the heightened salience of religion in American politics? Overall, how large a role do you think a particular religion's beliefs should play in elections and in determining national policy?*

Economic Class

Economic class has less influence on political opinion in the United States than in Europe, but income and education levels do affect Americans' opinions on some issues. Welfare assistance programs and business regulation, for example, have more support among lower-income Americans, whereas higher-income Americans are more supportive of tax cuts.

An obstacle to class-based politics in the United States is that people with similar incomes but differing occupations do not share the same outlook. Support for collective bargaining, for example, is higher among factory workers than among small farmers, white collar workers, and workers in the skilled crafts, even though the average income of each of these groups is similar. The interplay of class and opinion is examined more closely in Chapter 9, which discusses interest groups.

Region

For a period in U.S. history, region was the defining dimension in American politics. The North and South were divided over the issues of race and states' rights. Racial progress has diminished the regional divide, as has the relocation to the South of millions of Americans from the Northeast and Midwest. The newcomers are generally less conservative than natives to the region. Nevertheless, regional differences continue to exist on some issues, including social welfare and civil rights. The differences are large enough that when analysts talk about "red states" (Republican bastions) and "blue states" (Democratic bastions), they are generally referring to regions. The red states are clustered in the South, Great Plains, and Rocky Mountains, whereas the blue states are found mostly in the Northeast, the northern Midwest, and the West Coast.

Race and Ethnicity

As was discussed in Chapters 4 and 5, race and ethnicity affect opinions on civil rights and civil liberties issues. Blacks and Hispanics, for example, are generally more supportive of affirmative action and less trusting of police and the judicial system than are non-Hispanic whites. Blacks and Hispanics also tend to differ from non-Hispanic whites on economic assistance programs, although this difference mostly reflects differences in their income and education levels.

Gender

Men and women tend to think alike on many issues, including abortion rights, but tend to disagree on others.[24] Polls have found, for example, a consistent difference of about ten percentage points between women and men on support for affirmative action. The difference is even larger on some social welfare issues, such as poverty and education assistance. Women tend to have more liberal opinions on these issues, reflecting in part their greater economic vulnerability and their greater role in child care. A recent *Washington Post*/ABC News poll found, for example, that women were 20 percent more likely than men to favor increased spending for public education. Women and men also differ on national security policies, with men more likely than women to support the use of military force. Support for the Iraq and Afghanistan wars, for example, was consistently higher among men than women.

Generations and Age

As a generation comes of age, it encounters a different political environment than its predecessors, with the result that its political views will differ somewhat from those of earlier generations. Those Americans who came of age during World War II, for example, acquired a sense of civic duty unmatched by the preceding generation or by any generation since. On the other hand, those who came of age during the Vietnam War era were more mistrustful of government than the generation before them or the one that followed. Americans of different ages also respond differently to age-related policies. Today's young adults are no exception to the pattern. They came of age at a time when circumstances differed from those of earlier generations and have developed somewhat different political views as a result. Unlike senior citizens, for example, a substantial majority of today's young adults believe that gays and lesbians should have the right to marry.[25]

Crosscutting Groups

Although group loyalties have an impact on people's opinions, this influence is diminished when identification with one group is offset by identification with other groups. In a pluralistic society such as the United States, groups tend to be "crosscutting"—that is, each group includes individuals who also belong to other groups, where they can encounter different people and opinions. Crosscutting groups encourage individuals to appreciate and understand political differences, which fosters political moderation. By comparison, in societies such as Northern Ireland, where group loyalties are reinforcing rather than crosscutting, opinions are intensified by personal interactions. Catholics and Protestants in Northern Ireland live largely apart from each other, differing not only in their religious beliefs but also in their income levels, residential neighborhoods, ethnic backgrounds, and loyalties to the government. The result has been widespread mistrust between Northern Ireland's Catholics and Protestants and a willingness on the part of some on each side to resort to violence.

In the past few decades in the United States, the overlap between groups has diminished. Although the situation is still far different than in a place like Northern Ireland, Americans today interact less with those of a different background. Residential neighborhoods, for example, are now less diverse. Americans increasingly live alongside those of the same income level. Workplaces are also less diverse today than in the past. Many office workers and professionals, for example, spend their workday interacting almost entirely with others of the same occupation. Even Americans' "virtual" interaction has narrowed. Through the 1980s, Americans were exposed through television to a version of news that included Republican and Democratic arguments in roughly equal amount. Today, many Americans get their news from a cable outlet or Internet site that plays up one side of the partisan debate while dismissing the other (see Chapter 10).

"Information cocoons" is legal scholar Cass Sunstein's description of the increased tendency of Americans to interact with like-minded associates and to pay attention to like-minded information sources.[26] The tendency has contributed to the party polarization that is now a defining characteristic of American politics. Partisan differences are sharper and harder to bridge when people lack an understanding of the opinions of those that think differently than they do (see "Party Polarization" boxes throughout this book).

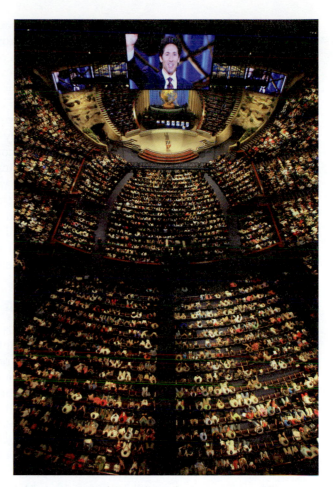

Religion is a powerful socializing force in American life. Churches, synagogues, mosques, and temples are places where Americans acquire values and beliefs that can affect their opinions about politics. Pictured here is the interior of the Lakewood Church in Houston, Texas. It is the largest of America's "megachurches"—those that hold thousands of worshipers.

The Measurement of Public Opinion

In a democracy, the central issue of public opinion is its impact on the governing process. Does government heed public opinion? Before addressing this question, it is helpful to discuss how political leaders find out about public opinion. Woodrow

Wilson once said that he had spent much of his adult life in government and yet had never seen a "government." What Wilson was saying, in effect, was that government is a system of relationships. A government is not tangible in the way that a building is. So it is with public opinion. No one has ever seen a "public opinion," and thus it cannot be measured directly. It must be assessed indirectly.

Election returns are a traditional method for assessing public opinion. Politicians routinely draw conclusions about what citizens are thinking by whether they voted and how they voted. Letters to the editor in newspapers and the size of crowds at mass demonstrations are among the other means of judging public opinion. All these indicators are useful guides for policymakers. Each of them, however, is a limited guide to what is on people's minds. Election returns indicate how many votes each candidate received but do not indicate why voters acted as they did. As for letter writers and demonstrators, their opinions tend to be atypical of the population as a whole. Fewer than 5 percent of Americans each year participate in a mass demonstration or write a letter to the editor. Studies have found that their opinions are more intense and often more extreme than those of other citizens.[27]

Public Opinion Polls

Today, opinion polls or surveys are the primary method for estimating public sentiment.[28] In a **public opinion poll,** a relatively few individuals—the **sample**—are interviewed in order to estimate the opinions of a whole **population,** such as the residents of a city or country.

How is it possible to measure the thinking of a large population on the basis of a relatively small sample of that population? How can interviews with, say, one thousand Americans provide a reliable estimate of what millions of them are thinking? The answer is found in the laws of probability. Consider the hypothetical example of a huge jar filled with a million marbles, half of them red and half of them blue. If a blindfolded person reaches into the jar, the probability of selecting a marble of a given color is fifty-fifty. And if one thousand marbles are chosen in this random way, it is likely that about half of them will be red and about half will be blue. Opinion sampling works in the same way. If respondents are chosen at random from a population, their opinions will approximate those of the population as a whole.

Random selection is the key to scientific polling, which is theoretically based on *probability sampling*—a sample in which each individual in the population has a known probability of being chosen at random for inclusion. The key is random selection. Individuals do not step forward to be interviewed; they are selected at random to be part of the sample. A scientific poll is thereby different from an Internet survey that invites visitors to a site to participate. Any such survey is biased because it includes only individuals who use the Internet, who happen for one reason or another to visit the particular site, and who decide to complete the survey. A scientific poll is also different from the "people-in-the-street" interviews that news reporters sometimes conduct. Although a reporter may say that the opinions of those interviewed represent the views of the local population, this claim is clearly faulty. Interviews conducted on a downtown street at the noon hour, for example, will include a disproportionate number of business employees on their lunch breaks. Stay-at-home mothers, teachers, and factory workers are among the many groups that would be underrepresented in such a sample.

The science of polling is such that the size of the sample, as opposed to the size of the population, is the key to accurate estimates. Although it might be assumed that a much larger sample would be required to poll accurately the people of the United States as opposed to, say, the residents of Georgia, the sample requirements are nearly the same. Consider again the example of a

---

public opinion poll

A device for measuring public opinion whereby a relatively small number of individuals (the sample) are interviewed for the purpose of estimating the opinions of a whole community (the population).

---

sample

In a public opinion poll, the relatively small number of individuals who are interviewed for the purpose of estimating the opinions of an entire population.

---

population

In a public opinion poll, the people (for example, the citizens of a nation) whose opinions are being estimated through interviews with a sample of these people.

huge jar filled with marbles, half of them red and half of them blue. If one thousand marbles were randomly selected, about half would be red and about half would be blue, regardless of whether the jar held one million, ten million, or one-hundred million marbles. On the other hand, the size of the sample—the number of marbles selected—would matter. If only ten marbles were drawn, it might happen that five would be of each color but, then again, it would not be unusual for six or seven of them to be of the same color. In fact, the odds are about one in twenty that eight or more would be of the same color. However, if one thousand marbles were drawn, it would be highly improbable for six hundred of the marbles, much less seven or eight hundred of them, to be of the same color. The odds of drawing even six hundred of the same color are about one in one-hundred thousand.

The accuracy of a poll is expressed in terms of **sampling error**—the degree to which the sample estimates might differ from what the population actually thinks. The larger the sample, the smaller the sampling error, which is usually expressed as a plus-or-minus percentage. For example, a properly drawn sample of one thousand individuals has a sampling error of roughly plus or minus 3 percent. Thus, if 55 percent of a sample of one thousand respondents say they intend to vote for the Republican presidential candidate, there is a high probability that between 52 percent and 58 percent (55 percent plus or minus 3 percent) of all voters actually plan to vote Republican. It should be noted that if the poll had found the candidates separated by one percentage point, it would be mathematically incorrect to claim that one of them is "leading." The one-point difference is smaller than the poll's three-point sampling error.

The impressive record of the Gallup poll in predicting the outcome of presidential elections indicates that the theoretical accuracy of polls can be matched in practice. The Gallup Organization has polled voters in every presidential election since 1936 (nineteen elections in all) and has erred badly only once: it stopped polling several weeks before the 1948 election and missed a late voter shift that carried Harry Truman to victory.

sampling error
A measure of the accuracy of a public opinion poll; mainly a function of sample size and usually expressed in percentage terms.

President Harry Truman holds up the early edition of the *Chicago Tribune* with the headline "Dewey Defeats Truman." The *Tribune* was responding to analysts' predictions that Dewey would win the 1948 election. A Gallup poll a few weeks before the election had shown Dewey with a seemingly insurmountable lead. The Gallup Organization decided that it did not need to do another poll closer to the election, a mistake that it has not since repeated.

Problems with Polls

Although pollsters assume that their samples are drawn from a particular population, such as all citizens of adult age, pollsters rarely have a list of all individuals in the population from which to sample. An expedient alternative is a sample based on telephone numbers. Pollsters use computers to randomly pick telephone numbers (including now also cell-phone numbers), which are dialed by interviewers to reach households. Within each of these households, a respondent is then randomly selected. Because the computer is as likely to pick one telephone number as any other, a sample selected in this way is assumed to be representative of the whole population. Nevertheless, some Americans do not have phones, and many of those who are called will not be home or refuse to participate. Such factors reduce the accuracy of telephone polling. Indeed, pollsters are concerned about the future of telephone polling. The refusal rate has increased sharply in recent decades.

The accuracy of polling is also diminished when respondents are asked about unfamiliar issues. Although respondents may answer the question anyway in order not to appear uninformed, their responses cannot be regarded as valid. Scholars label such responses "non-opinions." Less often, respondents will have an opinion but choose not to reveal it. On sensitive topics, interviewees will sometimes give what they regard as the socially correct response. For example, although turnout in presidential elections rarely exceeds 60 percent, 75 percent or more of respondents in post-election polls will claim to have voted. Some of them are not being truthful, but they are unwilling to tell the interviewer that they neglected to vote. Respondents are also not always truthful when it comes to expressing opinions that relate to race, gender, or ethnicity.

Question order and wording can also affect poll results. If respondents are asked their candidate preference at the outset of a survey, the results can differ from those obtained when they are asked at the end of the survey, after they have responded to other questions about the campaign. These questions can trigger thoughts that affect the choice of respondents who have a weak candidate preference at the start of the interview. In addition, how a question is framed, whether it is accompanied by relevant facts, and how the alternatives are worded can affect people's responses. Consider the issue of the death penalty. Do Americans favor or oppose its use? As it turns out, the answer depends to some extent on how the issue is worded. Respondents in some Gallup polls have been asked the question: "Are you in favor of the death penalty for a person convicted of murder?" Respondents in other Gallup polls have been asked a different version: "If you could choose between the following two approaches, which do you think is the better penalty for murder—the death penalty or life imprisonment, with absolutely no possibility of parole?" The two versions produce different results. When asked the first question, Americans by roughly two-to-one say they favor the death penalty. When asked the second question, Americans are evenly divided on whether the death sentence is the proper penalty.[29] Of the limits on polls, however, perhaps none is greater than pollsters' tendency—mostly for reasons of cost—to oversimplify the questions. On some topics, a simple yes-no type question is sufficient. When it comes to most issues, however, citizens often have conflicting thoughts. Rarely in surveys are they given the opportunity to talk at length about how they feel. They are asked only whether they "agree" or "disagree" with a particular issue position. In this sense, most survey questions provide only a rough approximation of what is on people's minds.

Despite these and other issues of polling, the poll or survey is the most relied-upon method of measuring public opinion. More than one hundred organizations are in the business of conducting public opinion polls. Some, like the Gallup

Organization, conduct polls that are released to the news media by syndication. Most large news organizations also have their own in-house polls; one of the most prominent of these is the CBS News/*New York Times* poll. Other polling firms specialize in conducting surveys for candidates and officeholders.

The Influence of Public Opinion on Policy

As yet unaddressed in the discussion is a central question about public opinion: what is its impact on the policies of government? The question does not have a firm or simple answer, either in theory or in practice.

Writers have long disagreed about the impact that public opinion *should* have on government. Some have contended that almost any opinion that citizens hold, except the most fleeting or malignant, deserves to be taken into account by officials, who otherwise would promote policies that are out of line with the public's thinking. This tradition was expressed pointedly by George Gallup, a pioneer in the field of polling: "The task of the leader is to decide how best to achieve the goals set by the people." Other writers have argued that public opinion is too whimsical and uninformed to be a basis for sound government. "Effective government," journalist Walter Lippmann wrote, "cannot be conducted by legislators and officials who, when a question is presented, ask themselves first and last not what is the truth and which is the right and necessary course, but 'What does the Gallup Poll say?'"

There is also disagreement over the impact public opinion actually has on government. Policies are complex, as are the factors that go into them. It is not a simple matter to pinpoint the influence of public opinion on particular public policies, and analysts do not entirely agree on what the evidence indicates. Nevertheless, most studies have concluded that public opinion exerts a strong influence on policymakers, though it varies across situations and issues.

Limits on the Public's Influence

Even if officials were intent on governing by public opinion, they would face obstacles, including inconsistencies in citizens' policy preferences. In polls, for example, Americans say they want a balanced federal budget. Yet only a minority say they would support the cuts in costly programs like social security and defense that would be necessary to bring the budget into closer balance. Nor are most citizens willing to balance the budget through a large tax increase. In the entire history of polling, there has never been a national survey in which a majority of respondents said their taxes should be raised significantly. In a 2011 Gallup poll, for example, 50 percent of respondents claimed that taxes were too high, and only 5 percent said taxes were too low.[30]

Many citizens also lack an understanding of issues, even vitally important ones. In the buildup to the U.S. invasion of Iraq in 2003, for example, polls revealed that more than half of adult Americans wrongly believed that Iraq had close ties to the al Qaeda terrorist network. Moreover, despite widespread opposition to the American invasion in most other countries, one in four Americans believed that world opinion supported the invasion. Americans who held these mistaken views were more likely than other Americans to support sending U.S. troops into Iraq.[31]

Only a minority of citizens can truly be said to be politically well informed. Even a college education is no guarantee that a citizen will have more than a passing familiarity with public affairs. The Intercollegiate Studies Institute surveyed

DEBATING THE ISSUES POLITICAL THINKING IN ACTION

Should Politicians Base Their Stands on Opinion Polls?

A fundamental principle of democracy is that public opinion ought to be the foundation of government. However, the role that public opinion should play in specific policy decisions is, and always has been, a subject of dispute. James Madison distinguished between the public's momentary passions and its enduring concerns, arguing that government is obliged to represent only the latter. In contrast, the Jacksonians and Progressives had a strong faith in the judgment of ordinary citizens and a distrust of entrenched elites. With the advent of the public opinion poll, it became possible to measure citizens' policy views more directly. Here are opposing views on whether policymakers should pay close attention to the polls in making their decisions.

YES Some analysts have held that leaders should act in close accord with the polls. Other analysts have argued that polls measure fleeting opinions about topical issues and that leaders are obliged to respond only to the people's enduring beliefs.

Sixty-eight percent of Americans think they should have a great deal of influence on the decisions of elected and government officials in Washington, but fewer than one in ten (9 percent) believe they do.... Who instead do Americans think bends the ears of the politicians and officials in the Capitol? According to the public, money talks. Nearly six in ten [say] that politicians pay a great deal of attention to their campaign contributors when making decisions about important issues.... Fifty-four percent of Americans expect their officials to follow what the majority wants, even if it goes against the officials' knowledge and judgment. Fewer (42 percent) want officials to use their own judgment if it goes against the wishes of the majority.... If we all lived in small New England towns, then perhaps town hall meetings would be a realistic means of injecting public opinion into the national debate. However, when it takes one western senator a whole year to travel to every single county in his or her home state, it is clear that the limits imposed by geography and time necessitate a continuing place for polling in public policy.

—Bill McInturff and Lori Weigel, pollsters

NO True statesmen are not merely mouthpieces for opinion polls. British historian Lord Acton recognized that the will of the majority could be and often is just as tyrannical as the will of a monarch, and in some cases more dangerous because the error has the support of the masses. Thus he observes, "It is bad to be oppressed by a minority, but it is worse to be oppressed by a majority," and "The will of the people cannot make just that which is unjust." ... In the United States we have compelling historical and contemporary examples of the majority siding with what were, in retrospect, clear-cut cases of injustice. The legalization and promotion of slavery by governments are a prime example, and stand as a stark rebuke to elected officials who think they ought to represent the people without regard to their own conscience. Today, there are a number of hotly contested issues—such as abortion, stem cell research, and, now, marriage—whose partisans often make appeals based on poll data. Our elected officials follow the shifting temper of the electorate with rapt attention. But is this how we ask our elected officials to lead? ... [T]oo many political leaders have settled on an inadequate answer: the will of the people (and the pollsters).

—Jordon J. Ballor, Acton Institute

Q: What's your view on this question? Should politicians try to follow public opinion in their decisions, or should they exercise independent judgment about what is best for the people they represent?

fourteen thousand college students in 2007, giving them a multiple-choice exam to test their "civic literacy." The average college student received a grade of F, answering barely half of the questions correctly. Even historical facts of great moment eluded many students. Only 46 percent of college seniors, for example, could identify the phrase "We hold these truths to be self-evident, that all men are created equal" as being part of the Declaration of Independence.[32] An earlier survey of Ivy League students found that one-third could not identify the British prime minister, half could not name both U.S. senators from their state, and three-fourths could not identify Abraham Lincoln as the author of the phrase "a government of the people, by the people, and for the people."[33]

POLITICAL THINKING   Are Citizens Fit for Democracy?

Nearly a century ago, two of America's leading thinkers—the journalist Walter Lippmann and the philosopher John Dewey—engaged in a spirited debate on whether citizens could play the role that democracy assigns to them. Lippmann and Dewey were in agreement that citizens' ability to think sensibly about politics was undermined by the numbing distraction of the entertainment media, the inattentiveness of many citizens to public affairs, and the propaganda efforts of political elites and special interests. But Lippmann and Dewey diverged sharply on the public's potential. Lippmann doubted that the public could live up to democracy's demands. Dewey contended that advances in public education and communication would enable citizens to realize their public potential. Which argument comes closer to your own thinking?

Of course, citizens do not have to be fully informed to have a reasonable opinion about some issues.[34] Knowing only that the economy is performing poorly, a citizen could reasonably believe that government should take action to fix it. The fact that the citizen is unaware of the government's economic policy options would not render his or her opinion irrelevant. As one research team noted: "It is true that individual Americans have a weak grasp on the essentials of economics and economic policy, and it is also true that Americans, in the aggregate, are highly sensitive to real economic performance."[35]

On the other hand, there are issues where information is nearly a prerequisite to a sound opinion. The health care reform legislation that Congress debated in 2009–2010, for example, had cost and coverage provisions that affected people in different ways. Yet many Americans had no awareness of these provisions or were misinformed about them. A Gallup poll found, for instance, that nearly a third of the public mistakenly believed that the legislation included government committees (the so-called death panels) that would decide which elderly patients would receive life-saving treatment and which would not. Those who held this erroneous belief were more likely than other citizens to oppose the legislation. Many of these individuals might have opposed it anyway for other reasons, but mistaken beliefs are not the basis for sound judgment.

Public Opinion and the Boundaries of Action

Such considerations led political scientist V. O. Key to conclude that the role of public opinion is to place boundaries on the actions of political leaders.[36] The public is seldom attentive enough or informed enough to dictate exactly what officials will do. However, politicians must operate within the limits of what the public deems reasonable and acceptable.

Certain policy actions are outside the boundaries of public acceptability. Opinions on some issues are so settled that officials have little chance of success if they try to work against them. During his first presidential term, Ronald Reagan proposed a major overhaul of the social security system, but he quickly backed down in the face of widespread public opposition from senior citizens. During his second term, George W. Bush attempted to privatize aspects of social security, only to back down in face of determined resistance. The founder of social security, Franklin D. Roosevelt, understood that public opinion would preserve the program. "No damn politician," he reportedly said, "can ever scrap my social security program." Roosevelt recognized that, by having social security benefits funded by payroll taxes, workers would feel they had rightfully earned their retirement benefits and would fight to keep them.

Although public opinion does not always drive government policy, it sets boundaries on what officials can do.

Issues vary in the degree to which they engage the public and the extent to which they provoke strong feelings. The greater the level of public involvement, the more likely officials will respond to public sentiment. In a study spanning four decades, Benjamin Page and Robert Shapiro found that changes in public opinion were usually followed by a corresponding change in public policy. As the public shifted its view, policy tended to shift in the same direction, particularly on issues that engaged large numbers of citizens.[37] Political scientist John Kingdon reached a similar conclusion, saying that when public opinion is intense and unmistakable as to a preferred course of action, politicians nearly always follow it.[38]

Nevertheless, even on issues that substantially engage the public, leaders usually have a degree of discretion. As political scientists Jeff Manza and Fay Lomax Cook noted from their study of public opinion: "[W]ithin the broad parameters established by public opinion, politicians and policy entrepreneurs often have substantial room to maneuver."[39] When the economy goes into a tailspin, for example, Americans expect officials to take action. However, Republican leaders typically like to respond with measures such as tax cuts and interest-rate adjustments, whereas Democratic leaders tend to rely on measures such as increased unemployment benefits and spending-level adjustments. Each approach can boost the economy, but they differ in their impact. The Republican approach helps mainly business interests and upper-income citizens whereas the Democratic approach helps mainly labor interests and lower-income citizens.

Officials also acquire latitude when the public is divided in its opinions. When significant numbers of citizens are aligned on each side of an issue, officials cannot easily satisfy both sides. However, this situation often is not politically difficult because the split falls largely along party lines. The 2009–2010 health care reform issue was of this type, enabling most members of Congress to take positions aligned with the views of most of their party's voters. A February 2010 Gallup poll, for example, found that Republican identifiers by more than three-to-one opposed comprehensive health care reform whereas Democratic identifiers by more than three-to-one favored it.

On issues that do not attract widespread public attention, leaders have considerable room to maneuver. On most policy issues, "the public"—if one means by that the whole citizenry—has no discernible opinion. The typical issue does not attract the attention of anywhere near a majority of citizens, much less provoke most of them to form an opinion about the proper course of action. Agricultural conservation programs, for example, are of keen interest to some farmers, hunters, and environmentalists but of little or no concern to most people. The pattern is so common that opinion analysts have described America as a nation of *many* publics.[40] The "public" for agricultural policy is a different one than, say, the "public" for financial regulation policy. Not surprising, in deciding such issues, political leaders are usually more responsive to the smaller number that are keenly interested in the issue than they are to the larger number that don't feel intensely about it, and may not think about it at all.[41]

Leaders and Public Opinion

The fact that public opinion and public policy coincide at points does not necessarily mean that officials are choosing policies on the basis of what citizens would prefer. Officials often go to great lengths to win public support for their policies.[42]

If leaders succeed in persuading the public to accept their point of view, policy and opinion will coincide but they will do so because leaders have been able to influence public opinion. A case in point is the period leading up to the U.S. invasion of Iraq in 2003. Although Americans had been hearing about Iraqi leader Saddam Hussein for years and had concluded that he was a tyrant and a threat, they were unsure whether an attack on Iraq made sense. Polls indicate that some Americans preferred to give United Nations inspectors ample time to investigate Iraq's weapons program before an invasion decision was made. Other Americans expressed support for an invasion only if the United States had the backing of its European allies. Still others thought that, if a war was launched, it should be conducted entirely through the air. However, over the course of a roughly six-month period, the Bush administration pressed the case for war, which gradually increased public support for it.[43] When the war began, polls showed that President Bush's decision to use ground and air forces against Iraq had the backing of 70 percent of Americans.

Such instances have led some analysts to claim that major policies more fully reflect the preferences of leaders than those of citizens.[44] The linguist Noam Chomsky, for example, claims that public opinion is largely the product of elite manipulation or, as he calls it, "manufactured consent."[45] Nevertheless, systematic studies have found that policy on high-profile issues usually changes in the direction of public opinion, rather than the reverse. President Obama had little choice but to accept public demands for spending cuts. Although he would have preferred an economic stimulus bill, the public had no appetite for a large increase in government spending. The public's support had been there two years earlier when Congress at Obama's urging enacted a $787 billion stimulus bill. By 2011, however, the federal budget deficit was at an all-time high, and Americans were in a budget-cutting mood. Such examples are commonplace. On the basis of their study of more than 350 policy-opinion relationships, Page and Shapiro concluded, "When Americans' policy preferences shift, it is likely that congruent changes in policy will follow."[46] In their more recent but similarly extensive study of the opinion-policy linkage, Robert Erikson, Michael MacKuen, and James Stimson found the same pattern, concluding that "public opinion influences policy."[47]

Summary
Self-Test www.mhhe.com/ pattersontadtx11e

The process by which individuals acquire their political opinions is called political socialization. During childhood, the family, schools, and church are important sources of basic political attitudes, such as beliefs about the parties and the nature of the U.S. political and economic systems. Many of the basic orientations that Americans acquire during childhood remain with them in adulthood, but socialization is a continuing process. Adults' opinions are affected mostly by peers, the news media, and political leaders. Events themselves also have a significant short-term influence on opinions.

The frames of reference that guide Americans' opinions include political ideology, although most citizens do not have a strong and consistent ideological attachment. In addition, individuals develop opinions as a result of group orientations—notably, religion, economic class, region, race and ethnicity, gender, and age. Partisanship is a major source of political opinions; Republicans and Democrats differ in their voting behavior and views on many policy issues.

Public opinion can be defined as those opinions held by ordinary citizens that they openly express. Public officials have many ways of assessing public opinion, such as the outcomes of elections, but they have increasingly come to rely on public opinion polls. There are many possible sources of error in polls, and surveys sometimes present a misleading portrayal of the public's views. However, a properly conducted poll can be an accurate indication of what the public is thinking.

Public opinion has a significant influence on government but seldom determines exactly what government will do in a particular instance. Public opinion serves to constrain the policy choices of officials but also is subject to their efforts to mold and channel what the public is thinking. Evidence indicates that officials are particularly attentive to public opinion on highly visible and controversial issues of public policy.

CHAPTER 6

Study Corner

Key Terms

agents of socialization (p. 145)
cultural (social) conservatives (p. 151)
cultural (social) liberals (p. 151)
economic conservatives (p. 151)
economic liberals (p. 151)
ideology (p. 151)

libertarians (p. 151)
party identification (p. 148)
political socialization (p. 144)
population (p. 156)
populists (p. 151)
public opinion (p. 144)
public opinion poll (p. 156)
sample (p. 156)
sampling error (p. 157)

Self-Test: Multiple Choice

1. The process by which individuals acquire political opinions is called
   a. public opinion polling.
   b. efficacy.
   c. selective incorporation.
   d. political socialization.
   e. sampling error.

2. Studies on the influence of ideology on public opinion agree that
   a. it is useless to apply ideological terms to patterns of opinion in America.
   b. most Republicans think of themselves as economic conservatives and social liberals.
   c. most people think of themselves as isolationists.
   d. only a minority of Americans have a true ideology in the sense of having consistent attitudes on public issues.

3. Public officials increasingly rely on which method to assess public opinion?
   a. talk show ratings
   b. election outcomes
   c. public opinion polls
   d. editorials in newspapers
   e. mail received by elected representatives in Washington, D.C.

4. Compared to Europeans, Americans are substantially more likely to form political opinions based on their
   a. religious beliefs.
   b. economic class.
   c. party identification.
   d. occupation.
   e. age.

5. Which of the following factors is most strongly and consistently related to differences in the opinions that Americans hold?
   a. party identification
   b. gender
   c. economic class
   d. ethnicity

6. In regard to the influence of public opinion on policy, it is accurate to say that
   a. most public opinion is the result of manipulation by political leaders.
   b. people tend to be highly informed about the issues on which they form opinions.
   c. in making their policy choices, politicians are particularly likely to follow public opinion when people's opinions are intense and unmistakable.
   d. politicians have almost no leeway in how they respond to public opinion.

7. Other things being equal, the larger the size of the sample in a poll, the more accurate the poll. (T/F)

8. Of the various agents of political socialization, political leaders are by far the most important one. (T/F)

9. People's party identification is measured by asking them to identify the party that they voted for in the most recent presidential election. (T/F)

10. Most Americans pay close attention to and are highly informed about politics and public affairs. (T/F)

Self-Test: Essay

What factors limit the influence of public opinion on the policy choices of public officials?

Suggested Readings

Alvarez, R. Michael, and John Brehm. *Hard Choices, Easy Answers: Values, Information, and American Public Opinion.* Princeton: Princeton University Press, 2002. An analysis arguing that what citizens know about politics is assessed in the context of their values and beliefs.

Asher, Herbert. *Polling and the Public,* 8th ed. Washington, D.C.: CQ Press, 2010. A guide to public opinion poll methods and analysis.

Canes-Wrone, Brandice. *Who Leads Whom? Presidents, Policy, and the Public.* Chicago: University of Chicago Press, 2005. A look at recent presidents and their policies in the context of public opinion.

Enns, Peter K., and Christopher Wlezien, eds. *Who Gets Represented?* New York: Russell Sage Foundation, 2011. A thoughtful assessment of the opinions that Americans hold and how these opinions affect policy.

Erikson, Robert S., Michael B. MacKuen, and James A. Stimson. *The Macro Polity.* New York: Cambridge University Press, 2008. A careful and thorough analysis of the influence of public opinion on policy.

Jacobs, Lawrence, and Robert Shapiro. *Politicians Don't Pander.* Chicago: University of Chicago Press, 2000. An analysis concluding that politicians are not driven by polls.

Stimson, James. *Tides of Consent: How Public Opinion Shapes American Politics.* New York: Cambridge University Press, 2004. An analysis of trends in public opinion and their political impact.

Whitaker, Lois Duke, ed. *Voting the Gender Gap.* Urbana: University of Illinois Press, 2008. An edited volume that explores the voting divide between men and women.

List of Websites

www.gallup.com
The website of the Gallup Organization, America's oldest and best-known polling organization.

www.people-press.org
The website of the Pew Research Center for the People and the Press; includes an abundance of recent polling results, including cross-national comparisons.

www.realclearpolitics.com
A site that has numerous up-to-date polls from a variety of organizations and on a variety of topics.

www.publicagenda.org
The nonpartisan Public Agenda's site; provides opinions, analyses, and educational materials on current policy issues.

Participate!

Studies have regularly found that Americans, in relative and in absolute terms, are substantially uninformed about the issues affecting their state, their nation, and the world. As a result, Americans' opinions about policy issues and problems are not as informed as they could and should be. Citizenship entails responsibilities, one of which is to stay informed about problems and developments that affect the community, the state, and the nation. As an informed citizen, you will be better able to make judgments about policy issues, to choose wisely when voting during elections, and to recognize situations that call for greater personal involvement. Fortunately, you have access to one of the most substantial news systems in the world. News about public affairs is virtually at your fingertips—through your computer, on television, and in the newspaper. Spending only a small amount of time each day following the news will help you to be a more effective and involved citizen.

Extra Credit

For up-to-the-minute *New York Times* articles, interactive simulations, graphics, study tools, and more links and quizzes, visit the text's Online Learning Center at **www.mhhe.com/pattersontad11e**.

Self-Test Answers

1. d, 2. d, 3. c, 4. a, 5. a, 6. c, 7. T, 8. F, 9. F, 10. F

Political Participation: Activating the Popular Will

political participation

Involvement in activities intended to influence public policy and leadership, such as voting, joining political groups, contacting elected officials, demonstrating for political causes, and giving money to political candidates.

We are concerned in public affairs, but immersed in our private ones. Walter Lippmann[1]

At stake in the 2012 elections was control of the White House and Congress. Which party would have the most say on issues of education and national security, much less the nation's economic policies? With so much at stake, it might be thought that Americans would have rushed to the polls to vote for the party of their choice. In fact, more than a third of American adults did not bother to vote. Despite a concerted effort by the candidates, the news media, and public service groups to get Americans to go to the polls, as many people stayed away as voted for the winning side.

Voting is a form of **political participation**—involvement in activities intended to influence public policy and leadership. Political participation involves other activities in addition to voting, such as joining political groups, writing to elected officials, demonstrating for political causes, and giving money to political candidates. Such activities contribute to a properly functioning democratic society. The concept of self-government is based on the idea that citizens have a right and a duty to participate in public affairs. Democracies differ, however, in their levels of political participation. The United States is an unusual case. Compared with other Western democracies, it has relatively low levels of voter participation. Yet it has relatively high levels of citizen participation in political and civic organizations. This chapter describes and explains this participation paradox. The chapter's main points are below:

- *Voter turnout in U.S. elections is low in comparison with that of other Western democracies.* The reasons include U.S. election laws, particularly those pertaining to registration requirements and the scheduling of elections.

- *Most citizens do not participate actively in politics in ways other than voting.* Only a minority of Americans can be classified as political activists. Nevertheless, Americans are more likely than citizens of other democracies to contribute time and money to political and community organizations.

■ *Most Americans make a distinction between their personal lives and public life.* This outlook reduces their incentive to participate and contributes to a pattern of participation dominated by citizens of higher income and education.

Voter Participation

suffrage
The right to vote.

At the nation's founding, **suffrage**—the right to vote—was limited to property-owning males. Thomas Paine ridiculed this restriction in *Common Sense*. Observing that a man whose only item of property was a jackass would lose his right to vote if the jackass died, Paine asked, "Now tell me, which was the voter, the man or the jackass?" Fifty years elapsed before the property restriction was lifted in all the states.

African Americans appeared to have gained suffrage after the Civil War with passage of the Fifteenth Amendment, which says that the right to vote cannot be abridged "on account of race, color, or previous condition of servitude." Nevertheless, African Americans were disenfranchised throughout the South by intimidation and electoral trickery, including rigged literacy tests as a precondition of being allowed to register to vote. The tests contained questions so difficult that often the examiner had to look up the answers. If that was not enough of an obstacle, the names of those that took the test were sometimes published in the local newspaper so that employers, the local police, and even the KKK would know the identity of the "troublemakers." It is no surprise that some counties in the South had almost no black registrants. Not until the 1960s did Congress and the courts sweep away the last legal barriers to equal suffrage for African Americans (see Chapter 5). Women did not secure the vote until 1920, with the ratification of the Nineteenth Amendment. Decades earlier, Susan B. Anthony had tried to vote in her hometown of Rochester, New York, claiming that as a U.S. citizen she had a right to vote. She was arrested for "illegal voting" and told that her proper place was in the home.

After a hard-fought, decades-long campaign, American women finally won the right to vote in 1920.

By 1920, men had run out of excuses for denying the vote to women. As Senator Wendell Phillips observed, "One of two things is true: either woman is like man—and if she is, then a ballot based on brains belongs to her as well as to him. Or she is different, and then man does not know how to vote for her as she herself does."[2]

The nation's youngest adults are the most recent beneficiaries of a suffrage amendment. Ratified during the Vietnam War—a time when the military draft was in full swing and the minimum voting age in nearly every state was twenty-one years—the Twenty-sixth Amendment lowered the voting age to eighteen years. "If you're old enough to die, you're old enough to vote" was the rallying cry of its proponents.

Factors in Voter Turnout: The United States in Comparative Perspective

Today, nearly any American adult—rich or poor, man or woman, black or white—who is determined to vote can legally and actually do so. Nearly all Americans embrace the symbolism of the vote, saying that they have a duty to vote in elections. Nevertheless, many Americans shirk their duty. Millions choose not to vote regularly, a tendency that sets Americans apart from citizens of most other Western democracies. In the past two decades, **voter turnout**—the proportion of adult citizens who actually vote in a given election—has averaged roughly 60 percent in presidential elections (see Figure 7-1). In other words, about three in five eligible citizens have gone to the polls in recent presidential elections while two in five have stayed away.

Although turnout in presidential elections is not particularly high, it is significantly higher than the turnout in the midterm congressional elections that take place between presidential elections. Midterm turnout has not reached 50 percent since 1920 and has hovered around 40 percent in recent decades. Turnout in local elections is lower still. In many places, only about 20 percent of eligible citizens—a mere one in five—bother to vote.

Voter participation is lower in the United States than in most other democracies (see "How the U.S. Differs"). For example, turnout in recent national elections has averaged more than 90 percent in Belgium and more than 75 percent in Germany and Denmark.[3] America's lower turnout is partly the result of its more demanding registration requirements and the greater frequency of its elections.

voter turnout

The proportion of persons of voting age who actually vote in a given election.

Percentage of eligible adults who voted

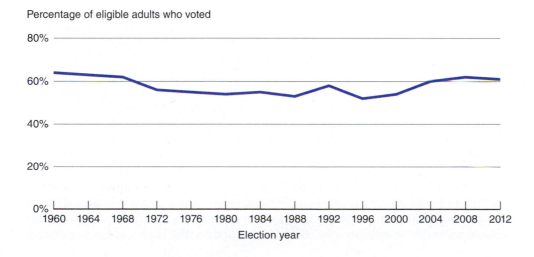

FIGURE 7-1

Voter Turnout in Presidential Elections, 1960–2012

During the three decades after 1960, turnout steadily declined. In the three most recent presidential elections, turnout has been high relative to the two preceding elections—1996 and 2000.

Source: U.S. Census Bureau. Figures are based on percentage of vote-eligible adults who voted. The 2012 percentage is an unofficial estimate.

HOW THE U.S. DIFFERS POLITICAL THINKING THROUGH COMPARISONS

Voter Turnout

The United States ranks near the bottom among the world's democracies in the percentage of eligible citizens who participate in national elections. One reason for the low voter turnout is that individual Americans are responsible for registering to vote, whereas in most other democracies voters are registered automatically by government officials. In addition, unlike some other democracies, the United States does not promote voting by holding elections on the weekend or by imposing penalties, such as fines, on those who do not participate.

Another factor affecting voter turnout rate in the United States is the absence of a major labor or socialist party, which would serve to bring lower-income citizens to the polls. America's individualist culture and its electoral system (see Chapter 8) have inhibited the establishment of a major labor

or socialist party. In democracies where such parties exist, the turnout difference between upper- and lower-income groups is relatively small. In the United States, the gap in the turnout levels of lower- and upper-income persons is substantial.

Q: How might American election campaigns differ if voter turnout were as high in the United States as in most European democracies?

A: If turnout in U.S. elections were in the 80-percent to 90-percent range, voters with less income and education would make up a much larger share of the electorate, and candidates would have to pay more attention to their policy concerns. As it stands, most candidates aim their appeals at middle-income voters. Such voters constitute a substantially larger share of the electorate in the United States than in Europe.

Country	Approximate voter turnout (%)	Automatic registration?	Social Democrat, Socialist, or Labor Party?	Election day a holiday or weekend day?
Belgium	90	Yes	Yes	Yes
Italy	80	Yes	Yes	Yes
Denmark	75	Yes	Yes	No
Germany	75	Yes	Yes	Yes
Austria	75	Yes	Yes	Yes
France	70	No	Yes	Yes
Great Britain	70	Yes	Yes	No
Japan	65	Yes	Yes	Yes
Canada	65	Yes	Yes	No
United States	60	No	No	No

Source: Developed from multiple sources. Turnout percentages are a rough average of national elections during the past two decades.

Registration Requirements

registration

The practice of placing citizens' names on an official list of voters before they are eligible to exercise their right to vote.

Before Americans are allowed to vote, they must be registered—that is, their names must appear on an official list of eligible voters. **Registration** began around 1900 as a way of preventing voters from casting more than one ballot on Election Day. Multiple balloting had become a tactic of big-city party machines—"vote early and often" was their mantra. Although registration reduced illegal voting, it also placed a burden on honest citizens. Because they had to register beforehand, citizens who forgot or otherwise failed to do so were unable to vote. Turnout in U.S. elections declined steadily after registration began.

Although other democracies also require registration, most of them place the responsibility on government. When someone moves to a new address, for example, the postal service will notify registration officials of the change. The United States—in keeping with its individualistic culture—is one of the few democracies in which registration is the individual's responsibility. Moreover, registration requirements have traditionally been determined by the state governments, and

Volunteers at a community event attempt to interest citizens in registering so that they can vote in the next election. Nearly all democracies have automatic voter registration. The United States does not, which makes voter registration efforts an important factor in election turnout.

some states make it relatively difficult for citizens to qualify. Although the 1993 Motor Voter Act requires all states to allow people to register when they apply for a driver's license or public assistance,[4] some states make little effort otherwise to inform citizens about registration times and locations.[5] Scholars estimate that turnout would be roughly ten percentage points higher in the United States if it had European-style registration.[6]

States with a tradition of convenient registration laws have higher turnout than other states. A few states, including Idaho, Maine, and Minnesota, allow people to register at their polling places on Election Day. Their turnout rates are more than ten percentage points above the national average. States with the most restrictive registration laws—for example, those that require residents to register at least two or three weeks before Election Day—have turnout rates well below the national average. Several of these states are in the South, which, even today, has the lowest turnout rate of any region (see "How the 50 States Differ").

A recent device, voter identification cards, serves to discourage voter turnout. Legislatures in a growing number of states have enacted laws requiring citizens to have a government-issued photo ID in order to register and vote. Proponents of these laws—most of whom are Republicans—say government-issued photo identification is needed to prevent voter fraud. Opponents of these laws—most of whom are Democrats—say the voter ID requirement is a thinly disguised effort to keep lower-income people, many of whom don't have a driver's license or passport, from voting. In nearly every instance, the voter identification card requirement has been enacted by a Republican-controlled state legislature.

Indiana and Georgia were the first states to enact such laws. Georgia's law required citizens without a government-issued photo ID, such as a driver's license or passport, to obtain a voter identification card, which would cost them twenty dollars and expire after five years. To obtain the card, they had to go to a Department of Motor Vehicles office and present a certified copy of their birth certificate and other documents. Georgia Democrats challenged the law, citing

HOW THE 50 STATES DIFFER POLITICAL THINKING THROUGH COMPARISONS

VOTER TURNOUT IN PRESIDENTIAL ELECTIONS

The United States has a lower rate of voter turnout than most Western democracies. Within the United States, however, the state-to-state variation is substantial. In a few states, including Minnesota and New Hampshire, nearly seven in ten adults vote in presidential elections. In contrast, there are a few states, including Hawaii and Texas, where barely more than four in ten adults vote in presidential elections.

Q: Why do states in the South and Southwest have relatively low turnout rates?

A: Southern states have more poverty and a tradition of more restrictive registration laws (dating to the Jim Crow era of racial segregation). Both factors are associated with lower voting rates. A large immigrant population is also associated with lower turnout, which helps to account for the lower voting rate in southwestern states.

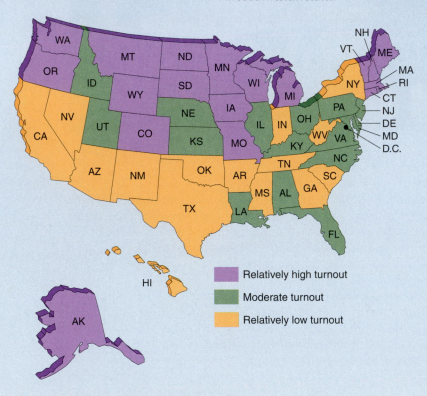

Relatively high turnout

Moderate turnout

Relatively low turnout

Source: Compiled by author from various sources; based on recent midterm and presidential elections.

scholarly studies that have found that fraudulent voting due to false identity claims is rare.[7] A federal judge invalidated Georgia's twenty-dollar fee requirement, which the Georgia legislature then eliminated while retaining the photo ID requirement. In 2008, the U.S. Supreme Court ruled on a case involving Indiana's voter identification card law, which is similar to Georgia's. Writing for the Court's 6-3 majority, Justice John Paul Stevens said states have a "valid interest" in improving election procedures and deterring fraud. The Court acknowledged that Indiana's Republicans had a partisan interest in enacting the law but argued that the law "should not be disregarded simply because partisan interests may have provided one motivation for the votes of individual legislators." In a dissenting opinion that focused on Indiana's poorer residents, Justice David Souter said the law "threatens to impose nontrivial burdens on [their] voting rights."[8]

DEBATING THE ISSUES POLITICAL THINKING IN ACTION

Should Citizens Be Required to Have a Government-issued Photo Identification Card in Order to Register and Vote?

Registration and voting rules are a necessary part of conducting free and fair elections. States have a legitimate interest in restricting the ballot to residents who are eligible to vote. Moreover, election administration is expensive and time consuming. If the polls or registration offices were open all hours of the day and night, the cost would be prohibitive. In recent years, several states have enacted laws requiring individuals to have a government-issued photo identification card in order to register and vote. For citizens with a driver's license or passport, this requirement is easily met. Other citizens, in order to vote, must produce an official birth certificate and documentary proof of residency in order to get from the state government a voter identification card that includes their photo. Proponents see the photo ID requirement as protection against fraud, whereas opponents see it as a device for reducing turnout among poorer citizens, many of whom don't have a driver's license or passport. Here are opposing arguments on the issue, one by the Heritage Foundation, a conservative think tank, and one by the liberal-minded Brennan Center at New York University's School of Law.

YES Every individual who is eligible to vote should have the opportunity to do so. It is equally important, however, that the votes of eligible voters are not stolen or diluted by a fraudulent or bogus vote cast by an ineligible or imaginary voter. The evidence from academic studies and actual turnout in elections is also overwhelming that—contrary to the shrill claims of opponents—voter ID does *not* depress the turnout of voters, including minority, poor, and elderly voters. . . . Photo IDs currently are needed to board a plane, enter federal buildings, and cash a check. Voting is equally important. . . . The potential for abuse and the casting of fraudulent ballots by ineligible voters (like illegal aliens or persons registered in more than one state) or in the names of fake voters, dead voters, or voters who have moved but whose names remain on the registration list exists, and such fraud has occurred in many reported cases. . . . As the U.S. Supreme Court has noted, voter ID protects the integrity and reliability of the electoral process.

—*Heritage Foundation*

NO Restrictive voter ID policies—especially those that require state-issued photo ID cards–threaten to exclude millions of eligible voters. . . . Approximately ten percent of voting-age Americans today do not have driver's licenses or state-issued non-driver's photo ID. . . . And getting ID costs substantial time and money. . . up to $45 for a birth certificate . . . and over $200 for naturalization papers. The voter may also have to take several hours off of work and travel significant distances to visit government offices open only during select daytime hours. . . . The impact of ID requirements is even greater for the elderly, students, people with disabilities, low-income individuals, and people of color. Thirty-six percent of Georgians over 75 do not have a driver's license. Fewer than 3 percent of Wisconsin students have driver's licenses listing their current address. The same study found that African Americans have driver's licenses at half the rate of whites . . . . There is no evidence that the type of fraud addressed by stricter voter ID—individual voters who misrepresent their identities at the polls—is anything but an anomaly. In Ohio, a statewide survey found four instances of ineligible persons voting or attempting to vote in 2002 and 2004 out of 9,078,728 votes cast—a rate of 0.00004%.

—*Brennan Center for Justice, New York University School of Law*

Q: Which of the two arguments do you find more persuasive? Do you think your position on the issue is affected by your party loyalty?

Frequency of Elections

Just as America's registration system places a burden on voters, so, too, does its election schedule. The United States holds elections more often than other nations. No other democracy has elections for the lower chamber of its national legislature (the equivalent of the U.S. House of Representatives) as often as every two years, and no democracy schedules elections for chief executive more frequently than every four years.[9] In addition, most local elections in the United States are held in odd-numbered years, unlike the even-year schedule of federal

Susan B. Anthony is nearly synonymous with women's right to vote. Her first crusade was with the temperance movement, which sought to ban the sale of alcohol because of the hardship alcoholism imposed on women and children. She next joined the antislavery movement. After the Civil War, Anthony teamed up with fellow activist Elizabeth Cady Stanton to demand equal pay and voting rights for women. She was twice arrested for trying to vote in her hometown of Rochester, New York. She died a decade before women gained the right to vote in the United States.

elections and most state elections. Finally, the United States uses primary elections to select the party nominees. In other democracies, party leaders pick them.

At an earlier time, most statewide elections coincided with the presidential election, when turnout is highest. This scheduling usually worked to the advantage of the party that won the presidential race—its candidates got a boost from the strong showing of its presidential nominee. In an effort to eliminate "presidential coattails," states began in the 1930s to hold their gubernatorial elections in nonpresidential years. Over three-fourths of the states have adopted this schedule, and two states—Virginia and New Jersey–elect their governors in odd-numbered years, insulating them even further from the turnout effects of federal elections.

Americans are asked to vote two to three times as often as Europeans, which increases the likelihood that they will not participate every time.[10] Moreover, elections in the United States have traditionally been scheduled on Tuesday, forcing most adults to find time before or after work to get to the polls. Many European nations hold their elections on Sunday or make Election Day a national holiday, making it easier for working people to vote.

Why Some Americans Vote and Others Do Not

Even though turnout is lower in the United States than in other major Western democracies, some Americans vote regularly while others seldom or never vote. Among the explanations for these individual differences are education and income, age, and civic attitudes.

Education and Income

College-educated and upper-income Americans have above-average voting rates. They have the financial resources and communication skills that encourage participation and make it personally rewarding. Nevertheless, the United States is unusual in the degree to which education and income are related to voter participation. Europeans with less education and income vote at only slightly lower rates than those with more education and income. By comparison, Americans with a college degree or high income are 50 percent more likely to vote in a presidential election than are those who did not finish high school or have a low income (see Figure 7-2).

FIGURE 7-2
Voter Turnout and Level of Income, 2012
Americans of lower income are much less likely to vote than those of higher income. The gap in these voting rates is greater in the United States than in other Western democracies.
Source: U.S. Census Bureau, 2012.

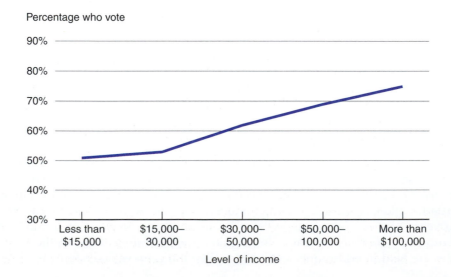

Why the great difference between the United States and Europe? For one thing, Europeans with less income and education are encouraged to participate by the presence of class-based organizations and appeals—socialist or labor parties, politically oriented trade unions, and class-based political ideologies. The United States has never had a major socialist or labor party. Although the Democratic Party represents the working class and the poor to a degree, it is chiefly responsive to middle-class voters, who hold the balance of power in U.S. elections.[11] In addition, Americans with less income and education are the people most adversely affected by the country's registration system. Many of them do not own cars or homes and are thus less likely to be registered in advance of an election. They are also less familiar with registration locations and requirements.[12]

POLITICAL

THINKING   Does the Party System Affect Turnout?

Most European democracies have three or more significant political parties that are shaped around class and social divisions, and sometimes along religious and ethnic divisions as well. Labor and socialist parties abound in Europe, as do middle-class, environmental, and right-wing parties. Accordingly, European voters have a broad range of choices, which some analysts cite as a reason why voter turnout in Europe is higher than in the United States, where voters basically have only two choices, the Republican and Democratic parties. Moreover, most European democracies have proportional representation systems, In such a system, parties get legislative seats according to their percentage of the total vote. The United States has a plurality system where representatives are chosen by legislative district, with the winner in each district getting the seat. Some district races are so lopsided that the outcome is a forgone conclusion, thereby reducing the incentive for voters to go to the polls. By comparison, every vote in a proportional representation system counts in the sense that it contributes to the party's percentage of the vote. What significance do you attach to these difference in the European and American party systems? Would you be more inclined to vote if you had more choices? What type of alternative party—religious, environmental, labor, or whatever—might be particularly attractive to you?

Age

Young adults are substantially less likely than middle-aged and older citizens to vote. Even senior citizens, despite the infirmities of old age, have a far higher turnout rate than do voters under the age of thirty. The difference is greater in local and state elections than in presidential elections. Only a small percentage of young adults vote regularly in local elections. Younger adults are less likely to live in the same residence from one election to the next and are more likely to have to reregister in order to establish their eligibility to vote. Nevertheless, the turnout rate of young adults has been higher in recent presidential elections than it was in those of the 1980s and 1990s. Young adults have developed a more positive attitude about voting. They have increasingly thought that "it's my duty as a citizen always to vote" (see Figure 7-3).

Civic Attitudes

Apathy—a lack of interest in politics—typifies some citizens. They rarely if ever vote. Just as some people would not attend the Super Bowl even if it was free and being played across the street, some Americans would not bother to vote even if a ballot were delivered to their door. Still other Americans refrain from

apathy
A feeling of personal disinterest in or lack of concern with politics.

FIGURE 7-3

American's Opinions on Voting as a Duty, by Age

In the past quarter century, there has been a substantial increase in the number of adults—particularly young adults—who "completely agree" that "it's my duty as a citizen always to vote."

Source: Pew Research Center for the People and the Press (2009).

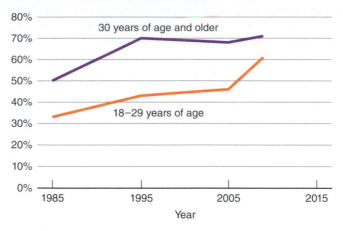

Percentage completely agreeing on voting as a duty

alienation

A feeling of personal powerlessness that includes the notion that government does not care about the opinions of people like oneself.

civic duty

The belief of an individual that civic and political participation is a responsibility of citizenship.

Turnout in presidential elections is higher than in other U.S. elections. Here, voters stand in a long line waiting to cast their presidential ballot at a polling place in Fort Mill, South Carolina.

voting because of **alienation**—a feeling of powerlessness rooted in the belief that government pays no attention to their interests. Many of these citizens regard voting as a waste of time, convinced that government won't respond to their concerns even if they do vote.

On the other hand, some Americans have a keen sense of **civic duty**—a belief that they ought to participate in public affairs. Citizens who hold this belief tend to vote more regularly. Civic duty and apathy are attitudes that are usually acquired from one's parents. When parents vote regularly and take an active interest in politics, their children usually grow up thinking they have a duty to participate. When parents never vote and show no interest in public affairs, their children are likely to be politically apathetic. Alienation can be traced to childhood socialization but often has adult roots. For example, when the Democratic Party took the lead on civil rights issues in the 1960s, some working-class white Democrats felt left out, believing that gains for African Americans would come at their expense. Some

of these Democrats switched parties, but others simply stopped voting. Voter turnout among working-class whites dropped sharply in 1968 and in 1972—two presidential elections in which civil rights issues were paramount.[13]

Political Interest and Party Identification

Finally, the likelihood that citizens will vote varies with their interest in politics. As would be expected, citizens with a strong or moderate interest in politics are much more likely to vote than those with little or no interest. What makes this fact noteworthy is that political interest is in large part a consequence of partisanship. Although "independents" are sometimes idealized in high school civics classes, they have much lower voting rates than citizens who identify with a political party. In recent presidential elections, party identifiers have turned out at a rate in excess of 75 percent, compared with a mere 50 percent for independents.

A reason that party loyalists are more likely to vote than independents is that they are more familiar with the policy differences between the parties and therefore more likely to be aware of the election's consequences. Moreover, party loyalty is like people's other loyalties—it deepens their involvement. Although party loyalists have but one vote to case, it is a way of expressing their commitment (see "Party Polarization").

PARTY POLARIZATION　Political Thinking in Conflict

The Role of Voter Turnout

Strong Republicans tend to be substantially more conservative than independents or weak Republican identifiers, while strong Democrats tend to substantially more liberal than independents or weak Democratic identifiers. In addition, strong partisans are substantially more likely to vote than independents or weak identifiers. As a result (see graph below). the voting public is more polarized in its political positions than is the public as a whole. This situation prods candidates to take more extreme positions in order to secure the votes of those on their side of the partisan divide. If candidates had to pitch their appeals to the full public, they might be inclined to take more moderate positions. This possibility is what led William Galston of the University of Maryland and the Brookings Institution to propose mandatory voting. Galston notes that some democracies, including Australia and Italy, require citizens to vote or pay a fine. These countries have exceptionally high turnout levels. "Our low turnout rate," Galston says, "pushes American politics toward increased polarization."*

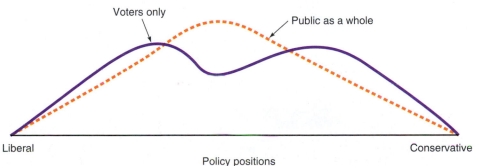

Q. *Would you favor a law requiring Americans to vote or pay a fine if they fail to do so? If the United States had such a policy do you think, as William Galston does, that it would significantly reduce the level of party polarization?*

*William A. Galston, "Telling Americans to Vote, or Else," New York Times, November 5, 2011, p. SR9.

Conventional Forms of Participation Other Than Voting

No form of political participation is as widespread as voting. Nevertheless, voting is a limited form of participation. Citizens have the opportunity to vote only at a particular time and only for the choices listed on the ballot. Fuller opportunities for participation exist, including contributing time and money to political and civic causes.

Campaign and Lobbying Activities

Compared with voting, working for a candidate is more time consuming. Not surprisingly, only a small percentage of citizens engage in such activities. Nevertheless, the number is substantially higher in the United States than in Europe (see Figure 7-4). One reason Americans are more active in campaigns, even though they vote less, is that the United States is a federal system with campaigns for national, state, and local offices. A citizen who wants to participate can easily find an opportunity at one level of office or another. Most of the European governments are unitary in form (see Chapter 3), which means that there are fewer elective offices and thus fewer campaigns. (Election campaigns are discussed further in Chapter 8.)

Americans are also more likely than citizens elsewhere to support the activities of political groups. This support usually takes the form of a monetary contribution but also includes more active forms, such as contacting lawmakers or attending public rallies. Among the hundreds of groups that depend on citizen contributions are Greenpeace, Common Cause, AARP (formerly known as the American Association of Retired Persons), the Christian Coalition of America, and the National Conservative Political Action Committee. (Lobbying groups are discussed further in Chapter 9.)

FIGURE 7-4

Campaign Activity

Although Americans are less likely to vote in elections than citizens elsewhere, they are more likely to engage in other campaign activities, such as trying to influence the vote choice of others.

Source: From Russell J. Dalton, "The Myth of the Disengaged American," *CSES Report* (October 25, 2005). Reprinted with permission.

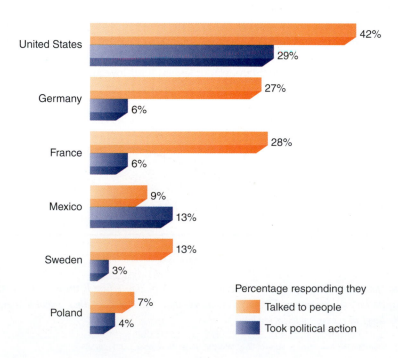

Virtual Participation

The introduction of the World Wide Web in the 1990s opened up an entirely new venue for political participation—the Internet. Through e-mails, chat rooms, social networks, and the like, the Internet has created participation possibilities previously unimaginable. Although this participation is "virtual" rather than face-to-face, much of it involves contact with friends, acquaintances, and activists. Internet participation peaks during presidential campaigns and now easily outstrips conventional participation. During the 2012 campaign, millions of Americans sent e-mails and text messages to family members, friends, and others in an attempt to promote their favorite candidate. Internet fundraising also flourished in 2012. More than five million Americans contributed online to a candidate, usually in an amount of $100 or less.[14]

A number of groups have built extensive online organizations. MoveOn.org, for example, has a network of more than three million "online activists." When MoveOn's leaders make a concerted appeal—whether on behalf of a candidate, a cause, or a bill before Congress—it gets a swift response. MoveOn was instrumental, for example, in helping Barack Obama defeat Hillary Clinton in their race for the 2008 Democratic presidential nomination. The Tea Party also has a huge online following. Relying on its hundreds of local coordinators, the Tea Party organized countless gatherings and rallies during the 2010 and 2012 elections, nearly always on behalf of Republican candidates.

The democratizing effect of the Web has been noted widely and, as Internet use and technology continue to advance, an era of unprecedented citizen involvement and influence could result.[15] Social networking is a powerful grassroots organizing force even in nondemocratic societies. Egyptians, Tunisians, Libyans, and Syrians took to the streets in 2011 and 2012 to protest their country's authoritarian regimes, coordinating their actions through Twitter, Facebook, and other networking tools. (The Internet is discussed further in Chapter 10.)

Tea Party protestors stage a rally at the Capitol against federal spending and taxes.

HOW THE 50 STATES DIFFER POLITICAL THINKING THROUGH COMPARISONS

VOLUNTEER ACTIVITY

Volunteer work in the community is an American tradition and occurs through a variety of groups. At the top of the list are church groups, followed by education groups such as parent-teacher associations. Many Americans also get involved in their communities through social service, health, and civic groups. The volunteer rate varies considerably by state, however, as indicated by a recent study by the Corporation for National and Community Service, the government corporation that manages federally funded service programs such as AmeriCorps. Utah has the highest volunteer rate; 44 percent of its residents sixteen years of age or older are engaged yearly in community volunteer work of one type or another. Nebraska (39 percent), Minnesota and Alaska (each at 38 percent), and Iowa (37 percent) are the other states in the top five.

Q: Why does the Upper Midwest region (which includes Iowa, Minnesota, Nebraska, and the Dakotas) have the highest volunteer rate?

A: Political scientist Daniel Elazar found that states in the Upper Midwest have a strong community orientation, reflecting the values of the Scandinavians and others who settled in the region. In addition to their more active community life, states in the regions spend more heavily on community-centered policies, such as the public schools, than do most other states. Utah's high participation rate stems from a different tradition. A majority of its population is Mormon, a religious faith that emphasizes the individual's community responsibilities.

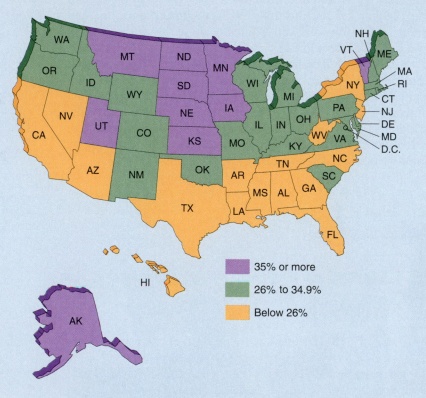

35% or more
26% to 34.9%
Below 26%

Source: Corporation for National and Community Service, 2010.

Community Activities

Political participation extends beyond campaigns and elections to involvement in the community. Citizens can join community groups, work to accomplish community goals, and let officials know their opinions on community matters. These forms of participation offer citizens a substantial degree of control over the timing and extent of their participation. The chief obstacle to participation is not opportunities, which are abundant, but the motivation to join in. Most people choose not to get involved, particularly when it comes to time-consuming activities.

Nevertheless, many Americans are involved in community affairs through local organizations such as parent-teacher associations, neighborhood groups, business clubs, church-affiliated groups, and hospital auxiliaries. The actual number of such participants is difficult to estimate, but they surely number in the tens of millions, reflecting in part a tradition of local participation that dates to colonial times. Moreover, compared with cities and towns in Europe, those in the United States have greater authority over local policies, giving their residents a motive to participate actively. Because of increased mobility and other factors, Americans may be less tied to their local communities than in the past and therefore less involved in community activity. Nevertheless, Americans are more than twice as likely as Europeans to work together in groups on issues of community concern.[16]

In a widely discussed book titled *Bowling Alone*, Harvard's Robert Putnam claims that America has been undergoing a long-term decline in its **social capital** (the sum of the face-to-face civic interactions among citizens in a society).[17] Putnam attributes the decline largely to television and other activities that draw people away from involvement in civic and political groups. Some scholars dispute Putnam's claim, but it appears to hold for older citizens. On the other hand, young adults have become more involved in their communities in recent decades, partly because of high school and college internship and volunteer programs.[18] According to a University of Maryland study, volunteering among young people has increased by roughly 20 percent since 1990.[19]

social capital
The sum of the face-to-face interactions among citizens in a society.

Unconventional Activism: Social Movements and Protest Politics

During the predemocratic era, people resorted to protest as a way of expressing displeasure with their rulers. Tax and food riots were the typical forms of protest. When democratic governments came into existence, citizens had a regular and less disruptive way to express themselves—through their votes. Voting is double-edged, however. Although the vote gives citizens control over government, *the vote also gives government control over citizens.*[20] Elections empower officials to pursue even those policies that, if given a choice, a majority of voters would not support. When voters go to the polls, they select only among candidates, and not also among policy options. The candidates that get elected are the ones that determine exactly what government will do.

Social movements, or **political movements** as they are sometimes called, are a way for citizens disenchanted with government policy to actively express their opposition.[21] These efforts are channeled through conventional forms of participation, such as political lobbying, but citizens sometimes take to the streets in protest against government. No protest movement in modern time had a larger or more lasting effect than the black civil rights movement. Beginning in the 1950s with boycotts of businesses that gave African Americans second-class treatment, the movement grew to include mass demonstrations and marches. It succeeded on a level beyond what even its leaders might have imagined. The landmark 1964 Civil Rights Act and 1965 Voting Rights Act were a direct result of the pressure the movement placed on lawmakers (see Chapter 5).

Political protests have taken on new forms in recent years. Protest was traditionally a desperate act that began, often spontaneously, when a group had lost hope of succeeding by more conventional methods. Today, however, protest is usually a planned event—a means of bringing added attention to a cause.[22] These tactical protests often involve a great deal of planning, including, in some

social (political) movements
Active and sustained efforts to achieve social and political change by groups of people who feel that government has not been properly responsive to their concerns.

instances, the busing of thousands of people to Washington for a rally staged for television. Civil rights, environmental, agricultural, and pro-choice and anti-abortion groups are among the many groups that have recently staged large tactical protests.

The Tea Party and Occupy Wall Street Protest Movements

The past few years have witnessed two of the best organized and most sustained protest movements in decades—the Tea Party and Occupy Wall Street movements. They each started from anger at established interests but otherwise have little in common.

The Tea Party came to the public's attention on April 15, 2009—the date that federal income taxes were due. The timing was not a coincidence, nor was the movement's name. Like the participants in the legendary Boston Tea Party, those that took to the streets in hundreds of cities and towns on that April day were expressing their opposition to high taxes. In Washington, D.C., the protesters hurled tea bags over the White House fence.

Backed by wealthy conservative donors, the Tea Party quickly became a major force in American politics. Although it was aligned from the start with factions of the Republican Party, its initial target was Republican lawmakers who had supported the bailout of banks in the aftermath of the 2008 financial crisis. Tea Party activists successfully challenged establishment GOP candidates in the 2010 primaries, prevailing in several states, including Utah, Alaska, Delaware, and South Carolina. Their platform, which was labeled a "Contract from America" called for sharp reductions in federal spending: "Our moral, political, and economic liberties are inherent, not granted by our government. It is essential to the practice of these liberties that we be free from restriction over our peaceful political expression and free from excessive control over our economic choices."

The Tea Party played a key role in the Republican takeover of the House of Representatives in the 2010 elections, and its influence carried into Congress. The representatives it supported took a hard line on fiscal issues, demanding large cuts in government spending and no increase in federal taxes. Their uncompromising position contributed to a congressional deadlock that nearly put the U.S. government into default on its debt for the first time in history. The resulting turmoil weakened the Tea Party's standing with the American public.[23] Polls indicated sharp declines in its popular support (see Figure 7-5).

FIGURE 7-5

Americans' Changing Opinions of the Tea Party and Occupy Wall Street Movements

Public support for the Tea Party and Occupy Wall Street movements weakened as they pressed their messages more forcefully.

Sources: Gallup Poll, January 2011, August 2011 (for Tea Party); Public Policy Polling, October 2011, November 2011 (for Occupy Wall Street).

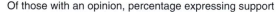

Of those with an opinion, percentage expressing support

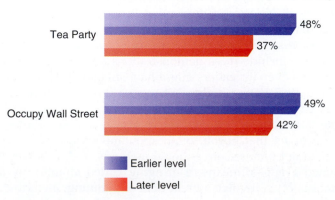

Tea Party — 48% / 37%

Occupy Wall Street — 49% / 42%

■ Earlier level
■ Later level

The Occupy Wall Street movement would also see its public support decline but for a different reason—Americans' unease with movements that pit protesters against the police. When the Occupy Wall Street movement (OWS) emerged in 2011, it began small—a single encampment in New York City's Zuccotti Park, adjacent to Wall Street. Within a few weeks, however, it had spread to dozens of other American cities, and even some abroad. Like the Tea Party, OWS was angry at the government's bailout of the financial industry and its failure to hold the bankers accountable for their role in the country's financial crisis. Unlike the Tea Party, however, OWS's target was private wealth. It aimed to curb the political influence of large donors and to rescind the Bush-era tax policies that benefitted the wealthiest 1 percent of Americans. "We are the 99%" soon became the movement's slogan.

OWS succeeded in directing public attention toward the widening gap between rich and poor in America and, for a time, support for OWS and its message was on the rise.[24] Its momentum slowed and then reversed when local officials began to disband OWS encampments, citing safety, convenience, and health concerns. In most locations, the process was peaceful, but in some locations the protesters clashed with police. As the headlines shifted from the issue of wealth to the issue of public order, OWS's public support weakened.[25]

Although the Tea Party and Occupy Wall Street movements served to mobilize hundreds of thousands of Americans, their futures are uncertain. Tea Party followers have been largely absorbed by the Republican Party, and their movement could have difficulty resurrecting itself as an independent force if a need should arise. Occupy Wall Street's uncertain future has a different basis. The movement resisted ties with liberal organizations and the Democratic Party, which meant that much of its momentum was completely lost when its encampments were disbanded. OWS is attempting to redefine itself as a more conventional movement but the success of the effort is by no means assured. Whatever their futures, the Tea Party and Occupy Wall Street movements represent the largest wave of political protest since the civil rights and antiwar movements of the 1960s. In this sense at least, their political legacy is assured.

Occupy Wall Street protesters rallying against policies that favor the wealthy. The building in the background is home to the New York Stock Exchange.

FIGURE 7-6
Protest Activity
Despite the significance of protest activity in U.S. history, Americans are less likely to protest than are citizens of many other democracies. Of twenty-three countries surveyed, the United States ranked eighteenth in level of protest activity. Only selected countries are included in this figure.

Source: From Russell J. Dalton, "The Myth of the Disengaged American," *CSES Report* (October 25, 2005). Reprinted with permission.

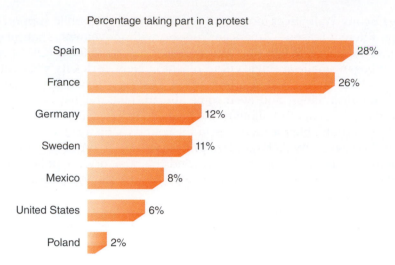

Percentage taking part in a protest

Spain	28%
France	26%
Germany	12%
Sweden	11%
Mexico	8%
United States	6%
Poland	2%

The Public's Response to Protest Activity

Protest politics has a long history in America. Indeed, the United States was founded on a protest movement that sparked a revolution against Britain. Despite this tradition, protest activity is less common today in the United States than in many Western democracies (see Figure 7-6). Spain, France, Germany, Sweden, and Mexico are among the countries that have higher rates of protest participation.

Public support for protest activity is also relatively low in the United States. The Vietnam War protests, which in some cases were accompanied by the burning of draft cards and the American flag, had only marginal public support. When unarmed student protesters at Kent State University and Jackson State University were shot to death in May 1970 by members of the National Guard, most American polls faulted the students. In a *Newsweek* poll, 58 percent of respondents blamed the Kent State killings on the student demonstrators, while only 11 percent said the guardsmen were at fault. The general public was more accepting of the Iraq war protest in 2003. Even after the fighting had begun, three in every five Americans said they saw the protests as "a sign of a healthy democracy." Still, almost two in five respondents felt that "opponents of the war should not hold antiwar demonstrations" and half of these respondents said that antiwar demonstrations should be outlawed.

In short, although most Americans recognize that protest is part of America's tradition of free expression, they do not embrace it in the way they do voting or community work. In this sense, protest is seen as something to be accepted but not necessarily to be admired.

Participation and the Potential for Influence

Most Americans are not highly active in politics. The emphasis that the American culture places on individualism is a reason. Most Americans under most conditions expect to solve their problems on their own rather than through political action. "In the United States, the country of individualism *par excellence*," William Watts and Lloyd Free write, "there is a sharp distinction in people's minds between their own personal lives and national life."[26]

POLITICAL THINKING Is the Country Better Off?

Some writers claim that the country is better off if less-interested and less-knowledgeable citizens—most of whom are near the bottom of the economic ladder—stay home on Election Day. In a cover story in the December 1997 issue of *The Atlantic Monthly*, Robert Kaplan wrote, "The last thing America needs is more voters—particularly badly educated and alienated ones." On the other hand, every citizen has the right to vote, and studies show that elected officials are truly responsive only to those who do go to the polls, which works to the disadvantage of the poor and less-well-educated. Where do you stand on the question of whether the country would be better off or worse off if nearly everyone voted?

Paradoxically, given their greater need for government help, lower-income Americans are the least likely to vote or to otherwise engage in collective action. They lack the financial resources and communication skills that encourage participation in politics and make it personally rewarding.[27] As a consequence, their political influence is relatively limited. In *Unequal Democracy*, political scientist Larry Bartels demonstrates that elected officials are substantially more responsive to the concerns of their more affluent constituents than to those of their poorer constituents.[28] In other words, the pattern of individual political participation in the United States parallels the distribution of influence that prevails in the private sector. Those who have the most power in the marketplace also have the most power in the political arena. However, the issue of individual participation is only one piece of the larger puzzle of how power in America is distributed. Subsequent chapters will furnish additional pieces.

Summary

Self-Test www.mhhe.com/pattersontadtx11e

Political participation is involvement in activities designed to influence public policy and leadership. A main issue of democratic government is the question of who participates in politics and how fully they participate.

Voting is the most widespread form of active political participation among Americans. Yet voter turnout is significantly lower in the United States than in other democratic nations. The requirement that Americans must personally register in order to establish their eligibility to vote is one reason for lower turnout among Americans; other democracies place the burden of registration on government officials rather than on individual citizens. The fact that the United States holds frequent elections also discourages some citizens from voting regularly.

Only a minority of citizens engage in the more demanding forms of political activity, such as work on community affairs or on behalf of a candidate during a political campaign. Nevertheless, the proportion of Americans who engage in these more demanding forms of activity exceeds the proportion of Europeans who do so. Most political activists are individuals of higher income and education; they have the skills and material resources to participate effectively and tend to take a greater interest in politics. More than in any other Western democracy, political participation in the United States is related to economic status.

Social movements are broad efforts to achieve change by citizens who feel that government is not properly responsive to their interests. These efforts sometimes take place outside established channels; demonstrations, picket lines, and marches are common means of protest. Protesters are younger and more idealistic on average than are other citizens, but they are a small proportion of the population. Despite America's tradition of free expression, protest activities do not have a high level of public support.

Overall, Americans are only moderately involved in politics. Although they are concerned with political affairs, they are mostly immersed in their private pursuits, a reflection in part of a cultural belief in individualism. The lower level of participation among low-income citizens has particular significance in that it works to reduce their influence on public policy and leadership.

Study Corner

Key Terms

alienation (*p. 176*)

apathy (*p. 175*)

civic duty (*p. 176*)

political participation (*p. 167*)

registration (*p. 170*)

social capital (*p. 181*)

social (political) movements (*p. 181*)

suffrage (*p. 168*)

voter turnout (*p. 169*)

Self-Test: Multiple Choice

1. Low voter turnout in U.S. elections compared to other democracies is explained by all of the following, *except*
   a. differences in registration requirements.
   b. use of the secret ballot.
   c. frequency of elections.
   d. differences in the political party systems.

2. Unconventional political activism includes all of the following, *except*
   a. participating in a social movement.
   b. taking part in a political demonstration or march.
   c. practicing civil disobedience.
   d. doing volunteer work for a political candidate or party.

3. Which group has the lowest voter turnout level?
   a. high-income Americans
   b. college-educated Americans
   c. young adult Americans
   d. Americans with a strong sense of civic duty

4. In European democracies, voting registration is
   a. purely an individual's responsibility.
   b. the responsibility of government officials.
   c. taxed, although the tax is only a small amount in most European countries.
   d. open only to citizens thirty years of age or older in most European countries.

5. In comparison with citizens of European democracies, Americans are more likely to
   a. vote in national elections.
   b. join labor unions.
   c. participate in community activities.
   d. regard protest as the most patriotic form of participation.

6. Which of the following statements does *not* describe political participation in America?
   a. Many people who participate in politics often do so from a sense of civic duty.
   b. America's culture of individualism discourages a reliance on political involvement.
   c. There are more barriers to regular participation in elections in the United States than in Europe.

   d. Americans place more emphasis on the public (political) sphere as a means of attaining their social and economic goals than they place on the private (economic) sphere.

7. More than in other Western democracies, political participation in the United States is related to income level. (T/F)

8. People who participate in social movements tend to be younger than nonparticipants. (T/F)

9. The Internet has increasingly been an important medium of election participation, including as a vehicle for contributing money to candidates' campaigns. (T/F)

10. With regard to election campaigns, Americans are more likely than Europeans to contribute money and to volunteer their time to help a candidate or party. (T/F)

Self-Test: Essay

Why does economic class—differences in people's education and income—make such a large difference in political participation levels? Why does it make a larger difference in the United States than in most European democracies?

Suggested Readings

Bartels, Larry. *Unequal Democracy*. Princeton, N.J.: Princeton University Press, 2008. An analysis that shows just how fully lower-income Americans are neglected by policymakers because of their low participation rates.

Burns, Nancy, Kay Lehman Schlozman, and Sidney Verba. *The Private Roots of Public Action: Gender, Equality, and Public Action*. Cambridge, Mass.: Harvard University Press, 2001. An analysis of gender differences in political participation.

Dalton, Russell J. *The Good Citizen: How a Younger Generation Is Reshaping American Politics*, rev. ed. Washington, D.C.: CQ Press, 2008. A study of the recent increase in young people's civic and political participation.

Franklin, Mark N. *Voter Turnout and the Dynamics of Electoral Competition in Established Democracies since 1945*. New York: Cambridge University Press, 2004. A comparison of voter participation and its correlates in advanced democracies.

Leighley, Jan. *Strength in Numbers: The Political Mobilization of Racial and Ethnic Minorities*. Princeton, N.J.: Princeton University Press, 2001. A study of the factors that motivate blacks and Hispanics to participate.

Putnam, Robert. *Bowling Alone*. New York: Simon & Schuster, 2000. A provocative analysis of the trend in civic participation.

Sunstein, Cass R. *Going to Extremes: How Like Minds Unite and Divide.* New York: Oxford University Press, 2009. A study of the effect of social interaction, including Internet networking, on how people position themselves politically.

Zukin, Cliff, Scott Keeter, Molly Andolina, Krista Jenkins, and Michael X. Delli Carpini. *A New Engagement: Political Participation, Civic Life, and the Changing American Citizen.* New York: Oxford University Press, 2006. A comprehensive study concluding that young adults are finding ways other than election politics to exercise citizenship.

List of Websites

www.rockthevote.org
The website of Rock the Vote, an organization dedicated to helping young people realize and utilize their power to affect the civic and political life of their communities.

www.electionstudies.org
The University of Michigan's American National Election Studies site; provides survey data on voting, public opinion, and political participation.

www.civicyouth.org
The website of a Tufts University institute dedicated to the study of young adults' civic engagement.

www.votesmart.org
The website of Project Vote Smart; includes information on Republican and Democratic candidates and officials, as well as the latest in election news.

Participate!

If you are not currently registered to vote, consider registering. You can obtain a registration form from the election board or clerk in your community of residence. Several websites contain state-by-state registration information. One such site is https://electionimpact3.votenet.com/declareyourself/voterreg2_ret/. If you are already registered, consider participating in a registration or voting drive on your campus. Although students typically register and vote at relatively low rates, they will often participate if encouraged by other students to do so.

Extra Credit

For up-to-the-minute *New York Times* articles, interactive simulations, graphics, study tools, and more links and quizzes, visit the text's Online Learning Center at **www.mhhe.com/pattersontad11e**.

Self-Test Answers

1. b, 2. d, 3. c, 4. b, 5. c, 6. d, 7. T, 8. T, 9. T, 10. T

Political Parties, Candidates, and Campaigns: Defining the Voter's Choice

political party

An ongoing coalition of interests joined together to try to get their candidates for public office elected under a common label.

Political parties created democracy and . . . modern democracy is unthinkable save in terms of the parties. E. E. Schattschneider[1]

Six hundred miles and a week apart, they faced off, each offering its own plan for a better America.

The Republicans met first, in Tampa, Florida. Their platform included the promise to cut government spending, lower taxes, limit abortions, expand school choice, stimulate the business sector, expand offshore drilling, and strengthen the armed forces. The Republicans picked former Massachusetts governor Mitt Romney as their presidential nominee, the first Mormon ever chosen for the position. Their vice presidential nominee was Paul Ryan, U.S. Representative from Wisconsin and a leading voice within the Republican Party on government spending issues. The Democrats met in North Carolina's largest city, Charlotte. They renominated Barack Obama as their presidential candidate and Joe Biden as their vice presidential candidate. Their 2012 platform included pledges to draw down U.S. forces in the Middle East, protect social security and Medicare, raise taxes on the wealthy, expand educational opportunities, promote clean energy, and create job programs.

The political parties, as their 2012 presidential nominees and platforms illustrate, are in the business of offering the voting public a choice. A **political party** is an ongoing coalition of interests joined together in an effort to get its candidates for public office elected under a common label.[2] By offering a choice between policies and leaders, parties give voters a chance to influence the direction of government. "It is the competition of [parties] that provides the people with an opportunity to make a choice," political scientist E. E. Schattschneider wrote. "Without this opportunity popular sovereignty amounts to nothing."[3]

This chapter examines political parties and the candidates who run under their banners. U.S. campaigns are **party centered** in the sense that the Republican and Democratic parties compete across

Republican Party presidential nominee Mitt Romney is surrounded by party faithful during the 2012 presidential campaign.

party-centered campaigns
Election campaigns and other political processes in which political parties, not individual candidates, hold most of the initiative and influence.

candidate-centered campaigns
Election campaigns and other political processes in which candidates, not political parties, have most of the initiative and influence.

linkage institution
An institution that serves to connect citizens with government. Linkage institutions include elections, political parties, interest groups, and the media.

the country election after election. Yet campaigns are also **candidate centered** in the sense that individual candidates devise their own strategies, choose their own issues, and form their own campaign organizations. The following points are emphasized in this chapter:

■ *Political competition in the United States has centered on two parties, a pattern that is explained by the nature of America's electoral system, political institutions, and political culture.* Minor parties exist in the United States but have been unable to compete successfully for governing power.

■ *To win an electoral majority, candidates of the two major parties must appeal to a diverse set of interests.* This necessity has typically led them to advocate moderate and somewhat overlapping policies, although this tendency has weakened in recent years.

■ *U.S. party organizations are decentralized and fragmented.* The national organization is a loose collection of state organizations, which in turn are loose associations of local organizations. This feature of U.S. parties can be traced to federalism and the nation's diversity, which have made it difficult for the parties to act as instruments of national power.

■ *The ability of America's party organizations to control nominations and election to office is weak, which strengthens the candidates' role.*

■ *Candidate-centered campaigns are based on money and media and utilize the skills of professional consultants.*

Party Competition and Majority Rule: The History of U.S. Parties

Through their numbers, citizens can exert influence, but it cannot be realized unless they act together. Parties give them that capacity. Parties are **linkage institutions;** they serve to connect citizens with government. When Americans go to the polls, they have a choice between candidates representing the Republican and Democratic parties. This **party competition** narrows voters' options to two and in the process enables people with different backgrounds and opinions to act together. In casting a majority of its votes for one party, the electorate chooses that party's candidates, philosophy, and policies over those of the opposing party.

The history of democratic government is intertwined with the history of parties. When the people of Tunisia, Egypt, and Libya in 2011 overthrew their authoritarian regimes, one of their first steps was to form political parties. When the United States was founded over two centuries ago, the formation of parties was also a first step toward building its democracy. The reason is simple: it is the competition among parties that gives popular majorities a choice over how they will be governed.[4] If there were no mechanism like the party to enable citizens to act as one, they would be powerless—each too weak to influence government.

The First Parties

Many of America's early leaders mistrusted parties. George Washington in his farewell address warned the nation of the "baneful effects" of parties, and James Madison likened parties to special interests. However, Madison's misgivings about parties slowly gave way to grudging admiration as he came to realize that parties were a means by which like-minded leaders and citizens could work together to achieve their common goals.

America's first parties originated in the rivalry between Alexander Hamilton and Thomas Jefferson, who opposed Hamilton's attempts to strengthen the federal government through national commerce. To advance his goal, Hamilton organized his followers into the Federalist Party, taking the name from the faction that had spearheaded the ratification of the Constitution (see Figure 8-1). Jefferson responded by creating the Democratic-Republican Party. The name harkened to the spirit behind the Declaration of Independence and reflected the party's strength among small farmers and states' rights advocates. The Federalists' preoccupation with commercial and moneyed interests fueled Jefferson's

party competition

A process in which conflict over society's goals is transformed by political parties into electoral competition in which the winner gains the power to govern.

FIGURE 8-1
A Graphic History of America's Major Parties
The U.S. party system has been remarkable for its continuity. Competition between two major parties has been a persistent feature of the system.

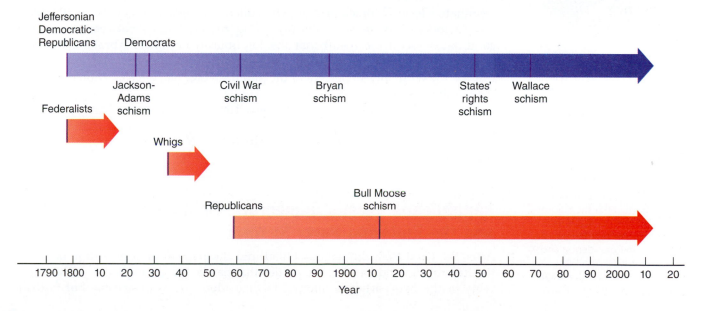

claim that they were bent on establishing a government of the rich and wellborn. After Jefferson in the election of 1800 defeated John Adams, who had succeeded Washington as president, the Federalists never again controlled the White House or Congress.

During the so-called Era of Good Feeling, when James Monroe ran unopposed in 1820 for a second presidential term, it appeared as if the political system might operate without competing parties. Yet by the end of Monroe's second term, policy differences had split the Democratic-Republicans. The dominant faction, under the leadership of Andrew Jackson, embraced Jefferson's commitment to the common people and adopted the label "Democrats." Thus, the party of Jefferson is the forerunner of today's Democratic Party rather than of today's Republican Party.

Andrew Jackson and Grassroots Parties

grassroots party

A political party organized at the level of the voters and dependent on their support for its strength.

Jackson's goal was to wrest political power from the established elite—the previous presidents had all come from old-line Virginia and Massachusetts families. Jackson saw a reorganized Democratic Party as the vehicle for change. Whereas Jefferson's party had operated largely at the leadership level, Jackson sought a **grassroots party.** As such, it was organized chiefly at the local level and was open to all citizens, The efforts of the local party organizations, along with the extension of voting rights to citizens without property, contributed to a nearly fourfold rise in election turnout during the 1830s.[5] Writing at the peak of Jacksonian democracy, Alexis de Tocqueville claimed that, "The People reign in the American political world as the Deity does in the universe."[6]

During this period, a new opposition party emerged to challenge the Democrats. The Whigs were a catchall party whose followers were united less by a coherent philosophy than by their opposition for one reason or another to Jackson and his followers. Competition between the Whigs and the Democrats was relatively short-lived, however. During the 1850s, the slavery issue began to tear both parties apart. The Whig Party disintegrated, and a northern-based new party, calling itself Republican, emerged as the Democrats' main challenger. In the 1860 presidential election, the Democratic Party's northern faction nominated Stephen A. Douglas, who held that the question of whether slavery would be allowed in a new state was for its voters to decide, while the southern faction nominated John C. Breckinridge, who called for legalized slavery in all states. The Democratic vote split sharply along regional lines between these two candidates—with the result that the Republican nominee, Abraham Lincoln, who had called for the gradual elimination of slavery, was able to win the presidency with only 40 percent of the popular vote. Lincoln's election prompted the southern states to secede from the Union.

Abraham Lincoln had been a member of Congress from Illinois before he was elected to the presidency in 1860. In the view of many historians, Lincoln ranks as America's greatest president, a feat that is all the more remarkable in that Lincoln as a child was poor and largely self-taught. He was assassinated at Ford's Theatre in the nation's capital shortly after the start of his second presidential term. Lincoln was the first Republican elected to the presidency, and his pursuit of the Civil War resulted in a party realignment favoring the Republican Party.

The Civil War was the first and only time in the nation's history that the party system failed to peacefully settle Americans' political differences. The issue of slavery was simply too explosive to be settled through electoral competition.[7]

Republicans versus Democrats: Realignments and the Enduring Party System

After the Civil War, the nation settled into the pattern of competition between the Republican and Democratic parties that has lasted through today. The durability of the two parties is due not to their ideological consistency but to their remarkable ability to adapt during periods of crisis. By abandoning at these crucial times their old ways of doing things, the Republican and Democratic parties have reorganized themselves—with new bases of support, new policies, and new public philosophies.

These periods of extraordinary party change are known as **party realignments.** A realignment involves three basic elements:

1. The emergence of unusually powerful and divisive issues
2. An election contest or contests in which the voters shift their partisan support
3. An enduring change in the parties' policies and coalitions

Realignments are rare. They do not occur simply because one party takes control of government from the other in a single election. Realignments result in deep and lasting changes in the party system that affect subsequent elections as well. By this standard, there have been four realignments since the 1850s.

The first was a result of the nation's Civil War and worked to the advantage of the Republicans. Called the "Union Party" by many, the Republicans dominated elections in the larger and more populous North, while the Democrats, who were widely blamed in the North for the Civil War, acquired a stronghold in what became known as "the Solid South." During the next three decades, the Republicans held the presidency except for Grover Cleveland's two terms in office and had a majority in Congress for all but four years.

The 1896 election also resulted in realignment. Three years earlier, an economic panic following a bank collapse had resulted in a severe depression. The Democrat Cleveland was president when the crash happened, and people blamed him and his party. In the aftermath, the Republicans made additional gains in the Northeast and Midwest, solidifying their position as the nation's dominant party. During the four decades between the 1890s realignment and the next one in the 1930s, the Republicans held the presidency except for Woodrow Wilson's two terms and had a majority in Congress for all but six years.

The Great Depression of the 1930s triggered a third realignment. The Republican Herbert Hoover was president when the stock market crashed in 1929, and many Americans blamed Hoover, his party, and its business allies for the economic catastrophe that followed. The Democrats became the country's majority party. Their political and policy agenda called for an expanded role for the national government. Franklin D. Roosevelt's presidency included unprecedented policy initiatives in the areas of business regulation and social welfare (see Chapter 3). Roosevelt's election in 1932 began a thirty-six-year period of Democratic presidencies that was interrupted only by Dwight D. Eisenhower's two terms in the 1950s. In this period, the Democrats also dominated Congress, losing control only in 1947–1948 and 1953–1954.

The reason these realignments had such a lasting effect on subsequent elections is that they affected voters' party loyalties (see Chapter 6). Young voters in particular embraced the newly ascendant party, giving it a solid base of support for years to come. First-time voters in the 1930s, for example, came to identify with the Democratic Party by a two-to-one margin, establishing it as the

party realignment

An election or set of elections in which the electorate responds strongly to an extraordinarily powerful issue that has disrupted the established political order. A realignment has a lasting impact on public policy, popular support for the parties, and the composition of the party coalitions.

The new order begins: Franklin D. Roosevelt rides to his inauguration with outgoing president Herbert Hoover after the realigning election of 1932.

nation's majority party and enabling it to dominate national politics for the next three decades.[8]

The Nature and Origins of Today's Party Alignment

A party realignment gradually loses strength as the issues that gave rise to it decline in importance. By the late 1960s, with the Democratic Party divided over the Vietnam War and civil rights, it was apparent that the era of New Deal politics was ending.[9]

The change was most dramatic in the South. The region had been solidly Democratic at all levels since the Civil War, but the Democratic Party's leadership on civil rights alienated white conservatives. In the 1964 presidential election, five southern states voted Republican, an indicator of what was to come. The South gradually became the most heavily Republican region in the country. Republicans routinely win the large majority of the region's presidential electoral votes and hold most of its top elected offices. More slowly and less completely, the northeastern states have become increasingly Democratic. The shift has been partly attributable to the declining influence of the Republican Party's moderate wing, which was concentrated in the region. As southern conservatives came to dominate Republican politics, the party's stands on social issues such as abortion and affirmative action shifted to the right, cutting into the party's following in the Northeast.[10]

The net result of these and other regional changes has been a remaking of the party landscape. Rather than occurring abruptly in response to a disruptive issue, as was the case in the 1860s, 1890s, and 1930s realignments, the change took place gradually and is the product of several issues rather than an overriding one. Nevertheless, the result has been much the same. The parties' coalitions and platforms have changed markedly. In effect, America's parties have realigned without going through the sudden shock of a single realigning election.

The GOP (short for "Grand Old Party" and another name for the Republican Party) has gained the most from the change. In the decades following the 1930s Great Depression, the GOP was decidedly the weaker party. Since 1968, however, Republicans have held the presidency more often than the Democrats, and have controlled one or both houses of Congress more than a third of the time. However, the Republican Party has not duplicated the success that the advantaged party had in the realignments of the 1860s, 1890s, and 1930s, partly because of missteps by two of its presidents. After winning the presidency in 1968 and 1972, Republican Richard Nixon became embroiled in the Watergate affair and was forced to resign, the first and only president to do so. The Republicans lost a huge number of congressional seats in the 1974 midterm election and did not recover the lost ground until the 1980s. After the 2000 election, the GOP for the first time in a half-century held the presidency and both houses of Congress. However, President George W. Bush's decision to invade Iraq in 2003 proved increasingly unpopular, contributing to his party's loss of the House and Senate in the 2006 midterm elections and its loss of the presidency in the 2008 election.

Analysts differ in their judgment on where the party system is heading in the long run. The two parties are now rather evenly matched in terms of voters' party loyalties but that could easily change in the coming years (see Figure 8-2). Some observers foresee a period of Republican resurgence if the GOP is able to refocus the public's attention on the issues, such as taxes and smaller

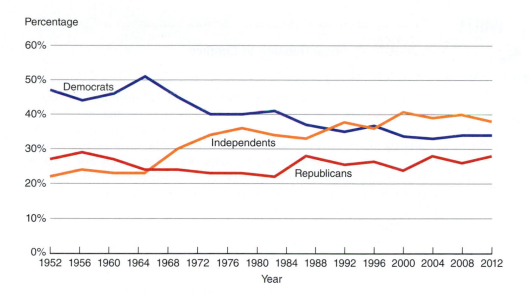

FIGURE 8-2
Partisan Identification
Of the roughly one-third of
voters who describe themselves
as independents, most say they
"lean" toward one of the two
major parties and tend to vote
for that party's candidates.
Source: American National Election
Studies, 1952–2008; Pew survey, 2012.

government, that worked for it before the Iraq war derailed its momentum.[11] Other observers foresee a period of Democratic dominance if the Democratic Party continues to receive strong support from Hispanics and young adults.[12] They are the major emerging voting blocs and, if they consistently cast the large majority of their votes for Democratic candidates, the GOP will struggle to keep up.

Parties and the Vote

The power of party is at no time clearer than when, election after election, Republican and Democratic candidates reap the vote of their party's identifiers. In the 2012 presidential election, both Barack Obama and Mitt Romney had the support of roughly 90 percent of their party's identifiers. It is relatively rare—in congressional races as well as in the presidential race—for a party nominee to get less than 80 percent of the partisan vote.

Even "independent" voters are less independent than might be assumed. When Americans are asked in polls if they are a Republican, a Democrat, or an independent, about a third say they are independents. However, in the follow-up question that asks if they lean toward the Republican Party or toward the Democratic Party, about two in three independents say they lean toward one of the parties. Most of these independents vote in the direction they lean. In recent presidential elections, more than eight in ten leaners have backed the candidate of the party toward which they lean. Less than 15 percent of all voters are "true" independents in the sense that party loyalty plays little to no part in the votes they cast.

The power of partisanship can be seen in the tendency of most voters to cast a *straight ticket*—meaning that they uniformly support their party's candidates. Most voters who cast a ballot for the Republican or Democratic presidential candidate also vote for that party's congressional candidate. Less than 20 percent of voters cast a *split-ticket*, voting for one party's presidential candidate and for the other party's congressional candidate (see "Party Polarization").

PARTY
POLARIZATION Political Thinking in Conflict

Voting a Straight Ticket

The 1970s were marked by what political scientists called *dealignment*—a movement of voters away from partisan commitments. One indicator was the prevalence of split-ticket voting. More than a fourth of voters supported one party's candidate for president and the other party's candidate for Congress. Many voters also divided their vote when it came to state offices, such as governor and state legislator. In recent elections, however, straight-ticket voting (supporting candidates of the same party at all levels of office) has reasserted itself. As the gap in the policy positions of Democratic and Republican candidates has widened, and as candidates within each party have become more alike in their positions, voters have faced a clearer choice during elections. Moreover, the gap in the policy opinions of Democratic and Republican party identifiers has widened. The net effect of these changes has been to increase the likelihood that Democratic and Republican voters will look less favorably on the policy positions of the other party's candidates and thus less likely to vote for them. As can be seen in the figure below, the percentage of voters that split their ticket has declined substantially in recent decades.

Percentage who split ticket (presidential and congressional vote only)

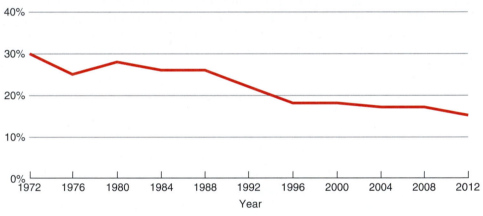

Source: American National Election Studies, 1972-2008. The 2012 figure is estimated from exit polls.

Q. *How might the decline in split-ticket voting have contributed to the increased level of polarization in Congress?*

A. *Moderate congressional candidates benefit from split-ticket voting. Compared with candidates that take more extreme positions, their issue positions are more likely to appeal to the other party's voters. However, as the gap in the partisan attitudes of voters has widened, even the other party's moderate candidates hold less appeal with the result that fewer of them get elected. Many analysts believe that the declining number of congressional moderates is a major reason why Republican and Democratic lawmakers have found it harder to reach compromise positions on legislative issues.*

Electoral and Party Systems

two-party system

A system in which only two political parties have a real chance of acquiring control of the government.

Throughout nearly all of its history, the United States has had a **two-party system**: Federalists versus Jeffersonian Democratic-Republicans, Whigs versus Democrats, Republicans versus Democrats. A two-party system, however, is the exception rather than the rule (see "How the U.S. Differs"). Most democracies

HOW THE U.S. DIFFERS POLITICAL THINKING THROUGH COMPARISONS

Party Systems

Since 1860, electoral competition in the United States has centered on the Republican and Democratic parties. By comparison, most democracies have a multiparty system, in which three or more parties receive substantial support from voters. The difference is significant. In a two-party system, the parties tend to have overlapping coalitions and programs, because each party must appeal to the middle-of-the-road voters who provide the margin of victory. In multiparty systems, particularly those with four or more strong parties, the parties tend to separate themselves as each tries to secure the enduring loyalty of a particular set of voters.

Whether a country has a two-party or a multiparty system depends on several factors, but particularly the nature of its electoral system. The United States has a single-member, plurality district system in which only the top vote getter in a district is elected. This system is biased against smaller parties; even if they have some support in a great many races, they win nothing unless one of their candidates places first in an electoral district. By comparison, proportional representation systems enable smaller parties to compete; each party acquires legislative seats in proportion to its share of the total vote. All the countries in the chart that have four or more parties also have a proportional representation system of election.

Q: Like the United States, Canada and Great Britain have the single-member district system of election. Yet, unlike the United States, they have more than two parties. Why?

A: Canada's third parties have stemmed from regional differences and resentments. French-speaking Quebec has a strong regional party, and from time to time, strong regional parties have appeared

in the western provinces. Britain's strongest third party (currently the Liberal Democrats) has been able to survive because the British House of Commons is much larger than the U.S. House of Representatives (659 seats versus 435 seats) and the population of Britain is much smaller than that of the United States. As a result, British election districts have only about a tenth as many voters as U.S. House districts. Britain's Liberal Democrats have enough concentrated strength in some of these districts to win the seat.

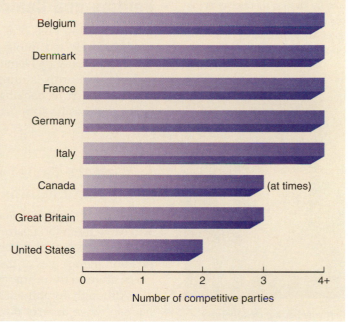

Number of competitive parties

have a **multiparty system,** in which three or more parties have the capacity to gain control of government, separately or in coalition. Why the difference? Why are there three or more major parties in most democracies but only two major parties in the United States?

The Plurality (Single-Member-District) System of Election

America's two-party system is largely the result of the nation's choosing its officials through plurality voting in **single-member districts.** Each constituency elects a single member to a particular office, such as U.S. senator or state representative; the candidate with the most votes (*the plurality*) in a district wins the office. The **plurality system** (sometimes called the **winner-take-all system**) discourages minor parties by reducing their chances of winning anything, even if they perform well by minor-party standards. Assume, for example, that a minor party receives exactly 20 percent of the vote in each of America's 435 congressional races. Even though one in five voters nationwide backed the minor party, it would not win any seats in Congress because none of its candidates would

multiparty system

A system in which three or more political parties have the capacity to gain control of government separately or in coalition.

single-member districts

The form of representation in which only the candidate who gets the most votes in a district wins office.

Plurality (winner-take-all) system

An electoral system in which the candidate who gets the most votes (the plurality) is an election district is elected to office from that district.

proportional representation system

A form of representation in which seats in the legislature are allocated proportionally according to each political party's share of the popular vote. This system enables smaller parties to compete successfully for seats.

median voter theorem

The theory that parties in a two-party system can maximize their vote by locating themselves at the position of the median voter—the voter whose preferences are exactly in the middle.

Germany has a mixed-member proportional representation system that allocates legislative seats on the basis of both single-district voting and the overall proportion of votes a party receives. Half the seats go to the candidates who finish first in their respective districts. The other half are allocated to the parties so that, in the end, each party gets roughly as many legislative seats as the percentage of the votes it received. This system requires that the German voter cast two ballots in legislative races: one to choose among the candidates in the particular district and one to choose among the parties. Shown here is a ballot from a German election. The left column lists the candidates for the legislative seat in a district, and the right column lists the parties. (Note the relatively large number of parties on the ballot.)

have placed first in any of the 435 single-member-district races. The winning candidate in each race would be the major-party candidate with the larger share of the remaining 80 percent of the vote.

By comparison, most European democracies use some form of a **proportional representation system,** in which seats in the legislature are allocated according to a party's share of the popular vote. This type of electoral system enables smaller parties to compete for power. In the most recent German election, for example, the Green Party received nearly 11 percent of the national vote and thereby won more than 60 seats in the 603-seat Bundestag, the German parliament. If the Greens had been competing under American electoral rules, they would not have won any seats.

Politics and Coalitions in the Two-Party System

The overriding goal of a major American party is to gain power by getting its candidates elected to office. Because there are only two major parties, however, the Republicans or Democrats can win consistently only by attracting majority support. In Europe's multiparty systems, a party can hope for a share of power if it has the firm backing of a minority faction. In the United States, if either party confines its support to too narrow a slice of voters, it can forfeit its chance of victory.

Seeking the Center, Without Losing the Support of the Party Faithful

A two-party system usually requires the major parties to avoid positions that will carry them too far from the political center. The **median voter theorem** holds that, if there are two parties, the parties can maximize their vote only if they position themselves at the location of the median voter—the voter whose preferences are exactly in the middle.[13]

Although hypothetical, the median voter theorem helps explain what can happen when a party makes a pronounced shift away from the center, leaving it open to the other party. In 1964, the Republican nominee, Barry Goldwater, proposed the elimination of mandatory social security and said he might consider the tactical use of small nuclear weapons in wars such as the Vietnam conflict—extreme positions that cost him many votes. Eight years later, the Democratic nominee, George McGovern, took positions on Vietnam and income security that alarmed many voters; like Goldwater, he was buried in one of the biggest landslides in presidential history.

The balance of power in American elections sometimes rests with the moderate voters in the center rather than with those who hold more extreme positions. When congressional Republicans mistook their 1994 landslide victory as a mandate to trim assistance programs for the elderly, the poor, and children, they alienated many of the moderate voters who had contributed to their 1994 victory. These voters had wanted "less" government but not a government that was indifferent to the needs of the economically disadvantaged. The net result was costly defeats for Republican candidates in the 1996 and 1998 elections. In similar fashion, Democratic lawmakers overplayed their hand after winning control of the presidency and Congress in 2008. Although the moderate voters that had fueled the Democratic Party's victory expected it to pursue policies that would restore the nation's economy, they didn't anticipate that it would go on a spending spree. In the 2010 congressional elections, moderate voters swung sharply toward the Republicans, contributing to its landslide victory.

DEBATING THE ISSUES POLITICAL THINKING IN ACTION

Is Party Polarization a Good Thing?

America's major parties have become more polarized. The gap in their policy positions has widen. The gap is more pronounced at the leadership level than among the voters, but it is evident at both levels. Taking note of this development, analysts have reached different opinions about whether the change is a desirable one. Although few analysts endorse the petty aspects of polarization, such as the decline in civility among congressional Republicans and Democrats, they are split on the question of whether the country is better off now than when the parties were less polarized. Below are two different views on the issue. The first is the view of Emory University professor Alan Abramowitz, author of *The Disappearing Center: Engaged Citizens, Polarization and American Democracy* (2010). The second is the view of Fareed Zakaria, who is an author, CNN contributor, and editor-at-large for *Time* magazine.

YES In the past, . . . the differences between Democrats and Republicans weren't nearly as sharp as they are today. Today, there are almost no liberal Republicans. . . and there aren't very many truly conservative Democrats. In fact, in Congress, there's basically no overlap at all between the parties. This makes any kind of bipartisan cooperation very difficult and reinforces that if members of Congress are viewed as cooperating with the other side, that can get them in trouble at home with the party base. . . . [Yet] people are actually more interested [in politics] now than they were 10 or 20 years ago. They're getting involved to a greater degree. More people are voting. More people also are talking about politics, and giving money, and putting out yard signs, and doing things like that. All the indicators we have show that polarization has actually contributed to increased engagement in politics, because people do perceive important differences and they think that there are big stakes in elections. . . . [A]certain degree of polarization is healthy in a democracy. It clarifies the choices people have in elections, and it helps voters to hold the parties accountable for their performance. It's healthier to have parties that actually stand for something than to have the situation that we had 50 or 40 years ago, when you really didn't know what the parties stood for because there was so much overlap between them.

—*Alan Abramowitz, professor, Emory University*

NO [At one time] the system encouraged compromise and governance. Over the last few decades, however, what has changed are the rules organizing American politics. They now encourage small interest groups—including ideologically charged ones—to capture major political parties as well as Congress itself. Call it 'political narrowcasting'. . . . Redistricting has created safe seats so that for most House members, their only concern is a challenge from the right for Republicans and the left for Democrats. The incentive is to pander to the base, not the center. . . . Party primaries have been taken over by small groups of activists who push even popular senators to extreme positions. . . . Changes in Congressional rules have also made it far more difficult to enact large, compromise legislation. . . . Political polarization has also been fueled by a new media, which is also narrowcast. . . . Some political scientists long hoped that American parties would become more ideologically pure and coherent, like European parties. They seem to have gotten their wish—and the result is abysmal. Here's why: America does not have a parliamentary system like Europe's, in which one party takes control of all levers of political power—executive and legislative—enacts its agenda and then goes back to the voters. Power in the United States is shared by a set of institutions with overlapping authorities—Congress and the presidency. People have to cooperate for the system to work.

—*Fareed Zakaria, author and journalist for CNN and Time*

Q: Abramowitz and Zakaria emphasize different aspects of polarization. For Abramowitz, the key consideration is the empowering effect of polarization on citizen choice and participation. For Zakaria, it is the crippling effect of polarization on America's governing institutions—congressional gridlock particularly. Which of these considerations do you see as more important, and why?

However, bold policies do not always result in electoral defeat. When Ronald Reagan won the presidency in 1980, for example, the voters were thoroughly discouraged with the nation's direction and wanted a new approach. Reagan moved the policy agenda to the right, opposed at each step by liberal Democrats. In this case, the moderates shifted toward the president's direction. The lesson of such periods is that, although the parties risk a crushing defeat by straying too far from the center during normal times, they may do so with some success during turbulent times.

The rising level of party polarization over the past two decades has altered the parties' electoral strategies somewhat. When the bulk of the electorate was clustered in the middle of the political spectrum, the parties usually converged on the center, knowing that defeat could result from straying too far from it. But as the voters themselves have moved away from the center, the parties have also had to worry about keeping their regular voters happy. If these voters think the party nominee is too moderate, they might choose not to vote. Mitt Romney took this possibility into account when running for president in 2012. Although Romney did not ignore moderate voters, he pitched his campaign toward conservatives and then organized a massive effort to get them to the polls on Election Day.

Party Coalitions

party coalition

The groups and interests that support a political party.

The groups and interests that support a party are collectively referred to as the **party coalition.** The Republican and Democratic coalitions are relatively broad. Each includes a substantial proportion of voters of nearly every ethnic, religious, regional, and economic grouping. Only a few groups are tightly aligned with a party. African Americans are the clearest example; more than 80 percent of them regularly vote Democratic.

Although the Republican and Democratic coalitions overlap, they are hardly identical (see Figure 8-3).[14] The party coalitions have been forged largely around conflict over the federal government's role in solving social and economic problems. Each party has supported government action to promote economic security

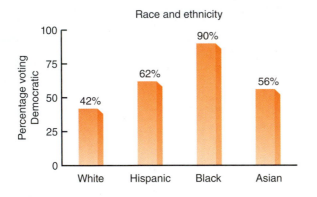

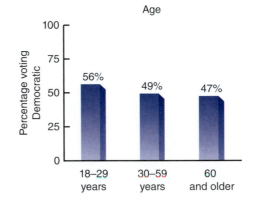

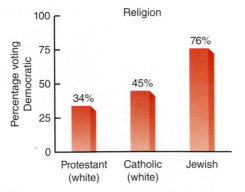

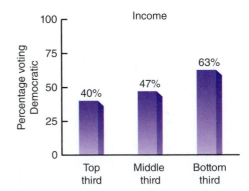

FIGURE 8-3

The Vote of Selected Demographic Groups in Recent Presidential Elections

Although the Democratic and Republican coalitions overlap substantially, there are important differences, as illustrated by the Democratic Party's percentage of the two-party vote among some major demographic groups in recent elections.

Source: Compiled by author from American National Election Studies and other surveys.

and social equality, but the Democrats have favored a greater level of government involvement. Virtually every major assistance program for the poor, the elderly, and low-wage workers since the 1930s has been initiated by the Democrats. Accordingly, the Democratic coalition draws support disproportionately from society's underdogs—blacks, union members, the poor, city dwellers, Hispanics, Jews, and other "minorities."[15] The Democratic Party also draws more support from women than men, although the **gender gap** is characteristic of white voters only. Whereas the Democratic vote is equally strong among minority-group women and men, it is usually 5 to 10 percentage points higher among white women than among white men. On a number of policy issues, including education and social welfare, white women hold opinions that are more liberal on average than those held by white men.[16]

The Republican coalition consists mainly of white middle-class Americans. The GOP has historically been the party of tax cuts and business incentives. It has also been more supportive of traditional values, as reflected, for example, in its opposition to same-sex marriage. Not surprisingly, the GOP is strongest in the suburbs and in regions where belief in traditional values and low taxes is prevalent, such as in the South, the Great Plains, and the Rocky Mountains. The Republican Party has made major gains in recent decades among white fundamentalist Christians, who are attracted by its positions on abortion, school prayer, same-sex marriage, stem cell research, and other social issues.[17] In recent presidential elections, the Republican nominee has garnered the votes of roughly three-fourths of white fundamentalist Christians.

A key to the future of both parties is the Hispanic vote. With the exception of Cuban Americans, who are concentrated in southern Florida, Hispanics lean heavily Democratic. Hispanics who call themselves Democrats outnumber those who call themselves Republicans by more than two to one. However, compared with African Americans, Hispanics are a less cohesive voting bloc. Whereas blacks of all income levels are solidly Democratic, lower-income Hispanics vote Democratic at substantially higher rates than do upper-income Hispanics. Polls show Hispanics to be relatively liberal on economic issues and relatively conservative on social issues, providing both parties a basis for appealing for their support.[18]

In the recent elections, however, Hispanics have sided heavily with the Democratic Party, seeing it as more closely aligned with their interests (see Figure 8-4). This perception has been heightened by recent Republican efforts to identify and

gender gap
The tendency of white women and men to differ in their political attitudes and voting preferences.

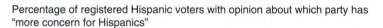
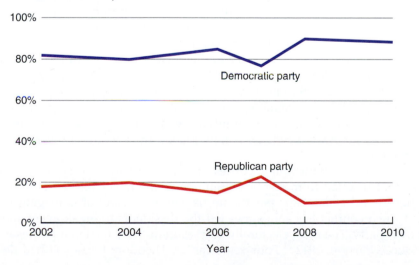

FIGURE 8-4
Hispanics' Opinions of the Democratic and Republican Parties
By a wide margin, Hispanics believe the Democratic Party has "more concern for Hispanics" than does the Republican Party.
Source: Created from 2002-2010 surveys of the Pew Hispanic Center, a project of The Pew Research Center.

deport illegal immigrants, most of whom are Hispanic. In late 2005, for example, the Republican majority in the House of Representatives passed a bill that would have authorized the mass deportation of illegal immigrants and imposed heavy penalties on employers that hire illegal immigrants. Seeing the bill as targeted at their community, Hispanics responded with huge protest rallies—ones reminiscent of the 1960s civil rights movement. The rally in Los Angeles drew an estimated half million marchers, reputedly the largest such gathering in the city's history. In the subsequent 2006 congressional election, two-thirds of Hispanics voted Democratic—a 10 percent increase from the 2004 level.

Then, starting with Arizona in 2010, Republican-controlled state legislatures enacted laws authorizing police to check for evidence of legal status whenever in the course of duty they stop a person for another reason. If the individual is an illegal alien, he or she is to be detained, charged with a state crime, and then turned over to federal authorities for deportation. Although the Supreme Court invalidated provisions of these laws in 2012, the legislation provoked a negative reaction in the Hispanic community that contributed to a lopsided vote in favor of Democratic candidates in the 2010 and 2012 elections.

Minor (Third) Parties

Although the U.S. electoral system discourages the formation of third parties (or, as they are more properly called, minor parties), the nation has always had them—more than a thousand over its history.[19] Most minor parties have been short lived, and only a few have had a lasting impact. Only one minor party, the Republican Party, has achieved majority status.

Minor parties in the United States have formed largely to promote policies that their followers believe are not being represented adequately by either of the two major parties. A major party is always somewhat captive to its past, which is the source of many of its ideas and most of its followers. When conditions change, major parties can be slow to respond, and a minor party can try to capitalize on neglected issues. Whatever success it achieves, however, is usually temporary. If a minor party gains a following, one or both major parties typically awaken to its issue, at which time the minor party begins to lose support. Nevertheless, the minor party will have served the purpose of making the major parties more responsive to the public's concerns.

single-issue (minor) party

A minor party formed around a single issue of overriding interest to its followers.

Minor parties were at their peak in the nineteenth century, when the party system was still in flux.[20] Many of these parties were **single-issue parties** formed around a lone issue of overriding interest to their followers. Examples are the Free Soil Party, which fought the extension of slavery into new territories, and the Greenback Party, which sought a currency system based on paper money rather than gold and silver. One nineteenth-century party, the Prohibition Party, persisted into the twentieth century and contributed to the ratification in 1919 of the Eighteenth Amendment, which prohibited the manufacture, sale, and transportation of alcoholic beverages (but which was repealed in 1933). Although single-issue parties (for example, the Right to Life Party) exist today, they do not have large followings or much influence. The role that single-issue parties played in the nineteenth century is now played by single-issue interest groups (see Chapter 9).

factional (minor) party

A minor party created when a faction within one of the major parties breaks away to form its own party.

The most important minor parties of the twentieth century were **factional parties** that resulted from a split within one of the major parties. Although the Republican and Democratic parties are usually successful at managing internal dissent, such conflict has sometimes led the dissidents to break away and form their own party. The most electorally successful of these factional parties was the Bull Moose Party in 1912.[21] Four years earlier, Theodore Roosevelt had declined to seek another presidential term, but he became disenchanted with the conservative policies of his handpicked successor, William Howard Taft, and challenged him for the 1912 Republican nomination. After losing out in the nominating race, Roosevelt proceeded to form the progressive Bull Moose Party (a reference to Roosevelt's claim that he was "as strong as a bull moose"). Roosevelt won 27 percent of the presidential vote to Taft's 25 percent, which enabled the Democratic nominee, Woodrow Wilson, to win the 1912 presidential election with 42 percent of the vote.. The States' Rights Party in 1948 and George Wallace's American Independent Party in 1968 are other examples of strong factional parties. They were formed by white southern Democrats angered by northern Democrats' support of black civil rights.

POLITICAL THINKING   Which System Makes More Sense—Proportional or Plurality?

Politics is conducted by predetermined rules. Although these rules are often portrayed as neutral, they affect who wins and who loses. An example is electoral systems. The United States has a single-member-district plurality system in which the election winners are the candidates who get the most votes in the district in which they run. Most European countries, by comparison, have proportional representation systems in which legislative seats are distributed to each party according to its share (proportion) of the popular vote. The European rule makes it possible for smaller parties to win legislative seats. In contrast, the American rule discourages smaller parties. A party that wins 15 percent of the national vote would end up with no seats in Congress if none of its candidates placed first in a congressional district. Which rule—proportional representation or the single-member district—do you prefer, and why?

Other minor parties have been characterized by their ideological commitment to a broad and noncentrist ideological position, such as redistribution of economic resources. The strongest ideological party was the Populists, whose 1892 presidential nominee, James B. Weaver, won 9 percent of the national vote and carried six western states on a radical platform that included a call for government takeover of the railroads. His strong showing was fueled by the anger of small farmers over low commodity prices, tight credit, and the high rates charged by railroad monopolies to transport their goods.[22] The strongest of today's **ideological parties** is the Green Party. A liberal party that emphasizes environmental and related issues, the Green Party won 3 percent of the presidential vote in 2000.

Some minor parties have been virtually "antiparties" in the sense that they arose out of a belief that partisan politics is a corrupting influence. The strongest of these **reform parties** was the Progressive Party, which in the early 1900s successfully pressured a number of states and localities into adopting primary elections, recall elections, nonpartisan elections, initiatives, and popular referendums (see Chapter 2). A more recent reform party was titled just that—the Reform Party. Created by Texas businessman Ross Perot after he garnered an astonishing 19 percent of the vote in 1992 as an independent presidential candidate (second only to Roosevelt's 27 percent in 1912), the Reform Party nominated Perot as its 1996 presidential candidate. Although he won 8 percent of the vote, he chose not to run again in 2000. The ensuring fight for the Reform Party's presidential nomination was so bitter that it destroyed the party.

ideological (minor) party

A minor party characterized by its ideological commitment to a broad and noncentrist philosophical position.

reform (minor) party

A minor party that bases its appeal on the claim that the major parties are having a corrupting influence on government and policy.

Party Organizations

The Democratic and Republican parties have organizational units at the national, state, and local levels. These **party organizations** concentrate on the contesting of elections.

party organizations

The party organizational units at national, state, and local levels; their influence has decreased over time because of many factors.

The Weakening of Party Organizations

A century ago, party organizations enjoyed nearly complete control of elections. Although today's party organizations perform all the activities in which parties formerly engaged—candidate recruitment, fundraising, policy development, canvassing—they do not control these activities as fully as they once did. For the most part, the candidates now have the lead role.[23]

Nomination refers to the selection of the individual who will run as the party's candidate in the general election. Until the early twentieth century, the party organizations picked the nominees, who, if elected, were expected to share with it the spoils of office—government jobs and contracts. The party built its organization by giving the jobs to loyalists and by granting contracts to donors. Bribes and kickbacks were part of the process in some locations. New York City's legendary Boss Tweed once charged the city twenty times what a building had actually cost, amassing a personal fortune before winding up in prison. Reform-minded Progressives invented primary elections as a way to deprive party bosses of their power over nominations (see Chapter 2).

nomination

The designation of a particular individual to run as a political party's candidate (its "nominee") in the general election.

primary election (direct primary)

A form of election in which voters choose a party's nominees for public office. In most primaries, eligibility to vote is limited to voters who are registered members of the party.

A **primary election** (or **direct primary**) gives control of nominations to the voters (see Chapters 2 and 12). The candidate who gets the most votes in a party's primary gets its nomination for the general election. In some states, the nominees are chosen in *closed primaries*, in which participation is limited to voters registered or declared at the polls as members of the party whose primary is being held. Voters of the other party are not allowed to "cross over" to vote in the primary. The logic of a closed primary is that a party's voters should have the power to choose its general election candidate without interference from voters that might not have its best interests in mind. In contrast, some states use *open primaries*, which allow independents and sometimes voters of the other party to vote in the party's primary (although they cannot vote simultaneously in both parties' primaries). The logic of the open primary is that it gives all voters a say in the choices they will have in the general election. California, Louisiana, Nebraska, and Washington conduct *top-two primaries*. Candidates are listed on the same ballot without regard to party; the top two finishers become the general election candidates.

Primaries hinder the building of strong party organizations. If there were no primaries, candidates would have to seek nomination through the party organization, and they could be denied renomination if they were disloyal to the party's policy goals. Because of primaries, however, candidates can seek office on their own and create a personal following that places them beyond the

Although the United States has long had a two-party system, numerous minor parties have surfaced. A few of them have been influential, including the Free Soil Party, which emerged before the Civil War with a platform that called for the abolition of slavery in new states and territories. Shown here is a Free Soil Party poster from the 1848 election. The party's presidential nominee was Martin Van Buren, who had been president from 1837 to 1841 as a member of the Democratic Party.

HOW THE 50 STATES DIFFER   POLITICAL THINKING THROUGH COMPARISONS

PRIMARY ELECTIONS

Primary elections were introduced in the United States in the early 1900s as a way of reducing the power of party organizations. Although some states resisted their use, primaries have gradually come to be employed in all states for at least some elections. However, the states differ in the type of primary they use. Nearly a fourth of them have *open primaries,* which allow any registered voter to vote in the primary (though not in the primary of both parties simultaneously). Another fourth have *closed primaries,* which are limited to voters registered as members of the party holding the primary. Other states have *partially open primaries* that allow independents but not registered voters of the other party to participate or that allow the parties to choose the type of primary they will conduct. In recent Alaska elections, for example, Democrats have held open primaries while Republicans have operated closed pri-

maries. Finally, four states—California, Louisiana, Nebraska, and Washington—employ *top-two primaries* in which candidates of both parties are on the same ballot and the top-two finishers compete in the general election.

Q: The relatively new top-two primary was recently adopted in California and Washington and is under consideration in other states. What do you think are the chief arguments for and against this type of primary?

A: Proponents argue that top-two primaries give independent voters a larger say in the selection of nominees and may result is the selection of more moderate nominees. Opponents say that this type of primary hurts the state's weaker party and narrows voters' choice in the general election when two candidates of the same party are the nominees.

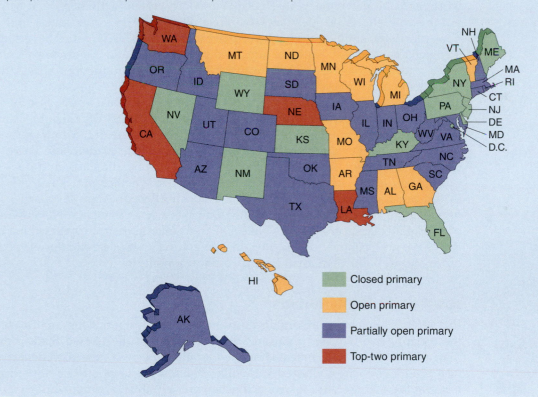

Closed primary
Open primary
Partially open primary
Top-two primary

Source: National Council of State Legislatures, 2012.

party's direct control. Candidates also have more control over campaign money than do the parties. At the turn of the twentieth century, when party machines were at their peak, most campaign funds passed through the hands of party leaders. Today, most of the money goes to the candidates directly, without first passing through the parties.

Party organizations were also weakened by the decline of patronage jobs. A century ago, when a party won control of government, it acquired control of nearly all public jobs, which were doled out to loyal party workers. However, as government jobs in the early twentieth century shifted from patronage to the merit system (see Chapter 13), the party organizations controlled many fewer positions. Today, because of the large size of government, thousands of patronage jobs still exist. These government employees help staff the party organizations (along with volunteers), but most patronage appointees are indebted to an individual politician rather than to a party organization. Congressional staff members, for example, are patronage employees, but they owe their jobs and their loyalty to their senator or representative, not to the party organization.

In Europe, where there are no primary elections, the parties are stronger. They control their nominations, and because of this, they also control campaign money and workers. A party's candidates are expected to support the national platform. A candidate or officeholder who fails to do so is likely to be denied renomination in the next election.

The Structure and Role of Party Organizations

Although party organizations have lost influence, parties are in no danger of extinction. Candidates and activists need an organization through which to work, and the party meets that need. Moreover, certain activities, such as get-out-the-vote efforts on Election Day, affect all of a party's candidates and are done more efficiently through the party organization. Indeed, parties have staged a comeback of sorts.[24] National and state party organizations now assist candidates with fundraising, polling, research, and media production, all essential ingredients of a successful modern campaign.

U.S. parties are organized at the national, state, and local levels, but there is no chain of command that connects them. The national party organization cannot tell the state organizations what to do and, in turn, the state organizations cannot tell the local organizations what to do. The Texas state Democratic Party, for example, does not take orders from the national Democratic Party and does not give orders to the state's local Democratic parties, whether in a large city like Dallas or Houston or in a smaller one like McAllen or Amarillo. Each party organization is largely autonomous and free to act as it wants. Nevertheless, party organizations at all levels have a shared stake in their party's success and thus have an incentive to work together to get the party's candidates elected to office and to build up a loyal base of support among the voters.[25]

Local Party Organizations

In a sense, U.S. parties are organized from the bottom up, not the top down. Of the roughly five hundred thousand elective offices in the United States, fewer than five hundred are contested statewide and only two—the presidency and vice presidency—are contested nationally. The rest are local offices; not surprisingly, at least 95 percent of party activists work within local organizations. Local parties vary greatly in their structure and activities. Only a few of them, including the Democratic organizations in Philadelphia and Chicago, bear even a faint resemblance to the fabled old-time party machines that, in return for jobs and even welfare services, were able to deliver the vote on election day. In many urban areas, and in most suburbs and towns, the party organizations today do not have enough activists to do organizing work outside the campaign period, at which time—to the extent their resources allow—they conduct registration drives, hand out leaflets, and help get out the vote. Local parties tend to concentrate on elections that coincide with local boundaries, such as races for mayor, city council, state legislature, and county offices. Local parties take part in congressional, statewide, and presidential contests, but in these cases, their role is

"SO, CAN I PUT YOU DOWN AS UNDECIDED?"

Door-to-door canvassing for votes is a time-honored though not always welcomed component of political party activity during elections.

Brian Fray/www.CartoonStock.com

typically secondary to that of the candidates' personal campaign organizations, which are discussed later in the chapter.

State Party Organizations

At the state level, each party is headed by a central committee made up of members of local party organizations and local and state officeholders. State central committees do not meet regularly and provide only general policy guidance for the state organizations. Day-to-day operations are directed by a chairperson, who is a full-time, paid employee of the state party. The state party organizations engage in activities, such as fundraising and voter registration, that can improve their candidates' chances of success. State party organizations concentrate on statewide races, including those for governor and U.S. senator, and also focus on races for the state legislature. They play a smaller role in campaigns for national or local offices, and in most states, they do not endorse candidates in their statewide primaries.

National Party Organizations

The national Republican and Democratic party organizations, which are located in Washington, D.C., are structured much like those at the state level: they have a national committee and a national party chairperson. Although the national parties in theory are run by their committees, neither the Democratic National Committee (DNC) nor the Republican National Committee (RNC) has great power. The RNC (with more than 150 members) and the DNC (with more than 300 members) are too large and meet too infrequently to actually run the national organization. Their power is largely confined to setting organizational policy, such as determining the site of the party's presidential nominating convention and deciding the rules governing the selection of convention delegates. They have no power to pick nominees or to dictate candidates' policy positions. The national party's day-to-day operations are directed by a national chair chosen by the national committee, although the committee defers to the president's choice when the party controls the White House.

The RNC and DNC, among other things, run training programs for candidates and their staffs, raise money, seek media coverage of party positions and activities, conduct issue and group research, and send field representatives to help state and local parties with their operations. In some cases, the national parties also try to recruit potentially strong candidates to run in House and Senate races.

The national parties' major role in campaigns is the raising and spending of money. The RNC and the DNC are major sources of campaign funds, but they are not the only national-level party units involved in fundraising. There are also House and Senate party campaign committees, which raise funds and provide advice to the parties' congressional candidates. For a long period, the Republican national organizations consistently outraised their Democratic counterparts, but they have been more evenly matched recently, with the Democrats sometimes coming out ahead (see Figure 8-5). In any case, the amount of money the national party organizations raise is staggering. During the 2011–2012 cycle (an election cycle is the two-year period from one federal election to the next), the various Democratic and Republican national party organizations raised a combined total of more than $1 billion.

Party money is spent mostly on the parties' own operations, such as their get-out-the-vote, fundraising, and advertising efforts. However, some of the money is given directly to House or Senate candidates for their campaigns. The

FIGURE 8-5
National Party Fundraising, 1999–2012

The national Democratic and Republican parties raise huge sums of money to spend on campaigns during each two-year election cycle.

Source: Center for Responsive Politics, 2012. The figures include fundraising by the DNC and RNC, as well as the parties' Senate-based organizations (DSCC and NRSC) and House-based organizations (DCCC and NRCC). The 2011–2012 figures are author's projections from unofficial reports.

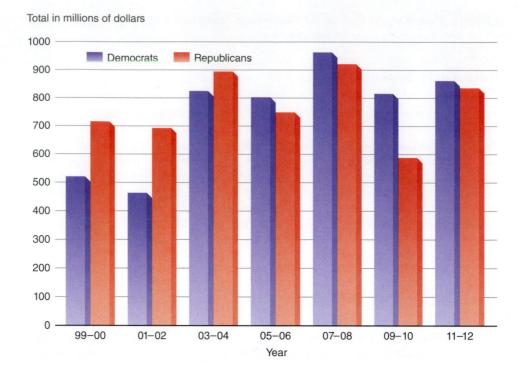

Total in millions of dollars

legal limit on these contributions is greater for Senate candidates than for House candidates, but the amount is relatively small (about $40,000 for Senate candidates) given the high cost of congressional campaigns.

Limits on party and other campaign contributions were established when campaign finance laws were rewritten in the early 1970s in the wake of the Watergate scandal that led to President Nixon's resignation. However, a loophole in the laws developed when a court ruling allowed the parties to raise unlimited funds provided they were not then given directly to candidates. Thus, whereas a wealthy contributor could legally give a candidate only a limited amount, that same contributor could give an unlimited amount to the candidate's party. In 2002, Congress prohibited these so-called *soft money* contributions. Nevertheless, the parties had become so proficient at fundraising that it didn't stop the money flow. In the next election cycle, the national party organizations raised $1.7 billion, compared with $1.3 billion in the final cycle of the soft-money era.

The Candidate-Centered Campaign

service relationship

The situation in which party organizations assist candidates for office but have no power to require them to support the party's main policy positions.

Party committees have more of a **service relationship** than a power relationship with their party's candidates. Because the party nominees are chosen through primaries, and because many of the potential candidates already have a power base at the local or state level, the national committees are unable to handpick the party nominees. Accordingly, the party organizations tend to back whichever candidate wins the primary. If the candidate then wins the general election, the party at least has denied the office to the opposing party.

Today's campaigns are largely controlled by the candidates, particularly in congressional, statewide, and presidential races. Each candidate has a personal organization, created especially for the campaign and disbanded once it is over. The candidates are entrepreneurs who play what political consultant Joe Napolitan labeled "the election game."[26] The game begins with money—lots of it.

Campaign Funds: The Money Chase

Campaigns for high office are expensive, and the costs keep rising. In 1980, about $250 million was spent by Senate and House candidates in the general election. The figure had jumped to $425 million by 1990. In 2012, the figure exceeded $2 billion—eight times the 1980 level.[27] As could be expected, incumbents have a distinct advantage in fundraising. They have contributor lists from past campaigns and the policy influence that donors seek. House and Senate incumbents outspend their challengers by more than two to one.

Because of the high cost of campaigns, candidates spend much of their time raising funds, which come primarily from individual contributors, interest groups (through PACs, discussed in Chapter 9), and political parties. The **money chase** is relentless.[28] A U.S. senator must raise nearly $20,000 a week on average throughout the entire six-year term in order to raise the minimum $5 million it takes to run a competitive Senate campaign in most states. A Senate campaign in one of the larger states can easily cost more than that amount. In the 2010 Massachusetts Senate race, incumbent Scott Brown and his Democratic challenger, Elizabeth Warren. spent more than $20 million each. House campaigns are less costly, but expenditures of $1 million or more have become commonplace. As for presidential elections, even the nominating race is expensive. During the competitive stage of the 2012 Republican race, Mitt Romney spent over $75 million while Newt Gingrich's expenditures topped $20 million. (In presidential races, but not congressional ones, candidates are eligible to receive federal funds, although none of the major contenders in 2012 did so. Public funding is discussed in Chapter 12.)

The money that political parties, individuals, and interest groups donate to an individual candidate is subject to legal limits (for example, $2,500 from an individual contributor and $5,000 from a group per election). These contributions are termed **hard money**—the money is given directly to the candidate and can be spent as he or she chooses.

Candidates are also the beneficiaries (and sometimes the casualties) of spending by super PACs. Although super PACs will be discussed more fully in Chapter 9, it should be noted here that these entities can legally raise and spend unlimited amounts of money as long as they do not coordinate their efforts with the candidate they support. (If they could coordinate their efforts, the legal limits on what candidates can personally raise would be meaningless.) Super PACs are an outgrowth of the Supreme Court's decision in *Citizens United v. Federal Election Commission* (2010), which held that corporations and unions can raise and spend money freely on campaigns (see Chapter 1). Although the Court upheld limits on what corporate and union donors can contribute directly to a candidate or party, it ruled that their spending could not otherwise be restricted.[29] (Unlike unions and corporations, individual donors already had the option of spending freely on campaigns.)

The level of independent spending by super PACs skyrocketed in the 2012 elections. However, much of the money was spent in ways the candidates and parties had not envisioned—to tear down candidates of the same party. During the Republican presidential primaries, pro-Romney super PACs spent more than $40 million on attacks on his Republican opponents, while their super PACs spent more than $20 million attacking him. And unlike the candidates' own messages, the super PACs pulled few punches. For example, one anti-Romney ad carried the following message: "The contradictions. The tax returns. The Cayman Islands. The Obamacare inventor. The $100 million IRA. The exclusive tax rate. The Swiss bank. The serial flip-flopper. The progressive." After Romney emerged from the primaries as the Republican presidential nominee, some

money chase
A term used to describe the fact that U.S. campaigns are very expensive and candidates must spend a great amount of time raising funds in order to compete successfully.

hard money
Campaign funds given directly to candidates to spend as they choose.

of the attacks directed at him by the Obama campaign echoed those of his Republican opponents.

Organization and Strategy: Political Consultants

political consultants

The professionals who advise candidates on various aspects of their campaigns, such as media use, fundraising, and polling.

The key operatives in today's campaigns—congressional as well as presidential—are highly paid **political consultants**: campaign strategists, pollsters, media producers, and fundraising and get-out-the-vote specialists. "The new king-makers" is the way writer David Chagall characterizes them.[30] They include campaign strategists who help the candidate to plot and execute a game plan. Over the years, some of these strategists, including James Carville and Roger Ailes, developed legendary reputations. Fundraising specialists are also part of the new politics. They are adept at tapping donors and interest groups that regularly contribute to election campaigns. The consultant ranks also include experts on polling and focus groups (the latter are small groups of voters brought together to discuss at length their thoughts on the candidates and issues). Polls and focus groups are used to identify issues and messages that will resonate with voters.[31] Media consultants are another staple of the modern campaign. They are adept at producing televised political advertising, generating news coverage, and developing Internet-based strategies.

packaging

A term of modern campaigning that refers to the process of recasting a candidate's record into an appealing image.

Campaign consultants are skilled at **packaging** a candidate—highlighting those aspects of the candidate's partisanship, policy positions, personal background, and personality that are thought most attractive to voters. Packaging is not new to politics. Andrew Jackson's self-portrayal in the nineteenth century as "the champion of the people" is an image that any modern candidate could appreciate. What is new is the need to fit the image to the requirements of a world of sound bites, thirty-second ads, televised debates, and Internet messages, and to do it in a persuasive way. In the old days, it was sometimes enough for candidates to drive home the point that they were a Republican or a Democrat, playing on the tendency of voters to choose a candidate on that basis. Party appeals are still critical, but today's voters also expect to hear about a candidate's personal life and policy proposals.

Over the course of a campaign, voters usually hear more about the candidates' weaknesses than about their strengths.[32] Of course, negative campaigning is as old as American politics. Thomas Jefferson, Andrew Jackson, and Abraham Lincoln were the target of vicious attacks. Lincoln was portrayed as "a hick" and "a baboon" for his gangly look and backwoods roots. But today's version of attack politics is unprecedented in its reach and scale (see Figure 8-6). Negative television ads were once the exception, but they have increased to the point where they now constitute the largest share of political ads.[33] Many of the ads are "badly misleading," according to Fact Check.org, which monitors ads and assesses their accuracy. During the 2012 presidential campaign, FactCheck.org identified several Obama and Romney ads that distorted the opposing candidate's record.[34]

Voter Contacts: Pitched Battle

Today's elections for high office have no historical parallel in their length and penetration. Candidates start their active campaigning much earlier—often two years in advance of election day—than they did in times past. The modern campaign is relentless. Voters are bombarded with messages that arrive by air, by land, and by Web.

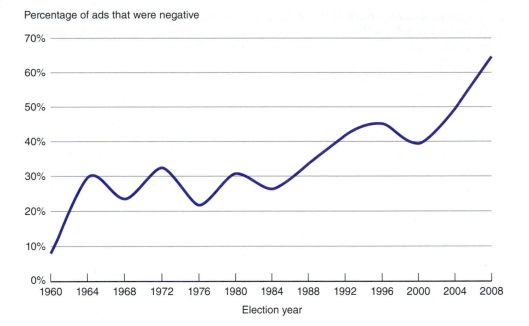

Percentage of ads that were negative

Election year

FIGURE 8-6
The Rise in Negative Campaigning, 1960–2008
In the past half-century, negative televised ads in presidential campaigns have increased to the point where they now constitute a majority of the televised ads.
Source: John G. Geer, *Fanning the Flames: The News Media's Role in the Rise of Negativity in Presidential Campaigns,* Discussion Paper #D55, Joan Shorenstein Center on the Press, Politics, and Public Policy, Kennedy School of Government, Harvard University, February 2010, p. 4. Reprinted with permission.

Air Wars

The main battleground of the modern campaign is the mass media, particularly television. Television emerged in the 1960s as the major medium of campaign politics and has remained so ever since.

Candidates spend heavily on televised political advertising, which enables them to communicate directly—and on their own terms—with voters. **Air wars** is the term that political scientist Darrell West applies to candidates' use of televised ads.[35] Candidates increasingly play off each other's ads, seeking to gain the strategic advantage. Modern production techniques enable well-funded candidates to get new ads on the air within a few hours' time, which allows them to rebut attacks and exploit fast-breaking developments, a tactic known as *rapid response.* The production and airing of televised political ads accounts for roughly half of campaign spending. Indeed, televised ads are the main reason for the high cost of U.S. campaigns. In most democracies, televised campaigning takes place through parties, which receive free air time to make their pitch. Many democracies, including France and Great Britain, prohibit the purchase of televised advertising time by candidates.

Candidates also use the press to get their message across, although the amount of news coverage they get varies widely by location and office. Many House candidates are almost completely ignored by local news media. The New York City media market, for example, includes more than a score of House districts in New York, New Jersey, Pennsylvania, and Connecticut, and candidates in these districts get little or no coverage from the New York media. They also get little exposure through televised ads because it is too expensive to buy ads in a metropolitan area where the congressional district is only a small fraction of the audience. Such candidates campaign the old-fashioned way, through leafleting, door-to-door canvassing, and the like. In contrast, presidential candidates get daily coverage from both national and local media. Between these extremes are Senate races, which always get some news coverage and, if hotly contested may get close coverage.

air wars
A term that refers to the fact that modern campaigns are often a battle of opposing televised advertising campaigns.

Debates are also part of the media campaign. Although many House candidates find it impossible to convince local television stations to carry debates, they are routine occurrences in Senate and presidential races. Debates can be risky encounters, because they give viewers a chance to compare the candidates directly. A weak or bumbling performance can hurt a candidate. Yet debates can also present a golden opportunity for a candidate who needs a boost.. In the 2012 Republican presidential race, Gingrich trailed Romney by double digits in the polls in South Carolina until he turned the debate moderator's question about his marital history into an attack on the media. His response energized South Carolina's conservatives, contributing to his victory in the state's primary. In contrast, the televised general election debates that attract tens of millions of viewers do not ordinarily change the minds of large numbers of voters. The 2012 presidential debates were atypical. Before the first debate, Romney was slipping in the polls. His strong performance in that debate, and Obama's weak performance, combined to dramatically tighten the presidential race.

Ground Wars

Candidates' first priority in a close election is "swing voters"—those voters who conceivably could be persuaded to vote for either side. As Election Day nears, however, candidates concentrate on getting their supporters to the polls. Get-out-the-vote efforts traditionally have been conducted by the parties and other organizations, such as labor unions. Although these groups remain the cornerstone of the effort, the candidates are also involved, and increasingly so. As partisanship has intensified in recent years, candidates have found it more difficult to persuade voters to switch sides. It is therefore important for them to get as many of their supporters as possible to the polls. Some campaign funds that formerly would have been spent on televised advertising are now spent on voter turnout efforts. In the final phase of the 2012 presidential election, millions of potential voters were contacted by phone or in person by the Republican and Democratic campaigns.

Web Wars

New communication technology usually makes its way into campaign politics, and the Internet is no exception. All the presidential and nearly all of the congressional candidates in 2012 had elaborate websites dedicated to providing information, generating public support, attracting volunteers, and raising money. Barack Obama's website was the most successful at fundraising, bringing in more than $100 million.

Although television is still the principal medium of election politics, some analysts believe that the Internet will eventually overtake it. Internet messaging is less expensive than television advertising. Because it is a targeted medium, the Internet could become the channel through which candidates reach identifiable voting groups. However, the Internet also has some disadvantages relative to television, especially in the greater control that individual users have over the message. With television, when a brief political ad appears during a favorite program, many viewers will sit through it. An unsolicited message on the Internet is more easily ignored or deleted. In general, the Internet has shown itself to be the better medium for fundraising and mobilizing supporters while television has proven to be the better medium for building name recognition and reaching less-interested voters.

In Retrospect: The Consequences of the Last War

A strong campaign effort can be the difference between winning and losing.[36] In the end, however, nothing so tips the balance in close races as voters' satisfaction with the party that holds power as a result of the previous election. Although some voters are swayed by what candidates promise to do if elected (a form of voting known as *prospective voting*), a greater number respond to past performance (*retrospective voting*). National economic conditions are particularly important in voters' judgments about whether to support the party in power. A weak economy, in conjunction with an unpopular war in Iraq, contributed heavily to the GOP's loss of Congress in 2006 and its loss of the presidency in 2008. When Americans think the country is headed in the wrong direction, the in-party has nearly always lost support in the next election. When times are good, the in-party has less to fear. The 2012 presidential elections was a departure from the usual pattern. Although voters were less than pleased with President Obama's handling of the economy, they narrowly elected him to a second term, partly because they doubted that Romney could do any better.

Parties, Candidates, and the Public's Influence

Candidate-centered campaigns have some distinct advantages. First, they can infuse new blood into electoral politics. Candidate recruitment is typically a slow process in party-centered systems. Would-be officeholders pay their dues by working in the party and, in the process, tend to adopt the outlook of those already there. By comparison, a candidate-centered system is more open and provides opportunities for newcomers to gain office quickly. Barack Obama is a case in point. He had run unsuccessfully for the U.S. House of Representatives in 2000 before winning the 2004 U.S. Senate race in Illinois. Barely two years later, Obama announced his candidacy for president of the United States, winning his party's 2008 nomination against the more experienced U.S. senator Hillary Clinton and then beating the even more experienced U.S. senator John

Republican vice-presidential nominee Paul Ryan on the campaign trail during the 2012 campaign. In America's candidate-centered system, party nominees have wide latitude in deciding how they will conduct their campaigns. Mitt Romney had nearly a free hand in choosing the little-known Ryan as his running mate, instantly making him a major political figure, which is a rarity in a party-centered system.

McCain in the general election. Obama's quick rise from political obscurity to the highest office in the country would be almost unthinkable in a party-centered democracy. Nor is he the only example. In 1976, Jimmy Carter went from being an obscure one-term governor of Georgia to winning the presidency two years later. In 2012, after being chosen as the Republican vice-presidential nominee, Wisconsin's Paul Ryan quickly went from being a little-known congressman to one of his party's most prominent leaders and, in the eyes of many Republicans, a future presidential nominee.

Candidate-centered campaigns also lend flexibility to electoral politics. When political conditions and issues change, self-directed candidates adjust quickly, bringing new ideas into the political arena. Strong party organizations are rigid by comparison. Until the early 1990s, for example, the British Labour Party was controlled by old-line activists who refused to concede that changes in the British economy called for changes in the party's trade unionist and economic policies. The result was a series of humiliating defeats at the hands of the Conservative Party that ended only after Tony Blair and other proponents of "New Labour" successfully recast the party's image.

POLITICAL THINKING Does It Make More Sense to "Vote the Person?"

It is sometimes said that it is better to "vote the person, not the party." Is that good advice, or bad? In voting for a president, Americans are choosing more than the person who will sit behind the desk in the Oval Office. They are also selecting scores of other top executives, including the secretary of state, the attorney general of the United States, and the director of the Central Intelligence Agency. The president also picks federal judges and justices. In all of these cases, presidents typically choose members of their party. The election of a senator or a representative is also more than a decision about which individual will occupy a seat in Congress. No single member of Congress has control over legislation. On vote after vote in Congress, most Republicans are aligned on one side while most Democrats are aligned on the other side. In light of these considerations, do you think it makes more sense "to vote the person" or more sense "to vote the party?"

Also, candidate-centered campaigns encourage national officeholders to be responsive to local interests. In building personal followings among their state or district constituents, members of Congress respond to local needs. Nearly every significant domestic program enacted by Congress is adjusted to accommodate the interests of states and localities that otherwise would be hurt by the policy. Where strong national parties exist, national interests take precedence over local concerns. In both France and Britain, for example, the pleas of legislators from underdeveloped regions have often gone unheeded by their party's majority.

In other respects, candidate-centered campaigns have distinct disadvantages. They provide abundant opportunities for powerful interest groups to shower money on the candidates. The role of campaign money, and the influence it buys, has long been an issue in American politics and has achieved new heights as a result of the Supreme Court's *Citizens United* decision. In no other Western democracy does money play as large a role as does in American elections.

Candidate-centered campaigns also weaken accountability by making it easier for officeholders to deny personal responsibility for government's actions. If national policy goes awry, an incumbent can always say that he or she represents only one vote out of many and that the real problem resides with the president or with "others" in Congress. The problem of accountability is apparent from surveys that have asked Americans about their confidence in Congress. Many citizens have a low opinion of Congress as a whole but say they have confidence in their local representative in Congress. This paradoxical attitude is so prevalent that the large majority of incumbents are reelected time and again (see Chapter 11). Party-centered campaigns are different in this respect. When problems surface, voters tend to hold the majority party responsible and vote large numbers of its members out of office.

In short, candidate-centered campaigns strengthen the relationship between the voters and their individual representatives while weakening the relationship between the full electorate and their representative institutions. Whether this arrangement serves the public's interest is debatable. Nevertheless, it is clear that Americans do not favor party-centered politics. Parties survived the shift to candidate-centered campaigns and will persist, but their organizational heyday has passed. (Congressional and presidential campaigns are discussed further in Chapters 11 and 12, respectively.)

Summary
Self-Test www.mhhe.com/pattersontadtx11e

Political parties serve to link the public with its elected leaders. In the United States, this linkage is provided by the two-party system; only the Republican and Democratic parties have any chance of winning control of government. The fact that the United States has only two major parties is explained by several factors: an electoral system—characterized by single-member districts—that makes it difficult for third parties to compete for power; each party's willingness to accept differing political views; and a political culture that stresses compromise and negotiation rather than ideological rigidity.

Because the United States has only two major parties, each of which seeks to gain majority support, their candidates typically avoid controversial or extreme political positions. Sometimes, Democratic and Republican candidates do offer sharply contrasting policy alternatives, particularly during times of crisis. Ordinarily, however, Republican and Democratic candidates pursue moderate and somewhat overlapping policies. Each party can count on its party loyalists, but U.S. elections can hinge on swing voters, who respond to the issues of the moment either prospectively, basing their vote on what the candidates promise to do if elected, or retrospectively, basing their vote on their satisfaction or dissatisfaction with what the party in power has already done.

America's parties are decentralized, fragmented organizations. The national party organization does not control the policies and activities of the state organizations, and these in turn do not control the local organizations. Traditionally, the local organizations have controlled most of the party's workforce because most elections are contested at the local level. Local parties, however, vary markedly in their vitality. Whatever their level, America's party organizations are relatively weak. They lack control over nominations and elections. Candidates can bypass the party organization and win nomination through primary elections. Individual candidates also control most of the organizational structure and money necessary to win elections. The state and national party organizations have recently expanded their capacity to provide candidates with modern campaign services. Nevertheless, party organizations at all levels have few ways of controlling the candidates who run under their banners. They assist candidates with campaign technology, workers, and funds, but they cannot compel candidates to be loyal to organizational goals.

American political campaigns, particularly those for higher office, are candidate centered. Most candidates are self-starters who become adept at "the election game." They spend much of their time raising campaign funds, and they build their personal organizations around campaign consultants: pollsters, media producers, fundraisers, and election consultants. Strategy and image making are key components of the modern campaign, as is televised political advertising, which accounts for half or more of all spending in presidential and congressional races.

The advantages of candidate-centered politics include a responsiveness to new leadership, new ideas, and local concerns. Yet this form of politics can result in campaigns that are personality driven, depend on powerful interest groups, and blur responsibility for what government has done.

Study Corner

Key Terms

air wars (*p. 211*)

candidate-centered campaigns (*p. 190*)

factional (minor) party (*p. 202*)

gender gap (*p. 201*)

grassroots party (*p. 192*)

hard money (*p. 209*)

ideological (minor) party (*p. 203*)

linkage institution (*p. 190*)

median voter theorem (*p. 198*)

money chase (*p. 209*)

multiparty system (*p. 197*)

nomination (*p. 204*)

packaging (*p. 210*)

party-centered campaigns (*p. 190*)

party coalition (*p. 200*)

party competition (*p. 191*)

party organizations (*p. 204*)

party realignment (*p. 193*)

plurality (winner-take-all) system (*p. 197*)

political consultants (*p. 210*)

political party (*p. 189*)

primary election (direct primary) (*p. 204*)

proportional representation system (*p. 198*)

reform (minor) party (*p. 203*)

service relationship (*p. 208*)

single-issue (minor) party (*p. 202*)

single-member districts (*p. 197*)

two-party system (*p. 196*)

Self-Test: Multiple Choice

1. The formation of political parties
   a. acts as a support for an elitist government.
   b. makes it difficult for the public to participate in politics.
   c. can mobilize citizens to collective action to compete for power with those who have wealth and prestige.
   d. can function as an alternative to free and open media.

2. A major change in party activity in the South since the 1960s is
   a. the emergence of a viable third party.
   b. a sharp decline in voter turnout.
   c. a decline in the level of two-party competition in state and local elections.
   d. a switch to support of Republican candidates in presidential elections.

3. The chief electoral factor supporting a two-party system in the United States is
   a. proportional representation.
   b. multimember election districts.
   c. single-member districts with proportional voting.
   d. single-member districts with plurality voting.

4. The high cost of campaigns in the United States is largely related to
   a. running televised ads.
   b. developing an effective website.

c. organizing door-to-door canvassing efforts.
d. paying the legal and accounting expenses related to filing information about campaign donors and expenditures with the Federal Elections Commission.

5. In recent decades, state political party organizations in the United States have
   a. become weaker and less effective.
   b. taken over control and direction of the national parties.
   c. been hurt by services provided by the national party organizations.
   d. become more professional in staffing and support of statewide races.

6. European and American political parties differ in which of the following ways?
   a. the degree to which they are party centered as opposed to candidate centered
   b. the nature of their party organizations: the extent to which they are organized at the local and national levels, and the amount of power that exists at each of these levels
   c. the type of electoral system in which they elect their candidates to office
   d. all of the above

7. The coalitions of voters that make up the Republican and Democratic parties are virtually identical. (T/F)

8. Primary elections help strengthen party organizations in the United States. (T/F)

9. U.S. political parties are organized largely from the bottom up, not the top down. (T/F)

10. Modern-day parties in the United States are described in the text as having more of a service than a power relationship with candidates. (T/F)

Self-Test: Essay

Why are elections conducted so differently in the United States than in European democracies? Why are American campaigns so much longer, more expensive, and more candidate centered?

Suggested Readings

Brewer, Mark D., and Jeffrey M. Stonecash. *Dynamics of American Political Parties*. New York: Cambridge University Press, 2009. A careful assessment of party change and its impact.

Craig, Stephen C. *The Electoral Challenge: Theory Meets Practice*. Washington, D.C.: CQ Press, 2006. A comprehensive assessment of the impact of election campaigns.

Farrar-Myers, Victoria A., and Diana Dwyer. *Limits and Loopholes: The Quest for Money, Free Speech, and Fair Elections.* Washington, D.C.: CQ Press, 2008. A careful look at the development of campaign finance legislation.

Flanigan, William H., and Nancy H. Zingale. *Political Behavior of the American Electorate*, 12th ed. Washington, D.C.: CQ Press, 2009. A concise but insightful look at the American voter.

Geer, John. *In Defense of Negativity.* Chicago: University of Chicago Press, 2006. A provocative and award-winning analysis of televised political ads.

Hillygus, D. Sunshine, and Todd G. Shields. *The Persuadable Voter: Wedge Issues in Presidential Campaigns.* Princeton, N.J.: Princeton University Press, 2008. A careful analysis of the use of wedge issues, such as abortion, in campaign strategy.

Kaufmann, Karen M., John R. Petrocik, and Daron R. Shaw. *Unconventional Wisdom: Facts and Myths about American Voters.* New York: Oxford University Press, 2008. An illuminating assessment of how America's voters actually behave.

Trautman, Karl G. *The Underdog in American Politics: The Democratic Party and Liberal Values.* New York: Palgrave Macmillan, 2010. A careful analysis of the underdog's place in American politics.

List of Websites

www.democrats.org
The Democratic National Committee's site; provides information on the party's platform, candidates, officials, and organization.

www.gp.org
The Green Party's site; contains information on the party's philosophy and policy goals.

www.rnc.org
Home page of the Republican National Committee; offers information on Republican leaders, policy positions, and organizations.

www.texasgop.org
Website of the Texas Republican Party. The Republican and Democratic parties in each state have similar sites.

Participate!

Consider becoming a campaign or political party volunteer. The opportunities are numerous. Parties and candidates at every level from the national on down seek volunteers to assist in organizing, canvassing, fundraising, and other activities. As a college student, you have communication and knowledge skills that would be valuable to a campaign or party organization. You might be pleasantly surprised by the tasks you are assigned.

Extra Credit

For up-to-the-minute *New York Times* articles, interactive simulations, graphics, study tools, and more links and quizzes, visit the text's Online Learning Center at **www.mhhe.com/pattersontad11e**.

Self-Test Answers

1. c, 2. d, 3. d, 4. a, 5. d, 6. d, 7. F, 8. F, 9. T, 10. T

Interest Groups: Organizing for Influence

The flaw in the pluralist heaven is that the heavenly chorus sings with a strong upper-class bias. E. E. Schattschneider[1]

The insurance companies began their effort to undermine the health care reform effort nearly as soon as the meeting ended. President Barack Obama had organized the meeting to hear what health industry groups had to say about reform of the nation's medical-care system. Insurance industry representatives attended the meeting and spoke favorably about the need for change. Insurance companies were determined, however, to block any change that would erode their profits. They ran a national advertising campaign that claimed they were "supporting bipartisan reforms that Congress can build on." In that congressional Republicans were united in their opposition to a major overhaul of the health care system, "bipartisan reforms" could only mean something less than what Obama had in mind. As the legislation worked its way through Congress, the insurance industry stepped up its attack. One day before a crucial Senate vote on the legislation, for instance, an industry trade group, America's Health Insurance Plans (AHIP), issued a report claiming the typical American family would wind up paying $4,000 more in premiums if the reform were enacted, a figure that was substantially higher than other projections.[2] All told, the insurance industry spent over $200 million on advertising and lobbying in its effort to derail legislation that would threaten its hold on America's health care system.[3]

The insurance industry's campaign against comprehensive health care reform suggests why interest groups are both admired and feared. Insurance companies have legitimate interests that are affected by public policy. It is perfectly appropriate for them to lobby on policy issues. The same can be said of farmers, consumers, minorities, college students—indeed, of virtually every interest in society. In fact, the *pluralist* theory of American politics (see Chapter 1) holds that society's interests are represented most effectively through group action.

This 1873 lithograph illustrates the benefits of membership in the National Grange, an agricultural interest group. Throughout their history, Americans have organized to influence government policy.

single-issue politics

The situation in which separate groups are organized around nearly every conceivable policy issue and press their demands and influence to the utmost.

interest group

Any organization that actively seeks to influence public policy.

Yet groups can wield too much power, getting their way at an unreasonable cost to the rest of society. When Obama launched his health care initiative, polls indicated that most Americans thought a major change in the nation's medical care system was needed. They were not necessarily behind Obama's plan. In fact, most of them were not exactly sure of what he had in mind, or what the leading alternatives might be. That said, the time was ripe for a fruitful public debate about the advantages, and the drawbacks, of an alternative health care system. Did the insurance industry, in pursuit of its self-interest, help to derail that debate?

Opinions differ on the answer to this question, but there is no doubt that groups have considerable influence over public policy. Indeed, most observers believe that group influence has increased significantly in recent decades. The situation has been described as the rise of **single-issue politics:** groups that are organized around nearly every conceivable policy issue, with each group pressing its demands to the utmost through lobbying and other forms of political pressure. The situation raises a perennial issue, one that James Madison addressed in his famous essay *Federalist* No. 10. Madison warned against "the dangers of faction," by which he meant a polity where factions (groups) become so powerful that they trample on the legitimate interests of other groups and society as a whole. Madison acknowledged that society has an obligation to protect the right of groups to organize and petition government but also said that society suffers if groups become overly powerful.

An **interest group**—also called a "faction," "pressure group," "special interest," or "organized interest"—can be defined as any organization that actively seeks to influence public policy.[4] Interest groups are similar to political parties in some respects but differ from them in important ways.[5] Like parties, groups are a linkage mechanism: they serve to connect citizens with government. However, political parties address a broad range of issues so as to appeal to diverse blocs of voters. Above all, parties are in the business of trying to win elections. Groups, on the other hand, concentrate on policies directly affecting their interests. A group may involve itself in elections, but its major purpose is to influence the policies that affect it.

This chapter examines the degree to which various interests in American society are represented by organized groups, the process by which interest groups exert influence, and the costs and benefits of group politics. The main points made in the chapter are:

■ *Although nearly all interests in American society are organized to some degree, those associated with economic activity, particularly business activity, are by far the most thoroughly organized.* Their advantage rests on their superior financial resources and on the private goods (such as wages and jobs) they provide to those in the organization.

■ *Groups that do not have economic activity as their primary function often have organizational difficulties.* These groups pursue public or collective goods (such as a safer environment) that are available even to individuals who are not group members, so individuals may free ride, choosing not to pay the costs of membership.

- *Lobbying and electioneering are the traditional means by which groups communicate with and influence political leaders.* Recent developments, including grassroots lobbying and political action committees, have heightened interest groups' influence.

- *The interest-group system overrepresents business interests and fosters policies that serve a group's interest more than the society's broader interests.* Thus, although groups are an essential part of the policy process, they also distort that process.

The Interest-Group System

In the 1830s, the Frenchman Alexis de Tocqueville wrote that the "principle of association" was nowhere more evident than in America.[6] His description still holds. Americans are more likely than citizens of other nations to join organized groups (see "How the U.S. Differs"). However, not all of these organizations are interest groups. Book clubs, softball teams, social clubs, and most church groups are examples of groups that are not in the interest-group category because they do not seek to influence the policy process. Even so, no other nation has as many organized interest groups as does the United States. The country's tradition of free association makes it natural for Americans to join together for political purposes, and their diverse interests give them reason to pursue policy influence through group action.

The nation's political structure also contributes to group action. Because of federalism and the separation of powers, groups have multiple points of entry through which to influence policy. The structure of the American system even contributes to a type of lobbying that is sometimes overlooked. While the vast majority of organized interests represent private interests, some represent governments. Most states and major cities have at least one Washington lobbyist. Intergovernmental lobbying also occurs through groups such as the Council of State Governments, the National Governors Association, the National Association of Counties, the National League of Cities, and the U.S. Conference of Mayors. These organizations sometimes play a significant role in national policy debates. For example, as Congress was preparing in 2011 to renew and amend the antiterrorism legislation that had gone into effect in 2001, the National Governors Association and the U.S. Conference of Mayors lobbied to ensure that the changes reflected their concerns. Even foreign governments lobby in Washington. Arms sales, foreign aid, immigration, and trade practices are among the U.S. policies they target.[7]

The extraordinary number of interest groups in the United States does not mean that the nation's various interests are equally well organized. Groups develop when people with a shared interest have the opportunity and the incentive to join together. Some individuals or organizations have the skills, money, contacts, or time to participate in group politics; others do not. Moreover, some groups are inherently more attractive to potential members than others and thus find it easier to organize. Groups also differ in their financial resources and thus in their capacity for political action.

Therefore, a first consideration in regard to group politics in America is the issue of how thoroughly various interests are organized. Interests that are highly organized stand a good chance of having their views heard by policymakers. Those that are poorly organized run the risk of being ignored.

HOW THE U.S. DIFFERS POLITICAL THINKING THROUGH COMPARISONS

Groups: "A Nation of Joiners"

"A nation of joiners" is how the Frenchman Alexis de Tocqueville described the United States during his visit to this country in the 1830s. Tocqueville was stunned by the group and community activity he saw, suggesting that Europeans would find it hard to comprehend. "The political activity that pervades the United States," said Tocqueville, "must be seen to be understood." Even today, Americans are more fully involved in groups and community causes than are Europeans. Among the reasons are the nation's tradition of free association, the openness of American society, and the prominence of religion and public education. Much of the nation's group life revolves around its churches and its schools.

Such differences are reflected in citizens' participation rates. Americans are more likely to belong to groups than are the French, Italians, British, or Germans, as the accompanying figures from the World Values Survey indicate.

Q: How does the structure of the U.S. government contribute to the proliferation of interest groups in America?

A: Because of federalism and the separation of powers, the American system offers numerous points at which groups can try to influence public policy. If unsuccessful with legislators, groups can turn to executives or to the courts. If thwarted at the national level, groups can turn to state and local governments. By comparison, the governments of most other democratic nations are not organized in ways that facilitate group access and influence. Great Britain's unitary government, for example, concentrates power at the national level. Moreover, in the British House of Commons, power is concentrated in the top leadership to a far greater degree that it is in the U.S. Congress (see Chapter 11).

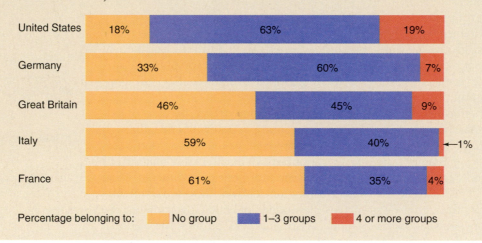

Percentage belonging to: No group / 1–3 groups / 4 or more groups

United States: 18% No group, 63% 1–3 groups, 19% 4 or more groups
Germany: 33% No group, 60% 1–3 groups, 7% 4 or more groups
Great Britain: 46% No group, 45% 1–3 groups, 9% 4 or more groups
Italy: 59% No group, 40% 1–3 groups, 1% 4 or more groups
France: 61% No group, 35% 1–3 groups, 4% 4 or more groups

Source: World Values Survey Association, 2012.

Economic Groups

No interests are more fully or effectively organized than those that have economic activity as their primary purpose. Corporations, labor unions, farm groups, and professional associations, among others, exist primarily for economic purposes—to make profits, provide jobs, improve pay, or protect an occupation. For the sake of discussion, we will call such organizations **economic groups.** Almost all such organizations engage in political activity as a means of promoting and protecting their economic interests. An indicator of this is the fact that Washington lobbyists who represent economic groups outnumber those of all other groups by more than two to one.

Among economic groups, the most numerous are *business groups.* Writing in 1929, political scientist E. Pendleton Herring noted, "Of the many organized groups maintaining offices in [Washington], there are no interests more fully, more comprehensively, and more efficiently represented than those of American industry."[8] Although corporations do not dominate lobbying as thoroughly as they once did, Herring's general conclusion still holds: more than half of all

economic groups

Interest groups that are organized primarily for economic reasons but that engage in political activity in order to seek favorable policies from government.

groups formally registered to lobby Congress are business organizations. Virtually all large corporations and many smaller ones are politically active.

Business firms are also represented through associations. Some of these "organizations of organizations" seek to advance the broad interests of business. One of the oldest associations is the National Association of Manufacturers, which was formed in 1894, and today represents fourteen thousand manufacturers. Another large business association is the U.S. Chamber of Commerce, which represents nearly three million businesses of all sizes. Other business associations, such as the American Petroleum Institute and the National Association of Home Builders, are confined to a single trade or industry.

Economic groups also include those associated with organized labor. *Labor groups* seek to promote policies that benefit workers in general and union members in particular. Although there are some major independent unions, such as the United Mine Workers and the Teamsters, the dominant labor group is the AFL-CIO, which has its national headquarters in Washington, D.C. The AFL-CIO has twelve million members in its nearly sixty affiliated unions, which include the International Brotherhood of Electrical Workers, the Sheet Metal Workers, and the Communications Workers of America.

At an earlier time, about a third of the U.S. workforce was unionized. Today, only about one in eight workers is a union member (see "How the 50 States Differ"). Historically, skilled and unskilled laborers constituted the bulk of organized labor, but their numbers have decreased as the economy has changed, while the number of professionals, technicians, and service workers has increased. Professionals have shown little interest in union organization, perhaps because they identify with management or consider themselves economically secure. A mere 2 percent of professionals are union members. Service workers and technicians can also be difficult for unions to organize because they work closely with managers and, often, in small offices. Nevertheless, unions have made inroads in their efforts to organize service and public employees. In fact, most union members today work in the public sector, despite the fact that it has only a fifth as many workers as does the private sector. The most heavily unionized employees are those who work for local government, such as teachers, police officers, and firefighters—roughly 40 percent of them are union members. State and federal employees are also heavily unionized. All told, more than a third of public-sector workers are union members, compared with less than a tenth of private-industry workers. Even the construction industry, which ranks high by comparison with most private-sector industries, has a unionization rate of less than 15 percent.[9]

Farm groups represent another large economic lobby. The American Farm Bureau Federation is the largest of the farm groups, with more than four million members. The National Farmers Union, the National Grange, and the National Farmers Organization are smaller farm lobbies. Agricultural groups do not always agree on policy issues. For instance, the Farm Bureau sides with agribusiness and owners of large farms, while the Farmers Union promotes the interests of smaller "family" farms. There are also numerous specialty farm associations,

Economic groups, which include business firms and labor unions, get the resources for their political activities from their economic activity. This source of support gives them an organizational advantage over citizens' groups, which depend on voluntary contributions to fund their lobbying. Shown here are members of the United Auto Workers (UAW), one of the nation's most powerful labor unions.

HOW THE 50 STATES DIFFER   POLITICAL THINKING THROUGH COMPARISONS

UNION MEMBERSHIP

For a long period in the twentieth century, labor unions were among the most powerful groups in America, and union leaders like George Meany and Walter Reuther were more widely known than most U.S. senators. Today, few Americans could name the top union leaders, and union membership has fallen to an eighth of the nation's workforce, down from a third at its peak. Most union members today are public employees—teachers, police officers, firefighters, and the like. Union membership has fallen most dramatically in industry and craft occupations, such as factory workers and carpenters. However, there is considerable variation among the fifty states in the level of union membership, reflecting differences in their economies and traditions. When unions were first getting organized, they made their largest inroads in industrialized and

mining states, and these states—most of which are located in the North—continue to rank high on union membership. The southern and mountain states have traditionally ranked low on union membership, as have the agricultural states of the Midwest.

Q: Looking only at the western third of the United States, can you suggest why the coastal states might have higher levels of union membership than the states located further inland?

A: These two areas differ in their economies. The coastal states are more industrialized and depend less heavily on agriculture and tourism, which are economic sectors that have low unionization levels.

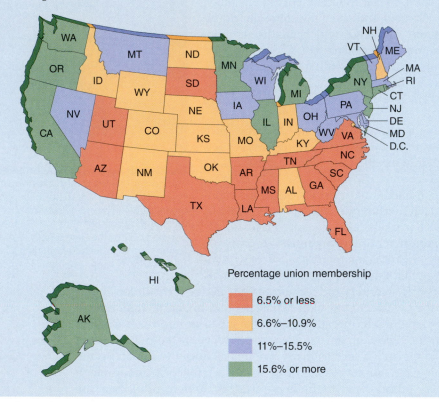

Percentage union membership

- 6.5% or less
- 6.6%–10.9%
- 11%–15.5%
- 15.6% or more

Source: U.S. Department of Labor, 2012.

including the Association of Wheat Growers, the American Soybean Association, and the Associated Milk Producers. Each association acts as a separate lobby, seeking to obtain policies that will serve its members' particular interests.

Most professions also have lobbying associations. Among the most powerful of these *professional groups* is the American Medical Association (AMA), which includes more than 200,000 physicians. Other professional groups include the American Bar Association (ABA) and the American Association of University Professors (AAUP).

Citizens' Groups

Economic groups do not have a monopoly on lobbying. There is another category of interest groups—**citizens' groups** (or **noneconomic groups**). Group members in this category are joined together not by a *material incentive*—such as jobs, higher wages, or profits—but by a *purposive incentive*, the satisfaction of contributing to what they regard as a worthy goal or purpose.[10] Whether a group's purpose is to protect the environment, return prayer to the public schools, or feed the poor at home or abroad, there are citizens who are willing to participate simply because they believe the cause is a worthy one.

Nearly every conceivable issue or problem has its citizens' group, often several of them. Some citizens' groups work to advance the interests of a particular social grouping; examples are the National Association for the Advancement of Colored People (NAACP), the National Organization for Women (NOW), and La Raza, which is the largest Hispanic American lobbying group. Other citizens' groups are dedicated to the promotion of a political ideology. Such groups have a broad agenda that derives from a philosophical or moral position. The American Conservative Union (ACU) is the largest conservative organization and lobbies on issues like taxation and national defense. MoveOn is a liberal counterpart to the ACU, as is Americans for Democratic Action (ADA). Another example is the Christian Coalition of America, which describes itself as "America's leading grassroots organization defending our godly heritage." The group addresses a wide range of issues, including school prayer, abortion, and television programming. Ideology is also a component of the state-level Public Interest Research Groups (PIRGs), such as NYPIRG (New York), CALPIRG (California), and TexPIRG (Texas). Almost every state has a PIRG, which usually has chapters on college campuses. Drawing on their network of researchers, students, and advocates, they address issues from a public interest angle. Ideological groups on both the left and the right have increased substantially in number since the 1960s. Most citizens' groups, however, have an issue-specific policy agenda. *Single-issue*

citizens' (noneconomic) groups
Organized interests formed by individuals drawn together by opportunities to promote a cause in which they believe but that does not provide them significant individual economic benefits.

Public Interest Research Groups (PIRGs) exist in about half the states. One of them is CalPIRG (California Public Interest Research Group). PIRG has student chapters on more than 100 college campuses, including several in California. Consumer protection and campaign reform are among PIRG's top issues.

groups have risen sharply in number in the past half century and now pressure government on almost every conceivable policy, from nuclear arms to drug abuse. Notable current examples are the National Rifle Association and the various right-to-life and pro-choice groups. Most environmental groups can also be seen as single-issue organizations in that they seek to influence public policy in a specific area, such as pollution reduction, wilderness preservation, or wildlife protection. The Sierra Club, one of the oldest environmental groups, was formed in the 1890s to promote the preservation of scenic areas. Also prominent are the National Audubon Society, the Wilderness Society, the Environmental Defense Fund, Greenpeace U.S.A., and the Izaak Walton League. Since 1960, membership in environmental groups has more than tripled in response to increased public concern about the environment.[11]

PARTY POLARIZATION Political thinking in conflict

The Impact of Ideological Interest Groups

After the Watergate scandal in the early 1970s, Congress enacted campaign finance reforms that opened the door to a larger funding role for interest groups through provisions that relaxed legal restrictions on political action committees (PACs). Many of the citizen-based PACs that formed at that time were more ideological than were the parties or most of the voters. At first, these PACs concentrated on general election races, but then also became heavily involved in primary election contests, working to defeat moderate candidates within their party. Their efforts have contributed to the election of senators and representatives that hold uncompromising conservative or liberal views, which has contributed to the party polarization that has characterized Congress in recent years. Examples of such groups are Emily's List, which supports liberal candidates, and the Family Research Council, which supports conservative candidates. In recent elections, Emily's List has given virtually 100 percent of its PAC contributions to Democratic candidates, while Family Research Council has given virtually 100 percent of its PAC contributions to Republican candidates. The tendency of ideological groups to support one side of the partisan divide can also be seen in the figures below, which show how ideological PACs in a few selected categories divided their contributions between Republican and Democratic candidates during a recent election cycle.

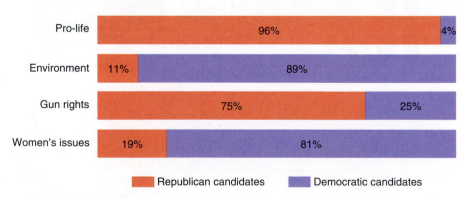

Source: Center for Responsive Politics, 2012.

Q. *Why do you think politically active citizen groups are generally more ideological—whether conservative or liberal—than is the society as a whole? Are citizens with strong views somehow more attracted to organized political activity than those with more moderate opinions?*

Citizens' groups are difficult to classify precisely because they differ so widely in their focus and goals. Some single-issue groups, for example, are ideological whereas others are pragmatic. A simple but precise way to describe citizens' groups is that they are "groups anyone can join." This does not mean that everyone would want to join a particular group. A conservative would not choose to join the ADA, just as a liberal would not join the ACU. But there is no barrier to joining a citizens' group if one is willing to contribute the required time or money. In this way, citizens' groups are distinct from business firms, which are closed to all but their employees, and distinct also from labor groups, farm groups, and professional associations, whose members have a particular type of training or vocation.[12]

The Organizational Edge: Economic Groups versus Citizens' Groups

Although the number of citizens' groups has mushroomed in recent decades, they are substantially outnumbered by economic groups. By most accounts, they also have less influence on government than do economic groups. The predominance of economic interests was predicted in *Federalist* No. 10, in which James Madison declared that property is "the most common and durable source of factions." Stated differently, nothing seems to matter quite so much to people as their economic self-interest. Several factors (summarized in Table 9-1) give economic groups an organizational advantage, including their resources and their size.

Unequal Access to Resources

One reason for the abundance of economic groups is their access to financial resources. Political lobbying does not come cheap. If a group is to make its views known, it typically must have a headquarters, an expert staff, and communication facilities. Economic groups pay for these things with money generated by their economic activity. Corporations have the greatest built-in advantage. They

TABLE 9-1 | Advantages and Disadvantages Held by Economic and Citizens' Groups

Economic groups	Citizens' groups
Advantages	*Advantages*
Economic activity provides the organization with the resources necessary for political action.	Members are likely to support leaders' political efforts because they joined the group in order to influence policy.
Individuals are encouraged to join the group because of economic benefits they individually receive (such as wages).	*Disadvantages*
In the case of firms within an industry, their small number encourages organization because the contribution of each firm can make a difference.	The group has to raise funds, especially for its political activities.
Disadvantages	Potential members may choose not to join the group because they get collective benefits even if they do not join (the free-rider problem).
Persons within the group may not support leaders' political efforts because they did not join the group for political reasons.	Potential members may choose not to join the group because their individual contribution may be too small to affect the group's success one way or the other.

do not have to charge membership dues or conduct fundraisers to support their lobbying. Their political money comes from their business profits.

Some economic groups rely on dues rather than profits to support their lobbying, but they have something of economic value to offer in exchange. Labor unions, for example, provide their members access to higher-paying jobs in return for the dues they pay. Such groups offer what is called a **private (individual) good**—a benefit, such as a job, that is given directly to a particular individual. An important feature of a private good is that it can be held back. If an individual is unwilling to pay organizational dues, the group can withhold the benefit.

Citizens' groups do not have these inherent advantages. They do not generate profits or fees as a result of economic activity. Moreover, the incentives they offer prospective members are not exclusive. As opposed to the private or individual goods provided by many economic groups, most noneconomic groups offer **collective (public) goods** as an incentive for membership. Collective goods are, by definition, goods that belong to all; they cannot be granted or withheld on an individual basis. The air people breathe and the national forests people visit are examples of collective goods. They are available to one and all, those who do not pay dues to a clean-air group or a wilderness preservation group as well as those who do.

The shared characteristic of collective goods creates what is called the **free-rider problem:** individuals can obtain the good even if they do not contribute to the group's effort. Take the case of National Public Radio (NPR). Although NPR's programs are funded primarily through listeners' donations, those who do not contribute can listen to the programs. The noncontributors are free riders: they receive the benefit without paying for it. About 90 percent of regular NPR listeners are noncontributors.

In a purely economic sense, as economist Mancur Olson noted, it is not rational for an individual to contribute to a group when its benefit can be obtained for free.[13] Moreover, the dues paid by any single member are too small to affect the group's success one way or another. Why pay dues to an environmental group when any improvements in the air, water, or wildlife from its lobbying efforts are available to everyone and when one's individual contribution is too small to make a real difference? Although many people do join such groups anyway, the free-rider problem is one reason citizens' groups are organized less fully than economic groups.

The free-rider problem has been lessened, but not eliminated, in recent decades by communication technologies that enable citizens' groups to easily contact prospective members. Computer-assisted direct mail is one of these technologies. Group organizers buy mailing lists and flood the mails with computer-typed "personal" letters asking recipients to pay a small annual membership fee. For some individuals, a fee of $25 to $50 annually represents no great sacrifice and offers the satisfaction of supporting a cause in which they believe. "Checkbook membership" is how political scientist Theda Skocpol describes such contributions.[14] Until the computer era, citizens' groups had great difficulty identifying and contacting potential members.

The Internet has also been a boon to citizens' groups. Virtually every such group of any size has its own website and e-mail list. MoveOn illustrates the Internet's organizing capacity. MoveOn was started by a handful of liberal activists working out of a garage. It now has well over one million members. During the 2012 campaign, MoveOn repeatedly prompted its members to contribute time and money to elect Democratic candidates, a strategy it has pursued in every election since its founding in 1998.

private (individual) goods
Benefits that a group (most often an economic group) can grant directly and exclusively to individual members of the group.

collective (public) goods
Benefits that are offered by groups (usually citizens' groups) as an incentive for membership but that are nondivisible (such as a clean environment) and therefore are available to nonmembers as well as members of the particular group.

free-rider problem
The situation in which the benefits offered by a group to its members are also available to nonmembers. The incentive to join the group and to promote its cause is reduced because nonmembers (free riders) receive the benefits (for example, a cleaner environment) without having to pay any of the group's costs.

The Advantages and Disadvantages of Size

Although citizens' groups have proliferated in recent decades, the organizational muscle in American politics rests primarily with economic groups. Business interests in particular have an advantage that economist Mancur Olson calls "the size factor."[15] Although it might be thought that the interests of groups with large memberships would typically prevail over the interests of smaller groups, the reverse is more often true. Olson notes that small groups are ordinarily more united on policy issues and often have more resources, enabling them to win out against large groups. Business groups in a specific industry are usually few in number and have an incentive to work together to influence government on issues of joint interest. The U.S. automobile industry, for example, has its "Big Three"—

The Internet has made it easier for citizens' groups to organize and increase their membership. One of the most successful examples is MoveOn. Founded by a small group of liberal activists, it has well over a million followers. MoveOn was instrumental in mobilizing opposition to the war in Iraq.

General Motors, Ford, and Chrysler. Although they compete for car sales, they usually work together on policy issues. They have succeeded at times, for example, in persuading government to delay or reduce higher fuel efficiency and safety standards, which has meant billions in additional profits for them at an incalculable cost to car owners.

Business associations testify to the advantage of small size. The business sector is divided into numerous industries, most of which include only a small number of major firms. Virtually every one of these industries, from oil to cereals to bow ties, has its own trade association. More than one thousand trade associations are represented in Washington, and they spend hundreds of millions of dollars annually on lobbying.

Their situation is far different from that of, say, taxpayers, who number in the tens of millions. Although taxpayers would be enormously powerful if they all joined together in a single cohesive group, most taxpayers have no real interest in paying dues to a taxpayers' group that would lobby on their behalf. In 2008, these differences came together in ways that conceivably hurt taxpayers while helping leading financial institutions. At issue was a government bailout aimed at protecting major investment banks from bankruptcy as a result of their purchase of mortgage-backed securities, which had declined sharply in value as the U.S. housing market weakened. With the backing of policymakers in the Federal Reserve, the Treasury Department, the White House, and Congress, troubled financial institutions received $700 billion in taxpayers' money to rescue them from bankruptcy, even though their risky investments had brought them to that point. Getting millions of taxpayers to work together to influence policy is infinitely more difficult than getting top financial firms to collaborate. "[T]he larger the group," Olson wrote, "the less it will further its common interests."[16]

Nevertheless, there is strength in numbers. No group illustrates this better than AARP (formerly known as the American Association of Retired Persons). Although not every retired person belongs to AARP, its membership dues are so low (five dollars annually) that millions do. AARP has a staff of more than one thousand and is a formidable lobby on social security, Medicare, and other issues affecting retirees. A *Fortune* magazine survey of 2,200 Washington insiders,

TABLE 9-2 | The Fifteen Top-Spending Lobbying Groups, 2011

Group	Lobbying expenditure
U.S. Chamber of Commerce	$46,240,000
General Electric	21,010,000
National Association of Realtors	16,234,310
American Medical Association	16,190,000
ConocoPhillips	16,134,043
AT&T	15,990,000
Blue Cross/Blue Shield	15,845,834
Comcast	14,785,000
American Hospital Association	14,637,047
Pharmaceutical Research and Manufacturers of America (PhRMA)	14,060,000
National Cable & Telecommunication Association	13,080,000
United Technologies	12,650,000
AARP	12,430,000
Verizon Communications	12,290,000
Boeing	12,280,000

Source: Center for Responsive Politics, 2012.

including members of Congress and their staffs, ranked AARP as the nation's most powerful lobbying group.[17] AARP is the only citizens' group that ranks among the top fifteen groups in terms of lobbying expenditures (see Table 9-2). All others in the top fifteen are corporations or business associations.[18]

Inside Lobbying: Seeking Influence through Official Contacts

Modern government is involved in so many issues—business regulation, income maintenance, urban renewal, cancer research, and energy development, to name only a few—that hardly any interest in society could fail to benefit significantly from having influence over federal policies or programs. Moreover, modern government is action oriented. Officials are more inclined to solve problems than to let them fester. When forest fires in Colorado destroyed property worth millions in 2012, the federal government contributed funds to meet the cleanup and other costs to the state and its residents.

Groups seek government's support through **lobbying,** a term that refers broadly to efforts by groups to influence public policy through contact with public officials.[19] Lobbying in America is a big business. An area of the nation's capital known as K Street is populated by lobbying firms. More than twenty thousand lobbyists work in Washington. They are regulated by the Honest Leadership and Open Government Act of 2007 (which amended the Lobbying Disclosure Act of 1995). The legislation requires lobbyists to register and to file detailed reports on their lobbying activities and expenditures.

Interest groups rely on two main lobbying strategies, which have been called *inside lobbying* and *outside lobbying.*[20] Each strategy involves communication with public officials, but the strategies differ in what is communicated and who does the communicating. This section discusses **inside lobbying**, which is based on

lobbying

The process by which interest-group members or lobbyists attempt to influence public policy through contacts with public officials.

inside lobbying

Direct communication between organized interests and policymakers, which is based on the assumed value of close ("inside") contacts with policymakers.

group efforts to develop and maintain close ("inside") contacts with policymakers. (Outside lobbying is described in the next section.)

Acquiring Access to Officials

Through inside lobbying, groups seek to gain direct access to officials in order to influence their decisions. Lobbying once depended significantly on tangible inducements, sometimes including bribes. This old form of lobbying survives, but modern lobbying generally involves subtler methods than simply slipping a cash-filled envelope to a public official. Lobbyists concentrate on contacting policymakers to supply them with information that supports the group's position on pending policy.[21] "If I don't explain what we do . . . Congress will make uninformed decisions without understanding the consequences to the industry," said one lobbyist.[22] For the most part, inside lobbying is directed at policymakers who are inclined to support the group rather than at those who have opposed it in the past. This tendency reflects both the difficulty of persuading opponents to change long-held views and the advantage of working through trusted officials. Thus, union lobbyists work mainly with pro-labor officeholders, just as corporate lobbyists work mainly with policymakers who support business interests.

For lobbyists to be fully persuasive, they must understand the policy process as well as the issue under consideration. For this reason, a "revolving door" exists between lobbying firms and government. Many lobbyists worked previously in government, and some top officials were once lobbyists. Upon retirement, many members of Congress join lobbying firms. Although they are prohibited by law from lobbying Congress for a set period of time after leaving office, they are free to do so thereafter and they usually lobby for groups or on issues they handled during their time in Congress.[23]

POLITICAL THINKING Should the Door Revolve So Freely?

The term *revolving door* is used to describe the tendency for policymakers to become lobbyists, and for lobbyists to become policymakers. There are a few constraints on this practice. High-ranking executives and members of Congress are required, after leaving office, to wait for a period of time before they are allowed to lobby. Nevertheless, there is a substantial interchange between lobbyists and policymakers. Do you think this practice results in better public policy, or worse? What constraints, if any, would you put on the practice?

Money is a key element in inside-lobbying efforts. Many groups have a Washington office and a staff of lobbyists and public relations specialists to convey their message to lawmakers. The amount of money spent on lobbying is staggering—more than $3 billion a year. The Center for Responsive Politics divided the amount of money spent on lobbying in 2009 ($3.47 billion) by the number of hours Congress was in session (2,688) to get a clearer idea of the extent of lobbying. The figure turned out to be a whopping $1.3 million per hour.[24] Consistently among the top spenders is the U.S. Chamber of Congress with an annual lobbying budget of well over $15 million. Other groups get by on much less, but it is hard to lobby effectively on a tiny budget. Given the costs of maintaining a Washington lobby, the domination by corporations and trade associations is understandable. These economic groups have the money to retain high-priced lobbyists, while many other interests do not.

Inside lobbying offers groups a chance to make their policy views known. Access to public officials is critical to the inside-lobbying strategy.

Lobbying Congress

The targets of inside lobbying are officials of all three government branches—legislative, executive, and judicial. The benefits of a close relationship with members of Congress are the most obvious. With support in Congress, a group can obtain the legislative help it needs to achieve its policy goals. By the same token, members of Congress benefit from ties to lobbyists. The volume of legislation facing Congress is heavy, and members rely on trusted lobbyists to identify bills that deserve their attention. When Republican lawmakers took control of the House of Representatives in 2011, they consulted closely with corporate lobbyists on legislative issues affecting business. Congressional Democrats complained, but Republicans said they were merely getting advice from those who best understood business's needs and noted that Democrats had worked closely with organized labor when they were in power.

Lobbyists' effectiveness depends in part on their reputation for fair play. Lobbyists are expected to play it straight. Said one congressman, "If any [lobbyist] gives me false or misleading information, that's it—I'll never see him again."[25] Bullying is also frowned upon. During the debate over the North American Free Trade Agreement in 1993, the AFL-CIO threatened to campaign against congressional Democrats who supported the legislation. The backlash from Democrats on both sides of the issue was so intense that the union withdrew its threat. The safe lobbying strategy is the aboveboard approach: provide information, rely on trusted allies in Congress, and push steadily but not too aggressively for favorable legislation.

Lobbying the Executive Branch

As the range of federal policy has expanded, lobbying of the executive branch has grown in importance. Some of this lobbying is directed at the president and presidential staff, but they are less accessible than top officials in the federal agencies, who are the chief targets.

Group influence is particularly strong in the regulatory agencies that oversee the nation's business sectors. Pharmaceutical companies, for example, provide much of the scientific evidence used by the Food and Drug Administration (FDA) in deciding whether a new drug is safe to market. The potential for influence is high, as are the stakes. After the FDA approved the marketing of the arthritis drug Vioxx, it generated $2.5 billion a year in sales for Merck, the pharmaceutical company that invented and patented it. As it turned out, Vioxx was unsafe. Its users suffered an abnormally high number of strokes and heart attacks. A review panel concluded that the FDA had been lax in testing the drug's safety, bowing to pressure from Merck and its political friends to approve Vioxx for sale.[26]

The FDA is sometimes cited as an example of "agency capture." The capture theory holds that, over time, regulatory agencies side with the industries they are supposed to regulate rather than with the public, which they are supposed to protect. Studies have found that capture theory explains some group-agency relationships, but not all of them. Agency officials are aware that they can lose support in Congress, which controls agency funding and program authorization, if they show too much favoritism toward an interest group.[27] In response to the

Vioxx controversy, as well as problems with other new drugs, Congress passed legislation in 2007 that forced the FDA to toughen its pre- and post-marketing safety tests.

Lobbying the Courts

Judicial rulings in areas such as education and civil rights have made interest groups recognize that they may be able to achieve their policy goals through the courts.[28] Interest groups have several judicial lobbying options, including efforts to influence the selection of federal judges. Right-to-life groups have pressured Republican administrations to make opposition to abortion a prerequisite for nomination to the federal bench. Democratic administrations have in turn faced pressure from pro-choice groups in their judicial nominations.[29] Judicial lobbying also includes lawsuits. For some organizations, such as the American Civil Liberties Union (ACLU), legal action is the primary means of lobbying. The ACLU often takes on unpopular causes, such as the free-speech rights of fringe groups. Such causes have little chance of success in legislative bodies but may prevail in a courtroom.

As interest groups have increasingly resorted to legal action, they have often found themselves facing one another in court. Environmental litigation groups such as the Earthwise Legal Defense Fund and the Environmental Defense Fund have fought numerous court battles with oil, timber, and mining corporations. Even when groups are not a direct party to a lawsuit, they sometimes get involved through amicus curiae ("friend of the court") briefs. An amicus brief is a written document in which a group explains to a court its position on a legal dispute the court is handling.

Webs of Influence: Groups in the Policy Process

To get a fuller picture of how inside lobbying works, it is helpful to consider two policy processes—iron triangles and issue networks—in which many groups are enmeshed.

Iron Triangles

An **iron triangle** consists of a small and informal but relatively stable set of bureaucrats, legislators, and lobbyists who seek to develop policies beneficial to a particular interest. The three "corners" of one such triangle are the Department of Agriculture (bureaucrats), the agriculture committees of Congress (legislators), and farm groups such as the Associated Milk Producers and the Association of Wheat Growers (lobbyists). Together they determine many of the policies affecting farmers. Although the support of the president and a majority in Congress is needed to enact new policies, they often defer to the judgment of the agricultural triangle, whose members are intimately familiar with farmers' needs.

Groups embedded in iron triangles have an inside track to well-positioned legislators and bureaucrats. They can count on getting a full hearing on issues affecting them. Moreover, because they have something to offer in return, the relationship tends to be clad in "iron." The groups provide lobbying support for agency programs and campaign contributions to members of Congress. Agricultural groups, for instance, donate millions of dollars to congressional campaigns during each election cycle. Most of the money goes to the campaigns of House and Senate incumbents who sit on the agriculture committees. Figure 9-1 summarizes the benefits that flow to each member of an iron triangle.

iron triangle

A small and informal but relatively stable group of well-positioned legislators, executives, and lobbyists who seek to promote policies beneficial to a particular interest.

FIGURE 9-1
How an Iron Triangle Benefits Its Participants
An iron triangle works to the advantage of each of its participants—an interest group, a congressional subgroup, and a government agency.

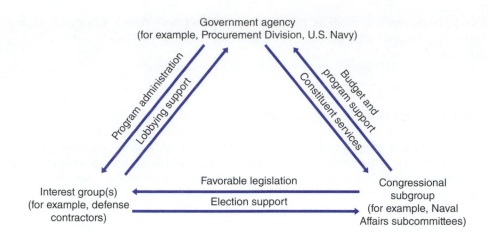

FIGURE 9-1
How an Iron Triangle Benefits Its Participants
An iron triangle works to the advantage of each of its participants—an interest group, a congressional subgroup, and a government agency.

issue network

An informal and relatively open network of public officials and lobbyists who come together in response to a proposed policy in an area of interest to each of them. Unlike an iron triangle, an issue network disbands after the issue is resolved.

Issue Networks

Iron triangles represent the pattern of influence in only certain policy areas and are less common now than in the past. A more frequent pattern of influence today is the **issue network**—an informal grouping of officials, lobbyists, and policy specialists (the "network") who come together *temporarily* around a policy problem (the "issue").

Issue networks are a result of the increasing complexity of policy problems. Participants must have a precise knowledge of the issue at hand in order to address it effectively. Thus, unlike iron triangles, in which a participant's position is everything, an issue network is built around specialized interests and knowledge. On any given issue, the participants might come from a variety of executive agencies, congressional committees, interest groups, and institutions such as universities or think tanks. Compared to iron triangles, issue networks are less stable. As the issue develops, new participants may join the debate and old ones may drop out. Once the issue is resolved, the network disbands.[30]

An example of an issue network is the set of participants who would come together over the issue of whether a large tract of old forest should be opened to logging. A few decades ago, this issue would have been settled in an iron triangle consisting of the timber companies, the U.S. Forest Service, and relevant members of the House and Senate agriculture committees. But as forestlands have diminished and environmental concerns have grown, such issues can no longer be contained within the cozy confines of an iron triangle. Today, an issue network would form that included logging interests, the U.S. Forest Service, House and Senate agriculture committee members, research scientists, and representatives of environmental groups, the housing industry, and animal-rights groups. Unlike the old iron triangle, which was confined to like-minded interests, this issue network would include opposing interests (for example, the loggers and the environmentalists). And unlike an iron triangle, the issue network would dissolve once the issue that brought the parties together was resolved.

In sum, issue networks differ substantially from iron triangles. In an iron triangle, a common interest brings the participants together in a long-lasting and mutually beneficial relationship. In an issue network, an immediate issue brings together the participants in a temporary network that is based on their ability to knowledgeably address the issue and where they play out their separate interests before disbanding once the issue is settled. Despite these differences, iron triangles and issue networks do have one thing in common: they are arenas in which organized groups exercise influence. The interests of the general public may be taken into account in these webs of power, but the interests of the participating groups are foremost.

U.S. Forest Service rangers start a controlled-burn fire to clear ground for the planting of new-growth trees. The U.S. Forest Service, which is part of the Department of Agriculture, oversees the national forests, as well as their use by logging, mining, and other industries. At an earlier time, decisions about the use of national forests typically would have been made in an iron triangle consisting of forest service bureaucrats, Senate and House agricultural committee members, and industry representatives. However, ever since the environmental movement raised awareness of how the national forests are managed, decisions about their use have involved issue networks that include environmentalists, research specialists, community leaders, and others in addition to the traditional decision makers.

Outside Lobbying: Seeking Influence through Public Pressure

Although an interest group may rely solely on inside lobbying, this approach is not likely to be successful unless the group can demonstrate that it represents an important constituency. Accordingly, groups also engage in **outside lobbying,** which involves bringing constituency ("outside") pressure to bear on policymakers (see Table 9-3).[31]

Constituency Advocacy: Grassroots Lobbying

One form of outside pressure is **grassroots lobbying**—that is, pressure designed to convince government officials that a group's policy position has popular support. Grassroots lobbying is a specialty, for example, of AARP. When major legislation affecting retirees is pending, AARP swings into action. Congress receives more mail from members of AARP than it does from members of any other group. AARP's

outside lobbying
A form of lobbying in which an interest group seeks to use public pressure as a means of influencing officials.

grassroots lobbying
A form of lobbying designed to persuade officials that a group's policy position has strong constituent support.

TABLE 9-3 | Tactics Used in Inside and Outside Lobbying Efforts

Inside lobbying	Outside lobbying
Developing contacts with legislators and executives	Encouraging group members to write, phone, or e-mail their representatives in Congress
Providing information and policy proposals to key officials	Seeking favorable coverage by news media
Forming coalitions with other groups	Encouraging members to support particular candidates in elections
	Targeting group resources on key election races
	Making political action committee (PAC) contributions to candidates

support was instrumental, for example, in the enactment in 2003 of a controversial prescription drug program for the elderly. Until AARP's last-minute endorsement, the program seemed headed for a narrow defeat in Congress.

Grassroots lobbying seeks to get members of the public to take action—for example, by participating in a demonstration or sending an e-mail—that will get policymakers' attention and convince them that a policy position has broad support. A case in point is the 2000 legislation that resulted in the permanent normalization of trade relations with China. Most business lobbies supported the proposed legislation, and several of them launched grassroots lobbying efforts. Boeing Corporation, for example, asked its employees, subcontractors, and suppliers—more than 40,000 in all—to contact members of Congress. Motorola was among the other corporations that engaged in grassroots lobbying on the issue of trade with China. Motorola spent more than $1 million on media advertising that highlighted a toll-free number through which people could contact members of Congress.[32]

Electoral Action: Votes and Money

An "outside" strategy can also include election activity. "Reward your friends and punish your enemies" is a political adage that loosely describes how interest groups view elections. One lobbyist said it directly: "Talking to politicians is fine, but with a little money they hear you better."[33] The possibility of campaign opposition from a powerful group can restrain an officeholder. Opposition from the three-million-member National Rifle Association, for example, is a major reason the United States has lagged behind other Western societies in its handgun control laws, despite polls indicating that a majority of Americans favor such laws.

political action committee (PAC)

The organization through which an interest group raises and distributes funds for election purposes. By law, the funds must be raised through voluntary contributions.

Political Action Committees (PACs)

A group's contributions to candidates are funneled through its **political action committee (PAC).** A group cannot give organizational funds (such as corporate profits or union dues) directly to candidates, but through its PAC, a group can solicit voluntary contributions from members or employees and then donate this money to candidates. A PAC can back as many candidates as it wants but is legally limited in the amount it can contribute to a single candidate. The ceiling is $10,000 per candidate—$5,000 in the primary campaign and $5,000 in the general election campaign. (These financial limits apply to candidates for federal office. State and local campaigns are regulated by state laws, and some states allow PACs to make unlimited contributions to individual candidates.)

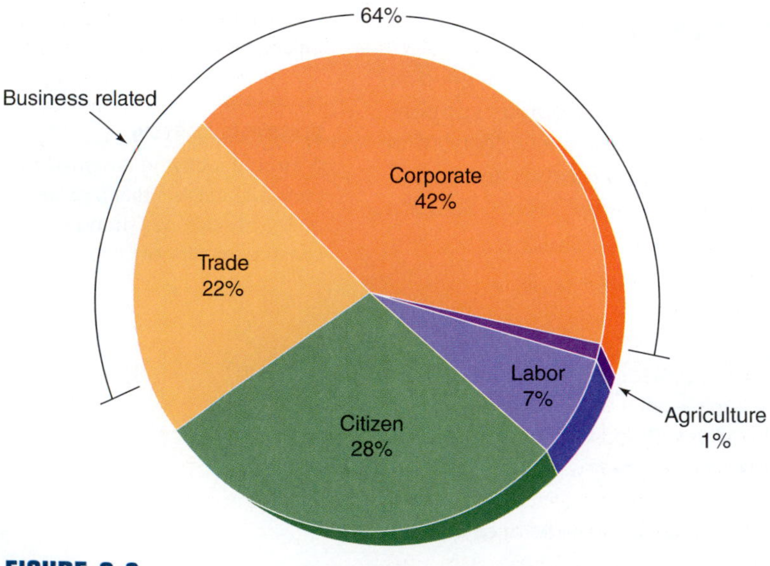

There are more than four thousand PACs, and PAC contributions account for roughly a third of total contributions to congressional campaigns. Their role is less significant in presidential campaigns, which are bigger in scale and depend largely on individual contributors.

More than 60 percent of all PACs are associated with businesses (see Figure 9-2). Most of these are corporate PACs, such as the Ford Motor Company Civic Action Fund, the Sun Oil Company Political Action Committee, and

FIGURE 9-2
Percentage of PACs by Category
Most PACs represent business. Corporate and trade association PACs make up roughly three out of every five PACs.
Source: Federal Election Commission, 2010.

the Coca-Cola PAC. The others are tied to trade associations, such as RPAC (National Association of Realtors). The next-largest set of PACs consists of those linked to citizens' groups (that is, public-interest, single-issue, and ideological groups), such as the liberal People for the American Way and the conservative National Conservative Political Action Committee. Labor unions, once the major source of group contributions, constitute less than 10 percent of PACs.

PACs contribute roughly eight times as much money to incumbents as to their challengers. PACs recognize that incumbents are likely to win and thus to remain in positions of power. One PAC director, expressing a common view, said, "We always stick with the incumbent when we agree with them both."[34] To some extent, the tendency of PACs to back incumbents has blurred long-standing partisan divisions in campaign funding. Business interests are especially pragmatic. Although they tend to favor Republican candidates, they are reluctant to anger Democratic incumbents. The result is that Democratic incumbents, particularly in House races, have received substantial support over the years from business-related PACs.[35] Other PACs, of course, are less pragmatic. The Christian Coalition of America, for example, backs only candidates who take conservative stands on issues such as school prayer and abortion.

Super PACs

A few short years ago, the term "super PAC" was not part of the political lexicon. That changed when the Supreme Court ruled in *Citizens United v. Federal Election Commission* (2010) that federal laws restricting campaign spending by corporations and unions violated their right of free expression. The Court held that corporations and unions can spend an unlimited amount of their funds on elections, as long as the spending is not coordinated directly with that of candidates and parties (see Chapters 1 and 8).[36] In a follow-up case, a lower federal court ruled that political activists can form independent campaign committees to solicit and spend corporate, union, and individual contributions,

These rulings spawned **super PACs** or, as they are officially called, *independent-expenditure-only-committees* (IEOCs). These campaign groups are not allowed to give money directly to candidates or parties, but they are otherwise more or less free to spend as much as they want. Moreover, the Federal Election Commission (FEC) has ruled that candidates can participate to a degree in super PAC activities. They can, for example, speak at super PAC fundraisers as long as they do not solicit contributions in excess of the amount they can legally take directly from groups. More than seventy-five super PACS were involved in the 2010 congressional elections, spending a combined total of $75 million. During the 2012 campaigns for president and Congress, their numbers more than doubled, as did their spending.

Super PACs have been the subject of hot debate. Although regular PACs have been criticized as giving groups too much influence over lawmakers, the criticisms have been muted by the fact that these PACs raise their money through small contributions and are strictly limited in how much they can give to a single candidate. Not so for super PACs. They can accept contributions of any size and can focus their spending entirely on the election or defeat of a single candidate. Unlike regular PACs, they are also not required by law to disclose in a timely way the sources of their funds. In the 2010 campaign, roughly half of the spending by Republican-aligned super PACs came from undisclosed donors. Democrats protested but found themselves on the losing end of the campaign and changed their approach in 2012. Said one Democratic organizer: "In 2010 . . . we sat on our hands in protest and got stomped on the airwaves and at the ballot box. Politics is a prize fight, and when you're getting pounded in the ring, you don't complain to the ref, you fight back."[37]

super PACs
Election committees that are unrestricted in their fundraising and spending as long as they do not coordinate their campaign efforts with that of a candidate.

DEBATING THE ISSUES POLITICAL THINKING IN ACTION

Are Super PACs a Good Thing?

The Supreme Court's decision in *Citizens United* opened the door to so-called super PACs that can raise and spend unlimited amounts of money on campaigns as long as they do not coordinate their activities with those of the candidate they support. Super PACs are controversial. To some observers, they corrupt the electoral process by giving big-money contributors too much influence in U.S. elections. Critics also point out that the campaign messages of some super PACs bear little relationship to the truth. Other observers say that super PACs bring additional voices and views into the campaign, thus widening the debate, which helps voters to better understand what's at issue. Here are two opposing opinions on the issue of super PACs, one by John Samples of the CATO Institute, a conservative think tank, and one by Fred Wertheimer, a liberal activist who headed Common Cause and is now president of a campaign-reform group, Democracy 21.

YES Everyone loves to hate super PACs. One critic said they were "a new political animal that is ugly, loud, anti-democratic." In fact, super PACs enhance democracy. . . . Consider what super PACs actually do. In [the 2012] Iowa [caucus campaign], a super PAC associated with Mitt Romney charged Newt Gingrich with ethical lapses and hypocrisy. In the South Carolina fight, a Gingrich super PAC [used] a $5 million donation to accuse Romney of destroying jobs. In other words, super PACs fund political speech. The First Amendment protects such speech. Are these charges against Gingrich and Romney correct? That's the wrong question. If government could suppress "false" speech, the First Amendment would be meaningless. Those in power would find that their critics are lying and suppress their criticisms. A better question: Do super PACs inform voters? Romney's attack on Gingrich questions his fitness for the GOP nomination and for office. Gingrich's response raises questions about Romney's character and his competence. The information is relevant. Voters must decide if the criticisms are true.

—John Samples, CATO Institute

NO Super PACs are the [latest] campaign finance scandal. . . . They allow influence-seeking individuals, corporations, labor unions and other donors to give unlimited, corrupting contributions to support federal candidates. In particular, the presidential candidate-specific super PACs are serving as vehicles for presidential candidates and donors to massively evade and circumvent restrictions on contributions to the candidates. These restrictions have been enacted over a period of more than a century to prevent the corruption of federal officeholders and combat the undue influence of big money on government decisions. . . . Each presidential candidate-specific super PAC is raising unlimited contributions from individuals and/or from corporations and unions and spending the contributions to directly support its favored presidential candidate. Such contributions would be illegal if given directly to the presidential candidate. Instead they are being given to super PACs that are controlled by close political and personal associates of the presidential candidate who are spending the money only to support that candidate. . . . In effect, candidate-specific super PACS are eviscerating candidate contribution restrictions and restoring the system of legalized bribery that existed in our country in the pre-Watergate era.

—Fred Wertheimer, Democracy 21

Q: Where do you stand on the question of super PACs? If you believe their activities should be curtailed, what changes in the rules governing them would you propose, keeping in mind that free political expression is also a consideration?

A criticism of super PACs is that they cannot be held accountable in any significant way for what they do. When candidates engage in deceptive campaigning, the voters at least have the option of voting against them, Not so for super PACs, They can make outrageous claims without paying a price. Early in the 2012 Republican presidential nominating race, some super PAC televised ads were so untruthful that they were criticized even by the candidates they were intended to help. During South Carolina's primary, Newt Gingrich asked a pro-Gingrich super PAC to stop airing its phony attacks on his Republican opponents. Said Gingrich: "Just as candidates must be certain to accurately present their own records, they also have a responsibility to describe the records of their fellow candidates accurately. And they have a responsibility to make sure that their supporters are doing the same."

Advocates of super PACs argue that the value of free expression cannot be judged by those that abuse it. As they see it, super PACs bring voices and views into the campaign that might otherwise be ignored and that the voters have a right to hear. The result, they say, is a more robust election debate that helps voters to better understand their choices.

The Group System: Indispensable but Biased

As noted in the chapter's introduction, pluralist theory holds that organized groups are a source of sound governance. On one level, this claim is indisputable. Groups are a means of getting government to pay attention to people's needs and interests. Yet the issue of representation through groups is also a question of whether the various interests in society are fairly represented, and here the pluralist argument is less compelling.

The Contribution of Groups to Self-Government: Pluralism

Government does not exist simply to serve majority interests. The fact that most people are not retirees or union members or farmers or college students is not an indication that the interests of such "minorities" are unworthy of government's attention. What better instrument exists for promoting their interests than lobbying groups working on their behalf?

Some pluralists even question the usefulness of terms such as the *public interest*. If people disagree on society's goals and priorities, as they always do, how can anyone claim that their goal or priority represents the public interest? As an alternative, pluralists say that society is best seen as a collection of separate interests and is best served by a process that serves a wide array of these interests. Thus, if manufacturing interests prevail on one issue, environmentalists on another, farmers on a third, minorities on a fourth, and so on until a great many interests are served, the "public interest" will have been served. Pluralists also note that the promotion of the special interest often benefits others as well. Tax incentives for corporations that encourage research and capital investment, for example, can result in job creation and improved goods and services.

Finally, interest groups expand the range of issues that come to lawmakers' attention. Party leaders sometimes shy away from issues that are controversial and, in any case, concentrate on those that have broad impact, which leaves hundreds of issues unaddressed through the party system. Interest groups advocate for and against many of these issues. As political scientist Jack Walker noted, the party and group systems together produce a more responsive and inclusive type of politics than would be the case if one of the systems somehow did not exist.[38]

Flaws in Pluralism: Interest-Group Liberalism and Economic Bias

Pluralist theory has questionable aspects. Political scientist Theodore Lowi points out that there is no concept of the public interest in a system that gives special interests the ability to determine the policies affecting them.[39] Nor can it be assumed that what a lobbying group receives is what the majority would also want. Consider the case of the federal law that required auto dealers to list the known defects of used cars on window stickers. The law was repealed after the

National Association of Automobile Dealers contributed more than $1 million to the reelection campaigns of members of Congress. Auto dealers won another victory when their loans to car buyers were exempted from regulation by the new consumer protection agency that was created as part of the Restoring American Financial Stability Act of 2010.

Lowi uses the term **interest-group liberalism** to describe the tendency of officials to support the policy demands of the interest group or groups that have a special stake in a policy. It is "liberal" in the sense that Republican and Democratic lawmakers alike are in the habit of using government to promote group interests. Each party has its favorites—for example, business groups usually do better when Republicans are in power, and labor groups usually do better when Democrats are in power. But neither party is "conservative" in the sense of being reluctant to use the power of government on behalf of groups. An effect is a weakening of majority rule. Rather than policymaking by the majority acting through its elected representatives, interest-group liberalism involves policymaking by narrow segments of society acting on their own behalf with the help of lawmakers. Another adverse effect is an inefficient use of society's resources: groups get what they want, whether or not their priorities match those of society as a whole.

Another flaw in the pluralist argument resides in its claim that the group system is representative. Although pluralists acknowledge that well-funded interests have more clout, they say that the group process is relatively open and few interests are entirely left out. This claim contains an element of truth, but it is not the full story. As this chapter has shown, organization is an unequally distributed resource. Economic interests, particularly corporations, are the most highly organized, and studies indicate that group politics works chiefly to the advantage of moneyed interests.[40] Of course, economic groups do not dominate everything, nor do they operate unchecked. Many of the citizens' groups formed since the 1960s were created as checks on the power of corporate lobbies. Most environmental groups, for example, work to shield the environment from threats posed by business activity. Activist government has also brought the group system into closer balance; the government's poverty programs have spawned groups that act to protect the programs. Nevertheless, the power of poverty-related groups is a pittance compared with the power of moneyed interests. Nearly two-thirds of all lobbying groups in Washington are business related, and their political clout is enormous.

---

interest-group liberalism
The tendency of public officials to support the policy demands of self-interested groups (as opposed to judging policy demands according to whether they serve a larger conception of "the public interest").

Although Wall Street in New York City is the traditional symbol of financial power in the United States, business firms also dominate political lobbying in Washington. Pluralism theory has traditionally underestimated the power of the business lobby. As political scientist E. E. Schattschneider expressed it, "The flaw in the pluralist heaven is that the heavenly chorus sings with a strong upper-class bias."

A Madisonian Dilemma

James Madison recognized the dilemma inherent in group activity. Although he worried that interest groups would have too much political influence, he argued in *Federalist* No. 10 that a free society must allow the pursuit of self-interest. Unless people can promote the separate opinions that stem from differences in their needs, values, and possessions, they are not a free people.

POLITICAL THINKING   Can Group Power Be Limited?

"Liberty is to faction what air is to fire," wrote James Madison in *Federalist* No. 10. Madison was lamenting the self-interested behavior of factions or, as they are called today, interest groups. Yet Madison recognized that the only way to suppress this behavior was to destroy the liberty that allows people to organize. Numerous efforts have been made to restrict the power of groups without infringing on free expression rights. Laws have been enacted that restrict group contributions to candidates and that require lobbyists to register and report their expenditures. Yet nothing in the end seems to be all that effective in harnessing the self-interested actions of groups. Do you think there is an answer to Madison's concern? Or are the excesses of group politics simply one of the costs of living in a free society?

Ironically, Madison's constitutional solution to the problem of factions is now part of the problem. The American system of checks and balances, with a separation of powers at its core, was designed to prevent a majority faction from trampling on the interests of smaller groups. This same system, however, makes it relatively easy for minority factions—or, as they are called today, special-interest groups—to gain government support. If they can get the backing of even a small number of well-placed policymakers, as in the case of iron triangles, they are likely to get many of the benefits they seek. Because of the system's division of power, they have numerous points at which to gain access and exert influence. Often, they need only to find a single ally, whether it is a congressional committee or an executive agency or a federal court, to get at least some of what they seek. And once they obtain a government benefit, it is likely to endure. Benefits are hard to eliminate because concerted action by the executive branch and both houses of Congress is usually required. If a group has strong support in even a single institution, it can usually fend off attempts to eliminate a policy or program that serves its interest. Such support ordinarily is easy to acquire, because the group has resources—information, money, and votes—that officeholders want.

Economist Mancur Olson concluded that groups ultimately exercise too much power in the American system. When groups are examined individually, their influence is not all that significant. In the aggregate, however, groups receive a huge share of government benefits and have nearly an unbreakable hold on them. Any attempt to trim a group's benefits is met by strenuous political opposition that in nearly every case blocks the attempt. In the process, government loses its flexibility. Resources that might be used to meet new challenges are tied up in previous commitments to organized interests.[41] (Chapters 11 and 13 discuss further the issue of interest-group power.)

Summary

Self-Test www.mhhe.com/pattersontadtx11e

A political interest group is composed of a set of individuals organized to promote a shared concern. Most interest groups owe their existence to factors other than politics. These groups form for economic reasons, such as the pursuit of profit, and maintain themselves by making profits (in the case of corporations) or by providing their members with private goods, such as jobs and wages. Economic groups include corporations, trade associations, labor unions, farm organizations, and professional associations. Collectively, economic groups are by far the largest set of organized interests. The group system tends to favor interests that are already economically and socially advantaged.

Citizens' groups do not have the same organizational advantages as economic groups. They depend on voluntary contributions from potential members, who may lack interest and resources or who recognize that they will get the collective good from a group's activity even if they do not participate (the free-rider problem). Citizens' groups include public-interest, single-issue, and ideological groups. Their numbers have increased dramatically since the 1960s despite their organizational problems.

Organized interests seek influence largely by lobbying public officials and contributing to election campaigns. Using an inside strategy, lobbyists develop direct contacts with legislators, government bureaucrats, and members of the judiciary in order to persuade them to accept the group's perspective on policy. Groups also use an outside strategy, seeking to mobilize public support for their goals. This strategy relies in part on grassroots lobbying—encouraging group members and the public to communicate their policy views to officials. Outside lobbying also includes efforts to elect officeholders who will support group aims. Through political action committees (PACs), organized groups now provide nearly a third of all contributions received by congressional candidates. A more recent development is the emergence of super PACs. They are independent campaign committees that can raise and spend nearly unrestricted amounts of money on elections as long as they do not coordinate their efforts with those of the candidate they are supporting.

The policies that emerge from the group system bring benefits to many of society's interests and often serve the collective interest as well. But when groups can essentially dictate policies, the common good is rarely served. The majority's interest is subordinated to group (minority) interests. In most instances, the minority consists of individuals who already enjoy a substantial share of society's benefits.

CHAPTER 9

Study Corner

Key Terms

citizens' (noneconomic) groups (*p. 225*)
collective (public) goods (*p. 228*)
economic groups (*p. 222*)
free-rider problem (*p. 228*)
grassroots lobbying (*p. 235*)
inside lobbying (*p. 230*)
interest group (*p. 220*)
interest-group liberalism (*p. 240*)

iron triangle (*p. 233*)
issue network (*p. 234*)
lobbying (*p. 230*)
outside lobbying (*p. 235*)
political action committee (PAC) (*p. 236*)
private (individual) goods (*p. 228*)
single-issue politics (*p. 220*)
super PACs (*p. 237*)

Self-Test: Multiple Choice

1. Interest groups tend to do all of the following, *except*
   a. try to influence the political process.
   b. pursue members' shared policy goals.
   c. contribute support to candidates and officials who favor their goals.
   d. change policy positions in order to win elections.

2. If an interest group wants to influence policy decisions at the implementation stage, efforts should be directed primarily toward the
   a. judiciary.
   b. bureaucracy.
   c. White House.
   d. Congress.

3. Interest-group politics is aligned with the political theory of
   a. elitism.
   b. inclusion.
   c. communitarianism.
   d. pluralism.

4. When lobbyists supply policymakers with information and indications of group strength to persuade them to adopt the group's perspective, the activity is called
   a. arm twisting.
   b. wrangling.
   c. outside lobbying.
   d. inside lobbying.

5. Economic interest groups have an advantage over other groups chiefly because of their
   a. ability to muster large numbers of members.
   b. emphasis on training people to run for Congress.
   c. devotion to promoting the broad public interest.
   d. access to financial resources.

6. Compared with super PACs, regular political action committees (PACs) differ in that they:
   a. raise money for election campaigns by soliciting voluntary contributions..
   b. have increased sharply in number since the Supreme Court ruled that corporations and unions can spend unlimited amounts on campaigns.
   c. are restricted in how much they can spend to promote the election of a particular candidate.
   d. play an insignificant role in campaigns.

7. The free-rider problem results when individuals can benefit from the activities of an interest group even if they do not contribute to the group's activities. (T/F)

8. The key tactic of outside-lobbying activity is to put public pressure on officeholders. (T/F)

9. *Interest-group liberalism* is a term used by Theodore Lowi to express the tendency of lawmakers to cater to narrow interests over majority interests. (T/F)

10. Affluent citizens and business groups dominate the interest-group system. (T/F)

Self-Test: Essay

Why are there so many more organized interests in the United States than elsewhere? Why are so many of these groups organized around economic interests—particularly business interests?

Suggested Readings

Baumgartner, Frank R., Jeffrey M. Berry, Marie Hojnacki, David C. Kimball, and Beth L. Leech. *Lobbying and Policy Change: Who Wins, Who Loses, and Why*. Chicago: University of Chicago Press, 2009. A thorough assessment of the impact of lobbying.

Garrett, R. Sam. *"Super PACs" in Federal Elections*. Washington, D.C.: Congressional Research Service, 2011. A first look at the campaign role of super PACs.

Herrnson, Paul S., Ronald G. Shaiko, and Clyde Wilcox, eds. *The Interest Group Connection: Electioneering, Lobbying, and Policymaking in Washington*, 2d ed. Washington, D.C.: CQ Press, 2004. Essays and commentaries on groups and officials and the linkages between them.

Lowery, David, and Holly Brasher. *Organized Interests and American Government*. Long Grove, Ill.: Waveland Press, 2011. A thoughtful overview of interest-group politics.

Lowi, Theodore J. *The End of Liberalism*, 2d ed. New York: Norton, 1979. A thorough critique of interest groups' influence on American politics.

Nownes, Anthony J. *Total Lobbying: What Lobbyists Want (and How They Try to Get It)*. New York: Cambridge University Press, 2006. An up-to-date, thoughtful assessment of the lobbying process.

Olson, Mancur, Jr. *The Logic of Collective Action*, rev. ed. Cambridge, Mass.: Harvard University Press, 1971. A pioneering analysis of why some interests are more fully and easily organized than others.

Rozell, Mark J., Clyde Wilcox, and David Madland. *Interest Groups in American Campaigns*, 2d ed. Washington, D.C.: Congressional Quarterly Press, 2005. An assessment of the role of interest groups in elections.

List of Websites

www.opensecrets.org
The Center for Responsive Politics site; offers information on elections, voting, campaign finance, parties, and PACs.

www.pirg.org
The Public Interest Research Group (PIRG) site; PIRG has chapters on many college campuses, and the site provides state-by-state policy and other information.

www.sierraclub.org
The website of the Sierra Club, one of the oldest environmental protection interest groups, which promotes conservation; provides information on its activities.

www.townhall.com
The website of the American Conservative Union (ACU); includes policy and political information, and has a lively chat room.

Participate!

Consider contributing to a citizens' interest group. Such groups depend on members' donations for operating funds. Citizens' groups cover the political spectrum from right to left and touch on nearly every conceivable public issue. You will not have difficulty locating a group through the Internet that has policy goals consistent with your beliefs and values. If you are interested in contributing your time instead, some citizens' groups (for example, PIRG) have college chapters that might provide opportunities for you to work on issues of personal interest.

Extra Credit

For up-to-the-minute *New York Times* articles, interactive simulations, graphics, study tools, and more links and quizzes, visit the text's Online Learning Center at **www.mhhe.com/pattersontad11e**.

Self-Test Answers

1. d, 2. b, 3. d, 4. d, 5. d, 6. c, 7. T, 8. T, 9. T, 10. T

The News Media: Communicating Political Images

The press in America . . . determines what people will think and talk about, an authority that in other nations is reserved for tyrants, priests, parties, and mandarins. Theodore H. White[1]

The news flashed across America. Mark Sanford, governor of South Carolina, was missing. Neither his wife nor the state troopers in charge of his security knew where he was. Repeated calls to his cell phone went unanswered. As concern mounted, Sanford's press secretary announced that the governor was hiking the Appalachian Trail and would be out of contact until his return.

As it turned out, Sanford was in Argentina visiting a woman with whom he was having a relationship. At a press conference after his return, Sanford admitted to the extramarital affair, saying that it had begun years before as an innocent relationship, only to turn romantic a year earlier. He called her his "soul mate." His admission led state officials to demand his resignation, but Sanford refused. In turn, the South Carolina legislature appointed a committee, granting it the power to hold impeachment hearings. Although impeachment proceedings were eventually dropped, the committee unanimously passed a censure motion and ethics charges were filed against Sanford.

Sanford was elected after having first made a reputation as a tough-minded conservative in the U.S. House of Representatives. In early 2009, he had made headlines by announcing that he would reject the stimulus funds due to his state from the economic recovery bill that Congress had enacted. He was among a half-dozen Republicans whose name cropped up whenever discussion turned to possible 2012 GOP presidential nominees. Nevertheless, nothing that Sanford had done previously—not as a member of Congress, not as governor, and not as a potential presidential contender—generated anything like the headlines accompanying his extramarital affair. It was front-page news throughout the country, the lead story on television newscasts, and the leading topic of conversation on talk shows and Internet blogs. It was also grist for the late-night TV shows. David Letterman, after noting in his opening monologue

news

The news media's version of reality, usually with an emphasis on timely, dramatic, and compelling events and developments.

press (news media)

Print, broadcast, cable, and Internet organizations that are in the news-reporting business.

that Sanford was having an affair with a woman from another country, quipped: "Once again, foreigners taking jobs that Americans won't do."

Although reporters sometimes compare the news to a mirror held up to reality, the news is described more accurately as a refracted version of reality. The **news** is mainly an account of obtruding events, particularly those that are *timely* (new or unfolding developments rather than old or static ones), *dramatic* (striking developments rather than commonplace ones), and *compelling* (developments that arouse people's emotions).[2] These tendencies have their origins in a number of factors, the most significant of which is that news organizations need to attract an audience in order to make a profit. Thus, compared with Sanford's sexual liaison, his work as a top public official was less newsworthy. It was part of the ongoing business of government and did not lend itself to the vivid storytelling of a sex scandal.

News and public affairs outlets are known collectively as the **press** or the **news media.** The news media include broadcast networks (such as ABC and NPR), cable networks (such as CNN and Fox), newspapers (such as the *Chicago Tribune* and *Dallas Morning News*), news magazines (such as *Time* and *Newsweek*), and Internet sites that provide news and commentary (such as Instapundit and the Drudge Report).

This chapter examines the news media's role in American politics. The media are a key intermediary between Americans and their leaders, but they are a different kind of intermediary than political parties and interest groups. The latter seek influence in order to promote particular leaders or policies. Although some members of the press do the same, the media's basic goal is to inform the public about politics and government. Yet, because news organizations also seek to attract an audience in their pursuit of a profit, their news coverage often centers on events of secondary importance. The main ideas presented in the chapter are:

- *The American press was initially tied to the nation's political party system (the partisan press) but gradually developed an independent position (the objective press). In the process, the news shifted from a political orientation, which emphasizes political values and ideas, to a journalistic orientation, which stresses newsworthy information and events.*

- *In recent years, traditional news organizations have faced increased competition for people's attention from cable and the Internet, which has contributed to audience fragmentation and an increase in opinionated and entertainment-laced journalism.*

- *The news media have several functions—signaling (the press brings relevant events and problems into public view), common-carrier (the press serves as a channel through which leaders and citizens can communicate), watchdog (the press scrutinizes official behavior for evidence of deceitful, careless, or corrupt acts), and partisan (the press promotes particular interests and values).*
The traditional media (print and broadcast) contribute mainly to the first three functions whereas the "new" news media (cable and the Internet) contribute mainly to the last one.

At a press conference, South Carolina governor Mark Sanford announces the real reason he had gone missing for several days. His office had claimed he was hiking the Appalachian Trail. As it turned out, Sanford was in Argentina to see a woman with whom he was having an affair. The news media, as their coverage of Sanford illustrates, presents a refracted version of reality, in which sensational developments typically get more attention than the day-to-day problems affecting Americans' lives.

■ *The news audience has been shrinking and fragmenting, partly as a result of new technology and partly because young adults are less likely than older ones to pay attention to news.* One consequence has been a widening gap in the information levels of America's more-attentive and less-attentive citizens.

Historical Development: From the Nation's Founding to Today

Democracy depends on a free flow of information,[3] a fact not lost on America's early leaders. Alexander Hamilton persuaded John Fenno to start a newspaper, the *Gazette of the United States*, as a means of publicizing the policies of George Washington's administration. To finance the paper, Hamilton, as secretary of the treasury, granted it the Treasury Department's printing contracts. Hamilton's political rival, Thomas Jefferson, dismissed the *Gazette*'s reporting as "pure Toryism" and convinced Philip Freneau to start the *National Gazette* as an opposition paper. Jefferson, as secretary of state, gave Freneau the authority to print State Department documents.

Early newspapers were printed a page at a time on flat presses, a process that limited production and kept the cost of each copy beyond the reach of the ordinary citizen. Leading papers such as the *Gazette of the United States* had fewer than fifteen hundred readers and could not have survived without party support. Not surprisingly, the "news" they printed was laced with partisanship.[4] In this era of the **partisan press**, publishers openly backed one party or the other.

Technological innovation in the early 1800s helped bring about the gradual decline of partisan newspapers. With the invention of the telegraph, editors had access to breaking news about events outside the local area, which led them to substitute news reports for opinion commentary. The invention in the late nineteenth century of the power-driven printing press was equally important in that it enabled publishers to print the newspapers more cheaply and quickly. As circulations rose, so did advertising revenues, reducing newspapers' dependence on government patronage. By 1900, some American newspapers had daily circulations in excess of a hundred thousand copies. The period marked the height of newspapers' power and the low point in their civic contribution. A new style of reporting—"yellow journalism"—had emerged as a way of selling papers. It was "a shrieking, gaudy, sensation-loving, devil-may-care kind of journalism which lured the reader by any possible means."[5] A circulation battle between William Randolph Hearst's *New York Journal* and Joseph Pulitzer's *New York World* may have contributed to the outbreak of the Spanish-American War through sensational (and largely inaccurate) reports on the cruelty of Spanish rule in Cuba. A young Frederic Remington (who later became a noted

partisan press
Newspapers and other communication media that openly support a political party and whose news tends to follow the party line.

Yellow journalism was characterized by its sensationalism. William Randolph Hearst's *New York Journal* whipped up public support for a war in Cuba against Spain through inflammatory reporting on the sinking of the battleship *Maine* in Havana Harbor in 1898.

painter and sculptor), working as a news artist for Hearst, planned to return home because Cuba appeared calm and safe, but Hearst supposedly cabled back: "Please remain. You furnish the pictures and I'll furnish the war."[6]

The Objective-Journalism Era

objective journalism

A model of news reporting that is based on the communication of "facts" rather than opinions and that is "fair" in that it presents all sides of partisan debate.

The excesses of yellow journalism led some publishers to devise ways of reporting the news more responsibly. One step was to separate the newspaper's advertising department from its news department, thus reducing the influence of advertisers on news content. A second development was **objective journalism,** which is based on the reporting of "facts" rather than opinions and is "fair" in that it presents both sides of partisan debate. A chief advocate of this new model of reporting was Adolph Ochs of the *New York Times.* Ochs bought the *Times* in 1896, when its circulation was nine thousand; four years later, its readership had grown to eighty-two thousand. Ochs told his reporters that he "wanted as little partisanship as possible . . . as few judgments as possible."[7] The *Times* gradually acquired a reputation as the country's best newspaper. Objective reporting was also promoted through newly formed journalism schools, such as those at Columbia University and the University of Missouri. Within a few decades, objective journalism had become the dominant reporting model.

Until the twentieth century, the print media were the only form of mass communication. By the 1920s, however, hundreds of radio stations were broadcasting throughout the nation. At first the government did not regulate radio broadcasting. The result was chaos. A common problem was that nearby stations often used the same or adjacent radio frequencies, interfering with each other's broadcasts. Finally, in 1934, Congress passed the Communications Act, which regulated broadcasting and created the Federal Communications Commission (FCC) to oversee the process. Broadcasters had to be licensed by the FCC, and because broadcasting frequencies are limited in number, licensees were required to be impartial in their political coverage and were prohibited from selling or giving airtime to a political candidate without offering to sell or give an equal amount of airtime to other candidates for the same office. (An exception was later made for election debates; broadcasters can televise them even if third-party candidates are excluded.)

Television followed radio, and by the late 1950s, more than 90 percent of American homes had a TV set. In this period, the FCC imposed a second restriction— the Fairness Doctrine—on broadcasters. The Fairness Doctrine required broadcasters to "afford reasonable opportunity for the discussion of conflicting views of public importance." Broadcasters were prohibited from using their news coverage to promote one party or issue position at the expense of another. In effect, the objective-reporting model practiced voluntarily by the newspapers was imposed by law on broadcasters.

The Rise of the "New" News

During the era of objective journalism, the news was not entirely devoid of partisanship. Although broadcasters were prohibited by law from editorializing, newspapers were not. Most of them backed one political party or the other on their editorial and opinion (op-ed) pages. Nevertheless, it was usually difficult to tell from their news pages which party they backed editorially. Nearly all of them highlighted the same national stories each day, and if a high-ranking public official got embroiled in a scandal or policy blunder, they played it up, whether the official was a Republican or a Democrat.

The introduction of cable television did not at first change this pattern. Since cable television was transmitted by privately owned wire rather than broadcast over the public airways, it was not required by law to comply with the Fairness Doctrine. Nevertheless, when media mogul Ted Turner started CNN in 1980, he chose to abide by it, instructing his correspondents to pursue a path of partisan neutrality.

In 1987, the FCC concluded that the emergence of cable television and the expansion of FM radio had alleviated the problem of scarce frequencies and rescinded the Fairness Doctrine. Radio stations were the first to respond to the opportunity. They had previously been required to air a liberal or conservative talk show if they aired one of the opposite type. The elimination of the Fairness Doctrine freed broadcasters from this constraint, and scores of radio stations switched from playing music to airing political talk shows.

In the 1990s, the Internet emerged as yet another source of news and political commentary. Unlike a newspaper, broadcast station, or cable company, where the capital investment can run into the tens or even hundreds of millions of dollars, the Internet has a low cost of entry. Anyone with a computer and technical savvy can create a website or blog devoted to news and public affairs. Thousands of such sites now exist. Such sites resemble political talk radio in that they freely mix news and partisanship.

Shown here is the official seal of the Federal Communications Commission (FCC), which oversees the nation's communication policies. In 1987, the FCC rescinded the Fairness Doctrine, a decision that opened the airwaves to partisan talk shows. The FCC also oversees Internet policy, although it has chosen to let the Internet operate in a largely unregulated way.

Journalism and Politics

The news media are Americans' window into the world of politics. For most people, politics is a secondhand experience, something they observe through the media rather than directly. People's mental pictures of events and policy problems, and even their images of political institutions and leaders, stem largely from what they see and hear through the media. Although the media are not the main source of citizens' political *opinions* (such as their opinion on gun control), they are the main source of people's political *perceptions* (such as their perception of the level of crime in their community).

The news media operate as *gatekeepers*. Among the countless story possibilities each day, they determine which events will be covered and which ones will not. These selections, in turn, will influence what citizens are thinking and talking about. What determines these selections? What determines whether a story will make the news, and thus become known to the public, or will not make the news, and thus remain largely out of sight except to those affected directly?

For one thing, the news is shaped by the need of news organizations "to attract and hold a large audience for advertisers."[8] Without advertising or other revenue sources, news organizations would quickly go out of business. The very definition of news—what it is and what it is not—is built around the need to attract the audience's attention. This need leads journalists to cover what they call "hard events"—developments that have taken a clear and definable shape within the past twenty-four hours.[9] It is a reason, for example, that policy issues are not the main focus of political coverage. Issues don't change all that much from one day to the next, which reduces their news value. The first time that a political leader talks about a major policy issue, it is likely to be reported, and it may even make the front page. Thereafter, it's looked upon by journalists as "old news." Journalists are attentive primarily to the things that do change regularly, such as politicians' tactical moves and their level of political support. Almost daily in the last months of a presidential campaign, for example, journalists will report the latest poll results—a level of attention never accorded the campaign's issues.[10]

Yet journalists do not completely neglect their duty to inform the public. They perform four functions—the signaling, common-carrier, watchdog, and partisan functions—that contribute to the public's information needs. We'll look first at the signaling function.

The Signaling Function

The media's responsibilities include a **signaling function—alerting** the public to important developments as soon as possible after they happen. The American media are well equipped to play a signaling role. With their large staffs of experienced reporters, they are uniquely positioned to converge on developing events anywhere in the country and nearly anywhere in the world. The signaling function is performed largely by the traditional media—the wire services, the daily newspapers, and the television networks. Occasionally, an event enters the news stream through the Internet. It was bloggers who first recognized that a racially laden comment by Senate Republican leader Trent Lott in 2002 was big news—big enough that it would eventually force Lott to resign his leadership post. Nevertheless, hundreds of news stories enter the news stream daily, and the great bulk of them are generated by traditional news outlets.

In their capacity as signalers, the media have the power to focus the public's attention. The term **agenda setting** has been used to describe the media's ability to influence what is on people's minds.[11] By covering the same events, problems, issues, and leaders—simply by giving them space or time in the news—the media place them on the public agenda. The press, as Bernard Cohen notes, "may not be successful much of the time in telling people what to think, but it is stunningly successful in telling them what to think about."[12]

Even when media portrayals are out of synch with reality, they have an agenda-setting effect. A striking example occurred in the early 1990s when local television stations, in an attempt to bolster sagging news ratings, upped their crime coverage. "If it bleeds it leads" became the mantra of local TV news. Meanwhile, the national media were playing up several high-profile murder cases including the kidnap-murder of twelve-year-old Polly Klaas in California. Crime was the most heavily reported national issue, overshadowing even coverage of the nation's struggling economy. The effect on public opinion was dramatic. In the previous decade, no more than 5 percent of Americans had believed at any time that crime was the country's biggest problem. By 1994, however,

The norms of objective journalism lead most U.S. news outlets to report the news in similar ways. Also contributing to this tendency is the fact that news organizations assign their reporters to cover many of the same stories.

HOW THE 50 STATES DIFFER   POLITICAL THINKING THROUGH COMPARISONS

IN THE NEWS, OR OUT?

Most of the news that reaches Americans, no matter where they live, originates with a handful of news outlets, such as NBC News. This coverage, however, concentrates on events in a few places. The map shows the relative frequency with which each of the fifty states was mentioned on NBC News during a one-year period.

Q: Why do some states get more coverage than other states?

A: The heavily covered states are usually the more populous ones, which increases the likelihood that a newsworthy event will occur. In NBC's case, coverage is also heavier in states where its permanent correspondents are based. NBC has correspondents stationed in New York, Washington, Los Angeles, Miami, Houston, Atlanta, and Chicago.

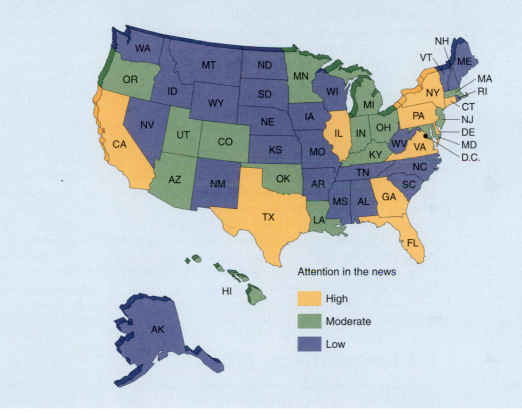

Source: Data compiled by the author from Nexis.

more than 40 percent of Americans said that crime was the top issue facing the nation. Lawmakers got caught up in the public's anxiety by enacting tough new sentencing policies and building new prisons at the fastest rate in the nation's history. The irony was that the level of crime in America was actually *declining* during this period. According to U.S. Justice Department statistics, the rate of violent crime had dropped by 5 percent since 1990.[13]

The press is a powerful agenda setter in part because nearly all major news organizations focus on the same stories and interpret them in pretty much the same way. In view of the freedom and great number of news organizations—there are roughly fifteen hundred daily newspapers and a thousand local television outlets in the United States—it might be expected that Americans would be exposed to widely different versions of national news. The opposite is true. Each day, newspapers and broadcast outlets from coast to coast tend to highlight the same national issues and events.

Objective journalism is one reason the national news is everywhere pretty much the same. Unlike some European news systems, in which journalism norms allow and even encourage reporters to present the news through a partisan lens, reporters at most U.S. news organizations are expected to treat the political parties and their leaders in a balanced way. They do not always do so, but in their quest for balance, American reporters tend toward a common interpretation of political developments, as opposed to a Republican version or a Democratic version. In addition, most news outlets lack the resources to gather news outside their own location and rely for this coverage on the wire services, particularly the Associated Press (AP), which has three thousand reporters stationed throughout the country and the world to gather news stories and transmit them to subscribing news organizations. More than 95 percent of the nation's dailies (as well as most broadcast news stations) subscribe to the AP, which, because it serves the full range of American news outlets, studiously avoids partisanship in preparing its stories. Even the top U.S. newspapers—including the *New York Times, Wall Street Journal, Los Angeles Times, Washington Post,* and *Chicago Tribune*—give similar coverage to the same top stories each day. They differ mostly in their feature and follow-up reports, which usually appear on the inside pages rather than the front page.

Local television stations also depend on outside sources for their national news coverage. Television production is hugely expensive, which limits the ability of local stations to produce anything except local news. For their national coverage, they rely on video feeds from the leading television networks—ABC, CBS, NBC, CNN, Fox, and MSNBC. Even the national networks have a similar lineup of stories. Most network newscasts are a half hour in length, with ten minutes devoted to advertising. With so little time for news, the day's top stories tend to dominate the newscasts of all networks. Moreover, network correspondents cover the same beats and rely on many of the same sources, which lead them to report more or less the same things. After filming a congressional hearing, for example, network correspondents are likely to agree on what was most newsworthy about it—often a testy exchange between a witness and one of the committee members.

The Common-Carrier Function

common-carrier function

The media's function as an open channel through which political leaders can communicate with the public.

The press also exercises a **common-carrier function,** serving as a conduit through which political leaders communicate with the public. The justification for this role is straightforward. Citizens cannot support or oppose a leader's plans and actions if they do not know about them, and leaders require news coverage if they are to get the public's attention and support.

Indeed, national news focuses largely on the words and actions of top political leaders, particularly the president (see Chapter 12). Presidents pursue what has come to be known as the "Rose Garden strategy"—so-called because many of their pronouncements are delivered in the flower garden just outside the Oval Office. More than two hundred reporters are assigned to cover the White House, where they receive daily briefings.[14]

Although officials sometimes succeed in getting favorable coverage, two things blunt their efforts to manage the news. One is journalists' norm of partisan neutrality. Although reporters depend heavily on official sources, they often present the positions of leaders of both parties—the "he said, she said" style of reporting. If the president, secretary of defense, Senate majority leader, or other high-ranking official says or does something newsworthy, the news report often includes a contrary statement or action by another individual, usually of the opposite party.

HOW THE U.S. DIFFERS   POLITICAL THINKING THROUGH COMPARISONS

Public Broadcasting

Public broadcasting got off to a slow start in the United States. Unlike the case in Europe, where public broadcasting networks (such as Britain's BBC) were created at the start of the radio age, the U.S. government in the 1930s handed control of broadcasting to commercial networks, such as NBC and CBS. By the time Congress decided in the 1960s that public broadcasting was needed, the commercial networks were so powerful that they convinced Congress to assign it second-class status. Public broadcasting was poorly funded and was denied access to the most powerful broadcast frequencies. In fact, most television sets in the 1960s had tuners that could not dial in the stations on which public broadcast programs were aired. Not surprisingly, public broadcasting faltered at the beginning and still operates in the shadow of commercial broadcasting.

Nevertheless, public broadcasting does have a success story—NPR. Since the early 1990s, NPR's audience has more than tripled. Each week, more than twenty million Americans listen to NPR, many of them on a regular basis. NPR's growth is a stark contrast to what has happened to commercial newscasts during the same period. The combined audience of the ABC, CBS, and NBC evening newscasts is now half that of the early 1980s. NPR has built its audience through a strategy opposite to that of the commercial networks. As the news audiences of these networks declined in the face of widening competition

from cable television, they "softened" their newscasts—boosting entertainment content in the hope of luring viewers away from cable programs. Former FCC chairman Newton Minow derided the change as "pretty close to tabloid." In contrast, NPR has held to the notion that news is news and not also entertainment. Although NPR carries features, they are typically tied to news developments. Studies indicate that NPR's audience is more politically interested and informed than any other broadcast news audience. Many of its listeners are refugees from the broadcast network news they used to watch but now find to be lacking in substance.

Q: What effect on public information might have resulted from the U.S. government's decision in the 1930s to base the nation's broadcasting system on commercial stations rather than public stations?

A: In countries like Britain, where public broadcasting has been well funded from the start, it has set a standard for high-quality news that conditions the public to prefer it and to expect it from other news providers as well. In the United States, public broadcasting depends on stories reported first by commercial outlets, where the profit motive can lead to news based more on its audience appeal than its social relevance. Accordingly, many Americans have become accustomed to, and even prefer, news that has an entertainment component.

Second, although news typically originates in the words and actions of political leaders, they do not monopolize the news, particularly on television. TV news is now more journalist centered than it is newsmaker centered.[15] In an effort to keep their viewers tuned in, television newscasts use a fast-paced format in which each story has multiple pieces woven together in story form, with the journalist acting as the storyteller. One indicator of this format is the "shrinking sound bite" in presidential campaigns. In the 1960s, a candidate's sound bite (the length of time within a television story that a candidate speaks without interruption) was more than forty seconds on average.[16] In recent campaigns, the average sound bite has been less than ten seconds, barely enough time for the candidate to utter a long sentence (see Figure 10-1). It is the journalists, not the candidates, who do most of the talking. For every minute that presidential candidates spoke on the network evening newscasts during recent campaigns, the journalists who were covering them spoke for more than five minutes.[17]

Journalists frame politics differently than do officials. **Framing** is the process of selecting certain aspects of a situation and using them as the framework for shaping the message.[18] Whereas officials frame politics primarily in the context of policy problems and issues, journalists frame it mainly in the context of the "political game."[19] They focus on political strategy and infighting, portraying politics largely as a struggle for personal power and competitive advantage. For the journalist, the strategic frame has a clear advantage over the

framing

The process by which the media play up certain aspects of a situation while downplaying other aspects, thereby providing a particular interpretation of the situation.

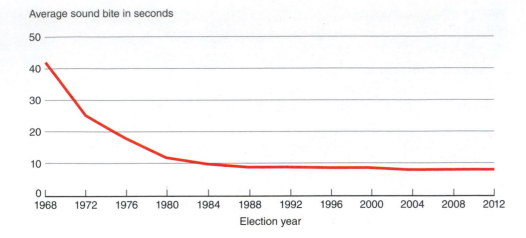

FIGURE 10-1

The Shrinking Sound Bite of Television Campaign Coverage
The average length of time that presidential candidates are shown speaking without interruption on broadcast television newscasts has declined sharply in recent elections.

Source: Adapted from various sources.

watchdog function

The accepted responsibility of the media to protect the public from incompetent or corrupt officials by standing ready to expose any official who violates accepted legal, ethical, or performance standards.

policy frame.[20] Journalists can report the game—telling the story of which side is winning and which is losing in an election campaign or policy dispute—without stepping outside the bounds of objective journalism. This portrayal "primes" the audience to view politicians more as strategists than as leaders. (*Priming* refers to the process by which a message's content activates certain opinions but not others.)[21]

The Watchdog Function

The American press has assumed responsibility for exposing incompetent, hypocritical, and corrupt officials. In this **watchdog function,** the press stands ready to expose officials who violate accepted legal, ethical, or performance standards. The American news media have rightfully been called a fourth branch of government—part of the political system's checks on abuses by those in power.

American journalists have not always vigorously fulfilled their watchdog function. After the terrorist attacks of September 11, 2001, the news media stepped back from their watchdog role. Press oversight of political leaders and institutions fell sharply, as journalists sought to contribute to a newfound sense of national unity and purpose. NBC News outfitted its peacock logo with stars and stripes after the World Trade Center and Pentagon attacks, and computer-generated flags festooned the other networks. Although there was some critical reporting during the lead-up to the 2003 invasion of Iraq, news organizations did not closely scrutinize the Bush administration's arguments in favor of war and downplayed the arguments of those that questioned whether Iraq was enough of a threat to U.S. security to justify an invasion.[22]

However, the Iraq invasion was the exception rather than the rule. Journalists are typically skeptical of politicians' motives and actions, an outlook that deepened during the Vietnam War. A turning point was the *New York Times*'s publication in 1970 of the so-called Pentagon Papers—classified documents revealing that government had deceived the public by claiming that the war in Vietnam was going well when in fact it was going badly. The Nixon administration tried to block publication of the documents but was overruled by the Supreme Court (see Chapter 4). The Watergate scandal gave journalists further reason to believe that they should not take politicians at their word. Led by investigative reporting of the *Washington Post*, the press uncovered evidence that high-ranking officials in the Nixon administration had lied about their role in the 1972 burglary of the Democratic National Committee's headquarters and the subsequent cover-up. President Richard Nixon was forced to resign, as was his attorney general, John Mitchell.

Ever since Watergate, the press usually has been quick to pounce on any sign of public wrongdoing. An example is the *Washington Post* exposé of neglect at the Walter Reed Army Hospital in the handling of wounded U.S. soldiers from the Iraq and Afghanistan conflicts. The *Post*'s reporters conducted stakeouts at the hospital, talked with dozens of patients and staff, and secured hundreds of documents in the course of their investigation. The *Post*'s stories led to congressional hearings and eventually forced the Department of Veterans Affairs to change health care practices at all medical facilities.

The Internet, with citizens acting in the role of journalists, has expanded the media's watchdog capacity. Virtually any public event involving a major politician today is likely to be filmed or taped by someone in attendance, which can land a politician in trouble. At a private campaign fundraiser during the 2012 presidential election, for example, Mitt Romney was asked about his strategy for winning the election. "There are 47 percent of the people who will vote for [Obama] no matter what," Romney said. "[They] believe that they are entitled to health care, to food, to housing, to you-name-it." Dismissing them as people "who pay no taxes," Romney went on to say: "[M]y job is not to worry about those people. I'll never convince them they should take personal responsibility and care for their lives." Romney was unaware that someone at the fundraiser was recording his remarks on a cell phone, which ended up in the hands of the media. Pundits had a field day, asking whether the multi-millionaire Romney was completely out of touch with ordinary people, that the non-taxpayers he was talking about included retirees on social security and members of the armed services.

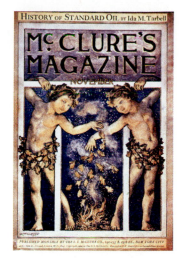

Watchdog reporting in the United States traces to the Progressive Era of the early 1900s, when journalists began to aggressively pursue public and private sector wrongdoing, such as unsafe factory conditions. Known as muckrakers, several of these reporters gained national fame, including Ida Tarbell, Upton Sinclair, and Lincoln Steffens. The now-defunct *McClure's* magazine was the primary outlet for their stories. This particular issue featured Tarbell's detailed account of Standard Oil's monopolistic practices.

POLITICAL THINKING   Is Press Freedom a Right *and* a Responsibility?

Freedom of the press is guaranteed by the First Amendment, making the press the only private institution that has a specific constitutional right designed for its benefit. Does press freedom bestow on the news media an obligation to act in the public interest? If so, what is that obligation and do you think the media are fulfilling it?

The Partisan Function

Traditionally, the **partisan function**—acting as an advocate for a particular viewpoint or interest—has been the responsibility of political leaders, institutions, and organizations. Today, however, the news media—particularly the newer of these media—also function in that capacity.

partisan function

Efforts by media actors to influence public response to a particular party, leader, issue, or viewpoint.

Traditional Media: Mostly Neutral

During the era of the partisan press, newspapers sought to guide their readers' opinions. In the presidential election campaign of 1896, for example, the *San Francisco Call*, a Republican newspaper, devoted 1,075 column-inches of photographs to the Republican ticket of McKinley-Hobart and only 11 inches to their Democratic opponents, Bryan and Sewell.[23] San Francisco Democrats had their own oracle, the Hearst-owned *Examiner*, which touted William Jennings Bryan as the savior of working men. The emergence of objective journalism brought an end to that style of reporting. Rather than slanting the news to favor the Republican or Democratic side, journalists sought to give their audience both sides, leaving it to them to decide which one was better.

The traditional media—the daily newspapers and broadcast networks—still operate largely in this way. Even their editorial pages, though slanted toward one party or the other, carry at least some opposing opinions so as not to alienate a portion of their readers. Most newspapers also make the safe choice in elections; they endorse incumbents of both parties with much greater frequency than they endorse their challengers.[24]

The traditional broadcast television networks—ABC, CBS, and NBC—do not endorse candidates and claim to be unbiased, although conservatives dispute the claim. In a best-selling book, a former network correspondent, Bernard Goldberg, accused the networks of having a liberal agenda.[25] Such allegations are not completely baseless. Until recently, for example, the concerns of evangelical Christians were rarely a subject of broadcast news except in the context of conflict-ridden issues like creationism and abortion. Also, most broadcast news journalists, as well as most journalists generally, lean Democratic in their personal beliefs.[26]

Nevertheless, scholarly research does not support the allegation that the traditional media have a substantial and systematic liberal bias. Communication scholars David D'Alessio and Mike Allen examined fifty-nine academic studies of media bias and found almost no pattern of bias in newspapers, a slight but insignificant bias in the Democratic direction on television news, and a slight but insignificant bias in the Republican direction in news magazines.[27] In fact, the television-age president with the worst press coverage was a Democrat, Bill Clinton. The Center for Media and Public Affairs found that Clinton's negative coverage exceeded his positive coverage in every quarter of every year of his two-term presidency—a dubious record that no president before or since has equaled.[28]

Instead of a strong partisan bias, scholars have highlighted a different kind of network bias—the networks' preference for the negative.[29] The news turned negative at the time of Vietnam and Watergate and has stayed that way. The networks' preference for "bad news" can be seen, for example, in their coverage of presidential candidates. Nearly all nominees since the 1980s have received mostly negative coverage during the course of the campaign. "Bad news" has characterized network coverage of Democratic and Republican nominees alike.[30] Congress has fared no better. Congressional coverage has been steadily negative since the 1970s, regardless of which party controlled Congress or how much or little was accomplished. "Over the years," concluded scholar Mark Rozell, "press coverage of Congress has moved from healthy skepticism to outright cynicism."[31] (Studies indicate that the press's negative bent is a prime reason why Americans have an unfavorable view of politicians and political institutions.[32])

The networks' negativity helps to explain why they are widely perceived as biased. Research indicates that negative news is perceived differently by those who support and those who oppose the politician being attacked. Opponents tend to see the criticism as valid whereas supporters tend to see it as unjustified and therefore biased.[33] It is not surprising, then, that Democrats during Bill Clinton's presidency thought that the networks favored the Republicans while Republicans during George W. Bush's presidency thought that the networks favored the Democrats. Such findings do not mean that the networks are completely unbiased, for they are not. The findings do indicate, however, that much of the perceived bias is in the eye of the beholder.[34]

DEBATING THE ISSUES   POLITICAL THINKING IN ACTION

Do the News Media Have a Liberal Bias?

A long-running debate about the mainstream news media is whether they have a liberal bias. The charge first surfaced in a large way with the publication of Edith Efron's *The News Twisters* in the late 1960s. Ever since, pundits have gone back and forth on the issue, with conservatives claiming that the press is biased and liberals saying that it is not. In an online debate hosted by National Review Online, Brent Bozell III and Eric Alterman faced off on the issue. Excerpts of their written statements are provided below. Bozell is a conservative pundit who founded the Media Research Center, which is dedicated to publicizing examples of liberal bias in the mainstream press. Alterman is a liberal pundit who writes critically of the mainstream press but rejects the claim that its faults include a liberal bias.

YES Just don't ask a liberal if there is a liberal bias in the national news media. . . . No matter how many times the obvious is proven, and no matter how many ways that evidence is documented, the response from the liberal elites is always the same. Noise. For decades conservatives have charged that a liberal bias dominated the press; at every turn the liberals in the press have denied it. But when irrefutable evidence is presented—say, a national survey . . . showing that . . . by 50–14 percent [journalists] see themselves as Democrats over Republicans; and that while 61 percent describe themselves as liberal, only two percent dare call themselves "conservative"—how do they respond? OK, they concede, we may be philosophically liberal, but it doesn't prove our philosophy affects our performance. But how can such an overwhelming bias *not* affect the work product? Noise. What, exactly, is a liberal denying when he denies a liberal bias in the media? Most journalists continue to promote the mythology that bias is nonexistent in the news business, an amazing proposition given that it is *impossible* not to be biased. What is news? What is the day's top news story? What is to be the lead? Who is to be cited? What ought to be the conclusion? These and so many others are the daily questions a reporter faces, and every single one demands a subjective, biased response. So why do so many journalists deny the obvious? First and foremost, because they really do believe their liberalism is mainstream. . . . Making noise.

—*L. Brent Bozell III, president, Media Research Center*

NO That the so-called liberal media were biased against the administration of Ronald Reagan is an article of faith among Republicans. Yet [Reagan advisor] James Baker, perhaps the most media savvy of them, owned up to the fact that any such complaint was decidedly misplaced. "There were days and times and events we might have had some complaints [but] on balance I don't think we had anything to complain about," he explained to one writer. Patrick Buchanan, among the most conservative pundits and presidential candidates in Republican history, found that he could not identify any allegedly liberal bias against him during his presidential candidacies. "I've gotten balanced coverage, and broad coverage—all we could have asked. For heaven sakes, we kid about the 'liberal media,' but every Republican on earth does that." And even William Kristol, without a doubt the most influential Republican/neoconservative publicist in America today, has come clean on this issue. "I admit it," he told a reporter. "The liberal media were never that powerful, and the whole thing was often used as an excuse by conservatives for conservative failures." Nevertheless, Kristol apparently feels no compunction about exploiting and reinforcing ignorant prejudices of his own constituency. In a 2001 subscription pitch to conservative potential subscribers of his Rupert Murdoch-funded magazine, Kristol complained, "The trouble with politics and political coverage today is that there's too much liberal bias. . . . There's too much tilt toward the left-wing agenda. Too much apology for liberal policy failures. Too much pandering to liberal candidates and causes." (It's a wonder he left out "Too much hypocrisy.")

—*Eric Alterman, author of What Liberal Media?*

Q: What biases—liberal, conservative, or otherwise—do you detect in the way journalists cover public affairs?

Talk Shows: Mostly Conservative

The broadcast networks' partisan bias—real and perceived—has been an issue for conservatives at least since 1970 when Republican vice president Spiro Agnew called the networks "nattering nabobs of negativism." Nevertheless, Republicans could only pressure the networks to cover politics differently in that there was

Broadcast news dominated television until the advent of cable. Today, the ABC, CBS, and NBC newscasts compete for viewers with those of Fox News, CNN, and MSNBC. Cable news organizations have also developed new models of journalism. For example, CNN specializes in live coverage of events while Fox News pursues a politically conservative news agenda. Shown here is Bill O'Reilly of Fox News, who has the largest audience among the TV talk show hosts.

no ready alternative. Cable television and the rescinding of the Fairness Doctrine changed that situation by providing a host of new options, including partisan talk shows.

On both radio and television, most of the successful partisan talk shows have been hosted by conservatives. The host with the largest audience is radio's Rush Limbaugh. In the top twenty-five radio markets, Limbaugh's show has more listeners, in all age groups, than the listenership of all the top liberal talk shows combined. Limbaugh built his following in the early 1990s with attacks on Bill Clinton, whom Limbaugh variously characterized as a draft dodger, womanizer, and wimp. Limbaugh's success prompted billionaire media mogul Rupert Murdoch to start Fox News in 1996. Murdoch reasoned that hard-core conservatives, because of their distrust of the established networks, would embrace a conservative alternative. He hired Roger Ailes, a Republican political consultant, to run Fox News. Ailes in turn hired a number of conservative talk show hosts, including Bill O'Reilly. Within a few years, propelled by a largely Republican audience, Fox News was the most heavily watched cable news network.

The other two cable news outlets, CNN and MSNBC, responded by hiring talk show hosts of their own, although they chose different marketing strategies. CNN has had a diverse set of hosts while MSNBC has cast itself as the liberal alternative to Fox. MSNBC's lineup features Rachel Maddow, a self-described "liberal policy wonk." The most heavily watched of the liberal talk shows, however, are on Comedy Central rather than a news channel. Jon Stewart's *The Daily Show* and Stephen Colbert's *The Colbert Report* are each seen by more than a million viewers a day.

The Internet: Mostly Liberal

Although the First Amendment protects each individual's right to press freedom, this right in practice was once reserved for a tiny few. Journalist A. J. Liebling wrote that freedom of the press belonged to those with enough money to own a news organization.[35]

Today, because of the Internet, freedom of the press is actively enjoyed by a larger number of Americans than ever before. Although access to the Internet is no substitute for owning a newspaper or a television station, it does provide the ordinary citizen with an opportunity to be part of the news system. Through their websites, citizens can post news and information about public affairs, harangue officials, and argue for public policies. The Internet has reduced the barriers to public communication to a level not seen since colonial days, when pamphleteers like Thomas Paine dominated political communication. Thomas Paine's pamphlet, *Common Sense*, sold over a hundred thousand copies and mobilized American opposition to British rule. "We have the power to begin the world over again," wrote Paine, who also penned the famous line "These are the times that try men's souls."

As was discussed in Chapter 7, the Internet has been a boon for political activists. It has allowed them to engage in unprecedented levels of organizing and fundraising. When it comes to news, however, the Internet's contribution is not as unique. Although there are literally hundreds upon hundreds of websites where news is regularly posted and examined, Internet news is characterized by what analysts call "the long tail." When news-based websites are arrayed by the number of visitors to each site, there are a few heavily visited sites on one end

Unlike talk shows, where conservative viewpoints dominate, Internet blogs and comedy-based news shows are bastions of liberal sentiment. Shown here is *The Colbert Report's* Stephen Colbert, who ran a tongue-in-cheek presidential campaign in 2012. He appointed *The Daily Show's* Jon Stewart to head his Super PAC, which he called his "Definitely Not Coordinated with Stephen Colbert Super PAC."

and thousands of lightly visited sites on the other end—the long tail. As it happens, most of the heavily visited sites are those of the traditional media, including CNN.com, and nytimes.com. In addition, most of the other heavily visited sites, such as Google News, carry news that was gathered and reported first by the established media. In other words, most Americans who go to the Internet for news are seeing news generated by the same sources they otherwise tap. A notable exception is the Huffington Post, which was started in 2005 by liberal activist Arianna Huffington and now has more than fifty journalists on staff. The site has more than fifty million unique visitors a month.

Some blogs also have substantial audiences, although nothing on the scale of the largest traditional outlets. The most successful ones—such as the Drudge Report, Instapundit, Daily Kos, and Boing Boing—are closer in form to talk shows than to news programs in that they freely mix opinion with information about current events. Unlike talk shows, however, most of the successful blogs have a liberal bias.[36] An example is the Daily Kos, which was founded by Markos Moulitsas Zúniga and draws several hundred thousand visitors a day. There, they encounter news reports that are mixed with commentary, sometimes including requests for donations to liberal causes or candidates. An exception to the liberal bent of the blogosphere is the conservative Drudge Report, founded by Matt Drudge, which gained fame in 1998 when it revealed that President Bill Clinton had an affair with a White House intern, Monica Lewinsky.

The News Audience

The news media today are a far different political intermediary than they were only a few decades ago, and the political consequences are substantial. The old media system was dominated by the broadcast networks. They had huge daily audiences, enabling them to alert Americans of all ages and classes to the same events. They also provided a platform for political leaders who, through a single statement or event, could reach tens of millions of citizens. Today's media system is different. The traditional media are still the major players, but their audiences are smaller and their influence has weakened. The audience for news and public affairs is far more fragmented than it was a few decades ago. The audience is spread across dozens of outlets that vary widely in how they present politics, how they portray political leaders, and what aspects of politics they highlight. America today has a **high-choice media system**, one in which people's media exposure—what they see and hear, as well as what they choose not to see and hear—is largely within their control. A result has been the widening of two divides, one relating to partisanship and one relating to public information.

high-choice media system

A media system in which audiences have such a wide range of choices that they can largely control the type of information to which they are exposed.

The Partisan Divide

When cable and the Internet expanded people's options, some observers thought the change would result in a public exposed to a wider set of opinions. The opposite has happened.[37] The Pew Research Center for the People and the Press has been tracking Americans' media preferences for two decades and finds that Americans' news choices are narrowing. Traditional news outlets still have much larger audiences but outlets that convey a partisan point of view are gaining in popularity, particularly among younger adults. Americans increasingly rely on sources that communication information that supports what they already believe.[38] Conservatives tune to right-wing talk shows while liberals tune to those on the left.[39] Political blogs also have like-minded followings.[40] It is rare to find a political blog where people of differing partisan views congregate.[41]

As political scientist Marcus Prior demonstrates in *Post-Broadcast Democracy*, these tendencies contribute to party polarization.[42] Partisan outlets play up partisan differences, praising their side while tearing down the other, contributing to the widening divide in the opinions of liberals and conservatives (see "Party Polarization").

The Information Divide

The U.S. news system now has more outlets—including newspapers, television stations, talk shows, and bloggers—than at any time in its history. Although it might be assumed as a consequence that Americans are more informed about public affairs than ever before, it is not the case. The same media system that makes news available on demand at any time also makes it easy for people to avoid the news. America today has many citizens who consume copious amounts of news. It also has many citizens who consume very little news.

Through the 1970s, most Americans shared a common news experience. In most television markets at the dinner hour, the only choices available to viewers were the ABC newscast, the CBS newscast, and the NBC newscast. Viewers who were intent on watching television in this time period—and 85 percent of households had their TV sets turned on—had no alternative but to sit through the news. Many of them were "inadvertent news viewers"—brought to the news less by a strong preference for it than by an addiction to television.[43] This exposure rubbed off on the children. The evening news was a ritual in many families, and though the children might have preferred something else, they also watched it. By the time these children finished school, many of them had acquired a television news habit of their own.

PARTY
POLARIZATION   Political Thinking in Conflict

Living in Different Media Worlds

Until the 1980s, Americans were immersed in what political scientist Matthew Baum calls "an information commons." The three television broadcast networks—ABC, CBS, and NBC—had huge daily audiences and their newscasts varied only slightly. Each headlined the same stories and interpreted them in much the same way. Viewers were exposed equally to the views of leaders of both political parties. The emergence of cable TV and the rescinding of the Fairness Doctrine disrupted the pattern. Today, Americans have a range of choices, including outlets that convey information through a partisan lens, heaping praise on one party and criticizing the other. Research indicates that this form of communication contributes to partisan polarization. It reinforces citizens' preexisting views while at the same time convincing them that the other side's opinions lack merit.

Shown below are findings from a recent Pew survey of news and political preferences. Respondents were classified by ideology based on their answers to poll questions about policy issues. Two of the resulting classifications were "staunch conservatives" and "strong liberals." As can be seen from the graph, individuals in these two categories have markedly different media preferences, choosing like-minded outlets over those that play up the opposing party.

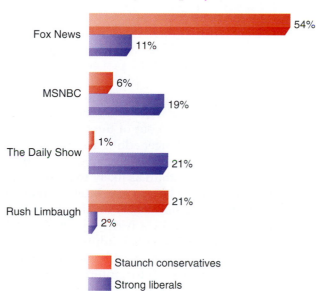

Percentage who regularly watch/listen to:

Outlet	Staunch conservatives	Strong liberals
Fox News	54%	11%
MSNBC	6%	19%
The Daily Show	1%	21%
Rush Limbaugh	21%	2%

■ Staunch conservatives
■ Strong liberals

Source: Pew Research Center for the People & the Press, May 4, 2011.

Q. *Do you find it troubling that partisan media outlets contribute to party polarization or do you think they play an indispensable role in clarifying the differences between the parties? Do you personally rely mostly on the traditional news media or mostly on outlets of the type shown in the above graph?*

Television's capacity to generate an interest in news declined sharply in the 1980s with the rapid spread of cable. Viewers no longer had to sit through the news while waiting for entertainment programs to come on. And television's capacity to generate news interest in children was greatly diminished. Fewer of their parents were watching the dinner-hour news, and even if they were watching, the children, as a Kaiser Family Foundation study revealed, were often in another room watching entertainment shows.[44]

The effect has been to divide Americans in how much attention they pay to news and how much they know about politics. Some Americans get more news than was possible in earlier times. Round-the-clock news is available to anyone with cable TV or the Internet. Yet today's high-choice media system also makes it possible for people to avoid the news with ease. As a result, large numbers of Americans, mostly younger adults, have neglected news in favor of movies, sitcoms, comedy shows, computer games, and other content.[45]

POLITICAL THINKING Are the "New" Media to Blame?

Research indicates that the level of public "misinformation" is increasing. During the lead up to the U.S. invasion of Iraq in 2003, for example, a large portion of the American public falsely believed that the Iraqi regime was allied with the al Qaeda terrorist network. Do you think the slanted messaging of the "new" media—political talk shows, blogs, social networks, and the like—is largely to blame for the increase in misinformation? If not, what else might explain this development?

A few decades ago, the news habits of younger and older adults were similar, as political scientist Martin Wattenberg has shown. In the late 1950s, for example, 53 percent of those in the 21–29 age group regularly read news coverage of national politics, compared with 61 percent in the 30–44 age group, 60 percent in the 45–60 age group, and 57 percent of those over 60. Wattenberg found a similar pattern for television news. "There was little variation in news viewing habits by age," Wattenberg writes. "TV news producers could hardly write off young adults, given that two out of three said they had watched such broadcasts every night."[46] Today, younger adults are substantially less likely than older adults to follow the news regularly. Compared with adults over fifty years of age, those under thirty are only a third as likely to follow public affairs closely through a newspaper, only half as likely to watch television news regularly, and even somewhat less likely to consume news on the Internet.[47] This widening attention gap has been accompanied by a widening "information gap." Wattenberg found that, until the early 1970s, young adults were nearly as knowledgeable about current events and leaders as older adults. Since the 1980s, and increasingly so, young adults have been less informed than older ones. In 2004, for example, adults sixty-five years of age and older could answer correctly 55 percent of factual questions about politics contained in the American National Election Studies (ANES) survey, however, adults under thirty years of age could answer only 36 percent of the questions accurately. In fact, young adults scored lower than all other age groups on every ANES question, whether it was identification of current political leaders, information about the presidential candidates, knowledge of which party controlled Congress, or basic civic facts. The chapter of Wattenberg's book in which these findings are presented is titled pointedly, "Don't Ask Anyone Under 30."[48]

The widening attention and information gaps are most pronounced when comparing across age groups but cut across every age groups. The high-choice media environment of today enables citizens of whatever age to pursue their interests, whether these are news, entertainment, or social networking. For citizens with an interest in news, there's a never ending supply. For those who lack this interest, there are endless other selections. The choices that Americans make affect what they know and don't know about politics. Although the information gap is not new, the gap is widening because today's news system makes it easier for citizens without an interest in news to avoid it.

Summary

Self-Test www.mhhe.com/ pattersontadtx11e

In the nation's first century, the press was allied closely with the political parties and helped the parties mobilize public opinion. Gradually, the press freed itself from this partisan relationship and developed a form of reporting known as objective journalism, which emphasizes fair and accurate accounts of newsworthy developments. That model still governs the news reporting of the traditional media—daily newspapers and broadcasters—but does not hold for the newer media—radio talk shows, cable TV talk shows, and Internet blogs. Although some of them cover politics in the traditional way, many of them transmit news through a partisan lens.

The press performs four basic functions. First, in their signaling function, journalists communicate information to the public about breaking events and new developments. This information makes citizens aware of developments that affect their lives. However, because of the media's need to attract an audience, breaking news stories often focus on developments, such as celebrity scandals, that have little to do with issues of politics and government. Second, the press functions as a common carrier in that it provides political

leaders with a channel for addressing the public. Increasingly, however, the news has centered nearly as much on the journalists themselves as on the newsmakers they cover. In a third function, that of watchdog, the press acts to protect the public by exposing deceitful, careless, or corrupt officials. Finally, the press functions as a partisan advocate. Although the traditional media perform this function to a degree, the newer media—the talk shows and blogs—specialize in it. Their influence has contributed to a rising level of political polarization in the United States.

The news audience has changed substantially in the past few decades. Daily newspapers and broadcast news have lost audiences to cable television and the Internet. At the same time, the emergence of cable television and the Internet has made it easier for citizens to avoid news when using the media. Although some citizens today consume more news than was possible at an earlier time, other citizens—young adults, in particular—consume less news than was previously typical. A consequence is that young adults are less informed politically relative to both older adults and to earlier generations of young adults.

CHAPTER 10

Study Corner

Key Terms

agenda setting (*p. 250*)
common-carrier function (*p. 252*)
framing (*p. 253*)
high-choice media system (*p. 260*)
news (*p. 246*)
objective journalism (*p. 248*)
partisan function (*p. 255*)
partisan press (*p. 247*)
press (news media) (*p. 246*)
signaling (signaler) function (*p. 250*)
watchdog function (*p. 254*)

Self-Test: Multiple Choice

1. Recent trends in the news media include
   a. increased government regulation of news content.
   b. combining the activities of the news and advertising departments.
   c. an increase in partisan news outlets.
   d. an increase in newspaper readership.

2. When the media are playing the role of watchdog, they are primarily
   a. protecting the public from deceitful, careless, incompetent, or corrupt public officials.
   b. conveying objective information about an event and minimizing reporting bias.
   c. trying to get their audience more interested in world affairs.
   d. trying to help their favorite political party at the expense of the other.

3. The news is said to provide a selective depiction of reality because it
   a. emphasizes dramatic events rather than the slow and steady social, economic, and political developments that typically have a larger impact on the nation.
   b. is biased in favor of a Democratic point of view.
   c. emphasizes the daily lives of ordinary Americans rather than the actions of public officials.
   d. places more emphasis on international affairs than on national affairs.

4. The Internet has revolutionized the American media because
   a. it creates a news habit among millions of young adults who otherwise would not care about the news.
   b. it has lowered dramatically the cost of starting a news-based operation, thus opening up the news system to thousands of new outlets.
   c. people are willing to devote hours to news on the Internet, whereas they tend to spend only minutes when reading a newspaper or watching television news.
   d. all of the above.

5. In its signaling function, the news media are trying to
   a. lure an audience.
   b. advance a particular partisan interest.
   c. help leaders to communicate effectively with the public.
   d. bring important events, developments, and issues to the public's attention.

6. The fragmentation of the media system has resulted in all the following except:
   a. increased attention to news among young adults.
   b. increased party polarization.
   c. increased opportunities for citizen journalism, such as blogging.
   d. a high-choice media environment.

7. Objective journalism is based on the reporting of opinions in preference to "facts." (T/F)

8. On television, newsmakers' "sound bites" have gotten shorter over the past half century. (T/F)

9. Studies reveal that much of the perceived bias in television news is due to the viewers' partisanship as opposed to slanted news coverage. (T/F)

10. Liberals tend to prefer talk radio whereas conservatives tend to prefer bloggers. (T/F)

Self-Test: Essay

What are the consequences of the fact that the press is charged with informing the public but at the same time needs to attract an audience in order to make a profit and fund its newsgathering operations?

Suggested Readings

Baum, Matthew A., and Tim J. Groeling. *War Stories: The Causes and Consequences of Public Views of War*. Princeton, N.J.: Princeton University Press, 2009. A study of the public's perceptions of war that includes an examination of the media's role.

Bennett, W. Lance, Regina G. Lawrence, and Steven Livingston. *When the Press Fails: Political Power and the News Media from Iraq to Katrina*. Chicago: University of Chicago Press, 2008. A revealing account of news coverage, particularly during the buildup to the Iraq conflict.

Davis, Richard. *Typing Politics: The Role of Blogs in American Politics*. New York: Oxford University Press, 2009. A thoughtful study of blogging's political impact.

Farnsworth, Stephen J., and S. Robert Lichter. *The Nightly News Nightmare: Media Coverage of U.S. Presidential Elections*. Lanham, Md.: Rowman & Littlefield, 2010. An empirical study of television coverage of elections.

Kerbel, Matthew R. *Netroots: Online Progressives and the Transformation of American Politics*. Boulder, Colo.: Paradigm Publishers, 2009. A look at how the Internet is changing politics in the United States.

Prior, Markus. *Post-Broadcast Democracy: How Media Choice Increases Inequality in Political Involvement and Polarizes Elections*. New York: Cambridge University Press, 2007. A thoughtful assessment of how the new media system is widening the information and partisan divides.

Wattenberg, Martin. *Is Voting for Young People?* 2d ed. New York: Longman, 2007. A careful look at how young adults' political attention and information have changed.

List of Websites

www.drudgereport.com
The website pioneer, through which Matt Drudge (The Drudge Report) has challenged the traditional media's control of the news.

www.fcc.gov
The Federal Communications Commission website; provides information on broadcasting regulations and current issues.

www.mediatenor.com
The website for Media Tenor, a nonpartisan organization that analyzes news coverage on a continuing basis; useful to anyone interested in the media's political coverage.

www.newslink.org
A website that provides access to more than a thousand
news organizations, including most U.S. daily
newspapers.

Participate!

Before the Internet opened new channels of communication,
freedom of the press, which is granted by the First Amendment to all Americans, was enjoyed for the most part only by
the very few who owned or worked in the news media. With
the Internet, the opportunity for citizen communication,
though not unlimited, is greater than at any time in the
nation's history. Take advantage of the opportunity. Meetup.
com is one of literally thousands of Internet sites where you
can participate in discussion forums about politics and
issues. A more ambitious alternative is to start your own Web

log. Blogging is time consuming, but it allows you to create
an agenda of news, information, and opinion—an activity
previously reserved for newspaper editors and broadcast
producers. Either of these options will enable you to make
your voice heard and also help you to hone your citizenship
skills—the ability to communicate, to defend your own
views, and to learn the opinions of others.

Extra Credit

For up-to-the-minute *New York Times* articles, interactive
simulations, graphics, study tools, and more links and quizzes, visit the text's Online Learning Center at **www.mhhe.
com/pattersontad11e**.

Self-Test Answers

1. c, 2. a, 3. a, 4. b, 5. d, 6. a, 7. F, 8. T, 9. T, 10. F

CHAPTER 11

Congress: Balancing National Goals and Local Interests

There are two Congresses. . . . The tight-knit complex world of Capitol Hill is a long way from [the member's district], in perspective and outlook as well as in miles. Roger Davidson and Walter Oleszek[1]

It was a fight the likes of which Washington had never seen. Dozens of times, Congress had routinely raised the debt ceiling, giving the federal government the authority to borrow money to pay its debt obligations. In 2011, however, House Republicans decided to use the ceiling limit to force Democrats into accepting steep cuts in federal spending. As other countries watched, worried that the U.S. government might default on its debt for the first time in history, Democratic and Republican lawmakers stubbornly refused to budge from their positions.

The House Republicans included five dozen newly elected members of Congress, nearly all of whom had campaigned on a pledge to cut government spending and oppose tax increases. Many of their senior colleagues had also received Tea Party backing in the campaign and had likewise pledged to hold the line on taxes and spending. Mindful of the backlash they might face in their next campaign, they were not about to go back on their promise. For his part, Republican House Speaker John Boehner was willing to cut a deal with the Democrats but was handcuffed by opposition within his own party. The Democrats in Congress were also in tough spot. Even though they expressed a willingness to accept some spending cuts, they insisted that a tax increase on wealthy Americans had to be part of the bargain. To do otherwise would be to put them at risk with their constituents, who expected them to protect the government programs upon which they depended.

In the end, Congress reached a compromise that prevented a government shutdown but otherwise left few members happy. The legislative package included modest spending cuts spread over a ten-year period and the formation of a joint bipartisan congressional committee (the so-called "super committee") that would negotiate a larger budget-deficit reduction package and submit it to the House and Senate for an up or down vote. Three months later, the committee disbanded,

The U.S. Capitol in Washington, D.C., with the House wing in the foreground. The Senate meets in the wing at the right of the central rotunda (under the dome). The offices of the House and Senate party leaders—Speaker, vice president, majority and minority leaders and whips—are located in the Capitol. Other members of Congress have their offices in nearby buildings.

having failed to reach agreement. As with the earlier effort, negotiations broke down over whether tax increases would be part of the package.

The story of the debt ceiling negotiations illustrates the dual nature of Congress. It is both a lawmaking institution for the country and a representative assembly for states and districts.[2] Members of Congress have a duty to serve both the interests of their constituencies and the interests of the nation as a whole. The nation's needs sometimes come first, but not always, because the support of the voters back home is necessary to members' reelection.[3] The question of how constituent groups will react to their stands on legislative issues is a persistent concern of members of Congress.

The framers of the Constitution regarded Congress as the preeminent branch of the federal government and granted it the most important of all the powers of government, the power to make the laws: "All legislative powers herein granted shall be invested in a Congress, which shall consist of a Senate and House of Representatives." Congress is granted the authority even to decide the form and function of the executive departments and the lower courts. No executive agency or lower court can exist unless authorized by Congress.

The positioning of Congress as the first among equals in a system of divided powers reflected the framers' trust in representative institutions. Congress was to be the branch where the interests of the people, through the House of Representatives, and the interests of the states, through the Senate, would find their fullest expression. Of course, the framers had an innate mistrust of political power and were not about to give Congress free rein. The Congress was to be subject to checks by the president and the courts (see Chapter 2). Yet the government's most important functions—lawmaking and representation—were granted largely to Congress. The framers' vision of a preeminent Congress has not fully met the test of time, however. Developments in the twentieth century served to shift power from Congress to the presidency and, today, both institutions have a central role in lawmaking. The points emphasized in the chapter are:

■ *Congressional elections have a local orientation and usually result in the reelection of the incumbent.* Congressional office provides incumbents with substantial resources (free publicity, staff, and legislative influence) that give them (particularly House members) a major advantage in election campaigns.

- *Leadership in Congress is provided by party leaders, including the Speaker of the House and the Senate majority leader. Party leaders are in a more powerful position today than a few decades ago because the party caucuses in Congress are more cohesive than in the past.*

- *The work of Congress is done mainly through its committees and subcommittees, each of which has its own leadership and its designated policy jurisdiction.*

- *Congress lacks the central direction and hierarchical organization required to provide consistent leadership on major national policies, which has allowed the president to assume this role. On the other hand, Congress is well organized to handle policies of narrower scope.*

- *Republicans and Democrats in Congress have become more polarized in recent decades with legislative deadlock and delay among the consequences.*

- *Congress's policymaking role is based on three major functions: lawmaking, representation, and oversight.*

Congress as a Career: Election to Congress

In the nation's first century, service in Congress was not a career for most of its members. Before 1900, at least a third of the seats in Congress changed hands at each election. Most members left voluntarily. Because travel was slow and arduous, serving in the nation's capital meant spending months away from one's family. Moreover, the national government was not the center of power that it is today; many politicians preferred to serve in state capitals.

The modern Congress is a different kind of institution. Most of its members are professional politicians, and a seat in the U.S. Senate or House is as high as most of them can expect to rise in politics. The pay (about $175,000 a year) is substantial, as is the prestige of their office, particularly if they serve in the Senate. Not surprisingly, most members of Congress seek to make it a career, which requires them to keep the voters happy. Members of Congress, says political scientist David Mayhew, are "single-minded seekers of reelection."[4] Most of them succeed in their quest (see Figure 11-1). **Incumbents** (as officeholders are called) have a roughly 90 percent probability of winning reelection. Even in congressional elections where an abnormally large number of incumbents lose, a much greater number win. In the 2010 congressional elections, for example, 54 House incumbents lost their reelection bids—more than twice the normal level. In the same election, 334 House incumbents were reelected—six times the number that lost.

incumbent

The current holder of a particular public office.

Using Incumbency to Stay in Congress

The main reason incumbents run so strongly is that many congressional districts and some states are so lopsidedly Democratic or Republican that candidates of the stronger party seldom lose. No more than 75 of the 435 House seats—about one in six—is competitive enough that the weaker party has a realistic chance of victory. In any case, whether their constituency is lopsided or competitive, incumbents have substantial advantages over their challengers, as will now be explained.

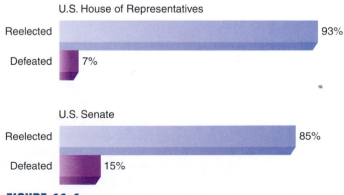

FIGURE 11-1 **Recent Reelection Rates of House and Senate Incumbents** Congressional incumbents have a very good chance of winning another term, as indicated by the reelection rates of U.S. representatives and senators who sought reelection during the last five congressional elections.

constituency

The people residing within the geographical area represented by an elected official.

pork (pork-barrel spending)

Spending whose tangible benefits are targeted at a particular legislator's constituency.

service strategy

Use of personal staff by members of Congress to perform services for constituents in order to gain their support in future elections.

The Service Strategy: Taking Care of Constituents

An incumbent promotes his or her reelection prospects by catering to the **constituency:** the people residing in the incumbent's state or district. Members of Congress pay attention to constituency opinions when choosing positions on legislation, and they work hard to get their share of federal spending projects. Such projects are often derided as **pork** (or **pork-barrel spending**) by outsiders but are embraced by those who live in the state or district that gets a federally funded project, such as a new hospital, research center, or highway. Incumbents also respond to their constituents' individual requests, a practice known as the **service strategy.** Whether a constituent is seeking information about a government program or looking for help in obtaining a federal benefit, the representative's staff is ready to assist.

At times, constituency service has reached nearly incredible heights. In September 2005, for example, Congress faced the question of how to come up with the billions of dollars that would be required to rebuild New Orleans and the other Gulf Coast communities devastated by hurricane Katrina. One option was to trim the $286-billion transportation bill that Congress had enacted a little more than a month earlier. In it were hundreds of pork-barrel projects that members of Congress had secured for their home states and districts. One such project was a bridge that came to be known as "the bridge to nowhere." Nearly the length of the Golden Gate Bridge, it would link the town of Ketchikan, Alaska (population nine thousand), to Gravina Island (population fifty). Its inclusion in the transportation bill was due to the power of its sponsor, Representative Don Young (R-Alaska), who chaired the House Transportation and Infrastructure Committee that oversaw the legislation. When a reporter asked Representative Young whether he was willing to cancel the Ketchikan-Gravina bridge, he replied, "They can kiss my ear! That's the dumbest thing I've ever heard." Young later relented, but the money for the bridge, rather than being spent in the Gulf Coast area, was handed to Alaska transportation officials to use on other projects in the state.

Congressional staffers spend most of their time not on legislative matters but on constituency service and public relations—efforts that can pay off on Election Day.[5] Each House member receives an office allowance of roughly $800,000 a year with which to hire up to eighteen permanent staff members.[6] Senators receive office allowances that range between $2 million and $4 million a year, depending on the population size of their state. Smaller-state senators have staffs in the range of thirty people whereas larger-state senators have staffs closer in number to fifty people.[7] Each member of Congress is also allowed free trips back to their home state and free mailings to constituent households (a privilege known as the "frank"). These trips and mailings, along with press releases and other public relations efforts, help incumbents build name recognition and constituent support—major advantages in their reelection campaigns.

It is worth noting that European legislators do not have the large personal staffs or the travel and publicity budgets of members of Congress. Not surprisingly, European incumbents have much lower reelection rates than members of Congress. In the 2010 British elections, for example, nearly half of the candidates elected to the House of Commons were newcomers. No U.S. congressional election of the past eight decades has produced anywhere near this level of turnover.

Campaign Fundraising: Raking in the Money

Incumbents also have a decided advantage when it comes to raising campaign funds. Congressional elections are expensive because of the high cost of TV advertising, polling, and other modern campaign techniques (see Figure 11-2).

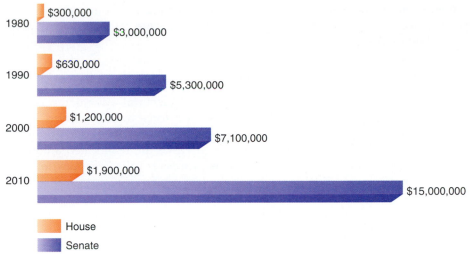

FIGURE 11-2
Congressional Campaign Expenditures, by Decade
Each decade, the cost of running for congressional office has risen sharply as campaign techniques—TV advertising, opinion polling, and so on—have become more elaborate and sophisticated. The increase in spending can be seen from a comparison of the approximate average spending by both candidates per House or Senate seat at ten-year intervals, beginning in 1980. Roughly speaking, the cost has doubled each decade.
Source: Federal Election Commission.

Today a successful House campaign in a competitive district costs more than a million dollars. The price of victory in competitive Senate races is much higher, ranging from several million dollars in small states to $20 million or more in larger states. Rarely do incumbents say they had trouble raising enough money to conduct an effective campaign, whereas challengers usually complain that their fundraising fell far short of their needs.[8] In the most recent election cycle, House incumbents raised on average about $1.5 million in campaign funds compared to less than half a million dollars for their challengers.[9]

Incumbents' past campaigns and constituent service enable them to develop mailing lists of potential contributors. Individual contributions, most of which are $100 or less, account for about 60 percent of all funds received by congressional candidates and are obtained mainly through fundraising events, websites, and direct-mail solicitation. Incumbents also have an edge with political action committees (PACs), which are the fundraising arm of interest groups (see Chapter 9). Most PACs are reluctant to oppose an incumbent unless the candidate appears beatable. More than 85 percent of PAC contributions in recent elections have gone to incumbents (see Figure 11-3). "Anytime you go against an incumbent, you take a minute and think long and hard about what your rationale is," said Desiree Anderson, director of the Realtors PAC.[10] (A race without an incumbent—called

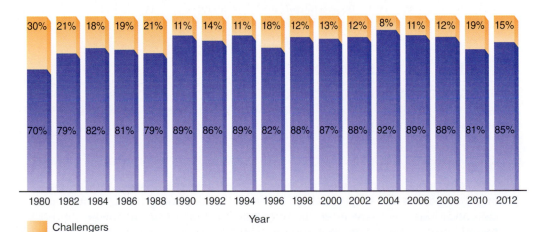

FIGURE 11-3
Allocation of PAC Contributions between Incumbents and Challengers in Congressional Races That Included an Incumbent, 1980–2012
In allocating campaign contributions, PACs favor incumbent members of Congress over their challengers by a wide margin.
Source: Federal Elections Commission. Figures for 2012 based on preliminary data.

open-seat election

An election in which there is no incumbent in the race.

reapportionment

The reallocation of House seats among states after each census as a result of population changes.

redistricting

The process of altering election districts to make them as nearly equal in population as possible. Redistricting takes place every ten years, after each population census.

gerrymandering

The process by which the party in power draws election district boundaries in a way that enhances the reelection prospects of its candidates.

an **open-seat election**—often brings out a strong candidate from each party and involves heavy spending, especially when the parties are rather evenly matched in the state or district.)

Redistricting: Favorable Boundaries for House Incumbents

House members, but not senators, have a final electoral advantage. Because incumbents are hard to unseat, they are always a force to be reckoned with, a fact that is apparent during redistricting. Every ten years, after each population census, the 435 seats in the House of Representatives are reallocated among the states in proportion to their population. This process is called **reapportionment.** States that have gained population since the last census may acquire additional House seats, while those that have lost population may lose seats. After the 2010 census, for example, Texas and Florida were among the states that gained House seats and New York and Ohio were among those that lost seats.

States are required by law to have House districts that are as nearly equal in population as possible. As a result, they must redraw their district boundaries after each census to account for population shifts within the state during the previous ten years. (The Senate is not affected by population change, because each state has two senators regardless of its size.) The responsibility for redrawing House election districts—a process called **redistricting**—rests with the respective state legislatures. The party that controls the legislature typically redraws the boundaries in a way that favors candidates of its party—a process called **gerrymandering.** (One of the few exceptions to this practice is Iowa, which entrusts redistricting to a nonpartisan commission.)

Incumbents are the chief beneficiaries of gerrymandering. When redistricting, the majority party in the state legislature places enough of its party's voters in its incumbents' districts to ensure their reelection. Most of the minority party's incumbents are also given a safe district. Because they have a solid base of support, and are difficult to defeat, the optimal strategy is to pack their districts with as many voters of their party as possible, so that in effect the party "wastes" votes, reducing its competitiveness elsewhere in the state.

For a few House incumbents, redistricting is a threat to reelection. When a state loses a congressional seat or seats, there may be fewer seats than there are incumbents, who end up running against each other. Moreover, the party in control of the state legislature might conclude that a particular incumbent of the opposite party is vulnerable and will redraw the boundaries of the incumbent's district to the incumbent's disadvantage. By and large, however, incumbents do not suffer greatly from redistricting, and the large majority of them wind up in districts that nearly assure their reelection.

Pitfalls of Incumbency

Incumbency is not without its risks. Senate and House incumbents can fall victim to disruptive issues, personal misconduct, turnout swings, strong challengers, and campaign money.

Disruptive Issues

Most elections are not waged in the context of disruptive issues, but when they are, incumbents are at greater risk. When voters are angry about existing political conditions, they are more likely to believe that those in power should be tossed out of office. The 2006 congressional election, which was waged in the context of Republican president George W. Bush's leadership of an unpopular war in Iraq, saw the defeat of more than twice the usual number of incumbents. Virtually all of them were Republicans, enabling the Democrats to seize control of both chambers. The parties' fortunes swung the other way in the 2010 congressional elections when public anger over economic conditions and the mushrooming federal deficit contributed to the defeat of an unusually high number of incumbents, nearly all of them Democrats.

Personal Misconduct

Members of Congress can also fall prey to scandal. Life in Washington can be fast paced, glamorous, and expensive, and some members of Congress get caught up in influence peddling, sex scandals, and other forms of misconduct. "The first thing to being reelected is to stay away from scandal, even minor scandal," says political scientist John Hibbing.[11] Roughly a fourth of House incumbents who lost their bid for reelection in the past two decades were shadowed by ethical questions. In 2005, for example, Representative William Jefferson demanded $100,000 in cash from a firm in return for helping it obtain government contracts. The firm alerted authorities to Jefferson's acceptance of the money, and the FBI raided Jefferson's congressional office, finding $90,000 hidden in a small freezer. In the 2008 election, Jefferson lost to his Republican opponent, even though his Louisiana district was heavily Democratic. Sexual misconduct proved to be the downfall of two married New York congressmen in 2011. Chris Lee, a Republican, resigned from Congress after it was discovered he had solicited sex on the Internet. A few months later, Anthony Weiner, a Democrat, resigned when lewd photographs he had posted on the Internet became public.

When Massachusetts was redistricted in 1812, Governor Elbridge Gerry had the lines of one district redrawn in order to ensure that a candidate of his party would be elected. Cartoonist Elkanah Tinsdale, noting that the strangely shaped district resembled a salamander, called it a "Gerry-mander."

Turnout Variation: The Midterm Election Problem

In twenty-one of the last twenty-five **midterm elections**—those that occur midway through a president's term—the president's party has lost House seats. The 2010 midterm elections, when the Democratic Party lost seats, fit the normal pattern. The pattern is partly attributable to the drop-off in turnout that accompanies a midterm election. The midterm electorate is substantially smaller than the presidential electorate. People who vote only in the presidential election tend to have weaker party ties and are more responsive to the issues of the moment. These issues are likely to favor one party, which contributes to the success not only of its presidential candidate but also of its congressional candidates. Two years later in the midterm elections, many of these voters stay home while those who do go the polls vote largely along party lines. Accordingly, the congressional candidates of the president's party do not get the boost they enjoyed in the previous election, and House seats are lost as a result.[12] The pattern also owes to the fact some voters treat the midterm elections as a referendum on the president's performance. Presidents usually lose popularity after taking office as a result of the policy positions they take. As the president's support declines, so does voters' support of congressional candidates from the president's party.[13]

midterm election

The congressional election that occurs midway through the president's term of office.

DEBATING THE ISSUES   POLITICAL THINKING IN ACTION

Should Partisan Gerrymandering Be Abolished?

Most U.S. House districts are electorally uncompetitive, and partisan gerrymandering is a reason. In redrawing election district boundaries after the census, the states tend to draw the lines in ways designed to create safe Democratic or Republican districts. Of the 435 House districts today, more than 300 are totally beyond the reach of one party. An issue is whether partisan gerrymandering puts election of House members in the hands of the states rather than in the hands of the voters. A lawsuit to that effect challenged the district boundaries that Pennsylvania established after the 2000 census. Fewer than 10 percent of the state's House districts were competitive. In *Vieth v. Jubelirer* (2004), the Supreme Court by a 5-4 vote refused to overturn Pennsylvania's redistricting arrangement, saying that, although there might be constitutional limits on partisan redistricting, the judiciary was not positioned to determine what the rules should be. The following are excerpts from two amicus curiae briefs (see Chapter 14) filed in the Pennsylvania case:

YES Challengers to incumbents and third-party voters and candidates are disadvantaged when the two political parties create safe seats for themselves. "[Partisan]" gerrymandering violates the Constitution's Equal Protection Clause by intentionally discriminating against identifiable groups and diminishing those groups' political power. Congressional elections are becoming less competitive every year. . . . Over 90 percent of Americans live in congressional districts that are essentially one-party monopolies. The situation is even worse in some states. For example, in California, 50 out of 53 races were decided by margins of greater than 20 percent. In a related phenomenon, incumbents are now more than ever nearly guaranteed reelection. . . . This situation is not mere happenstance, but rather the result of carefully orchestrated political gerrymandering—sometimes by one of the major political parties to the disadvantage of the other, and sometimes by the two parties colluding to protect their seats and their incumbents. . . . [E]ven though most states are close to evenly divided between the two major political parties, the vast majority of districts for the U.S. House of Representatives are drawn so as to prevent any real competition.

—*Center for Voting and Democracy*

NO Fairness in the redistricting process [has evaded] resolution for generations. Scholars cannot even agree on such foundational points as (1) whether there is a problem at all with respect to the ability of Republicans and Democrats to compete for control of the legislature; (2) if there is a problem, whether redistricting is to blame for it; (3) whether creation of safe seats is a bad thing, and, if so, whether it can be avoided; and (4) whether neutral, nonpartisan redistricting standards are either theoretically or practically possible. . . . Justice White [once]cited the work of the late Robert G. Dixon Jr., "one of the foremost scholars of reapportionment," for the proposition "that there are no neutral lines for legislative districts . . . every line drawn aligns partisans and interest blocs in a particular way different from the alignment that would result from putting the line in some other place." Elsewhere, Professor Dixon rebuked . . . his colleagues who aspire to discover universal principles of fair representation: "My own experience tells me that although I may find nonpartisanship in heaven, in the real world, and especially in academia, there are no nonpartisans, although there may be noncombatants."

—*Leadership of the Alabama Senate and House of Representatives*

Q: Which view is closer to your opinion? Do you think there should be limits to partisan gerrymandering? Or do you think there is no fair way to restrict the practice, even though the practice itself may be unfair to the voters?

Primary Election Challengers

Primary elections can also be a time of risk for incumbents, especially if they hold politically moderate views. If they are confronted with a strong challenger from the extreme wing of their party, they stand a chance of losing because strong partisans are more likely than party moderates to vote in primary elections.[14] In 2012, Richard Luger, a six-term incumbent and widely respected member of the Senate, was trounced in Indiana's GOP primary by conservative Richard Mourdock, who portrayed Lugar as too moderate and too much of a Washington insider. In 2010, incumbent U.S. senator Bob Bennett of Utah did not even get a chance to run in his state's Republican primary. At the state nominating convention, Republican delegates rejected Bennett's bid to compete in the GOP primary. Although Bennett had a conservative record, it wasn't conservative

Mike Lee exemplifies the type of primary election challenger that congressional incumbents increasingly fear. Lee, a lawyer and son of the founding dean of Brigham Young University's law school, challenged incumbent Bob Bennett in 2010 for Utah's Republican Senate nomination. Backed by staunch conservatives, Lee won the GOP nomination and then went on to win the general election.

enough for the delegates. They were angry at his support of the 2008 bill that authorized the use of federal funds to bail out the nation's troubled banks and auto companies.

General Election Challengers: A Problem for Senators

Incumbents, particularly those in the Senate, are also vulnerable to strong challengers. Senators often find themselves running against a high-ranking politician, such as the state's governor or attorney general. Such opponents have the voter base, campaign organization, fundraising ability, public recognition, and credentials to mount a strong campaign. The U.S. Senate also lures wealthy challengers. Maria Cantwell spent $10 million of her own money to defeat Senator Slade Gorton in the state of Washington's Senate race in 2000. Cantwell made her fortune as an executive with RealNetworks, a high-tech company. Running again in 2006, Cantwell found herself in a tighter-than-expected race, partly because her opponent, Mike McGavick, was himself a millionaire executive. In 2012, Cantwell won more easily. Her opponent, Michael Baumgartner, did not have a large personal fortune upon which to base his campaign.

House incumbents have less reason to fear strong challengers. A House seat is often not attractive enough to induce a prominent local politician, such as a mayor or state legislator, to risk taking on the incumbent.[15] As a result, most House incumbents face weak opponents. The situation changes somewhat when voters are deeply unhappy with the way government is performing. Then, the party out of power has an easier time persuading strong challengers to run. In 2006, when the political mood favored the Democrats, they fielded a stronger than usual slate of challengers, which helped them unseat an unusually large number of Republican incumbents. In 2010, with the parties' roles reversed, the Republican Party recruited a strong group of challengers, which contributed to the defeat of an unusually large number of Democratic incumbents.

A New Threat: Super PACs

Although incumbents ordinarily have a funding advantage over their challengers, the situation can change when they appear vulnerable. Contributors from outside the state or district may target the race and donate money to the challenger. Although this threat has existed for years, it has become larger with the emergence of super PACs, which have the capacity to pour millions of dollars into a race (see Chapters 8 and 9). This scenario played itself out in the 2010 Colorado Senate race, which pitted the Democratic incumbent Michael Bennett against Ken Buck, a Republican district attorney. Their race turned out to be one of the most expensive Senate campaigns in history. Although the Bennett and Buck campaigns spent a combined total of less than $15 million—about average for a contested Senate race in a midsized state—independent groups and super PACs spent an additional $22 million, mostly on behalf of Buck. Bennett survived the inflow of money, although narrowly. His margin of victory was less than two percentage points.

Who Are the Winners in Congressional Elections?

The Constitution places a few restrictions on who can be elected to Congress. House members must be at least twenty-five years of age and have been a citizen for at least seven years. For senators, the age and citizenship requirements are thirty years and nine years, respectively. Senators and representatives alike must be residents of the state from which they are elected.

But if the formal restrictions are minimal, the informal limits are substantial. Congress is not a microcosm of the population. Although lawyers constitute less than 1 percent of the population, they make up a third of Congress. Attorneys enter politics in large numbers in part because knowledge of the law is an asset in Congress and also because campaign publicity—even if a candidate loses—is a good way to build up a law practice. Along with lawyers, professionals such as business executives, educators, bankers, and journalists account for roughly 90 percent of congressional membership.[16] Blue-collar workers, clerical employees, and home-makers are seldom elected to Congress. Farmers and ranchers are less rare; a fair number of House members from rural districts have agricultural backgrounds.

Finally, members of Congress are disproportionately white and male. Although the number of women in Congress is nine times that of four decades ago, they account for only about 15 percent of the membership (see Chapter 5). Minorities account for an even smaller proportion—less than 10 percent—of the members of Congress. Women and minorities are also less likely than white men to attempt a run for Congress, even though the winning percentage of those who do is roughly the same as that of nonincumbent white males.[17] In local and state legislative elections, where running for office is less onerous, women and minority candidates have made greater inroads.[18]

Parties and Party Leadership

The U.S. Congress is a **bicameral legislature**, meaning it has two chambers, the House and the Senate. Both chambers are organized largely along party lines. At the start of each two-year congressional term, party members in each chamber meet to elect their **party leaders**—the individuals who will lead their party's

bicameral legislature

A legislature that has two chambers (the House and the Senate, in the case of the United States).

party leaders

Members of the House and Senate who are chosen by the Democratic or Republican caucus in each chamber to represent the party's interests in that chamber and who give some central direction to the chamber's work.

TABLE 11-1 | The Number of Democrats and Republicans in the House of Representatives and the Senate, 2001–2014

	2001–2	2003–4	2005–6	2007–8	2009–10	2011–12	2013-14
House							
Democrats	213	208	203	235*	257	192	197
Republicans	222	227	232	200	178	243*	238*
Senate							
Democrats	51*	49	45	51*	60	53	55
Republicans	49	51	55	49	40	47	45

*Chamber not controlled by the president's party. Senate and House members who are independents are included in the total for the party with which they caucused. Figures based on party totals that result from the congressional elections as opposed to subsequent totals that result, for example, because of the death or resignation of seated members.

efforts in the chamber. Party members also meet periodically in closed session, which is called a **party caucus,** to plan strategy, develop issues, and resolve policy differences. (Table 11-1 shows the party composition in Congress during the past two decades.)

Party Unity in Congress

Political parties are the strongest force within Congress. They are the greatest source of unity among members of Congress, as well as the greatest source of division.

The partisan divide in Congress has intensified since the mid-1980s, partly as a result of changes in the composition of the parties. At an earlier time, congressional Republicans were divided almost evenly between the party's conservative and progressive wings, and congressional Democrats consisted of a liberal northern wing and a conservative southern wing. Today, the large majority of congressional Republicans are conservative and the large majority of congressional Democrats are liberal. In fact, there is now little overlap in the ideologies of congressional Democrats and Republicans. In a recent study based on legislative votes, political scientists Keith Poole and Howard Rosenthal found that, in both the House and the Senate, the most liberal Republican was farther to the right than the most conservative Democrat.[19] As a result, each congressional party has found it easier to achieve **party unity**—in which members of a party band together on legislation and stand against the opposite party.[20]

The heightened level of party unity in Congress can be seen by looking at the party distribution on *roll-call votes* (these are votes on which each member's vote is officially recorded, as opposed to voice votes, where the members simply say "aye" or "nay" in unison and the presiding officer indicates which side prevails without tallying individual members' positions). Since the mid-1980s, party-line voting on roll calls has increased considerably (see "Party Polarization"). In the 1970s, roll-call votes generally did not pit most Republicans against most Democrats. More recently, most roll-call votes have divided along party lines. The ideological split in the congressional parties is most pronounced on major domestic legislation. When the $787 billion economic stimulus bill went through Congress in 2009, it did so almost entirely on Democratic votes. No House Republican and only three Senate Republicans voted for the bill. The health care reform bill enacted in 2010 was passed without a single Republican vote in the House or Senate. (The effect of heightened partisanship on the congressional process is discussed later in the chapter.)

party caucus

A group that consists of a party's members in the House or Senate and that serves to elect the party's leadership, set policy goals, and plan party strategy.

party unity

The degree to which a party's House or Senate members act as a unified group to exert collective control over legislative action.

HOW THE 50 STATES DIFFER   POLITICAL THINKING THROUGH COMPARISONS

WOMEN IN THE STATE LEGISLATURES

Women have had more success in gaining election to state legislatures than to Congress, partly because there is more turnover and less incumbency advantage at the state level, which creates more opportunities for newcomers to run and to win. More than one in five state legislators are women, a fourfold increase since 1970. Colorado, with 41 percent, has the highest proportion of women legislators. South Carolina, with 9 percent, has the lowest.

Q: Why do the northeastern and western regions have the most women legislators?

A: The northeastern and western regions have a higher proportion of college-educated women in the workforce than do other regions. College-educated women are more likely to run for public office and to actively support those who do run.

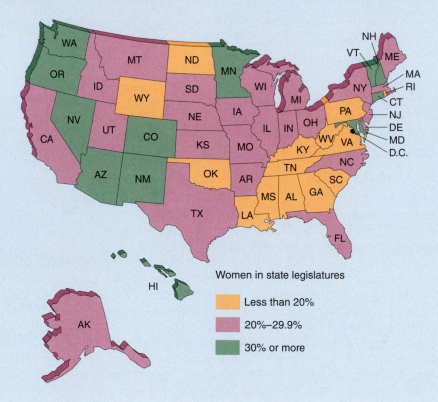

Women in state legislatures

- Less than 20%
- 20%–29.9%
- 30% or more

Source: Created from data gathered by the Center for the American Woman and Politics (CAWP); National Information Bank on Women in Public Office; and Eagleton Institute of Politics, Rutgers University, 2010.

Party Leadership in Congress

Party leaders in Congress are usually chosen for their demonstrated leadership ability, as well as their ability to work effectively with other members. In European parliaments, party leaders can count on the backing of party members (see "How the U.S. Differs" on page 280). The members depend on the party for nomination to office and can be denied nomination in the next election if they fail to support the party on key legislative votes. In contrast, members of the U.S. Congress depend on themselves for reelection, which gives them the freedom to selectively back or oppose the party's position on key votes. Accordingly, the power of party leaders in Congress depends to a considerable extent on their ability to gain the trust of party members and to forge positions that bridge their policy views.

PARTY
POLARIZATION   Political Thinking in Conflict

Congress, the Keystone of Partisan Conflict?

To some observers, the partisan acrimony that has characterized American politics in recent years had its origins in Congress. In *The Broken Branch* (2008), congressional scholars Thomas Mann and Norman Ornstein argue that both congressional parties are at fault. The House Democrats started the partisan wars in the 1980s by employing rules that denied House Republicans a meaningful lawmaking role. The House Republicans institutionalized the arrangement upon taking control of Congress in 1994. Underlying these developments was the eclipse of the Democratic Party's conservative wing and the Republican Party's progressive wing. As the congressional Democrats became more uniformly liberal and the congressional Republicans became more uniformly conservative, the overlap between the congressional parties diminished, making it harder to bridge party differences and easier for each side to attack the other. As the graph below indicates, party-line voting on roll-call votes has substantially increased since the 1980s. Before then, most roll-call votes did not pit a majority of Republicans against a majority of Democrats. Since then, roll-call votes have increasingly divided along party lines. When only major bills are considered (the graph is based on all roll-call votes), the partisan divide is even clearer. Voting on the 2009 stimulus bill, the 2010 health care reform bill, and the 2011 budget ceiling bill, for example, divided almost exactly along party lines.

Percentage of roll-call votes in the House and Senate in which a majority of Democrats voted against a majority of Republicans

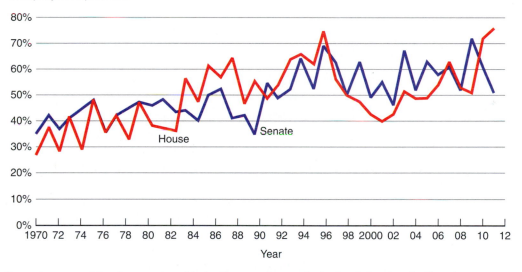

Q. *Some observers claim that partisanship in Congress has reached a level that is crippling the institution as an effective policymaking body. Party disputes on everything from health care to tax policy have produced legislative deadlock and delay. Do you share the view that excessive partisanship is warping the congressional process, or do you think members of Congress should stick to their partisan principles, whatever the consequences?*

Source: Congressional Quarterly Weekly, various dates.

House Leaders

The Constitution specifies that the House of Representatives will be presided over by a Speaker, elected by the vote of its members. Since the majority party has the largest number of members, it also has the most votes, and the Speaker

HOW THE U.S. DIFFERS   POLITICAL THINKING THROUGH COMPARISONS

Legislative Structure

The U.S. House and Senate are separate and coequal chambers, each with its own leadership and rules. This type of legislative structure is not found in most democracies. Many democracies, for example, have a single legislative chamber, which is apportioned by population. If the United States had an equivalent legislature, it would consist only of the House of Representatives.

Even democracies that have bicameral (two-chamber) legislatures tend to structure them differently than the U.S. Congress is structured. The U.S. Senate is apportioned strictly by geography: there are two senators from each state. Germany is among the democracies that have a chamber organized along geographical lines, but Germany's upper house (the Bundesrat) differs from the U.S. Senate. Each of the German states (known as Länder) has at least three representatives in the Bundesrat, but the more populous states have more than three representatives. Moreover, in most bicameral legislatures, one legislative chamber has substantially less power than the other. In the British Parliament, for example, the House of Lords in some instances can slow down legislation that is passed by the House of Commons but cannot stop it from becoming law. In the German Parliament, the Bundesrat has a voice on constitutional policy issues but not on most other issues, and its vote can in some cases be overridden by the population-based chamber (the Bundestag). In the United States, the Senate and House are equal in their legislative powers; without their joint agreement, no law can be enacted.

The U.S. Congress is fragmented in other ways as well: it has elected leaders with limited formal powers, a network of relatively independent and powerful committees, and members who are free to follow or ignore other members of their party. It is not uncommon for a fourth or more of a party's

legislators to vote against their party's position on legislative issues. In contrast, European legislatures have a centralized power structure. Top leaders have substantial authority, the committees are weak, and the parties are unified. European legislators are expected to support their party unless granted permission to vote otherwise on a particular bill.

Q: In terms of the enactment of legislation, what is the relative advantage and disadvantage of the way in which Congress is structured, compared with a national legislature that has a single dominant chamber in which the majority party can count on its members to support its legislative agenda?

A: Congress is structured in a way that slows the passage of legislation, which can be a safeguard against hastily prepared, ill-considered, or weakly supported laws. On the other hand, the structure of Congress can permit a determined minority to block legislation that has majority support within and outside Congress.

Country	Form of legislature
Canada	One house dominant
France	One house dominant
Germany	One house dominant (except on certain issues)
Great Britain	One house dominant
Israel	One house only
Japan	One house dominant
Mexico	Two equal houses
Sweden	One house only
United States	Two equal houses

is invariably a member of the majority party. Thus, when the Republicans took control of the House after the 2010 election, John Boehner, the Republicans' leader in the chamber, replaced Democrat Nancy Pelosi as Speaker. Boehner, an Ohio representative, was first elected to the House in 1991.

Next to the president, the Speaker of the House is sometimes said to be the most powerful national official. The Speaker is active in developing the party's positions on issues and in persuading party members in the House to support them. Although the Speaker cannot require party members to support the party's program, they look to the Speaker for leadership. The Speaker also has certain formal powers, including the right to speak first during House debate on legislation and the power to recognize members—that is, to grant them permission to speak from the floor. Because the House places a time limit on floor debate, not everyone has a chance to speak on a given bill, and the Speaker can sometimes influence legislation simply by exercising the power to decide who will speak and when. The Speaker also chooses the chairperson and the majority-party members of the powerful House Rules Committee, which controls the scheduling of bills. Those that the Speaker wants passed are likely to reach the floor under conditions favorable to their enactment; for example, the Speaker may ask the Rules Committee to delay sending a bill to the floor until there is sufficient support for its passage. The Speaker also has other ways of influencing the work of the House. The Speaker assigns bills to committees, places time limits on the reporting of bills out of committees, and assigns members to conference committees. (The importance of these committee-related powers will become apparent later in this chapter.)

Although powerful, the Speaker is ultimately beholden to the party's membership. The Speaker cannot force them to vote for or against a particular bill. House members are separately elected and will normally not cast a vote that could jeopardize their reelection chances. In this sense, the Speaker must consider what party members will accept when taking positions on legislative issues. In the 1990s, Newt Gingrich was deposed as Speaker after House Republicans concluded he was pursuing a personal agenda rather than one that aligned with their policy and reelection concerns. In 2011, John Boehner also discovered the limits to the Speaker's power when he tried unsuccessfully to convince House Republicans to support budget compromises he had negotiated with President Obama.

The Speaker of the House is chosen by the majority party in the House of Representatives and has been called the second most powerful national official (after the president). The Speaker's power owes to the large size of the House and the restrictive rules under which it operates. Shown here are the two most recent Speakers, John Boehner (R-Ohio) and Nancy Pelosi (D-California).

The Speaker is assisted by the House majority leader and the House majority whip, who are also chosen by the majority party's members. The majority leader acts as the party's floor leader, organizing the debate on bills and lining up legislative support. The whip has the job of informing party members when critical votes are scheduled. As voting is getting under way on the House floor, the whip will sometimes stand at a location that is easily seen by party members and let them know where the leadership stands on the bill by giving them a thumbs-up or thumbs-down signal.

The minority party also has its House leaders. The House minority leader heads the party's caucus and its policy committee and plays the leading role in developing the party's legislative positions. The minority leader is assisted by a minority whip.

Senate Leaders

In the Senate, the most important party leadership position is that of the majority leader, who heads the majority-party caucus. The majority leader's role resembles that of the Speaker of the House in that the Senate majority leader formulates the majority party's legislative agenda and encourages party members to support it. Like the Speaker, the Senate majority leader chairs the party's policy committee and acts as the party's voice in the chamber. The majority leader is assisted by the majority whip, who sees to it that members know when important votes are scheduled. The minority party in the Senate also has its leaders. The minority leader and minority whip have roles comparable to those of their House counterparts.

For several reasons, the Senate majority leader's position is less powerful than that of the Speaker of the House. Unlike the Speaker, the Senate majority leader is not the chamber's presiding officer. The Constitution assigns this position to the vice president of the United States. But because the vice president is allowed to vote only in case of a tie, the vice president rarely attends Senate sessions. In the absence of the vice president, the president pro tempore (temporary president) has the right to preside over the Senate. By tradition, the majority party's most senior member serves as president pro tempore. The position is largely honorary because the Senate's presiding officer has no real power. Unlike the House, where the Speaker directs the floor debate, the Senate has a tradition of unlimited debate. Ordinarily, any senator who wishes to speak on a bill can do so.

Compared with the House Speaker, the Senate majority leader's power is also limited by the fact that individual senators have more power and freedom of action than do individual House members. The Senate is smaller in size—100 members versus 435 members in the House—which leads senators to see themselves as co-equals in a way that House members do not. As well, senators serve six-year terms and do not face the unrelenting reelection pressures on House members, who serve two-year terms. Bob Dole of Kansas, who served as Republican Senate leader, remarked: "There's a lot of free spirits in the Senate. About 100 of them."[21]

Committees and Committee Leadership

standing committees

Permanent congressional committees with responsibility for a particular area of public policy. An example is the Senate Foreign Relations Committee.

Most of the work in Congress is conducted through **standing committees,** which are permanent committees with responsibility for particular areas of public policy. At present there are twenty standing committees in the House and sixteen in the Senate (see Table 11-2). Each chamber has, for example, a standing committee that handles foreign policy issues. Other important standing committees are those that deal with agriculture, commerce, the interior (natural resources and public lands), defense, government spending, labor, the judiciary, and taxation. House committees, which average about thirty-five to forty members each, are about twice the size of Senate committees. Each standing committee has legislative authority in that it can draft and rewrite proposed legislation and can recommend to the full chamber the passage or defeat of the bills it handles.

Most of the standing committees have subcommittees, each of which has a defined jurisdiction. The House Foreign Affairs Committee, for instance, has seven subcommittees: Oversight and Investigations; Africa, Global Health, and Human Rights; Asia and the Pacific; Europe and Eurasia; Middle East and South Asia; Terrorism, Nonproliferation, and Trade; and Western Hemisphere. Each House and Senate subcommittee has about a dozen members. These few individuals do most of the work and have a leading voice in the disposition of bills in their policy area.

Congress could not manage its workload without the help of its committee system. About ten thousand bills are introduced during each two-year session of Congress. This amount of legislation would overwhelm the institution if it did not divide the work among its standing committees, each of which has its own staff. Unlike the members' personal staffs, which concentrate on constituency relations, the committee staffs perform an almost entirely legislative function. They help draft legislation, gather information, and organize hearings.

In addition to its permanent standing committees, Congress also has a number of *select committees* that have a designated responsibility but, unlike the

TABLE 11-2 | The Standing Committees of Congress

House of Representatives	Senate
Agriculture	Agriculture, Nutrition, and Forestry
Appropriations	Appropriations
Armed Services	Armed Services
Budget	Banking, Housing, and Urban Affairs
Education and the Workforce	Budget
Energy and Commerce	Commerce, Science, and Transportation
Ethics	Energy and Natural Resources
Financial Services	Environment and Public Works
Foreign Affairs	Finance
Homeland Security	Foreign Relations
House Administration	Health, Education, Labor, and Pensions
Judiciary	Homeland Security and Governmental Affairs
Natural Resources	Judiciary
Oversight and Government Reform	Rules and Administration
Rules	Small Business and Entrepreneurship
Science and Technology	Veterans' Affairs
Small Business	
Transportation and Infrastructure	
Veterans' Affairs	
Ways and Means	

standing committees, do not produce legislation. An example is the Senate Select Committee on Intelligence, which receives periodic classified briefings from the intelligence agencies. Congress also has *joint committees*, composed of members of both houses, which perform advisory functions. The Joint Committee on the Library, for example, oversees the Library of Congress, the largest library in the world. Finally, Congress has *conference committees*—joint committees formed temporarily to work out differences in House and Senate versions of a particular bill. The role of conference committees is discussed more fully later in the chapter.

Committee Jurisdiction

The 1946 Legislative Reorganization Act requires that each bill introduced in Congress be referred to the proper committee. An agricultural bill introduced in the Senate must be assigned to the Senate Agriculture Committee, a bill dealing with foreign affairs must be sent to the Senate Foreign Relations Committee, and so on. This requirement is a source of each committee's power. Even if a committee's members are known to oppose certain types of legislation, bills clearly within its **jurisdiction**—the policy area in which it is authorized to act—must be sent to it for deliberation.

Jurisdiction is not always clear cut, however. Which House committee, for example, should handle a major bill addressing the role of financial institutions in global trade? The Financial Services Committee? The Energy and Commerce Committee? The Foreign Affairs Committee? All committees seek legislative influence, and each is jealous of its jurisdiction, so a bill that overlaps

jurisdiction (of a congressional committee)

The policy area in which a particular congressional committee is authorized to act.

committee boundaries can provoke a "turf war" over which committee will handle it.[22] Party leaders can take advantage of these situations by assigning the bill to the committee that is most likely to handle it in the way they would like. But because party leaders depend on the committees for support, they cannot regularly ignore a committee that has a strong claim to a bill. At times, party leaders have responded by dividing up a bill, handing over some of its provisions to one committee and other provisions to a second committee.

Committee Membership

Each committee has a fixed number of seats, with the majority party holding most of them. The ratio of Democrats to Republicans on each committee is approximately the same as the ratio in the full House or Senate, but there is no fixed rule on this matter, and the majority party determines the ratio (mindful that at the next election it could become the chamber's minority party). Members of the House typically serve on only two committees. Senators often serve on four, although they can sit on only two major committees, such as the Finance Committee or the Foreign Relations Committee. Once appointed to a committee, the member can usually chose to stay on it indefinitely.

Each committee has a fixed number of seats, and a committee must have a vacancy before a new member can be appointed. Most vacancies occur after an election as a result of the retirement or defeat of committee members. Each party has a special committee in each chamber that decides who will fill the vacancies. A variety of factors influence these decisions, including members' preferences. Most newly elected members of Congress ask for and receive assignment to a committee on which they can serve their constituents' interests and at the same time enhance their reelection prospects. For example, when John Boozman was elected to the Senate in 2010 from Arkansas, a state that depends heavily on the farm sector, he asked for and received an appointment to the Senate Agriculture Committee.

POLITICAL THINKING   Whose Interest Is Served?

The membership of congressional committees is not representative of Congress as a whole. The House and Senate agricultural committees, for example, are filled with farm-state senators and representatives. This type of arrangement clearly serves the interests of members of Congress and their constituencies. But how might it also serve the interests of the country as a whole, or doesn't it?

Some members of Congress prefer a seat on the most prestigious committees, such as the Senate Foreign Relations Committee or the House Ways and Means (taxation) Committee. Although these committees do not align closely with constituency interests, they have responsibility for prominent policy issues. Factors such as party loyalty, level of knowledge, willingness to work hard, and length of congressional service determine whether a member is granted a seat on one of these committees.[23]

Subcommittee assignments are handled differently. The members of each party on a committee decide who among them will serve on each of its subcommittees. The members' preferences and seniority, as well as the interests of their constituencies, are key factors in subcommittee assignments.

Committee Chairs

Each committee (as well as each subcommittee) is headed by a chairperson. The position of committee chair is a powerful one. The chair schedules committee meetings, determines the order in which committee bills are considered, presides over committee discussions, directs the committee's majority staff, and can choose to lead the debate when a committee bill goes to the floor of the chamber for a vote.

Committee chairs are always members of the majority party and usually the party member with the most **seniority** (consecutive years of service) on the committee. Seniority is based strictly on time served on a committee, not on time spent in Congress. Thus, if a member switches committees, the years spent on the first committee do not count toward seniority on the new one. The seniority system has

Senators Orrin Hatch (R-Utah) and Patrick Leahy (D-Vt.) confer at a Judiciary Committee hearing. Most of the legislative work of Congress is done in committees and their subcommittees.

advantages: it reduces the number of power struggles that would occur if the chairs were decided each time by open competition, it places committee leadership in the hands of experienced members, and it enables members to look forward to the reward of a position as chair after years of service on the same committee.

seniority
A member of Congress's consecutive years of service on a particular committee.

The seniority system is not absolute, however, and is applied less strictly than in the past. There was a period when seniority was a strict rule, which led to abuses. Although most chairs were responsive to the concerns of other members, some were dictatorial. Howard Smith, an arch segregationist, chaired the House Rules Committee from 1955 to 1965 and used his position to keep civil rights legislation from reaching the House floor for a vote. During that era, a committee could not meet unless its chair called it into session, and Smith would leave Washington for his Virginia farm when a civil rights bill came to the Rules Committee, returning only if committee members agreed to withdraw the bill from consideration. Abuses by Smith and other chairs led to reforms in the 1970s that reduced the power of committee chairs. Seniority was no longer an absolute rule, and a committee majority was given the power to call a committee into session if the chair refused to do so.

Committees and Parties: Which Is in Control?

In one sense, committees are an instrument of the majority party, in that it controls most of each committee's seats and appoints its chair. In another sense, each committee is powerful in its own right. Committees have been described as "little legislatures," each secure in its jurisdiction and membership, and each wielding considerable control over the legislation it handles.

Committees decentralize power in Congress and serve individual members' power and reelection needs. Less than a dozen members hold a party leadership position, but several hundred serve as committee or subcommittee chairs or are *ranking members*, the term for the minority party's committee and subcommittee leaders. In these positions, they exercise authority, often in ways that serve local constituencies or personal policy agendas—actions that may or may not coincide with the party leadership's goals. The result is an institution very different from European parliaments, where party leaders hold nearly all the power (an arrangement reflected even in the name for rank-and-file members: "backbenchers").

When Republicans took control of Congress in 1995, they sought to reduce the power of committees and their chairs, in an effort to strengthen the party's role. The Republicans passed over some senior party members in selecting the committee chairs and placed term limits on the rest. After six years, a chair or ranking member must relinquish the post. Each chair was to use the position's power to promote the goals of the party as opposed to those of individual committee members. When the Democrats took over Congress in 2007, they left the term limits in place. When Republicans retook control of the House in 2011, they instituted several reforms that were intended to strengthen party leaders' control, including measures aimed at making it easier for party leaders to monitor the work of the standing committees.

Although the parties have more influence in Congress than they did a few decades ago, the balance between party power and committee power is always an ongoing issue. The institution is at once a place for pursuing the parties' national agendas and a venue for promoting the interests of members' constituencies. At times, the balance has tipped toward the committees and their leadership. At other times, it has tipped toward the parties and their leadership. At all times, there has been an effort to strike a workable balance between the two. The distinguishing feature of congressional power is its division among the membership, with provision for added power—sometimes more and sometimes less—in the hands of the top party leaders.

How a Bill Becomes Law

Parties, party leaders, and committees are critical actors in the legislative process. Their roles and influence, however, vary with the nature of the legislation under consideration. The formal process by which bills become law is shown in Figure 11-4. A **bill** is a proposed legislative act. Many bills are prepared by executive agencies, interest groups, or other outside parties, but members of Congress also draft bills, and they alone can formally submit a bill for consideration by their chamber.

bill

A proposed law (legislative act) within Congress or another legislature.

Committee Hearings and Decisions

When a bill is introduced in the House or Senate, it receives a bill number and is sent to the relevant committee, which assigns it to one of its subcommittees. Less than 10 percent of the bills referred to committee will get to the floor for a vote; the others are "killed" when committees decide they lack merit. The full House or Senate can overrule such decisions, but this rarely occurs. Most bills die in committee because they are poorly conceived or of little interest to anyone other than a few members of Congress. Some bills are not even supported by the members who introduce them. A member may submit a bill to appease a powerful constituent group and then quietly inform the committee to ignore it.

The fact that committees kill more than 90 percent of the bills submitted in Congress does not mean that they exercise 90 percent of the power in Congress. Committees do not operate in a vacuum. They rarely decide the fate of major bills that are of keen interest to other members. They also have to take into account the fact that their decisions can be reversed by the full chamber, just as subcommittees must recognize that the full committee can override their decisions.[24]

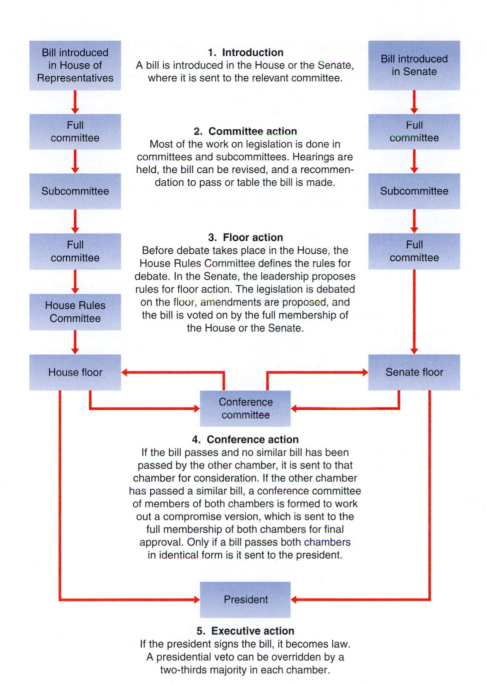

1. Introduction
A bill is introduced in the House or the Senate, where it is sent to the relevant committee.

Bill introduced in House of Representatives

Bill introduced in Senate

Full committee

2. Committee action
Most of the work on legislation is done in committees and subcommittees. Hearings are held, the bill can be revised, and a recommendation to pass or table the bill is made.

Full committee

Subcommittee

Subcommittee

Full committee

3. Floor action
Before debate takes place in the House, the House Rules Committee defines the rules for debate. In the Senate, the leadership proposes rules for floor action. The legislation is debated on the floor, amendments are proposed, and the bill is voted on by the full membership of the House or the Senate.

Full committee

House Rules Committee

House floor

Senate floor

Conference committee

4. Conference action
If the bill passes and no similar bill has been passed by the other chamber, it is sent to that chamber for consideration. If the other chamber has passed a similar bill, a conference committee of members of both chambers is formed to work out a compromise version, which is sent to the full membership of both chambers for final approval. Only if a bill passes both chambers in identical form is it sent to the president.

President

5. Executive action
If the president signs the bill, it becomes law. A presidential veto can be overridden by a two-thirds majority in each chamber.

FIGURE 11-4
How a Bill Becomes Law
Although the legislative process can be short-circuited in many ways, this diagram describes a normal way a bill becomes law.

If a bill appears to have merit, the subcommittee will schedule hearings on it. After the hearings, if the subcommittee still feels that the legislation is needed, members will recommend the bill to the full committee, which might hold additional hearings. In the House, both the full committee and a subcommittee can **mark up** a bill—that is, they have the authority to change its content. In the Senate, mark up usually is reserved for the full committee.

From Committee to the Floor

If a majority of the committee vote to recommend passage of the bill, it is referred to the full chamber for action. In the House, the Rules Committee has the power to determine when the bill will be voted on, and how long the debate on it will last. On most House bills, only a small number of legislators are granted the

mark up
The authority of congressional committees (and subcommittees in some cases) to change the content of a bill.

cloture

A parliamentary maneuver that, if a three-fifths majority votes for it, limits Senate debate to thirty hours and has the effect of defeating a filibuster.

filibuster

A procedural tactic in the U.S. Senate whereby a minority of legislators prevent a bill from coming to a vote by holding the floor and talking until the majority gives in and the bill is withdrawn from consideration.

opportunity to speak on the floor; in most cases, the bill's chief sponsor and one of the bill's leading opponents will choose speakers. The Rules Committee also decides whether a bill will receive a "closed rule" (no amendments will be permitted), an "open rule" (members can propose amendments relevant to any of the bill's sections), or something in between (for example, only certain sections of the bill will be subject to amendment). The rules are a means by which the majority party controls legislation. When they had a majority in the House in the period before 1995, Democrats employed closed rules to prevent Republicans from proposing amendments to major bills, a tactic House Republicans said they would forgo when they took control in 1995. Once in control, however, the Republicans applied closed rules to a number of major bills. The tactic was too effective to ignore.

The Senate also has a rules committee, but it is less important than its House counterpart because the Senate has less restrictive rules on debate and amendments. In the Senate, the majority leader, usually in consultation with the minority leader, schedules bills. All Senate bills are subject to unlimited debate unless a three-fifths majority (60 of the 100 senators) vote for **cloture,** which limits debate to thirty hours. Cloture is a way of defeating a Senate **filibuster,** which is a procedural tactic whereby a minority of senators can block a bill by talking until other senators give in and the bill is withdrawn from consideration or altered to fit opponents' demands. In 2010, for example, Senate Republicans twice used the filibuster to block a bill that would tighten the regulations governing financial institutions. The bill passed only after Democrats granted enough concessions to get the Republican votes they needed to break the filibuster.

POLITICAL THINKING Eliminate the Filibuster?

Of all the impediments to congressional action, perhaps none is more imposing than a Senate filibuster, which can be ended only if three-fifths of the senators agree to end it. In effect, a minority of Senators has the power to kill legislation, even if it is backed by the president and the House of Representatives. No other democratic legislature has a rule that allows the minority so much power. Should the filibuster be kept or eliminated? Why?

rider

An amendment to a bill that deals with an issue unrelated to the content of the bill. Riders are permitted in the Senate but not in the House.

In the House, proposed amendments must directly relate to the bill's contents. In the Senate, however, members can propose any amendment to any bill. For example, a senator may propose an antiabortion amendment to a bill dealing with defense expenditures. Such amendments are called **riders.**

Leadership and Floor Action

A bill that emerges from committee with the support of all or nearly all of its members is usually passed by an overwhelming majority of the full chamber. On the other hand, when the committee vote is closely divided, other members may conclude that they need to give the bill a close look before deciding whether to support it. Other members are also less deferential to committee action on major bills and on those that affect their constituents.

On major bills, the majority party's leaders (particularly in the House) have increasingly assumed the lead.[25] They shape the bill's broad content and work closely with the relevant committee during the committee phase. Once the bill clears the committee, they often direct the floor debate. In these efforts, they depend on the ongoing support of their party's members. To obtain it, they consult their members informally and through the party caucus. (The role of parties in Congress is discussed further in the section on Congress's representation function.)

Conference Committees and the President

For a bill to pass, it must have the support of a simple majority (50 percent plus one) of the House or Senate members voting on it. To become law, however, a bill must be passed in identical form by both the House and the Senate. About 10 percent of the bills that pass both chambers differ in important respects in their House and Senate versions. These bills are referred to conference committees to resolve the differences. Each **conference committee** is formed temporarily for the sole purpose of handling a particular bill; its members are usually appointed from the House and Senate standing committees that drafted the bill. The conference committee's job is to develop a compromise version, which then goes back to the House and Senate floors for a vote. There it can be passed, defeated, or returned to conference, but not amended.

A bill that is passed in identical form by the House and the Senate is not yet a law. The president also has a say. If the president signs the bill, it becomes a **law.** If the president rejects the bill through use of the **veto,** the bill is sent back to Congress with the president's reasons for not signing it. Congress can override a veto by a two-thirds vote of each chamber; the bill then becomes law without the president's signature. A bill also becomes law if Congress is in session and the president fails to sign or veto the bill within ten days (Sundays excepted). However, if Congress has concluded its term and the president fails to sign a bill within ten days, the bill does not become law. This last situation, called a *pocket veto*, forces Congress in its next term to start over from the beginning: the bill again must pass both chambers and again is subject to presidential veto.

Congress's Policymaking Role

The framers of the Constitution expected that Congress, as the embodiment of representative government, would be the institution to which the people looked for policy leadership. During most of the nineteenth century, Congress had that stature. Aside from a few strong leaders such as Andrew Jackson and Abraham Lincoln, presidents did not play a major legislative role (see Chapter 12). However, as national and international forces combined to place greater policy demands on the federal government, the president assumed a central role in the legislative process. Today Congress and the president share the legislative effort, although their roles differ.[26]

Congress's policymaking role revolves around its three major functions: lawmaking, representation, and oversight (see Table 11-3). In practice, the three functions overlap, but they are conceptually distinct.

Republican Susan Collins was first elected to the U.S. Senate from Maine in 1996. Collins is among the growing number of women who sit in the U.S. Congress. Collins easily won reelection to a third term in 2008, gathering more than 60 percent of the vote.

conference committee
A temporary committee formed to bargain over the differences in House and Senate versions of a bill. A conference committee's members are usually appointed from the House and Senate standing committees that originally worked on the bill.

law (as enacted by Congress)
A legislative proposal, or bill, that is passed by both the House and the Senate and is not vetoed by the president.

veto
The president's rejection of a bill, thereby keeping it from becoming law unless Congress overrides the veto.

TABLE 11-3 | The Major Functions of Congress

Function	Basis and Activity
Lawmaking	Through its constitutional grant to enact law, Congress makes the laws authorizing federal programs and appropriating the funds necessary to carry them out.
Representation	Through its elected constitutional officers—U.S. senators and representatives—Congress represents the interests of constituents and the nation in its deliberations and its lawmaking.
Oversight	Through its constitutional responsibility to see that the executive branch carries out the laws faithfully and spends appropriations properly, Congress oversees and sometimes investigates executive action.

The Lawmaking Function of Congress

lawmaking function

The authority (of a legislature) to make the laws necessary to carry out the government's powers.

Under the Constitution, Congress is granted the **lawmaking function**: the authority to make the laws necessary to carry out the powers granted to the national government. The constitutional powers of Congress are substantial; they include the power to tax, to spend, to regulate commerce, and to declare war. However, whether Congress takes the lead in the making of laws usually depends on the type of policy at issue.

Broad Issues: Fragmentation as a Limit on Congress's Role

Congress is structured in a way that can make agreement on large issues difficult to obtain. Congress is not one house but two, each with its own authority and constituency base. Neither the House nor the Senate can enact legislation without the other's approval, and the two chambers are hardly identical. California and North Dakota have exactly the same representation in the Senate, but in the House, which is apportioned by population, California has fifty-three seats compared to North Dakota's one.

Congress also includes a lot of lawmakers: 100 members of the Senate and 435 members of the House. They come from different constituencies and represent different and sometimes opposing interests, which leads to disagreements. Nearly every member of Congress, for example, supports the principle of global free trade. Yet when it comes to specific trade provisions, members often disagree. Foreign competition means different things to manufacturers who produce automobiles, computer chips, or underwear; it means different things to farmers who produce corn, sugar, or grapes; and it means different things to firms that deal in international finance, home insurance, or student loans. Because it means different things to different people in different areas of the country, members of Congress who represent these various areas have conflicting views on when free trade makes sense.

For such reasons, Congress often has difficulty taking the lead on broad issues of national policy. Although an increase in party unity in Congress has strengthened the role of the chamber's majority party and its leaders, the fact remains that House and Senate members are largely free to vote as they please. As a result, Congress sometimes struggles when faced with the task of crafting major legislation. In 2009, for example, Congress thrashed about for months in the process of trying to draft a comprehensive health care reform bill. Even though the Democrats had substantial majorities in both chambers, the Senate's filibuster rule and a set of divisive issues, including whether federal health care funds could be used for abortions, kept the Democrats from mustering the necessary votes. Both the House and the Senate eventually passed a health care bill, although the House and Senate versions differed substantially on key provisions. At that point, because Senate Democrats could not garner the three-fifths majority necessary to hold a vote on a compromise version of the legislation, the House passed the Senate version, even though it was widely acknowledged to have significant flaws.

As an institution, the presidency is better suited to the task of providing leadership on major national issues. First, whereas Congress's authority is divided, executive power is vested constitutionally in the hands of a single individual—the president. Unlike congressional leaders, who must bargain with their party's members when taking a stand on legislation, the president has less need to negotiate with other executive officials in taking a position. Second, whereas members of Congress often see issues from the perspective of their state or constituency, presidents have a national constituency and tend to look at policy from that perspective. Third, news coverage tilts national policy leadership toward the presidency and away from Congress. In the national press, the presidency gets twice the news coverage of Congress. Former House Speaker Thomas P. "Tip" O'Neill complained that the news media seem oblivious to the fact that Congress is a coequal branch of the national government.

Presidential leadership means that Congress will listen to White House proposals, not that it will act on them. It may reject a proposal outright, particularly when the president is from the opposing party. In 2011 and 2012, most of President Obama's major legislative initiatives were pronounced "dead on arrival" when they reached Congress. Republicans controlled the House of Representatives and were determined to block his agenda. On the other hand, when a presidential proposal is somewhat close to what a congressional majority might find acceptable, the proposal becomes the starting point for congressional negotiations, saving Congress the time and trouble of developing the legislation from scratch. (The legislative roles of Congress and the president are discussed further in Chapter 12.)

In its lawmaking activities, Congress has the support of three congressional agencies. One is the Congressional Budget Office (CBO), which has a staff of 250 employees. The CBO provides Congress with general economic projections, overall estimates of government expenditures and revenues, and specific estimates of the costs of proposed programs. A second congressional agency is the Government Accountability Office (GAO). With three thousand employees, the GAO is the largest congressional agency. Formed in 1921, it has primary responsibility for overseeing executive agencies' spending of money that has been appropriated by Congress. The programs that the executive agencies administer are authorized and funded by Congress. The GAO's responsibility is to ensure that executive agencies operate in the manner prescribed by Congress. The third and oldest congressional agency is the Congressional Research Service (CRS), which has a staff of one thousand employees and operates as a nonpartisan reference agency. CRS conducts research and responds to information requests from congressional committees and members.

Shown here is the logo of a congressional agency, the Government Accountability Office (GAO). It oversees the spending of executive agencies to check for their compliance with congressional mandates.

Congress in the Lead: Fragmentation as a Policymaking Strength

Congress occasionally takes the lead on major issues. Labor legislation, environmental law, federal aid to education, and urban development are policy areas in which Congress has taken an initiating role.[27] Nevertheless, Congress does not routinely develop broad policy programs and carry them through to passage. "Congress remains organized," James Sundquist notes, "to deal with narrow problems but not with broad ones."[28]

Not surprisingly, then, the great majority of the hundreds of bills that Congress considers each session deal with narrow issues. Congress takes the lead on these bills, which are handled largely through the standing committees. The same fragmentation that makes it difficult for Congress to lead on broad issues enables Congress to tackle scores of smaller issues simultaneously. Most of the legislation passed by Congress is "distributive"—that is, it confers a benefit on a particular group while spreading the cost across the taxpaying public. An example is the veterans' jobs bill that Congress enacted in late 2011. The bill extended tax credits to businesses that hire jobless veterans and provided funding for retraining older unemployed veterans. At the time, Congress was embroiled in a bitter partisan dispute over how to reduce the size of the federal deficit. Yet, when the veterans' bill was considered, despite the fact that it would add to the deficit, not a single member of Congress voted against it. The final vote was 95-0 in Senate and 422-0 in the House.

Distributive policies have a clear political advantage. The benefit is large enough that members of the recipient group will recognize and appreciate it, while the cost to each taxpayer is less noticeable. Such policies are also the type that Congress, through its committee system, is organizationally best suited to handle. Most committees parallel a major constituent interest, such as agriculture, commerce, labor, or veterans.

The Representation Function of Congress

representation function

The responsibility of a legislature to represent various interests in society.

In the process of making laws, the members of Congress represent various interests within American society, giving them a voice in the national legislature. The proper approach to the **representation function** has been debated since the nation's founding. A recurrent issue is whether the representative should respond to the interests of the nation as a whole or those of the constituency. These interests overlap to some degree but do not coincide exactly. Policies that have broad benefits are not necessarily advantageous to particular localities. Free trade in steel is an example. Although U.S. manufacturers as a whole benefit from access to low-priced steel from abroad, domestic steel producers and the communities where they are located are hurt by it.

Representation of States and Districts

The choice between national and local interests is not a simple one, even for a legislator who is inclined toward one or the other orientation. To be fully effective, members of Congress must be reelected time and again, a necessity that compels them to pay attention to local demands. Yet, they serve in the nation's legislative body and cannot ignore national needs. In making the choice, most members of Congress, on narrow issues at least, vote in a way that will not antagonize local interests.[29] Opposition to gun control legislation, for example, is stronger among members of Congress representing rural areas where hunting is prevalent than it is among those from urban areas where guns are more likely to be perceived as a threat to public safety.

Local representation occurs in part through the committee system. Although studies indicate that the preferences of most committees are not radically different from those of the full House or Senate,[30] committee memberships roughly coincide with constituency interests. For example, farm-state legislators dominate the membership of the House and Senate Agriculture Committees, and westerners dominate the Interior Committees (which deal with federal lands and natural resources, most of which are concentrated in the West). Committees are also the site of most **logrolling**—the practice of trading one's vote with another member's so that both get what they want. For example, it is not uncommon in the agricultural committees

logrolling

The trading of votes between legislators so that each gets what he or she most wants.

for members from livestock-producing states of the North to trade votes with members from the cotton- and peanut-producing states of the South.

Local representation also shapes how Congress distributes funds for federal programs. If a program has a local element, members of Congress will often withhold their support unless their locality gets a share of the money, even if the effect is to make the program less efficient. An example is the State Homeland Security Program that helps states to buy security equipment and train security personnel. Even though the threat of a terrorist attack is much higher in cities like New York, Washington, and Los Angeles, the act specifies that 40 percent of the money is to be spread across all the states.

Nevertheless, representation of constituency interests has its limits. Constituents have little awareness of most issues that come before Congress. Whether Congress appropriates a few million dollars in foreign aid to Chad or Bolivia is not the sort of issue that local residents will hear about. Moreover, members of Congress often have no choice but to go against the wishes of a significant portion of their constituency. The interests of workers and employers in a district or state, for example, can differ considerably. In the case of conflicting interests within their constituencies, members of Congress typically side with those that align with their party. When local business and labor groups take opposing sides on issues before Congress, for example, Republican members tend to back business's position, whereas Democratic members tend to line up with labor.

Moreover, constituent groups are not the only groups that get legislators' support. The nation's capital is filled with powerful lobbies that contribute funds to congressional campaigns. Some of these lobbies represent interests that coincide with those of the legislator's state or district but many of them do not—for example, American Crystal Sugar, a firm that produces sugar from sugar beets grown in the Red River Valley between Minnesota and the Dakotas, contributed money during 2011–2012 election cycle to dozens of congressional candidates, most of whom were from states and districts outside American Crystal Sugar's home area.

POLITICAL THINKING   Local or National?

Members of Congress represent both the nation and a particular state or district. These representational roles often complement each other but sometimes conflict. When should a representative place the interest of the nation ahead of that of the particular state or district? When should the local interest dominate? Try to place your answer in the context of specific policy issues, such as energy, trade, immigration, or defense spending.

Representation of the Nation through Parties

When a clear-cut and vital national interest is at stake, members of Congress can be expected to respond to that interest. With the economy showing signs of a recession in early 2008, Congress enacted legislation that provided most taxpayers a rebate of several hundred dollars in the hope that they would spend it, thereby giving the economy a boost. The House voted 380–34 in favor of the tax rebate; the Senate vote was 81–16.

In most cases, however, members of Congress, though agreeing on a need for national action, disagree on the course of action. Most Americans believe, for example, that the nation's education system requires strengthening. The test scores of American schoolchildren on standardized reading, math, and science examinations are substantially below those of children in many other industrial democracies. This situation creates pressure for political action. But what action is necessary and desirable? Does more money have to be funneled into public schools, and if so, which level of government—federal, state, or local—should provide it? Or does the problem rest with teachers? Should they be subject to higher performance standards? Or is the problem a lack of competition for excellence? Should schools be required to compete for students and the tax dollars they represent? Should private schools be part of any such competition, or would their participation wreck the public school system? There is no general agreement on such issues.

In Congress, disagreements over national goals occur primarily along party lines. Republican and Democratic lawmakers have different perspectives on national issues because their parties differ philosophically and politically. Differences in the parties' approach to education policy, for example, played out in the legislative debate on No Child Left Behind (NCLB), which President George W. Bush was pushing. NCLB would tie federal education grants to public schools to their students' performance on standardized national tests. Republicans stressed a need for tough testing standards. Democrats stressed a need to provide schools, particularly those in poorer communities, with the financial support necessary for them to meet NCLB testing requirements.

Partisan divisions have increasingly defined congressional action. In the past, the diversity of the congressional parties—the presence of a large number of conservatives within Democratic ranks and a large number of progressives within Republican ranks—was a barrier to legislation rooted in party ideology. Neither party could muster the support of enough of its members to pursue such legislation on a regular basis. Democratic lawmakers from the South, for example, did not share the liberal outlook of Democratic lawmakers from the North. Today, as was discussed earlier, the large majority of congressional Democrats are liberal and the large majority of congressional Republicans are conservative, which has enabled each group to pursue a legislative agenda rooted in its ideology. Local differences still matter in Congress but less so, as national party ideologies have taken center stage. On small and large issues alike, Republican and Democratic lawmakers have been deeply split.

A positive aspect of this development is that party differences are increasingly apparent to voters. At times in the past, many voters believed that the parties did not offer a clear choice. In the view of some political scientists, this situation was a barrier to accountability. They argued that America's voters deserve to have the choice between "responsible parties"—parties that take clear-cut and opposing policy positions and seek to enact them when in office so that voters can more easily hold them to account for their actions.

Critics of this view say that it fails to account for the structure of U.S. institutions. In a European parliamentary system, the majority party has full control of legislative and executive power and can enact its agenda. At the next election, the voters can decide whether they approve or disapprove of what it has accomplished. In the American system, however, executive and legislative powers are divided, and legislative power is further divided between the House and the Senate. These divisions were put in place to foster compromise and cooperation. But when the two parties are strong and closely divided in strength, the division of powers enables each

SOUTHERN CHIVALRY — ARGUMENT versus CLUB'S.

Although party polarization in Congress has reached a modern high, it pales alongside the partisan rancor of the period leading up to the Civil War. In 1856 on the Senate floor, Preston Brooks of South Carolina severely beat Charles Sumner of Massachusetts with a cane, causing brain injuries that kept Sumner out of the Senate for three years. Brooks was incensed by an abolitionist speech that Sumner had made and was greeted by cheering crowds when he returned to South Carolina after the assault.

party to prevent the other from acting. The result can be policy deadlock and delay, even in the face of pressing policy needs.[31] In *Beyond Ideology*, political scientist Frances Lee shows that, even on low-stake issues, lawmakers exploit negotiation and floor debate to attack opponents and promote their party's image. Lee also notes that the congressional agenda is increasingly shaped by partisan considerations rather than policy priorities. Parties shape some of their legislative agenda around nonsense bills that provoke the type of fight that catches journalists' attention and excites their partisan base.[32]

As congressional partisanship has intensified, the public's image of Congress has plummeted. In a 2011 Pew Research Center poll, only one in four Americans expressed approval of Congress—the lowest level ever recorded in a Pew survey (see Figure 11-5). In the 1980s, before Congress became polarized, two in three Americans approved of how Congress was doing its job.

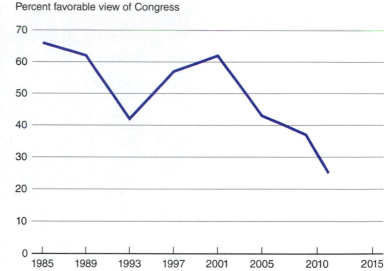

Percent favorable view of Congress

FIGURE 11-5   **Public Approval of Congress**   Partisan polarization in Congress has been accompanied by declining public approval of Congress.
Source: Pew Research Center for the People and the Press surveys.

The Oversight Function of Congress

Although Congress enacts the nation's laws, their administration is entrusted to the executive branch. Congress has the responsibility to see that the executive branch carries out the laws faithfully, a supervisory activity referred to as the **oversight function** of Congress.[33]

Oversight is carried out largely through the committee system of Congress and is facilitated by the parallel structure of the committees and the executive bureaucracy: the House and Senate judiciary committees oversee the work of the Department of Justice, the House and Senate Agriculture Committees monitor the Department of Agriculture, and so on. The Legislative Reorganization Act of 1970 spells out each committee's responsibility for overseeing its parallel agency: "Each standing committee shall review and study, on a continuing basis, the application, administration, and execution of those laws, or parts of laws, the subject matter of which is within the jurisdiction of that committee."

Oversight is a demanding task. The bureaucracy has hundreds of agencies and thousands of programs. Congress gets some leverage from the fact that federal agencies have their funding renewed each year, which provides an opportunity for congressional committees to review agency activities. Congress also gets leverage from its committee staffs, which interact regularly with the top bureaucrats in the agencies within their committee's jurisdiction.[34] Nevertheless, because the task is so large, oversight is not pursued vigorously unless members of Congress are annoyed with an agency, have discovered that a legislative authorization is being abused, or are intending to modify an agency program.

When an agency is alleged to have acted improperly, committee hearings into the allegations can occur. Congress's investigative power is not listed in the Constitution, but the judiciary has upheld this power as a reasonable extension of Congress's power to make the laws. Except in cases involving *executive privilege* (the right of the executive branch to withhold confidential information affecting national security), executive branch officials are required to testify when called by Congress to do so. If they refuse, they can be cited for contempt of Congress, a criminal offense.

oversight function
A supervisory activity of Congress that centers on its constitutional responsibility to see that the executive branch carries out the laws faithfully.

Surrounded by Democratic lawmakers, President Obama signs into law the 2010 health care reform bill. The legislation provoked an intensely partisan fight in Congress. In the end, the bill was enacted without the support of a single Republican senator or representative.

Congressional interest in oversight increases substantially when the White House is the target, and the president is from the opposite party. Until they gained control of the House and Senate in the 2006 congressional elections, Democratic lawmakers were unable to probe deeply into the Bush administration's handling of the Iraq war. After they gained control, they held scores of hearings, examining everything from the administration's justification for the war to its treatment of enemy prisoners. Through their oversight hearings, they exposed activities that were politically damaging to Bush and the Republicans.

Congress: An Institution Divided

Of all U.S. political institutions, Congress most closely reflects aspects of American culture. The individualism that pervades American society is evident in the independence of members of Congress. They are self-reliant politicians who are both part of and apart from the institution they serve. This characteristic is especially evident when candidates for Congress attack the institution for its failings and then, once in office, use the institution's resources to keep themselves there.

The diversity of American society is also reflected in Congress. This is not to say that the members of Congress are a microcosm of the U.S. population. Far from it. But Congress is diverse in the sense that it is a vast network of power centers. Each committee has its separate leaders and members and has jurisdiction over an area of American life; agriculture, labor, education, commerce, and other economic sectors have their own committees. It is hard to conceive of a national legislature structured to parallel the economic sectors of society more closely than the Congress of the United States. There is also the fact that individual representatives and senators are keenly attuned to the interests of their separate districts and states.

Congress is not an institution where majorities rule easily. Separate majorities in the two chambers, and sometimes within the relevant committees, are required for enactment of significant legislation. For this reason Congress is sometimes portrayed as a weak institution. However, the power to prevent change can be as powerful as the power to accomplish change. This was the intention of the framers of the Constitution. They designed the institution in a way that the majority could rule but only if that majority was exceptionally strong.

What the writers of the Constitution did not anticipate was the degree to which members of Congress, out of self-interest and because of their local base, would cater to the demands of special interests. The framers were intent on designing an institution that would forestall majority tyranny; in doing so, they created an institution that facilitates access and influence by special interests. The writers of the Constitution also did not anticipate how intense partisanship would interact with the structure of Congress. Party unity is the clearest way for the majority to overcome the obstacles to action inherent in Congress's fragmented structure. At the same time, party unity is the most direct way for the minority to block action. And because Congress's structure makes it easier to block legislation than to enact it, a determined minority party can act in ways that foster deadlock and delay, even in the face of urgent national problems.

Conflicting opinions on Congress are inevitable. The strength of Congress is its representativeness, its attention to local interests, and its function as an arena in which compromise is normally an ingredient of legislative accomplishment. The weakness of Congress lies in the fact that the minority—whether acting on behalf of a special interest or to block the majority from acting—has disproportionate influence. Thus, in a sense, the source of Congress's strength is also the source of its weakness. Congress could not at once be structured as an institution where power is concentrated in the hands of the majority and an institution where power is divided.

Summary

Self-Test www.mhhe.com/
pattersontadtx11e

Members of Congress, once elected, are likely to be reelected. Members of Congress can use their office to publicize themselves, pursue a service strategy of responding to the needs of individual constituents, and secure pork-barrel projects for their states or districts. House members gain a greater advantage from these activities than do senators, whose larger constituencies make it harder for them to build close personal relations with voters and whose office is more likely to attract strong challengers. Incumbency does have some disadvantages. Members of Congress must take positions on controversial issues, may blunder into political scandal or indiscretion, must deal with changes in the electorate, or may face strong challengers; any of these conditions can reduce members' reelection chances. By and large, however, the advantages of incumbency far outweigh the disadvantages. Incumbents' advantages extend into their reelection campaigns: their influential positions in Congress make it easier for them to raise campaign funds from PACs and individual contributors.

Congress is a fragmented institution. It has no single leader; rather, the House and Senate have separate leaders, neither of whom can presume to speak for the other chamber. The principal party leaders of Congress are the Speaker of the House and the Senate majority leader. They share leadership power with committee and subcommittee chairpersons, who have influence on the policy decisions of their committee or subcommittee.

It is in the committees that most of the day-to-day work of Congress is conducted. Each standing committee of the House or the Senate has jurisdiction over congressional policy in a particular area (such as agriculture or foreign relations), as does each of its subcommittees. In most cases, the full House and Senate accept committee recommendations about the passage of bills, although amendments to bills are quite common and committees are careful to take other members of Congress into account when making legislative decisions. Congress is a legislative system in which influence is widely dispersed, an arrangement that suits the power and reelection needs of its individual members. However, partisanship is a strong and binding force in Congress. It is the basis on which party leaders are able to build support for major legislative initiatives. On this type of legislation, party leaders and caucuses, rather than committees, are the central actors.

The major function of Congress is to enact legislation. Yet the role it plays in developing legislation depends on the type of policy involved. Because of its divided chambers and committee structure, as well as the concern of its members with state and district interests, Congress, through its party leaders and caucuses, only occasionally takes the lead on broad national issues. Congress instead typically looks to the president for this leadership. Nevertheless, presidential initiatives are passed by Congress only if they meet its members' expectations and usually only after a lengthy process of compromise and negotiation. Congress is more adept at handling legislation that deals with problems of narrow interest. Legislation of this sort is decided mainly in congressional committees, where interested legislators, bureaucrats, and groups concentrate their efforts on issues of mutual concern.

A second function of Congress is the representation of various interests. Members of Congress are highly sensitive to the state or district on which they depend for reelection. They do respond to overriding national interests, but for most of them local concerns generally come first. National or local representation often operates through party representation, particularly on issues that divide the Democratic and Republican parties and their constituent groups, which is increasingly the case.

Congress's third function is oversight—the supervision and investigation of the way the bureaucracy is implementing legislatively mandated programs. Although oversight is a difficult process, it is an important means of legislative control over the actions of the executive branch.

Study Corner

Key Terms

bicameral legislature (*p. 276*)
bill (*p. 286*)
cloture (*p. 288*)
conference committees
   (*p. 289*)
constituency (*p. 270*)
filibuster (*p. 288*)
gerrymandering (*p. 272*)
incumbent (*p. 269*)
jurisdiction (of a
   congressional committee)
   (*p. 283*)
law (as enacted by
   Congress) (*p. 289*)
lawmaking function (*p. 290*)
logrolling (*p. 292*)
mark up (*p. 287*)

midterm election (*p. 273*)
open-seat election (*p. 272*)
oversight function (*p. 295*)
party caucus (*p. 277*)
party leaders (*p. 276*)
party unity (*p. 277*)
pork (pork-barrel spending)
   (*p. 270*)
reapportionment (*p. 272*)
redistricting (*p. 272*)
representation function
   (*p. 292*)
rider (*p. 288*)
seniority (*p. 285*)
service strategy (*p. 270*)
standing committees (*p. 282*)
veto (*p. 289*)

Self-Test: Multiple Choice

1. Which of the following is *not* a general characteristic of the U.S. Congress?
   a. Congress is a fragmented institution.
   b. Influence in Congress is widely dispersed.
   c. Congress rather than the president usually takes the lead in addressing broad national issues.
   d. Both the House and the Senate are directly elected by the voters.

2. In Congress, the role of representation of the nation through political parties is illustrated by all of the following, *except*
   a. conflicts over national goals occurring primarily along party lines.
   b. the emphasis that members of Congress place on pork-barrel legislation.
   c. a common division of votes along party lines in committee voting.
   d. Republicans aligned against Democrats on roll-call votes.

3. Which of the following give(s) the president a policymaking advantage over Congress on broad national issues?
   a. the public's expectation that the president will take the lead on such issues
   b. the fragmented leadership structure of Congress
   c. the president's position as the sole chief executive and thus the authoritative voice of the executive branch
   d. all of the above

4. Which of the following factors usually plays the largest role in the reelection of members of Congress?
   a. incumbency
   b. positions taken on issues
   c. close ties to the president
   d. gender

5. Most bills that are introduced in Congress
   a. are defeated in committee.
   b. are passed in committee and defeated on the floor.
   c. are passed and become law.
   d. are sent to executive agencies for review.

6. The most important party leadership position in the U.S. Senate is that of
   a. Speaker.
   b. majority leader.
   c. president pro tempore.
   d. vice president of the United States.

7. Congressional incumbents receive fewer campaign contributions from PACs than their opponents do. (T/F)

8. The Speaker is the only officer of the House of Representatives provided for in the Constitution. (T/F)

9. Most of the work done in Congress is conducted through standing committees. (T/F)

10. A bill must be passed in identical form by both chambers of Congress before it can be sent to the president for approval or veto. (T/F)

Self-Test: Essay

How does the structure of Congress—for example, its two chambers and its committee system—affect its policymaking role?

Suggested Readings

Anthony, Steve. *Witness to History: A Memoir—Tom Murphy and His Role in Georgia Politics.* New York: McGraw-Hill Learning Solutions, 2010. A readable and riveting account of a legendary state legislative leader.

Burden, Barry C. *Personal Roots of Representation.* Princeton, N.J.: Princeton University Press, 2007. An analysis that reveals how representatives' personal preferences affect their legislative votes.

Dwyre, Diana, and Victoria Farrar-Myers. *Legislative Labyrinth: Congress and Campaign Finance Reform.* Washington, D.C.: CQ Press, 2001. An inside look at the mix of Congress and campaign money.

Herrnson, Paul S. *Congressional Elections: Campaigning at Home and in Washington,* 5th ed. Washington, D.C.: CQ Press, 2008. A study arguing that members of Congress run two campaigns, one at home and one in Washington.

Lee, Frances E. *Beyond Ideology: Politics, Principles, and Partisanship in the U.S. Senate.* Chicago: University of Chicago Press, 2009. A careful account of the sources of discord in the U.S. Senate.

Smith, Steven S., Jason M. Roberts, and Ryan J. Vander Wielen. *The American Congress*, 7th ed. New York: Cambridge University Press, 2011. An insightful and comprehensive examination of Congress.

Strahan, Randall. *Leading Representatives: The Agency of Leaders in the Politics of the U.S. House.* Baltimore, Md.: Johns Hopkins University Press, 2007. A study arguing that congressional leaders are powerful in their own right.

Theirault, Sean M. *Party Polarization in Congress.* New York: Cambridge University Press, 2008. A careful accounting of the various sources of the increased level of party polarization in Congress.

List of Websites

www.usafmc.org/default.asp?pagenumber=8
The website of the United States Association of Former Members of Congress, which has a "Congress to Campus" program that upon request brings former congressional members to campuses for talks.

http://thomas.loc.gov/
The Library of Congress site, named after Thomas Jefferson; provides information about the congressional process, including the status of pending legislation.

www.house.gov
The U.S. House of Representatives' website; has information on party leaders, pending legislation, and committee hearings, as well as links to each House member's office and website.

www.senate.gov
The U.S. Senate's website; similar to that of the House and provides links to each senator's website.

Participate!

Each year, thousands of college students serve as interns in Congress or a state legislature. Many internships are unpaid, but students can ordinarily receive college credit for the experience. Internships are not always a great adventure. Many legislative interns envision themselves contributing ideas and research that might influence public policy, only to find that they are answering letters, developing mailing lists, or duplicating materials. Nevertheless, few interns conclude that their experience has been a waste of time. Most find it rewarding and ultimately memorable. Information about internships can be obtained from the American Political Science Association (www.apsa.org). In addition, there are organizations in Washington that arrange internships in Congress and the executive agencies. These organizations frequently charge a fee for their services, so you might want to contact a legislative office or executive agency directly. It is important to make your request as early as possible in the college year, because some internship programs have deadlines and nearly all offices receive more requests than they can accommodate. You could also check with the student services office at your college or university. Some of these offices have information on internship programs and can be of assistance.

Extra Credit

For up-to-the-minute *New York Times* articles, interactive simulations, graphics, study tools, and more links and quizzes, visit the text's Online Learning Center at **www.mhhe.com/pattersontad11e**.

Self-Test Answers

1. c, 2. b, 3. d, 4. a, 5. a, 6. b, 7. F, 8. T, 9. T, 10. T

The Presidency: Leading the Nation

[The president's] is the only voice in national affairs. Let him once win the admiration and confidence of the people, and no other single voice will easily overpower him. Woodrow Wilson[1]

Barack Obama was sinking in the polls. Unemployment remained high, and the federal deficit was mounting. The mood in the White House was downcast compared with the first months of his presidency when his public approval rating topped 70 percent and pundits were comparing him to Franklin D. Roosevelt. His election as the first African American president had been historic, and he had campaigned on the promise of change. "We are the ones we've been waiting for," he exclaimed. "We are the change we seek."

He successfully steered his first major presidential initiative, a nearly $800 billion economic stimulus bill, through Congress. It was a legislative triumph, but it came at a price. The stimulus bill had contributed to the ballooning federal deficit, which increased the likelihood of a tax hike. The stimulus bill was followed by a knock-down, drag-out partisan battle over health care reform. Although Obama was able in the end to get a health bill through Congress, it, too, came at a price. Many Americans had doubts about the legislation's content and cost, and were confused and angered by the partisan bickering that accompanied its passage. By early 2010, Obama's approval rating had sunk below 50 percent. In a widely cited *New Yorker* article, George Packer wrote about "Obama's Lost Year." His first year in office, Packer said, bore little resemblance to the fabled "One Hundred Days" that had marked the start of Franklin D. Roosevelt's presidency.[2] Even then, the worst was yet to come. In the 2010 midterm elections, which were widely portrayed as a referendum on the Obama presidency, Republicans won a landslide victory. They captured control of the House of Representatives and proceeded to block nearly every major bill he proposed.

The Obama story is but one in the saga of the ups and downs of the modern presidency. Lyndon Johnson's and Richard Nixon's dogged pursuit of the Vietnam War led to talk of "the imperial presidency," an office so powerful that constitutional checks and balances were no longer an effective constraint on it. Within a few years, because of the

The White House contains, on the first floor, the president's Oval Office, other offices, and ceremonial rooms. The First Family's living quarters are on the second floor.

Watergate scandal and intractable international problems during the Ford and Carter presidencies, the watchword became "the imperiled presidency," an office too weak to meet the nation's need for executive leadership. Ronald Reagan's policy successes prior to 1986 renewed talk heard in the Roosevelt and Kennedy years of "a heroic presidency," an office that is the inspirational center of American politics. After the Iran-Contra scandal in 1986, Reagan was more often called a lame duck. George H. W. Bush's handling of the Gulf crisis—leading the nation in 1991 into a major war and emerging from it with a stratospheric public approval rating—bolstered the heroic conception of the office. A year later, Bush was defeated in his campaign for a second term. Bill Clinton overcame a fitful start to his presidency to become the first Democrat since Franklin D. Roosevelt in the 1930s to win reelection. As Clinton was launching an aggressive second-term policy agenda, however, he got entangled in an affair with a White House intern, Monica Lewinsky, which led to his impeachment by the House of Representatives and weakened his claim to national leadership. After the terrorist attacks of September 11, 2001, George W. Bush's job approval rating soared to a record high. By the time he left office, Americans had turned against his economic and war policies and only a third of the public had a positive view of his leadership.

No other political institution has been subject to such varying characterizations as the modern presidency. One reason is that the formal powers of the office are relatively modest and so presidential power changes with political conditions and the personal capacity of the office's occupant. The American presidency is always a central office in that its occupant is a focus of national attention. Yet the presidency operates in a system of divided powers, which means that presidential power is conditional. It depends on the president's own abilities but even more on circumstances—on whether the situation demands strong leadership and whether there is public and congressional support for that leadership. When circumstances are favorable, the president exercises considerable power. When circumstances are unfavorable, the president struggles to exercise power effectively.

This chapter examines the roots of presidential power, the presidential selection process, the staffing of the presidency, and the factors associated with the success and failure of presidential leadership. The main ideas of this chapter are:

■ *Over time, the presidency has become a more powerful office.* This development owes largely to the legacy of strong presidents and to domestic and international developments that have increased the need for executive leadership.

- *The modern presidential campaign is a marathon affair in which self-selected candidates seek a strong start in the nominating contests and a well-run media campaign in the general election.*

- *The president could not control the executive branch without a large number of presidential appointees—advisors, experts, and skilled managers—but the sheer number of these appointees is itself a challenge to presidential control.*

- *The president's election by national vote and position as sole chief executive make the presidency the focal point of national politics.* Nevertheless, whether presidents are able to accomplish their goals depends on their personal capacity for leadership, national and international conditions, the stage of their presidency, the partisan composition of Congress, and whether the issue is foreign or domestic.

Foundations of the Modern Presidency

The framers of the Constitution knew what they wanted from the presidency—national leadership, statesmanship in foreign affairs, command in time of war, enforcement of the laws—but they did not have a precise sense of how the office would work in practice. Accordingly, they chose to describe the powers of the president in general terms. Compared with Article I of the Constitution, which contains a precise listing of Congress's powers, Article II defines the president's powers in general terms (see Table 12-1).[3]

Over the course of American history, each of the president's constitutional powers has been expanded in practice beyond the framers' expectation. For example, the Constitution grants the president command of the nation's military, but only Congress can declare war. In *Federalist* No. 69, Alexander Hamilton wrote that a surprise attack on the United States was the only justification for war by presidential action. Nevertheless, presidents on their own authority have launched military attacks abroad on more than two hundred occasions. Of the roughly fifteen major wars included in that figure, only five were formally declared by Congress.[4] None of America's most recent major conflicts—the Korean, Vietnam, Persian Gulf, Balkans, Afghanistan, and Iraq wars—have been waged on the basis of a congressional declaration of war.

TABLE 12-1 | The Constitutional Authority for the President's Roles

Commander in chief: Article II, Section 2: "The President shall be commander in chief of the Army and Navy of the United States, and of the militia of the several states."

Chief executive: Article II, Section 2: "He may require the opinion, in writing, of the principal officer in each of the executive departments, upon any subject relating to the duties of their respective offices, and he shall have power to grant reprieves and pardons for offences against the United States, except in cases of impeachment."

Article II, Section 2: "He shall have power, by and with the advice and consent of the Senate, to make treaties, provided two thirds of the senators present concur; and he shall nominate, and by and with the advice and consent of the Senate, shall appoint ambassadors, other public ministers and consuls, judges of the Supreme Court, and all other officers of the United States, whose appointments are not herein otherwise provided for, and which shall be established by law."

Article II, Section 2: "The President shall have power to fill up all vacancies that may happen during the recess of the Senate, by granting commissions which shall expire at the end of their next session."

Article II, Section 3: "He shall take care that the laws be faithfully executed, and shall commission all the officers of the United States."

Chief diplomat: Article II, Section 2: "He shall have power, and with the advice and consent of the Senate, to make treaties, provided two thirds of the senators present concur."

Article II, Section 3: "He shall receive ambassadors and other public ministers."

Legislative leader: Article II, Section 3: "He shall from time to time give to the Congress information of the state of the Union, and recommend to their consideration such measures as he shall judge necessary and expedient; he may, on extraordinary occasions, convene both houses, or either of them, and in case of disagreement between them, with respect to the time of adjournment, he may adjourn them to such time as he shall think proper." (Article I, Section 7, which defines the president's veto power, is also part of his legislative authority.)

Knowing that his presidency would define future ones, George Washington wrote, "it is devoutly wished on my part that these precedents may be fixed on true principles." Washington sought a national government strong enough to keep the nation from disintegrating over sectional rivalries. Washington retired after two terms, saying that the presidency was a citizen's office and not a monarchy. The two-term precedent is now institutionalized through the Constitution's Twenty-second Amendment.

The Constitution also empowers the president to act as diplomatic leader with the authority to appoint ambassadors and to negotiate treaties with other countries, subject to approval by a two-thirds vote of the Senate. The framers anticipated that Congress would define the nation's foreign policy objectives, while the president would oversee their implementation. However, presidents gradually took charge of U.S. foreign policy and have even acquired the power to make treaty-like arrangements with other nations. In 1937, the Supreme Court ruled that *executive agreements*—which are formal agreements that presidents make on their own with foreign nations—are legally binding in the same way that treaties are.[5] Since World War II, presidents have negotiated over fifteen thousand executive agreements—more than ten times the number of treaties ratified by the Senate during the same period.[6]

The Constitution also vests "executive power" in the president. This power includes the responsibility to execute the laws faithfully and to appoint major administrators, such as the heads of federal agencies. In *Federalist* No. 76, Hamilton indicated that the president's real authority as chief executive was to be found in this appointive capacity. Presidents have indeed exercised power through their appointments, but they have also found their administrative authority—the power to execute the laws—to be significant, because it enables them to decide how laws will be implemented. President George W. Bush used his executive power to *prohibit* the use of federal funds by family-planning clinics that offered abortion counseling. President Barack Obama exerted the same power to *permit* the use of federal funds for this purpose. The same act of Congress was the basis for each of these decisions. The act authorizes the use of federal funds for family-planning services, but it neither requires nor prohibits their use for abortion counseling, enabling the president to decide the issue.

Finally, the Constitution provides the president with legislative authority, including use of the veto and the ability to propose legislation to Congress. The framers expected this authority to be used in a limited way. George Washington acted as the framers anticipated: he proposed only three legislative measures and vetoed only two acts of Congress. Modern presidents have assumed a more active legislative role. They regularly submit proposals to Congress and do not hesitate to veto legislation they dislike.

The Changing Conception of the Presidency

The presidency, for many reasons, is a more powerful office than the framers envisioned. But two features of the office in particular—*national election* and *singular authority*—have enabled presidents to make use of changing demands on government to claim national policy leadership. It is a claim that no other elected official can routinely make. Unlike the president, who is elected by nationwide vote and is the sole chief executive, members of Congress are elected from separate states or districts and operate in an institution where they share power with the other members. Unlike the president, no member of Congress can fully claim to be the nation's leader.

The first president to forcefully assert a broad claim to national policy leadership was Andrew Jackson, who was elected in 1828 on a tide of popular support that broke the upper class's hold on the presidency (see Chapter 2). Jackson used his popular backing to challenge Congress's claim to national policy leadership, contending that he was "the people's tribune." This view, however, was not shared by his immediate successors. The nation's major issues were of a sectional nature (especially the North-South split over slavery) and were suited to action by Congress, which represented state interests. In fact, throughout most of the nineteenth century (the Civil War presidency of Abraham Lincoln was an exception), Congress jealously guarded its constitutional authority over national policy. James Bryce wrote in the 1880s that Congress paid no more attention to the president's policy pronunciations than it did to the editorial stands of newspaper publishers.[7]

The nineteenth-century conception of the presidency was expressed in the **Whig theory**, which holds that the presidency is a limited or constrained office whose occupant is empowered to act only within the confines of expressly granted constitutional authority. According to this "weak presidency" theory, the president is primarily an administrator, charged with carrying out the will of Congress. "My duty," said President James Buchanan, a Whig adherent, "is to execute the laws . . . and not my individual opinions."[8]

Upon taking office in 1901, Theodore Roosevelt cast aside the Whig tradition.[9] He embraced what he called the **stewardship theory**, which calls for a "strong presidency" that is limited, not by what the Constitution allows, but by what it prohibits. The stewardship theory holds that presidents are free to act as they choose, as long as they do not take actions denied them by law. In his autobiography, Roosevelt wrote: "I declined to adopt the view that what was imperatively necessary for the nation could not be done by the President unless he could find some specific authorization for it. My belief was that it was not only his right but his duty to do anything that the needs of the nation demanded unless such action was forbidden by the Constitution or by the laws."[10] Acting on his belief, Roosevelt challenged the power of business monopolies. When coal mine owners refused to bargain with miners, he threatened to seize the mines, forcing owners to improve mine safety and increase miners' wages. He also opened world markets to American goods, using the navy and marines to project U.S. influence southward into the Caribbean and Latin America and westward toward Hawaii, the Philippines, and China (the "Open Door" policy). When congressional leaders objected, he forced a showdown, knowing that the American people would support the troops. Roosevelt said: "I have the money to send [the navy's ships] halfway around the world—let Congress bring them back."

Theodore Roosevelt's conception of a strong presidency was not shared by most of his immediate successors.[11] Herbert Hoover was slow to respond to the human misery caused by the Great Depression, saying that he did not have the constitutional authority to take strong action. His successor, Franklin D. Roosevelt (a distant cousin of Theodore Roosevelt) felt no such constraint. His New Deal policies included unprecedented public works projects, social welfare programs, and economic regulatory actions (see Chapter 3). The New Deal effectively marked the end of the limited (Whig) presidency. FDR's successor, Harry S Truman, wrote in his memoirs: "The power of the President should be used in the interest of the people and in order to do that the President must use whatever power the Constitution does not expressly deny him."[12]

Theodore Roosevelt is regarded by many historians and political scientists as the first of the "modern" presidents. Operating from an activist view of the presidency, Roosevelt ignored the nation's isolationist tradition and extended America's influence into Latin America and the Pacific. On the domestic front, he battled the business trusts, believing that unfettered capitalism was incompatible with social justice. Roosevelt held the presidency as a Republican from 1901 to 1908 and was defeated when he tried to recapture it as a third-party candidate in 1912.

Whig theory

A theory that prevailed in the nineteenth century and held that the presidency was a limited or restrained office whose occupant was confined to expressly granted constitutional authority.

stewardship theory

A theory that argues for a strong, assertive presidential role, with presidential authority limited only at points specifically prohibited by law.

The Need for a Strong Presidency

Today the presidency is an inherently strong office, made so by the federal government's increased policy responsibilities. Although individual presidents differ in their capacity for leadership, the office they hold is one that requires active involvement in a broad range of policy areas.

Modern government consists of thousands of programs and hundreds of agencies. Congress is ill suited to directing and coordinating them. Congress is a fragmented institution that acts through negotiation, bargaining, and compromise. It is simply not structured in a way that would enable it to easily and regularly oversee government activity and develop comprehensive approaches to policy. The presidency is structured in a way that enables it to do so. Final authority rests with a single individual, the president, who is thereby able to direct the actions of others and to undertake large-scale planning.[13] As a result, major domestic policy initiatives since the New Deal era have usually come from the White House, as exemplified by Lyndon Johnson's Great Society and Ronald Reagan's New Federalism (see Chapter 3). In fact, as the size of government has increased, all democracies have seen a shift in power from their legislature to their executive. In Britain, for example, the prime minister has taken on policy responsibilities that once belonged to the cabinet or the Parliament.

The presidency has also been strengthened by the expanded scope of foreign policy. World War II fundamentally changed the nation's international role and the president's role in foreign policy. The United States emerged from the war as a global superpower, a giant in world trade, and the recognized leader of the noncommunist world—a development that had a one-sided effect on America's institutions.[14] Because of the president's constitutional authority as chief diplomat and military commander and the special demands of foreign policy leadership, the president, not Congress, assumed the dominant role.[15] Foreign policy requires singleness of purpose and, at times, fast action. Congress—a large, divided, and often unwieldy institution—is poorly suited to such a response. In contrast, the president, as sole head of the executive branch, can act quickly and speak authoritatively for the nation as a whole in its relations with other nations. After the terrorist attacks of September 11, 2001, for example, President Bush took the lead in obtaining international support for U.S. military, intelligence, and diplomatic initiatives. Although Congress backed these actions, it had little choice but to

Harry S Truman's presidency was characterized by bold foreign policy initiatives. He authorized the use of nuclear weapons against Japan in 1945, created the Marshall Plan as the basis for the economic reconstruction of postwar Europe, and sent U.S. troops to fight in Korea in 1950. Truman is shown here greeting British prime minister Winston Churchill at a Washington airport in early 1952.

TABLE 12-2 | The Four Systems of Presidential Selection

Selection System	Period	Features
1. Original	1788–1828	Party nominees are chosen in congressional caucuses. Electoral College members act somewhat independently in their presidential voting.
2. Party convention	1832–1900	Party nominees are chosen in national party conventions by delegates selected by state and local party organizations. Electoral College members cast their ballots for the popular-vote winner in their respective estates.
3. Party convention, primary	1904–1968	As in system 2, except that a *minority* of national convention delegates are chosen through primary elections (the majority still being chosen by party organizations).
4. Party primary, open caucus	1972–present	As in system 2, except that a *majority* of national caucus convention delegates are chosen through primary elections.

support Bush's decision. Americans wanted decisive action and looked to the president, not to Congress, for leadership in combating terrorism. (The changing shape of the world and its implications for presidential power and leadership are discussed more fully later in the chapter.)

Choosing the President

As the president's policy and leadership responsibilities changed during the nation's history, so did the process of electing presidents. The public's role in selecting the president has grown ever more direct.[16] The United States in its history has had four systems of presidential selection, each more "democratic" than the previous one in the sense that it gave ordinary citizens a larger role in the president's election (see Table 12-2).

The delegates to the constitutional convention of 1787 feared that popular election of the president would make the office too powerful and accordingly devised an electoral vote system (the so-called Electoral College). The president was to be chosen by electors picked by the states, with each state entitled to one elector for each of its members of Congress (House and Senate combined). This system was modified after the election in 1828 of Andrew Jackson, who believed that the people's will had been denied four years earlier when he got the most popular votes but failed to receive an electoral majority. Although Jackson was unable to persuade Congress to support a constitutional amendment to eliminate the Electoral College, he championed the next-best alternative. Under Jackson's reform, which is still in effect today, the candidate who wins a state's popular vote is awarded its electoral votes (see Chapter 2). Thus, the popular vote for the candidates directly affects their electoral vote, and one candidate is likely to win both forms of the presidential vote. Since Jackson's time, only Rutherford B. Hayes (in 1876), Benjamin Harrison (in 1888), and George W. Bush (in 2000) have won the presidency after having lost the popular vote.

Jackson also championed the national party convention as a means of nominating the party's presidential candidate (before this time, nominations were made by party caucuses in Congress and in state legislatures). Jackson saw the national convention—where each state is represented by delegates who select the party nominee—as a means of strengthening the link between the presidency and the people. Since Jackson's time, all presidential nominees have been formally chosen at national party conventions.

Jackson's system of presidential nomination remained intact until the early twentieth century, when the Progressives devised the primary election as a means of curbing the power of the party bosses (see Chapter 2). State party leaders had taken control of the nominating process by handpicking their states' convention delegates. The Progressives sought to give voters the power to select the delegates. Such a process is called an *indirect primary* because the voters are not choosing the nominees directly (as they do in House and Senate races) but rather are choosing delegates who in turn select the nominees. However, the Progressives were unable to persuade most states to adopt presidential primaries, which meant that party leaders continued to control a majority of the convention delegates.

That arrangement held until 1968 when Democratic Party leaders ignored the strength of anti–Vietnam War sentiment in the primaries and nominated Vice President Hubert Humphrey, who had not entered a single primary and was closely identified with the Johnson administration's Vietnam policy. After Humphrey narrowly lost the 1968 general election to Richard Nixon, reform-minded Democrats forced changes in the nominating process. The new rules gave the party's voters more control by requiring states to select their delegates through either primary elections or **open party caucuses** (meetings open to any registered party voter who wants to attend). Although the Democrats initiated the change, the Republicans also adopted it. Today it is the voters in state primaries and open caucuses who choose the Democratic and Republican presidential nominees.[17] (About forty states choose their delegates through a primary election; the others use the caucus system.)

In sum, the presidential election system has changed from an elite-dominated process to one based on voter support. This arrangement has strengthened the presidency by providing the office with the added authority that the vote of the people confers. By virtue of having been chosen in a national election, the president has a claim to national leadership that no other U.S. official is in a position to make.

The Nominating Campaign: Primaries and Caucuses

The fact that voters pick the party nominees has opened the nominating races to nearly any prominent politician with the energy, resources, and desire to run. The competition is intense, except in the case of an incumbent president seeking renomination. The list of candidates is always a long one, as the 2012 Republican contest illustrates. The contenders included Michele Bachmann, Herman Cain, Newt Gingrich, Ron Paul, Tim Pawlenty, Rick Perry, Mitt Romney, and Rick Santorum.

Candidates for nomination have no choice but to start early and run hard. The year before the first contest in Iowa is a critical period, one that has been called the **invisible primary**. Although no votes are cast in this period, it is the time when candidates demonstrate through their fundraising ability, poll standing, and debate performance that they are serious contenders for the nomination. A candidate that fails to show strength in these areas is quickly dismissed as an also-ran. In fact, in almost every nominating race of the past three decades, the winner has been the candidate who, before a single vote was cast, had raised the most money or ranked first in the opinion polls.[18] The 2012 Republican race was no exception. On the eve of the Iowa caucuses, Romney was ahead in the national polls and had easily outpaced his Republican rivals in fundraising.

Once the state caucuses and primaries get under way, a key to success is **momentum**—a strong showing in the early contests that contributes to voter support in subsequent ones. Nobody—not the press, not donors, not the voters—has an interest in candidates who are at the back of the pack. No candidate in recent

open party caucuses

Meetings at which a party's candidates for nomination are voted on and that are open to all the party's rank-and-file voters who want to attend.

invisible primary

The critical period before the first presidential primaries and caucuses when the candidates compete for the public support, media attention, and financial contributions that can spell the difference between winning and losing once the voting begins.

momentum (in campaigns)

A strong showing by a candidate in early presidential nominating contests, which leads to a buildup of public support for the candidate.

Shown here are the contenders for the 2012 Republican presidential nomination during one of their many television debates. The eventual winner of the GOP's nominating race, Mitt Romney, is the fourth candidate from the left.

decades has got off to a lousy start in the first few contests and then picked up enough steam to win nomination. The advantage rests with the fast starters. They get more attention from the press, more money from contributors, and more consideration by the voters. It's not surprising that presidential contenders strive to do well in the early contests, particularly the first caucus in Iowa and the first primary in New Hampshire. In 2012, Romney finished in a near tie with Santorum for first place in Iowa and then won New Hampshire's primary. Although he did not lock up the nomination until much later, his fast start launched him on the way to victory.

POLITICAL

THINKING   Should There Be a National Primary?

The nomination of presidential candidates is a marathon affair. The campaign goes from state to state until the voters of each state have had their turn to cast a ballot. An alternative system would be a national primary in which, on a single day, voters throughout the nation cast their ballots. What would be the advantages and disadvantages of a national primary? Why do you think the political parties have opposed the adoption of a national primary? Would you personally prefer a national primary to the current state-by-state system?

Money is a crucial factor in presidential nominating races. Observers estimate that it takes $25 million to run a halfway respectable (though not a winning) nominating campaign. Although primary-election candidates have increasingly declined federal funding, they are eligible for it if they meet the eligibility criteria. Under the Federal Election Campaign Act of 1974 (as amended in 1979), the government matches the first $250 of each private donation received by a primary election candidate if the candidate raises at least $5,000 in individual contributions of up to $250 in at least twenty states. This provision is designed to restrict matching funds to candidates who can demonstrate that they have a reasonable level of public support. In addition, any candidate who receives matching funds must agree to limit expenditures for the nominating phase to a set amount both overall (roughly $50 million in 2012) and in individual states (the 2012 limits in Iowa and New Hampshire, for example, were roughly $1.4 million and $800,000, respectively). The limits are adjusted upward each election year to account for inflation.

Until the 2000 election, when George W. Bush declined matching funds so that he could spend an unrestricted amount of money, candidates had routinely accepted matching funds, which required them to abide by the spending limits. In 2004, Bush again turned down matching funds, as did the two leading Democratic contenders, Howard Dean and John Kerry. In 2008, an even larger number of candidates declined public funds. Obama was easily the leading fundraiser, garnering in excess of $300 million for his nominating campaign—more than four times the amount allowed if he had accepted matching funds. In 2012, none of the major Republican contenders accepted matching funds, leading some observers to conclude that the public funding level should be increased, perhaps to as much as $100 million per candidate. Otherwise, they say, the only candidates that will accept matching funds are those with no chance of victory. This development would defeat the purpose of the public funding system, which is to free the nominees from the obligations that come from taking money from wealthy individuals and groups.

The National Party Conventions

The summertime national party conventions mark the end of the nominating campaign. In an earlier era, the delegates from the various states actually bargained and negotiated over the choice of a presidential nominee. However, after the delegate selection process was changed in 1972, the strongest candidate in every case has acquired enough delegates through the primaries and caucuses to secure nomination in advance of the convention. Despite the lack of suspense, the convention remains a major event. It brings together the delegates elected in the state caucuses and primaries, who approve a party platform and formally nominate the party's presidential and vice presidential candidates. It also serves as a time for the party to heal any divisions created by the nominating race and to persuade the party faithful to rally behind its presidential candidate. Studies indicate that the conventions are a point in the campaign when large numbers of voters settle on their choice of a candidate, usually the one nominated by their preferred party.[19]

The convention is also the time when the parties choose their vice-presidential nominees. By tradition, this choice rests with the presidential nominee. In 2012, Romney selected Wisconsin representative Paul Ryan, a rising star in the Republican

Although the national party conventions are not the tumultuous and decisive events they once were, they offer the parties a showcase for their candidates and platforms. Shown here is a scene from the 2012 Democratic convention, which renominated Barack Obama and Joe Biden for president and vice president, respectively.

Party and also someone who could shore up Romney's support among social and fiscal conservatives. Ryan was a vocal opponent of abortion and a strong advocate in the House for deep cuts in government spending.

The General Election Campaign

The winner in the November general election is certain to be the Republican or the Democratic candidate. Two-thirds of the nation's voters identify with the Republican or Democratic Party, and most independents lean toward one or the other party. As a result, the major-party presidential nominees have a reservoir of votes. Even Democrat George McGovern, whose level of party support was the lowest in the past half-century, was backed in 1972 by 60 percent of his party's identifiers. Because the Democratic and Republican nominees have this built-in advantage, a third-party candidate has no realistic hope of victory. Even Ross Perot, who in 1992 ran the most successful third-party campaign in nearly a century, attracted only a fifth of the vote. On the other hand, a third-party candidate can create problems for a major party by drawing votes away from its nominee. In 2000, third-party candidate Ralph Nader received 3 percent of the popular vote, most of it from voters who otherwise preferred Al Gore, the Democratic nominee. If Nader had not been in the race, Gore, rather than George W. Bush, would have won the 2000 presidential election.

Election Strategy

The candidates' strategies in the general election are shaped by several considerations, none more so than the Electoral College (see Chapter 2). Each state has two electoral votes for its Senate representation and a varying number of electoral votes depending on its House representation. Altogether, there are 538 electoral votes, including 3 for the District of Columbia, even though it has no voting representatives in Congress. To win the presidency, a candidate must receive at least 270 votes, an electoral majority. (If no candidate receives a majority, the election is decided in the House of Representatives. No president since John Quincy Adams in 1824 has been elected in this way.)

The importance of electoral votes is magnified by the **unit rule**: all states except Maine and Nebraska grant all their electoral votes as a unit to the candidate who wins the state's popular vote. For this reason, candidates are concerned with winning the most populous states, such as California, Florida, Illinois, Michigan, New York, Ohio, Pennsylvania, and Texas. Nevertheless, a larger strategic factor than a state's size is its competitiveness. Because of the unit rule, candidates have no incentive to campaign in a lopsidedly Republican or Democratic state because its electoral votes are not in doubt. As a result, the fall campaign becomes a fight to win the toss-up states (see "How the 50 States Differ"). In 2012, only a third of the states were of this type, and they were the places where Obama or Romney spent their time and money. Other states might as well have been located in Canada for the amount of attention they received.

unit rule
The rule that grants all of a state's electoral votes to the candidate who receives the most popular votes in the state.

Media and Money

At an earlier time, candidates based their campaigns on the party organizations. Today, they rely on the media, particularly the Internet and television. The Internet is used mostly for fundraising and organizing. Television is used mostly as a way to persuade undecided voters. Through appearances on news and interview programs, as well as through their televised advertising (which accounts for most of their spending), the nominees try to win over those voters who are undecided or wavering in their choice (see Chapter 8).[20] The televised presidential

HOW THE 50 STATES DIFFER POLITICAL THINKING THROUGH COMPARISONS

ELECTORAL VOTE STRATEGY IN THE 2012 ELECTION

The Constitution of the United States specifies that the president is to be chosen by electoral votes. The candidate receiving a majority of the electoral vote, even if receiving fewer popular votes than the opponent, becomes president. The Constitution further specifies that states have authority to determine how their electors will be chosen. Today, all states except two (Maine and Nebraska, which give one electoral vote to the winner of each congressional district and two electoral votes to the statewide winner), give all their electoral votes to the popular-vote winner in the state—the so-called unit rule. This winner-take-all feature of the electoral vote system leads presidential candidates to focus on toss-up states—those that conceivably could be won by either party. These battleground states are the only ones where the candidates spend any appreciable amount of time and money during the general election. One-sided states—those that are solidly Republican or Democratic—are more or less ignored during the fall campaign. The map below identifies the potential battleground states in the 2012 presidential race, based on an analysis of states' voting patterns in recent elections.

Q: The unit rule is only one of the possible ways of allocating electoral votes. As indicated above, Maine and Nebraska use a different method. Some state legislatures are considering yet a third method: allocating their state's electoral votes among the candidates in proportion to the popular votes they each receive. What's your view? Do you think the unit rule is a fair way for states to distribute their electoral votes, or do you prefer one of the alternatives?

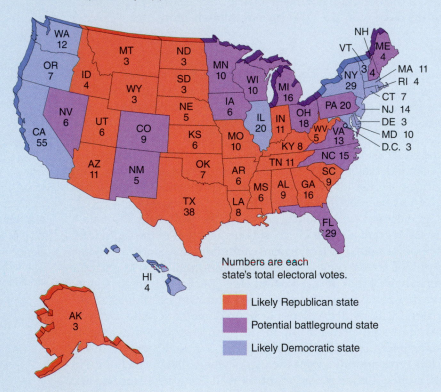

Numbers are each state's total electoral votes.

🟧 Likely Republican state

🟪 Potential battleground state

🟦 Likely Democratic state

Note: Electoral votes shown for each state are based on 2000 census.

debates are part of this effort, although the debates normally do not have a large impact on the candidates' support, largely because most voters have already picked their candidate by this point in the campaign. The 2012 debates, the first one particularly, did not follow the normal pattern. Before the first debate, Romeny had been dropping in the polls. However, he won the opening debate decisively, which energized Republican voters and helped him to pick up support among undecided and wavering voters.

The Republican and Democratic nominees are eligible for federal funding of their general election campaigns even if they do not accept it during the primaries. The amount was set at $20 million when the policy was instituted in 1976 and has been adjusted for inflation in succeeding elections—the figure for the 2012 election is roughly $90 million. The only string attached to this money is that a nominee who accepts it cannot spend additional funds on the general election campaign (although each party is allowed to spend some money—in 2012, roughly $5 million—on behalf of its nominee). In 2008, Barack Obama declined public funding, becoming the first major-party nominee to do so. Obama had promised to run on public funds but went back on his promise upon realizing that he could raise a much larger sum on his own. John McCain accepted public funding for his general election campaign and was outspent three to one by Obama. In 2012, neither Obama nor Romney accepted public funding. (Minor-party and independent presidential candidates can qualify for federal funding if they receive at least 5 percent of the vote. Their funding is proportional to the votes they attract. If, for example, a third-party candidate receives half the number of votes as the average for the major-party nominees, that candidate would get half the federal funding that each of them was eligible to receive.)

The Winners

The Constitution specifies that the president must be at least thirty-five years old, be a natural-born U.S. citizen, and have been a U.S. resident for at least fourteen years. Except for four army generals, all presidents to date have served previously as vice presidents, members of Congress, state governors, or top federal executives. Historians have devised rankings of the presidents, and their rankings reveal that there is no template for a successful presidency (see Table 12-3). The

TABLE 12-3 | **The Path to the White House**

President	Years in office	Highest previous office	Second highest office
Theodore Roosevelt	1901–1908	Vice president*	Governor
William Howard Taft	1909–1912	Secretary of war	Federal judge
Woodrow Wilson	1913–1920	Governor	None
Warren G. Harding	1921–1924	U.S. senator	Lieutenant governor
Calvin Coolidge	1925–1928	Vice president*	Governor
Herbert Hoover	1929–1932	Secretary of commerce	War relief administrator
Franklin D. Roosevelt	1933–1945	Governor	Assistant secretary of Navy
Harry S Truman	1945–1952	Vice president*	U.S. senator
Dwight D. Eisenhower	1953–1960	None (Army general)	None
John F. Kennedy	1961–1963	U.S. senator	U.S. representative
Lyndon Johnson	1963–1968	Vice president*	U.S. senator
Richard Nixon	1969–1974	Vice president	U.S. senator
Gerald Ford	1974–1976	Vice president*	U.S. representative
Jimmy Carter	1977–1980	Governor	State senator
Ronald Reagan	1981–1988	Governor	None
George H. W. Bush	1989–1992	Vice president	Director, CIA
Bill Clinton	1993–2000	Governor	State attorney general
George W. Bush	2001–2008	Governor	None
Barack Obama	2009–	U.S. senator	State senator

*Became president on death or resignation of incumbent.

DEBATING THE ISSUES POLITICAL THINKING IN ACTION

Should the Electoral College Be Abolished?

The president is chosen by an indirect system of election. Voters cast ballots for candidates, but their votes choose only each state's electors, whose subsequent ballots result in the actual selection of the president. Electoral votes are apportioned by states based on their representation in Congress, which creates the possibility that the candidate who receives the most popular votes will not receive the most electoral votes and thus will not be elected president. The 2000 election was of this type. Although George W. Bush trailed Al Gore by 550,000 votes nationally, he won Florida by 537 votes, thereby getting the state's twenty-five electoral votes, which gave him a slim majority of the electoral vote. Bush's victory renewed the debate about retaining the electoral vote system. The following are two of the arguments that were heard, the first by Congressman William Delahunt (D-Massachusetts) and the second by Congressman and two-time presidential candidate Ron Paul (R-Texas).

YES It's time to abolish the Electoral College and to count the votes of all Americans in presidential elections.... Two centuries ago the Constitutional Convention considered many ways to select the president of the emerging republic, from popular election to assigning the decision to the Congress. The Electoral College was a compromise that reflected a basic mistrust of the electorate—the same mistrust that denied the vote to women, African-Americans, and people who did not own property. The Electoral College may or may not have made sense in 1787. But through 21st-century eyes it is as anachronistic as the limitations on suffrage itself. Whether or not you like the results of a particular election . . . your vote should count. . . . If the Electoral College merely echoes the election results, then it is superfluous. If it contradicts the voting majority, then why tolerate it? It is a remarkable and enduring virtue of our political system that our elections are credible and decisive—and that power changes hands in a coherent and dignified manner. . . . Every other public official is chosen by majority vote. That's the way it's supposed to work in a democracy. For reasons both philosophical and practical, that's also how we should elect the president.

—*William D. Delahunt, U.S. representative (D-Mass.)*

NO The pundits will argue that it is not fair to deny the presidency to the man who received the most total votes. After all, to do so would be "undemocratic." This argument ignores the fundamental nature of our constitutional system. The Founding Fathers sought to create a loose confederacy of states, joined together by a federal government with very little power. They created a constitutionally limited republic, not a direct democracy. They did so to protect fundamental liberties against the whims of the masses. The Electoral College likewise was created in the Constitution to guard against majority tyranny in federal elections. The President was to be elected by the states rather than the citizenry as a whole, with votes apportioned to states according to their representation in Congress. The will of the people was to be tempered by the wisdom of the Electoral College. By contrast, election of the President by pure popular vote totals would damage statehood. Populated areas on both coasts would have increasing influence on national elections, to the detriment of less populated southern and western states. A candidate receiving a large percentage of the popular vote in California and New York could win a national election with very little support in dozens of other states! A popular vote system simply would intensify the populist pandering which already dominates national campaigns.

—*Ron Paul, U.S. representative (R-Texas)*

Q: Which argument do you find most persuasive? Can you think of other reasons for why the Electoral College should or should not be abolished?

strong presidents have differed considerably in their backgrounds, as have the weak ones. Of the four army generals, for example, two of them (George Washington and Dwight D. Eisenhower) are in the upper ranks while the other two (Ulysses S. Grant and Zachary Taylor) are in the lower ranks.

Until Obama's election in 2008, all presidents had been white. No woman has won the presidency, though it is only a matter of time before the nation elects its first woman president. Until the early 1950s, a majority of Americans polled said they would not vote for a woman for president. Today, fewer than 5 percent hold this view. A similar change of opinion preceded John F. Kennedy's election to the presidency in 1960. Kennedy was the nation's first Catholic president and only the second Catholic to receive a major party's nomination. By the time of

Kennedy's candidacy, anti-Catholic sentiment had declined to the point where it did not prevent his election. If he had won in 2012, Romney would have been the first Mormon elected to the presidency. Polls indicated that Romney's religion played only a small part in voters' decisions in the general election, although it cost him support among some Protestant denominations during the GOP nominating race.

Staffing the Presidency

When Americans go to the polls on Election Day, they are electing more than a president. They are also picking a secretary of state, the director of the FBI, and hundreds of other federal executives. Each of these is a presidential appointee, and each of these is an extension of the president's authority. Although the president cannot be in a hundred places at once, the president's appointees collectively can be. Not surprisingly, presidents typically appoint party loyalists who are committed to the administration's policy goals.

Roughly a thousand of these appointments require Senate approval and, reflecting the increased level of party polarization in Washington, the confirmation process has grown more contentious. Senators of the opposing party have sought to slow down and block the appointment of individuals they see as having unacceptable policy views. An example is Senate Republicans' opposition in 2010 to the appointment of Elizabeth Warren to head the newly created Consumer Financial Protection Bureau (CFPB). Warren was a staunch consumer advocate and had helped design the CFPB. After he withdrew her nomination, Obama nominated former Ohio attorney general Richard Cordray to head the agency. Senate Republicans then proceeded to block his appointment, forcing Obama to use a *recess appointment* to place Cordray in the position. (The Constitution permits the president to fill executive openings without Senate approval after the Senate concludes its business at the end of the year. These recess appointments expire at the end of the subsequent Senate session.)

The Vice President

The vice president holds a separate elective office from the president but, in practice, is part of the presidential team. Because the Constitution assigns no executive authority to the office, the vice president's duties within the administration are determined by the president. At an earlier time, presidents largely ignored their vice presidents, who did not even have an office in the White House. Nomination to the vice presidency was declined by several leading politicians, including Daniel Webster and Henry Clay. Said Webster, "I do not propose to be buried until I am really dead."[21] When Jimmy Carter assumed the presidency in 1977, he redefined the office by assigning important policy duties to his vice president and relocating him to an office in the White House. The vice president is now entrenched in the White House and is supported by a staff of policy advisors (the Office of the Vice President). Some observers believe that George W. Bush gave his vice president, Dick Cheney, too much power.[22] Cheney was a vigorous advocate of the Iraq invasion and other policies that ultimately weakened Bush's public and congressional support.

The Executive Office of the President (EOP)

The key staff organization is the Executive Office of the President (EOP), created by Congress in 1939 to provide the president with the staff necessary to coordinate the activities of the executive branch.[23] The EOP has since become the

The Constitution assigns no policy authority to the vice president, whose role is determined by the president. Recent vice presidents have been assigned major policy responsibilities. Earlier vice presidents played smaller roles. No vice president in history was more powerful or more controversial than Dick Cheney, shown here with President George W. Bush. Cheney played a leading role in Bush's decision to invade Iraq.

command center of the presidency. Its exact configuration is determined by the president, but some of its organizational units have carried over from one president to the next. These include the White House Office (WHO), which consists of the president's closest personal advisors; the Office of Management and Budget (OMB), which consists of experts who formulate and administer the federal budget; and the National Security Council (NSC), which advises the president on foreign and military affairs.

Of the EOP's organizational units, the **White House Office (WHO)** serves the president most directly. The WHO includes the Communications Office, the Office of the Press Secretary, the Office of the Counsel to the President, and the Office of Legislative Affairs. As these labels suggest, the WHO consists of the president's personal assistants, including top advisors, press agents, legislative and group liaison aides, and special assistants for domestic and international policy. These individuals do much of the legwork for the president and are a main source of advice. They tend to be skilled at developing political strategy and communicating with the public, the media, and other officials. They are among the most powerful individuals in Washington because of their closeness to the president.

Most of the EOP's other organizational units are staffed by policy experts. These include economists, legal analysts, national security specialists, and others. The president is advised on economic issues, for example, by the National Economic Council (NEC).

Cabinet and Agency Appointees

The heads of the fifteen executive departments, such as the Department of Defense and the Department of Agriculture, constitute the president's **cabinet.** They are appointed by the president, subject to confirmation by the Senate. Although the cabinet once served as the president's main advisory group, it has not played this role since Herbert Hoover's administration. As issues have increased in complexity, presidents have relied more heavily on presidential advisors and individual cabinet members rather than on the cabinet as a whole. Cabinet meetings are no longer the scene of lengthy debates over policy. Nevertheless, cabinet members, as individuals who head major departments, are important figures in any

White House Office (WHO)

A subunit of the Executive Office of the President, the White House Office is the core of the presidential staff system in that it includes the president's closest and most trusted personal advisors.

cabinet

A group consisting of the heads of the executive (cabinet) departments, who are appointed by the president, subject to confirmation by the Senate. The cabinet was once the main advisory body to the president, but it no longer plays this role.

administration. The president selects them for their prominence in politics, business, government, or the professions.[24] The office of secretary of state is generally regarded as the most prestigious cabinet post.

In addition to cabinet secretaries, the president appoints the heads and top deputies of federal agencies and commissions, as well as the nearly two hundred ambassadors. There are more than two thousand full-time presidential appointees, a much larger number than are appointed by the chief executive of any other democracy.[25]

The Problem of Control

Although the president's appointees are a major asset, their large number poses a control problem for the president. President Truman kept a wall chart in the Oval Office that listed the more than one hundred officials who reported directly to him. He often told visitors, "I cannot even see all of these men, let alone actually study what they are doing."[26] Since Truman's time, the number of bureaucratic agencies has more than doubled, compounding the problem of presidential control over subordinates.[27]

The president's problem is most severe in the case of appointees who work in the departments and agencies. Their offices are located outside the White House, and their loyalty is sometimes split between a desire to promote the president's goals and an interest in promoting themselves or the agencies they lead. In 2005, when Hurricane Katrina devastated New Orleans, FEMA director Michael Brown, a Bush appointee, took control even though he had no appreciable experience with disaster relief. Intent on taking the lead, Brown ignored the chain of command, withholding information from his immediate superior, the Homeland Security secretary, thereby making a coordinated relief effort harder to achieve. Brown's incompetence was initially obscured by the scale of the disaster. Two days into the relief effort, President Bush said publicly, "Brownie, you're doing a heck of a job." Several days later, however, Brown's missteps had become headline news, leading the White House to force him to resign.

Lower-level appointees within the departments and agencies pose a different type of problem. The president rarely, if ever, sees them, and many of them are political novices (most have less than two years of government or

Presidents rely on trusted advisors in making critical policy decisions. During the Cuban missile crisis in 1962, this group of advisors to President John F. Kennedy helped him decide on a naval blockade as a means of forcing the Soviet Union to withdraw its missiles from Cuba.

policy experience). They are sometimes "captured" by the agency in which they work because they depend on the agency's career bureaucrats for advice and information (see Chapter 13).

In short, the modern presidential office is a mixed benefit. Although presidential appointees enable presidents to extend their influence into every executive agency, these appointees do not always act in ways that serve the president's interest. (The subject of presidential control of the executive branch is discussed further in Chapter 13.)

Factors in Presidential Leadership

All presidents are expected to provide national leadership, but not all presidents are equally adept at it.[28] Strong presidents, as political scientist Stephen Skowronek notes, have usually had a strategic vision of where they want to lead the country, as well as a clear sense of how their ideas intersect with Americans' aspirations.[29] As a result, they have been able to communicate their goals in a way that generates public support and confidence. Ronald Reagan had this capacity, which helped him to alter the direction of domestic and foreign policy. Jimmy Carter lacked it. In what was arguably the most important speech of his presidency, Carter lamented "the malaise" that he said was infecting American life. At a time when Americans were struggling with rising inflation and unemployment and were seeking strong leadership, Carter lectured them on their lack of confidence.

Although effective leadership is a key to presidential success, it is only one component. The president operates within a system of separate institutions that share power (see "How the U.S. Differs"). Significant presidential action typically depends on the approval of Congress, the cooperation of the bureaucracy, and sometimes the acceptance of the judiciary. Because other officials have their own priorities, presidents do not always get their way. Congress in particular—more than the courts or the bureaucracy—holds the key to presidential success. Without congressional authorization and funding, most presidential proposals are nothing but ideas, empty of action. Dwight D. Eisenhower, whose personal integrity made him perhaps the most trusted president of the twentieth century, had a keen awareness of the need to win over Congress. "I'll tell you what leadership is," he said. "It's persuasion, and conciliation, and education, and patience. It's long, slow, tough work."[30]

Whether a president's initiatives succeed depends substantially on several factors, including the force of circumstance, the stage of the president's term, the nature of the particular issue, the president's support in Congress, and the president's standing with the American people. The remainder of this chapter discusses the importance of these factors.

The Force of Circumstance

During his first months in office and in the midst of the Great Depression, Franklin D. Roosevelt accomplished the most sweeping changes in domestic policy in the nation's history. Congress moved quickly to pass nearly every New Deal initiative he proposed. In 1964 and 1965, Lyndon Johnson pushed landmark civil rights and social welfare legislation through Congress on the strength of the civil rights movement, the legacy of the assassinated President Kennedy, and large Democratic majorities in the House and Senate. When Ronald Reagan assumed the presidency in 1981, inflation and high unemployment had greatly weakened the national economy and created a mood for change, enabling Reagan

HOW THE U.S. DIFFERS POLITICAL THINKING THROUGH COMPARISONS

Systems of Executive Leadership

The United States instituted a presidential system in 1789 as part of its constitutional checks and balances. This form of executive leadership was copied in Latin America but not in Europe. European democracies adopted parliamentary systems, in which executive leadership is provided by a prime minister, who is a member of the legislature. In recent years, some European prime ministers have campaigned and governed as if they were a singular authority rather than the head of a collective institution. In the 2010 British election, the three main parties' candidates for prime minister even engaged in televised debates, almost as if they were running against each other rather than as heads of their respective parties.

The policy leadership of a president can differ substantially from that of a prime minister. As a singular head of an independent branch of government, a president does not have to share executive authority but nevertheless depends on the legislative branch for support. By comparison, a prime minister shares executive leadership with a cabinet, but once agreement within the cabinet is reached, he or she is almost assured of the legislative support necessary to carry out policy initiatives.

On the other hand, the American president has the advantage of being both the head of state and the head of government. Most democracies divide the executive office between a head of state, who is the ceremonial leader, and the head of government, who is the policy leader. In Great Britain, these positions are filled by the queen and the prime minister, respectively. In democracies without a hereditary monarchy, the position of head of state is usually held by an individual chosen by the legislature. Germany's head of state, for example, is the president, who is elected by the Federal Assembly. The head of government is the chancellor, who is chosen by the majority party in the lower house (Bundestag) of the Federal Assembly. A disadvantage of the American system is that the president must devote considerable time to ceremonial functions, such as hosting visiting heads of state. An offsetting advantage is that the president alone is the center of national attention.

Q: Which executive leadership do you think is better—a presidential system, in which the chief executive heads only the executive branch, or a parliamentary system, in which the chief executive heads both the executive and the legislative branches? Why?

to persuade Congress to enact some of the most substantial taxing and spending changes in history.

From presidencies such as these has come the popular impression that presidents single-handedly decide national policy. However, each of these presidencies was marked by a special set of circumstances—a decisive election victory that gave added force to the president's leadership, a compelling national problem that convinced Congress and the public that bold presidential action was needed, and a president who was mindful of what was expected and championed policies consistent with expectations.

When conditions are favorable, the power of the presidency is remarkable. The problem for most presidents is that they serve at a time when conditions are not conducive to ambitious goals. Political scientist Erwin Hargrove suggests that presidential influence depends largely on circumstance.[31] Some presidents serve in periods when resources are scarce or when important problems are surfacing in American society but have not yet reached a critical stage. Such situations, Hargrove notes, work against the president's efforts to accomplish significant policy changes. In 1994, reflecting on the constraints of budget deficits and other factors beyond his control, President Clinton said he had no choice but "to play the hand that history had dealt" him. Even Abraham Lincoln admitted as much: "I claim not to have controlled events, but confess plainly that events controlled me."[32]

The Stage of the President's Term

If conditions conducive to great accomplishments occur irregularly, it is nonetheless the case that nearly every president has favorable moments. Such moments often come during the first months in office. Most newly elected presidents enjoy

honeymoon period

The president's first months in office, a time when Congress, the press, and the public are more inclined than usual to support presidential initiatives.

a **honeymoon period** during which Congress, the press, and the public anticipate initiatives from the Oval Office and are more predisposed than usual to support them. Most presidents propose more new programs in their first year in office than in any subsequent year.[33] Later in their terms, presidents may have run out of good ideas or depleted their political resources; meanwhile, the momentum of their election is gone, and sources of opposition have emerged. Even successful presidents like Johnson and Reagan had weak records in their final years. Franklin D. Roosevelt began his presidency with a remarkable period of achievement—the celebrated "Hundred Days"—that he was unable to duplicate later in his presidency.

An irony of the presidency, then, is that presidents are often most powerful when they are least experienced—during their first months in office. These months can, as a result, be times of risk as well as times of opportunity. An example is the Bay of Pigs fiasco during the first year of John F. Kennedy's presidency, in which a U.S.-backed invasion force of anticommunist Cubans was easily defeated by Fidel Castro's army.

The Nature of the Issue: Foreign or Domestic

In the 1960s, political scientist Aaron Wildavsky wrote that the nation has only one president but two presidencies: one domestic and one foreign.[34] Wildavsky was referring to Congress's greater deference to presidential leadership on foreign policy than on domestic policy. He had in mind the broad leeway Congress had granted Truman, Eisenhower, Kennedy, and Johnson in their foreign policies. Wildavsky's thesis is now regarded as a somewhat time-bound conception of presidential influence. Today, many of the same factors that affect a president's domestic policy success, such as the partisan composition of Congress, also affect foreign policy success.

Nevertheless, presidents still have an edge when the issue is foreign policy, because they have more authority to act on their own and are more likely to have congressional support.[35] The president is recognized by other nations as America's voice in world affairs, and members of Congress will sometimes defer to the president in order to maintain America's credibility abroad. In some cases, presidents can literally dictate the direction of foreign policy. In 2009, Obama delayed for weeks a decision on a new strategy for the war in Afghanistan, saying that "it is a matter of making certain . . . that it's making us safer." When he finally announced his strategy, which included an increase in troop levels and a timetable for withdrawal, there was some dissent in Congress, but it did not materially affect Obama's war plans.

Presidents also acquire leverage in foreign and defense policy because of their special relationship with the defense, diplomatic, and intelligence agencies. Other agencies are sometimes more responsive to Congress than to the president. The Department of Agriculture, for example, relies more heavily on the support of farm-state senators and representatives than on the president's backing. The defense, diplomatic, and intelligence agencies are a different matter. Their missions closely parallel the president's constitutional authority as commander in chief and chief diplomat. In the period before the Iraq invasion in 2003, for example, U.S. intelligence agencies provided assessments that bolstered President Bush's assertion that Iraq's weapons systems threatened American interests. Only later did Congress discover that some of the assessments were tailored to fit Bush's claims about Iraq's capabilities.

A president's domestic policy initiatives usually encounter stiffer opposition than their foreign policy efforts. The Republican and Democratic parties differ sharply in their domestic policy philosophies, and there are strong interest groups on each side of nearly every important domestic issue. Attempts at significant action in the domestic policy realm invariably activate contending forces. A case in point is President Obama's promise to reform the nation's immigration system. Obama said he would take up the issue in early 2010, but as opposition intensified, it became clear that he had little chance of getting a reform bill through Congress. Although Hispanic groups and liberal Democrats in Congress urged him to make the push anyway, believing it would mobilize the Hispanic vote in the 2010 midterm election, Obama chose not to make the fight.

Relations with Congress

Although the power of the presidency is not nearly as substantial as some Americans assume, the president's ability to set the national agenda is unrivaled. Whenever the president directs attention to a particular issue, members of Congress take notice. But will they take action? The answer is sometimes yes and sometimes no, depending in part on whether the president takes their interests into account.

Seeking Cooperation from Congress

As the center of national attention, presidents can start to believe that their ideas should prevail over those of Congress. This reasoning invariably gets the president into trouble. Jimmy Carter had not held national office before he was elected president in 1976 and lacked a sense of how Washington operates.[36] Soon after taking office, Carter cut from his budget nineteen public works projects that he regarded as a waste of taxpayers' money, ignoring the determination of members of Congress to obtain federally funded projects for their constituents. Carter's action set the tone for a conflict-ridden relationship with Congress.

To get the help of members of Congress, the president must respond to their interests.[37] The most basic fact about presidential leadership is that it takes place in the context of a system of divided powers. Although the president gets most of the attention, Congress has lawmaking authority, and presidents need its cooperation to achieve their legislative goals. In 2011, after the so-called "super committee"—a bipartisan committee of House and Senate members—failed to reach agreement on a plan to reduce the federal budget deficit, President Obama was criticized for not pressuring the committee into a decision. This criticism ignored the fact that members of Congress are separately elected and serve in a different branch of government. Presidents can cajole them but cannot force them to act. President Truman expressed the situation in blunt terms: "The people can never understand why the President does not use his supposedly great power to make 'em behave. Well, all the President is, is a glorified public relations man who spends his time flattering, kissing and kicking people to do what they are supposed to do anyway."[38]

Even the president's most direct legislative tool, the veto, has limits. Congress can seldom muster the two-thirds majority in each chamber required to override a presidential veto, so the threat of a veto can make Congress bend to the president's demands. Yet, as presidential scholar Richard Neustadt argued, the veto is as much a sign of presidential weakness as it is a sign of strength, because it arises when Congress refuses to accept the president's ideas.[39] An example is the first veto cast by George W. Bush. Until then, Bush was on track to join Thomas Jefferson as the only two-term president not to veto a bill. In 2006, however, Bush vetoed a bill that would have expanded federal support for embryonic-stem-cell research. He had announced his opposition to such research early in his presidency and succeeded for a time in getting congressional Republicans to back him. As Bush's popularity plummeted in 2005, however, some congressional Republicans separated themselves from the president out of concern for their reelection chances. Enough Republicans defected on the stem-cell bill to get it through Congress, setting the stage for Bush's first veto. Bush was weakened further when his party lost control of the House and Senate in the 2006 midterm elections. He increasingly resorted to actual and threatened vetoes in dealing with Congress.

Congress is a constituency that all presidents must serve if they expect to have its support. Neustadt concluded that presidential power, at base, is "the power to persuade."[40] Like any singular notion of presidential power, Neustadt's has limitations. Presidents at times have the power to command and to threaten. They can also appeal directly to the American people as a means of pressuring Congress. But Congress can never be taken for granted. Theodore Roosevelt expressed the wish that he could "be the president and Congress too for just ten minutes." Roosevelt would then have had the power to enact as well as to propose legislation.

Benefiting from Partisan Support in Congress

For most presidents, the next best thing to being "Congress, too" is to have a Congress filled with members of their own party. The sources of division within Congress are many. Legislators from urban and rural areas, wealthier and poorer constituencies, and different regions of the country often have conflicting policy views. To obtain majority support in Congress, the president must find ways to overcome these divisions.

No source of unity is more important to presidential success than partisanship. Presidents are more likely to succeed when their own party controls Congress (see Figure 12-1). Between 1954 and 1992, each Republican president—Eisenhower, Nixon, Ford, Reagan, and Bush—had to contend with a Democratic majority in one or both houses of Congress. Congress passed a smaller percentage of the initiatives backed by each of these presidents than those supported by any Democratic president of the period: Kennedy, Johnson, or Carter. In Clinton's first two years in office, backed by Democratic majorities in the House and Senate, more

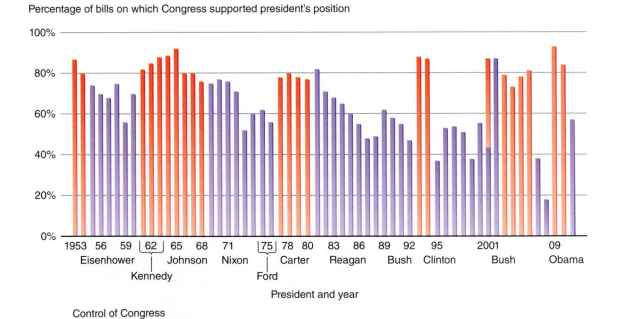

FIGURE 12-1 **Percentage of Bills Passed by Congress on Which the President Announced a Position, 1953–2011** In most years, presidents have been supported by Congress on a majority of policy issues on which they have taken a stand. Nevertheless, presidents fare much better when their party controls Congress than when the other party has a majority in one or both chambers.

Source: Congressional Quarterly Weekly Report, various dates.

than 80 percent of the bills that he supported were enacted into law. After Republicans took control of Congress in 1995, Clinton's legislative success rate sank below 40 percent. George W. Bush suffered a similar fate. He had a legislative success rate of more than 80 percent in 2006, but when control of Congress shifted from the Republicans to the Democrats in 2007, it fell to less than 40 percent. Obama's success rate followed a similar downward trajectory after Republicans captured control of House in the 2010 midterm elections. Unquestionably, presidential power depends significantly on which party controls Congress. As the historian Arthur Schlesinger put it: "In the end, arithmetic is decisive."[41] (*Unified government* is the term used to describe the situation where one party controls the presidency and both houses of Congress, whereas *divided government* is used to describe the situation where control is split between the parties.)

Few recent policy issues illustrate the importance of partisan support more than does President Obama's ability, and then his inability, to convince Congress to enact spending legislation aimed at stimulating the economy. In 2009, the Democrats had a solid majority in the House and a sizeable one in the Senate. Less than a month after the proposed legislation was introduced in Congress, it passed. Only three Republicans, all in the Senate, voted for the $787 billion spending package. In 2011 and 2012, with the Republicans now in control of the House of Representatives, Obama repeatedly asked Congress for a second spending package. In one instance, he even asked for, and was granted, the opportunity to make his argument directly to a joint session of Congress. It was all to no avail. House Republicans ignored his plea.

Colliding with Congress

On rare occasions, presidents have pursued their goals so zealously that Congress has taken steps to curb their use of power. Congress's ultimate sanction is its constitutional authority to impeach and remove the president from office. The House of Representatives decides by majority vote whether the president should be impeached (placed on trial), and the Senate conducts the trial and then votes on the president's case, with a two-thirds vote required for removal from office. In 1868, Andrew Johnson came within one Senate vote of being removed from office for his opposition to Congress's harsh Reconstruction policies after the Civil War. In 1974, Richard Nixon's resignation halted congressional proceedings on the Watergate affair that almost certainly would have ended in his impeachment and removal from office. In 1998, the House of Representatives impeached President Clinton on grounds he had lied under oath about a sexual relationship with intern Monica Lewinsky and had obstructed justice by trying to conceal the affair. The Senate acquitted Clinton, partly because polls indicated that most Americans did not think Clinton's behavior constituted "treason, bribery, or other high crimes and misdemeanors," which is what the Constitution specifies as the grounds for removing a president from office.

The gravity of impeachment action makes it an unsuitable basis for curbing presidential action except in rare instances. More often, Congress has responded legislatively to what it sees as unwarranted assertions of executive power. An example is the Budget Impoundment and Control Act of 1974, which prohibits a president from indefinitely withholding funds that have been appropriated by Congress. The legislation grew out of President Nixon's practice of withholding funds from programs he disliked. A similar controversy erupted in 2006 when it was revealed that President Bush had used so-called signing statements to challenge the constitutionality of more than seven hundred bills. These statements, appended to a bill when the president signs it, are meant to indicate that the president does not necessarily intend to abide by particular provisions of a law. Although Bush was not the first president to use this device, he had attached

The Senate votes on an article of impeachment during its 1999 trial of President Bill Clinton. He was acquitted of all charges. No president was been removed from office by action of the House and Senate, although Richard Nixon resigned the presidency in 1974 when it became clear that he would be the first.

signing statements to more bills than all his predecessors combined and had done so in secrecy. Even congressional Republicans expressed concern about the practice. At Senate Judiciary Committee hearings, Senator Arlen Specter (R-Penn.), chair of the committee, argued that presidents do not have the authority to pick and choose among legislative provisions, accepting those they like and disregarding the rest. The president's choice is to accept or reject a bill in its entirety. Said Specter, "The president has the option under the Constitution to veto or not."[42]

Congress's most ambitious effort to curb presidential power is the War Powers Act. During the Vietnam War, Presidents Johnson and Nixon misled Congress, supplying it with intelligence estimates that painted a falsely optimistic picture of the military situation. Believing the war was being won, Congress regularly voted to provide the money to keep it going. However, congressional support changed abruptly in 1971 with publication in the *New York Times* of classified documents (the so-called Pentagon Papers) that revealed the Vietnam situation to be more perilous than Johnson and Nixon claimed.

In an effort to prevent future presidential wars, Congress in 1973 passed the War Powers Act. Nixon vetoed the measure, but Congress overrode his veto. The act does not prohibit the president from sending troops into combat, but it does require the president to consult with Congress whenever feasible before doing so and requires the president to inform Congress within forty-eight hours of the reason for the military action. The War Powers Act also requires hostilities to end within sixty days unless Congress extends the period. The act gives the president an additional thirty days to withdraw the troops from hostile territory, although Congress can shorten the thirty-day period. Presidents have claimed that the War Powers Act infringes on their constitutional power as commander in chief, but the Supreme Court has not ruled on the issue, leaving open the question of whether it constrains the president's war-making powers.

POLITICAL

THINKING Can the President's War Power Be Checked?

The U.S. government is based on a system of checks and balances. In practice, there is an area where the system is deficient—the president's power to wage war. As commander in chief of the armed forces, the president has the authority to order troops into combat. Once this action occurs, Congress is almost powerless to reverse it. Congress could conceivably withhold funding for the conflict but in doing so might risk the lives of the troops. Moreover, even if a war is going badly, the president is unlikely to withdraw the troops. To do so would be an admission that the decision to go to war was a mistake. The War Powers Act of 1973 is an attempt by Congress to assert more control over America's wars. Do you think Congress should have more say in this area? How do you think the Supreme Court would rule if Congress invoked the War Powers Act and the president defied it, citing as the basis the constitutional provision that establishes the president as commander in chief of the armed forces?

TABLE 12-4 | Percentage of Public Expressing Approval of President's Performance

President	Years in office	Average during presidency (%)	First-year average (%)	Final-year average (%)
Harry S Truman	1945–1952	41	63	35
Dwight D. Eisenhower	1953–1960	64	74	62
John F. Kennedy	1961–1963	70	76	62
Lyndon Johnson	1963–1968	55	78	40
Richard Nixon	1969–1974	49	63	24
Gerald Ford	1974–1976	46	75	48
Jimmy Carter	1977–1980	47	68	46
Ronald Reagan	1981–1988	53	58	57
George H. W. Bush	1989–1992	61	65	40
Bill Clinton	1993–2000	57	50	60
George W. Bush	2001–2008	51	68	33
Barack Obama	2009–	—	58	—

Source: Averages compiled from Gallup polls.

In sum, the effect of presidential efforts to circumvent congressional authority has been to heighten congressional opposition. Even if presidents gain in the short run by acting on their own, they undermine their capacity to lead in the long run if they fail to keep in mind that Congress is a coequal branch of the American governing system.

Public Support

Presidential power rests in part on a claim to national leadership, and the strength of that claim is roughly proportional to the president's public support. **Presidential approval ratings** are predictably high at the start of the president's time in office. When asked in polls whether they "approve or disapprove of how the president is doing his job," most Americans express approval during a president's first months in office. The honeymoon rarely lasts long, however. Difficult issues and adverse developments inevitably cut away at the president's public support, and more than half of post–World War II presidents have left office with an approval rating of less than 50 percent (see Table 12-4).

With public backing, the president's leadership cannot be dismissed easily by other Washington officials. When the president's public support sinks, however, officials are less inclined to accept that leadership. In the early years of his presidency, for example, Congress gave George W. Bush most of what he asked for, which is the main reason that five years elapsed before his first veto. During Bush's first two years, Congress enacted seventeen major legislative acts, the second highest for this period among postwar presidents.[43] However, congressional opposition mounted as Bush's popularity fell in response to a deteriorating economy and a worsening of the Iraq conflict. Among the Bush initiatives rejected by Congress were his social security and immigration reform proposals.

presidential approval ratings
A measure of the degree to which the public approves or disapproves of the president's performance in office.

Events and Issues

Public support for the president is conditioned by developments at home and abroad. International crises tend to produce a patriotic "rally 'round the flag" reaction that builds support for the president. Virtually every foreign policy crisis

PARTY
POLARIZATION Political Thinking in Conflict

President of All the People, or Just Those of the Same Party?

Unlike senators and representatives, the president is elected by the vote of the whole electorate and is vested with the full authority of a branch of government. The president is also the spokesperson for the nation in in international affairs and speaks on behalf of the nation during times of crisis, at home as well as abroad. In this sense, the president represents all Americans. Increasingly, however, Americans have diverged sharply in their opinions about the president's performance. As would be expected, Democrats have always been more likely to approve of the performance of a Democratic president and disapprove of that of a Republican president, while the reverse has been true of Republicans. However, the gap in Democrats and Republicans' opinions of the president has widened significantly in recent years. During the three-decade period from Harry Truman's presidency in the late 1940s to Jimmy Carter's presidency in the late 1970s, the difference in the presidential approval level of Republicans and Democrats was roughly 35 percent on average. The difference now exceeds 60 percent, as can be seen in the figure below. As two *Washington Post* commentators put it: "We are simply living in an era in which Democrats dislike a Republican president (and Republicans dislike a Democratic one) even before [he]has taken a single official action."

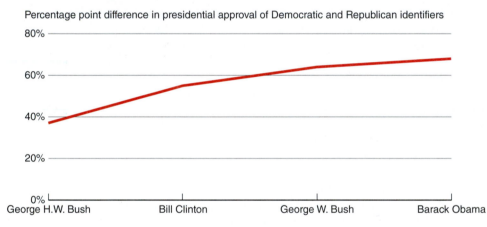

Percentage point difference in presidential approval of Democratic and Republican identifiers

Q. Why do you think the approval gap between Republicans and Democrats has widened?

A. The reasons are many but one of them is that Democrats and Republicans are now further apart in their opinions on controversial policy issues. When it comes to these issues, presidents usually take positions that are in line with prevailing opinion within their party. As a result, their positions please most of their party's followers while displeasing, even angering, most of the other party's followers.

Source: Compiled by author from various Gallup poll reports. Figure for Obama is based on Gallup polls through 2011.

of the past four decades has followed this pattern. Although Americans were divided in 2003 over the wisdom of war with Iraq, for example, President Bush's approval rating rose when the fighting began. On the other hand, public support tends to erode if the crisis is not resolved successfully or in a relatively short period. Bush's support fell steadily as U.S. casualties mounted in Iraq. By 2006, his approval rating had dropped below 40 percent, contributing to his party's heavy losses in that year's midterm election.

Economic conditions play a large part in a president's public support. Economic downturns invariably reduce public confidence in the president.[44] Ford, Carter, and the first President Bush lost their reelection bids when their popularity plummeted after the economy dipped. In contrast, Clinton's popularity rose in 1995 and 1996 as the economy strengthened, contributing to his 1996 reelection. In 2012, Obama benefited from an improving economy, which helped him win election to a second term. The irony, of course, is that presidents do not have all that much control over the economy. If they did, it would always be strong.

The Televised Presidency

An advantage that presidents have in their efforts to nurture public support is their access to the media, particularly television. Only the president can expect the networks to provide free airtime to address the nation, and in terms of the amount of news coverage, the presidency receives twice as much news coverage as Congress.

Political scientist Samuel Kernell calls it "going public" when the president bypasses bargaining with Congress and promotes "his policies by appealing to the American public for support."[45] Such appeals are at least as old as Theodore Roosevelt's use of the presidency as a "bully pulpit," but they have increased substantially in recent decades. Television has made it easier for presidents to go public with their programs, though the public's response depends partly on the president's rhetorical skill. President Reagan was so adept at the use of television that he was labeled the "Great Communicator." Nevertheless, presidents are unable to control everything that reporters say about them.[46] Journalists are adept at putting their own spin on what political leaders say and generally place a lot more emphasis on adverse developments than on positive ones.

President Ronald Reagan became known as the "Great Communicator" because of his adept use of television. Reagan acquired many of his on-camera skills during his years as a movie and television actor.

The Illusion of Presidential Government

Presidents have no choice but to try to counter negative press portrayals by putting their own spin on developments. Such efforts can carry a president only so far, however. No president can fully control his communicated image, and national conditions ultimately have the largest impact on a president's public support. No amount of public relations can disguise adverse developments at home or abroad. Indeed, presidents run a risk by building up their images through public relations. By thrusting themselves into the limelight, presidents contribute to the public's belief that the president is in charge of the national government, a perception political scientist Hugh Heclo calls "the illusion of presidential government."[47] If they are as powerful as they project themselves to be, they will be held responsible for policy failures as well as policy successes.

Because the public's expectations are high, presidents get too much credit when things go well and too much blame when things go badly. Therein rests an irony of the presidential office. More than from any constitutional grant, more than from any statute, and more than from any crisis, presidential power derives from the president's position as the sole official who can claim to represent the entire American public. Yet because presidential power rests on a popular base, it erodes when public support declines. The irony is that the presidential office typically grows weaker as problems mount, which is the time when strong presidential leadership is needed most.[48]

Summary

Self-Test www.mhhe.com/ pattersontadtx11e

The presidency has become a much stronger office than the framers envisioned. The Constitution grants the president substantial military, diplomatic, legislative, and executive powers, and in each case the president's authority has increased measurably over the nation's history. Underlying this change is the president's position as the one leader chosen by the whole nation and as the sole head of the executive branch. These features of the office have enabled presidents to claim broad authority in response to the increased demands placed on the federal government by changing global and national conditions.

During the course of American history, the presidential selection process has been altered in ways intended to make it more responsive to the preferences of ordinary people. Today, the electorate has a vote not only in the general election but also in the selection of party nominees. To gain nomination, a presidential hopeful must win the support of the electorate in state primaries and open caucuses. Once nominated, the candidates are eligible to receive federal funds for their general election campaigns, which today are based on Internet and televised appeals.

Although the campaign tends to personalize the presidency, the responsibilities of the modern presidency far exceed any president's personal capacities. To meet their obligations, presidents have surrounded themselves with large staffs of advisors, policy experts, and managers. These staff members enable the president to extend control over the executive branch while at the same time providing the information necessary for policymaking. All recent presidents have discovered, however, that their control of staff resources is incomplete and that some things that others do on their behalf can work against what they are trying to accomplish.

As sole chief executive and the nation's top elected leader, presidents can always expect that their policy and leadership efforts will receive attention. However, other institutions, particularly Congress, have the authority to make presidential leadership effective. No president has come close to winning approval of all the programs he has placed before Congress, and presidents' records of success have varied considerably. The factors in a president's success include whether national conditions that require strong leadership from the White House are present and whether the president's party has a majority in Congress.

Presidential success stems from the backing of the American people. Recent presidents have made extensive use of the media to build public support for their programs, yet they have had difficulty maintaining that support throughout their terms of office. A major reason is that the public expects far more from its presidents than they can deliver.

CHAPTER 12

Study Corner

Key Terms

cabinet (*p. 316*)
honeymoon period (*p. 320*)
invisible primary (*p. 308*)
momentum (in campaigns)
  (*p. 308*)
open party caucuses
  (*p. 308*)

presidential approval
  ratings (*p. 325*)
stewardship theory (*p. 305*)
unit rule (*p. 311*)
Whig theory (*p. 305*)
White House Office (WHO)
  (*p. 316*)

Self-Test: Multiple Choice

1. Which two features of the presidency have enabled it to become more powerful than the framers envisioned?
   a. the powers to disregard the Supreme Court and Congress during national emergencies
   b. the power to use presidential resources to defeat members of Congress and the power to veto acts of Congress
   c. election by national vote and the president's position as sole chief executive
   d. the powers to appoint federal judges and to appoint high-ranking executives

2. Key presidential appointees who are responsible for coordinating the activities of the executive branch are located in the
   a. Office of the General Counsel.
   b. Attorney General's Office.
   c. Government Accountability Office.
   d. Executive Office of the President.

3. A president is most successful passing legislative initiatives when Congress is
   a. in recess.
   b. acting in an election year as opposed to a year when no federal election is scheduled to be held.
   c. controlled by the president's own party.
   d. concentrating on domestic policy issues as opposed to foreign policy issues.

4. Which of the following is *not* an important factor in the success that presidents have had in getting their policy proposals enacted into law?
   a. the force of circumstance, such as war or economic instability
   b. stage of the president's term
   c. level of public support for the president's leadership
   d. ability to raise campaign funds

5. Which of the following systems has *not* been used in the United States for presidential selection?
   a. national party convention
   b. direct election by popular vote
   c. combination of national convention and primary elections
   d. party primary and open party caucus

6. From their appointment power, newly elected presidents gain all of the following, *except*
   a. expert advice on policymaking.
   b. total assurance that appointees will always act in the president's best interests.
   c. an opportunity to extend their influence into the federal bureaucracy.
   d. an opportunity to appoint like-minded individuals to executive offices.

7. A candidate running for president has to accept federal campaign funding. (T/F)

8. Under the War Powers Act, the president must have the formal consent of Congress to send U.S. troops into combat. (T/F)

9. National conditions, such as the state of the economy, rarely affect the level of public confidence in the president. (T/F)

10. Big government after the Roosevelt era has favored the growth of legislative authority at the expense of executive authority. (T/F)

Self-Test: Essay

Why is presidential power "conditional"—that is, why is it affected so substantially by circumstance, the nature of the issue, the makeup of Congress, and popular support? (The separation of powers should be part of your answer.)

Suggested Readings

Campbell, James E. *The American Campaign: U.S. Presidential Campaigns and the National Vote.* College Station: Texas A & M University Press, 2008. An analysis that reveals the predictability of presidential campaign outcomes.

Cohen, Jeffrey E. *The Presidency in the Era of 24-Hour News.* Princeton, N.J.: Princeton University Press, 2008. A look at how changes in the media have affected presidential communication and politics.

Hargrove, Erwin C. *The Effective Presidency.* Boulder, Colo.: Paradigm Publishers, 2008. An assessment of presidential leadership through an examination of the Kennedy through George W. Bush presidencies.

Milkis, Sidney, and Michael Nelson. *The American Presidency: Origins and Development, 1776–2002,* 5th ed. Washington, D.C.: CQ Press, 2007. A thoughtful assessment of the factors and conditions that have molded the presidential office.

Neustadt, Richard E. *Presidential Power and the Modern Presidents: The Politics of Leadership from Roosevelt to Reagan.* New York: Free Press, 1990. The classic analysis of the limitations on presidential power.

Norrander, Barbara. *The Imperfect Primary: Oddities, Biases and Strengths in U.S. Presidential Nomination Politics.* New York: Routledge, 2010. A thoughtful analysis of the nominating process.

Pika, Joseph A., and John Anthony Maltese. *The Politics of the Presidency,* 7th ed. Washington, D.C.: CQ Press, 2008. An insightful look at the leadership skills demanded of presidents.

Skowronek, Stephen. *Presidential Leadership in Political Time: Reprise and Reappraisal.* Lawrence: University of Kansas Press, 2008. An assessment of how conditions of the time have affected presidents' role and power.

List of Websites

www.ibiblio.org/lia/president
A site with general information on specific presidents and links to the presidential libraries.

www.ipl.org/div/potus
A site that profiles the nation's presidents, their cabinet officers, and key events during their time in office.

www.usa.gov
A site that gives information on the presidency and the Executive Office of the President, as well as links to key executive agencies and organizations.

www.whitehouse.gov
The White House's home page; has an e-mail guest book and includes information on the president, the vice president, and current White House activities.

Participate!

Consider writing a letter or sending an e-mail to the president or a top presidential appointee that expresses your opinion on an issue that is currently the object of executive action. You can inform yourself about the administration's policy or stance on the issue through the website of the White House (www.whitehouse.gov) or of the agency in question (for example, the State Department's site, www.state.gov).

Extra Credit

For up-to-the-minute *New York Times* articles, interactive simulations, graphics, study tools, and more links and quizzes, visit the text's Online Learning Center at **www.mhhe.com/pattersontad11e**.

Self-Test Answers

1. c, 2. d, 3. c, 4. d, 5. c, 6. b, 7. F, 8. F, 9. F, 10. F

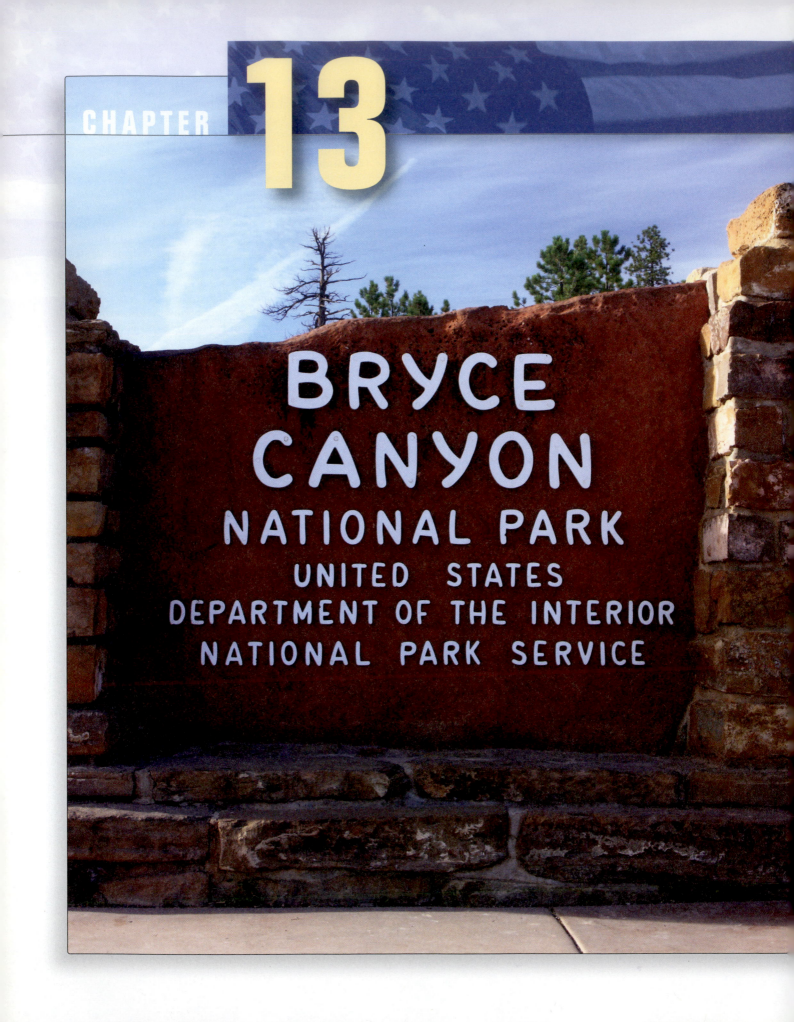

BRYCE
CANYON
NATIONAL PARK
UNITED STATES
DEPARTMENT OF THE INTERIOR
NATIONAL PARK SERVICE

The Federal Bureaucracy: Administering the Government

Origin and Structure of the Federal Bureaucracy

Types of Federal Agencies
Federal Employment

The Budgetary Process

The President and Agency Budgets
Congress and the Agency Budgets

Policy and Power in the Bureaucracy

The Agency Point of View
Sources of Bureaucratic Power

Democracy and Bureaucratic Accountability

Accountability through the
    Presidency
Accountability through Congress
Accountability through the Courts
Accountability within the
    Bureaucracy Itself

From a purely technical point of view, a bureaucracy is capable of attaining the highest degree of efficiency, and is in this sense formally the most rational known means of exercising authority over human beings. Max Weber[1]

On April 20, 2010, as the *Deepwater Horizon* was drilling an exploratory oil well nearly a mile deep in the Gulf of Mexico, methane gas shot out from the drilling pipe and exploded, engulfing the oil platform in flames, killing eleven workers and forcing the rest to jump into the rig's lifeboats. Two days later, still aflame, the *Deepwater Horizon* sank, collapsing the drilling pipe, which sent oil from the well gushing into the Gulf. Nearly three months elapsed before the oil well could be capped, resulting in the worst environmental disaster in the nation's history. The resulting oil spill forced closure of much of the Gulf to fishing, damaged hundreds of miles of beaches and wetlands, and killed unknown quantities of marine life.

The U.S. government blamed the disaster on the oil firm BP, which owned the drilling rights and was supervising the ill-fated drilling operation. But the government itself had a hand in the disaster. Oversight of offshore drilling was the responsibility of the Minerals Management Service (MMS), a bureau within the Department of the Interior. MMS had been lax, or worse, in its responsibilities. Rather than closely regulating offshore drilling, top MMS managers had given oil companies wide latitude in meeting safety and environmental standards. When this information became known in the days following the sinking of the *Deepwater Horizon*, MMS's top officials were forced to resign and a reorganization of MMS was undertaken. In announcing this action, President Barack Obama said: "For a decade or more, the cozy relationship between the oil companies and the federal agency was allowed to go unchecked. That allowed drilling permits to be issued in exchange not for safety plans, but assurances of safety from oil companies. That cannot and will not happen anymore."

Government agencies are seldom in the headlines unless they do something wrong, as in the case of MMS. Nor do federal agencies rank high in public esteem. Even though most Americans respond favorably

As one of thousands of services provided by the federal bureaucracy, the National Oceanic and Atmospheric Administration monitors hurricane activity and provides early warning to affected coastal areas.

bureaucracy

A system of organization and control based on the principles of hierarchical authority, job specialization, and formalized rules.

hierarchical authority

A basic principle of bureaucracy that refers to the chain of command within an organization whereby officials and units have control over those below them.

job specialization

A basic principle of bureaucracy holding that the responsibilities of each job position should be defined explicitly and that a precise division of labor within the organization should be maintained.

formalized rules

A basic principle of bureaucracy that refers to the standardized procedures and established regulations by which a bureaucracy conducts its operations.

to personal encounters with the federal bureaucracy (as, for example, when a senior citizen applies for social security), they have a low opinion of the bureaucracy as a whole. A Pew Research Center poll found, for example, that roughly two-thirds of Americans see the bureaucracy as "inefficient and wasteful."

Yet, ambitious programs like space exploration, social security, interstate highways, and universal postal service would be impossible without the federal bureaucracy. In fact, the bureaucratic form of organization is found wherever there is a need to manage large numbers of people and tasks. Its usefulness is clear from the fact that virtually every large private organization is also a bureaucracy, although such organizations typically operate by a different standard than do most public organizations. Efficiency is the chief goal of private organizations but is only sometimes the goal of public organizations. The most efficient way to administer government loans to college students, for instance, would be to give money to the first students who apply and then shut down the program when the money runs out. College loan programs, like many other government programs, operate on the principles of fairness and need, which require that each application be judged on its merit.

In formal terms, **bureaucracy** is a system of organization and control that is based on three principles: hierarchical authority, job specialization, and formalized rules. These features are the reason bureaucracy, as a form of organization, is the most efficient means of getting people to work together on tasks of large magnitude. **Hierarchical authority** refers to a chain of command whereby the officials and units at the top of a bureaucracy have authority over those in the middle, who in turn control those at the bottom. Hierarchy speeds action by reducing conflict over the power to make decisions: those higher in the organization have authority over those below them. **Job specialization** refers to explicitly defined duties for each job position and to a precise division of labor within the organization. Specialization yields efficiency because each individual concentrates on a particular job and becomes proficient at the tasks it involves. **Formalized rules** are the established procedures and regulations by which a bureaucracy conducts its operations. Formalized rules enable workers to make quick and consistent judgments because decisions are based on preset rules rather than on a case-by-case basis.

The noted German sociologist Max Weber (1864–1920) was the first scholar to systematically analyze the bureaucratic form of organization. Although Weber admired the bureaucratic form of organization for its efficiency, he recognized that its advantages carried a price. Bureaucrats' actions are dictated by position, specialty, and rule. In the process, they can become insensitive to circumstance. They often stick to the rules even when it's clear that bending them would produce a better result. "Specialists without spirit," was Weber's unflattering description of the bureaucratic mindset.[2]

This chapter examines both the need for bureaucracy and the problems associated with it. The chapter describes the bureaucracy's responsibilities, organizational structure, and management practices. The chapter also explains the "politics" of the bureaucracy. Although the three constitutional branches of government impose a degree of accountability on the bureaucracy, its sheer size confounds their efforts to control it fully. The main points discussed in this chapter are:

- *Bureaucracy is an inevitable consequence of complexity and scale.* Modern government could not function without a large bureaucracy. Through authority, specialization, and rules, bureaucracy provides a means of managing thousands of tasks and employees.

- *Bureaucrats naturally take an "agency point of view," seeking to promote their agency's programs and power.* They do this through their expert knowledge, support from clientele groups, and backing by Congress or the president.

- *Although agencies are subject to oversight by the president, Congress, and the judiciary, bureaucrats exercise considerable power in their own right.*

Origin and Structure of the Federal Bureaucracy

The federal bureaucracy was initially small (three thousand employees in 1800, for instance). The federal government's role was confined largely to defense and foreign affairs, currency and interstate commerce, and the delivery of the mail. In the latter part of the 1800s, the bureaucracy began to grow rapidly in size (see Figure 13-1), largely because economic growth was generating new demands on government. Farmers were among the groups clamoring for help, and Congress in 1889 created the Department of Agriculture. Business and labor interests also pressed their claims, and Congress in 1903 established the Department of Commerce and Labor. (A decade later, the department was split into separate commerce and labor departments.) The biggest spurt in the bureaucracy's growth, however, took place in the 1930s. Franklin D. Roosevelt's New Deal included creation of the Securities and Exchange Commission (SEC), the Social Security Administration (SSA), the Federal Deposit Insurance Corporation (FDIC), the Tennessee Valley Authority (TVA), and numerous other federal agencies. Three decades later, Lyndon Johnson's Great Society initiatives, which thrust the federal government into policy areas traditionally dominated by the states, resulted in the creation of additional federal agencies, including the Department of Transportation and the Department of Housing and Urban Development.

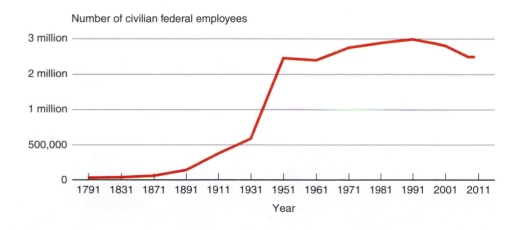

FIGURE 13-1

Number of Full-Time Federal Employees

The federal bureaucracy grew slowly until the 1930s, when an explosive growth began in the number of programs that required ongoing administration by the federal government.

Source: Historical Statistics of the United States and Statistical Abstract of the United States, 1986, 322; recent figures from U.S. Office of Personnel Management. Figure excludes military personnel.

Although the federal bureaucracy is sometimes portrayed as an entity that grows larger by the year, the facts say otherwise. Federal employment today is at roughly the same level as it was fifty years ago, despite the fact that the U.S. population has nearly doubled in size since then.

Types of Federal Agencies

At present, the U.S. federal bureaucracy has about 2.5 million employees, who have responsibility for administering thousands of programs. The president and Congress get far more attention in the news, but the federal bureaucracy has a more direct impact on Americans' everyday lives. It performs a wide range of functions; for example, it delivers the daily mail, oversees the national forests, administers social security, enforces environmental protection laws, maintains the country's defense systems, provides foodstuffs for school lunch programs, operates the airport flight-control systems, and regulates the stock markets.

The U.S. federal bureaucracy is organized along policy lines. One agency handles veterans' affairs, another specializes in education, a third is responsible for agriculture, and so on. No two units are exactly alike. Nevertheless, most of them take one of five forms: cabinet department, independent agency, regulatory agency, government corporation, or presidential commission.

The leading administrative units are the fifteen **cabinet (executive) departments** (see Figure 13-2). Except for the Department of Justice, which is led by the attorney general, the head of each department is its secretary (for example, the secretary of defense), who also serves as a member of the president's cabinet. Cabinet departments vary greatly in their visibility, size, and importance. The Department of State, one of the oldest and most prestigious departments, is also

cabinet (executive) departments

The major administrative organizations within the federal executive bureaucracy, each of which is headed by a secretary or, in the case of Justice, the attorney general. Each department has responsibility for a major function of the federal government, such as defense, agriculture, or justice.

FIGURE 13-2
Cabinet (Executive) Departments
Each executive department is responsible for a general policy area and is headed by a secretary or, in the case of Justice, the attorney general, who serves as a member of the president's cabinet. Shown is each department's year of origin. (The Office of the Attorney General was created in 1789 and was reorganized as the Justice Department in 1870.)

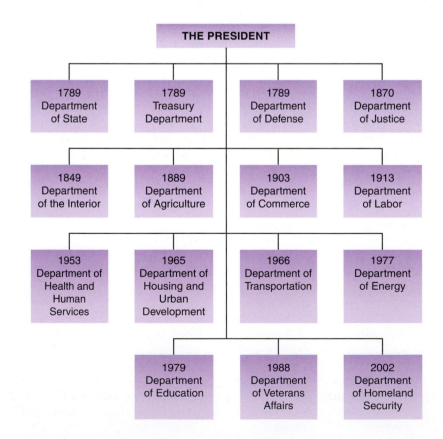

one of the smallest, with approximately 25,000 employees. The smallest with a mere 5,000 employees is the Department of Education. The Department of Defense has the largest budget and workforce, with more than 600,000 civilian employees (apart from the more than 1.4 million uniformed active service members). The Department of Health and Human Services has the second largest budget, most of which goes for Medicaid and Medicare payments (but not social security payments, which are handled by the Social Security Administration, an independent agency). The Department of Homeland Security is the newest department, dating from 2002.

Each cabinet department has responsibility for a general policy area, such as defense or law enforcement. This responsibility is carried out within each department by semiautonomous operating units that typically carry the label "bureau," "agency," "division," or "service." The Department of Justice, for example, has thirteen such operating units, including the Federal Bureau of Investigation (FBI), the Civil Rights Division, the Tax Division, and the Drug Enforcement Administration (DEA).

Independent agencies resemble the cabinet departments but typically have a narrower area of responsibility. They include organizations such as the Central Intelligence Agency (CIA) and the National Aeronautics and Space Administration (NASA). The heads of these agencies are appointed by and report to the president but are not members of the cabinet. Some independent agencies exist apart from cabinet departments because their placement within a department would pose symbolic or practical problems. NASA, for example, could conceivably be located in the Department of Defense, but such positioning would suggest that the space program exists solely for military purposes and not also for civilian purposes, such as space exploration and satellite communication.

The largest and also the oldest independent agency is the U.S. Postal Service, with roughly seven hundred thousand employees. Established at the nation's founding, the postal service delivers a first-class letter for the same low price to any postal address in the United States, a policy made possible by its status as a government agency. If the postal service were a private firm, the price of a first-class stamp would vary by location, with remote areas of states like Wyoming and the Dakotas paying extremely high rates.

Regulatory agencies are created when Congress recognizes the need for ongoing regulation of a particular economic activity. Examples of such agencies are the Securities and Exchange Commission (SEC), which oversees the stock and bond markets, and the Environmental Protection Agency (EPA), which regulates industrial pollution. In addition to their administrative function, regulatory agencies have a legislative function and a judicial function. They develop lawlike regulations and then judge whether individuals or organizations are complying with them. The EPA, for example, can impose fines and other penalties on business firms that violate environmental regulations.

Government corporations are similar to private corporations in that they charge clients for their services and are governed by a board of directors. However, receive federal funding to help defray operating expenses, and their directors are appointed by the president with Senate approval. Government corporations include the Federal Deposit Insurance Corporation (FDIC), which insures individuals' savings accounts against bank failures, and the National Railroad Passenger Corporation (Amtrak), which provides passenger rail service.

Presidential commissions provide advice to the president. Some of them are permanent bodies; examples include the Commission on Civil Rights and the Commission on Fine Arts. Other presidential commissions are temporary and

independent agencies
Bureaucratic agencies that are similar to cabinet departments but usually have a narrower area of responsibility. Each such agency is headed by a presidential appointee who is not a cabinet member. An example is the National Aeronautics and Space Administration.

regulatory agencies
Administrative units, such as the Federal Communications Commission and the Environmental Protection Agency, that have responsibility for the monitoring and regulation of ongoing economic activities.

government corporations
Government bodies, such as Amtrak, which are similar to private corporations in that they charge for their services but differ in that they receive federal funding to help defray expenses. Their directors are appointed by the president with Senate approval.

presidential commissions
Advisory organizations within the bureaucracy that are headed by commissioners appointed by the president. An example is the Commission on Civil Rights.

HOW THE 50 STATES DIFFER   POLITICAL THINKING THROUGH COMPARISONS

THE SIZE OF STATE BUREAUCRACIES

Although the federal bureaucracy is often criticized as being "too big," it is actually smaller on a per-capita basis than even the smallest state bureaucracy. There are 83 federal employees for every 1,000 Americans. Illinois, with 103 state employees for every 1,000 residents, has the smallest state bureaucracy on a per-capita basis. Hawaii has the largest—428 state employees per 1,000 residents.

Q: What do the states with larger per-capita bureaucracies have in common?

A: In general, the less populous states, especially those that cover a large geographical area, have larger bureaucracies on a per-capita basis. This pattern reflects the fact that a state, whatever its population or area, must perform basic functions (such as highway maintenance and policing).

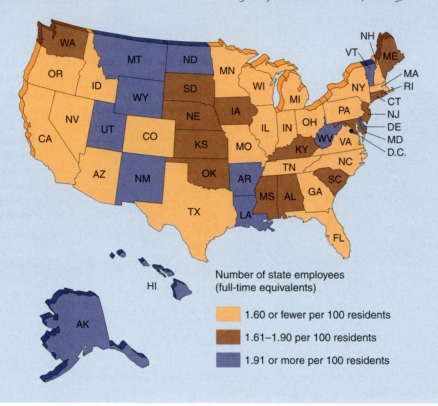

Number of state employees
(full-time equivalents)

■ 1.60 or fewer per 100 residents
■ 1.61–1.90 per 100 residents
■ 1.91 or more per 100 residents

Source: U.S. Census Bureau, 2010.

disband after making recommendations on specific issues. An example is the President's Commission to Strengthen Social Security, which was created by President George W. Bush in 2001 to study ways of reforming social security.

Federal Employment

The roughly 2.5 million full-time civilian employees of the federal government include professionals who bring their expertise to the problems involved in governing a large and complex society, service workers who perform such tasks as the typing of correspondence and the delivery of mail, and middle and top managers who supervise the work of the various federal agencies. Most civil servants are hired through the government's **merit system,** whereby they have to score high on a competitive exam (as in the case of postal service, civil service, and foreign service employees) or have specialized training (as in the case of

merit system

An approach to managing the bureaucracy whereby people are appointed to government positions on the basis of either competitive examinations or special qualifications, such as professional training.

lawyers, engineers, and scientists). The merit system is overseen by two independent agencies. The Office of Personnel Management supervises the hiring and job classification of federal employees. The Merit Service Protection Board hears appeals from career civil servants who have been fired or face other disciplinary action.

The merit system is an alternative to the **patronage system** that governed federal employment during much of the nineteenth century. Patronage was the postelection practice of filling administrative offices with people who had supported the winning party. In the view of President Andrew Jackson, its chief advocate, the patronage system was a way to tie the administration of government to the people it served. Later presidents extended patronage to all levels of administration without much regard for its impact on the quality of administration, which led critics to label it a **spoils system**—a device for the awarding of government jobs to friends and party hacks. In any case, as the federal government grew in size and complexity, the need for a more skilled workforce emerged. In 1883, Congress passed the Pendleton Act, which established a merit system for certain positions. By 1885, roughly 10 percent of federal positions were filled on a merit basis. The proportion increased sharply when the Progressives championed the merit system as a way of eliminating partisan corruption (see Chapter 2). By 1920, as the Progressive Era was concluding, more than 70 percent of federal employees were merit appointees. Today, they make up more than 90 percent of the federal workforce.[3] (Among the nonmerit employees are patronage appointees, who include those holding presidential and congressional staff positions—see Chapters 11 and 12.)

The assassination of President James A. Garfield in 1881 by Charles Guiteau, a disappointed office seeker, did much to end the spoils system of distributing government jobs.

The administrative objective of the merit system is **neutral competence.**[4] A merit-based bureaucracy is "competent" in the sense that employees are hired and retained on the basis of their skills, and it is "neutral" in the sense that employees are not partisan appointees and are expected to be of service to everyone, not just those who support the incumbent president. Although the merit system contributes to impartial and proficient administration, it has its own biases and inefficiencies. Career bureaucrats tend to place their agency's interests ahead of those of other agencies and typically oppose efforts to trim their agency's programs. They are not partisans in a Democratic or Republican sense, but they are partisans in terms of protecting their own agencies, as will be explained more fully later in the chapter.

The large majority of federal employees have a GS (Graded Service) job ranking. The regular civil service rankings range from GS-1 (the lowest rank) to GS-15 (the highest). College graduates who enter the federal service usually start at the GS-5 level, which provides an annual salary of roughly $27,000 for a beginning employee. With a master's degree, employees begin at level GS-9 with a salary of roughly $40,000 a year. Federal employees' salaries increase with rank and length of service. Although federal employees are underpaid in comparison with their counterparts in the private sector, they receive better fringe benefits—including full health insurance, secure retirement plans, and substantial vacation time and sick leave—than do most private-sector employees.

Federal employees can form labor unions, but their unions by law have limited scope; the government has full control of job assignments, compensation, and promotion. Moreover, the Taft-Hartley Act of 1947 prohibits strikes by

patronage system

An approach to managing the bureaucracy whereby people are appointed to important government positions as a reward for political services they have rendered and because of their partisan loyalty.

spoils system

The practice of granting public office to individuals in return for political favors they have rendered.

neutral competence

The administrative objective of a merit-based bureaucracy. Such a bureaucracy should be "competent" in the sense that its employees are hired and retained on the basis of their expertise and "neutral" in the sense that it operates by objective standards rather than partisan ones.

federal employees and permits the firing of striking workers. When federal air traffic controllers went on strike anyway in 1981, President Reagan fired them. There are also limits on the partisan activities of civil servants. The Hatch Act of 1939 prohibited them from holding key jobs in election campaigns. Congress relaxed this prohibition in 1993, although some high-ranking administrators are still barred from taking such positions.

The Budgetary Process

budgetary process

The process through which annual federal spending and revenue determinations are made.

The Constitution mentions executive agencies but does not grant them authority. Their authority derives from grants of power to the three constitutional branches: Congress, the president, and the courts. Of special importance to executive agencies is the **budgetary process**—the process through which annual federal spending and revenue decisions are made. It is no exaggeration to say that agencies live and die by their budgets. No agency or program can exist without funding.

Agencies play an active role in the budgetary process, but the elected branches have final authority. The Constitution assigns Congress the power to tax and spend, but the president, as chief executive, also has a major role in determining the budget (see Chapter 12). The budgetary process involves give-and-take between Congress and the president as each tries to influence how federal funding will be distributed among various agencies and programs.[5] From beginning to end, the budgetary process lasts a year and a half (see Figure 13-3).

The President and Agency Budgets

The budgetary process begins in the executive branch when the president, in consultation with the Office of Management and Budget (OMB), establishes general budget guidelines. OMB is part of the Executive Office of the President (see Chapter 12) and takes its directives from the president. Hundreds of agencies are covered by the budget, and OMB uses the president's directives to issue

FIGURE 13-3

Federal Budgetary Process
The budget begins with the president's instructions to the agencies and ends when Congress enacts the budget. The entire process spans about eighteen months.

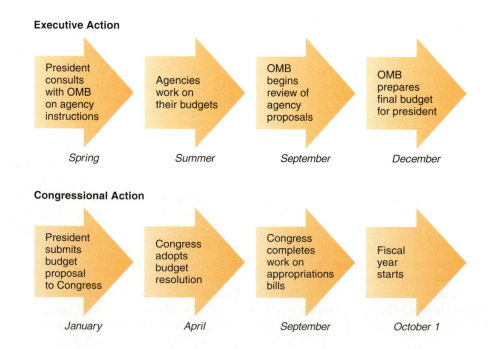

Executive Action

President consults with OMB on agency instructions	Agencies work on their budgets	OMB begins review of agency proposals	OMB prepares final budget for president
Spring	Summer	September	December

Congressional Action

President submits budget proposal to Congress	Congress adopts budget resolution	Congress completes work on appropriations bills	Fiscal year starts
January	April	September	October 1

guidelines for each agency's budget preparations. Each agency, for example, is assigned a budget ceiling that it cannot exceed in developing its budget proposal.

The agencies receive their guidelines in the spring and then work through the summer to create a detailed agency budget, taking into account their existing programs and new proposals. Agency budgets are then submitted to OMB in September for a full review that invariably includes further consultation with each agency and the White House. OMB then finalizes the agency budgets and combines them into the president's budget proposal.

The agencies naturally seek additional funding for their programs, whereas OMB has the job of matching the budget to the president's priorities. However, the president does not have any real say over most of the budget, about two-thirds of which involves mandatory spending. This spending is required by law, as in the case of social security payments to retirees. The president has no authority to suspend or reduce such payments. Accordingly, OMB focuses on the one-third of the budget that involves discretionary spending, which includes spending on defense, foreign aid, education, national parks, space exploration, and highways. In reality, even a large part of this spending is not truly discretionary. No president would slash defense spending to almost nothing or cut off funding for the national parks.

The president, then, works on the margins of the budget. In most policy areas, the president will propose a modest spending increase or decrease over the previous year. There are always a few areas, however, where the president will seek a substantial adjustment. In his 2010 budget, for example, President Barack Obama requested an additional $45 billion in defense spending for a troop buildup in Afghanistan.

Congress and the Agency Budgets

In January, the president's budget is submitted to Congress. During its work on the budget, the president's recommendations undergo varying degrees of change. Congress has constitutional authority over government spending and its priorities are never exactly the same as the president's, even when the congressional majority is of the same political party. When it is of the opposite party, its priorities will differ substantially from those of the president.

Upon reaching Congress, the president's budget proposal goes to the House and Senate budget committees. Their job is to recommend overall spending and revenue levels. Once approved by the full House and Senate, the levels are a constraint on the rest of Congress's work on the budget.

The House and Senate appropriations committees take over at this point. As with the executive branch, these committees focus on discretionary spending programs, which are basically the only budget items subject to change (see Figure 13-4). The House Appropriations Committee through its thirteen subcommittees reviews the budget, which includes hearings with officials from each federal agency. Each subcommittee has responsibility for a particular substantive area, such as defense or agriculture. A subcommittee may cut an agency's budget if it concludes that the agency is overfunded or may increase the budget if it concludes that the agency is underfunded. The subcommittees' recommendations are then reviewed by the House Appropriations Committee as a whole. The budget is also reviewed by the Senate Appropriations Committee and its subcommittees. However, the Senate is a smaller body, and its review of agency requests is less exacting than

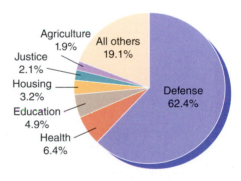

FIGURE 13-4   **Discretionary Federal Spending, by Category**
About two-thirds of the federal budget involves mandatory spending, as in the case of social security payments to retirees. As a result, the annual budget process focuses on discretionary (nonmandatory) spending—funding that at least in theory can be adjusted during negotiations between the White House, Congress, and the agencies. The largest discretionary spending category is national defense. Health and human services is a distant second, followed by education, housing and urban development, the justice system (courts and corrections), and agriculture. All other policy areas combined account for less than a fifth of the discretionary spending budget.
Source: Office of Management and Budget, 2012.

that of the House. To a degree, the Senate Appropriations Committee serves as a "court of last resort" for agencies that have had their funding requests cut by OMB or by the House Appropriations Committee.

Throughout this process, members of the House and Senate rely on the Congressional Budget Office, which, as discussed in Chapter 11, is the congressional equivalent of OMB. If the Congressional Budget Office believes that OMB or an agency has miscalculated the amount of money needed to carry out its mandated programs, it will alert Congress to the discrepancy.

After the House and Senate appropriations committees have completed their work, they submit their recommendations to the full chambers for a vote. If approved by a majority in the House and in the Senate, differences in the Senate and House versions are then reconciled in conference committee (see Chapter 11). The reconciled version of the budget is then voted upon in the House and Senate and, if approved, is sent to the president to sign or veto. The threat of a presidential veto can be enough to persuade Congress to accept many of the president's recommendations. In the end, the budget inevitably reflects both presidential and congressional priorities. Neither branch gets everything it wants, but each branch always gets some of what it seeks.

POLITICAL

THINKING Balanced Budget, Good Idea or Bad Idea?

A constitutional amendment to require a balanced federal budget has been proposed from time to time. The amendment would force lawmakers to bring spending and revenues into line each year. Do you think a balanced budget amendment is a good idea? Would you make an exception in time of war or economic recession? If such an amendment were enacted, what *combination* of spending cuts and tax increases would you suggest in order to balance the budget? (Even if some politicians say otherwise, every serious analyst that's looked at the issue has concluded that the budget cannot be balanced only by cutting spending or by raising taxes.)

After the budget has been signed by the president, it takes effect on October 1, the starting date of the federal government's fiscal year. If agreement on the budget has not been reached by October 1, temporary funding legislation is required in order to maintain government operations. In 2011, for instance, Democrats and Republicans deadlocked on budgetary issues to such an extent that they twice almost missed the deadline that would have forced a shutdown of nonessential government services, such as the national parks.

Policy and Power in the Bureaucracy

policy implementation

The primary function of the bureaucracy; it refers to the process of carrying out the authoritative decisions of Congress, the president, and the courts.

Administrative agencies' main task is **policy implementation**—that is, the carrying out of decisions made by Congress, the president, and the courts. When a directive is issued by Congress, the president, or the courts, the bureaucracy is charged with executing it. In implementing these decisions, the bureaucracy is constrained by the budget. It cannot spend money on an activity unless Congress has appropriated the necessary funds.

Some of what the bureaucracy does is fairly straightforward, as in the case of delivering the mail, processing government loan applications, and imprisoning those convicted of crime. Yet the bureaucracy often has broad discretion when implementing policy. Consider the example of the Consumer Financial Protection Bureau (CFPB) that Congress created in 2010 to protect consumers from financial institutions that exploit consumers in the granting of home mortgages, credit cards, and the like. The legislation that created the CFPB instructed the agency to:

- Conduct rule-making, supervision, and enforcement for Federal consumer financial protection laws
- Restrict unfair, deceptive, or abusive acts or practices
- Take consumer complaints
- Promote financial education
- Research consumer behavior
- Monitor financial markets for new risks to consumers

However, the legislation did not spell out in detail how the CFPB was to implement these tasks. What type of enforcement would it conduct? Which unfair practices would it restrict, and how would this be done? What action would be taken on consumer complaints? How would financial education occur? What consumer behaviors would be studied? How would financial markets be monitored and new risks identified? It was left to CFPB bureaucrats to devise the answers to these questions.

As the CFPB example illustrates, the bureaucracy is far more than an administrative extension of the three branches. Administrative agencies make policy in the process of determining how to implement congressional, presidential, and judicial decisions. FBI agents, for example, pursue organized crime more vigorously than they pursue white-collar crime, even though the law does not say that white-collar crime should be pursued less aggressively.[6] Or consider the U.S. Forest Service, which is required by law to employ a "multiple use" policy of forest land—preserving the forests as an environmental heritage while also opening up the forests for harvesting by lumber companies. The Forest Service's decisions have sometimes favored environmental interests and at other times have favored logging interests. The Federal Communications Commission (FCC) provides yet another example. It has a broad mandate under the Federal Communication Act to regulate various forms of communication. On its own authority, it has developed different regulatory regimes for telephones, broadcast television, cable television, and the Internet. For a lengthy period, for example, the FCC required broadcasters to adhere to a fairness standard; if they aired one side of a political issue, they were also required to air opposing sides. The FCC later rescinded this doctrine. Both of these FCC rulings were based on the same legislative act. Such *rulemaking*—determining how a law will work in practice—is the chief way administrative agencies exercise control over policy.[7]

The Old Executive Office Building is adjacent to the West Wing of the White House. Its occupants include the Office of Management and Budget (OMB), which plays a key role in the budgetary process.

In the course of their work, administrators also develop policy ideas that they then propose to the White House or Congress. The origin of the Occupational Safety and Health Act is an example. A bureaucrat believed that worker safety was not receiving enough attention and encouraged his brother, a presidential speechwriter, to bring it to the attention of the White House. Department of Labor officials then picked up the issue, as did some labor unions and members of Congress. When the legislation was under consideration by congressional committees, bureaucrats who had pressed for the creation of an occupational safety and health program were among those invited to testify.[8]

In sum, administrators initiate policy, develop it, evaluate it, apply it, and decide whether others are complying with it. The bureaucracy does not simply administer policy. It also *makes* policy.

The Agency Point of View

agency point of view

The tendency of bureaucrats to place the interests of their agency ahead of other interests and ahead of the priorities sought by the president or Congress.

A key issue about bureaucratic policymaking is the perspective that bureaucrats bring to their decisions. Do they operate from the perspective of the president or do they operate from the perspective of Congress? The answer is that, although bureaucrats are responsive to both of them, they are even more responsive to the needs of the agency in which they work, a perspective called the **agency point of view.** This outlook comes naturally to most high-ranking civil servants. More than 80 percent of top bureaucrats reach their high-level positions by rising through the ranks of the same agency.[9] As one top administrator said when testifying before the House Appropriations Committee, "Mr. Chairman, you would not think it proper for me to be in charge of this work and not be enthusiastic about it . . . would you? I have been in it for thirty years, and I believe in it."[10] One study found, for example, that social welfare administrators are three times as likely as other civil servants to believe that social welfare programs should be a top spending priority.[11]

Professionalism also cements agency loyalties. High-level administrative positions have increasingly been filled by scientists, engineers, lawyers, educators, physicians, and other professionals. Most of them take a job in an agency whose mission they support, as in the case of the aeronautical engineers who work for NASA or the doctors who work for the National Institutes of Health (NIH).

Although the agency point of view distorts government priorities, bureaucrats have little choice but to look out for their agency's interests. The president and members of Congress differ in their constituencies and thus in the agencies to which they are most responsive. Republican and Democratic officials also differ in their priorities, a reality that is never more apparent than when party control of the presidency or Congress changes. Some agencies rise or fall in their level of political support for that reason alone. In sum, if an agency is to operate successfully in America's partisan system of divided power, it must seek support wherever it can find it. If the agency is a low priority for the president, it needs to find backing in Congress. If Republican lawmakers want to cut the agency's programs, it must turn to Democratic lawmakers for help. In other words, agencies are forced to play politics if they want to protect their programs.[12] An agency that sits on the sidelines while other agencies seek support from the White House and Congress is likely to lose out in budget negotiations.

Sources of Bureaucratic Power

In promoting their agency's interests, bureaucrats rely on their specialized knowledge, the support of interests that benefit from their programs, and the backing of the president and Congress.

HOW THE U.S. DIFFERS POLITICAL THINKING THROUGH COMPARISONS

Educational Backgrounds of Bureaucrats

To staff its bureaucracy, the U.S. government tends to hire persons with specialized educations to hold specialized jobs. This approach heightens the tendency of bureaucrats to take the agency point of view. By comparison, Great Britain tends to recruit its bureaucrats from the arts and humanities, on the assumption that general aptitude is the best qualification for detached professionalism. The continental European democracies also emphasize detached professionalism, but in the context of the supposedly impartial application of rules. As a consequence, high-ranking civil servants in Europe tend to have legal educations. The college majors of senior civil servants in the United States and other democracies reflect these tendencies.

Q: Why might the hiring pattern for the U.S. bureaucracy make it more likely that civil servants in the United States will take an agency point of view than will civil servants in some other democracies?

A: Compared with the bureaucracies of other western democracies, the U.S. bureaucracy has a higher proportion of employees with a specialized education. They tend to take jobs in agencies where their specialty is particularly desirable, as in the case of the aeronautical engineers who work at NASA. Accordingly, their training would incline them to support their agency's mission—the agency point of view. European civil servants are more likely to have a type of education, as in the case of law or the humanities, that is less specific to the work of a particular agency, which presumably would make them less likely to deeply embrace their agency's mission.

College major of senior civil servants

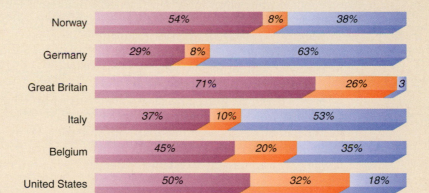

Norway	54%	8%	38%
Germany	29%	8%	63%
Great Britain	71%	26%	3
Italy	37%	10%	53%
Belgium	45%	20%	35%
United States	50%	32%	18%

■ Social science, humanities, business, other
■ Natural science, engineering
■ Law

Source: Adapted from B. Guy Peters, *The Politics of Bureaucracy,* 5th ed. (New York: Routledge, 2001), p. 118.

The Power of Expertise

Most of the policy problems confronting the federal government are extraordinarily complex. Whether the problem relates to space travel or hunger in America, a solution requires deep knowledge of the problem. Much of this expertise is provided by bureaucrats. They spend their careers working in a particular policy area, and many of them have had scientific, technical, or other specialized training (see "How the U.S. Differs").[13] Elected officials, on the other hand, are generalists, none more so than the president, who must deal with dozens of issues. Members of Congress acquire some expertise through their committee work, but most of them lack the time, training, or inclination to become deeply knowledgeable of the issues they handle. It's not surprising that Congress and the president rely heavily on career administrators for policy advice.

All agencies acquire some influence over policy through their careerists' expertise. No matter how simple a policy issue may appear at first, it nearly always has layers of complexity. The recognition that the United States has a trade deficit with China, for example, can be the premise for policy change, but this recognition does not begin to address basic issues such as the form the new policy might take, its probable cost and effectiveness, and its links to other issues, such as America's standing in Asia. Among the officials most likely to understand these issues are the career bureaucrats in the Treasury Department, the Department of State, the Commerce Department, and the Federal Trade Commission.

The Power of Clientele Groups

Most federal agencies were created for the purpose of promoting, protecting, or regulating a particular interest. Indeed, nearly every major interest in society—commerce, labor, agriculture, banking, and so on—has a corresponding federal agency. In most cases, these interests are **clientele groups** in the sense that they benefit directly from the agency's programs. As a result, clientele groups can be counted on to lobby Congress and the president on behalf of the agency when its programs and funding are being reviewed.[14] Even a relatively weak or loosely organized clientele group can be of help to an agency if its programs—and therefore, the group's benefits—are threatened with cuts or elimination. When House Speaker Newt Gingrich threatened in 1995 to "zero out" funding for the Corporation for Public Broadcasting, Congress was inundated by complaints from listeners of National Public Radio (NPR) and viewers of the Public Broadcasting System (PBS) who worried that programs like *Sesame Street* and *All Things Considered* might be canceled. Many of the complaints came from Republicans in rural areas where the local NPR station is a leading source of local news and information. Within a few weeks, Gingrich had retreated from his position, saying that a total funding cut was not what he had in mind.

The relationship between an agency and its clientele group is a reciprocal one. Just as a clientele group can be expected to protect its agency, the agency will work to protect the group.[15] The Department of Agriculture, for instance, is a dependable ally of farm interests year after year. The same cannot be said of the president or Congress as a whole, which must balance farmers' demands against those of other groups.

clientele groups

Special interest groups that benefit directly from the activities of a particular bureaucratic agency and therefore are strong advocates of the agency.

The popular children's program *Sesame Street* is produced through the Corporation for Public Broadcasting, a government agency that gains leverage in budgetary deliberations from its public support. Shown here in a photo of a display at the Smithsonian National Museum of American History is Oscar the Grouch, a *Sesame Street* puppet whose home is a garbage can.

DEBATING THE ISSUES   POLITICAL THINKING IN ACTION

Did the CIA Play Politics?

The federal bureaucracy is a storehouse of knowledge that informs national policy. Though major policy decisions are made primarily by elected officials, these officials rely on agencies for policy-related information. Seldom has this relationship created more controversy than in the case of Iraq's weapons programs. The Bush administration justified its invasion of Iraq in 2003 by saying that intelligence agencies had confirmed Iraq's possession of large stockpiles of weapons of mass destruction and its willingness to use them. After U.S. military forces invaded Iraq, investigators could not find evidence of an Iraqi weapons program of the scale portrayed by the administration. Suddenly, the intelligence agencies themselves were on the spot. Had they misread their intelligence or slanted it to fit the Bush administration's agenda? Or had they offered their best judgment based on the intelligence they had? There were sharply conflicting views on this issue, including those of Senator Carl Levin, a member of the Senate Select Committee on Intelligence, and George Tenet, the director of the CIA.

YES   There is now confirmation from the administration's own leading weapons inspector that the intelligence community produced greatly flawed assessments about Iraq's weapons of mass destruction in the months leading up to the invasion of Iraq. It is my opinion that flawed intelligence and the administration's exaggerations concerning Iraq's weapons of mass destruction resulted from an effort to make the threat appear more imminent and the case for military action against Iraq appear more urgent than they were. . . . Director Tenet, after 12 months of indefensible stonewalling, recently relented and declassified the material that I requested, which makes clear that his public testimony before the Congress on the extent to which the United States shared intelligence with the United Nations on Iraq's weapons of mass destruction programs was false. . . . In other words, honest answers by Director Tenet might have undermined the false sense of urgency for proceeding to war and could have contributed to delay, neither of which fit the administration's policy goals. . . . We rely on our intelligence agencies to give us the facts, not to give us the spin on the facts. The accuracy and objectivity of intelligence should never be tainted or slanted to support a particular policy.

—*Carl Levin, U.S. senator (D-Mich.)*

NO   Much of the current controversy centers on our prewar intelligence on Iraq, summarized in the National Intelligence Estimate of October 2002. . . . This Estimate asked if Iraq had chemical, biological, and nuclear weapons and the means to deliver them. We concluded that in some of these categories, Iraq had weapons. And that in others—where it did not have them—it was trying to develop them. Let me be clear: analysts differed on several important aspects of these programs and those debates were spelled out in the Estimate. They never said there was an "imminent" threat. Rather, they painted an objective assessment for our policymakers of a brutal dictator who was continuing his efforts to deceive and build programs that might constantly surprise us and threaten our interests. No one told us what to say or how to say it. . . . Did these strands of information weave into a perfect picture—could they answer every question? No—far from it. But, taken together, this information provided a solid basis on which to *estimate* whether Iraq did or did not have weapons of mass destruction and the means to deliver them. It is important to underline the word *estimate*. Because not everything we analyze can be known to a standard of absolute proof.

—*George J. Tenet, director of central intelligence*

Q: How would you explain the fact that U.S. intelligence agencies provided flawed assessments of Iraq's weapons systems?

The Power of Friends in High Places

Although the goals of the president or Congress can conflict with those of the bureaucracy, they need it as much as it needs them. An agency's resources—its programs, expertise, and group support—can help elected officials achieve their policy goals. When President Obama early in his presidency announced the goal of making the United States less dependent on foreign oil, he needed the help of the Department of Energy's experts to develop programs that would further that objective. At a time when other agencies were feeling the pinch of a tight federal budget, the Department of Energy's budget nearly doubled.

Agencies also have allies in Congress. Agencies with programs that benefit important key voting blocs are particularly likely to have congressional support. A prime example is the Department of Agriculture. Although the agricultural sector is just one of the president's many concerns, it is a primary concern of farm-state senators and representatives. They can be counted on to support Department of Agriculture funding and programs.

Democracy and Bureaucratic Accountability

Studies have found that the U.S. federal bureaucracy compares favorably to government bureaucracies elsewhere. "Some international bureaucracies," Charles Goodsell writes, "may be roughly the same [as the U.S. bureaucracy] in quality of performance, but they are few in number."[16] The U.S. Postal Service, for example, has an on-time and low-cost record that few national postal services can match.

Nevertheless, the federal bureaucracy's policy influence is at odds with democratic principles. The bureaucratic form of governing is the antithesis of the democratic form. Bureaucracy entails hierarchy, command, permanence of office, appointment to office, and fixed rules, whereas self-government involves equality, consent, rotation of office, election to office, and open decision making. The president and members of Congress are accountable to the people through elections. Bureaucrats are not elected and yet exercise a significant degree of independent power.

Their influence raises the question of **bureaucratic accountability**—the degree to which bureaucrats are held accountable for the power they exercise. To a small degree, they are accountable directly to the public. In some instances, for example, agencies are required to hold public hearings before issuing new regulations. For the most part, however, bureaucratic accountability occurs largely through the president, Congress, and the courts.[17]

Accountability through the Presidency

Periodically, presidents have launched broad initiatives aimed at making the bureaucracy more responsive. The most recent was the National Performance Review, which Bill Clinton began when he assumed the presidency in 1993. He had campaigned on the issue of "reinventing government" and assembled "reinventing teams" that produced 384 specific recommendations grouped into four broad imperatives: reducing red tape, putting customers first, empowering administrators, and eliminating wasteful spending.[18] Although different in its particulars, the National Performance Review was like earlier reform panels, including the Brownlow, Hoover, and Volcker commissions,[19] which sought with some success to improve the bureaucracy's efficiency, responsiveness, and accountability.

Presidents can also intervene more directly through *executive orders* to force agencies to pursue particular administrative actions. In the closing days of his presidency, for example, Bill Clinton ordered federal agencies to take the steps necessary to ensure that eligible individuals with limited English proficiency obtained full access to federal assistance programs.

Nevertheless, presidents do not have the time or knowledge to exercise personal oversight of the federal bureaucracy. It is far too big and diverse. Presidents rely instead on management tools that include reorganization, presidential appointees, and the executive budget.[20]

Reorganization

The bureaucracy's size—its hundreds of separate agencies—makes it difficult for presidents to coordinate its activities. Agencies pursue independent and even conflicting paths. For example, the United States spends more than $50 billion annually to gather intelligence on threats to the nation's security and does so through several

bureaucratic accountability
The degree to which bureaucrats are held accountable for the power they exercise.

agencies. Each of them has its own priorities and a desire to retain control of the intelligence information it has gathered. A lack of communication between the CIA and the FBI contributed to the failure to prevent the terrorist attacks on the World Trade Center and the Pentagon on September 11, 2001. Each agency had information that might have disrupted the attack if the information had been shared.

Presidents have sought to streamline the bureaucracy in an attempt to make it more accountable. After the intelligence breakdown in 2001, for example, President Bush commissioned a study of the intelligence agencies that resulted in the creation of the Office of

Although studies indicate that its performance compares favorably with other government bureaucracies, the U.S. federal bureaucracy is often criticized. One of the most frequent complaints is that it is wasteful of taxpayers' money.

the Director of National Intelligence in 2004. Fifteen intelligence agencies, including the CIA and the FBI, now report directly to the director of national intelligence, who has responsibility for coordinating their activities.

Such reorganization efforts usually improve the bureaucracy's performance, but not dramatically so.[21] On Christmas Day 2009, for example, Umar Farouk Abdulmutallab boarded a plane in Amsterdam that was headed for Detroit. As the plane prepared to land in Detroit, Abdulmutallab attempted to detonate plastic explosives hidden in his underwear. Quick action by other passengers might have been all that prevented him from blowing up the plane and killing all aboard. After his arrest, it was revealed that his father had contacted CIA officials to tell them of his son's extremism and that U.S. intelligence officials had earlier obtained information tying Abdulmutallab to terrorist groups. Nevertheless, U.S. intelligence officers had failed to revoke his visa to enter the United States and had failed to enter his name on the "no-fly list," enabling him to escape detection when he went through airport security in Amsterdam. The episode led to presidential and congressional investigations that sought to discover how America's reorganized intelligence system could have performed so poorly.

Presidents have had more success in controlling the bureaucracy by moving activities out of the agencies and into the Executive Office of the Presidency (EOP). As explained in Chapter 12, EOP is directly under White House control and functions to a degree as the president's personal bureaucracy. The EOP now makes some policy decisions that at an earlier time would have been made in the agencies. For example, the office of the United States Trade Representative, which is part of the EOP, has assumed some of the policy authority that once belonged to the Department of Commerce.

Presidential Appointments

For day-to-day oversight of the bureaucracy, presidents rely on their political appointees. The president has about three thousand partisan appointees. Some appointees fill part-time positions and some must satisfy specified criteria, such as legal training, Even so, presidents appoint a large number of handpicked executive officials—more than ten times the number appointed, for example, by the British prime minister.

The top positions in every agency are held by presidential appointees. Their influence is greatest in agencies that have substantial discretionary authority. Some agencies, like the Social Security Administration (SSA), operate within guidelines that limit what agency heads can do. Although the SSA has a huge budget and makes monthly payments to more than 40 million Americans, recipient eligibility is determined by fixed rules. The head of the SSA does not have the option, say, of granting a retiree an extra $100 a month because the retiree is facing financial hardship. At the other extreme are the regulatory agencies, which have considerable latitude in their decisions. For example, Republican Ronald Reagan's appointee to chair the Federal Trade Commission (FTC), James Miller III, shared Reagan's belief that consumer protection policy had gone too far and was hurting business interests. In Miller's first year as head of the FTC, it dropped one-fourth of its pending cases against business firms. During Miller's full tenure at the FTC, it pursued only half as many cases as it had under his predecessor, who was appointed by a Democratic president, Jimmy Carter.[22]

As party polarization has increased in Washington, the presidential appointment process has become more contentious. Presidents have increasingly sought to appoint individuals who can be trusted to advance the White House's agenda while senators of the opposing have increasingly sought to block those that they think are overly partisan (see "Party Polarization"). Although presidents usually prevail in these showdowns, there are limits to what they can accomplish through their appointees. Presidential appointees number in the hundreds, and many of them lack detailed knowledge of the agencies they head, making them dependent on agency careerists. By the time they come to understand the agency's programs, many of them leave. The typical presidential appointee stays on the job for about two years before moving on to other employment.[23]

PARTY

POLARIZATION   Political Thinking in Conflict

The Politicization of the Bureaucracy

The appointment process for high-ranking federal executives has heated up in recent decades. Presidents naturally want to appoint well-qualified individuals to these positions but they also want them to follow the White House's policy goals. As the division between the parties has widened in the past few decades, these goals have become increasingly at odds with those of the opposing party's senators, making the Senate confirmation process increasingly slow and contentious. Many high-ranking executive posts have gone unfilled for lengthy periods because of senators' delaying tactics. Moreover, by seeking loyal appointees, presidents have sometimes downplayed qualifications, resulting in the appointment of headstrong or incompetent individuals. When Hurricane Katrina devastated New Orleans in 2005, for example, President Bush's appointee at the head of the Federal Emergency Management Agency (FEMA) had no experience in emergency management and worsened an already bad situation. Finally, when the presidency changes hands from one party to the other, the new appointees at the head of an agency can have radically different agendas than those they replaced, disrupting the agency's operations.

These problems are substantial enough to lead some observers to conclude that the federal bureaucracy has been weakened by them. They would prefer a bureaucracy in which neutral competence—impartial and expert administration—is the overriding principle. Other observers dismiss this claim, arguing that the bureaucracy needs to be responsive to partisan politics—that the will of the voters should be reflected in administrative staffing and policymaking. They do not deny the need for competent administrators but argue that strong political leadership at the top is the key to a more accountable and responsive bureaucracy.

Q. *What's your view of the increased politicization of the bureaucracy? On balance, do you regard it as a favorable development? Would you have the same opinion if control of the presidency were to change to the other party?*

OMB: Budgets, Regulations, and Legislative Proposals

Of the management tools available to the president, few are more direct than the Office of Management and Budget. Funding and policy are the mainstays of every agency, and OMB has substantial control over each. In addition to OMB's role in overseeing the preparation of agency budgets, it acts as a review board for agency regulations and policy proposals. No agency can issue a major regulation without OMB's verification that the benefits of the regulation outweigh its costs, and no agency can propose legislation to Congress without OMB's approval. In making these decisions, OMB operates from a presidential perspective. A proposed regulation or bill that conflicts with the president's policies is unlikely to be approved.

Accountability through Congress

A common misperception is that the president, as the chief executive, has sole authority over executive agencies. In fact, Congress also claims ownership because it is the source of each agency's programs and funding. One presidential appointee asked a congressional committee whether it had a problem with his plans to reduce an agency's programs. The committee chairman replied, "No, you have the problem, because if you touch that bureau I'll cut your job out of the budget."[24]

The most substantial control that Congress exerts over the bureaucracy is through its "power of the purse." Congress has constitutional authority over spending; it decides how much money will be appropriated for agency programs. Without funding, a program simply does not exist, regardless of how important the agency believes it is. Congress can also void an administrative decision through legislation that instructs the agency to follow a different course of action. Congress can also exert control by taking authority away from the bureaucracy. In 1978, as a first step in what would become a decades-long wave of deregulation, Congress passed the Airline Deregulation Act, which took away the Civil Aeronautics Board's authority to set airfares and gave it to the airlines.

POLITICAL

THINKING Who Is the Problem?

No institution is an easier target for politicians than the bureaucracy. In election campaigns, politicians often run against government, saying it is wasteful. Yet it is the politicians themselves who create and fund the programs that administrative agencies run. On the other hand, once a program is created, the bureaucrats in charge of it try to protect it. Where would you place most of the blame for government waste and duplication? Does it rest with the administrators who run the programs or with the lawmakers who create them?

Congress also has control through its oversight function, which involves monitoring the bureaucracy's work to ensure its compliance with legislative intent.[25] If any agency steps out of line, Congress can call hearings to ask tough questions and, if necessary, take legislative action to correct the problem. Bureaucrats are required by law to appear before Congress when asked to do so, and the mere possibility of being grilled by a congressional panel can lead administrators to stay in line. The effect is not altogether positive. Bureaucrats are sometimes reluctant to try innovative approaches out of a fear that particular members of Congress will disapprove.[26]

The U.S. Postal Service is regarded by many as the best entity of its kind anywhere. It delivers more mail to more addresses than any other postal administration in the world, and it does so inexpensively and without undue delay. Yet, like many other government agencies, it is often criticized for its inefficiency and ineptness.

Nevertheless, Congress lacks the time and expertise to define in detail how programs should be run.[27] Accordingly, Congress has delegated much of its oversight responsibility to the Government Accountability Office (GAO). At an earlier time, the GAO's role was limited largely to keeping track of agency spending. The GAO now also monitors whether agencies are implementing policies in the way that Congress intended. When the GAO finds a problem with an agency's handling of a program, it notifies the appropriate congressional committees, which can then take corrective action.

Oversight cannot correct mistakes or abuses that have already occurred. Recognizing this limit, Congress has devised ways to constrain the bureaucracy *before* it acts. The simplest method is to draft more detailed laws. Legislation typically contains *enabling provisions* that give administrators the authority to implement the law. By including specific instructions in these provisions, Congress limits bureaucrats' options. *Sunset provisions* are another restrictive device. These provisions establish specific dates when all or part of a law will expire unless it is extended by Congress. Sunset provisions are a method of countering the bureaucracy's reluctance to give up outdated programs. However, because members of Congress usually want the programs they create to last, most legislation does not include a sunset provision.

Accountability through the Courts

The bureaucracy is also overseen by the judiciary. Legally, the bureaucracy derives its authority from acts of Congress, and an injured party can bring suit against an agency on the grounds that it has failed to carry out a law properly. If the court agrees, the agency must change its policy.[28] In 1999, for example, a federal court approved a settlement in favor of African American farmers who demonstrated that the Department of Agriculture had systematically favored white farmers in granting federal farm loans.[29]

Nevertheless, the courts tend to support administrators if their actions are at least somewhat consistent with the law they are administering. The Supreme Court has held that agencies can apply any reasonable interpretation of statutes unless Congress has stipulated something to the contrary and that agencies in some instances have discretion in deciding whether to enforce statutes.[30] These rulings reflect the judiciary's recognition that administrators must have flexibility if they are to operate effectively. The bureaucracy and the judiciary would both grind to a crunching halt if administrators were constantly in court defending their agency's decisions.

Accountability within the Bureaucracy Itself

The recognition of the difficulty of ensuring adequate accountability of the bureaucracy through the presidency, Congress, and the courts has led to the development of mechanisms of accountability within the bureaucracy itself. Four of these mechanisms—the Senior Executive Service, administrative law judges, whistleblowing, and demographic representativeness—are particularly noteworthy.

Senior Executive Service

The agency point of view within the bureaucracy is partly a result of career patterns. Most civil servants work in the same agency throughout their time in government service. As they acquire the skills and knowledge associated with a particular agency, they rise through its ranks and derive job satisfaction and security from supporting its mission.

Recognizing that the bureaucracy's employment system encourages an agency point of view, Congress in 1978 established the **Senior Executive Service (SES)**. Enacted at the urging of President Jimmy Carter, the SES represents a compromise between a president-led bureaucracy and an expert one.[31] The SES consists of roughly seven thousand top-level career civil servants who qualify through a competitive process to receive a higher salary than their peers but, in return, can be assigned by the president to any position within the bureaucracy. They are intended to be the intermediaries between the regular presidential appointees at the top of federal agencies and the regular civil servants who work in these agencies. Unlike the president's regular appointees, SES bureaucrats cannot be fired; if the president relieves them of their jobs, they have "fallback rights" to their former rank in the regular civil service.

The SES has been less successful in practice than its proponents anticipated. A 2009 study found that most senior executives are assigned to work within their original agency. The study concluded that most SES employees "have been viewed primarily as agency-specific assets, not federal or national assets." The major obstacle to moving SES members from one agency to another is that much of their value rests on their knowledge of a particular agency's programs. Although SES employees undergo development training designed to strengthen their leadership ability, their real strength is their intimate knowledge of an agency and its programs. "Part of the reason that people don't move is they get comfortable in a particular agency, they learn the policy issues and the policy challenges in a particular area, and they feel like that's their comfort zone," a former senior executive said. "I got promoted because I became an expert in the policies in that area, not because I'm such a great executive who can go anywhere and do anything."[32]

Administrative Law Judges

Every day, bureaucrats make tens of thousands of decisions affecting individuals. Occasionally, an individual will believe that he or she was unfairly disadvantaged by a bureaucrat's decision and will contest it. Such disputes are usually handled by an **administrative law judge**. These judges are empowered to administer oaths, seek evidence, take testimony, make factual and legal determinations, and render decisions. However, they operate through a less formal process than do regular federal judges. Administrative law hearings usually take place in an office or meeting room rather than a courtroom, and administrative law judges do not wear a robe or sit on a high bench. The system is designed to provide a less formal, less expensive, and faster method of resolving administrative disputes than would be the case if they were handled through the regular federal courts. Under some circumstances, the decision of an administrative law judge can be appealed to such a court, although this seldom occurs.

Administrative law judges typically work within the confines of a particular agency and specialize in the laws and regulations governing its activities. Although they are employees of their agency, they are charged with protecting individuals from arbitrary, prejudicial, or incorrect decisions by the agency. Accordingly, their positions are insulated from agency pressure. Administrative law judges are not subject to performance or salary review by agency heads, and their superiors are prohibited from interfering with their hearings or undermining their rulings.

Senior Executive Service (SES)
Top-level career civil servants who qualify through a competitive process to receive higher salaries than their peers but who can be assigned or transferred by order of the president.

administrative law judge
An official who presides at a trial-like administrative hearing to settle a dispute between an agency and someone adversely affected by a decision of that agency.

Richard Clarke, arguably the most famous whistleblower since the Watergate era, testifies about Bush administration antiterrorism policies in the months before the September 11, 2001, attacks on the World Trade Center and the Pentagon. In high-profile appearances before Congress and the 9/11 Commission, Clarke accused the Bush administration, in which he had served as the top terrorist advisor, of ignoring warnings of a possible large-scale terrorist attack on the United States. "I believe the Bush administration in the first eight months considered terrorism an important issue, but not an urgent issue," Clarke told the 9/11 Commission, a bipartisan commission formed by Congress to investigate the attacks. The White House countered with Vice President Dick Cheney's claim that Clarke "wasn't in the loop" and could not possibly have known what was going on in the Bush administration's inner circle. The White House slowed its attack on Clarke after documents surfaced supporting some of his allegations. In a pre-9/11 memo prepared for National Security Advisor Condoleezza Rice, Clarke had expressed alarm at the slow pace of the administration's antiterrorism planning, saying "Imagine a day after hundreds of Americans lay dead at home or abroad after a terrorist attack."

Whistleblowing

Although the bureaucratic corruption that is commonplace in some countries is rare in the United States, a certain amount of fraud and abuse is inevitable in any large bureaucracy. One way to stop these prohibited practices is **whistleblowing**—the act of reporting instances of official mismanagement. To encourage whistleblowers to come forward with their information, Congress enacted the Whistleblower Protection Act. It protects whistleblowers from retaliation by their superiors and gives them a financial reward in cases where their information results in a savings to government.

Nevertheless, whistleblowing is not for the fainthearted. Many federal employees are reluctant to report instances of mismanagement because they fear retaliation. Their superiors might claim that they are malcontents or liars and find ways to ruin their careers. A case in point is Bunnatine Greenhouse who filed a complaint alleging that the U.S. Army Corps of Engineers was greatly overpaying a contractor because it had accepted the contractor's multiyear no-bid cost estimates rather than conducting its own assessment. Her complaint was ignored by the Corps of Engineers and she was demoted, stripped of her top-secret security clearance, and subjected to on-the-job harassment after she took her complaint to Congress. In 2011, more than six years after her initial complaint, she was vindicated when a U.S. district court ruled in her favor. Said Greenhouse: "I hope that the plight I suffered prompts the administration and Congress to move dedicated civil servants from second-class citizenry and to finally give federal employees the legal rights that they need to protect the legal trust."[33]

whistleblowing

An internal check on the bureaucracy, whereby employees report instances of mismanagement that they observe.

Demographic Representativeness

Although the bureaucracy is an unrepresentative institution in the sense that its officials are unelected, it can be representative in the demographic sense. The concept of a demographically representative civil service was endorsed in 1961 by the President's Commission on Equal Employment Opportunity, which was created by President John F. Kennedy. The commission concluded that, if civil servants were a demographic microcosm of the general public, they would treat the various groups and interests in society more responsibly.[34]

The federal government has made progress in improving the employment status of women and, to a lesser extent, minorities. If all employees are taken into account, the federal bureaucracy comes reasonably close to being representative of the nation's population (see Table 13-1). Moreover, women and minorities are better represented among the top ranks of administrators than they are in Congress or the judiciary. Nevertheless, the bureaucracy is not demographically representative at the top levels. About three in every five managerial and professional positions are held by white males, a marked improvement over earlier periods but less than fully representative.

In any case, **demographic representativeness** is only a partial answer to the problem of bureaucratic accountability. The careerists in the defense and welfare agencies, for example, have similar demographic backgrounds, but they differ markedly in their opinions about policy. Each group believes that the goals of

demographic representativeness

The idea that the bureaucracy will be more responsive to the public if its employees at all levels are demographically representative of the population as a whole.

TABLE 13-1 | Federal Job Rankings (GS) of Various Demographic Groups

Grade level*	Women (%) 1982	Women (%) 2011	Blacks (%) 1982	Blacks (%) 2011	Hispanics (%) 1982	Hispanics (%) 2011
GS 13–15 (highest ranks)	5	37	5	13	2	6
GS 9–12	20	46	10	17	4	8
GS 5–8	60	61	19	26	4	9
GS 1–4 (lowest ranks)	78	66	23	25	5	9

*In general, the higher-numbered grades are managerial and professional positions, and the lower-numbered grades are clerical and manual labor positions.
Source: Office of Personnel Management, 2012.

its agency should be a top priority. In this sense, agency loyalty trumps demographics. Once in an agency, civil servants—whatever their demographic background—become advocates for its programs.

Summary
Self-Test www.mhhe.com/ pattersontadtx11e

Bureaucracy is a method of organizing people and work, based on the principles of hierarchical authority, job specialization, and formalized rules. As a form of organization, bureaucracy is the most efficient means of getting people to work together on tasks of great magnitude and complexity. It is also a form of organization that is prone to waste and rigidity, which is why efforts are always being made to reform it.

The United States could not be governed without a large federal bureaucracy. The day-to-day work of the federal government, from mail delivery to provision of social security to international diplomacy, is done by federal agencies. Federal employees work in roughly four hundred major agencies, including cabinet departments, independent agencies, regulatory agencies, government corporations, and presidential commissions. Yet the bureaucracy is more than simply an administrative giant. Administrators have discretion when making policy decisions. In the process of implementing policy, they make important policy and political choices.

Administrative agencies operate within budgets established by the president and Congress, and they participate in the budgetary process. The process begins with the president's budget instructions, conveyed through OMB, to the agencies. They then develop their budgets, which are consolidated and sent by the president to Congress, where the House and Senate budget and appropriations committees do the bulk of the work, including holding hearings involving agency heads. Throughout, Congress, the president, and the agencies seek to promote their respective budgetary goals. Once the annual budget has been passed by the House and Senate and signed by the president, it takes effect on October 1, the starting date of the federal government's fiscal year.

Administrators are actively engaged in politics and policymaking. The fragmentation of power and the pluralism of the American political system result in a contentious policy process, which leads government agencies to compete for power and resources. Accordingly, civil servants tend to have an agency point of view: they seek to advance their agency's programs and to repel attempts by others to weaken them. In promoting their agencies, civil servants rely on their policy expertise, the backing of their clientele groups, and the support of the president and Congress.

Administrators are not elected by the people they serve, yet they wield substantial independent power. Because of this, the bureaucracy's accountability is a central issue. The major checks on the bureaucracy occur through the president, Congress, and the courts. The president has some power to reorganize the bureaucracy and the authority to appoint the political head of each agency. The president also has management tools (such as the executive budget) that can be used to limit administrators' discretion. Congress has influence on bureaucratic agencies through its authorization and funding powers and through various devices (including enabling provisions, sunset provisions, and oversight hearings) that can increase administrators' accountability. The judiciary's role in ensuring the bureaucracy's accountability is smaller than that of the elected branches, but the courts have the authority to force agencies to act in accordance with legislative intent, established procedures, and constitutionally guaranteed rights. Internal checks on the bureaucracy—the Senior Executive Service, administrative law judges, whistleblowing, and demographic representativeness—are also mechanisms for holding the bureaucracy accountable.

Study Corner

Key Terms

administrative law judge (p. 351)

agency point of view (p. 342)

budgetary process (p. 338)

bureaucracy (p. 332)

bureaucratic accountability (p. 346)

cabinet (executive) departments (p. 334)

clientele groups (p. 344)

demographic representativeness (p. 352)

formalized rules (p. 332)

government corporations (p. 335)

hierarchical authority (p. 332)

independent agencies (p. 335)

job specialization (p. 332)

merit system (p. 336)

neutral competence (p. 337)

patronage system (p. 337)

policy implementation (p. 340)

presidential commissions (p. 335)

regulatory agencies (p. 335)

Senior Executive Service (p. 351)

spoils system (p. 337)

whistleblowing (p. 352)

Self-Test: Multiple Choice

1. Which of the following is *not* an internal check that can lead to greater bureaucratic accountability?
   a. whistleblowing
   b. agency point of view
   c. administrative law judges
   d. demographic representativeness

2. The strength of bureaucracy as a form of organization is that it
   a. leads to flexibility in the completion of tasks.
   b. can be used only in the public sector.
   c. is the most efficient means of getting people to work together on tasks of great magnitude.
   d. allows individuals great latitude in making decisions.

3. Bureaucratic accountability through the presidency includes all of the following *except*
   a. appointment of agency heads.
   b. budgetary oversight through the Office of Management and Budget.
   c. the power to fire at will any civil servant the president chooses to fire.
   d. the president's authority to recommend the reorganization of federal agencies.

4. Which of the following is *not* an advantage of merit hiring?
   a. a more competent workforce through use of competitive exams
   b. ability to hire people with special qualifications
   c. greater responsiveness to presidential leadership
   d. employees who are likely to treat clients and customers the same whether they are Republicans or Democrats

5. Which of the following is *not* a source of bureaucratic power in the federal bureaucracy?
   a. power of broad public support and esteem
   b. power of expertise
   c. power of clientele groups
   d. power of friends in Congress and the White House

6. The primary function of America's federal bureaucracy is
   a. oversight of the executive branch.
   b. developing laws for review by Congress.
   c. bringing cases for trial before the Supreme Court.
   d. policy implementation.

7. Bureaucracies are found only in the governmental sector of society and not in the private and corporate sectors. (T/F)

8. Regulatory agencies such as the Securities and Exchange Commission are permitted only to issue advisory opinions to the firms they regulate. Only the judiciary and Congress are allowed to take more decisive action if a firm disregards the law. (T/F)

9. Congress holds the bureaucracy accountable in part through its power to authorize and fund agency programs. (T/F)

10. Once they are in place, federal programs are often terminated at the request of their clientele groups. (T/F)

Self-Test: Essay

What are the major sources of bureaucrats' power? What mechanisms for controlling that power are available to the president and Congress?

Suggested Readings

Aberbach, Joel D., and Bert A. Rockman. *In the Web of Politics: Two Decades of the U.S. Federal Executive.* Washington, D.C.: Brookings Institution, 2000. An evaluation of the federal bureaucracy and its evolving nature.

Huber, Gregory A. *The Craft of Bureaucratic Neutrality: Interests and Influence in Governmental Regulation of Occupational Safety.* New York: Cambridge University Press, 2007. An argument that claims political neutrality is the best political strategy, as well as the proper administrative approach, for agencies.

Ketti, Donald F. *System under Stress: Homeland Security and American Politics.* Washington, D.C.: CQ Press, 2007. An award-winning study of executive reorganization that focuses on the Department of Homeland Security.

Lewis, David E. *The Politics of Presidential Appointments: Political Control and Bureaucratic Performance.* Princeton, N.J.: Princeton University Press, 2008. An assessment of the trade-off between competency and loyalty in presidential appointments.

Meier, Kenneth J., and Laurence J. O'Toole Jr. *Bureaucracy in a Democratic State.* Baltimore, Md.: Johns Hopkins University Press, 2006. A careful assessment of the relationship between bureaucracy and democracy.

Osborne, David, and Ted Gaebler. *Reinventing Government: How the Entrepreneurial Spirit Is Transforming the Public Sector.* New York: Addison-Wesley, 1992. The book that Washington policymakers in the 1990s regarded as the guide to transforming the bureaucracy.

Sagini, Meshack M. *Organizational Behavior: The Challenges of the New Millennium.* Lanham, Md.: University Press of America, 2001. A comprehensive assessment of bureaucratic structures and behaviors.

List of Websites

www.census.gov
The website of the U.S. Census Bureau, the best source of statistical information on Americans and the government agencies that administer programs affecting them.

www.whistleblower.org
The Government Accountability Project's website; designed to protect and encourage whistleblowers by providing information and support to federal employees.

www.whitehouse.gov/government/cabinet.html
A website that lists the cabinet secretaries and provides links to each cabinet-level department.

Participate!

If you are considering a semester or summer internship, you might want to look into working for a federal, state, or local agency. Compared with legislative interns, executive interns are more likely to get paid and to be given significant duties. (Many legislative interns spend the bulk of their time answering phones or responding to mail.) Internship information can often be obtained through an agency's website. You should apply as early as possible; some agencies have application deadlines.

You might consider a career in government. President John F. Kennedy said that government is "the highest calling." A study by Harvard's Kennedy School of Government found that public-sector managers get more intrinsic satisfaction from their work, which focuses on improving public life, than do private-sector managers. For people who want to pursue a government career, a first step is often a master's degree program in public administration or public policy. Many of these programs require only a year of study after the bachelor's degree. For an entry-level employee with a master's degree rather than a bachelor's degree, the initial salary is 40 percent higher. Appointees with master's degrees enter the civil service at a higher rank (GS-9 rather than GS-5) and are placed in positions that entail greater responsibility than those assigned to newly hired appointees with bachelor's degrees. Those who enter the civil service at the higher rank also are more likely to advance to top positions as their careers develop.

Extra Credit

For up-to-the-minute *New York Times* articles, interactive simulations, graphics, study tools, and more links and quizzes, visit the text's Online Learning Center at **www.mhhe.com/pattersontad11e**.

Self-Test Answers

1. b, 2. c, 3. c, 4. c, 5. a, 6. d, 7. F, 8. F, 9. T, 10. F

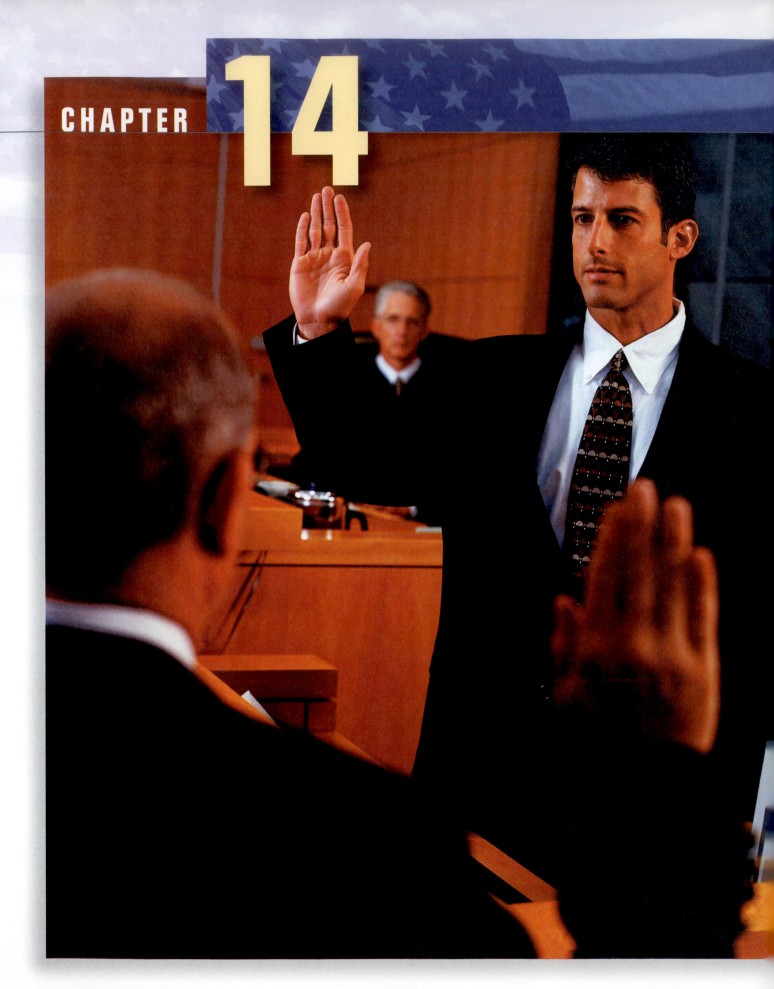

The Federal Judicial System: Applying the Law

It is emphatically the province and duty of the judicial department to say what the law is. Those who apply the rule to particular cases, must of necessity expound and interpret that rule. If two laws conflict with each other, the courts must decide on the operation of each. John Marshall[1]

Through its ruling in *Citizens United v. Federal Election Commission* (2010), the Supreme Court opened the door to unrestricted corporate and union spending in federal election campaigns. At issue was a provision of the 2002 Bipartisan Campaign Reform Act that banned corporations and unions from using organization funds to pay for broadcasts or other advertisements that were designed to promote a political candidate. The ban applied thirty days before a primary and sixty days before the general election and extended a century-old policy of limiting election contributions by economic organizations on grounds that such spending would give them undue influence with lawmakers.

The Supreme Court concluded that Congress had overstepped its constitutional boundaries, holding that that spending restrictions infringed on the free speech rights of corporations and unions. Writing for the five justices in the majority, Justice Anthony Kennedy said: "If the First Amendment has any force, it prohibits Congress from fining or jailing citizens, or associations of citizens, for simply engaging in political speech." Kennedy went on to say: "When government seeks to use its full power . . . to command where a person may get his or her information or what distrusted source he or she may not hear, it uses censorship to control thought. This is unlawful." The four justices in the minority took issue with this argument, saying that allowing powerful organizations to spend freely on elections could corrupt the political process. "While American democracy is imperfect," Justice John Paul Stevens wrote, "few outside the majority of this court would have thought its flaws included a dearth of corporate money in politics. The court's ruling threatens to undermine the integrity of elected institutions across the nation." Stevens added that the First Amendment was intended to protect the free speech rights of individuals and not of corporations or unions.[2]

The Court's campaign finance ruling illustrates three key points about court decisions. First, the judiciary is an important policymaking body. Some of its rulings are as consequential as a law of Congress or an executive order of the president. Second, the judiciary has considerable discretion in its rulings. The *Citizens United* decision was not based on any literal reading of the law or else the justices would have been in full agreement on the proper ruling. Third, the judiciary is a political as well as legal institution. The campaign finance ruling was a product of contending political forces, had political content, and was decided by political appointees. All five justices that voted to allow unlimited corporate spending were appointed to the Court by a Republican president. Of the four justices that voted to ban such spending, three were Democratic appointees.

POLITICAL

THINKING   Is the Issue Political or Judicial?

The Supreme Court has made a distinction between political issues (which are to be decided by elected officials) and judicial issues (which can be ruled on by the judiciary). At times, however, the Supreme Court has ruled on issues that it had previously left in the hands of elected officials. An example is the 2010 campaign finance ruling in which the Court held that Congress could not prevent corporations and unions from spending freely on elections. The Court had previously held that Congress had the power to regulate such spending. Is the line between political questions and judicial questions therefore an artificial one? Is it a line the Court can cross whenever it chooses, and therefore a line without substantial meaning?

This chapter describes the federal judiciary. Like the executive and legislative branches, the judiciary is an independent branch of the U.S. government, but unlike the other two branches, its top officials are not elected by the people. The judiciary is not a democratic institution, and its role is different from and, in some ways, more controversial than the roles of the executive and legislative branches. This chapter explores this issue in the process of discussing the following main points:

The Supreme Court has issued a number of controversial rulings in recent years. As a result, protesters have become an increasingly common sight outside the Supreme Court building.

- *The federal judiciary includes the Supreme Court of the United States, which functions mainly as an appellate court; courts of appeals, which hear appeals; and the district courts, which hold trials.* Each state has a court system of its own, which for the most part is independent of supervision by the federal courts.

- *Judicial decisions are constrained by applicable constitutional law, statutory and administrative law, and precedent.* Nevertheless, political factors have a major influence on judicial appointments and decisions; judges are political officials as well as legal ones.

- *The judiciary has become an increasingly powerful policymaking body in recent decades, raising the question of the judiciary's proper role in a democracy.* The philosophies of judicial restraint and judicial activism provide different answers to this question.

The Federal Judicial System

The Constitution establishes the judiciary as a separate and independent branch of the federal government. The Constitution provides for the Supreme Court of the United States but gives Congress the power to determine the number and types of lower federal courts.

All federal judges are nominated and appointed to office by the president, subject to confirmation by majority vote in the Senate. Unlike the office of president, senator, or representative, the Constitution places no age, residency, or citizenship requirements on the office of federal judge. Nor does the Constitution require judges to have legal training, though by tradition they do. Once seated on the bench, as specified in the Constitution, they "hold their offices during good behavior." This has meant, in effect, that federal judges serve until they die or retire voluntarily. No Supreme Court justice and only a handful of lower-court judges have been removed through impeachment and conviction by Congress, the method of early removal specified by the Constitution.

Alexander Hamilton argued forcefully for life tenure for federal judges in *Federalist* No. 78. Responding to arguments by anti-Federalists that unelected, life-appointed judges would be a threat to the republic, Hamilton argued that the judicial branch would be the weakest of the three branches. Whereas congressional power rests on spending authority ("the power of the purse") and presidential power rests on control of military force ("the power of the sword"), judicial power rests on what Hamilton called "judgment"—the reasonableness and fairness of its decisions. The best way to ensure that judicial decisions meet this standard, Hamilton claimed, is to grant life tenure to federal judges so that they are free of all allegiances except to the rule of law.

The Supreme Court of the United States

The Supreme Court of the United States is the nation's highest court. It has nine members—the chief justice and eight associate justices. The chief justice presides over the Court but has the same voting power as each of the other justices.

Article III of the Constitution grants the Supreme Court both original and appellate jurisdiction. A court's **jurisdiction** is its authority to hear cases of a particular type. **Original jurisdiction** is the authority to be the first court to hear a case. The Supreme Court's original jurisdiction includes legal disputes involving foreign diplomats and cases in which the opposing parties are state governments. The Court has convened as a court of original jurisdiction only a few hundred times in its history and has seldom done so in recent decades. One of the rarities was

jurisdiction (of a court)
A given court's authority to hear cases of a particular kind. Jurisdiction may be original or appellate.

original jurisdiction
The authority of a given court to be the first court to hear a case.

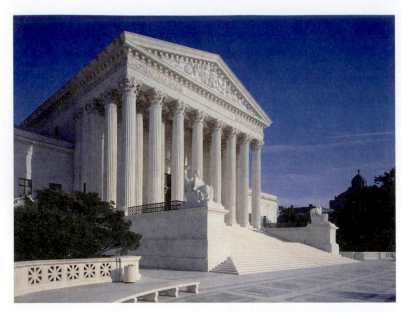

The Supreme Court building is located across from the Capitol in Washington, D.C. Sixteen marble columns support the pediment. Two bronze doors, each weighing more than six tons, lead into the building. The courtroom, the justices' offices, and the conference room are on the first floor. Administrative staff offices and the Court's records and reference materials occupy the other floors.

South Carolina v. North Carolina (2010), which involved a dispute between the two states over the distribution of water in the Catawba River, which flows through the two states.[3]

The Supreme Court does its most important work as an appellate court. **Appellate jurisdiction** is the authority to review cases that have already been heard in lower courts and are appealed to a higher court by the losing party. These higher courts are called *appeals courts* or *appellate courts*. Appellate courts do not retry cases; rather, they determine whether a trial court in hearing a case has acted in accord with applicable law. The Supreme Court's appellate jurisdiction extends to cases arising under the Constitution, federal law and regulations, and treaties. The Court also hears appeals involving legal controversies that cross state or national boundaries. Article III of the Constitution gives Congress the power to create "exceptions" to the Supreme Court's appellate jurisdiction, whereas its original jurisdiction is unalterable by Congress.

Selecting and Deciding Cases

The Supreme Court's power is most apparent when it declares another institution's action to be unconstitutional. This power, called **judicial review,** was first asserted by the Supreme Court in *Marbury v. Madison* (1803), when the Court rebuked both Congress and the president (see Chapter 2). It is a power that the Supreme Court has used sparingly; it has usually deferred to Congress and the president when there is reasonable doubt as to whether their actions fall inside or outside the bounds of the Constitution.[4]

Although judicial review is its most dramatic power, the Supreme Court's primary responsibility is to establish legal precedents that will guide the decisions of lower courts. A **precedent** is a judicial decision that serves as a rule for settling subsequent cases of a similar nature. Lower courts are expected to follow precedent—that is, to resolve cases in ways consistent with upper-court rulings.

Nearly all cases that reach the Supreme Court do so after the losing party in a lower-court asks the Court to hear its case. If at least four of the justices agree to do so, the Court issues a **writ of certiorari,** which is a request to the lower court to submit to the Supreme Court a record of the case. Each year roughly eight thousand parties apply for certiorari, but the Court grants certiorari to fewer than a hundred cases (see Figure 14-1).

The Supreme Court is most likely to grant certiorari when the U.S. government through the solicitor general (the high-ranking Justice Department official who serves as the government's lawyer in Supreme Court cases) requests it.[5] When the government loses a case in a lower court, the solicitor general decides whether to appeal it. Such cases often make up half or more of the cases the Supreme Court hears in a term.

The Supreme Court seldom accepts a routine case, even if the justices believe that a lower court has made a mistake. The Court's job is not to correct the errors of other courts but to resolve substantial legal issues. The Court's own guidelines say that there must be "compelling reasons" for accepting a case, which include

appellate jurisdiction

The authority of a given court to review cases that have already been tried in lower courts and are appealed to it by the losing party; such a court is called an *appeals court* or *appellate court.*

judicial review

The power of courts to decide whether a governmental institution has acted within its constitutional powers and, if not, to declare its action null and void.

precedent

A judicial decision that serves as a rule for settling subsequent cases of a similar nature.

writ of certiorari

Permission granted by a higher court to allow a losing party in a legal case to bring the case before it for a ruling; when such a writ is requested of the U.S. Supreme Court, four of the Court's nine justices must agree to accept the case before it is granted certiorari.

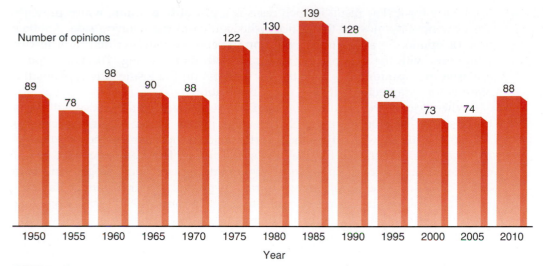

FIGURE 14-1 **Supreme Court Opinions, 1950–2010** The number of signed Supreme Court opinions each term is relatively small. The Court has considerable control over the cases it selects. The cases that are heard by the Supreme Court tend to be ones that have legal significance beyond the particular case itself. The Courts term runs from October 1 to June 30; the year indicated is the closing year of the term.
Source: Supreme Court of the United States.

resolving issues that are being decided inconsistently by the lower courts, correcting serious departures from accepted standards of justice, settling key questions of federal law, and reviewing lower-court rulings that conflict with a previous Supreme Court decision. When the Court does accept a case, chances are that most of the justices disagree with the lower court's ruling. About three-fourths of Supreme Court decisions reverse the lower court's judgment.[6]

During a Supreme Court hearing, the attorneys for the two sides present their oral arguments, which typically are limited to thirty minutes for each side.[7] Each side also provides the Court a written **brief**, which contains its full argument. The oral session is followed by the **judicial conference**, which is attended only by the nine justices and in which they discuss and vote on the case. The chief justice has the option of speaking first on the case and can sometimes influence the decision by framing the choice in a persuasive way. Regardless, the conference's proceedings are secret, which allows the justices to speak freely about a case and to change their positions as the discussion progresses.[8]

Issuing Decisions and Opinions

After a case has been decided, the Court issues its ruling, which consists of a decision and one or more opinions. The **decision** indicates which party the Court supports and by how large a margin. The most important part of the ruling, however, is the **opinion**, which explains the legal basis for the decision. In the landmark *Brown v. Board of Education* opinion, for instance, the Court held that government-sponsored school segregation was unconstitutional because it violated the Fourteenth Amendment provision that guarantees equal protection under the law to all citizens (see discussion in Chapter 5). This opinion became the legal basis by which public schools throughout the South were ordered by lower courts to end their policy of racial segregation.

When a majority of the justices agree on the legal basis of a decision, the result is a **majority opinion.** In some cases there is no majority opinion because, although a majority of the justices agree on the decision, they disagree on the

brief
A written statement by a party in a court case that details its argument.

judicial conference
A closed meeting of the justices of the U.S. Supreme Court to discuss and vote on the case before them; the justices are not supposed to discuss conference proceedings with outsiders.

decision
A vote of the Supreme Court in a particular case that indicates which party the justices side with and by how large a margin.

opinion (of a court)
A court's written explanation of its decision, which serves to inform others of the legal basis for the decision. Supreme Court opinions are expected to guide the decisions of lower courts.

majority opinion
A court opinion that results when a majority of the justices are in agreement on the legal basis of the decision.

plurality opinion

A court opinion that results when a majority of justices agree on a decision in a case but do not agree on the legal basis for the decision. In this instance, the legal position held by most of the justices on the winning side is called a *plurality opinion*.

concurring opinion

A separate opinion written by one or more Supreme Court justices who vote with the majority in the decision on a case but who disagree with its reasoning.

dissenting opinion

The opinion of a justice in a Supreme Court case that explains his or her reasons for disagreeing with the majority's decision.

legal basis for it. The result in such cases is a **plurality opinion,** which presents the view held by most of the justices who vote with the winning side. Another type of opinion is a **concurring opinion,** a separate view written by a justice who votes with the majority but disagrees with its reasoning. The final type is a **dissenting opinion;** in it, a justice (or justices) on the losing side explains the reasons for disagreeing with the majority position.

When part of the majority, the chief justice decides which justice will write the majority opinion. Otherwise, the senior justice in the majority picks the author. The justice who writes the Court's majority opinion has the responsibility to express accurately the majority's reasoning. The vote on a case is not considered final until the opinion is written and agreed upon, so give-and-take can occur during the writing stage. In rare instances, the writing stage has produced a change in the Court's decision. In *Lee v. Weisman* (1992), a case involving prayer at a public school graduation, Justice Anthony Kennedy originally sided with the four justices who said the prayer was permissible. While writing the 5-4 majority opinion, Kennedy found that he could not make a persuasive case for allowing it. He switched sides, resulting in a 5-4 majority the other way. Kennedy's switch was dramatic in its effect, but strategic considerations are a component of the workings of the Court. Justices have been known, for example, to vote with the majority even when disagreeing with it in order to have a say in the draft opinion that circulates during preparation of the final version.[9]

Other Federal Courts

The Supreme Court's position at the top of the judicial system gives it unrivaled importance. Nevertheless, the Supreme Court is not the only court that matters. Judge Jerome Frank once wrote of the "upper-court myth," which is the view that lower courts dutifully follow the rulings handed down by the courts above them.[10] The reality is different, as the following discussion explains.

U.S. District Courts

The lowest federal courts are the district courts (see Figure 14-2). There are ninety-four federal district courts altogether—at least one in every state and as many as four in some states. Each district includes several judges, who number roughly seven hundred in all. The federal district courts are the chief trial courts of the federal system. Virtually all criminal and civil cases arising under federal law are argued first in the district courts. They are the only courts in the federal system where the two sides present their case to a jury for a verdict. Cases at this level are usually presided over by a single judge.

Lower federal courts rely on and follow Supreme Court decisions in their own rulings. The Supreme Court reiterated this requirement in a 1982 case, *Hutto v. Davis:* "Unless we wish anarchy to prevail within the federal judicial system, a precedent of this Court must be followed by the lower federal courts no matter how misguided the judges of those courts may think it to be."[11] However, the idea that lower courts are rigidly bound to Supreme Court rulings is part of the upper-court myth. District court judges might misunderstand the Supreme Court's position and deviate

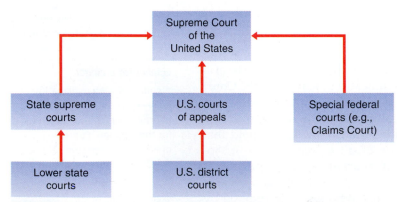

FIGURE 14-2 **The Federal Judicial System** The simplified diagram shows the relationships among the various levels of federal courts and between state and federal courts. The losing party in a case can appeal a lower-court decision to the court at the next-highest level, as the arrows indicate. Decisions normally can be moved from state courts to federal courts only if they raise a constitutional question.

from it for that reason. In addition, the facts of a case before a district court are seldom identical to those of a case settled by the Supreme Court. The lower-court judge must decide whether a different legal judgment is appropriate. Finally, ambiguities or unaddressed issues in Supreme Court rulings give lower courts some flexibility in deciding cases.

Another indication of the significant role of district court judges is that most federal cases end with the district court's decision. Typically, the losing party decides not to appeal the decision to a higher court.

U.S. Courts of Appeals

Cases appealed from district courts go to federal courts of appeals, which are the second level of the federal court system. Courts of appeals do not use juries. Ordinarily, no new evidence is submitted in an appealed case; rather, appellate courts base their decision on a review of the lower court's records. Appellate judges act as supervisors in the legal system, reviewing trial court decisions and correcting what they consider to be legal errors. Facts (that is, the circumstances of a case) found by district courts are ordinarily presumed to be correct.

The United States has thirteen courts of appeals. Eleven of them have jurisdiction over a "circuit" made up of the district courts in anywhere from three to nine states (see Figure 14-3). Of the remaining two, one has jurisdiction over the District of Columbia (the D.C. "circuit") and the other (the U.S. Court of Appeals for the Federal Circuit) has jurisdiction over appeals involving patents and international trade, regardless of the circuit in which they arise. Between four and twenty-six judges sit on each court of appeals, but each case usually is heard by a panel of three judges. On rare occasions, all the judges of a court of appeals

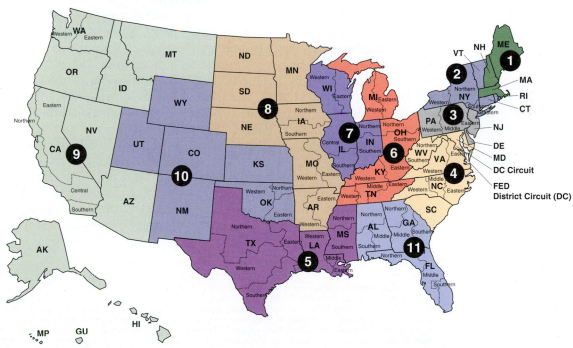

FIGURE 14-3   **Geographic Boundaries of U.S. Courts of Appeals**   The United States has thirteen courts of appeals, each of which serves a "circuit." Eleven of these circuit courts serve anywhere from three to nine states, as the map shows. The other two are located in the District of Columbia: the Court of Appeals for the District of Columbia and the Court of Appeals for the Federal Circuit, which specializes in appeals involving patents and international trade. Within each circuit are federal trial courts, most of which are district courts. Each state has at least one district court within its boundaries. Larger states, such as California (which has four district courts, as can be seen on the map), have more than one.

Source: Administrative Office of the U.S. Courts.

sit as a body (*en banc*) in order to resolve difficult controversies, typically ones that have resulted in conflicting decisions within the same circuit. Each circuit is monitored by a Supreme Court justice, who typically takes the lead in reviewing appeals originating in that circuit. Conflict or inconsistency in how the different circuits are applying a law can lead the Supreme Court to review such cases.

Courts of appeals offer the only real hope of reversal for many appellants, because the Supreme Court hears so few cases. The Supreme Court reviews less than 1 percent of the cases heard by federal appeals courts.

Special U.S. Courts

In addition to the Supreme Court, the courts of appeals, and the district courts, the federal judiciary includes a few specialty courts. Among them are the U.S. Claims Court, which hears cases in which the U.S. government is being sued for damages; the U.S. Court of International Trade, which handles cases involving appeals of U.S. Customs Office rulings; and the U.S. Court of Military Appeals, which hears appeals of military courts-martial. Some federal agencies and commissions also have judicial powers (for example, the issuing of fines), and their decisions can be appealed to a federal court of appeals.

The State Courts

The American states are separate governments within the U.S. political system. The Tenth Amendment protects each state in its sovereignty, and each state has its own court system. Like the federal courts, state court systems have trial courts at the bottom level and appellate courts at the top.

Each state decides for itself the structure of its courts and the method of selecting judges. In some states the governor appoints judges, but in most states judges are elected to office. The most common form involves competitive elections of either a partisan or a nonpartisan nature. Other states use a mixed system called the *merit plan* (also called the "Missouri Plan" because Missouri was the first state to use it), under which the governor appoints a judge from a short list of acceptable candidates provided by a judicial selection commission. In the first scheduled election after a year in office, the selected judge is reviewed by the voters who simply decide by a "yes" or "no" vote whether the judge should be allowed to stay in office (see "How the 50 States Differ").

Besides the upper-court myth, there exists a "federal court myth," which holds that the federal judiciary is the most significant part of the judicial system and that state courts play a subordinate role. This view is also inaccurate. More than 95 percent of the nation's legal cases are decided by state or local courts. Most cases arising under *criminal law* (from shoplifting to murder) and most cases arising under *civil law* (such as divorces and business disputes) are defined by state laws or by local ordinances, which are derived from state laws.*

---

*Laws fall into three broad categories—procedural, civil, and criminal. *Procedural law* refers to rules that govern the legal process. In some cases, these rules apply to government, as in the example of the obligation of police to inform suspects of their right to an attorney. In other cases, the rules apply to private parties. For example, in some states, a homeowner cannot take an insurance company to court over a policy claim without first having that claim heard, and possibly resolved, by an arbitration board. *Civil law* governs relations with and between private parties as when a person injured in an accident sues the other party for monetary damages. Marriage, divorce, business contracts, and property ownership are examples of relations covered by civil law. The losing party in a civil suit might be ordered to pay or otherwise compensate the other party but would not face jail unless he or she refuses to comply with a court order, which can be a punishable offense. Government can also be a party to a civil suit, as when the IRS sues a taxpayer in a dispute over how much the taxpayer owes the government. *Criminal law* deals with acts that government defines as illegal, which can result in a fine, imprisonment, or other punishment. Murder, assault, and drunk driving are examples of acts covered by criminal law. The government is always a party to a criminal law case; the other party is the individual alleged to have broken the law. (Legal relationships between government and private parties, whether criminal or civil, are defined as *public law*. The term *private law* is used to refer to the legal rights and relationships between private parties.)

HOW THE 50 STATES DIFFER   POLITICAL THINKING THROUGH COMPARISONS

PRINCIPAL METHODS OF SELECTING STATE JUDGES

The states use a variety of methods for selecting the judges on their highest court, including the merit plan, election, and political appointment. The states that appoint judges grant this power to the governor, except in Virginia, Connecticut, and South Carolina, where the legislature makes the choice.

Q: What might explain why several states in the middle of the nation use the merit plan for selecting judges?

A: The merit plan originated in the state of Missouri. Innovations in one state sometimes spread to adjacent states with similar political cultures.

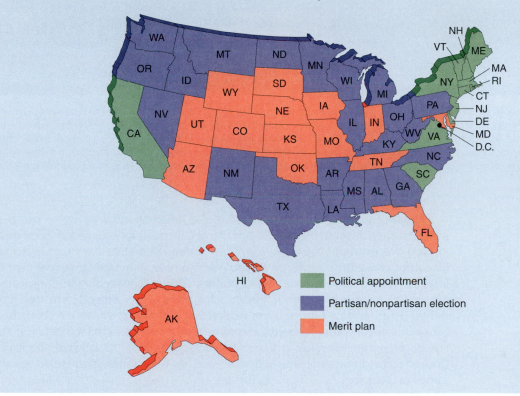

Political appointment

Partisan/nonpartisan election

Merit plan

Source: The Council of State Governments. Reprinted with permission.

Moreover, nearly all cases that originate in state or local courts also end there. The federal courts do not come into the picture because the case does not involve a federal issue. The losing party in a divorce suit, for example, cannot appeal the decision to federal court because no federal law is involved. In most state criminal cases, there is also no federal issue, unless state authorities are alleged to have violated a right protected by the U.S. Constitution, such as the right of the accused to remain silent (see Chapter 4). In such instances, an individual convicted in a state court can, after exhausting the avenues of appeal in the state system, appeal to a federal court. If the federal court accepts such an appeal, it ordinarily confines itself to the federal aspects of the matter, such as whether the defendant's constitutional rights were violated. In addition, the federal court accepts the facts determined by the state court unless such findings are clearly in error. Federal courts are also disinclined, when a provision of federal law does not clearly resolve a case, to substitute their own interpretation of a state's law for that applied by the state court. In short, legal and factual determinations of state courts can bind the federal courts—a clear contradiction of the federal court myth.

Pictured here is the courtroom of the Supreme Court of Texas, which is one of two high courts in the state and has final say in civil and juvenile cases. The other high court in Texas is the Court of Criminal Appeals, which hears appeals of criminal cases. Each court has nine judges, elected to staggered six-year terms. More than 95 percent of the nation's legal cases are decided entirely by state courts, a refutation of the federal court myth, which wrongly holds that the federal courts are all that matter in the end. The United States has a federal system of government, and the division of power between the national and state governments affects the courts as well as other governing institutions.

However, issues traditionally within the jurisdiction of the states can become federal issues through the rulings of federal courts. In its *Lawrence v. Texas* decision in 2003, for example, the Supreme Court invalidated state laws that had made it illegal for consenting adults of the same sex to engage in private sexual relations.[12] John Lawrence had been convicted under a Texas sodomy law and appealed his conviction on grounds that it violated his Fourteenth Amendment due process rights. By grounding his appeal in federal law, Lawrence was able to have his case heard in federal court. When the Supreme Court then decided in his favor, federal law became the governing authority in such cases. Until its *Lawrence* decision, the Court had held that states could decide whether to prohibit sexual relations among same-sex partners.[13]

Federal Court Appointees

Appointments to the Supreme Court and the lower federal courts are controlled by the president, who selects the nominees, and the Senate, which confirms or rejects them. The quiet dignity of the courtroom and the lack of fanfare with which a court delivers its decisions give the impression that the judiciary is as far removed from the world of politics as a governmental institution can possibly be. In reality, federal judges and justices bring their political views with them to the courtroom and have opportunities to promote their political beliefs through the cases they decide. Not surprisingly, the process by which federal judges are appointed is a partisan one.

Supreme Court Nominees

A Supreme Court appointment is a significant opportunity for a president.[14] Most justices retain their positions for many years, enabling presidents to influence judicial policy through their appointments long after they have left office. The careers of some Supreme Court justices provide dramatic testimony to the enduring nature of judicial appointments. For example, Franklin D. Roosevelt appointed William O. Douglas to the Supreme Court in 1939, and for thirty years after Roosevelt's death in 1945, Douglas remained a strong liberal influence on the Court.

Presidents usually appoint jurists who have a compatible political philosophy. Although Supreme Court justices are free to make their own decisions, their legal positions can usually be predicted from their background. A study by judicial scholar Robert Scigliano found that about three of every four appointees have behaved on the Supreme Court approximately as presidents could have expected.[15] Of course, a president has no guarantee that a nominee will actually do so. Justices Earl Warren and William Brennan, for example, proved to be more liberal than President Dwight D. Eisenhower had anticipated. Asked whether he had made any mistakes as president, Eisenhower replied, "Yes, two, and they are both sitting on the Supreme Court."[16]

In 2010, President Barack Obama nominated Elena Kagan to replace the retiring John Paul Stevens on the Supreme Court. Kagan is shown here testifying before the Senate Judiciary Committee during her confirmation hearings.

Although presidents seek nominees who share their political philosophy, they also must take into account a nominee's acceptability to others. Every nominee is scrutinized closely by the legal community, interested groups, and the media; must undergo an extensive background check by the FBI; and then must gain the approval of a Senate majority. Within the Senate, the key body is the Judiciary Committee, whose members have responsibility for conducting hearings on judicial nominees and recommending their confirmation or rejection by the full Senate.

Nearly 20 percent of presidential nominees to the Supreme Court have been rejected by the Senate on grounds of judicial qualification, political views, personal ethics, or partisanship. Most of these rejections occurred before 1900, and partisan politics was the usual reason. Today a nominee with strong professional and ethical credentials is less likely to be blocked for partisan reasons alone. Nominees can expect confirmation if they have a clean personal record and a strong professional record, and are able to demonstrate during Senate confirmation hearings that they have the temperament and intellect expected of a Supreme Court justice. President Bush's nomination of John Roberts in 2005 to be chief justice is a case in point. Roberts faced tough questioning during Senate hearings, but nothing startlingly new or disturbing came out, and he was confirmed by a 78-22 vote. The Senate vote in 2010 on Elena Kagan, who was nominated by President Obama, was closer, even though the Senate hearings went smoothly. Although Kagan was confirmed by a 63-37 vote, most GOP senators voted against her. Expressing a view held by many Senate Republicans, Orrin Hatch of Utah said she lacked an "appropriate judicial philosophy," which was his way of saying that her legal views were at odds with his own.

POLITICAL THINKING   Partisanship or Merit?

Partisan considerations have increasingly influenced the selection of federal judges. Interest groups on the right and the left have insisted on the appointment of judges who hold compatible views. Presidents and members of Congress have also increasingly sought appointees who will decide issues in ways they prefer. What is your view? Should politics play such a large role in judicial appointments? Or should merit be given greater weight?

Lower-Court Nominees

The president typically delegates to the deputy attorney general the task of identifying potential nominees for lower-court judgeships, a process that includes seeking recommendations from U.S. senators of the president's party, and sometimes House members as well. **Senatorial courtesy,** a tradition that dates back to the 1840s, holds that a senator from the state in which a vacancy has arisen should be consulted on the choice of the nominee if the senator is of the same party as the president.[17] If not consulted, the senator can request that confirmation be denied. Other senators usually grant the request as a "courtesy" to their colleague.

Although presidents are not as personally involved in selecting lower-court nominees as in naming potential Supreme Court justices, lower-court appointments are collectively significant. A president who serves two terms can shape the federal judiciary for years to come. By the time he left office, George W. Bush had appointed more than a third of the seated federal judges. Bill Clinton appointed a similar number during his two terms.

Presidents typically select members of their own party for lower-court judgeships. More than 90 percent of recent district and appeals court nominees have been members of the president's political party.[18] This fact does not mean that federal judges engage in blatant partisanship while on the bench. They are officers of a separate branch of government and prize their judicial independence. All Republican appointees do not vote the same way on cases, nor do all Democratic appointees. Nevertheless, partisanship influences judicial decisions. A study of the voting records of appellate court judges, for example, found that Democratic appointees were more likely than Republican appointees to side with parties who claim the government has violated their civil liberties.[19]

senatorial courtesy

The tradition that a U.S. senator from the state in which a federal judicial vacancy has arisen should have a say in the president's nomination of the new judge if the senator is of the same party as the president.

Personal Backgrounds of Judicial Appointees

In recent years, increasing numbers of federal justices and judges have had prior judicial experience on the assumption that such individuals are best qualified for appointment to the federal bench.[20] Elective office (particularly a seat in the U.S. Senate) was once a common route to the Supreme Court,[21] but recent appointees, with the exception of Elena Kagan, who was solicitor general, have come from the appellate courts (see Table 14-1).

TABLE 14-1 | Justices of the Supreme Court

Justice	Year of appointment	Nominating president	Position before appointment
Antonin Scalia	1986	Reagan	Judge, D.C. Circuit Court of Appeals
Anthony Kennedy	1988	Reagan	Judge, 9th Circuit Court of Appeals
Clarence Thomas	1991	G. H. W. Bush	Judge, D.C. Circuit Court of Appeals
Ruth Bader Ginsburg	1993	Clinton	Judge, D.C. Circuit. Court of Appeals
Stephen Breyer	1994	Clinton	Judge, 1st Circuit Court of Appeals
John Roberts Jr.*	2005	G. W. Bush	Judge, D.C. Circuit Court of Appeals
Samuel Alito Jr.	2006	G. W. Bush	Judge, 3rd Circuit Court of Appeals
Sonia Sotomayor	2009	Obama	Judge, 2nd Circuit Court of Appeals
Elena Kagan	2010	Obama	Solicitor general of the United States

*Chief justice.

White males are overrepresented on the federal bench, just as they dominate in Congress and at the top levels of the executive branch. However, the number of women and minority-group members appointed to federal judgeships has increased significantly in recent decades. The number of such appointees has varied according to which party controls the presidency. Women and minority-group members are key constituencies of the Democratic Party, and Democratic presidents have appointed more judges from these groups than have Republican presidents (see Figure 14-4). In the first three years of his presidency, three-fourths of Barack Obama's appointees were women or minorities, an all-time high.[22] Of Democratic President Bill Clinton's appointees, half were women or minority-group members, compared with a third for his Republican successor George W. Bush.

The Supreme Court has a degree of diversity. Of the nine current justices, three are women (Ruth Bader Ginsburg, Sonia Sotomayor, and Elena Kagan) and two are minority-group members (Clarence Thomas and Sotomayor). The historical pattern is more one-sided. Until 1916, when Louis D. Brandeis was appointed to the Court, no Jewish justice had ever served. Prior to the twentieth century, only one Catholic, Roger Taney, had served on the Court. Six of the current justices are Catholic and three are Jewish, marking the first time the Court has been without a Protestant member. Thurgood Marshall in 1967 was the first black justice, and Sandra Day O'Connor in 1981 was the first woman justice. Antonin Scalia in 1986 was the Court's first justice of Italian descent. Sotomayor, who was appointed in 2009, is the first Hispanic justice. No person of Asian descent has been appointed to the Supreme Court.

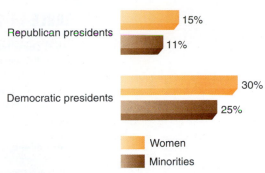

Republican presidents — Women 15%, Minorities 11%

Democratic presidents — Women 30%, Minorities 25%

FIGURE 14-4 **Political Parties, Presidents, and Women and Minority Judicial Appointees** Reflecting differences in their parties' coalitions, recent Republican and Democratic presidents have quite different records in terms of the percentage of their judicial appointees who have been women or minority-group members.

Source: Various sources. Data based on appointees of Presidents Carter, Reagan, G. H. W. Bush, Clinton, G. W. Bush, and Obama (2009–2011).

The Nature of Judicial Decision Making

Unlike the president or members of Congress, federal judges make their decisions within the context of a legal system. Yet, they are also political officials: they constitute one of three coequal branches of the national government. As a result, their decisions, though rooted in law, also have a political component.

Legal Influences on Judicial Decisions

Article III of the Constitution bars a federal court from issuing a decision except in response to a case presented to it. This restriction is a substantial one. For one thing, it limits judges to issues that arise from actual legal disputes. As federal judge David Bazelon noted, a judge "can't wake up one morning and simply decide to give a helpful little push to a school system, a mental hospital, or the local housing agency."[23]

The facts of a particular case also limit judicial action. The **facts** of a case are the relevant circumstances of a legal dispute or offense. In the case of a person accused of murder, for example, key facts would include evidence about the crime and whether the rights of the accused had been upheld by police. A judge must treat a murder case as a murder case, applying to it the laws that define murder and the penalties for it. A murder case cannot be used as an occasion for a judge to pronounce judgment on free speech rights or campaign finance laws.

Judicial decisions are also restricted in their breadth. Technically, a court ruling is binding only on the parties involved. Its broader impact depends on the willingness of others to accept it. If a court were to decide, for example, that a

facts (of a court case)
The relevant circumstances of a legal dispute or offense as determined by a trial court. The facts of a case are crucial because they help determine which law or laws are applicable in the case.

TABLE 14-2 | Sources of Law That Constrain the Decisions of the Federal Judiciary

U.S. Constitution: The federal courts are bound by the provisions of the U.S. Constitution. The sparseness of its wording, however, requires the Constitution to be applied in the light of present circumstances. Thus, judges are accorded some degree of discretion in their constitutional judgments.

Statutory law: The federal courts are constrained by statutes and by administrative regulations derived from the provisions of statutes. Many laws, however, are somewhat vague in their provisions and often have unanticipated applications. As a result, judges have some freedom in deciding cases based on statutes.

Precedent: Federal courts tend to follow precedent (or stare decisis), which is a legal principle developed through earlier court decisions. Because times change and not all cases have a clear precedent, judges have some discretion in their evaluation of the way earlier cases apply to a current case.

school was bound by law to spend more on programs for the learning disabled, the ruling would extend to other schools in the same situation only if those schools voluntarily complied or were forced by subsequent court action to do so. By comparison, if Congress were to pass legislation granting funds to schools for programs for the learning disabled, all eligible schools would receive the funding.

The major constraint on the courts is the law itself. Although a president or Congress can make almost any decision that is politically acceptable, the judiciary must work within the confines of the law. When asked by a friend to "do justice," Justice Oliver Wendell Holmes Jr. said that he was bound to follow the law rather than his personal sense of right and wrong.[24]

The judiciary works within the context of three main sources of law: the Constitution, legislative statutes, and legal precedents (see Table 14-2). The Constitution of the United States is the nation's highest law, and judges and justices are sworn to uphold it. When a case raises a constitutional issue, a court has the duty to apply the Constitution to it. For example, the Constitution prohibits the states from printing their own currency. If a state decided that it would do so anyway, a federal judge would be obligated to rule against the practice.

The large majority of cases that arise in courts involve issues of statutory and administrative law rather than constitutional law. *Statutory law* is legislative (statute) law. *Administrative law* is based on statutory law but is set by government agencies rather than by legislatures. Administrative law consists of the rules, regulations, and judgments that agencies make in the process of implementing and enforcing statutory law. All federal courts are bound by federal statutory and administrative laws, as well as by treaties, and judges must work within the confines of these laws. A company that is charged with violating an air pollution law, for example, will be judged within the context of that law—what it permits and what it prohibits, and what penalties apply if the company is found to have broken the law. When hearing such a case, a judge will typically try to determine whether the meaning of the statute or regulation can be determined by common sense (the "plain meaning rule"). The question for the judge is what the law or regulation was intended to safeguard (such as clean air). In most cases, the law or regulation is clear enough that when the facts of the case are determined, the decision is fairly straightforward.

The U.S. legal system developed from the English common-law tradition, which includes the principle that a court's decision on a case should be consistent with previous judicial rulings. This principle, known as precedent, reflects the philosophy of stare decisis (Latin for "to stand by things that were previously decided"). Precedent holds that principles of law, once established, should be applied in subsequent similar cases. Judges and justices often cite past rulings as justification for their decisions in the cases before them. Deference to precedent gives predictability to the application of law. Government has an obligation to make clear what its laws are and how they are being applied. If courts routinely ignored how similar cases had been decided in the past, they would create confusion and uncertainty about what is lawful and what is not. A business firm that is seeking to comply with environmental protection laws, for example, can develop company policies that will keep the company safely within the law if court decisions in this area are consistent. If courts routinely ignored precedent, a firm could unintentionally engage in an activity that a court might conclude was unlawful.

Political Influences on Judicial Decisions

Adherence to the law in the judging of cases is what gives substance to the claim that the United States is governed by "the rule of law." If judges were to ignore or downplay their obligation to uphold the law, the public's respect for the law and willingness to comply with it would diminish accordingly.

Nevertheless, the law is not always a precise guide to judicial decisions, with the result that judges often have some leeway in their rulings.[25] The Constitution, for example, is a sparsely worded document and must be adapted to new and changing situations. The judiciary also has no choice at times but to impose meaning on statutory law. Statutes are typically more detailed in their provisions than is the Constitution, but Congress cannot always anticipate the specific applications of a legislative act and often defines statutory provisions in general terms. The judiciary is then required to determine what the language means in the context of a specific case. Precedent is even less precise as a guide to decisions in that it is specific to particular cases. A new case may differ in important ways from its closest precedent or rest at the intersection of competing precedents. In such instances, a judge must determine which precedent, if any, applies to the case at hand.

The Supreme Court's ruling in *Faragher v. City of Boca Raton* (1998), involving sexual harassment in the workplace, illustrates the ambiguity that can exist in the law. The Court developed its ruling in the context of the antidiscrimination provisions of the Civil Rights Act of 1964. However, the act itself contains no description of, or even reference to, job-related sexual harassment. Yet the act does prohibit workplace discrimination, and the Court was unwilling to dismiss sexual harassment as an irrelevant form of job-related discrimination. In this sense, the Court was "making" law; it was deciding how legislation enacted by Congress applied to behavior that Congress had not specifically addressed when it wrote the legislation. In the end, the Court decided that sexual harassment on the job is among the types of job-related discrimination prohibited by the Civil Rights Act.[26]

Political influences affect how judges decide cases in which they have leeway. These influences come from both inside and outside the judicial system.

Inside the Court: Judges' Political Beliefs

Although the judiciary symbolizes John Adams's description of the U.S. political system as "a government of laws, and not of men," court rulings are not simply an extension of the laws. They are also influenced by the political beliefs of the men and women who sit on the federal bench.[27] Changes in the

Rule by law is idealized by a scale, where the weight of the evidence on each side of a case determines the outcome. In reality, court decisions are affected by politics, as well as by the law.

Supreme Court's membership, for example, can bring about a change in its position. Samuel Alito's appointment to the Court in 2006 produced that kind of change. Although the justice he replaced, Sandra Day O'Connor, usually voted with the Court's four most conservative justices, she sometimes switched sides. Voting with the Court's four most liberal justices, she cast the deciding vote, for example, in the 2000 Nebraska case that upheld the use of partial-birth abortion when the mother's life is endangered. In contrast, Alito cast the deciding vote in the 2007 decision to uphold a congressional ban on the use of partial-birth abortion. Alito's decision in this case and others prompted observers to say that the Supreme Court had swung to the right. Even one of the Supreme Court justices admitted as much. "It is not often in the law," wrote Justice Stephen Breyer, "that so few have so quickly changed so much."[28]

Studies by political scientists Jeffrey Segal and Harold Spaeth show that justices tend to vote in line with their political attitudes. Segal and Spaeth examined thousands of non-unanimous Court decisions, looking at the extent to which each justice voted on the same side or the opposite side from each of the other justices. Clear patterns emerged, such as the tendency of Antonin Scalia and Clarence Thomas, who are Republican appointees, to vote the same way and opposite that of Stephen Breyer and Ruth Bader Ginsburg, who are Democratic appointees. Compared with Democratic appointees to the Court, Republican appointees were found to be more likely to side with employers rather than with employees, with law enforcement officials rather than with the criminally accused, with corporations rather than with unions, and with government rather than with those claiming discrimination. Segal and Spaeth conclude that the "[policy] preferences of the justices go a long way toward explaining their decisions."[29]

It is true, of course, that disputes that reach the Supreme Court are anything but clear-cut. If they were, they would have been settled in the lower federal courts. It is also true that Supreme Court justices have less leeway in making their decisions than elected officials have in making their choices. Justices operate within the confines of established laws and legal principles, which constrain their choices. The fact that Republican appointees to the Supreme Court are more likely than Democratic appointees to side with law enforcement officials than with the criminally accused does not mean that they invariably do so or that they are unmindful of legal restraints on law enforcement officials. In *United States v. Jones* (2012), for example, the Supreme Court held that law enforcement officials had exceeded their authority under the law by placing a GPS tracking device on a suspect's car without first obtaining a search warrant from a judge (see Chapter 4). The ruling was unanimous, meaning that the Court's Republican appointees sided with its Democratic appointees in concluding that police had violated the suspect's constitutional rights.

Nevertheless, when viewed as a whole, Supreme Court decisions are a mix of law and politics. Arguably, partisanship was never more evident than in the Supreme Court's *Bush v. Gore* (2000) decision that blocked a manual recount of the Florida presidential vote in 2000, thereby assuring the election of the Republican nominee, George W. Bush.[30] The five justices in the majority—Chief Justice William Rehnquist and associate justices Sandra Day O'Connor, Anthony Kennedy, Antonin Scalia, and Clarence Thomas—were Republican appointees and were the same justices who in previous decisions had deferred to state authority and had opposed new applications of the Fourteenth Amendment's equal protection clause. Yet they rejected the authority of Florida's highest court, which had ordered a statewide manual recount of the vote. They also devised a never-before-used application of the equal protection clause, concluding that the recount could not go forward because no uniform standard for counting the ballots existed. Justice John Paul Stevens, who thought the Florida high court had acted properly in ordering a recount, accused the Court's majority of devising a ruling based on their partisanship rather than on the law, saying the majority had ignored "the basic principle, inherent in our Constitution and our democracy, that every legal vote should be counted."[31] Stevens noted that different standards for casting and counting ballots are used throughout the country, even within the same state.

Outside the Court: The Public, Groups, and Elected Officials

The courts can and do make unpopular decisions. In the long run, however, judicial decisions must be seen as fair if they are to be obeyed. In other words, the judiciary cannot routinely ignore the expectations of the general public, interest groups, and elected officials.

Judges are less responsive to public opinion than are elected officials. Nevertheless, the Supreme Court in some instances has tempered its rulings in an effort to get public support or reduce public resistance. The Supreme Court usually stays close enough to public opinion to reduce the likelihood of outright defiance of its decisions.[32] In the 1954 *Brown* case, for example, the justices, recognizing that school desegregation would be an explosive issue in the South, required only that desegregation take place "with all deliberate speed" rather than immediately or on a fixed timetable. After its *Swann v. Charlotte-Mecklenburg Board of Education* (1971) school busing decision led to riots in several cities, the Court held in *Milliken v. Bradley* (1974) that busing across school district lines would not be permitted. The *Milliken* decision effectively insulated suburban school districts from busing, which served to reduce white suburbanites' opposition to the policy.[33]

Interest groups also have an influence on the judiciary. Groups petition the White House and Congress to appoint judges and justices who share their outlook on legal disputes. More directly, they submit amicus curiae ("friend of the court") briefs to make their positions known on court cases (see Chapters 5 and 9) and file lawsuits to advance their policy goals. Groups that rely on a judicial strategy pick their cases carefully, choosing those that offer the greatest chance of success. They also carefully pick the courts in which they file their lawsuits, knowing that some judges are more sympathetic than others to their argument. In fact, some groups rely almost entirely on legal action, knowing they have a better chance of success in the courts than in Congress or the White House. The American Civil Liberties Union (ACLU), for example, has filed hundreds of lawsuits over the years on issues of individual rights, including a recent suit aimed at forcing federal agents to meet constitutional requirements for search and seizure before they are allowed to examine documents stored on travelers' laptop computers.

Elected officials also have ways of influencing the courts. Congress can rewrite legislation that it feels the judiciary has misinterpreted. Meanwhile, the president is responsible for enforcing court decisions and has some influence over the cases that come before the courts. Under President Reagan, for example, the Justice Department vigorously pursued lawsuits

Even though the Supreme Court tried to temper the public response to its 1954 *Brown v. Board of Education* decision by ruling that desegregation of public schools should proceed with "all deliberate speed" rather than immediately or on a fixed timetable, the delay in implementation did little to quell the anger of many white southerners. Shown here is one of the many billboards in the South that called for the impeachment of Chief Justice Earl Warren.

that challenged the legality of affirmative action programs, a strategy consistent with Reagan's determination to limit their use.

Judicial appointments offer the president and Congress their biggest opportunity to influence the courts. In 2008, when it became clear that their party was likely to win the presidency, Senate Democrats slowed action on the confirmation of President Bush's judicial nominees. When Barack Obama took office in 2009, scores of judgeships were vacant, which he filled with loyal Democrats. It was a tactic Senate Republicans had employed in 2000. They had delayed action on President Clinton's nominees, enabling Bush to appoint Republicans to existing vacancies when he took office in 2001.

As a result of heightened partisanship in Congress during the past two decades, the judicial appointment process has become increasingly contentious (see "Party Polarization"). Democratic and Republican lawmakers alike recognize the power of the courts to determine policy in areas such as affirmative action and environmental protection, and each party's lawmakers have been determined to confirm judicial appointees whose policy views align with their own. Nevertheless, the influence of elected officials on the judiciary is never total. Judges prize their independence, and their lifetime appointment insulates them from political pressures. In 2004, for example, the Republican-laden Supreme Court rejected the Bush administration's claim that it had the authority to jail suspected terrorists indefinitely without a court hearing (see Chapter 4).

PARTY POLARIZATION   Political Thinking in Conflict

Has the Supreme Court Confirmation Process Become Too Partisan?

In the nineteenth century, Supreme Court confirmation hearings in the Senate were often partisan slugfests and the nominees were often confirmed or rejected on the basis of partisanship. For most of the twentieth century, the process worked differently. Senate confirmation hearings were typically polite and dignified and centered on the nominees' legal qualifications. The rejection of Robert Bork's nomination in 1987 ended that practice. Picked by President Ronald Reagan, Bork was attacked in Senate hearings as holding extreme legal positions that were driven by a conservative ideology. The Democrats had control of the Senate and his nomination went down to defeat. Since then, reflecting the increase in party polarization, Supreme Court nominees have routinely been subject to partisan attack, within and outside the Senate. Organized groups on the wings of the parties have mounted intense—often downright nasty—lobbying and public relations campaigns to defeat objectionable nominees. Senators have used the confirmation hearings to score political points and curry political favor. More "heat" than "light" is how some observers have characterized the hearings. Other observers say that the intense partisanship surrounding the Senate hearings has made nominees so careful in what they say that they say almost nothing meaningful about their judicial philosophy. Said Senator Jon Kyl (R-Arizona): "I don't know what to do. I am not one for being a nasty questioner. Whereas somebody might be able to bore in and finally get something from a witness by just sheer, brute force, I am not suggesting that that is a good technique."

Q. *In* Electing Justices *(2005), Brigham Young University political scientist Richard Davis notes that the Supreme Court appointment process is now more like an election campaign than the more dignified process that the writers of the Constitution had in mind when they established the procedure. Do you think it's a good thing, or a bad thing, that partisanship is now such a large part of the process?*

Judicial Power and Democratic Government

Federal judges are unelected officials with lifetime appointments, which places them beyond the reach of the voters. Because the United States has a constitutional system that places limits on the power of the majority, the judiciary has a legitimate role in the system. Yet court decisions reflect in part the personal political beliefs of the judges. A basic question is how far judges should go in substituting their judgments for those of elected officials.

This power is most dramatically evident when courts declare laws enacted by Congress to be unconstitutional. In such instances, unelected judges substitute their judgment for that of the people's elected representatives. In almost every case, their judgment is the final word. The difficulty of amending the Constitution (approval by two-thirds majorities in the House and Senate and by three-fourths of the states) makes it an impracticable means of reversing Supreme Court decisions. The Sixteenth Amendment, which grants the federal government the power to levy income taxes, is one of the few times that a Supreme Court decision has been reversed through constitutional amendment.

The judiciary's power has been a source of controversy throughout the nation's history, but the debate has seldom been livelier than during recent decades. The sheer number of legal disputes is among the reasons. Federal cases have increased threefold (and federal appeals have increased tenfold) over the past half century as Americans have increasingly turned to the courts to settle their disputes. The judiciary at times has acted almost legislatively by addressing broad social issues, such as abortion, busing, affirmative action, church-state relations, campaign finance, and prison reform. During the 1990s, for example, the prison systems in forty-two states were operating under federal court orders that mandated improvements in health care or reductions in overcrowding. Through such actions the judiciary has restricted the policymaking authority of the states, has narrowed legislative discretion, and has made judicial action an effective political strategy for some groups.[34]

The judiciary has become more extensively involved in policymaking for many of the same reasons that Congress and the president have been thrust into new policy areas and become more deeply involved in old ones. Social and economic changes have required government to play a larger role in society, and this development has generated a seemingly endless series of new legal controversies. Environmental pollution, for example, was not a major issue until the 1960s; since then, it has been the subject of innumerable court cases.

How far should judges go in asserting their interpretations of the law, as opposed to those put into effect by the people's elected representatives? What is the proper role of an unelected judiciary in a system rooted in the principle of majority rule? There are competing schools of thought on this issue, none of which is definitive. The Constitution is silent on the question of how it should be interpreted, which has left the judiciary's proper role open to dispute. Nevertheless, a brief review of the major competing theories is instructive.

Originalism Theory versus Living Constitution Theory

Originalism theory, a prominent philosophy of conservatives, holds that the Constitution should be interpreted in the way that a reasonable person would have interpreted it at the time it was written.[35] Originalists emphasize the wording of the law, arguing that the words of the framers are the only reliable indicator of how the law should be interpreted. As Supreme Court justice Antonin Scalia,

originalism theory
A method of interpreting the Constitution that emphasizes the meaning of its words at the time they were written.

Judicial Power

U.S. courts are highly political compared to the courts of most other democracies. First, U.S. courts operate within a common-law tradition, in which judge-made law becomes (through precedent) a part of the legal code. Many democracies have a civil-law tradition, in which nearly all law is defined by legislative statutes. Second, because U.S. courts operate in a constitutional system of divided powers, they are required to rule on conflicts between state and nation or between the executive and the legislative branches, which thrusts the judiciary into the middle of political conflicts. Not surprisingly, then, federal judges and justices are appointed through an overtly political process in which partisan views and activities are major considerations. Many federal judges, particularly at the district level, have no significant prior judicial experience. In fact, the United States is one of the few countries that does not require formal training for judges.

The pattern is different in most European democracies, where judgeships tend to be career positions. Individuals are appointed to the judiciary at an early age and then work their way up the judicial ladder largely on the basis of seniority. Partisan politics does not play a large role in appointment and promotion. By tradition, European judges see their job as the strict interpretation of statutes, not the creative application of them.

The power of U.S. courts is nowhere more evident than in the exercise of judicial review—the voiding of a legislative or executive action on the grounds that it violates the Constitution. Judicial review had its origins in European experience and thought, but it was first formally applied in the United States at the federal level when, in *Marbury v. Madison* (1803), the Supreme Court declared an act of Congress unconstitutional. Some democracies, including Great Britain, still do not allow broad-scale judicial review, but most democracies now provide for it.

In the so-called American system of judicial review, all judges can evaluate the applicability of constitutional law to particular cases and can declare ordinary law invalid when it conflicts with constitutional law. By comparison, the so-called Austrian system restricts judicial review to a special constitutional court. Judges in other courts cannot declare a law void on the grounds that it is unconstitutional; they must apply ordinary law as it is written. In the Austrian system, moreover, constitutional decisions can be made in response to requests for judicial review by elected officials when they are considering legislation. In the American case, judges can act only within the framework of actual legal cases; thus, their rulings are made only after laws have been enacted.

Q: Do you think it would be advantageous if the U.S. Supreme Court, in response to queries by Congress or the president, could issue advisory opinions on the constitutionality of policies under consideration? Or do you prefer the current American system, whereby the Supreme Court can issue opinions only in the context of an actual court case, which means that legislative or executive action must take place in advance of any court ruling?

---

living constitution theory

A method of interpreting the Constitution that emphasizes the principles it embodies and their application to changing circumstances and needs.

---

an avowed originalist, has said: "You figure out what [the Constitution] was understood to mean when it was adopted and that's the end of it." The difficult part, Scalia claims, is trying to figure out what the words meant to those who wrote and ratified them. "It requires immersing oneself in the political and intellectual atmosphere of the time—somehow placing out of mind knowledge that we have which an earlier age did not."[36]

An opposing theory, embraced more often by liberals, holds that the Constitution is a living document that should be interpreted in light of changing circumstances. Proponents of the **living constitution theory** claim that the framers, through the use of broad language and basic principles, intended the Constitution to be an adaptable instrument. They cite the preamble of the 1787 Constitutional Convention's Committee of Detail, which says the Constitution "ought to be accommodated to times and events." Supreme Court justice Stephen Breyer embraces this view, saying that the judiciary should promote in today's world the kind of government the Constitution was meant to establish. "The Constitution," Breyer argues, "provides a framework for the creation of democratically determined solutions, which protect each individual's basic liberties . . . while securing a democratic form of government."[37]

Critics of the living constitution theory argue that, in practice, it allows judges to promote their personal views by enabling them to devise arguments that support the rulings they prefer. Such judges are said to turn the law into what they want it to say, rather than what it actually says. On the other hand, critics of originalism theory say that the framers in using broad terms such as "search and seizure" could not possibly have had the practices of their time solely in mind. If that was their intention, they would have provided detailed information on how such terms were to be interpreted.

Judicial Restraint versus Judicial Activism

A longer standing debate over the judiciary's proper role has pitted the advocates of judicial restraint against the advocates of judicial activism. This debate centers on the degree to which judges should defer to precedent and elected officials.

The doctrine of **judicial restraint** holds that judges should generally defer to precedent and to decisions made by legislatures. The restraint doctrine holds that in nearly every instance policy issues should be decided by elected lawmakers and not by appointed judges. The role of the judge is to apply the law rather than determine it. Advocates of judicial restraint say that when judges substitute their views for those of elected representatives, they undermine the fundamental principle of self-government—the right of the majority, through its elected representatives, to determine how they will be governed.[38] Underlying this argument is the idea that policy is the result of conflicts between contending interests and that elected representatives, because they have to deal directly with these interests, are better positioned than judges to determine how these conflicts should be resolved.[39]

In contrast, the doctrine of **judicial activism** holds that judges should actively interpret the Constitution, statutes, and precedents in light of fundamental principles and should intervene when elected representatives fail to act in accord with these principles. Although advocates of judicial activism acknowledge the importance of majority rule, they claim that the courts should not blindly defer to the decisions of elected officials when core principles—such as liberty, equality, and self-government—are threatened. They also contend that precedent should be respected only if it is based on legal reasoning that is as sound today as it was when the precedent was decided.

Over its history, the Supreme Court has had strong proponents of each doctrine. Chief Justice John Marshall was an avowed activist who used the Court to enlarge the judiciary's power and to promote the national government (see Chapters 2 and 3). Judicial review—the most substantial form of judicial power—is not granted explicitly by the Constitution but was claimed through Marshall's opinion in *Marbury v. Madison*. Associate Justice Oliver Wendell Holmes Jr. was Marshall's philosophical opposite. One of the nation's most influential jurists, Holmes argued that the judiciary should defer to the elected branches unless they blatantly overstep their authority.[40] An example of judicial restraint is the Supreme Court's 2012 ruling upholding the individual mandate provision of the health care reform bill enacted by Congress in 2010. The Court's majority creatively invoked Congress's taxing power in order to uphold the provision (see Chapter 3). "Because the Constitution permits such a tax, it is not our role to forbid it, or to pass upon its wisdom or fairness," said the Court's majority.[41]

Although judicial activism is sometimes associated with liberal justices, history indicates it has also been practiced by conservative justices. During the period between the Civil War and the Great Depression, the Supreme Court was dominated by conservatives and had an activist agenda, striking down most state and congressional legislation aimed at economic regulation (see Chapter 3). In the period after World War II, the Court was again in an activist mode, but this time in a different direction. Dominated by liberal justices, the Court struck

judicial restraint

The doctrine that the judiciary should follow closely the wording of the law, be highly respectful of precedent, and defer to the judgment of legislatures. The doctrine claims that the job of judges is to work within the confines of laws set down by tradition and lawmaking majorities.

judicial activism

The doctrine that the courts should develop new legal principles when judges see a compelling need, even if this action places them in conflict with precedent or the policy decisions of elected officials.

John Marshall served thirty-four years as chief justice of the Supreme Court, the longest tenure in that position in U.S. history. An ardent nationalist who saw himself as a guardian of federal authority, Marshall led the Court to a series of activist rulings that established it as a powerful institution and helped lay the foundation for a strong Union. Marshall saw himself as a framer of the Constitution, acting as the ongoing architect of the work begun in Philadelphia during the summer of 1787.

Should Originalism Guide Court Decisions?

The Constitution is silent on the question of how it should be interpreted, which has left the issue a subject of dispute. One theory—originalism—emphasizes the wording of the law. As Justice Antonin Scalia expressed it: "You figure out what [the Constitution] was understood to mean when it was adopted and that's the end of it." Proponents of the living constitution theory, including Justice Stephen Breyer, reject this argument, saying that the framers deliberately chose general phrases and principles so that the Constitution could be adapted to the changing needs and values of society. The following segments pit the view of Scalia against that of Breyer. Scalia's argument comes from a speech he gave at the Woodrow Wilson International Center for Scholars, while Breyer's argument is taken from a speech he gave at the New York University School of Law.

YES I am [among the judges] who are known as originalists. Our manner of interpreting the Constitution is to begin with the text, and to give that text the meaning that it bore when it was adopted by the people.... If you don't believe in originalism, then you need some other principle of interpretation. Being a non-originalist is not enough. You see, I have my rules that confine me. I know what I'm looking for. When I find it—the original meaning of the Constitution—I am handcuffed. If I believe that the First Amendment meant when it was adopted that you are entitled to burn the American flag, I have to come out that way even though I don't like to come out that way.... Now, if you're not going to control your judges that way, what other criterion are you going to place before them? What is the criterion that governs the Living Constitutional judge? What can you possibly use, besides original meaning? . . . [W]hen the Senate interrogates nominees to the Supreme Court, or to the lower courts—you know, "Judge so-and-so, do you think there is a right to this in the Constitution? You don't? Well, my constituents think there ought to be, and I'm not going to appoint to the court someone who is not going to find that"—when we are in that mode, you realize, we have rendered the Constitution useless, because the Constitution will mean what the majority wants it to mean.

—Antonin Scalia, Supreme Court justice

NO [My] approach to constitutional interpretation . . . places considerable weight upon consequences—consequences valued in terms of basic constitutional purposes. It disavows a contrary constitutional approach, a more "legalistic" approach that places too much weight upon language, history, tradition, and precedent alone while understating the importance of consequences.... The Constitution, considered as a whole, creates a framework for a certain kind of government. Its general objectives can be described abstractly as including: (1) democratic self-government; (2) dispersion of power (avoiding concentration of too much power in too few hands); (3) individual dignity (through protection of individual liberties); (4) equality before the law (through equal protection of the law); and (5) the rule of law itself. . . . Literalist judges who emphasize language, history, tradition, and precedent cannot justify their practices by claiming that is what the Framers wanted, for the Framers did not say specifically what factors judges should emphasize when seeking to interpret the Constitution's open language. Nor is it plausible to believe that those who argued about the Bill of Rights, and made clear that it did not contain an exclusive detailed list, had agreed about what school of interpretive thought should prove dominant in the centuries to come. Indeed, the Constitution itself says that the "enumeration" in the Constitution of some rights "shall not be construed to deny or disparage others retained by the people." Professor [Bernard] Bailyn [properly] concludes that the Framers added this language to make clear that "rights, like law itself, should never be fixed, frozen, that new dangers and needs will emerge, and that to respond to these dangers and needs, rights must be newly specified to protect the individual's integrity and inherent dignity."

—Stephen Breyer, Supreme Court justice

Q: Which theory, Scalia's or Breyer's, is closer to your own? Why do you think this theory is the better one?

down numerous state statutes in the course of expanding fair-trial rights and civil rights (see Chapters 4 and 5).

In recent years, the conservative-dominated Supreme Court has also been an activist court. In the past fifteen years or so, the Supreme Court has struck down more acts of Congress than were invalidated during the previous half-century.[42] A case in point is the Court's recent ruling on campaign spending. In deciding that corporations and unions could spend freely on election campaigns, the Court overturned congressional action, thus substituting its judgment for that of elected officials. The ruling also overturned precedent—in earlier cases, the Court had held that Congress could regulate election spending by corporations and unions.

What Is the Judiciary's Proper Role?

Like the debate between originalism and living Constitution theorists, the debate between advocates of judicial restraint and activism is a normative one. There is no conclusive way of settling the issue because the Constitution does not specify the method by which judges should arrive at their decisions.

Nevertheless, the debates are important because they address the fundamental question of the role of judges in a governing system based on the often-conflicting concepts of majority rule and individual rights. The United States is a constitutional democracy that recognizes both the power of the majority to rule and the claim of the minority to protection of its rights and interests. The judiciary was not established as the nation's final authority on all things relating to the use of political power. Yet the judiciary was established as a coequal branch of government charged with responsibility for protecting individual rights and constraining political authority. The question of how far the courts should go in asserting their authority is one that every student of government should ponder.

Summary

Self-Test www.mhhe.com/ pattersontadtx11e

At the lowest level of the federal judicial system are the district courts, where most federal cases begin. Above them are the federal courts of appeals, which review cases appealed from the lower courts. The U.S. Supreme Court is the nation's highest court. Each state has its own court system, consisting of trial courts at the bottom and one or two appellate levels at the top. Cases originating in state courts ordinarily cannot be appealed to the federal courts unless a federal issue is involved, and then the federal courts can choose to rule only on the federal aspects of the case. Federal judges at all levels are nominated by the president, and if confirmed by the Senate, they are appointed by the president to the office. Once on the federal bench, they serve until they die, retire, or are removed by impeachment and conviction.

The Supreme Court is unquestionably the most important court in the country. The legal principles it establishes are binding on lower courts, and its capacity to define the law is enhanced by the control it exercises over the cases it hears. However, it is inaccurate to assume that lower courts are inconsequential (the upper-court myth). Lower courts have considerable discretion, and the great majority of their decisions are not reviewed by a higher court. It is also inaccurate to assume that federal courts are far more significant than state courts (the federal court myth).

The courts have less discretionary authority than elected institutions do. The judiciary's positions are constrained by the facts of a case and by the laws as defined through the Constitution, legal precedent, and statutes (and government regulations derived from statutes). Yet existing legal guidelines are seldom so precise that judges have no choice in their decisions. As a result, political influences have a strong impact on the judiciary. It responds to national conditions, public opinion, interest groups, and elected officials, particularly the president and members of Congress. Another political influence on the judiciary is the personal beliefs of judges, who have individual preferences that affect how they decide issues that come before the courts. It's not surprising that partisan politics plays a significant role in judicial appointments.

In recent decades, as the Supreme Court has crossed into areas traditionally left to lawmaking majorities, the issue of judicial power has become more pressing, which has prompted claims and counterclaims about the judiciary's proper role. Advocates of originalism theory argue that judges should apply the law in terms of the words of the law as they were understood at the time of enactment. Advocates of the living constitution theory hold that the law should be interpreted in light of changing circumstances. Judicial restraint and activism are two additional theories of the judiciary's proper role. Advocates of judicial restraint claim that the justices' personal values are inadequate justification for exceeding the proper judicial role; they argue that the Constitution entrusts broad issues of the public good to elective institutions and that the courts should ordinarily defer to the judgment of elected officials. Judicial activists counter that the courts were established as an independent branch and should not hesitate to promote general principles when necessary, even if this action brings them into conflict with elected officials.

Study Corner

Key Terms

appellate jurisdiction (*p. 360*)
brief (*p. 361*)
concurring opinion (*p. 362*)
decision (*p. 361*)
dissenting opinion (*p. 362*)
facts (of a court case) (*p. 369*)
judicial activism (*p. 377*)
judicial conference (*p. 361*)
judicial restraint (*p. 377*)
judicial review (*p. 360*)

jurisdiction (of a court) (*p. 359*)
living constitution theory (*p. 376*)
majority opinion (*p. 361*)
opinion (of a court) (*p. 361*)
original jurisdiction (*p. 359*)
originalism theory (*p. 375*)
plurality opinion (*p. 362*)
precedent (*p. 360*)
senatorial courtesy (*p. 368*)
writ of certiorari (*p. 360*)

Self-Test: Multiple Choice

1. When nominating a justice to the U.S. Supreme Court, presidents
   a. are required by law to consult with the American Bar Association.
   b. in accordance with senatorial courtesy have usually decided the choice by finding out who a majority of the senators in their party would like the nominee to be.
   c. tend to select a nominee who shares their political philosophy.
   d. get their nominee confirmed by the Senate only about half the time.

2. Judges in the U.S. judiciary
   a. after issuing a ruling are personally responsible for seeing that the ruling is carried out by other officials.
   b. by law must attend public meetings from time to time and, while at these meetings, advise the public on judicial matters.
   c. are prohibited from issuing decisions except on actual cases that come to their court.
   d. have greater freedom than legislators or executives to choose the issues they will address.

3. The federal district courts are
   a. courts of original jurisdiction.
   b. the only federal courts that regularly use juries to determine the outcome of cases.
   c. the courts that, in practice, make the final decision in most federal cases.
   d. the lowest level of federal courts.
   e. all of the above.

4. Most cases reach the U.S. Supreme Court through
   a. appeal of cases that the Court is bound by the Constitution or by act of Congress to hear even if it would prefer not to hear them.

   b. grant of a writ of certiorari.
   c. plea bargaining.
   d. its power of original jurisdiction.

5. Which constitutional power does Congress have in relation to the Supreme Court?
   a. Congress can change the number of justices on the Supreme Court.
   b. Congress can change the Supreme Court's original jurisdiction.
   c. By two-thirds vote of both chambers, Congress determines which justice will become Chief Justice when that office becomes vacant.
   d. Congress can refuse to implement Supreme Court decisions when it disagrees with those decisions.

6. A court exercising judicial activism would likely
   a. totally disregard judicial precedent.
   b. totally disregard legislative and executive action.
   c. not hesitate to act when it thought an important constitutional principle was at issue, even if such action would bring the court into conflict with public opinion or the elected branches.
   d. none of the above.

7. State court systems in the United States are lower-level administrative units of the federal court system and not independent judicial units. (T/F)

8. The U.S. judiciary is not influenced by either public opinion or the actions of interest groups. (T/F)

9. The "federal court myth" implies that the federal courts are far more important than state courts. (T/F)

10. According to the text, social and economic changes have required the government, including the judiciary, to play a larger role in resolving societal problems and conflicts. (T/F)

Self-Test: Essay

Discuss the influence of politics in the selection and decisions of Supreme Court justices.

Suggested Readings

Breyer, Stephen. *Active Liberty: Interpreting the Democratic Constitution*. New York: Vintage, 2006. A treatise on constitutional interpretation by one of the Supreme Court's most liberal justices.

Davis, Richard. *Electing Justices: Fixing the Supreme Court Nomination Process*. New York: Oxford University Press, 2005. An examination of the now-contentious process through which Supreme Court justices are nominated and confirmed.

Hansford, Thomas G., and James F. Spriggs II. *The Politics of Precedent on the Supreme Court*. Princeton, N.J.: Princeton University Press, 2006. An examination of how the Court interprets precedent to suit new situations and goals.

Maltzman, Forest, Paul Wahlbeck, and James Spriggs. *The Collegial Game: Crafting Law on the U.S. Supreme Court*. New York: Cambridge University Press, 2000. A fascinating look at the strategic considerations that go into Supreme Court justices' interactions and decisions.

O'Brien, David M. *Storm Center: The Supreme Court in American Politics*, 9th ed. New York: Norton, 2011. A thorough assessment of the Supreme Court.

Scalia, Antonin. *A Matter of Interpretation: Federal Courts and the Law*. Princeton, N.J.: Princeton University Press, 1998. A treatise on constitutional interpretation by one of the Supreme Court's most conservative justices.

Segal, Jeffrey A., and Harold J. Spaeth. *The Supreme Court and the Attitudinal Model Revisited*. New York: Cambridge University Press, 2002. A study of inter-justice agreement on Supreme Court decisions that reveals the influence of political attitudes.

List of Websites

www.supremecourt.gov/
The website of the U.S. Supreme Court; it includes information on the Court, as well as on its previous and pending cases.

www.fjc.gov
The home page of the Federal Judicial Center, an agency created by Congress to conduct research and provide education on the federal judicial system.

www.lib.umich.edu/govdocs/fedjudi.html
A University of Michigan web page that provides detailed information on the federal judicial system.

www.law.cornell.edu
The Cornell University Legal Information Institute's website includes full-text versions of historic and recent Supreme Court decisions, as well as links to state constitutions and other subjects.

Participate!

The right to a jury trial is one of the oldest features—dating to the colonial period—of the American political experience. Jury trials also offer the average citizen a rare opportunity to be part of the governing structure. Yet Americans increasingly shirk jury duty. When summoned, many of them find all sorts of reasons why they should be excused from jury duty. In some areas of the country, the avoidance rate exceeds 50 percent. Some citizens even give up their right to vote because they know that jurors in their area are selected from names on voter registration lists. There are reasons, however, to look upon jury duty as an opportunity as well as a responsibility. Studies indicate that citizens come away from the jury experience with a fuller appreciation of the justice system. Jurors acquire an understanding of the serious responsibility handed to them when asked to decide upon someone's guilt or innocence. The legal standard in American courts—"guilty beyond a reasonable doubt"—is a solemn one. The fairness of the jury system also requires full participation by the community. Studies show that jurors' life experiences can affect the decisions they reach. If everyone on a jury is from the same background and one that is different from the defendant's, the odds of a wrongful verdict increase. "A jury of one's peers" should mean just that—a jury of individuals who, collectively, represent the range of groups in the community. If you are called to serve on a jury, you should answer the call. You would want nothing less from others than if you, a family member, or a friend were the person on trial.

Extra Credit

For up-to-the-minute *New York Times* articles, interactive simulations, graphics, study tools, and more links and quizzes, visit the text's Online Learning Center at **www.mhhe.com/pattersontad11e**.

Self-Test Answers

1. c, 2. c, 3. e, 4. b, 5. a, 6. c, 7. F, 8. F, 9. T, 10. T

WALL STREET IN DESPAIR

stocks plunge anew

MARKETS IN TURMO

Dow down nearly 778 in its biggest one-day point decline in history

A-5

Yet another precipitous

Economic and Environmental Policy: Contributing to Prosperity

We the people of the United States, in order to . . . insure domestic tranquility. Preamble, U.S. Constitution

The economy was in turmoil. The housing market was collapsing from the inability of homeowners with subprime adjustable-rate mortgages to make their monthly payments. Then, on September 15, 2008, after its stock had dropped precipitously, Lehman Brothers, one of the nation's oldest and largest commercial banks, went out of business. Its bankruptcy sent shock waves through Wall Street—the Dow Jones Industrial Average plunged 500 points, followed soon thereafter by an even larger one-day drop. Was the United States headed for an economic meltdown that would rival the Great Depression of the 1930s?

Although some pundits suggested another Great Depression might be in the offing, few economists predicted as much, and for good reason. When the Great Depression began in 1929, there were no government programs in place to stabilize and stimulate the economy. Back then, panic had swept through society, worsening the downturn. Businesses cut back on production, investors fled the stock market, depositors withdrew their bank savings, and consumers slowed their spending—all of which accelerated the downward spiral. In 2008, by contrast, government programs were in place to protect depositors' savings, slow the drop in home and stock prices, and steady the economy through adjustments in interest rates and government spending. Among the government initiatives was the Troubled Asset Relief Program (TARP) of 2008 that made $700 billion available to bolster shaky financial institutions. By 2010, job loss had lessened, the financial markets were beginning to stabilize, and businesses were starting to recover. The turnaround was slower and more fitful than many economists had predicted, but government intervention had helped prevent a repeat of the 1930s, a decade when unemployment rose as high as 25 percent and never dropped below 10 percent.

This chapter examines economic and environmental policy. As was discussed in Chapter 1, public policy is a decision by government to follow a course of action designed to produce a particular result. In this vein, economic policy aims to promote and regulate economic interests and, through fiscal and monetary actions, to foster economic growth and stability. The main ideas presented in this chapter are:

■ *Through regulation, the U.S. government imposes restraints on business activity for the purpose of promoting economic efficiency and equity.*

■ *Through regulatory and conservation policies, the U.S. government seeks to protect and preserve the environment from the actions of business firms and consumers.*

■ *Through promotion, the U.S. government helps private interests achieve their economic goals. Business in particular benefits from the government's promotional efforts, including, for example, tax breaks and loans.*

■ *Through its taxing and spending decisions (fiscal policy), the U.S. government seeks to generate a level of economic supply and demand that will maintain economic prosperity.*

■ *Through its money supply decisions (monetary policy), the U.S. government—through the Federal Reserve System (the "Fed")—seeks to maintain a level of inflation consistent with sustained, controllable economic growth.*

Government as Regulator of the Economy

economy

A system for the exchange of goods and services between the producers of those goods and services and the consumers of them.

An **economy** is a system of production and consumption of goods and services that are allocated through exchange. When a shopper selects an item at a store, and pays for it with cash or credit card, the transaction is one of the millions upon millions of exchanges that make up the economy.

In *The Wealth of Nations* (1776), Adam Smith advanced the doctrine of **laissez-faire economics,** which holds that private firms should be free to make their own production and distribution decisions. Smith reasoned that firms will supply a good when there is a demand for it (that is, when people are willing and able to buy it). Smith argued that the profit motive is the "invisible hand" that guides supply decisions in a capitalist system. He acknowledged that laissez-faire capitalism had limits. Certain areas of the economy, such as roadways, are natural monopolies and are better handled by government than by private firms. Government is also needed to impose order on private transactions by regulating banking, currency, and contracts. Otherwise, Smith argued, the economy should be left largely in private hands.

laissez-faire economics

A classic economic philosophy holding that owners of business should be allowed to make their own production and distribution decisions without government regulation or control.

Although laissez-faire economics prevailed in the United States during the nineteenth century, government was not sidelined completely. Through the Pacific Railways Act of 1862, for example, Congress authorized the issuance of government bonds and the use of public lands to build the transcontinental railroad, which, though operated by private firms, was subject to government regulation. Nevertheless, it was not until the Great Depression of the 1930s that government assumed a large economic role. Today, the United States has what is described as a *mixed economy.* Although the economy operates mainly through private transactions, government plays a substantial role. The stock market, for example, is regulated by the Securities and Exchange Commission (SEC), which requires publicly traded companies to disclose their assets to investors. The U.S. government even owns some industry (for example, the Tennessee Valley Authority, which produces electricity). Nevertheless, in comparison, say, with the Scandinavian countries, where government provides health care to all citizens and controls a number of major industries, including the airlines, the United States relies more

TABLE 15-1 | The Main Objectives of Regulatory Policy

Objective	Definition	Representative actions by government
Efficiency	Fulfillment of as many of society's needs as possible at the cost of as few of its resources as possible. The greater the output for a given input, the more efficient the process.	Preventing restraint of trade; requiring producers to pay the costs of damage to the environment; reducing restrictions on business that cannot be justified on a cost-benefit basis.
Equity	When the outcome of an economic transaction is fair to each party.	Requiring firms to bargain in good faith with labor; protecting consumers in their purchases; protecting workers' safety and health.

heavily on free-market mechanisms to make its production, distribution, and consumption decisions.

One way the U.S. government participates in the economy is through the **regulation** of privately owned businesses.[1] U.S. firms are not free to act as they please but instead operate within the limit of government regulation, which is designed to promote economic *efficiency* and *equity* (see Table 15-1).

Efficiency through Government Intervention

Economic efficiency results when the output of goods and services is the highest possible given the amount of input (such as labor and material) that is used to produce it.[2] Efficiency is desirable. It means that society is getting as many goods and services as possible from the resources expended on their production.

Promoting Competition

Adam Smith and other classical economists argued that the free market is the optimal means of achieving efficiency. In producing goods and services, firms will try to use as few resources as possible in order to keep their prices low, which will make their products more attractive to consumers. To compete, less-efficient producers will have to cut their production costs or face the loss of customers to lower-priced competitors.

Markets are not always competitive, however. If a producer can acquire a monopoly on a particular product or can successfully conspire with other producers to fix the price of the product at an artificially high level, the producer does not have to be concerned with efficiency. Consumers who need or want a good have no choice but to pay the seller's price. Price fixing was prevalent in the United States in the late nineteenth century when large trusts came to dominate many areas of the economy, including the oil, steel, railroad, and sugar industries. Railroad companies, for example, had no competition on short routes and charged such high rates that many farmers went broke because they could not afford to ship their crops to markets. In 1887, Congress enacted the Interstate Commerce Act, which created the Interstate Commerce Commission (ICC) and assigned it responsibility for regulating railroad practices, including shipping rates.

The goal of such regulatory activity is to improve efficiency by restoring market competition or by placing a limit on what monopolies can charge for goods and services. Business competition today is overseen by a wide range of federal agencies, including, for example, the Federal Trade Commission and the Antitrust Division of the Justice Department. These agencies—The Federal Trade Commission, particularly—blocked the attempted merger of Office Depot and

regulation
A term that refers to government restrictions on the economic practices of private firms.

economic efficiency
An economic principle holding that firms should fulfill as many of society's needs as possible while using as few of its resources as possible. The greater the output (production) for a given input (for example, an hour of labor), the more efficient the process.

PARTY
POLARIZATION Political Thinking in Conflict

Business Regulation

There is barely an economic issue on which Republican and Democratic lawmakers now agree. It was not always that way. When Republican President Richard Nixon took the United States off the gold standard in 1971, he said "I am now a Keynesian in economics," embracing an economic theory that had been associated with the Democratic Party. Nixon also issued the executive order that created the Environmental Protection Agency (EPA)—an action that was applauded by lawmakers from both parties. This bipartisan spirit began to unravel in the 1980s when Republican President Ronald Reagan, despite Democratic opposition, got Congress to cut taxes on upper incomes and deregulate key industries, including banking. Reagan argued that the policies would unleash the private sector as a source of jobs and profits. Democrats said the policies would impose costs on consumers and the less wealthy. The divide has persisted, with Republicans advocating policies that would reduce government regulation of business activity and Democrats advocating policies that would allow for close oversight of business. The differences surfaced, for example, in the passage of the 2010 Dodd-Frank Wall Street Reform and Consumer Protection Act, which broadened government oversight of financial institutions and created a new consumer agency to protect borrowers against abuses by credit card companies, mortgage companies, and other lenders. The bill was enacted along party lines, with Democrats overwhelmingly voting for it and Republicans overwhelmingly voting against it—positions that meshed with the parties' ideologies and constituencies. President Obama said the legislation would "protect consumers and lay the foundation for a stronger and safer financial system." Senate Republican leader Mitch McConnell took an opposing view. "The White House will call this a victory," he said. "But as credit tightens, regulations multiply and job creation slows even further as a result of this bill, they'll have a hard time convincing the American people that this is a victory for them."

Q. *What's your view on business regulation? Would you prefer less regulation, even though it could subject some consumers to unfair business practices, or would you prefer more regulation, even though it could slow economic growth?*

Staples, on grounds that it would undermine competition in the sale of office supplies. On the other hand, the government allows concentrated ownership in industries, such as oil and automobiles, where the capital costs are so high that small firms cannot hope to compete.[3] Government acceptance of corporate giants also reflects the realization that market competition is no longer simply an issue of domestic firms. For example, the major U.S. automakers—Chrysler, Ford, and General Motors—compete for customers not only with each other but also with Asian and European auto manufacturers, such as Honda and BMW.

Making Business Pay for Indirect Costs

Economic inefficiencies also result when businesses or consumers fail to pay the full costs of resources used in production. Consider companies whose industrial wastes seep into nearby lakes and rivers. The price of these companies' products does not reflect the cost to society of the resulting water pollution. Economists label these unpaid costs **externalities**.

externalities

Burdens that society incurs when firms fail to pay the full costs of production. An example of an externality is the pollution that results when corporations dump industrial wastes into lakes and rivers.

Until the 1960s, the federal government did not require firms to pay such costs. The impetus to begin doing so came from the scientific community and environmental groups. The Clean Air Act of 1963 and the Water Quality Act of 1965 required firms to install antipollution devices in order to reduce air and water pollution. In 1970, Congress created the Environmental Protection Agency to monitor firms and ensure their compliance with federal regulations governing air and water quality and the disposal of toxic wastes. (Environmental policy is discussed more fully later in the chapter.)

Deregulation and Underregulation

Although government regulation is intended to increase economic efficiency, it can have the opposite effect if it unnecessarily increases the cost of doing business.[4] Firms have to devote work hours to monitor and implement government regulations, which in some instances (for example, pollution control) also require companies to buy and install expensive equipment. These costs are efficient to the degree that they produce corresponding benefits. Yet if government places excessive regulatory burdens on firms, they waste resources in the process of complying. The result of overregulation is higher-priced goods that are more expensive for consumers and less competitive in the domestic and global markets.

To curb overregulation, Congress in 1995 enacted legislation that prohibits administrators in some instances from issuing a regulation unless they can show that its benefits outweigh its costs. A more concerted response is **deregulation**— the rescinding of regulations already in force for the purpose of improving efficiency. This process began in 1977 with passage of the Airlines Deregulation Act, which eliminated the requirement that airlines provide service to smaller-sized cities and gave them the authority to set ticket prices (before then, the prices were set by a government agency). The change had its intended effect. Competition between airlines increased on routes between larger-sized cities, resulting in cheaper airfares on these routes. Congress followed airline deregulation with partial deregulation of, among others, the trucking, banking, energy, and communications industries.

Deregulation can be carried too far.[5] Freed of regulatory restrictions, firms can engage in reckless or unethical practices out of a belief that they can get away with it. Such was the case with the recent subprime mortgage crisis. Mortgage firms lured marginally qualified homebuyers by offering low interest rates and small down payments. After pocketing the up-front profit, they sold the mortgages to unsuspecting investors in order to reduce their risk. When the economy weakened, many homeowners defaulted on their mortgages, precipitating the 2008 financial crisis. Expressing a view held by political leaders of both parties, Barack Obama said that government had failed to properly oversee the financial sector. "The free market," said Obama, "was never meant to be a free license to take whatever you can get." In 2010, Congress enacted the most substantial regulation of financial institutions since the New Deal. Designed to curb the abuses that contributed to the financial crisis, the Dodd-Frank Wall Street Reform and Consumer Protection Act empowers government to more closely oversee financial activities. It also created a new federal agency (the Consumer Financial Protection Bureau) to protect consumers from exploitation by credit card companies, lending institutions, and other creditors.

deregulation
The rescinding of excessive government regulations for the purpose of improving economic efficiency.

A meltdown in the subprime mortgage sector in 2008 contributed to falling home prices and a rise in foreclosures. This development rippled through the economy and the financial markets, contributing to the recent economic downturn.

The crisis in America's financial system demonstrates that the issue of business regulation is not a simple question of whether or not to regulate. Too much regulation can burden firms with excessive implementation costs, whereas too little regulation can give firms the leeway to engage in risky or unethical practices. Either too little or too much regulation can result in economic inefficiency.

Equity through Government Intervention

economic equity

The situation in which the outcome of an economic transaction is fair to each party. An outcome can usually be considered fair if each party enters into a transaction freely and is not unknowingly at a disadvantage.

The government intervenes in the economy to bring equity as well as efficiency to the marketplace. **Economic equity** occurs when an economic transaction is fair to each party.[6] A transaction can be considered fair if each party enters into it freely and ethically. For example, if a seller knows that a product is defective, equity requires that the buyer also know of the defect.

The Progressive Era was marked by some equity efforts, including the creation of the Food and Drug Administration (FDA) in 1907. Unsafe food and drugs were being widely marketed, and the FDA was charged with keeping adulterated food and dangerous or worthless drugs off the market. The New Deal era produced another wave of equity measures, including financial regulation. The Securities and Exchange Act of 1934, for example, was designed in part to protect investors from dishonest or imprudent stock and bond brokers. The New Deal also provided greater equity for organized labor, which had been in a weak position in dealing with management. The Fair Labor Standards Act of 1938, for example, required employers to pay workers a minimum wage and placed limits on the use of child labor.

The 1960s and 1970s produced the greatest number of equity reforms. Ten federal agencies, including the Consumer Product Safety Commission, were established to protect consumers, workers, and the public from harmful business activity. Among the products declared to be unsafe in the 1960s and 1970s were cigarettes, leaded paint, and gasoline. This regulatory activity has produced remarkable improvements in public health. Brain damage in children from lead poisoning, for example, has declined sharply in the past few decades.[7]

POLITICAL THINKING Thank You for Smoking?

Jason Reitman's *Thank You for Smoking* is a satirical film about the efforts of big tobacco companies to hook young people on smoking. Cigarettes were one of the first targets of the wave of regulatory reform that began in the late 1960s. Recently, the FDA ordered tobacco makers to place graphic warning labels on cigarette packs. One such label is a picture of diseased lungs. R.J. Reynolds and other tobacco companies sued the FDA, saying that the label requirement infringes on their free speech rights (the case is currently being heard in federal court). What's your view on this issue? Should the government have the regulatory authority to require firms to warn consumers of the dangers associated with the use of a product, even to the extent of requiring them to display graphic warnings?

The Politics of Regulatory Policy

Economic regulation has come in waves, as changes in national conditions have created social awareness. The first wave came during the Progressive Era, when reformers sought to stop the unfair business practices of the new monopolies, such as the railroads. The second wave came during the Great Depression, when reformers sought to regulate troubled economic sectors, such as banking.

Although business firms fought the Progressive Era and New Deal reforms, their opposition diminished gradually as they adapted to the idea that the new regulatory agencies were charged with overseeing particular industries, such as banking or pharmaceuticals. This arrangement enabled a regulated industry to develop a close relationship with the agency overseeing its activities. Pharmaceutical firms, for example, established a working relationship with the FDA that at times has served their interest. In the 1990s, for instance, drug companies convinced the FDA to streamline its drug-safety reviews in order to speed the marketing of new drugs.[8] In some cases, the FDA's fast-track reviews were harmful to consumers. One fast-tracked drug, Vioxx, had to be taken off the market in 2004 after it was found to cause strokes and heart attacks.

The third wave of regulatory reform, in the 1960s and 1970s, differed from the Progressive and New Deal phases in both its form and its politics. This third wave has been called the era of "new social regulation" because of the broad social goals it addressed in three policy areas: environmental protection, consumer protection, and worker safety. Most of the regulatory agencies established during the third wave were granted a broader mandate than those created earlier. They have responsibility not for a single industry but for firms of all types, and their policy scope covers a wide range of activities. The Environmental Protection Agency (EPA), for example, is charged with regulating environmental pollution of almost any kind by almost any firm.

Because newer agencies such as the EPA have a broad mandate, no one firm or industry can easily influence agency decisions. Group competition also exists within the newer regulatory spheres. For example, environmental groups such as the Sierra Club and Greenpeace compete with business lobbies for influence with the EPA.[9] Business lobbies face much less competition when it comes to the older regulatory agencies. For example, although patients have a stake in the FDA's decisions, they are not an organized group, which limits their ability to counter the influence of the pharmaceutical lobby on the FDA.

Most of the older agencies, including the Federal Communications Commission (FCC) and the Securities and Exchange Commission (SEC), are run by a commission whose members are nominated by the president and serve fixed terms but cannot be removed by the president during their term of office. Most of the newer agencies, including the EPA, are headed by a single director who can be removed from office at the president's discretion. As a result, the newer agencies tend to be more responsive to the president than to the firms they regulate.

Government as Protector of the Environment

Few changes in public opinion and policy during recent decades have been as dramatic as those relating to the environment. Most Americans today recycle some of their garbage, and roughly two-thirds say they are either an active environmentalist or sympathetic to environmental concerns. In the 1960s, few Americans sorted their trash, and few could have answered a polling question that asked them whether they were an "environmentalist." The term was not widely used, and most people would not have understood its meaning.

The publication in 1962 of Rachel Carson's *Silent Spring* helped launch the environmental movement.[10] Written at a time when the author was dying of breast cancer, *Silent Spring* revealed the threat to birds and animals of pesticides such as DDT. Carson's appearance at a Senate hearing contributed to legislative action that produced the 1963 Clean Air Act and the 1965 Water Quality Act—the first major federal laws aimed at protecting the environment from man-made pollution. Today, environmental protection extends to nearly two hundred harmful forms of emission.

Silent Spring brought lasting fame to Rachel Carson. Even before the book was published in 1962, chemical companies were threatening lawsuits and portraying her as mentally unstable and scientifically untrained. Despite the attacks, *Silent Spring* became a huge best-seller and contributed to passage of the first federal safe air and water legislation.

Conservationism: The Older Wave

Although antipollution policy is relatively new, the government has been involved in land conservation for more than a century.[11] The first national park was created at Yellowstone in 1872 and, like the later ones, was established to preserve the nation's natural heritage for generations to come. Today, the national park system serves more than one hundred million visitors each year and includes a total of eighty million acres, an area larger than every state except Alaska, Texas, California, and Montana. The national parks are run by the National Park Service, an agency within the Department of the Interior. Another agency, the U.S. Forest Service, located within the Department of Agriculture, manages the national forests, which cover an area more than twice the size of the national parks. They too have been established in order to protect America's natural heritage.

The nation's parks and forests are subject to a "multiple use" policy. They are nature preserves and recreation areas, but they are also rich in natural resources—minerals, timber, and grazing lands. The federal government sells permits to ranchers, logging companies, and mining firms that authorize them to take some of these resources, which can bring them into conflict with conservationists. A case in point is Alaska's Arctic National Wildlife Refuge (ANWR). The refuge is home to numerous species, including caribou and moose, but it also contains substantial oil and natural gas reserves. Oil companies have long wanted to drill in ANWR, whereas environmental groups have sought to block drilling. Over the past few decades, ANWR has periodically been the focus of intense political debate and lobbying. President George W. Bush sought to open ANWR to drilling while President Obama acted to oppose it.

Conservation is more than an issue of protecting nature's unspoiled beauty. Also involved is the protection of species that cannot survive outside their natural habitat. Some species, such as the deer and the raccoon, adapt easily to human encroachment. Other species are harmed by it. These species are covered by the Endangered Species Act (ESA) of 1973, which requires federal agencies to protect threatened and endangered species. Hundreds of mammals, birds, fishes, insects, and plants are currently on the ESA's protection list.

ESA administrators have frequently clashed with companies that extract natural resources. One such dispute centered on the northern spotted owl, which inhabits the old-growth forests of Oregon and Washington. Federal administrators had banned logging in the owl's habitat, precipitating a legal battle that ended with a compromise in which logging was permitted in some old-growth timber areas and prohibited in others. Although the outcome left neither side fully satisfied, it is typical of how most such disputes are settled.

Some of the nation's untapped oil reserves are on public lands. Oil companies and conservationists often clash when the question arises as to whether a particular site should be opened for drilling.

Environmentalism: The Newer Wave

The 1960s were pivotal to the federal government's realization of the harmful effects of air, water, and ground pollutants. The period was capped by the first Earth Day. Held in the spring of 1970, it was the brainchild of Senator Gaylord Nelson (D-Wis.), who had devoted nearly ten years to finding ways to create public interest in environmental issues. With Earth Day, Nelson succeeded to a degree not even he might have imagined: ten thousand grade and high schools, two thousand colleges, and one thousand communities participated in the event, which included public rallies and environmental cleanup efforts. Earth Day has been held every year since 1970 and is now a worldwide event.

Environmental Protection

The year 1970 also marked the creation of the Environmental Protection Agency. Within a few months, the EPA was issuing new regulations at such a rapid pace that business firms had difficulty implementing them. Corporations eventually found an ally in President Gerald Ford, who in a 1975 speech claimed that business regulation was costing $150 billion annually, or $2,000 for every American family.[12] Although Ford's estimate was disputed by economic analysts, his point was not lost on policymakers or the public. The economy was in a slump, and the costs of complying with the new regulations were slowing the recovery. Polls indicated declining public support for regulatory action.

Since then, environmental protection policy has not greatly expanded, nor has it greatly contracted. The emphasis has been on implementation of laws put into effect in the 1960s and 1970s. In a 2001 decision, for example, the Supreme Court ruled unanimously that public health is the only thing that the EPA should take into account in establishing air quality standards; the costs to industry are not to be considered.[13]

Environmental regulation has led to dramatic improvements in air and water quality. Pollution levels today are far below their levels of the 1960s, when yellowish-gray fog ("smog") hung over cities like Los Angeles and New York and when bodies of water like the Potomac River and Lake Erie were open sewers. In the past four decades, toxic waste emissions have been halved, hundreds of polluted lakes and rivers have been revitalized, energy efficiency has increased, food supplies have been made safer, and urban air pollution has declined by 60 percent.[14]

Badly contaminated toxic waste sites are also a problem. These sites pollute local water supplies, resulting in increased rates of cancer and other illnesses. Although Congress in the 1980s established the so-called Superfund program to rid these sites of their contaminants, the cleanup process has been slow and contentious. Firms that caused the pollution are liable for some of the cleanup costs, but many of these firms are no longer in business, have since been purchased by other companies, or lack the funds. Firms that could pay the costs have often chosen to fight the issue in court, further delaying the cleanup. According to EPA figures, more than a third of the most dangerous sites are still contaminated.

Global Warming and Energy Policy

No environmental issue receives more attention than global warming. The earth's temperature level has been rising and the rate of increase has accelerated (see Figure 15-1). Most scientists theorize that the temperature rise is attributable to emissions from carbon-based fuels, such as oil and coal. They hypothesize that the emissions produce a "greenhouse effect"—heat gets trapped in the atmosphere

Degrees Fahrenheit

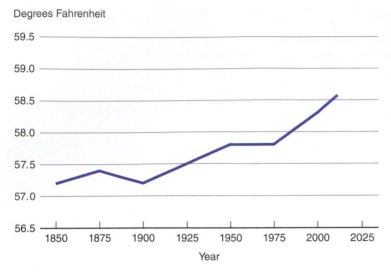

FIGURE 15-1   **Average Temperature of the Earth's Surface,**
1850-2010 The average surface temperature of the earth has risen
substantially in the past century and has done so at an accelerating pace in
the past three decades.

Source: National Weather Service, Great Britain, 2010.

rather than escaping into space, resulting in rising temperature levels. This theory has not gone unchallenged. Although virtually all credible scientists accept as fact the increase in temperature, some of them think it's due primarily to the earth's natural cycle of warming and cooling.

As would be expected, there is greater disagreement on climate change among U.S. lawmakers. Some hold to the view that climate change is a problem that needs to be addressed urgently and in a substantial way. Others say that a substantial response should be delayed until the consequences of global warming are more clearly understood. Still others say that the remedies for global warming, such as requiring companies to reduce their carbon emissions, would slow economic growth to an unacceptable level.

This lack of consensus has led U.S. lawmakers to prefer clean energy sources and energy conservation as answers to global warming. In 2007, a bipartisan majority in Congress enacted the Energy Independence and Security Act, which established higher fuel-efficiency standards for vehicles and set a goal of eliminating incandescent light lightbulbs within a decade. President Bush said the legislation was a "major step . . . toward confronting global climate change." Some provisions of the American Recovery and Reinvestment Act of 2009 were also designed to address the problem of global warming. Roughly $40 billion was appropriated for energy-related projects, including funds for the development of renewable fuels such as wind and solar and the development of alternative fuel vehicles.

Nevertheless, the United States lags behind most Western countries, including Germany, France, and Great Britain, in reducing its greenhouse gas emissions. The reasons are several, including the structure of the U.S. political system. The division of power between the president, the House, and the Senate makes it difficult to garner the support necessary to implement policies that impose economic costs. In 1997, after helping to negotiate an international agreement on carbon emissions (the Kyoto Protocol), President Clinton was unable to persuade the Senate to ratify it. When George W. Bush assumed office in 2001, he rejected the agreement, saying that it would blunt economic growth. A congressional effort in 2010 to reduce greenhouse gases also failed to gain the necessary support. Although Democrats in the House of Representatives passed a bill that capped carbon emissions, the legislation died when Senate Republicans and Democrats were unable to reach agreement on key provisions.

Global warming is shrinking the polar ice caps, as can be seen from these two photos of the Arctic ice cap taken in 1979 (left) and 2003 (right). Within the foreseeable future and for the first time in recorded history, ships are expected to be able to travel in summer between Europe and Asia via the Arctic Ocean.

HOW THE U.S. DIFFERS POLITICAL THINKING THROUGH COMPARISONS

Carbon-Fuel Emissions and Global Warming

The United States, as the chart indicates, is the world's single largest source of carbon-fuel emissions on a per-capita basis. The United States emits about 20 percent of the world total. Carbon-fuel emissions have been linked to global warming and have increasingly drawn the attention of the international community. Most scientists believe global warming can be retarded only by curbing greenhouse gas emissions. Politics stands in the way of such action. Curbs on emissions would slow a country's economic growth, and no country by itself has the capacity to reduce global warming significantly. These realities have blocked full-scale international agreement on how to address the problem. The United Nations Framework Convention on Climate Change, which met in Copenhagen in 2009, broke down when the nearly two hundred participating nations could not agree on a binding method for allocating the costs associated with reducing carbon-based emissions. The United States and other advanced industrialized countries argued that global warming can be retarded only by significant action on the part of rapidly developing countries, China and India particularly. For their part, China and India argued that the largest burden should be borne by the United States and other advanced industrialized countries because they have been the largest source of carbon-fuel emissions.

Q: Why might it make sense to place most of the burden for reducing carbon fuel emissions on nations with developing economies such as China and India? How might advanced industrialized nations such as the United States and Germany contribute to this effort?

A: An argument for placing the burden on developing economies is that their carbon emissions are increasing at the fastest rate.

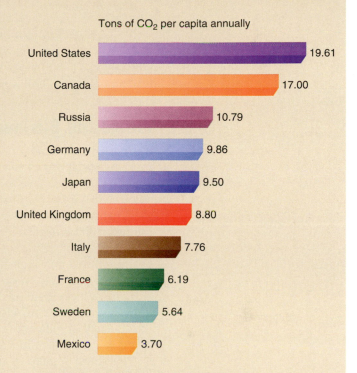

Tons of CO_2 per capita annually

United States	19.61
Canada	17.00
Russia	10.79
Germany	9.86
Japan	9.50
United Kingdom	8.80
Italy	7.76
France	6.19
Sweden	5.64
Mexico	3.70

Advanced industrialized nations such as the United States and Germany could then provide developing countries with clean-energy technology that can be used, for example, when they install new power plants, which are a major source of carbon emissions. Developed countries could also provide monetary assistance to ease the economic burden that would fall on developing countries as a result of implementing costly carbon-reduction measures.

Source: Organization for Economic Cooperation and Development, 2010.

The issue of climate change is complicated by the fact that no single nation can solve the problem on its own. When carbon emissions get into the atmosphere, they affect conditions elsewhere. The problem is also compounded by the rapid expansion of the economies of China, India, and other developing nations, which has increased the level of carbon emissions. Yet the less-developed countries claim they should not bear the burden of curbing global warming, arguing that the problem stems from decades-long carbon emissions by the industrialized nations, including the United States (see "How the U.S. Differs").

The obstacles to getting agreement on carbon-emissions policy was apparent at the United Nations Climate Change Conference held in 2009 in Copenhagen, Denmark. Disputes between the developed and developing nations over how to share the cost derailed any chance of securing a binding agreement. President Obama negotiated a last-minute nonbinding agreement on general principles, including a goal of reducing carbon-based emissions by 50 percent over a period of four decades.

Government as Promoter of Economic Interests

Congress in 1789 gave a boost to the nation's shipping industry by imposing a tariff on goods brought into the United States on foreign ships, which prompted importers to make greater use of American ships. Since that first favor, the U.S. government has provided thousands of direct and indirect benefits to economic interests. The following sections describe some of these benefits.

Promoting Business

Business firms are not opposed to government regulation as such. They object only to regulatory policies that harm their interests. At various times and in different ways, as in the case of the FCC and broadcasters, some regulatory agencies have sided with the very industries they are supposed to regulate in the public interest.

Loans and tax breaks are other ways that government promotes business interests. Firms receive loan guarantees, direct loans, tax credits for capital investments, and tax deductions for capital depreciation. Since the 1970s, the burden of federal taxation has shifted from corporations to individuals. A few decades ago, the revenue from corporate income taxes was roughly the same as the revenue from individual income taxes. Today, individual taxpayers carry a substantially heavier burden. However, some economists do not regard the change as particularly significant, claiming that higher corporate taxes would be passed along to consumers in the form of higher prices for goods and services.

The most significant contribution that government makes to business is in the traditional services it provides, such as education, transportation, and defense. Colleges and universities, which are funded primarily by government, furnish business with most of its professional and technical workforce and with much of the basic research that goes into product development. The nation's roadways, waterways, and airports are other public-sector contributions without which business could not function. In short, America's business has no bigger booster than government.

Promoting Labor

Laissez-faire thinking dominated government's approach to labor well into the twentieth century. Union activity was held by the courts to be illegal because it interfered with the rights of business. Government hostility toward labor included the use of police and soldiers to break up strikes. In 1914 in Ludlow, Colorado, state militia attacked a tent colony of striking miners and their families, killing nineteen, including eleven children.

The 1930s Great Depression brought about a change in labor's position. The National Labor Relations Act of 1935, for example, gave workers the right to bargain collectively and prohibited business from disrupting union activities or discriminating against union employees. Government support for labor now also includes minimum-wage and maximum-work-hour guarantees, unemployment benefits, safer and more healthful working conditions, and nondiscriminatory hiring practices. Although the federal government's support of labor extends beyond these examples, its support is much less extensive than its support of business.

Striking janitors march in Beverly Hills, California. Although the U.S. government supports labor interests, it does so less fully than it supports business and agricultural interests.

Promoting Agriculture

Government support for agriculture has a long history. The Homestead Act of 1862, for example, opened government-owned lands to settlement. The federal government provided 160 acres of land free to any family that staked a claim, built a house, and farmed the land for five years.

Government programs today provide billions of dollars of assistance annually to farmers, small and large. Federal payments account for more than a fifth of net agricultural income, making America's farmers among the most heavily subsidized in the world. This assistance is intended in part to reduce the market risks associated with farming. Weather, global conditions, and other factors can radically affect crop and livestock prices, and federal subsidies lend stability to farm incomes.

Farm subsidies traditionally have had strong support in Congress, particularly from rural-state senators and representatives. In 2008, Congress passed a five-year, $300-billion farm bill that would put farmers in line for hefty government assistance in future years. President Bush vetoed it, but Congress overrode his veto. An appeal by President Obama in 2009 to cut subsidies for large farms also was rejected by Congress. As a result of the large federal budget deficit and record-high farm incomes, it is generally believed that farmers will not fare as well when the next five-year farm bill is enacted. Analysts expect Congress to cut what are called "direct subsidies"—those that are paid regardless of crop yield or price in a given year—while retaining subsidies that kick in when crop prices drop dramatically as a result of conditions beyond farmers' control, such as adverse weather.

Fiscal Policy as an Economic Tool

Before the 1930s, prevailing economic theory held that the economy was self-regulating, that it would correct itself after a downturn. The greatest economic collapse in the nation's history—the Great Depression of the 1930s—shattered that idea. The economy did not recover on its own, but instead continued to decline. President Franklin D. Roosevelt's spending and job programs, which stimulated the economy and put Americans back to work, ushered in the modern era.[15] Today, government is expected to intervene when the economy dips.

The government's efforts to maintain a thriving economy occur in part through its taxing and spending decisions (see Figure 15-2), which together are

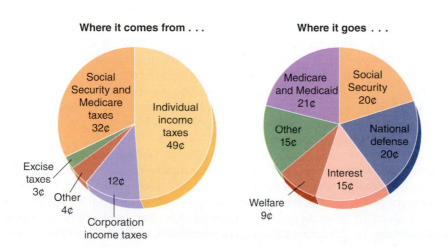

FIGURE 15-2
The Federal Budget Dollar, Fiscal Year 2013
Source: Congressional Budget Office.

TABLE 15-2 | Fiscal Policy: A Summary of the Government's Role

Problem	Fiscal policy actions
Low productivity and high unemployment	Demand side: increase spending
	Supply side: cut business taxes
Excess production and high inflation	Decrease spending
	Increase taxes

referred to as its **fiscal policy.** Through changes in its level of spending and taxation, government can stimulate or slow the economy (see Table 15-2).

Demand-Side Policy

fiscal policy

A tool of economic management by which government can attempt to maintain a stable economy through its taxing and spending policies.

Fiscal policy has origins in the economic theories of John Maynard Keynes. Noting that employers tend to cut their production and workforce when the economy begins to weaken, Keynes challenged the traditional idea that government should also cut back on its spending. Keynes claimed that a downturn could be shortened only if government compensates for the slowdown in private spending by increasing its spending level. In doing so, the government pumps money into the economy, which stimulates consumer spending, which in turn stimulates business production and creates jobs, thereby hastening the economic recovery.[16]

economic depression

A very severe and sustained economic downturn. Depressions are rare in the United States; the last one was in the 1930s.

Keynesian theory holds that the level of the government's response should be commensurate with the severity of the downturn. During an **economic depression**—an exceptionally steep and sustained decline in the economy—the government should engage in massive new spending programs to speed the recovery. During an **economic recession,** which is a less-severe downturn, government spending should also be increased but by a lesser amount.

economic recession

A moderate but sustained downturn in the economy. Recessions are part of the economy's normal cycle of ups and downs.

Keynes's theory is based on **demand-side economics.** It emphasizes the consumer "demand" component of the supply–demand equation. When the economy is sluggish, the government, by increasing its spending, places additional money in consumers' hands. With more money in their pockets, consumers spend more, which boosts economic activity. The theory is that if more goods and services are being purchased, whether for groceries or for new construction projects, firms will have to retain or hire workers to produce the goods and services, which will lessen the severity of the downturn. This line of reasoning was behind the $787 billion American Economic Recovery and Reinvestment Act that Congress passed in 2009 as a means of combating the steep economic slide precipitated by the near collapse of the financial markets. The legislation included, for example, funding for construction projects and an extension of unemployment benefits.

demand-side economics

A form of fiscal policy that emphasizes "demand" (consumer spending). Government can use increased spending or tax cuts to place more money in consumers' hands and thereby increase demand.

budget deficit

The situation in which the government's expenditures exceed its tax and other revenues.

Although increased government spending can promote economic recovery, it is a tool that needs to be applied with discretion. Excessive spending results in a **budget deficit**—in which the federal government spends more in a year than it receives in tax and other revenues. The shortfall increases the **national debt,** which is the total cumulative amount the federal government owes to its creditors. The government pays interest on the debt, which consumes money that would otherwise remain in taxpayers' pockets.

national debt

The total cumulative amount that the U.S. government owes to creditors.

It is widely agreed that the United States faces a looming fiscal crisis because of a combination of high spending and low taxation. Federal programs are funded largely by taxes on individuals and businesses and by money the government borrows. In recent years, the government has spent far more than it has received in taxes, which has required it to borrow in order to make up the difference. In 2012, the federal government's budget deficit was roughly

HOW THE 50 STATES DIFFER   POLITICAL THINKING THROUGH COMPARISONS

FEDERAL TAXING AND SPENDING: WINNERS AND LOSERS

Fiscal policy (the federal government's taxing and spending policies) varies in its effect on the states. The residents of some states pay a lot more in federal taxes than they receive in benefits. The biggest loser is New Jersey, whose taxpayers get back in federal spending in their state only $0.61 for every dollar they pay in federal taxes. Nevada taxpayers ($0.65 for every dollar) are the next-biggest losers. In contrast, the residents of some states get back more from federal spending programs than they contribute in taxes. The biggest winners are New Mexico and Mississippi, whose taxpayers get back $2.03 and $2.02, respectively, in federal spending in their states for every dollar they pay in federal taxes.

Q: Why are most of the "losers" in the northeastern section of the country?

A: The federal taxes that originate in a state reflect its wealth, and the northeastern states are generally the wealthier ones. Because they are wealthier, they also get less federal assistance for programs designed to help lower-income people and areas. Finally, most federal lands and military installations—sources of federal money—lie outside the northeastern region.

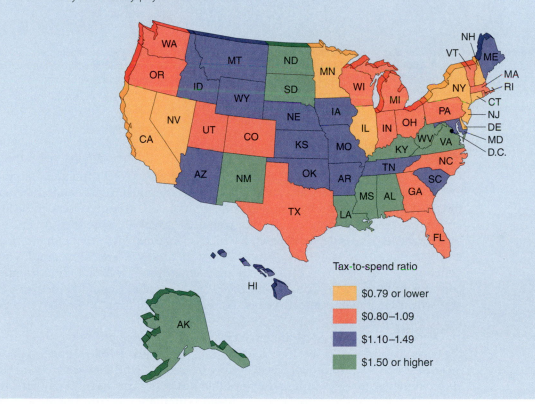

Tax-to-spend ratio

- $0.79 or lower
- $0.80–1.09
- $1.10–1.49
- $1.50 or higher

Source: Adapted from Tax Foundation Calculations, 2007.

$1.1 trillion, the fourth year in a row it had topped $1 trillion. Projections indicate that high deficits will continue into the future (see Figure 15-3), which will add to the national debt, which already exceeds $16 trillion. The U.S. government spends an enormous amount each year just to pay the interest on the debt. In fact, interest on the national debt accounts for nearly 15 percent of the federal budget. The interest payments are roughly the total of all federal income taxes paid by Americans living west of the Mississippi. Only rarely in recent decades has the U.S. government had a **balanced budget** (in which revenues are equal to government expenditures) or a **budget surplus** (in which the federal government receives more in tax and other revenues than it spends).

balanced budget

The situation in which the government's tax and other revenues for the year are roughly equal to its expenditures.

budget surplus

The situation in which the government's tax and other revenues exceed its expenditures.

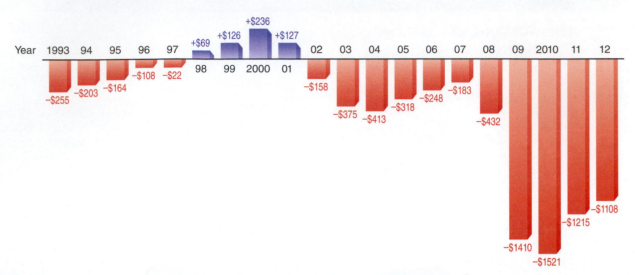

FIGURE 15-3 **The Federal Budget Deficit/Surplus** The federal government ran a budget deficit until 1998, at which time a surplus emerged that was expected to last for years. In 2001, however, the surplus disappeared as a result of an economic downturn, the cost of the war on terrorism, and the Bush tax cuts. The deficit has ballooned recently because of the declining tax revenues and stimulus spending associated with the economic recession.

Source: Office of Management and Budget, 2012.

Supply-Side Policy

Demand-side stimulation has been the preferred policy of Democratic lawmakers. Lower-income Americans are a core Democratic constituency and are usually the most deeply affected by rising unemployment. Accordingly, Democratic leaders have typically responded to a sluggish economy with increased government spending (demand-side fiscal policy), which offers direct help to the unemployed and stimulates consumption. Almost every increase in federal unemployment benefits, for example, was initiated by the Democrats. The $787 billion economic stimulus bill passed by Congress in 2009 was filled with demand-side programs and was ostensibly a Democratic bill. No House Republican and only three Senate Republicans voted for it.

Republican Party leaders are more likely to see an economic downturn through the lens of business firms. Republicans have typically resisted large spending increases because government has to borrow the money, which creates upward pressure on interest rates, including the rates that business firms have to pay for loans.

A fiscal policy alternative to demand-side stimulation is **supply-side economics,** which emphasizes the business (supply) component of the supply-demand equation. Supply-side theory was a cornerstone of President Ronald Reagan's response to the economic downturn that began before he took office in 1981. Rather than relying on government spending programs to boost consumer spending, Reagan turned to tax cuts as a means of stimulating business activity. "Reaganomics" included large tax breaks for firms and upper-income individuals.[17] These supply-side measures were intended to encourage business investment with resulting increases in employment and income. As jobs and wages increased, consumer spending was also expected to increase, fostering economic growth.

Supply-side theory was also the basis of President George W. Bush's economic initiatives, which included reductions in the personal income tax and in the **capital-gains tax** (the tax that individuals pay on gains in capital investments such as property and stocks). Claiming that taxes on the wealthy were stunting

supply-side economics

A form of fiscal policy that emphasizes "supply" (production). An example of supply-side economics is a tax cut for business.

capital-gains tax

The tax that individuals pay on money gained from the sale of a capital asset, such as property or stocks.

economic growth, Bush persuaded Congress to reduce the capital-gains tax rate from 28 percent to 15 percent and to cut the highest marginal tax rate on personal income from 39 percent to 35 percent. The savings to Americans in the top 1 percent of income was $54,493 per year, compared with an average of $67 for those in the bottom 20 percent and $611 for those in the middle 20 percent.[18] (In contrast to the philosophy behind the Bush tax cuts, Democratic policymakers have pursued tax policies that favor working-class and lower-middle-class Americans. Democrats typically advocate a progressive, or **graduated**, **personal income tax**, in which the tax rate increases significantly as income rises, thus shifting more of the tax burden to wealthier individuals. A progressive tax differs from a *regressive tax*, where lower-income individuals pay a higher rate. An example is the social security tax. After a worker's income reaches roughly $110,000, it is no longer subject to the social security tax. Accordingly, those with incomes above this level have a lower social security tax rate on their total income than do those with incomes below the level.)

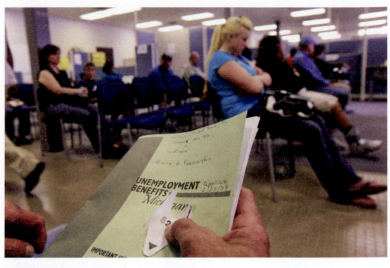

The unemployment office is an all-too-familiar scene for jobless Americans during an economic downturn. Through demand-side or supply-side policies, U.S. policy makers seek to stimulate the economy in order to reduce the unemployment rate.

progressive (graduated) personal income tax

A tax on personal income in which the tax rate increases as income increases; in other words, the tax rate is higher for higher income levels.

POLITICAL

THINKING   Who Should Get the Tax Cuts?

Few issues spark more controversy than taxes. When a tax cut is being debated, the argument usually centers on how the cut should be divided. Supply-side economists have one answer to the question: the taxpayers who are personally least in need of tax relief are the ones who should get the biggest share of the cut. Supply-side theory holds that high-income taxpayers will invest the extra income, which gives the economy a boost and thereby helps others. Warren Buffett, one of America's richest individuals, has a different answer to the question. He argues that tax cuts should be targeted for the less well off, because they have less income, which means they spend nearly every dollar they receive through a tax cut, thereby giving the economy a boost. Which of the two views is closer to your own?

As with demand-side stimulation, supply-side policy has its costs. President Bush argued that his tax cut would boost economic activity to such an extent that government revenue would actually increase. The prediction was faulty. The loss in revenue from the tax cut exceeded the gain in revenue from heightened economic activity. In combination with the costs of the Iraq war, the Bush tax cut led to a ballooning of the budget deficit and the national debt.[19] When Bush took office, the budget was balanced and the national debt stood at $5.7 trillion. By the time he left office, the budget deficit had reached nearly $500 billion and the national debt had risen to more than $10 trillion.[20]

Like demand-side policy, supply-side policy is intensely partisan. Whereas Republican lawmakers tend to balk at demand-side measures, Democratic lawmakers tend to balk at supply-side measures. Bush's supply-side tax cuts had the support of 90 percent of congressional Republicans and only 20 percent of congressional Democrats.[21]

Fiscal Policy: Practical and Political Limits

Demand-side stimulation as an economic tool emerged in the era when the federal government had a relatively small and mostly balanced budget. As a result, it was feasible for government to boost spending during an economic downturn without going so deeply in debt as to jeopardize longer-term economic growth. Supply-side stimulation had a similar early history. Today, however, the use of either tool—as the Bush and Obama presidencies illustrate—produces large budget deficits that could dampen long-term growth.

This practical limit is not the only barrier to the application of fiscal policy during economic downturns. Republican and Democratic lawmakers are miles apart on how best to deal with recessionary periods. For reasons stated earlier, Democrats are inclined toward deficit spending whereas Republicans lean toward tax cuts on business and upper incomes. When a second stimulus package (as a follow-up to the one enacted in 2009) was debated in Congress in 2011, partisan deadlock brought the issue to a standstill. Unless one party or the other gains a substantial majority in Congress, and also controls the presidency, fiscal policy is unlikely to be a tool readily available in the future.

Monetary Policy as an Economic Tool

monetary policy

A tool of economic management based on manipulation of the amount of money in circulation.

Fiscal policy is not the only instrument of economic management available to government. A second is **monetary policy,** which is based on adjustments in the amount of money in circulation. Monetarists, as economists who emphasize monetary policy are called, contend that the money supply is the key to sustaining a healthy economy. Their leading theorist, the American economist Milton Friedman, held that supply and demand are best controlled by manipulating the money supply.[22] Too much money in circulation contributes to inflation because too many dollars are chasing too few goods, which drives up prices. Too little money in circulation results in a slowing economy and rising unemployment, because consumers lack the ready cash and easy credit required to maintain spending levels. Monetarists believe in increasing the money supply when the economy needs a boost and decreasing the supply when it needs to be slowed down.

The economist Milton Friedman helped devise the theory of monetary policy, arguing that control of the money supply is the key to sustaining a healthy economy. *Time* magazine named Friedman "the economist of the century," ranking him ahead of John Maynard Keynes, who devised fiscal policy theory.

The Fed

Control over the money supply rests not with the president or Congress but with the Federal Reserve System ("the Fed"). Created by the Federal Reserve Act of 1913, the Fed was designed to be the "lender of last resort" for banks that did not have enough cash on hand to pay their depositors during a bank panic. Lawmakers had the Panic of 1907 in mind when creating it. The panic had begun after a sudden drop in the stock market spooked depositors, who rushed to withdraw their bank savings. A banking catastrophe was averted when a group of wealthy financiers pooled their capital to provide temporary loans to troubled banks. Congress decided that the United States needed a permanent central bank—the Federal Reserve—to serve that purpose.

Headquartered in Washington, D.C., the Fed is directed by a board of governors whose seven members serve for fourteen years, except for the chair and vice chair, who serve for four years. All members are appointed by the president with the approval of the Senate. The Fed regulates the activities of all national banks and those state banks that chose to become members of the Federal Reserve System—about six thousand banks in all. The policies of the Fed's board are carried out through twelve regional Federal Reserve banks, each of which has responsibility for the member banks in its district (see Figure 15-4). Most of the checks and electronic financial transactions that take place in the U.S. banking system are coordinated through the regional banks, which also conduct research that informs the Fed's board of governors. The federal reserve bank for the Ninth District, for example, is located in Minneapolis and serves member banks in Montana, North and South Dakota, Minnesota, and northern areas of Wisconsin and Michigan.

From its inception, the Federal Reserve has been the depository bank for federal funds and is the instrument through which the federal government borrows money, pays federal employees, makes payments on the national debt, and transfers funds between banks. When the government is running a budget deficit, for example, the Federal Reserve sells treasury bonds on the open market to private investors in order to raise the money to cover the deficit (a process called "monetizing" the debt).

Over time, the Fed has also become became the instrument through which monetary policy is applied. The Fed decides how much money to add to or subtract from the economy, seeking a balance that will permit steady growth without causing an unacceptable level of inflation (see Table 15-3). One method the Fed uses is to raise or lower the percent of funds that that member banks are required to hold—meaning they cannot loan or invest these funds. The reserve rate is the proportion of a bank's funds that it must keep on hand. When the Fed raises the reserve rate, member banks are required to keep more of their money out of circulation, thereby reducing the money supply. When it lowers the reserve rate, the Fed allows banks to use more of their money for loans to consumers and firms. During the 2008 subprime mortgage crisis, the Fed slashed the reserve rate several times so that member banks would have more money available to deal with the shortfall resulting from failed mortgages.

A second and more publicly visible way in which the Fed affects the money supply is by lowering or raising the interest rate that member banks pay when they borrow money from the Federal Reserve. When the Fed raises the interest rate for banks, they in turn will raise the rate they charge their customers for new loans,

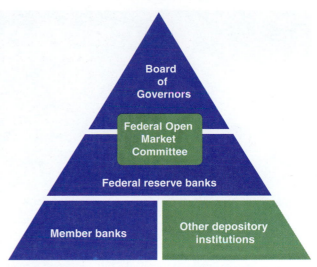

FIGURE 15-4 **The Federal Reserve System** The Federal Reserve is the central bank of the United States. It is directed by a board of governors and its day-to-day operations are conducted through twelve regional Federal Reserve banks, each of which services and oversees the member banks in its district.

TABLE 15-3 | Monetary Policy: A Summary of the Fed's Policy Tools

Problem	Fed Actions
Low productivity and high unemployment (requires increase in money supply)	Decrease interest rate on loans to member banks
	Lower percentage (reserve rate) of funds banks must hold in reserve
	Buy securities
Excess productivity and high inflation (requires decrease in money supply)	Increase interest rate on loans to member banks
	Raise percentage (reserve rate) of funds banks must hold in reserve
	Sell securities

Federal Reserve chairman Ben Bernanke testifies before a congressional committee. The Fed chairman has sometimes been called the second-most powerful official in Washington.

which discourages borrowing, thereby reducing the amount of money entering the economy. Conversely, when the Fed lowers the interest rate on its loans to member banks, they are able to lower the rate they charge for their loans, which leads to additional borrowing by firms and consumers, resulting in an increase in the money supply. As the economy slowed in 2008, for example, the Fed began a series of adjustments that dropped the interest rate by several percentage points, enabling member banks to lower their rates, making loans more affordable for firms and consumers.

The Fed's reserve and interest rate decisions are made its Board of Governors. There is also a third mechanism that the Fed uses— the buying and selling of government securities. In this case, the decisions are made by the Fed's Open Market Committee, which consists of the seven members of the Board of Governors and the presidents of five of the regional reserve banks. The president of the Federal Reserve Bank of New York (which is the largest of the regional reserve banks due to the concentration of major financial institutions in New York City) serves continuously on the Open Market Committee while the presidents of the other regional banks serve one-year terms on a rotating basis.

When it sells government securities in exchange for cash, the Fed is taking that money out of circulation, thereby reducing the amount of money available for consumption and investment. On the other hand, when it buys government securities, the Fed is putting the money used to purchase the securities into private hands to be spent or invested, thus stimulating the economy.

The Fed's Open Market Committee meets eight times annually to determine and announce the monetary policies that will govern until the next meeting. At times, the Fed will also announce a longer-range policy, which is meant to provide investors with information that can guide the timing and scale of their financial decisions.

The Fed and Control of Inflation

inflation

A general increase in the average level of prices of goods and services.

Although the meltdown of financial markets in 2008 placed the Fed in the role of trying to stimulate the economy, a sluggish economy is not the only problem the Fed is expected to address. Another is **inflation**—an increase in the average level of prices of goods and services. Before the late 1960s, inflation was a minor problem, rising by less than 4 percent annually. However, inflation jumped during the last years of the Vietnam War and remained high throughout the 1970s, reaching a postwar high of 13 percent in 1979. The impact was substantial. Prices were rising but personal income was stagnant. Many Americans were forced to cut back on basics, such as food purchases and medical care. Personal and business bankruptcies increased as a result of rising costs and skyrocketing borrowing rates. The interest rate on business loans and home mortgages topped 15 percent—up from 5 percent a few years earlier.

To fight inflation, the Fed applies policies exactly the opposite of those used to fight an economic downturn. By increasing interest and reserve rates and by selling government securities, the Fed takes money out of the economy, which has the effect of reducing economic demand. As demand weakens, the price of goods

Inflation rate since 1979 (Consumer Price Index)

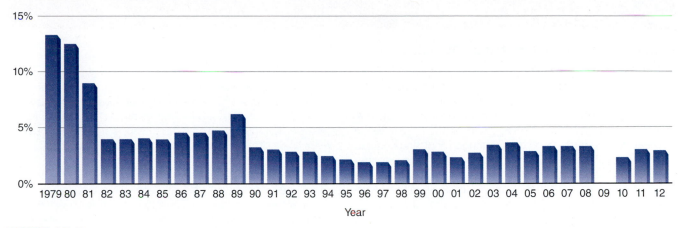

FIGURE 15-5   **The Annual Rate of Inflation, 1979–2012**   Price increases have been low in recent years compared with those of the late 1970s and early 1980s. In 2009, because of declining consumer demand associated with the economic recession, the inflation rate fell to 0 percent for the first time in the postwar era.

Source: U.S. Department of Labor, 2008.

and services drop, thereby easing inflationary pressures. During the inflationary period of the late 1970s and early 1980s, the Fed kept the prime interest rate above 10 percent for seven years, an action that is widely credited with bringing inflation under control. (In 1980, the interest rate hit an all-time high—21.5 percent.) Since the 1980s, inflation has been kept largely in check. The inflation rate has not topped 5 percent in any year during the past two decades (see Figure 15-5).

Ironically, through its recent stimulus policies, the Fed may have set the stage for another inflationary period. Its actions included a controversial device. Known as quantitative easing (QE), it involves the buying of financial assets strictly for the purpose of injecting more money into the economy and paying for them through the simple act of printing more money. This device came into use after the Fed had lowered interest rates almost to the point of zero and therefore could not lower them further as a means of injecting money into the economy. So it turned to quantitative easing, buying assets that were paid for by printing more money, taking advantage of the fact that the government can print as much money as it wants. The Fed used this approach, for example, to buy billions of dollars in problematic mortgages from financial institutions. The purchases had the effect of strengthening these institutions by relieving them of questionable assets while putting cash in their hands that they could then lend out, thereby increasing the money supply.

If the Fed were to pursue this policy endlessly, there would be so many dollars in circulation that the dollar at some point would lose most of its value. For this reason, quantitative easing is considered the tool of "last resort," to be used only when other devices have reached the point where they are no longer effective.[23] Some analysts are critical of all quantitative easing, saying it amounts to nothing more than creating money out of nothing. Other analysts think the Fed went too far with it—roughly $2 trillion dollars were dispersed. Even Ben Bernanke, the chair of the Federal Reserve, conceded that the recession-driven policies of Congress and the Fed had pushed the limits of what was sustainable. Testifying at a Senate Banking Committee hearing in 2012, Bernanke said: "The United States is on an unsustainable fiscal path looking out over the next couple of decades. If we continue along that path, eventually we will face a fiscal and financial crisis that will be very bad for growth and sustainability."

DEBATING THE ISSUES   POLITICAL THINKING IN ACTION

Should the Government Bail Out Troubled Financial Institutions?

When the subprime mortgage crisis hit in 2008, a number of venerable financial institutions found themselves in trouble. One of these institutions was the investment bank Bear Stearns, which was established in 1923 and had managed to survive the Great Depression. More recently, during the housing boom in the United States, Bear Stearns made a fortune in mortgage-backed securities. However, the firm had overinvested in these securities and found itself in a liquidity crisis when the investments turned sour. As it was teetering on the edge of bankruptcy, the Federal Reserve stepped in with a huge loan guarantee that enabled JP Morgan Chase, another financial institution, to buy Bear Stearns to keep it from folding. The govern-ment also stepped in to keep AIG, Fanny Mae, and other large financial institutions from bankruptcy. But should the Fed have done it? The federal government does not bail out small businesses or individuals who make risky financial decisions. Should huge financial firms be an exception? Here are two opposing views on the subject. In congressional testimony, Federal Reserve chairman Ben Bernanke argued that the government should intervene when the failure of financial institutions would threaten the entire economy. In a 2010 Senate floor speech during a debate on financial reform legislation, Richard Shelby argued that financial institutions should live or die in the marketplace rather than by government action.

YES Government assistance should be given with the greatest of reluctance and only when the stability of the financial system, and, consequently, the health of the broader economy, is at risk. In the cases of Fannie Mae and Freddie Mac, however, capital raises of sufficient size appeared infeasible and the size and government-sponsored status of the two companies precluded a merger with or acquisition by another company. To avoid unacceptably large dislocations in the financial sector, the housing market, and the economy as a whole, the Federal Housing Finance Agency (FHFA) placed Fannie Mae and Freddie Mac into conservatorship, and the Treasury used its authority, granted by the Congress in July, to make available financial support to the two firms. . . . The Federal Reserve and the Treasury attempted to identify private-sector approaches to avoid the imminent failures of AIG and Lehman Brothers, but none was forthcoming. In the case of AIG, the Federal Reserve, with the support of the Treasury, provided an emergency credit line to facilitate an orderly resolution. The Federal Reserve took this action because it judged that, in light of the prevailing market conditions and the size and composition of AIG's obligations, a disorderly failure of AIG would have severely threatened global financial stability and, consequently, the performance of the U.S. economy.

—*Ben Bernanke, Federal Reserve chairman*

NO Did we explain Bear Stearns and the causes of its collapse? . . . Did we take time to learn lessons from the debacle of the AIG Financial Products division, or securities lending operations, or of overheated tri-party repo activity? Did we analyze how maturity transformation allowed the shadow banking system to, in effect, create money out of AAA rated securities? Did we analyze how activities in the shadow banking system led to an increased concentration of inherently ruinable activities? . . . [T]he answer to all of these questions is: No. . . . The American people expect more, and certainly deserved more from us. . . . [T]he most incredulous shortcoming of this bill is the lack of any serious attention being paid to the Government Sponsored Enterprises, Fannie Mae and Freddie Mac. . . . [T]he bill does nothing to affect the ongoing, unlimited bailouts of Fannie Mae and Freddie Mac that, to date, have cost the American taxpayer $146 billion—one of the largest bailouts in history. . . . Hardworking Americans in Alabama and throughout the Nation will be asked to pony up again and again until we do something to stop it. When will it stop? . . . [W]ho will back up those clearinghouses at the end of the day should market stresses prove to be severe? The Federal government and the Federal Reserve will back them up, promising even more bailouts in the future. . . . I urge my colleagues to oppose final passage of this bill.

—*Richard Shelby, U.S. senator (R-Ala.)*

Q: Which view—Bernanke's or Shelby's—comes closer to your own? Do you see any merit in the opposing view?

The Politics of the Fed

Compared with fiscal policy, monetary policy can be implemented more quickly. The Fed can adjust interest and reserve rates on short notice, thus providing the economy with a psychological boost to go along with the actual effect of a change in the money supply. In contrast, changes in fiscal policy usually take months to implement. Congressional action is relatively slow, and new taxing and spending programs ordinarily require a preparation period before they can be put into effect. In early 2010, a full year after Congress passed the $787 billion economic stimulus bill, half of the money had not yet been spent. The greater flexibility of monetary policy is a reason the Fed has emerged as the institution that has primary responsibility for keeping the U.S. economy on a steady course.[24]

When the Fed was created in 1913, no one imagined that it would have such a prominent role. Economists had not yet "invented" the theory of monetary policy. All that has changed, which has raised questions about the power the Fed wields. One concern is the issue of representation: whose interest should the Fed serve—that of the public as a whole or that of the banking sector? The Fed is not a wholly impartial body. Although it makes decisions in the context of economic theories and projections, it is "the bankers' bank" and as such tends to be protective of financial institutions. In 2008, the Fed provided emergency loans to keep banking institutions, including Citibank and JP Morgan Chase, from bankruptcy. The Fed justified its intervention by saying that the financial markets might otherwise have collapsed, adversely affecting every American. Many taxpayers saw it differently. A Pew Research Center national poll found that 87 percent of Americans opposed the use of taxpayer money to bail out the banks.

Another question about the Fed is the issue of its accountability. Should the Fed, an unelected body, have so much power? Though appointed by the president, members of the Federal Reserve Board are not subject to removal. They serve for fixed terms and are relatively insulated from political pressure. The Fed's policies are not always popular with elected officials. Some members of Congress, for example, were sharply critical of the Fed when it sharply increased interest rates in the late 1970s and then kept them there, even as the rate of inflation fell. The high rates discouraged borrowing by consumers and business firms, which dampened economic growth. During the recession that began in 2008, the Fed was again the target of criticism—its bailout of major financial institutions being a case in point.

Regardless, the Fed is part of the new way of thinking about the federal government and the economy that emerged during the Great Depression of the 1930s. Before then, the federal government's economic role was confined largely to the provision of a limited number of public services, such as the currency and mail delivery. Roosevelt's New Deal permanently changed how Americans thought about the government and the economy. Through its economic management and regulatory activities, the government assumed an ongoing role in managing the economy. The overall result is impressive. Although the American economy has suffered from economic downturns during the roughly three-quarters of a century in which the U.S. government has played a significant policy role, none of them has matched the severity of the depressions of earlier times. (The economic policies of the federal government in the areas of social welfare and national security are discussed in the next two chapters.)

Summary

Self-Test www.mhhe.com/pattersontadtx11e

Although private enterprise is the main force in the American economic system, the federal government plays a significant role through its policies to regulate, promote, and stimulate the economy.

Regulatory policy is designed to achieve efficiency and equity, which require the government to intervene, for example, to maintain competitive trade practices (an efficiency goal) and to protect vulnerable parties in economic transactions (an equity goal). Many of the regulatory decisions of the federal government, particularly those of older agencies (such as the Food and Drug Administration), are made largely in the context of group politics. Business lobbies have an especially strong influence on the regulatory policies that affect them. In general, newer regulatory agencies (such as the Environmental Protection Agency) have policy responsibilities that are broader in scope and apply to a larger number of firms than those of the older agencies. As a result, the policy decisions of the newer agencies are more often made in the context of party politics. Republican administrations are less vigorous in their regulation of business than are Democratic administrations.

Business is the major beneficiary of the federal government's efforts to promote economic interests. A large number of these programs, including those that provide loans and research grants, are designed to assist business firms, which are also protected from failure through measures such as tariffs and favorable tax laws. Labor, for its part, obtains government assistance through laws covering areas such as worker safety, the minimum wage, and collective bargaining. Yet America's individualistic culture tends to put labor at a disadvantage, keeping it less powerful than business in its dealings with the government. Agriculture is another economic sector that depends substantially on government's help, particularly in the form of income stabilization programs such as crop subsidies.

The U.S. government pursues policies that are designed to protect and conserve the environment. A few decades ago, the environment was not a policy priority. Today, there are many programs in this area, and the public has become an active participant in efforts to conserve resources and prevent exploitation of the environment. The continuing challenge is to find a proper balance between the nation's natural environment, its economic growth, and its energy needs.

Through its fiscal and monetary policies, Washington attempts to maintain a strong and stable economy—one characterized by high productivity, high employment, and low inflation.

Fiscal policy is based on government decisions in regard to spending and taxing, which are aimed at either stimulating a weak economy or dampening an overheated (inflationary) economy. Fiscal policy is worked out through Congress and the president and consequently is responsive to political pressures. However, because it is difficult to raise taxes or cut programs, the government's ability to apply fiscal policy as an economic remedy is somewhat limited. Monetary policy is based on the money supply and works through the Federal Reserve System, which is headed by a board whose members hold office for fixed terms and operates through the work of its twelve regional Federal Reserve banks.. The Fed, as the Federal Reserve is commonly called, has become the primary instrument from managing the economy. It can affect the amount of money circulating in the economy by raising or lowering the interest rate that banks are charged for borrowing from the Fed, by raising or lowering the percentage of their funds (reserve rate) that member banks are required to keep on hand, and by buying and selling securities.

CHAPTER 15

Study Corner

Key Terms

balanced budget (*p. 397*)
budget deficit (*p. 396*)
budget surplus (*p. 397*)
capital-gains tax (*p. 398*)
demand-side economics (*p. 396*)
deregulation (*p. 387*)
economic depression (*p. 396*)
economic efficiency (*p. 385*)
economic equity (*p. 388*)
economic recession (*p. 396*)
economy (*p. 384*)

externalities (*p. 386*)
fiscal policy (*p. 396*)
inflation (*p. 402*)
laissez-faire economics (*p. 384*)
monetary policy (*p. 400*)
national debt (*p. 396*)
progressive (graduated) personal income tax (*p. 399*)
regulation (*p. 385*)
supply-side economics (*p. 398*)

Self-Test: Multiple Choice

1. Supply-side economic stimulus policy includes
   a. reliance on the Fed.
   b. reliance on business regulation.
   c. reliance on business tax cuts.
   d. reliance on government spending programs.

2. The challenge for policymakers in devising and implementing regulatory and deregulatory policies is to
   a. simply remove all regulations.
   b. not be concerned about economic inefficiency in protecting the public interest.
   c. favor equity at the expense of efficiency.
   d. strike a proper balance between regulatory measures and free-market mechanisms.

3. The institutions of the U.S. government involved in determining fiscal policy are
   a. the executive and legislative branches.
   b. the Fed and the regulatory agencies.
   c. the judicial branch and the states.
   d. the legislative branch and the Fed.

4. The era of new social regulation in the 1960s and 1970s differed from that of previous eras in
   a. narrowing the scope and range of activities regulated.
   b. concentrating on financial and banking reform.
   c. expanding regulation into areas such as the environment and consumer protection.
   d. pioneering the idea of cost-benefit analysis as a regulatory standard.

5. Examples of services provided by government that aid business include
   a. loan guarantees and direct loans to business.
   b. funding of public colleges and universities.
   c. subsidizing the building of roads, waterways, and airports.
   d. all of the above.

6. Which of the following is *not* an action taken by the Federal Reserve Board to affect the economy?
   a. meeting periodically to evaluate the economy and to decide on a proper response
   b. lowering or raising interest charged on money borrowed by banks
   c. raising or lowering the cash reserve that member banks are required to deposit with regional Federal Reserve banks
   d. submitting monetary legislation to Congress for a vote

7. Early in the development of America's economy, there was hostility toward labor union activity. (T/F)

8. In times when the economy needs a quick fix, one would be better off to use fiscal policy than monetary policy because fiscal policy can be implemented within a shorter time frame. (T/F)

9. Rachel Carson's *Silent Spring* encouraged the growth of the modern environmental movement. (T/F)

10. Fiscal policy has its origins in the economic theories of John Maynard Keynes. (T/F)

Self-Test: Essay

What are the tools of fiscal policy and monetary policy? What are the advantages and disadvantages of each of these two approaches to managing the economy?

Suggested Readings

Duncan, Richard. *The Dollar Crisis: Causes, Consequences, Cures,* rev. ed. New York: John Wiley, 2005. A look at the problem of budget and trade deficits.

Fisher, Patrick. *The Politics of Taxing and Spending.* Boulder, Colo.: Lynne Rienner Publishers, 2009. An assessment of the policies of taxing, spending, and the federal budget.

Lindbloom, Charles E. *The Market System: What It Is, How It Works, and What to Make of It.* New Haven, Conn.: Yale University Press, 2001. A clear analysis of the advantages and disadvantages of the market system.

Mayer, Martin. *Fed: The Inside Story of How the World's Most Powerful Financial Institution Drives the Markets.* New York: Free Press, 2001. A look at the Fed's impact on the economy and politics.

Miller, Norman. *Environmental Politics: Stakeholders, Interests, and Policymakers.* New York: Routledge, 2008. A careful look at the politics of environmental policymaking.

Sheingate, Adam D. *The Rise of the Agricultural Welfare State.* Princeton, N.J.: Princeton University Press, 2003. A penetrating analysis of farm policy in the United States, France, and Japan.

List of Websites

www.federalreserve.gov/default.htm
The Federal Reserve System website describes the Fed, provides information about its current activities, and has links to some of the Fed's national and international information sources.

www.epa.gov
The Environmental Protection Agency website provides information on environmental policy and regulations, EPA projects, and related subjects.

www.ftc.gov
The website of the Federal Trade Commission, one of the older regulatory agencies, describes the range of the FTC's activities.

www.whitehouse.gov/omb
The home page of the Office of Management and Budget contains a summary of the level of federal taxing, borrowing, and spending.

Participate!

The environment is a policy area in which individual citizens can make a difference by reducing waste and pollution. If you have a car, you will burn significantly less fuel if you drive and accelerate more slowly. Choosing a fuel-efficient car, keeping your car properly tuned, walking rather than driving short distances to stores, and living closer to work or school are other ways to cut gas consumption. In your residence, the simplest steps are to use lights sparingly and keep the thermostat lower during cold periods and higher during hot periods. Smaller but meaningful savings can be achieved through simple things such as using low-flow shower heads and replacing incandescent bulbs with fluorescent lights, which require less energy and last longer. Even a change in eating habits can make a difference. Frozen convenience foods are wasteful of energy. They are cooked, frozen, and then cooked again—not to mention the resources used up in packaging. Fresh foods are more nutritious and less wasteful. And if you prefer bottled water to tap water, consider using a water filter system instead. Nearly all of the cost of bottled water is due to the plastic container, which is a nonbiodegradable petroleum product. The recycling of paper, plastics, and bottles also conserves natural resources. However, the recycling process itself requires the use of energy. By cutting back on your use of recyclables and by recycling those you do use, you will contribute twice to a cleaner environment.

Extra Credit

For up-to-the-minute *New York Times* articles, interactive simulations, graphics, study tools, and more links and quizzes, visit the text's Online Learning Center at **www.mhhe.com/pattersontad11e.**

Self-Test Answers

1. c, 2. d, 3. a, 4. c, 5. d, 6. d, 7. T, 8. F, 9. T, 10. T

CHAPTER **16**

Welfare and Education Policy: Providing for Personal Security and Need

We the people of the United States, in order to . . . promote the general welfare. Preamble, U.S. Constitution

President Barack Obama had been in office only a few weeks when he proposed a plan to change the nation's health care system. Obama vowed to cut rising medical costs and to increase Americans' access to health insurance. He had plenty of eager Democrats in the House and Senate on his side. The idea of extending health coverage to the millions of uninsured Americans had long been a Democratic Party goal. A half-century earlier, President Harry S Truman had tried but failed to create a universal health insurance system.

Although congressional Republicans agreed with Obama that the nation's health care system has flaws, the agreement stopped at that point. Republicans were dead-set against any reform that would give the federal government broad control over health insurance. They were willing to countenance a few restrictions on insurance companies but wanted to leave the rules and rates of health insurance largely in the hands of private companies. They were also concerned about increases in federal health care spending. For their part, Democrats expressed dismay that anyone could look at how insurance companies operate and conclude that the status quo was acceptable. They pointed to such industry practices as voiding the insurance of policyholders after they became sick. According to Democrats, insurance industry profits and practices are the primary reason the United States has the most expensive health care system in the world and yet by statistical indicators ranks below many other countries in quality of health care.

At several points in the months-long policy debate, a majority of Americans sided with Obama and Democratic lawmakers on the desirability of comprehensive health care reform. At other times, a majority sided with congressional Republicans. Throughout the debate, however, confirmed liberals were strongly in favor of having the federal government play a larger role in health care insurance whereas confirmed conservatives were strongly opposed to it.

The health care reform legislation that was passed by Congress in 2010 was bitterly contested. No Senate or House Republican voted for the bill. The dispute was not confined to the halls of Congress. Shown here is a rally held to protest the bill.

Health policy issues, like other social welfare policy issues, activate opposing philosophies of government. Some Americans hold that government should intervene in the marketplace to assist disadvantaged individuals. Others hold that government assistance discourages personal effort and creates dependency. America's federal system of government also fuels conflict over welfare policies. Welfare was traditionally a responsibility of state governments. Only since the 1930s has the federal government also played a major role, which has sometimes brought it into conflict with the states over the best course of action. The health care reform bill enacted by the Democratic-controlled Congress in 2010 is a case in point. Almost as quickly as the bill was signed into law, Republican attorney generals in several states filed suit to have it declared unconstitutional. (As discussed in Chapter 3, the Supreme Court upheld the law in a 2012 ruling.)

This chapter examines the problems that federal social welfare programs are designed to alleviate and describes how these programs operate. It also addresses public education policies. This chapter seeks to provide an informed basis for understanding issues of social welfare and education and to show why disagreements in these areas are so substantial. The issues involve hard choices that inevitably require trade-offs between federal and state power and between the values of individual self-reliance and egalitarian compassion. The main points of the chapter are:

■ *Poverty is a large and persistent problem in America, affecting about one in eight Americans, including many of the country's most vulnerable—children, female-headed families, and minority-group members.*

■ *Welfare policy has been a partisan issue, with Democrats taking the lead on government programs to alleviate economic insecurity and Republicans acting to slow down or restrict these initiatives.*

■ *Social welfare programs are designed to reward and foster self-reliance or, when this is not possible, to provide benefits only to those individuals who are truly in need. U.S. welfare policy is not based on the assumption that every citizen has a right to material security.*

■ *Americans favor social insurance programs (such as social security) over public assistance programs (such as food stamps).* As a result, most social welfare expenditures are not targeted toward the nation's neediest citizens.

■ *A prevailing principle in the United States is equality of opportunity, which in terms of policy is most evident in the area of public education.* America invests heavily in its public schools and colleges.

Poverty in America: The Nature of the Problem

In the broadest sense, social welfare policy includes any effort by government to improve social conditions. In a narrower sense, which is the way the term is used in this chapter, social welfare policy refers to government programs that help individuals meet basic needs, including food, clothing, and shelter. Social welfare

DEBATING THE ISSUES POLITICAL THINKING IN ACTION

Is the 2010 Health Care Reform Good Policy?

In 2010, Congress passed the Patient Protection and Affordable Care Act. The legislation was tied up for months in Congress, with Democratic and Republican lawmakers on opposite sides of the issue. They argued over everything from the cost of the program to its requirement that individuals either obtain insurance or pay an annual penalty. In the end,

the bill was enacted solely on the basis of Democratic votes. No Senate or House Republican voted for it. In the House, the differences between the parties were voiced in speeches on the floor by Speaker Nancy Pelosi, a Democrat, and by minority leader John Boehner, a Republican. The following are portions of their speeches.

YES I believe that this legislation will unleash tremendous entrepreneurial power into our economy. Imagine a society and an economy where a person could change jobs without losing health insurance, where they could be self-employed or start a small business. Imagine an economy where people could follow their passions and their talent without having to worry that their children would not have health insurance, that if they had a child with diabetes who was bipolar or [had a] pre-existing medical condition in their family, that they would be job-locked. Under this bill, their entrepreneurial spirit will be unleashed. We all know, we all know that the present health care system and insurance system in our country is unsustainable. We simply cannot afford it. It simply does not work for enough people in terms of delivery of service, and it is bankrupting the country with the upward spiral of increasing medical costs. . . . With this action tonight, with this health care reform, 32 million more Americans will have health care insurance. And those who have insurance now will be spared of being at the mercy of the health insurance industry with their obscene increases in premiums, their rescinding of policies at the time of illness, their cutting off of policies even if you have been fully paying but become sick, the list goes on and on about the health care reforms that are in this legislation: insure 32 million more people, make it more affordable for the middle class, end insurance company discrimination based on pre-existing conditions . . . create 4 million jobs in the life of the bill and doing all that by saving the taxpayer 1.3 trillion dollars.

—*Nancy Pelosi, Speaker of the U.S. House of Representatives*

NO [W]e're standing here looking at a health care bill that no one in this body believes is satisfactory. . . . We have failed to listen to America. And we have failed to reflect the will of our constituents. And when we fail to reflect that will—we fail ourselves and we fail our country. Look at this bill. Ask yourself: do you really believe that if you like the health plan you have, that you can keep it? No, you can't. In this economy, with this unemployment, with our desperate need for jobs and economic growth, is this really the time to raise taxes, to create bureaucracies, and burden every job creator in our land? The answer is no. Can you go home and tell your senior citizens that these cuts in Medicare will not limit their access to doctors or further weaken the program instead of strengthening it? No, you cannot. . . . And look at how this bill was written. Can you say it was done openly, with transparency and accountability? Without backroom deals, and struck behind closed doors, hidden from the people? Hell no, you can't! . . . [T]his bill is not what the American people need, nor what our constituents want. Americans are out there making sacrifices and struggling to build a better future for their kids. And over the last year as the damn-the-torpedoes outline of this legislation became more clear, millions lifted their voices, and many for the first time, asking us to slow down, not try to cram through more than the system could handle. Not to spend money that we didn't have. In this time of recession, they wanted us to focus on jobs, not more spending, not more government, and certainly not more taxes.

—*John Boehner, minority leader, U.S. House of Representatives*

Q: *Which argument—Pelosi's or Boehner's—do you find more persuasive? To what extent is your opinion based on your partisanship as opposed to your familiarity with provisions of the legislation?*

policy can differ markedly even among countries that are similar in many other respects. As this chapter shows, U.S. social welfare policy is distinctive, even by comparison with Canada and other Western industrialized nations.

The Poor: Who and How Many?

Americans' social welfare needs are substantial. Although Americans are far better off economically than most of the world's peoples, poverty is a significant and persistent problem in the United States. The government defines the **poverty line** as the annual cost of a thrifty food budget for an urban family of four, multiplied

poverty line
As defined by the federal government, the annual cost of a thrifty food budget for an urban family of four, multiplied by three to allow also for the cost of housing, clothes, and other expenses. Families below the poverty line are considered poor and are eligible for certain forms of public assistance.

HOW THE 50 STATES DIFFER POLITICAL THINKING THROUGH COMPARISON

POVERTY RATES

Relative to other Western democracies, the United States has an unusually high proportion of poor people. Based on the government-defined poverty line, about one in eight Americans lives in poverty. However, poverty is spread unevenly among the states. At one extreme are Louisiana, Mississippi, and New Mexico, each of which has a poverty rate above 18 percent. New Mexico has the highest rate. At the other extreme are New Hampshire and Utah, which have poverty rates that are less than half that of the highest states.

Q: What might explain the difference in poverty levels between the states?

A: States differ considerably in their natural wealth, level and type of economic activity, level of education, number of newer immigrants, and percentage of minority-group members. Each of these factors is correlated with level of poverty.

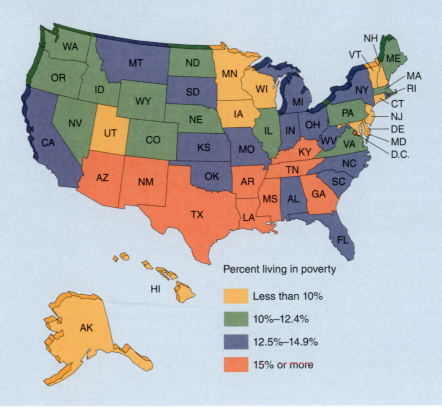

Percent living in poverty

- Less than 10%
- 10%–12.4%
- 12.5%–14.9%
- 15% or more

Source: U.S. Census Bureau, 2012.

by three to include the cost of housing, clothes, and other necessities. Families whose incomes fall below that line are officially considered poor. In 2012, the poverty line was set at an annual income of roughly $23,000 for a family of four. One in seven Americans—roughly 45 million people—live below the poverty line. If they could all join hands, they would form a line stretching from New York to Los Angeles and back again.

America's poor include individuals of all ages, races, religions, and regions (see "How the 50 States Differ"), but poverty is concentrated among certain groups. Children are one of the largest groups of poor Americans. One in every five children—more than ten million in total—live in poverty. Most poor children live in families with a single parent, usually the mother. Single-parent, female-headed families are roughly five times as likely as two-income families to fall below the poverty line, a situation referred to as "the feminization of poverty."[1]

Poverty is also widespread among minority-group members. Compared with whites, African Americans and Hispanics are more than twice as likely to live below the poverty line. Poverty is also geographically concentrated. Although poverty is often portrayed as an urban problem, it is somewhat more prevalent in rural areas. About one in seven rural residents—compared with one in nine urban residents—lives in a family with income below the poverty line. The urban figure is misleading, however, in that the level of poverty is very high in some inner-city areas. Suburbs are the safe haven from poverty. Because suburbanites are far removed from it, many of them have no sense of the impoverished condition of what Michael Harrington called "the other America."[2]

The "invisibility" of poverty is evident in polls showing that most Americans greatly underestimate the level of poverty in the United States. Nothing in the daily lives of many Americans or in what they see on television would lead them to think that poverty rates are uncommonly high. Yet the United States has the highest level of poverty among the advanced industrialized nations. Moreover, its rate of child poverty is twice the average rate of these other nations (see Figure 16-1).

Child poverty rate

United States	22%
Great Britain	16%
Italy	16%
Canada	14%
Germany	12%
Sweden	4%

FIGURE 16-1 **Child Poverty Rates** The United States has the highest child poverty rate among Western democracies. One in five American children lives in poverty; in most other Western democracies, the number is fewer than one in seven. Households with incomes less than half that of the median household are classified as living in poverty. *Source:* United Nations Childrens Fund, 2010.

Living in Poverty: By Choice or Chance?

Many Americans hold to the idea that poverty is largely a matter of choice—that most low-income Americans are unwilling to make the effort to hold a responsible job and get ahead in life. In his book *Losing Ground*, Charles Murray argues that America has a permanent underclass of unproductive citizens who prefer to live on welfare and whose children receive little educational encouragement at home and grow up to be copies of their parents.[3] There are, indeed, many such people in America. They number in the millions. They are the toughest challenge for policymakers because almost nothing about their lives equips them to escape from poverty and its attendant ills.

Yet most poor Americans are in their situation as a result of circumstance rather than choice. Economists Signe-Mary McKernan and Caroline Ratcliffe found that most of the poor are poor only for a while, and then for reasons largely beyond individual control—such as a job layoff or desertion by the father—rather than because they prefer not to work.[4] When the U.S. economy goes into a tailspin, the impact devastates many families. According to U.S. Department of Labor figures, more than seven million Americans lost their jobs during the recent economic downturn. The unemployment rate doubled as a result of the recession.

The Politics and Policies of Social Welfare

At one time in the nation's history, the federal government was not involved in social welfare policy. Poverty and other welfare problems were deemed to fall within the powers reserved to the states by the Tenth Amendment and to be adequately addressed by them, even though they offered few welfare services. Individuals were expected to fend for themselves, and those unable to do so were usually supported by relatives and friends. This approach reflected the

negative government

The philosophical belief that government governs best by staying out of people's lives, giving individuals as much freedom as possible to determine their own pursuits.

positive government

The philosophical belief that government intervention is necessary in order to enhance personal liberty and security when individuals are buffeted by economic and social forces beyond their control.

idea of **negative government**, which holds that government governs best by staying out of people's lives, so that they can determine their own pursuits and become self-reliant.

The Great Depression changed that outlook. The unemployment level reached 25 percent, and many of those with jobs were working for pennies an hour. Americans looked to the federal government for help. Franklin D. Roosevelt's New Deal brought economic relief in the form of public jobs and assistance programs and altered Americans' view of the federal government's welfare role.[5] The new attitude was a belief in **positive government**—the idea that government intervention is necessary in order to enhance personal liberty and security when individuals are buffeted by economic and social forces beyond their control.

Not all Americans of the 1930s embraced the new philosophy. Many Republican leaders clung to traditional ideas about self-reliance and free markets. A key vote in the House of Representatives on the Social Security Act of 1935, for example, had 85 percent of Democrats voting in favor of it and 99 percent of Republicans voting against it.[6] Republicans gradually accepted the idea that the federal government has a social welfare role but argued that it should be kept as small as practicable. Thus, in the 1960s, Republican opposition to President Lyndon Johnson's Great Society was substantial. His programs included federal initiatives in health care, education, public housing, nutrition, and other areas traditionally dominated by state and local governments. More than 70 percent of congressional Republicans voted against the 1965 Medicare and Medicaid programs, which provide government-paid medical assistance for the elderly and the poor, respectively. In contrast, the 1996 Welfare Reform Act, which was designed to cut welfare rolls and costs, had the overwhelming support of congressional Republicans, whereas a majority of congressional Democrats voted against it.

The health care reform bill that Congress passed in 2010 also brought out partisan divisions. No Senate or House Republican voted for the bill, and Republican lawmakers have said they intend to repeal it if they gain full control of Congress. They have also promised to cut social welfare spending as part of a broader effort to reduce federal spending. In 2011, Congress was nearly brought to a standstill over fiscal issues, with Republicans refusing to budge on demands for cuts in welfare spending and Democrats refusing to accept even modest cuts in the absence of tax increases on the wealthy.

Although the Republican and Democratic parties have been at odds on social welfare issues, they have also had reason to work together. Millions of Americans depend on the federal government to provide benefits to ease the loss of income caused by retirement, disability, unemployment, and the like. Some social welfare programs, such as federal grants for health research, benefit all of society. Other spending is aimed at helping particular individuals. *Transfer payments* are government benefits given directly to individual recipients, such as retirees' monthly social security checks. Most programs that support individuals are **entitlement programs,** meaning that any individual who meets the eligibility criteria is entitled to the benefit. For example, upon reaching the legal retirement age, any senior citizen who has paid social security taxes for the required amount of time is entitled to receive social security benefits. In this sense, entitlement programs have the same force of law as taxes. Just as individuals are required by law to pay taxes on the income they earn, they are entitled by law to receive government benefits for which they qualify.

Individual-benefit programs fall into two broad groups: social insurance programs and public assistance programs. Social insurance programs enjoy broader public support, are more heavily funded, and provide benefits to individuals of all income levels. Public assistance programs have less public support, receive

entitlement programs

Any of a number of individual-benefit programs, such as social security, that require government to provide a designated benefit to any person who meets the legally defined criteria for eligibility.

PARTY POLARIZATION   Political Thinking in Conflict

Government's Social Welfare Role

The two major ways that economic benefits are distributed in America is through the economic marketplace in the form of jobs, wages, dividends, and the like and through the government in the form of programs such as social security, Medicaid, and food stamps. In few areas have the differences between the Republican and Democratic parties been more consistent over the years than their positions on the use of government as an instrument of economic security. Although both parties have seen a need for some sort of safety net for the economically vulnerable, the Democratic Party has taken the lead on extending it. Nearly every major U.S. social insurance and public assistance program was put into place by Democratic presidents and Congresses. In recent years, conflict between the parties over the government's social welfare role has intensified. Democratic lawmakers have pushed to extend the economic safety net, as in the case of the 2010 health care reform act, while Republicans have sought to reduce social welfare spending as a means of reducing the federal deficit. The policy conflicts in Washington are aligned with how the parties' identifiers see the issue of government's role in providing assistance to the economically disadvantaged, as the figure below indicates.

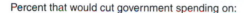

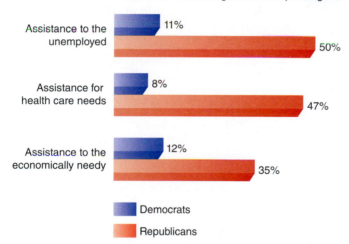

Percent that would cut government spending on:

- Assistance to the unemployed: Democrats 11%, Republicans 50%
- Assistance for health care needs: Democrats 8%, Republicans 47%
- Assistance to the economically needy: Democrats 12%, Republicans 35%

Democrats
Republicans

Q. *What's your opinion on how far government should go in providing economic assistance to the less-well-off?*

Source: Pew Research Center for the People & the Press survey, February 10, 2011.

less funding, and are restricted to people of low income. The next sections discuss these two types of programs.

Social Insurance Programs

More than fifty million Americans receive monthly benefits from social insurance programs—including social security, Medicare, unemployment insurance, and workers' compensation. The cost of the two major programs, social security and Medicare, exceeds one trillion dollars a year. Such programs are labeled **social insurance** because eligibility is restricted to individuals who paid special payroll taxes during their working years.

social insurance

Social welfare programs are based on the "insurance" concept, requiring that individuals pay into the program in order to be eligible to receive funds from it. An example is social security for retired people.

With the possible exception of Franklin D. Roosevelt, no American president had a greater impact on social welfare policy than Lyndon B. Johnson. Johnson's Great Society programs included Medicare and Medicaid, as well as increased federal spending in areas such as education, childhood nutrition, and poverty alleviation. Johnson was also instrumental in passage of the 1964 Civil Rights Act and the 1965 Voting Rights Act.

Social Security

The main social insurance program is social security for retirees. Social security is one of the few welfare programs run entirely by the federal government. Washington collects the payroll taxes that fund the program and sends monthly checks directly to social security recipients, who receive on average about $1,200 a month.

The program began with passage of the Social Security Act of 1935 and is funded through payroll taxes on employees and employers (currently set at 6.2 percent). Franklin D. Roosevelt emphasized that retiring workers would receive an insurance benefit they had earned through their payroll taxes, not a handout from the government. This method of financing has resulted in broad public support for the social security program.[7] Polls indicate that a large majority of Americans favor current or higher levels of social security benefits for the elderly.

Although people qualify for social security by paying payroll taxes during their working years, the money they receive upon retirement is funded by payroll taxes on current workers' salaries. This arrangement poses a threat to the long-term viability of the social security program because people are living longer than they once did. As a result, there will be fewer workers relative to the number of retirees, and the inflow of payroll taxes from workers will be less than the outflow of social security benefits to retirees. There is broad agreement among policymakers that adjustments in the social security program will be necessary in the near future in order to ensure its solvency. The year 2010 provided a look into the future if no action is taken. As a result of the economic recession, fewer people than normal were employed and the revenue from their payroll taxes was temporarily insufficient to cover the cost of social security payments to retirees.

POLITICAL THINKING What's the Future of Social Security?

Social security for retirees is paid through payroll taxes on the current workforce. However, because retirees are living longer and increasing in number, the inflow of payroll tax revenue from workers at some point will be insufficient to fund the outflow of social security payments. One solution to the problem would be to increase taxes on workers. Another solution would be to reduce retiree benefits and require workers to wait longer before they become eligible for social security benefits (the earliest eligibility is currently 62 years of age). If you were asked to solve the problem, what would you propose?

Unemployment Insurance

The 1935 Social Security Act provides for unemployment benefits for workers who lose their jobs involuntarily. Unemployment insurance is a joint federal-state program. The federal government collects the payroll taxes that fund unemployment benefits, but states have the option of deciding whether the taxes will be paid by both employees and employers or by employers only (most states use the latter option). Individual states also set the tax rate, conditions of eligibility, and benefit level, subject to minimum standards established by the federal government. Although unemployment benefits vary widely among states, they average about $300 a week, roughly a fourth of what an average worker makes while employed. The benefits are usually terminated after twenty-six weeks, but Congress, as it did in the recent economic downturn, sometimes extends the eligibility period in recessionary periods.

The unemployment program does not have the broad public support that social security enjoys. This situation reflects the widespread assumption that the loss of a job, or the failure to find a new one right away, is often a personal failing. Unemployment statistics indicate otherwise. A U.S. Bureau of Labor study found that only about one in seven workers who lost their jobs were fired or quit voluntarily. The rest became unemployed because of either a temporary layoff or the permanent elimination of a job position.

Medicare

After World War II, most European democracies created government-paid health care systems, and Democratic president Harry S Truman proposed a similar program for Americans. The American Medical Association (AMA) called Truman's plan "un-American" and vowed to mobilize local physicians to campaign against members of Congress who supported "socialized medicine." Truman's proposal never came to a vote in Congress. In 1961, President John F. Kennedy, also a Democrat, proposed a health care program restricted to social security recipients, but the AMA, the insurance industry, and congressional conservatives succeeded in blocking the plan.[8]

The 1964 elections swept a tide of liberal Democrats into Congress, and the result was Medicare. Enacted in 1965, the program provides medical assistance to retirees and is funded primarily through payroll taxes. Medicare is based on the insurance principle, and because of this, it has gained as much public support as social security. Medicare does not cover all hospital, nursing home, or physicians' fees, but enrollees in the program have the option of paying an insurance premium for fuller coverage of these fees. Enrollees who cannot afford the additional premium can apply to have the government pay it. In 2006, a prescription drug benefit was added to the Medicare program, though it included restrictions on eligibility and the amount of the benefit. The health care reform bill that Congress enacted in 2010 reduced the restrictions but did not eliminate them entirely. The reform bill also included provisions designed to increase the solvency of the Medicare program, which was otherwise projected to run out of money within a few years.

Public Assistance Programs

Unlike social insurance programs, **public assistance** programs are funded through general tax revenues and are available only to the financially needy. Eligibility for these programs is established by a **means test**; that is, applicants must prove that they are poor enough to qualify for the benefit. Once they have done so, they are entitled to the benefit, unless their personal situation changes or government changes the eligibility criteria. These programs often are referred to as "welfare" and the recipients as "welfare cases."

Americans are far less supportive of public assistance programs than they are of social insurance programs. Americans tend to look upon social insurance benefits as having been earned by the recipient, whereas they see public

public assistance

A term that refers to social welfare programs funded through general tax revenues and available only to the financially needy. Eligibility for such programs is established by a means test.

means test

The requirement that applicants for public assistance must demonstrate that they are poor in order to be eligible for the assistance.

Supplemental Security Income (SSI) is a combined federal-state program that provides public assistance to the disabled.

assistance benefits as handouts. Support for public assistance programs is weakened further by Americans' perception that the government is already spending vast amounts on welfare. A poll found that Americans believe public assistance programs to be the second costliest item in the federal budget. These programs actually rank much farther down the list. In fact, the federal government spends hundreds of billions more on its two major social insurance programs—social security and Medicare—than it does on all public assistance programs combined.

Supplemental Security Income (SSI)

Supplemental Security Income (SSI) is a major public assistance program that originated as federal assistance to the blind and elderly poor as part of the Social Security Act of 1935. Although SSI is primarily a federal program, the states have retained some control over benefits and eligibility and provide some of the funding. Because SSI recipients (who now include the disabled in addition to the blind and elderly poor) have physical limitations on their ability to provide fully for themselves, SSI is not widely criticized.

Temporary Assistance for Needy Families (TANF)

Before passage of the 1996 Welfare Reform Act, needy American families had an open-ended guarantee of cash assistance. As long as their income was below a certain level, they were assured of government support. The program (Aid for Families with Dependent Children, or AFDC for short) was created in the 1930s as survivors' insurance to assist children whose fathers had died prematurely. Relatively small at the outset, the program became controversial as Americans increasingly linked it to welfare dependency and irresponsibility. AFDC was an entitlement program, which meant that any single parent (and in some states two parents) living in poverty could claim the benefit and keep it for as long as a dependent child was in the household. Some AFDC recipients were content to live on this assistance, and in some cases their children also grew up to become AFDC recipients, creating what was called "a vicious cycle of poverty." By 1995, AFDC was supporting 14 million Americans.

The 1996 Welfare Reform Act abolished AFDC, replacing it with the program titled Temporary Assistance for Needy Families (TANF). TANF's goal is to reduce long-term welfare dependency by limiting the length of time recipients can receive assistance and by giving the states an incentive to place welfare recipients into jobs. Each state is given an annual federal block grant that it uses to help poor families meet their subsistence needs and to develop programs that will help the parents find employment. The state programs operate within strict federal guidelines, including the following:

■ Americans' eligibility for federal cash assistance is limited to no more than five years in their lifetime.

■ Within two years, the head of most families on welfare must find work or risk the loss of benefits.

■ Unmarried teenage mothers qualify for welfare benefits only if they remain in school and live with a parent or legal guardian.

■ Single mothers lose a portion of their benefits if they refuse to cooperate in identifying for child support purposes the father of their children.

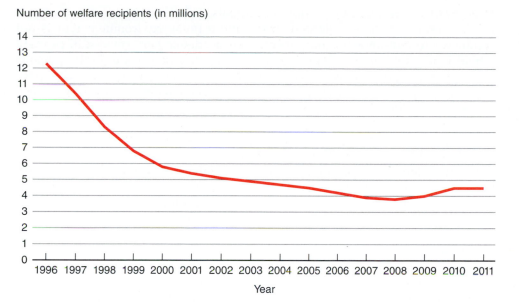

Number of welfare recipients (in millions)

Year

FIGURE 16-2
Number of Welfare Recipients, 1996–2011
The number of welfare recipients dropped sharply after the Temporary Assistance for Needy Families (TANF) program was instituted. The last year of the Aid for Families with Dependent Children (AFDC) program was 1996; it was replaced by TANF.
Source: U.S. Department of Health and Human Services, 2012.

Although states can grant exceptions to some of the rules (for example, an unmarried teenage mother who faces sexual abuse at home is permitted to live elsewhere), the exceptions are limited. States can even choose to impose more restrictive rules in some areas. For example, states have the option of denying increased benefits to unwed mothers who give birth to another child. The biggest challenge facing the states, however, has been the creation of welfare-to-work programs that are effective enough to qualify people for secure jobs. Most welfare recipients who have found employment since 1996 had enough skills that they required little or no job training from the state. In contrast, most of those who have been unable to find stable long-term employment have limited education and few job-related skills.[9]

TANF has dramatically reduced the size of the welfare rolls (see Figure 16-2). Within five years of its enactment, the number of people on welfare had dropped by 50 percent. In only three states—Hawaii, Rhode Island, and New Mexico—was the drop less than 20 percent. However, the decline was not simply the result of TANF. The American economy expanded at a rapid rate in the late 1990s, which created millions of new jobs. Nevertheless, even as the economy weakened in 2000, the number of welfare recipients continued to decline. The downward trend was reversed during the recent economic recession. Even so, the number of American families receiving TANF payments is only about a third of the number that were receiving assistance before TANF was enacted.

Head Start

Education programs for the poor are not limited to job training. In the 1960s, as part of Lyndon Johnson's Great Society, the federal government started an education program, Head Start, aimed at helping poor children at an early age. Head Start provides free preschool education to low-income children in order to help them succeed when they begin kindergarten. Roughly a million children are currently enrolled in Head Start, at an average annual cost of about $7,500 per child.

At no time in its history has the Head Start program been funded at a level that would allow all eligible children to participate. The low point was reached in the 1980s, when there was only enough money to enroll one in ten of those eligible. Today, less than half of all eligible children get to participate. In addition,

Head Start has not met the performance goals expected when it was founded. Because many of the enrolled children have a home environment that is not conducive to educational achievement, their academic performance in primary school is not substantially higher than that of other poor children. Proponents of Head Start argue that its real contribution is a less tangible one: it places poor children, for part of the day, in an environment where their nutritional and social needs receive attention.

Earned Income Tax Credit (EITC)

A full-time job does not guarantee that a family will rise above the poverty line. A family of four with one employed adult who works forty hours a week at $8 an hour (slightly higher than the federal minimum wage) has an annual income of about $16,000, which is $7,000 below the poverty line. Millions of Americans—mostly household workers, service workers, unskilled laborers, and farm workers—are in this position. The U.S. Bureau of Labor Statistics estimates that roughly 10 percent of full-time workers, the so-called working poor, do not earn enough to lift their family above the poverty line.[10]

Some of these workers are eligible to receive the Earned Income Tax Credit (EITC). Enacted in 1975 under President Gerald Ford and expanded during the presidencies of Ronald Reagan and Bill Clinton, EITC now covers about 10 million low-income American families. The maximum yearly payment for a family with one child is $3,100, and eligibility is limited to families that include a wage earner. EITC payments occur when the wage earner files a federal income tax return. Those whose incomes are sufficiently low receive an EITC payment, the amount of which depends on their income level and number of dependents. The EITC program is now the federal government's largest means-tested cash assistance program. According to U.S. Census Bureau calculations, the EITC lifts about a third of low-income Americans above the poverty line.

Although the EITC is subject to budgetary and political pressures, it has more public support than most assistance programs. The reason is simple: EITC is tied to employment. Only those who work are eligible to receive the payment. Polls that span more than a half-century reveal that Americans have consistently favored work-based assistance to welfare payments as the answer to poverty. Work is widely believed to foster initiative and accountability; welfare is widely held to breed dependency and irresponsibility.

In-Kind Benefits: Food Stamps and Housing Vouchers

in-kind benefit

A government benefit that is a cash equivalent, such as food stamps or rent vouchers. This form of benefit ensures that recipients will use public assistance in a specified way.

The Food Stamps program, which took its present form in 1961, is fully funded by the federal government. The program provides an **in-kind benefit**—not cash, but food stamps that can be spent only on grocery items. Food stamps are available only to people who qualify on the basis of low income. The program is intended to improve the nutrition of poor families by enabling them to purchase qualified items—mainly foodstuffs—with food stamps. Some critics say that food stamps stigmatize their users by making it obvious to onlookers in the checkout line that they are "welfare cases." More prevalent criticisms are that the program is too costly and that too many undeserving people receive food stamps.

Low-income persons are also eligible for subsidized housing. Most of the federal spending in this area is on rent vouchers, an in-kind benefit. The government gives the individual a monthly rent payment voucher, which the individual gives in lieu of cash to the landlord, who then hands the voucher over to the government in exchange for cash. About five million households annually receive a federal housing subsidy.

One of the many ironies of U.S. social welfare policy is that tax deductions for home mortgages for the middle and upper classes are government subsidies, just as are rent vouchers for the poor, but only the latter are stigmatized as a government "handout."

Like other public assistance programs, housing subsidies are criticized as being too costly. Nevertheless, the federal government spends less on public housing for the poor than it gives in tax breaks to homeowners, most of whom are middle- and upper-income Americans. Homeowners are allowed tax deductions for their mortgage interest payments and their local property tax payments. The total of these tax concessions is three times as much as is spent by the federal government on low-income housing. In many European democracies, there is no tax deduction for home mortgage payments.

Medicaid

When Medicare was created for retirees in 1965, Congress also established Medicaid, which provides health care for the poor. It is a public assistance program, rather than a social insurance program like Medicare, because it is based on need and funded by general tax revenues. More than 60 percent of Medicaid funding is provided by the federal government with the rest coming from the states. Over 40 million Americans receive Medicaid assistance. The figure will increase as a result of the health care reform bill that Congress enacted in 2010. The legislation expanded the eligibility criteria for Medicaid recipients. Most single adults without children, for example, were not eligible under the old rules but are eligible under the new ones. (In addition, beginning in 2014, the new law will provide a subsidy to individuals and families with incomes below four times the poverty rate to help them pay for health insurance premiums, although in most cases they will have to bear the larger share of the cost.)

As health care costs have spiraled far ahead of the inflation rate, so have the costs of Medicaid. It absorbs roughly half of all public assistance dollars spent by the U.S. government and has forced state and local governments to cut other services to meet their share of the costs. Medicare is now the first or second biggest budget item for most states. "It's killing us" is how one official described the impact of Medicaid on the annual budget.[11] As is true of other public assistance programs, Medicaid has been criticized for supposedly helping too many people who could take care of themselves.

The SCHIP Program

Enacted in 1997 at the urging of President Bill Clinton, the State Children's Health Insurance Program (commonly called CHIP) provides health insurance for uninsured children of lower-income families that do not qualify for Medicaid insurance. CHIP is a matching program with he federal government providing some of the funds and the states providing the rest. States can opt out of the program and have some flexibility in setting eligibility criteria. Arizona is the only state not enrolled in the program. Arizona closed out its CHIP program in 2010, although it continued to insure those already enrolled.

A decade after the CHIP program began, enrollment has risen to more than six million children. When the program was reauthorized in 2009 at the urging of President Obama, it was expanded to include an additional four million children and also pregnant women. An increase in taxes on tobacco products was used to fund the expansion.

The 2010 Health Care Reform Act

Although the health care reform bill (the Patient Protection and Affordable Care Act) passed by Congress in 2010 expanded the Medicaid program, it aims to increase health insurance coverage primarily through mandates on individuals and companies. Starting in 2014, individual Americans will face a tax penalty if they don't have health insurance. Low-income individuals will be eligible for a federal subsidy in order to enable them to afford insurance coverage. At the same time, most companies with more than two hundred employees will be required to provide their employees with health insurance and most companies with fifty to two hundred employees will have to provide insurance or pay a tax penalty.

The bill includes mechanisms designed to hold down insurance costs in order to ease the burden on individuals and firms. The chief mechanism is state-based insurance exchanges that will negotiate with insurance companies to obtain the lowest insurance rates possible. The legislation also prohibits a number of insurance practices, such as placing lifetime limits on insurance payments and canceling policies when people become sick, that have the effect of depriving people insurance when they most need it.

The Congressional Budget Office (CBO) estimates that the health care reform act, when fully implemented, will increase the number of insured Americans by roughly thirty million persons. It is expected to cost about $100 billion a year, which will be financed by new taxes and fees and by cost savings in other federal health care programs. The CBO estimates that these payment mechanisms will fully cover the program's cost. Critics have challenged the CBO's estimate and have derided the program as the "federalization" of health insurance.

Culture and Social Welfare

Surveys repeatedly show that most Americans are convinced that people on welfare could get along without it if they tried. As a consequence, there is constant political pressure to reduce welfare expenditures and to weed out undeserving recipients. The unwritten principle of social welfare in America, reflecting the country's individualistic culture, is that the individual must somehow earn a social welfare benefit or, barring that, demonstrate a convincing need for it.

The result is a welfare system that is both inefficient, in that much of the money spent on welfare never reaches the intended recipients, and inequitable, in that less than half of social welfare spending goes to the people most in need.[12]

Inefficiency

The United States has the most inefficient welfare system in the Western world. Scores of separate programs have been established to address different, often overlapping needs. A single individual in need of public assistance may qualify for many, one, or none of these programs, and the eligibility criteria can be mystifying. For some programs, there is no sliding eligibility scale. A person who makes $495 a month in wages might be eligible to receive a particular benefit, whereas a person making $500 might be ineligible.

Beyond the question of the fairness of such rules is the issue of their efficiency. The unwritten principle that the individual must somehow earn or be in absolute need of assistance makes the U.S. welfare system heavily bureaucratic. For example, the 1996 Welfare Reform Act—which limits eligibility to families with incomes below a certain level and, in most instances, to families with a single parent living in the home—requires that the eligibility of each applicant be checked periodically by a caseworker. This procedure makes such programs doubly expensive; in addition to making payments to recipients, the programs must pay local caseworkers, supervisors, and support staffs (see Figure 16-3). These costs do not include the administrative costs of the state and federal agencies that oversee the programs.

The bureaucratic costs of welfare are substantially lower in Europe because most European countries have unitary rather than federal systems, which eliminates a layer of government, and also because eligibility is often universal, as in the case of government-paid health care. Caseworkers do not have to pore over records to determine who is and who is not eligible for government-provided medical treatment—everyone is.[13]

Inequity

European welfare programs are also more equitable in the sense that the major beneficiaries are those individuals most in need. In contrast, the United States spends as much, or more, on assistance programs for the nonpoor than it does for the poor.

Social security and Medicare provide an example. Spending on these programs, which assist rich and poor alike, exceeds the total of all spending on public assistance programs, which help only the needy. Many social security recipients are in the higher-income categories, and thus have no absolute economic need for the benefit. In fact, their monthly social security income is substantially higher than that of those in the lower-income categories as a result of the formula for determining social security payouts—the higher your income while working, the larger your social security benefit upon retirement. To be sure, social security

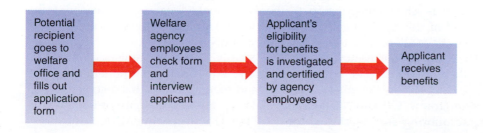

FIGURE 16-3

The Welfare Bureaucracy
Because U.S. social welfare benefits are distributed on the basis of demonstrated need, a large bureaucracy is required to ascertain applicants' eligibility and to monitor whether changes in recipients' circumstances render them ineligible for further assistance.

recipients, regardless of their wealth, have a claim to the benefit as a result of having paid payroll taxes during their working years. Nevertheless, most retirees receive more in social security benefits than they contributed in payroll taxes while working. The excess payment could be regarded as public assistance and has been increasing as a result of lengthening life spans. The prime beneficiaries of the extra years on social security assistance are the more affluent. Poverty takes a toll on people's health and cuts short their retirement years. The poorest 10 percent of Americans live five fewer years on average than the wealthiest 10 percent.

Of course, social insurance programs do help many who are needy. Monthly social security checks keep millions of Americans, mostly widows, out of poverty. About one-fourth of America's elderly have no significant monthly income aside from what they receive from social security. Nevertheless, families in the top fifth of the income population receive more in social security and Medicare benefits than the government spends in total on TANF, SSI, food stamps, and housing subsidies for the poor.

Education as Equality of Opportunity

Although few Americans would support economic equality for all, most Americans endorse the principle of **equality of opportunity**—the idea that people should have a reasonable chance to succeed if they make the effort. The concept includes a commitment to equality in the narrow sense that everyone should have a fair chance to get ahead. But it is a form of equality shaped by liberty because the outcome—personal success or personal failure—depends on what individuals do with that opportunity. The expectation is that people will end up differently— some will make a good living and some will be poor. It is sometimes said that equality of opportunity gives individuals an equal chance to become unequal.

Equality of opportunity is an ideal. Americans do not start life on an equal footing. It was said of one successful American politician, whose father before him was a successful politician and a millionaire, that "he was born on third base and thought he hit a triple."[14] Some Americans are born into privilege, and others start life in such abject poverty that few of them escape it. Nonetheless, equality of opportunity is more than a catchphrase. It is the philosophical basis for a number of government programs, none more so than public education.

Until the 1960s, the federal government's role in education was relatively small. Education was largely the responsibility of state and local governments, and they continue to provide more than 90 percent of school funding and to determine the bulk of school policies, from the length of the academic year to teachers' qualifications. However, the federal government also has an ongoing role in education policy, largely through financial assistance to states and localities. The grant money is split almost evenly between support for colleges and support for elementary and secondary schools.

The 1964 Elementary and Secondary Education Act is the cornerstone of the federal government's public-school efforts. The legislation authorizes funding for items such as school construction, textbooks, special education, and teacher training. Most of this spending is not uncontroversial, largely because members of Congress have all insisted that their states and districts have a share of the funds.

The 1964 Higher Education Act is the basis for federal assistance aimed at strengthening the higher education system. Among its components are Pell Grants, federal loans to college students, and federally subsidized college work-study programs. Of these, Pell Grants make up the largest share of federal support, accounting for roughly a third of the U.S. Department of Education's discretionary spending budget (see Figure 16-4). Millions of college students have been the recipients of Pell Grants, which are designed to make college affordable to students from modest and low income families. The federal student loan program has also helped millions of students, although it is a relatively small spending item in that most of the money is recouped through loan repayments. In 2010, as a cost-saving measure, the federal government completely took over the government-guaranteed student loan program. Before then, some student loans were issued by banks, which had the safety of a government-insured loan while being paid a fee for handling the loans.

Public Education: Leveling through the Schools

During the nation's first century, the question of a free education for all children was a divisive issue. Wealthy interests feared that an educated public would challenge their power. Egalitarians, on the other hand, saw education as a means of enabling ordinary citizens to get ahead. The egalitarians won out. Public schools sprang up in nearly every community and were free of charge.[15]

Equality continues to be a guiding principle of public education. Unlike the situation in countries that divide children even at the grade school level into different tracks that lead ultimately to different occupations, the curriculum in U.S. schools is relatively standardized. Of course, public education has never been a uniform experience for American children. Cities in the late nineteenth century neglected the education of many immigrant children, who were thereby placed at a permanent disadvantage. During the first half of the twentieth century, southern public schools for black children were designed to keep them down, not lift them up. Today, many children in poorer neighborhoods attend overcrowded, understaffed, and underfunded public schools. The quality of education depends significantly on the wealth of the community in which a child resides. The Supreme Court has upheld this arrangement, saying that the states are obliged to give all children an "adequate" education as opposed to one that is "equal" across communities.

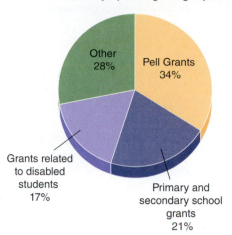

Discretionary Spending Budget ($68 billion)

Other 28%, Pell Grants 34%, Grants related to disabled students 17%, Primary and secondary school grants 21%

FIGURE 16-4   Discretionary Federal Spending on Education   Pell Grants to college students account for the largest share of the federal discretionary budget for higher education. (College loans, which are provided for under the Department of Education's mandatory spending budget, are not included in the figure.)

Source: U.S. Department of Education, 2012.

The Supreme Court has held that American children are entitled to an "adequate" education but do not have a right to an "equal" education. America's public schools differ greatly in quality primarily as a result of differences in the wealth of the communities they serve. Some public schools are overcrowded and have few facilities and little equipment. Others are very well equipped, have spacious facilities, and offer small class sizes.

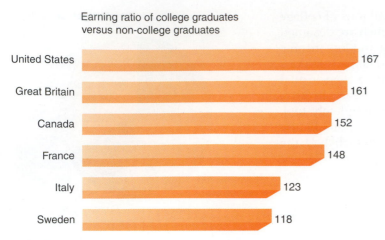

Earning ratio of college graduates
versus non-college graduates

United States   167
Great Britain   161
Canada   152
France   148
Italy   123
Sweden   118

FIGURE 16-5 **The Earning Power of a College Degree** College graduates in every Western democracy earn more on average then do non-college graduates. The difference is more pronounced in the United States than elsewhere.

Source: Organization for Economic Development and Cooperation, 2010.

Nevertheless, the United States through its public schools seeks to broadly educate its children. Public education in America was labeled "the great leveler" when it began in the early nineteenth century, and the tradition has been maintained. Arguably, no country makes an equivalent effort to give children, whatever their parents' background, an equal opportunity in life through education. Per-pupil spending on public elementary and secondary schools is substantially higher in the United States than it is in Europe. America's commitment to broad-based education extends to college. The United States has the world's largest system of higher education—it has nearly four thousand two- and four-year colleges.[16]

The nation's education system preserves both the myth and the reality of an equal-opportunity society. The belief that success is within the reach of anyone who works for it could not be sustained if the public education system were designed to serve the privileged few. Moreover, educational attainment is related to personal success, at least as measured by income. In fact, the gap in income between those with and those without a college degree is greater now than at any time in the country's history. On average during their lifetime, college graduates will earn about 65 percent more than those without a college degree. This difference is greater than in European democracies; workers without college degrees in those countries receive higher wages than their American counterparts because they have the benefit of higher minimum-wage laws and stronger labor unions (see Figure 16-5).

Improving America's Schools

Because America's public schools play such a key role in creating an equal-opportunity society, they are scrutinized closely. Parents of schoolchildren are not shy about saying what they think of their local schools. Interestingly, parents tend to rate their own children's schools more highly than they rate other schools. A national survey found that most parents gave their children's schools a grade of A or B while giving schools as a whole a grade of C or lower.[17]

By objective indicators, America's students are not high performers. U.S. students rank below students in Canada and most European countries on standardized reading, math, and science tests (see "How the U.S. Differs"). One reason is that the United States has a larger portion of non-native-speaking children. American students for whom English is a second language have lower standardized test scores on average than do other students.[18] The United States is also more segregated residentially by income than are European countries. As a result, poor children are more likely to go to schools where most of the other students are also poor. Moreover, because the wealth of a community affects the level of school funding, schools with a high proportion of poor students tend to have fewer resources. In fact, the best predictor of a school's overall performance on standardized tests is the wealth of the community in which it is located; schools in poorer areas have much lower scores on average than do schools in more affluent areas.[19]

The weak performance of many U.S. schools has led to policies aimed at strengthening education in America. The most contentious of these policies are school choice and mandatory high-stakes testing.

School Choice

Advocates of school choice say that a student should have the option of leaving a poorly performing school in favor of one that might provide a better education. They also argue that the student's new school should get the funding that otherwise would have gone to the student's former school. This policy, it is claimed,

HOW THE U.S. DIFFERS POLITICAL THINKING THROUGH COMPARISON

Education Performance

Although the United States spends more heavily on its public schools than do nearly all other advanced industrialized democracies, its students perform less well on standardized tests than do students in most of these countries. In fact, American students do not rank even in the top ten countries in terms of academic performance. Some of the cross-national surveys have been conducted by the Organization for Economic Cooperation and Development (OECD). Its surveys are administered periodically in more than three dozen countries. The surveys in each case are given to a sample of fifteen-year-olds, by which age students in most countries are nearing the end of their compulsory time in school. Every OECD survey covers reading, mathematical, and scientific literacy in terms of general competencies—that is, how well students can apply the knowledge and skills they have learned at school to real-life situations. Only those questions that are approved unanimously by the participating countries

are used in the survey. The chart below shows the average OECD test scores in selected countries.

Q: Why might the United States lag behind other advanced industrialized democracies in student performance, even though it spends more heavily on public education?

A: Although the blame for the relatively poor performance of U.S. students on standardized tests is often directed at teachers, other factors have been found to be more important. Compared with most Western democracies, the United States has a relatively high proportion of non-native-speaking children, who on average do less well in school than other students. In addition, the United States has more residential segregation by income and more poor children than do other Western democracies. Poor children, particularly those residing in poor neighborhoods or communities, tend to perform less well in school than do their peers.

Source: Organization for Economic Cooperation and Development, 2010.

forces school administrators and teachers to do a better job, or face the continued loss of students and funding.[20] Opponents of the policy do not defend poorly performing schools but instead argue that school choice will only serve to weaken these schools further. They claim that the policy benefits middle- and upper-income students because the parents of poor children lack the means to transport them to a better but more distant school.[21]

School choice has gained momentum in recent years. The emergence of charter schools is a case in point. Although charter schools are publicly funded, they operate by different standards than other public schools. They have greater freedom, for example, in determining their curricula and in picking their students. In return, they must meet specified accountability criteria in order to remain open. Backed primarily by conservatives, charter schools have faced opposition from public school teachers and administrators on grounds that these schools drain the regular public schools of funding and top students. In 2009, President Obama broke with the Democratic-aligned teachers unions by endorsing charter schools. Obama said charter schools are leaders in innovation and argued that state-imposed limits on the number of charter schools are not "good for our children, our economy, and our country."

School vouchers are another way of expanding student choice. Parents receive a voucher from the government that they can give to a private or parochial school to cover part of the cost of their child's tuition. Proponents say that vouchers force failing public schools to improve their instructional programs or face a permanent loss of revenue. For their part, opponents argue that vouchers weaken the public schools by siphoning off revenue and say that vouchers subsidize many families that would have sent their children to private or parochial schools anyway. They also note that vouchers are of little use to students from poor families because vouchers cover only part of the tuition costs at a private or parochial school and poor families do not have the money to pay the rest.

Although the courts have upheld the constitutionality of vouchers in some circumstances, polls indicate that Americans are divided over the issue of school vouchers.[22] The question gets majority support when it is framed in the context of giving students a choice among public schools but is opposed by the majority when private and parochial schools are included among the choices. The issue of vouchers reflects the tensions inherent in the concept of equal opportunity. Vouchers expand opportunity by increasing the number of choices available to students. Yet not all students are able to take advantage of the choice, and not all taxpayers want their tax dollars used to support private and parochial schools.

Mandatory High-Stakes Testing

In 2001, President George W. Bush persuaded Congress to pass the No Child Left Behind Act (NCLB). The legislation requires national testing in reading, math, and science and ties federal funding to the test results. Schools that show no improvement in students' test scores after two years receive an increased amount of federal aid. If these schools show no improvement by the end of the third year, however, their students become eligible to transfer elsewhere, and their school's federal assistance is reduced.

NCLB has been a source of contention since inception.[23] Whereas the federal government had previously used financial aid as a means of influencing education policy, NCLB thrust the federal government directly into the classroom. The national testing process has nearly forced public schools to concentrate on tested subjects, such as math and science. The National Education Association (NEA)

POLITICAL THINKING   Does High-Stakes Testing Improve Learning?

Few education issues have provoked such sharply different reactions as mandatory high-stakes testing of public school students. Advocates say that it is the best way to hold schools and teachers accountable. If they repeatedly fail to perform, they, rather than their students, will suffer the consequences, as in the case of a school that loses funding because its students fail to improve on standardized tests. Opponents argue that mandatory high-stakes testing distorts what happens in the classroom. Teachers devote their time to "teaching to the test"—preparing their students to do well on the test, at whatever the cost to other forms of learning. What's your view on mandatory high-stakes testing? Is your opinion the result of being required to take such tests while you were in primary or secondary school?

has argued that the law forces teachers to teach to the national tests, undermining true learning. Congressional Democrats have claimed that the program has failed to provide struggling schools with enough funds to improve the quality of classroom education. For their part, congressional Republicans have generally supported the law, saying that it holds teachers and schools accountable for student performance. House Republican leader John Boehner said: "Money alone is not the answer to the problems facing our children's schools. High standards and accountability for results—not just spending—are the key to erasing the achievement gap in education."[24] Opinion polls show that Americans are divided over the issue of whether NCLB is an effective program, with Republicans being somewhat more supportive of NCLB than are Democrats.[25]

In 2009, at President Obama's urging, the Democratic-controlled Congress enacted the Race to the Top program, which rewards states for school performance and innovation. States that score high by the program's criteria are eligible to receive federal funds that can be used to further strengthen their schools. A distinguishing feature of the program is that it requires the states to compete for funding. In the first round of competition, only Delaware and Tennessee were awarded funds. Ten additional states received funds in the second round. Although most states have chosen to compete for the funds, which has required them to align their education systems with the program's criteria, some states have opted not to do so. Texas governor Rick Perry, who was a candidate for the 2012 Republican presidential nomination, said: "We would be foolish and irresponsible to place our children's future in the hands of unelected bureaucrats and special interest groups thousands of miles away in Washington."[26]

Thus, many of the partisan and philosophical differences that affect federal welfare policy also affect federal education policy. Democrats are more inclined to find the answer to how to improve schools in increased federal spending on education, particularly in less affluent communities, whereas Republicans are more inclined to look to market-like mechanisms such as school choice and achievement tests.

The American Way of Promoting the General Welfare

All democratic societies promote economic security, but they do so in different ways and to different degrees. Economic security has a higher priority in European democracies than in the United States. European democracies have

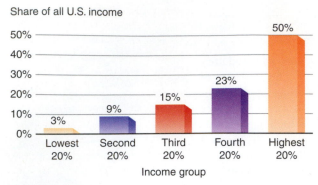

Share of all U.S. income

FIGURE 16-6 **Income Inequality in the United States**
The United States has the highest degree of income inequality of any industrialized democracy. Citizens in the top fifth by income get half of all income; those in the bottom fifth get less than a twentieth of all income.
Source: U.S. Census Bureau, 2012.

instituted programs such as government-paid health care for all citizens, compensation for all unemployed workers, and retirement benefits for all elderly citizens. As this chapter shows, the United States provides these benefits only to some citizens in each category. On the other hand, the American system of higher education dwarfs those in Europe.

The differences between the European and American approaches to welfare stem from historical and cultural differences. Democracy in Europe developed in reaction to centuries of aristocratic rule, which brought the issue of economic privilege to the forefront. European democracies initiated sweeping social welfare programs designed to bring about greater economic equality. Social inequality was harder to root out because it was thoroughly embedded in European society, shaping everything from social manners to education. Private schools and university training were the preserve of the elite, a tradition that, though now in the past, continues to affect how Europeans think about educational opportunity.

The American experience was a different one. Democracy in America grew out of a tradition of limited government that emphasized personal liberty, which included a belief in self-reliance. This belief contributed to Americans' strong support for public education, their weak support for public assistance, and their persistent preference for low tax rates. Unlike political equality, the idea of economic equality has never captured Americans' imagination. Political scientists Stanley Feldman and John Zaller found that Americans' support for public assistance programs rests more on compassion for the poor than on an ideological belief in economic sharing.[27] Or, as the political scientist Robert Lane expressed it, Americans have a preference for market justice, meaning that they prefer that society's material benefits be allocated through the economic marketplace rather than through government policies.[28] It's thus not surprising that the United States has a high level of income inequality (see Figure 16-6). Americans in the top fifth by income receive roughly 50 percent of total U.S. income, whereas those in the bottom fifth get about 3 percent. This 17-to-1 income difference between the top and bottom earners is easily the highest among Western democracies.

Summary

Self-Test www.mhhe.com/ pattersontadtx11e

The United States has a complex social welfare system of multiple programs addressing specific welfare needs. Each program applies only to those individuals who qualify for benefits by meeting the specific eligibility criteria. In general, these criteria are designed to encourage self-reliance or, when help is necessary, to ensure that laziness is not rewarded or fostered. This approach to social welfare reflects Americans' traditional belief in individualism.

Poverty is a large and persistent problem in the United States. About one in nine Americans falls below the government-defined poverty line, including a disproportionate number of children, female-headed families, minority-group members, and rural and inner-city dwellers. The ranks of the poor are increased by economic recessions and are reduced through government assistance programs.

Welfare policy has been a partisan issue, with Democrats taking the lead on government programs to alleviate economic insecurity and Republicans acting to slow down or decentralize these initiatives. Changes in social welfare have usually resulted from presidential leadership in the context of public support for the change. Welfare policy traditionally has involved programs to provide jobs and job training, education programs, income measures, and especially individual-benefit programs.

Individual-benefit programs fall into two broad categories: social insurance and public assistance. The former includes programs such as social security for retired workers and Medicare for the elderly. Social insurance programs are funded by payroll taxes paid by potential recipients, who, in this sense, earn the benefits they later receive. Because of this arrangement, social insurance programs have broad public support. Public assistance programs, in contrast, are funded by general tax revenues and are targeted toward needy individuals and families. These programs are not controversial in principle; most Americans believe that government should assist the truly needy. However, because of a widespread belief that most welfare recipients could get along without assistance if they tried, these programs do not have universal public support, receive only modest funding, and are politically divisive.

Social welfare is a contentious issue. In one view, social welfare is too costly and assists too many people who could help themselves; another view holds that social welfare is not broad enough and that too many disadvantaged Americans live in poverty. Because of these irreconcilable beliefs and because of federalism and the widely shared view that welfare programs should target specific problems, the existing system of multiple programs, despite its administrative complexity and inefficiency, has been the only politically feasible solution.

The balance between economic equality and individualism tilts more heavily toward individualism in the United States than in other advanced industrialized democracies. Other democracies, for example, have government-paid health care for all citizens. The United States does not, although the recently enacted health care reform bill provides coverage to many of the previously uninsured.

Compared to other democracies, the United States attempts to more equally educate its children, a policy consistent with its cultural emphasis on equality of opportunity. Like social welfare, however, education is a partisan issue involving disputes over the federal government's role, school choice, spending levels, and mandatory high-stakes testing.

CHAPTER 16

Study Corner

Key Terms

entitlement programs (p.414)

equality of opportunity (p. 424)

in-kind benefit (p. 420)

means test (p. 417)

negative government (p. 414)

positive government (p. 414)

poverty line (p. 411)

public assistance (p. 417)

social insurance (p. 415)

Self-Test: Multiple Choice

1. The shape of the U.S. welfare policy system has been influenced strongly by
   a. the cultural emphasis placed on economic equality.
   b. the fact that the United States has a federal system of government.
   c. the fact that the United States is the wealthiest nation on earth and thus can afford the most generous benefit system.
   d. a and b only.

2. The 1996 Welfare Reform Act that Congress passed provides
   a. an end to the federal guarantee of cash assistance to needy families.
   b. a limitation of five years in most cases for a person to receive assistance.
   c. that states must train and help welfare recipients find employment.
   d. all of the above.

3. Which of the following programs is based on the social insurance principle?
   a. subsidized housing
   b. unemployment benefits
   c. Medicaid
   d. food stamps

4. Regarding American education, which of the following statements is *not* true?
   a. The United States invests more heavily in public education than any other nation.
   b. U.S. law requires states to spend roughly equal amounts on each public school student, regardless of whether that student is going to school in a city, suburb, or rural area.

c. Free public education provides a way for more people to gain the foundation needed for economic advantage.

d. The curriculum in U.S. schools is relatively standardized on the assumption that children should be given an equal opportunity to get ahead in life.

5. Administrative costs of welfare are substantially lower in Europe than in the United States because

a. European eligibility is universal for certain programs, such as health care, and thus money does not have to be spent on the paperwork necessary to determine eligibility, which is the case in the United States.

b. European eligibility for most programs is restricted to providing services to only the poorest 5 percent of the population.

c. Europe has primarily unitary governments, which means they have to administer only one set of rules, rather than fifty different sets as is the case in the United States because of state involvement in social welfare programs.

d. both a and c.

6. Regarding unemployment,

a. according to research, the loss of a job or failure to immediately find a new job is in most cases the fault of the individual.

b. U.S. Bureau of Labor statistics indicate that of those who have lost jobs, the large majority made the decision on their own to stop working rather than being terminated as part of a larger job layoff.

c. government unemployment payments enjoy high levels of public support.

d. none of the above.

7. The United States has one of the lowest poverty rates of any Western democracy. (T/F)

8. The Republican Party has initiated nearly all major federal welfare programs. (T/F)

9. Social security and Medicare have widespread public support because they cost less than other welfare programs. (T/F)

10. There is a wide gap in income levels between the top and bottom fifths of the American population. (T/F)

Self-Test: Essay

How has U.S. policy on welfare and education been influenced by Americans' belief in individualism and by America's federal system of government?

Suggested Readings

Alesina, Alberto, and Edward Glaeser. *Fighting Poverty in the U.S. and Europe: A World of Difference.* New York: Oxford University Press, 2006. A comparison of poverty policies in the United States and Europe.

Howard, Christopher. *The Welfare State Nobody Knows: Debunking Myths about U.S. Social Policy.* Princeton, N.J.: Princeton University Press, 2006. A critical assessment of the U.S. social welfare system.

Jacobs, Lawrence R., and Theda Skocpol, *Health Care Reform and American Politics.* New York: Oxford University Press, 2010. A careful look at the passage and implications of the health care reform bill.

Koretz, Daniel. *Measuring Up: What Educational Testing Really Tells Us.* Cambridge, Mass.: Harvard University Press, 2009. A comprehensive look at standardized testing performance and its correlates.

Patterson, James T. *America's Struggle against Poverty in the Twentieth Century.* Cambridge, Mass.: Harvard University Press, 2000. A careful study of poverty and its history.

Reed, Douglas S. *On Equal Terms: The Constitutional Politics of Educational Opportunity.* Princeton, N.J.: Princeton University Press, 2003. An insightful analysis of school reform issues.

Van Dunk, Emily, and Anneliese M. Dickman. *School Choice and the Question of Accountability.* New Haven, Conn.: Yale University Press, 2003. A careful look at the voucher system as applied in the Milwaukee school system.

List of Websites

www.doleta.gov
The U.S. Department of Labor's website on the status of the welfare-to-work program, including state-by-state assessments.

www.nea.org
The home page of the National Education Association provides information on the organization's membership and policy goals.

www.dhhs.gov
The website of the Department of Health and Human Services—the agency responsible for most federal social welfare programs.

www.npc.umich.edu
The website of the University of Michigan's National Poverty Center, which seeks to stimulate interest in policy issues and to transmit research findings to policymakers.

Participate!

When it comes to partisan politics, poverty is a contentious issue. Republicans and Democrats disagree mightily on the question of how far government should go in helping the poor. On the other hand, virtually all Americans—on the right and on the left—support private efforts to help the poor. Numerous local religious, civic, social, and economic groups run programs for the poor, such as food kitchens and clothing drives. Also, many national organizations work locally to assist the poor. An example is Habitat for Humanity, which builds modest houses with volunteer labor and then makes them available to low-income families, which assist in the construction and receive low-interest or no-interest mortgages to pay for the cost of construction materials. Consider volunteering some of your time to a group that gives a helping hand to those in need—whether a church or a community group or a nonprofit organization like Habitat for Humanity. Habitat for Humanity has a website that makes it easy for you to volunteer.

Extra Credit

For up-to-the-minute *New York Times* articles, interactive simulations, graphics, study tools, and more links and quizzes, visit the text's Online Learning Center at **www.mhhe. com/pattersontad11e**.

Self-Test Answers

1. b, 2. d, 3. b, 4. b, 5. d, 6. d, 7. F, 8. F, 9. F, 10. T

Foreign Policy: Protecting the American Way

We the people of the United States, in order to . . . provide for the common defense. Preamble, U.S. Constitution

In announcing on national television his decision to send thirty thousand additional troops to Afghanistan, President Barack Obama declared the action to be "in our vital national interest." Terrorism, he said, cannot be quelled without stopping it in Afghanistan. "I make this decision," he stated, "because I am convinced our national security is at stake. . . . Afghanistan is the epicenter of violent extremism." Yet Obama went on to say that America's commitment in Afghanistan was not open-ended. He announced that American troops would train Afghan military forces at an accelerated pace so that U.S. forces could begin withdrawing in 2011. In justifying the timetable, Obama spoke of America's other pressing needs. "I must weigh all the challenges that our nation faces," he said. "Over the past several years we have lost that balance. We've failed to appreciate the connection between national security and our economy. . . . So we can't simply afford to ignore the price of these wars."

The cornerstone of foreign policy is the **national interest**—what is best for the nation in terms of protecting its physical security and way of life. Americans may disagree on the specific policies that will serve the national interest. President Obama's decision to escalate the war in Afghanistan was praised by many, but it was also criticized widely. Nonetheless, though the national interest is difficult to define in practice, it is the underlying objective of foreign policy. The national interest is promoted through adequate military preparedness and through productive trade relations.

Foreign policy, unlike other areas of government policy, rests on relations with actors outside rather than within the country. As a result, the chief instruments of national security policy differ from those of domestic policy. One of these instruments is diplomacy—the process of negotiation between countries. The lead agency in U.S. diplomatic efforts is the Department of State, which is headed by the secretary of state and coordinates the efforts of U.S. embassies abroad, each of which is directed by a U.S. ambassador. American diplomacy also takes place through international organizations—such as the

national interest

That which is best for the nation in its dealings with the world in terms of protecting its security and its way of life.

United Nations—to which the United States belongs. A second instrument of foreign policy is military power. The lead agency in military affairs is the Department of Defense, which is headed by the secretary of defense and oversees the military services—the army, air force, navy, and marine corps. Here, too, the United States sometimes works through alliances, the most important of which is the North Atlantic Treaty Organization (NATO). NATO has nearly thirty member nations, including the United States, Canada, and most Western and Eastern European countries. A third instrument of world politics is intelligence gathering, or the process of monitoring other countries' activities. For many reasons, but primarily because all countries pursue their self-interest, each nation keeps a watchful eye on other nations. In the United States, the task of intelligence gathering falls to specialized federal agencies including the Central Intelligence Agency (CIA) and the National Security Agency (NSA). Economic exchange, the fourth instrument of foreign affairs, involves both international trade and foreign aid. U.S. interests in this area are promoted by a range of U.S. agencies, such as the Agriculture, Commerce, Labor, and Treasury Departments, as well as specialty agencies such as the Federal Trade Commission. The United States also pursues its economic goals through international organizations of which it is a member, including the World Trade Organization, the World Bank, and the International Monetary Fund.

The national security policies of the United States include an extraordinary array of activities—so many, in fact, that they could not possibly be addressed adequately in an entire book, much less a single chapter. There are roughly two hundred countries in the world, and the United States has relations of one kind or another—military, diplomatic, economic—with all of them. This chapter narrows the subject by concentrating on a few main ideas:

- *Since World War II, the United States has acted in the role of world leader, which has substantially affected its military, diplomatic, and economic policies.*

- *The United States maintains a high degree of defense preparedness, which requires a substantial level of defense spending and a worldwide deployment of U.S. conventional and strategic forces.*

- *Changes in the international marketplace have led to increased economic interdependence among nations, which has had a marked influence on the U.S. economy and on America's security planning.*

isolationist

The view that the country should deliberately avoid a large role in world affairs and instead concentrate on domestic concerns.

The Roots of U.S. Foreign and Defense Policy

Before World War II, except within its own hemisphere, the United States was a mostly **isolationist** country. It was preoccupied with its internal development and intent on avoiding European entanglements. A different America emerged from the devastation of World War II. It had more land, sea, and air power than any other country; a huge armaments industry; and more than a hundred military installations overseas. The United States had become a fully **internationalist** country—a nation deeply involved in world affairs.[1]

internationalist

The view that the country should involve itself deeply in world affairs.

The United States was also a nation not fully at peace. It was locked in a wide-reaching conflict with the Soviet Union, which, after World War II, had engineered the communist takeover of Poland, Hungary, Czechoslovakia, and other Eastern European nations. President Harry S Truman and other American leaders regarded communist Russia as an implacable foe, a view that led to adoption of the doctrine of **containment**—the notion that Soviet aggression could be stopped only by the determined use of American power.[2] This doctrine had

containment

A doctrine, developed after World War II, based on the assumption that the Soviet Union was an aggressor nation and that only a determined United States could block Soviet territorial ambitions.

roots in the failed efforts to appease Germany's Adolf Hitler in the years leading up to World War II. At the 1938 Munich conference, Germany was allowed to annex Czechoslovakia's Sudetenland, which had a substantial German population. The annexation whetted Hitler's expansionist goals. The "Lesson of Munich" was that totalitarian leaders could not be appeased; they had to be confronted.

The Cold War Era and Its Lessons

Developments in the late 1940s embroiled the United States in a **cold war** with the Soviet Union.[3] The term refers to the fact that the two countries were not directly engaged in actual combat (a "hot war") but were locked in deep-seated hostilities that lasted forty-five years. The structure of international power was **bipolar**—the United States versus the Soviet Union. Each side was supreme in its sphere and was blocked by the power of the other from expanding its influence. A first application of containment policy was a massive aid program for Greece, where communists were gaining headway. President Truman believed that if Greece went communist, Turkey would be the next "domino" to fall, which would give control of the eastern Mediterranean to the Soviets. Then, in June 1950, when the Soviet-backed North Koreans invaded South Korea, Truman sent U.S. forces into the conflict in an attempt to stop the spread of communism in Northeast Asia. Nearly thirty-five thousand U.S. troops lost their lives in the Korean War, which ended in stalemate.

The turning point in U.S. foreign policy was the Vietnam War. Responding to the threat of a communist takeover in Vietnam, the United States became ever more deeply involved. Washington policymakers were driven by the "domino theory"—the claim that if Vietnam fell to the communists, so too would Laos, Cambodia, and the rest of Southeast Asia. By the late 1960s, 550,000 Americans were fighting in South Vietnam. Although U.S. forces were technically superior in combat to the communist fighters, Vietnam was a guerrilla war, with no front lines and few set battles.[4] U.S. public opinion, most visibly among the young, gradually turned against the war. U.S. combat troops left Vietnam in 1973, and two years later North Vietnamese forces completed their takeover of the country. Vietnam was the most painful and costly application of the containment doctrine: fifty-eight thousand Americans lost their lives in the fighting.

America's failure in Vietnam led U.S. policymakers to reconsider the country's international role. The "Lesson of Vietnam" was that there were limits to the country's ability to assert its will in the world. President Richard Nixon proclaimed that the United States could no longer act as the free world's "Lone Ranger" and sought to reduce tensions with communist countries. In 1972, Nixon visited the People's Republic of China, the first official contact with that country since the communists seized power in 1949. Nixon also initiated the Strategic Arms Limitation Talks (SALT), which resulted in reductions in the nuclear arsenals of the United States and the Soviet Union. This spirit of cooperation lasted until the Soviet invasion of Afghanistan in 1979, which convinced U.S. leaders that the Soviet Union had not changed its ways. Ronald Reagan, elected president in 1980, called for a renewed hard line toward the Soviet Union, which he described as the "evil empire."

Although U.S. policymakers did not realize it, the Soviet Union was collapsing under the weight of its heavy defense expenditures, its isolation from Western technology, and its inefficient centralized economy. In 1985, Soviet leader Mikhail Gorbachev undertook a restructuring of Soviet society, an initiative known as

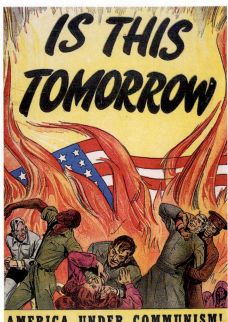

IS THIS TOMORROW

AMERICA UNDER COMMUNISM!

Cold war propaganda, like this poster warning of the danger of communism, contributed to a climate of opinion in the United States that led to public support for efforts to contain Soviet power.

cold war
The lengthy period after World War II when the United States and the Soviet Union were not engaged in actual combat (a "hot war") but were locked in a state of deep-seated hostility.

bipolar (power structure)
A power structure dominated by two powers only, as in the case of the United States and the Soviet Union during the cold war.

In the jungle warfare of Vietnam, American soldiers had difficulty finding the enemy and adapting to guerrilla tactics.

---

unipolar (power structure)

A power structure dominated by a single powerful actor, as in the case of the United States after the collapse of the Soviet Union.

---

perestroika. Gorbachev's reforms came too late to prevent the Soviet Union's collapse. In 1988, the Soviet Union withdrew its troops from Afghanistan, followed a year later by a withdrawal from Eastern Europe. Within the next two years, nearly all of the Soviet republics declared their independence, marking the end of the Soviet Union as a governing entity. The bipolar power structure that had defined world politics since the end of World War II was finished. The new structure was **unipolar**—the United States was now the world's unrivaled military superpower.

POLITICAL

THINKING Friend or Foe?

A long-standing debate among foreign policy analysts has been the emphasis the United States should place on the internal politics of other countries. Some analysts argue that foreign relations should be based strictly on mutual interests. This view dominated U.S. foreign policy during the cold war period when the United States aligned itself with anticommunist dictators in Africa and Latin America. Other analysts claim that America's long-term national interest is best served by aligning the country with governments that share a commitment to democratic values. Which view is closer to your own, and why?

The Post-Cold War Era and Its Lessons

The end of the cold war prompted the first President Bush in 1990 to call for a "new world order." George H. W. Bush advocated **multilateralism**—the idea that major nations should act together in response to problems and crises. Included in Bush's plan was a stronger role for multinational organizations such as the United Nations and NATO.

The Air Wars of the 1990s

Multilateralism defined America's response to the Iraqi invasion of Kuwait in August 1990. President Bush secured UN resolutions ordering Iraq to withdraw

---

multilateralism

The situation in which nations act together in response to problems and crises.

from Kuwait and authorizing the use of force if it failed to do so. Five months later, a half million troops, mostly American but including contingents from nearly two dozen nations, were lined up to attack Iraq. The war began with a week-long aerial bombardment that decimated Iraqi forces. When the ground troops then entered Iraq under cover of air power, the fighting ended in four days during which nearly four hundred U.S. service members were killed.

The Gulf operation was a military triumph, prompting President Bush to declare that the United States had "kicked the Vietnam syndrome [the legacy of America's defeat in Vietnam] once and for all." The Gulf War, however, was less successful in another way. Believing that an overthrow of Hussein's regime would destabilize Iraq, President Bush ordered a halt to the hostilities after Iraqi forces retreated. Hussein remained in power but was ordered by a UN resolution to dismantle his weapons programs, subject to UN inspections. However, Hussein repeatedly interfered with the inspectors' attempts to verify the status of his weapons programs, raising concern about his intentions.

Multilateralism carried over into the Clinton administration. Confronting Serb atrocities in Bosnia—where tens of thousands of Muslims and Croats were murdered, raped, or driven from their homes—President Bill Clinton pursued UN economic sanctions as a means of halting Serb aggression. When sanctions failed, the United States and its NATO allies attacked Serb forces with air power in 1995, which culminated in a U.S.-negotiated peace agreement (the Dayton Accords) that included the deployment to Bosnia of nearly sixty thousand peace-keeping troops, including twenty thousand Americans. War in the Balkans flared again in 1999 when the Serbs undertook a campaign of "ethnic cleansing" in the Serbian province of Kosovo, whose population was 90 percent Albanian. When attempts at a negotiated settlement failed, NATO planes, including U.S. aircraft, attacked Serbia.[5] After nearly three months of intensive bombing, Serb president Slobodan Milosevic (who died in 2006 while on trial for war crimes) pulled his troops out of Kosovo. Ethnic Albanians moved back in and, despite the presence of UN peacekeeping troops, launched revenge attacks on Serbs who remained. (In 2008, Kosovo became an independent state.)

As these examples indicate, multilateralism was not a wholly successful strategy for resolving international conflicts. With the deployment of enough resources, the world's major powers showed that they could act together with some success. However, these interventions offered no guarantee of long-term success. Regional and internal conflicts typically stem from enduring ethnic, religious, factional, or national hatreds or from chronic problems such as famine, overcrowding, or government corruption. Even if these hatreds or problems can be eased momentarily, they are often too deep-seated to be settled permanently.

The War on Terrorism

Upon assuming the presidency in 2001, George W. Bush rejected his father's multilateral approach to foreign policy. He announced plans to reduce America's military presence abroad. His position changed when terrorists attacked the World Trade Center and the Pentagon on September 11, 2001. In a televised address, Bush urged other nations to join the United States in a multilateral "war on terrorism."

The war on terrorism resulted in the first major reorganization of the U.S. national security bureaucracy since the Department of Defense was formed from the War and Navy Departments after World War II. This time, the new agency was the Department of Homeland Security (DHS), which was created in 2002 to coordinate domestic antiterrorism efforts. The DHS's responsibilities include securing the nation's borders, enhancing defenses against biological attacks,

In a nationally televised address shortly after the terrorist attacks of September 11, 2001, President George W. Bush announced that the United States was at war with terrorists. Few observers at the time believed that the war would be as long-lasting and costly as it has been.

preparing emergency personnel (police, firefighters, and rescue workers) for their roles in responding to terrorist attacks, and coordinating efforts to stop domestic terrorism.[6]

The first U.S. military action in the war on terrorism was an attack on Afghanistan, which commenced barely a month after the September 11 attacks. Afghanistan's Taliban-led government had granted sanctuary and training sites to the al Qaeda terrorists who carried out the attacks. Supported by troops from other NATO countries, U.S. forces quickly toppled the Taliban government, but failed to capture al Qaeda leader Osama bin Laden and his top lieutenants.

The Iraq War

preemptive war doctrine

The idea, espoused by President George W. Bush, that the United States could attack a potentially threatening nation even if the threat had not yet reached a serious and immediate level.

In 2002, President Bush labeled Iraq, Iran, and North Korea "the axis of evil." A few months later, he announced a new national security doctrine: the **preemptive war doctrine**.[7] Speaking at West Point, Bush asserted that the United States would not wait until it was attacked by hostile nations. Instead, America would take "preemptive action."[8] The concept was not entirely new—U.S. officials had long maintained a right to strike first if faced with an imminent attack. What was new in the Bush Doctrine was its embrace of a first-strike option before a threat became imminent.

In the summer of 2002, Bush targeted the regime of Iraq's Saddam Hussein, claiming that it was stockpiling weapons of mass destruction (WMDs)—chemical and biological weapons, and possibly nuclear weapons—for use against U.S. interests. That October, Congress authorized the use of military force against Iraq if it did not disarm voluntarily. Facing the possibility of an unwanted war in Iraq, America's European allies urged UN weapons inspectors to undertake the disarmament of Iraq, which had blocked earlier UN attempts to verify its weapon stockpiles. In late 2002, the United Nations passed a resolution requiring Iraq to accept weapons inspections. A two-track policy ensued. UN weapons inspectors entered Iraq in search of WMDs, while the United States deployed combat units to Iraq's borders.

Despite the UN's refusal to authorize a military attack and in the face of strenuous opposition from France, Germany, and Russia, President Bush in

March 2003 ordered U.S. forces to invade Iraq. British troops were also involved, but the attack was essentially an act of **unilateralism**—the situation in which one nation takes action against another state or states.[9] The Iraqi regime collapsed quickly, but the postcombat phase proved costlier than the Bush administration had anticipated. Age-old animosities between Sunni, Shiite, and Kurdish groups within Iraq blocked political compromise and fueled internal violence. Improvised explosive devices and suicide bombers took a heavy toll on U.S. troops. Moreover, weapons inspectors did not find the WMDs that the Bush administration had claimed were in Iraq's possession. In early 2004, the chief U.S. weapons inspector, David Kay, testified before Congress that U.S. intelligence agencies had vastly overstated the extent and purpose of Iraq's weapons program. The revelations undermined public support for the war. At the beginning, Americans by three-to-one had expressed support for the invasion. Two years later, the public was evenly split on the question of whether the invasion was a wise decision.[10]

In 2007, President Bush authorized a "surge" to give the struggling Iraqi government an opportunity to govern more effectively. Some 30,000 U.S. combat troops were added to the 130,000 military personnel already there. The surge contributed to a significant reduction in the violence, leading Bush to announce a phased withdrawal of U.S. combat forces from Iraq. President Obama stayed with the plan when he came into office and the last of America's combat units left Iraq in late 2011. Nearly nine years of war there had resulted in the deaths of more than 4,500 American troops and had cost nearly a trillion dollars—all with no assurance that the new Iraqi government would be on friendly terms with the United States over the long run.

Thus, as is true of multilateralism, unilateralism has limits. Even with the world's most powerful military, the United States found it difficult to bear the brunt of the Iraq conflict. Wars of this type do not lend themselves to quick and tidy battlefield solutions. It is one thing to defeat a conventional army in open warfare and quite another to prevail in a conflict in which the fight is not so much a battle for territory as it is a struggle for people's loyalties, especially when they distrust each other, as in the case of Iraq's Sunnis, Shiites, and Kurds.

POLITICAL

 ### THINKING Has It Been Worth It?

After a dozen years of war in Iraq and Afghanistan, the United States is slowly withdrawing its combat units from that troubled region of the world. Observers agree that much has been accomplished in this period but also that the costs have been high—over a trillion dollars spent and nearly seven thousand U.S. troops killed. Based on your understanding of these wars, do you think they were worth the cost, or do you think the United States would have been better off if it had chosen not to go to war? Do you have the same opinion of both wars, or do you feel differently about the Iraq war than about the Afghan war?

The Afghanistan Escalation and Pakistan

When the United States shifted its main theater of military operations to Iraq in 2003, the situation in Afghanistan began to deteriorate. The newly installed Afghan government, headed by Hamid Karzai, proved to be ineffective and corrupt, and the Taliban regrouped, slowly reasserting control over parts of the country, while using neighboring Pakistan as a safe haven.

During the 2008 presidential campaign, Obama argued that Afghanistan was America's "war of necessity." A month after taking office, he ordered twenty

unilateralism

The situation in which one nation takes action against another state or states.

In late 2011, the last U.S. combat troops left Iraq, crossing the border into neighboring Kuwait.

thousand additional troops to be deployed to Afghanistan. Nine months later, after a months-long series of meetings with top advisors, he ordered the deployment of thirty thousand more troops, while urging America's NATO allies to also increase their troop levels. The escalation had a threefold purpose: to disrupt the Taliban resurgence, to speed the training of Afghan army and police, and to provide a level of security that would strengthen Afghans' confidence in their government. At the same time, Obama rejected an open-ended commitment in Afghanistan, setting 2011 as the year in which troop withdrawals would begin and establishing 2014 as the year in which the last units would leave.

The Afghan surge reversed the Taliban's gains and weakened its fighting capacity but also had the effect of increasing tensions between NATO forces and the Afghan government and people. The heightened combat associated with the surge resulted in an increase in the number of innocent civilians killed and each such incident sparked public protests. In 2012, riots broke out when Afghans discovered that an American unit had incinerated copies of the Muslim holy book, the Koran. As in Iraq, it had become clear that tolerance of America's presence in Afghanistan was wearing thin and that the strategic goal—a stable and peaceful Afghanistan—was proving to be elusive.

The Afghan conflict is complicated by America's uneasy relationship with Pakistan, which shares a porous border with Afghanistan. Afghan rebels hide out in Pakistan and stage cross-border raids from there, supported covertly by factions within the Pakistani military and government. Although the Pakistan government has assisted American forces in some areas, it has resisted getting drawn more deeply into the conflict, fearing that any such commitment would spark domestic protests, even terrorist acts. Pakistan reacted angrily when the United States failed to alert it to the raid into Pakistan in 2011 that resulted in the killing of Osama bin Laden. Later in the same year, the Pakistani government shut down NATO supply routes through Pakistan after a U.S. air strike accidentally killed two dozen Pakistani soldiers stationed near the Afghan border.

Many analysts regard Pakistan as a larger security concern than is Afghanistan. Pakistan is a Muslim nation and has a large nuclear arsenal. If radical Islamists should come to power in Pakistan, the threat to U.S. interests would increase exponentially.

The Arab Spring and the Iranian Nuclear Threat

In late 2010, demonstrators flooded the streets of Tunisia's capital to protest government corruption and oppression. Within a month, Tunisia's authoritarian president had been forced from office. The unrest spread to Egypt where demonstrators overthrew Hosni Mubarak, who had been the country's authoritarian president for three decades. He, too, was soon forced from office. Similar protests erupted in nearly every Arab country, leading observers to proclaim an "Arab Spring"—the demand of Arab populations for a larger say in their governing.

The United States had been on friendly terms with most of these Arab regimes and was caught off guard by the scale of the uprisings. Eventually, the United States pressured its Arab allies to undertake political reforms. In the case of Libya, a long-time adversary, the United States intervened militarily, joining other NATO countries in an aerial bombardment that helped overthrow the regime of Muammar Gaddafi, who had sponsored the bombing of an American commercial airliner in 1988 that killed all 243 passengers and 16 crew members. The United States also intervened actively on behalf of dissidents in Syria, although relying on economic and diplomatic sanctions rather than military force.

As the Arab Spring was unfolding, Iran was moving ever closer to developing a nuclear weapons capacity, which would have a destabilizing effect on the Middle East. In an effort to force Iran to end its nuclear program, the United States took the lead in imposing UN-backed economic sanctions on Iran. The United States also froze Iranian financial assets in U.S. banks and their overseas branches and, along with its European allies, imposed an embargo on Iranian oil. Simultaneously, the United States pressured Israel to refrain from a preemptive attack on Iran's nuclear facilities, concerned that any such attack would disrupt the supply of Middle East oil and could provoke a regional war. (In recent years, as Figure 17-1 indicates, Iran has emerged as the nation that Americans regard as their country's "greatest enemy.")

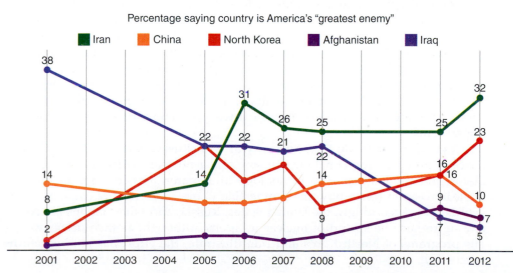

Percentage saying country is America's "greatest enemy"

FIGURE 17-1

Americans' Perception of the Nation's "Greatest Enemy"
In recent years, Iran has emerged as the country that Americans see as the "greatest enemy," a perception that owes partly to the threat posed by Iran's nuclear weapons program.
Source: Gallup Poll Organization, February 20, 2012. The survey question asked: "What one country anywhere in the world do you regard to be the United States' greatest enemy today?"

Even if Iran's nuclear program was the only problem facing U.S. policymakers, the challenge would be substantial. When combined with the ongoing war in Afghanistan, the uprising in the Arab world, the continuing threat of international terrorism, and instability in the global economy, the challenge is truly enormous. Ambassador Nicholas Burns, one of America's most respected diplomats, has called the current period "the most challenging time for the United States since World War II."[11] It is by no means clear, for example, that the Arab Spring will result in governments friendly to the United States, any more than it is certain that the Afghanistan government, which the United States has underwritten for a dozen years, will be a reliable partner in the years ahead.

The Military Dimension of National Security Policy

Defense spending by the United States is far higher than that of any other nation. In fact, the United States accounts for more than 40 percent of all military spending worldwide (see "How the U.S. Differs"). The U.S. defense budget exceeded $600 billion in 2010, a level of military spending that is five times that of China and more than eight times that of Russia.

Military Power, Uses, and Capabilities

U.S. military forces are trained for different types of military action, ranging from nuclear conflict to terrorism.

Nuclear War

Although the possibility of all-out nuclear war declined dramatically with the collapse of the Soviet Union, the United States retains a nuclear arsenal designed to prevent such a war. **Deterrence policy** is based on the concept of mutually assured destruction (MAD). The assumption is that any nation would be deterred from launching a full-scale nuclear attack by the knowledge that, even if it destroyed the United States, it too would be obliterated.

America's nuclear weapons are deployed in what is called the "nuclear triad." This term refers to the three ways—by land-based missiles, submarine-based missiles, and bombers—that nuclear weapons can be launched. The triad provides a second-strike capability—that is, the ability to absorb a first-strike nuclear attack and survive with enough nuclear capacity for a massive retaliation (second strike). Since the end of the cold war, the United States and Russia have negotiated substantial reductions in their nuclear arsenals and have established monitoring systems designed to reduce the possibility that either side could launch an effective surprise attack. In 2010, for example, the two countries signed a pact reducing their nuclear weapons and tightening the monitoring systems.

A greater fear today than nuclear war with Russia is the possibility that a terrorist group or rogue nation will smuggle a nuclear device into the United States and detonate it. The technology and materials necessary to build a nuclear weapon (or to buy one clandestinely) are more readily available than ever before. Accordingly, the United States, Russia, and other nations are cooperating to halt the spread of nuclear weapons, although, as the nuclear weapons programs of North Korea and Iran illustrate, the effort has not been fully successful.

deterrence policy

The idea that nuclear war can be discouraged if each side in a conflict has the capacity to destroy the other with nuclear weapons.

HOW THE U.S. DIFFERS POLITICAL THINKING THROUGH COMPARISONS

Worldwide Military Spending

The United States spends more than 40 percent of all the money spent worldwide on the military. The U.S. military establishment is huge and deployed across the globe. More than half a trillion dollars each year are spent on national defense. China is second in military spending, but its expenditures are only a fifth of those of the United States. Russia spends about an eighth of what the United States spends. Even on a per-capita basis, the United States ranks far ahead of other nations in military spending.

The United States has pressured its Western allies to carry a larger share of the defense burden, but many of them have resisted, contending that the cost would be too high and that their security would not improve substantially. Of America's European allies, Britain and France spend the most on their military.

Q: What do you make of the disparity in military spending between the United States and its military allies? Do you think they spend too little on defense, relying too heavily on the United States for their security? Or do you think the United States spends *too much on defense, placing too much emphasis on military force as an instrument of foreign policy?*

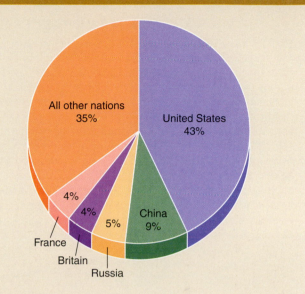

Source: From Center for Arms Control and Non-Proliferation (2008).

Conventional War

Not since World War II has the United States fought an all-out conventional war, nor at present does it have the capacity to do so. Such a war would require the reinstatement of the military draft and the full mobilization of the nation's industrial capacity. Instead, the U.S. armed forces are structured to be capable of fighting two medium-sized wars simultaneously if necessary. The U.S. military clearly has the capacity to fight a limited conventional war. When U.S. forces invaded Iraq in 2003, they were outnumbered three to one by Iraqi army units. Nevertheless, U.S. ground forces seized control of Baghdad within three weeks, at which time the remaining Iraqi military units quit the field.

The United States today relies on an all-volunteer military force (see "How the 50 States Differ") that is second to none in its destructive power. The U.S. Navy has a dozen aircraft carriers, scores of attack submarines, and hundreds of fighting and supply ships. The U.S. Air Force has thousands of high-performance aircraft, ranging from fighter jets to jumbo transport planes. The U.S. Army has roughly five hundred thousand regular troops and more than three hundred thousand Reserve and National Guard soldiers, who are supplied with tanks, artillery pieces, armored personnel carriers, and attack helicopters. This armament is doubly lethal because it is linked to sophisticated surveillance, targeting, and communication systems. No other nation has anywhere near the advanced weapons systems that the United States possesses.

In 2012, Leon Panetta, the secretary of defense, announced that the United States would be restructuring its military in response to budget pressures and changing security needs. Conventional forces—soldiers and marines—will be reduced by one hundred thousand while the military's special forces units and quick-strike capacities will be increased. The United States, said Panetta, is aiming for "a smaller, leaner force" while "retaining the ability to defeat any enemy on land."[12]

HOW THE 50 STATES DIFFER POLITICAL THINKING THROUGH COMPARISONS

THE ALL-VOLUNTEER MILITARY'S RECRUITS

Until 1973, the United States had an active military draft. Upon reaching age eighteen, males were required to register for the draft. Local draft boards would then pick the draftees based on quotas that varied with the size of the local population. Accordingly, each state contributed equally to the military's manpower needs relative to its population size. Today's military is an all-volunteer force, and the states' contributions vary significantly. The map below indicates the degree to which each state is over- and underrepresented in the military, as indicated by the ratio of military recruits from a state to the number of males aged eighteen to thirty-four in that state's population. Montana has the largest number of recruits relative to its population, followed in order by Alaska, Wyoming, and Maine. Utah, Rhode Island, and Massachusetts rank lowest, in that order.

Q: What might explain why military recruits come disproportionately from states like Montana, Alaska, Wyoming, and Maine, as well as from the southern states?

A: According to Department of Defense data, recruits are more likely to come from rural areas, particularly areas where few well-paying jobs are available to young adults. The four states with the highest recruitment ratios have these characteristics. As for the South, higher recruitment levels have been explained in terms of its stronger military tradition and its numerous military installations. Individuals from areas near these installations, as well as the sons and daughters of military personnel, are more likely to enlist in the military. (Mississippi and Tennessee, with the South's lowest recruitment rates, have relatively few military installations.)

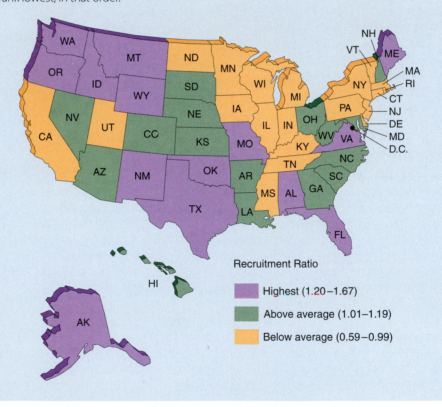

Recruitment Ratio

■ Highest (1.20–1.67)

■ Above average (1.01–1.19)

■ Below average (0.59–0.99)

Source: Adapted from Tim Kane, "Who Bears the Burden? Demographic Characteristics of U.S. Military Recruits before and after 9/11", Heritage Foundation, Center for Data Analysis Report #05-08, November 7, 2005. Used by permission of The Heritage Foundation.

Unconventional (Guerrilla) War

America's military firepower is not a large advantage in so-called unconventional wars of the type taking place in Afghanistan. The insurgents employ guerrilla tactics including hit-and-run attacks, roadside explosive devices, and suicide bombings, as well as the killing and intimidation of civilians who side with the Afghan government. Such tactics are extremely difficult to defend against and virtually impossible to stop by conventional means.

Unlike a conventional war, in which the measures of success are territory gained, casualties inflicted, and combat units destroyed, an unconventional war requires winning the support of the people or, as it is described, "winning their hearts and minds." Insurgents depend on the local population for recruits, intelligence, hiding places, and food. If they can be denied access to these resources, their military capability falls dramatically. Tactically, an unconventional war is fought with small and highly mobile combat units that can provide security to local populations and can seek out insurgent forces. A successful counterinsurgency also involves providing indigenous military and police forces with the training and equipment they need in order to gradually assume responsibility for their nation's security.[13]

Although the U.S. military has special operations units (such as the U.S. Army's Special Forces), and provides its regular units with some training in counterinsurgency warfare, the U.S. military for the most part is not structured to fight unconventional wars. As a consequence, it had difficulty adapting to the wars in Iraq and Afghanistan, just as it struggled to adapt to the war in Vietnam four decades earlier. The restructuring of the armed services that is now under way is designed to correct this imbalance.

Transnational Terrorism

The terrorist attacks of September 11, 2001, thrust the U.S. military into a new kind of war—a war on terrorism. The United States was not prepared for a terrorist war when it was attacked in 2001. Its intelligence agencies had not focused their efforts on terrorist activity, and its military units had few linguists who spoke the terrorists' languages.

Shown here is one of the many wanted posters that the U.S. government circulated in its hunt for Osama bin Laden, who planned the deadly attacks of September 11, 2001. He was killed in a clandestine U.S. operation in Pakistan in 2011.

FBI TEN MOST WANTED FUGITIVE

MURDER OF U.S. NATIONALS OUTSIDE THE UNITED STATES; CONSPIRACY TO MURDER U.S. NATIONALS OUTSIDE THE UNITED STATES; ATTACK ON A FEDERAL FACILITY RESULTING IN DEATH

USAMA BIN LADEN

Date of Photograph Unknown

Aliases: Usama Bin Muhammad Bin Ladin, Shaykh Usama Bin Ladin, the Prince, the Emir, Abu Abdallah, Mujahid Shaykh, Hajj, the Director

DEBATING THE ISSUES POLITICAL THINKING IN ACTION

Should U.S. Military Spending Be Reduced?

In 2012, President Barack Obama announced reductions in defense spending, partly because Congress was seeking ways to reduce federal spending and partly because his national security advisors had concluded that the U.S. military could be restructured in ways that would make it more cost effective. Conventional army and marine units would be cut from seven hundred thousand personnel to six hundred thousand, while the military's technology, quick-strike capacity, and special forces units would be increased. Obama's plan was attacked by Republican presidential nominee Mitt Romney. He accused Obama of being weak on national defense and of failing to understand America's special role in the world. Here are excerpts of their remarks that highlight some of the differences in their views on military spending.

YES Even as our troops continue to fight in Afghanistan, the tide of war is receding. Even as our forces prevail in today's missions, we have the opportunity—and the responsibility—to look ahead to the force that we are going to need in the future. . . . That's why I called for this comprehensive defense review—to clarify our strategic interests in a fast-changing world, and to guide our defense priorities and spending over the coming decade—because the size and the structure of our military and defense budgets have to be driven by a strategy, not the other way around. . . . As we look beyond the wars in Iraq and Afghanistan—and the end of long-term nation-building with large military footprints—we'll be able to ensure our security with smaller conventional ground forces. We'll continue to get rid of outdated Cold War–era systems so that we can invest in the capabilities that we need for the future, including intelligence, surveillance and reconnaissance, counterterrorism, countering weapons of mass destruction and the ability to operate in environments where adversaries try to deny us access. So, yes, our military will be leaner, but the world must know the United States is going to maintain our military superiority with armed forces that are agile, flexible and ready for the full range of contingencies and threats. . . . I'd encourage all of us to remember what President Eisenhower once said—that "each proposal must be weighed in the light of a broader consideration: the need to maintain balance in and among national programs." After a decade of war, and as we rebuild the source of our strength—at home and abroad—it's time to restore that balance.

—Barack Obama, President of the United States

NO President Obama is shrinking our military and hollowing out our national defense. I will insist on a military so powerful that no one in the world would ever think of challenging us. President Obama seems to believe that America's role as leader in the world is a thing of the past. I believe the 21st century will be and must be an American century. . . . It is only American power--conceived in the broadest terms—that can provide the foundation of an international system that ensures the security and prosperity of the United States and our friends and allies around the world. . . . America is not destined to be one of several equally balanced global powers. America must lead the world, or someone else will. Without American leadership, without clarity of American purpose and resolve, the world becomes a far more dangerous place, and liberty and prosperity would surely be among the first casualties. The United States should always retain military supremacy to deter would-be aggressors and to defend our allies and ourselves. If America is the undisputed leader of the world, it reduces our need to police a more chaotic world. [We must reverse] Obama-era cuts to national missile defense. [I will] prioritize the full deployment of a multilayered national ballistic missile defense system. . . .This is America's moment. We should embrace the challenge, not shrink from it, not crawl into an isolationist shell, not wave the white flag of surrender, nor give in to those who assert America's time has passed. That is utter nonsense. An eloquently justified surrender of world leadership is still surrender.

—Mitt Romney, Republican presidential nominee

Q: What is your view of this issue? What military structure and spending level do you think are appropriate for the challenges the United States will face in the coming years?

---

transnational terrorism

Terrorism that transcends national borders and often targets people and locations other than the ones directly at issue.

Terrorism is not by itself a new form of warfare. It has been employed in many places over the centuries, but it has become a broader threat in recent years. Historically, terrorism was a domestic problem, employed by disgruntled groups against their own government. Terrorism today has an international dimension. **Transnational terrorism** is terrorism that transcends national borders and includes attacks on nonmilitary targets.[14] When terrorists attacked the United States in 2001, or bombed the Madrid commuter system in 2004, they were not seeking to take over the United States or Spain. They were seeking to alter the balance of power in the Middle East by forcing Western nations to rethink their presence in the region.

America's war on terrorism is aimed at groups, such as al Qaeda, rather than nations. Al Qaeda is a nonstate actor without clearly defined borders, which complicates the task of locating and destroying it. Moreover, transnational terrorists have become adept at waging "asymmetric war," so called because they lack the strength to directly engage opposing military forces. In fighting their wars, terrorists resort to improvised weapons, including suicide bombers.

The war on terrorism lacks sharply defined battlefronts and is being waged through a variety of instruments, including military force, intelligence gathering, law enforcement, foreign aid, international cooperation, and immigration control. In reality, the main responsibility for rooting out terrorist cells rests with law enforcement and intelligence agencies in the United States and abroad rather than with military units. Recent arrests of suspected terrorists in the United States, Europe, Africa, Asia, and South America have usually been the result of the work of nonmilitary agencies.

The Politics of National Defense

Policy elites, public opinion, and special interests all play significant roles in national defense policy. The American public usually backs the judgment of its political leaders on the use of military force. In nearly all military initiatives of the past half-century, Americans have supported the action at the outset. When President Bush ordered U.S. forces to invade Iraq in 2003,[15] two-thirds of Americans supported his decision. The rest were split between those who opposed the war and those who were unsure about the proper course of action.

On the other hand, if a war begins to seem endless, public support inevitably erodes.[16] A swing in public opinion against the Vietnam War forced U.S. policymakers to withdraw American troops in 1973. Public opinion on the Iraq war soured more quickly, partly because the stated reason for the war—the threat of Iraq's WMDs—proved faulty. Public support for the Afghan war has eroded to the point where most Americans now think that U.S. troops should be withdrawn from Afghanistan.[17]

Although the public has an influence on war policy, it is not informed or interested enough to affect most national security policies, which are decided largely by the president and Congress in consultation with top experts and military officers. Of these various actors, the president has the most say, as indicated by President Obama's unilateral decision in 2011 to commit U.S. airpower to assist rebel forces in Libya.

The defense industry also has a say in national security policy. In his 1961 farewell address, President Dwight D. Eisenhower, who had commanded U.S. forces in Europe during World War II, warned Americans against "the unwarranted influence" and "misplaced power" of what he termed "the military-industrial complex." Eisenhower was referring to the fact that national defense is big business, involving the annual expenditure of hundreds of billions of dollars.[18] As Eisenhower described it, the **military-industrial complex** has three main components: the military establishment, the arms industry, and the members of Congress from states and districts that depend heavily on the arms industry. All three benefit from a high level of defense spending, whether needed or not. The defense industry suffered a rare defeat in 2009 when Congress, backed by President Obama and Defense Secretary Robert Gates, refused to appropriate funds for building additional F-22 fighter jets. The F-22 is the world's most sophisticated fighter jet, but it is hugely expensive and excels at air-to-air combat, a type of warfare that the United States has not fought on any scale since the

military-industrial complex

The three components (the military establishment, the industries that manufacture weapons, and the members of Congress from states and districts that depend heavily on the arms industry) that mutually benefit from a high level of defense spending.

Dwight D. Eisenhower was Supreme Commander of Allied Forces in Europe during World War II and was elected president in 1952. Though trained in the art of war, Eisenhower sought throughout his presidency to reduce cold war tensions. As his presidency was ending, he used his farewell address to warn of the dangers of the military-industrial complex, arguing that sustained high levels of military expenditure and secrecy would weaken America in the long run.

Korean War. Secretary Gates said the military would be better served by less expensive aircraft suited to wars of the type fought in Iraq and Afghanistan. Nevertheless, forty-two senators voted to continue production of the F-22. Some of them were less concerned with the F-22's cost and capabilities than with the fact that tens of thousands of jobs in more than forty states would be lost if production were stopped.

The Economic Dimension of National Security Policy

National security is more than an issue of military might. It is also a question of maintaining a strong position in the global economy. Geographically, the world has three major economic centers. One is the United States, which produces roughly 25 percent of the world's goods and services. Another center, also responsible for about 25 percent of the world's economy, is the European Union (EU), which includes most European countries. The EU is dominated by Germany, Britain, and France, which together account for roughly half its economy. The third center is the Pacific Rim, anchored by the economies of Japan and China, which together account for more than 15 percent of the world's economy.

By some indicators, the United States is the weakest of the three economic centers. Its trade deficit is easily the world's largest. The United States imports substantially more goods and services than it exports. In fact, the United States has not had a trade surplus since 1975 and over the past decade its deficit has exceeded $300 billion annually (see Figure 17-2).

In other ways, however, the United States is the strongest of the three centers. According to the Switzerland-based World Economic Forum, the United States is economically more competitive than its major rivals. The United States owes this position to several factors, including its technological innovation, financial institutions, and extensive higher education system.[19] The U.S. economy is also the most diversified of the three. In addition to its industrial base, the United States has a strong agricultural sector and abundant natural resources. Its vast fertile plains and advanced farming methods have made it the world's leading agricultural producer. The United States ranks among the top three countries worldwide in production of wheat, corn, soybeans, peanuts, cotton, eggs, cattle, and pigs. As for natural resources, the United States ranks among the top five nations in deposits of copper, uranium, lead, sulfur, zinc, coal, gold, iron ore, natural gas, silver, and magnesium.[20]

Nevertheless, the United States does not have the option of "going it alone" economically. To meet Americans' production and consumption needs, the country depends on other countries' raw materials, finished goods, markets, and capital. This imperative requires the United States to exert global economic influence. The broad goals of the United States in the world economy include the following:[21]

■ Sustaining a stable and open system of trade that will promote prosperity at home

■ Maintaining access to oil and other natural resources vital to the strength of the U.S. economy

■ Preventing the widening gap between rich and poor countries from disrupting the world economy

■ Contributing to the stability of the global economy

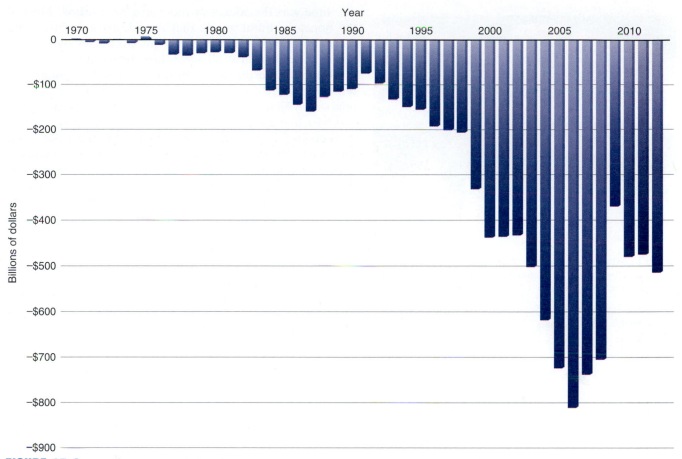

FIGURE 17-2 **The U.S. Trade Deficit** Not since 1975 has the United States had a trade surplus; the annual deficit has not dropped below $300 billion at any time during the past decade.

Source: U.S. Bureau of Economic Analysis, 2012.

Promoting Global Trade

After World War II, the United States helped enact a global trading system with itself at the center. The U.S. dollar had become the leading currency of international trade, replacing the English pound, which held that position for more than a century. World War II had weakened Britain's global economic position and elevated that of the United States, which quickly asserted its dominance. A key initiative was the European Recovery Plan, better known as the Marshall Plan. It included an unprecedented amount of aid (more than $100 billion in today's dollars) for the postwar rebuilding of Europe. Apart from enabling the countries of Western Europe to better confront the perceived Soviet threat, the Marshall Plan served America's economic needs. Wartime production had lifted the United States out of the Great Depression, but the immediate postwar period was marked by a recession and renewed fears of hard times. A rebuilt Western Europe would become a much-needed market for American products.

Since then, major shifts have taken place in the world economy. Germany is now a trading rival of the United States, as is Japan, which also received substantial postwar reconstruction aid from the United States. More recently, China and the European Union have taken their place as trading giants, and Russia, propelled by its huge oil and gas reserves, has the potential to become one.

Today, the American economy depends more heavily on international commerce than in any period in history. The domestic manufacturing sector that at

Some U.S. firms are now as recognizable in other countries as they are in the United States. Shown here is a Pepsi billboard alongside a road in Vietnam.

multinational (transnational) corporations

Business firms with major operations in more than one country.

economic globalization

The increased interdependence of nations' economies. The change is a result of technological, transportation, and communication advances that have enabled firms to deploy their resources around the globe.

free trade

The condition in which tariffs and other barriers to trade between nations are kept to a minimum.

tariffs

The taxes that a country levies on goods shipped into it from other countries.

protectionism

The placing of the immediate interests of domestic producers (through, for example, protective tariffs) above that of free trade between nations.

one time was the source of most jobs has shrunk. Most of the nonagricultural goods that Americans now buy, from television sets to automobiles, are produced by foreign firms. Indeed, nearly all large U.S. firms are themselves **multinational corporations** (or **transnational corporations**), with operations in more than one country. From a head-quarters in New York City, a firm has no difficulty managing a production facility in Thailand that is filling orders for markets in Europe and South America. Money, goods, and services today flow freely and rapidly across national borders, and large U.S. firms increasingly think about markets in global terms. As a result, they sometimes engage in activities that conflict with America's foreign policy goals. In Africa, for example, U.S. oil companies have sometimes supported dictatorial regimes in order to maintain access to oil fields.

Economic globalization is a term that describes the increased interdependence of nations' economies. This development is both an opportunity for and a threat to U.S. economic interests. The opportunity rests with the possibility of increased demand abroad for U.S. products and lower prices to U.S. consumers as a result of inexpensive imports. The threat lies in the fact that foreign firms also compete in the global marketplace and may use their competitive advantages, such as cheaper labor, to outposition U.S. firms.

In general, international commerce works best when countries trade freely with one another. This situation keeps the price of traded items, whether finished goods or raw materials, at their lowest level, resulting in economic efficiency (see Chapter 15). However, global trade is a political issue as well as an economic one, and there are conflicting views on international trade. **Free trade** holds that barriers to international trade should be kept to a minimum. Proponents of free trade claim that the long-term economic interests of all countries are advanced when **tariffs** (taxes on imported goods) and other trade barriers are kept to a minimum. Most free-trade advocates couple their advocacy with fair-trade demands, but they are committed, philosophically and practically, to the idea that free trade results in a net gain for firms and consumers. The 1993 North American Free Trade Agreement (NAFTA) was a product of this thinking. It created a largely free market between the United States, Canada, and Mexico.

Since then, the United States has negotiated free-trade agreements with several countries. The most recent are bilateral agreements with Panama, Columbia, and Korea, which were negotiated during the Bush administration and ratified under the Obama administration. In 2011, President Obama proposed yet another such agreement, perhaps the most ambitious yet. If approved by Congress, the Trans Pacific Partnership (also called the Pacific Rim Trade Agreement) would include Australia, Brunei, Chile, Malaysia, New Zealand, Peru, Singapore, Vietnam, and the United States and could eventually include other Pacific nations. The United States has also been deeply involved in the World Trade Organization (WTO). Created in 1995, the WTO is the formal international institution through which most nations negotiate general rules of trade.[22] The WTO's mission is to promote global free trade through reductions in tariffs, protections for intellectual property (copyrights and patents), and other policies. Trade disputes among WTO members are settled by arbitration panels, which consist of representatives from the member nations.

Although the United States has clearly been a leader in promoting free trade, some Americans advocate **protectionism,** which holds that domestic producers should be protected from foreign competitors. The classic protectionist measure is a tariff on a particular import, which raises the market price of the product, thereby giving domestic producers of the same product a competitive advantage. For some protectionists, the issue is a simple matter of defending domestic firms against their foreign competitors. For others, the issue is one of fair trade. They are protectionists in those instances where foreign firms have an unfair competitive advantage as a result, for example, of a subsidy from their government that enables them to market their goods at an artificially low price.

Protectionist sentiment is usually stronger in Congress than in the White House. Although most members of Congress say they support free trade, many of them act differently when a key economic interest in their state or district is threatened by foreign competition. In such cases, they seek protective measures, such as a tariff on the competitor's products. Often, they find public support for their position. Although many Americans regard free trade as a net benefit for the United States in terms of less-expensive products and export opportunities, many others think that free trade harms American firms and workers by opening the U.S. market to goods from countries that have cheap labor and poor environmental standards (see Figure 17-3).

Economists argue that economic disruption is an inevitable result of market change and that firms should try to adapt to the change rather than turn to government for protection. Elected officials, however, cannot take the long-range view so easily because they face immediate pressures from constituents who have lost jobs and from communities that have lost firms. In response to such pressures, U.S. officials have insisted that foreign governments halt practices that put American firms at an unfair disadvantage. In 2009, for example, President Obama placed a 35 percent tariff on the import of Chinese tires on the grounds that the Chinese government was subsidizing their production. However, other countries are not convinced that the United States itself always plays fair. In 2006, international trade talks collapsed in part because the United States refused to reduce its hefty farm subsidies, which enable U.S. agricultural producers to sell their products at a low price in world markets, thereby giving them a competitive advantage.

Trade with China is a particularly vexing issue.[23] In the past decade, America's trade deficit with China has increased more than thirtyfold, surpassing $250 billion annually. The United States has provided China with a marketplace for its goods, which has helped fuel China's economic growth. In turn, China has provided the United States with inexpensive goods, which has satisfied the demands of America's consumers and kept inflation in check. Nevertheless, the trade deficit with China is a growing concern. The United States has pressured China to increase the value of its currency (the yuan), which would increase the price of the goods it exports for sale, thereby making American goods more competitive with those produced in China.

China is also a key to the future of the U.S. dollar as the world's preferred reserve currency. Because of its trade advantage with the United States, China holds more than $1 trillion in U.S. treasury bonds—the largest such holding in the world. The value of China's holding declines as the dollar declines in value, which is a realistic prospect given America's huge national debt (see Chapter 15). China and other countries, including Russia and Japan, have threatened to reduce their holdings in dollars, which would put additional pressure on the value of the dollar. "We have lent a huge amount of money to the U.S.," Chinese premier Wen Jiabao said in 2009. "Of course we are concerned about the safety of our assets." If the dollar should decline sharply in value, the United States would be

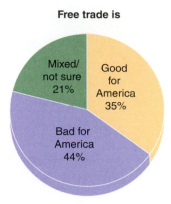

Free trade is

FIGURE 17-3
Americans' Opinions on Free Trade
Americans are divided in their opinions on free trade, with some thinking that it helps the country and others thinking that it harms American firms and workers.
Source: Pew Research Center survey, October 2010.

Although the Chinese yuan (also called the renminbi) will not rival the American dollar as the dominant international currency any time soon, it has become a symbol of China's rise to global economic prominence.

forced to pay a higher rate of interest to get other countries to buy its bonds, which would raise the cost of borrowing and add to America's debt problem.

China's growing economy has enabled it to enlarge its navy, which had been structured to protect China's territorial waters but is now being configured to operate throughout the Pacific. China launched its first aircraft carrier in 2011 and is in the process of building attack submarines and missile ships. In response to China's naval buildup, the United States has enlarged its Pacific fleet and has increased the number of joint naval exercises with Asian countries, including in 2011 a naval exercise with its one-time opponent, Vietnam.

Maintaining Access to Oil and Other Natural Resources

For decades, America has used its economic and military power to protect its access to natural resources, particularly oil. Although the United States produces a significant amount of oil domestically, it provides only about half of what the nation consumes. The United States gets most of its oil imports from Canada and Latin America, but the price of oil is determined by worldwide production and demand. The demand for oil has risen as a result of rapid economic growth in China, India, Brazil, and other developing countries, which has created upward pressure on oil prices and has intensified efforts to increase oil production.[24]

The key oil-producing region is the Middle East, which has substantially larger oil reserves than elsewhere in the world. After World War II, the United States acquired a foothold in the region when its oil companies, with their technical capacity and huge amounts of capital, acquired a stake in Middle Eastern oil fields. Since then, U.S. firms have been leaders in worldwide oil exploration and production. Underpinning their activities is the military might of the United States. The U.S. Navy patrols the world's shipping routes to ensure that oil tankers reach their destinations safely.

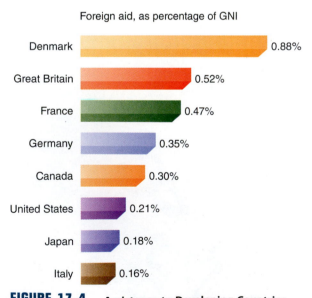

Foreign aid, as percentage of GNI

Denmark	0.88%
Great Britain	0.52%
France	0.47%
Germany	0.35%
Canada	0.30%
United States	0.21%
Japan	0.18%
Italy	0.16%

FIGURE 17-4 **Assistance to Developing Countries, as a Percentage of Gross National Income** The United States ranks highest in terms of total amount spent on foreign aid to developing countries but ranks lower in terms of percentage of gross national income (GNI).

Source: Organization for Economic Cooperation and Development, 2012.

Assisting Developing Nations

Industrialized nations have a stake in helping developing nations to grow. With growth comes greater political stability as well as markets for the goods and services that industrialized nations produce. For such reasons, the United States provides developmental assistance to poorer countries. Contributions include direct foreign aid and also indirect assistance through international organizations, such as the International Monetary Fund (IMF) and the World Bank, which were created by the United States and Great Britain at the Bretton Woods Conference near the end of World War II. The IMF makes short-term loans to keep countries experiencing temporary problems from collapsing economically or resorting to destructive practices such as the unrestricted printing of paper money. For its part, the World Bank makes long-term development loans to poor countries for capital investment projects such as dams, highways, and factories.

Since World War II, the United States has been the leading source of aid to developing countries. Although the United States still contributes the most in terms of total dollars, Canada and European countries now spend more on a per capita basis than does the United States (see Figure 17-4). America's fiscal problems, and its costly wars in Iraq and

PARTY

POLARIZATION Political Thinking in Conflict

Hard Power or Soft Power?

Until the Vietnam War, there was little partisan difference in Americans' views on national security. A bipartisan consensus prevailed with Republicans and Democrats alike convinced of the need to contain Soviet communism, by force if necessary. America's defeat in Vietnam disrupted the consensus. Since then, nearly every American conflict has been less strongly supported by Democrats, who have placed more emphasis on diplomacy, economic sanctions, and foreign aid as the means of protecting U.S. interests. Joseph Nye, who served in national security positions in the Carter and Clinton administrations, coined the term "soft power" to describe this approach, contrasting it with the use of military force, which he characterized as "hard power."

It must be noted that the difference between Republicans and Democrats is one of degree rather than of kind. Democrats and Republicans alike recognize that military action, diplomacy, sanctions, and foreign aid all have a part to play in protecting the United States. Nevertheless, there are clear partisan differences when it comes to the instruments of national security policy, as indicated by the response of Republicans and Democrats in recent polls that have asked Americans which programs they would prefer to cut as a means of reducing the federal budget deficit.

Percent supporting cuts in:

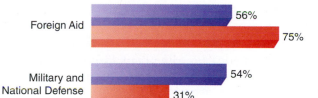

Foreign Aid 56%
75%

Military and National Defense 54%
31%

■ Democrats
■ Republicans

Sources: For foreign aid and military spending, respectively: Pew Research Center survey, January 26, 2011; Gallup survey, February 11, 2011.

Q. *Where do you stand on the question of the relative use of "hard power" and "soft power" as instruments of national security policy? What do you think might explain the different tendencies of Republicans and Democrats on this issue?*

Afghanistan, have weakened it ability to strengthen its position in the world through the use of foreign aid. Public opinion is also an obstacle to increased foreign aid spending. Most Americans believe the United States is already spending too much on foreign aid. In a poll that asked Americans to name the largest federal programs, foreign aid topped the list, with 27 percent identifying it as the most expensive program.[25] In reality, foreign aid is far down the list, accounting for only about 1 percent of federal spending.

As the United States has cut back on foreign aid spending, China has stepped up its spending. Through loans and grants, China is spending heavily on infrastructure and commercial projects in scores of countries in Africa, South America, and Asia. It is also pursuing mining and drilling projects in many of these countries, seeking to secure the raw materials needed to sustain its economic growth.

In a sense, China is following the path laid out by the United States after World War II, when it pursued a similar strategy as a means of extending its influence to other parts of the globe.

Stabilizing the Global Economy

When U.S. financial markets teetered on the edge in 2008, the impact was felt around the globe. Stock markets tumbled and governments rushed to institute policies that could stem the fall. The crisis taught policymakers a critical lesson: economic turbulence in one part of today's global economy spreads quickly to other parts as a result of increased economic interdependency.[26]

Policymakers around the globe also drew another lesson from the crisis: the need for cooperative mechanisms by which nations can coordinate their economic policies in order to reduce the likelihood that problems in one country will spill over to other countries. This responsibility has fallen largely on the G20, a group of twenty leading nations that includes the United States. Before the 2008 economic downturn, the G20 was a forum through which member nations' finance ministers (the secretary of treasury in the case of the United States) met periodically to share information and ideas. After the economic downturn, the G20 was upgraded to act as a council that could address issues related to the management of global economic and financial shocks. At the 2011 G20 meeting, for example, the members agreed to develop indicators to measure economic imbalances, such as the level of public debt that can place a country into default on its debt obligations,[27] as happened recently with Greece.

The United States has also led other efforts to stabilize the global economy. In 2009, for example, America's leading banks were subjected to a "stress test" to determine their ability to withstand defaults on the debt they are owed. Banks that failed the test were provided government loans to protect them from such defaults. U.S. policymakers urged other nations to do the same, recognizing that major financial institutions operate around the globe and that the collapse of even one of them can send a shock through the world economy.

As the example illustrates, the new global economy poses risks as well as benefits to the United States. At the end of World War II, the U.S. economy accounted for half of the world's economic output, and the United States was in a position to nearly define the terms of its economic relations with other countries. Today, it operates in a global economy marked by mutual dependence. The United States depends on the economic health of other nations, just as they are dependent on the health of the American economy. Thus, just as the United States faces a set of nearly unprecedented military challenges around the globe, it is confronting a set of nearly unprecedented economic ones. In the end, its national security will rest on its ability to respond effectively to both sets of challenges.

Summary

Self-Test www.mhhe.com/pattersontadtx11e

The chief instruments of national security policy are diplomacy, military force, economic exchange, and intelligence gathering. These are exercised through specialized agencies of the U.S. government, such as the Departments of State and Defense that are largely responsive to presidential leadership. National security policy has also relied on international organizations, such as the United Nations and the World Trade Organization, that are responsive to the global concerns of major nations.

From 1945 to 1990, U.S. foreign and defense policies were dominated by a concern with the Soviet Union. During most of this period, the United States pursued a policy of containment based on the premise that the Soviet Union was an aggressor nation bent on global conquest. Containment policy led the United States to enter into wars in Korea and Vietnam and to maintain a large defense establishment.

A first response to the end of the cold war period was multilateralism—the idea that major nations could achieve common goals by working together, including the use of force to restrain regional conflicts. The interventions in the Persian Gulf and the Balkans during the 1990s are examples. They demonstrated that major nations can intervene with some success in global hot spots but also showed that the ethnic, religious, and national conflicts that fuel these conflicts are not easily resolved.

The terrorist attacks on the World Trade Center and the Pentagon in 2001 led to broad changes in national security organization and strategy. Increased defense and homeland security spending has been coupled with a partial reorganization of U.S. intelligence, law enforcement, and immigration agencies, as well as new laws affecting the scope of their activities. However, the defining moment of the post–September 11 period was America's invasion of Iraq in 2003, which was rooted in President George W. Bush's preemptive war doctrine and his willingness to commit the United States to unilateral action. The locus of Middle East conflict has shifted recently to Afghanistan.

In recent decades, the United States has increasingly taken economic factors into account in its national security considerations, which has meant, for example, that trade has played a larger part in defining its relationships with other countries. The trading system that the United States helped erect after World War II has given way to one that is global in scale and more competitive. Changes in communication, transportation, and computing have altered the way large corporations operate, and as businesses have changed their practices, nations have had to adapt. The changes include the emergence of regional and international economic structures, such as the European Union, NAFTA, and the WTO. Nevertheless, nations naturally compete for economic advantage, including access to natural resources; accordingly, trade is a source of conflict as well as a source of cooperation.

CHAPTER 17

Study Corner

Key Terms

bipolar (power structure) (p. 437)

cold war (p. 437)

containment (p. 436)

deterrence policy (p. 444)

economic globalization (p. 452)

free trade (p. 452)

internationalist (p. 436)

isolationist (p. 436)

military-industrial complex (p. 449)

multilateralism (p. 438)

multinational (transnational) corporations (p. 452)

national interest (p. 436)

preemptive war doctrine (p. 440)

protectionism (p. 452)

transnational terrorism (p. 448)

tariffs (p. 452)

unilateralism (p. 441)

unipolar (power structure) (p. 438)

Self-Test: Multiple Choice

1. Diplomacy is distinct from military power as a foreign policymaking instrument in that diplomacy
   a. is effective only when used in conjunction with other instruments.
   b. requires a bilateral relationship; it cannot be employed unilaterally.
   c. is subject to direction by the president.
   d. is sometimes applied through an international intermediary, such as the United Nations.

2. International economic exchange takes place primarily through
   a. entering into military alliances that then turn into trading alliances.
   b. monitoring other countries' economic activities and enacting tariffs if necessary.
   c. developing trade relations with nations that are premised on the assumption that these relations will benefit both sides.
   d. military takeovers of countries that have raw materials of value.

3. Drawbacks to the pursuit of a policy of multilateralism include which of the following?
   a. Multilateral interventions are almost always less successful than when the United States acts unilaterally.
   b. Multilateral intervention does not guarantee long-term success in solving situations.

c. Multilateral interventions abroad almost always reduce the president's popularity at home.

d. All of the above.

4. The formal organization through which nations administer and negotiate the general rules governing international trade is
a. the United Nations.
b. NATO.
c. the World Bank.
d. the WTO.

5. The lesson of Vietnam for the United States was that
a. there are limits to America's ability to assert its will on the world.
b. America's military arsenal was obsolete and needed updating.
c. appeasement only encourages further aggression.
d. an isolationist foreign policy is the only safe direction for U.S. policy.

6. After World War II, the United States emerged as
a. an economically impoverished country.
b. the major country with the least amount of domestic oil reserves.
c. an internationalist country.
d. the world's only superpower.

7. The main threat to the physical security of the United States since the attacks on the World Trade Center and the Pentagon is international terrorists who fight on behalf of causes. (T/F)

8. High levels of congressional support for an expensive weapons program are sometimes linked more to the jobs it creates than to its overall usefulness to the U.S. arsenal. (T/F)

9. The United States spends more on foreign aid as a percentage of its total national budget than do most Western democracies. (T/F)

10. U.S. military intervention both in the Persian Gulf and in Kosovo not only punished the aggressor party in each case but also settled the underlying dispute once and for all. (T/F)

Self-Test: Essay

What are the major objectives of U.S. national security policy? What are the mechanisms for pursuing these objectives?

Suggested Readings

Clarke, Richard A. *Against All Enemies: Inside America's War on Terror.* New York: Free Press, 2004. A best-selling book by the nation's former top-ranking presidential advisor on terrorism.

Deese, David A. *World Trade Politics: Power, Principles, and Leadership.* New York: Routledge, 2007. A meticulous study of the politics of international trade negotiations.

Hixson, Walter L. *The Myth of American Diplomacy: National Identity and U.S. Foreign Policy.* New Haven, Conn.: Yale University Press, 2008. An analysis of the influence of America's cultural ideals on its foreign policy.

Klare, Michael T. *Rising Powers, Shrinking Planet: The New Geopolitics of Energy.* New York: Holt, 2009. An assessment of the energy and environmental challenges posed by global economic development.

Nye, Joseph S. *Soft Power: The Means to Success in World Politics.* New York: PublicAffairs, 2004. An argument for making diplomacy, assistance, and other forms of "soft power" the basis of U.S. foreign policy.

Pearlstein, Richard. *Fatal Future? Transnational Terrorism and the New Global Disorder.* Austin: University of Texas Press, 2004. A penetrating look at the dangers posed by transnational terrorism.

Sobel, Richard, Peter Furia, and Bethany Barratt, eds. *Public Opinion and International Intervention: Lessons from the Iraq War.* Dulles, Virginia: Potomac Books, 2012. A careful assessment of the impact of public opinion on foreign policy.

List of Websites

www.defenselink.mil
The U.S. Department of Defense website provides information on each of the armed services, daily news from the American Forces Information Service, and other material.

www.cfr.org
A website that includes reports and assessments of the Council of Foreign Relations and transcripts of speeches by U.S. and world political leaders on topics of international interest.

www.igc.org/igc
The website of the Institute for Global Communications (IGC) provides information and services to organizations and activists on a broad range of international issues, including human rights.

www.wto.org
The World Trade Organization (WTO) website contains information on the organization's activities and has links to related sites.

Participate!

In his 1961 inaugural address, President John F. Kennedy said, "Ask not what your country can do for you. Ask what you can do for your country." Kennedy called America's young people to service on behalf of their country. His call was not just a call to military service. One of Kennedy's early initiatives, the Peace Corps, offered Americans the opportunity to apply their skills to development projects in other countries. Under Kennedy's successor, President Lyndon Johnson, a domestic version of the Peace Corps—Volunteers in Service to America (VISTA)—was established. Before the military draft ended in 1973, male Americans were expected to serve their country. Not all did so, but millions served in the army, navy, air force, or marine corps. Since the end of the draft, Congress has from time to time considered establishing a national service that would require every young American man and woman to serve the country in one way or another for a set period of time. However, you do not need an act of Congress if you want to serve your country. A range of alternatives are available, including the all-volunteer military, the Peace Corps, and AmeriCorps (a network of local, state, and national service programs).

Extra Credit

For up-to-the-minute *New York Times* articles, interactive simulations, graphics, study tools, and more links and quizzes, visit the text's Online Learning Center at **www.mhhe. com/pattersontad11e**.

Self-Test Answers

1. b, 2. c, 3. b, 4. d, 5. a, 6. c, 7. T, 8. T, 9. F, 10. F

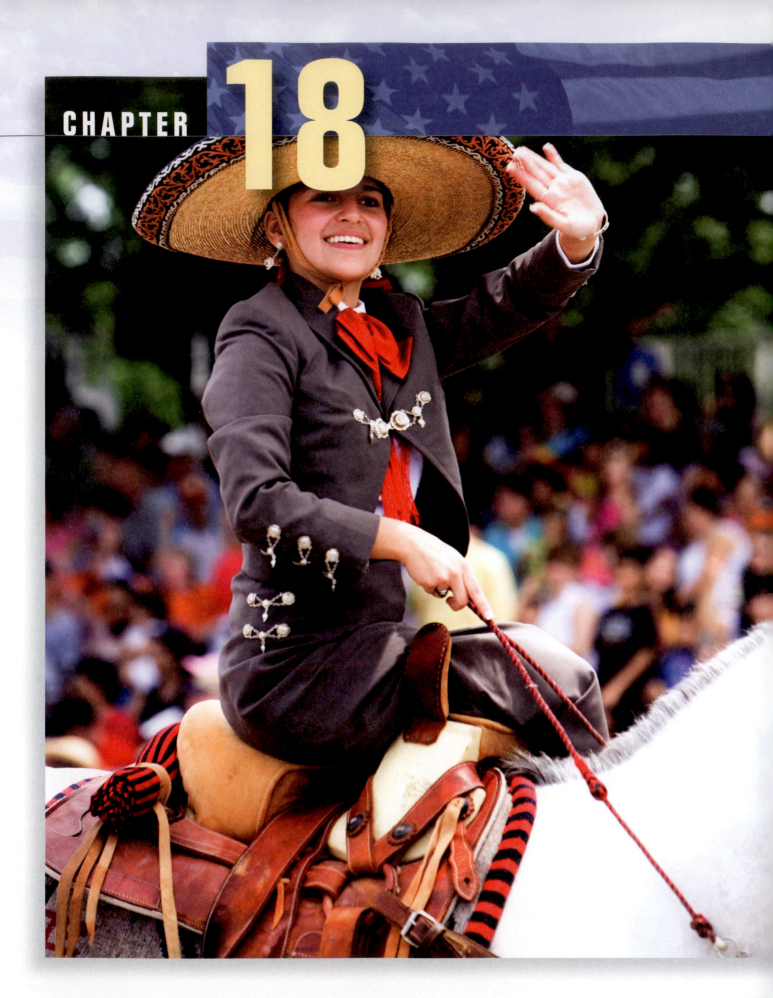

Introduction to Texas Government

Texas Society

Population Growth and the Changing Political Climate

The Political Culture of Texas

The Economy of Texas

In the past half century, Texas has changed greatly. Today, although the white, conservative society continues to thrive in a land first settled by the Spanish, social and economic diversity has turned Texas into a state of growing contrasts. Minorities have become a majority of the population, and urban professionals have built high-tech industries in the major cities. If Texas is still "a nation in every sense of the word,"[1] then it is a different nation, and these changes are having a profound impact on the politics of the state.

In this chapter, we trace settlement of Texas by different groups and analyze how economic development eventually created tremendous contrasts between regions and between urban and rural areas. We explore the ethnic makeup of Texas and analyze how the demographics are changing. We assess how different groups combined to form a political culture in Texas that is cautious of a powerful, centralized government. Finally, we examine the drastic economic changes Texas has undergone in recent decades as it transformed itself from an agrarian state to a leader in trade and technology. The following points are emphasized in this chapter:

- Regional variations arise from settlement patterns in different parts of Texas.

- The ethnic makeup of Texas is changing. While the African-American population has remained stable, the Hispanic population has increased making Texas one of four majority-minority states, one in which the white population makes up less than half of the total population.

- Despite regional and ethnic variations, Texans share a political culture that values traditionalism and individualism.

- Since the 1980s, Texas has replaced its dependence on oil and agriculture with a highly diversified economy. Texas has become a leader in technological development and a center of international trade.

Texas Society

Several years ago, Texas state tourism promotion literature used the theme "Texas, a Land of Contrasts." Texas is very much a land of contrasts, and this is reflected in its government and politics.

Texas is rural and urban, southern and western, Anglo, African American, and Latino. A southern state with a southern heritage, Texas is also a western state with a western heritage and a very strong Spanish and Mexican heritage.

The diversity of Texas history is reflected in the name of a popular theme park in the Dallas/Fort Worth area—Six Flags over Texas. Texas has been a Spanish colony, partially under French control; a Mexican state; an independent republic; a state in the United States; and a Confederate state. Each of these periods of its history has influenced what the state is today.

Settlement Patterns in Texas History

The contrasts in Texas society are better understood and take on meaning if we examine the history of **settlement patterns** in the state. The many origins of first settlers to the state have a significant impact on Texas politics today. This large state (268,601 square miles) has been a crossroads where the cultures of Mexico, the Old South, the West, and the Midwest have met and clashed (see Figure 18-1).

settlement patterns

the many origins of first settlers to the state

FIGURE 18-1   Settlement Patterns in Texas

The Tejanos, European settlers from Mexico, dance the fandango in the Spanish governor's house in San Antonio in 1844.

The Tejanos, Or Mexican Settlers

The Rio Grande Valley was the first area of the state to be settled by Europeans. In the late 1600s, Spaniards developed settlements along the Rio Grande and as far north and east as San Antonio. Of the Spanish settlements in other parts of the state, only Nacogdoches lasted for more than a few years. Although permanent Spanish settlements did not penetrate much beyond San Antonio, the influence of Spain extends throughout the state. Most of the major rivers have Spanish names. Many other geographic features and a number of cities and counties also have Spanish names. Texas state laws are still very much influenced by past Spanish law, especially laws on land ownership and rights.

Anglo Settlers

Southern Anglos and African Americans began settling East Texas in the 1820s. The southern white Protestant settlers were decidedly different from the resident Spanish Catholic settlers. These two groups clashed in 1836 during the Texas Revolutionary War, with many of the Spanish remaining loyal to Mexico while the Anglos formed the Republic of Texas (1836–1845).

   The settlements of Anglo southerners did not extend west much beyond a line running from the Red River to present-day Fort Worth and south through Waco and Austin to San Antonio. This line is a natural geological feature, known as the Balcones Escarpment, which separates the High Plains and pine forest regions of Texas from the middle and High Plains (Llano Estacado, which translates as "staked plains") regions of the state. For two reasons, most of the areas west of this line were not settled until after the Civil War. First, Comanche, Lipan Apache, Kiowa, and Tonkawa Indians inhabited this region. In the 1850s, the U.S. Army attempted to control this region by constructing a series of forts on

The Company E Frontier Battalion of the Texas Rangers poses in Alice, Texas. Formed from a volunteer corps in 1835, the Rangers protected Texans from both external and internal threats. Today, the Rangers are the oldest statewide law enforcement agency in the United States.

the edge of the Cross Timbers area. The forts were Belknap, Cooper, Phantom Hill, Chadborne, McKavett, and Terrett. During the Civil War, the U.S. government abandoned these forts, and the Indian presence in this region reemerged. Indian domination of the area did not end until 1875, when Chief Quanah Parker was captured in Palo Duro Canyon near present-day Amarillo. The second reason for the lack of settlement was that the southern wood, water, and plantation culture was not adaptable to the dry, arid, treeless plains west of the Balcones Escarpment.

Settlement in this area increased after 1875 and took the form of large ranches and, later, small farms. Many of these settlers migrated from northern states, mostly from the Midwest, and from foreign countries. These settlers lacked the southern culture and traditions that dominated East Texas.

German Immigrants

One other early immigrant group also contributed to the character of Texas politics. Owing to the efforts of the Adelsverein Society (established to promote German immigration to the United States), Germans began to immigrate to Texas in the 1840s. By 1847, the society had brought more than seven thousand Germans to Texas, most settling in and around the town of Fredericksburg.[2] By 1850, German settlers made up 5.4 percent of the state population.[3]

These German immigrants were not slave owners and objected to that institution. They lived apart from and often shunned contact with non-Germans. During the Civil War, many young German men refused to fight, and some fled to Mexico. From Reconstruction until the 1960s, a majority of the votes for Republicans in Texas were cast in areas settled by Germans.

Thus, Texas has four distinct and contrasting settlement periods and regions: Spanish South Texas, antebellum East Texas, frontier West Texas, and the German Fredericksburg Hill Country area. As we will see later, these regional differences still have an influence on Texas politics today.

Comparison of Growth Rates of the 15 Most Populous States

The accompanying graph shows the growth rate of the fifteen states with the largest populations.

Q: How do northern states compare to southern states? How does Texas compare to the others?

A: Southern states have much higher growth rates than northern states. Texas has the third highest growth rate.

State	Percentage change in population from 1998 to 2008
Michigan	1.9%
Ohio	2.2%
Pennsylvania	3.7%
Massachusetts	5.8%
Illinois	6.9%
New Jersey	7.3%
New York	7.3%
California	12.5%
United States	12.5%
Virginia	14.4%
Washington	15.1%
North Carolina	22.2%
Florida	22.9%
Texas	23.4%
Georgia	26.8%
Arizona	39.3%

Source: U.S. Census Bureau.

POLITICAL THINKING

Who influences political culture in Texas?

As each group of settlers arrived in the different regions that make up Texas, they brought with them their own set of political values. To what extent do settlement patterns and regionalism explain differences within the political culture of the state today? What other factors explain differences or similarities in political culture among Texans?

Urban and Rural Contrasts

Texas is the second most populous state, and over 80 percent of its 24.8 million people live in 53 urban counties.[4] The remaining 20 percent live in the other 201 counties. Texas has three of the ten largest cities in the United States (Houston, Dallas, and San Antonio). Texas is also a rural state. One does not have to travel far from an urban center to see the contrast. The young urban professional living in Dallas has very little in common with someone working in a sawmill in Diboll.

These contrasts often frame the conflicts of Texas politics. East Texas Anglos demanding English-only amendments to the state constitution view demands for bilingual education by South Texas Latinos with contempt. High Plains Republicans from Amarillo often clash with East Texas traditional Democrats. The urban legislator from Austin might see things quite differently from a colleague from Muleshoe in West Texas.

These regional, urban, and rural contrasts are less severe today than they were twenty-five years ago, but they are still important for understanding the unique character of politics in the Lone Star State.

Population Growth and the Changing Political Climate

In the past several decades, Texas has experienced tremendous growth in its population. This growth is due both to birthrates and to immigration of citizens from other states and countries. The fastest-growing segment of the population is Mexican Americans. Also, many northeastern states are losing population while southern states are gaining rapidly. Figure 18-2 shows how Texas ranks among the fourteen other most populous states.

For the last several decades, Texas has experienced a migration of people from other states, owing partly to its strategic location in the Sunbelt and its proximity to Mexico. The 1970s Texas oil boom also contributed to this migration. Some people migrated out of the state in 1987–1989, but by 1990 the population had increased to almost 17 million, up from 11.2 million in 1970. In 1996, the population of Texas was estimated to be 18.6 million, and today it stands at 24.8 million.

Many of these newcomers to Texas have caused a **changing political climate** in significant ways. From the end of Reconstruction until the mid-1970s, the Democratic Party dominated Texas politics, with only one person (U.S. Senator John Tower) winning statewide office as a Republican. The term Yellow Dog Democrat was used to describe the voting habits of many Texans ("He would vote for a yellow dog if it ran as a Democrat"). From the 1880s until the 1960s, straight ticket party voting was also necessitated by the absence of meaningful competition from Republicans in the November general election. Many new immigrants to the state, however, brought with them their Republican traditions and strengthened the Republican Party in the state. That,

changing political climate

changing national politics and immigration are changing the politics of the state from Democratic to Republican domination

FIGURE 18-2

Historical and Projected Population in Texas, 2005–2040, as a Percentage of Total Population

Source: U.S. Census Bureau.

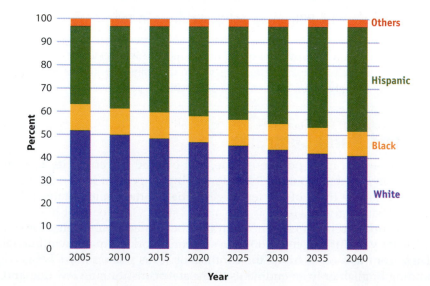

coupled with changing national politics, made it respectable to vote Republican.

Minority groups have played a significant role in changing the political climate in Texas. By the early twenty-first century, the majority of the state's population was Mexican American and African American, and Anglos became a minority: Texas had become a **majority-minority state** (see Figure 18-2). According to the Texas Education Agency, in 1987 Anglos made up 52.5 percent of all school attendees in Texas. In 2010, Anglos made up 34 percent of the school population. Higher birthrates for minorities and migration to urban areas, coupled with white migration to suburban areas, contributed to the concentration of minority groups in major cities of the state. Corpus Christi, Dallas, El Paso, Houston, and San Antonio have majority-minority populations. These changes in majority and minority status will have many implications for the politics of the state and public policy decisions.

Jakelin Galindo gets ready to celebrate her quinceañera, a "coming of age" party for girls who turn 15 years old, which is a Hispanic tradition.

Latinos—High Population Growth and Increasing Political Clout

majority-minority state
a state in which minority groups make up a majority of the population; a change from Anglos being the majority

Immigration of Latinos from Mexico to Texas has been a factor in population increases and in state politics. In 1960, Latinos were 15 percent of the total population of Texas. Their percentage increased to 18 percent by 1970, to 25 percent in 1990, and to a little over 36.5 percent in 2010. With liberalized voter registration procedures, Latinos began to dominate politics in the border areas, in some sections of the Gulf Coast, and in the San Antonio area. They have been successful in electing local officials to city and county government and school boards, to the state legislature, and to Congress. Dan Morales was elected the state's attorney general in 1990 and served until 1999. Raul Gonzales was appointed to serve on the Texas Supreme Court in 1984 and served until 1999.[5] Victor Morales, a newcomer to politics, won the Democratic Party nomination for the U.S. Senate in April 1996 to run against Senator Phil Gramm. In the 2002 governor's race, Tony Sanchez was the first Latino candidate for governor in a major party. The expectation was that Sanchez would produce a great increase in Latino votes. That did not happen, and he was soundly defeated. In fact, there is some evidence that Anglo voters, who would normally vote for Democratic candidates, failed to vote for Sanchez.

Despite Sanchez's loss, Latino voters remain a potential force in Texas politics in the years ahead. By 2036, they will outnumber Anglos and should be a major force in Texas politics.

African Americans—Steady Population and Political Participation

Unlike the Latino population, which has steadily increased as a percentage of the total population since the 1960s, the African American population has remained at about 10 to 12 percent since 1950. At the time of the Civil War, African Americans made up about 30 percent of the population, and that

Asian Americans in Texas rally in support of Hubert Vo, a Democratic member of the Texas House of Representatives.

percentage declined to about 20 percent by the turn of the twentieth century. Originally located in rural areas, African Americans moved to the cities. Today, they tend to be concentrated in three metropolitan areas—Houston, Dallas/Fort Worth, and Austin. They have had some political success at electing officials to local offices (school boards, city councils, and county offices), to the state legislature, and to a few seats in the U.S. Congress. In 1990, Democrat Morris Overstreet became the first African American to be elected to statewide office. Judge Overstreet served on the Texas Court of Criminal Appeals, the Supreme Court for criminal matters in the state until 1999. By 2010, three African Americans were serving in statewide office: Texas Supreme Court Chief Justice Wallace Jefferson, Texas Supreme Court Justice Dale Wainwright, and Railroad Chairman Michael Williams. All three are Republicans.

In 2002, Ron Kirk, a popular mayor of Dallas, ran for the U.S. Senate seat. Although polls showed Kirk to be in a dead heat with John Cornyn, he lost this race. Voting among African Americans was low, and some Anglos, who normally support Democrats, voted for Republican Cornyn. With their smaller population and low voter turnout, African Americans have not yet become as powerful a political force as the Latinos. Currently, three of Texas's thirty-two members of the U.S. House of Representatives are African American.

Asian Americans—Moderate Population Growth and Political Inroads

In 1980, Asian Americans constituted less than 1 percent of the population of Texas; by 2010, they were 2.6 percent. Projections are that by the year 2020, the Asian American population of Texas will increase to 4.5 percent. Most Asian Americans are concentrated in the Houston area. One section of Houston has such a large concentration of Chinese Americans that the City of Houston has placed Chinese writing on some of the street signs there. Asian Americans in the Houston area have had some success in electing local officials, including one city

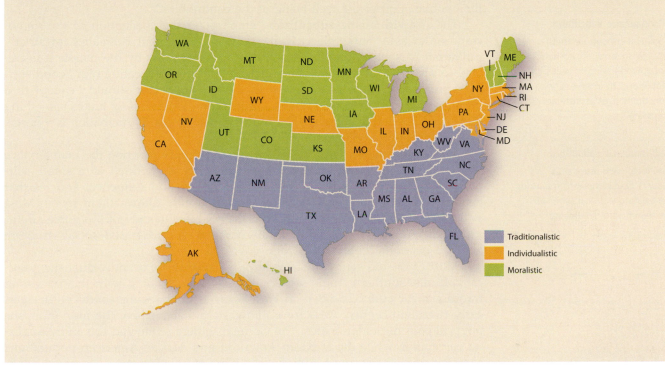

HOW TEXAS DIFFERS   POLITICAL THINKING THROUGH COMPARISONS

Dominant Political Culture in the States The accompanying map shows how the states compare based on the concept of political culture.

Q: What political culture dominates in the West, the Midwest, and the South? How does Texas compare with other southern states in terms of political culture?

A: States in the West are individualistic and sometimes moralistic as well. States in the Midwest tend to be moralistic or Individualistic. The South is dominated by traditionalistic political culture, and Texas is no exception. However, Texas is also individualistic.

Source: Daniel J. Elazar, *American Federalism: A View from the States*, pp. 124–125.

council member and a judge. In 2002, voters in the Houston area elected Martha Wong as a representative to the Texas state House of Representatives. She was only the second Asian to serve in the Texas House and the first Republican of Asian background. In 2004 and 2008, voters elected a Vietnamese, Hubert Vo, to the Texas House of Representatives.

The Political Culture of Texas

Thus far, we have discussed the historic settlement patterns, the changing makeup of the current population, and the ethnic mix of the population in the state. These factors have had a profound impact on the *political culture* of the state. Political culture consists of the people's collective beliefs and attitudes about government and political processes. It determines the values people expect the government to support and the roles they think government and ordinary citizens should play in the political process.

Daniel J. Elazar, in his book *American Federalism: A View from the States*, developed a system for applying the idea of political culture to the fifty states. Elazar found that there were three distinctive political subcultures in the United States—moralistic, individualistic, and traditionalistic.[6] (See "How Texas Differs.")

In the **moralistic subculture,** politics "is considered one of the great activities of [people in their] search for the good society . . . an effort to exercise power for the betterment of the commonwealth."[7] Government is a positive instrument for change and a means of promoting the general welfare of all citizens. Politics becomes the responsibility of all citizens, who have an obligation to participate in government. People seek government offices not for personal gain but out of a sense of serving the public. The government in turn has a right—an obligation—to intervene in the private affairs of citizens when it is necessary for the "public good or the well-being of the community."[8]

The **individualistic subculture** "emphasizes the conception of the democratic order as a marketplace. In its view, a government is created for strictly utilitarian reasons, to handle those functions demanded by the people it is created to serve."[9] Government is not concerned with the creation of a "good society," and government intervention in the private sector should be kept to a minimum. Politics is viewed not as a profession of high calling but as something that should be left to those willing to dirty their hands. Participation is a necessary evil but not an obligation of each citizen.

The **traditionalistic subculture** has as its primary function the maintenance of the existing political order, and participation is confined to a small, self-perpetuating elite. The public has limited power and influence. Policies that benefit the public are enacted only when the elite allows them to be. Most policies enacted by government benefit the ruling elite and not the public. Political participation by the public is discouraged. A class-based social structure helps to maintain the existing order.

Most of the old southern states have traditionalistic or individualistic political cultures. Southern Anglo settlers of East Texas brought with them a strong traditionalistic culture. Settlers in West Texas in the late nineteenth century and early twentieth century were from midwestern states where the individualistic political culture predominates. The German settlers reinforced this individualistic perception, while the Mexican American and African American populations contributed to the strong traditionalistic view of government.

These two political cultures (traditionalistic and individualistic) coexist and blend in the state. They share some common views regarding the role of government. Both see a limited role for government and discourage broad-based citizen participation in political processes. The two share a conservative view of government: Individuals should do things for themselves whenever possible, and government should do only those things that individuals cannot do for themselves—such as pave the roads, keep the peace, and put out fires—and leave the rest to the private sector. Government should keep taxes low, limit social services, and limit the advancement of civil rights. However, most government institutions and political processes are much more consistent with the traditionalistic political culture than with the individualistic political culture.

Patterns of political culture are slow to change, and they persist for very long periods of time. For example, these were the primary planks of the **party platform** of the Democratic governors in the 1940s and 1950s:

1. Opposition to expanding civil rights
2. Limits on the role of the federal government in state affairs
3. Opposition to federal control over natural resources (oil and gas)
4. Opposition to organized labor unions
5. No new taxes[10]

---

moralistic subculture

a political subculture that expects the government to act as a positive force to achieve a common good for all citizens

individualistic subculture

a political subculture that expects government to handle functions demanded of it by the people and to intervene in individuals' lives as little as necessary

traditionalistic subculture

a political subculture that expects government to maintain the existing political order for the benefit of a small elite

party platform

statement of the primary beliefs and goals of a political party

Except for minor differences, most of these planks would fit well into the platforms of former Republican Governor George W. Bush in 1994 and 1998 and Governor Rick Perry in 2002, 2004, and 2010. Also, a review of the platform of the Republican Party in Texas in 2004 showed support for all these points (www.texasgop.org). The party in control of the governor's mansion and most statewide offices has a different name; the political culture has not changed. Texas has gone from a state dominated by the Democratic Party to a state dominated by the Republican Party with no change in philosophy, ideology, or policy.

The basic structure of state government in Texas fits the traditionalistic-individualistic model quite well. Government is limited. Power is divided among many elected officials. Executive authority is weak, and most power rests with the state legislature. Few state regulations are placed on business, and many of those that exist benefit specific businesses. Regulation of the environment is modest. Despite the repeal of the poll tax, intervention by the federal government, and the passage of the Voting Rights Act, voter participation in Texas is still quite low, ranking near the bottom of the fifty states in the percentage of the population voting. Political corruption is often tolerated as the necessary cost of doing business.

Except on rare occasions, the state legislature protects the status quo and places few restrictions on lobbying and other activities of interest groups. The office of the governor is formally very weak. The state bar and business interest groups heavily control the selection of the state judiciary in partisan elections. State finances reflect the philosophy of limited government; Texas often ranks near the bottom of the fifty states on expenditures. Limited state expenditures are financed with a regressive tax system that relies on property taxes and sales taxes. Thus, the political culture of Texas helped establish a conservative, limited government.

The Economy of Texas

The economy of a state also plays a role in its politics. The economy of Texas has changed greatly in the past several decades. Texas is no longer a rural state with an economy dominated by cattle, cotton, and oil, although these are still important elements in the economy. The Texas economy has experienced rapid growth as large cities have become centers of international trade and technological innovation. The state's economy has significantly outperformed the U.S. economy since the 1970s. This transformation has facilitated the rise of the Republican Party, spurred debate, and placed many new issues on the political agenda.

Although agriculture is still a cornerstone of the Texas economy, the technology revolution has transformed this industry.

Land has always been an important factor in Texas's economy and politics. Many settlers were lured to Texas by offers of free land. The Spanish and later the Mexican government provided generous grants of land to any family that settled in the state. Each family could receive one *sitio*, or *legua* (Spanish for "league")—about 4,428 acres of land. A single person could receive 1,500 acres of land. In the 1820s, such a generous incentive was needed to get people to live in Texas, given the hardships of travel and simple survival. General P. H. Sheridan, best known for his remark "The only good Indian

I ever saw was dead," said in a letter from Fort Clark, Texas, dated 1855, "If I owned Hell and Texas, I'd rent out Texas and live in Hell."[11] Other people may have come to Texas from more comfortable environments to escape the law. "GTT" (Gone to Texas) was supposedly a common sign left by those escaping the long arm of the sheriff.

Land issues drove the Texas revolution in 1836 and the annexation of Texas by the United States in 1845. When Texas entered the Union, it kept its public debt and its public lands. The U.S. government had to purchase from Texans all land that was to be federal land. The U.S. government also purchased lands that were formerly the west and northwest parts of Texas and that now make up much of present-day New Mexico and some of Colorado, Utah, and Wyoming.[12]

For most of its history the Lone Star State has had a **land-based economy.** Cotton farming dominated from the 1820s to the 1860s. After the Civil War, cattle became the economic mainstay. In the early twentieth century, abundant oil was discovered in East Texas. However, agriculture continues to be the second-largest resource-based industry in the state, generating about $80 billion per year, accounting for about 9 percent of the state's gross product. One out of every seven Texans still works in agriculture. Texas leads the nation in cattle, cotton, hay, and wool production.[13] Although production peaked in 1972, Texas remains the country's leading producer of oil and gas.[14] Only in the past forty to fifty years has the economy begun to diversify and become less dependent on the land and its cotton, cattle, and oil. Some regions of the state remain more dependent on land economies than others, and vast differences can be found from one region to another.

Economic Regions

The State of Texas Comptroller's Office has divided Texas into a number of **economic regions,** based on their dominant economic activity, as a convenient way to collect data for a wide variety of purposes. For our discussion, we have combined them into six regions, shown in Figure 18-3.

The East Texas, or Piney Woods, region was traditionally dominated by agriculture, timber, and oil. Today, agriculture is less important and oil is declining. Timber is still important. Some diversification has occurred, with manufacturing becoming a more important element in the economy.

The Plains region of the state, with Lubbock and Amarillo as the major cities, was dominated by agriculture (especially cotton, wheat, and maize) and by ranching and cattle feedlots. In recent years, the economy of this region has become more diversified and less dominated by agriculture.

The Gulf Coast region, extending from Corpus Christi to Beaumont/Port Arthur/Orange, and including Houston, is dominated by petrochemical industries, manufacturing, shipping, and fishing. In recent years, this area has diversified into manufacturing and high-tech industries. It is also the area with the highest concentration of organized labor unions in the entire state.

The border area of South Texas and the Rio Grande Valley, stretching from Brownsville to El Paso, is noted primarily for its agricultural production of citrus fruits and vegetables. In recent years, trade with Mexican border cities has diversified the economy of this region, and this process has increased with the passage of the **North American Free Trade Agreement (NAFTA)**—an act passed by Congress in 1993 that established closer trade relations with Mexico and Canada. Some writers would distinguish the El Paso area and the border area as separate economic units because the two regions are several hundred miles apart and their economic contact is limited. Many citizens of El Paso often feel that they are not a part of Texas and identify themselves more closely with New Mexico.

land-based economy
an economic system in which most wealth is derived from the use of the land

economic regions
divisions of the state based on dominant economic activity

North American Free Trade Agreement (NAFTA)
an act passed by Congress in 1993 that established closer trade relations and economic cooperation between the United States, Canada, and Mexico

FIGURE 18-3   **Economic Regions Of Texas**

The Metroplex, or Dallas/Fort Worth area, is considered the financial center of the state. This economic region is the most diversified in the state, with a combination of banking, manufacturing, high-tech, and aerospace industries.

The Central Corridor, or midstate region, is an area stretching roughly from College Station in the east to Waco in the north and Austin and San Antonio in the southwest. This economic area is dominated by two large state universities (Texas A&M University and the University of Texas at Austin), high-tech industries in Austin and San Antonio, and major military bases in the Waco/Temple/Killeen and San Antonio areas.

Economic Sectors

During the 1970s and early 1980s, the state economy experienced tremendous growth because of the increase in the price of oil. In the mid-1980s, the price of oil declined, and as a result, the economy of the entire state fell into a deep recession. To many, the economic recession of the early 1980s showed a need for more **economic diversity** for the state. An economy based on many types of economic activity, rather than the old land-based economy, would be needed to carry the state into the twenty-first century. Since 1988, there has been significant restructuring of the state economy. Today, the service industry dominates the Texas economy. By 2007, this industry employed nearly 80 percent of the

economic diversity

an economy based on many types of economic activity rather than one or a few activities

States are in an inherently competitive position with regard to taxation. A state cannot raise taxes very high without losing firms and residents to a state where taxes are lower. This situation has led states to develop alternative sources of revenue. One of the most common is a state lottery. The payout to lottery winners is typically about half of the amount taken in. The remainder is used by governments to subsidize programs such as education and parks. The Powerball Lottery, which is sponsored jointly by thirty-three states, is the largest lottery.

private-sector workforce. Moreover, the industry accounted for 63 percent of output. The state's location, its proximity to Mexico, and its centrality within the continental United States has pushed the growth of this sector. Trade has expanded rapidly because of both NAFTA and globalization. Texas has become a transportation hub. Increased trade has also fueled the growth of professional and business services in areas such as accounting, legal, and computer services, as well as construction, engineering, and management. Meanwhile, the population expansion has also produced a marked increase in the need for health care and education services. Simultaneously, the rise in both trade and population has sparked the growth of the leisure and hospitality industry.[15]

By the turn of the twenty-first century, Texas had become a major international trading power. The passage of NAFTA in 1993 had promised significant economic growth for Texas because its border with Mexico held the potential for increased trade. Within a few years, that promise was fulfilled. Since 2001, Texas has been the leading U.S. exporter. In 2009, Texas exported $163 billion in goods, whereas California, in second place, exported $134 billion.[16] Texas's major trading partners are Mexico and Canada, followed by countries in Asia. Texas has become a portal to Latin America, with Mexico accounting for over 34 percent of all exports.[17]

Like the rest of the United States, Texas has been transformed by the information technology revolution. (See Figure 18-4.) New high-tech industries, especially in Austin, Dallas, and Houston, have significantly influenced the Texas economy. Whereas Texas Instruments helped turn the calculator into a common household item in the 1970s, the Texas of today boasts a thriving software, equipment, telecommunications, and semiconductor industry. To support this industry, Texas has become a leader in scientific and technological research and development. The number of international patent applications filed under the Patent Cooperation Treaty is a good indicator of technological innovation. By 2006, Texas ranked fourth in the United States in the number of patents filed, trailing California, New York, and Massachusetts.[18]

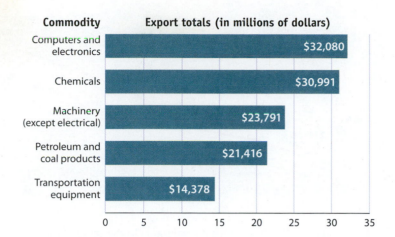

Commodity	Export totals (in millions of dollars)
Computers and electronics	$32,080
Chemicals	$30,991
Machinery (except electrical)	$23,791
Petroleum and coal products	$21,416
Transportation equipment	$14,378

FIGURE 18-4

Texas Exports Today

The graph shows the dollar value of the state's top five exports. How are the top exports today different from those of forty years ago?

Source: "Texas: Crossroads of the World," *Texas Ahead,* 2010, Issue 3 www.texasahead.org/economic _developer/downloads/1313-3TexasAhead_Global.pdf.

Consequences of Economic Changes

In the second decade of the twenty-first century, the economy of the state is far more diverse than it was even twenty years ago. Though energy and agriculture are still vital elements in the state's economy, they are balanced by many new elements. This diversification has affected Texas both economically and politically.

Today, the economy of Texas is more stable than it was prior to diversification. Texas did follow the nation into the economic downturn that resulted from the U.S. housing crisis of 2007–2008, reporting its highest unemployment rate in twenty years. However, Texas fared better than other regions, outperforming the nation in job growth and real gross domestic product (GDP) growth. In 2010, for example, Texas was among only three states whose employment growth rose above 1.5 percent. Although high oil and gas prices have allowed Texas to skirt three of the United States' six most recent recessions, rising gas prices had no impact whatsoever on employment rates and rising oil prices contributed only 0.5 percent.[19] The remaining growth was attributed to sectors such as professional and business service employment, which expanded by 4.8 percent, and the health care service workforce, which rose by 4 percent. Analysts cited Texas exports, its healthy banking system, its thriving IT industry, and relatively stable home prices as reasons for the state's economic success.[20] Overall, these observations suggest that the strategy of diversification that Texas pursued in the late twentieth century has accomplished more than its original goal, insulating Texas not only from boom and bust cycles in the energy industry but from other economic jolts as well.

With the rise of trade, technology, and urbanization, political changes have occurred. As we have seen, economic changes have spurred the rise of the Republican Party as the party acquired increasing support among the business community and as professionals from other states came to Texas to become part of these new and growing industries. However, economic transformation has also given rise to a host of political issues for the Texas government to address.

Chief among the political issues facing Texas is illegal immigration. In recent decades, the number of illegal immigrants who have come to the United States to work has been rising (see Figure 18-5). Because of its long border with Mexico, Texas bears the brunt of dealing with this issue. Since the early 1990s,

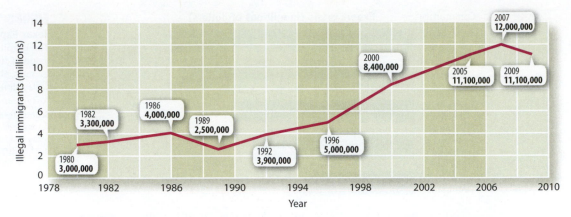

FIGURE 18-5   **Estimated Number of Illegal Immigrants in the United States**
How has the number of illegal immigrants coming into the United States changed since 1990? How has this influx affected Texas? What do you think accounts for the drop in the number of illegal immigrants between 2007 and 2009?

Source: Jeffrey S. Passel and D'Vera Cohn, "A Portrait of Unauthorized Immigrants in the United States," a Pew Research Center Project http://pewhispanic.org/reports/report.php?ReportID5107; "Unauthorized at New High—Details of Trend Uncertain" from *Background Brief Prepared for Task Force on Immigration: America's Future* by Jeffrey S. Passel. a Pew Research Center Project http://pewhispanic.org/files/reports/46.pdf; data for 2007 and 2009 from Jeffrey S. Passel and D'Vera Cohn, "U.S. Unauthorized Immigration Flows Are Down Sharply Since Mid-Decade," a Pew ResearchCenter Project, http://pewhispanic.org/files/reports/126.pdf.

fences have been built across high-traffic border areas. In 1996, Congress passed legislation authorizing increased funds for border patrols and stiffer penalties for smugglers. Some argue that these measures are responsible for the drop in illegal immigration from 2008 to 2010, but others attribute this decrease to the economic downturn. Despite the drop, approximately 300,000 illegal immigrants entered the country during this period, and many did so by crossing the border into Texas. Texas also has the financial burden of increased health care and education costs. A 2006 study in Harris County determined that the number of undocumented immigrants in the county's health care system had increased 44 percent in three years. Their care accounted for approximately 14 percent of the health care system's total operating costs.[21] In addition, many financially strapped school districts serve the children of illegal immigrants, offering programs for those with limited English proficiency. Yet illegal immigration also serves an important function within the Texas economy, providing a cheap workforce for its growing industry.

In addition to grappling with illegal immigration, the Texas government must come to terms with a number of controversies regarding how to accommodate a growing population and economy. Growth has placed new demands on the state's energy and transportation infrastructure and other public services. Issues such as the Trans-Texas Corridor and the granting of permits to build more coal-burning power plants have incited heated debate. The Trans-Texas Corridor has been especially controversial. The corridor is intended to be a vast network of toll roads, railroads, and utility lines built in part upon existing infrastructure. The government and those who support the corridor argue that it will relieve heavy traffic congestion, facilitate economic growth, and improve road safety. Some oppose it because they are anti-NAFTA, and the corridor will connect Texas and Mexico. Others worry that it will divert money from local governments. Still others argue that it will push pollution to rural areas and disrupt wildlife habitat, or that it will provide a soft target for terrorists. Governor Rick Perry and other politicians who support the corridor have been accused of accepting large campaign contributions from construction companies who will likely be awarded contracts from the Department of Transportation. As these economic changes create demands on infrastructure, the Texas government must try to find solutions that are acceptable to all.

Summary
Self-Test www.mhhe.com/ pattersontadtx11e

The settlers who came to Texas in the nineteenth and twentieth centuries shared similar views on politics. They feared powerful government and felt that the state should not interfere in the social or economic spheres. An Anglo elite held the reins of government and preserved the status quo. Following the recession in the 1980s, Texas began to diversify economically. People from other states and Mexican immigrants helped fuel economic growth, which centered on high tech, trade, and industry. Although the population shift contributed to the rise of the Republican Party, Texans' political values appear to have changed little. Texas is still one of the lowest-ranking states in areas such as school expenditures and levels of voter participation. The legislature continues to meet only once every two years, and the government remains weak and divided. As these factors indicate, Texans still share a traditionalistic-individualistic political culture.

As the Latino population increases and the urban professional sector also grows, will they change the political values of the state significantly? Immigrants from Mexico and Central America tend to hold traditionalistic views of government. However, urban professionals are accustomed to governments that provide a broader range of services.

Even if the influx of new populations does not fundamentally shift political values, economic development is creating new political problems that the state has been and will be forced to confront. For example, the state must meet the demand of these new industries for improved transportation, increased energy supplies, and a larger workforce. These new demands may force the government to take on greater responsibilities than it has in the past.

CHAPTER 18

Study Corner

Key Terms

changing political climate
(*p. 466*)
economic diversity (*p. 473*)
economic regions (*p. 472*)
individualistic subculture
(*p. 470*)
land-based economy (*p. 472*)
majority-minority state
(*p. 467*)

moralistic subculture
(*p. 470*)
North American Free Trade
Agreement (NAFTA)
(*p. 472*)
party platform (*p. 470*)
settlement patterns (*p. 462*)
traditionalistic subculture
(*p. 470*)

Self-Test: Multiple Choice

1. To date, what effects have the population increase and changing demographics had on Texas political culture?
   a. The political culture has become increasingly moralistic.
   b. The political culture has become less individualistic.
   c. The political culture has become less traditionalistic.
   d. The political culture has remained unchanged.

2. The Texas Democratic Party platforms of the 1940s and1950s included all of the following primary planks *except*
   a. opposition to organized labor.
   b. opposition to expanding civil rights.
   c. limitation of the role of government in state affairs.
   d. acceptance of federal oil and gas regulation and control.

3. The set of attitudes, values, and beliefs that most people in a state have that influence how they perceive the proper role of government is called
   a. political socialization.
   b. political culture.
   c. political behavior.
   d. politics.

4. All of the following play a critical role in Texas politics *except*
   a. state taxing policies.
   b. population growth and ethnic composition.
   c. political culture.
   d. urban versus rural demographics.

5. Of the three political subcultures suggested by Daniel Elazar, Texas is best described as
   a. moralistic and traditionalistic.
   b. individualistic and traditionalistic.
   c. moralistic and traditionalistic.
   d. idealistic and traditionalistic.

6. By the year 2020, the three largest ethnic groups in Texas, in descending order, will be
   a. Anglos, Hispanics, and African Americans.
   b. Hispanics, African Americans, and Anglos.
   c. Hispanics, Anglos, and Asian Americans.
   d. Hispanics, Anglos, and African Americans.

7. The growth of the service sector within the Texas economy is fueled primarily by which of the following?
   a. gambling
   b. agriculture
   c. trade
   d. oil

8. In Texas, government is limited, power is divided among many elected officials, executive authority is weak, and most power resides with the state legislature. (T/F)

9. Since the 1970s, Texas has experienced staggering population growth attributed to legal migration of people from other states and legal and illegal immigration from Mexico. (T/F)

10. The population of African Americans in Texas is concentrated in selected areas of the state and is expected to increase to nearly 20 percent. (T/F)

Critical Thinking

The political culture of Texas is described as traditionalistic/individualistic. How well does this characterization fit your idea of Texans and their political beliefs?

Suggested Readings

Calvert, Robert A., and Arnold DeLeon. *The History of Texas.* Arlington Heights, Ill.: Harland Davidson, 1990. A good general history of Texas.

Davidson, Chandler. *Race and Class in Texas Politics.* Princeton, N.J.: Princeton University Press, 1976. A good review of critical issues in Texas politics.

Elazar, Daniel J. *American Federalism: A View from the States.* New York: HarperCollins, 1984. A more detailed explanation of the concept of political culture.

Fehrendbach, T. R. *Lone Star: A History of Texas and Texans.* New York: Collier, 1980. An excellent history of Texas.

Jordon, Terry G. *German Seed in Texas Soil: Immigrant Farmers in Nineteenth-Century Texas.* Austin. University of Texas Press, 1966. An excellent review of the impact of German immigration.

Soukup, James R., Clifton McCleskey, and Harry Holloway. *Party and Factional Division in Texas.* Austin: University of Texas Press, 1964. A comprehensive review of the transition of Texas from a one-party to a two-party state.

List of Websites

http://www.lbb.state.tx.us/
The Legislative Budget Board site; gives information on Texas past and present and is a good source of data on the state budget.

http://www.tshaonline.org/handbook
The Texas Handbook, published online by the Texas Historical Society; contains a lot of information on the history of the state and its people.

www.texasonline.com
Texas Online, the official portal of Texas, with a link to state agencies and popular online services.

www.window.state.tx.us/
The Comptroller of Public Accounts website is a good source on state expenditures and economic regions.

www.usnpl.com/txnews.php
State newspaper links, with information on Texas newspapers.

Participate!

What kinds of activities could you become involved in that would change an individual's or a group's basic view of the proper role of government? You might consider forming a student political forum group at your campus and invite a political figure to appear.

Extra Credit

Find an article in your local newspaper that supports the idea of Texas as a conservative state. Editorials may be your best source of such information. Follow the newspaper's stories and editorials for a few days to see if an obvious political bias emerges.

Self-Test Answers

1. d, 2. d, 3. b, 4. a, 5. b, 6. a, 7. c, 8. T, 9. T, 10. F

19

The State Constitution

State constitutions vary greatly in length and longevity as well as in the type of government structure and amendment process they establish. In this chapter, we compare the constitutions that Texas has established in its early history. We then analyze the key values expressed by the current constitution, both as it was established in 1876 and as it has evolved through the amendment process. We isolate the basic principles shared by state and national constitutions, exploring the structure of constitutions and the types of governments they establish. Finally, we outline the amendment process and the role of different groups, then consider reasons that the constitution has not been significantly amended since 1876. The chapter's main points are the following:

- Many constitutions have governed the geographical area that is now the State of Texas.

- The provisions of the 1876 constitution represent a reaction against the centralist government under Reconstruction.

- The state constitution reflects key values that comprise Texas traditionalistic-individualistic political culture. Large-scale attempts at modernizing the Texas constitution have failed. Instead, the Texas constitution changes in a piecemeal manner as voters pass amendments during odd-year elections.

- State constitutions differ from one another and from the national constitution in length and longevity.

Texas Constitutions

Constitutions Under the Republic of Mexico

The first constitution to govern Anglos in Texas was the Republic of Mexico's constitution of 1824. This constitution was federalist in concept and a clear break with the Spanish centralist tradition.[1] Under the 1824 national constitution, Texas was governed by a provincial constitution of the state of Coahuila y Tejas that was approved in 1827. The 1827 constitution provided for a unicameral legislature, and Texas elected two representatives to the

FIGURE 19-1　**The Republic of Texas**　From 1836 until 1845, Texas was an independent nation known as the Republic of Texas. In the treaty forced on Mexico by Texas, Mexico ceded land stretching to the headwaters of the Rio Grande. Though it never fully occupied this land, Texas claimed parts of modern-day New Mexico, Oklahoma, Kansas, Colorado, and Wyoming.

A painting of the meeting at Washington-on-the-Brazo, where Texans wrote the 1836 constitution.

provincial legislature. This constitution, which lacked a bill of rights, provided a government structure with which the Anglos were comfortable. Texans ignored sections of the constitution of 1827, most notably those that required Catholicism as the state religion and those that did not recognize slavery.

Suspension of the Mexican national constitution of 1824, and with it the provincial constitution of 1827, by President Santa Anna of Mexico was a factor that led to the Texas Revolution. One of the early Texas flags, reportedly flown at the Alamo, had the number 1824 superimposed on a red, green, and white emblem of the Mexican flag. This was a demand that the constitution of 1824 be restored.[2]

The Republic of Texas Constitution of 1836

In 1836, when Texas declared itself a republic independent of Mexico, a new constitution was adopted (see Figure 19-1). This document was a composite of the U.S. Constitution and the constitutions of several southern states. It provided for a unitary, rather than federal, form of government. Signs of the distrust of government by the traditionalistic southerners who wrote the document are evident. They limited the term of the president to a single three-year term with prohibitions against consecutive reelection. The president was also prohibited from raising an army without the consent of the congress. There were other features, such as freedom of religion and property rights protection, that had been absent in the 1824 and 1827 constitutions. Slavery, which had been ignored by the Mexican government, was legalized.[3]

Statehood Constitution of 1845

When Texas joined the Union in 1845, a state constitution was adopted. This document also reflected the traditionalistic Southern culture, with a few notable exceptions that were adaptations of Spanish law. Women were granted property rights equal to those of men, especially in marriage, where women were given half the value of all property acquired during the marriage (community property). In addition, a person's homestead was protected from forced sale to pay debts. These ideas were later adopted by many other states.

The 1845 constitution also provided for limited executive authority, biennial sessions of the legislature, and two-year terms for most officials. Most of these features were included in later constitutions.

The Civil War and Reconstruction Constitutions of 1861, 1866, and 1869

In 1861, when Texas joined the Confederacy, another constitution was adopted. It was essentially the same as the 1845 document, with the exception of a prohibition against the emancipation of slaves, a provision to secede from the Union, and a provision to join the Confederacy.

In 1866, a third state constitution was approved as a condition for rejoining the Union following the Civil War. This document abolished slavery, nullified the ordinances of secession, renounced the right of future secession, and repudiated the wartime debts of the state. This constitution of 1866 was short-lived and overturned by Reconstruction acts of the U.S. Congress.

Military rule was again imposed on Texas, and a new constitution was adopted in 1869. This fourth state constitution, which was approved under the supervision of the federal government's military rule, is called the Reconstruction constitution, or the "carpetbagger's constitution." It represented a radical departure from past and future documents and reflected the centralization aspirations of the national Republicans. A four-year term was provided for the governor, who was also given strong appointive authority. The governor could appoint most state and many local officials. County courts were abolished, and much local authority and control were removed from the planter class. Public schools were centralized under state control and funded with a poll tax and the sale of public lands. African Americans were given the right to vote, and whites who had participated in the "rebellion" (Civil War) were disenfranchised.[4]

The Constitution of 1876

Texans approved the current constitution in 1876. In 1875, at the end of Reconstruction, a constitutional convention had assembled. The delegates included former Confederate generals who held positions within the Confederate government. These men were landowners who had objected strongly to the centralist

In this painting, a representative of the Freedmen's Bureau tries to prevent an armed conflict between whites and African Americans. The Freedmen's Bureau, created by the War Department to help freed slaves and refugees after the Civil War, was underfunded but nevertheless managed to provide needed services to many former slaves.

Six of the delegates to the Constitutional Convention of 1875 were African Americans. They fought to maintain their voting rights. Although the constitution did not restrict voting rights by race, none of the six delegates participated in later sessions of the state legislature.

government under Reconstruction. They were united by their concern over what the government could do to them, rather than a sense of what the government could do for them. The document reflected the antigovernment sentiments of the traditionalistic-individualistic political culture of the state. The new document reimposed shorter terms of office, reestablished many statewide and local elected offices, and severely restricted the ability of government to act. The powers of both the legislature and the governor were restricted.[5]

None of these changes were especially controversial. The controversial issues were the poll tax payment for the right to vote, women's suffrage, and public schools. The centralized state school system was abolished and replaced by local control of schools with some state funding provided. In addition, provisions were made for a state-funded university system.[6]

Thus Texas has been governed by a number of constitutions since the early 1800s: The Spanish constitutions contributed several key elements, including community property rights for women, which was a clear departure from English laws. The 1845 constitution provided for limited government with little centralized power. The constitutions of 1861 and 1866 continued these principles of limited government. The present constitution, approved in 1876, not only reinstated but also expanded the ideas of limited government. Only the Reconstruction constitution of 1869, which provided for a strong, centralized government, was a departure from these ideas. Its swift repeal at the end of Reconstruction indicates how utterly the southern whites rejected these concepts. Many Texans today would still not accept these concepts. In 1999, voters rejected two amendments that would have expanded the power of the governor to appoint and remove minor state officials.

Political Culture and Constitutions

To a large degree, political culture drives institutions. The Reconstruction constitution of 1869 was a fundamental departure from earlier constitutions and in conflict with the political culture of the state. This document centralized power in state government and reduced the authority of local governments, provided for four-year terms for many officeholders, and gave the governor the power to appoint most state and many local officials, including the state judiciary. In addition it provided for annual sessions of the legislature, gave African Americans the right to vote, and provided for state-controlled schools and a state police system. Most of these provisions are not supported by a traditionalistic-individualistic political culture that calls for decentralized, weak government while discouraging political participation and nonelite involvement in government.

Except for the four-year terms for governor and other statewide officials, most of these ideas (gubernatorial appointment of state and local officials, annual sessions of the legislature, and state control of local affairs) have little support in Texas today. The voters have rejected annual sessions of the legislature on several occasions, and despite widespread decentralization of local schools, there is demand for even greater decentralization of decisions down to the local level. Culture drives institutions by influencing the basic structure and organization of government. Thus, the current constitution is very compatible with the political culture of the state.

Although Texans created the current state constitution in 1876, they have continued to refine the power and structure of government through the amendment process. The Texas Constitution has changed as the state has developed from a sparsely populated rural frontier to a major economic player in the national and international arena. Yet, the same traditionalistic-individualistic culture still drives this change.

Texans generally oppose tax hikes and government spending. For example, in 2011 Texans stopped counties from gaining the same rights to issue bonds as cities and towns. Those Texans who opposed the proposition argued that bonds put state and local governments in debt and by enriching the government, would make it more powerful.[7] Two years earlier, Texans pushed through an amendment limiting the rights of local government to seize blighted or underdeveloped property from private owners. Property-rights advocates bristled at the exercise of this right, known as eminent domain. Others opposed it because they felt that local governments unfairly targeted African Americans and the underprivileged.

Texans tend to reject measures that grant state or local governments permission to take actions that they see as costly. For example, in 2011, Texans shot down an amendment that would have lowered taxes for landowners who implemented measures to conserve water and protect water quality. Texans cast this vote amidst the worst drought in the state's history, and the amendment's opponents argued that the measure would have been too costly.

FIGURE 19-2

Number of State Constitutions and Dates of Most Recent Ones
The average life span for a state constitution is ninety-five years. What do you notice about states that have had just one constitution? What do these states have in common?

Source: The Book of the States 2007, Vol. 38 (Lexington, KY: Council of State Governments 2007), Table 1.1, p. 10.

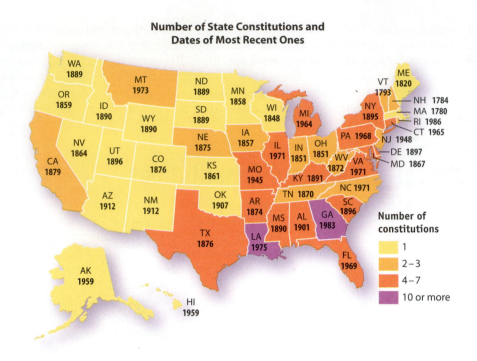

Number of State Constitutions and Dates of Most Recent Ones

Still, notable exceptions show that Texans demonstrate compassion for those who are disadvantaged. In 2007, Texans overwhelmingly supported a proposition that reduced property taxes for the disabled and the elderly, with 88 percent of the population voting in favor. That same year, when the famous cyclist Lance Armstrong campaigned across the state for a proposition to issue bonds in support of cancer research, 61 percent of voters approved the measure. In 2011, four propositions containing the phrase "ad valorem" tax or taxation were on the ballot. This phrase means taxes related to property values, and in each case they referred to an exemption of ad valorem taxes. Only one of the propositions passed: an exemption for the surviving spouse of a disabled veteran.[8] This trend demonstrates that although Texans, as individualists, are less inclined than most Americans to support government programs that provide for the disadvantaged, they do support measures that help the needy so long as they do not significantly expand government authority.

Successful amendments also reflect socially conservative values. In 2005, Texans passed an amendment prohibiting gay marriage. The amendment was a response to court rulings in other states declaring that limiting marriage to opposite-sex couples was unconstitutional. That same year, Texans added an amendment forcing judges to deny bail to accused persons whose release might put the crime victims at risk. As seen in Figure 19-2, these measures passed with overwhelming majorities.

Principles of State Constitutions

We have looked at the overall impact of history, culture, and traditions on constitutions, but several important principles specifically underpin the general idea of constitutional government. Constitutions are established on the principles of self-government, or *popular sovereignty,* and *limited government.* Popular sovereignty is the idea that all power rests with the people.[9] Constitutions are written by a popularly elected convention of citizens and not by state legislatures. Thus the citizens must also approve any changes in state constitutions—except in

Delaware, where the state legislature can amend the state constitution. The current Texas Constitution supports this idea very strongly in its preamble and bill of rights.

Second, constitutions are a contract, or compact, between the citizens and the government and cannot be violated. The laws passed by legislatures and carried out by the executive branch must fit within the framework of the constitution. Hence, constitutions are a limitation upon the power of government. Like the U.S. Constitution, state constitutions limit the scope of government by **grants of power**—explicitly listing the powers that governments may use—and **denials of power**—explicitly listing those they may not use.

The current (1876) Texas Constitution is very much an example of limitations upon the power of state government. When the current constitution was drafted in 1875, Governor Richard Coke said to the assembled constitutional convention:

> The accepted theory of American constitutional government is that State Constitutions are limitations upon, rather than grants of power: and as a rule, not without its exceptions, that power not prohibited exists in State government. Therefore, express prohibitions are necessary upon the power of state government . . . these restrictions . . . have multiplied in the more recently created instruments of fundamental law.

The current constitution heavily reflects those values, which are also a product of the state's individualistic-traditionalistic political culture.

In addition to the ideals of popular sovereignty, compact (or contract) theory, and limited government, other common characteristics of state constitutions serve to limit and clarify the authority of state governments.

Separation of Powers in State Constitutions

All state constitutions embrace the idea of *separation of powers* provided in the U.S. Constitution. Power is divided among an elected executive, an elected legislature, and the judiciary. The separation of powers provides a check on the actions of government. Fear of strong executive authority, experienced in Texas under Governor Edmund J. Davis and the Radical Republicans, led the framers of the 1876 document to fragment executive power. The voters elect a governor, a lieutenant governor, a comptroller, an attorney general, a commissioner of the land office, and, at that time, a state treasurer. The agricultural commissioner, railroad commissioners, and a state board of education were added later. The office of treasurer was abolished in 1995.

Bill of Rights in State Constitutions

Like the U.S. Constitution, most state constitutions include strong statements on civil liberties that grant basic freedoms. Most civil liberties protections in state constitutions duplicate those found in the U.S. document, but many state constitutions are more generous in the granting of liberties than is the U.S. Constitution. The Texas Constitution is no exception in this regard. The average citizen, upon reading the "Bill of Rights" section of the Texas Constitution, might well conclude that it is a very liberal document. Besides those rights provided by the federal document, the Texas Constitution grants equalities under the law to all citizens regardless of "sex, race, color, creed or national origin."[10] This is almost the exact wording of the failed Equal Rights Amendment to the U.S. Constitution. Citizens often have more freedoms provided in their state constitutions than in the national constitution, but most citizens are unaware of that fact. Attention more often focuses on the national Bill of Rights than on the state bill of rights.

---

grants of power

a way that Constitutions limit the power of government by explicitly listing the powers that governments may use

denials of power

a way that Constitutions limit the power of government by explicitly listing the powers that governments may not use

Independent consultant Delia Pompa testifies in 2004 during the *West-Orange Cove v. Neeley* case, which challenged the school finance system. The Texas Constitution guarantees all students the right to a public education. The Texas system had previously been found to be unconstitutional by the Texas Supreme Court. The decision in this case forced the legislature to propose a solution to the funding crisis.

Supreme Law of the State

Article VI of the U.S. Constitution contains the supremacy clause, which makes the U.S. Constitution the supreme law of the land. Most state constitutions have a similar statement that makes the state constitution superior to state law and actions by local governments. Any state or local law that conflicts with the state constitution is invalid.

A recent example of local laws potentially conflicting with a state law involves the state's issuing of permits to citizens to carry concealed handguns. Many local governments (cities, counties, and metropolitan transit authorities) passed regulations prohibiting the carrying of concealed handguns in some public places. Supporters of the "concealed carry law" have charged that these local regulations violate the state law. The state court system determined that these local regulations did not violate the concept of "supreme law of the state."

The Structure of State Constitutions

Although they have common characteristics, state constitutions also have some vast differences. According to legal experts and political theorists, there are some ideal characteristics that constitutions should possess and against which constitutions can be compared. Ideally, a constitution should be brief and explicit, embody only the general principles of government, and provide the broad outlines of government subject to interpretation, especially through the court's power of judicial review. Constitutions should not be detailed and specific but broad and flexible. Furthermore, constitutions should provide broad grants of power to specific agencies and hold government officials accountable for their actions. Last, formal amendments to the constitution should be infrequent, deliberate, and significant.

The U.S. Constitution meets these ideals. There are only 4,300 words in the original document. It broadly outlines the basic principles of government and has been amended only twenty-seven times. All but eight of these amendments involve questions of civil liberty, voting, and electoral issues. Very few of these amendments have altered the basic structure of the federal government.

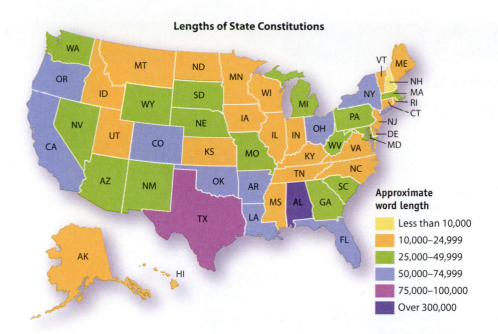

Lengths of State Constitutions

Approximate word length

- Less than 10,000
- 10,000–24,999
- 25,000–49,999
- 50,000–74,999
- 75,000–100,000
- Over 300,000

FIGURE 19-3
Lengths of States Constitutions
How does the length of the Texas Constitution compare with constitutions of other states?

Source: The Book of the States 2007, Vol. 38 (Lexington, KY: Council of State Governments 2007), Table 1.1, p. 10.

The U.S. Constitution is flexible enough to allow for change without altering the basic document.

Few state constitutions can meet these standards of brevity and few amendments. This is especially true of the Texas Constitution. If we compare the Texas Constitution with the "average" state constitution, we find that it is longer than most, at 93,000-plus words, and has more amendments. The Texas Constitution currently has 474 amendments.[11] Only five states have drafted more constitutions. One can easily conclude that most state constitutions, including the one used in Texas, do not meet the criteria outlined previously for an ideal constitution. Most are lengthy, detailed documents that require frequent alteration. Most state constitutions might be more accurately described as statutory or legislative acts than as constitutional law. This is especially true of the document that governs Texas. (See Figure 19-3.)

Several other generalizations can be made about state constitutions. First, most create weak executives and strong legislatures. Second, all state constitutions contain articles on taxation and finance that limit how funds can be spent. Taxes are often **earmarked taxes**—established for specific purposes. (A common example is the gasoline tax for state highways.) Third, all but a few constitutions prohibit deficit expenditures unless approved by voters in the form of a bond election. Finally, most state constitutions contain large amounts of trivia. For example, the original Texas Constitution contained a detailed list of items protected by the homestead protection provisions from forced sale for payment of debts. The list included the number of chickens, ducks, cows, pigs, dogs, and horses exempt from forced sale for payment of debts.

Revising State Constitutions

All state constitutions provide procedures for amending and revising the document. Except in the state of Delaware, changing constitutions involves two steps: proposing amendments and getting citizen approval. In Texas, two-thirds of each house of the legislature must propose amendments, and a majority of the voters who vote on the amendment must approve.

earmarked taxes

Taxes dedicated to a specific expenditure

HOW TEXAS DIFFERS   POLITICAL THINKING THROUGH COMPARISONS

Constitutional Amendments Among the States

The map below shows the number of amendments to state constitutions. Some western states have lots of amendments due to initiative provisions in their constitutions.

Q: How does Texas compare?

A: Texas is in the highest category, having passed 456 amendments to its state constitution.

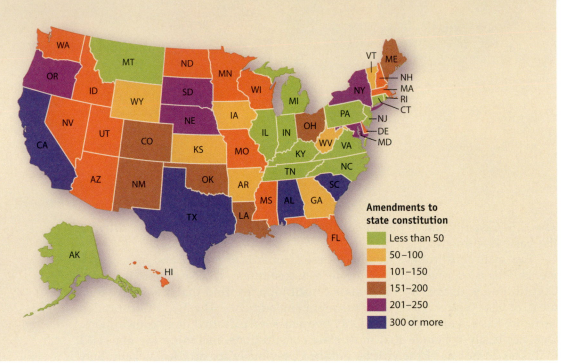

Source: The Book of the States 2010 (Lexington, KY: Council of State Governments, 2010), Table 1.1, p. 11.

initiative

a process that allows citizens to propose changes to the state constitution or state laws through the use of petitions signed by registered voters; Texas does not have these procedures at the state level

constitutional convention

an assembly of citizens who may propose changes to state constitutions for voter approval

Some states provide a variety of methods for proposing or recommending changes to the constitution. All state constitutions allow the legislature to propose changes. Most states require an extraordinary majority vote of both houses of the legislature to propose an amendment.[12]

A second method of proposing amendments to constitutions is by voter **initiative,** which requires the collection of a prescribed number of signatures on a petition within a set time. Seventeen states allow initiative. Most states with initiative are Western states that entered the Union in the late nineteenth century or early twentieth century when initiative was a popular idea. Only four states with initiative are east of the Mississippi River. Texas does not have initiative. The Texas Republican party pushed the idea of initiative for many years, but in 1996 it was dropped from the party platform. "How Texas Differs" compares the number of constitutional amendments among the states.

Most states, including Texas, allow the legislature to submit to the voters the question of calling a **constitutional convention** to propose amendments. This method is normally used for general revision and not for single amendments. Fourteen states have some provision for automatically submitting the question of a general convention to the voters periodically. If the voters approve, a convention is elected, assembles, and proposes amendments for voter approval.

Constitutional commissions are most often created by acts of the legislature, although other methods are provided. These commissions usually submit a report to the legislature recommending changes. If the legislature approves, the proposed amendments are submitted to the voters. In Florida, the commission can bypass the legislature and go directly to the voters. Texas last used a commission in 1973 when the legislature created a thirty-seven member commission.[13] This commission submitted recommendations to the Texas legislature, which acted as a constitutional convention.

Except for Delaware, where the state legislature can unilaterally amend the constitution, voters must approve amendments to the constitution in an election. Most states require a majority of those voting on the amendment to approve. Some states require a majority of the voters voting for some office (usually the governor) to approve. New Hampshire requires that two-thirds of the voters approve all amendments. Texas requires that a majority of those voting on the amendment approve.

Patterns of Amending

If we examine the amendment processes discussed previously, several patterns of state constitutional change can be observed. The first pattern involves the frequency of change. State constitutions are amended more frequently than the U.S. Constitution. One reason is that state constitutions deal with a wider range of functions. About 63 percent of the state amendments deal with issues not covered in the U.S. Constitution, such as education. However, even if we remove issues not covered in the U.S. Constitution, the rate of amendment is still three and a half times the national rate. Change is also related to length. Longer state constitutions are more likely to be amended.[14]

The second pattern involves the method used to amend. As indicated, most amendments (90 percent) are proposed by state legislatures. States that require large legislative majorities for initiation have fewer amendments proposed and approved. Most amendments proposed by legislatures also receive voter approval. About 63 percent of all amendments proposed since 1970 have been approved by the voters.[15]

In the seventeen states that allow voters to initiate amendments, two patterns emerge: More amendments are proposed, and the voter approval success rate for initiative-generated amendments is about half the rate for those proposed by state legislatures (32 percent versus 64 percent).[16] This tells us that the initiative process does not screen out amendments that lack broad public support. Proposal by legislature does. Amendments that gain support from super majorities are more likely to be politically acceptable. The legislature screens out unacceptable amendments.

Process of Amending

All amendments to the Texas Constitution have been proposed by a two-thirds vote of each house of the legislature. These proposed amendments are then submitted to voters. Since 2007, the Texas legislature has proposed thirty-eight amendments. Of these, voters passed thirty-five, or a whopping 92 percent. Most amendments appear on the ballot in November of odd-numbered years when no statewide offices are up for election and no national elections that draw media attention are held. As a result, many fewer voters turn out in these elections. Table 19-1 shows voter turnout in recent decades. In many elections, the turnout falls below 7 percent. In some years, when a controversial proposed amendment is placed on the ballot, turnout spikes into the teens. For example, in 1987, turnout doubled when a school tax amendment was placed on the ballot. In 2005, turnout rose again to almost 14 percent when the public was asked to consider an amendment prohibiting gay marriage. However, as little as 5 percent of the population has passed an amendment changing the constitution.

TABLE 19-1 | Voter Turnout in Odd-Year Constitutional Amendment Elections in Texas

Year	Percentage of Voting-Age Population Voting
2011	5.21
2009	5.90
2007	8.49
2005	13.80 (gay marriage amendment)
2003	9.30
2001	5.60
1999	6.69
1997	5.32
1995	5.55
1993	8.25
1991	16.6 (school tax reform)
1989	9.33
1987	18.6 (school tax reform)
1985	8.24
1983	6.19

Source: Texas Secretary of State, www.sos.state.tx.us/elections/historical/70-92.shtml.

ballot wording

description of a proposed amendment as it appears on the ballot, which can be noninstructive and misleading to voters

Ballot Wording

Ballot wording can also contribute to voter confusion and to levels of voter support for amendments. The state legislature dictates the ballot wording of all amendments. Sometimes this wording can be misleading or noninstructive unless the voter has studied the issue before the election.

For example, in 2011, Proposition 9 proposed a "constitutional amendment authorizing the governor to grant a pardon to a person who successfully completes a term of deferred adjudication community supervision." In order to make an informed decision, voters would have to understand what the phrase "deferred adjudication community supervision" meant. If they researched the proposition, they would discover that the proposed amendment refers to people who have pled guilty to a minor offense and received probation or community service. These people are not convicted of the crime, but the arrest stays on their record. As a result, they often have trouble getting jobs or renting housing when employers or apartment owners conduct background checks. The amendment allows the governor to grant a pardon, wiping the record clean, but only upon the recommendation of the Board of Pardons and Paroles and only after ten years have passed since the offense.[17] All of this information is not readily apparent from the wording of the ballot.

Ballot wording can also apparently be a significant factor in the passage or rejection of amendments. As we saw earlier, the words "ad valorem" may reduce a proposition's chances of passing. In 2011, voters solidly rejected an amendment that provides an "ad valorem" tax break to property owners who practiced water conservation during a drought. In the same election, voters approved an amendment allowing the Texas Water Development Board (TWDB) to issue bonds to promote water conservancy. The amendment just barely passed, but it did pass and ballot wording may well have been responsible. The ballot wording said that the board could issue bonds "in an amount not to exceed $6 billion at any time outstanding." Does this amendment limit the bond-issuing capability of the board, or does it grant the board new authority to issue bonds? A voter would have to research this issue prior to arriving at the polls to discover that the TWDB has had the authority to issue bonds since 1957. The bonds help local governments finance water-related infrastructure. Until the passage of Proposition 2, the TWDB could only issue up to $4.23 in bonds, but in the three years preceding the passage, the board had issued $1 billion. This steep hike in demand is a result of rapidly aging water infrastructure in the midst of rising water needs.[18] This information is not apparent from the ballot wording, and in fact, it may have appeared to voters that the amendment served to reduce rather than increase the dollar amount of the bonds the board is allowed to issue.

Confusing wording may also have unintended consequences. In 2009, the national media had a field day when Democratic candidate for state attorney general Barbara Ann Radnofsky pointed out that the Texas amendment prohibiting gay marriage may have accidentally banned all marriage. Radnofsky pointed to a phrase in Subsection B stating, "This state or a political subdivision of this state may not create or recognize any legal status identical or similar to marriage." Having previously defined marriage as a union between one man and one woman, Radnofsky argued that "you do not have to have a fancy law degree to read this and understand what it plainly says."[19]

The Role of Interest Groups

Several other observations can be made regarding the amendment processes in Texas. Most amendments pass and face little opposition. Texans have approved 470 amendments and rejected 173.[20] Most are supported by an organized interest group willing to spend money, gain support, and get the amendment passed. Interest groups attempt to protect their interests in the constitution because it is more difficult to alter than a state law, which can be easily changed in the next session of the legislature. The process of constitutional change requires a two-thirds vote of the legislature plus electoral approval. An old Texas saying goes, "Neither man nor property is safe as long as the legislature is in session."

An example of such a protection in the constitution is the Permanent University Fund (PUF). The University of Texas and Texas A&M University are the only state schools benefiting from this fund, which has a value of approximately $11 billion. Other state universities have long felt that they deserved a share of this protected fund. Texas A&M and the University of Texas wanted to protect their funds and formed a coalition with non-PUF schools to support an amendment that created the Higher Education Assistance Fund (HEAF). This fund provides money to non-PUF universities. In the end, higher education funding for all state universities became protected in the state constitution.

Odd-year elections, confusing or noninstructive ballot wording, issues that interest few voters, and voter ignorance all contribute to low voter turnout. A very small number of voters, stimulated by personal interests and supported by an active interest group, can amend the constitution without a majority of the voters becoming involved. Many Texans are not even aware that an election is being held.

Prospects for Amending

Many legal scholars have pointed out the need for a general revision of the current Texas Constitution, which was written in 1876 and has been amended many times over the years. In the 1970s, a serious effort at total revision was unsuccessful.

In 1999, two prominent members of the Texas legislature introduced a bill calling for general revision of the Texas Constitution. Bill Ratliff, who was the Republican senator from East Texas at the time, and Representative Robert Junell, Democrat from San Angelo, were the chairs of budget-writing committees in the Senate and the House in that session. Ratliff served as lieutenant governor of the state from 2000 to 2003. Their bill called for substantial changes in the current constitution. They proposed to increase the power of the legislature by lengthening the terms of state senators to six years and of house members to four years, raising the salary of the legislators, and giving the legislature the power to reconvene in a special fifteen-day session to override the governor's vetoes. They also augmented the power of the governor, making only the lieutenant governor, the comptroller, and the attorney general independently elected offices. This proposal also reduced the size of the current constitution, which has 93,000 words contained in 376 sections, to some 19,000 words in 150 sections. This proposal died in committees in both houses.

Hence, the piecemeal process of amending the constitution every two years will likely continue. The political culture of the state and the conservative nature of state politics stand in the way of

World-class cyclist Lance Armstrong campaigns for an amendment to the state constitution that would allow the state to issue $3 billion in bonds to support cancer research.

broad-scale change. The current constitution supports the traditionalistic-individualistic political culture of the state, carefully limiting the powers of the executive and legislative branches. Texans may also feel uncomfortable with reform that may lead to unintended consequences.

Another reason generally cited for this piecemeal amendment process is a lack of support for reform by significant political forces in the state. Strong political leadership from someone like the governor would be necessary, but powerful lobby groups whose interests are currently protected by the document would make change difficult, if not impossible.

Summary   Self-Test www.mhhe.com/ pattersontadtx11e

The Piecemeal Amendment Process: How It Prevents Big Government in Texas

Early in its history, Texas adopted a series of constitutions as it established a republic, joined the Union and then the Confederacy, and returned to the Union. With the exception of the Reconstruction constitution, all of these documents shared the goal of providing for a government with very limited powers. The current constitution of the state of Texas was written and adopted by people who wanted minimalist government. Yet the state has grown from a sparse rural outback to a thriving center of trade and industry. Texans continue to amend the constitution in a piecemeal process so that it gradually evolves to accommodate this development. When faced with propositions, Texans tend to favor those that don't expand the power of government. Why have Texans continued to be suspicious of big government for well over a century? Despite gradual demographic and economic changes, the individualistic-traditionalistic political culture has continued to dominate Texas society.

Moreover, only a small percentage of Texans vote in the constitutional amendment elections. These elections are held in odd-numbered years when no candidates for statewide or national offices are running. As few as 5 percent of the population can push through an amendment to the constitution. As a result, interest groups who work with legislators to formulate laws and propositions, and who campaign and galvanize their members in support of certain propositions, can play a major role in the passage of amendments. It's not surprising that these same interests oppose overhauling a constitution that has gradually evolved to meet their needs.

Those who argue for reform lament the weak governor and point to a legislature so constrained by amendments and laws that responding to crises is difficult. Can such a weak central government responsibly serve the needs of one of the leading economic powers in the world? Senator Ratliff and Representative Junell may well have been ahead of their time in proposing changes to the constitution. However, as Texas faces challenges such as water scarcity, skyrocketing demands for energy, and the ever-increasing needs of a growing population, its political culture and political system may be forced to adapt. But this change is likely to happen slowly, through a piecemeal amendment process.

CHAPTER 19

Study Corner

Key Terms

ballot wording (*p. 492*)
constitutional convention (*p. 490*)
denials of power (*p. 487*)

earmarked taxes (*p. 489*)
grants of power (*p. 487*)
initiative (*p. 490*)

Self-Test: Multiple Choice

1. Which of the following is *not* a general principle of the Texas Constitution?
   a. separation of powers
   b. limited government
   c. compact or contract theory
   d. annual elections

2. Passage of a proposed constitutional amendment in Texas requires
   a. approval by two-thirds of the house and senate and adoption by the citizens with a majority vote.
   b. approval by three-fifths of the house and senate and adoption by the citizens with a majority vote.
   c. approval by two-thirds of the house and senate and adoption by the citizens with a two-thirds vote.
   d. approval by a majority vote of the house and senate and adoption by the citizens with a majority vote.

3. Generally, most state constitutions do all of the following *except*
   a. contain provisions pertaining to taxation and finance.
   b. prohibit deficit spending without voter approval.
   c. require only infrequent alteration.
   d. create weak executives and strong legislatures.

4. Which of the following is a contributing factor to voter apathy toward proposed constitutional amendments in Texas?
   a. the number of amendments
   b. the two-party system
   c. clear and simple ballot wording
   d. elections in odd-numbered years

5. What does the supremacy clause in the Texas Constitution establish?
   a. the supremacy of the Texas Constitution over the U.S. Constitution
   b. the supremacy of the U.S. Constitution over the state constitution
   c. the supremacy of the state constitution over state and local laws
   d. the supremacy of local laws over state laws

6. The percentage of voters who participate in constitutional amendment elections in Texas is usually no higher than
   a. 10 percent.
   b. 20 percent.
   c. 30 percent.
   d. 40 percent.

7. Because Texans consistently have displayed characteristics of an individualistic subculture, all of the constitutions governing the state have included a bill of rights. (T/F)

8. The constitution of 1876 reimposed lengthier terms of office for government officials, eliminated many statewide and local elected offices, and empowered the government to act with few restrictions. (T/F)

9. Most state constitutions, including the Texas Constitution, grant more generous liberties to citizens than does the U.S. Constitution. (T/F)

10. Constitutions that are short and explicit tend to better serve the needs of the people over time. (T/F)

Critical Thinking

Go online and find the state constitutions of Delaware and Texas. Compare the documents. What major differences do you see?

Suggested Readings

Chandler, Davidson. *Race and Class in Texas Politics*. Princeton, N.J.: Princeton University Press, 1976. A good discussion of how race and class have played a role in state constitutional politics in Texas.

Lutz, Donald S. "Toward a Theory of Constitutional Amendments." *American Political Science Review* 88 (June 1994): 355–70. A review of changes in state constitutions.

May, Janice C. "State Constitutional Development in 2004," in *Book of the States 2005*, Vol. 37, 3–9. A summary of trends in the revision of state constitutions.

Websites

http://www.sos.state.tx.us/
The secretary of state's website; provides votes in all elections and recent votes on constitutional amendments.

http://www-camlaw.rutgers.edu/statecon/
The website of the Center for State Constitutional Studies; contains general information on state constitutional revisions among the states.

www.texasbar.com/
The website of one of the many state organizations that favor constitutional revision in Texas.

Participate!

Search online to find proposed amendments the legislature has passed or is hoping to pass for the next odd-year election. Study the issue and discuss whether you agree with the outcome.

Extra Credit
Search online to find editorials on the last proposed amendments to the Texas Constitution. Do you agree with the views expressed?

Self-Test Answers

1. d, 2. a, 3. c, 4. d, 5. c, 6. a, 7. F, 8. F, 9. T, 10. T

Participation and Interest Groups in Texas Politics

Texas ranks below all but a few states in voter participation in both national and state elections. This low level of participation helps to shape a political environment in which interest groups thrive and even dominate. In this chapter, we will search for clues that can explain the low levels of voting among Texans. We will assess the impact of political culture on participation and uncover the historic legacy of restricted access to the ballot for many groups within the voting-age population. We will turn to current policies and trends, and predict how recent changes in voting laws might affect voter turnout. We will then transition to interest groups, first characterizing the types of interest groups that are active in Texas and then analyzing the roles they play in the political process. We will evaluate whether interest groups in Texas contribute to democratic process or reinforce a political system in which elites dominate. The points emphasized in the chapter are these:

- Texas and other Southern states have used methods such as poll taxes, annual registration, and white primaries to limit voter eligibility in the past.

- Today socioeconomic factors, party competition, and election timing contribute to low levels of voter participation in Texas.

- Classify interest groups that are active in state politics.

- Texas places fewer limits on interest group activities than most states. As a result, interest groups in Texas have stronger political influence than they do in other states.

Legacy of Restricted Ballot Access

Like other southern states, Texas has a history of restrictive voter registration laws. In the past, those laws made it difficult to qualify to vote and limited avenues of political participation. Largely because of actions by the federal government, most legal restrictions to voter registration have been removed. Although the past restrictions have been removed from law, they still have an effect today. Political

TABLE 20-1 | Texas Rank as a Percentage of Voting-Age Population Voting in National Elections, 1976–2010

Year	Texas Rank*	National Turnout†	Texas Turnout‡
Presidential Election Years			
1976	44	53	47
1980	44	52	44
1984	45	53	47
1988	46	50	45
1992	46	55	49
1996	47	52	41
2000	47	50	43
2004	47	58.3	46.1
2008	47	57	46
Congressional/Statewide Office Elections			
1978	46	35	24
1982	46	38	26
1986	45	33	25
1990	42	33	27
1994	45	36	31
1998	47	38	24
2002	46	38	26
2006	49	42	26
2010	50	37	26

*Texas ranking compared with the other forty-nine and fifty states.

†Average turnout for all states as a percentage of voting-age population voting in the election.

‡Percentage of voting-age population in Texas elections.

Source: Statistical Abstracts of United States, 1976, 1978, 1980, 1982, 1984, 1985, 1991, 1993, 1995, 1998, 2004, 2006, and 2008 (Washington, DC: U.S. Government Printing Office).

voting-age population

all citizens who meet the formal requirements to register to vote; in Texas, you must be 18 years of age and a resident of the state for thirty days before the election

behavior does not change quickly, as Table 20-1 suggests. The following are a few examples of the many restrictions common in Southern political cultures.

Poll Tax and Annual Registrations

In 1902, the Texas legislature adopted, with voter approval, the payment of a poll tax as a requirement for voting. This law was aimed primarily at the Populist movement, which had organized low-income white farmers into a political coalition that threatened the establishment within the Democratic Party.[1] This tax ($1.75) was a large amount of money for poor farmers in their predominantly barter economy in the early 1900s. The poll tax also restricted ballot access for African Americans and Latinos, who were disproportionately poor.

In 1964, the poll tax was eliminated as a requirement for voting in federal elections by the passage of the Twenty-Fourth Amendment to the U.S. Constitution; however, Texas kept the poll tax as a requirement for voting in state elections.[2] In 1966, the poll tax as a requirement for voting was abolished by a decision of the U.S. Supreme Court.[3]

The poll tax had the intended effect of reducing qualified voters—2.4 million Texans paid the tax in order to vote in 1964–1965. In 1968, the first election cycle after the poll tax was abolished, voter registration rose to over 4 million, an increase of about 41 percent.[4]

Even after the 1966 elimination of the poll tax as a voter requirement, Texas retained a very restrictive system of **annual voter registration,** requiring citizens to reregister every year. This was eliminated in 1971, and in 1972, the first year that Texas used a **permanent registration system,** which allows citizens to remain registered if they vote regularly, voter registration increased by almost 1.4 million.[5] All states now use some form of permanent registration.[6]

annual voter registration

a system that requires citizens to reregister every year

permanent registration system

a system that allows citizens to remain on the voter registration list if they continue to vote at prescribed intervals

White Primary

Another past practice used by many Southern states, including Texas, to eliminate participation by African Americans was the white primary. Beginning in 1923 and continuing until 1945, the Texas legislature passed bills prohibiting African Americans from participating in the Democratic Party primary election. The U.S. Supreme Court declared those legislative acts unconstitutional.[7] In 1932, the state Democratic Party passed rules that prohibited African Americans from participating in any activity of the party, including voting in the Democratic Party primary. That action led to another U.S. Supreme Court ruling.[8] The issue before the court was whether or not a political party was an agent of government or a private organization. The Supreme Court ruled in 1935 that political parties are private organizations and can decide who may participate in primary elections. That effectively prevented African Americans from participating in the Democratic Party primary. Because there was no opposition by Republicans at that time in the general election, the primary became the "general election." Thus, from 1932 until 1945, African Americans in Texas were denied the right to vote by the rules of the Democratic Party and not by state law.

In 1944, the U.S. Supreme Court outlawed all white primaries in southern states in the case *Smith v. Allwright*.[9] That ruling overturned earlier rulings that political parties were private organizations. The Supreme Court ruled that political parties are agents of the state and cannot exclude people from participating in primary elections because of race.

Property Ownership Restrictions

As was common in many states, Texas used property ownership to restrict the right of people to vote. Those restrictions applied mostly to local elections, especially bond elections. The reason for restricting voting by property ownership was that local governments are financed primarily with property taxes, and supposedly renters did not pay property tax. However, renters might pay property tax, because landlords, when market conditions are favorable to them, do shift property taxes to renters as higher rents. Property ownership requirements were eliminated in the 1970s when permanent registration became effective in Texas. There was no way to effectively enforce the property ownership requirement.

Gender Discrimination in Voting

Women's access to voting was also restricted in Texas until 1920, when the Nineteenth Amendment to the U.S. Constitution was approved. By 1914, eleven states had granted women the right to

Texans vote on the campus of the University of Texas, Austin. Changes in Texas law since the 1960s and 1970s have made voting easier for all citizens in Texas, yet the turnout remains low compared with that of other states.

vote.[10] In 1915, the Texas legislature considered granting women the right to vote, but the measure failed. In 1918, women were given the right to participate in primary elections, and in 1919, Texas became the first southern state to approve the Nineteenth Amendment.[11]

Gender discrimination along with all the other restrictions combined to produce the state's tradition of discouraging participation. The elimination of those restrictions and today's easy access to voter registration have increased the number of registered voters in Texas, but that has not translated into a significant increase in the level of participation. Texas today still ranks near the bottom on voter turnout in elections. In time, the residual effect of restrictive practices may decline.

Factors That Affect Voter Participation Today

The increasing presence of minority candidates in elections is one factor that has been increasing voter participation by minorities. The 2002 election, in which the Democratic candidates for governor and U.S. senator were minorities, saw increased turnout by African Americans and Latinos. Other factors that influence voter turnout include socioeconomic status, party competition, regional differences, and timing of elections.

Effects of Social and Economic Status on Voting

On both the national and the state levels, rates of voter participation are strongly affected by socioeconomic factors such as educational level, family income, and minority status. High-income, well-educated citizens are more likely to vote than are lower-income, less-well-educated citizens. People of higher socioeconomic status are likely to be more aware of elections and to perceive themselves as having a higher stake in the outcomes of elections; therefore they are more likely to vote. They are also more likely to contribute financially to political campaigns and to become actively involved in elections and party activity.

Race is also a factor in voter turnout—African Americans and Latinos are less likely to vote than whites. Large minority populations in Texas may help explain the lower levels of voter participation in Texas than in other states. Voting by Latinos is lower for a variety of reasons, but in Texas, they are disproportionately younger than Anglos, and many are not citizens. As with Latinos, voter turnout among African Americans is lower in part because of lower income and educational levels and because of a high percentage of young people in this population groups.[12]

party competition

the principle that states with two active and competitive parties have higher rates of voter turnout than states, such as Texas, with weak or noncompetitive parties

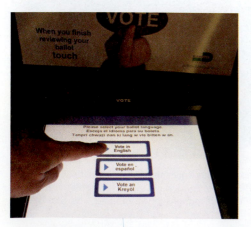

Party Competition and Voter Turnout

Although **party competition** in Texas—the condition of having two active parties—has increased in recent years, the state has a long history of being a one-party state, which partially accounts for the state's lower voter turnout. Studies have shown that party competition is a significant factor in voter turnout. In states where there are two strong, competitive political parties, voter turnout is much higher than in those with one strong and one weak party. Competition increases voter interest in the election because of campaign activities and because of a perception by voters that their vote counts.

Party competition also increases grassroots political organizations that stimulate participation and turn people out to vote.[13] Texans elected Republicans to all statewide offices from since 2002. It remains to be seen if this domination of state politics will be permanent.

HOW TEXAS DIFFERS   POLITICAL THINKING THROUGH COMPARISONS

Percentage of Eligible Voters Voting in the 2008 Presidential Election

This map shows the percentage of eligible voters in each state who voted in the 2008 presidential election.

Q: How does turnout in Texas compare to that in other states?

A: Less than half the voting-age population of Texas went to the polls in 2008, compared with 58 percent of all Americans. Of the fifty states, only Hawaii had a lower percentage of voters that year.

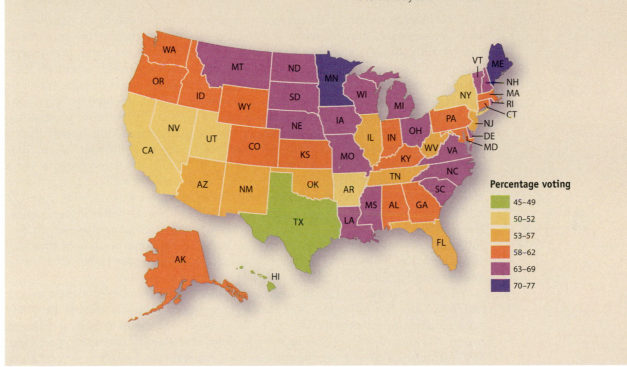

Percentage voting
- 45–49
- 50–52
- 53–57
- 58–62
- 63–69
- 70–77

Regional Variations in Voter Turnout

Some writers have suggested that region is the most reliable factor in predicting voter turnout. This is supported by an examination of voter turnout in the states of the Old South, where voter participation is the lowest. Region alone, however, does not explain individual voting behavior. The states of the Old South, including Texas, have a history of repressed voting activity for the reasons discussed earlier—the poll tax, white primaries, annual registrations, and lack of party competition. Also, income and educational levels in this region have historically been lower than in the rest of the country. These factors, combined with traditionalistic-individualistic political cultures, historically reduced political participation.

In recent years, voter turnout in Southern states has increased.[14] This is due in part to the elimination of many of the past restrictions. Income and educational levels have also increased, as has immigration from other regions of the country by people from other political cultures.

Timing of Elections

Voter turnout in Texas is higher in November general elections than in odd-year elections when we do not elect a president or other statewide or national offices. (See "How Texas Differs.") Also, local elections for city councils and school boards are generally not held in conjunction with general elections; the common time for these in Texas is in May. Turnout in local elections is always lower than in other elections. Because these elections are less visible and receive less attention by the media, voters do not perceive them as being important, and many of these races are not contested. In 1995, a constitutional amendment allowed cities and school boards to cancel elections if all races are uncontested. The governing body certifies the uncontested candidates as "winners."

Early Voting

In 2011, Florida angered civil rights organizations, the League of Women Voters, and Democrats in general when it passed a new law reducing the number of early voting days from 15 to 8, placed new restrictions on voter registration groups, and forced voters to cast provisional ballots if they failed to register their change of address prior to Election Day. These groups claimed that the new law would squelch voter turnout, particularly among low-income voters.[15]

In the late twentieth century, many states initiated early voting, absentee voting, and mail voting laws. Advocates of convenience voting hoped that it would increase overall voter turnout and help overcome turnout inequalities among ethnic, racial, and income groups. In 1987, the Texas legislature passed a no-excuse absentee voting law. Any qualified voter can cast a ballot 17 days prior to Election Day with no excuse. The purpose of this policy is not only to make voting more convenient for all registered voters, but also to better accommodate the elderly and disabled. Texans can vote early in person or by mail or fax. Individuals who have trouble walking or standing for long periods of time can call ahead and vote at the curbside. Individuals who expect to be out of their county on Election Day can also apply for a ballot in person.

A large number of researchers have explored these voting policies, asking questions like the following: Are states getting their money's worth? Do these reforms actually increase turnout or equalize voter participation among different groups? Is there evidence to support the claim that Florida is constraining voter turnout? Studies diverge significantly in their assessment of impact on voter turnout, with one observing a 10 percent spike in participation while others report significantly less or no effect on turnout. Recent research suggests that convenience voting measures produce a short-lived increase in turnout that dissipates over several years. Electoral reforms do not have a clear impact on turnout inequalities. Early voters tend to be older, more partisan, and more ideologically extreme than other voters, rather than members of a particular demographic group.

In Texas, although an increasing number of residents are taking advantage of early voting as shown in a How Texas Differs box, the policy has had no significant impact on turnout. Although early voting hasn't helped to overcome voter turnout inequalities, it hasn't exacerbated them either. The primary benefit of early voting has been to make voting more convenient for elderly and disabled persons. In elections, between 10 and 15 percent more individuals aged 65 and up vote early than vote on Election Day.[16]

Voter Identification Laws

In May 2008, *The New York Times* published an article accusing Hillary Clinton of hiring "electoral soldiers of fortune" in the Texas primary. Along border towns, these campaign workers were known as *politiqueras*, individuals paid to go door to door, distribute flyers, and help people get to the polls to vote. They guarantee votes for the candidate who has hired them at the going rate of $100 to $200 a day.[17] Politiqueras are mostly women with a ready network of friends, family,

DEBATING THE ISSUES   POLITICAL THINKING IN ACTION

Should Voter ID Cards Be Required?

In the past, poll taxes, grandfather clauses, annual registration, and other tactics have been used to keep citizens from voting. Today, some claim that a new method will accomplish the same result: voter ID cards. Texas passed a law requiring voter ID cards in 2011. Although the majority of states have now passed some type of voter ID laws, Texas is one of only six states that require photo identification. Hence, critics view the Texas law as among the strictest. The U.S. Justice Department, however, has approved the law, ruling that it did not violate the Voting Rights Act. The U.S. Supreme Court also approved an Indiana voter ID card law. Hence, the federal government has affirmed the legality of these laws,

YES Texas has long lacked the ability to detect in-person voter fraud. Today, with the number of non-citizens living in Texas on the rise, the problem of voting fraud may increase significantly. These laws would inconvenience very few voters. In fact, in Indiana and Georgia voter turnout actually increased following the passage of such laws.

—*Texas Republicans*

NO Requiring photo IDs effectively disenfranchises the elderly, the homeless, the urban poor, and the disabled who are less likely to have government-issued photo IDs such as driver's licenses. Requiring citizens to travel to government offices and pay for ID cards creates a barrier to voting. It will likely cause a significant drop-off in the number of citizens voting for Democratic candidates in state and national elections.

—*Texas Democrats*

Q: Why do Texas Republicans believe the state should require voter ID cards? Why do Texas Democrats oppose it?

A: Without any evidence of voter fraud, Republicans believe it will reduce the number of Democratic voters. Democrats know the number of votes for their party will be reduced.

and neighbors. A big factor in local elections in South Texas, experienced politiqueras can "deliver" over 200 votes on or by Election Day. However, politiqueras are attracting an increasing amount of criticism. Some Texas candidates have even pledged not to use them.

This practice, however, is not unique to South Texas. In cities across the United States, campaigns give out "street money" or "walk around money," and in Northern states, campaign workers can earn considerably more than politiqueras do. In Philadelphia, the rate can be as high as $400 per day.[18] The controversial practice of hiring campaign workers is safeguarded by the First Amendment right to freedom of speech.

Yet some Texans feel that politiqueras cross the line between what is legal and what is not by stealing mail-in ballots and sometimes even paying people for their votes. In 2005, Texas Republican Attorney General Greg Abbott led a crackdown on voter fraud. Over the course of two years, 26 arrests were made. In 18 of these instances, the campaign workers were charged with mishandling mail-in ballots. Of the 26 people arrested, all were Democrats and almost all were Latino or African American.[19]

Meanwhile, the Texas legislature began to the debate on a voter identification law. Voter ID laws require citizens who do not possess a government-issued identity card, such as a driver's license, to obtain a voter ID card. Republicans argued that requiring Texans to show an identification card before voting would cut down on voter fraud. Democrats believed that these laws would impede ballot access and unfairly target low-income or disadvantaged voters, who were less likely to have a driver's license. In 2011, after two previous sessions that featured shouting matches and walkouts, the Texas legislature passed such a law.

Types of Interest Groups

The lack of citizen involvement in elections increases the importance and the influence of interest groups in Texas politics. Being an active member of an interest group is another form of political participation and a way to increase one's influence on government. Frequently, it is not the individual, or the more broadly defined "public opinion," that influences government officials, but the opinions of these attentive publics, organized in interest groups, who often have the ear of public officials. Involvement in interest groups is a more influential form of participation than the simple act of voting, especially in Texas where these groups wield considerable power. Interest groups in Texas can be divided into economic, citizens', and government groups.

Economic Organizations—Promoting Business and Professionalism

A few different types of economic interest groups are active in Texas politics. **Peak business organizations** are interest groups that represent statewide interests, such as the state Chamber of Commerce, the Texas Association of Manufacturers, and the National Federation of Independent Business Owners. These groups advocate for their members' interests and present a united front against policies that do not promote a "good business climate" in the state. They are often the most active at the state level and are generally well financed.

Texas business groups also include nonmembership organizations, which do not have active members and generally represent a single company, organization, corporation, or individual. These form the largest category of interest groups. Examples include Chili's Grill and Bar in Dallas, El Chico Corporation, and H. Ross Perot.

Trade associations differ from peak business organizations in that they represent more specific business interests. In Texas, examples of these groups abound. Two trade associations that are often classified as among the more powerful are the Mid-Continent Oil and Gas Association, representing oil and gas producers, and the Good Roads Association, which represents highway contractors. Some groups represent more specific economic interests.

Examples of retail trade groups are the Texas Apartment Association, the Texas Automobile Dealers Association, the Texas Restaurant Association, and the Association of Licensed Beverage Distributors. The primary goal of these groups is to protect their trades from state regulations deemed undesirable by the groups and to support regulations favorable to the groups' interests.

Agriculture groups are prominent because of the importance of agriculture to the Texas economy. There are three types of **agricultural associations.** First are those that represent general farm interests. The Texas Farm Bureau represents large agricultural producers in the state. The Texas Farmers Union represents family farms and ranches. Second are organizations that represent commodity groups, such as cotton growers, cattle raisers, chicken raisers, and mohair producers. The third type of agriculture interest group represents suppliers of services to agriculture producers. Such groups include cotton ginners, seed and fertilizer producers, and manufacturers and sellers of farm equipment.

peak business organizations
interest groups that represent statewide business organizations, such as a state's Chamber of Commerce

trade associations
interest groups that represent specific business interests, such as oil producers and highway contractors

agricultural associations
interest groups that represent different types of farmers and businesses that provide farming supplies

Professional associations differ from trade associations in two ways: (1) generally a professional license is issued by the state, and (2) the state controls their scope of practice. They represent such professions as physicians (the Texas Medical Association) and attorneys (the Texas Trial Lawyers Association, which represents some attorneys). There are also organizations representing the interests of architects, landscape architects, engineers, surveyors, plumbers, accountants, librarians, barbers, hairdressers, cosmetologists, funeral directors, dentists, nurses, chiropractors, optometrists, pharmacists, podiatrists, clinical psychologists, veterinarians, and many other professional groups.

In Texas, public employees are not granted the right of **collective bargaining**—the right to negotiate wages, hours, and other working conditions with their employer—as they are in many states. In collective bargaining, the government must enter negotiations with an organization representing government workers, and both sides must reach an agreement. State law in Texas does not grant this right to state or local employees.

Because of this lack of collective bargaining in Texas, public-sector employee organizations are professional associations rather than labor unions. In other states, such groups are classified as public-sector labor unions.

The Texas State Teachers Association (TSTA) is the largest professional group in the state. Affiliated with the National Education Association, TSTA is generally considered the more liberal teachers' group. TSTA is well organized and sometimes presents a united front. At other times, TSTA members have been known to fight among themselves. The Association of Texas Professional Educators is a more conservative organization that represents some teachers in the state. It was formed to counter the TSTA and has strong associations with the Texas Republican Party.

Labor unions in Texas exist only in the private sector, are not powerful, and represent a small fraction of the workers. Strong labor unions are anathema to the traditionalistic-individualistic political culture of Texas. In many industrialized states, organized labor unions are important and powerful interest groups, although their influence has been declining in recent years. Except in a few counties on the Texas Gulf Coast, where organized labor represents petrochemical workers and longshoremen, organized labor in Texas is very weak. In 2010, only 9.6 percent of the total Texas workforce belonged to labor unions.[20] As in most of the South, strong anti-union feelings are very much a part of the political culture. Texas is one of twenty-two states with "right-to-work" laws. These laws prohibit union shops where all workers, based on a majority vote of the workers, are forced to join the union within ninety days of employment to retain their jobs.

Austin teachers protest budget cuts at the Capitol. The Texas State Teachers Association, the largest professional group in Texas, represents teachers but lacks the right to collective bargaining under Texas law.

professional associations

organizations of people in professions such as teaching, medicine, law, architecture, cosmetology, and many others that generally require a license, have an element of state control, and lack the right to collective bargaining

collective bargaining

negotiations on wages, hours, and other working conditions between employers and employees

Citizens' Groups—Promoting Ideas and Causes

Ideological interest groups in Texas consist largely of both ethnic and religious groups. African Americans and Latinos are the two most active ethnic groups in the state. Latinos are represented by a variety of groups that are sometimes at odds with one another. The League of United Latin American Citizens (LULAC) is the largest such group in the state. Other such organizations include Mexican American Democrats (MAD), the Mexican American Legal Defense and Education Fund (MALDEF), and the Political Association of Spanish-Speaking Organizations (PASSO). The National Association for the Advancement of Colored People (NAACP) and the Congress of Racial Equality (CORE) represent African Americans in Texas.

These groups are primarily concerned with advancing civil rights, ending discrimination, improving government services, and gaining political power.

The National Firearms Association demonstrates against gun control in Austin. Public interest groups such as this one represent a range of causes that are important to Texans.

Although they do not always share common interests, gaining economic and political equality is an interest they do share.

Texas has a history of active religious groups. As in the rest of the Old South, Protestant churches fought to eliminate the sale of alcoholic beverages in the state. Even today, large sections of the state are "dry," meaning that alcohol is not sold there. In areas where alcohol can be sold, only beer and wine can be sold on Sunday, and only after noon.

The Catholic Church is also active in state politics. This activity, primarily among Latino Catholics, is driven by concerns about economic advancement, local services, and the abortion issue. In San Antonio, the Catholic Church was a driving force for the creation of Communities Organized for Public Service (COPS). This organization successfully challenged the Good Government League, which had dominated city elections for decades.[21] In the Rio Grande Valley, the Catholic Church was a driving force in the formation of the Interfaith Alliance. In the El Paso area, the Inter-Religious Sponsoring Organization was created to advance Latino interests.

In recent years, fundamentalist religious groups have increased their activities on the national level and in Texas. In 1994, they gained control of the Republican Party State Executive Committee in Texas and maintain control today. Organizations such as the Christian Coalition attempt to promote antiabortion campaigns, abstinence-based sex education, homeschooling, a school voucher system, prayer in school, and, of course, "family values." These groups have had some success at electing local school boards and now control the Texas State Board of Education, which governs some aspects of school policy statewide.

In 2010, these conservatives drew national attention when they overhauled the Texas grade school curriculum standards to deemphasize the civil rights movement, religious freedoms, and hundreds of other topics. They removed Thomas Jefferson as one of the great political thinkers introduced in world history. The decision sparked intense criticism nationwide because some feared that textbook companies, catering to the new Texas standards, would make these changes in new editions of their social studies textbooks that were slated to be used by other states.[22]

Public interest groups represent causes or ideas rather than economic, professional, or governmental interests. Many of these Texas organizations have national counterparts—for instance, Mothers Against Drunk Driving (MADD), the National Organization for Women (NOW), the National Right to Life Association, the Sierra Club, the American Civil Liberties Union (ACLU), Common Cause, the League of Women Voters, and Public Citizen. These groups usually limit their support or opposition to a narrow range of issues.

Government Organizations—Promoting Local Interests

On the state level, government organizations include **state and local interest groups (SLIGs)** consisting of government employees and officials who organize to protect and advance their interests. Examples of these groups are the Texas Municipal League, the Texas Association of Police Chiefs, the Combined Law Enforcement Association of Texas, the Texas Association of Fire Fighters, the City Attorneys Association, the Texas Association of County Officials, and the Texas School Board Association. These groups share the goals of protecting local government interests from actions of the state legislature, the governor, and state agencies.

state and local interest groups (SLIGs)

interest groups that represent state government employees, such as the Texas Association of Police Chiefs, and local governments, such as the Texas Association of County Officials

Interest Group Tactics and Their Regulation

Most states have laws that regulate two kinds of activities of interest groups: lobbying and making financial contributions to political campaigns. Lobby regulations generally consist of requiring organizations that have regular contacts with legislators to register and provide reports on their activities. Often, this requirement is weak, and the reports might not reflect the true activities of such organizations.

Texas first required the registration of interest groups in 1907. This statute prohibited "efforts to influence legislation 'by means other than appeal to reason' and provided that persons guilty of lobbying were subject to fines and imprisonment."[23] The act was never enforced. In 1957, a new law was passed that required lobbyists to register and disclose information about their activities; however, the law had many loopholes and was ineffective. In 1973, a new law was passed that called for more stringent reporting. The act was again amended in 1983. Under current law, three kinds of persons must register as lobbyists: individuals who lobby as professionals; "individuals who receive more than $200.00 in one calendar quarter as pay for lobbying"; and individuals who spend more than $200 for gifts, awards, or entertainment to influence legislation.[24] Each year about 1,500 groups and persons register. Government officials who lobby for state agencies and universities are exempt from registration. Also, some lawyers do not register because they claim they are representing clients and are not lobbying. Thus the total number of persons who actually lobby the legislature is much higher.

Interest groups attempt to gain influence by lobbying government officials, launching grassroots campaigns, and galvanizing voters and financial support for candidates. The type of technique depends on the type of group and the resources available to that group.

Lobbying

In Texas, the legislature meets every two years for 140 days, and the most intense lobby activity takes place during the regular session (see Figure 20-1). Lobbying does not stop when the legislature adjourns. Most legislation

A lobbyist communicates by e-mail in the "owner's box" in the Texas House of Representatives. Lobbyists provide information to legislators and the governor, and they also attempt to influence administrative agencies once legislation is passed.

FIGURE 20-1

Each year, lobbyists spend money during the legislative session to have their issues presented to the members. Ideological and single-issue clients account for 15 percent of all spending. Business interests spend most of the money. Does this kind of money buy legislation that is slanted toward business and against consumers?

Source: Texans for Public Justice, *Austin's Oldest Profession: Texas' Top Lobby Clients and Those Who Serve Them,* September 2008, www.tpj.org.

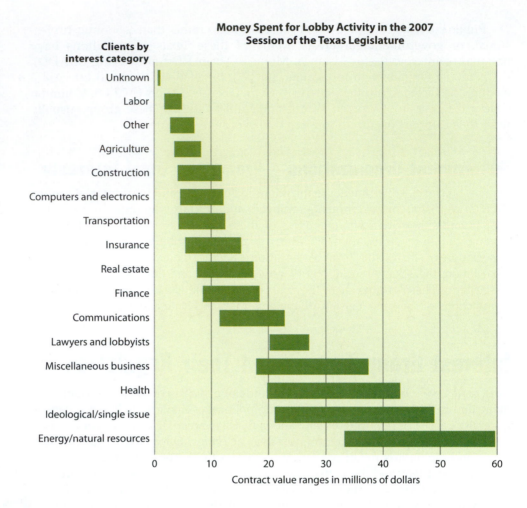

Money Spent for Lobby Activity in the 2007 Session of the Texas Legislature

requires a signature by the governor. Persuading the governor to either sign or veto a bill is an important part of lobbying activity.

If the governor signs a bill, an administrative agency must enforce it. Administrative discretion in enforcement of a law can also be the object of lobbying. Interest groups devote great efforts to influencing how agencies interpret and enforce laws, and they try to secure appointments to governing boards and commissions of people who favor their interests.

Lobbying tactics have changed in recent years. In the past, the process was described primarily as "booze, bribes, and broads." There is much less of that today. Lobbyists emphasize information and public relations over the old tactics, but entertaining members of the legislature is still very much a part of the process.

Interest groups often provide research information to members of the Texas legislature. This information can be self-serving but is often accurate and can be a valuable resource for state legislators. An interest group that provides high-quality research and information can have an impact on public policy. Over the years, several business-sponsored groups in Texas have developed a reputation for producing quality research and providing information of value to the Texas legislature.[25] Today, the dominance of these groups is countered by citizen groups who work to further private or public interests. Texans for Public Justice, for example, tracks PAC contributions, supplying a wealth of information to the media. MALDEF tracks election irregularities that target minority voters and analyzes the potential impact of redistricting measures on minority representations.

Electioneering

Interest groups devote considerable time and effort trying to influence the out-come of elections through political action committees (PACs). Most states require some formal registration of PACs. In Texas, a PAC created by corpora-tions or labor unions must be formed exclusively to support or oppose a ballot issue and may not be created to support or oppose a candidate for office. "However, employees, members or families of corporation employees, unions and associations may form a PAC and make individual donations."[26] PACs must register with the **Texas Ethics Commission,** the agency that enforces regulations for interest groups and candidates, and they must designate a trea-surer and file periodic reports. These reports must give the names of persons donating more than $50 to campaigns. PACs are also prohibited from making a contribution to members of the legislature during the period beginning 30 days before the start of a regular session and ending 30 days after the regular 140-day session. In Texas, except for voluntary limits in judicial campaigns, state law does not limit how much an individual or a PAC may contribute to a candidate.

The process of electioneering is much broader than making a monetary con-tribution to a campaign. It begins with candidate recruitment. Interest groups work to recruit candidates for office many months before the election. They encourage individuals who will be sympathetic to their cause to seek nomina-tions in party primaries. This encouragement takes the form of promises of sup-port and money in the election. Some interest groups might cover their bets by encouraging both Democratic and Republican candidates to seek nomination in their respective parties. No matter which candidate wins, they win.

After the primary election, interest groups often give money to candidates in the general election. They might give money to both Democratic and Republican candidates, hoping to have access and influence regardless of who wins the general election. Some writers have observed that PAC money has undermined party loyalty and weakened political parties in this country. Candidates no longer owe their loyalty to the party that helped elect them but to interest groups.

Interest groups might also become directly involved in campaigns. The amount of spending on campaigns doubled between 1998 and 2006 and contin-ues to escalate. This can involve running television and newspaper ads explain-ing the record of officials or the virtues of a nonincumbent, or working in voter registration drives and get-out-the-vote campaigns. Interest groups might also aid candidates by helping to write speeches and organize rallies, and by staging political events such as fundraisers. Some groups keep track of legislators' voting records and circulate "good guy/bad guy score cards" to members of the orga-nization, instructing members to vote for or against candidates.

Grassroots Lobbying

Interest groups also attempt to influence public policy through public education and public relations activities. These efforts portray the organization in the best possible light by creating a favorable public image of the group. Obviously, much of this information can be very self-serving and can be called propaganda. Not all such information is wrong, but some filtering of the information by public officials is necessary. Competing interest groups often counter the information provided by another interest group. In a mass media society, with much public scrutiny, an interest group's credibility can be compromised if it frequently pro-vides inaccurate or misleading information.

Texas Ethics Commission
state agency responsible for enforcing requirements to report information on money collected and activities by interest groups and candidates for public office

Besides presenting a favorable image of themselves to the public, interest groups curry favor with public officials. Inviting public officials to address organizational meetings is another technique to advance the group's standing in the eyes of public officials. Giving awards to public officials at such gatherings, thanking them for their service to the public, is also a common technique.

POLITICAL

THINKING The Energy Crisis

To combat an impending energy crisis, the 2005 Texas legislature decided to run power lines from windy West Texas to cities in the east. In 2009 the Texas Public Utility Commission began awarding contracts—for three times the estimated costs. The largest contract, for $1.34 billion, went to Energy Future Holdings, a company that had spent nearly $3 million on campaign contributions to Texas politicians between 2005 and 2010. What measures do you think should be taken to ensure that the costs of this project are reasonable? What guidelines do you think the Public Utility Commission should follow in awarding contracts? Who do you think should appoint/elect member to this commission—the governor or the voters?

The Strength of Interest Groups in Texas

The strength and influence of interest groups vary among the states. Most writers explain this variation based on four factors: economic diversity, party strength, professionalism of the legislature, and government fragmentation.[27]

Economic Diversity

States that are highly industrialized and have a great variety of industries will have a multitude of interest groups. Because of the diversity and the complexity of the state's economy, no single industry or group can dominate. The many interests cancel each other out. In other states with less diversity, a single or a few industries dominate the economy.

In the past, the Texas economy was dominated by a few industries: cotton, cattle, banking, and oil. Today, the Texas economy is more diversified, and the number of interest groups has grown accordingly. It has become much more difficult for one or a few interests to dominate state politics.

Political Party Competition

The strength of the political parties in the state can influence the strength of the interest groups. States with two strong competitive parties that recruit and support candidates for office can offset the influence of interest groups. Members of the legislature in competitive party states might owe their election to the political party and be less influenced by interest groups. In Texas, a history of weak party structure has contributed to the power of interest groups. (see "How Texas Differs").

Professionalism of the State Legislature

A professional legislature is one that has a full-time staff, is well paid, serves full-time, and has high-quality research and advisory services. Full-time, well-paid legislators with a professional staff are less dependent upon information

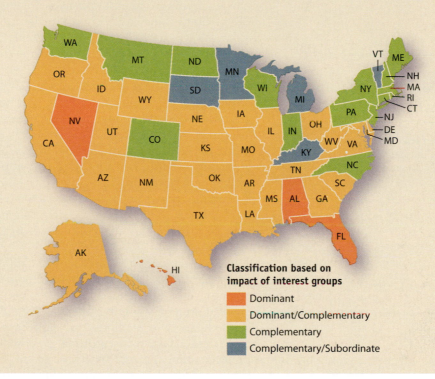

HOW TEXAS DIFFERS POLITICAL THINKING THROUGH COMPARISONS

Classification of States Based on the Overall Impact of Interest Groups

Clive S. Thomas and Ronald J. Hrebenar have classified interest group patterns in the fifty states according to their degree of influence. This map illustrates these patterns.

Q: How does Texas compare to other states?

A: In Texas, interest groups are dominant but must negotiate with state agencies and the legislature.

Classification based on impact of interest groups
- Dominant
- Dominant/Complementary
- Complementary
- Complementary/Subordinate

Source: Clive S. Thomas and Ronald J. Hrebenar, "Interest Groups in the States." In Virginia Gray and Russell L. Hanson (Eds.), *Politics in the American States: A Comparative Analysis* (8th ed.) (Washington, DC: Congressional Quarterly Press, 2004). Reprinted by permission.

supplied by interest groups, and the exchange of information between the lobbyist and the legislator is reduced. The Texas legislature has improved the quality of its staff in recent years; most members have full-time staff in Austin and in local offices. In addition, committee staff has increased. The Texas legislature now provides more money than any other state for staff salaries. The Texas Legislative Council also provides excellent staff assistance in research and information.

Fragmented Government Structure

The degree to which interest groups succeed in influencing the administration of state laws depends upon the structure of the state government. If the government is centralized under a governor who appoints and removes most of the heads of departments, interest groups will find it necessary to lobby the governor directly and the agencies indirectly. Texas has a **fragmented government structure** with power dispersed to many agencies and little central control. The governor of Texas makes few significant appointments of agency heads. Each interest group tries to gain access to and influence the state agency that deals with its area of interest. Often, these agencies are created to regulate the industry

fragmented government structure

a government structure in which power is dispersed to many state agencies with no central control

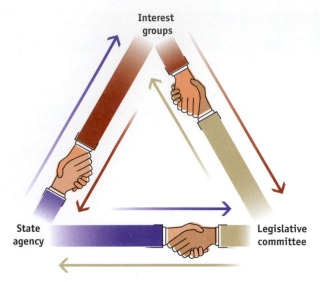

FIGURE 20-2 **The Iron Triangle** There is often a close relationship between the state agency created to regulate an industry, the legislative oversight committee, and interest groups.

capture

the situation in which a state agency or board falls under the heavy influence of its constituency interest groups

that the interest group represents. For example, the Texas Railroad Commission, originally created to regulate railroads, also regulates the oil industry in Texas. Historically, the oil industry lobby groups have dominated the three members who serve on the Railroad Commission and the decisions of that commission.[28]

Similar relationships exist between many state agencies and interest groups. Until the Texas Sunset Commission was created in 1977 to review most state agencies every ten years, the members of most state licensing boards (such as the Texas State Bar, State Board of Medical Examiners, State Board of Morticians) were professionals in that field. Members of the profession still dominate these boards. These licensing boards were created to "protect the public interest," but they often spend most of their time protecting the profession by limiting the number of persons who can be licensed and by making rules favorable to the group. For example, in Texas when a person dies, he or she must be dead for seventy-two hours before cremation. However, if the body is not buried within twenty-four hours, it must be embalmed. According to authorities, the reason for embalming before cremation is to protect the public from the spread of diseases. Others have suggested that the procedure is unnecessary and demonstrates the degree to which interest groups control rule making to increase the amount of money a group makes.

When the relationship between the state agency and the interest group becomes very close, it is referred to as **capture:** The interest group has "captured" the agency. However, capture of the agency by the interest group is probably more the exception than the rule. Competing interest groups often vie for influence with the agency, reducing the likelihood of capture by a single interest group. The iron triangle model shown in Figure 20-2 provides a more accurate explanation of the policy making process in Texas. In this model, the interest group, the state agency, and the legislative committee (with oversight of the agency) share in the process of making policy.

In Texas, the fragmented nature of the state government, the many independent boards and commissions, and the separately elected state agency heads all increase the strength and influence of interest groups on state government.

Summary

Self-Test www.mhhe.com/pattersontadtx11e

Voting restrictions such as poll taxes, white primaries, and annual registration historically limited political participation in Texas. Once the federal government forced the state to lift these restrictions, the level of participation and voter turnout should have jumped. Why didn't it? Texas still lags substantially behind the rest of the nation in voter turnout rates. Some argue that the traditionalistic-individualistic political culture of Texas does not encourage participation by nonelite groups. Minorities and low-income groups still have lower voter participation rates than other groups. Others argue that groups lacking a tradition of civic participation take time to adopt new behaviors. Recent voting laws have not significantly increased turnout but have facilitated voter turnout of an already overrepresented population: individuals over 65 years of age.

Yet as more minority candidates run for office, it is possible that these groups will mobilize in support of those who demographically represent them.

Low rates of voter participation lay the groundwork for the influential role of interest groups. The fragmented structure of Texas government means both the legislative and the executive branch look to interest groups to provide expertise they need to create policies. Yet, as Texas has developed economically, new interest groups have arisen and it is no longer fair to say that the government is dominated by agriculture, oil, and banking groups. New public, economic, and citizen interest groups have emerged in recent decades to challenge the dominance of business, and although they may not displace a well-positioned elite, they have begun to put a check on their influence.

Study Corner

Key Terms

agricultural associations
(*p. 504*)

annual voter registration
(*p. 499*)

capture (*p. 512*)

collective bargaining
(*p. 505*)

fragmented government
structure (*p. 511*)

party competition (*p. 500*)

peak business organizations
(*p. 504*)

permanent registration
system (*p. 499*)

professional associations
(*p. 505*)

state and local interest
groups (SLIGs) (*p. 507*)

Texas Ethics Commission
(*p. 509*)

trade associations (*p. 504*)

voting-age population
(*p. 498*)

Self-Test: Multiple Choice

1. All of the following were restrictions that once limited voter participation in Texas elections *except*
   a. political affiliation.
   b. the white primary.
   c. the poll tax.
   d. annual registration.
   e. property ownership.

2. In 1944 the U.S. Supreme Court held that all-white primaries in southern states were unconstitutional, in the case of
   a. *Painter v. Sweatt.*
   b. *NAACP v. Alabama.*
   c. *Smith v. Allwright.*
   d. *Brown v. Board of Education.*
   e. *Dred Scott v. Sandford.*

3. Which of these groups has the lowest voter turnout in Texas?
   a. high-income earners
   b. younger voters
   c. moralistic subculture advocates
   d. African Americans and Hispanics

4. Which of the following individuals do *not* have the right to vote in Texas today?
   a. anyone under the age of 21
   b. any citizen who does not register annually
   c. any person who cannot afford to pay the poll tax
   d. a convicted felon serving his or her sentence

5. Why do interest groups wield considerable power in Texas?
   a. the lack of limitations on campaign contributions
   b. the fragmented structure of state government

c. the absence of a well-paid and professional legislative staff
d. a long history of intense two-party competition

6. Which of the following is an example of an ideological interest group that is active in Texas?
   a. the Texas Farm Bureau
   b. the National Federation of Independent Business Owners
   c. the Texas State Teachers Association
   d. the Christian Coalition

7. Wealthier Texans are more likely to vote because they are more likely to be aware of elections, to believe that they have a higher stake in election outcomes, and to contribute money, effort, and time to campaigns. (T/F)

8. Texas legislation requires most lobbyists to register and to disclose information about their activities. (T/F)

9. An "iron triangle" exists when the relationship between a state agency and the interest group that the agency was created to regulate becomes too close. (T/F)

10. When the relationship between a state agency and an interest group becomes very close, it is referred to as capture. (T/F)

Critical Thinking

Examine the neighborhood you live in. How would you assess the social and economic status of your neighborhood? Compare your assessment with the factors that affect voter turnout, and predict how many citizens will turn out to vote in elections in your area.

Suggested Readings

Chavez, Linda. *Out of the Barrio: Toward a New Politics of Hispanic Assimilation.* New York: Basic Books, 1992. A good overview of the shifting political landscape in Texas.

Davidson, Chandler. *Race and Class in Texas Politics.* Princeton, N.J.: Princeton University Press, 1990. A discussion of how race and class have played a role in state constitutional politics in Texas.

Leighley, Jan. *Strength in Numbers: The Political Mobilization of Racial and Ethnic Minorities.* Princeton, N.J.: Princeton University Press, 2001. A review of the increasing politicization of Hispanics, African Americans, and other groups.

Patterson, Thomas E. *The Vanishing Voter.* New York: Knopf, 2002. An examination of trends in voting in the United States.

514 ■ **PART FIVE** Texas Government and Politics

Websites

http://www.sos.state.tx.us/

The Texas secretary of state's website; contains information on current ballot issues, where to vote, and election dates.

http://www.ethics.state.tx.us/

The Texas Ethics Commission website; provides information on campaign contributions and interest group registrations.

http://www.tpj.org/

The website of Texans for Public Justice, an advocacy group that compiles information on many aspects of Texas state government, including listings of lobbyist and campaign contributions by PACs and money contributed to judicial candidates.

http://www.nraila.org/

The National Rifle Association website; presents information to the public regarding the group's positions.

Participate

Go to the County Tax Assessor's Office in your county, and register to vote. You can then ask to become a deputy voter registrar, which will allow you to register other citizens as voters.

Extra Credit

Collect data on voter turnout in your county for the last two general elections. See how it compares with statewide data.

Self-Test Answers

1. a, 2. c, 3. d, 4. d, 5. b, 6. d, 7. T, 8. T, 9. F, 10. T

Political Parties and Elections in Texas

State party systems vary widely, and often the only common link is the name Democrat or Republican. Although state-elected officials might carry common party labels—Democratic and Republican—there is little interaction between these officials and two U.S. senators and thirty-two U.S. representatives. The national and state party organizations often act independently, and for a long period of Texas history, they did just that. This chapter examines the evolution of the party system in Texas, the state's political parties, and the process by which candidates from these parties are elected to office. We will compare the party system in Texas with other state party systems, explore the history of political parties in Texas, and determine whether Texas policy changed when the Republican Party took control of the state government. We will outline permanent party organization in Texas and evaluate whether parties are playing a weaker role in state politics. We will examine primary elections and assess the significance of crossover voting. Finally, we will determine the role of professional consultants and money in campaigns. The following points are emphasized in this chapter:

- At the end of the twentieth century, Texas completed a transition from Democratic to Republican dominance on the state level without undergoing a significant change in political ideology. Texas remained true to its traditionalistic-individualist political values.

- State laws limit the viability of third party movements in Texas. Although the Libertarian Party has been the strongest third party in recent decades, its candidates have been unable to capture statewide offices.

- Texas state party organizations are relatively weak. Texas holds semiopen primaries in a process known as the Texas two-step.

- The cost of political campaigns in Texas has skyrocketed as candidates employ professional campaign workers and pay for costly media ads. As a result, candidates rely heavily on campaign contributions.

State Party Systems

States can be classified according to the strength of each party within the state. States in which parties switch control of the statewide elected offices and control of the state legislature are called

Party Competition in the United States

The map below shows party competition in the fifty states.

Q: Where are the Democratic strongholds? Where are the Republican strongholds? How do you explain this pattern?

A: Southern states are strongholds for the Republican Party whereas in the past they were solid Democratic states. The Democratic Party dominates in New England states, which were a stronghold for the Republicans in the past.

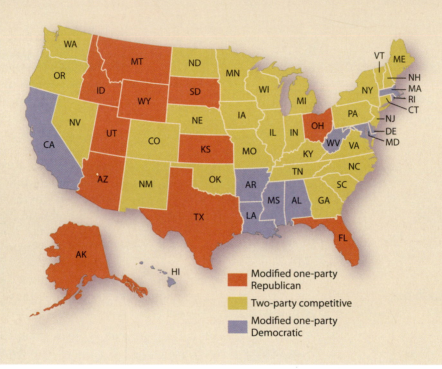

Modified one-party Republican

Two-party competitive

Modified one-party Democratic

Source: Thomas M. Holbrok and Raymond La Raja, "Parties and Elections," *Politics in the American States: A Comparative Analysis,* 9th ed., ed. Virginia Gray and Russell L. Hanson (Washington, DC: Congressional Quarterly Press, 2009), Table 3.4, p. 84.

two-party competitive state

a state in which parties switch control of the statewide elected offices and control of the state legislature

modified one-party state

a state in which one party regularly wins elections

two-party competitive states. States in which one party generally wins elections are called **modified one-party states.** The term *modified* is used to differentiate between the political system of these states and one-party systems in which only one party is allowed to participate in elections.

Most studies of competition between the parties, including the ones used to construct the map provided in "How Texas Differs: Party Competition in the United States," rely on several measures: (1) the percentage of votes won by each party in races for governor and the state legislature; (2) the length of time each party controls the legislature and the office of governor; and (3) the frequency with which parties divide control of the governorship and the legislature. These studies do not rely on voting for the president of the United States. The vote for presidential candidates is not a valid measure of party strength within a state.

The map in "How Texas Differs" shows current party competition in the fifty states, but since 1946, state-party competitive patterns have changed. Three patterns emerge. First, one-party Democratic states have disappeared and are now classified as modified one-party Democratic, two-party competitive states, or modified one-party Republican states. Second, modified one-party Republican states have increased slightly in the past five years. Third, the number of two-party competitive states increased from twenty-five to twenty-six in 2006. From 1946 to 1994, thirteen states remained two-party competitive states, while others began to change. Most of those changes in party competitive patterns are explained by changes in southern states, where one-party Democratic states have become two-party competitive states or modified one-party Republican states. In most other parts of the country, changes in party competitiveness have been less dramatic.

In Texas and other southern states, the Democratic Party dominated state politics from Reconstruction in the 1870s until the 1960s. Few Republicans placed their names on the ballot. The Republican Party in Texas has been gaining strength for the past thirty years. It now controls both houses of the Texas legislature, and it has captured the governor's office seven times in the last eight elections. Republicans hold all statewide elected offices. These victories have changed the classification for Texas from a modified one-party Democratic state, to a two-party competitive state, to a modified one-party Republican state.

State Party Ideologies

The party labels *Democratic* and *Republican* do not necessarily indicate ideology. **Party ideology** is the basic belief system that guides the party. The Democratic Party in one state can be quite different ideologically from the Democratic Party in another state. For many years in Texas, the Democratic Party has had very strong conservative leanings. The Democratic Party in Massachusetts has a liberal orientation. The conservatism of Texas Democrats shows in voter support for presidential candidates. Since the end of World War II, Texans have most often supported Republican candidates. Texas supported Dwight Eisenhower in 1952 and 1956, Richard Nixon in 1972, Ronald Reagan in 1980 and 1984, George H. W. Bush in 1988 and 1992, Bob Dole in 1996, George W. Bush in 2000 and 2004, and John McCain in 2008. Since 1960, Texas has voted Democratic only four times; in two of those cases, a native-son Democrat was on the ballot. Texans voted Democratic in 1960 and 1964 for Lyndon Johnson, and for Hubert Humphrey, vice president under Johnson, in 1968. Texans supported Jimmy Carter in 1976, in part because he was a southerner and in part because of the backwash from the Watergate scandal. This strong support for Republican presidential candidates results from ideological differences between the more conservative Texas Democratic Party and the more liberal national Democratic Party organization.

In Texas in recent years, a change in the person holding the office of governor has not resulted in any policy changes. The policies under Democrat Dolph Briscoe did not change when Republican Bill Clements was elected governor in 1976, nor did policies change much when Democrat Mark White replaced Bill Clements in 1982, or when Clements in turn replaced White in 1986. When Ann Richards was elected governor as a Democrat in 1990, replacing Bill Clements, a few policy changes occurred. George W. Bush, a Republican, defeated Ann Richards in 1994 and was reelected in 1998. In 2001, Rick Perry continued the conservative policies of the past. A close examination of the actions in the 1995, 1997, 1999, 2001, and 2003 sessions of the Texas legislature shows little change from the conservative policies of the past. The traditionalistic-individualistic political culture of the state preserves the status quo and protects elite interests, regardless of the party of the governor or the majority party in the legislature. Bipartisan cooperation, so evident during the three Bush sessions of the legislature,

party ideology
basic belief system that guides a political party

was made easier because of philosophical agreements between the governor and the leadership of the House and Senate. Texas has gone from a one-party Democratic-controlled state to one dominated by the Republicans with no significant change in philosophy or policy.

Political Parties in Texas

The two major political parties in Texas have had a long and varied history, with periods of weakness and strength for both. In this section, we trace their history and discuss third-party movements as well.

Democratic and Republican Party Strength in Texas

Texas's movement from a one-party Democratic state to a modified one-party Republican state is reflected in public opinion polls, as shown in Figure 21-1.[1] The question is, why did this change occur, and who supports each party today? To understand this, we need to examine the traditional areas of support for the Democratic and Republican parties in Texas.

The One-Party Era in Texas

From the end of Reconstruction in 1874 until the 1960s, Texas was a one-party Democratic state. This anti-Republicanism can be traced to the Civil War and Reconstruction. Following the Civil War and the experiences of Reconstruction, southerners felt a strong resentment toward the rest of the nation. That resentment bonded the South together as a unit, and it voted against all Republicans.[2] From the end of Reconstruction until at least the 1950s, Republicans were held in disrespect and were the subject of jokes. Calling someone a Republican was an insult. Some termed the Republican Party the "party of Yankee aggression." While living in Austin in the 1890s, the famous writer O. Henry once said, "We have only two or three laws [in Texas], such as against murder before witnesses and being caught stealing horses and voting Republican."

Several second-party movements developed during the last three decades of the nineteenth century, and the conservative Democrats who controlled the party effectively destroyed all opposition. In 1877, the Greenback Party (initially, Greenback Clubs) formed in the South and the West in reaction to declining farm prices. In Texas, the Greenbackers were recruited from the more radical farmers. They demanded currency expansion ("greenbacks") to drive up agricultural prices, an income tax, the secret ballot, direct election of U.S. senators, better schools, and reduced railroad freight rates. In the governor's race in 1880, the Greenback Party's candidate received about 12 percent of the vote. By 1884, the organization had faded out of existence. Also formed at that time was the Texas Farmers' Alliance, which became known as

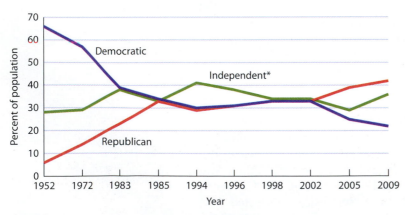

FIGURE 21-1 Party Realignment in Texas, 1952–2009

*Data on independents include those identified as "other party" and "don't know."

Source: Data for 1952–1985 from James A. Dyer, Arnold Vedlitz, and David B. Hill, "New Voters, Switches and Political Party Realignment in Texas," in *The Western Political Quarterly 41:* 156, March 1988. Data for 1994 from The Texas Poll, 1994, Harte-Hanks Communications. Figures for 1996 and 1998 from Texas Poll data, Scripps Howard Inc., University of Texas at Austin. Figures for 2002 and 2005: Texas Poll Data, Scripps Howard Inc. Data for 2009 from Earl Survey Research Laboratory, Texas Tech University, Spring 2009, www.orgs.ttu.edu/earlsurveyresearchlab/data.php.

the Grange. This organization also represented small farmers and made an uneasy alliance with African Americans, who were the primary supporters of the Republican Party.[3] The large landowners and businesses of Texas controlled the state Democratic Party and successfully destroyed these party movements, allowing the Democratic Party to dominate state politics from the late 1880s until the 1960s.

Party Realignment in Texas

Until the late 1960s, Texas politics revolved almost exclusively around personality and economic issues. Race issues, which dominated many southern states, were less important in Texas.[4] The period from 1940 to 1960 might even be characterized as an era of nonpartisan politics, with domination by the conservative business community. Factional issues within the party, between liberals and conservatives, were driven by economics.

Businesspeople, oilmen, wealthy farmers, and cattle ranchers formed the backbone of the conservative element.

> The liberal element in Texas was also based on economic consideration. Liberalism in Texas encouraged welfare spending by means of deficit spending if necessary; promoted equal treatment for Negroes, Latin Americans, and other minorities; increased government regulation of business in accordance with the preceding aims, the expansion of the national government powers; trade union organization; and taxes on business—especially on large, interstate corporations—rather than on sales or individuals. Furthermore, liberals in Texas at this time made loyalty to the national Democratic Party a part of their creed.[5]

From 1940 to 1960, political conflicts and competition were confined to the Democratic Party. Party primary elections replaced November general elections because there was no competition from Republicans. On the few occasions when Republicans mounted a challenge to Democrats in the November general election, most Texans still voted a **straight ticket.** The old saying "I would vote for a yellow dog before I'd vote for a Republican" summarizes the attitude of many voters, who came to be known as **Yellow Dog Democrats.** Yellow dogs ranked above Republicans.

The Beginning of Change

In the 1952 and 1956 presidential elections, many Yellow Dog Democrats broke with tradition and voted for Eisenhower. Democratic governor Allan Shivers, of the conservative faction of the party, led this movement. This faction chose to dissociate themselves from the New Deal/Fair Deal element of the national Democratic Party and any of its candidates.

The Republican state party convention also nominated Shivers and most statewide Democratic candidates as the Republican Party's nominees. Thus, Shivers and most statewide office seekers were candidates for both political parties in 1952. This group became known as the **Shivercrats.** The liberal faction of the Democratic Party became known as the "Loyalists" and were associated with the national Democratic Party.[6]

This action began the Texas tradition of supporting Republican presidential candidates while retaining Democratic Party dominance over state offices. Presidential politics in 1952 broke the tradition of voting a straight ticket, at least for the top of the ticket.

The Election of John Tower

In a special election in 1961, John Tower was elected U.S. senator to fill the seat formerly held by Lyndon Johnson and became the first Republican statewide

straight ticket voting
casting all votes for candidates of one party

Yellow Dog Democrats
people who voted straight ticket for Democrats—they would vote for a yellow dog if it ran as a Democrat

Shivercrats
Democrats who followed Governor Allan Shivers's example and voted for Eisenhower in 1952 and 1956

officeholder since the 1870s. The election was originally heralded as the beginning of a new era of two-party politics in the state. In the 1962 elections, Republicans managed to field candidates for many statewide, congressional, and local races. There were few successes.

The Election of Bill Clements

The election of Bill Clements as governor in 1978 marked the real beginning of two-party politics in Texas. Governor Clements used his power to make appointments to boards, commissions, and judgeships and to recruit people who would publicly declare their Republicanism. Some referred to these new converts as "closet Republicans" who had finally gone public. These appointments helped build the Republican Party in Texas, the start of **party realignment** in the state.

The loss of the governorship by Clements in 1982 to Democrat Mark White was a blow to the Republicans because the party also had little success in gaining other statewide offices. In 1986, Republican fortunes improved when Bill Clements returned to the governor's office. He defeated Mark White in what many termed a "revenge match."

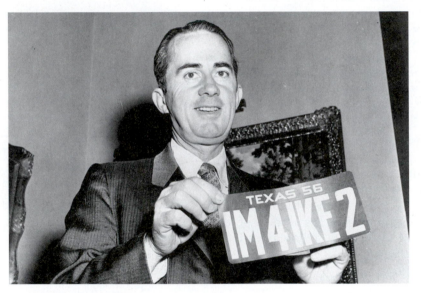

Democratic governor Allan Shivers led a group of Democrats, the "Shivercrats," who endorsed Republican candidate Dwight D. Eisenhower.

party realignment

the change from a state dominated by one political party to the two-party system operating today

The "Conversion" and Election of Phil Gramm

In 1983, John Tower announced that he would not seek reelection to the U.S. Senate in 1984. Phil Gramm, the Democratic representative from the sixth Congressional District, used Tower's retirement to advance from the U.S. House to the Senate. Gramm had first been elected as a Democrat in 1976. By early 1981, Gramm had gained some national prominence by helping President Reagan "cut the federal budget."[7] Gramm, who served as a member of the House Budget Committee, was accused of leaking Democratic strategy to the White House budget office. David Stockman, budget director under Ronald Reagan, confirmed that he had.[8] Because of his disloyalty to the party and because of House rules, Gramm was not reappointed to another term on the Budget Committee.

In a smart political move, Gramm used this loss of his committee seat as an excuse to convert to the Republican Party. In 1983, Gramm resigned his seat in the U.S. House. Outgoing Republican Governor Clements called a special election, which was held thirty days after Gramm's resignation. Since no other candidate could possibly put together a successful campaign in so short a time, Gramm easily won reelection to Congress as a Republican. In 1984, "fully baptized" as a Republican, Gramm won election as U.S. senator, pulled along on the coattails of President Ronald Reagan. The Republican Party retained the seat in the U.S. Senate. Gramm easily won reelection in 1990 and 1996 but chose not to run for reelection in 2002, thus ending a long political career in Texas politics.

The Move Toward Parity, 1988–1994

In 1988, the Republicans made significant gains, aided by Bill Clements's return in 1987 and George H. W. Bush's election to the presidency. The party won four statewide offices. Three Republicans won election to the Texas Supreme Court, and Kent Hance was elected to the Texas Railroad Commission.

In 1990, Republicans captured the offices of state treasurer and agricultural commissioner and another seat on the state supreme court. The big setback for the Republicans in 1990 was the loss of the governor's office. Bill Clements did not seek reelection. Clayton Williams, a political newcomer, used his considerable wealth to win the Republican nomination. His campaign for governor was something of a disaster, and he managed to lose to Democrat Ann Richards.

In 1992, Democrat Lloyd Bentsen, after serving as U.S. senator from Texas for twenty years, resigned to become secretary of the treasury under President Clinton. His resignation allowed Republicans to capture their second seat in the U.S. Senate with the election of Kay Bailey Hutchison. In 1996, Republican Phil Gramm was elected to a third term as U.S. senator from Texas.

In 1994, the Republicans captured all three seats on the Railroad Commission and a majority of the seats on the state supreme court, and they retained control of the agriculture commissioner's office. In addition, Republicans captured three additional seats on the state board of education, for a total of eight seats. More important, George W. Bush was elected governor. When the dust cleared, Republicans controlled a total of twenty-three statewide offices. Those wins, coupled with additional seats in the Texas House and Senate, substantially changed Texas party structure. Texas had moved to a two-party competitive system.

Governor Bush and Republican Dominance, 1995–2001

In 1994, the son of former president George H. W. Bush ran for governor of Texas and beat the Democratic incumbent, Ann Richards. Governor George W. Bush, to a large degree, won because of family name recognition rather than political experience. Governor Bush had no statewide electoral experience before running for governor. In 1976, he ran for Congress in his "hometown" of Midland. He lost to Kent Hance, who later changed parties and won a seat on the Texas Railroad Commission as a Republican. During the 1995 and 1997 sessions of the Texas legislature, Governor Bush developed a reputation as a bipartisan leader. This was in part due to the rather noncontroversial nature of his programs and prosperous economic times in the state. The legislature was faced not with the need to raise taxes but with the decision about what to do with a surplus.

In 1998, Governor Bush won reelection. His popularity also helped down-ballot candidates win election for all statewide executive offices and many judicial offices. For the first time in over 120 years, Texas voters elected Republicans to all but one statewide elected office. Figure 21-2 illustrates the gradual shift in power from the Democrats to the Republicans since the 1970s.

Democratic Representative Steve Wolens and Republican senator David Sibley look on as Texas Governor George W. Bush signs a bipartisan bill to deregulate the state's energy industry in 1999.

1974

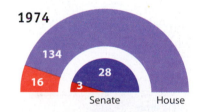

134   28   16   3
Senate   House

1988

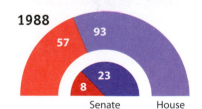

57   93   8   23
Senate   House

2008

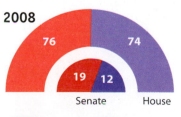

76   74   19   12
Senate   House

■ Republican   ■ Democrat

FIGURE 21-2 Republican and Democratic Party Strength in the Texas Legislature, 1974, 1988, and 2008

TABLE 21-1	Total County Offices Held by Republicans, 1974–2008	

Year	County Office*
1974	53
1976	67
1978	87
1980	166
1982	270
1984	377
1986	504
1988	608
1990	717
1992	814
1994	900
1996	950
1998	973
2000	1,231
2002	1,327+
2004	1,390
2006	1,410
2008	1,345

*Estimates by the author. 2008 data were estimated by author on the basis of Democratic gains in Harris and Dallas counties.

Sources: *Houston Chronicle*, November 13, 1994, 16A. Figures for 1996 and 1998 from own sources. Data for 1996–2000 generated by the author. Data for 2002, 2004, and 2006 from the secretary of state's Web page.

ballot form

the forms used by voters to cast their ballot; in Texas, each county, with approval of the secretary of state, determines the form of the ballot

Republican Dominance after Bush

With the election of Governor George W. Bush as president, some speculated that his absence from state politics could make it easier for Democrats to regain some offices. Bush had received 67 percent of the popular vote in 1998. Rick Perry, who as lieutenant governor had succeeded Bush as governor in December 2000, had limited success filling the void left by Bush's departure. In 2002, Perry won the governorship in his own right with 57 percent of the vote. Facing conflict and controversy over issues such as school financing, redistricting, environmental issues, and the trans-Texas corridor, Perry's first term proved rocky. In 2006, with one Democratic and two independent challengers garnering significant electoral support, Perry won reelection with only 39 percent of the vote.

Speculations about the decline of the Republican Party proved false, however, with the party instead securing its dominant position in the state during this period. In the 2002 election, the Republican Party captured all statewide elected offices, controlled the Texas Senate, and, for the first time in 125 years, controlled the Texas House. In both the 2004 and the 2006 elections, Republicans maintained control over statewide offices and the legislatures.

In addition to electing statewide officeholders, the Republicans have made inroads into controlling locally elected offices, especially at the county level. As shown in Table 21-1, in 1990, Republicans controlled 717 local offices; by 2006, that number had increased to approximately 1,410.

Straight Ticket Voting

Each county in Texas decides the **ballot form** and method of casting ballots. In 2008, all counties in Texas used electronic voting systems. Formerly, paper ballots usually used a *party column format,* which lists candidates by party and by office. This type of ballot encouraged straight ticket voting and was strongly advocated by the Democratic Party for many years. Most computer ballots are *office block.* This ballot form lists the office (for example, president), followed by the candidates by party. The office block format is often advocated as a way of discouraging straight ticket voting. However, Texas law allows computer-readable ballots to enable voters to vote a straight ticket. By marking a single place on the ballot, the voter can vote for all candidates for that party. In recent years, straight ticket voting has worked to the advantage of the Republicans in some elections.

Democrats have increasingly been ousted through straight ticket voting. In Harris County in 1994, sixteen contested Democratic incumbents for district and county judges were replaced by straight ticket voting for Republican judges. By 2000, not one Democratic judge remained in office in Harris County. Straight ticket voting for the Republican Party continued to unseat even long-standing, experienced Democratic judges until 2006, when voters in Dallas County replaced most countywide elected officials with Democrats. Harris County followed suit in 2008, in part because of straight ticket voting.

Socioeconomic Factors in the Political Parties

Party realignment in Texas is in part the result of regional and national trends. There is more support nationally for Republicans, and this has an impact on Texas. Texas voters, like voters elsewhere in the Old South, have switched from the Democratic to the Republican Party. Immigration to Texas from other states has also helped the growth of the Republican Party. In addition, socioeconomic factors contribute to the dominance of the party.

In the 1950s and 1960s, Republicans began to gain strength in the suburban areas of Dallas and Houston, in oil-producing counties in East Texas, and in the Midland-Odessa area of West Texas. Voters in oil-producing areas supported Republican candidates largely because of national Republican Party policies that favored the oil industry. The suburban areas of Houston and Dallas contained many people who relocated from states with Republican loyalties.

Republican support is found today in the traditional areas and among young professionals and new immigrants to the state who have settled in the suburbs of Dallas/Fort Worth, Houston, and San Antonio. These new residents are not socialized into voting a straight Democratic ticket as older native Texans were. Republicans also draw disproportionately from young voters (see Table 21-2). The profile of the average Republican supporter in Texas would include the following: young, high income, well educated, Anglo, professional, living in the suburbs of a large metropolitan area. In addition, Republican voters are likely to be newcomers to the state. One study concluded that about one-fourth of Texas Republicans are new arrivals in the state.[9]

By contrast, the Democratic Party draws support from older residents, native Texans, the lower-income groups, the less educated, and minority groups, especially Mexican Americans in South Texas and African Americans in urban areas and East Texas. There is also some variation among religious groups, with Catholics, especially Catholic Mexican Americans, showing strong support for the Democratic Party and Protestant fundamentalists showing more support for the Republican Party.

Some Texans are concerned that party realignment will produce race-based political parties. The Republican Party's appeals to whites, especially appeals that have racial overtones, could drive most Mexican Americans and African Americans into the Democratic Party. According to Dick Murray, a political scientist at the University of Houston, in past elections, Democrats managed to get about 35 percent of the white vote. In 2002, Ron Kirk, the Democratic candidate for senator (who is black) received 31 percent of the white vote, and gubernatorial candidate Tony Sanchez received 27 percent of the white vote. Murray estimates that for every Latino voter the Democrats gain, they lose one white one.[10]

In the 1998 election, Governor Bush seemed to realize that Republicans must appeal to minority voters in order to remain the dominant party. He especially made appeals to Mexican American voters, and that effort may have paid off. He received about 40 percent of the Mexican American votes. That was not a significant change in how Mexican Americans vote, however. It was more a vote for Bush; to some degree the percentage Bush received was magnified by low voter turnout. Voter turnout is discussed further in "Political Thinking: Balance of Power."

As Texas becomes ever more a majority-minority state, these new participants (Latinos, African Americans, and Asians) may help Democratic candidates challenge the dominance of the Republican Party. Though Republicans claim to have made strong inroads into the Latino community, most Latinos and African Americans still show strong support for Democratic candidates. Historically, these groups have not voted in large numbers; yet in 2006, Latino and African American support allowed Democrats to capture most countywide offices in Dallas County for the first time in twenty years. Although some blamed a poor Republican turnout that was due to anger over immigration issues, Democratic straight ticket voting had been growing 2 to 3 percent every two-year election cycle since 1994. Whether Dallas County represents the beginning of a Democratic revival remains to be seen.

TABLE 21-2 | Party Identification Among Texans by Socioeconomic Factors

	Republican, 39%	Democrat, 25%	Independent, 23%	Other, 10%
AGE				
18–29	41	25	22	7
30–39	43	23	19	13
40–49	43	21	18	15
50–59	39	24	26	9
60 and older	36	30	26	7
RACE/ETHNICITY				
Hispanic	26	34	29	8
Anglo	47	21	22	9
Black	8	58	17	12
GENDER				
Male	40	20	27	10
Female	29	30	18	10
REGION				
East	39	23	26	9
West	43	25	27	5
South	34	31	22	11
North	42	24	22	9
Gulf	47	28	18	7
Central	33	27	30	8
INCOME				
Less than $10,000	27	42	22	7
$10,001–$20,000	27	38	19	12
$20,001–$30,000	33	34	26	7
$30,001–$40,000	33	27	25	14
$40,001–$50,000	40	22	23	11
$50,001–$60,000	41	32	16	9
$60,001 and above	52	16	21	9
EDUCATION				
Some high school	29	40	20	8
High school grad	34	30	22	9
Some college	43	25	16	14
College grad	45	18	29	7
Graduate school	40	22	26	11

Source: Texans poll, Scripps Howard News Service. Reprinted by permission.

The Death of the Yellow Dog Democrat?

In 1995, Rick Perry, the Republican governor who was then state agricultural commissioner, pronounced, "Yellow Dog Democrats are dead."[11] Some Democrats disagree. Ed Martin, executive director of the Texas Democratic Party at that time, said, "Anybody who thinks Yellow Dogs are dead may be looking for tooth marks." Martin attributes much of the success of the Republicans in the Democratic stronghold of East Texas to hot-button issues: "They focus on

POLITICAL
THINKING   Balance of Power

In 2008, the percentage of registered voters who turned out for the elections was higher for African Americans than for any other ethnic group, standing at 88.1 percent. This represented an increase of over 30 percent from 2006. White registered voters turned out at a rate of 82.8 percent, an increase of over 20 percent from 2006. Latino turnout stood at 69.5 percent. During the 2002, 2004, 2006, and 2008 elections, the Latino turnout fluctuated from 43.8 percent to 70.6 percent. How do you think these fluctuations in turnout affect the balance of power between the two major parties?

---

hot-button issues, get Texans to look the other way while picking their pockets. The old saw is that Republicans have successfully used guns, gays, and God as polarizing wedges to define themselves. We have nothing equally emotional to define ourselves."[12]

If the Republican efforts to encourage straight ticket voting are successful, especially with younger Texans, perhaps Yellow Dogs are not so much dead as changed from Yellow Dog Democrats to **Yellow Pup Republicans**—a nickname for younger voters who tend to vote straight ticket for Republicans. In the final analysis, this might not mean much in terms of a change in state policy. The traditionalistic-individualistic political culture has not changed and will not change any time soon. Texas is experiencing party realignment while maintaining continuity of political ideology.[13] The change can be described as a change in party label rather than change in ideology or policy.

An alternative view of party realignment, known as **party dealignment,** holds that the growing number of voters who do not identify with either party, but instead call themselves independent, indicates the low esteem for political parties and politics in general among American voters.[14] Many citizens do not see any difference in the two major parties and do not identify with either one.

Yellow Pup Republicans
younger voters who tend to vote straight ticket for Republican candidates

party dealignment
the change from identifying with either major political party to identifying as independents

Third-Party Movements in Texas

To date, third parties have not had much impact on Texas politics. The rules governing elections in Texas, as in many other states, do not make it easy for third parties to gain access to the ballot. To appear on the November general election ballot, candidates must meet criteria established by state law. These criteria prevent the lists of candidates from being unreasonably long. The Texas Election Code specifies three ways for names to be on the ballot through petitions, minor-party caucuses, and major-party conventions. Independents and third-party candidates either file petitions or are members of a minor party.

Petitions to Run for Office

To run as an **independent candidate,** with no party affiliation, a person must file a petition with a specified number of signatures. For statewide office, signatures equal to 1 percent of the votes cast for governor in the last general election are required. For example, in the 2002 governor's race, a total of 4.5 million votes were cast. An independent candidate for statewide office in 2004 would have to collect 45,000 signatures. For multicounty offices, such as state representative, signatures equal to 5 percent of the votes cast for that office in the last election are needed. On the average, 30,000 to 40,000 votes are cast in House races.[15] For county offices, signatures equal to 5 percent of votes cast for those

independent candidate
a person who has collected a required number of signatures on a petition to have her or his name appear on the ballot without a political party designation

offices are needed. That may seem like a large number of signatures, but the process is intended to weed out people who do not have a serious chance of getting elected. Few candidates file for statewide office as independents. However, it is not uncommon for independents to run for Texas House and Senate races.

Getting signatures on a petition is not easy. Each signer must be a registered voter and must not have participated in the primary elections of other parties in that electoral cycle. For example, persons who voted in either the Democratic or the Republican Party primary in 1996 were not eligible to sign a petition to have Ross Perot's Reform Party on the ballot. Signing a petition is considered the same as voting. This provision of state law makes it all the more difficult for independents to get signatures and get on the ballot.

The 2006 governor's race in Texas was an exception to this. Both Carole Keeton Strayhorn, the current comptroller, and Kinky Friedman, a country-western singer and mystery writer, qualified for positions on the ballot as independents. Friedman and Strayhorn suffered the same fate as most independent and third-party candidates: They pulled enough votes away from the major-party candidates to upset the election outcome. Governor Perry won with a plurality of 38.1 percent, whereas Friedman had just 12.6 percent and Strayhorn, 18 percent. Chris Bell, the Democratic candidate, did better than expected with 30 percent. The role of the independent candidates was to help reelect an unpopular governor who, after six years in office, managed to get less than 40 percent of the votes.

Candidates defeated in the primary election may not file as independents in that year's general election. This is the "sore loser" law. In 2006, rather than run against Governor Perry in the Republican primaries, Carole Keeton Strayhorn chose to run as an independent.

Though they are sometimes confused with candidates who file and are listed on the ballot as independents, **write-in candidates** are not listed on the ballot, and the process of filing is a separate procedure. To be "official" write-in candidates, individuals must file their intention before the election. This is true for all elections, including local, city, and school board elections. If a person does not file before the election, votes for that person are not counted. For some state offices, a filing fee may be required to have a candidate's name listed on the ballot. The amount varies from $3,000 for statewide office to as little as $300 for local justices of the peace. People sometimes write in things like "Mickey Mouse" and "None of the above." These are recorded but not counted. In 1990, nineteen write-in candidates filed for governor. Bubbles Cash, a retired Dallas stripper, led the pack with 3,287 out of a total of 11,700 write-in votes.[16]

MINOR-PARTY CAUCUS

The state election code defines a **minor party** (sometimes called a third party) as any political organization that receives between 5 and 19 percent of the total votes cast for any statewide office in the last general election. In the last fifty years, there have been three minor parties: the Raza Unida Party in South Texas in the 1970s,[17] the Socialist Workers Party in 1988, and the Libertarian Party in recent decades. Parties that achieve minor-party status must nominate their candidates in a party caucus or convention and are exempt from the petition requirement discussed previously.

Founded in 1971, the Libertarian Party of Texas has grown over the years to become a fairly stable third party. Over the past fifteen years, Libertarian candidates have served locally as city mayors and on city councils as well as

write-in candidate
a person whose name does not appear on the ballot; voters must write in the name, and the person must have filed formal notice before the election that she or he is a write-in candidate

minor party
a party that receives 5 to 19 percent of the vote in any statewide election; candidates from minor parties are not required to file petitions to get on the ballot

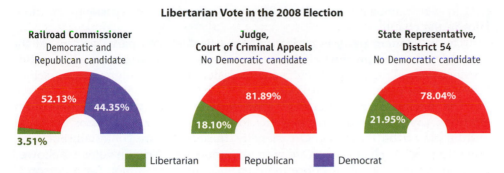

Libertarian Vote in the 2008 Election

Railroad Commissioner	Judge,	State Representative,
Democratic and	Court of Criminal Appeals	District 54
Republican candidate	No Democratic candidate	No Democratic candidate

Railroad Commissioner: 52.13%, 44.35%, 3.51%

Judge, Court of Criminal Appeals: 81.89%, 18.10%

State Representative, District 54: 78.04%, 21.95%

Libertarian   Republican   Democrat

FIGURE 21-3   In the competitive race for Railroad Commissioner, the Libertarian candidate only received 3.1 percent of the vote. In races where Democrats and Republicans competed, Libertarians received between about 2 percent and 5 percent of the vote. But in many races in which only one candidate from a major party competed, Libertarians sometimes garnered 20 percent or more of the vote. Why do you think this is so?

Source: Office of the Secretary of State, Race Summary Report, 2008 General Election, http://elections.sos.state.tx.us/elchist.exe.

other boards and commissions. In 2006, several statewide candidates received over 20 percent of the vote, securing their minor-party status for 2008. In 2008, the Libertarians once again secured their minor party status by receiving 18.1 percent of the vote in a statewide race for the Court of Criminal Appeals, as shown in Figure 21-3.

The success of the Libertarian Party may be due in part to alignment of its platform with the individualistic political culture of the state. Libertarians oppose government spending and support the legalization of "open carry" firearms. However, the party's advocacy of other issues, such as the legalization of gambling, may not appeal to socially conservative Texans.[18]

Party Organization in Texas

Political parties in all states have formal organizations. Their organizational structure is partly determined by state law, but parties have some discretion in deciding specific arrangements. Additionally, rules established by the national Democratic and Republican Party organizations might dictate state party actions in selected areas, such as the number of delegates to the national convention and how they are selected. In Texas, the Texas Election Code decides many aspects of party activity, especially the conduct of primary elections. Aside from these variations from state to state, party organization is basically the same for the Democratic and Republican parties.

In the past, the state executive committees of both parties were likely to be part-time organizations with limited staff. Today, both parties have a permanent headquarters, a full-time paid professional staff, and financial resources to help party development. They are actively engaged in organizing and building the party through voter identification and registration, candidate recruitment, candidate education, and get-out-the-vote drives, and in supporting candidates during the general election.

In all states, party organization falls into two broad categories: the permanent party organization and the temporary party organization. The **temporary party organization,** for both parties, consists of a series of conventions (caucuses)

temporary party organization

the series of conventions, or caucuses, that occur every two years at the precinct, county, and state levels held in even-numbered years. We will examine this in the discussion of elections later in the chapter.

The **permanent party organization** consists of elected party officers. At the lowest level is the **precinct chair.** Each county in Texas is divided into voting precincts, or polling places. When voters register, they are assigned to a precinct-based polling place near their home.

The precinct chair is elected for a two-year term during the party's primary election. Any registered voter may file for precinct chair, and his or her name will be placed on the ballot. Occasionally, these races are contested, but more often the precinct chair is reelected without opposition. Write-in votes are allowed with no pre-election filing notice required. It is not uncommon for a person to win election by writing in his or her name. In 1976, Paul Van Riper, a professor of political science at Texas A&M, was elected precinct chair in Brazos County with one write-in vote, his own. In 1978, his name appeared on the ballot, and he was reelected with three votes.

Ideally, the role of the precinct chair is to organize the precinct, identify party supporters, make sure they are registered to vote, turn out voters on Election Day, and generally promote and develop the interests of the party at this level. In the one-party Democratic era in Texas, few precinct chairs performed those duties; generally their only duty was to serve as election judge during primary and general elections. As Texas developed into a two-party state, the role of the precinct chair changed from election judge to party organizer at the grassroots level in some counties; but neither party is well organized at the grassroots level. Precinct chairs often remain vacant.

The next office in the party hierarchy is **county chair.** This position is also filled during the primary election, and the person elected serves a two-year term. Any registered voter may file for the office. In large urban counties, this office is usually contested. Informally, the county chair's duties consist of representing the party in the county, serving as the official spokesperson for the party, maintaining a party headquarters (in some counties), and serving as a fund-raiser. Formally, the county chair is responsible for receiving formal filings from persons seeking to have their names placed on the party's primary election ballot, conducting the primary election, filling election judge positions, and officially counting the ballots in the primary election.

In large urban counties, the county chair is often a full-time paid employee whose job is to organize the party at the county level. This involves voter registration, fund-raising, candidate recruitment and education, and aiding in the election of candidates in the general election.

The **county executive committee** is the next level in the permanent party organization. It is composed of all precinct chairs and the county chair. The degree of organization of this committee varies greatly from county to county. In some counties, the executive committee is an active organization that works to promote the party's interests. In many counties, especially in rural areas, this committee is more a paper organization that fulfills the formal duties of canvassing the election returns and filling vacancies in party offices when they occur.

Many large metropolitan counties use, instead of the county executive committee, a district executive committee for some functions. This is an organizational convenience because these counties have such large county committees. District committees are organized around the state senatorial districts.

permanent party organization
the series of elected officers in a political party who keep the party organization alive between elections

precinct chair
party official elected in each voting precinct who organizes and supports the party

county chair
party official elected in each county to organize and support the party

county executive committee
committee made up of the county chair and all precinct chairs in the county; serves as the official organization for the party in each county

The role of precinct chair can sometimes lead in unexpected directions. In the March 2008 Democratic primary, for example, an angry group of Barack Obama supporters chased Dallas Precinct Chairwoman Sandra Crenshaw, who sought refuge in a police station. The crowd claimed Crenshaw was making off with sign-in sheets to the precinct convention. Crenshaw said she had been trying to make sure they were filled out correctly.

The next level of permanent party organization is the **state executive committee.** From each of Texas's *thirty-one senatorial* districts, each party, by tradition, elects one man and one woman to serve on the state executive committee. Their election usually occurs during the state convention, which is traditionally held in June of even-numbered election years. Delegates to this convention caucus by senatorial district and elect their representative to the state executive committee; the state convention, as a whole, ratifies these choices.

Being selected to serve on the state executive committee is considered an honor, usually reserved for those who have strong political ties and who have supported the party for many years. Occasionally, a maverick group will surface and take control of the party, electing their people, who might not be the longtime party faithful. The Texas Republican Party experienced this type of insurgency from 1994 to 2002, when the Christian Right took control of the party; it has maintained that control for the last decade.

The state convention also elects a state party chair and vice chair; one must be a woman. Traditionally in the Democratic Party, the governor or gubernatorial candidate chose the state chair and vice chair, and the state chair office was often filled by the governor's campaign manager. With the rise of the Republican Party, the state chair is not the automatic choice of the governor; however, the party candidate for governor still has influence in deciding who the state party chair will be.

At the state level, the functions of the state chair and the state executive committee are very similar to those of the county chair and the county executive committee. They have similar informal duties of organizing the party and formal duties of conducting primary elections. Both parties in Texas have permanent, full-time, paid professional staffs that do most of the work at the state level. The state chair and executive committee are policy-making positions. Their main function should be to provide leadership for the party.

state executive committee
a committee that is made up of one man and one woman elected from each state senatorial district and functions as the governing body of the party

Party Strength

As discussed in Chapter 8, party strength has plummeted over the past century. In Texas, neither party has a strong party organization or a strong grassroots organization. Candidates can operate independently of any party and capture a nomination without party support. One high-profile example of this independence came in 1996 when unknown Dallas schoolteacher Victor Morales gained the Democratic Party nomination for the U.S. Senate without support from party officials. Crisscrossing the state in his beat-up pickup truck, he presented a serious challenge to Republican senator Phil Gramm. Despite his loss in this race and a few that followed, in 2008 Morales ran unsuccessfully for a seat in the Texas House of Representatives. Morales's case points to the role of media attention in the Texas electoral system.

A number of factors contribute to the reduced role parties play today in state politics. The primary system and changes in this system have weakened the parties. Not only do parties no longer control candidate selection, but parties also no longer perform traditional functions pertaining to campaigning, fundraising, and elections. Other institutions, such as interest groups, professional campaign managers, and the media, have assumed those functions. Figure 21-4 shows the amount of donations to campaigns provided by parties versus those provided by other institutions. This changing nature of parties in Texas is not unique to the state but part of a much larger national change in the role played by political parties.

FIGURE 21-4 Percentage of Top Donations by Group

Source: Texans for Public Justice, "Money in PoliTex, A Guide to Money in the 2008 Texas Legislative Elections," http://info.tpj.org/reports/politex08/donors08.html#topinstitutionaldonors.

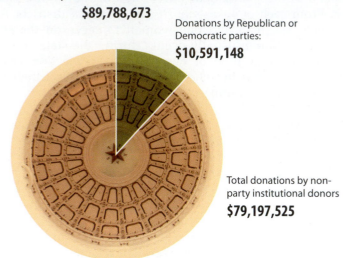

Total donations by institutional donors of $150,000 or more:
$89,788,673

Donations by Republican or Democratic parties:
$10,591,148

Total donations by non-party institutional donors
$79,197,525

Primary Elections

major party

any organization receiving 20 percent or more of the total votes cast for governor in the last election

semiclosed primary

a primary that allows voters to register or change their party registration on Election Day; registration as a member of a party is required on Election Day

semiopen primary

a nominating election in which registered voters can choose which primary to vote in on Election Day

The Texas Election Code defines a **major party** as any organization receiving 20 percent or more of the total votes cast for governor in the last election. Obviously, only the Democratic and Republican parties hold this status today. By law, these party organizations must nominate their candidates in primary elections. Chapter 9 discussed open primaries, in which all registered voters can vote regardless of party affiliation, and closed primaries, which are closed to all voters except those who have registered as a member of the party holding the primary. In addition, **semiclosed primaries** allow voters to register or change their party registration on Election Day. Registration as a member of a party is required on Election Day. Texas holds a **semiopen primary,** in which the voter may choose to vote in the primary of either party on Election Day. Voters are considered "declared" for the party in whose primary they vote. If you vote in the Republican Party primary, you are in effect declaring that you are a member of that party. You may not participate in any activity of any other party for the remainder of that election year.

In the past, Alaska, California, and Washington used a blanket primary, which allowed voters to switch parties between offices. A voter might vote in the Republican primary for the races for governor and U.S. House, and in the Democratic primary for the U.S. Senate race. The U.S. Supreme Court has ruled such primaries unconstitutional. Alaska currently uses a closed primary with voter registration by party, and California has adopted an open primary system. Washington has adopted Louisiana's system of a nonpartisan primary for all statewide and U.S. House and Senate races. Under this system, all candidates are listed on the ballot by office. The voter can choose one candidate per office. If no person receives a majority, the top two candidates face each other in a runoff. "How Texas Differs" shows the different types of primaries held in the fifty states.

Crossover Voting

The primary system used in a state may affect the party system in the state. Advocates of the closed primary system say that it encourages party identifica-

HOW TEXAS DIFFERS   POLITICAL THINKING THROUGH COMPARISONS

Primary Systems Used in State Elections

The map shows the different types of primary elections used among the states. Southern states tend to have open or semiopen primaries due to their history of modified one-party systems in which winning the primary election was tantamount to winning the general election.

Q: Do southern states tend to have open or semiopen primaries? How does Texas compare to other southern states?

A: Most southern states tend to have open or semiopen primaries because of their history of modified one-party systems in which winning the primary election was tantamount to winning the general election. Texas holds semiopen primaries like most other southern states.

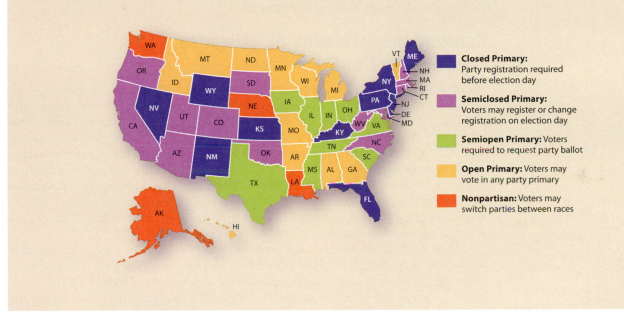

Source: From *Politics in the American States: A Comparative Analysis,* 8th ed. ed. Virginia Gray and Russell L. Hanson (Washington, D.C.: Congressional Quarterly Press, 2004).

tion and loyalty, and therefore helps build stronger party systems. Open primary systems, they say, allow participation by independents with no loyalty to the party, which weakens party organization. There is no strong evidence that this is the case.

Open primaries do allow voters to leave their party and vote in the other party's primary—a practice known as **crossover voting.** Occasionally, voters in one party might vote in the other party's primary in hopes of nominating a candidate from the other party whose philosophy is similar to their own. For example, Republicans have been accused of voting in the Democratic primary in Texas to ensure that a conservative will be nominated. In 2008, well-known right-wing radio host Rush Limbaugh urged Texas Republicans to cross over and vote for Democratic presidential candidate Hillary Clinton. Exit polls showed that approximately 9 percent of voters in the Democratic primary were Republican; however, 53 percent of them favored Democratic presidential candidate Barack Obama, not Clinton.[19]

From 1996 to 2002, more Texans voted in the Republican primaries than in the Democratic primaries. Republicans claimed that this was evidence that their party was the majority party. Democrats suggest that these differences in turnout are explained by the low levels of opposition in the Democratic primaries. For

crossover voting

a voting pattern in which voters from one party vote in the primaries of another party instance, President Clinton did not have any opposition in his primary election, whereas Bob Dole and Pat Buchanan were still actively seeking the Republican nomination; some Democratic Party leaders claim that many traditional Democratic Party voters, therefore, crossed over and voted in the Republican primary in an attempt to affect who would be the Republican nominee. As it turns out, the Democrats' explanation may be the more accurate. In the 2002 primary election, 400,000 more people voted in the Democratic Party primary than in the Republican Party primary. The difference is due almost entirely to the lack of contested races in the Republican primary and the highly contested races for U.S. Senate and governor in the Democratic primary. Governor Perry had no opponents, and John Cornyn had little opposition for the U.S. Senate seat. Elections since that time have shown this same tendency: Crossover voting seems to be caused by voters' attraction to competitive races.

Conventions—Election of Delegates, from Precinct to State Level

As discussed earlier, the temporary party organization, for both parties, consists of a series of conventions (caucuses) held in even-numbered years. The precinct convention is held on the same day as the party primary. Any voter who has voted in that party's primary is eligible to attend the precinct convention. This primary/precinct convention has been dubbed "the Texas two-step," essentially giving voters a chance to vote twice. Usually, the precinct chair is elected permanent chair of the convention, and her or his temporary appointees for vice chair and secretary are usually selected as permanent officers. Sometimes, especially during presidential election years, control of the convention's officers becomes an issue.

After officers are elected, the most important function of the convention is the selection of delegates to the county convention, or the district convention in large metropolitan counties. The number of delegates a precinct sends to the county convention is based on party support in that precinct—the higher the turnout in previous elections, the larger the number of delegates. If a candidate is represented by a larger number of convention attendees than her or his rival, more delegates will be pledged to that candidate. During presidential election years, many people are interested in attending the county convention, and the seats can be hotly contested. In 2008, Hillary Clinton won nearly 51 percent of the popular vote in the primary, yet Barack Obama's supporters managed to capture 56 percent of the state's precinct convention delegates. The Clinton campaign contested the results, citing over 2,000 complaints of violations and requesting that the eligibility of the 1 million attendees be double-checked.[20]

The county or district convention is a replay of the precinct convention. Selection of delegates to the state convention is its most important function. The state convention is normally held in June of even-numbered years. Normally, the convention is held in a major city and moved around to different cities for political reasons. At the state convention during presidential election years, the most important event is the selection of delegates to the national convention that nominates the party's candidate for president. Texas uses a **presidential preference primary,** held in March. The primary decides the presidential preference of most, but not all, of the delegates from Texas at the national convention. Without presidential preference primary elections, all delegate preferences would be decided at the state convention.

In addition to the state party officers chosen at these state conventions, during presidential election years these conventions also elect the representatives (electors) who will serve in the Electoral College if their party candidate wins

presidential preference primary

election held every four years by political parties to determine the preferences of delegates for presidential candidates

Democratic presidential candidates Barack Obama and Hillary Clinton debate before the Texas primary in March 2008. The Texas primary was widely anticipated and closely watched, with Clinton winning the popular vote yet Obama winning the majority of the state's precinct convention delegates.

the popular vote in Texas. By tradition, Texas Democratic delegates caucus by senatorial districts at the state convention and choose their elector. Republicans caucus by U.S. congressional districts. These decisions are ratified by the convention as a whole.[21] Those chosen to serve in the Electoral College are generally longtime party supporters. The electors of the party winning the popular vote meet in Austin, in the Senate Chamber, on the first Monday after the second Wednesday in December following their election, and cast their vote.[22]

Runoff Primary Elections

Eleven southern and border states, plus South Dakota, hold **runoff primaries,** which are required if no candidate receives a majority in the first primary. Until recently in the South, winning the Democratic Party primary was the same as winning the general election, and the runoff primary became a fixture, supposedly as a way of requiring the winner to have "majority" support. In reality, voter turnout in the runoff primary is always lower than in the first primary, sometimes substantially lower. The "majority" winner is often selected by a small percentage of the electorate, those who bother to participate in the runoff primary.

Racial and ethnic minority candidates have challenged the runoff primary system in these eleven states. They charge that because voter turnout decreases in the runoff and minorities are less likely to vote in runoff elections, the system is racially biased. The only evidence available suggests that this might not be the case. A study in Georgia examined 215 runoff elections between 1965 and 1982 and found no support for racial bias in runoff primary elections.[23]

Delegate Selection Systems

For the past seven presidential elections, Texas has used a primary system to determine the preferences of most, but not all, of the state delegates to the national convention. In states without presidential preference primaries, such as Iowa, precinct conventions (also called caucuses) take on greater significance.

runoff primary
election required if no person receives a majority in the primary election; primarily used in southern and border states

Democratic candidate for the U.S. House of Representative campaigns at an art fair in San Antonio.

Delegates selected at the precinct level go to the county level and eventually to the state and national conventions. A well-organized group, such as the Moral Majority, can take control of these caucuses. In 1988, Republican presidential hopeful Pat Robertson used his organization and worked with local churches to win more delegates than any other candidate in the Iowa caucuses. Republican presidential candidate Pat Buchanan also benefited from these organizations in the 1996 Iowa caucuses. Churches become a rallying point before the evening caucus. Potluck dinners, child care services, and church buses that help deliver voters to precinct conventions produce a turnout that exceeds the candidate's actual support among the voting population. By contrast, the Iowa media campaign of Buchanan's Republican rival, Steve Forbes, had little effect in 1996.

Thus, a caucus system can be an effective way to win delegates to conventions. However, it requires an organization of active volunteers to produce results. Win enough delegates to enough precinct conventions, and you can take over the county. Win enough counties, and you control the state. Control the state, and you select the delegates to the national convention. Control enough states, and you might win the nomination for president.

If Texas were to change from a preference primary to a caucus system, different campaign organization and strategies would be required. Preference primaries are mass media events that require big money and professional organizations. Caucus systems require grassroots organizations and dedicated volunteers. In Texas, during a number of Republican state conventions, some Christian organizations have called for an end to preference primaries and a return to a caucus system of selecting delegates to the national convention. Obviously, the caucus system is in their best interest and would allow them to control most of the delegates to the national convention. If the Texas caucus were held early enough in the election process, it might affect the direction of the Republican presidential race or, at least, give the winner some early exposure.

The Administration of Primary Elections

In the past, primary elections were considered functions of private organizations, and the state did not regulate them. As we discussed in Chapter 20, courts have ruled that political parties are not private organizations and their functions are subject to control by state law. The Texas Election Code governs primary elections. Technically, elections are administered by the local county chair and executive committee and by the state party officials at the state level; however, the Texas Election Code and the secretary of state oversee administration of elections to ensure that rules are followed, and the party has only limited discretion in these elections.

Although voter fraud is a significant concern for many Texans, few individuals have been charged with violating the Texas Election Code. In early 2006, an election held in Duval County for county judge attracted statewide concern: A whopping 55 percent of voters had turned out for the local election. A high voter turnout is usually welcomed in democratic systems, but this large turnout was not. A highly contested sheriff's race in Nueces County had recently inspired only 11 percent of registered voters to go the polls.[24] Voting fraud was suspected, and eventually, four women in Duval County were charged with mail-in ballot fraud.

Texas holds general elections every two years. During nonpresidential years, voters elect candidates to statewide offices: governor, lieutenant governor, attorney general, land commissioner, agricultural commissioner, comptroller, some members of the Texas Railroad Commission and the Texas State Board of Education, and some members of the two supreme courts in the state. Every two years, voters also elect all 150 members of the Texas House of Representatives (for two-year terms), half of the members of the Texas Senate (for four-year terms), many judges to various courts, and local county officials.

Campaigns and Elections

Campaign activity in Texas has changed considerably in the past two or three decades. These changes are not unique to Texas but are part of a national trend. Norman Brown, in his book on Texas politics, describes the form of political campaigning that once took place in the state as "local affairs."[25] Candidates would travel from county seat to county seat and give "stump" speeches to political rallies arranged by local supporters. Brown devotes special attention to the campaigns of Governors Jim and Miriam Ferguson ("Ma" and "Pa" Ferguson). Jim Ferguson, when campaigning for himself and later for his wife, would travel from county to county, telling each group what they wanted to hear—often saying different things in different counties. Brown contends that Ferguson and other candidates could do this because of the lack of a statewide press to report on these inconsistencies in such political speeches.

The Role of the Media

In modern-day Texas, the media play a significant role in political campaigns. Reporters often follow candidates for statewide office as they travel the vast expanses of Texas. Political rallies are still held but are most often used to gain media attention and convey the candidate's message to a larger audience. Candidates hope these events will attract media attention and convey a favorable image of them to the public.

Heavy media coverage can have its disadvantages for the candidates. For instance, in 1990 Clayton Williams, the Republican candidate for governor, held a media event on one of his West Texas ranches. He and "the boys" were to round up cattle for branding in a display designed to portray Williams as a hardworking rancher. Unfortunately for Williams, rain spoiled the event and it had to be postponed. Resigned to the rain delay, Williams told the reporters, "It's like rape. When it's inevitable, relax and enjoy it." The state press had a field day with that remark, and it probably hurt Williams's chances with many voters. The fact that his opponent was a woman (Ann Richards) helped to magnify the significance of the statement. In June 2008, Republican presidential candidate John McCain hastily canceled a fund-raiser that was to be hosted by Williams after learning of the remark.

In 1994, George W. Bush was the Republican candidate for governor running against incumbent Ann Richards. In Texas, the opening day of dove season is in September, and the event marks the beginning of the fall hunting season. Both Bush and Richards participated in opening-day hunts in an attempt to appeal to the strong hunting and gun element in the state. Unfortunately for Bush, by mistake he shot a killdeer rather than a dove. Pictures of Bush holding the dead bird appeared in most state papers and on television. He was fined for shooting a migratory bird. A Texas Democratic group in Austin produced bumper stickers reading "Guns don't kill killdeer. People do." In 1998, Governor Bush did not have a media event for the opening day of dove season. He was so far ahead in the polls that even opening the issue could result in nothing but a painful reminder.

Television Ads

Most campaign events are not as disastrous as the cattle-branding and dove-hunting incidents. Some gain attention and free media coverage for the candidate; however, free media attention is never enough. Candidates must purchase time on television and radio and space in newspapers. In a state as large as Texas, this can be quite costly. Candidates try to make the most of the expensive time they purchase by conveying simple messages. This has led to the **sound-bite commercial,** a thirty-second message that the candidate hopes will be remembered by the voters. This is not unique to Texas but occurs nationwide.

These sound bites can be classified into at least five types. The feel-good spot lacks substance or issues and is designed to make the public feel good about the candidate or the party. In 1988, President George H. W. Bush told us he saw "a thousand points of light." Others, including Clayton Williams, say, "Share my vision." In 1998, Governor George W. Bush ran a number of TV spots that asked voters to support his effort to have every child read and become a productive member of society.

Sainthood spots try to depict the candidate as having saintly qualities:[26] "Senator Smith is a Christian family man, Eagle Scout, Little League coach, Sunday School teacher, involved, concerned, committed, community leader who fights the people's fights. Let's keep him working for us."

Good ol' boy (or good ol' girl) spots are testimonials from other citizens about the candidate. In a staged "person on the street" interview, the citizen says something like, "Senator Smith is the most effective leader this state has seen since Sam Houston. He's so effective it's frightening. He is committed to his job, and we need him to fight the coming battles with the liberals." In Texas, cattle and horses in the background provide a down-to-earth backdrop for ranchers' good ol' boy testimonials.

NOOTS ("No one's opposed to this") commercials are also common. In these ads, candidates take courageous stands on issues everyone supports: sound fiscal management, planned orderly growth, good schools, open government, getting tough on crime, no new taxes, and so on.

---

sound-bite commercial

a brief, usually thirty-second, TV political advertisement that conveys a simple and memorable message about the candidate or the opponent

Basher spots are the last type. In these, candidates play on voters' emotions by painting their opponent in a very unfavorable light. If the opponent is a lawyer, the candidate can point out that he or she defends criminals. Candidates can point out that their opponent has received money from controversial organizations. Governor Rick Perry, running for secretary of agriculture in 1990, defeated Democratic incumbent Jim Hightower. In one of his commercials, Perry claimed that Hightower had once visited the home of Jane Fonda, often used as a symbol for the radical war protesters of the 1960s because of her visit to Hanoi during the Vietnam War. When pressed for details on the visit, Perry said that Hightower had visited Los Angeles and that Los Angeles was the home of Jane Fonda.

Basher spots have developed into a fine art. Newt Gingrich, former speaker of the U.S. House, extended the art when he used his GOPAC political action committee to help "train local Republican candidates." In 1990, GOPAC mailed a 131-word glossary to over 4,000 state Republican candidates. This glossary included a list of "optimistic positive governing words" that Republican candidates should use to describe themselves and a list of "contrasting negative words" they should use to describe their opponents. Republicans are described as having common sense and Democrats as big-spending liberals, for example.

These types of advertisements are used because most often they work to the advantage of the candidate. Occasionally, basher spots can backfire on the candidate. These ads plant in the voter's mind a simple message that they

In a 2003 runoff election, U.S. Representative Henry Bonilla charged Democratic challenger Ciro Rodriguez with meeting with and taking contributions from Islamic radicals. In a surprising upset, Rodriguez won the election. Here, Rodriguez responds to Bonilla's charges. How does Rodriguez make use of symbols in his response?

carry into the voting booth. Most citizens do not spend much time studying issues or candidates' backgrounds. They often depend entirely on advertisements for information. Though the news media often denounce such ads, the media (which receives most of the money spent in campaigns) do not refuse to run them.

The Internet

Texas candidates have been increasingly turning to the Internet to raise funds and widen their base of support. When Democrat Mark Strama ran for the Texas House of Representatives in 2004, he started a summer program directed primarily at high school and college students called Mark Strama's Campaign Academy. Strama attracted students by organizing luncheons with prominent speakers involved in different aspects of local, state, and national politics. In exchange, students campaigned for Strama, utilizing the Internet to galvanize support. They came up with campaign slogans such as "No Drama with Strama: Mark Represents ALL of District 50!" and posted them on their blog. They figured out how to use social-networking websites such as Facebook and MySpace to spread the word. Strama's Campaign Academy has been a key factor in his success in subsequent elections.

Political Consultants

As discussed in Chapter 8, the use of professional campaign consultants, or "hired guns," is becoming more common both nationally and in Texas. Most candidates find it necessary to have such professionals help run their campaigns. If their opponents use professionals, candidates might be at a disadvantage without one. Among the many techniques professional campaign consultants use are public opinion polls, which measure voter reaction to issues so the candidate knows what stands to take. They run **focus groups,** in which a panel of "average citizens" is asked to react to issues or words. Consultants also help the candidate in the design of written and visual advertisements, "packaging" the candidate to the voters. In 2002, David Dewhurst filmed a TV spot for his consulting firm in which he praised its effectiveness in making him look professional during his campaign.

Money in Campaigns

Using media advertisements, professional consultants, and a full-time paid campaign staff increases the cost of running for state office. The cost can run into the millions even for a race for the Texas House of Representatives. The amount of money spent in campaigns is increasing each election cycle. Most of this money comes from PACs. Figure 21-5 shows the increase in the total amount of money contributed by PACs from 1996 to 2008. As you can see, the amount more than doubled during this twelve-year period.

Money supplied by PACs obviously has an impact on elected officials. At the least, PAC money buys the group access to the official. At the worst, PAC money buys the vote of the elected official. Distinguishing between the two is almost impossible. Most states, including Texas, have passed laws designed to regulate campaign finances. Many other states have passed laws limiting the amount of money that could be spent on campaigns, but these laws have been invalidated by the U.S. Supreme Court.

Statewide races can be so costly that few candidates have the resources to self-finance their campaigns. One notable exception is Tony Sanchez, the Democratic candidate for governor in 2002. In that year, Sanchez self-financed $27 million (89 percent of his total campaign costs) and received campaign contributions totaling $3.5 million.[27] In that same election year, Governor Rick Perry raised almost $31.5 million from PACs.[28]

Candidates sometimes lend themselves money that they can later repay with what are sometimes called "late train" contributions. Special interest groups will seldom retire the debt of losers. The law limits the amount of money that a candidate can collect to retire personal campaign debts for each election (primary, runoff, general) to $500,000 in personal loans. In 2002, several candidates far exceeded this amount in personal loans.

focus group

opinion research technique in which a panel of "average citizens" is asked to react to issues or words

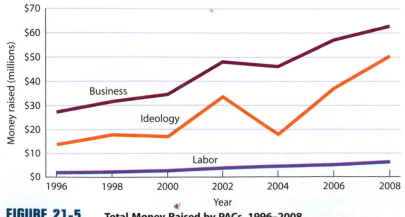

FIGURE 21-5 **Total Money Raised by PACs, 1996–2008**
Source: Texans for Public Justice, "Texas PACs: 2008 Election Cycle Spending," www.tpj.org.

HOW TEXAS DIFFERS   POLITICAL THINKING THROUGH COMPARISONS

Limitations on Campaign Contributions by Pacs in Statewide Races

The map shows the types of spending limitations states place on PACs.

Q: How does Texas compare to other states in terms of limiting campaign expenses?

A: Texas places a limit on corporate contributions but imposes no other limits. About one-third of states do the same.

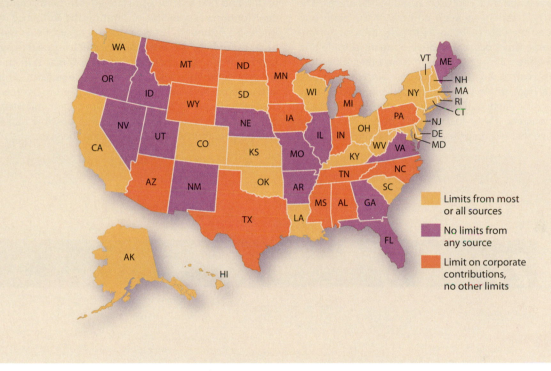

Limits from most or all sources

No limits from any source

Limit on corporate contributions, no other limits

Source: National Conference of State Legislatures, Limits on Contributions to Political Parties, updated February 5, 2008, www.ncsl.org/default.aspx?tabid=16552.

The leaders were gubernatorial candidate Tony Sanchez with $22,262,662 in personal loans and lieutenant governor–elect David Dewhurst with $7,413,887 in outstanding debt.[29]

All elected officials hope to keep part of the money they raise in a war chest, which can have the effect of forcing likely opponents to think twice before running against them. Also, candidates without opponents for many years, such as speaker of the house, may contribute part of their war chests to House candidates in hope of getting or keeping their support.

Today, the regulation of campaign finances in Texas is limited to requiring all candidates and PACs to file reports with the Texas State Ethics Commission. All contributions of over $50 must be reported with the name of the contributor. An expenditure report must also be filed. These reports must be filed before and after the election. The idea behind the reporting scheme is to make public the sources of the funds received by candidates and how the candidates spend their funds. Sometimes these reports are examined closely by the news media and are given significant media coverage, but this is not common. Citizens mostly are left to find out such information on their own, which is difficult for the average citizen. Texas has no limit on the amount of money candidates can spend for statewide races, but many states do.

Summary

Self-Test www.mhhe.com/pattersontadtx11e

Texas election results have sharply demonstrated the independence of state and national party systems. Throughout the twentieth century, Democrats dominated statewide elections. In the 1950s, however, the national Republican Party began drawing conservatives away, and Texas became a state that voted Republican in presidential elections but Democratic in all statewide elections. After the turn of the twenty-first century, Republicans for the first time captured all statewide offices. The Republican Party's ability to keep control of the state will depend in part on the vote of Texas's growing minority population. At the same time, economic development in trade and industry is attracting a large population from other states that represents conservative business interests. Since this group tends to have a high voter turnout, it could counteract any gains the Democratic Party makes because of the minority vote.

As the Democratic Party lost ground, minor parties also arose to challenge its hold on power—at least at the local level.

Since the 1970s, the Libertarian Party has established increasingly strong roots in Texas. The party's ideology appeals to those who espouse an individualistic political culture. However, the electoral system and the growing expense of political campaigns make it unlikely that a third party will be able to gain and maintain control over statewide offices.

In the past several years, the American public has begun to demand that federal and state governments cap campaign contributions as a means of limiting the influence of special interests. Although Texas is not a leader in this movement, more candidates are using the Internet to appeal to individual voters for smaller campaign contributions. Will this loosen the grip of the two major parties on state politics? Third-party and independent candidates will still need to overcome other obstacles placed on the road to ballot access and media attention, but if these trends continue, it is possible that elections will become more competitive within the state.

CHAPTER 21

Study Corner

Key Terms

ballot form (*p. 524*)
county chair (*p. 530*)
county executive committee (*p. 530*)
crossover voting (*p. 533*)
focus group (*p. 540*)
independent candidate (*p. 527*)
major party (*p. 532*)
minor party (*p. 528*)
modified one-party state (*p. 518*)
party dealignment (*p. 527*)
party ideology (*p. 519*)
party realignment (*p. 522*)
permanent party organization (*p. 530*)
precinct chair (*p. 530*)
presidential preference primary (*p. 534*)

runoff primary (*p. 535*)
semiclosed primary (*p. 532*)
semiopen primary (*p. 532*)
Shivercrats (*p. 521*)
sound-bite commercial (*p. 538*)
state executive committee (*p. 531*)
straight ticket voting (*p. 521*)
temporary party organization (*p. 529*)
two-party competitive state (*p. 518*)
write-in candidate (*p. 528*)
Yellow Dog Democrats (*p. 521*)
Yellow Pup Republicans (*p. 527*)

Self-Test: Multiple Choice

1. Which of the following describes the Texas political system from the 1880s to the 1960s?
   a. modified one-party Democratic state
   b. modified two-party Republican state
   c. two-party competitive state
   d. none of the above

2. What national policy first led Texas voters to vote for Republican presidential candidates?
   a. the Civil War   c. the civil rights movement
   b. the New Deal   d. Reaganomics

3. When did Texas become a two-party state?
   a. in the late 1960s   c. in the late 1980s
   b. in the early 1970s   d. in the late 1990s

4. Who was the first Republican governor of the state of Texas?
   a. Rick Perry   c. Ann Richards
   b. George W. Bush   d. Bill Clements

5. Texas has what type of primary system?
   a. semiclosed   d. nonpartisan
   b. blanket   e. semiopen
   c. closed

6. Who provides most of the funding for political campaigns in Texas?
   a. political consultants
   b. political parties
   c. special interest groups
   d. the candidates themselves

7. Because the Republican Party in Texas now controls both houses of the Texas legislature, the governor's mansion, and all statewide elected offices, Texas has officially been redesignated a two-party competitive state. (T/F)

8. In Texas the governor appoints the most important members of the executive branch including the attorney general, the comptroller, and the land commissioner. (T/F)

9. The election of 2002 was critical in Texas because it marked the first time in 125 years that all elected statewide executive offices were held by Republicans. (T/F)

10. Texas holds a two-step primary in which a general election and precinct conventions determine the number of delegates each candidate will receive. (T/F)

Critical Thinking

Go the websites for both the Democratic and the Republican parties in Texas, and look at the party platforms. What are the major differences between the two parties in Texas? Which party platform do you most agree with?

Suggested Readings

Anderson, James E., Richard W. Murray, and Edward L. Farley. *Texas Politics: An Introduction.* New York: Harper & Row, 1989.

Key, V. O., Jr. *Southern Politics in State and Nation.* New York: Knopf, 1949.

Key, V. O., Jr. *Politics and Pressure Groups,* 4th ed. New York: Thomas Y. Crowell, 1958.

Soukup, James R., Clifton McCleskey, and Harry Holloway. *Party and Factional Division in Texas.* Austin: University of Texas Press, 1962.

Weeks, Douglas O. *Texas Presidential Politics in 1952.* Austin: University of Texas, Institute of Public Affairs, 1953.

List of Websites

http://www.txdemocrats.org/
The Texas Democratic Party website.

http://www.texasgop.org/
The Texas Republican Party website.

http://www.ethics.state.tx.us
The website of the Texas Ethics Commission; has information on campaign contributions reported by candidates for office and by interest groups.

http://www.sos.state.tx.us/
The Texas Secretary of State website; provides information on election laws and voter turnout.

www.tpj.org
The website of Texans for Public Justice; provides information on campaign spending and lobbying.

http://www.fairvote.org
The website of the Center for Voting and Democracy, an organization promoting other election systems. This organization has a slight Republican lean.

Participate!

Both political parties are always looking for volunteers to work at their headquarters. In larger cities, these party offices will be open much of the year. Volunteer at the headquarters of the party of your choice. As elections approach, there is much work you can do, from very exciting—helping to organize events—to very boring—stuffing envelopes. As you "do your time in the trenches," you will be given more responsibilities and more interesting jobs.

Extra Credit

After working in a campaign as a volunteer, write a paper describing your experiences. Which experiences were positive, and which negative? Did your work leave you with a positive view of the political process?

Self-Test Answers

1. a, 2. b, 3. c, 4. d, 5. e, 6. c, 7. F, 8. F, 9. T, 10. T

CHAPTER 22

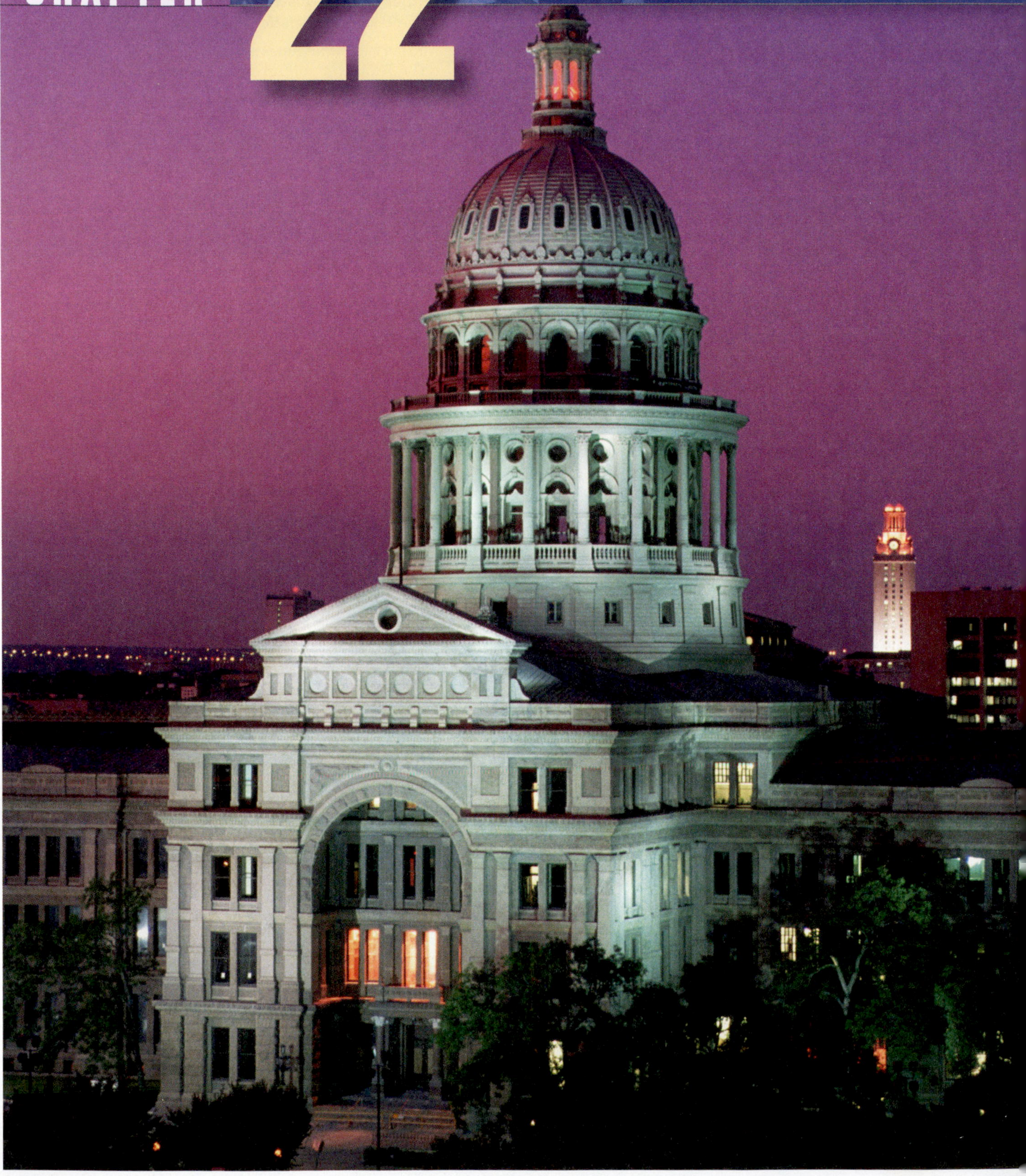

The Texas Legislature

The Texas Constitution makes the legislature the most important decision-making body in the state. Without approval of the legislature, money cannot be spent, taxes cannot be levied, state laws cannot be enacted or changed, and the constitution cannot be amended. This chapter examines how the legislature is elected and how legislators create laws. We evaluate the different methods that are used to elect representatives and the impact of controversial attempts to change district boundaries. We then discuss the process of getting elected, including the qualifications candidates must have and the obstacles they must overcome to get elected and remain in office. We consider legislative procedures, specifically, how a bill becomes a law, and explore the roles played by leaders and committees. Finally, we rate the Texas legislature, comparing it with other state legislatures to analyze its strengths and weaknesses. This chapter will focus on these points:

- The Texas legislature consists of the House of Representatives and the Senate, both of which are elected from single-member districts.

- In recent decades, major controversies have surrounded reapportionment and redistricting. As Texas has grown in population, it has gained seats in Congress. Republican control of the state legislature has led the party to implement redistricting plans that help Republican candidates gain more seats.

- Because of the low pay and the biennial nature of the Texas legislature, it rates lower on the scale of "professionalism" than other state legislatures.

Methods of Election

The Texas legislature consists of two houses. The Texas Senate has 31 members elected for four-year overlapping terms; half the membership is elected every two years. The Texas House of Representatives now consists of 150 members elected for two-year terms. The size of legislatures raises several issues. Large bodies might promote the representation of diverse interests within the state; however, statewide interests might go unrepresented. Large legislatures can become inefficient at decision making or, in part because of their inefficiency, become dominated by a few members. There is no doubt that decision-making dynamics depend on the size of the legislative body. The smaller Texas Senate is generally regarded as more sedate and genteel in its proceedings than the House of Representatives. Historically, few people have dominated the Senate, and members act more independently. Although the lieutenant governor is powerful, the power of the office comes from the Senate rules. The House, on the other hand, is generally more "disputatious" in its proceedings, and historically the speaker of the house dominates.

Members of legislative bodies most often are elected from **single-member districts.** Under this system, each legislative district has one member in the legislative body. In Texas, there are 31 senatorial districts and 150 House districts (see Figures 22-1 and 22-2). The voters living in these districts elect one House and one Senate member to represent the district. This system allows for geographical representation—all areas of the state get to choose representatives to the state legislature.

Some states use **multimember districts** for some legislative elections. Methods of electing representatives in multimember districts vary widely, but the most common method is to elect two or three members per district. Voters get one vote for each seat in the multimember district, so more than one state representative represents each voter. Under a single-member-district system, districts can be drawn to the advantage of ethnic and political minorities

single-member district

district having one member elected to the legislature

multimember district

district having more than one member elected to the legislature

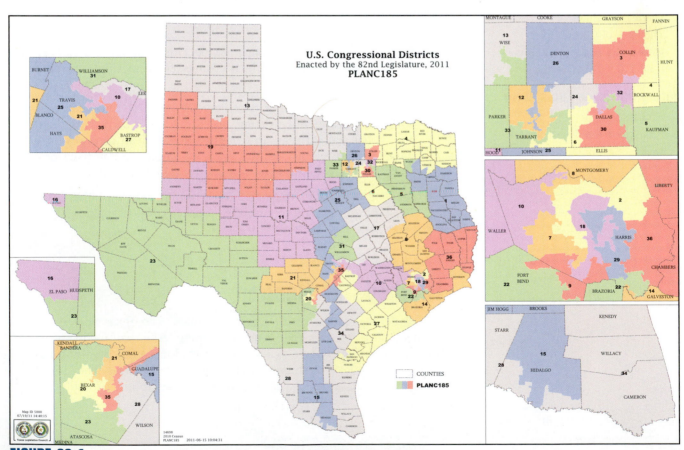

FIGURE 22-1   **Congressional Districts Proposed by the Texas State Legislature**

Source: Data from the Texas Legislative Council

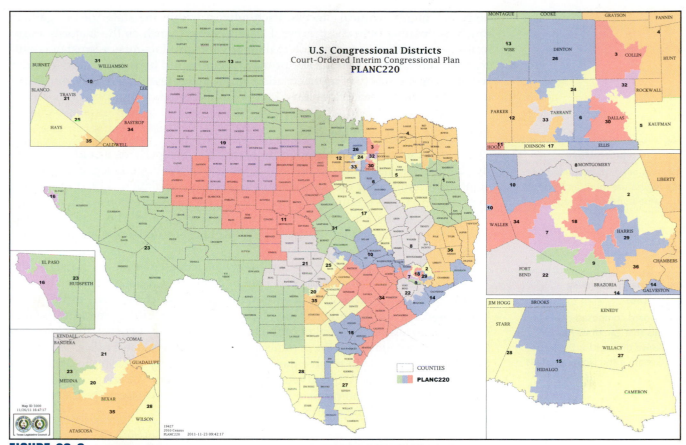

FIGURE 22-2 Interim Congressional Districts Decided by the Federal Judicial Panel. Compare the two maps. How has the panel changed the map of Congressional districts to include more minority-majority districts?

Source: Data from the Texas Legislative Council.

within the county. Multimember districts promote majority representation or domination.

Texas last used multimember districts to create eleven large urban counties during the 1970s. The Legislative Redistricting Board, which is discussed later in this chapter, drew up this plan after the plan drawn by the Texas legislature was invalidated by federal court action. In 1971, the courts invalidated the Legislative Redistricting Board's multimember plan. Minority groups contested the plan, pointing out that the system allowed for a majority to elect all the representatives and for minorities to be frozen out. Some writers have called this the "Matthew effect" after the words of Matthew 13:12: "For whoever has to him more will be given, and he will have abundance; but whoever does not have, even what he has will be taken away from him."[1]

Reapportionment and Redistricting Issues

The U.S. Constitution requires that Congress reapportion the seats in the U.S. House of Representatives among the states following each federal census (every ten years). The Texas Constitution likewise requires the state legislature to reapportion the seats following each federal census.[2] The terms *reapportionment* and *redistricting* are usually used to describe this process. As discussed in Chapter 11, reapportionment refers to the process of allocating representatives to districts; redistricting is the drawing of district lines. Apportioning seats in any legislative body is a highly political process. Each interest within the state tries to gain as much as possible from the process. Existing powers, such as the majority party in the legislature, will try to protect their advantages. Incumbent legislators will try to ensure their reelection. The primary issues raised by reapportionment and redistricting are equity of representation, minority representation, and gerrymandering (drawing district boundary lines for political advantage).

Equity of Representation

equity of representation

situation in which each member of a legislature represents about the same number of people

The issue of **equity of representation** is not new; it is perhaps as old as legislative bodies. Thomas Jefferson noted the problem in the Virginia legislature in the eighteenth century.[3] In the early twentieth century, population shifted from rural to urban areas, and gradually the rural areas were overrepresented in many state legislatures. In the 1960s, only two states (Wisconsin and Massachusetts) had rural/urban representation in the legislature that equaled population distributions in the state.[4]

In an attempt to resolve the inequality of representation in the state, the Texas Constitution was amended in 1948 to create the **Legislative Redistricting Board (LRB),** which was given the authority to redistrict the seats in the Texas House and Senate if the legislature failed to act. The LRB is made up of the lieutenant governor, the speaker of the house, the attorney general, the comptroller of public accounts, and the commissioner of the general land office.[5] Although the LRB was not able to resolve the issue early on, equity of representation is no longer an issue today. With advancements in computers, drawing districts with approximately the same number of people is easy. Other issues, just as contentious, have replaced the equity issue.

Legislative Redistricting Board (LRB)

state board composed of elected officials that can draw new legislative districts for the House and Senate if the legislature fails to act

Minority Representation

minority representation

requirement that in drawing legislative districts, the legislature should create districts that give members of minority groups an opportunity to be elected

The second issue raised by reapportionment is **minority representation.** Not only should legislative districts be approximately equal in population, they should also allow for minority representation.

The 1981 session of the legislature produced a redistricting and reapportionment plan that advanced minority representation in both houses. However, Bill Clements, the Republican governor, vetoed the Senate plan, and the Texas Supreme Court invalidated the House plan. That forced the Legislative Redistricting Board to draw new districts. The new plan was challenged in federal courts and by the U.S. Justice Department, which ruled that the plan violated the federal Voting Rights Act because it did not achieve maximum minority representation. African Americans and Mexican Americans felt that the plan diluted their voting strength. A new plan, drawn up by federal courts, maximized minority representation by creating districts that contained a majority of ethnic minorities—"majority-minority" districts.

Similar battles took place in the 1990s. Minorities gained many seats, as did Republicans, who managed to take control of the Texas Senate for the first time in over one hundred years. In the 2001 session of the legislature, minorities did not gain significantly. Later in this chapter, the effects of this redistricting are discussed in detail.

Political and Racial Gerrymandering

As noted in Chapter 11, the practice of gerrymandering dates to the early days of the Republic. Political parties drew legislative districts to achieve the political advantage of one party over another. The term has also been applied to the practice of creating minority districts—racial gerrymandering.

With the rise of the Republican Party, political gerrymandering in Texas has intensified. Until 2003, Republicans repeatedly charged that the Democrats have reduced the number of potential Republican districts, especially in suburban areas. In the 1980s, the Republicans forged alliances with minority groups. Republicans support the creation of **racially gerrymandered majority-minority districts,** and minority groups support the Republican efforts. As we shall see, the creation of majority-minority districts aids both groups.

In 1996, the U.S. Supreme Court reviewed a legal challenge to the practice of creating majority-minority districts.[6] In ruling against three majority-minority districts, the Court determined that these districts "are ultimately unexplainable on grounds other than the racial quotas established for these districts," resulting in "unconstitutional racial gerrymandering."

In April 2001, the U.S. Supreme Court placed further limitation on the use of racial gerrymandering in drawing legislative districts.[7] The Court said that although race can be a factor, it must not be the primary factor in determining the makeup of legislative districts. Partisan makeup can be a primary factor, but race cannot. This court ruling reduced the practice of racial gerrymandering but makes it possible to pack minority Democrats into districts so long as the intent is not based on race.

Redistricting in the 2000s

Redistricting efforts in the 1990s increased the number of majority-minority districts, and this concentration of minority populations in districts also had the effect of increasing the number of legislative districts that are majority Anglo and that vote Republican.

In the 2001 session of the legislature, several issues surfaced. Both parties hoped to gain seats through the redistricting process. Texas gained two U.S. congressional seats, for a total of thirty-two, and the fight over these seats between Democrats and Republicans added to the controversy in the legislature. The Texas House and Senate adjourned without approving new redistricting plans. As a result of this inaction by the Senate, the Legislative Redistricting Board had to establish new districts for the Texas legislature. Only one member of this board was a Democrat—Speaker Laney, who was effectively frozen out of the discussion. Lt. Governor Ratliff objected to the proceeding. The remaining three members, Attorney General Cornyn, Land Commissioner Dewhurst, and Comptroller Rylander, proceeded to draw districts that greatly favor Republicans. Because of these redistricting efforts by the LRB, in 2003 Republicans gained control of both houses of the Texas legislature for the first time in over one hundred years.

Normally, redistricting takes place every decade following the new federal census. In the 2003 session, Republicans used their new control over the Texas legislature to redistrict the state's thirty-two congressional districts. This mid-decade redistricting, or re-redistricting, was unprecedented.

In 2001, the LRB drew districts that greatly favored Republicans in both House and Senate elections. This board cannot in fact redistrict congressional districts, and Governor Perry refused to call a special session in 2001 to consider the issue. Instead, he stated that the matter was best left to the courts.

The congressional district map used in the 2002 election cycle was drawn by a special three-judge federal court. Though this map may have favored Republicans in a majority of the districts, Democrats managed to win election in seventeen of the thirty-two districts, leaving the Republicans with fifteen districts. Five districts that heavily favored Republicans were won by Democrats. With these unexpected results, U.S. House majority leader Tom DeLay, a Republican

racially gerrymandered majority-minority districts
legislative districts that are drawn to the advantage of a minority group

from Sugarland, forwarded a plan to the Texas legislature in the 2003 session to redraw the 2001 court-ordered congressional district map.

The Texas House, under the direction of newly elected Speaker Tom Craddick, took up the cause, and a new congressional district map was reported out of committee. The Democrats were incensed, but they did not have enough votes to block the passage of the bill. Instead, they decided to deprive the Texas House of a quorum. The Texas House rules state that a quorum, two-thirds of the whole membership—one hundred representatives—must be present for the House to act. During the last week of the regular session in 2003, fifty-two Democrats crossed the border and took up residence at a Holiday Inn in Ardmore, Oklahoma. The Democratic exodus infuriated state and national Republican leadership. Texas Rangers were sent to get the renegades back to Austin, but to no avail. The absence of these Democrats effectively prevented the House from passing the redistricting legislation and the bill died.

Meanwhile, the Texas Senate, under the direction of newly elected Lt. Governor David Dewhurst, did not debate the issue during the regular session because of the Senate's two-thirds rule, which required that twenty-one members of the Senate agree to allow a bill to be considered by the whole Senate. Senate Democrats, with twelve members, refused to consider any bills.

The First Special Session

Despite much statewide opposition to continuing the re-redistricting battle, on June 19, 2003, Governor Rick Perry called a special session of the legislature, to begin June 30, to reconsider the re-redistricting proposal. Despite many misgivings, on July 8, 2003, the Texas House quickly passed a new congressional map by a highly partisan vote of eighty-three to sixty-two. The battle now moved to the Texas Senate.

In this first special session, Lt. Governor Dewhurst left in place the two-thirds rule required to consider a bill on the Senate floor. As long as the Democrats held twelve seats, they could block the House-passed bill from being considered by the Senate; however, several Democrats at first withheld their support for blocking the legislation. Some minority Democratic senators were offered passage of legislation favorable to their districts. Others were offered

Senator Leticia Van de Putte arranged for the two private planes that secretly flew the Texas Eleven to New Mexico. Standing with the ten other Democratic senators, she speaks to reporters during a press conference in August 2003.

"safe" congressional seats in exchange for favoring re-redistricting. On July 15, 2003, Senator Bill Ratliff, a Republican from Mount Pleasant, joined ten Democrats in blocking the re-redistricting bill.

Great pressure was applied to Lt. Governor Dewhurst to drop the two-thirds rule; however, many senators, both Democratic and Republican, opposed the change. Newspapers across the state urged Dewhurst to hold the line and not change the rules. Statewide polls showed Governor Perry losing support over the redistricting issue.

On July 28, 2003, eleven Texas senators (the "Texas Eleven") fled to Albuquerque, New Mexico. Two things prompted this action. First, they anticipated that the governor was going to adjourn the first special session early and call a second special session immediately thereafter (which he did). The rumor was that the Senate sergeant-at-arms had been ordered to lock the senators in the Senate chamber as soon as the session was called to prevent them from busting a quorum. Second, Lt. Governor Dewhurst had stated he would suspend the two-thirds rule for future sessions.

The Texas governor and lieutenant governor were livid at the actions of these Democratic senators, but the Democratic governor and lieutenant governor of New Mexico were delighted and welcomed the eleven to the state. Republicans and Democrats held dueling press conferences, each accusing the other of wrongdoing. Governor Perry at one point blamed the absent senators for preventing consideration of a bill to fund Medicaid benefits for child health care. Perry had earlier vetoed part of the state budget that would have allowed this funding.

The Second Special Session

A few hours after the second special session began and a quorum was present, the House passed the same redistricting bill passed in the first special session. The quick passage of the bill led some Democrats to question the fairness of the process, since no debate or discussion was allowed.

The Republican senators in Austin attempted to force the return of the eleven Democrats by imposing fines. In the end, the fines amounted to $57,000 for each of the stray senators. The Republicans also took away the parking spaces of the boycotting senators. Some have questioned the legality of that action, since a quorum was not present and technically the Senate could not take action. The fines were later removed on the condition that there would be no more boycotts until the end of the term in January 2005.

The eleven Democratic senators stayed in New Mexico until the thirty-day special session expired on August 26, 2003. They did not immediately return to the state because they thought they would be arrested and taken to Austin for a third special session call. On September 3, 2003, however, the stalemate was broken when Senator John Whitmire, Democrat from Houston, broke the boycott and returned to the state. The Texas Senate now had a quorum.

The Third Special Session

On September 10, 2003, Governor Perry called a third special session of the legislature to consider redistricting. Some were surprised that a third session was called, since a state poll by Montgomery and Associates, an independent research firm, found that most Texans were opposed to redistricting. In fact, 47.9 percent of self-identified Republicans supported redistricting. The poll also showed the governor with a negative rating on job performance.

The House and the Senate quickly passed different redistricting bills, which went to a conference committee. These differences quickly led to infighting among the Republicans, with the main issue being congressional districts in West Texas. House Speaker Tom Craddick wanted a district dominated by his hometown of Midland, but Senator Robert Duncan, Republican from Lubbock, wanted to keep Midland in a district with Lubbock.

The fight over the West Texas districts became so intense that Governor Perry and U.S. Congressman Tom DeLay became involved. In the end, an entirely new map unseen before DeLay's arrival, was produced by the conference committee and accepted by both houses in mid-October 2003.

Outcome of the Redistricting Wrangle

Although many predicted that the DeLay redistricting map would be found in violation of the federal Voting Rights Act because it split minority voters rather than concentrating them into majority-minority districts, they were wrong. U.S. Attorney General Ashcroft issued a one-sentence letter saying that he did not object to the new map. At the time, Democratic Texas House members claimed that the professional staff of the U.S. Justice Department objected to the map, and they asked that the report be made public, but it was not released. When it was later released, they were proved right.

A three-judge special court consisting of two Republicans and one Democrat approved the map, voting along party lines. The logic that prevailed in essence sets aside the Voting Rights Act by allowing minority voters to be divided into many congressional districts so long as the intention is to divide Democrats and not to divide minority voters. Partisan gerrymandering is considered legal. Since most minorities vote for Democrats, they can be split into many districts so long as the gerrymandering is partisan in intent. This established a new standard for redistricting. The U.S. Supreme Court later forced a change in four of these districts because the redistricting plan had diluted the voting strength of minorities.

Governor Perry, Congressman Tom DeLay, and the Republicans were successful in their redistricting efforts. In the 2004 election, the Republicans gained five congressional seats and now control the Texas delegation to Congress, with twenty-one Republicans to eleven Democrats. Democrats entered the decade with a seventeen-to-fifteen majority. All targeted Democrats either were defeated or chose not to run. Only Congressman Chet Edwards won reelection in District 17.

In July 2006, the U.S. Supreme Court heard an appeal to the DeLay redistricting and ruled that nothing in the Constitution prohibited redistricting at mid-decade. However, they did order the redrawing of three congressional districts because of concerns over minority representation.

On the national level, Republicans increased their control of the U.S. House of Representatives in 2004 by six seats. Five of these came from the redistricting effort in Texas. Without this redistricting, the Republicans might not have retained control of the House of Representatives in the 109th Congress.

The Texas mid-decade redistricting contributed to a nationwide controversy that eventually led some states to move away from allowing state legislatures to develop new redistricting maps. Instead, this responsibility has been handed over to independent commissions. In 2008, California voters passed an initiative creating the Citizen's Redistricting Committee. The committee consists of five Democrats, five Republicans, and four independents or third-party members that are selected from a pool of individual applicants by the state auditor's office. In ten states, the redistricting commissions cannot include members of the state legislature, state employees, or elected officials. It is doubtful, however, that Texas will move in that direction anytime soon.

Redistricting in the 2010s

Between 2000 and 2010, the population of Texas grew faster than other states. As a result of the 2010 Census, the state of Texas gained four seats in the U.S. House of Representatives, giving it a total of thirty-six congressional districts. Although rise in population was mostly attributable to the growth of the Hispanic and other minority populations, the Texas legislature adopted a 2011 redistricting plan that created no new minority-majority districts.

Due to provisions within the Voting Rights Act of 1965, either the U.S. Department of Justice or a special federal Appeals Court panel of three judges must approve the Texas redistricting plan. Unlike all other states subject to these provisions, Texas chose not to seek approval through the Obama administration-controlled Department of Justice and appealed directed to the court. All three federal judges, two of whom were appointed by President George W. Bush, rejected the plan in its entirety. They ordered a panel of three federal judges in San Antonio to draft an alternative plan that would meet the guidelines of the Voting Rights Act. The three judge panel returned a plan that created three new minority-majority districts, bringing the total of minority-majority district in Texas to thirteen. The state of Texas immediately appealed the plan to the U.S. Supreme Court. In the meantime, Texas must abide by the plan created by the judicial panel.

Getting Elected

Formal qualifications for state office include age, citizenship, state residency, district residency, and qualified voter status. Among the states, the lowest minimum age for House membership is eighteen years and the upper minimum age is twenty-five. Most states require U.S. citizenship, residency in the state from one to five years, and district residency for a year or less.

A Texas House member must be a U.S. citizen, a registered voter, and at least twenty-one years of age, and must have lived in the state for two years and in the district for one year. To be a Texas state senator, a person must be at least twenty-six years of age and reside in the district for one year preceding her or his election and have resided in the state for five years before the election.

The Impact of Informal Qualifications

Formal requirements are minimal and keep few citizens from serving. More important are informal qualifications that limit many people's ability to serve. These include income, education, occupation, ethnicity, and gender. On these dimensions, state legislators tend not to represent the general population. Similar to members of the U.S. Congress, state legislators tend to be male, well educated, and professionals (often lawyers). (See Table 22-1.)

Other dimensions, sometimes called **"birthright" characteristics,** include race, ethnicity, religion, and national background. On these dimensions, representatives tend to represent their district.[8] If the legislative district is predominantly Mexican American, the representative will likely be Mexican American; the same is true for African American districts. Even though legislators generally represent their constituents on these characteristics, they are usually better educated and from selected occupational groups.

"birthright" characteristics

social and economic characteristics of legislators that match certain demographic characteristics of many people in their district

TABLE 22-1 | Characteristics of Members of the Texas Legislature (2009)

	House	Senate
Sex		
Male	113	25
Female	37	6
Race		
Anglo	105	22
Hispanic	30	7
African American	14	2
Asian	1	0
Longevity		
Incumbent	128	29
Freshman	20	2
Party		
Democrat	74	12
Republican	76	19

Source: www.capitol.state.tx.us/.

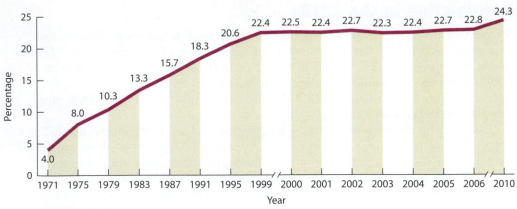

FIGURE 22-3 **Women in State Legislatures** How adequately are women represented in state legislatures? What impact might this have on legislation?

Source: Center for American Women and Politics, Eagleton Institute of Politics, Rutgers University, www.cawp.rutgers.edu. Reprinted with permission.

An African American legislator, for example, is generally better educated than his or her constituents and is drawn from a selected occupational group. In the 2001 session of the Texas House, nine of the fourteen African Americans were attorneys, and sixteen of the thirty-one Mexican Americans were attorneys. All had a higher level of education than their constituents.[9] The same is true for Anglo legislators.

In the case of women, in 2010, 24.3 percent of all state legislators nationwide were women. Few women served until the early 1970s. The number of women increased steadily until 2000 but has remained at about that level since then, as shown in Figure 22-3. In Texas, the number of women legislators has increased from one in each chamber in 1971 to forty-three in 2009. Six are senators and thirty-seven are state representatives.

The numbers of Latinos and African Americans have also increased in legislatures across the nation, in part because of reapportionment. Both ethnic groups are underrepresented in the Texas legislature when compared with their numbers in the population. In 2009, Latinos made up 36.5 percent of the population of Texas and held 20 percent of the House seats and 22.5 percent of the Senate seats. African Americans made up 13.4 percent of the Texas population and held 9.3 percent of the seats in the legislature.

Even with the changes in apportionment, most legislators are upwardly mobile white males. Most are from old, established, often very wealthy families. The legislature is a good place to begin a political career. Having family and money helps launch that career. In addition, some professions, especially law, allow a person time to devote to legislative duties. As we shall see later, most states do not pay their legislators well, and having other sources of income is essential. Also, unlike the U.S. Congress, most state legislatures are part-time bodies, meeting for a set number of days annually or biennially.

The percentage of attorneys in the Texas legislature (35 percent in 2009) is much higher than in the average legislature (16.5 percent). In addition, Texas has fewer who identify themselves as full-time legislators. Texas legislators are not well paid ($7,200 per year), and this might contribute to their feeling that their legislative jobs are only part-time. There is a higher-than-average percentage of business-men and women in the Texas legislature, and a lower-than-average percentage of schoolteachers. In some states, state employees can serve in the state legislature and keep their jobs as teachers. This is prohibited in Texas. A Texas state employee may not hold an elective and an appointive office and receive pay for both.

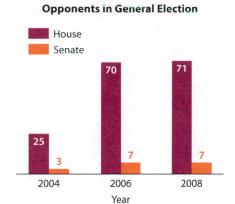

Opponents in General Election

FIGURE 22-4 **Competition In Texas House and Senate Races.** The graph shown here depicts the number of competitive races in recent general elections. It should be noted that only half of the Senate (16 or 15) members are up for election every two years. In the House, all 150 members are up for election every two years.

What trend does this graph illustrate?

Do you think this trend will continue in the future? Explain your answer.

If this trend continues, what impact might increased competition have on the length of tenure in the legislature, party strength, and third parties in the future?

Competition for Office

As noted in earlier chapters, in the one-party Democratic era in Texas, most of the competition for offices was in the Democratic Party primary. Today, competition is more likely to be in the general election. (See Figure 22-4)

Historically, most candidates for the House and Senate races faced little opposition in either the primary or the general election. This lack of competition in Texas legislative races is the result of several factors, but the major reason is the degree to which districts are politically and racially gerrymandered, creating **safe election districts** for both parties. This can be seen by comparing two characteristics of Texas legislative districts in 2004: the strength of party voting in the district and the percentage of minority population in the district. As Figures 22-5 and 22-6 clearly show, House and Senate seats are clustered into safe Democratic and safe Republican districts with only a few competitive seats.

Party voting is a measure of the strength of a political party in the legislative district based on voter support for the party's candidates in previous elections. This is also a measure of party competition. Studies of party competition in the U.S. House and Senate seats define noncompetitive as any district in which either party receives 55 percent or more of the votes. Thus, a district in which the party vote is between 44 and 54 percent is considered competitive.[10] The measure used here to gauge party competitiveness is the combined vote received by either party for all offices/candidates in the district in the 2000 general election. This is the composite party vote. Thus, a House or Senate district in which the Republican Party candidates for statewide office collectively received 55 percent or more of the votes is considered a safe Republican district.

The second variable is the racial composition of the district. This is simply the percentages of minority and nonminority population of the district. If we compare these two characteristics (party competition and minority population in the district) using some simple statistics, we can see that most Texas House and Senate seats fall into two categories—noncompetitive Republican Anglo districts and noncompetitive Democratic minority districts. Since minority support for

safe election districts

noncompetitive districts that can be won only by the party with 55 percent or more of the votes in the district

FIGURE 22-5
Political Inquiry
This map shows the districts based on 2000 Census and voting data. Since 2000, both the demographics and the voting patterns have changed, and some districts have become more competitive, especially for Democrats in South Texas and in inner-city districts. How is this map likely to change as a result of the 2010 Census?

Texas House of Representatives Party Competition in 2002–2010

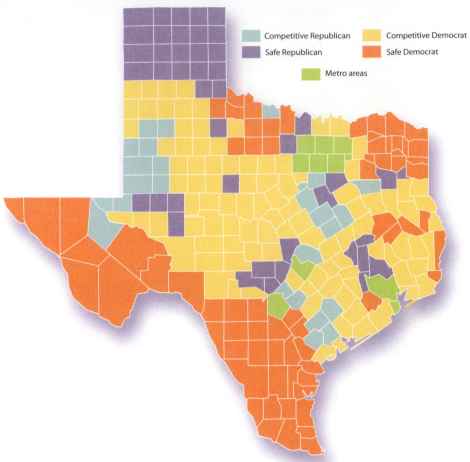

Democratic candidates is always very high, concentrating minorities in districts also concentrates Democratic party support in these districts. Many remaining districts are noncompetitive Republican districts. Other studies have found the same is true for U.S. congressional districts.[11]

Safe Democratic districts exist primarily in two places: South Texas, where there are concentrations of Mexican Americans, and East Texas, the traditional stronghold of Democrats. Republicans are strong in the Panhandle and the German Hill Country. Metropolitan areas of the state also contain both safe Democratic and safe Republican districts—Democrats in the inner city and Republicans in the suburbs.

Thus, one reason for the low competition in Texas legislative races is racial and political gerrymandering. In addition, members of the legislature get money from PACs because they are incumbents. They face little opposition in either the primary or the general elections. Having a war chest of money keeps competition at a low level. Competition in districts is most likely to occur at the primary level and when there is no incumbent.

In the last eight years, however, there has been an increase in the level of competition in the Republican Party primary elections. Some of this competition is related to House Speaker Craddick, who has been known to seek opponents for those members who oppose his agenda and may threaten his continuation as speaker.

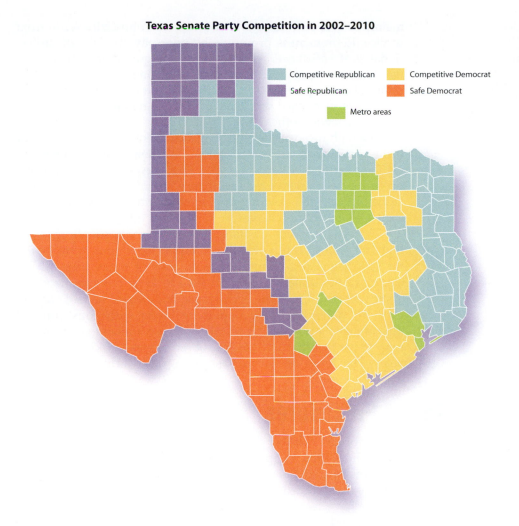

Texas Senate Party Competition in 2002–2010

Competitive Republican   Competitive Democrat

Safe Republican   Safe Democrat

Metro areas

FIGURE 22-6
Political Inquiry
This map shows the districts based on 2000 Census and voting data. Since 2000, both the demographics and the voting patterns have changed, and some districts have become more competitive, especially for Democrats in South Texas and in inner-city districts. What might this mean for future races and the composition of the Texas Senate?

Even when candidates do not face opposition, they are likely to collect large amounts of money from various groups, especially from PACs. In the 2006 races for the legislature, House winners collected an average of $208,000, and Senate winners collected an average of $917,000. Most money comes from contributors who live outside the senator's or representative's district. The upper right gallery of the Texas House chamber, looking toward the speaker's podium, is "reserved" for the most powerful members of the lobbies. Some lobbyists are almost always there when business is being conducted on the floor. They watch members of the House, and the House members know they are being watched. Members are sometimes contacted by these lobbyists and are "encouraged" to vote in the right way. Members of the House call this space the "Owners' Box."

Legislative Turnover

One could conclude from the relatively low level of competition for Texas legislative seats that there would be low turnover of the membership. This is not the case. **Turnover**—the number of new members of the legislature each session—is high in all state legislatures, and normally it is higher for the lower house than for the upper chamber.[12]

Figure 22-7 shows the number of years of service for members of the Texas legislature. Over time, turnover rates in Texas are very high. Turnover is not due

turnover

the number of new members of the legislature each session

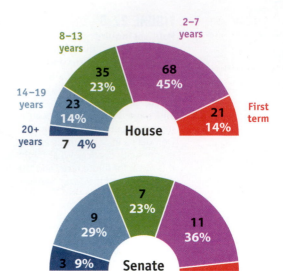

FIGURE 22-7

Years of Service of the Members of the 2009 Legislature

Source: Legislative Reference Library, www.lrl.state.tx.us/legis/members/roster.crm?leg=81.

term limits

limits on the number of times a person can be elected to the same office

speaker of the house

member of the Texas House, elected by the other House members, who serves as presiding officer and generally controls the passage of legislation

mainly to electoral defeat; most members voluntarily retire from service. Retirement is prompted by poor pay, the lack of professional staff assistance, redistricting, the requirements of the job, the demands upon one's family, fund-raising demands, and the rigors of seeking reelection.[13] Some use the office as a stepping-stone to higher office and leave to become members of Congress or take statewide office.

The high turnover rate has a political fallout. If 20 to 25 percent of the members are new each session, these new members are learning the rules and finding their way. This allows a few "old-timers" to control the legislative process. Even with only nine new members in the House, a few "old-timers" can still control the process, as we shall see later in this chapter.

Though turnover in state legislatures nationwide is quite high, in recent years voters have supported formal **term limits** for state legislators, limiting the number of times they can be elected to the same office. From 1990 to 1996, twenty-one states approved term limits for both House and Senate seats. Fourteen of those states have imposed these limits with constitutional amendments and seven by statutes.[14] These limits were approved despite the fact that self-limiting of terms was working for many years. The Texas legislature has self-imposed term limits.

Legislative Procedures

All legislatures have formal rules of procedure that govern their operations. These rules prescribe how bills are passed into law and make the process of passing laws more orderly and fair. These rules also make it difficult to pass laws. A bill must clear many hurdles before it becomes a law. Rules that make it difficult to pass bills have two results: They prevent bills from becoming law without careful review, and they preserve the status quo. In the traditionalistic-individualistic political culture of Texas, these rules protect the ruling elite and enable them to control the legislative process. Thus, it is more important to understand the impact of rules on legislation than to have a detailed understanding of the actual rules. We use this basic approach here to explain how laws are made in Texas.

Leadership Roles

In any legislative body, those holding formal leadership positions possess considerable power to decide the outcome of legislation. In the Texas legislature, power is very much concentrated in the hands of two individuals: the speaker of the house and the lieutenant governor. These two individuals control the output of legislation.

Speaker of the House

The members of the House elect the speaker of the Texas House of Representatives by majority vote to preside over the House. The election of the **speaker of the house** is the first formal act of the members. The secretary of state presides over the election. Only occasionally is the outcome of this election in doubt. Who the speaker will be is generally known far in advance of the beginning of the session, and this individual spends considerable time lining up supporters before the session begins. In all but a few cases, the person elected is a longtime member of the House and has support from current members. When a third of the members are new, the person elected speaker may also have to gain support from some of these new members. It is illegal for candidates for speaker to formally promise members something in exchange for their vote, but key players in the election of the speaker often receive choice **committee assignments,** since the speaker decides which members sit on which committees.

Many feel that speaker of the house is the most powerful position in Texas government. There is no doubt that the speaker is extremely powerful. Generally, speakers have the power to direct and decide what legislation passes the House. The speaker gains power from the formal rules adopted by the House at the beginning of each session. These rules allow the speaker to do the following:

- Appoint the chairs of all committees.
- Appoint most of the members of each standing committee. About half of these committee seats are assigned according to a limited seniority system. In reality, the backers of the speaker often use their seniority to choose a committee assignment, thus freeing up an appointment for the speaker.
- Appoint members of the calendar and procedural committees, conference committees, and other special and interim committees.
- Serve as presiding officer over all sessions. This power allows the speaker to recognize members on the floor who wish to speak, generally interpret House rules, decide when a vote will be taken, and decide the outcome of voice votes.
- Refer all bills to committees. As a rule, bills go to subject matter committees. However, the speaker has discretion in deciding what committee will receive a bill. Some speakers used the State Affairs Committee as a "dead bill committee." Bills assigned to this committee usually had little chance of passing. Also, the speaker can assign a bill to a favorable committee to enhance its chances of passing.

These rules give the speaker control over the House agenda. The selected chairs are members of the "speaker's team." Few bills pass the House without the speaker's approval. For example, in the 2005 session of the legislature, House Bill 1348, which would have limited campaign contributions from corporations and labor unions, was being cosponsored by two-thirds of the members of the House, both Democrats and Republicans. The bill was not given a hearing by the Elections Committee because of the influence of Speaker Tom Craddick.

For many years, the Texas House of Representatives operated on a bipartisan basis. In the 2001 session of the legislature, Democrats controlled the House and Democrat Pete Laney was speaker. Bipartisanship was much more apparent in committee assignments and the overall tone of the session. In the 2003 session, much of this bipartisanship disappeared when the Republicans held a majority of the seats in the House and Tom Craddick became speaker. Dawnna Dukes (Democrat from Houston) stated that the Republicans did not feel the need to compromise on issues, since they controlled a majority of the seats. As we have seen, this was especially evident on the issue of the redistricting of the U.S. House seats.

Incumbent speakers are almost always reelected. A new speaker is chosen only after the death, retirement, or resignation of a sitting speaker. Traditionally, speakers served for two terms and retired or moved to higher offices.

committee assignments
decisions by the speaker of the house on which members of the House sit on each committee; some committees, such as appropriations, are more powerful than others

From 1951 to 1975, no speaker served more than two terms. In 1975, Billy Clayton broke with that tradition and served four terms. Gib Lewis, who succeeded Clayton, served five terms, as did Pete Laney.[15] Tom Craddick was elected speaker for the 2003 session. He was the first Republican speaker since Reconstruction.

In the 2007 session, an attempt was made to remove Tom Craddick as speaker, in large degree because of his partisanship and actions that many felt were arbitrary. Several attempts were made to advance a motion to vacate the chair, but Craddick exercised his power as speaker and refused to recognize anyone wanting to make that motion. When Craddick was overruled by the two **parliamentarians,** the experts in legislative procedure, he forced them to resign and brought in two former House members and colleagues to act as parliamentarians. These two upheld the speaker's decision not to recognize any member wanting to vacate the chair.

In the 2009 session, Democrats and Republicans finally succeeded in ousting Craddick, replacing him with a less autocratic, compromise speaker, Joe Straus. Straus was elected with the backing of sixty-two of the seventy-four Democrats. In November 2010, Republicans increased their majority in the House from seventy-eight to ninety-nine. Subsequently, two Democrats switched ranks to join the Republicans. At this point, about thirty Christian social conservatives led an initiative to replace Straus, whom they regarded as a moderate. They pointed out that a coalition of the Democratic caucus and eleven moderate Republicans pushed through Straus' original election to the speakership. The social conservatives nominated Ken Paxton, who received a mere 15 of the 101 Republican votes.

During the 2011 legislative session, Straus ushered through many major bills that advanced the conservative agenda including the new voter ID law, the redistricting plan, and further restrictions on abortions. Despite these successes, Democrats still see Straus as likeable, accessible, and largely nonpartisan.

Lieutenant Governor

Unlike the speaker of the house, the **lieutenant governor** is elected by the voters for a four-year term in the general election. The lieutenant governor does not owe his or her election to the legislative body, is not formally a senator, and cannot vote except in cases of a tie. One might assume that the office is not a powerful legislative office. In most states, that is true; however, the lieutenant governor in Texas possesses powers very similar to those of the speaker. Lieutenant governors can do the following:

- Appoint the chairs of all Senate committees.
- Select all members of all Senate committees. The Senate has no formal seniority rule.
- Appoint members of the conference committees.
- Serve as presiding officer and interpret rules.
- Refer all bills to committees.

On the surface, it appears that the lieutenant governor is more powerful than the speaker. Lieutenant governors do not owe their election to the Senate, and they have all powers possessed by the speaker. The reality is different. The powers of the lieutenant governor are assigned by the formal rules of the Senate, which are adopted at the beginning of each session. What the Senate gives, it can take away. Lieutenant governors must play a delicate balancing role of working with powerful members of the Senate and often

parliamentarian
expert in legislative procedures

lieutenant governor
presiding officer of the Texas Senate, elected by the voters of the state

compromising in the assignment of chairs of committees and committee membership. The same is true for all other powers held by the lieutenant governor: He or she must forge an alliance with key senators to use those powers effectively.[16]

From 1876 to 1999, the Democrats controlled the lieutenant governor's office. They controlled the Senate from 1876 to 1997. Until recently, party control was not a factor. It is often suggested that if the lieutenant governor and the Senate are ever of opposite parties, the powers of the lieutenant governor could be diminished. Such concerns have been voiced in the past few years, and given the pattern in other states, this development seems quite likely. Having such a powerful lieutenant governor is unusual among the states. Only five other states (Alabama, Georgia, Mississippi, South Carolina, and Vermont) give the lieutenant governor the power to appoint committee members and assign bills to committees.[17]

Most lieutenant governors are figureheads, who stand in when the governor is out of state. In states where the lieutenant governor is a figurehead, or when there is no lieutenant governor, the Senate elects one of its members to be the presiding officer, called the pro tempore, president of the Senate, or speaker of the senate.

Thus, the office of lieutenant governor in Texas is quite different from the office in most other states, but this has not always been true. J. William Davis, in his book *There Shall Also Be a Lieutenant Governor*, traces the concentration of power in this office to the actions of Allen Shivers and Ben Ramsey during the 1940s and 1950s. Over a period of several years, the office gained power in the Senate.[18]

The speaker and the lieutenant governor also have other significant powers outside the legislature. They appoint members of other state boards, or they serve as members of such boards. For example, they appoint the members of the Legislative Budget Board, which writes the state budget, and they serve as the chair and the vice chair, respectively, of this board. The budget determines what agencies and programs will be funded and in what amounts.

The Role of Committees

Similar to the U.S. Congress, most of the work of the legislature is done in standing committees established by House and Senate rules. Besides the standing committees, there are subcommittees of the standing committees, conference committees to work out differences in bills passed by the two houses, temporary committees to study special problems, and **interim committees** to study issues between sessions of the state legislature.

Of these, the standing committees are the most important. In the 2007 session, there were seventeen standing committees in the Senate and forty-four in the House. These are listed in Table 22-2.

The chairs of these standing committees have powers similar to those of the speaker and the lieutenant governor, but at the committee level. They decide the times and the agendas for meetings of the committee. In doing so, they decide the amount of time devoted to bills and which bills get the attention of the committee. A chair that strongly dislikes a bill can often prevent the bill from passing. Even if the bill is given a hearing, the chair can decide to give that bill to a subcommittee that might kill the bill.

Thus, as in most legislative bodies, in Texas the power is concentrated in a few powerful individuals who control the agendas and the actions of the legislature. Few bills can pass the legislature without the support of these individuals.

interim committees

temporary committees of the legislature that study issues between regular sessions and make recommendations on legislation

TABLE 22-2 | Standing Committees of the Texas House and Senate, 2009 Session

Senate Committees	House Committees
Administration	Agriculture & Livestock
Agriculture & Rural Affairs	Appropriations
Business & Commerce	Border & Intergovernmental Affairs
Committee of the Whole Senate	Business & Industry
Criminal Justice	Calendars
Economic Development	Corrections
Education	County Affairs
Finance	Criminal Jurisprudence
Government Organization	Culture, Recreation, & Tourism
Health & Human Services	Defense & Veterans' Affairs
Higher Education	Elections
Intergovernmental Relations	Emergency Preparedness, Select
International Relations & Trade	Energy Resources
Jurisprudence	Environmental Regulation
Natural Resources	Federal Economic Stabilization Funding, Select
Nominations	Federal Legislation, Select
State Affairs	Fiscal Stability, Select
Transportation & Homeland Security	General Investigating & Ethics
Veteran Affairs & Military Installations	Government Efficiency & Accountability, Select
	Higher Education
	House Administration
	Human Services
	Insurance
	Judiciary & Civil Jurisprudence
	Land & Resource Management
	Licensing & Administrative Procedures
	Local & Consent Calendars
	Natural Resources
	Pensions, Investments, & Financial Services
	Public Education
	Public Health
	Public Safety
	Redistricting
	Rules & Resolutions
	Special Purpose Districts, Select
	State Affairs
	Technology, Economic Development, & Workforce
	Transportation
	Transportation Funding, Select
	Urban Affairs
	Ways & Means

Source: Texas Legislature Online, www.capitol.state.tx.us.

How a Bill Becomes a Law

Figure 22-8 lists the formal procedures in the Texas House and Senate for passing a bill. Each bill, to become law, must clear each step. The vast majority of bills that are introduced fail to pass. Few bills of major importance are passed in any given legislative session. Most bills make only minor changes to existing law. At each stage in the process, the bill can receive favorable or unfavorable actions. At each step, a bill can die by either action or inaction. There are many ways to kill a bill, but only one way to pass a bill. To pass, a bill must clear all hurdles.

The rules of the Texas Senate in effect provide a number of constraints on legislation. Before the sixtieth day of the legislative session, a bill can clear the Senate with a simple majority vote. Few bills pass before the sixtieth day. After the sixtieth day, before a bill can be considered on the floor of the Senate, a two-thirds vote is required. Technically, after the sixtieth day, Senate rules state that bills must be considered in the order they are reported out of committees. If bills are not considered in the order reported out of committees, a two-thirds vote is required to consider a bill. By design, bills are never considered in the order reported out of committee. If two-thirds of the senators agree to consider the bill, it can pass by a simple majority. Because of these rules, few bills clear the Senate that are not supported by more than a simple majority of the senators.

In some cases, the formal rules can be used to hide actions of the legislature. It is not uncommon in legislative bodies to attach riders to appropriations bills. A **rider** can be a subject matter item (creation of a new state regulatory board) or a money item (money for a park in a legislator's district). In the Texas legislature, the practice adds a new twist. **Closed riders** can be attached to appropriations, and they are closed to public inspection and appear only after the appropriation bills have passed the House and the Senate and go to conference committee. In the conference committee, the cloak is removed, and they appear for public inspection for the first time. At this stage, which is always near the end of the session, the likelihood of change is remote. Unless the governor vetoes the bill, these closed riders become law without public comment.

A recent example of a closed rider dealt with the Bush School at Texas A&M University. In the 1999 session of the legislature, the Bush School was separated from the College of Liberal Arts and made a separate school within the university, and its budget was increased by several million dollars. This was done at the request of Governor George W. Bush.

Calendars and Bills

To fully understand the legislative process, we must distinguish between major and minor bills, because state legislators treat them very differently. State legislatures use different **calendars** to distinguish between major, controversial bills and minor or local bills. By using different calendars, legislatures can better manage their limited time and devote attention to important matters. Texas is one of thirty-six states that use both a local and a consent calendar in both chambers.[19]

The Texas House uses the local and consent calendars for minor bills. To be assigned to these calendars, a bill must meet tests established by House rules. Local bills must not have an effect upon more than one of the 254 counties in the state. Bills for the consent calendar must be minor, noncontroversial bills. To be placed on either the local or the consent calendar, bills must meet two further criteria. First, they must receive unanimous support in the substantive House committee handling the bill. Second, the **Local and Consent Calendars Committee,** the committee that handles minor bills, must approve them. If this committee does not approve the bill, it is sent to the **Calendars Committee** (which decides which bills will be considered for floor debate) for assignment to another

rider

provision attached to a bill that may not be of the same subject matter as the main bill

closed rider

provision attached to appropriations bills that is not made public until the conference committee meets

calendars

procedures in the House used to consider different kinds of bills: Major bills and minor bills are considered under different procedures

Local and Consent Calendars Committee

committee handling minor and noncontroversial bills that normally apply to only one county

Calendars Committee

standing committee of the House that decides which bills will be considered for floor debate and to which committee they will be assigned

FIGURE 22-8
Political Inquiry

This diagram displays the sequential flow of a bill from the time it is introduced in the Texas House of Representatives to final passage and transmittal to the governor. A bill introduced in the Senate follows the same procedure, flowing from Senate to House. How does this procedure compare with the route a bill follows through the U.S. House of Representatives and Senate (see Chapter 11)?

Basic Steps in the Texas Legislative Process

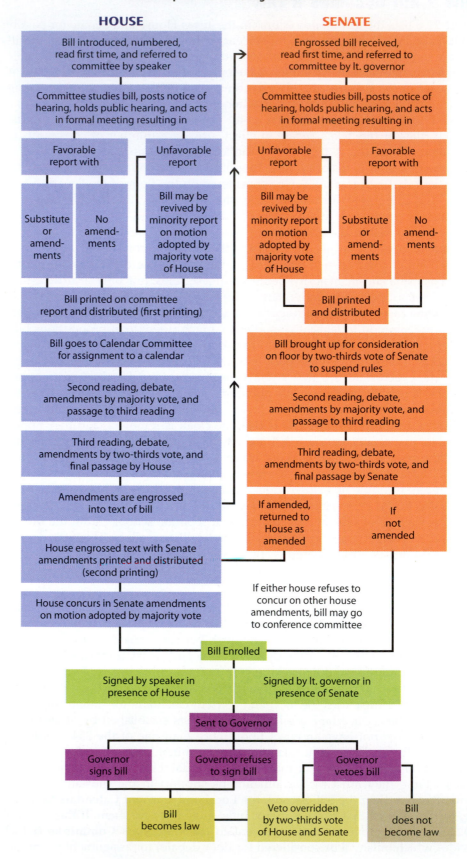

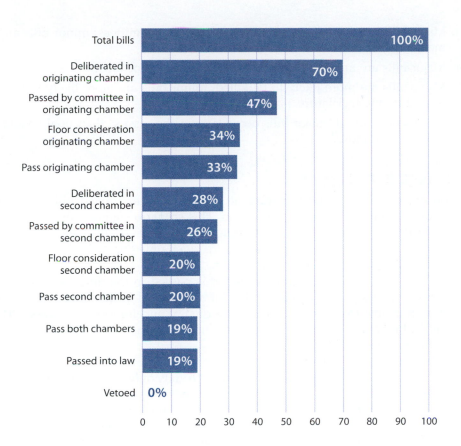

FIGURE 22-9   Where do most bills die? Bill Survival Rate in the Eighty-first Session of the Texas Legislature (2009)

Source: Adapted from Harvey J. Tucker, "Legislation Deliberation in the Texas House and Senate." Paper presented at Annual Meeting of Midwest Political Science Association, Chicago, April 15–18, 2004. Data updated for the 2009 session by Harvey J. Tucker.

calendar. A bill may be removed from the local or consent calendar if five members object during floor debate. Also, if debate exceeds ten minutes, the bill is withdrawn and effectively killed.[20] These procedures safeguard against important bills being approved without adequate review by the whole House.

Figure 22-9 demonstrates the fate of bills in the eighty-first session of the Texas legislature. As can be seen, only about 25 percent of all bills introduced in the House and Senate make it into law. Most bills are introduced in the House. Most make it to a committee for deliberation but die at the committee level. Some bills are introduced to satisfy a constituency, and the member has no intention of working to pass the bill.

There are three calendars for major bills: the emergency calendar, the major state calendar, and the general state calendar. The Calendars Committee only has the authority to assign bills to these calendars. This power is rarely challenged. The distinction among the major calendars is not important until the final days of the legislative session, when time is limited.

There are a few similarities and differences between major and minor bills. The bills are identical in three ways:

1. They originate in either chamber.
2. They are equally likely to be vetoed.
3. They receive final action toward the end of the legislative session.

Major and minor bills are treated differently in six ways:

1. Major bills are introduced earlier in the session than minor bills.
2. Companion bills are introduced in the other chamber more frequently for major bills than for minor bills.

3. Major bills are more evenly distributed across committees; minor bills are more concentrated in a few committees.

4. Major bills are amended more frequently than minor bills.

5. Major bills are more likely to be killed; minor bills are more likely to be passed by the legislature.

6. Final actions to kill major bills occur later in the session than final actions to kill minor bills.[21]

Workload and Logjams

According to much of the literature on state legislatures, most bills pass the legislature in the final days of the session. This scenario suggests that the legislature "goofs off" for most of the session and then frantically passes bills just before adjournment, producing laws that are given only "hasty consideration, of poor quality and are confused and inferior."[22]

In Texas, it is true that most legislation is passed in the final two weeks of the session. In 1985, almost 80 percent of all bills passed in this time period. The question remains: Does this result in poor quality and inferior legislation? The answer is, Probably not. One must understand the process of setting the agenda in the Texas legislature.

First, bills may be introduced at any time before the session and up until the 60th day of the 140-day session. After the 60th day, only local bills, emergency appropriations, emergency matters submitted by the governor, and bills with a four-fifths vote of the House may be introduced. Thus, for the first 60 days, the agendas for both houses are being set. After the 60th day, the legislature begins to clear those agendas. As indicated, most bills die in committees and are never assigned to a calendar. Killing a bill in committee is an action by the legislature, and it occurs at a regular rate during the session.[23] The bill is dead if it does not make it out of committee. That leaves only about a third of all bills for further consideration late in the session.

Thus, the image of the legislature as goofing off for 120 days is not accurate. The nature of the legislative process requires the passage of major legislation near the end of the session. Also, about half the bills that pass toward the end of the session are minor bills, and they are cleared late for different reasons than are major bills.

We have seen that the formal rules of the House and the Senate govern how and what kind of legislation gets passed. These rules have the effect of preserving the status quo because killing a bill is easy and passing one is very difficult. Although the Texas legislature is not remarkably different from most other legislatures in this respect, in Texas these rules protect the traditionalistic-individualistic political culture of the state.

Rules, Roles, and Styles

In addition to the formal rules regarding procedures, such as how bills become laws and how legislators are appointed to committees, informal rules, expected roles, and leadership styles come into play within legislative procedure. **Informal rules** are legislative norms that all state legislators must learn if they are to be successful. Examples include the following:

informal rules

set of norms or values that govern legislative behavior

Do not:
- conceal the real purpose of a bill.
- deal in personalities in floor debate.
- be a thorn in the side of the majority by refusing unanimous consent.

speak on issues you know nothing about.

seek publicity from the press to look good to the people back home.

talk to the press about decisions reached in private.[24]

Each legislature will have a different set of norms and place different value on them. In Texas, dealing in personalities during floor debate has been viewed as acceptable behavior by a large number of Texas legislators, whereas in the other states, only a few members usually view this as acceptable behavior.[25] Legislators must learn the norms of their legislature and adhere to them, or they might find themselves isolated and ineffective. The informal rules are as important as the formal rules governing the legislature.

Styles of Leadership

Each speaker approaches the job in different ways. Historically, most speakers have exerted tight control over the House. This was true of Billy Clayton, speaker from 1975 to 1983. However, Gib Lewis, who followed Clayton, exerted much less control. He allowed the members of his team—namely, committee chairs—to control the process, and he took a much more "laid-back" attitude. Pete Laney was more like Billy Clayton in that he controlled the House. Tom Craddick, speaker from 2003 to 2009, followed a style similar to that of Speakers Laney and Clayton.

Lieutenant governors can also differ greatly in their leadership styles. For instance, Bill Hobby, the son of a former governor, served as lieutenant governor for eighteen years (1972–1990). A soft-spoken, low-key person, Hobby seldom forced his will on the members of the Senate. He preferred to work behind the scenes and forge compromises.

Hobby chose not to run for reelection in 1990, and Bob Bullock succeeded him. Bullock had served for sixteen years as the state comptroller and had developed a reputation for strong, effective leadership, but he often went out of his way to make enemies. Bullock's leadership style as lieutenant governor is almost the opposite of Hobby's. Stories have circulated of shouting matches and angry behavior, sometimes even in open sessions of the Senate. The Senate seemed to adjust to Bullock's style of leadership, and he managed to get much of his agenda passed. Hobby and Bullock illustrate very different ways to be effective leaders of the Senate.

Rick Perry, while serving as the Texas agricultural commissioner, did not have the reputation of a compromiser; however, as lieutenant governor, he performed quite effectively in the 1999 session. Lt. Governor Dewhurst was something of a political unknown, having served only four years as land commissioner before his election. Dewhurst's performance received mixed reviews. He was an effective leader in the regular sessions and was partisan in the three special sessions. Powerful Republican leaders have ensured that he will keep the broad powers normally given to lieutenant governors.

Leadership in legislative bodies can take many forms. In addition to formal leadership roles, some members develop reputations as experts in some

After being elected for the first time to the House of Representatives, Democrat Patrick Rose received a good deal of publicity when PBS chronicled his experience during the 2002 election in the documentary *Last Man Standing: Politics Texas Style*. Here, he sits on Republican senator Jeff Wentworth's wastebasket during a Senate discussion.

areas of legislation, and others look to them as leaders in those areas. Being recognized by other members as the expert in some area of legislation obviously increases one's influence. For instance, a person who is a recognized expert on taxation issues can use this reputation to forge coalitions and pass tax legislation.

Representational Roles

Constituencies have expectations about their legislators' roles. As noted in Chapter 11, for centuries members of legislatures have argued about the representational role of a legislator. Are they *delegates,* sent by the voters to represent the voters' interests, or are they *trustees,* entrusted by the voters to make decisions based on their best judgment? The delegate role is perceived as being more democratic—as doing what the people want. The trustee role can be characterized as elitist—as doing what one thinks is best.

In reality, members may play both the delegate and the trustee role, depending upon the issue before them. For example, in 1981 the Texas legislature passed a bill prohibiting the catching of redfish by commercial fishermen in some waters in the Gulf of Mexico. The bill was written and advanced by sport fishermen. Representatives from coastal communities in Texas voted as delegates—with the commercial fishermen and against the bill. Representatives from the Panhandle, however, were free to vote as trustees. In matters affecting the livelihood of Panhandle ranchers but not coastal fisheries, these representatives would reverse their voting roles. Which role representatives play is largely dependent on how the issues affect their district. The problem with this is that local interests can take the forefront, leading legislators to neglect long-term statewide or larger public interests.

Rating the Texas Legislature

How does the Texas legislature compare with legislatures of other states? Making comparisons is always difficult, but several political scientists have developed indexes to measure the "professionalism" of state legislatures. Most of these indexes of professionalism rely on several measures. Two important measures are annual salary and number of days the legislature is in session. A third measure that is often employed is the amount of money available for staff assistance. Of these three measures, the last, salary and staff assistance, is most significant.

Other writers have also used "percent metropolitan" as a factor in explaining professional development of state legislatures. The argument goes that large, metropolitan states will cause an increase in the number of bills introduced because of the increased problems that come with urban growth. More bills require more time, which results in longer sessions. When sessions become longer, lasting most of the year, pay and staff assistance tend to increase.[26]

Given these criteria, how does the professionalism of the Texas legislature stack up when compared with that of legislatures in other states? Texas is a mixed bag when judged on these criteria.

Staff Assistance

Texas provides more money for legislative staff than any other state. Most members keep open offices on a full-time basis in their district, and many do in the state capital as well. The recent renovations of the state capitol building have provided each senator and House member with excellent office and committee hearing space. Texas senators receive $25,000 per month for staff salary support plus office expenses. House members each receive $8,500 per month for staff salary plus office expenses. In addition, standing committees have staff salary support during and between legislative sessions. California provides $20,000 to both House and Senate members. New York provides staff support similar to Texas for its legislature. The Texas Legislative Council has a large, professional staff to assist the legislature. It has produced one of the best Web pages of any of the states and provides easy access to the citizens during and between legislative sessions. The House also has the House Research Organization, which produces professional assistance to the legislature.

Salary and Building Facilities

As a result of the renovations to the state capitol building, the members of the Texas legislature have excellent facilities for their staff, committee hearings, and legislative work. In this area, the Texas legislature compares favorably with other state legislatures. Salaries, however, are considerably lower than those in other states, and on this important indicator of professionalism, Texas does not score well.

Some citizens feel that because the legislature meets for only 140 days every two years, it is part-time and members should be paid accordingly. The pay reflects that attitude. Texas pays the 181 members of the legislature $7,200 a year plus an additional $139 per day for the first 140 days the legislature is in session. In years when the legislature meets, the total compensation is $26,600. In years when the legislature is not in session, legislators receive their $7,200 in salary and may receive some additional per diem pay for off-session committee work.

The salary of Texas legislators has not been increased in the past thirty years. Several attempts to change the state constitutional limit have been rejected by the voters. The current pay qualifies legislators who have no other income for food stamps and other federal assistance. Obviously, most legislators have other sources of income. Many are attorneys or successful businessmen and businesswomen. Lack of compensation is very much in keeping with the traditionalistic political culture of the state, according to which only the elite should serve in the legislature. Also, note in "How Texas Differs" that other southern states (Florida, Georgia, and North Carolina) also have low salaries.

Most citizens are excluded from being legislators because they would not be able to devote the large amount of time to legislative work and still earn a living. Service in the Texas legislature is possible only for the independently wealthy, "political consultants," and people who can find a person or a group to support them while they are in the legislature. In Texas, attorney-legislators who have cases in courts while the legislature is in session can have their cases delayed until the legislature adjourns. Some attorney-legislators receive cases from people who want to delay court action. Unlike many other states, Texas does not have a financial disclosure law that forces members to disclose their sources of income. This leaves the sources of members' income an open question. Some might receive income as "consultants" to businesses with interests in current legislation. The objectivity of members under these circumstances is questionable.

HOW TEXAS DIFFERS POLITICAL THINKING THROUGH COMPARISONS

Legislative Salaries in the Ten Most Populous States

Texas currently pays members of the state legislature $600 per month. Among the ten largest states, Texas has the lowest pay.

Q: Should members of the legislature be paid a living-wage salary?

A: Because the legislature meets for only 140 days every two years, and because most legislators are attorneys or successful businesspeople, the need for a living-wage salary is not high. Further, lack of compensation is very much in line with the traditionalistic/individualistic political culture of the state.

Annual salary 2009

California	$116,208
Michigan	$79,650
New York	$79,500
Pennsylvania	$73,315
Illinois	$67,835
Ohio	$60,584
Florida	$30,336
Georgia	$17,342
North Carolina	$14,951
Texas	$7,200

Source: Council of State Governments, *The Book of the States 2009* (Lexington, KY: Council of State Governments, 2009), Vol. 41, 99–100, table 3.9.

Annual Sessions

biennial session

meeting of the legislature every two years

The Texas legislature meets in **biennial sessions** (every two years) of 140 days in odd-numbered years, beginning in January. At the end of World War II, only four states held annual sessions. As state legislatures assumed more power during the second half of the twentieth century, legislatures transitioned to annual sessions. As state budgets expanded and become more complicated, with economic development and federal grants-in-aid during the 1960s and 1970s, states also moved from biennial budgets to annual budgets. Today, Texas is one of only four states that holds biennial legislative sessions (see Figure 22-10).[27]

Voters in Texas, in the past, have rejected initiatives to move to annual sessions. In keeping with the traditionalistic-individualistic political culture of the state, there is some concern that the more often the legislature meets, the more damage it can do. One political wag once remarked that there was a typographical error in the original Texas Constitution, and the founders had intended the legislature to meet for two days every 140 years.

sine die

adjourned; the legislature must adjourn at end of its regular session and cannot continue to meet

At the end of the 140-day session, the Texas legislature must adjourn (**sine die**) and cannot call special or longer sessions (known as **extraordinary sessions**). In recent years, many state governments have placed limits on the number of days a legislature can stay in session. Thirteen states do not place a limit on the length of legislative sessions.[28] The inability to call itself into special session,

extraordinary session

legislative session called by the legislature, rather than the governor; not used in Texas

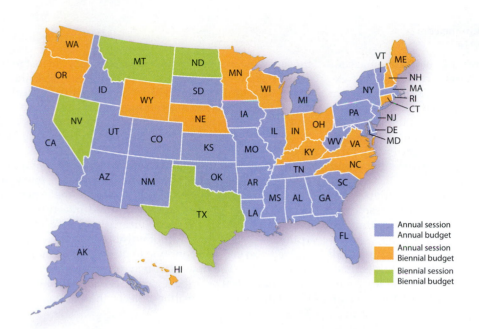

FIGURE 22-10 Legislative Session and Budget Cycle
Source: Ronald K. Snell, "State Experiences with Annual and Biennial Budgeting," National Conference of State Legislatures, April 2011, see at http://www.ncsl.org/documents/fiscal/BiennialBudgeting_May2011.pdf.

*Biennial budget states that enact a consolidated two-year budget. Other biennial budget states enact two annual budgets at one time.
+Annual budget states where smaller agencies receive biennial budgets.

which Texas shares with seventeen other states, makes the limit on the regular session even more meaningful. The legislature must finish its work in the prescribed time and leave.

In Texas, only the governor may call **special sessions,** of not more than thirty days each. There is no limit on the number of special sessions the governor may call. Also, in Texas, the governor decides the subject matter of the session, thus limiting the range of topics the legislature can consider. This gives the governor tremendous power to set the agenda of the legislature during special sessions and a bargaining chip to get the legislature to do what the governor wants.

The Texas legislature's inability to call itself into special session also gives the governor stronger veto powers. If the governor vetoes a bill and the legislature has adjourned, the veto stands. This in part helps to explain why so few vetoes of the governor are overridden.

States such as Texas that limit the number of days of regular sessions are often forced to resort to special sessions. Budgetary problems, reapportionment issues, school finance, and prison funding have forced the Texas legislature to have many special sessions in the past decades. Many critics of the Texas biennial sessions point to the frequency of special sessions as evidence that the state needs to go to annual sessions. Budgeting for two years is extremely difficult, since it involves predicting state revenues.

The National Conference of State Legislatures produced a professionalism ranking based on four factors: full-time or part-time, pay, staff size, and turnover. In this ranking, Texas was classified as a moderate professional/citizen legislature.[29] Texas is a large urban state with many problems, and many bills are introduced each session. Although biennial budgeting reduces the cost of the process to executive agencies, legislatures are not able to forecast income and expenditure with as much accuracy. The question remains as to whether economic development will force Texans to act against the dictates of their political culture and establish a more professional legislature.

special session

session called by the governor to consider legislation proposed by the governor only

Summary

Self-Test www.mhhe.com/
pattersontadtx11e

State legislatures tend to mirror the socioeconomic conditions within their states. As Texas's economy has expanded, the level of professionalism within the legislature and the amount of interest group activity have risen. A larger, better-paid staff and the renovations to the state capitol, which included introducing high-tech hardware and software applications, certainly point to an increasing level of professionalism within the Texas legislature. No doubt rapid economic development within the state has helped drive these changes. Yet despite legislative initiatives to move toward annual sessions, Texans remain resolutely against attempts to empower the state legislature through increased frequency or duration of the sessions.

State legislatures also tend to represent local interests rather than statewide interests. Legislators are recruited, elected, and reelected locally. Local interests will always be the dominant factor in determining how legislators vote on proposed legislation. As a result, the leadership must push

for statewide interests, which otherwise may get lost in the zeal to protect and promote local interests. Despite the high turnover rate of individual representatives, speakers of the Texas House and committee chairs do tend to hold on to their positions. As the legislative body becomes more professional, legislators may also start to rise above local interests.

As the Texas legislature redraws district boundaries, the membership shifts. The federal "one person, one vote" law increased the power of urban areas at the expense of rural districts. As new residents flowed into urban areas from out of state, the Republican Party rose to power within the legislature. Yet minority representation has increased also and will continue to do so with the new redistricting plan. The new plan may or may not weaken the Republic control over the legislature, but it will ensure that the state legislature better reflects the contrasts within Texas society.

CHAPTER 22

Study Corner

Key Terms

biennial sessions (*p. 570*)
"birthright" characteristics
(*p. 553*)
calendars (*p. 563*)
Calendars Committee
(*p. 563*)
closed rider (*p. 563*)
committee assignments
(*p. 559*)
equity of representation
(*p. 548*)
extraordinary session
(*p. 570*)
informal rules (*p. 566*)
interim committees (*p. 561*)
Legislative Redistricting
Board (LRB) (*p. 548*)
lieutenant governor (*p. 560*)
Local and Consent Calendars
Committee (*p. 563*)

minority representation
(*p. 548*)
multimember district
(*p. 546*)
parliamentarian
(*p. 560*)
racially gerrymandered
majority-minority
districts (*p. 549*)
rider (*p. 563*)
safe election districts
(*p. 555*)
sine die (*p. 570*)
single-member district
(*p. 546*)
speaker of the house
(*p. 558*)
special session (*p. 571*)
term limits (*p. 558*)
turnover (*p. 557*)

Self-Test: Multiple Choice

1. Which of the following explains the high turnover rate in the Texas legislature?
   a. the frequent defeat of incumbents
   b. recently established term limits
   c. the refusal of PACs to contribute to political campaigns
   d. the rigorous demands of a low-paying job

2. Which of the following is *not* true about sessions of the Texas legislature?
   a. The governor may call special sessions.
   b. The legislature may call extraordinary sessions.
   c. Sessions occur biennially.
   d. The duration of a regular session is 140 days.

3. Which of the following is *not* a power shared by the Texas speaker of the house and the lieutenant governor?
   a. appointing chairs of committees
   b. voting on all bills after the third reading
   c. serving as presiding officer
   d. referring all bills to committees

4. In which areas does the Texas legislature rate favorably compared to other state legislatures?
   a. annual salary and length of sessions
   b. length of session and staff assistance
   c. building facilities and annual salary
   d. staff assistance and building facilities

5. Which of the following is true regarding legislative bills?
   a. Most bills are assigned to a calendar.
   b. Throughout the session, bills require a two-thirds majority to pass.
   c. Most bills are passed in the final days of the session.
   d. Bills may not be introduced prior to the session.

6. Which group is overrepresented in the Texas state legislature?
   a. Anglos
   b. women
   c. Hispanics
   d. African Americans

7. Redistricting efforts during the 2003 session favored Democrats and minorities. (T/F)

8. Political and racial gerrymandering in Texas has created safe party districts for both Republicans and Democrats. (T/F)

9. Speaker of the House Tom Craddick ushered in a new era of nonpartisanship by assigning important committee positions to both Republican and Democrat members of the house. (T/F)

10. Minor, noncontroversial bills can be assigned to the local calendar or consent calendar. (T/F)

Critical Thinking

Think about an issue that is important to you. Research bills that have been filed on this issue in the Texas legislature website (www.capitol.state.tx.us/). Have the bills died in committee or become law? How would you write a bill to address this issue? What could you do to increase the chances that this bill would pass in both houses?

Suggested Readings

Hamm, Keith E., and Gary F. Moncrief. "Legislative Politics in the States," in *Politics in the American States: A Comparative Analysis*, 8th ed., Virginia Gray and Russell L. Hanson, eds. Washington, D.C.: Congressional Quarterly Press, 2004.

Jewell, Malcolm E., and Samuel C. Patterson. *The Legislative Process in the United States*. New York: Random House, 1985.

Websites

http://www.capitol.state.tx.us/
The website of the Texas legislature; lets you find your state representative or senator if you know your zip code, as well as look up bills by subject matter or by bill number, author, and session.

http://www.lrl.state.tx.us/
The website of the Texas Legislative Reference Library; has an excellent collection of information about current and past legislatures.

http://www.ncsl.org/
The website of the National Conference of State Legislatures; contains information on state legislatures.

www.tlc.state.tx.us/
The Texas Legislative Council Web page; gives access to redistricting plans and to maps and reports.

Participate!

Go to the Texas legislature Website (www.capitol.state.tx.us), and find your state representative and senator. Look at the information provided in their biographies, and decide if they represent you. Are you typical of other people living in your house and residents of your legislative district? Do they have "birthright" characteristics? How important is it that your legislator have these characteristics?

Extra Credit

Go to the Texas legislature website, and find your state representative and senator. Do a bill search, and find out how many bills he or she has introduced. What subject matter do these bills cover? Does the bill have any direct reference to problems in your area of the state? Write an essay explaining these bills and their implications.

Self-Test Answers

1. d, 2. b, 3. b, 4. d, 5. c, 6. a, 7. F, 8. T, 9. F, 10. T

The Office of Governor and State Agencies in Texas

The governor is the most salient political actor in state government. Whether the true power center of the state is embodied in the office or elsewhere in self-government, the office is the focal point of media and public attention. The governor is expected to accomplish many goals and is blamed for not achieving others, even if the office is formally very weak. The power and respect accorded to governors have varied greatly over time. During the colonial period, little power or respect was afforded the office—some have argued that the American Revolution was a war against colonial governors. The experiences of southern states following Reconstruction led to a return of weak governors in the South. There is an old Texas saying: "The governor should have only enough power to sign for his paycheck." In recent times, the power and prestige of the office have increased, as the U.S. Congress has returned some power and responsibility to state governments and allowed states more flexibility in administering programs funded by the federal government. Even though many governors have little formal power, governors are important players in state politics.

This chapter examines the structure and the functions of the offices and agencies within the executive branch. Initially, we investigate the roles of the governor within the Texas political system. We explore the governor's powers, both formal and informal. We categorize the governor's powers into formal executive, legislative, judicial, and military authority. Then we explore how the governor uses informal influence as party leader and head of government. Finally, we analyze the administrative agencies of state government in Texas and compare their structure with the structures of executive branches of other states. The chapter's main points are the following:

- Although citizens expect governors to play many roles and hold them responsible for the successes and failures of the state, many governors, including the governor of Texas, enjoy very limited power.

- In Texas, the governor's position is weakened by the plural executive, an executive branch in which most of the important offices are elected rather than appointed.

- There are formal and informal qualifications for the office—most governors have been white, male, Protestant, and well educated. Texas places no term limits on governors, yet few have served longer than four years.

- In Texas, there are three main types of administrative agencies: agencies with elected heads, agencies with a single appointed head, and multimember boards and commissions. These agencies carry out much of the work of state government.

- The governor has little authority over these agencies, and each state board and commission operates independently from the others, with no central controlling authority.

The Roles of the Governor

Citizens expect governors to play many roles. They should be the chief policy makers, formulating long-term goals and objectives. This requires selling the program to state legislators and coordinating with state agencies that administer the programs.

chief legislator

a role of governors in which they spend time and energy presenting an active agenda of legislation to the legislature and working to pass that agenda

The governor is also expected to act as **chief legislator.** Governors do not formally introduce bills, but because they need the support of significant members of the legislature who will carry their program, they must spend considerable time and energy developing those relationships. If the governor is a member of one party and the other party dominates the legislature, getting legislation passed can be difficult. The governor might have to spend considerable resources to accomplish his or her goals.

party chief

a role of governors that calls for them to aid their fellow party members in their reelection efforts, raise money for the party, and create a favorable party image

The governor must also act as **party chief.** As the most important party official in the state, the governor helps legislators and other elected officials in their reelection efforts, raises money for the party, and creates a favorable image of the party in the state.

The governor also serves as the ceremonial leader of the state. The demands of **ceremonial duties** are extreme. "Where two or more are gathered together," there also is the governor expected to be. The governor will receive many invitations to speak, make presentations, and cut ribbons. Some governors become trapped in the safe, friendly environment of ceremonial duties and neglect or avoid the other duties of their office. For governors with an agenda for action, ceremony is a diversion from more important and difficult objectives.

ceremonial duties

a governor's duties to attend many functions and represent the state

Governors can use ceremonial duties as communication opportunities to promote their programs. They must wisely choose which invitations to accept and which to delegate to others or decline. Ceremonial appearances, such as graduation speaker, provide an opportunity to generate favorable press coverage and support for programs. Former governor Bush used these opportunities both to promote his state programs and as an avenue to promote his run for the presidency.

intergovernmental coordinator

a role of governors in which they coordinate activities with other state and federal officials

The governor is also the chief **intergovernmental coordinator,** working with federal officials and officials in other states. The governor must work with congressional delegations of U.S. senators and representatives, the president, and cabinet officials to promote the interests of the state.

Thus, many roles are assigned to governors. In Texas, the formal powers of the governor are very weak, and this complicates things. The governor cannot rely on formal authority but must develop and use the power and prestige of the office to persuade others to accept his or her program. This informal leadership trait, the power to persuade others, is perhaps the most necessary "power" of all.

Rules of the Gubernatorial Office

The rules of the Texas governor's office include both formal and informal qualifications as well as regulations regarding salary, succession to office, removal from office, and tenure.

Qualifications

In most states the formal qualifications to be governor are minimal. All but six states set a minimum age requirement, and most require a candidate to be a resident of the state for five to ten years preceding election. Also, most states require governors to be U.S. citizens and qualified voters.

In Texas, the formal qualifications are simple: One must be at least thirty years of age, a citizen of the United States, and a resident of the state for five years preceding election. There is no requirement to be a registered voter. In the 1930s, W. Lee O'Daniel ran for governor stressing that he was not a "professional politician." To prove this, he made a point of not being a registered voter.

Informal qualifications are more important than formal qualifications. Nationwide, most governors have held elected office before becoming governor. An examination of the 933 people serving as governor between 1900 and 1997 reveals that the most common career path to that office is to begin in the legislature, move to statewide office, and then move to the governor's office.[1] Others who are elected governor have served as U.S. senator or representative, and a few have served in local elected offices (such as mayor). Thus, having held elected office emerges as an informal qualification for becoming governor. Some governors gain experience as appointed administrators or as party officials. Between 1970 and 1999, only 10 percent of all people elected governor had no prior political office experience.[2]

These observations about governors generally apply to Texas governors. Table 23-1 lists those who have served as governor in Texas since 1949 and their prior office experience. Most had served in elected office, five in statewide offices. Only two had not held elected office. The current governor, Rick Perry, followed a rather typical pattern before becoming governor. He served in the

TABLE 23-1 | Previous Office Experience of Texas Governors, 1949–Present

Governor	Terms of Office	Previous Offices
Allan Shivers	1949–1957	State Senate, lieutenant governor
Price Daniel	1957–1963	U.S. Senate
John Connally	1963–1969	U.S. secretary of the navy*
Preston Smith	1969–1973	Texas House and Senate, lieutenant governor
Dolph Briscoe	1973–1979	Texas House
Bill Clements	1979–1983 1987–1991	Assistant U.S. secretary of defense*
Mark White	1983–1987	Attorney general
Ann Richards	1991–1995	County office, state treasurer
George W. Bush	1995–2001	None
Rick Perry	2001–present	State legislature, agricultural commissioner, and lieutenant governor

*Appointive offices. No electoral experience before becoming governor.

Source: James Anderson, Richard W. Murray, and Edward L. Farley, *Texas Politics: An Introduction*, 6th ed. (New York: HarperCollins, 1992), 166–88. Governors Bush and Perry from other sources.

FIGURE 23-1 **Women Governors** Whereas Miriam Ferguson and Lurleen Wallace were stand-in governors for husbands ineligible for re-election, an increasing number of women besides Wyoming's Nellie T. Ross have been elected in their own right. The map at right shows which states have current or past women governors. How many states have had women governors? Are there any regional patterns?

Source: Center for Women and Politics, Rutgers University, www.cawp.rutgers.edu/.

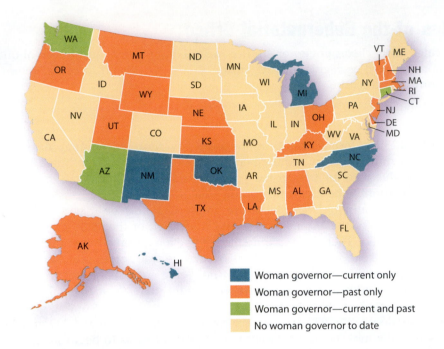

■ Woman governor—current only
■ Woman governor—past only
■ Woman governor—current and past
☐ No woman governor to date

state legislature, as agricultural commissioner, and as lieutenant governor before becoming governor when George Bush resigned to assume the office of president of the United States. He was elected governor in his own right in 2002.

Besides electoral experience, many informal qualifications play a role in winning a governor's seat. Nationwide, most people who have served as governors have been white, male, Protestant, well-educated, wealthy individuals. Four African Americans and several Latinos have served as governors. The number of women governors has increased in recent years. In 1924, Wyoming elected the first woman governor, Nellie T. Ross, who served one term. She succeeded her husband, who died in office. Later in 1924, Texas elected Miriam A. Ferguson governor, and she was reelected in 1932. Mrs. Ferguson was a "stand-in" for her husband, Jim Ferguson, who had been impeached, removed from office, and barred from seeking reelection. Similarly, in 1968, Lurleen Wallace was elected governor of Alabama as a stand-in for her husband, George Wallace, who could not be reelected because of term limits.

Historically, the men who have served as governor of Texas have generally had one thing in common—wealth. A few, such as Dolph Briscoe and Bill Clements, were very wealthy. If not wealthy, most have been successful in law, business, or politics before becoming governor. Ann Richards was an exception to these informal qualifications. She was not wealthy or from a wealthy family and had no business or law experience. Governor Perry, while claiming the status of a sharecropper's son, came from a family with a moderate, middle-class background.

Salary

Governors receive much higher pay than state legislators. As of 2010, salaries ranged from a low of $70,000 in Maine to a high of $179,000 in New York. The Texas salary of $150,000 per year is above the mean salary of $90,000.[3] In addition, Texas provides the governor with a home in Austin, an automobile with a driver, an airplane, and reimbursement for actual travel expenses. Texas governors also receive a budget for entertaining and maintaining the Governor's Mansion.

Compared with members of the state legislature, the governor in Texas is extremely well paid. Given the demands and responsibilities of the job, however, the governor is not overpaid compared with executives of large corporations, who receive many times this amount.

Succession to Office

Most states provide for a successor if the governor dies or leaves office for any reason. Forty-three states have lieutenant governors who advance to the office if it is vacant for any reason. In the seven states without lieutenant governors, another officeholder, usually the leader of the state Senate, succeeds to the governor's office. In some states, the lieutenant governor and the governor are separately elected. In others, the governor and lieutenant governor run as a "team," much as candidates for president and vice president do. In these cases, the candidate for governor picks the lieutenant governor.

When the governor leaves the state, the lieutenant governor becomes **acting governor.** This is unlike the office of vice president of the United States, who does not become acting president if the president leaves the country. Some governors have experienced problems with their lieutenant governor when they have left the state. For instance, in 1995 Jim Guy Tucker of Arkansas had problems with Senate President Pro Tem Jerry Jewell, who was acting as governor in the absence of the lieutenant governor. Jewell "granted two pardons and executive clemency to two prison inmates."[4] Also, the Arkansas lieutenant governor, Republican Mike Huckabee, "signed a proclamation for a Christian Heritage Week after Tucker declined to do so earlier."[5]

acting governor
the position held by the lieutenant governor, who performs the functions of the office of governor when a governor leaves a state

Removal from Office

All states except Oregon have a procedure for removing governors by a process generally called impeachment. In this procedure, the lower House of the legislature adopts articles of impeachment, and then the Senate holds a trial on these articles of impeachment. If the Senate finds the governor guilty, he or she is removed from office. Sixteen governors have had impeachment trials, and eight have been removed from office.[6]

Technically, impeachment is a judicial process, but it is also a very political process. Impeached governors have generally been guilty of some wrongdoing, but they are often removed for political reasons. For example, one of the eight impeached governors was Jim Ferguson of Texas (1915–1917). Ferguson was indicted by the Texas House, technically for misuse of state funds, and was convicted and removed from office by the Senate. In reality, he was impeached because of his fight with the University of Texas board of regents. When the governor could not force the board of regents to terminate several professors who had criticized the governor, or force the resignation of board members, he line-item vetoed the entire appropriations bill for the University of Texas.[7] This veto led to his removal from office.

Ferguson tried to prevent his impeachment by calling the legislature into special session. Since only the governor may decide the agenda of a special session, Governor Ferguson told the legislature it could consider any item it wanted, except impeachment. That ploy did not work, and he was removed from office. Courts later upheld Ferguson's impeachment.

A few years after the Ferguson affair in Texas, Oklahoma impeached two consecutively elected governors. These two impeachments were as political as the one in Texas. In 1921, there were several race riots, in which many African Americans were killed. The most noted of these was in the Greenwood area of Tulsa, Oklahoma. Thirty-five square blocks of this segregated African American community were burned and destroyed, and over forty people were killed.

In 1922, John C. Walton was elected governor as a member of the Farmer-Laborite party. Walton tried to break up the Ku Klux Klan in the state, and that led to his impeachment.

The lieutenant governor, Martin Trapp, served out the remainder of Walton's term but was unable to run for reelection because Oklahoma had a limit of one term at that time. Henry S. Johnson was elected governor in 1926 as a pro-KKK candidate and refused to use his office to quell Klan activity in the state. Johnson used the National Guard to try to prevent the legislature from meeting to consider his impeachment. The legislature was kept out of the state capitol building and had to meet in a hotel in Oklahoma City. Johnson was convicted and removed from office. He had been indicted on eighteen counts and found not guilty on all but on "general incompetence" for which he was impeached.[8]

The impeachment of Evan Mecham in Arizona in 1988 was equally political. Mecham made a number of racist remarks and had become a source of embarrassment in the state. Technically, he was impeached for misuse of state funds during his inaugural celebration.

POLITICAL THINKING   A Long-Standing Governor

Lt. Governor Rick Perry stepped into the governor's seat in 2001, when Texas Governor George W. Bush resigned to become U.S. president. Perry is now one of the longest-serving governors in the history of the United States. In March 2010, Perry won the a third full term—despite a 33-percent job approval rating. What do you think are the advantages and disadvantages of long-serving governors? Should Texas consider instituting term limits for the office of governor?

recall of the governor

the removal of the governor (or another elected official) by a petition signed by the required number of registered voters, followed by an election in which a majority votes to remove the person from office

Fifteen states also allow **recall of the governor.** Texas does not provide for recall of state officials. Many Texas home-rule cities do allow recall of city councils and mayors. Recall involves getting petitions signed by some number of voters, followed by an election in which, if a majority approves, the governor can be recalled or removed from office. Two governors have been recalled: Lynn J. Frazier of North Dakota was recalled in 1921, the same time when governors were being impeached in Texas and Oklahoma. In 1988, Governor Mecham of Arizona was spared a recall election when he was impeached by the legislature.[9] In 2003, Gray Davis of California was recalled.

Tenure

tenure of office

the legal ability of governors to succeed themselves in office and the length of their term

The legal ability of governors to succeed themselves in office and the length of their term is known as **tenure of office.** Historically, the tenure of governors has been less than that for most other statewide elected state officials, in part because of term limits.[10] Term limits for governors have been a fixture since the beginning of the Republic. Ten of the governors in the original thirteen states had one-year terms. States first moved to two-year terms, then four-year terms. In the 1960s, states borrowed from the federal Constitution the idea of limiting governors to two four-year terms.[11] Southern states were the last to move to longer terms. Many southern states once prohibited the governor from serving consecutive terms in office. Today, only Virginia retains that provision.

Tenure is an important determinant of power. If governors can be continually reelected, they retain the potential to influence government until they decide to leave office. Only fourteen states do not limit how long a person can serve as

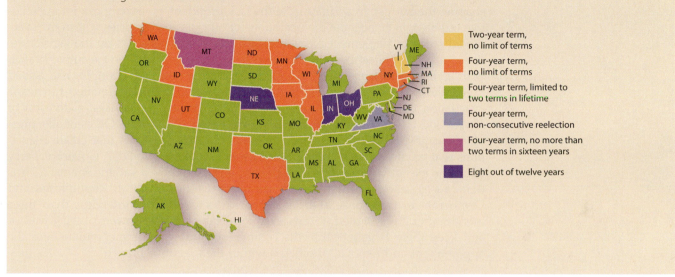

HOW TEXAS DIFFERS POLITICAL THINKING THROUGH COMPARISONS

Term Limits for Governors

Although term limits for legislators are a recent phenomenon, governors have always been limited in the number of terms they could serve. As the map shows, most states limit the governor to two terms, just like the president of the United States. Texas is one of twelve states that do not limit the number of terms a governor can serve.

Q: Do most states limit the number of terms a governor can serve? How does Texas compare?

A: Most states limit a governor to two four-year terms. Texas places no term limits on the governor.

Legend:
- Two-year term, no limit of terms
- Four-year term, no limit of terms
- Four-year term, limited to two terms in lifetime
- Four-year term, non-consecutive reelection
- Four-year term, no more than two terms in sixteen years
- Eight out of twelve years

Source: Council of State Governments, The Book of the States 2009 (Lexington, Ky.: Council of State Governments, 2004), Vol. 41, Table 4.1, 185–186.

governor. When prevented from being reelected by term limits, governors suffer as "lame ducks" toward the end of their terms. Long tenure also enables governors to carry out their programs. Short terms (two years) force governors to continually seek reelection and make political compromises. Only two states retain the two-year term—Vermont and New Hampshire.

Length of tenure also influences the governor's role as intergovernmental coordinator. Building up associations with officials in other states and in Washington, D.C., takes time. Short tenure makes it difficult for governors to gain leadership roles in this area and has the effect of shortchanging the state that imposes it.[12] The map in "How Texas Differs: Term Limits for Governors" details state term limits. The Texas governor has the strongest tenure—four-year terms with no limit on the number of terms.

Still, few Texas governors have served more than four years in office. Governor Perry is the first governor to serve three consecutive four-year terms. The length of his service has raised calls for new limits. During the contentious 2010 Republican primary, Governor Perry's main opponent, U.S. Senator Kay Bailey Hutchison, unveiled a plan to limit Texas governors to two terms. A poll conducted less than a month after Senator Hutchison's proposal reported that 75 percent of Texans surveyed do support term limits. Perry's campaign, however, retorted that Hutchison's proposition lacked credibility, since she herself was serving a third term in the U.S. Senate after pledging to step down after two.[13] Hutchison lost to Perry in the March 2010 primary. Governor Perry is Texas's longest-serving governor. At the end of his current term, he will have served a total of fourteen years as governor.

The Governor's Powers

As indicated previously, most governors do not have great formal powers. Nevertheless, many duties fall under the formal executive, legislative, judicial, and military powers of the office. How governors use their informal powers can contribute to their success in office.

Executive Powers

Governors exercise executive powers by appointing and removing officials and shaping the budget. In addition, like the U.S. president, governors can issue executive orders, which facilitate the operations of officials and agencies within the executive branch or implement measures specified by laws enacted by the legislature. These orders in effect become law, and hence they provide the executive branch with a degree of legislative authority. Governor Perry, for example, has issued executive orders that have ensured schools be paid on time, detailed hurricane evacuation procedures, and reorganized Adult Protective Services, a division of Health and Human Services that is part of the executive branch. Occasionally, presidents or governors overstep their authority by issuing orders that create regulations that would not have been passed by the legislature. In 2007, Governor Perry issued an executive order requiring preteen girls to receive a vaccine against a virus that causes cervical cancer. In the uproar that followed, both Republicans and Democrats in the House and Senate voted to revoke the order less than three months after it was signed. Texans acted to curtail executive powers of the governor and keep them largely within the confines of budget recommendations and the appointment and removal of officials within the executive branch.

Appointive and Removal Powers

appointive power

the ability of a governor to appoint and remove important state administrators

Jacksonian statehouse democracy

a system in which most of the major department heads in state government are chosen by the voters at the ballot box

plural executive

system in which voters elect many statewide officeholders to serve as heads of departments

More important than tenure of office is the **appointive power** of the governor to make appointments and control the agencies of state government. By appointing and removing the heads of most state agencies, the governor gains some control over the administration of programs. But we will see that control is often mitigated by the way government is structured.

Historically, governors have not had strong appointive powers. For most of the nineteenth century, the traditional method of selecting the heads of state agencies was by election. This is called **Jacksonian statehouse democracy.** President Andrew Jackson expressed ultimate faith in the ballot box for selecting administrators. Toward the end of the nineteenth century, there was a proliferation of agencies headed by appointed or elected boards and commissions. The governor was just one of many elected state officials and had little formal control over state administration.[14] Governors often share power with many other elected individuals. Such arrangements are known as **plural executive** structures.

The ability of the Texas governor to control administrative functions through formal appointive and removal powers is exceptionally weak because of Texas's plural executive structure. Voters elect a lieutenant governor, an attorney general, a comptroller of public accounts, a state land commissioner, an agricultural commissioner, the Railroad Commission, and the Texas State Board of Education.[15]

The governor does appoint a few agency heads, the most significant being the secretary of state, who serves as the chief record keeper and election official for the state. The governor also appoints the executive directors of the Departments of Commerce, Health and Human Services, Housing and Community Affairs, and Insurance, the Office of State-Federal Relations, and the Fire Fighters

Pension Commission. The governor appoints the head of the Texas National Guard and appoints the executive director of the Texas Education Agency from recommendations made by the elected Texas State Board of Education. The governor also appoints the chief counsels for the Public Utility Commission, the Insurance Commission, and the State Office of Administrative Hearings. This leaves significant portions of state government beyond the control of the governor, because several agency heads are elected.

Most agencies are controlled by independent boards and commissions. These independent state agencies are usually governed by three-, six-, or nine-member boards or commissions appointed by the governor for six-year, overlapping, staggered terms. Usually, one-third of the membership of boards is appointed every two years. In total, the number of governing and policy-making positions filled by gubernatorial appointment is about 2,600.[16] If the governor stays in office for two terms (eight years), she or he will have appointed all members of these agencies and boards and might therefore have indirect influence over them. The governing board chooses the heads of these agencies. As an example, the president of a state university is selected by the board of regents, the members of which are appointed by the governor. The governor often exercises influence with his or her appointees on the board of regents.

The governor also appoints a number of persons to non-policy-making and governing boards that recommend policy and programs to the governor or other state officials. Many of these non-policy-making boards recommend changes in policy and programs. Others are simply window dressing and allow the governor to reward supporters. Most often, these non-policy-making boards do not require Senate approval.

Some gubernatorial appointments are subject to approval by a two-thirds vote of the Senate. In these cases, the governor must clear his or her appointments with the state senator from the appointee's home district. This process, known as senatorial courtesy, limits the discretion of the governor. If the senator from an appointee's home district disapproves of the appointment, the Senate might not confirm the appointee.

Other factors limit the discretion of the governor. For example, some boards require geographic representation. Members of river authority boards, such as the Trinity River Authority and the Lower Colorado River Authority, must live in the area covered by the river authority. Other boards require specified professional backgrounds. Membership on the Texas Municipal Retirement Board, for instance, is limited to certain types of city employees—such as firefighters, police, and city managers.[17]

Of course, there are always political limits placed on the governor's ability to appoint people. Interest groups pay close attention to the governor's appointments to these boards and commissions and try to influence the governor's choices. The governor may have to bend to demands from such groups.

Equally important to the appointive power is the power to remove administrators. Without the power of removal, the appointive powers of the governor are greatly diminished. U.S. presidents may remove many of their appointees, but state governors are often very restricted by the state constitution, or statutes creating the agency, or term limits set for appointees. Some states allow the governor to remove a person only for cause. This requires the governor to make a case for wrongdoing by the individual. The governor can force the resignation of a person without formal hearings, but the political cost of such forced resignations can be quite high and beyond what the governor is willing to pay.

Beginning in the early twentieth century, the powers of the governor to appoint and remove officials were increased in some states. This expansion of executive authority has increased in the last three decades in many states.[18] This has not been the pattern for much of the South or for the office of governor in Texas. In 2001, the voters in Texas even rejected an amendment that would have made the adjutant general of the Texas National Guard subject to removal by the governor. The traditionalistic culture does not support the idea of strong executive authority even for relatively minor offices.

As with other powers, the removal power of the Texas governor is very weak. Before 1981, Texas state law was silent on the issue of removal. In 1981, the constitution was amended to allow governors to remove any person they personally appointed, with a two-thirds vote of the Senate. Governors may not remove any of their predecessors' appointees. To date, no person has been formally removed from office using this procedure, but it does provide the governor with some leverage to force an appointee to resign. It might also be used to force a policy change that the governor wants. It does not, however, allow the governor to control the day-to-day administration of state government.

In Texas, the appointive power of the governor, even with these formal limitations, allows him or her to indirectly influence policy. A governor is unlikely to select men and women to serve on these boards and commissions who do not agree with him or her on major policy issues. Ann Richards used her appointive powers to increase the number of women and minorities serving on these boards and commissions. This broad appointive power allows the governor to influence policy even after leaving office, since some of the appointees will remain on these boards and commissions. Richards's successor, George W. Bush, appointed some women and minorities, but tended mainly to appoint businessmen to these positions. Governor Perry, for the most part, appoints business leaders as well.

Thus, the governor exerts indirect, not direct, control over policy by appointing people with similar policy views. This influence will continue for some time after the governor leaves office, since her or his appointee will remain in office for four to six years after the governor's term ends.

Governors have also been known to appoint people to governing boards and commissions who were supporters in their campaigns. Loyal supporters, especially those giving big campaign contributions, are often rewarded with appointments to prestigious state boards and commissions. University governing boards are especially desired positions. Table 23-2 lists the contributions given by individuals appointed to state boards and commissions by then Governor Bush.

TABLE 23-2 | Campaign Contributions and Appointment to Boards and Commissions by Governor Rick Perry (Top Five)

State Body	Total Contributions	Number of Appointments
Commission for Women	$159,978	13
Higher Education Coordinating Board	$162,943	11
Historical Commission	$194,010	10
Texas Tech Board of Regents	$515,664	9
Rock Crushers/Quarries Adv. Com.	$103,779	9

Source: "Governor Perry's Patronage," Texans for Public Justice, April 2006, http://info.tpj.org/docs/pdf/perrypatronagereport.pdf.

Budgetary Powers

Along with tenure of office and appointive/executive authority, the budgetary powers determine the extent of executive authority. Control over how money is spent is at the heart of the policy-making process. Some writers define a budget as a statement of policy in monetary terms. If the **budgetary powers** allow the governor to control budget formation and development (the preparation of the budget for submission to the legislature) and budget execution (deciding how money is spent), he or she can have a significant influence on state policy. There are four kinds of constraints that can undercut the governor's budgetary authority:

- The extent to which the governor must share budget formation with the legislature or with other state agencies
- The extent to which funds are earmarked for specific expenditures and the choice on how to spend money is limited by previous actions
- The extent to which the governor shares budget execution authority with others in state government
- The limits on the governor's use of a line-item veto for the budget

In forty states, the governor is given "full" authority over budget formation and development.[19] In those states where the governor is given authority for budget formation, agencies must present their requests for expenditures to the governor's office, which then combines them and presents a unified budget to the legislature. In some states, the governor is limited in how much he or she can reduce the budget requests of some state agencies. If the governor can change the requests of agencies, this gives the governor tremendous control over the final form of the budget submitted to the legislature. A common practice of state governments is to earmark revenue for specific purposes. For example, funds received through the gasoline tax are commonly earmarked for state highways. This also limits the discretion of the governor. In Texas, many funds are earmarked by the previous actions of the legislature. One estimate is that more than 80 percent of all funds are earmarked for specific expenditures, such as highways, teachers' retirement, parks, and schools.

Budget execution authority is more involved. Governors and others control budget execution in a variety of ways. If the governor controls the appointment of the major department heads of state government, he or she will have some discretion in how money is spent. The governor may decide not to spend all the money appropriated for a state park. Administrative discretion over how money is spent is a time-honored way to expand executive authority over the budget.

In Texas, the governor's budgetary powers are exceptionally weak except in the area of the line-item veto, discussed below. The governor is not constitutionally mandated to submit a budget. This power is given to the **Legislative Budget Board (LBB),** an agency governed by the speaker of the

budgetary powers
the ability of a governor to formulate a budget, present it to the legislature, and execute or control it

Legislative Budget Board (LBB)
Texas state agency that is controlled by the leadership in the state legislature and writes the state budget

In 2003, the $10 billion state budget deficit pitched Governor Rick Perry and Texas Comptroller Carole Keeton Strayhorn against each other. Perry wanted to make good on his promised tax cuts. Strayhorn wanted to balance the budget and keep Texas out of debt. Here, they share a rare moment of cordiality during the budget crisis—just before their battle divided the social and fiscal conservatives within the Republican Party.

house and the lieutenant governor. Agencies of the state must present budget requests to the LBB, and the LBB produces a budget that is submitted to the legislature. Historically, governors have submitted budget messages to the legislature, often in the form of reactions to the LBB's proposed budget. Someone once said that the "governor's budget" has the same effect as a letter to Santa Claus, since it has little effect on the final budget form.

During the 2003 financial crisis in which Texas faced a $10 billion shortfall, Governor Perry presented a budget with all zeros. In 2003–2004, spending for Health and Human Services (HHS) stood at $38.7 billion. For 2004–2005, Perry recommended an HHS budget of $0, an education budget of $0, and so forth for all state spending categories. In creating this "zero-based" budget, Perry argued that all agencies had first to justify their expenditure before any money was allocated. Some critics had a good laugh, but others argued that it was an attempt to depart from the tradition of basing budgets on current services. Perry and other prominent Republicans insisted that it was a gesture meant to call attention to the need for increased accountability. In the meantime, the LLB quietly submitted its own budget.

The Texas governor also has very limited authority over budget execution, but it does extend to cases of fiscal crisis. A constitutional amendment approved in 1985 created the Budget Execution Committee, composed of the governor, the lieutenant governor, the comptroller, the speaker of the house, and chairs of the Finance and Appropriations Committees in the Senate and House. The Budget Execution Committee can exercise restraints over the budget if there is a fiscal crisis such as a shortfall in projected revenue.

Another way the Texas governor influences budget decisions is with the line-item veto. The governor can veto part of the appropriations bill without vetoing the entire bill. The legislature determines what a line item is. It can be a department within an agency, or the entire agency. Rick Perry used the line-item veto to reduce the 2008–2009 state budget by $288.9 million, although some claimed that most of those cuts were due to technical corrections.

The legislature can override this veto by a two-thirds vote of each house. However, appropriations bills generally pass in the last days of the session, so the legislature has adjourned by the time the governor vetoes items. Since the legislature cannot call itself back into session ("extraordinary" sessions), overriding a line-item veto is in practice almost impossible.

Legislative Powers

legislative powers

the formal powers, especially the veto authority and power to call special sessions, of the governor to force the legislature to enact his or her legislation

The governor's **legislative powers** include the right to veto and to call special sessions of the legislature. Before exercising these powers, the governor can use them as a threat to pressure the legislature to forward his or her agenda. In addition, the governor presents a State of the State address at the beginning of each legislative session in which he or she requests that the legislature address specific issues.

Vetoes and the Threat of A Veto

partial veto

a veto that allows the legislature to recall a bill to answer a governor's objections to it; Texas does not have a formal partial veto process

Although the line-item veto can be viewed as a budgetary power, it is also a legislative power. There are also other types of vetoes. All governors possess some form of veto authority, but this varies among the states (see Table 23-3). Forty-three states have formalized **partial vetoes,** whereby the legislature can recall a bill from the governor so that objections raised by the governor can be changed and a veto avoided.[20] Texas does not have a formal partial veto process; however, the governor can still state objections to a bill before it is passed and

TABLE 23-3 | Veto Authority of State Governors with Override Provisions

Type of Veto	Number of Governors
General veto and item veto: two-thirds needed to override	37
General veto and item veto: majority elected needed to override	6
General veto, no item veto: special legislative majority to override*	6
General veto, no item veto: simple majority to override	1

*Most common is three-fifths vote. Data change slightly.

Source: Thad L. Beyle, "Governors: The Middlemen and Women in Our Political System," in *Politics in the American States* (8th ed.), ed. Virginia Gray and Russell L. Hanson (Washington, DC: Congressional Quarterly Press, 2004).

thus seek to effect changes in legislation. Formalizing the process would shift some power to the office of governor and give the governor more say in the legislative process.

Requirements for overriding a governor's veto also vary widely among the states. Most states require a two-thirds vote to override, although a few allow a simple majority.[21] In Texas, the governor has very strong veto authority. The office possesses a general veto and line-item veto, with a two-thirds vote of each house required for override. Very few vetoes have been overturned. From 1876 to 1968, the legislature overrode 25 of 936 vetoes. Most of those vetoes occurred before 1940. This low number of veto overrides is primarily due to late passage of bills and adjournment of the legislature. Only one veto has been overturned in recent years, and it was not a significant bill. In 1979 during his first term, Bill Clements vetoed fifty-two bills. The legislature, in an attempt to get the governor's attention, overrode the veto on a bill that limited the ability of county governments to prohibit hunters from killing female deer.[22] Since 1979, no votes have been overridden by the legislature.

Some governors have a pocket veto, meaning that they can veto a bill by not signing it. The governor just "puts the bill in a pocket" and forgets about it. The Texas governor does not have a pocket veto. If the legislature is in session, the governor has ten days to sign a bill or it becomes law without his or her signature. If the legislature has adjourned, the governor has twenty days to sign a bill or it becomes law without a signature. Sometimes governors do not like a bill but do not want to veto it for some reason. Letting the bill become law without a signature can be a way of expressing displeasure short of an actual veto.

More important than the actual veto is the threat of a veto. Typically, governors do not veto many bills. Historically in Texas, governors have used the threat of a veto to discipline the legislature. It is not uncommon for the governor to threaten to veto a local line item, such as an item creating a new state park in a legislator's district. This threat to veto local appropriations can be used to gain legislative support for items important to the governor but unrelated to the park.

Special Sessions

The governor may call a special session of the legislature and prescribe its agenda. The session lasts thirty days. During the long period of bipartisan cooperation in Texas, from 1993 to 2001, no special sessions were called. That period ended in 2003 when Governor Perry called special sessions to deal with the budget shortfall, redistricting, and educational reform.

The fact that the governor can call a special session but the legislature cannot increases the governor's veto power. In states where legislatures can call "extraordinary" sessions, the legislature has the power to reconvene to override

Two governors for the price of one: "Ma and Pa" Ferguson in 1924.

the governor's vetoes. Governor Perry has set a new record by vetoing eighty-two bills in one session. If the Texas legislature could have called an extraordinary session, there is little doubt that it would have happened and that some vetoes would have been overridden.

Judicial Powers

judicial powers

the ability of a governor to issue pardons, executive clemency, and parole for citizens convicted of a crime

Governors also have limited **judicial powers** to grant pardons, executive clemency, and parole. Historically, governors have misused this power, which has led to the creation of checks on this authority. James "Pa" Ferguson was accused of misusing judicial powers by selling pardons and paroles to convicted felons during the second term of his wife, Miriam Amanda "Ma" Ferguson (1933–1935).[23] Those charges led to the creation of the state Pardons and Paroles Board. This eighteen-member board, appointed by the governor, recommends the actions the governor can take and serves as a check on the process. Independent of board action, the governor may grant only one thirty-day stay of execution for any condemned prisoner. This board recommends all other actions by the governor.

In the Fergusons' defense, many of the pardons were given to people who were in prison because they had violated the Prohibition laws. Laws prohibiting the use of alcoholic liquor were the "war on drugs" of several generations ago. Former lieutenant governor Hobby put it this way: "Prohibition's laws filled the prisons and ruined lives then just as marijuana laws do now. The Fergusons may have rightly concluded that the state was better served by these men being home supporting their families."[24]

Military Powers

military powers

the governor's authority to use the National Guard in times of natural disaster or civil unrest

The **military powers** of the governor are quite limited and come into play only in times of natural disaster or civil unrest. The governor appoints the adjutant general of the National Guard and can direct the Guard to protect the lives and property of Texas citizens. The most common use of this power is during natural disasters, when the Guard is employed to help evacuate people, protect property, and supply food and water to victims.

HOW TEXAS DIFFERS POLITCAL THINKING THROUGH COMPARISONS

Powers of the Governor

If we take six indexes of governors' power—election of other statewide executives, tenure of office, appointive powers, budgetary powers, veto powers, and control over party—we can compare the Texas governor with those in the other forty-nine states. The higher the score, the stronger the powers. As the accompanying map shows, the Texas office is comparatively weak in formal powers. The office is formally weak because of the limitations placed on administrative and budgetary powers (though the office is strong on tenure and veto authority).

Q: How does the Texas governor compare? Is this in keeping or not in keeping with the traditionalistic/individualistic political culture of the state? Explain your answer.

A: The Texas governor is comparatively weak. A weak government in general—and a weak governor in particular—is in keeping with the traditionalistic/individualistic political culture of the state.

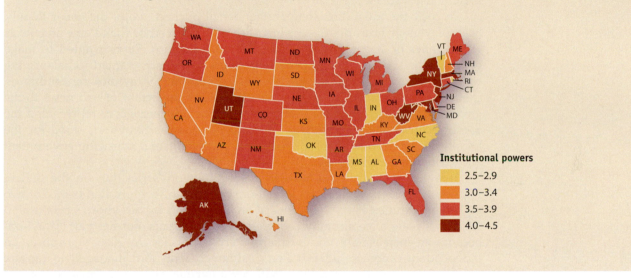

Institutional powers

- 2.5–2.9
- 3.0–3.4
- 3.5–3.9
- 4.0–4.5

Source: Thad L. Beyle, "Governors," in *Politics in the American States* (9th ed.), ed. Virginia Gray and Russell L. Hanson (Washington, DC: Congressional Quarterly Press, 2004).

Informal Powers

Although the office of Texas governor is formally very weak, the office can be strong politically. The governor's primary political resource is the ability to exert influence. The governor is the most visible officeholder in the state and can command the attention of the news media, holding press conferences and announcing new decisions on policy issues. Such news conferences are usually well covered and reported by the press and other media. This enables the governor to have an impact on the direction of state government. The governor can also stage events that are newsworthy to emphasize things she or he is interested in changing.

The popularity of the governor in public opinion polls is another aspect of informal leadership. Governors who consistently rank high in popularity polls can use this fact to overcome opposition to their policies and reduce the likelihood of opposition, to both policies and electoral challenges. A governor who is weak in public opinion polls becomes an easy target for political opponents.

In very general ways, governors are judged on their leadership abilities. Some governors develop reputations as being indecisive, and others become known as effective, decisive leaders. The characterization attached to the governor will in turn affect his or her ability to be effective. The press will begin to repeat the description of the governor's reputation, and if that happens often enough, the reputation will become "fact." Therefore, image is a factor in how much power a governor has. In addition to these informal powers, governors can make use of their staff and position as party leader to forward their agenda.

Party Leadership

As indicated earlier, governors are expected to be leaders of their political party and in most states are in fact recognized as the leader of the party. In the one-party era in Texas, the Democratic candidate for governor picked the state party chair and controlled the state party organization. Today, party chairs are elected, and although the governor still fulfills a vital role, the parties have experienced increasing division within their ranks. The Republican Party is increasingly divided between the social conservatives who recently wrestled control from the fiscal conservatives.

In 2003, the $10 billion state budget deficit pitched two of the major Republican players in Texas politics against each other: Governor Rick Perry and Texas Comptroller of Public Funds Carole Keeton Strayhorn. Perry wanted to make good on the tax cuts he had promised voters. Strayhorn wanted to balance the budget and keep Texas out of debt. As comptroller, Strayhorn ran audits on executive branch agencies and frequently became the bearer of bad news to the governor, but the core of their conflict was much deeper. Perry represented the socially conservative Republican newcomers, whereas Strayhorn stood for the fiscally conservative wing of the party that was intent on downsizing government and reducing expenditures.

In what some called a retaliation for Strayhorn's position on the deficit, Republican leaders in the Texas legislature stripped the comptroller's office of two high-profile duties. Perry also reneged on his support for Strayhorn's proposal to fund two years of community college for Texas students. For her part, Strayhorn became an increasingly vocal critic of Perry's policies. In 2006, she ran as an independent candidate against Perry. Although Strayhorn managed to capture only 18 percent of the vote, Perry suffered a pyrrhic victory: He became the first governor in over a century to be elected with less than 40 percent of the vote.

Similarly, in the 2010 primary, Governor Perry reached for the support of social conservatives to try to defeat the formidable opponent Senator Kay Bailey Hutchison. He criticized her for being a weak pro-life advocate. By rallying the support of Tea Party activists, he managed to win the gubernatorial nomination with 48 percent of the vote to Hutchison's 27 percent.

The Governor's Staff

In Texas, the trend in recent years has been to expand the staff of the governor's office. When John Connally became governor in 1963, he made the first use of a professional staff of advisers. Previous governors often appointed only a handful of individuals who were loyal to them politically, but not necessarily highly professional. Other governors since Connally have added to the governor's staff. Today, an organizational chart is necessary to maintain lines of authority and responsibility. Currently, the governor has a staff of about two hundred.

Each governor makes different uses of her or his staff. In recent years, most governors have used their staff to keep track of state agencies over which the governor has little or no direct control. The staff also gathers information and makes recommendations on changes in policy that affect most areas of state government. A message from a member of the governor's staff to a state agency is taken seriously. A report issued by the governor's office automatically attracts the attention of significant state leaders and the news media. Often the governor must use the information gathered to wage a public relations war with the legislature or state agencies. In Texas, the increases in the size, professionalism, and complexity of the governor's staff have become necessary to offset the limited formal control the governor has over state government.

Administrative Agencies of State Government

In addition to the office of governor, a number of other state agencies make up what might be called the state bureaucracy. The term *bureaucracy* often implies a hierarchy of offices with levels of power leading to a centralized controlling authority. This term does not describe the overall structure of state government in Texas, since there is no overall central governing, controlling authority. Government authority in Texas is much decentralized and resides within many independent state agencies. As we have seen, in the plural executive structure, the governor is not the only executive; she or he must share power with other elected officials. In addition, many independent boards, commissions, and agencies operate independently of the governor.

There are three basic kinds of state agencies in Texas, as illustrated in Figure 23-2. First are the agencies headed by an elected official; second are the appointed single-head agencies; and finally, and the most numerous, are those headed by a multimember appointed board or commission. The governor obviously has little or no authority over agencies headed by other elected officials who are responsible to the voters who elected them. As indicated earlier, although the Texas governor appoints citizens to these three-hundred-plus state boards and commissions, he or she has very limited removal authority. Each state board and commission operates independently and there is no

VOTERS IN STATE ELECT	GOVERNOR APPOINTS		
	Agency Heads	Boards and Commissions	
Lieutenant Governor	Secretary of State	General Government	Licensing and Professional Examining Boards
Attorney General	Adjutant General of the National Guard	Health and Human Services	Public Safety and Criminal Justice
Comptroller of Public Accounts	Director of Housing and Community Affairs	Higher Education Boards of Regents	Natural Resources
Commissioner of the General Land Office	Director of Office of State-Federal Relations	Other Education	Employee Retirement Boards
Commissioner of Agriculture	Executive Director of Texas Education Agency	Business Regulation	Interstate Compact Commissions
Railroad Commission (three members)	Commissioner for Health and Human Services	Business and Economic Development	Water and River Authorities
State Board of Education (fifteen members)	Eight other minor agencies	Regional Economic Development	Judicial

FIGURE 23-2   **The Administrative Structure of State Government in Texas**   What officers are elected independently? Do these officers have more power than the officers the governor appoints?

Note: The governor makes about 1,000 appointments to task forces or ad hoc advisory committees whose members make recommendations to the governor or other state officials. They are not governing or policy-making bodies.

Sources: Guide to Texas State Agencies, 9th ed. (Austin: University of Texas, LBJ School); Legislative Budget Board, "Fiscal Size-up," 1999–2000 Biennium; Legislative Budget Board, Austin; some information supplied by Governor's Appointments Office.

Employment for the Top Four State Agencies

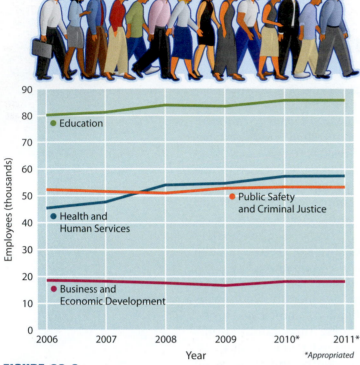

FIGURE 23-3 Approximately 76 percent of Texas state employees work in the five major areas of state government: corrections, highways, public welfare, hospitals, and higher education. Among the fifteen most populous states, Texas ranks tenth in the number of state employees per 10,000 population. Still, the state of Texas is the largest single employer in Texas. What is the fastest-growing agency in state government? What areas are losing jobs?

Source: Legislative Budget Board, "Fiscal Size-up, 2010–2011," www.lbb.state.tx.us/Fiscal _Size-up/Fiscal%20Size-up%202010-11.pdf.

central controlling authority. The governor's greatest authority is over the single-head agencies that he or she appoints, but except for the secretary of state, these are of limited significance.

Most of the work of state government is conducted by agencies controlled by either elected officials or boards and commissions that operate independently of the governor. Only the legislature, through oversight and budgetary authority, exercises control over all state agencies. Figure 23-3 illustrates the growth, decline, or stability in employment in the top five state agencies from 1998 to 2003.

Agencies with Elected Officials

Some agencies in Texas government are headed by elected officials, who are accountable to the voters.

Office of the Attorney General

The **attorney general** serves as the legal counsel to the governor, the legislature, and most of the other agencies, boards, and commissions in state government. Most of the work of the attorney general involves civil law and not criminal law. Criminal functions of the office are primarily limited to those cases appealed to federal courts. The most common example of these criminal cases is death penalty appeals. Occasionally, the attorney general's office may assist local criminal prosecutors when invited to do so.

Most of the resources of this office are devoted to collection of child support payments, collection of delinquent state taxes, administration of the

attorney general

chief counsel to the governor and state agencies; the attorney general has limited criminal jurisdiction

Crime Victims Compensation program, and investigation of Medicare fraud. Despite this rather "mundane" list of functions, the office has political functions that can have an impact on the course of legislation. The most important of these is to issue so-called AG opinions on legal questions. Often when the legislature is in session, the attorney general (AG) will be asked for an opinion on a pending piece of legislation. A negative AG opinion can kill a bill's chances of passing.

In 2007, the ultraconservative chairperson of the House State Affairs Committee, David Swinford, surprised Texans by killing a series of anti-immigration bills. Swinford had sought the advice of Attorney General Greg Abbott, who suggested that these bills, which would have deprived illegal aliens and their American-born children of certain rights, were unconstitutional. Swinford decided that the bills were a waste of money because the courts would strike them down.

comptroller of public accounts

chief tax collector, revenue forecaster, and investor of state funds; the comptroller does not perform financial audits

Comptroller of Public Accounts

The **comptroller of public accounts** has been assigned many additional duties over the years and currently functions as the chief fiscal and revenue forecasting officer. Generally in government, the controller has a preaudit responsibility for

In 2004, Comptroller Carole Keeton Strayhorn denied the church of Unitarian Universalism tax-exempt status of a religious organization. She argued that the church does not have one system of belief and so did not qualify. The comptroller's office reversed its decision shortly after media reports suggested that she might be overreaching her earthly authority.

Reprinted by permission of Doug Potter. From *The Austin Chronicle* (May 28, 2004).

ensuring that funds can be spent for specific functions. In Texas, the comptroller not only has the preaudit responsibility but also serves as the chief tax collector (a function normally associated with the office of treasurer), revenue forecaster, and investor of state funds.

Former governor Bob Bullock served as comptroller for many years. During his tenure, the office expanded the information and management functions and developed a fiscal forecasting model essential to projecting revenues in a two-year budget cycle. John Sharp, who followed Bob Bullock as comptroller, continued and expanded the information management programs of the office. Also under Sharp, the office developed the Texas Performance Review teams to evaluate the effectiveness of government operations and ensure the most efficient use of state funds. These reviews were estimated to have saved the state over $1.3 billion in the 1998–1999 biennium fiscal years. Similar management information and efficiency audits are available to assist local governments. Most of these programs have been kept in place.

The office also assists the private sector through the provision of information. The State of Texas Econometric Model is used to forecast state economic growth, keep track of business cycles, and generally provide information on the health of the economy of the state.

Commissioner of the General Land Office

Texas is one of only four states to have a **land commissioner** to administer state-owned land.[25] When Texas entered the Union in 1845, the agreement between the former republic and the U.S. government was that Texas would keep its public debt and its public land. When Texas became a state, most of the land was state owned. Today, the state of Texas owns and manages 20.3 million acres of land, including open beaches and submerged land 10.3 miles into the Gulf of Mexico.[26]

The land commissioner's office is responsible for leasing state lands and generating funds from oil and gas production. The office is also responsible for overseeing the Veterans Land Board and Veterans Land Fund. This fund lends money to Texas veterans to purchase rural land. Finally, the land office is responsible for maintaining the environmental quality of the state's open beaches along the Gulf Coast.

land commissioner

elected official responsible for administration and oversight of state-owned lands and coastal lands extending 10.3 miles into the Gulf of Mexico

Commissioner of Agriculture

Elected by the voters in a statewide election, the commissioner of agriculture heads the Texas Department of Agriculture (TDA). The agency has the dual, and sometimes contradictory, roles of promoting agriculture products and production and regulating agricultural practices, while protecting the public health from unsafe agricultural practices. For example, the TDA must promote cotton production and sales in the state while regulating the use of pesticides.

The TDA has six major functions: marketing of Texas agriculture products, development and promotion of agricultural businesses' production, pesticide regulation, pest management, product certification and safety inspection, and inspection and certification of measuring devices (including gasoline pumps, electronic scanners, and scales).

Although the TDA and the agricultural commissioner are not as publicly visible as the other statewide agencies with elected officials, the office is vital to a large section of the state's economy—those engaged in agriculture. The economy of Texas has become more diversified in recent years, but agriculture is still a significant player in the state's economy. Major agribusinesses and others in agriculture in the state pay close attention to who serves as the agricultural commissioner.

The Texas Railroad Commission

Texas Railroad Commission (RRC)
state agency, with a three-member elected board, that regulates some aspects of transportation and the oil and gas industry of the state

The three-member **Texas Railroad Commission (RRC)** was created in 1891 to regulate the railroad monopolies that had developed in the state. The commission's authority has expanded greatly since that time. In the 1920s, when oil and natural gas production developed in the state, the task of regulating the exploration, drilling, and production of oil and natural gas was assigned to the RRC in part because it was the only regulatory agency in the state at the time. When motor truck transport developed in the state, regulation of the trucking industry was also assigned to the RRC. In part because of federal rules and regulations, the original role of regulating railroads and the later role of regulating trucking have diminished to a minor role of the agency, reduced primarily to concern with safety issues. The regulation of the oil and gas industry is its primary function today.

Many have been critical of the RRC over the years because of close ties between the elected commissioners and the oil and gas industry they regulate. Large campaign contributions from oil and gas PACs have raised questions about the commission being co-opted by the industry it regulates. Also, like the agricultural commissioner, the RRC board has the dual role of promoting oil and gas production in the state and regulating the safety and environmental aspects of the industry (for example, promoting the development of pipelines to carry petroleum products as well as the safety of such pipelines). A similar conflict may exist between the RRC's task of regulating and promoting mining of minerals (especially lignite coal) in the state.

The role of the RRC that most directly affects Texas citizens is that of setting the rates charged by local natural gas companies. Natural gas companies must get RRC approval for the rates they charge residential and commercial customers. The RRC also regulates the safety of natural gas systems.

The State Board of Education

Unlike the other offices discussed in this section, the governing body for public elementary and secondary education in the state has varied greatly in form and structure over the years. In 1986, the board was changed from appointed to elected from districts. The current board, called the State Board of Education (SBOE), nominates one of its members to be commissioner of education.

In recent years, the authority of the board has been greatly reduced by actions of the state legislature. The political battle over the power of the board revolved around the social conservatives' (Christian Right) success in electing members to the board and the actions taken in setting curriculum standards and textbook selection issues. Public infighting among members of the board diminished its effectiveness. The legislature has removed several functions, most significantly the selection of textbooks, from the Board of Education in part because of the infighting and control by this faction. In 2010, the SBOE's revision of Texas curriculum standards drew national criticism when the board removed Thomas Jefferson from the list of philosophers studied in world history courses—and attempted to push through over two hundred amendments that introduced conservative values into the curriculum.

Single-Head Agencies

In some states, an individual appointed and serving at the pleasure of the governor heads most agencies. The structure is much like that of the federal government in which the president appoints his own cabinet, whose members serve at the president's pleasure. Only a handful of state agencies in Texas meet this model, and few are of great importance.

Secretary of State

Appointed by the governor with approval of the state Senate, the **secretary of state (SOS)** heads an office with duties assigned by the constitution and state statutes. Duties can be lumped into three broad categories: elections, records keeping/information management, and international protocol. As the chief election official, the SOS is responsible for overseeing voter registration, preparation of election information, and supervision of elections. The SOS issues rules, directives, and opinions on the conduct of elections and voter registration. These duties allow the secretary some latitude in the interpretation and application of the state Election Code. For example, the SOS has some latitude in how vigorously she or he encourages citizens to register and vote.

secretary of state (SOS)
chief election official and keeper of state records—appointed by the governor

A second duty of the SOS is to serve as the official keeper of state records. This includes records on business corporations and some other commercial activities. The office also publishes the Texas Register, which is the source of official notices or rules, meetings, executive orders, and opinions of the attorney general that are required to be filed by state agencies. Through the protocol functions of the office, the SOS provides support services to state officials who interact with representatives of foreign countries.

Commissioner for Health and Human Services

This office was created in 1991 to coordinate a number of health-related programs and agencies. The governor appoints the commissioner for a two-year term with the approval of the state Senate. The commissioner has oversight and review functions, but not direct responsibility, for eleven separate health and welfare programs, which are directed by boards, councils, or commissions. The programs include aging; alcohol and drug abuse; the blind, deaf, and hard-of-hearing; early childhood intervention; juvenile probation; mental health and retardation; rehabilitation; and departments of Health, Human Services, and Protective and Regulatory Services. This office has little direct administrative control, but it can and often does have an impact on policy. The commissioner serves as a spokesperson for the governor in health and welfare matters.

Office of State-Federal Relations

The governor appoints the executive director of the Office of State-Federal Relations. As the name suggests, this office coordinates relations between state and federal officials. The office has existed since 1971 and is the primary liaison between the governor's office and federal officials. To some degree, this office becomes an advocate (lobbyist) for the state in dealing with the Texas congressional delegation and federal agencies.

Adjutant General of the National Guard

This office is created by the Texas Constitution and is responsible for directing the state military force under the direction of the governor. The governor serves as commander in chief of the Guard. The size of the National Guard (nationwide and in Texas) is determined and funded by Congress as a reserve force to the regular army. The Guard also provides emergency aid and protection of property and persons in times of natural disaster.

In the November 1999 election, Texas voters rejected a constitutional amendment that would have allowed the governor to appoint and remove the head of the National Guard. As with other appointees, the governor may appoint the head of the National Guard, but not remove him or her except on approval of the state Senate.

Boards and Commissions

state boards and commissions
administrative units for many state agencies that carry out most of the work of state government; members are appointed by the governor for fixed terms

In addition to the elected and appointed officials, about 2,800 people are appointed by the governor for fixed terms to about three hundred **state boards and commissions.** These administrative units carry out most of the work of state government. The board or commission usually appoints the head of the agency (for example, chancellor of a university or executive director of a state agency) and in varying degrees is responsible for policy and administration of the agency. Most operate quite independently from other agencies of state government, except the legislature.

Given the lack of central control and the decentralized nature of state government in Texas, it is surprising that things work as well as they do. For example, there are thirty-one agencies that provide health and welfare services. In addition to the Department of Agriculture, the General Land Office, and the Railroad Commission—all having some control over environmental and natural resources— at least seven other agencies with independent boards or commissions have some authority in this area. These include the Texas Commission of Environmental Quality, the Texas Parks and Wildlife Department, the Soil and Water Conservation Board, and the Water Development Board.

In this conservative state with a strong belief in the free market, there are, nonetheless, no fewer than thirty-eight professional licensing and examining boards. Think of a profession, and there is probably a state agency that licenses and regulates it. Just a few examples are accountants, architects, barbers, chiropractors, cosmetologists, dentists, exterminators, funeral directors, land surveyors, medical doctors, two kinds of nurses, pharmacists, physical therapists, podiatrists, and veterinarians. Most often, the professional group asks for regulation by the state. When such groups advocate government regulation and licensing, they claim they are primarily interested in protecting the public from incompetent or dishonest practitioners. This may be partially true; however, regulation also has the added benefits of limiting entry into the profession and allowing the development of rules favorable to the group. Two professions that have benefited from regulation are the water well drillers and landscape architects.

Also, professionals frequently argue that the people appointed to the boards by the governor should be knowledgeable about the profession they are governing. Although knowledge is one factor, the danger is that these boards and commissions, dominated by members of the profession, will be more inclined to make rules and regulations that favor the group rather than the public. Because of that fear, in recent years, the appointment of at least some members of the board from outside the profession has become the norm—for example, nonphysicians on the State Board of Medical Examiners.

Twelve college governing boards oversee the institutions of higher education in the state. These boards are required to coordinate their activities and gain approval for some activities and programs from the State Higher Education Coordinating Board. Within these broad guidelines, each governing board is relatively free to set policy, approve budgets, and govern its university. Once again, governance is decentralized, with only a minimum of control from the state and almost none from the governor.

Legislative Agencies

In addition to the previous executive agencies, there are several legislative agencies. These are units controlled by the leadership in the Texas House and Senate. Their purpose is to provide legislative oversight of the "executive" agencies and to assist the legislature in its lawmaking functions.

Legislative Budget Board (Lbb)

As discussed earlier in the chapter, this agency is primarily responsible for preparing the state budget. It is composed of the lieutenant governor, the speaker of the house, four senators, and four state representatives. All agencies that receive state funds from the state budget must submit their requests for appropriations to the LBB. The LBB reviews these requests and proposes a budget to the state legislature. As indicated before, unlike most other states, in Texas the governor plays a very limited role in budgeting.

Texas Legislative Council

The speaker, the lieutenant governor, four senators, and four state representatives control this agency. They appoint the executive director. This agency was created in 1949 to assist the legislature in drafting bills, conducting research on legislation, producing publications, and providing technical support services. This is a highly professional agency that produces information for the legislature that is made available to the public in various ways.

Legislative Audit Committee and State Auditor's Office

The **Legislative Audit Committee** consists of the lieutenant governor, the speaker of the house, and the chairs of the Senate Finance Committee and State Affairs Committee, and the House Appropriations Committee and Ways and Means Committee. This committee appoints the state auditor, who is responsible for auditing state agencies and assisting the legislature in its oversight functions.

Legislative Audit Committee
legislative agency that performs audits on all state agencies

Legislative Reference Library

This organization assists the legislature in doing research and serves as a depository of records for the legislature. The library, located in the state capitol, is open to members of the public who wish to do research on the Texas legislature.

Other Agencies

Other agencies in Texas government handle judicial matters, oversee redistricting and budgetary matters, and deal with ethics issues.

Judicial Agencies

There are several agencies that can be called judicial agencies and are under the supervision of the State Supreme Court (civil matters). Except for budgeting of money by the legislature, these agencies are relatively free of legislative oversight. The State Bar, which licenses attorneys, receives no state appropriations. The remaining agencies are responsible for court administration (Office of Court Administration), operations of the state law library, and certification of legal licenses and specializations.

Ex Officio Boards and Commissions

A number of state agencies are headed by boards whose membership is completely or partially made up of designated state officials who are members because of the position they hold. Examples of these officials are the statewide elected officials—governor, lieutenant governor, speaker of the house, attorney general, and land commissioner. Examples of these agencies are the Bond Review Board, the Legislative Redistricting Board, and the Budget Execution Committee.

Multiappointment Boards

Finally, there are some state agencies that have governing boards whose members are appointed by more than one elected official. The reason for this is to prevent one individual from dominating the selection process and the outcome of decisions. Examples of these agencies are the Texas Ethics Commission and the Criminal Justice Policy Council. For example, the Texas Ethics Commission has four members appointed by the governor and two each by the lieutenant governor and the speaker of the house.

Citizen Control and the Sunset Review

Part of the concept of democracy requires that state agencies be responsible to the people—that is, that state agencies respond to demands placed on them by citizens. With Texas state administrative agencies operating independently of one another and overall administrative control being absent from state government, agencies are often able to respond only to clientele groups they serve and not the public generally. Thus, most state agencies are accountable only to small groups of attentive citizens. See Chapter 21 on interest groups for a more complete discussion of agency capture.

State government in Texas is so fragmented and responsibility so divided that holding anyone responsible for state government is almost impossible. Although citizens may blame the governor when things go wrong, and governors may claim credit when things go right, in truth the governor is responsible for very little and deserves credit for much less than most claim.

Given the lack of overall central control in state government and the limited and weak authority of the governor, in 1977 the Texas legislature created the ten-member **Sunset Advisory Commission** to review most state agencies every twelve years and recommend changes. This commission consists of five state

Sunset Advisory Commission
agency responsible for making recommendations to the legislature for change in the structure and organization of most state agencies

senators, five members of the House of Representatives, and two public members.

The sunset process is basically the "idea that legislative oversight of government operations can be enhanced by a systematic evaluation of state agencies."[27] The process works by establishing a date when an agency is abolished if the legislature does not pass a law providing for its continuance. The act does not apply to agencies created in the Texas Constitution or to some exempt agencies, such as state universities. Sunset asks this basic question: "Do the policies carried out by an agency need to be continued?"[28]

As Table 23-4 shows, in more than thirty years of sunset review, very few state agencies have been abolished. Most were minor state agencies with few functions. Most notable were the Boll Weevil Commission, the Battle Ship Texas Commission, and the Stonewall Jackson Memorial Board. More important than abolition is the review process. By forcing a review of an agency every twelve years, the legislature has the opportunity to recommend changes to improve the efficiency and effectiveness of state government. In many cases, functions of state agencies are transferred to other agencies, and agencies are combined or merged.

Sunset review has also forced public evaluation of many agencies that operate out of the public eye. This is especially true of those agencies that license professions. Sunset review resulted in the appointment of nonprofessionals to these agencies in an effort to promote the broader interests of the public over the narrow interests of the agency and its clientele.

TABLE 23-4 | Agencies Abolished by Sunset Review, 1979–2009

Year	Number of Agencies Abolished
1979	8
1981	2
1983	3
1985	6
1987	1
1989	3
1991	3
1993	1
1995	0
1997	0
1999	1
2001	1
2003	3
2005	6
2007	2
2009	1
Total	**41**

Summary
Self-Test www.mhhe.com/ pattersontadtx11e

Even though governors in most states do not have much formal power, the office has great importance in state politics. In recent years, the office has grown in stature. Many U.S. presidents have been former governors, and the office has become increasingly visible in both state and national politics. The need for strong leadership in this office will continue to increase.

Although citizens expect governors to play many roles and hold them responsible for the successes and failures of the state, many governors, including the governor of Texas, enjoy very limited power. In Texas, the governor's position is weakened by the plural executive, an executive branch in which most of the important offices are elected rather than appointed.

Although the Texas governor appoints some agency directors and the members of some boards, other agencies have elected heads and important multimember boards are also elected. These institutions carry out much of the work of state government. The governor has little authority over them, and each state board and commission operates independently from the others, with no central controlling authority.

Texas is now the second-largest state in population and one of the leading states in industrial growth. Because the governor lacks formal power and the executive branch is so divided, however, the task of governing this large, diverse, and economically vital state is challenging. Will the Texas governor and executive branch have enough authority and cohesion to fulfill the state's future needs? The Sunset Commission has led the reform of the executive branch. Will the commission ensure the effective implementation of state regulations and services? Will the governor be able to wield control over the agencies and boards to advance sound policy? The political culture of the state does not support increasing the authority of the governor's office. Hence, leadership will have to come from force of will and personality rather than from formal, large-scale changes in structure.

Study Corner

Key Terms

acting governor (*p. 579*)
appointive power (*p. 582*)
attorney general (*p. 592*)
budgetary powers (*p. 585*)
ceremonial duties (*p. 576*)
chief legislator (*p. 576*)
comptroller of public accounts (*p. 592*)
intergovernmental coordinator (*p. 576*)
Jacksonian statehouse democracy (*p. 582*)
judicial powers (*p. 588*)
land commissioner (*p. 593*)
Legislative Audit Committee (*p. 597*)
Legislative Budget Board (LBB) (*p. 585*)

legislative powers (*p. 586*)
military powers (*p. 588*)
partial veto (*p. 586*)
party chief (*p. 576*)
plural executive structure (*p. 582*)
recall of the governor (*p. 580*)
secretary of state (SOS) (*p. 595*)
state boards and commissions (*p. 596*)
Sunset Advisory Commission (*p. 598*)
tenure of office (*p. 580*)
Texas Railroad Commission (RRC) (*p. 594*)

Self-Test: Multiple Choice

1. Why are Texas governors typically held responsible for the performance of the state government?
   a. because they have a great deal of power within the government
   b. because they control the state budget
   c. because they have high visibility
   d. because they appoint the heads of all the executive branch offices

2. Which of the following is *not* true regarding the Texas governor's appointive and removal powers?
   a. Many of the governor's proposed appointees must be confirmed by the senate.
   b. The governor appoints many individuals to non-policy-making and governing boards that recommend policy and programs.
   c. The governor must give geographic and political consideration to his or her appointments.
   d. The governor's appointive powers do not allow him or her to influence policy after leaving office.

3. Which of the following accurately describes the Texas governor's budgetary powers?
   a. The governor has the authority to create and implement the state budget.
   b. The governor controls the budget through appointment and removal power.

c. The governor's strongest budgetary power is the line-item veto.
   d. The governor controls only funds that are earmarked for special purposes.

4. Which of the following is a state executive officer who is appointed by the Texas governor?
   a. attorney general
   b. secretary of state
   c. comptroller of public accounts
   d. commissioner of agriculture

5. Which of the following describes the tenure of the Texas governor?
   a. two-year term with a two-term limit
   b. two-year term with no limit
   c. four-year term with a two-term limit
   d. four-year term with no limit

6. Which of the following forms the basis of the governor's legislative powers?
   a. veto power and the right to call special sessions
   b. control of the National Guard
   c. powers of appointment and removal
   d. the authority to pardon prisoners

7. The lieutenant governor becomes the acting governor when the governor leaves the state. (T/F)

8. Removal of the governor requires a two-step process in which formal articles of impeachment are adopted by the house and conviction occurs in the senate. (T/F)

9. If the legislature is in session and the governor chooses not to sign a bill forwarded by the legislature, the bill becomes law after twenty days. (T/F)

10. The governor of Texas has full independent pardoning power of condemned prisoners. (T/F)

Critical Thinking

The office of governor in Texas is relatively weak in terms of formal power. What would be the advantages and disadvantages of making this office stronger? What arguments could be used to persuade the legislature to give up power to the executive?

Suggested Readings

Anderson, James, Richard W. Murray, and Edward L. Farley. *Texas Politics: An Introduction*, 6th ed. New York: HarperCollins, 1992.
Beyle, Thad. "Governors: The Middlemen and Women in Our Political System," in *Politics in the American States*, 8th ed., ed. Virginia Gray and Russell L. Hanson. Washington, D.C.: Congressional Quarterly Press, 2004.

Brown, Norman D. *Hood, Bonnet and Little Brown Jug: Texas Politics 1921–1928*. College Station: Texas A&M Press, 1983.

Gantt, Fred, Jr. *The Chief Executive in Texas: A Study in Gubernatorial Leadership*. Austin: University of Texas Press, 1964.

List of Websites

www.governor.state.tx.us/
The website of the Texas governor's office; contains useful general information.

www.lbb.state.tx.us/
The website of the state Legislative Budget Board; provides information on governor's budget proposals.

www.csg.org/
The Council of State Governors website; provides up-to-date information on state government and governors.

www.nga.org/
The National Governors Association website; contains information about governors.

Each of the state agencies has its own Web page. They can be found at www.texasonline.state.tx.us. There are also links to other organizations.

Participate!

Send a letter to the governor of Texas and express your opinion on some current issue—for example, school finance. The legislature and governor are at odds on this issue. Ask the governor what tax increases he might be willing to support to adequately fund education in Texas. Ask specifically about an income tax.

Extra Credit

Go to the Web page for Texans for Public Justice—www.tpj.org. Here you will find a report on Governor Perry's patronage. Read this article and write an essay giving your opinion on it. Do you think the governor is influenced by campaign contributions in his appointment of members of state boards and commissions? What are the implications of this practice for state policy produced by these boards and commissions?

Self-Test Answers

1. c, 2. d, 3. c, 4. b, 5. d, 6. a, 7. T, 8. T, 9. F, 10. F

The Court System in Texas

The Structure of State Courts

Local Trial Courts
County Courts
District Courts
Appellate and Supreme Courts

Judicial Selection and Removal

Issues in Judicial Selection
Removing and Disciplining Judges

Juries

Grand Jury
Petit Jury

Issues in the Justice System

Racial Disparity
The Effect of Punishment
  on Crime Rates
Death Penalty
Tort Reform

The nine justices on the Texas high court are chosen by voters in partisan elections. The majority of campaign money for judicial candidates is donated by lawyers and interest groups, many of whom can reasonably expect to have litigation reach the court. This apparent conflict of interest raises the obvious question: under such a system, is justice for sale?

In this chapter, we explore issues that may impact the judicial system. We study the structure of the judiciary branch of state government, the authority of different courts and juries, and the major political issues within the justice system. First, we examine the structure of state courts and describe the role and authority of each type of court. We then evaluate the process of judicial selection and removal in Texas, determining the advantages and disadvantages of this system relative to those used in other states. We also consider the role played by grand and petit juries in the court system. Finally, we explore issues in the justice system, such as tort reform, the death penalty, and the effect of punishment on crime rates. The points emphasized in the chapter are:

- State court systems consist of trial, appellate, and supreme courts. In addition, the Texas court system holds two types of trials: criminal and civil.

- Texas nominally uses partisan elections to select many judges, but in fact many candidates are appointed to their positions before being elected. Most states have moved away from partisan elections, as a preference for some type of merit system is emerging.

- The Texas selection system has a number of disadvantages: Voters tend to pick candidates with familiar names without any other knowledge of the candidate. They also tend to vote a straight ticket, which often replaces experienced judges with inexperienced judges. In addition, campaign contributions may have an impact on the impartiality of judges.

- High incarceration rates in Texas have achieved only a small reduction in crime. Although Texas leads the nation in the number of individuals executed, the number sentenced to death has dropped significantly in recent years.

The Structure of State Courts

Like the federal system, most state court systems provide for three levels of courts: trial courts, appellate courts, and a supreme court. Texas has several levels of trial courts and appellate courts. Figure 24-1 illustrates their structure and main characteristics. Trial courts differ from appellate courts in several important ways. First, they are localized. Jurisdiction is limited to a geographic area, such as a county.[1] Second, one judge presides over a trial court, and each court is considered a separate court. Third, citizens participate in trial court activity. They serve as members of juries and as witnesses during trials. Fourth, trial courts are primarily concerned with establishing the facts of a case (such as a determination that a person is guilty). Fifth, trial courts announce decisions immediately after the trial is finished.[2] In Texas, trial courts are the justices of the peace, municipal courts, county courts, district courts, and special-purpose courts such as probate, juvenile, and domestic relations courts.

Appellate courts decide whether proper procedures have been followed, and they are centralized, often at the state level. More than one judge presides; citizen participation is virtually absent. Texas has fourteen intermediate appellate courts and two "supreme" appellate courts: one for civil cases (Supreme Court) and one for criminal cases (the Court of Criminal Appeals).

Local Trial Courts

All states provide for some type of minor or magistrate court, usually called the justice of the peace. These courts hear cases involving misdemeanors, most often traffic violations and minor civil cases. In Texas, there are two courts at this level: justices of the peace (JPs) and municipal courts. Municipal courts hear cases involving violations of city ordinances, most often, traffic tickets.

These courts also have **magistrate functions,** involving preliminary hearings for persons charged with a serious offense. These persons are informed of the charges against them and told of their rights, and bail is set. As magistrates, municipal judges and JPs can also issue search-and-arrest warrants. JP courts also serve as small claims courts in Texas. Municipal courts do not.[3] Jurisdiction in small claims is limited to a maximum of $15,000.

County Courts

In Texas, there are two kinds of county courts: constitutional county courts and county courts at law. County courts at law are created in large urban counties. In those counties, the constitutional county court ceases to function as a court, and the "county judge" becomes the administrative officer or county executive but retains the title of judge and some limited judicial functions.

County courts primarily hear intermediate criminal and civil cases. Most criminal cases are misdemeanors. The most common types of cases are DWI, worthless check, and drug and traffic appeals.

County courts also serve as appellate courts for cases heard by JP and municipal courts. All JP and most municipal courts in Texas are not courts of record but **trial *de novo* courts,** in which no record of the proceeding is kept and cases may be appealed for any reason. It is common practice in Texas to appeal traffic tickets to the county court, where, because of heavy caseloads, they get buried. If a person has the resources to hire a lawyer, there is a good chance the ticket will be "forgotten" in case overload.

magistrate functions

preliminary hearings for persons charged with a serious criminal offense

trial *de novo* courts

courts that do not keep a written record of their proceedings; cases on appeal begin as new cases in the appellate courts

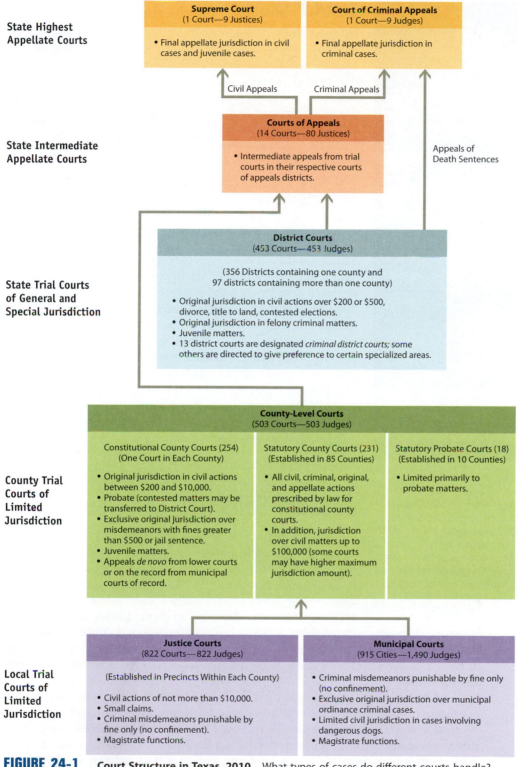

FIGURE 24-1   **Court Structure in Texas, 2010**   What types of cases do different courts handle?

Source: http://www.courts.state.tx.us

In 2008 officers from the Texas Department of Family and Protective Services removed some 4,000 children from the Yearning for Zion Ranch, part of the Fundamentalist Church of Jesus Christ of the Latter-day Saints. The group practiced polygamy, and several underage girls were pregnant. A month later, an appellate court ruled that the seizure was illegal since the department's Family Code justifies the removal only in cases where there was an urgent need to help children in physical danger and where the department had made previous attempts to prevent the threat.

merit system (Missouri system)

a system of selecting judges in which the governor appoints judges from a list submitted by a screening committee, and after appointment, a judge serves for a set term and is then subjected to a retention election in which the voters decide whether the judge stays in office

partisan election

method used to select all judges (except municipal court judges) in Texas by using a ballot showing party identification

District Courts

In most states, major trial courts are called district or superior courts. These courts hear major criminal and civil cases. Examples of major criminal cases (felonies) are murder, armed robbery, and car theft. Whether a civil case is major is generally established by the dollar amount of damages claimed in the case. Large urban counties generally have several district courts. In rural areas, one district court may serve several counties. The jurisdiction of these courts often overlaps with that of county courts, and cases may be filed in either court. Other cases must begin in district courts.

Appellate and Supreme Courts

Ten states do not have courts of appeals, and twenty-three states have only one court of appeals. The other states, primarily large urban states, have several courts of appeals.[4] Texas has fourteen courts of appeals, with eighty judges elected by districts in the state. Only California has more judges and courts at this level. These courts hear all civil appeals cases and all criminal appeals except those involving the death penalty, which go directly to the Court of Criminal Appeals. All states have a supreme court, or court of last resort. Texas has two supreme courts, one for civil matters and one for criminal cases. Each court consists of nine judges elected statewide for six-year overlapping terms.

Judicial Selection and Removal

Different states use a variety of methods to select judges. Some allow certain judges to be appointed by the governor and serve for life. Some allow the legislature to elect judges.[5] Some states use partisan elections and nonpartisan elections to select certain judges. Last, some states use the **merit system,** or **Missouri system.** Under this plan, the governor appoints judges from a list submitted by a screening committee of legal officials. After appointment, a judge serves for a set term and is then subjected to a retention election in which the voters decide whether the judge stays in office.

The method of selection also varies between courts within some states. For example, appellate court judges are chosen by a merit system, and the voters elect trial court judges. Figure 24-2 shows the number of states using each selection method for appellate and trial courts. Most states have moved away from partisan election of judges and use either a nonpartisan election or a merit system.

In Texas, trial court judges are elected in **partisan elections** for four-year terms, and all appellate court judges are elected in partisan elections for six-year terms. The only exceptions to this are municipal court judges. Most municipal judges are appointed by the mayor or the city council (1,435 are appointed, and 16 are elected). Some have argued, however, that Texas really has an

appointive-elective system, because the governor can fill any seat for district or appellate court that becomes vacant due to death or resignation or any new district court position created by the legislature. Vacancies in the county courts and justice of the peace courts are filled by the county governing body, the County Commissioners Court. Persons appointed to fill vacancies serve until the next regular election for that office, when they must stand for regular election.

Historically, many judges in Texas initially receive their seats on the courts by appointment. Although not complete for all time periods, enough data are available to show that this is a common practice. Between 1940 and 1962, about 66 percent of the district and appellate judges were appointed by the governor to their first term on the court. In 1976, 150 sitting district court judges were appointed.[6] Table 24-1 shows data on appointments of sitting judges in 2010. As you can see, many judges in all state courts get an initial appointment to serve.

Issues in Judicial Selection

In Texas, the question of judicial selection has been an issue for the last fifteen to twenty years. Several highly political issues have driven demands for change in the way Texas selects its judges. Voting based on name recognition and party label has resulted in the election of persons of questionable qualifications. Campaign contributions from groups with vested interests in cases before the courts have raised the specter of judicial bias, or "justice for sale." This issue has attracted much attention and will be discussed later in the chapter. Last, in large urban counties, minority representation on state district and county courts is affected by at-large elections at the county level. As we shall see, the legislature has not acted to correct any of these problems.

Voting for Familiar Names

Several events have brought the issue of judicial selection to the forefront in Texas today. The first of these is electoral problems. Although elections are at the heart of any democracy, they are imperfect instruments for deciding the qualifications

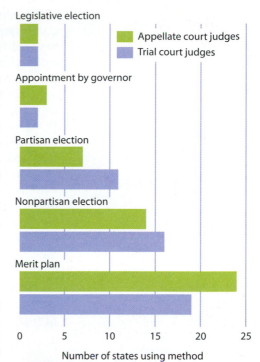

FIGURE 24-2 Methods of Selecting Judges
What are the most popular methods of selecting judges?

Note: The number of states does not add up to fifty because some states use more than one method to select judges. For example, district judges are elected; appellate judges are appointed.

Source: *The Book of the States 2006* (Lexington, KY: Council of State Governments, 2006), 256–58, table 5.9.

appointive-elective system
the Texas system in which many judges are initially appointed to a seat on the court and later must stand for election

TABLE 24-1 | Texas Judges Serving in 2010 Who Were Appointed to Their Initial Seat

	APPOINTED		ELECTED	
	Number	Percentage	Number	Percentage
Supreme Court	5	56	4	44
Court of Criminal Appeals	1	11	8	89
Courts of appeals	44	56	35	44
District courts	168	38	272	62
County courts at law	72	32	156	68
Probate courts	8	44	10	56
Constitutional county courts	48	19	203	81
Justice of the peace courts	235	29	586	71
Municipal courts	1,435	99	16	1

Note: Appellate and district court judges are appointed by the governor. County court judges and JPs are appointed by the county commissioners.

Source: "Profile of Appellate and Trial Judges," Office of Court Administration, www.courts.state.tx.us.

of the persons seeking office. This is especially true for judicial offices, for which qualifications are extremely important. The average voter in Texas will be asked to vote for judges for the Texas Supreme Court and the Court of Criminal Appeals, and, in large urban counties, several district judges, county judges, and JPs. Most voters go to the election booth with scant knowledge about the qualifications of judicial candidates, and they often end up voting by name familiarity. This happened in Texas in the 1976 election, when voters elected Don Yarbrough to the Texas Supreme Court. Yarbrough was an unknown attorney from Houston who won nomination as the Democratic candidate and claimed after the election that God had told him to run. Many voters had thought he was Don Yarborough, who had run unsuccessfully for governor. Still others thought he was Ralph Yarborough, who had served in the U.S. Senate for two terms. Judge Yarbrough was forced to resign after about six months because criminal charges were filed against him. He was later convicted of perjury and sentenced to five years in jail, but jumped bond. He then attended medical school in Grenada, which refused extradition to the United States. He was arrested on St. Thomas, Virgin Islands, while attending medical school classes and returned to Texas, where he was eventually sentenced to five years in prison.[7]

Straight Ticket Voting

Another electoral problem that has surfaced in recent years is straight ticket voting. Texas is one of fourteen states that allow straight ticket voting. Straight ticket voting allows a voter to vote for all candidates in a party by making a single mark. A study by Richard Murray at the University of Houston demonstrated that about 54 percent of the votes cast in Harris County in both 1998 and 2002 were straight ticket votes. A Republican running for countywide office had a 14,000-vote head start.[8]

Many incumbent judges have lost their seats in large urban counties to unknown challengers because of straight ticket voting. In Harris County in 1994, only one incumbent Democrat was reelected, and Republicans defeated sixteen Democrats because of straight ticket voting. Many of the Republican replacements lacked judicial experience, and one had no courtroom experience. In the 2006 elections in Dallas County, straight ticket voters turned the tables on Republicans, placing many inexperienced Democrats in office. This reversal occurred again in 2008—this time in Harris County.

These recent cases of straight ticket voting have caused some to call for **nonpartisan election** of judges—changing the ballots to show no party identification. Yet another suggestion is to prohibit straight ticket voting in judicial races, which has been considered in past sessions of the legislature. This would force voters to mark the ballot for each judicial race.

Costly Campaigns and Campaign Contributions

Under the Texas partisan election system, judges must win nomination in the party primary and then win in the general election. Two elections, stretching over ten months (January to November), can be a costly process. In 1984, Chief Justice John L. Hill spent over $1 million to win the chief justice race. The cost of that race and other experiences caused

nonpartisan election

election of judges in which party identification does not appear on the ballot

Ignorance about candidates often leads voters to vote by name familiarity.

POLITICAL

THINKING   Was Justice Served?

Twice convicted of murder, Michael Richard, 49, was scheduled to be executed on the evening of September 25, 2007. His lawyers were racing to complete the last minute paperwork necessary for an appeal to the Texas Court of Criminal Appeals (CCA) when they allegedly ran into computer problems. When the general counsel of the CCA called the presiding chief justice, Sharon Keller, to explain the predicament, she responded with four words: "We close at five." The appeal was never submitted, Michael Richard was executed, and a public uproar ensued.

Eighteen months later, the Texas State Commission on Judicial Conduct charged Judge Keller with failing to follow execution day protocol. In 2010, the judge presiding over Keller's trial recommended that she neither lose her job nor receive further punishment. However, a bill was submitted to the Texas legislature to impeach Keller. Do you think Keller should continue to serve as the presiding chief justice of the CCA? Would changing the judicial selection process help avoid this type of controversy?

Hill and two other Democratic justices to resign from the Supreme Court in 1988. They called for a merit system to replace partisan elections. Those resignations, along with other openings on the court, resulted in six of the nine seats on the Supreme Court being up for election. The total cost of the six races exceeded $10 million. One candidate spent over $2 million.[9] Races for district judgeships can also be very costly.

Money often comes from law firms that have business before the judges who receive the money. Other money comes from interest groups such as the Texas Medical Association, which has an interest in limiting malpractice tort claims in cases before the courts. In the 2002 election cycle, five of nine seats on the Supreme Court were up for election, including the chief justice. Close to $5 million had been raised by November 2002. Many of these contributions came from large law firms that had cases before the court.

The basic question raised by these contributions is their impact on judicial impartiality. Do these contributions influence the decisions made by judges? According to a poll by the Citizens for Public Justice, the average Texan thinks this money influences judges (73 percent). Even court personnel (69 percent) felt that the money influences judges. Lawyers were even more certain (77 percent), and since they contribute about 40 percent of the money, they may be in a position to know. About half of the judges (47 percent) thought the money influences their decisions. When people lose confidence in courts, respect for the law declines, and this should be of concern to all citizens.

In June 1995, the Texas legislature passed a law that aimed to reduce abuses of campaign contributions. This law limits the amount of money that individuals, PACs, law firms, and political party organizations can contribute to judicial races. Under this act, corporations are prohibited from making campaign contributions.

The amount of money an individual, PAC, law firm, or party organization can contribute is proportional to the population of the district or county from which the judge is seeking election and is highest for statewide offices. Unlike state representatives and senators, judges are elected from districts that vary greatly in the number of people voting. Judges in Dallas County must run countywide and appeal to several hundred thousand potential voters. Judges in rural counties might have only a few thousand voters in their district. The total amount of money a candidate may spend in seeking office is also limited. The limits are as follows:

- $2 million for candidates for statewide judicial office
- $500,000 for candidates for courts of appeals where the population is more than a million
- $350,000 for candidates for chief justice of courts of appeals where the population in the district is less than a million
- $200,000 for candidates for district or county courts where the population of the district or county is between 250,000 and a million
- $100,000 for candidates for district or county courts where the population is less than 250,000

All provisions of this law are voluntary. A candidate may file a declaration of intention not to comply with the provisions of this act. Candidates who file such a declaration must place a notice of noncompliance on all their campaign literature and advertisements. Candidates who comply may state in their literature that they are complying. Noncompliance by an opponent would supposedly become an issue in the campaign, and this is the intent of the act. However, the effect of this act has been marginal at best. Since the law went into effect, no one has made an issue of noncompliance. It has had no effect on campaign contributions or expenditures. Unless these provisions are made mandatory, this law will have no effect.

Minority Representation

minority representation in judgeships

election of judges from single-member districts in major urban counties to allow minority judges to be elected

A fourth electoral issue is **minority representation in judgeships,** which some feel would require election of judges from single-member districts. District and county court judges all run for election on a countywide basis. Countywide races for judgeships create the same problem for minorities as multimember legislative districts do. Minority judges have not been successful in races for these at-large, countywide offices. The problem is especially difficult in nine urban counties (Harris, Dallas, Bexar, Tarrant, Jefferson, Lubbock, Ector, Midland, and Travis). In 1989, the League of United Latin American Citizens (LULAC) sued, claiming that at-large election of judges in these counties was a violation of the Voting Rights Act. In 1989, the federal district court in Midland ruled the Texas system in violation of the Voting Rights Act. On appeal, the Fifth Federal Circuit Court, in 1994, reversed that decision, and the U.S. Supreme Court refused to hear the case, thus upholding the federal circuit court.[10]

Opponents of single-member-district elections in urban counties claim that partisan voting was more significant than ethnicity in these judicial elections. The two are obviously related. One could make the same argument that if all twenty-four delegates from Harris County to the Texas House of Representatives were elected at large, few minorities would be elected, because of straight ticket voting. The issue of minority representation in the state judiciary remains politically active but as a legal matter is dead. Any change would have to come from the legislature.

Is There a Best System for Selection of Judges?

Reformers, who include some of the best legal minds in the state, are calling for change from the current partisan election system. The Texas legislature has introduced many bills in the past decade calling for nonpartisan elections for judges or the implementation of a merit system, but none have passed.

Judicial selection revolves around three basic issues. Citizens expect judges to be (1) competent, (2) independent and not subject to political pressures, and (3) responsive, or subject to democratic control. Each method used by the states to select judges has strengths and weaknesses regarding each of these issues.

When judicial selection is by appointment by the governor, there is great potential for the selection of judges who are competent, but it does not ensure competence. Governors can use judicial appointments to reward friends and repay political debts. All U.S. presidents, some more than others, have used their judicial appointive powers to select federal judges with political philosophies similar to their own. Governors do the same thing. In such cases, questions of judicial competence are sometimes raised.

Governors are not likely to select unqualified people for judicial appointments; however, governors might not be able to persuade the best candidates to agree to serve. The appointive system probably rules out the complete incompetents, but it does not necessarily result in the appointment of the most competent people to serve as judges. Once appointed, judges are not responsive to voters and can exercise great independence in their decisions.

Election by the legislature is a system left over from colonial America, when much power rested with the state legislature. It is used only in South Carolina and Virginia. This system tends to result in the selection of former legislators as judges. In South Carolina, the number of judges who formerly were legislators is very close to 100 percent. Appointment is viewed as a capstone to a successful legislative career.[11]

Nonpartisan election is one system being given serious consideration in Texas. It would reduce the cost of campaigns and the problem of straight ticket voting. Voters would be more likely to base their decisions on something other than party label. It would not necessarily result in the selection of more competent judges, but it would prevent the kind of large-scale changes in judgeships that happened in Harris County in 1994. As indicated earlier, it has also been suggested that Texas prohibit straight ticket voting for judicial candidates, requiring voters to mark the ballot for each judicial race.

The merit, or Missouri, plan is also being considered as a method of selecting judges. Under this system, the governor would appoint judges from a list of acceptable (and, it is hoped, competent) candidates supplied by a judicial panel and perhaps ranked by the state bar association. Once appointed, the judge would serve for a set term and stand for retention in an election. In this retention election, voters could vote to either retain or remove the judge. The system is used by twenty-one states for appellate judges and fifteen for trial judges.

The merit plan seems strong on the issues of competency and responsiveness; however, there is little evidence that it results in the selection of more competent judges.[12] There is also evidence that it is weak on responsiveness. In retention elections, the judge does not have an opponent.[13] Voters vote to retain or remove. Several writers have pointed out the difficulty of defeating someone with no one.[14] In the states that use this system, most judges are retained; less than 1 percent are ever removed.[15] One study showed that between 1964, when the system was first used, and 1984, only 22 of 1,864 trial judges were defeated.[16] When judges are removed, it is usually because of either an organized political effort to remove them or gross incompetence.

Some variations on these plans are worth considering in Texas. In Illinois, judges are elected using a partisan ballot, but they must win 60 percent of the vote in a retention election to remain in office. In Arizona, judges in rural

Supreme Court Justice Nathan Hecht arrives at a meeting of the Texas Ethics Commission in 2008, where he defended himself against charges that he broke campaign finance laws by accepting $16,000 from homebuilder Bob Perry's HillCo PAC to help pay his legal fees to fight charges that he abused his office. Would another system of selecting judges—such as nonpartisan elections or the Missouri system—help to avoid such situations?

counties are elected in nonpartisan elections, but judges in the most populous counties are appointed.

In short, there is no best, or perfect, system for selecting judges. All methods have problems. Also, there is no evidence that compared with the other methods, any one of these judicial selection methods results in the selection of judges with "substantially different credentials."[17] The only exception to this is that in the states where the legislature elects judges, more former legislators serve as judges.

Removing and Disciplining Judges

Most states provide some system to remove judges for misconduct. Impeachment, a little used and very political system, is provided for in forty-three states, including Texas. Five states allow for recall of judges by the voters.[18] One state, New Hampshire, allows the governor to remove a judge after a hearing. In five states, the legislature can remove judges by a supermajority vote (a two-thirds vote is most common). In recent years, the trend in the states has been to create a commission on judicial conduct to review cases of misconduct by judges and remove them from office. To date, forty-nine states have established judicial conduct commissions. Also, the method of removal of judges can depend on the level of the judgeship—for instance, trial judges versus appellate judges.

In Texas, the state Supreme Court may remove any judge from office. District judges may remove county judges and justices of the peace. The State Commission on Judicial Conduct may recommend the removal of judges at all levels. This twelve-member commission conducts hearings and decides whether "the judge in question is guilty of willful or persistent conduct that is inconsistent with the proper performance of a judge's duties."[18] The commission can privately reprimand, publicly censure, or recommend that the state Supreme Court remove the judge. The use of review commissions to reprimand, discipline, and remove judges acts as a check on the actions of judges.

Juries

In general, Texas convenes two types of juries: grand juries and petit juries. Every defendant in a criminal case has the right to a trial by jury. However, defendants can choose to waive this right.

Grand Jury

grand jury
a jury of citizens that determines whether a person will be charged with a crime

information (administrative hearing)
a hearing before a judge who decides whether a person must stand trial; used in place of a grand jury

Any citizen may file a civil suit in court, but a screening body must review criminal cases. The U.S. Constitution requires the use of a **grand jury** to serve as a screening mechanism to prevent arbitrary actions by federal prosecutors. Some states use the grand jury system for some criminal cases, although in recent years the use of a formal hearing before a judge, called an **information,** or an **administrative hearing,** has become more common. The judge reviews the facts and decides whether there is enough evidence to try the case.

Texas uses both grand juries and administrative hearings. A citizen may waive his or her right to review by a grand jury and ask that a judge review the charges. In Texas, grand juries consist of twelve citizens chosen by district judges in one of two ways. The district judge may appoint a grand jury commission that consists of three to five people.[20] Each grand jury commissioner supplies the judge with three to five names of citizens qualified to serve on a grand jury. From these names, the judge selects twelve citizens to serve on a grand jury. In the other method, the district judge can have twenty to seventy-five prospective grand jurors summoned in the same manner used for petit juries. From this group, the district judge selects twelve citizens who are called grand jurors.[21]

Most grand juries serve for six months. They often screen the major criminal cases to decide whether enough evidence exists to go to trial. Grand juries are supposed to serve as filters to prevent arbitrary actions by prosecuting attorneys, but they do not always serve that function. The district attorney often dominates grand juries. Most grand jury members are laypeople who have never served before, and they frequently follow the advice of the prosecuting attorney. Although grand juries may conduct investigations on their own, few do. Those that do conduct investigations are sometimes termed "runaway grand juries" by the media.

A study by the *Houston Chronicle* presented evidence that some judges in Harris County had been given names of citizens for the grand jury by prosecutors from the district attorney's office. The study also demonstrated that many of the same citizens serve on grand juries year after year. Judges justified the repeated use of the same people for grand juries based on the difficulty of getting people to serve. Often, older, retired citizens volunteer to serve.[22]

Thus, a grand jury might not always serve the function of protecting the citizen from arbitrary action by prosecutors. For that reason, a person may ask for an administrative hearing before a judge. During grand jury proceedings, the accused is not allowed to have an attorney present during the hearing; during an administrative hearing, the attorney is present and can protect the accused.

In Texas, the prosecuting attorney files minor criminal cases in county courts. The county court judge, who determines whether the case should proceed to trial, holds an "administration" hearing. Criminal cases in the county court are generally less serious than those filed in district courts. They consist of DWI/DUI, minor theft, drug, assault, and traffic cases.

Petit Jury

Both criminal and civil cases can be decided by a petit (pronounced "petty") jury. Members of a **petit jury** are randomly selected from voter registration lists or, more recently in Texas, lists of licensed drivers. In criminal and civil cases, the defendant has the right to a trial by jury but may waive this right and let the judge decide the case.

Very few cases involve jury trials. In 2009, Texas county courts heard 611,231 cases, and 2,818 were jury trials. In district courts, 280,059 cases were disposed of, and 2,670 were jury trials. The lack of jury trials in criminal cases is often the subject of concern to some citizens. In a process known as plea bargaining, most people charged with crimes agree to plead guilty in exchange for a lesser sentence agreed to by the accused and the prosecuting attorney. The judge hearing the case can accept or reject the agreement.

If all criminal cases were subject to jury trials, the court system would have to be greatly expanded. Many additional judges, prosecuting attorneys, and public defenders would be needed. In addition, many more citizens would have to serve on juries. The cost of this expanded process would be excessive, and even though citizens support "getting tough on criminals," they would balk at paying the bill.

Issues in the Justice System

The Texas justice system hears three types of cases: civil, criminal, and juvenile. Civil cases are those between individual citizens and are brought to court when a lawsuit is filed. Criminal cases are those brought against individuals for violating laws. Juvenile cases resemble criminal cases but involve children aged ten to

petit jury
a jury of citizens selected randomly from voter registration lists or lists of licensed drivers that determines the guilt or innocence of a person during a criminal trial

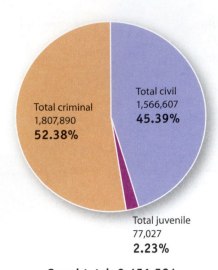

Grand total: 3,451,524

FIGURE 24-3 **Total Crimes in County and District Courts (2009)** How does the number of civil cases compare to the number of criminal cases? What initiatives might reduce the number of civil cases?

Source: The Texas Office of Court Administration Trial Court Judicial Data Management System, "County Level Courts Activity by Case Type, January 1, 2009 to December 31, 2009," and "District Courts Summary by Case Type from January 1, 2009 to December 31, 2009," http://dm.courts.state.tx.us/OCA/ReportSelection.aspx.

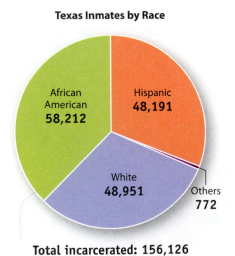

Total incarcerated: 156,126

FIGURE 24-4 **Texas Inmates by Race** Which demographic groups are overrepresented and underrepresented among the prison population?

Source: Fiscal Year 2008 Statistical Report, Texas Department of Criminal Justice, www.tdcj.state.tx.us/publications/executive/FY08%20Stat%20Report.pdf.

seventeen, and thus are considered civil in nature. Children cannot be tried as adults in Texas. Figure 24-3 illustrates the percentage of cases in each category.

Texas laws and judicial policies have a powerful impact on the number of cases, the types of cases, and the types of punishments. Many ordinary citizens advocate for victims' rights or against the death penalty. Texans have voted on a constitutional amendment fast-tracking tort reform in the state. As a result, the number of motor vehicle and personal injury cases has dropped. The values and the attitudes of juries and justices also affect who is sentenced and how long they serve.

Racial Disparity

Racial disparities within the criminal justice system are readily apparent both in Texas and in the United States in general. Minorities are significantly overrepresented among the group of individuals who are arrested each year in Texas. Texan juries arrive at a guilty verdict more frequently when the defendant is a member of a minority. As shown in Figure 24-4, in 2008 Texas jails and prisons housed almost 10,000 more African Americans than Anglos. Yet, in that same year, almost three times the number of Anglos were arrested in Texas.[23]

The issue of racial disparity in the Texas judicial system attracted national attention because of a case that occurred in Tulia, a small farming town in the Texas panhandle with a population of about five thousand. On July 23, 1999, police officers and state troopers carried out an early-morning drug raid in the town. The raid was part of a federal and state war on drugs in rural areas. It was the fruit of an eighteen-month investigation on the part of undercover narcotics officer Tom Coleman, and it was a major operation: forty-six partially-dressed residents were dragged to the courthouse and charged with selling one to four grams of cocaine. The offense carried only a 20-year penalty, but many of those arrested were charged with more than one count or with selling cocaine in close proximity to a park or a school yard. So, of the thirty-eight who were convicted, twenty-two received long prison sentences—some as long as 60, 99, and 434 years. The case was widely acclaimed, and Coleman became the Department of Public Safety's Outstanding Lawman of the Year.

But some aspects of the case didn't sit right with a handful of Texans. For one, Tulia had a very small African American population, and yet all but a few of the forty-six arrested were African American, and they had been convicted by an almost all-white jury. Only five of those sentenced had previous convictions. Then, those who admitted selling to Coleman insisted they dealt only in marijuana and crack, narcotics that are more prevalent among low-income groups. Dealing in these drugs carries a lighter sentence in Texas. Finally, no drugs, paraphernalia, or stashes of money were found during the raid. The convictions were based entirely on the testimony of Coleman.

Jeff Blackburn, an Amarillo attorney and ACLU member working pro bono proved that Tanya White had been in Oklahoma City on the day and time Coleman claimed to have bought cocaine from her. As a result, in 2000, the ACLU filed a lawsuit with the U.S. Department of Justice. The *New York Times* picked up the story, and the national media turned to Coleman's shady past. Former friends and associates described him as unreliable and as racist. Coleman had committed theft in Cochran County, where he had previously worked as a deputy sheriff, and he pinned the department with thousands of dollars of debt. Finally, in early 2003, the Texas Court of Appeals arranged for an evidentiary hearing. Judge Ron Chapman determined that apart from Coleman's notes on the buys, he had collected no physical evidence to corroborate his testimony: no fingerprints, no photos—nothing.

By August 2003, all thirty-eight prisoners were released. Coleman, meanwhile, was indicted for perjury on multiple counts.

The Effect of Punishment on Crime Rates

As Figure 24-5 shows, the crime rate decreased in the United States and Texas from 1990 through 2006. Texas ranks third among the fifteen most populous states in total crimes committed per 100,000 population.[24] Total violent crime has increased, but the increase is not as great as suggested by the news media or by campaign rhetoric. Crime has increased in Texas less than in the nation as a whole.

Many factors contribute to the crime rate. Most crimes are committed in larger cities. If we compare the fifty states, we find a strong correlation between the percentage of the population living in urban (metropolitan) areas and crime rates. This in part explains the crime rate in Texas, because about 80 percent of the population lives in metropolitan areas. There is also a strong relationship between age, sex, and crime. See Table 24-2 People below twenty-five years of age commit almost 45 percent of the crimes, and males commit 75 percent of all crimes. In Texas, the number of young men aged 18 to 24 has 25 decreased in recent years. This has contributed to the reduced crime rate since 1989 in Texas.[25]

The attitude among most Texans is "if you do the crime, you should do the time." Juries in Texas give longer sentences than the average nationwide. However, the average time served in Texas is less than the national average, and the percentage of sentence served by violent offenders in Texas is also lower than the national average, because of the longer sentences imposed by juries. The length of time served has increased in recent years, because of an increase in available prison space.

Texas has one of the highest rates of incarceration in the country. (See "How Texas Differs: Incarceration Rates.") The argument advanced for more incarceration is that it will lead to a reduction in crime rates. Studies of Texas crime show that between 1989 and 1993, when the incarceration rate increased by 4 percent, there

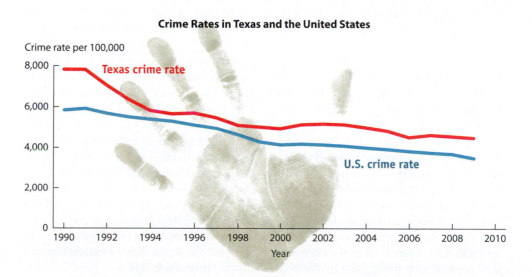

Crime Rates in Texas and the United States

Crime rate per 100,000

Texas crime rate

U.S. crime rate

Year

FIGURE 24-5
Political Inquiry
How does the Texas crime rate compare with the average rate in the United States? What factors might explain this difference?

Source: www.disastercenter.com/crime/uscrime.htm.

TABLE 24-2 | Persons Arrested for Crime by Sex, Race, and Age

	PERCENTAGE OF ARRESTS, 2007
SEX	
Male	75.8
Female	24.2
RACE	
White	69.7
Black	28.2
Others	2.1
AGE	
Under 18	15.4
18–24	28.9
25–34	23.9
35–44	17.6
45–54	10.9
55 and over	3.3

Sources: The 2010 Statistical Abstract, Persons Arrested by Charge and Selected Characteristics: 2007, table 314, www.census.gov/prod/2009pubs/10statab/law.pdf; Arrests by Age, 2007, www.fbi.gov/ucr/cius2007/data/table_38.html.

was a 1 percent decrease in the crime rate. Even if no other factors affecting crime rates were involved, this seems a high cost for such a small reduction in crime.

Death Penalty

Political values and attitudes influence not only the number of people sentenced but also the type of punishment they receive.

It has often been suggested that the death penalty can reduce crime. As discussed earlier in the book, the death penalty was outlawed in the United States in 1972 (*Furman v. Georgia*) because it was unfairly applied to many crimes and because of the lack of safeguards in place in many states. In 1976, the U.S. Supreme Court established guidelines under which a state could reinstate the death penalty (*Gregg v. Georgia*). To date, thirteen states do not have the death penalty: Alaska, Hawaii, Iowa, Maine, Massachusetts, Michigan, Minnesota, North Dakota, Rhode Island, Vermont, West Virginia, New Jersey, and Wisconsin.

Most executions (82 percent; 822 of 1,006) have been in southern states. The death penalty fits well within the dominant traditionalistic culture of the South. In Texas and many other southern states, juries can set the sentence for all crimes, and juries might be more inclined than judges to impose the death penalty.

Although Texas is still the leading state in the number of prisoners executed, the number of people sentenced to death has been in decline in recent years. Since the death penalty was reinstated in 1976, Texas has executed 452 of the 1,200 people executed nationwide. There is no shortage of people waiting to be executed. As of April 2010, 342 people sat on death row. However, Harris County, which was once known as the death penalty capital of the United States, has passed that title on to Los Angeles County in California, where in 2009 more people were sentenced to death than in the entire state of Texas.[26] In April 2010, a Harris County jury sentenced a defendant to death for the first time since 2007.

HOW TEXAS DIFFERS   POLITICAL THINKING THROUGH COMPARISONS

Incarceration Rates

Spending more on incarceration means less funding for juvenile justice and other crime prevention programs.

Q: How does Texas compare to other states in terms of its incarceration rate?

A: Texas has one of the highest incarceration rates in the nation.

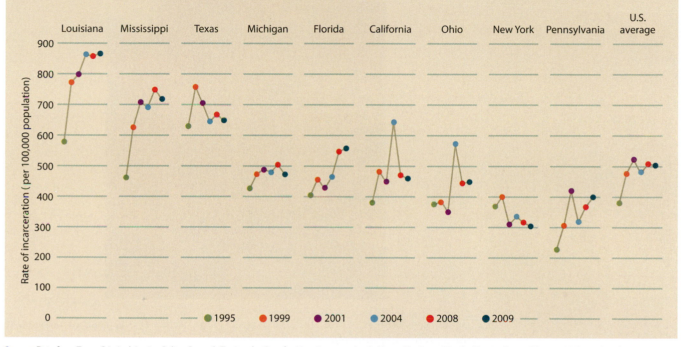

Sources: Data from Texas Criminal Justice Policy Council, *Testing the Case for More Incarceration in Texas: The Record So Far* (Austin: State of Texas, 1995), 29; data for 1999, Texas Criminal Justice Policy Council Web page; data for 2001 and 2004, "Fiscal Size-up," table 56, www.lbb.state.tx.us; data for 2004, U.S. Department of Justice, Bureau of Judicial Studies, www.ojp.usdoj.gov/bjs/abstract/po4.htm; data for 2008 and 2009, "Prison Inmates at Midyear 2009—Statistical Tables NCJ," Bureau of Justice Statistics.

In 2001, the *Houston Chronicle* reported that nearly 70 percent of Texans supported the death penalty. Have Texans suddenly had a change of heart? It is more likely that there are other issues involved.

Money is often a factor in determining whether the prosecuting attorney will ask for a death sentence. Small rural counties often lack the money to prosecute a death sentence case. Even large urban counties often find that death sentence cases will strain their budgets. Until just a few years ago, the wealth of Harris County was seen as a reason it led the country in executions. Harris County could afford it. However, the economic crisis seems to have spurred prison reform across the nation as counties and states scramble to pinch pennies. During this time, the number of death sentences has also declined nationally. Harris County has implemented cost-saving "in-reach programs" that aim to reduce the number of repeat offenders by encouraging inmates to turn their lives around.

Another factor may simply be the negative attention that Harris County and Texas have received of late. The state had gained a reputation for showing little mercy or leniency regarding death penalty sentencing. The Texas Court of Criminal Appeals almost never reverses a death sentence, and the Texas Board of Pardons and Paroles, often the final recourse for those with failed

Jean Dember protests outside a Texas prison in February 2000 just before the execution of Betty Lou Beets, who was charged with murdering her fourth and fifth husbands. Beets became only the second woman to be executed in Texas since the 1860s.

appeals, is even less apt to make changes. Then, in 2007, one case in particular incited statewide and even national outrage.

In 2010, a federal district court judge in Harris County made, and later rescinded, a ruling that the manner in which the death penalty is administered is unconstitutional. Some in the media accused the judge of "judicial activism" and questioned whether a judge should be allowed to make a ruling that contradicted the values of those living within his jurisdiction.[27] Thus, it seems that although Texans may be moving away from death sentencing, they are still determined to keep their options open.

Tort Reform

In February 1992, 79-year-old Stella Liebeck ordered a cup of coffee at a McDonald's drive-through. She placed the Styrofoam cup between her knees to remove the plastic lid and add cream and sugar. The very hot coffee spilled, causing third-degree burns. In what became known as the "McDonald's coffee case," a jury awarded Liebeck $2.7 million in **punitive damages**—damages meant as a punishment or a deterrent. The case brought national attention to frivolous civil lawsuits—personal injury, medical malpractice, and other lawsuits that end in excessive monetary awards to the plaintiff. Opponents of such suits argue that they are wasteful, clog the legal system, and extract a terrible financial and emotional price from both individuals and businesses. These people advocate **tort reform**—changes in the rules regarding compensation for damages—to limit the amount of damages that can be awarded and to define or restrict the circumstances under which a plaintiff can sue for damages.

Critics of tort reform argue that personal injury lawsuits are a means of holding large, powerful corporations accountable for practices that endanger

punitive damages

damages awarded in a legal case as a punishment or a deterrent

tort reform

changing the legal rules regarding compensation for damages done by one party to another worker safety and hurt consumers. They point to the role of asbestos lawsuits in establishing safe guidelines when it became clear that asbestos caused lung cancer. Other opponents of tort reform argue that it limits the power of the judiciary and its ability to act as a check on the other branches of government.

In the 2002 elections, tort reform became a major issue in Texas. The state was in the midst of an economic crisis, and Governor Perry and Republican candidates argued that frivolous civil lawsuits were preventing it from attracting new businesses, large industries, and potential employers. Because of the rise of these suits, they argued, Texas had gained a reputation as a "judicial hell hole." In fact, the number of personal injury and damage cases had risen in the 1990s. This was due in large part to the Supreme Court ruling in *Dow Chemical Co. v. Alfaro*, which determined that the legislature had abolished *forum non conveniens*, a doctrine that allows a court to refuse to hear a case if there is a more appropriate forum in which the matter may be settled.[28]

In addition, Governor Perry argued that Texas was in the midst of a medical crisis, with severe doctor shortages particularly in rural areas and in high-risk specializations, such as obstetrics and gynecology. Because of medical malpractice suits, doctors' insurance rates had skyrocketed. Only a few insurance companies still offered insurance to doctors in Texas. Governor Perry recounted personal testimonies of physicians closing their practices and moving to other states. The pro–tort reform lobby, which included HMOs, hospitals, doctors' associations, and nursing homes as well as insurance and pharmaceutical companies, had contributed a whopping $5.3 million to the 2002 campaign.[29]

In January 2003, Governor Perry officially designated medical malpractice reform as an emergency issue, directing legislators to address this problem within the first sixty days of the session. The legislature passed a bill to cap punitive damages for civil suits at $250,000. However, this was not the first time the legislature had tried to cap punitive damages. In 1977, the legislature had passed a similar law, but it had been struck down by the Texas Supreme Court on the grounds that the Texas Constitution did not give the legislature the power to limit the judicial process in this way. Therefore, the 2003 legislature passed another bill calling for a constitutional amendment providing the legislature with this authority. This amendment became known as Proposition 12. Citizens' rights groups such as Public Citizen staunchly opposed the proposition, but the amendment was approved by a narrow majority.

These laws and other lower-profile tort reforms have helped lower the number of injury and damage cases (see Figure 24-6). By 2005, fifteen new insurance companies had moved in, and insurance rates were becoming more affordable.[30]

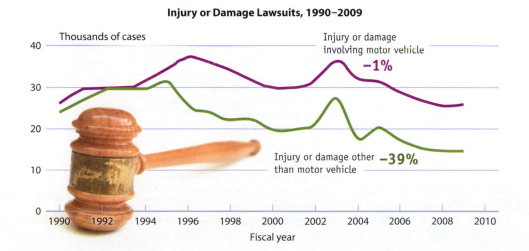

Injury or Damage Lawsuits, 1990–2009

Thousands of cases

Injury or damage involving motor vehicle −1%

Injury or damage other than motor vehicle −39%

Fiscal year

FIGURE 24-6

Political Inquiry

After a steady increase in injury and damage cases in the early 1990s, tort reform legislation has had an impact, decreasing the number of such lawsuits. What impact, if any, will this have on Texas citizens who seek access to the courts? On product safety? On professional standards?

Source: Texas Courts Online, www. courts.state.tx.us/pubs/AR2007/trends/ Caseload%20Trends%20by%20Case% 20Type.pdf.

Between 2003 and 2007, the number of new medical licenses granted climbed by 18 percent.[31] But critics argue that the number of patient complaints and disciplinary actions are up and that relief from the doctor shortage is coming mainly to urban areas. These critics lament the loss of the one big stick citizens had to keep big business from injuring those less powerful.

Summary

Self-Test www.mhhe.com/ pattersontadtx11e

In the twenty-first century, the court system in Texas faces many challenges. Is justice for sale? Certainly, partisan elections have undermined the impartiality of justices in the past. Voters also tend to pick candidates with familiar names without any other knowledge of the candidate, and to vote a straight ticket and thus replace experienced judges with inexperienced judges. Most states have moved away from partisan elections, as a preference for some type of merit system is emerging. Texans have rejected such a move. However, because judges often resign or retire from their positions midterm, many judges are in fact appointed prior to being elected.

The judicial system is bogged down with increasingly heavier caseloads. Texas has made progress in adopting methods to make the system more effective. In 1995, the state legislature established the Commission on Judicial Efficiency. One of the committee's four principal goals was to spearhead the adoption of information technologies. This included a statewide court filing system for attorneys to file documents in civil cases. Dozens of counties are implementing these systems.[32] This and other measures should decrease the pressure on the county-level courts. As the population continues to grow rapidly, the Texas judicial system will have to find more ways to handle its increasing caseload.

Texans may also need to reconsider their approach to dealing with the high crime rates in the state. Although voters seem eager to approve bonds for the construction of more prisons, they have been reluctant to consider other approaches to crime control. Budgetary constraints may force them to weigh the long-term costs of a high prison population and high execution rate—with the attendant costs of appeals—against the costs of alternatives, such as expanded supervision and treatment programs, that might reduce crime more effectively. High incarceration rates in Texas have achieved only a small reduction in crime. Hence, cost and efficiency issues may lead Texas toward reform.

CHAPTER 24

Study Corner

Key Terms

appointive-elective system (*p. 607*)

grand jury (*p. 612*)

information (administrative hearing) (*p. 612*)

magistrate functions (*p. 604*)

merit system (Missouri system) (*p. 606*)

minority representation in judgeships (*p. 610*)

nonpartisan election of judges (*p. 608*)

partisan election of judges (*p. 606*)

petit jury (*p. 613*)

punitive damages (*p. 618*)

tort reform (*p. 618*)

trial *de novo* courts (*p. 604*)

Self-Test: Multiple Choice

1. Where would a small-claims case be tried?
   a. in a justice of the peace court
   b. in a county-level court
   c. in a district court
   d. in the courts of appeals

2. Where would a felony criminal case be tried?
   a. in a justice of the peace court
   b. in a county-level court
   c. in a district court
   d. in the courts of appeals

3. Which of the following phenomena tend to unseat experienced judges in the judicial system?
   a. straight-ticket voting
   b. campaign contributions
   c. minority representation
   d. merit systems

4. Which of the following judges tend to demonstrate strong competence and independence but weak responsiveness to voters?
   a. judges elected in nonpartisan elections
   b. judges appointed by the governor
   c. judges selected by the merit system or Missouri method
   d. judges elected in partisan elections

5. In Texas how can a judge be removed from office?
   a. by criminal indictment
   b. by a vote of the legislature
   c. by order of a supreme or district court judge
   d. by order of the lieutenant governor

6. Which of the following is *not* a factor contributing to the large number of death sentences in Texas in general and in Harris County in particular?
   a. the reluctance of state and federal courts to overturn verdicts
   b. a traditionalistic subculture
   c. an almost complete public consensus in support of the death penalty
   d. the availability of funds to prosecute cases

7. Texas judicial elections are costly, but these funds often are provided by businesses and other interest groups. (T/F)

8. Texas has an appointive-elective system of selecting judges because the governor, county governing bodies, and city councils fill seats that become vacant due to death or resignation. (T/F)

9. Supporters of tort reform argue that it will increase the accountability of large companies and improve consumer and worker safety. (T/F)

10. Texas is one of the leading states in both the number of people sentenced to death and the number of prisoners executed. (T/F)

Critical Thinking

How are Americans' attitudes toward the courts shaped by mass communications? Many citizens think that courts should not legislate but should make decisions based on the law. If courts reverse decisions made by previous courts, are they legislating or basing their decisions on the law? If the Bush appointments swing the balance of the Supreme Court to the conservative side and reverse *Roe v. Wade*, would that be legislating or interpreting the law?

Suggested Readings

Abramson, Jeffrey. *We, The Jury.* New York: Basic Books, 1994.
Cheek, Kyle, and Anthony Champagne."Money in Texas Supreme Court Elections," *Judicature* 84 (2000): 20–25.
Eisenstein, James, and Herbert Jacob. *Felony Justice.* Boston: Little, Brown, 1977.
Jacob, Herbert,"Courts: The Least Visible Branch," in *Politics in the American States,* 8th ed., eds. Virginia Gray and Russell L. Hanson. Washington, D.C.: Congressional Quarterly Press, 2004.
Lawrence, Susan. *The Poor in Court.* Princeton, N.J.: Princeton University Press, 1990.

List of Websites

www.pbs.org/wgbh/pages/frontline/shows/justice/howshould
The website of the PBS show *Frontline;* provides information on campaign finances in Texas judicial races.
www.deathpenaltyinfo.org/
The website of the Death Penalty Information Center; keeps track of the death penalty in all states.
www.courts.state.tx.us
The Office of Court Administration website, a good source of information on state courts in Texas; keeps track of court data and serves as a watchdog agency for all state courts.
www.tpj.org/
The website of Texans for Public Justice, an advocacy group; keeps track of many aspects of state government including state courts and campaign contributions.

Participate!

Attend a session of a local county or district court. It might be helpful to call before you attend and ask about what might be covered in court on the days you can attend. Write an essay describing what happened in court that day. What kinds of cases were heard, and what was the disposition of these cases?

Extra Credit

Go to www.courts.state.tx.us. Use the judicial directory to research the courts in your area. Explore other information on this site to find out about the courts and judges in your area.

Self-Test Answers

1. a, 2. c, 3. a, 4. b, 5. c, 6. c, 7. T, 8. T, 9. F, 10. T

Public Policy in Texas

Public Policy in Texas

Public policy can be any rule or regulation or the lack of rules and regulations that influence how government affects the lives of citizens. When the state legislature passes a law requiring that all students take two political science courses to graduate from a public university, that is a public policy. Had the legislature not passed such a rule, most students would not have registered for a course in state and local government. In this chapter, we explore some major public policies in Texas state government and take a look at how Texas has implemented those policies. First, we examine economic policies, asking key questions about where the money comes from and where it goes. We then turn to education policies and consider who determines tuition rates, where college funding comes from, and how affirmative action is being pursued within the state. We examine social policies and how civil liberties, such as the right of privacy, fare in Texas. Finally, we analyze Texas's environmental policies in view of the demands that arise from an increasing population and a booming economy. This chapter will explore the following points:

- A state pursues its priorities by deciding how much money to spend on a variety of governmental programs. The budgetary process in Texas restricts its ability to create and implement innovative policies.

- How a state taxes individuals and businesses is a political policy. Most state tax systems are regressive, with lower-income individuals and families paying a greater percentage of their income to the state. Texas has one of the ten most regressive state tax systems in the nation.

- Texas public policy also determines who is admitted to public universities and how much they will have to pay.

- Texas is conservative in other areas of public policy besides the economy and education. Where privacy rights support conservative family values, Texans favor privacy. Where privacy rights undermine those values, Texans tend to oppose them.

- Texas has not considered innovative policies that states such as California have enacted, even though Texas faces rising energy demands and health issues caused by pollution.

Economic Policies

A budget can be thought of as a statement of policy in monetary terms, but where a state secures its revenue and how much it chooses to secure also reflect the state's values and political culture. Although a state may set priorities through laws that originate in any legislative committee, a state pursues its priorities by allocating funds to executive and legislative branch organizations that are then charged with executing those laws. An underfunded or unfunded law cannot be implemented. In this section, we analyze how the state's expenditures, sources of revenue, tax policies, and budgeting issues shape and produce its public policies.

Expenditures: Where Does the Money Go?

Today, much attention is focused on federal spending, and not all citizens realize that state governments also spend large sums of money to supply services to their citizens. In 2007, state and local governments, combined, spent $1.785 trillion. That amounted to $6,821 for each U.S. citizen. During the same year, the federal government spent $6,917 per citizen.[1] Some money spent by state and local governments comes from the federal government as grants, but state governments generate about 77 percent of their revenue from their own sources, and local governments generate about 67 percent of their revenue from their own sources.

What a state spends money for and how much it spends largely express its priorities. The budget becomes a statement of the dominant values in the state. The pattern of expenditures for Texas differs little from that of most states in terms of the items funded. In most states, three items consume most of the state budget—education, health and welfare, and transportation. In recent years, an increase in the prison population has greatly increased the amount spent for public safety, which includes prison operations. After those items, everything else pales in comparison. Figure 25-1 shows the major expenditure items in the state of Texas 2010–2011 biennium budget.

Whereas education eats up the lion's share of the state budget (about 42 percent), local school districts contribute about 60 percent of the funds for local schools. The state currently finances about 38 percent of the cost of elementary and secondary education. This is a decline in state contributions from a decade ago. The state's contribution has been steadily decreasing, and school districts have been forced to pick up a greater share of the cost of local education, which they are covering by assessing higher local property taxes.

Health and human services, about 33 percent of the state budget, is funded primarily with federal grants to the state. About 36 percent of the Texas budget comes from federal funds, most of which (about 52 percent) goes for health and human services (welfare and Medicare). Texas contributes less than most states to the cost of providing these services. The Texas Constitution prohibits spending more than an amount equal to 1 percent of the state budget on welfare.

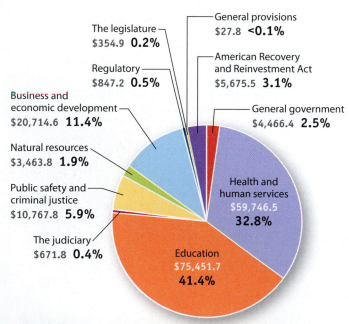

Total Expenditures in Texas for 2010–2011

The legislature — $354.9 **0.2%**

General provisions $27.8 **<0.1%**

Regulatory — $847.2 **0.5%**

American Recovery and Reinvestment Act $5,675.5 **3.1%**

Business and economic development — $20,714.6 **11.4%**

General government $4,466.4 **2.5%**

Natural resources — $3,463.8 **1.9%**

Public safety and criminal justice $10,767.8 **5.9%**

Health and human services $59,746.5 **32.8%**

The judiciary $671.8 **0.4%**

Education $75,451.7 **41.4%**

FIGURE 25-1 **Political Inquiry** The total expenditure was $182,880 million. What is most of this money spent on?

Source: Legislative Budget Board.

A comparison of Texas with other large industrial states on the primary budget items will tell us more about what Texans value. Among the fifteen most populous states, Texas ranks near the bottom in expenditures for welfare and transportation. In education, Texas still ranks below the mean. Although Texas spends much money in total dollars, it spends less than the average comparable state in per capita dollars for most items. In recent years, most of the growth in state expenditures has been driven by population.

Revenue Sources: Where Does the Money Come From?

In addition to how a state spends its money, how a state funds its programs and how much funding it collects reveal a great deal about its public policy positions. To pay for the many services a state government provides, revenue must be raised from many sources. For state governments, the primary source of revenue is taxes paid by citizens and not service charges and fees. The most common single source of revenue for state governments is **consumer taxes,** such as sales and excise taxes on gasoline, tobacco, and liquor. Figure 25-2 shows the break-down for Texas state tax revenue in 2010–2011, which totaled $77,726.7 billion for the two-year period. As you can see, most revenue comes from consumer taxes paid by individuals when they make purchases. Over 80 percent of all tax revenue comes from consumer taxes (sales, motor vehicle sales, motor fuels, alcoholic beverages, tobacco taxes).

Because of high sales taxes, most of the taxes in Texas are paid by consumers and not by businesses. There is only a limited tax on businesses, in the form of a corporate franchise tax. When compared with taxes on consumers, business taxes in Texas pale to insignificance at present. Texas has a form of corporate "income tax" that is called a **franchise fee.** Originally, it was assessed only on corporations doing business in the state. Some businesses changed to limited liability companies and other types of business structures to avoid the tax. The legislature was forced to eliminate many of these loopholes in 2007 and apply the franchise fee to most businesses in the state. In part, these loopholes were closed because of the school finance crisis. These reforms were implemented for the first time in 2008. The franchise fee is now the third largest source of tax revenue.

Texas is one of a handful of states without any form of personal income tax. Being in such a limited company of states without an income tax is not troublesome to most Texans. Politically there is great resistance to imposing such a tax. In 1992, the voters approved a constitutional amendment preventing the legislature from enacting an income tax without voter approval.

Service charges and fees are a source of **nontax revenue** for state governments. Governments often charge service charges and assess fees when a person can be excluded from receiving the service for nonpayment. When this exclusion is not possible, tax revenue is usually used to finance the service. Examples of these fees include tuition, driver's license fees, water bills, and fees for garbage collection. Figure 25-3 shows nontax revenue by source for the state of Texas in 2008–2009.

The trend in recent years has been to increase service charges and fees as a way to increase revenue and avoid raising taxes. All students attending state colleges and universities in Texas have experienced these increases as higher

consumer taxes
taxes that citizens pay when they buy goods and services, such as sales taxes

franchise fee
a type of business income tax levied in Texas

nontax revenue
governmental revenue derived from service charges, fees (tuition), the lottery, and other sources

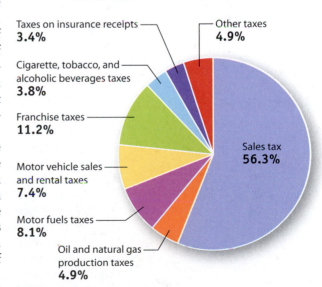

Tax Revenue in Texas for 2010–2011

Taxes on insurance receipts 3.4%
Other taxes 4.9%
Cigarette, tobacco, and alcoholic beverages taxes 3.8%
Franchise taxes 11.2%
Motor vehicle sales and rental taxes 7.4%
Motor fuels taxes 8.1%
Oil and natural gas production taxes 4.9%
Sales tax 56.3%

FIGURE 25-2   Political Inquiry The total tax revenue was $77,726.7 million. Where does most of this revenue come from?
Source: Texas Fact Book 2010–2011.

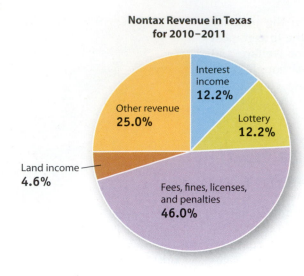

Nontax Revenue in Texas for 2010–2011

- Interest income 12.2%
- Lottery 12.2%
- Other revenue 25.0%
- Land income 4.6%
- Fees, fines, licenses, and penalties 46.0%

FIGURE 25-3 **Political Inquiry** The total nontax revenue was $29,600 million. Where does most of this revenue come from?

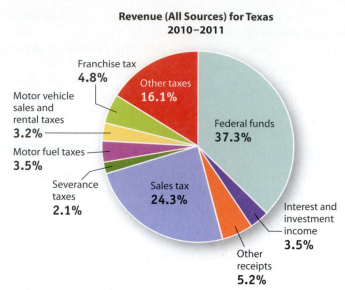

Revenue (All Sources) for Texas 2010–2011

- Franchise tax 4.8%
- Other taxes 16.1%
- Motor vehicle sales and rental taxes 3.2%
- Motor fuel taxes 3.5%
- Severance taxes 2.1%
- Federal funds 37.3%
- Sales tax 24.3%
- Interest and investment income 3.5%
- Other receipts 5.2%

FIGURE 25-4 **Political Inquiry** Total revenue was $180,316.2 million. Where does most of this revenue come from?
Source: Legislative Budget Board, "Fiscal Size-up 2010–2011," figure 33.

tuition and service charges. In total dollars in the state budget, the various service charges and fees provide 15 percent of total state revenue. The state lottery and interest income generates about 4 percent of total state revenue. (See Figure 25-4.) Federal aid made up about 35.5 percent of the Texas 2008–2009 biennium budget.

Taxation: Who Is Targeted?

The question of who should pay the taxes raises many issues. The state shapes public policy by deciding whom to take money from, how to take it, and how much to take. In the following sections, we examine three additional categories of tax policy and show how Texas implements mostly conservative policies in line with its political culture.

Benefit-Based Taxes and Ability to Pay

benefit-based taxes

taxes for which there is a relationship between the amount paid in taxes and services received, such as gasoline taxes

ability to pay

taxes that are based not on the benefit received but on the wealth, or ability to pay, of an individual

Should those who benefit from public services pay taxes (**benefit-based taxes**), or should those who can most afford it pay the taxes? Some taxes are based more on the benefit a person receives, and others are based more on the **ability to pay.** For example, the excise tax on gasoline is an example of a tax based on benefit received rather than on ability to pay. A large portion of the gasoline tax is earmarked for highway construction. The more gasoline people buy, the more tax they pay and the more benefit they receive from using the streets and highways.

For most taxes, other than the gasoline tax, showing direct benefit is problematic. Benefit received is more applicable to service charges and fees than to taxes. Sometimes the service charge covers the actual cost of providing the service, such as a service charge for garbage collection. In other cases, the service charge might cover only part of the cost of providing the service. College students receive most of the benefit from attending classes, and they pay tuition and fees to attend. In state-supported universities and colleges, however, not all of the cost of a college education is covered by tuition and fees paid by students. Most of the cost is still paid by taxpayers.

State Tax Capacity

The amount of tax money available for any given state depends on the wealth of the citizens of that state. Some states, like some individuals, have a higher income capacity than others. The measure of a state's "wealth" is called the state tax capacity.

Q: How does Texas's tax capacity compare to that of other states?

A: Texas has a fairly high tax capacity relative to other states.

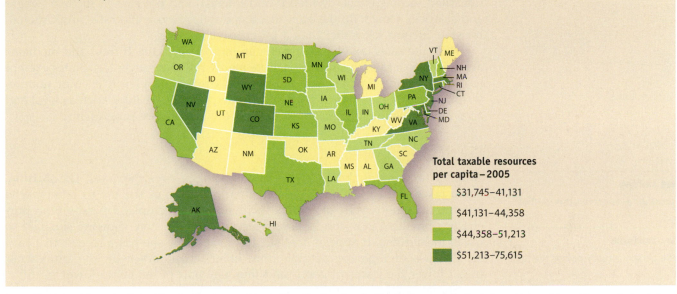

Total taxable resources per capita – 2005

$31,745–41,131
$41,131–44,358
$44,358–51,213
$51,213–75,615

Source: The National Center for Higher Education Management Systems, "State Tax Capacity—Total Taxable Resources Per Capita," www.higheredinfo.org/dbrowser/index.php?submeasure=132&year=2005&level=nation&mode=map&state=0. Reprinted by permission of the National Center for Higher Education Management Systems (NCHEMS). www.higheredinfo.org

Generally, when individual benefit can be measured, at least part of the cost of the service is paid as fees. People using a public golf course pay a green's fee, hunters pay for hunting licenses, and drivers pay a driver's license and tag fee. Often these funds go directly to the government unit providing the service. Taxpayers may pick up part of the cost through money paid in taxes. For example, green's fees paid by golfers often do not cover the total capital and operating costs of running a golf course. The difference is paid from revenue from other sources, typically from property tax revenues.

Other taxes, such as the federal income tax, are based more on ability to pay. The higher your net income, the higher your income tax bracket, and the higher the percentage of your net income you pay in federal income taxes. Most taxes, especially at the state level, are not based on ability to pay.

Regressive and Progressive Taxes

Using the criterion of ability to pay, taxes can be ranked as regressive or progressive. A *regressive tax* takes a higher percentage of income from lower-income persons, and a *progressive tax* takes a higher percentage from higher-income people. Economists also talk about so-called proportional taxes, in which the tax paid is a fixed percentage of each person's income.

Texas has one of the most regressive tax structures of all the states. The Institute for Taxation and Economic Policy, a Washington, D.C., advocacy group, issued a report in 2007 that ranked the fifty states based on how progressive or regressive their tax systems are. Texas made the "Terrible Ten" list, the list of states with the most regressive tax systems in the country.[2] Although all state tax structures are regressive, the tax structure in Texas is more regressive than average. States such as Texas that have no personal income tax have the most regressive tax systems. These states also have the lowest taxes on the rich.[3]

The degree to which taxes are regressive or progressive depends upon many factors. It is affected not only by the mix of taxes used in a state (income, sales, excise, property) but also by taxation rates and what is subject to tax. What is subject to taxation is called the *tax base*. For example, some states tax only unearned income (stock dividends and interest) and not earned income (wages and salaries). Others do the opposite. Some states have a flat rate (proportional) for state income tax rather than a progressive tax rate.

With the sales tax, the tax base is an important factor. If food and medicine are subject to a sales tax, the tax is more regressive. Only seventeen states exempt food items, forty-four exempt prescription drugs, and eleven exempt nonprescription drugs. If services used predominantly by the wealthy, such as legal and accounting fees, are subject to a sales tax, the tax is more progressive.

Tax Shifting

Another tax issue is the question of who actually pays the taxes: **tax shifting.** Some taxes can be shifted from the apparent payer of the tax to others, who become the true payers, or the **tax incidence.** For example, a person who purchases something in a store obtains a receipt from the store showing she paid so much in sales tax. It appears that she has paid a tax; she has a receipt that says so. Because of high competition from other stores, however, the storeowner might lower the prices of goods and thus pay part of the tax in lower profits.

Students who rent apartments near their campus never receive a property tax bill. The landlord pays the tax each year; however, the landlord will try to pass along the property tax as part of the rent. Market conditions will determine when 100 percent of the tax gets passed along to the renter and when the landlord has to lower the rent and absorb part of the tax in lower profits.

tax shifting

passing taxes on to other parties

tax incidence

the person actually paying the tax

Texans protest tax increases proposed by the state legislature. Texas has one of the most regressive tax systems in the country, yet Texans are resistant to a state income tax. Why are Texans—and citizens of other states—more willing to pay taxes on consumer goods than on their income?

Except for personal income tax, all taxes can be shifted to others. Market conditions will decide when taxes are shifted. People sometimes argue against business tax increases, advancing the argument that such increases will "simply result in higher prices to the customer." If taxes on businesses could always be shifted forward to customers as higher prices, no business would object to tax increases. Except for the inconvenience of collecting the tax and forwarding it to the government, there would be no cost involved. Obviously, taxes cannot always be shifted to the customer as higher prices, and businesses resist tax increases.

Budgeting and Crises

Because the legislature meets in regular sessions every other year (biennially), the Texas legislature approves budgets for two-year periods, called biennium budgets. In recent years, the Texas budget has been characterized by budget crises and an inability to pursue new policies.

The Budget "Fix"

The legislature has a limited amount of discretion in spending money. Much of the revenues are earmarked for specific items, called fixed revenues, or **budget fixes.** Revenues are fixed in three ways: by constitutional or statutory provisions, by funding formulas, and by federal government rules. Although the legislature could change the statutory and funding formula rules, these are often politically fixed by past actions and, except in extraordinary circumstances, are not changed. Interest groups have a strong attachment to these appropriations and will fight to maintain them. Examples of fixes are the proceeds from the state lottery, which go to education, and the motor fuel tax, which goes primarily to state and local road programs.

budget fix
a provision of the budget, mandated by state laws and constitutional amendments, that sets aside money to be spent on specific items

The earmarking of revenues obviously limits the ability of the legislature to change budget priorities or to react to emergencies. If one fund is short, movement of money from another fund may not be possible. Last year's budget becomes the best predictor of next year's budget. Changes in the budget occur incrementally over a long period of time.

Most funds in Texas are fixed, earmarked, or restricted. Only 19.5 percent of the moneys in the general fund are nonrestricted and available for change. That does not give the legislature much leeway in making changes in the budget. Similar patterns are found in most state budgets. Except for the Permanent University Fund, which applies only to the University of Texas and Texas A&M, university funding is part of the **discretionary funding.** That is why student tuition has increased in recent years. In per capita expenditures, the state has remained at about the same level over the past decade.

discretionary funding
those funds in the state budget that are not earmarked for specific purposes

Dealing with Budget Crises

Over the past twenty years, Texas has experienced a number of fiscal shortfalls, and the legislature has been forced to meet in special sessions to correct those problems. Many of the fixes have been short-term, but there is a need for a long-term solution.

During the 1980s, there were ten special sessions of the legislature to attempt to correct revenue shortfalls. These shortfalls were caused primarily by a decline in the state economy attributable to a drop in oil prices from a high of $40 per barrel to a low of less than $10. The fiscal crisis was worsened by the state's tax structure. Texas depends heavily on **income-elastic taxes** (85 to 90 percent),

income-elastic taxes
taxes that rise and fall quickly relative to changes in economic conditions; the Texas tax system is very income-elastic

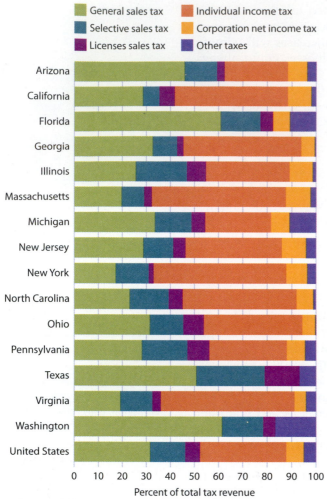

■ General sales tax	■ Individual income tax	
■ Selective sales tax	■ Corporation net income tax	
■ Licenses sales tax	■ Other taxes	

Percent of total tax revenue

FIGURE 25-5   How States and the National Government Raise Revenues   The bar graph compares the sources of tax revenue for the fifteen most populous states as well as the federal government. Note that Texas, Washington, and Florida rely most heavily on the total sales tax, whereas other populous states, such as California and New York, derive a large part of their revenue from an individual income tax, although both states also levy sales taxes. Based on what you've learned about state revenue, which states would you expect to experience the most severe budget crises? Explain your answer.

Source: Legislative Budget Board, "Fiscal Size-up 2010–2011," 50, figure 59.

which rise or fall very quickly relative to changes in economic conditions. When the economy is growing or contracting, tax revenue grows or contracts proportionately with the growth or contraction in the economy. For example, as retail sales grow, the sales tax grows. Texas is also very dependent on sales and excise taxes, which are also highly income-elastic. The same is true for the tax on oil and gas extracted in Texas. As the price of oil increases on world markets, the economy of the state booms and tax revenue increases. When an oil bust occurs, the opposite happens, and Texas finds itself extremely short of revenue. People quit buying goods and services subject to the sales and excise tax, and revenue falls accordingly.

Figure 25-5 compares the tax dependency of the fifteen most populous states. As you can see, Texas is far more dependent on sales taxes than most other large states. Only Florida and Washington are about as dependent as Texas on consumer taxes. Washington, like Texas, lacks both a personal and a corporate income tax, and Florida lacks a personal income tax. Many states faced severe problems balancing their budgets in the wake of the global economic crisis that came to a climax in the fall of 2008.

In the 2003 session of the legislature, Texas faced at least a $10 billion revenue shortfall because of a downturn in the economy, and it will face another fiscal crisis so long as it remains dependent on consumer taxes. What recourses are available to the state? During past crises, the problem of revenue shortfall was often solved by raising sales and gasoline taxes and by increasing fees. Can those taxes be tapped again? Texas currently has one of the highest sales tax rates. The state tax is 6.25 percent and local tax is 2 percent, for a total of 8.25 percent. Raising the rate might not be possible. Only four states (Washington, Nevada, Rhode Island, and Mississippi) have higher state (excluding local) sales taxes.

POLITICAL THINKING --

Planning and Implementing the State Budget

In late 2006, the media reported a wave of grisly deaths of Texas children under foster care. The Texas legislature quickly passed bills that tightened regulations on foster care providers, shortened the time children stayed with these providers, and encouraged the involvement of extended family in the care of these children. The result was a savings of one-hundred million dollars to the Texas state budget. Then in 2009, the media ran a series of stories on the deaths of children left in the home, the economic downturn placed greater stress on struggling families, and the number of children in foster care rose steeply. By 2010, a thousand more children than expected had been removed from their homes, which meant that the state would have to furnish an additional $150 million for foster care. These events certainly serve to underscore the complexity of planning and implementing the state budget. What other noneconomic factors are likely to impact the state budget? How should Texas respond to these demands?

Education Policies

The state regulates many education issues, but many are handled locally by special districts. We explore local issues in Chapter 26. Here, we look at state education policies pertaining to higher education, such as tuition, funding, and access.

College Tuition and Funding

For many years, the costs of college tuition and fees in Texas were very low and affordable to most people. Nonresidents of Texas often found it cheaper to come to Texas and pay a small out-of-state fee than to attend college in their own states. In the 1970s, the legislature began gradually to increase tuition and tie the amount students paid to semester hours taken. For most of the 1970s, the cost was four dollars per semester hour, or about twelve dollars per course, with a few fees for labs attached to some courses.

Universities approached the legislature for more money during most of the 1980s and 1990s. For most of that time, the legislature refused to allow universities to set their own tuition rates but did allow the universities to charge additional fees for services provided to students. That included such charges as computer access fees, recreational fees, and transportation fees.

Texas A&M and the University of Texas at Austin approached the legislature about allowing the two "flagship" universities to charge a higher rate of tuition. They claimed flagship status as the lead universities in the state. Their request met considerable opposition in the legislature, especially from members who were graduates of "non-flagship" universities. Both schools continued to press this issue with the legislature, and in the 2003 session, the newly installed Republican majority and Republican Speaker Craddick agreed to allow what was called **deregulated tuition** for all state universities—a policy allowing them to set their own tuition. The legislature faced a $10 billion shortfall in revenues, and this seemed an easy solution to part of the problem. In 2002, the average cost for fifteen student credit hours for tuition and fees was $1,685. By 2007–2008, tuition had increased to an average of $6,000 per year.[4]

deregulated tuition
a policy allowing universities to set their own tuition

Students demonstrate in support of affirmative action, which remains a controversial issue in higher education.

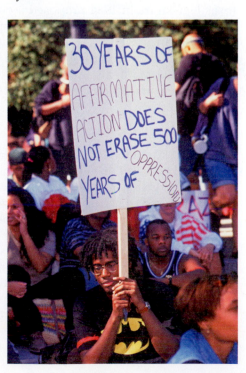

After the legislature changed the tuition policy, constituents began to complain about the increases. In the next session, the legislature held hearings and asked university officials to justify the increases. One wag called the hearings "How dare you do what we told you to do" hearings.

As indicated earlier in the chapter, operating funds for higher education are not part of the budget fix but, rather, are discretionary funds. This means that every session of the legislature must decide how much or how little to allocate for this expenditure, and so the cost of higher education may be funded with tuition and fee increases. Just as the cost of elementary and secondary education has been increasingly funded by local property taxes, which now equal almost half the total taxes collected at the state and local levels in Texas, the cost of higher education will increasingly fall to individual students and their parents, unless there is a drastic change in tuition policy.

Although the operating budgets for higher education in Texas are part of the regular budget, funds for capital projects are fixed in two funds. The Permanent University Fund (PUF), established by the Texas Constitution of 1876, is divided between the University of Texas and Texas A&M University. Originally, these lands were located in East Texas and were rather good farmland that generated much income. The state legislature later transferred these lands in East Texas to 2.1 million acres of land, primarily in West Texas. In the early part of the twentieth century, oil was discovered on these lands, and the income became substantial over time. The current value of the fund is $11.4 billion.[5] The University of Texas and some of its branch campuses receive two-thirds of the money from this fund, and Texas A&M and some of its branches and divisions receive one-third of the fund. Most of the money is committed to capital items and not operating budgets.[6]

Needless to say, many other colleges and universities in the state were upset that this policy did not give them any portion of these funds. The constitution specifically states that the money could be spent only at the University of Texas and its branch at College Station. The division of the money into two-thirds for the University of Texas and one-third for Texas A&M was an earlier agreement between the two schools.[7]

Because of pressure from other universities for a share in the PUF, the Texas legislature in 1984 proposed a policy change with an amendment to the state constitution, which the voters approved, that created the Higher Education Assistance Fund (HEAF). Beginning in 1985, the legislature set aside annual appropriations of $100 million for this fund. This was later increased to $175 million. Today, this fund provides about $275 million each year for colleges and universities not included within the PUF.[8]

Affirmative Action

From the 1950s to the 1970s, access to state colleges and universities in Texas was what could be called open enrollment, in which all students who were high school graduates and Texas residents would be automatically admitted without consideration of their high school standing or standardized test scores. Almost anyone could enroll in the university of his or her choice. In the 1980s, many schools, but especially Texas A&M and the University of Texas, began to impose higher standards for acceptance, primarily based on SAT scores and high school class standing.

This action to increase enrollment standards to some degree conflicted with the need to increase minority enrollment in the state's colleges and universities. Latinos and African Americans make up a majority of the state's population, but only about 20 percent were enrolled in colleges and fewer still at the top two state universities. This discrepancy was also true of law and other professional schools, where minority students were underrepresented.

Many colleges and universities began an affirmative action program to attempt to increase opportunities for members of minority groups to enroll in colleges and universities. These programs resulted in a lawsuit concerning the admission of minority students to the University of Texas law school. In 1996, the federal courts ended affirmative action practices at the University of Texas law school in the *Hopwood* decision.[9]

The attorney general of Texas, Daniel Morales, a beneficiary of affirmative action programs while a student in Texas higher education institutions, expanded the reach of the *Hopwood* case in Texas, effectively eliminating affirmative action admission policies in all colleges and universities in Texas. Thus, under the Morales interpretation, *Hopwood* was extended to prevent the consideration of race in areas beyond admissions.

In June 2003, *Hopwood* was overturned in a case originating in Michigan. The U.S. Supreme Court, in *Grutter v. Bollinger*, 539 U.S. 306 (2003), ruled that the U.S. Constitution does not prohibit the use of race as a factor in an admissions decision or policy. (For more on court decisions and affirmative action, see Chapter 5.)

Before the *Grutter v. Bollinger* decision, the Texas legislature, in an attempt to provide both equal opportunity and minority representation in higher education, changed the standards. It prevented admissions decisions and financial awards from being based primarily on any standardized test score such as the SAT, ACT, or GRE. Instead, the legislature allowed any student who graduated in the upper 10 percent of his or her high school class to gain automatic admission to any state college or university without consideration of other factors such as SAT scores. This ruling had the greatest impact on the University of Texas, where currently 81 percent of the freshman class has been admitted under the 10 percent rule. To a lesser degree, this is also the case at Texas A&M University.[10]

The 10 percent rule was supposed to increase minority enrollment by allowing students from inner-city minority high schools to attend the top schools in the state. There is some evidence that the 10 percent rule has increased minority enrollment, especially at the University of Texas and to a lesser degree at Texas A&M. It has created a problem for some high-performing students in the better high schools in the state, however, where students with SAT scores of 1,500 and higher often do not make the top 10 percent. There are also a few students with very low SAT scores from small rural schools who have been accepted under the 10 percent rule. Some people think the 10 percent rule needs to be changed.

Hopwood decision
a controversial 1996 case in which a federal court reversed affirmative action at the University of Texas law school

Social Policies

Each session, the Texas legislature introduces bills relating to social issues. Compared with those of other states, the laws that are passed engender conservative social and economic policy. (See "How Texas Differs: Policy Liberalism.") This conservative approach to public policy becomes very clear when looking at the state's approach to right to privacy issues. Where infringement of privacy upholds conservative values, Texas laws have supported the right to privacy. Where the same type of infringement violates conservative values, Texas laws have opposed it.

Sex and Abortion: Upholding Texas's Conservative Tradition

Privacy and abortion were discussed in Chapter 4. As noted there, after the U.S. Supreme Court decided in the landmark *Roe v. Wade* case that the Texas law banning abortions was unconstitutional, *Planned Parenthood v. Casey* allowed

State Rank on Policy Liberalism Index, 2005

Policy Liberalism

This index of policy liberalism examines state indicators of policy positions in three areas: gun control, abortion, and tax progressivity. From these policy areas, the index of policy liberalism was constructed for each state. Notice that some states rank high on some indicators of policy liberalism and near the bottom on others.

Q: Are there patterns among western states, southern states, or eastern states? How does Texas rank in each of these categories? Is that what you would expect?

State	Policy Liberalism	Gun Law Index	Abortion Index	Taxes Progressively
California	1	2	1	10
Hawaii	2	4	12	34
New York	3	7	9	19
Vermont	4	27	6	3
New Jersey	5	6	16	21
Connecticut	6	9	3	24
Oregon	7	18	7	6
Massachusetts	8	1	17	18
Maine	9	35	5	5
Rhode Island	10	8	28	27
Maryland	11	3	4	12
Montana	12	50	11	2
Illinois	13	5	20	39
Minnesota	14	17	20	8
New Mexico	15	31	14	26
Delaware	16	21	22	1
Alaska	17	26	10	28
Washington	18	23	2	50
West Virginia	19	29	15	13
Pennsylvania	20	14	47	40
Wisconsin	21	15	32	14
Missouri	22	16	41	20
New Hampshire	23	41	13	43
Iowa	24	10	19	22
Michigan	25	11	43	37
Ohio	26	25	38	11
Kentucky	27	48	49	16
Colorado	28	33	25	33
Nebraska	29	13	36	7
Nevada	30	29	8	47
Kansas	31	32	31	25
South Carolina	32	19	37	4
Indiana	33	24	34	36

State	Policy Liberalism	Gun Law Index	Abortion Index	Taxes Progressively
Tennessee	34	40	23	48
Arizona	35	29	18	38
Louisiana	36	37.5	50	41
North Carolina	37	20	24	15
Virginia	38	22	40	17
Utah	39	45	42	31
Florida	40	12	27	49
Texas	41	35	33	44
Idaho	42	37.5	35	9
Arkansas	43	44	43	23
Alabama	44	49	38	42
Oklahoma	45	39	30	29
Georgia	46	46	28	30
Mississippi	47	42	43	32
North Dakota	48	43	48	35
South Dakota	49	35	46	45
Wyoming	50	47	25	46

Note: The policy liberalism index also includes right-to-work laws that were not included in this table because the law is a binary variable.

Source: Virginia Gray, "The Socioeconomic and Political Context of States," in *Politics in the American States: A Comparative Analysis* (9th ed.), ed. Virginia Gray and Russell Hanson (Washington, DC: Congressional Quarterly Press, 2008). Constructed by the author from data from the Brady Campaign to Prevent Gun Violence (for the gun law index), NAM Pro-Choice America (abortion index), Urban Institute (TAW index), and Institute on Taxation and Economic Policy (tax progressively).

states to impose regulations on women seeking an abortion, so long as those laws do not constitute an "undue burden." Many states have tried in a variety of ways to limit and restrict abortions. Texas is no exception. In the 2007 session of the legislature, twenty-five bills were introduced to restrict or define abortions and limit abortion rights. Each session of the legislature finds about this same number of bills filed that could have an impact on women's right to abortion. Often these bills restrict the right of a woman to have an abortion unless she obtains the consent of her parents or the father of the child grants permission. The legislature has passed bills that have required parental consent for minors, necessitated consent form both parents, and instituted a twenty-four-hour waiting period once the pregnant woman is shown an ultrasound and given a booklet with facts about abortions.

The legislature has also altered the rules in the state budget to make it easier for pro-life groups to receive funds for abortion counseling, and it has reduced the availability of funds for organizations such as Planned Parenthood that support a woman's right to choose.

Many legislators who file these bills do so out of strong religious convictions that abortions are wrong. They have a lot of vocal company supporting these actions. At the Planned Parenthood clinic in Bryan/College Station, the local Coalition for Life group keeps a constant vigil. They have a camera set up to photograph the license plates of everyone who visits the clinic. Parents of students who go to the clinic sometimes get a letter informing them that their daughter has visited the "abortion" clinic.

Some bills involving sex and teen behavior have been known to make the national news. One such bill in the 2005 session, introduced by former Representative Al Edwards of Houston, became known as the "Booty Bill." This bill

Youth from a San Marcos Catholic church march to an anti-abortion rally in Austin to hear Governor Rick Perry speak on the issue.

would have prevented cheerleaders at high school events, such as football games, from doing dances and body movements that are sexually suggestive. Testifying before the committee when the bill was given a hearing, Edwards was unable to provide the words to describe what constituted such suggestive behavior. He knew what it looked like when he saw it but could not put it into words.

The Texas State Board of Education, however, has succeeded in introducing abstinence-only sex education curriculum in Texas high schools. In 2004, the SBE approved only textbooks that adopted this approach. By 2009, one study reported that 94 percent of Texas school districts provided only abstinence-only sex education and 2.3 percent skipped sex education altogether.[11]

Recent studies found no difference in sexual participation rates between students who received abstinence-only sex education and those who received no sex education at all. In both groups, 48 percent of students had sexual relations within 72 months.[12] In addition, students in abstinence-only programs had significantly higher rates of sexually transmitted diseases and lower contraceptive use than those with no sex education at all.[13]

In 2005, Texas had the fourth highest teenage pregnancy rate and the highest live birth rate in the nation. Perhaps not surprisingly, Texas has one of the most restrictive birth control policies for minors. In almost one-third of the state's family planning clinics and in all school-based clinics, minors must obtain parental consent to obtain a prescription. Even teens who have already had a child of their own must obtain permission. The vast majority of teenagers who gave birth were unwed mothers: 81 percent of teens who give birth to their first child and 72 percent of teens who give birth to subsequent children. The percentage of unwed teens that have given birth, however, falls below the national average, suggesting that more teens marry prior to giving birth.[14]

On other privacy issues, however, the Texas legislature has come down firmly on the side of the "get your laws off my body" argument—in cases where such an argument upholds conservative values. At the beginning of the 2007 session of the legislature, the governor, on very slim authority, issued an executive order requiring all schoolgirls to be vaccinated against the human papillomavirus to prevent cervical cancer later in life. Several members of the legislature expressed concern that if young women were to get the vaccine, it would encourage teen sex because they would not have to worry about getting cancer. In part, this logic assumed that teen behavior is rational when it comes to sex. Other legislators doubted this. Conservative groups also argued that requiring the vaccine was a violation of privacy and that Governor Perry had overstepped his authority. Several members of the House and Senate introduced legislation, which passed, preventing the vaccinations from taking place.

In March 2008, the Centers for Disease Control and Prevention (CDC) released a study that found one in four young women was infected with the virus. According to the *Houston Chronicle,* "Texas Gov. Rick Perry was right. Members of the Texas Legislature who last year shot down his plan to require schoolgirls be vaccinated against the human papillomavirus were shortsighted. This groundbreaking study shows how pressing is the need for sound public policy on teen sexual health—policy based on data and demonstrated best practices rather than emotion."[15]

Gay Rights and Gender Equality

One of the first rights won by gays and lesbians in the United States was the overturning of sodomy laws that ban this form of private consensual sex between adults of the same sex or the opposite sex. At one time, all states had antisodomy laws. However, by 2003 the number had decreased to thirteen states. Texas was one of the thirteen. In 2003, these laws were invalidated by the Supreme Court.[16]

The Texas legislature proposed an amendment to ban same-sex marriage, which was approved in the 2005 session. In November 2005, the voters overwhelmingly approved this amendment. Texas joined eighteen other states that had added amendments banning gay marriage to their constitutions.[17] Many of these bans follow the same language as the Defense of Marriage Act passed in 1996 by Congress that said states do not have to honor same-sex marriages performed in other states. This act goes against the Full Faith and Credit provision of the federal Constitution that requires states to recognize the acts and judicial proceedings of other states. There is no doubt that this amendment, which was primarily symbolic, has the support of most Texans, including many minority voters in the state.

Texas also lags slightly behind the other states in issues of gender equality. Regarding women's and men's salaries, for example, the median salary of a college-educated woman falls at 76 percent of the median salary of a college-educated man in the United States. In Texas, the earnings gap is higher, with women's median salary at 71 percent.[18] Although most other southern states fare no better with this indicator, other southern states that have well-developed high-tech industries like Texas, such as North Carolina and Georgia, rank well above Texas.

Environmental Policies

Texas not only ranks number one in greenhouse gas emissions but also produces more carbon dioxide than California and Pennsylvania, the next two biggest polluters. If Texas declared itself an independent nation, it would rank seventh in the world among the top greenhouse gas polluters. Some point their finger at Texans' attachment to big gas-guzzling cars and air-conditioners, and others blame population growth and a booming economy that increases energy demands. Whatever the reason, the state's reliance on coal-burning power plants has loaded lakes and rivers with enough mercury to generate fish consumption

FIGURE 25-6
City Water Demand Projections in Acre-Feet (Acft)

Source: City Water Demand Projections: 2010–2060, The Texas Water Development Board, www.twdb.state.tx.us/wrpi/data/proj/popwaterdemand/2011Projections/Demand/5CityDemands.pdf. How can Texas meet its growing demand for clean water?

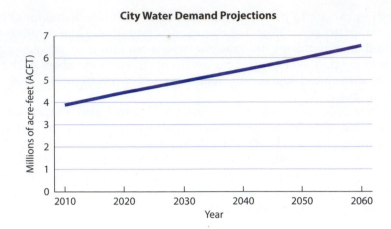

City Water Demand Projections

warnings for hundreds of acres across the state, and about one in five U.S. women of child-bearing age has mercury levels that are high enough to injure her unborn child.[19]

The nature of Texas politics and political culture does not support efforts to reduce pollution. In a state where the petrochemical and oil industries have been a mainstay of the economy, pollution has often been viewed as a sign of prosperity. In the past, if someone objected to the smell of oil production, the comeback was often, "Smells like money to me." ·

When George Bush was running for president in 2000, Texas already ranked as the top polluter among the states. Karen Hughes, a spokesperson for then governor Bush, was asked about the high pollution ranking of the state, and she said, "Governor Bush has done more than any governor in the history of Texas to hold the polluters' feet to the fire and force them to voluntarily comply." The news media reported that statement. No one in the news media asked the obvious question—"How many polluters have complied?" The press simply reported it. To a large degree, state leaders often deal with the problems by denying that they exist and thus foreclosing any need for a change in policy. Former congressman Tom DeLay called global warming data "political science," meaning that the data are driven by politics and not science.

In 2006, Environmental Defense Fund (EDF), an organization that works with governments, businesses, and communities to implement practical solutions to environmental problems, issued a report predicting the effects of global warming on Texas. As weather conditions change, the plant and animal life that inhabit the different regions of Texas will shift. Mosquito-borne diseases will therefore migrate from the tropics northward. Malaria will spread. By 2006, Texas had already experienced its first cases of dengue fever. Over six hundred miles of low-lying coastal lands will be inundated by rising sea levels. Some crops, such as cotton, will fare well, but others, such as corn, will fare badly. In general, however, longer droughts and surface-water evaporation will tax the water supply.[20]

Even if none of those predictions materialize, Texas still faces severe water shortages. Population growth, especially within urban areas, will mean a skyrocketing demand. Figure 25-6 shows projected demand, based solely on population estimates drawn from data from the U.S. census. Municipalities are already preparing for this eventuality. San Antonio and El Paso are leaders in this effort. San Antonio runs water conservation consumer education programs, provides rebates for water-efficient toilets and washing machines, and employs a four-person team to repair leaks quickly. The city's $5.5 million water conservation program reported a $4–7 savings on every $1 spent.[21]

Some entrepreneurs in Texas have been buying up rural lands in close proximity to urban areas to acquire water rights. Texas oilman T. Boone Pickens purchased land overlying the Ogallala aquifer, the largest underground water reservoir in North America. Pickens hopes to pump as much as two-hundred thousand acre-feet of groundwater into municipalities such as Dallas. Environmental groups, however, have argued that pumps are already pulling water out of the aquifer ten times faster than it can be replaced.[22]

The water crisis is not the only challenge, presented by the rising number of Texans. As both industries and the population expand, Texas faces a steep rise in energy demands. To accommodate this growing need, Texas energy companies began applying for permits to build more coal-burning power plants. In 2005, Governor Perry issued an executive order to speed up the construction of seventeen of these new plants. Environmentalists and local government officials, who feared the new plants would put them out of compliance with federal law, joined together to fight this initiative and were successful in part. Energy companies agreed to cut the number of plants down and applied to build new nuclear power plants. The power companies agreed, as well, to pursue alternative energy schemes, and wind energy in particular. Today, Texas leads all fifty states in wind power generation. In 2009, Texas generated 9,400 megawatts of electricity, as compared with its closest competitor, Iowa, which produced 3,600.[23]

Despite the state's embrace of wind power, Texas shows little sign of changing its high-polluting ways. By contrast, California is a leader in pollution legislation. Its standards for auto emissions have forced the auto industry to reduce emissions nationwide. California is also leading efforts to reduce other emissions through the Global Warming Solutions Act. This act will require a reduction of carbon emissions from all sources by 25 percent by 2020.[24] Meanwhile, many Texas public officials deny that global warming is a problem. Texas's environmental policy is an example of how public policy can be created not by legislation but by the lack of it.

Summary
Self-Test www.mhhe.com/pattersontadtx11e

As a state much influenced by its past and the dominant traditionalistic political culture, Texas tends to pursue conservative public policy choices in comparison with other states. The state of Texas spends a great deal of money, but measured in total dollars, it still ranks toward the bottom on per capita expenditures. School funding, discussed further in Chapter 26, will continue to be an issue. Prison funding will also become a major problem in the future if the state persists in its policy of increasing the number of state prisoners. The need for more health and human services will keep growing as the population increases. These expenditures cannot be funded through bonds, and yet they will have to be cut to repay bond debt in lean years.

State revenue is at or near capacity from most sources, and there is little room to raise existing state taxes. Tax revenue is highly dependent on income, and the current downturn in the economy can erase the surplus that existed in earlier sessions of the legislature. Perhaps this situation will force the state to evaluate the current tax system and its impact on the many segments of the state's economy. Politically, the prospects for change in the state tax structure are dim. The traditionalistic-individualistic political culture of the state does not support radical change. Without a major crisis, the status quo will probably prevail, and the current tax and spending structure in the state will continue.

Texas also faces challenges in the area of energy and environment. As Texas's population and economy grow, the state's energy needs will continue to expand. Yet, the state is already one of the world's top polluters. Public policy is an outcome of legislative initiatives, interest group activities, court decisions, executive branch decisions, and public opinion. Although business interests push for deregulation, federal mandates and public health issues may force Texas to move toward environmentally safer solutions in the future. Texas today is a national leader in wind power generation. Recent large-scale opposition to the granting of permits to coal-burning power plants may be indicative of evolving public opinion.

Study Corner

Key Terms

ability to pay (*p. 626*)
benefit-based taxes (*p. 626*)
budget fix (*p. 629*)
consumer taxes (*p. 625*)
deregulated tuition (*p. 631*)
discretionary funding
  (*p. 629*)
franchise fee (*p. 625*)

Hopwood decision (*p. 633*)
income-elastic taxes
  (*p. 629*)
nontax revenue (*p. 625*)
public policy (*p. 624*)
tax incidence (*p. 628*)
tax shifting (*p. 628*)

Self-Test: Multiple Choice

1. Which of the following describes the taxation system of Texas compared to most states?
   a. highly regressive
   b. somewhat regressive
   c. somewhat progressive
   d. highly progressive

2. What is the result of Texas's policy of earmarking revenues?
   a. Texas has no stable source of revenue and many budget crises.
   b. The Texas legislature has a limited ability to set budget priorities.
   c. Texas tends to enact conservative taxation policies.
   d. Texas relies heavily on business taxes such as franchise fees.

3. Which of the following characterizes Texas's taxation system?
   a. no sales tax
   b. no property tax
   c. no business tax
   d. no personal income tax

4. What factor is at least partly responsible for the fact that Texas universities have become increasingly competitive with other top U.S. universities?
   a. rising tuition
   b. the establishment of the National Educational Assessment Program
   c. the 10 percent rule
   d. the breakup of the Permanent University Fund

5. What is the significance of the *Hopwood* decision?
   a. It established the tax on corporations.
   b. It provided tuition refunds for dissatisfied university students.
   c. It reversed affirmative action in Texas universities.
   d. It led to a quota system in higher education.

6. What happened in Texas following *Planned Parenthood v. Casey?*
   a. Texas increased low-income women's access to abortion clinics.
   b. Texas outlawed late-term abortions.
   c. Texas submitted numerous bills requiring parental or spousal consent for abortions.
   d. The state supreme court system reversed *Roe v. Wade.*

7. Texas will require a reduction of carbon emissions by 25 percent by the year 2020. (T/F)

8. Texas has passed a constitutional amendment banning same-sex marriage. (T/F)

9. Texas overturned its sodomy law in 2003. (T/F)

10. Texas budget crises could be mitigated by establishing a personal income tax. (T/F)

Critical Thinking

Texas is undergoing major changes, such as the growth in trade and high-tech industry, the population boom, and Anglos' new majority–minority status. What effect do you think these changes will have on public policy?

Suggested Readings

Aronson, J. Richard, and John L. Hilley. *Financing State and Local Governments.* Washington, D.C.: Brookings Institution, 1986.

Mikesell, John L. *Fiscal Administration: Analysis and Applications for the Public Sector.* Pacific Grove, Calif.: Brooks/Cole, 1991.

Websites

http://www.thecb.state.tx.us/
The website of the Texas Higher Education Coordinating Board, which was established to help Texas meet its higher education goals; contains information on its Closing the Gaps program, college readiness, and financial aid.

http://www.window.state.tx.us/
The Texas Comptroller's website; provides information on sales, franchise, and property taxes, as well as on state finances and the economy.

http://www.texaspolicy.com/
The website of the Texas Public Policy Foundation, a research institute that provides research and data on state issues; also makes recommendations to state policymakers based on the foundation's research.

http://www.cppp.org
The website of the Center for Public Policy Priorities, a research organization dedicated to improving the conditions of low- and moderate-income families and individuals within Texas, with a focus on economic and social issues.

Participate!

Consider one issue that is of vital concern to you. Explore how the state or local government creates laws that establish public policy concerning this issue. What steps could you take to influence policy in this area?

Extra Credit
Find an interest group that is involved in an issue of concern to you. Research the group on the Web, and find out what it does to influence public policy.

Self-Test Answers

1. a, 2. b, 3. d, 4. a, 5. c, 6. c, 7. F, 8. T, 9. F, 10. T

26

Local Governments in Texas

Local Governments in Texas

State and national governments have an undeniably large impact on our daily lives, however, local governments can have an even greater impact. Many services that local governments provide are taken for granted by citizens. We may notice local government only when it doesn't do its job—when the water mains fail, the garbage is not collected, the pothole is not filled, stray animals are not impounded. When things work, local government often goes unnoticed.

Citizens depend on local governments for many life-supporting services, such as water, sewers, and police and fire protection. Local governments also help maintain the environment and lifestyles of citizens by zoning restrictions and the regulation of land development. In addition, local governments assume the important, perhaps critical, function of educating children.

Though 20 percent of Texans live in rural areas without many services, the vast majority live in urban areas and are very dependent on local governments. In this chapter, we examine local government forms, their authority, and their challenges. First, we distinguish between state and local authority and identify local governments as "creatures of the state." We then explore types of municipal governments, municipal elections, and the challenges municipalities face. We consider the structure of county governments and analyze policies that might help these governments overcome the disadvantage of their weak authority. We examine special district governments and what they do. Finally, we take a look at school districts and how they deal with financing and quality of education. The chapter's main points are:

- The authority of local governments is derived solely from state constitutions and statutes.

- In Texas, cities are chartered as either general-law cities or home-rule cities. Most cities that are large enough to be eligible elect to become home-rule cities.

- County governments have resisted change and seem content to operate under a plural executive, a form of government designed by and for an agrarian society. With this weak authority, county governments frequently cannot pass ordinances and raise the funds necessary to provide services to county residents.

- Special districts are created to perform a single function (for example, fire protection) or multiple functions (for example, water, sewer, street repair). School districts are one type of special district government. They face many problems; the most pressing is school finance.

State and Local Authority

When citizens become involved in local governments, they do so under the power and authority given them by state governments. All local governments are creatures of the state, and whatever power or authority they possess is derived from state constitutions and statutes. Local governments are not mentioned in the U.S. Constitution. They are created under state constitutions to serve the interests of the state.

The amount of local authority granted and the degree to which governments can act independently of state government vary greatly from state to state and within states by type of government. One way to understand this variety is to distinguish between general-purpose and limited-purpose governments. **General-purpose governments** are those units given broad discretionary authority by the state government. They have the authority to perform many functions and can control their own finances, personnel, and government structure. **Limited-purpose governments** have very limited authority or control over their finances, and they are governed by a set structure. Personnel decisions are controlled by state law.[1]

An example of a limited-purpose government in Texas is a school district. It performs only one function (education), has limited revenue sources (property taxes and state funds), and is governed by a seven-member school board, with many personnel decisions (such as teacher certification) controlled by a state agency. Texas counties are also examples of limited-purpose governments. State laws limit their authority and revenue, they all operate under the same form of government, and state law often dictates personnel decisions.

Texas cities, on the other hand, are excellent examples of general-purpose governments. Under home rule (discussed next), Texas cities have the authority to pass any ordinance not prohibited by state law and have many sources of revenue. The structure of government varies greatly from city to city, and the state exerts limited control over personnel decisions.[2]

Thus, although all units of local government are creatures of the state, some units are granted more discretionary authority and operate relatively free of state control and supervision. Texas cities have very broad authority. Other units of

general-purpose government

a government given broad discretionary authority by the state government

limited-purpose government

a government that has very limited authority or control over its finances and is governed by a set structure

Natalie Villafranca and her mother protest an ordinance passed by Farmers Branch, a suburb of Dallas, that required renters to provide proof of citizenship or residency and penalized landlords for renting apartments to illegal aliens. In May 2008, a federal judge struck down the ordinance. Determining whether a person is an illegal alien falls within federal authority, and Texas cities, as creations of the state, have no authority to make laws in this matter.

local government in Texas are limited-purpose governments. This chapter examines cities, counties, special districts, and school districts in Texas and the differences among these units of government.

Municipal Governments

City governments are technically municipal corporations. The term *municipality* derives from the Roman *municipium,* which means "a free city capable of governing its local affairs, even though subordinate to the sovereignty of Rome."[3] In Texas, the state government grants charters to cities. A city charter is a document much like a state constitution, in that it provides the basic structure and organization of city government and the broad outlines of powers and authorities.

General-Law and Home-Rule Cities

Texas cities are chartered as either general-law cities or home-rule cities. A **general-law city** can choose from seven charters specified in state statutes.[4] These options allow considerable choice as to form of government. There are 938 general-law cities in Texas.[5]

Since the passage of a constitutional amendment in 1912, any city in Texas with a population of at least five thousand may be chartered as a **home-rule city.**[6] Most cities of this size adopt home-rule charters. Home rule means that the local citizens may adopt any form of government they want and pass any ordinance not prohibited by state law. For example, state law is silent on the number of members on city councils, but the state constitution limits the term of office to no more than four years.

A prohibition in state law might be an **implicit or explicit prohibition on city ordinance power.** For example, there is no explicit prohibition against cities passing an ordinance prohibiting open alcohol containers in vehicles. Several Texas cities passed such ordinances in the 1980s before there was a state law against open containers. However, state courts ruled that the regulation of alcohol was a state function, and by implication (implicitly) Texas cities could not pass no-open-container ordinances.

The home-rule provisions of the Texas Constitution allow great latitude in governing local affairs. Once approved, home-rule charters may be amended only with the approval of the city voters. Usually the city council or a charter commission proposes changes. However, many home-rule charters in Texas allow voters to initiate charter changes.

Incorporation

The process of creating a city is known as **incorporation** because, as mentioned earlier, technically cities are municipal corporations. Creating a city normally involves the following steps: Local citizens must petition the state and ask to be incorporated as a city; an election is held, and voters must approve the creation of the city; the state then issues a charter.

In Texas, the requirements are as follows:

- There must be a population of at least 201 citizens living within a two-square-mile area. (This is a measure of density.)
- Petitions requesting that an election be called must be signed by 10 percent of the registered voters and 50 percent of the landowners in the area to be incorporated.

general-law city
a city whose charter is created by state statutes

home-rule city
a city whose charter is created by the actions of local citizens

implicit or explicit prohibition on city ordinance power
limitation on the power of cities, preventing them from passing ordinances that are explicitly prohibited by state law and from passing ordinances that by implication may violate state law

incorporation
the process of creating a city government

- If the petition is valid, the county judge calls an election.
- If voters approve, the city is created and a general-law charter is adopted. A second election is held to elect officials.[7]

Although these procedures are not difficult, there are limitations about where cities can be created. Under Texas law, all cities have what is called **extra territorial jurisdiction (ETJ),** or power over an area that extends beyond the city limits of an existing city.[8] General-law cities have a half mile of ETJ. The distance increases as population increases, for up to as much as five miles for cities above 250,000 in population.[9] A city may not be incorporated within the ETJ of an existing city unless that city approves. This provision is intended to prevent the growth of smaller cities on the fringe of larger cities and to allow existing cities room to grow.

In addition, cities may annex land within their ETJ. Cities annex land by taking adjoining land that is unincorporated (not a part of another city). Texas cities have broad annexation powers. The city council, by majority vote, can unilaterally annex land, and the residents living in the area being annexed have no voice or vote in the process. This provision in state law, coupled with the ETJ provisions, provides Texas cities with room to expand. In every session of the Texas legislature, many bills are introduced to restrict the ability of Texas cities to annex land. Some restrictions are placed on home-rule cities; however, they still have broad annexation authority when compared with many other states.

The Creation of Impact, Texas

The city of Abilene surrounds the small city of Impact, Texas, which was incorporated in February 1960. The primary purpose of this incorporation was to allow for the sale of liquor. Under Texas law, the citizens of a city may vote to allow the sale of alcohol—so-called wet-dry elections. Abilene is noted for being a center of Christian fundamentalism and is the home of three religious colleges. Some citizens of Abilene were scandalized at the prospect of liquor sales in this dry corner of the state and attempted to block the incorporation. After the courthouse battles, the incorporation was allowed, and liquor sales took place for many years. Impact was the only place for miles around where liquor could be purchased.

The city of Abilene, using its annexation powers, surrounded the city of Impact, eliminating any chance for it to grow. In 1963, the Texas legislature passed the law creating the ETJ for all Texas cities and limiting the incorporation of cities within the ETJ of an existing city. The incorporation of Impact was a factor in the passage of this act.

In the 1980s, Abilene allowed for the sale of liquor within the city limits. The liquor store in Impact is now closed.

Forms of Municipal Governments

Cities use two basic forms of government in the United States and Texas: mayor-council and council-manager. A third form, commission, was tried once in Galveston but is not used by any Texas city and is used by only a few cities nationwide.

Mayor-Council Government

The traditional form of city government that developed in the nineteenth century is mayor-council. There are two variations of mayor-council government—weak executive and strong executive. Under the weak executive, or weak mayor, form of government, the formal powers of the mayor are limited in much the same way that the Texas governor's formal powers are limited. First, the mayor shares power with other elected officials and with the city council, as shown in Figure 26-1.

---

extra territorial jurisdiction (ETJ)

city powers that extend beyond the city limits to an adjacent area

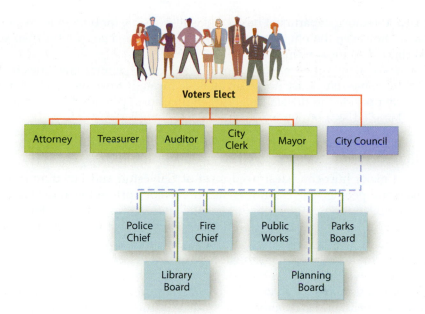

FIGURE 26-1
Mayor-Council Form of City Government, with a Weak Mayor
What powers does a mayor have in this form of city government?

The weak mayor's executive/administrative authority is limited. Second, the mayor has limited control over budget formation and execution. Third, the number of terms the mayor can serve is limited. Last, the mayor has little or no veto authority.[10]

Under a strong executive, or strong mayor, form of government, the mayor can appoint and remove the major heads of departments, has control over budget formation and execution, is not limited by short terms or term limits, and can veto actions of the city council. (See Figure 26-2.)

Only 39 of the 290 home-rule cities in Texas use the mayor-council form of government. Houston and Pasadena are the two largest cities using the form.[11] Of the two, only Houston has a strong mayor form. The Houston mayor can

FIGURE 26-2
Mayor-Council Form of City Government, with a Strong Mayor
Why is a mayor more powerful in this system of local government than in a mayor-council form with a weak mayor?

appoint and remove department heads and is responsible for budget formation and execution; however, the office has no veto authority, has a short term (two years), and is limited to three terms.

There are many more mayor-council forms in the general-law cities in Texas than in the home-rule cities; however, all have formally very weak mayors. Their powers are provided in the state statutes, and no form provided in the state laws can be classified as a strong executive.

Commissions and the Rebuilding of Galveston

In 1901, a major hurricane destroyed most of Galveston and killed an estimated five thousand people. Galveston was the only major port on the Texas Gulf Coast and a kingpin in the cotton economy of the state. It was in the interests of all Texans to rebuild the city and port. A delegation of Galveston citizens approached the Texas legislature for funds to help in the rebuilding. Joseph D. Sayers, the governor then, proposed establishment of a local government of five commissioners to oversee the rebuilding of the city. The new commission in Galveston worked in an expeditious manner and quickly rebuilt the port city. This efficiency attracted nationwide attention. Many other cities adopted this new form of government, illustrated in Figure 26-3, assuming that the form had caused the efficiency.

It was a very simple form when compared with the older weak mayor system, and it seemed to allow for quick action. However, it also created many problems. The first weakness was that voters did not always elect competent administrators. For example, a failed banker might run for finance commissioner and stress his banking experience.[12] With no way of knowing that his banking experience had been a failure, voters might elect him on apparent qualifications, and the bank where he worked might want to see him depart and not challenge his qualifications.

Second, the system combined executive and legislative functions into a single body of government. Though efficient, this system eliminated the separation of powers and its checks and balances. Commissioners were reluctant to scrutinize the budget and the actions of other commissioners for fear of retaliation. Logrolling set in: You look the other way on my budget and programs, and I will look the other way on yours. Third, initially the commission had no leader. The commissioners rotated the position of mayor among themselves. This "mayor" presided over meetings and served as the official representative of the city but was not in a leadership position.

FIGURE 26-3

Commission Form of City Government

What is the main weakness of the commission form of city government?

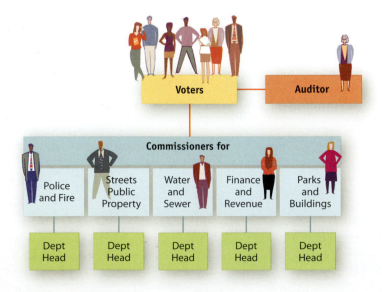

| Voters | | Auditor |

Commissioners for

| Police and Fire | Streets Public Property | Water and Sewer | Finance and Revenue | Parks and Buildings |

| Dept Head | Dept Head | Dept Head | Dept Head | Dept Head |

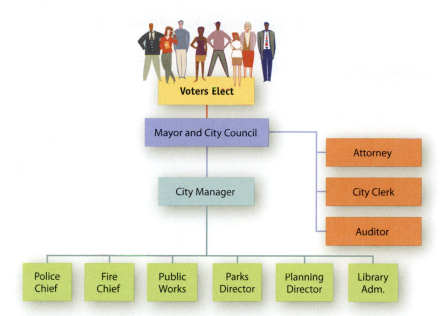

FIGURE 26-4
Council-Manager Form of City Government
Why is a council-management form of city government more responsive to public needs than other forms of city government?

The major contribution of the commission form of government was that it served as a transition between the old weak mayor form, with many elected officials and a large city council, and the council-manager form, with no elected executives and a small city council. Many cities altered their charters, stripping the administrative power from the commissioners and assigning it to a city manager. Many Texas cities retained the term *commission* as a name for the city council.

Council-Manager Government

The most popular form of government among Texas cities is the council-manager form, shown in Figure 26-4. Except Houston, all major cities in Texas use this form. Under the **council-manager** system, the voters elect a small city council (usually seven members), including a mayor. The council hires a city manager, who has administrative control over city government. The city manager appoints and removes the major heads of departments of government and is responsible for budget preparation and execution.

Administrative authority rests with the city manager, and the council is the policy-making body. The mayor and the city council are responsible for establishing the mission, policy, and direction of city government. Their roles in administration and management are greatly reduced. Figure 26-5 shows the roles of the council and the mayor on the four dimensions of city government: mission, policy, administration, and management. The council and the manager share in each of these areas, with the council dominating in mission and policy and the manager dominating in administration and management.

Roles of Mayors

The role of the mayor in city governments is often misunderstood because of the variations in strong mayor, weak mayor, and council-manager governments. This difference often escapes the average citizen.

In the strong mayor-council form, the mayor is the chief executive officer of the city, in charge of the city government. If the mayor possesses a veto authority, she or he can use the threat of a veto to extract some things from the council, just as the governor does with the legislature. There is a separation of powers between the mayor (the executive branch) and the city council (the legislative branch).

council-manager form of government

a form of government in which voters elect a mayor and a city council; the mayor and the city council appoint a professional administrator to manage the city

FIGURE 26-5

Political Inquiry

The curved line suggests the division between the council's and the manager's spheres of activity (the council's tasks to the left of the line, the manager's to the right). This division roughly approximates a "proper" degree of separation and sharing; shifts to the left or right would indicate improper incursions. What might cause the line to shift one way or the other?

Source: James Svara, "Dichotomy and Duality: Reconceptualizing the Relationship Between Policy and Administration in Council-Manager Cities," *Public Administration Review* 450, no. 1 (1985): 228. Reprinted with permission from Public Administration Review. Copyright Blackwell Publishing, Ltd.

Roles in the Council–Manager Form of Government

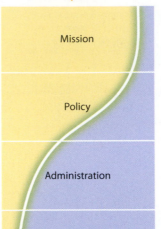

Dimensions of governmental process

Illustrative tasks for council	Council's sphere	Illustrative tasks for administrators
Determine "purpose," scope of services, tax level, constitutional issues.	Mission	Advise (what city "can" do may influence what it "should" do), analyze conditions and trends.
Pass ordinances, approve new projects and programs, ratify budget.	Policy	Make recommendations on all decisions, formulate budget, determine service distribution formulas.
Make implementing decisions, e.g., site selection, handle complaints, oversee administration.	Administration	Establish practices and procedures and make decisions for implementing policy.
Suggest management changes to manager, review organizational performance in manager's appraisal.	Management	Control the human, material, and informational resources of organization to support policy and administrative functions.

Manager's sphere

In a weak mayor form, the mayor is not the chief executive officer. The mayor may be the first among equals and the most visible member of city government but does not control administrative matters, although the mayor may have some administrative authority. The mayor's control over budgetary matters is limited and generally requires approval of the council even for minor matters such as paying bills. The mayor usually serves as a member of the council and generally lacks veto authority.

In council-manager government, the mayor is not the chief executive officer. The mayor does not control the city administration or the budget. Those powers rest with the city manager. The mayor is a member of the city council, and there is no separation of powers. The mayor serves as a leader of the council, presides over council meetings, usually helps set the council agenda, and serves as the official representative of the city. Some mayors in council-manager cities have been very successful leaders. They rule not from the formal powers granted in the charter but from personal abilities or informal leadership traits.

Henry Cisneros of San Antonio was one of the best examples of a successful mayor leader in a council-manager city. Cisneros led "by sheer personal magnetism and intellect, facilitating local successes through joint action of the total city council and professional staff."[13] Thus, mayors in council-manager cities are leaders, although the leadership style is quite different. They are not a driving force, as they can be in mayor-council governments, but they can serve as a guiding force.[14] No matter what the form of city government, the successful mayor must have political support within the community, the support and confidence of community leaders, popular support among the citizens, charisma, and the energy and stamina to lead, mold a coalition, and gain acceptance of his or her programs.

Roles of City Managers

Because so many cities in Texas use the council-manager form of government, some understanding of the role of the **city manager** is essential. Texas has always

city manager

official hired by the city council to manage the city and serve as chief administrative officer been a leader in the use of this form of government. In 1913, Amarillo became the first city in the state to adopt the form. O. M. Carr, the first city manager in Amarillo, strongly influenced the formation of the International City Managers (Management) Association.[15]

Under the council-manager form of government, the voters elect a city council and a mayor. Generally, these are the only elected officials in city government. The council in turn appoints the city manager and may remove the manager for any reason at any time; managers serve at the pleasure of the city council. In smaller general-law cities in Texas, the position may be called a city administrator rather than manager, but the duties are essentially the same.

Most managers are trained professionals. Today, many managers have a master's degree in public administration and have served as an assistant city manager for several years before becoming city manager. All but a few city managers are members of the International City Management Association (ICMA) and, in Texas, members of the Texas City Management Association (TCMA). These organizations have a code of ethics and help to promote professionalism in the management of local governments. This expertise and professionalism sets city governments apart from county governments in Texas. In county governments, the voters elect most officeholders, and professionalism is often absent. Because city managers appoint and can remove all major department heads and are in charge of the day-to-day management of city government, they can instill a high level of professionalism in the city staff.

Although the manager's primary role is to administer city government, managers can and do have an impact on the policies made by the city council. Managers provide information and advice to the council on the impact of policy changes in city government. Professional managers attempt to provide information that is impartial so that the council can make the final decision. Councils sometimes delegate this policy-making process to city managers, either openly or indirectly by failure to act. When that happens, councils are neglecting their duty of office and are not serving the citizens who elected them.

Over the last ninety years, the council-manager form of government has functioned well in Texas. Texas cities have a national reputation for being well managed and maintaining a high degree of professionalism in their operations.

Municipal Elections and Voter Turnout

The traditional method, used for most of the nineteenth century, to elect city council members was the **single-member district,** or ward system. The city is divided into election districts of approximately equal populations, and the voters in those districts elect a council member. There are a few cases of multimember districts, but none in Texas.

In the beginning of the twentieth century, many cities, led by early commission adoptions, moved away from the single-member-district system and began to elect council members at large by all voters in the city. There are several variations on the **at-large election system,** summarized in Figure 26-6. (For a thorough discussion of electoral systems in American cities, see Joseph Zimmerman in this chapter's "Suggested Readings.")

Some cities use a combination of at-large and single-member-district (SMD) systems. Houston is a prime example. Voters elect nine council members from single-member districts, and five council members and the mayor are elected at large by all voters in the city.[16]

Two other systems are used to elect council members. Under **cumulative voting,** each voter has votes equal to the number of city council seats open in the election. If five seats are open, each voter has five votes and may cast all five

single-member district
a system in which the city is divided into election districts and only the voters living in that district elect the council member from that district

at-large election system
system in which all voters in the city elect the mayor and city council members

cumulative voting
a system in which voters can concentrate (accumulate) all their votes on one candidate rather than casting one vote for each office up for election

At-large by place

This is the most common such system used in Texas. In this system, candidates file for at-large ballot positions, which are usually given a number designation—Place 1, Place 2, and so on. Voters cast one vote for each at-large ballot position, and the candidate with a majority is elected to that place on the city council.

At-large by place with residence wards required

In this system, candidates file for a specific place as in an at-large by place system; however, these candidates must live in a section, area, or ward of the city to file for a specific place. Mayors can live anywhere in the city. All voters in the city elect them at large.

At-large no place

This is the least common system used in Texas. In this system, all candidates seeking election to the council have their names placed on the ballot. If there are ten candidates seeking election and five open seats, each voter is instructed to cast one vote each for five candidates. The top five vote getters are elected. With this method it is not uncommon for a candidate to win with only a plurality (less than a majority) of the vote.

FIGURE 26-6   **At-Large Voting Systems**   How would each form of at-large system impact minority representation? Why?

preferential voting

a system that allows voters to rank candidates for the city council

votes for one candidate (accumulating their votes), one vote each for five candidates, or any combination or variation. Several cities have adopted this system as an alternative to SMDs. Since 1991, forty school districts and fourteen cities in Texas have adopted cumulative voting. The Amarillo Independent School District is the largest government body using the system in Texas (160,000 people).

Preferential voting, also called instant runoff voting, is another system, which works by allowing voters to rank the candidates for city council. All candidates' names are listed on the ballot, and the voter indicates the order of his or her preferences (first, second, third, and so on). Using a complicated ballot-counting system, the most-preferred candidates are elected. Although no city in Texas currently uses this system, San Francisco and fifteen other cities use preferential voting nationwide. Advocates believe that both cumulative voting and preferential voting increase minority representation, but there is little evidence to support that claim.

Since the Voting Rights Act was amended in 1975 and applied to Texas, many cities have changed from an at-large system to single-member districts. Before 1975, almost no Texas cities used the SMD system. Most major cities have been forced to change to SMD for at least some of their city council seats.

In cities that have changed from at-large to SMD systems, the number of minority candidates elected to the city council has increased substantially. There is some evidence that SMD council members approach their role differently than at-large council members do. A study of council members in Houston, Dallas, San Antonio, and Fort Worth found that council members from SMDs showed greater concern for neighborhood issues, engaged in vote trading, increased their contacts with constituents in their districts regarding service requests, and became more involved in administrative affairs of the city.[17]

Although SMD council members might view their job as representing their districts first and the city as a whole second, there is no evidence that the distribution of services changes dramatically. District representation may be primarily symbolic. Symbolism is not insignificant, though, because support for local governments can be increased as minority groups feel they are represented on city councils and feel comfortable contacting their council member with problems.

POLITICAL THINKING   Making History

In 2009, the city of Houston made U.S. history when it elected the first openly gay mayor, Annise Danette Parker. Parker had run on a platform of fiscal conservatism, winning over the Republican electorate. Could an openly gay candidate in the state of Texas win the race for governor or a seat in the U.S. Senate? How are local campaigns and politics different from those at the state and national level? How do voter demands on local officials differ from their expectations for state or national representatives?

Election of Mayors

The voters of the entire city generally elect mayors at large. During most of the nineteenth century, this was the prevailing system. With the coming of the commission form of government, and later the council-manager form, mayors were often selected by the members of the council, from among the members of the council. In recent years, the trend nationwide and in Texas has been toward at-large election of mayors in council-manager cities. In Texas, most mayors are elected at large. The election of mayors by the voters of the city gives the mayor some independence from the council and therefore the opportunity to function as the leader of the council.

Nonpartisan Elections

Nationwide, about 70 percent of city council members are elected in **nonpartisan elections.**[18] In Texas, all city elections are technically nonpartisan. Officially, in a nonpartisan election no party labels appear on the ballot, so voters cannot determine party affiliation by looking at the ballot. This differs from the general election ballot used in November.

    Nonpartisan elections were a feature of the reform movement in the early part of the twentieth century and were aimed at undercutting the power of partisan big-city political machines. Reformers said there is no Democratic or Republican way to pave streets or provide police and fire protection, so partisanship should not be a factor in city decisions.

    Texas cities adopted the nonpartisan system largely because the state was a one-party Democratic state for over a hundred years, and partisanship, even in state elections, was not a factor as long as you ran as a Democrat. It was only natural that city elections used nonpartisan ballots. The Texas Election Code allows for partisan city elections in home-rule cities. To date, no city has officially used partisan elections.[19]

    The use of a nonpartisan ballot does not eliminate partisanship from local politics. Partisanship simply takes new forms, and new labels are applied. For decades in several Texas cities, "nonpartisan organizations" successfully ran slates of candidates and dominated city politics. Most noted among these organizations were the Citizens Charter Association in Dallas, the Good Government League in San Antonio, and the Business and Professional Association in Wichita Falls and Abilene.[20] The influence of these groups has declined, but slate making is not unknown today in Texas city politics. Partisanship has been a factor in city elections recently in San Antonio, Houston, and Dallas, especially in mayoral races.

nonpartisan elections
ballot form in which voters are unable to determine the party of candidates by looking at the ballot

Voter Turnout in City Elections

Nationwide, voter turnout in city elections is quite low—often lower than in state elections. Turnout rates as low as 4 percent are not uncommon in Texas cities, and seldom do they exceed 25 percent. Off-year elections, a lack of contested races, and low levels of voter interest all contribute to low turnout in city elections.

    State law provides two dates during the year when Texas cities may hold city council elections. Known as **off-year elections,** these elections are never held at the same time as state or national elections. The lack of contested races is so common in Texas that in 1996 a new state law went into effect that allows cities and school boards to dispense with elections if all seats are uncontested. The city or the school board declares the uncontested candidates elected. A standard joke is often told about a person sitting on a bench by city hall with a sign reading, "Will run for mayor for food."

off-year elections
local elections held at a different time of year from state and national elections

The third factor in low turnout is a lack of publicity and interest in city elections. The news media might cover races in the major cities, especially in years when the mayor's office is up for election, but coverage of suburban city elections in a major metropolitan area is given scant attention by the press. Also, the average citizen does not think local elections are important. The races for president, governor, and other state offices are viewed as more important. These races are also given more attention by the news media.

Participation is largely class-based: The higher socioeconomic groups vote at higher rates. Thus, lower overall voter turnout tends to benefit the high-income, nonminority areas of a city. These groups often dominate city elections and city politics. The use of single-member district systems might overcome the class bias in voting and increase the number of minority members on the council, but there is little evidence that this produces great changes in policy. Also, SMD elections often lead to council members being elected with very small numbers of votes. For example, in a city with a population of twenty-five thousand and six council seats elected from districts, it is quite common to have someone elected with a few hundred votes.

Low voter turnout can also heavily affect towns with a large percentage of students in the population. Students generally do not participate in local city elections, even though city governments have a big impact on the student population. For example, in Denton, the home of the University of North Texas, most students live off campus, and the city provides electrical, water, sewer, and other services for which fees are charged. These services affect off-campus students just as they do nonstudents. One consequence of students' not voting or participating in city government is that others make decisions that can have profound effects on the cost and the availability of housing.

One could argue that the fact that most citizens pay scant attention to elections may mean that people who live in cities are satisfied with the levels and kinds of services they are receiving. The main Texas cities have a reputation of being well run by professionals. This is in stark contrast to county government in the state, in which professionalism is often quite lacking. Patronage and politics more accurately describe what happens in county government.

Challenges to Cities: Revenues and Mandates

Local governments in Texas collect taxes from two primary sources—property tax and local sales tax. Almost all units of local government collect property tax. For school districts, the property tax is the largest source of revenue, exceeding state contributions. For so-called rich school districts, all of the cost of running local schools may come from the property tax, and it is a significant source of revenue for cities and counties. In addition, most cities, many counties, and all local transit authorities collect a local sales tax. In Texas, the local sales tax is fixed by state law at no more than 2 percent of the value of sales. Thus, in most urban areas in Texas, there is a 6.25 percent state sales tax, plus a 2.0 percent local tax, for a total of 8.25 percent sales tax.

There is effectively no state-level property tax in Texas. All but a small portion of property taxes goes to local governments. In recent years, property taxes have increased dramatically. In 2005, the most recent year for which data are available, a total of 3,748 local governments in Texas assessed a property tax. The total property tax levy was $30.9 billion, an increase of about 27 percent since 2000. Figure 26-7 shows this change. Texas local governments, especially school districts, have become more dependent upon the property tax. Texas ranks tenth in property tax revenue per $1,000 of personal income among the fifty states. As you can see in "How Texas Differs: Property Taxes," among the top twelve states,

HOW TEXAS DIFFERS POLITICAL THINKING THROUGH COMPARISONS

Property Taxes

The accompanying chart shows the property tax revenues per $1,000 of personal income for the twelve most populous states in 2002.

Q: How does the property tax in Texas compare with the other most populous states? Take a look at the states that have high property tax rates and those that have lower property tax rates. What might cause some to have higher rates than others?

A: Only New York, New Jersey, Michigan, and Illinois have higher property tax rates than Texas. States that have low or no income taxes may have higher property tax rates.

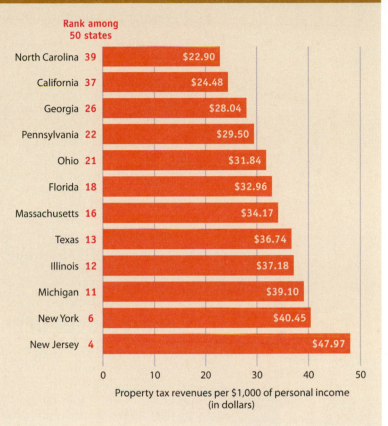

Rank among 50 states

State	Rank	Value
North Carolina	39	$22.90
California	37	$24.48
Georgia	26	$28.04
Pennsylvania	22	$29.50
Ohio	21	$31.84
Florida	18	$32.96
Massachusetts	16	$34.17
Texas	13	$36.74
Illinois	12	$37.18
Michigan	11	$39.10
New York	6	$40.45
New Jersey	4	$47.97

Property tax revenues per $1,000 of personal income (in dollars)

Source: Legislative Budget Board, "Fiscal Size-up 2009–2010," fig 60.

Texas has the second highest property tax per $1,000 of personal income. Only New Jersey is higher.

As taxes have climbed, local government must abide by an increasing number of mandates—laws passed by federal and state governments that apply to local governments. For example, the Texas Commission on Jail Standards inspects county jails to make sure the facilities and the personnel meet state laws. This state agency may require facilities to increase personnel or make other changes. On a federal level, the Clean Air Act forces city governments to comply with air quality standards. Yet municipalities cannot always control air quality in their jurisdiction. Although they can reduce pollution created by cars, buses, and other vehicles in their area, winds might blow air pollution from a power plant in the vicinity. Such considerations forced Dallas mayor Laura Miller to organize municipalities throughout the state to stop the building of over a dozen new coal-burning power plants in Texas. The efforts of municipalities and environmental groups eventually succeeded in reducing the number of new plants built.

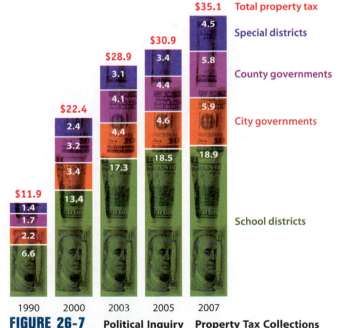

FIGURE 26-7 **Political Inquiry Property Tax Collections by Type of Local Governments in Texas (billions of dollars).** Which type of local governments have levied the highest hikes in property taxes? How can you explain this?

Source: Legislative Budget Board, "Fiscal Size-up" in 1990, 2000, 2003, 2005, 2010.

The problem, however, goes beyond the mandates themselves. The mandates dictated by the federal government as well as state governments are often **unfunded or underfunded mandates.** This means that they do not give local governments the money they need to abide by these laws, and hence local governments must come up with the funds themselves. In 1995, the U.S. Congress passed the Unfunded Mandates Reform Act. The act specified that Congress committees obtain an estimate of the costs imposed on lower governments by their legislation. If the amount exceeds $50 million per year, the information would have to be discussed by legislators before the bill could be passed into law. The act has not been effective in preventing the federal government from increasing the financial burden placed on state and local governments by federal laws. A similar law was passed by the Texas state legislature with similar results.

In addition, when city governments fail to comply with state and federal mandates such as the Clean Air Act or No Child Left Behind, they may face penalties or loss of funds. With property taxes already high, with a traditionalistic-individualistic political culture opposed to high taxes, and with taxation limitations imposed on local governments by the state legislature, local governments face challenges finding the revenue necessary to meet federal and state mandates.

County Governments

The oldest type of local government in the United States is **county government,** an adaptation of the British county unit of government that was transported to this country. County governments exist in all states except Connecticut, which abolished them in 1963, and Rhode Island (which never needed them). Louisiana calls them "parishes," from the French influence, and Alaska calls them "boroughs." The number of counties varies greatly among the states. Alaska, Delaware, and Hawaii each have three county governments, and Texas has 254.[21]

County governments were originally intended to be a subdivision, or arm, of state government to perform state functions at the local level. For example, counties in Texas still serve as voter registrar, a state function; voters register to vote with the local county government. Other services of counties include recording vital statistics, operating state courts and jails, administering elections, and maintaining roads and bridges. In issuing marriage licenses, birth certificates, and automobile registrations, and in operating state courts, county governments are acting as an arm of state government. Texas counties can also assist in the creation of rural fire protection districts.

Besides performing state functions, county governments provide local services—in some states they provide many local services. In Texas, however, counties provide very limited local services. All Texas counties provide road construction and repair and police protection through the sheriff's department. Some urban county governments operate hospitals or health units, libraries, and parks.

The distinguishing feature of county government is population. Of the 3,043 counties in the United States, most are rural with small populations. About 700 counties have populations of less than 10,000, and fewer than 200 have populations of over 250,000. In Texas, 56 percent of the population lives in the ten largest urban counties (see Table 26-1). Texas also has the distinction of having the smallest county in the United States. Loving County had a population of 70 in 2000, an increase from 18 in 1980 because of the oil boom.[22]

TABLE 26-1 | The Ten Largest Counties in Texas in 1990 and 2000

County and Major City	POPULATION	
	1990	**2000**
Harris (Houston)	2,925,965	3,400,578
Dallas (Dallas)	2,049,666	2,218,899
Bexar (San Antonio)	1,232,098	1,392,931
Tarrant (Fort Worth)	1,208,986	1,446,219
El Paso (El Paso)	614,927	679,622
Travis (Austin)	599,357	812,280
Hidalgo (McAllen)	398,648	569,463
Fort Bend (Richmond)	255,412	354,452
Denton (Denton)	212,792	432,976
Collin (Plano)	234,172	491,675
Total	**9,732,023**	**11,799,095**
Total state population	17,655,650	20,892,627
Percentage of population in the ten largest counties	55%	56%

Source: Texas State Data Center, University of Texas at San Antonio, www.txsdc.utsa.edu.

The Structure of County Government

All Texas county governments have the same basic structure, regardless of the county's size. This structure, illustrated in Figure 26-8, mirrors the fragmented structure of state government. It can most accurately be described as weak or plural executive. Voters elect the heads of major departments. These provisions appeared in the constitution of 1876. The writers of this document distrusted appointive authority and trusted the electorate to choose administrators.[23]

The governing body of the county is the **county commissioner's court,** which is not really a court but a legislative body composed of the constitutional county judge and four county commissioners. The county judge is elected at large, and each commissioner is elected from a single-member district called a *commissioner precinct*. Like most other state officeholders, these officials are elected for four-year terms in partisan elections. Their duties include passing local ordinances, approving budgets and new programs, and overseeing county government.

The **constitutional county judge** presides as the chair of the commissioner's court, participates as a full member in deliberations, and has a vote on all matters. The constitution assigns judicial duties to this office, but the occupant does not have to be a licensed attorney; the constitution states that she or he must be "well informed in the law." In seventy-two urban counties, where the state legislature has created county courts of law, the constitutional county judge performs very limited judicial functions. The judicial functions of county commissioner's courts are transferred to the county courts of law, and the constitutional county judge acts as the primary administrative officer of the county.

Like other legislative districts, commissioner precincts eventually became malapportioned. In 1968, the U.S. Supreme Court ruled that the one-person-one-vote rule applied to these election districts. The commissioner's court in Midland County claimed it was a court and not a legislative body, and therefore the one-person-one-vote rule did not apply. In *Avery v. Midland County,* the U.S. Supreme Court disagreed and ruled that it was a legislative body and not a court, and that election districts had to be equally apportioned.

county commissioner's court
legislative body made up of five elected officials that governs Texas counties

constitutional county judge
chief administrative officer of the county commissioner's court; may also have judicial duties in rural counties

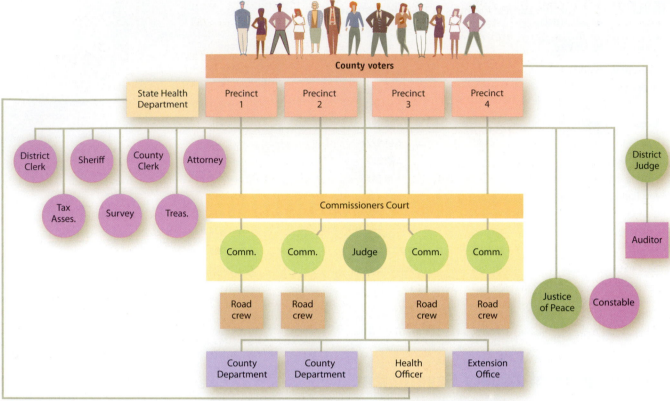

FIGURE 26-8 **Structure of County Government in Texas** Which officials do county voters elect?

Source: John A. Gilmartin and Joe M. Rothe, *County Government in Texas,* Issue 2, V. G. Young Institute of County Government, Texas Agricultural Extension Service, Texas A&M University.

county sheriff

the elected head law enforcement officer for a county who in smaller counties may act as the tax assessor collector

constables

elected county law enforcement and court officers

county and district attorneys

elected chief prosecuting attorneys for criminal cases

tax assessor collector

elected officer responsible for collecting revenue for the state and the county

The circled titles in Figure 26-8 indicate elected officials. Seven constitutionally prescribed officers are elected by the voters: sheriff, district attorney, county attorney, tax assessor collector, district clerk, county clerk, and county treasurer. These officials act as heads of departments of government. Some counties also have other minor elected officials, such as county surveyor and inspector of hides and wools.

The **county sheriff** is elected countywide for a four-year term and serves as the law enforcement officer for the county. Sheriffs can appoint deputy sheriffs. In rural counties, the sheriff may be the primary law enforcement officer. In urban counties, city police departments carry out most of these duties, and the sheriff's primary duty may be to operate the county jail. In the smaller counties (fewer than eighteen hundred residents), state law allows the sheriff to act as the tax assessor collector.[24] Some have suggested that combining sheriff and tax collector is a frightening leftover from Anglo-Saxon law, inspiring visions of Sherwood Forest, the Sheriff of Nottingham, and Robin Hood.

The voters also elect **constables,** who serve as law enforcement officers. Their primary function is to serve as court officers for the justice of the peace courts, delivering subpoenas and other court orders. Constables may also provide police protection in the precinct they serve.

The **county and district attorneys** are the chief prosecuting attorneys for criminal cases in the county. Not all counties have county attorneys. In those that have one, this office usually prosecutes the less serious criminal offenses before county courts, and the district attorney prosecutes major crimes before the district courts.

The **tax assessor collector** is responsible for collecting revenue for the state and the county. Before 1978, this office also assessed the value of all property in the county for property tax collection purposes. In 1978, these functions were transferred to a county-wide assessment district. There are 180 of these tax assessment districts in the state, and they are governed by a board elected by the governing bodies of all governments in the jurisdiction—counties, cities, school districts, and special districts. Though the tax assessor collector still has the title *assessor*, few occupants serve in that capacity today. Most still collect county property taxes, sell state vehicle licenses and permits, and serve as voter registrars. The voter registration function is a carryover from the days of the poll tax.[25]

The **county clerk** is the chief record keeper for the county and keeps track of all property records and issues marriage licenses, birth certificates, and other county records. Although normally the function of voter registration rests with the tax assessor collector, in some counties this function has been transferred to the county clerk, who in all counties is responsible for conducting elections. The **district clerk** is primarily a court official who maintains court records for county and district courts. The clerk schedules cases in these courts and maintains records. The **county treasurer** is responsible for receiving, maintaining, and disbursing county funds.

The **district judge** or judges in the county appoint the county auditor. The county auditor's responsibility is to oversee the collection and disbursement of county funds. The auditor reports to the district judge or judges. Not all counties have auditors. Counties with populations under ten thousand are not required to have auditors. In larger counties (populations above two-hundred and fifty thousand), the auditor acts as a budget officer unless the commissioner's court appoints its own budget officer.[26]

county clerk
elected chief record keeper for the county

district clerk
elected official who maintains county and district court records

county treasurer
elected official who manages county funds

district judge
elected official who appoints the county auditor

Challenges to Counties: Weak Authority and Limited Financial Resources

The major issues county governments face are inherent weaknesses in the plural executive form of government and lack of power to confront many problems in urban areas.

The plural executive structure of county government in Texas is a product of the nineteenth century and the general distrust of centralized executive authority. As with the plural executive structure in state government, it lacks centralized authority, and the elected officials can, and often do, act quite independently of one another. Although the county commissioner's court does exercise some control over these department heads, it is primarily limited to budgetary matters. After a budget is approved, elected officials can make many independent decisions.

Elected officials also hire their own staff. After each election, personnel at the county courthouse can change dramatically. For example, new sheriffs hire their own deputy sheriffs. The patronage ("spoils") system in some courthouses results in a less professional staff.

Elections are imperfect instruments for determining the qualifications of candidates, and voters do not always select the most competent person to administer departments. Appointment of department heads is more likely to result in the selection of competent persons. A lack of professionalism and competence is a frequently noted problem with county officials in some counties.

County government was designed to meet the needs of and provide services to a rural population, and in rural areas of the state it still functions adequately. In large urban counties, however, this form of government has many weaknesses. The first of these weaknesses is the inability to provide urban-type services. Dense urban populations demand and need services that are unnecessary in rural areas. Usually, county governments are powerless under state law to provide even the most basic services common to city governments, such as water and sewer services.

Citizens living on the fringes of cities are forced to provide these services themselves or to form other governments, such as a water district, to provide these services. In recent years, garbage (solid waste) collection and disposal have become a problem in the urban fringe areas. Many citizens must contract with private collectors for this service. Some counties help residents by providing collection centers, often operated by private contractors. In the area of fire protection, counties often help rural residents to establish volunteer fire departments. However, counties are not permitted to operate fire departments. Each rural fire department goes its own way, and there is often a lack of coordination between departments. Training and equipment are generally below the standards of full-time city fire departments. Counties sometimes contract with city governments in the county to provide fire protection for the county, although this practice has declined in recent years.

County governments also lack general ordinance authority. City governments in Texas may pass any ordinance not prohibited by state law, but county governments must seek legislative approval to pass specific ordinances. For example, county governments may not pass ordinances on land use (zoning) or building codes that regulate construction standards. A citizen buying a home in a rural area is largely dependent upon the integrity of the builder.

Finally, a problem for county governments related to their lack of power is the inequity of financial resources and expenditures. A few counties have a sales tax, but most rely almost exclusively on the property tax. Most of this tax is paid by citizens living inside cities and not in the unincorporated, rural areas of the county. Thus, most (89 percent) of the cost of county government is paid for by city residents paying county taxes. Although county residents pay little of the cost to operate county governments, they receive many services from county governments (such as road construction and repair, police protection) that are not provided to city residents by the county. City residents receive these services from their city and pay city taxes. City residents are paying twice for services they receive only once. This financial inequity goes unnoticed by most citizens.

Suggested Reforms of County Government

Since the 1930s, there have been suggestions to reform county government in Texas. The rhetoric often called for county government to be "brought into the twentieth century." In Texas, apparently all such reforms skipped the twentieth century and have to wait for the twenty-first century. While other states have modernized county governments, Texas has steadfastly refused all efforts at change. One suggestion that has been a frequent agenda item over the past seventy years is to allow for county home rule, which would allow the voters in each county to adopt a local option charter.[27] Voters could then approve any form of government not prohibited by state law; no county would be forced to change its form of government. This might result in the adoption of a strong executive form of government similar to the strong mayor or council-manager forms popular with Texas cities. Even though this suggestion seems quite reasonable, it has been strongly opposed by the many elected county officials in Texas who see this reform as a threat to their jobs.

The Texas Association of Counties (TAC) is an umbrella organization that represents elected county officials—sheriffs, tax collectors, treasurers, judges, commissioners, and so on. This politically powerful group has many supporters throughout the state and has opposed granting county governments home rule. One group within the TAC, the Conference of Urban Counties (CUC), has shown mild support for home rule. The CUC represents thirty metropolitan county governments in Texas where home rule would have the greatest impact. The CUC is not pushing home-rule issues and is more concerned with representing the unique interests of urban counties.

County officials have traditionally resisted changes in their powers to deal with urban problems. They have a provincial attitude toward providing service, and their view of county government does not extend much beyond that of a nineteenth-century official. This means that urban problems that are outside cities are often neglected. Even simple things such as the safety of home construction and septic systems are neglected. This lack of attention can have an effect on citizens' life and health.

County officials often will not even consider providing services that might enhance community amenities. For example, the city council in College Station once proposed that the city libraries be combined and made into a county library operated by Brazos County. A county commissioner was quoted as saying, "The last thing in the world we need is a bigger library. I was down at the Bryan Library once and they already got more books than anyone can read and every year they ask the county for more money to buy more books." The city council cooled on the idea of a county-run library with this provincial attitude among county officials.

At one time, county government was given the responsibility for inspecting septic systems in rural areas. One county never passed an ordinance or put in place an inspection system. When asked by a citizen why they did not have an ordinance and inspections, their reply was, "We just expect you to do it right." The state has since given this authority to the state health department, and septic installers must be licensed.

County government is often more concerned with problems of rural residents than with those living in cities. When the Brazos animal shelter confiscated a number of horses that it felt were malnourished and being mistreated, the county commissioner's court, at the request of rural residents, prevented the animal shelter from doing this in the future. They turned this function over to the sheriff, who is oriented toward policing in rural areas.

Improving the professionalism of county staff might prove difficult because each elected county official can hire his or her own people. Some county officials in some counties place great emphasis on professionalism. Other officials reward faithful campaign workers with appointments. In rural counties, these jobs are often well paid and much sought after by supporters.

Special District Governments

Another form of local government that provides services to local residents is known as special district government. Special districts have been referred to as *shadow governments* because they operate out of the view of most citizens. These governments are created for many reasons and perform many functions. Some districts are single function (such as fire) and others are multipurpose (such as water, sewer, street repair). Some special districts (such as metropolitan transit districts) cover several counties, and others (such as the municipal utility districts) are very small, covering only a few acres.

The primary reason special districts are created is to provide services when no other unit of government exists to provide that service. Sometimes the need extends beyond the geographical boundaries of existing units of government. Mass transportation is an example: Dallas/Fort Worth, Houston, San Antonio, Austin, El Paso, and other metropolitan areas have created transit districts that serve several counties. Sometimes the service involves natural boundaries that extend over county lines. Soil and water conservation and flood control are examples of this. In still other cases, the need for a service may be confined to a single county, but no government unit exists to provide the service. An excellent example of this is municipal utility districts (MUDs), which are multifunction districts generally created outside cities to provide water, sewage treatment,

Liberty Hill firefighters battle a blaze at a local beauty salon. They were part of Williamson County Emergency Service District #4, a special district government.

and other services. In Texas, these MUDs are created because county governments cannot provide these services. Finally, some districts are created for political reasons, when no existing unit of government wants to solve the service problem because of potential political conflicts. The creation of another unit of government to deal with a hot political issue is preferable. The Gulf Coast Waste Disposal Authority, created to clean up water pollution in the Houston area, is an example of this.

Special districts are often an efficient and expedient way to solve a problem, but they can also generate problems. One problem citizens face is keeping track of the many special districts that provide services to them. For example, a MUD, a soil and water conservation district, a flood control district, a fire protection district, a metropolitan transit authority, a hospital district, and a waste disposal district can govern a citizen living in the Houston suburbs. Most citizens have trouble distinguishing among a school district, a county, and a city. Dealing with seven or more units of government is even more complicated.

The governing boards of special districts in Texas are selected in two ways. Multicounty special districts (such as DART in Dallas and METRO in Houston) are governed by boards appointed by the governmental units (cities, counties) covered by the district. Single-county special districts (such as MUDs and flood control districts) usually have a board of directors elected by the voters.

Many special districts have taxation authority and can raise local property taxes. The remoteness of these districts from the electorate, their number, and their potential impact on the lives of citizens raise questions of democratic control.[28]

County jails are facing an overcrowding crisis. Many blame judges who are determined to "get tough on crime." One study found that the number of people incarcerated prior to conviction has increased substantially in the past decade—suggesting that judges are setting bail too high. Others argue that the jails are being filled up with nonviolent drug offenders who should be in treatment programs rather than behind bars.

The average citizen cannot be expected to know about, understand, and keep track of the decisions made by these remote governments. The alternatives are to consolidate governments, expand cities through the annexation of land, or expand the power of county governments. None of these alternatives is generally acceptable. Citizens demand and expect local governments to be decentralized. This is true even if they have only limited ability to watch and control the actions of local government and the government is ineffective. Big government is something most Texans want to avoid.

School Districts

A type of special district government that citizens generally watch and control very closely is the school district. One controversy that has gained a great deal of attention, for example, is the issue of whether to teach alternatives to the theory of evolution in the public schools; Because school districts play such an important role in the lives of all citizens, we distinguish them from other special districts for discussion.

Texas experienced a slight decline in number of school districts in the 1990s and the first decade of the twenty-first century: from 1,100 in 1992 to 1,062 in 2007.[29] This decline is the result of consolidation, which has been driven by several factors. First, there have been demands for improved curriculum, especially in science and math, and many small rural school districts were unable to provide the desired range and diversity of curriculum. Second, there has been increased state financial aid to school districts that consolidate. Third, road conditions have continued to improve. For example, Texas developed the farm-to-market road system in the 1950s. This system, coupled with improved all-weather county roads, made it possible to bus students to urban schools, a trend that continues.

In the rural areas of Texas, there are still many school districts with a small student body that could consolidate with neighboring districts. Sometimes resistance to consolidation is driven by considerations for the school football program and the realization that closing the school will lead to the death of the town. Often the school is the only glue that holds a community together. Football and community pride are powerful forces, even if the football team has only six players.

The future will see few additional consolidations. The demand today is not for consolidation but for decentralization with the "open-enrollment charter school." In 1995, the legislature authorized the creation of "up to 20 charters for open-enrollment charter schools. These schools can be operated in school districts or non-school district facilities, by public or private higher education institutions, non-profit organizations or governmental entities."[30] Additional charter schools were authorized in the 1997 and 1999 sessions of the legislature. In 1998–1999, there were 89 charter schools operating in the state, and by 2010–2011, the number had increased to about 500. The exact implication of these charter schools is not known. Some preliminary reports and data are available from the Texas Education Agency, but whether these schools will produce substantial improvements in student achievement is unclear.[31] Thirty-two other states have some version of home-rule or charter schools. What is clear from the passage of these laws is that many citizens want to decentralize control over local schools. Further consolidation seems unlikely.

All but one of the 1,089 school districts in Texas are called **independent school districts,** meaning that they are independent of any other unit of government. In seventeen states, 1,400 school systems are attached to, or dependent upon, another unit of government, most commonly a city or a county.[32] Most are located in the East and the Midwest, with few in the West and the South. In Texas, the Stafford School District in the Houston suburbs is the only school district attached to a city government. Reformers advocated making the school district independent of city government. Such independence was supposed to isolate the schools from evil political influences of city government.

A seven-member elected school board governs most independent school districts in Texas. School board elections are often held in April or May, at the same time as city elections. Some school boards are elected from single-member districts; most are at large, and all are chosen in nonpartisan ballot elections.

Challenges to School Districts: Financing, Quality, and Curriculum

Although the creation of independent school districts may have reduced the influence of city politics, school district elections are still quite political. Over the past several decades, many issues have dominated school politics, and we examine those of finance, quality, and certain areas of curriculum.

School Finance

The first and perhaps most difficult issue for school districts to resolve is school finance. The state of Texas pays for part of the cost of education. Over the past twenty years, the state's share of the cost of education has declined, and local school districts have been forced to pick up a larger part of the cost. Today, the state pays about 38 percent of the cost of education, and local districts provide the remainder.[33] Because the only source of local financial support is the property tax, some school districts have been better able than others to absorb the higher local share. Some school districts have a high per-pupil property tax base (so-called rich districts), and others have a low per-pupil property tax base (so-called poor districts). Though the state does show preference to poor districts by providing increased funding, this support is still inadequate, and great disparities exist in the amount of money available to school districts on a per-pupil basis.

These inequities became a statewide issue in 1968 when parents in the Edgewood School District in San Antonio filed a lawsuit challenging the financing of schools in Texas (*Rodriguez v. San Antonio Independent School District*). The U.S. Supreme Court found the system of school financing to be unfair but said that

independent school districts

school districts that are not attached to any other unit of government and operate schools in Texas it was a state problem and that its resolution rested with the state. Because of this case, the state did increase aid to poor school districts. However, severe inequities continued. In 1984, another lawsuit brought education finance to the forefront in Texas (*Edgewood v. Kirby*). This case was filed in state district court, and because of the efforts of the Mexican American Legal Defense and Education Fund and the Equity Center in Austin, the Texas Supreme Court in 1989 ruled the system of school finance in the state unconstitutional.

In an attempt to correct these inequities, the state legislature in 1991 consolidated property taxes within 188 units called *county education districts.* These districts collected property taxes to be used for school operations and distributed them to the school districts in their jurisdiction on a per-student basis. This system became known as the **"Robin Hood plan."** It was challenged in court by some rich districts, and the courts ruled that the plan violated the Texas Constitution. The state legislature proposed a constitutional amendment to make the system legal. In May 1993, the voters rejected this amendment by a large margin (63 percent against).[34]

The rejection of this issue had political implications in the 1994 governor's race. According to the *Dallas Morning News,* the Republican National Committee spent $400,000 to help defeat this amendment and to promote negative views about the governor, Ann Richards. The ads tied Richards to the amendment.[35] Richards was defeated by George W. Bush in 1994, although she may have lost even without the ads.

Following the defeat of this amendment, the legislature passed a new law that revised the Robin Hood plan by giving several options to rich districts. Under this plan, a school district's property tax wealth is capped at $305,000 per pupil. At that point, a district has several choices. It may send its excess wealth to the state, which will send the money to poor districts. It can also combine its wealth with a specific district. Most have sent the money to the state. After a district reaches the $305,000 per-pupil cap, it receives very little state money, although it still receives some federal funds. Ninety percent of the school districts in Texas are poor districts. Only 10 percent must give money to the state.

The 2003 session of the legislature again faced the problem of school finances. A new issue that has grown out of the present system is that school district taxes are capped by state law at no more than $1.50 per $100 of valuation for operations. Many districts reached the $1.50 limit and still did not have enough money to operate. In 2004, Governor Perry, intent on solving this crisis, called a special session of the legislature and proposed funding schools through gambling revenues. Public attention immediately focused on the pro-gambling lobby, which had contributed substantial sums to the campaigns of the governor and other top legislators. Many Republicans opposed gambling on moral grounds, and the 2004 legislative session failed to find a solution. The crisis was exacerbated when the so-called rich districts filed a lawsuit to throw out the Robin Hood plan in *Neeley v. West-Orange-Cove Consolidated Independent School District.* In September 2004, the district court ruled the current system unconstitutional on a number of grounds, including that school property taxes were so high that they constituted a virtual state income tax, which is forbidden by state law. Yet the 2005 legislative session was again unable to come to an agreement. In November 2005, the Texas Supreme Court upheld the district court's decision regarding the taxation and ordered the legislature to redo school finance before September 2006.

Under pressure from a decision by the Texas Supreme Court to close the schools in the fall of 2006, the legislature met in a special session to consider the changes in school finance. The legislature eventually produced a plan that

"Robin Hood plan"
a nickname for the provision in the education statutes that consolidated property taxes so that they are distributed among rich and poor districts; revised later to require rich districts with a property tax base per pupil in excess of $305,000 to share their wealth with other school districts

DEBATING THE ISSUES POLITICAL THINKING IN ACTION

Should an Alternative to Evolution Be Taught in Public Schools?

In 2005, President George W. Bush announced his belief that intelligent design (ID) should be taught as another point of view along with evolution in biology classes. Texas governor Rick Perry agreed. The Texas Board of Education is responsible for approving textbooks and supplemental materials. Several members of the board are creationists, and polls have shown that as many as two-thirds of Texans support teaching ID. Yet in 2007, 2009, and 2011, the board has overwhelmingly rejected the proposal to introduce intelligent design into the science curriculum.

YES The theory of intelligent design (ID) proposes that the earth and the universe can best be explained by proposing an intelligent cause instead of natural selection. Proponents claim that their theories are based on the principles of modern science. The movement challenges explanations of phenomena like the origins of life that are based on the theory of natural selection advanced by Darwin.

ID is a scientific theory with a following in many communities in the United States and so should be taught in science classes when topics such as the origins of life on earth and the human species are discussed. There are biological phenomena that cannot be explained by undirected forces, and students should be made aware of these deficiencies in the currently accepted theories. Moreover, teachers should be allowed the intellectual freedom to introduce ID as an alternative to widely accepted modern scientific theories, and students should be allowed to examine the evidence for both theories and decide for themselves which one has more credibility.

NO ID is an outgrowth of religious teachings. Since the dawn of modern science, religious groups have persecuted scientists and attempted to stifle new discoveries. Yet scientific investigation continued and scientific breakthroughs have made possible the wonders of our modern world: the fight against disease, the ability to communicate with people across the world, and an understanding of life forms in environments that we have just started to explore.

The U.S. Constitution guarantees the separation of church and state. As a result, it would be unconstitutional for public schools to force religious observance or teachings on their students. ID is a pseudoscience, nothing more than creationism in new clothing. Religion is a belief system, not a field of scientific exploration. It does not enjoy support or consensus within the scientific community and hence should not be taught in the classroom. Parents who want their children to learn about ID can teach it in their homes or through religious organizations. Today, the study of science and technology is critical to our country's economic and military success. These subjects are challenging, and national test scores in math and science are falling. Taking time away from the study of biology, chemistry, or physics would amount to throwing obstacles in the path of our nation's future achievements.

Q: What are the arguments in favor of introducing an alternative to evolution in public schools? Why do you think the Texas Board of Education rejected this idea?

provides some modest reduction of property tax for homeowners, additional property tax for businesses, a tax increase of a dollar per pack on cigarettes, and an increase in the franchise tax paid by businesses. This act solved the school finance issue temporarily. It cut the revenue taken from wealthier districts by almost half.[36] Some estimates, however, say that the state will face funding shortfalls of several million dollars over the next few years. In the meantime, wealthier districts are once again unhappy about the flow of funds out of their jurisdictions.

Quality of Education

A second issue for school districts is the quality of education given to students. In the early 1980s, Governor Mark White, a Democrat, raised the profile of this issue. Working with Lt. Governor Hobby and House Speaker Gib Lewis, White appointed a select committee on public education. Texas billionaire Ross Perot was appointed chair of this committee. The recommendations of this committee led to the passage of House Bill 72, which contained two very controversial provisions. Although it provided funding for a teacher pay raise, it also required the state's teachers to pass a test to prove their competency. There was great resistance to this test by the teachers, although it was apparently a rather simple test designed to weed out the completely unqualified. Some referred to the test as a literacy test. Despite the easiness of the test, many teachers resented taking it and took it as a personal affront. Many blame this test and the teachers' reactions to it for Mark White's loss to Republican Bill Clements in the 1986 governor's race.

The second controversial provision in House Bill 72 was the no-pass, no-play provision. This new rule prohibited students from participating in extracurricular activities if they were not passing all their courses. In a state where Friday night football is an institution and in many small towns the premier social event, preventing students from participating because they failed a course was viewed as not only un-Texan but also perhaps a little "communistic." Students were also prohibited from participating in band, tennis, soccer, swimming, and cheerleading, but no one really much cared beyond football (although some communities cared about baseball). The no-pass, no-play rule also contributed to Mark White's defeat in 1986. The effects of no-pass, no-play and teacher literacy tests were probably more symbolic than real.

The first school accountability program was set up under Democratic governor Ann Richards. When Republican George W. Bush was elected governor in 1994, many feared he would abolish this program. Instead, he championed school accountability. During his term, the first statewide achievement testing, Texas Assessment of Academic Skills (TAAS), for grades three through twelve was established. The tests were used to rank schools and hold them accountable for student progress. If schools scored high on these tests, they would receive financial rewards. If they scored too low, they could be subject to public hearings and risked being taken over by the state government. A study of test scores on the National Assessment of Educational Progress (NAEP) found that the quality of education improved measurably following the implementation of this new testing system. Detractors, however, argued that the study failed to look at important statistics that showed that the new system penalized low-income and minority students. In 2003, TAAS was replaced by Texas Assessment of Knowledge and Skills (TAKS), a new assessment system. Another way of determining progress is to examine completion rates, as considered in Figure 26-9.

Sex Education, Intelligent Design, and Bilingual Education

In school board elections in Texas and much of the nation, three curriculum issues have caused much controversy: sex education, intelligent design (ID), and bilingual education. Sex education (see Chapter 25) and ID are issues driven by members of the Christian Right, or Social Conservatives, who have a comfortable majority on the state board of education and are attempting to elect local school board members. Their aim is to limit sex education to abstinence-based programs and to require the teaching of ID as an alternative to evolution or along with evolution. The extent to which these groups have managed to control school boards is unknown, and the issues surrounding this are not likely to be resolved anytime soon. Members of the Christian Right have had an impact on choosing the state school board, which is elected by districts in the state. The legislature has reduced some authority of this board in the past ten years, and more restrictions are possible in future sessions, especially in the area of textbook content.

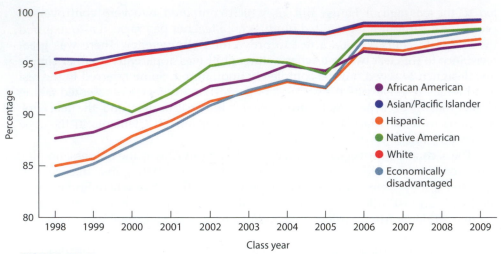

FIGURE 26-9 **Measuring Progress in Education** Test scores are just one of many indicators that measure the performance of public education in Texas. In addition to NAEP and TAKS scores, the Texas Education Agency tracks measures such as enrollment trends, school and class size, and completion, graduation, and drop-out rates. This graph provides completion rates for students from seventh to twelfth grade. Completion rate consists of the percentage of students who graduated, received General Educational (GED) certificates, or continued high school. How have completion rates changed over time? What does this say about the performance of public schools? What factors might explain this trend?

Source: Secondary School Completion and Dropouts in Texas Public Schools, 2008–2009, Texas Education Agency, p. 50, table 14, www.tea.state.tx.us/index4.aspx?id=4080#reports.

Bilingual education is a controversy dating to the early twentieth century, when Germans and Czechs in Texas wanted to teach their native languages in the schools. Following World War I, anti-German sentiment in the state killed those efforts, and in the 1920s the legislature prohibited the teaching of languages (other than English). There is an old story in the lore of Texas politics that claims when Governor Ma Ferguson signed the bill prohibiting the teaching of children in any language other than English, she reportedly said, "If English was good enough for Jesus Christ, it's good enough for the school children of Texas."

Currently, the bilingual issue revolves around teaching in Spanish and English to Latino children in the elementary schools. Many Anglo Texans object to using tax money for bilingual education. Some take the inconsistent position that everyone should speak English, but no tax money should be spent to ensure that they can. Governors Bush and Perry both helped soften the resistance to these education programs and reached out to Latino voters in the state.

Summary

Self-Test www.mhhe.com/ pattersontadtx11e

Although local governments do not generate the same degree of interest that national and state governments do, they have an extremely important impact on the daily lives of citizens. Without the services provided by local governments, modern urban life would not be possible.

In Texas, city governments are the principal providers of local services. Many federal and state mandates are implemented at the local level. The increasing number of unfunded mandates and the growing population and economy are new challenges for these governments.

The form of government used in most major cities is council-manager, a system that has brought a degree of professionalism to city government that is often lacking in counties and in some other units of local government. In many respects, the contrast between county and city government is remarkable. County governments have resisted change and seem content to operate under a form of government designed by and for an earlier, agrarian society. Given the political culture of Texas, it is a paradox that council-manager city government and plural executive county government exist in the same state. Economy, efficiency, and professionalism are not values supported by the traditionalistic political culture of the state, yet they are widely practiced in the council-manager form of government. The needs of an economically developing community have eclipsed the push of political culture toward weaker government, at least at the lower local level. Local governments will need to continue to find ways to increase efficiency in order to provide more, and improved, services to Texas's fast-growing population.

CHAPTER 26

Study Corner

Key Terms

at-large election system (p. 651)
city manager (p. 650)
constables (p. 658)
constitutional county judge (p. 657)
council-manager form of government (p. 649)
county and district attorneys (p. 658)
county clerk (p. 659)
county commissioner's court (p. 657)
county government (p. 656)
county sheriff (p. 658)
county treasurer (p. 659)
cumulative voting (p. 651)
district clerk (p. 659)
district judge (p. 659)
extra territorial jurisdiction (ETJ) (p. 646)
general-law city (p. 645)

general-purpose government (p. 644)
home-rule city (p. 645)
implicit or explicit prohibition on city ordinance power (p. 645)
incorporation (p. 645)
independent school districts (p. 664)
limited-purpose government (p. 644)
nonpartisan elections (p. 653)
off-year elections (p. 653)
preferential voting (p. 652)
"Robin Hood plan" (p. 665)
single-member district (p. 651)
tax assessor collector (p. 658)
unfunded or underfunded mandates (p. 656)

Self-Test: Multiple Choice

1. Most municipalities in the state of Texas with populations over five thousand are
   a. home-rule cities.
   b. general-law cities.
   c. weak mayor–council governments.
   d. strong mayor–council governments.

2. What is extraterritorial jurisdiction?
   a. the process of creating a city
   b. a form of special districts that provide services to residents of urban counties
   c. an extension of city authority to areas adjacent to city limits
   d. the legislative powers of a district judge

3. Which of the following describes the characteristics of a strong mayor in Texas?
   a. The number of terms the mayor may serve is limited.
   b. The mayor has little or no veto authority.
   c. The mayor has limited control over budget formation.
   d. The mayor shares power with other elected officials and with the city council.

4. Which of the following voting systems is most common in city council elections in Texas?
   a. single-member districts
   b. at-large by place
   c. cumulative voting
   d. preferential voting

5. Which of the following is an example of an underfunded or unfunded mandate?
   a. the incorporation of Impact, Texas
   b. the Texas Board of Education
   c. multicounty special districts like DART
   d. the Clean Air Act

6. What was the result of *Rodriguez v. San Antonio School District*?
   a. The state of Texas provided extra funds to poor school districts.
   b. The legislature passed the "Robin Hood plan."
   c. Property taxes increased dramatically.
   d. Taxes on businesses and cigarette sales increased.

7. In Texas county governments often are providers of urban-oriented services such as water supply, sewage disposal, planning and zoning, airports, building codes and enforcement, mass transit systems, and fire protection. (T/F)

8. Home-rule cities are inhabited by citizens who may adopt any form of government they want and pass any ordinance not prohibited by state law, as long as the city has a population of at least ten thousand. (T/F)

9. For cities with a population exceeding two-hundred and fifty thousand, the extraterritorial jurisdiction extends five miles beyond the limits of those cities. (T/F)

10. The city of Galveston popularized the commission form of government in the early 1900s. (T/F)

Critical Thinking

What aspects of local government are strongly influenced by the traditionalistic/individualistic political culture?

Suggested Readings

Blodgett, Terrell. *Texas Home Rule Charters*. Austin: Texas Municipal League, 1994.

Frank, Nancy. *Charter Schools: Experiments in Reform, an Update*. Austin: Texas Legislative Budget Board, Public Education Team, 1995.

Halter, Gary M., and Gerald L. Dauthery. "The County Commissioners Court in Texas." In *Governing Texas: Documents and Readings*, 3d ed., ed. Fred Gantt Jr. et al. New York: Thomas Y. Crowell, 1974.

Johnson, David R., John A. Booth, and Richard J. Harris. *The Politics of San Antonio: Community Progress and Power*. Lincoln: University of Nebraska Press, 1983.

Lyndon B. Johnson School of Public Affairs. *Local Government Election Systems*, Policy Research Report No. 62. Austin: University of Texas Press, 1984.

Martin, David L. *Running City Hall: Municipal Administration in the United States*. Tuscaloosa: University of Alabama Press, 1990.

Pernod, Virginia. *Special District, Special Purposes: Fringe Governments and Urban Problems in the Houston Area*. College Station: Texas A&M University Press, 1984.

Rice, Bradley Robert. *Progressive Cities: The Commission Government Movement in America, 1901–1920*. Austin: University of Texas Press, 1977.

Smith, Richard A. "How Business Failed Dallas." In *Governing Texas: Documents and Readings*, 2d ed., ed. Fred Gantt Jr. et al. New York: Thomas Y. Crowell, 1970.

Stillman, Richard. *The Rise of the City Manager: A Public Professional in Local Government*. Albuquerque: University of New Mexico Press, 1974.

Svara, James A. *Official Leadership in the City: Patterns of Conflict and Cooperation*. New York: Oxford University Press, 1990.

List of Websites

http://fairvote.org/
The website of the Center for Voting and Democracy.

http://usacitylink.com/
A website containing information on cities across the nation; lets you locate your hometown page and get information on your city government.

http://teep.tamu.edu/
The Texas Educational Excellence Project website providing data and reports about state education.

http://icma.org/
The website of the International City/County Management Association.

http://www.nlc.org/
The website of the National League of Cities, a national organization representing city governments in the United States.

http://www.county.org
The website of the Texas Association of Counties.

http://www.tml.org
The website of the Texas Municipal League.

www.txregionalcouncil.org
The website of the Texas Association of Regional Councils.

Participate!

Attend a meeting of your local city government, school board, or county commission. All meetings are open to the public, and most allow public comment. Observe what role the presiding officer (mayor, president of school board, county judge) plays in the meeting. What role does the city manager play? What role do legislators and citizens play in these meetings?

Extra Credit

Obtain a copy of the home-rule charter for your hometown. If you do not live in a home-rule city, you may pick another charter.

Prepare a written report on your city charter, including the following:

■ The form of government
■ The number of city council members and method of election

- Terms of office and term limits
- The method of electing the mayor
- Qualifications for holding office
- The way vacancies on the council are filled
- Compensation for council members and mayor—how determined or how much
- Procedures for initiative, referendum, and recall if provided in the charter
- Powers of the mayor

Self-Test Answers

1. a, 2. c, 3. c, 4. b, 5. d, 6. a, 7. F, 8. F, 9. T, 10. T

Appendixes

The Declaration of Independence

In Congress, July 4, 1776

The Unanimous Declaration of the Thirteen United States of America

When, in the course of human events, it becomes necessary for one people to dissolve the political bands which have connected them with another, and to assume, among the powers of the earth, the separate and equal station to which the laws of nature and of nature's God entitle them, a decent respect to the opinions of mankind requires that they should declare the causes which impel them to the separation.

We hold these truths to be self-evident, that all men are created equal; that they are endowed by their Creator with certain unalienable rights; that among these, are life, liberty, and the pursuit of happiness. That, to secure these rights, governments are instituted among men, deriving their just powers from the consent of the governed; that, whenever any form of government becomes destructive of these ends, it is the right of the people to alter or to abolish it, and to institute a new government, laying its foundation on such principles, and organizing its powers in such form, as to them shall seem most likely to effect their safety and happiness. Prudence, indeed, will dictate that governments long established, should not be changed for light and transient causes; and, accordingly, all experience hath shown, that mankind are more disposed to suffer, while evils are sufferable, than to right themselves by abolishing the forms to which they are accustomed. But, when a long train of abuses and usurpations, pursuing invariably the same object, evinces a design to reduce them under absolute despotism, it is their right, it is their duty, to throw off such government and to provide new guards for their future security. Such has been the patient sufferance of these colonies, and such is now the necessity which constrains them to alter their former systems of government. The history of the present King of Great Britain is a history of repeated injuries and usurpations, all having, in direct object, the establishment of an absolute tyranny over these States. To prove this, let facts be submitted to a candid world:

He has refused his assent to laws the most wholesome and necessary for the public good.

He has forbidden his governors to pass laws of immediate and pressing importance, unless suspended in their operation till his assent should be obtained; and, when so suspended, he has utterly neglected to attend to them.

He has refused to pass other laws for the accommodation of large districts of people, unless those people would relinquish the right of representation in the legislature; a right inestimable to them, and formidable to tyrants only.

He has called together legislative bodies at places unusual, uncomfortable, and distant from the depository of their public records, for the sole purpose of fatiguing them into compliance with his measures.

He has dissolved representative houses repeatedly for opposing, with manly firmness, his invasions on the rights of the people.

He has refused, for a long time after such dissolutions, to cause others to be elected; whereby the legislative powers, incapable of annihilation, have returned to the people at large for their exercise; the state remaining, in the meantime, exposed to all the danger of invasion from without, and convulsions within.

He has endeavored to prevent the population of these States; for that purpose, obstructing the laws for naturalization of foreigners, refusing to pass others to encourage their migration hither, and raising the conditions of new appropriations of lands.

He has obstructed the administration of justice, by refusing his assent to laws for establishing judiciary powers.

He has made judges dependent on his will alone, for the tenure of their offices, and the amount and payment of their salaries.

He has erected a multitude of new offices, and sent hither swarms of officers to harass our people, and eat out their substance.

He has kept among us, in time of peace, standing armies, without the consent of our legislatures.

He has affected to render the military independent of, and superior to, the civil power.

He has combined, with others, to subject us to a jurisdiction foreign to our Constitution, and unacknowledged by our laws; giving his assent to their acts of pretended legislation:

For quartering large bodies of armed troops among us:

For protecting them by a mock trial, from punishment, for any murders which they should commit on the inhabitants of these States:

For cutting off our trade with all parts of the world:

For imposing taxes on us without our consent:

For depriving us, in many cases, of the benefit of trial by jury:

For transporting us beyond seas to be tried for pretended offences:

For abolishing the free system of English laws in a neighboring province, establishing therein an arbitrary government, and enlarging its boundaries, so as to render it at once an example and fit instrument for introducing the same absolute rule into these colonies:

For taking away our charters, abolishing our most valuable laws, and altering, fundamentally, the powers of our governments:

For suspending our own legislatures, and declaring themselves invested with power to legislate for us in all cases whatsoever.

He has abdicated government here, by declaring us out of his protection, and waging war against us.

He has plundered our seas, ravaged our coasts, burnt our towns, and destroyed the lives of our people.

He is, at this time, transporting large armies of foreign mercenaries to complete the works of death, desolation, and tyranny, already begun, with circumstances of cruelty and perfidy scarcely paralleled in the most barbarous ages, and totally unworthy of the head of a civilized nation.

He has constrained our fellow citizens, taken captive on the high seas, to bear arms against their country, to become the executioners of their friends, and brethren, or to fall themselves by their hands.

He has excited domestic insurrections amongst us, and has endeavored to bring on the inhabitants of our frontiers, the merciless Indian savages, whose known rule of warfare is an undistinguished destruction of all ages, sexes, and conditions.

In every stage of these oppressions, we have petitioned for redress, in the most humble terms; our repeated petitions have been answered only by repeated injury. A prince, whose character is thus marked by every act which may define a tyrant, is unfit to be the ruler of a free people.

Nor have we been wanting in attention to our British brethren. We have warned them, from time to time, of attempts made by their legislature to extend an unwarrantable jurisdiction over us. We have reminded them of the circumstances of our emigration and settlement here. We have appealed to their native justice and magnanimity, and we have conjured them, by the ties of our common kindred, to disavow these usurpations, which would inevitably interrupt our connections and correspondence. They, too, have been deaf to the voice of justice and of consanguinity. We must, therefore, acquiesce in the necessity which denounces our separation, and hold them as we hold the rest of mankind, enemies in war, in peace, friends.

We, therefore, the representatives of the United States of America, in general Congress assembled, appealing to the Supreme Judge of the world for the rectitude of our intentions, do, in the name, and by the authority of the good people of these colonies, solemnly publish and declare, that these united colonies are, and of right ought to be, free and independent states: that they are absolved from all allegiance to the British Crown, and that all political connection between them and the state of Great Britain is, and ought to be, totally dissolved; and that, as free and independent states, they have full power to levy war, conclude peace, contract alliances, establish commerce, and to do all other acts and things which independent states may of right do. And, for the support of this declaration, with a firm reliance on the protection of Divine Providence, we mutually pledge to each other our lives, our fortunes, and our sacred honor.

The foregoing Declaration was, by order of Congress, engrossed, and signed by the following members:

John Hancock

New Hampshire
Josiah Bartlett
William Whipple
Matthew Thornton

Massachusetts Bay
Samuel Adams
John Adams
Robert Treat Paine

Elbridge Gerry

Rhode Island
Stephen Hopkins
William Ellery

Connecticut
Roger Sherman
Samuel Huntington

William Williams
Oliver Wolcott

New York
William Floyd
Philip Livingston
Francis Lewis
Lewis Morris

New Jersey
Richard Stockton
John Witherspoon
Francis Hopkinson
John Hart
Abraham Clark

Pennsylvania
Robert Morris
Benjamin Rush
Benjamin Franklin
John Morton
George Clymer
James Smith
George Taylor
James Wilson
George Ross

Delaware
Caesar Rodney
George Reed
Thomas M'Kean

Maryland
Samuel Chase
William Paca
Thomas Stone
Charles Carroll, of Carrollton

Virginia
George Wythe
Richard Henry Lee
Thomas Jefferson
Benjamin Harrison
Thomas Nelson, Jr.
Francis Lightfoot Lee
Carter Braxton

North Carolina
William Hooper
Joseph Hewes
John Penn

South Carolina
Edward Rutledge
Thomas Heyward, Jr.
Thomas Lynch, Jr.
Arthur Middleton

Georgia
Button Gwinnett
Lyman Hall
George Walton

Resolved, That copies of the Declaration be sent to the several assemblies, conventions, and committees, or councils of safety, and to the several commanding officers of the continental troops; that it be proclaimed in each of the United States, at the head of the army.

The Constitution of the United States of America[1]

We the People of the United States, in Order to form a more perfect Union, establish Justice, insure domestic Tranquility, provide for the common defence, promote the general Welfare, and secure the Blessings of Liberty to ourselves and our Posterity, do ordain and establish this CONSTITUTION for the United States of America.

Article I

Section 1

All legislative Powers herein granted shall be vested in a Congress of the United States, which shall consist of a Senate and House of Representatives.

Section 2

The House of Representatives shall be composed of Members chosen every second Year by the People of the several States, and the Electors in each State shall have the Qualifications requisite for Electors of the most numerous Branch of the State Legislature.

No Person shall be a Representative who shall not have attained to the Age of twenty-five Years, and been seven Years a Citizen of the United States, and who shall not, when elected, be an Inhabitant of that State in which he shall be chosen.

[Representatives and direct Taxes[2] shall be apportioned among the several States which may be included within this Union, according to their respective Numbers, which shall be determined by adding to the whole Number of free Persons, including those bound to Service for a Term of Years, and excluding Indians not taxed, three fifths of all other Persons.][3] The actual Enumeration shall be made within three Years after the first Meeting of the Congress of the United States, and within every subsequent Term of ten Years, in such Manner as they shall by Law direct. The Number of Representatives shall not exceed one for every thirty Thousand, but each State shall have at Least one Representative; and until such enumeration shall be made, the State of New Hampshire shall be entitled to chuse three, Massachusetts eight, Rhode-Island and Providence Plantations one, Connecticut five, New York six, New Jersey four, Pennsylvania eight, Delaware one, Maryland six, Virginia ten, North Carolina five, South Carolina five, and Georgia three.

When vacancies happen in the Representation from any State, the Executive Authority thereof shall issue Writs of Election to fill such Vacancies.

The House of Representatives shall chuse their Speaker and other Officers; and shall have the sole Power of Impeachment.

Section 3

The Senate of the United States shall be composed of two Senators from each State, chosen by the Legislature thereof, for six Years; and each Senator shall have one Vote.

Immediately after they shall be assembled in Consequence of the first Election, they shall be divided as equally as may be into three Classes. The Seats of the Senators of the first Class shall be vacated at the Expiration of the second Year, of the second Class at the Expiration of the fourth Year, and of the third Class at the Expiration of the sixth Year, so that one-third may be chosen every second Year; and if Vacancies happen by Resignation, or otherwise, during the Recess of the Legislature of any State, the Executive thereof may make temporary Appointments until the next Meeting of the Legislature, which shall then fill such Vacancies.

No Person shall be a Senator who shall not have attained to the Age of thirty Years, and been nine Years a Citizen of the United States, and who shall not, when

---

[1]This version, which follows the original Constitution in capitalization and spelling, was published by the United States Department of the Interior, Office of Education, in 1935.

[2]Altered by the Sixteenth Amendment.

[3]Negated by the Fourteenth Amendment.

elected, be an Inhabitant of that State for which he shall be chosen.

The Vice President of the United States shall be President of the Senate, but shall have no vote, unless they be equally divided.

The Senate shall chuse their other Officers, and also a President pro tempore, in the absence of the Vice President, or when he shall exercise the Office of President of the United States.

The Senate shall have the sole Power to try all Impeachments. When sitting for that purpose they shall be on Oath or Affirmation. When the President of the United States is tried, the Chief Justice shall preside: And no person shall be convicted without the Concurrence of two thirds of the Members present.

Judgment in Cases of Impeachment shall not extend further than to removal from Office, and disqualification to hold and enjoy any Office of honor, Trust, or Profit under the United States: but the Party convicted shall nevertheless be liable and subject to Indictment, Trial, Judgment and Punishment, according to Law.

Section 4

The Times, Place and Manner of holding Elections for Senators and Representatives, shall be prescribed in each State by the Legislature thereof; but the Congress may at any time by Law make or alter such Regulations, except as to the Places of Chusing Senators.

The Congress shall assemble at least once in every Year, and such Meeting shall be on the first Monday in December, unless they shall by Law appoint a different Day.

Section 5

Each House shall be the Judge of the Elections, Returns and Qualifications of its own Members, and a Majority of each shall constitute a Quorum to do Business; but a smaller number may adjourn from day to day, and may be authorized to compel the Attendance of absent Members, in such Manner, and under such Penalties, as each House may provide.

Each House may determine the Rules of its Proceedings, punish its Members for disorderly Behaviour, and, with the Concurrence of two thirds, expel a Member.

Each House shall keep a Journal of its Proceedings, and from time to time publish the same, excepting such Parts as may in their Judgment require Secrecy; and the Yeas and Nays of the Members of either House on any question shall, at the Desire of one fifth of those Present, be entered on the Journal.

Neither House, during the Session of Congress, shall, without the Consent of the other, adjourn for more than three days, nor to any other Place than that in which the two Houses shall be sitting.

Section 6

The Senators and Representatives shall receive a Compensation for their Services, to be ascertained by Law, and paid out of the Treasury of the United States. They shall in all Cases, except Treason, Felony, and Breach of the Peace, be privileged from Arrest during their Attendance at the Session of their respective Houses, and in going to and returning from the same; and for any Speech or Debate in either House, they shall not be questioned in any other Place.

No Senator or Representative shall, during the Time for which he was elected, be appointed to any civil Office under the Authority of the United States, which shall have been created, or the Emoluments whereof shall have been increased, during such time; and no Person holding any Office under the United States shall be a Member of either House during his continuance in Office.

Section 7

All Bills for raising Revenue shall originate in the House of Representatives; but the Senate may propose or concur with Amendments as on other bills.

Every Bill which shall have passed the House of Representatives and the Senate, shall, before it becomes a Law, be presented to the President of the United States; if he approve he shall sign it, but if not he shall return it, with his Objections, to that House in which it shall have originated, who shall enter the Objections at large on their Journal, and proceed to reconsider it. If after such Reconsideration two thirds of that House shall agree to pass the bill, it shall be sent, together with the objections, to the other House, by which it shall likewise be reconsidered, and if approved by two thirds of that House, it shall become a Law. But in all such Cases the Votes of both Houses shall be determined by Yeas and Nays, and the Names of the Persons voting for and against the Bill shall be entered on the Journal of each House respectively. If any Bill shall not be returned by the President within ten Days (Sundays excepted) after it shall have been presented to him, the Same shall be a Law, in like Manner as if he had signed it, unless the Congress by their Adjournment prevent its Return, in which Case it shall not be a Law.

Every Order, Resolution, or Vote to which the Concurrence of the Senate and House of Representatives may be necessary (except on a question of Adjournment) shall be presented to the President of the United States; and before the Same shall take Effect, shall be approved by him, or being disapproved by him, shall be repassed by two thirds of the Senate and House of Representatives, according to the Rules and Limitations prescribed in the Case of a Bill.

Section 8

The Congress shall have Power To lay and collect Taxes, Duties, Imposts and Excises, to pay the Debts and provide for the common Defence and general Welfare of the United States; but all Duties, Imposts and Excises shall be uniform throughout the United States;

To borrow money on the credit of the United States;

To regulate Commerce with foreign Nations, and among the several States, and with the Indian Tribes;

To establish a uniform rule of Naturalization, and uniform Laws on the subject of Bankruptcies throughout the United States;

To coin Money, regulate the Value thereof, and of foreign Coin, and fix the Standard of Weights and Measures;

To provide for the Punishment of counterfeiting the Securities and current Coin of the United States;

To establish Post Offices and post Roads;

To promote the Progress of Science and useful Arts, by securing for limited Times to Authors and Inventors the exclusive Right to their respective Writings and Discoveries;

To constitute Tribunals inferior to the Supreme Court;

To define and punish Piracies and Felonies committed on the high Seas, and Offenses against the Law of Nations;

To declare War, grant Letters of Marque and Reprisal, and make Rules concerning Captures on Land and Water;

To raise and support Armies, but no Appropriation of Money to that Use shall be for a longer Term than two Years;

To provide and maintain a Navy;

To make Rules for the Government and Regulation of the land and naval forces;

To provide for calling forth the Militia to execute the Laws of the Union, suppress Insurrections and repel Invasions;

To provide for organizing, arming, and disciplining the Militia, and for governing such Part of them as may be employed in the Service of the United States,

reserving to the States respectively, the Appointment of the Officers, and the Authority of training the Militia according to the discipline prescribed by Congress;

To exercise exclusive Legislation in all Cases whatsoever, over such District (not exceeding ten Miles square) as may, by Cession of particular States, and the acceptance of Congress, become the Seat of the Government of the United States, and to exercise like Authority over all Places purchased by the Consent of the Legislature of the State in which the Same shall be, for the Erection of Forts, Magazines, Arsenals, Dock-yards, and other needful Buildings;—And

To make all Laws which shall be necessary and proper for carrying into Execution the foregoing Powers, and all other Powers vested by this Constitution in the Government of the United States, or in any Department or Officer thereof.

Section 9

The Migration or Importation of such Persons as any of the States now existing shall think proper to admit, shall not be prohibited by the Congress prior The Constitution of the United States of America to the Year one thousand eight hundred and eight, but a tax or duty may be imposed on such Importation, not exceeding ten dollars for each Person.

The privilege of the Writ of Habeas Corpus shall not be suspended, unless when in Cases of Rebellion or Invasion the public Safety may require it.

No bill of Attainder or ex post facto Law shall be passed.

No capitation, or other direct, Tax shall be laid unless in Proportion to the Census or Enumeration herein before directed to be taken.

No Tax or Duty shall be laid on Articles exported from any State.

No Preference shall be given by any Regulation of Commerce or Revenue to the Ports of one State over those of another: nor shall Vessels bound to, or from, one State, be obliged to enter, clear, or pay Duties in another.

No Money shall be drawn from the Treasury, but in Consequence of Appropriations made by Law; and a regular Statement and Account of the Receipts and Expenditures of all public Money shall be published from time to time.

No Title of Nobility shall be granted by the United States: And no Person holding any Office of Profit or Trust under them, shall, without the Consent of the Congress, accept of any present, Emolument, Office, or Title, of any kind whatever, from any King, Prince, or foreign State.

Section 10

No State shall enter into any Treaty, Alliance, or Confederation; grant Letters of Marque and Reprisal; coin Money; emit Bills of Credit; make any Thing but gold and silver Coin a Tender in Payment of Debts; pass any Bill of Attainder, ex post facto Law, or Law impairing the Obligation of Contracts, or grant any Title of Nobility.

No State shall, without the Consent of the Congress, lay any Imposts or Duties on Imports or Exports, except what may be absolutely necessary for executing its inspection Laws; and the net Produce of all Duties and Imposts, laid by any State on Imports or Exports, shall be for the use of the Treasury of the United States; and all such Laws shall be subject to the Revision and Control of the Congress.

No state shall, without the Consent of Congress, lay any duty of Tonnage, keep Troops, or Ships of War in time of Peace, enter into any Agreement or Compact with another State, or with a foreign Power, or engage in War, unless actually invaded, or in such imminent Danger as will not admit of delay.

Article II

Section 1

The executive Power shall be vested in a President of the United States of America. He shall hold his Office during the Term of four years, and, together with the Vice President, chosen for the same Term, be elected, as follows:

Each State shall appoint, in such Manner as the Legislature thereof may direct, a Number of Electors, equal to the whole Number of Senators and Representatives to which the State may be entitled in the Congress: but no Senator or Representative, or Person holding an Office of Trust or Profit under the United States, shall be appointed an Elector.

[The Electors shall meet in their respective States, and vote by Ballot for two persons, of whom one at least shall not be an Inhabitant of the same State with themselves. And they shall make a List of all the Persons voted for, and of the Number of Votes for each; which List they shall sign and certify, and transmit sealed to the Seat of the Government of the United States, directed to the President of the Senate. The President of the Senate shall, in the Presence of the Senate and House of Representatives, open all the Certificates, and the Votes shall then be counted. The Person having the greatest Number of Votes shall be the President, if such Number be a Majority of the whole Number of Electors appointed; and if there be more than one who

have such Majority, and have an equal Number of Votes, then the House of Representatives shall immediately chuse by Ballot one of them for President; and if no Person have a Majority, then from the five highest on the List the said House shall in like Manner chuse the President. But in chusing the President, the Votes shall be taken by States, the Representation from each State having one Vote; a quorum for this Purpose shall consist of a Member or Members from two-thirds of the States, and a Majority of all the States shall be necessary to a Choice. In every Case, after the Choice of the President, the Person having the greatest Number of Votes of the Electors shall be the Vice President. But if there should remain two or more who have equal votes, the Senate shall chuse from them by Ballot the Vice President.][4]

The Congress may determine the Time of chusing the Electors, and the Day on which they shall give their Votes; which Day shall be the same throughout the United States.

No person except a natural-born Citizen, or a Citizen of the United States, at the time of the Adoption of this Constitution, shall be eligible to the Office of President; neither shall any Person be eligible to that Office who shall not have attained to the Age of thirty-five years, and been fourteen Years a Resident within the United States.

In Case of the Removal of the President from Office, or of his Death, Resignation, or Inability to discharge the Powers and Duties of the said Office, the same shall devolve on the Vice President, and the Congress may by Law provide for the Case of Removal, Death, Resignation, or Inability, both of the President and Vice President, declaring what Officer shall then act as President, and such Officer shall act accordingly, until the disability be removed, or a President shall be elected.

The President shall, at stated Times, receive for his Services a Compensation, which shall neither be increased nor diminished during the Period for which he shall have been elected, and he shall not receive within that Period any other Emolument from the United States, or any of them.

Before he enter on the execution of his Office, he shall take the following Oath or Affirmation:—"I do solemnly swear (or affirm) that I will faithfully execute the Office of President of the United States, and will, to the best of my Ability, preserve, protect, and defend the Constitution of the United States."

---

[4]Revised by the Twelfth Amendment.

Section 2

The President shall be Commander in Chief of the Army and Navy of the United States, and of the Militia of the several States, when called into the actual Service of the United States; he may require the Opinion, in writing, of the principal Officer in each of the executive Departments, upon any subject relating to the Duties of their respective Offices, and he shall have Power to Grant Reprieves and Pardons for Offenses against the United States, except in Cases of Impeachment.

He shall have Power, by and with the Advice and Consent of the Senate, to make Treaties, provided two-thirds of the Senators present concur; and he shall nominate, and by and with the Advice and Consent of the Senate, shall appoint Ambassadors, other public Ministers and Consuls, Judges of the supreme Court, and all other Officers of the United States, whose Appointments are not herein otherwise provided for, and which shall be established by Law: but the Congress may by Law vest the Appointment of such inferior Officers, as they think proper, in the President alone, in the Courts of Law, or in the Heads of Departments.

The President shall have Power to fill up all Vacancies that may happen during the Recess of the Senate, by granting Commissions which shall expire at the End of their next Session.

Section 3

He shall from time to time give to the Congress Information of the State of the Union, and recommend to their Consideration such Measures as he shall judge necessary and expedient; he may, on extraordinary occasions, convene both Houses, or either of them, and in Case of Disagreement between them, with respect to the Time of Adjournment, he may adjourn them to such Time as he shall think proper; he shall receive Ambassadors and other public Ministers; he shall take care that the Laws be faithfully executed, and shall Commission all the Officers of the United States.

Section 4

The President, Vice President and all civil Officers of the United States, shall be removed from Office on Impeachment for, and Conviction of, Treason, Bribery, or other high Crimes and Misdemeanors.

Article III

Section 1

The judicial Power of the United States, shall be vested in one supreme Court, and in such inferior Courts as the Congress may from time to time ordain and establish. The Judges, both of the supreme and inferior Courts, shall hold their Offices during good Behaviour, and shall, at stated Times, receive for their Services, a Compensation, which shall not be diminished during their Continuance in Office.

Section 2

The judicial Power shall extend to all Cases, in Law and Equity, arising under this Constitution, the Laws of the United States, and Treaties made, or which shall be made, under their Authority;—to all Cases affecting ambassadors, other public ministers and consuls;—to all cases of admiralty and maritime Jurisdiction;—to Controversies to which the United States shall be a Party;—to Controversies between two or more states;—between a State and Citizens of another State;[5]—between Citizens of different States—between Citizens of the same State claiming Lands under Grants of different States, and between a State, or the Citizens thereof, and foreign States, Citizens, or Subjects.

In all Cases affecting Ambassadors, other public Ministers and Consuls, and those in which a State shall be Party, the supreme Court shall have original Jurisdiction. In all the other Cases before mentioned, the supreme Court shall have appellate Jurisdiction, both as to Law and Fact, with such Exceptions, and under such Regulations as the Congress shall make.

The trial of all Crimes, except in Cases of Impeachment, shall be by Jury; and such Trial shall be held in the State where the said Crimes shall have been committed; but when not committed within any State, the Trial shall be at such Place or Places as the Congress may by Law have directed.

Section 3

Treason against the United States, shall consist only in levying War against them, or in adhering to their Enemies, giving them Aid and Comfort. No Person shall be convicted of Treason unless on the Testimony of two Witnesses to the same overt Act, or on Confession in open Court.

The Congress shall have power to declare the Punishment of Treason, but no Attainder of Treason shall work Corruption of Blood, or Forfeiture except during the Life of the Person attainted.

[5]Qualified by the Eleventh Amendment.

Article IV

Section 1

Full Faith and Credit shall be given in each State to the public Acts, Records, and judicial Proceedings of every other State. And the Congress may by general Laws prescribe the Manner in which such Acts, Records and Proceedings shall be proved, and the Effect thereof.

Section 2

The Citizens of each State shall be entitled to all Privileges and Immunities of Citizens in the several States.

A Person charged in any State with Treason, Felony, or other Crime, who shall flee from Justice, and be found in another State, shall on demand of the executive Authority of the State from which he fled, be delivered up, to be removed to the State having Jurisdiction of the crime.

No Person held to Service or Labour in one State, under the Laws thereof, escaping into another, shall, in Consequence of any Law or Regulation therein, be discharged from such Service or Labour, but shall be delivered up on Claim of the Party to whom such Service or Labour may be due.

Section 3

New States may be admitted by the Congress into this Union; but no new State shall be formed or erected within the Jurisdiction of any other State; nor any State be formed by the Junction of two or more States, or parts of States, without the Consent of the Legislatures of the States concerned as well as of the Congress.

The Congress shall have Power to dispose of and make all needful Rules and Regulations respecting the Territory or other Property belonging to the United States; and nothing in this Constitution shall be so construed as to Prejudice any Claims of the United States, or of any particular State.

Section 4

The United States shall guarantee to every State in this Union a Republican Form of Government, and shall protect each of them against Invasion; and on Application of the Legislature, or of the Executive (when the Legislature cannot be convened) against domestic Violence.

Article V

The Congress, whenever two-thirds of both Houses shall deem it necessary, shall propose Amendments to this Constitution, or, on the Application of the Legislatures of two-thirds of the several States, shall call a Convention for proposing Amendments, which, in either Case, shall be valid to all Intents and Purposes, as part of this Constitution, when ratified by the Legislatures of three-fourths of the several States, or by Conventions in three-fourths thereof, as the one or the other Mode of Ratification may be proposed by the Congress; Provided that no Amendment which may be made prior to the Year One thousand eight hundred and eight shall in any Manner affect the first and fourth Clauses in the Ninth Section of the first Article; and that no State, without its Consent, shall be deprived of its equal Suffrage in the Senate.

Article VI

All Debts contracted and Engagements entered into, before the Adoption of this Constitution, shall be as valid against the United States under this Constitution, as under the Confederation.

This Constitution, and the Laws of the United States which shall be made in Pursuance thereof; and all Treaties made, or which shall be made, under the Authority of the United States, shall be the supreme Law of the Land; and the Judges in every State shall be bound thereby, any Thing in the Constitution or Laws of any State to the Contrary notwithstanding.

The Senators and Representatives before mentioned, and the Members of the several State Legislatures, and all executive and judicial Officers, both of the United States and of the several States, shall be bound by Oath or Affirmation to support this Constitution; but no religious Tests shall ever be required as a qualification to any Office or public Trust under the United States.

Article VII

The Ratification of the Conventions of nine States shall be sufficient for the Establishment of this Constitution between the States so ratifying the same.

Done in Convention by the Unanimous Consent of the States present the Seventeenth Day of September in the Year of our Lord one thousand seven hundred and Eighty seven, and of the Independence of the United States of America the Twelfth. In Witness whereof We have hereunto subscribed our Names.[6]

---

[6]These are the full names of the signers, which in some cases are not the signatures on the document.

George Washington
*President and deputy from
Virginia*

New Hampshire
John Langdon
Nicholas Gilman

Massachusetts
Nathaniel Gorham
Rufus King

Connecticut
William Samuel Johnson
Roger Sherman

New York
Alexander Hamilton

New Jersey
William Livingston
David Brearley
William Paterson
Jonathan Dayton

Pennsylvania
Benjamin Franklin
Thomas Mifflin
Robert Morris
George Clymer
Thomas FitzSimmons
Jared Ingersoll
James Wilson
Gouverneur Morris

Delaware
George Read
Gunning Bedford, Jr.
John Dickinson
Richard Bassett
Jacob Broom

Maryland
James McHenry
Daniel of St. Thomas
 Jenifer
Daniel Carroll

Virginia
John Blair
James Madison, Jr.

North Carolina
William Blount
Richard Dobbs Spaight
Hugh Williamson

South Carolina
John Rutledge
Charles Cotesworth
 Pinckney
Charles Pinckney
Pierce Butler

Georgia
William Few
Abraham Baldwin

Articles in Addition to, and Amendment of, the Constitution of the United States of America, Proposed by Congress, and Ratified by the Legislatures of the Several States, Pursuant to the Fifth Article of the Original Constitution[7]

Amendment I

Congress shall make no law respecting an establishment of religion, or prohibiting the free exercise thereof; or abridging the freedom of speech, or of the press; or the right of the people peaceably to assem-

ble, and to petition the Government for a redress of grievances.

Amendment II

A well regulated Militia, being necessary to the security of a free State, the right of the people to keep and bear Arms shall not be infringed.

Amendment III

No Soldier shall, in time of peace, be quartered in any house, without the consent of the Owner, nor in time of war, but in a manner to be prescribed by law.

Amendment IV

The right of the people to be secure in their persons, houses, papers, and effects, against unreasonable searches and seizures, shall not be violated, and no Warrants shall issue, but upon probable cause, supported by Oath or affirmation, and particularly describing the place to be searched, and the persons or things to be seized.

Amendment V

No person shall be held to answer for a capital or otherwise infamous crime, unless on a presentment or indictment of a Grand Jury, except in cases arising in the land or naval forces, or in the Militia, when in actual service in time of War or public danger; nor shall any person be subject for the same offence to be twice put in jeopardy of life or limb; nor shall be compelled in any criminal case to be a witness against himself, nor be deprived of life, liberty, or property, without due process of law; nor shall private property be taken for public use, without just compensation.

Amendment VI

In all criminal prosecutions, the accused shall enjoy the right to a speedy and public trial, by an impartial jury of the State and district wherein the crime shall have been committed, which district shall have been previously ascertained by law, and to be informed of the nature and cause of the accusation; to be confronted with the witnesses against him; to have compulsory process for obtaining witnesses in his favour, and to have the Assistance of Counsel for his defence.

[7]This heading appears only in the joint resolution submitting the first ten amendments, which are collectively known as the Bill of Rights. They were ratified on December 15, 1791.

Amendment VII

In suits at common law, where the value in controversy shall exceed twenty dollars, the right of trial by jury shall be preserved, and no fact tried by a jury, shall be otherwise reexamined in any Court of the United States, than according to the rules of the common law.

Amendment VIII

Excessive bail shall not be required, nor excessive fines imposed, nor cruel and unusual punishments inflicted.

Amendment IX

The enumeration of the Constitution, of certain rights, shall not be construed to deny or disparage others retained by the people.

Amendment X

The powers not delegated to the United States by the Constitution, nor prohibited by it to the States, are reserved to the States respectively, or to the people.

Amendment XI [1795]

The Judicial power of the United States shall not be construed to extend to any suit in law or equity, commenced or prosecuted against one of the United States by Citizens of another State, or by Citizens or Subjects of any Foreign State.

Amendment XII [1804]

The Electors shall meet in their respective States and vote by ballot for President and Vice-President, one of whom, at least, shall not be an inhabitant of the same State with themselves; they shall name in their ballots the person voted for as President, and in distinct ballots the person voted for as Vice-President, and they shall make distinct lists of all persons voted for as President, and of all persons voted for as Vice-President, and of the number of votes for each, which lists they shall sign and certify, and transmit sealed to the seat of the government of the United States, directed to the President of the Senate;—The President of the Senate shall, in the presence of the Senate and House of Representatives, open all the certificates and the votes shall then be counted;—The person having the greatest number of votes for President, shall be the President, if such number be a majority of the whole number of Electors appointed; and if no person have such majority, then from the persons having the highest numbers not exceeding three on the list of those voted for as President, the House of Representatives shall choose immediately, by ballot, the President. But in choosing the President, the votes shall be taken by states, the representation from each state having one vote; a quorum for this purpose shall consist of a member or members from two-thirds of the states, and a majority of all the states shall be necessary to a choice. And if the House of Representatives shall not choose a President whenever the right of choice shall devolve upon them, before the fourth day of March next following, then the Vice-President shall act as President, as in the case of the death or other constitutional disability of the President—The person having the greatest number of votes as Vice-President, shall be the Vice-President, if such number be a majority of the whole number of Electors appointed, and if no person have a majority, then from the two highest numbers on the list, the Senate shall choose the Vice-President; a quorum for the purpose shall consist of two-thirds of the whole number of Senators, and majority of the whole number shall be necessary to a choice. But no person constitutionally ineligible to the office of President shall be eligible to that of Vice-President of the United States.

Amendment XIII [1865]

Section 1

Neither slavery nor involuntary servitude, except as a punishment for crime whereof the party shall have been duly convicted, shall exist within the United States, or any place subject to their jurisdiction.

Section 2

Congress shall have power to enforce this article by appropriate legislation.

Amendment XIV [1868]

Section 1

All persons born or naturalized in the United States, and subject to the jurisdiction thereof, are citizens of the United States and of the State wherein they reside. No State shall abridge the privileges or immunities of citizens of the United States; nor shall any State deprive any person of life, liberty, or property, without due process of law; nor deny to any person within its jurisdiction the equal protection of the laws.

Section 2

Representatives shall be apportioned among the several States according to their respective numbers, counting the whole number of persons in each State, excluding Indians not taxed. But when the right to vote at any election for the choice of electors for President and Vice-President of the United States, Representatives in Congress, the Executive and Judicial officers of a State, or the members of the Legislature thereof, is denied to any of the male inhabitants of such State, being twenty-one years of age, and citizens of the United States, or in any way abridged, except for participation in rebellion, or other crime, the basis of representation therein shall be reduced in the proportion which the number of such male citizens shall bear to the whole number of male citizens twenty-one years of age in such State.

Section 3

No person shall be a Senator or Representative in Congress, or elector of President and Vice-President, or hold any office, civil or military, under the United States, or under any State, who, having previously taken an oath, as a member of Congress, or as an officer of the United States, or as a member of any State legislature, or as an executive or judicial officer of any State, to support the Constitution of the United States, shall have engaged in insurrection or rebellion against the same, or given aid or comfort to the enemies thereof. But Congress may by a vote of two-thirds of each House, remove such disability.

Section 4

The validity of the public debt of the United States, authorized by law, including debts incurred for payment of pensions and bounties for services in suppressing insurrection or rebellion, shall not be questioned. But neither the United States nor any State shall assume or pay any debts or obligation incurred in aid of insurrection or rebellion against the United States, or any claim for the loss or emancipation of any slave; but all such debts, obligations, and claims shall be held illegal and void.

Section 5

The Congress shall have the power to enforce, by appropriate legislation, the provisions of this article.

Amendment XV [1870]

Section 1

The right of citizens of the United States to vote shall not be denied or abridged by the United States or by any State on account of race, color, or previous condition of servitude.

Section 2

The Congress shall have power to enforce this article by appropriate legislation.

Amendment XVI [1913]

The Congress shall have power to lay and collect taxes on incomes, from whatever source derived, without apportionment among the several States, and without regard to any census or enumeration.

Amendment XVII [1913]

The Senate of the United States shall be composed of two Senators from each State, elected by the people thereof, for six years; and each Senator shall have one vote. The electors in each State shall have the qualifications requisite for electors of the most numerous branch of the State legislatures.

When vacancies happen in the representation of any State in the Senate, the executive authority of such State shall issue writs of election to fill such vacancies: Provided, That the legislature of any State may empower the executive thereof to make temporary appointments until the people fill the vacancies by election as the legislature may direct.

This amendment shall not be so construed as to affect the election or term of any Senator chosen before it becomes valid as part of the Constitution.

Amendment XVIII [1919]

Section 1

After one year from the ratification of this article the manufacture, sale, or transportation of intoxicating liquors within, the importation thereof into, or the exportation thereof from the United States and all territory subject to the jurisdiction thereof for beverage purposes is hereby prohibited.

Section 2

The Congress and the several States shall have concurrent power to enforce this article by appropriate legislation.

Section 3

This article shall be inoperative unless it shall have been ratified as an amendment to the Constitution by the legislatures of the several States, as provided in the Constitution, within seven years from the date of the submission hereof to the States by the Congress.

Amendment XIX [1920]

The right of citizens of the United States to vote shall not be denied or abridged by the United States or by any State on account of sex.

Congress shall have power to enforce this article by appropriate legislation.

Amendment XX [1933]

Section 1

The terms of the President and Vice-President shall end at noon on the 20th day of January, and the terms of Senators and Representatives at noon on the 3d day of January, of the years in which such terms would have ended if this article had not been ratified; and the terms of their successors shall then begin.

Section 2

The Congress shall assemble at least once in every year, and such meeting shall begin at noon on the 3d day of January, unless they shall by law appoint a different day.

Section 3

If, at the time fixed for the beginning of the term of the President, the President elect shall have died, the Vice-President elect shall become President. If a President shall not have been chosen before the time fixed for the beginning of his term or if the President elect shall have failed to qualify, then the Vice-President elect shall act as President until a President shall have qualified; and the Congress may by law provide for the case wherein neither a President elect nor a Vice-President elect shall have qualified, declaring who shall then act as President, or the manner in which one who is to act shall be selected, and such

person shall act accordingly until a President or Vice-President shall have qualified.

Section 4

The Congress may by law provide for the case of the death of any of the persons from whom the House of Representatives may choose a President whenever the right of choice shall have devolved upon them, and for the case of the death of any of the persons from whom the Senate may choose a Vice-President whenever the right of choice shall have devolved upon them.

Section 5

Sections 1 and 2 shall take effect on the 15th day of October following the ratification of this article.

Section 6

This article shall be inoperative unless it shall have been ratified as an amendment to the Constitution by the legislatures of three-fourths of the several States within seven years from the date of its submission.

Amendment XXI [1933]

Section 1

The eighteenth article of amendment to the Constitution of the United States is hereby repealed.

Section 2

The transportation or importation into any State, Territory, or possession of the United States for delivery or use therein of intoxicating liquors, in violation of the laws thereof, is hereby prohibited.

Section 3

This article shall be inoperative unless it shall have been ratified as an amendment to the Constitution by conventions in the several States, as provided in the Constitution, within seven years from the date of the submission hereof to the States by the Congress.

Amendment XXII [1951]

No person shall be elected to the office of the President more than twice, and no person who has held the office of President, or acted as President, for more than two years of a term to which some other person was elected

President shall be elected to the office of the President more than once.

But this Article shall not apply to any person holding the office of President when this Article was proposed by the Congress, and shall not prevent any person who may be holding the office of President, or acting as President, during the term within which this Article becomes operative from holding the office of President or acting as President during the remainder of such term.

This article shall be inoperative unless it shall have been ratified as an amendment to the Constitution by the legislatures of three-fourths of the several states within seven years from the date of its submission to the states by the Congress.

Amendment XXIII [1961]

Section 1

The District constituting the seat of Government of the United States shall appoint in such manner as the Congress may direct:

A number of electors of President and Vice-President equal to the whole number of Senators and Representatives in Congress to which the District would be entitled if it were a State, but in no event more than the least populous State; they shall be in addition to those appointed by the States, but they shall be considered, for the purposes of the election of President and Vice-President, to be electors appointed by a State; and they shall meet in the District and perform such duties as provided by the twelfth article of amendment.

Section 2

The Congress shall have power to enforce this article by appropriate legislation.

Amendment XXIV [1964]

Section 1

The right of citizens of the United States to vote in any primary or other election for President or Vice President, for electors for President or Vice President, or for Senator or Representative in Congress, shall not be denied or abridged by the United States or any state by reason of failure to pay any poll tax or other tax.

Section 2

The Congress shall have the power to enforce this article by appropriate legislation.

Amendment XXV [1967]

Section 1

In case of the removal of the President from office or of his death or resignation, the Vice President shall become President.

Section 2

Whenever there is a vacancy in the office of the Vice President, the President shall nominate a Vice President who shall take office upon confirmation by a majority vote of both Houses of Congress.

Section 3

Whenever the President transmits to the President Pro Tempore of the Senate and the Speaker of the House of Representatives his written declaration that he is unable to discharge the powers and duties of his office, and until he transmits to them a written declaration to the contrary, such powers and duties shall be discharged by the Vice President as Acting President.

Section 4

Whenever the Vice President and a majority of either the principal officers of the executive departments or of such other body as Congress may by law provide, transmit to the President Pro Tempore of the Senate and the Speaker of the House of Representatives their written declaration that the President is unable to discharge the powers and duties of his office, the Vice President shall immediately assume the powers and duties of the office as Acting President.

Thereafter, when the President transmits to the President Pro Tempore of the Senate and the Speaker of the House of Representatives his written declaration that no inability exists, he shall resume the powers and duties of his office unless the Vice President and a majority of either the principal officers of the executive departments or of such other body as Congress may by law provide, transmit within four days to the President Pro Tempore of the Senate and the Speaker of the House of Representatives their written declaration that the President is unable to discharge the powers and duties of his office. Thereupon Congress shall decide the issue, assembling within forty-eight hours for that purpose if not in session. If the Congress, within twenty-one days after receipt of the latter written declaration, or, if Congress is not in session, within twenty-one days after Congress is required to assemble, determines by two-thirds vote of both Houses that the President is unable to discharge the powers and duties of his office, the Vice President shall continue to discharge the same as Acting President; otherwise, the President shall resume the powers and duties of his office.

Amendment XXVI [1971]

Section 1

The right of citizens of the United States, who are eighteen years of age or older, to vote shall not be denied or abridged by the United States or by any State on account of age.

Section 2

The Congress shall have the power to enforce this article by appropriate legislation.

Amendment XXVII [1992]

No law varying the compensation for the service of Senators and Representatives shall take effect until an election of Representatives shall have intervened.

Federalist No. 10 (James Madison)

Among the numerous advantages promised by a well-constructed union, none deserves to be more accurately developed than its tendency to break and control the violence of faction. The friend of popular governments never finds himself so much alarmed for their character and fate as when he contemplates their propensity to this dangerous vice. He will not fail, therefore, to set a due value on any plan which, without violating the principles to which he is attached, provides a proper cure for it. The instability, injustice, and confusion introduced into the public councils have, in truth, been the mortal diseases under which popular governments have everywhere perished, as they continue to be the favorite and fruitful topics from which the adversaries to liberty derive their most specious declamations. The valuable improvements made by the American constitutions on the popular models, both ancient and modern, cannot certainly be too much admired; but it would be an unwarrantable partiality to contend that they have as effectually obviated the danger on this side, as was wished and expected. Complaints are everywhere heard from our most considerate and virtuous citizens, equally the friends of public and private faith and of public and personal liberty, that our governments are too unstable, that the public good is disregarded in the conflicts of rival parties, and that measures are too often decided, not according to the rules of justice and the rights of the minor party, but by the superior force of an interested and overbearing majority. However anxiously we may wish that these complaints had no foundation, the evidence of known facts will not permit us to deny that they are in some degree true. It will be found, indeed, on a candid review of our situation, that some of the distresses under which we labor have been erroneously charged on the operation of our governments; but it will be found, at the same time, that other causes will not alone account for many of our heaviest misfortunes; and, particularly, for that prevailing and increasing distrust of public engagements and alarm for private rights which are echoed from one end of the confinent to the other. These must be chiefly, if not wholly, effects of the unsteadiness and injustice with which a factious spirit has tainted our public administration.

By a faction I understand a number of citizens, whether amounting to a majority or minority of the whole, who are united and actuated by some common impulse of passion, or of interest, adverse to the rights of other citizens, or to the permanent and aggregate interests of the community.

There are two methods of curing the mischiefs of faction: the one, by removing its causes; the other, by controlling its effects.

There are again two methods of removing the causes of faction: the one, by destroying the liberty which is essential to its existence; the other, by giving to every citizen the same opinions, the same passions, and the same interests.

It could never be more truly said than of the first remedy that it was worse than the disease. Liberty is to faction what air is to fire, an aliment without which it instantly expires. But it could not be a less folly to abolish liberty, which is essential to political life, because it nourishes faction than it would be to wish the annihilation of air, which is essential to animal life, because it imparts to fire its destructive agency.

The second expedient is as impracticable as the first would be unwise. As long as the reason of man continues fallible, and he is at liberty to exercise it, different opinions will be formed. As long as the connection subsists between his reason and his self-love, his opinions and his passions will have a reciprocal influence on each other; and the former will be objects to which the latter will attach themselves. The diversity in the faculties of men, from which the rights of property originate, is not less an insuperable obstacle to a uniformity of interest. The protection of these faculties is the first object of government. From the protection of different and unequal faculties of acquiring property, the possession of different degrees and kinds of property immediately results; and from the influence of these on the sentiments and views of the respective proprietors ensues a division of the society into different interests and parties.

The latent causes of faction are thus sown in the nature of man; and we see them everywhere brought into different degrees of activity, according to the different circumstances of civil society. A zeal for different opinions concerning religion, concerning government, and many other points, as well of speculation as of practice; an attachment to different leaders ambitiously contending for pre-eminence and power; or to persons of other descriptions whose fortunes have been interesting to the human passions, have, in turn, divided mankind into parties, inflamed them with mutual animosity, and rendered them much more disposed to vex and oppress each other than to co-operate for their common good. So strong is this propensity of mankind to fall into mutual animosities that where no substantial occasion presents itself the most frivolous and fanciful distinctions have been sufficient to kindle their unfriendly passions and excite their most violent conflicts. But the most common and durable source of factions has been the various and unequal distribution of property. Those who hold and those who are without property have ever formed distinct interests in society. Those who are creditors, and those who are debtors, fall under a like discrimination. A landed interest, a manufacturing interest, a mercantile interest, a moneyed interest, with many lesser interests, grow up of necessity in civilized nations, and divide them into different classes, actuated by different sentiments and views. The regulation of these various and interfering interests forms the principal task of modern legislation and involves the spirit of party and faction in the necessary and ordinary operations of government.

No man is allowed to be a judge in his own cause, because his interest would certainly bias his judgment, and, not improbably, corrupt his integrity. With equal, nay with greater reason, a body of men are unfit to be both judges and parties at the same time; yet what are many of the most important acts of legislation but so many judicial determinations, not indeed concerning the rights of single persons, but concerning the rights of large bodies of citizens? And what are the different classes of legislators but advocates and parties to the causes which they determine? Is a law proposed concerning private debts? It is a question to which the creditors are parties on one side and the debtors on the other. Justice ought to hold the balance between them. Yet the parties are, and must be, themselves the judges; and the most numerous party, or in other words, the most powerful faction must be expected to prevail. Shall domestic manufacturers be encouraged, and in what degree, by restrictions on foreign manufacturers? [These] are questions which would be differently decided by the landed and the manufacturing classes, and probably by neither with a sole regard to justice and the public good. The apportionment of taxes on the various descriptions of property is an act which seems to require the most exact impartiality; yet there is, perhaps, no legislative act in which greater opportunity and temptation are given to a predominant party

to trample on the rules of justice. Every shilling with which they overburden the inferior number is a shilling saved to their own pockets.

It is in vain to say that enlightened statesmen will be able to adjust these clashing interests and render them all subservient to the public good. Enlightened statesmen will not always be at the helm. Nor, in many cases, can such an adjustment be made at all without taking into view indirect and remote considerations, which will rarely prevail over the immediate interest which one party may find in disregarding the rights of another or the good of the whole.

The inference to which we are brought is that the *causes* of faction cannot be removed and that relief is only to be sought in the means of controlling its *effects*.

If a faction consists of less than a majority, relief is supplied by the republican principle, which enables the majority to defeat its sinister views by regular vote. It may clog the administration, it may convulse the society; but it will be unable to execute and mask its violence under the forms of the Constitution. When a majority is included in a faction, the form of popular government, on the other hand, enables it to sacrifice to its ruling passion or interest both the public good and the rights of other citizens. To secure the public good and private rights against the danger of such a faction, and at the same time to preserve the spirit and the form of popular government, is then the great object to which our inquiries are directed. Let me add that it is the great desideratum by which alone this form of government can be rescued from the opprobrium under which it has so long labored and be recommended to the esteem and adoption of mankind.

By what means is this object attainable? Evidently by one of two only. Either the existence of the same passion or interest in a majority at the same time must be prevented, or the majority, having such coexistent passion or interest, must be rendered, by their number and local situation, unable to concert and carry into effect schemes of oppression. If the impulse and the opportunity be suffered to coincide, we well know that neither moral nor religious motives can be relied on as an adequate control. They are not found to be such on the injustice and violence of individuals, and lose their efficacy in proportion to the number combined together, that is, in proportion as their efficacy becomes needful.

From this view of the subject it may be concluded that a pure democracy, by which I mean a society consisting of a small number of citizens, who assemble and administer the government in person, can admit of no cure for the mischiefs of faction. A common passion or interest will, in almost every case, be felt by a majority of the whole, a communication and concert result from the form of government itself; and there is nothing to check the inducements to sacrifice the weaker party or an obnoxious individual. Hence it is that such democracies have ever been spectacles of turbulence and contention; have ever been found incompatible with personal security or the rights of property; and have in general been as short in their lives as they have been violent in their deaths. Theoretic politicians, who have patronized this species of government, have erroneously supposed that by reducing mankind to a perfect equality in their political rights, they would at the same time be perfectly equalized and assimilated in their possessions, their opinions, and their passions.

A republic, by which I mean a government in which the scheme of representation takes place, opens a different prospect and promises the cure for which we are seeking. Let us examine the points in which it varies from pure democracy, and we shall comprehend both the nature of the cure and the efficacy which it must derive from the Union.

The two great points of difference between a democracy and a republic are: first, the delegation of the government, in the latter, to a small number of citizens elected by the rest; secondly, the greater number of citizens and greater sphere of country over which the latter may be extended.

The effect of the first difference is, on the one hand, to refine and enlarge the public views by passing them through the medium of a chosen body of citizens, whose wisdom may best discern the true interest of their country and whose patriotism and love of justice will be least likely to sacrifice it to temporary or partial considerations. Under such a regulation it may well happen that the public voice, pronounced by the representatives of the people, will be more consonant to the public good than if pronounced by the people themselves, convened for the purpose. On the other hand, the effect may be inverted. Men of factious tempers, of local prejudices, or of sinister designs, may, by intrigue, by corruption, or by other means, first obtain the suffrages, and then betray the interests of the people. The question resulting is, whether small or extensive republics are most favorable to the election of proper guardians of the public weal; and it is clearly decided in favor of the latter by two obvious considerations.

In the first place it is to be remarked that however small the republic may be the representatives must be raised to a certain number in order to guard against the cabals of a few; and that however large it may be they must be limited to a certain number in order to guard against the confusion of a multitude. Hence, the number of representatives in the two cases not being in proportion to that of the constituents, and being proportionally greatest in the small republic, it follows that if the proportion of fit characters be not less in the large than in the small republic, the former will present a greater option, and consequently a greater probability of a fit choice.

In the next place, as each representative will be chosen by a greater number of citizens in the large than in the small republic, it will be more difficult for unworthy candidates to practice with success the vicious arts by which elections are too often carried; and the suffrages of the people being more free, will be more likely to center on men who possess the most attractive merit and the most diffusive and established characters.

It must be confessed that in this, as in most other cases, there is a mean, on both sides of which inconveniencies will be found to lie. By enlarging too much the number of electors, you render the representative too little acquainted with all their local circumstances and lesser interests; as by reducing it too much, you render him unduly attached to these, and too little fit to comprehend and pursue great and national objects. The federal Constitution forms a happy combination in this respect; the great and aggregate interests being referred to the national, the local and particular to the State legislatures.

The other point of difference is the greater number of citizens and extent of territory which may be brought within the compass of republican than of democratic government; and it is this circumstance principally which renders factious combinations less to be dreaded in the former than in the latter. The smaller the society, the fewer probably will be the distinct parties and interests composing it; the fewer the distinct parties and interests, the more frequently will a majority be found of the same party; and the smaller the number of individuals composing a majority, and the smaller the compass within which they are placed, the more easily will they concert and execute their plans of oppression. Extend the sphere and you take in a greater variety of parties and interests; you make it less probable that a majority of the whole will have a common motive to invade the rights of other citizens; or if such a common motive exists, it will be more difficult for all who feel it to discover their own strength and to act in unison with each other. Besides other impediments, it may be remarked that, where there is a consciousness of unjust or dishonorable purposes, communication is always checked by distrust in proportion to the number whose concurrence is necessary.

Hence, it clearly appears that the same advantage which a republic has over a democracy in controlling the effects of faction is enjoyed by a large over a small republic—is enjoyed by the Union over the States composing it. Does this advantage consist in the substitution of representatives whose enlightened views and virtuous sentiments render them superior to local prejudices and to schemes of injustice? It will not be denied that the representation of the Union will be most likely to possess these requisite endowments. Does it consist in the greater security afforded by a greater variety of parties, against the event of any one party being able to outnumber and oppress the rest? In an equal degree does the increased variety of parties comprised within the Union increase this security. Does it, in fine, consist in the greater obstacles opposed to the concert and accomplishment of the secret wishes of an unjust and interested majority? Here again the extent of the Union gives it the most palpable advantage.

The influence of factious leaders may kindle a flame within their particular States but will be unable to spread a general conflagration through the other States. A religious sect may degenerate into a political faction in a part of the Confederacy; but the variety of sects dispersed over the entire face of it must secure the national councils against any danger from that source. A rage for paper money, for an abolition of debts, for an equal division of property, or for any other improper or wicked project, will be less apt to pervade the whole body of the Union than a particular member of it, in the same proportion as such a malady is more likely to taint a particular county or district than an entire State.

In the extent and proper structure of the Union, therefore, we behold a republican remedy for the diseases most incident to republican government. And according to the degree of pleasure and pride we feel in being republicans ought to be our zeal in cherishing the spirit and supporting the character of Federalists.

Federalist No. 51 (James Madison)

To what expedient, then, shall we finally resort, for maintaining in practice the necessary partition of power among the several departments as laid down in the Constitution? The only answer that can be given is that as all these exterior provisions are found to be inadequate, the defect must be supplied, by so contriving the interior structure of the government as that its several constituent parts may, by their mutual relations, be the means of keeping each other in their proper places. Without presuming to undertake a full development of this important idea I will hazard a few general observations which may perhaps place it in a clearer light, and enable us to form a more correct judgment of the principles and structure of the government planned by the convention.

In order to lay a due foundation for that separate and distinct exercise of the different powers of government, which to a certain extent is admitted on all hands to be essential to the preservation of liberty, it is evident that each department should have a will of its own; and consequently should be so constituted that the members of each should have as little agency as possible in the appointment of the members of the others. Were this principle rigorously adhered to, it would require that all the appointments for the supreme executive, legislative, and judiciary magistracies should be drawn from the same fountain of authority, the people, through channels having no communication whatever with one another. Perhaps such a plan of constructing the several departments would be less difficult in practice than it may be in contemplation appear. Some difficulties, however, and some additional expense would attend the execution of it. Some deviations, therefore, from the principle must be admitted. In the constitution of the judiciary department in particular, it might be inexpedient to insist rigorously on the principle; first, because peculiar qualifications being essential in the members, the primary consideration ought to be to select that mode of choice which best secures these qualifications; second, because the permanent tenure by which the appointments are held in that department must soon destroy all sense of dependence on the authority conferring them.

It is equally evident that the members of each department should be as little dependent as possible on those of the others for the emoluments annexed to their offices. Were the executive magistrate, or the judges, not independent of the legislature in this particular, their independence in every other would be merely nominal.

But the great security against a gradual concentration of the several powers in the same department consists in giving to those who administer each department the necessary constitutional means and personal motives to resist encroachments of the others. The provision for defense must in this, as in all other cases, be made commensurate to the danger of attack. Ambition must be made to counteract ambition. The interest of the man must be connected with the constitutional rights of the place. It may be a reflection on human nature that such devices should be necessary to control the abuses of government. But what is government itself but the greatest of all reflections on human nature? If men were angels no government would be necessary. If angels were to govern men, neither external nor internal controls on government would be necessary. In framing a government which is to be administered by men over men, the great difficulty lies in this: you must first enable the government to control the governed; and in the next place oblige it to control itself. A dependence on the people is, no doubt, the primary control on the government; but experience has taught mankind the necessity of auxiliary precautions.

This policy of supplying, by opposite and rival interests, the defect of better motives, might be traced through the whole system of human affairs, private as well as public. We see it particularly displayed in all the subordinate distributions of power, where the constant aim is to divide and arrange the several offices in such a manner as that each may be a check on the other—that the private interest of every individual may be a sentinel over the public rights. These inventions of prudence cannot be less requisite in the distribution of the supreme powers of the State.

But it is not possible to give to each department an equal power of self-defense. In republican government, the legislative authority necessarily predominates. The remedy for this inconveniency is to divide the legislature into different branches; and to render them, by different modes of election and different principles of action, as little connected with each other as the nature of their common functions and their common dependence on the society will admit. It may even be necessary to guard against dangerous encroachments by still further precautions. As the weight of the legislative authority requires that it should be thus divided, the weakness of the executive may require, on the other hand, that it should be fortified. An absolute negative on the legislature appears, at first view, to be the natural defense with which the executive magistrate should be armed. But perhaps it would be neither altogether safe nor alone sufficient. On ordinary occasions it might not be exerted with the requisite firmness, and on extraordinary occasions it might be perfidiously abused. May not this defect of an absolute negative be supplied by some qualified connection between this weaker department and the weaker branch of the stronger department, by which the latter may be led to support the constitutional rights of the former, without being too much detached from the rights of its own department?

If the principles on which these observations are founded be just, as I persuade myself they are, and they be applied as a criterion to the several State constitutions, and to the federal Constitution, it will be found that if the latter does not perfectly correspond with them, the former are infinitely less able to bear such a test.

There are, moreover, two considerations particularly applicable to the federal system of America, which place that system in a very interesting point of view.

First. In a single republic, all the power surrendered by the people is submitted to the administration of a single government; and the usurpations are guarded against by a division of the government into distinct and separate departments. In the compound republic of America, the power surrendered by the people is first divided between two distinct governments, and then the portion allotted to each subdivided among distinct and separate departments. Hence a double security arises to the rights of the people. The different governments will control each other, at the same time that each will be controlled by itself.

Second. It is of great importance in a republic not only to guard the society against the oppression of its rulers, but to guard one part of the society against the injustice of the other part. Different interests necessarily exist in different classes of citizens. If a majority be united by a common interest, the rights of the minority will be insecure. There are but two methods of providing against this evil: the one by creating a will in the community independent of the majority—that is, of the society itself; the other, by comprehending in the society so many separate descriptions of citizens as will render an unjust combination of a majority of the whole very improbable, if not impracticable. The first method prevails in all governments possessing an hereditary or self-appointed authority. This, at best, is but a precarious security; because a power independent of the society may as well espouse the unjust views of the major as the rightful interests of the minor party, and may possibly be turned against both parties. The second method will be exemplified in the federal republic of the United States. Whilst all authority in it will be derived from and dependent on the society, the society itself will be broken into so many parts, interests and classes of citizens, that the rights of individuals, or of the minority, will be in little danger from interested combinations of the majority. In a free government the security for civil rights must be the same as that for religious rights. It consists in the one case in the multiplicity of interests, and in the other in the multiplicity of sects. The degree of security in both cases will depend on the number of interests and sects; and this may be presumed to depend on the extent of country and number of people comprehended under the same government. This view of the subject must particularly recommend a proper federal system to all the sincere and considerate friends of republican government, since it shows that in exact proportion as the territory of the Union may be formed into more circumscribed Confederacies, or States, oppressive combinations of a majority will be facilitated; the best security, under the republican forms, for the rights of every class of citizen, will be diminished; and consequently the stability and independence of some member of the government, the only other security, must be proportionately increased. Justice is the end of government. It is the end of civil society. It ever has been and ever will be pursued until it be obtained, or until liberty be lost in the pursuit. In a society under the forms of which the stronger faction can readily unite and oppress the weaker, anarchy may as truly be said to reign as in a state of nature, where the weaker individual is not secured against the violence of the stronger; and as, in the latter state, even the stronger individuals are prompted, by the uncertainty of their condition, to submit to a government which may protect the weak as well as themselves; so, in the former state, will the more powerful factions or parties be gradually induced, by a like motive, to wish for a government which will protect all parties, the weaker as well as the more powerful. It can be little doubted that if the State of Rhode Island was separated from the Confederacy and left to itself, the insecurity of rights under the popular form of government within such narrow limits would be displayed by such reiterated oppressions of factious majorities that some power altogether independent of the people would soon be called for by the voice of the very factions whose misrule had proved the necessity of it. In the extended republic of the United States, and among the great variety of interests, parties, and sects which it embraces, a coalition of a majority of the whole society could seldom take place on any other principles than those of justice and the general good; whilst there being thus less danger to a minor from the will of a major party, there must be less pretext, also, to provide for the security of the former, by introducing into the government a will not dependent on the latter, or, in other words, a will independent of the society itself. It is no less certain than it is important, notwithstanding the contrary opinions which have been entertained, that the larger the society, provided it lie within a practicable sphere, the more duly capable it will be of self-government. And happily for the republican cause, the practicable sphere may be carried to a very great extent by a judicious modification and mixture of the federal principle.

Glossary

A

ability to pay Taxes that are based not on the benefit received but on the wealth, or ability to pay, of an individual.

acting governor The position held by the lieutenant governor, who performs the functions of the office of governor when a governor leaves a state.

administrative law judge An official who presides at a trial-like administrative hearing to settle a dispute between an agency and someone adversely affected by a decision of that agency.

affirmative action Refers to programs designed to ensure that women, minorities, and other traditionally disadvantaged groups have full and equal opportunities in employment, education, and other areas of life.

agency point of view The tendency of bureaucrats to place the interests of their agency ahead of other interests and ahead of the priorities sought by the president or Congress.

agenda setting The power of the media through news coverage to focus the public's attention and concern on particular events, problems, issues, personalities, and so on.

agents of socialization Those agents, such as the family and the media, that have significant impact on citizens' political socialization.

agricultural associations Interest groups that represent different types of farmers and businesses that provide farming supplies.

air wars A term that refers to the fact that modern campaigns are often a battle of opposing televised advertising campaigns.

alienation A feeling of personal powerlessness that includes the notion that government does not care about the opinions of people like oneself.

annual voter registration A system that requires citizens to reregister every year.

Anti-Federalists A term used to describe opponents of the Constitution during the debate over ratification.

apathy A feeling of personal disinterest in or lack of concern with politics.

appellate jurisdiction The authority of a given court to review cases that have already been tried in lower courts and are appealed to it by the losing party; such a court is called an appeals court or appellate court. (See also **original jurisdiction.**)

appointive power The ability of a governor to appoint and remove important state administrators.

appointive-elective system The Texas system in which many judges are initially appointed to a seat on the court and later must stand for election.

at-large election system System in which all voters in the city elect the mayor and city council members.

attorney general Chief counsel to the governor and state agencies; the attorney general has limited criminal jurisdiction.

authoritarian government A form of government in which leaders, though they admit to no limits on their powers, are effectively limited by other centers of power in the society.

authority The recognized right of officials to exercise power as a result of the positions they hold. (See also **power.**)

autocracy A form of government in which absolute control rests with a single person.

B

balanced budget The situation in which the government's tax and other revenues for the year are roughly equal to its expenditures

ballot form The forms used by voters to cast their ballot; in Texas, each county, with approval of the secretary of state, determines the form of the ballot.

ballot wording Description of a proposed amendment as it appears on the ballot, which can be noninstructive and misleading to voters.

benefit-based taxes Taxes for which there is a relationship between the amount paid in taxes and services received, such as gasoline taxes.

biennial session Meeting of the legislature every two years.

bill A proposed law (legislative act) within Congress or another legislature. (See also **law.**)

Bill of Rights The first ten amendments to the Constitution. They include rights such as freedom of speech and religion and due process protections (such as the right to a jury trial) for persons accused of crimes.

bipolar (power structure) A power structure dominated by two powers only, as in the case of the United States and the Soviet Union during the cold war.

"birthright" characteristics Social and economic characteristics of legislators that match certain demographic characteristics of many people in their district.

block grants Federal grants-in-aid that permit state and local officials to decide how the money will be spent within a general area, such as education or health. (See also **categorical grants.**)

brief A written statement by a party in a court case that details its argument.

budgetary powers The ability of a governor to formulate a budget, present it to the legislature, and execute or control it.

budgetary process The process through which annual federal spending and revenue determinations are made.

budget deficit The situation in which the government's expenditures exceed its tax and other revenues.

budget fix A provision of the budget, mandated by state laws and constitutional amendments, that sets aside money to be spent on specific items.

budget surplus The situation in which the government's tax and other revenues exceed its expenditures.

bureaucracy A system of organization and control based on the principles of hierarchical authority, job specialization, and formalized rules. (See also **formalized rules; hierarchical authority; job specialization.**)

bureaucratic accountability The degree to which bureaucrats are held accountable for the power they exercise.

bureaucratic rule The tendency of large scale organizations to develop into the bureaucratic form, with the effect that administrators make key policy decisions.

C

cabinet (executive) departments The major administrative organizations within the federal executive bureaucracy, each of which is headed by a secretary or, in the case of Justice, the attorney general. Each department has responsibility for a major function of the federal government, such as defense, agriculture, or justice. (See also **cabinet; independent agencies.**)

cabinet A group consisting of the heads of the (cabinet) executive departments, who are appointed by the president, subject to confirmation by the Senate. The cabinet was once the main advisory body to the president but no longer plays this role. (See also **cabinet (executive) departments.**)

Calendars Committee Standing committee of the House that decides which bills will be considered for floor debate and to which committee they will be assigned.

calendars Procedures in the House used to consider different kinds of bills: Major bills and minor bills are considered under different procedures.

candidate-centered campaigns Election campaigns and other political processes in which candidates, not political parties, have most of the initiative and influence. (See also **party-centered campaigns.**)

capital-gains tax The tax that individuals pay on money gained from the sale of a capital asset, such as property or stocks.

capitalism An economic system based on the idea that government should interfere with economic transactions as little as possible. Free enterprise and self-reliance are the collective and individual principles that underpin capitalism.

capture The situation in which a state agency or board falls under the heavy influence of its constituency interest groups.

categorical grants Federal grants-in-aid to states and localities that can be used only for designated projects. (See also **block grants.**)

ceremonial duties A governor's duties to attend many functions and represent the state.

changing political climate Changing national politics and immigration are changing the politics of the state from Democratic to Republican domination.

checks and balances The elaborate system of divided spheres of authority provided by the U.S. Constitution as a means of controlling the power of government. The separation of powers among the branches of the national government, federalism, and the different methods of selecting national officers are all part of this system.

chief legislator A role of governors in which they spend time and energy presenting an active agenda of legislation to the legislature and working to pass that agenda.

citizens' (noneconomic) groups Organized interests formed by individuals drawn together by opportunities to promote a cause in which they believe but that does not provide them significant individual economic benefits. (See also **economic groups; interest group.**)

city manager Official hired by the city council to manage the city and serve as chief administrative officer a system in which the city is divided into election districts and only the voters living in that district elect the council member from that district.

civic duty The belief of an individual that civic and political participation is a responsibility of citizenship.

civil law Laws governing relations with or between private parties where no criminal act is alleged and where the parties are making conflicting claims or are seeking to establish a legal relationship.

civil liberties The fundamental individual rights of a free society, such as freedom of speech and the right to a jury trial, which in the United States are protected by the Bill of Rights.

civil rights (equal rights) The right of every person to equal protection under the laws and equal access to society's opportunities and public facilities.

civil service system See **merit system.**

clear-and-present-danger test A test devised by the Supreme Court in 1919 to define the limits of free speech in the context of national security. According to the test, government cannot abridge political expression unless it presents a clear and present danger to the nation's security.

clientele groups Special interest groups that benefit directly from the activities of a particular bureaucratic agency and therefore are strong advocates of the agency.

closed rider A provision attached to appropriations bills that is not made public until the conference committee meets.

cloture A parliamentary maneuver that, if a three-fifths majority votes for it, limits Senate debate to thirty hours and has the effect of defeating a filibuster. (See also **filibuster.**)

cold war The lengthy period after World War II when the United States and the USSR were not engaged in actual combat (a "hot war") but were nonetheless locked in a state of deep-seated hostility.

collective (public) goods Benefits that are offered by groups (usually citizens' groups) as an incentive for membership but that are nondivisible (such as a clean environment) and therefore are available to nonmembers as well as members of the particular group. (See also **free-rider problem; private (individual) goods.**)

collective bargaining Negotiations on wages, hours, and other working conditions between employers and employees.

commerce clause The authority granted Congress in Article I, Section 8 of the Constitution "to regulate commerce" among the states.

committee assignments Decisions by the speaker of the house on which members of the House sit on each committee; some committees, such as appropriations, are more powerful than others.

common-carrier function The media's function as an open channel through which political leaders can communicate with the public. (See also **partisan function; signaling function; watchdog function.**)

communism An economic system in which government owns most or all major industries and also takes responsibility for overall management of the economy.

compliance The issue of whether a court's decisions will be respected and obeyed.

comptroller of public accounts Chief tax collector, revenue forecaster, and investor of state funds; the comptroller does not perform financial audits.

concurring opinion A separate opinion written by a Supreme Court justice who votes with the majority in the decision on a case but who disagrees with their reasoning. (See also **dissenting opinion; majority opinion; plurality opinion.**)

confederacy A governmental system in which sovereignty is vested entirely in subnational (state) governments. (See also **federalism; unitary system.**)

conference committees A temporary committee that is formed to bargain over the differences in the House and Senate versions of a bill. A conference committee's members are usually appointed from the House and Senate standing committees that originally worked on the bill.

constables Elected county law enforcement and court officers.

constituency The people residing within the geographical area represented by an elected official.

constitution The fundamental law that defines how a government will legitimately operate.

constitutional convention An assembly of citizens who may propose changes to state constitutions for voter approval.

constitutional county judge Chief administrative officer of the county commissioner's court; may also have judicial duties in rural counties.

constitutional democracy A government that is democratic in its provisions for majority influence through elections and constitutional in its provisions for minority rights and rule by law.

constitutional democratic republic A government that is constitutional in its provisions for minority rights and rule by law; democratic in its provisions for majority influence through elections; and a republic in its mix of deliberative institutions, which check and balance each other.

constitutionalism The idea that there are lawful limits on the power of government.

consumer taxes Taxes that citizens pay when they buy goods and services, such as sales taxes.

containment A doctrine, developed after World War II, based on the assumptions that the Soviet Union was an aggressor nation and that only a determined United States could block Soviet territorial ambitions.

cooperative federalism The situation in which the national, state, and local levels work together to solve problems.

corporate power The power that corporations exercise in their effort to influence government and maintain control of the workplace.

council-manager form of government A form of government in which voters elect a mayor and a city council; the mayor and the city council appoint a professional administrator to manage the city.

county and district attorneys Elected chief prosecuting attorneys for criminal cases.

county chair Party official elected in each county to organize and support the party

county clerk Elected chief record keeper for the county.

county commissioner's court Legislative body made up of five elected officials that governs Texas counties.

county executive committee Committee made up of the county chair and all precinct chairs in the county; serves as the official organization for the party in each county.

county government The oldest type of local government, adapted from the British, whose numbers vary greatly among states; it is the primary administrative arm of a state government, providing services such as voter registration, operation of courts and jails, and maintenance of roads and bridges.

county sheriff The elected head law enforcement officer for a county who in smaller counties may act as the tax assessor collector.

county treasurer Elected official who manages county funds.

criminal law Laws governing acts deemed illegal and punishable by government, such as robbery. Government is always a party to a criminal law case; the other party is the individual accused of breaking the law.

crossover voting A voting pattern in which voters from one party vote in the primaries of another party.

cultural (social) conservatives Those who believe government power should be used to uphold traditional values.

cultural (social) liberals Those who believe it is not government's role to buttress traditional values at the expense of unconventional or new values.

cumulative voting A system in which voters can concentrate (accumulate) all their votes on one candidate rather than casting one vote for each office up for election.

D

de facto discrimination Discrimination on the basis of race, sex, religion, ethnicity, and the like that results from social, economic, and cultural biases and conditions. (See also **de jure discrimination**.)

de jure discrimination Discrimination on the basis of race, sex, religion, ethnicity, and the like that results from a law. (See also **de facto discrimination**.)

decision A vote of the Supreme Court in a particular case that indicates which party the justices side with and by how large a margin.

deficit spending When the government spends more than it collects in taxes and other revenues.

delegates Elected representatives whose obligation is to act in accordance with the expressed wishes of the people they represent. (See also **trustees**.)

demand-side economics A form of fiscal policy that emphasizes "demand" (consumer spending). Government can use increased spending or tax cuts to place more money in consumers' hands and thereby increase demand. (See also **fiscal policy; supply-side economics**.)

democracy (according to the framers) A form of government in which the power of the majority is unlimited, whether exercised directly or through a representative body.

democracy A form of government in which the people govern, either directly or through elected representatives.

demographic representativeness The idea that the bureaucracy will be more responsive to the public if its employees at all levels are demographically representative of the population as a whole.

denials of power A way that constitutions limit the power of government by explicitly listing the powers that governments may not use.

deregulated tuition A policy allowing universities to set their own tuition.

deregulation The rescinding of excessive government regulations for the purpose of improving economic efficiency.

détente A French word meaning "a relaxing" and used to refer to an era of improved relations between the United States and the Soviet Union that began in the early 1970s.

deterrence policy The idea that nuclear war can be discouraged if each side in a conflict has the capacity to destroy the other with nuclear weapons.

devolution The passing down of authority from the national government to the state and local governments.

direct primary See **primary election**.

discretionary funding Those funds in the state budget that are not earmarked for specific purposes.

dissenting opinion The opinion of a justice in a Supreme Court case that explains his or her reasons for disagreeing with the majority's decision. (See also **concurring opinion; majority opinion; plurality opinion**.)

district clerk Elected official who maintains county and district court records.

district judge Elected official who appoints the county auditor.

dual federalism A doctrine based on the idea that a precise separation of national power and state power is both possible and desirable.

due process clause (of the Fourteenth Amendment) The clause of the Constitution that has been used by the judiciary to apply Bill of Rights protections to the actions of state governments.

E

earmarked taxes Taxes dedicated to a specific expenditure.

economic conservatives Those who believe government tries to do too many things that should be left to private interests and economic markets. (See also **economic liberals; libertarians; populists; social conservatives; social liberals.**)

economic depression A very severe and sustained economic downturn. Depressions are rare in the United States: the last one was in the 1930s.

economic diversity An economy based on many types of economic activity rather than one or a few activities.

economic efficiency An economic principle holding that firms should fulfill as many of society's needs as possible while using as few of its resources as possible. The greater the output (production) for a given input (for example, an hour of labor), the more efficient the process.

economic equity The situation in which the outcome of an economic transaction is fair to each party. An outcome can usually be considered fair if each party enters into a transaction freely and is not unknowingly at a disadvantage.

economic globalization The increased interdependence of nations' economies. The change is a result of technological, transportation, and communication advances that have enabled firms to deploy their resources across the globe.

economic groups Interest groups that are organized primarily for economic reasons but that engage in political activity in order to seek favorable policies from government. (See also **citizens' (noneconomic) groups; interest group.**)

economic liberals Those who believe government should do more to assist people who have difficulty meeting their economic needs on their own. (See also **economic conservatives; libertarians; populists; social conservatives; social liberals.**)

economic recession A moderate but sustained downturn in the economy. Recessions are part of the economy's normal cycle of ups and downs.

economic regions Divisions of the state based on dominant economic activity.

economy A system for the exchange of goods and services between the producers of those goods and services and the consumers of them.

effective tax rate The actual percentage of a person's income that is spent to pay taxes.

efficiency An economic principle that holds that firms should fulfill as many of society's needs as possible while using as few of its resources as possible. The greater the output (production) for a given input (for example, an hour of labor), the more efficient the process.

elastic clause See **"necessary and proper" clause.**

Electoral College An unofficial term that refers to the electors who cast the states' electoral votes.

electoral votes The method of voting used to choose the U.S. president. Each state has the same number of electoral votes as it has members in Congress (House and Senate combined). By tradition, electoral voting is tied to a state's popular voting. The candidate with the most popular votes in a state (or, in a few states, the most votes in a congressional district) receives its electoral votes.

elitism The notion that wealthy and well-connected individuals exercise power over certain areas of public policy.

entitlement program Any of a number of individual benefit programs, such as social security, that require government to provide a designated benefit to any person who meets the legally defined criteria for eligibility.

enumerated (expressed) powers The seventeen powers granted to the national government under Article I, Section 8 of the Constitution. These powers include taxation and the regulation of commerce as well as the authority to provide for the national defense.

equal rights See **civil rights.**

equality of opportunity The idea that all individuals should be given an equal chance to succeed on their own.

equality of result The objective of policies intended to reduce or eliminate the effects of discrimination so that members of traditionally disadvantaged groups will have the same benefits of society as do members of advantaged groups.

equality The notion that all individuals are equal in their moral worth and are thereby entitled to equal treatment under the law.

equal-protection clause A clause of the Fourteenth Amendment that forbids any state to deny equal protection of the laws to any individual within its jurisdiction.

equity (in relation to economic policy) The situation in which the outcome of an economic transaction is fair to each party. An outcome can usually be considered fair if each party enters into a transaction freely and is not knowingly at a disadvantage.

equity of representation Situation in which each member of a legislature represents about the same number of people.

establishment clause The First Amendment provision stating that government may not favor one religion over another or favor religion over no religion, and prohibiting Congress from passing laws respecting the establishment of religion.

exclusionary rule The legal principle that government is prohibited from using in trials evidence that was obtained by unconstitutional means (for example, illegal search and seizure).

executive departments See **cabinet (executive) departments.**

executive leadership system An approach to managing the bureaucracy that is based on presidential leadership and presidential management tools, such as the president's annual budget proposal. (See also **merit system; patronage system.**)

externalities Burdens that society incurs when firms fail to pay the full costs of production. An example of an externality is the pollution that results when corporations dump industrial wastes into lakes and rivers.

extraterritorial jurisdiction (ETJ) City powers that extend beyond the city limits to an adjacent area a city whose charter is created by state statutes.

extraordinary session Legislative session called by the legislature, rather than the governor; not used in Texas.

F

factional (minor) party A minor party created when a faction within one of the major parties breaks away to form its own party.

facts (of a court case) The relevant circumstances of a legal dispute or offense as determined by a trial court. The facts of a case are crucial because they help determine which law or laws are applicable in the case.

federalism A governmental system in which authority is divided between two sovereign levels of government: national and regional. (See also **confederacy; unitary system.**)

Federalists A term used to describe supporters of the Constitution during the debate over ratification.

filibuster A procedural tactic in the U.S. Senate whereby a minority of legislators prevents a bill from coming to a vote by holding the floor and talking until the majority gives in and the bill is withdrawn from consideration. (See also **cloture.**)

fiscal federalism A term that refers to the expenditure of federal funds on programs run in part through states and localities.

fiscal policy A tool of economic management by which government can attempt to maintain a stable economy through its taxing and spending policies. (See also **demand-side economics; monetary policy; supply-side economics.**)

focus group Opinion research technique in which a panel of "average citizens" is asked to react to issues or words.

formalized rules A basic principle of bureaucracy that refers to the standardized procedures and established regulations by which a bureaucracy conducts its operations. (See also **bureaucracy.**)

fragmented government structure A government structure in which power is dispersed to many state agencies with no central control.

framing The process by which the media play up certain aspects of a situation while downplaying other aspects, thereby providing a particular interpretation of the situation.

franchise fee A type of business income tax levied in Texas.

freedom of expression Americans' freedom to communicate their views, the foundation of which is the First Amendment rights of freedom of conscience, speech, press, assembly, and petition.

free-exercise clause A First Amendment provision that prohibits the government from interfering with the practice of religion.

free-market system An economic system based on the idea that government should interfere with economic transactions as little as possible. Free enterprise and self-reliance are the collective and individual principles that underpin free markets.

free-rider problem The situation in which the benefits offered by a group to its members are also available to nonmembers. The incentive to join the group and to promote its cause is reduced because nonmembers (free riders) receive the benefits (for example, a cleaner environment) without having to pay any of the group's costs. (See also **collective (public) goods.**)

free trade The condition in which tariffs and other barriers to trade between nations are kept to a minimum.

free-trade position The view that the long-term economic interests of all countries are advanced when tariffs and other trade barriers are kept to a minimum. (See also **protectionism.**)

G

gender gap The tendency of white women and men to differ in their political attitudes and voting preferences.

general-law city A city whose charter is created by state statutes.

general-purpose government A government given broad discretionary authority by the state government.

gerrymandering The process by which the party in power draws election district boundaries in a way that enhances the reelection prospects of its candidates.

government corporations Government bodies, such as the U.S. Postal Service and Amtrak, which are similar to private corporations in that they charge for their services but differ in that they receive federal funding to help defray expenses. Their directors are appointed by the president with Senate approval.

grand jury A jury of citizens that determines whether a person will be charged with a crime.

grants of power A way that Constitutions limit the power of government by explicitly listing the powers that governments may use; the method of limiting the U.S. government by confining its scope of authority to those powers expressly granted in the Constitution.

grants-in-aid Federal cash payments to states and localities for programs they administer.

grassroots lobbying A form of lobbying designed to persuade officials that a group's policy position has strong constituent support.

grassroots party A political party organized at the level of the voters and dependent on their support for its strength.

Great Compromise The agreement of the constitutional convention to create a two-chamber Congress with the House apportioned by population and the Senate apportioned equally by state.

H

hard money Campaign funds given directly to candidates to spend as they choose.

hierarchical authority A basic principle of bureaucracy that refers to the chain of command within an organization whereby officials and units have control over those below them. (See also **bureaucracy.**)

high-choice media system A media system in which audiences have such a wide range of choices that they can largely control the type of information to which they are exposed.

hired guns The professional consultants who run campaigns for high office.

home-rule city A city whose charter is created by the actions of local citizens.

honeymoon period The president's first months in office, a time when Congress, the press, and the public are more inclined than usual to support presidential initiatives.

***Hopwood* decision** A controversial 1996 case in which a federal court reversed affirmative action at the University of Texas law school.

I

ideological (minor) party A minor party characterized by its ideological commitment to a broad and noncentrist philosophical position.

ideology A general belief about the role and purpose of government.

imminent lawless action test A legal test that says government cannot lawfully suppress advocacy that promotes lawless action unless such advocacy is aimed at producing, and is likely to produce, imminent lawless action.

implicit or explicit prohibition on city ordinance power Limitation on the power of cities, preventing them from passing ordinances that are explicitly prohibited by state law and from passing ordinances that by implication may violate state law.

implied powers The federal government's constitutional authority (through the "necessary and proper" clause) to take action that is not expressly authorized by the Constitution but that supports actions that are so authorized. (See also **"necessary and proper" clause.**)

inalienable (natural) rights Those rights that persons theoretically possessed in the state of nature, prior to the formation of governments. These rights, including those of life, liberty, and property, are considered inherent and as such are inalienable. Since government is established by people, government has the responsibility to preserve these rights.

income-elastic taxes Taxes that rise and fall quickly relative to changes in economic conditions; the Texas tax system is very income-elastic.

incorporation The process of creating a city government.

incumbent The current holder of a particular public office.

independent agencies Bureaucratic agencies that are similar to cabinet departments but usually have a narrower area of responsibility. Each such agency is headed by a presidential appointee who is not a cabinet member. An example is the National Aeronautics and Space Administration.

independent candidate A person who has collected a required number of signatures on a petition to have her or his name appear on the ballot without a political party designation.

independent school districts School districts that are not attached to any other unit of government and operate schools in Texas.

individual goods See **private (individual) goods.**

individualism The idea that people should take the initiative, be self-sufficient, and accumulate the material advantages necessary for their well-being.

individualistic subculture A political subculture that expects government to handle functions demanded of it by the people and to intervene in individuals' lives as little as necessary.

inflation A general increase in the average level of prices of goods and services.

informal rules Set of norms or values that govern legislative behavior.

information (administrative hearing) A hearing before a judge who decides whether a person must stand trial; used in place of a grand jury.

initiative A process that allows citizens to propose changes to the state constitution or state laws through the use of petitions signed by registered voters. Texas does not have these procedures at the state level.

in-kind benefit A government benefit that is a cash equivalent, such as food stamps or rent vouchers. This form of benefit ensures that recipients will use public assistance in a specified way.

inside lobbying Direct communication between organized interests and policymakers, which is based on the assumed value of close ("inside") contacts with policymakers.

interest group Any organization that actively seeks to influence public policy. (See also **citizens' (noneconomic) groups; economic groups.**)

interest-group liberalism The tendency of public officials to support the policy demands of self-interested groups (as opposed to judging policy demands according to whether they serve a larger conception of "the public interest").

intergovernmental coordinator A role of governors in which they coordinate

activities with other state and federal officials.

interim committees Temporary committees of the legislature that study issues between regular sessions and make recommendations on legislation.

internationalist The view that the country should involve itself deeply in world affairs (See also **isolationist.**)

invisible primary The critical period before the first presidential primaries and caucuses when the candidates compete for the public support, media attention, and financial contributions that can spell the difference between winning and losing once the voting begins.

iron triangle A small and informal but relatively stable group of well-positioned legislators, executives, and lobbyists who seek to promote policies beneficial to a particular interest. (See also **issue network.**)

isolationist The view that the country should deliberately avoid a large role in world affairs and instead concentrate on domestic concerns (See also **internationalist.**)

issue network An informal and relatively open network of public officials and lobbyists who come together in response to a proposed policy in an area of interest to each of them. Unlike an iron triangle, an issue network disbands after the issue is resolved. (See also **iron triangle.**)

J

Jacksonian statehouse democracy A system in which most of the major department heads in state government are chosen by the voters at the ballot box.

job specialization A basic principle of bureaucracy holding that the responsibilities of each job position should be defined explicitly and that a precise division of labor within the organization should be maintained. (See also **bureaucracy.**)

judicial activism The doctrine that the courts should develop new legal principles when judges see a compelling need, even if this action places them in conflict with precedent or the policy decisions of elected officials. (See also **judicial restraint.**)

judicial conference A closed meeting of the justices of the U.S. Supreme Court to discuss and vote on the cases before them; the justices are not supposed to discuss conference proceedings with outsiders.

judicial powers of governors The ability of a governor to issue pardons, executive clemency, and parole for citizens convicted of a crime.

judicial restraint The doctrine that the judiciary should broadly defer to precedent and the judgment of legislatures. The doctrine claims that the job of judges is to work within the confines of laws set down by tradition and lawmaking majorities. (See also **judicial activism.**)

judicial review The power of courts to decide whether a governmental institution has acted within its constitutional powers and, if not, to declare its action null and void.

jurisdiction (of a congressional committee) The policy area in which a particular congressional committee is authorized to act.

jurisdiction (of a court) A given court's authority to hear cases of a particular kind. Jurisdiction may be original or appellate.

L

laissez-faire economics A classic economic philosophy holding that owners of business should be allowed to make their own production and distribution decisions without government regulation or control.

land commissioner Elected official responsible for administration and oversight of state-owned lands and coastal lands extending 10.3 miles into the Gulf of Mexico.

land-based economy An economic system in which most wealth is derived from the use of the land.

large-state plan See **Virginia (large-state) Plan.**

law (as enacted by Congress) A legislative proposal, or bill, that is passed by both the House and the Senate and is not vetoed by the president. (See also **bill.**)

lawmaking function The authority (of a legislature) to make the laws necessary to carry out the government's powers. (See also **oversight function; representation function.**)

laws (of a court case) The constitutional provisions, legislative statutes, or judicial precedents that apply to a court case.

legal action The use of courts of law as a means by which individuals protect their rights and settle their conflicts.

Legislative Audit Committee Legislative agency that performs audits on all state agencies.

Legislative Budget Board (LBB) Texas state agency that is controlled by the leadership in the state legislature and writes the state budget.

legislative powers of governors The formal powers, especially the veto authority and power to call special sessions, of the governor to force the legislature to enact his or her legislation.

Legislative Redistricting Board (LRB) State board composed of elected officials that can draw new legislative districts for the House and Senate if the legislature fails to act.

legitimacy (of judicial power) The issue of the proper limits of judicial authority in a political system based in part on the principle of majority rule.

Lemon test A three-part test to determine whether a law relating to religion is valid under the religious establishment clause. To be valid, a law must have a secure purpose, serve neither to advance nor inhibit religion, and avoid excessive government entanglement with religion.

libel Publication of false material that damages a person's reputation.

libertarians Those who believe government tries to do too many things that should be left to firms and markets, and who oppose government as an instrument for upholding traditional values. (See also **economic conservatives; economic liberals; populists; social conservatives; social liberals.**)

liberty The principle that individuals should be free to act and think as they choose, provided they do not infringe unreasonably on the rights and freedoms of others.

lieutenant governor Presiding officer of the Texas Senate, elected by the voters of the state.

limited government A government that is subject to strict limits on its lawful uses of power and, hence, on its ability to deprive people of their liberty.

limited-purpose government A government that has very limited authority or control over its finances and is governed by a set structure.

linkage institution An institution that serves to connect citizens with government. Linkage institutions include elections, political parties, interest groups, and the media.

living constitution theory A method of interpreting the Constitution that emphasizes the principles it embodies and their application to changing circumstances and needs.

lobbying The process by which interest group members or lobbyists attempt to influence public policy through contacts with public officials.

Local and Consent Calendars Committee Committee handling minor and noncontroversial bills that normally apply to only one county.

logrolling The trading of votes between legislators so that each gets what he or she most wants.

M

magistrate functions Preliminary hearings for persons charged with a serious criminal offense.

majoritarianism The idea that the majority prevails not only in elections but also in determining policy.

majority-minority state A state in which minority groups make up a majority of the population; a change from Anglos being the majority.

majority opinion A court opinion that results when a majority of the justices is in agreement on the legal basis of the decision. (See also **concurring opinion; dissenting opinion; plurality opinion.**)

major party Any organization receiving 20 percent or more of the total votes cast for governor in the last election.

mark up The authority of congressional committees (and subcommittees in some cases) to change the content of a bill.

means test The requirement that applicants for public assistance must demonstrate they are poor in order to be eligible for the assistance. (See also **public assistance.**)

median voter theorem The theory that parties in a two-party system can maximize their vote by locating themselves at the position of the median voter—the voter whose preferences are exactly in the middle.

merit system An approach to managing the bureaucracy whereby people are appointed to government positions on the basis of either competitive examinations or special qualifications, such as professional training. (See also **executive leadership system; patronage system.**)

merit system (Missouri system) A system of selecting judges in which the governor appoints judges from a list submitted by a screening committee, and after appointment, a judge serves for a set term and is then subjected to a retention election in which the voters decide whether the judge stays in office.

midterm election The congressional election that occurs midway through the president's term of office.

military-industrial complex The three components (the military establishment, the industries that manufacture weapons, and the members of Congress from states and districts that depend heavily on the arms industry) that mutually benefit from a high level of defense spending.

military powers of governors The governor's authority to use the National Guard in times of natural disaster or civil unrest.

minority representation Requirement that in drawing legislative districts, the legislature should create districts that give members of minority groups an opportunity to be elected.

minority representation in judgeships Election of judges from single-member districts in major urban counties to allow minority judges to be elected.

minor party A party that receives 5 to 19 percent of the vote in any statewide election; candidates from minor parties are not required to file petitions to get on the ballot.

modified one-party state A state in which one party regularly wins elections.

momentum (in campaigns) A strong showing by a candidate in early presidential nominating contests, which leads to a buildup of public support for the candidate.

monetary policy A tool of economic management based on manipulation of the amount of money in circulation. (See also **fiscal policy.**)

money chase A term used to describe the fact that U.S. campaigns are very expensive and candidates must spend a great amount of time raising funds in order to compete successfully.

moralistic subculture A political subculture that expects the government to act as a positive force to achieve a common good for all citizens.

multilateralism The situation in which nations act together in response to problems and crises.

multimember district District having more than one member elected to the legislature.

multinational (transnational) corporations Business firms with major operations in more than one country.

multiparty system A system in which three or more political parties have the capacity to gain control of government separately or in coalition.

N

national debt The total cumulative amount that the U.S. government owes to creditors.

national interest That which is best for the nation in its dealings with the world in terms of protecting its security and its way of life.

nationalization The process by which national authority has increased over the course of U.S. history as a result primarily of economic change but also of political action.

natural rights See **inalienable (natural) rights.**

"necessary and proper" clause (elastic clause) The authority granted Congress in Article I, Section 8 of the Constitution "to make all laws which shall be necessary and proper" for the implementation of its enumerated powers. (See also **implied powers.**)

negative government The philosophical belief that government governs best by staying out of people's lives, thus giving individuals as much freedom as possible to determine their own pursuits. (See also **positive government.**)

neutral competence The administrative objective of a merit-based bureaucracy. Such a bureaucracy should be "competent" in the sense that its employees are hired and retained on the basis of their expertise and "neutral" in the sense that it operates by objective standards rather than partisan ones.

New Jersey (small-state) Plan A constitutional proposal for a strengthened Congress but one in which each state would have a single vote, thus granting a small state the same legislative power as a larger state.

news The news media's version of reality, usually with an emphasis on timely, dramatic, and compelling events and developments.

news media See **press (news media).**

nomination The designation of a particular individual to run as a political party's candidate (its "nominee") in the general election.

noneconomic groups See **citizens' (noneconomic) groups.**

nonpartisan election Election of judges in which party identification does not appear on the ballot.

nonpartisan elections Ballot form in which voters are unable to determine the party of candidates by looking at the ballot.

nontax revenue Governmental revenue derived from service charges, fees (tuition), the lottery, and other sources.

North American Free Trade Agreement (NAFTA) An act passed by Congress in 1993 that established closer trade relations and economic cooperation between the United States, Canada, and Mexico.

North-South Compromise The agreement over economic and slavery issues that enabled northern and southern states to settle differences that threatened to defeat the effort to draft a new constitution.

O

objective journalism A model of news reporting that is based on the communication of "facts" rather than opinions and that is "fair" in that it presents all sides of partisan debate. (See also **partisan press.**)

off-year elections Local elections held at a different time of year from state and national elections.

oligarchy Government in which control rests with a few persons.

open party caucuses Meetings at which a party's candidates for nomination are voted on and that are open to all the party's rank-and-file voters who want to attend.

open-seat election An election in which there is no incumbent in the race.

opinion (of a court) A court's written explanation of its decision, which serves to inform others of the legal basis for the decision. Supreme Court opinions are expected to guide the decisions of lower courts. (See also **concurring opinion; dissenting opinion; majority opinion; plurality opinion.**)

original jurisdiction The authority of a given court to be the first court to hear a case. (See also **appellate jurisdiction.**)

originalism theory A method of interpreting the Constitution that emphasizes the meaning of its words at the time they were written.

outside lobbying A form of lobbying in which an interest group seeks to use public pressure as a means of influencing officials.

oversight function A supervisory activity of Congress that centers on its constitutional responsibility to see that the executive carries out the laws faithfully. (See also **lawmaking function; representation function.**)

P

packaging A term of modern campaigning that refers to the process of recasting a candidate's record into an appealing image.

parliamentarian Expert in legislative procedures.

partial veto A veto that allows the legislature to recall a bill to answer a governor's objections to it; Texas does not have a formal partial veto process.

partisan election of judges Method used to select all judges (except municipal court judges) in Texas by using a ballot showing party identification.

partisan function Efforts by media actors to influence public response to a particular party, leader, issue, or viewpoint.

partisan press Newspapers and other communication media that openly support a political party and whose news tends to follow the party line. (See also **objective journalism.**)

party (partisan) polarization The condition in which opinions and actions in response to political issues and situations divides substantially along political party lines.

party caucus A group that consists of a party's members in the House or Senate and that serves to elect the party's leadership, set policy goals, and plan party strategy.

party chief A role of governors that calls for them to aid their fellow party members in their reelection efforts, raise money for the party, and create a favorable party image.

party coalition The groups and interests that support a political party.

party-centered campaigns Election campaigns and other political processes in which political parties, not individual candidates, hold most of the initiative and influence. (See also **candidate centered campaigns.**)

party competition A process in which conflict over society's goals is transformed by political parties into electoral competition in which the winner gains the power to govern; the principle that states with two active and competitive parties have higher rates of voter turnout than states, such as Texas, with weak or noncompetitive parties.

party dealignment The change from identifying with either major political party to identifying as independents.

party discipline The willingness of a party's House or Senate members to act together as a cohesive group and lative action.

party identification The personal sense of loyalty that an individual may feel toward a particular political party. (See also **party realignment.**)

party ideology Basic belief system that guides a political party.

party leaders Members of the House and Senate who are chosen by the Democratic or Republican caucus in each chamber to represent the party's interests in that chamber and who give some central direction to the chamber's work.

party organizations The party organizational units at national, state, and local levels; their influence has decreased over time because of many factors. (See also **candidate-centered campaigns; party-centered campaigns; primary election.**)

party platform Statement of the primary beliefs and goals of a political party.

party realignment An election or set of elections in which the electorate responds strongly to an extraordinarily powerful issue that has disrupted the established political order. A realignment has a lasting impact on public policy, popular support for the parties, and the composition of the party coalitions; the change from a state dominated by one political party to the two-party system operating today. (See also **party identification.**)

party unity The degree to which a party's House or Senate members act as a unified group to exert collective control over legislative action. 11

patronage system An approach to managing the bureaucracy whereby people are appointed to important government positions as a reward for political services they have rendered and because of their partisan loyalty. (See also **executive leadership system; merit system; spoils system.**)

peak business organizations Interest groups that represent statewide business organizations, such as a state's Chamber of Commerce.

permanent party organization The series of elected officers in a political party who keep the party organization alive between elections.

permanent registration system A system that allows citizens to remain on the voter registration list if they continue to vote at prescribed intervals.

petit jury A jury of citizens selected randomly from voter registration lists or lists of licensed drivers that determines the guilt or innocence of a person during a criminal trial.

plural executive System in which voters elect many statewide officeholders to serve as heads of departments.

pluralism A theory of American politics that holds that society's interests are substantially represented through the activities of groups.

plurality (winner-take-all) system An electoral system in which the candidate who gets the most votes (the plurality) is an election district is elected to office from that district.

plurality opinion A court opinion that results when a majority of justices agrees on a decision in a case but do not agree on the legal basis for the decision. In this instance, the legal position held by most of the justices on the winning side is called a *plurality opinion*. (See also **concurring opinion; dissenting opinion; majority opinion.**)

policy Generally, any broad course of governmental action; more narrowly, a specific government program or initiative.

policy formation The stage of the policy process in which a policy is formulated for dealing with a policy problem.

policy implementation The primary function of the bureaucracy; it refers to the process of carrying out the authoritative decisions of Congress, the president, and the courts.

policy implementation (in reference to policy process) The stage of the policy process in which a policy is put into effect and evaluated.

political action committee (PAC) The organization through which an interest group raises and distributes funds for election purposes. By law, the funds must be raised through voluntary contributions.

political consultants The professionals who advise candidates on various aspects of their campaigns, such as media use, fundraising, and polling.

political culture The characteristic and deep-seated beliefs of a particular people.

political movements See **social (political) movements.**

political participation Involvement in activities intended to influence public policy and leadership, such as voting, joining political groups, contacting elected officials, demonstrating for political causes, and giving money to political candidates.

political party An ongoing coalition of interests joined together to try to get their candidates for public office elected under a common label.

political science The systematic study of government and politics.

political socialization The learning process by which people acquire their political opinions, beliefs, and values.

political system The various components of American government. The parts are separate, but they connect with each other, affecting how each performs.

political thinking Reflective thinking focused on deciding what can reasonably be believed and then using this information to make political judgments.

population In a public opinion poll, the people (for example, the citizens of a nation) whose opinions are being estimated through interviews with a sample of these people.

populists Those who believe government should do more to assist people who have difficulty meeting their economic needs and who look to government to uphold traditional values. (See also **economic conservatives; economic liberals; libertarians; social conservatives; social liberals.**)

pork (pork-barrel spending) Spending whose tangible benefits are targeted at a particular legislator's constituency.

pork-barrel projects Legislative acts whose tangible benefits are targeted at a particular legislator's constituency.

positive government The philosophical belief that government intervention is necessary in order to enhance personal liberty and security when individuals are buffeted by economic and social forces beyond their control. (See also **negative government.**)

poverty line As defined by the federal government, the annual cost of a thrifty food budget for an urban family of four, multiplied by three to allow also for the cost of housing, clothes, and other expenses. Families below the poverty line are considered poor and are eligible for certain forms of public assistance.

power The ability of persons or institutions to control policy. (See also **authority.**)

precedent A judicial decision that serves as a rule for settling subsequent cases of a similar nature.

precinct chair Party official elected in each voting precinct who organizes and supports the party.

preemptive war doctrine The idea, espoused by President George W. Bush, that the United States could attack a potentially threatening nation even if the threat had not yet reached a serious and immediate level.

preferential voting A system that allows voters to rank candidates for the city council.

presidential approval ratings A measure of the degree to which the public approves or disapproves of the president's performance in office.

presidential commissions Organizations within the bureaucracy that are headed by commissioners appointed by the president. An example is the Commission on Civil Rights.

presidential preference primary Election held every four years by political parties to determine the preferences of delegates for presidential candidates.

press (news media) Print, broadcast, cable, and Internet organizations that are in the news-reporting business.

primary election (direct primary) A form of election in which voters choose a party's nominees for public office. In most states, eligibility to vote in a primary election is limited to voters who designated themselves as party members when they registered to vote.

prior restraint Government prohibition of speech or publication before the fact, which is presumed by the courts to be unconstitutional unless the justification for it is overwhelming.

private (individual) goods Benefits that a group (most often an economic group) can grant directly and exclusively to individual members of the group. (See also **collective goods.**)

probability sample A sample for a poll in which each individual in the population has a known probability of being selected randomly for inclusion in the sample. (See also **public opinion poll.**)

problem recognition The stage of the policy process whereby conditions in society become recognized as a policy problem.

procedural due process The constitutional requirement that government must follow proper legal procedures before a person can be legitimately punished for an alleged offense.

procedural law Laws governing the legal process that define proper courses of action by government or private parties.

professional associations Organizations of people in professions such as teaching, medicine, law, architecture, cosmetology, and many others that generally require a license, have an element of state control, and lack the right to collective bargaining.

progressive (graduated) personal income tax A tax on personal income in which the tax rate increases as income increases; in other words, the tax rate is higher for higher income levels.

proportional representation system A form of representation in which seats in the legislature are allocated proportionally according to each political party's share of the popular vote. This system enables smaller parties to compete successfully for seats. (See also **single-member districts.**)

prospective voting A form of electoral judgment in which voters choose the candidate whose policy promises most closely match their own preferences. (See also **retrospective voting.**)

protectionism The placing of the immediate interests of domestic producers (through, for example, protective tariffs) above that of free trade between nations. (See also **free-trade position.**)

public assistance A term that refers to social welfare programs funded through general tax revenues and available only to the financially needy. Eligibility for such a program is established by a means test. (See also **means test; social insurance.**)

public goods See **collective (public) goods.**

public opinion poll A device for measuring public opinion whereby a relatively small number of individuals (the sample) is interviewed for the purpose of estimating the opinions of a whole community (the population). (See also **probability sample.**)

public opinion The politically relevant opinions held by ordinary citizens that they express openly.

public policies Decisions by government to pursue particular courses of action.

public policy Any action or inaction by the government that has an impact on the lives of its citizens.

public policy process The political interactions that lead to the emergence and resolution of public policy issues.

punitive damages Damages awarded in a legal case as a punishment or a deterrent.

purposive incentive An incentive to group participation based on the cause (purpose) that the group seeks to promote.

R

racially gerrymandered majority-minority districts Legislative districts that are drawn to the advantage of a minority group.

realignment See **party realignment.**

reapportionment The reallocation of House seats among states after each census as a result of population changes.

reasonable-basis test A test applied by courts to laws that treat individuals unequally. Such a law may be deemed constitutional if its purpose is held to be "reasonably" related to a legitimate government interest. develop

recall of the governor The removal of the governor (or another elected official) by a petition signed by the required number of registered voters, followed by an election in which a majority votes to remove the person from office.

redistricting The process of altering election districts in order to make them as nearly equal in population as possible. Redistricting takes place every ten years, after each population census.

reform (minor) party A minor party that bases its appeal on the claim that the major parties are having a corrupting influence on government and policy.

registration The practice of placing citizens' names on an official list of voters before they are eligible to exercise their right to vote.

regulation A term that refers to government restrictions on the economic practices of private firms.

regulatory agencies Administrative units, such as the Federal Communications Commission and the Environmental Protection Agency, that have responsibility for the monitoring and regulation of ongoing economic activities.

representation function The responsibility of a legislature to represent various interests in society. (See also **lawmaking function; oversight function.**)

representative democracy A system in which the people participate in the decision-making process of government not directly but indirectly, through the election of officials to represent their interests.

representative government A government in which the people govern through the selection of their representatives.

republic A form of government in which the people's representatives decide policy through institutions structured in ways that foster deliberation, slow the progress of decision making, and operate within restraints that protect individual liberty. To the framers, the Constitution's separation of powers and other limits on power were defining features of a republican form of government, as opposed to a democratic form, which places no limits on the majority.

reserved powers The powers granted to the states under the Tenth Amendment to the Constitution.

retrospective voting A form of electoral judgment in which voters support the incumbent candidate or party when their policies are judged to have succeeded and oppose the candidate or party when their policies are judged to have failed. (See also **prospective voting.**)

rider An amendment to a bill that deals with an issue unrelated to the content of the bill; provision attached to a bill that may not be of the same subject matter as the main bill. Riders are permitted in the Senate but not in the House.

right of privacy A right implied by the freedoms in the Bill of Rights that grants individuals a degree of personal privacy upon which government cannot lawfully intrude. The right gives individuals a level of free choice in areas such as reproduction and intimate relations.

"Robin Hood plan" A nickname for the provision in the education statutes that consolidated property taxes so that they are distributed among rich and poor districts; revised later to require rich districts with a property tax base per pupil in excess of $305,000 to share their wealth with other school district.

S

safe election districts Noncompetitive districts that can be won only by the party with 55 percent or more of the votes in the district.

sample In a public opinion poll, the relatively small number of individuals who are interviewed for the purpose of estimating the opinions of an entire population. (See also **public opinion poll.**)

sampling error A measure of the accuracy of a public opinion poll; mainly a function of sample size and usually expressed in percentage terms. (See also **probability sample.**)

secretary of state (SOS) Chief election official and keeper of state records—appointed by the governor.

selective incorporation The process by which certain of the rights (for example, freedom of speech) contained in the Bill of Rights become applicable through the Fourteenth Amendment to actions by the state governments.

self-government The principle that the people are the ultimate source and proper beneficiary of governing authority; in practice, a government based on majority rule.

semiclosed primary A primary that allows voters to register or change their party registration on Election Day; registration as a member of a party is required on Election Day.

semiopen primary A nominating election in which registered voters can choose which primary to vote in on Election Day.

senatorial courtesy The tradition that a U.S. senator from the state in which a federal judicial vacancy has arisen should have a say in the president's nomination of the new judge if the senator is of the same party as the president.

Senior Executive Service (SES) Top-level career civil servants who qualify through a competitive process to receive higher salaries than their peers but who can be assigned or transferred by order of the president.

seniority A member of Congress's consecutive years of service on a particular committee.

separated institutions sharing power The principle that, as a way to limit government, its powers should be divided among separate branches, each of which also shares in the power of the others as a means of checking and balancing them. The result is that no one branch can exercise power decisively without the support or acquiescence of the others.

separation of powers The division of the powers of government among separate institutions or branches.

service relationship The situation in which party organizations assist candidates for office but have no power to require them to support the party's main policy positions.

service strategy Use of personal staff by members of Congress to perform services for constituents in order to gain their support in future elections.

settlement patterns the many origins of first settlers to the state.

Shivercrats Democrats who followed Governor Allan Shivers's example and voted for Eisenhower in 1952 and 1956.

signaling (signaler) function The responsibility of the media to alert the public to important developments as soon as possible after they happen or are discovered. (See also **common-carrier function; partisan function; watchdog function.**)

sine die Adjourned; the legislature must adjourn at end of its regular session and cannot continue to meet.

single-issue (minor) party A minor party formed around a single issue of overriding interest to its followers.

single-issue politics The situation in which separate groups are organized around nearly every conceivable policy issue and press their demands and influence to the utmost.

single-member district District having one member elected to the legislature; a system in which the city is divided into election districts and only the voters living in that district elect the council member from that district.

single-member districts The form of representation in which only the

candidate who gets the most votes in a district wins office. (See also **proportional representation system.**)

slander Spoken falsehoods that damage a person's reputation.

small-state plan See **New Jersey (small-state) Plan.**

social (political) movements Active and sustained efforts to achieve social and political change by groups of people who feel that government has not been properly responsive to their concerns.

social capital The sum of the face-to-face interactions among citizens in a society.

social conservatives Those who believe government power should be used to uphold traditional values. (See also **economic conservatives; economic liberals; libertarians; populists; social liberals.**)

social contract A voluntary agreement by individuals to form a government that is then obligated to work within the confines of that agreement.

social insurance Social welfare programs are based on the "insurance" concept, requiring that individuals pay into the program in order to be eligible to receive funds from it. An example is social security for retired people. (See also **public assistance.**)

social liberals Those who believe it is not government's role to buttress traditional values at the expense of unconventional or new values. (See also **economic conservatives; economic liberals; libertarians; populists; social conservatives.**)

socialism An economic system in which government owns and controls many of the major industries.

soft money Campaign contributions that are not subject to legal limits and are given to parties rather than directly to candidates.

solicitor general The high-ranking Justice Department official who serves as the government's lawyer in Supreme Court cases.

sound-bite commercial A brief, usually thirty-second, TV political advertisement that conveys a simple and memorable message about the candidate or the opponent.

sovereignty The supreme (or ultimate) authority to govern within a certain geographical area.

speaker of the house Member of the Texas House, elected by the other House members, who serves as presiding officer and generally controls the passage of legislation.

special session Session called by the governor to consider legislation proposed by the governor only.

split ticket The pattern of voting in which the individual voter in a given election casts a ballot for one or more candidates of each major party.

spoils system The practice of granting public office to individuals in return for political favors they have rendered. (See also **patronage system.**)

standing committees Permanent congressional committees with responsibility for a particular area of public policy. An example is the Senate Foreign Relations Committee.

state and local interest groups (SLIGs) Interest groups that represent state government employees, such as the Texas Association of Police Chiefs, and local governments, such as the Texas Association of County Officials.

state boards and commissions Administrative units for many state agencies that carry out most of the work of state government; members are appointed by the governor for fixed terms.

state constitutional convention A state convention convened to amend the state constitution or draft a new one.

state executive committee A committee that is made up of one man and one woman elected from each state senatorial district and functions as the governing body of the party.

stewardship theory A theory that argues for a strong, assertive presidential role, with presidential authority limited only at points specifically prohibited by law. (See also **Whig theory.**)

straight ticket voting Casting all votes for candidates of one party.

strict-scrutiny test A test applied by courts to laws that attempt a racial or an ethnic classification. In effect, the strict-scrutiny test eliminates race or ethnicity as legal classification when it places minority-group members at a disadvantage. (See also **suspect classifications.**)

suffrage The right to vote.

Sunset Advisory Commission Agency responsible for making recommendations to the legislature for change in the structure and organization of most state agencies.

sunset law A law containing a provision that fixes a date on which a program will end unless the program's life is extended by Congress.

super PACs Election committees that are unrestricted in their fund raising and spending as long as they do not coordinate their campaign efforts with that of a candidate.

supply-side economics A form of fiscal policy that emphasizes "supply" (production). An example of supply-side economics would be a tax cut for business. (See also **demand-side economics; fiscal policy.**)

supremacy clause Article VI of the Constitution, which makes national law supreme over state law when the national government is acting within its constitutional limits.

suspect classifications Legal classifications, such as race and national origin, that hve invidious discrimination as their purpose and therefore are unconstitutional. (See also **strict-scrutiny test.**)

symbolic speech Action (for example, the waving or burning of a flag) for the purpose of expressing a political opinion.

T

tariffs The taxes that a country levies on goods shipped into it from other countries.

tax assessor collector Elected officer responsible for collecting revenue for the state and the county.

tax capacity The measure of wealth in taxable resources.

tax incidence The person actually paying the tax.

tax shifting passing taxes on to other parties.

temporary party organization The series of conventions, or caucuses, that occur every two years at the precinct, county, and state levels.

tenure of office The legal ability of governors to succeed themselves in office and the length of their term.

term limits Limits on the number of times a person can be elected to the same office.

Texas Ethics Commission State agency responsible for enforcing requirements to report information on money collected and activities by interest groups and candidates for public office.

Texas Railroad Commission (RRC) State agency, with a three-member elected board, that regulates some aspects of transportation and the oil and gas industry of the state.

Three-Fifths Compromise A compromise worked out at the 1787 convention between northern states and southern states. Each slave was to be counted as three-fifths of a person for purposes of federal taxation and congressional apportionment (number of seats in the House of Representative).

tort reform Changing the legal rules regarding compensation for damages done by one party to another.

totalitarian government A form of government in which the leaders claim complete dominance of all individuals and institutions.

trade associations Interest groups that represent specific business interests, such as oil producers and highway contractors.

traditionalistic subculture A political subculture that expects government to maintain the existing political order for the benefit of a small elite.

transfer payment A government benefit that is given directly to an individual, as in the case of social security payments to a retiree.

transnational terrorism Terrorism that transcends national borders and often targets people and locations other than the ones directly at issue.

trial *de novo* courts Courts that do not keep a written record of their proceedings; cases on appeal begin as new cases in the appellate courts.

trustees Elected representatives whose obligation is to act in accordance with their own consciences as to what policies are in the best interests of the public. (See also **delegates.**)

turnover The number of new members of the legislature each session.

two-party competitive state a state in which parties switch control of the statewide elected offices and control of the state legislature.

two-party system A system in which only two political parties have a real chance of acquiring control of the government.

tyranny of the majority The potential of a majority to monopolize power for its own gain and to the detriment of minority rights and interests.

U

unfunded or underfunded mandates Laws enacted by federal or state governments that impose responsibilities and financial burdens on city and county governments.

unilateralism The situation in which one nation takes action against another state or states.

unipolar (power structure) A power structure dominated by a single powerful actor, as in the case of the United States after the collapse of the Soviet Union.

unit rule The rule that grants all of a state's electoral votes to the candidate who receives most of the popular votes in the state.

unitary system A governmental system in which the national government alone has sovereign (ultimate) authority. (See also **confederacy; federalism.**)

V

veto The president's rejection of a bill, thereby keeping it from becoming law unless Congress overrides the veto.

Virginia (large-state) Plan A constitutional proposal for a strong Congress with two chambers, both of which would be based on numerical representation, thus granting more power to the larger states.

voter turnout The proportion of persons of voting age who actually vote in a given election.

voting-age population All citizens who meet the formal requirements to register to vote; in Texas, you must be 18 years of age and a resident of the state for thirty days before the election.

W

watchdog function The accepted responsibility of the media to protect the public from incompetent or corrupt officials by standing ready to expose any official who violates accepted legal, ethical, or performance standards. (See also **common-carrier function; partisan function; signaling function.**)

Whig theory A theory that prevailed in the nineteenth century and held that the presidency was a limited or restrained office whose occupant was confined to expressly granted constitutional authority. (See also **stewardship theory.**)

whistleblowing An internal check on the bureaucracy whereby employees report instances of mismanagement that they observe.

White House Office (WHO) A subunit of the Executive Office of the President, the White House Office is the core of the presidential staff system in that it includes the president's closest and most trusted personal advisors.

write-in candidate A person whose name does not appear on the ballot; voters must write in the name, and the person must have filed formal notice before the election that she or he is a write-in candidate.

writ of certiorari Permission granted by a higher court to allow a losing party in a legal case to bring the case before it for a ruling; when such a writ is requested of the U.S. Supreme Court, four of the Court's nine justices must agree to accept the case before it is granted certiorari.

Y

Yellow Dog Democrats People who voted straight ticket for Democrats—they would vote for a yellow dog if it ran as a Democrat.

Yellow Pup Republicans Younger voters who tend to vote straight ticket for Republican candidates.

Notes

Chapter 1

[1]John Stuart Mill, *On Liberty*, eds. Michael B. Mathias and Daniel Kolak (New York: Longman, 2006), 43.

[2]PIPA/Knowledge Networks Poll, "Misperceptions, the Media, and the Iraq War," Center on Policy Attitudes and the Center for International Security Studies, University of Maryland, October 2, 2003.

[3]This misperception persisted even into 2004 as an October 2004 Harris poll discovered.

[4]Ibid.

[5]Walter Lippmann, *Public Opinion* (New York: Free Press, 1997), 82.

[6]Bruce Ackerman and James Fishkin, *Deliberation Day* (New Haven, Conn.: Yale University Press, 2004), 5.

[7]"Take the Quiz: What We Don't Know," *Newsweek,* March 20, 2011.

[8]Clay Ramsey, Steven Kull, Evan Lewis, and Stefan Subias, "Misinformation and the 2010 Election: A Study of the US Electorate," The Program on International Policy Attitudes, University of Maryland, College Park, Maryland, December 10, 2010, pp. 20–23.

[9]Mark Bauerlein, *The Dumbest Generation* (New York: Penguin, 2008), 28.

[10]Mill, *On Liberty*, 224.

[11]James David Barber, "Characters in the Campaign," in James David Barber, ed. *Race for the Presidency* (Englewood Cliffs, N.J.: Prentice-Hall, 1978), 181.

[12]See, for example, Doris A. Graber, *Processing the News: How People Tame the Information Tide,* 2d ed. (New York: Longman, 1988), 107–15.

[13]Pew Internet and American Life survey, March 1, 2010.

[14]Ellen Hume, "Talk Show Culture," Web posting, 2009.

[15]Ramsey et al., "Misinformation and the 2010 Election," 13.

[16]See Bryant Welch, *State of Confusion: Political Manipulation and the Assault on the American Mind* (New York: Thomas Dunne Books, 2008).

[17]Martha Joynt Kumar, *Managing the President's Message* (Baltimore, Md.: Johns Hopkins University Press, 2007).

[18]Thomas E. Patterson, *News and Democracy; The Need for Knowledge-Based Journalism,* forthcoming, 2013.

[19]Marvin Kalb, "The Rise of the 'New News,'" Discussion Paper D-34, Joan Shorenstein Center on the Press, Politics, and Public Policy, John F. Kennedy School of Government, Harvard University, October 1998.

[20]Todd K. Hartman and Christopher R. Weber, "Who Said What? The Effects of Source Cues in Issue Frames." *Political Behavior* 31(2009): 537–58.

[21]Diana Mutz, *Hearing the Other Side: Deliberative versus Participatory Democracy* (New York: Cambridge University Press, 2006).

[22]Mill, *On Liberty,* 35.

[23]Intercollegiate Studies Association, "Greater Civic Knowledge Trumps a College Degree as the Leading Factor in Encouraging Active Civic Engagement," online report, 2011.

[24]See Michael Foley, *American Credo: The Place of Ideas in American Politics* (New York: Oxford University Press, 2007).

[25]James Bryce, *The American Commonwealth,* vol. 2 (New York: Macmillan, 1960), 247–54. First published in 1900.

[26]Bryce, *The American Commonwealth,* 132.

[27]Louis Hartz, *The Liberal Tradition in America* (New York: Harcourt, Brace, 1952), 12.

[28]Raymond T. Bond, ed., *The Man Who Was Chesterton* (Garden City, N. Y.: Image Books, 1960), 125.

[29]Alexis de Tocqueville, *Democracy in America, Volume 2* (New York: Vintage Classics), 89.

[30]William Watts and Lloyd A. Free, eds, *The State of the Nation* (New York: University Books, Potomac Associates, 1967), 97.

[31]Bryce, *The American Commonwealth,* 182.

[32]U.S. Census Bureau figures, 2012.

[33]Quoted in Ralph Volney Harlow, *The Growth of the United States,* vol. 2 (New York: Henry Holt, 1943), 497.

[34]*Tinker v. Colwell,* 193 U.S. 473 (1904).

[35]David Herbert Donald, *Lincoln* (New York: Simon & Schuster, 1996), 406.

[36]Martin Luther King Jr., Speech at Civil Rights March on Washington, August 28, 1963.

[37]Theodore H. White, "The American Idea," *New York Times,* August 3, 1986.

[38]Harold D. Lasswell, *Politics: Who Gets What, When, How* (New York: McGraw-Hill, 1936).

[39]Russell Hardin, *Liberalism, Constitutionalism, and Democracy* (New York: Oxford University Press, 1999).

[40]Foucault's phrasing was a deliberate inversion of von Clausewitz's famous line, "War is politics by other means." Foucault is not the only writer who has applied this inversion.

[41]Eric F. Goldman, *The Crucial Decade* (New York: Knopf, 1956), 116.

[42]Adam Przworski and José María Maravall, eds., *Democracy and the Rule of Law* (New York: Cambridge University Press, 2003).

[43]See Robert Dahl, *On Democracy* (New Haven, Conn.: Yale University Press, 2000).

[44]See Paul Steinhauser, "Poll: U.S. Split over Afghan Troop Buildup," CNN online, November 24, 2009.

[45]Seymour Martin Lipset, *American Exceptionalism: A Double-Edged Sword* (New York: W. W. Norton: 1996), 37.

[46]*Gideon v. Wainwright,* 372 U.S. 335 (1963).

[47]Figures based on American Bar Association and Council of European Lawyers data as of 2007.

[48]James Q. Wilson, "American Exceptionalism," AEI Online, August 29, 2006, 9.

[49]Figures are for 2008.

[50]See William G. Domhoff, *Who Rules America? Challenges to Corporate and Class Dominance,* 6th ed. (New York: McGraw-Hill, 2009).

[51]C. Wright Mills, *The Power Elite* (New York: Oxford University Press, 1965).

[52]See Joseph A. Schumpeter, *Capitalism, Socialism and Democracy* (New York: Harper, 1975).

[53]E. E. Schattschneider, *Two Hundred Million Americans in Search of a Government* (New York: Holt, Reinhart, and Winston, 1969), 42.

Chapter 2

[1] Quoted in Charles S. Hyneman, "Republican Government in America," in George J. Graham Jr. and Scarlett G. Graham, eds., *Founding Principles of American Government,* rev. ed. (Chatham, N.J.: Chatham House, 1984), 19.

[2] See John Harmon McElroy, *American Beliefs: What Keeps a Big Country and a Diverse People United* (Chicago: I. R. Dee, 1999).

[3] See Russell Hardin, *Liberalism, Constitutionalism, and Democracy* (New York: Oxford University Press, 1999); A. John Simmons, *The Lockean Theory of Rights* (Princeton, N.J.: Princeton University Press, 1994).

[4] Thomas Hobbes, *Leviathan* (1651).

[5] John Locke, *Second Treatise on Civil Government* (1690).

[6] Quoted in "The Constitution and Slavery," Digital History website, December 1, 2003.

[7] Gaillard Hunt, ed., *The Writings of James Madison* (New York: Putnam, 1904), 274; see also Garret Ward Sheldon, *The Political Philosophy of James Madison* (Baltimore, Md.: Johns Hopkins University Press, 2000).

[8] See Vincent Ostrom, *The Political Theory of a Compound Republic: Designing the American Experiment* (Lanham, Md.: Lexington Books, 2007).

[9] See *Federalist* Nos. 47 and 48.

[10] Richard Neustadt, *Presidential Power* (New York: Macmillan, 1986), 33.

[11] Henry J. Abraham, *The Judicial Process,* 6th ed. (New York: Oxford University Press, 1993), 320–22.

[12] *Marbury v. Madison,* 1 Cranch 137 (1803).

[13] Martin Diamond, *The Founding of the Democratic Republic* (Itasca, Ill.: Peacock, 1981), 62–71.

[14] *Federalist* No. 10.

[15] Leslie F. Goldstein, "Judicial Review and Democratic Theory: Guardian Democracy vs. Representative Democracy," *Western Political Quarterly* 40 (1987): 391–412.

[16] See Douglas Bradburn, *The Citizenship Revolution: Politics and the Creation of the American Union 1774–1804* (Charlottesville: University of Virginia Press, 2009).

[17] Benjamin Ginsberg, *The Consequences of Consent* (New York: Random House, 1982), 22.

[18] Robert Dahl, *Pluralist Democracy in the United States* (Chicago: Rand McNally, 1967), 92.

[19] This interpretation is taken from Walter Lippmann, *Public Opinion* (New York: Free Press, 1965), 178–79.

[20] Michael McGeer, *A Fierce Discontent: The Rise and Fall of the Progressive Movement in America, 1870–1920* (New York: Free Press, 2005).

[21] Charles S. Beard, *An Economic Interpretation of the Constitution* (New York: Macmillan, 1941). First published in 1913.

[22] John M. Scheb and John M. Scheb II, *Introduction to the American Legal System* (Clifton Park, N.Y.: Delmar Cengage Learning System, 2001), 6.

[23] See Randall G. Holcombe, *From Liberty to Democracy* (Ann Arbor: University of Michigan Press, 2002).

Chapter 3

[1] Woodrow Wilson, *Constitutional Government in the United States* (New York: Columbia University Press, 1908), 173.

[2] *National Federation of Independent Business v. Sebelius,* No. 11–393 (2012).

[3] See Samuel Beer, *To Make a Nation: The Rediscovery of American Federalism* (Cambridge, Mass.: The Belknap Press of Harvard University, 1993).

[4] *Antifederalist* No. 9. This essay appeared in the *Independent Gazetteer* on October 17, 1787, under the pen name "Montezuma."

[5] Alison L. LaCroix, *The Ideological Origins of American Federalism* (Cambridge, Mass.: Harvard University Press, 2010).

[6] *McCulloch v. Maryland,* 4 Wheaton 316 (1819).

[7] *Gibbons v. Ogden,* 22 Wheaton 1 (1824). [22 U.S. 1 (1824)].

[8] Oliver Wendell Holmes Jr., *Collected Legal Papers* (New York: Harcourt, Brace, 1920), 295–96.

[9] See John C. Calhoun, *The Works of John C. Calhoun* (New York: Russell & Russell, 1968).

[10] *Dred Scott v. Sanford,* 19 Howard 393 (1857).

[11] *U.S. v. Cruikshank,* 92 U.S. 452 (1876).

[12] *Slaughter-House Cases,* 16 Wallace 36 (1873); *Civil Rights Cases,* 109 U.S. 3 (1883).

[13] *Plessy v. Ferguson,* 163 U.S. 537 (1896).

[14] See, for example, Douglas A. Blackmon, *Slavery by Another Name: The Re-Enslavement of Black America from the Civil War to World War II* (New York: Anchor Books, 2009).

[15] *Santa Clara County v. Southern Pacific Railroad Co.,* 118 U.S. 394 (1886).

[16] *U.S. v. E. C. Knight Co.,* 156 U.S. 1 (1895).

[17] *Hammer v. Dagenhart,* 247 U.S. 251 (1918).

[18] *Lochner v. New York,* 198 U.S. 25 (1905).

[19] Alfred H. Kelly, Winifred A. Harbison, and Herman Belz, *The American Constitution,* 7th ed. (New York: Norton, 1991), 529; but also see Kimberley Johnson, *Governing the American State: Congress and the New Federalism, 1877–1929* (Princeton, N.J.: Princeton University Press, 2006).

[20] James E. Anderson, *The Emergence of the Modern Regulatory State* (Washington, D.C.: Public Affairs Press, 1962), 2–3.

[21] *Schechter Poultry Corp. v. United States,* 295 U.S. 495 (1935).

[22] *NLRB v. Jones and Laughlin Steel,* 301 U.S. 1 (1937).

[23] *American Power and Light v. Securities and Exchange Commission,* 329 U.S. 90 (1946).

[24] Louis Fisher, *American Constitutional Law,* 6th ed. (Durham, N.C.: Carolina Academic Press, 2005), 390.

[25] *North American Company v. Securities and Exchange Commission,* 327 U.S. 686 (1946).

[26] *Brown v. Board of Education,* 347 U.S. 483 (1954).

[27] See Thomas Anton, *American Federalism and Public Policy* (Philadelphia: Temple University Press, 1989).

[28] Morton Grodzins, *The American System: A New View of Government in the United States* (Chicago: Rand McNally, 1966).

[29] John D. Nugent, *Safeguarding Federalism: How States Protect Their Interests in National Policymaking* (Norman: University of Oklahoma Press, 2009).

[30] Rosella Levaggi, *Fiscal Federalism and Grants-in-Aid* (Brookfield, Vt.: Avebury, 1991).

[31] Beth Fouhy, "GOP Governors Press Congress to Pass Stimulus Bill," Associated Press wire story, January 31, 2009.

[32] Timothy J. Conlan, *From New Federalism to Devolution* (Washington, D.C.: Brookings Institution, 1998).

[33] *Garcia v. San Antonio Authority,* 469 U.S. 528 (1985).

[34] See Tinsley E. Yarbrough, *The Rehnquist Court and the Constitution* (New York: Oxford University Press, 2000); David L. Hudson, *The Rehnquist Court: Understanding Its Impact and Legacy* (Westport, Conn.: Praeger, 2006).

[35] *United States v. Lopez,* 514 U.S. 549 (1995).

[36] *Printz v. United States,* 521 U.S. 98 (1997).

[37] *Arizona v. United States,* No. 11-182 (2012).

[38] *Kimel v. Florida Board of Regents,* 528 U.S. 62 (2000).

[39] NCSL, "Task Force on No Child Left Behind," final report, National Council of State Legislators, Denver Colorado, February 2005.

[40] Andrew W. Dobelstein, *Politics, Economics, and Public Welfare* (Englewood Cliffs, N.J.: Prentice-Hall, 1980), 5.

[41] Lloyd A. Free and Hadley Cantril, *The Political Beliefs of Americans* (New York: Simon & Schuster, 1968), 21.

[42]Survey for the Times Mirror Center for the People and the Press by Princeton Survey Research Associates, July 12–27, 1994.

Chapter 4

[1]Julian P. Boyd, ed., *The Papers of Thomas Jefferson*, vol. 12 (Princeton, N.J.: Princeton University Press, 1955), 440.

[2]*United States v. Jones*, No. 10-1250 (2012).

[3]*Barron v. Baltimore*, 32 U.S. (7 Pet.) 243 (1833).

[4]*Gitlow v. New York*, 268 U.S. 652 (1925).

[5]*Fiske v. Kansas*, 274 U.S. 30 (1927); *Near v. Minnesota*, 283 U.S. 697 (1931); *Hamilton v. Regents, U. of California*, 293 U.S. 245 (1934); *DeJonge v. Oregon*, 299 U.S. 253 (1937).

[6]*Near v. Minnesota*, 283 U.S. 697 (1931).

[7]*Palko v. Connecticut*, 302 U.S. 319 (1937).

[8]*Powell v. Alabama*, 287 U.S. 45 (1932).

[9]*Mapp v. Ohio*, 367 U.S. 643 (1961).

[10]*Gideon v. Wainright*, 372 U.S. 335 (1963)

[11]*Malloy v. Hogan*, 378 U.S. 1 (1964).

[12]*Miranda v. Arizona*, 384 U.S. 436 (1966); see also *Escobedo v. Illinois*, 378 U.S. 478 (1964).

[13]*Pointer v. Texas*, 380 U.S. 400 (1965).

[14]*Klopfer v. North Carolina*, 386 U.S. 213 (1967).

[15]*Duncan v. Louisiana*, 391 U.S. 145 (1968).

[16]*Benton v. Maryland*, 395 U.S. 784 (1969).

[17]*United States v. Carolene Products Co.*, 304 U.S. 144 (1938).

[18]*Exparte McCardle*, 74 U.S. 506 (1869).

[19]*Schenck v. United States*, 249 U.S. 47 (1919).

[20]*Dennis v. United States*, 341 U.S. 494 (1951); for a broad look at the relationship between issues of national security and liberty, see Geoffrey Stone, *War and Liberty: An American Dilemma: 1790 to the Present* (New York: W. W. Norton, 2007).

[21]See, for example, *Yates v. United States*, 354 U.S. 298 (1957); *Noto v. United States*, 367 U.S. 290 (1961); *Scales v. United States*, 367 U.S. 203 (1961).

[22]*Brandenburg v. Ohio*, 395 U.S. 444 (1969).

[23]*R.A.V. v. St. Paul*, No. 90-7675 (1992).

[24]*Wisconsin v. Mitchell*, No. 92-515 (1993).

[25]*Snyder v. Phelps* No. 09-7571 (2011)

[26]*United States v. O'Brien*, 391 U.S. 367 (1968).

[27]*Texas v. Johnson*, 109 S. Ct. 2544 (1989).

[28]*National Socialist Party v. Skokie*, 432 U.S. 43 (1977).

[29]*Forsyth County v. Nationalist Movement*, No. 91-538 (1992).

[30]*New York Times Co. v. United States*, 403 U.S. 713 (1971).

[31]*Nebraska Press Assn. v. Stuart*, 427 U.S. 539 (1976).

[32]*Milkovich v. Lorain Journal*, 497 U.S. 1 (1990); see also *Masson v. The New Yorker*, No. 89-1799 (1991).

[33]*New York Times Co. v. Sullivan*, 376 U.S. 254 (1964).

[34]*Miller v. California*, 413 U.S. 15 (1973).

[35]*Barnes v. Glen Theatre*, No. 90-26 (1991).

[36]*Stanley v. Georgia*, 394 U.S. 557 (1969).

[37]*Osborne v. Ohio*, 495 U.S. 103 (1990); see also *Ashcroft v. Free Speech Coalition*, No. 00-795 (2002).

[38]*United States v. Williams*, No. 06-694 (2008).

[39]*Denver Area Consortium v. Federal Communications Commission*, No. 95-124 (1996); *Reno v. American Civil Liberties Union*, No. 96-511 (1997); *Ashcroft v. ACLU*, No. 03-0218 (2004).

[40]*Engel v. Vitale*, 370 U.S. 421 (1962).

[41]*Abington School District v. Schempp*, 374 U.S. 203 (1963).

[42]*Wallace v. Jaffree*, 472 U.S. 38 (1985).

[43]*Santa Fe Independent School District v. Does*, No. 99-62 (2000).

[44]*Van Orden v. Perry*, No. 03-1500 (2005).

[45]*McCreary County v. American Civil Liberties Union*, No. 03-1693 (2005).

[46]*Lemon v. Kurtzman*, 403 U.S. 602 (1971).

[47]*Board of Regents v. Allen*, 392 U.S. 236 (1968).

[48]*Zelman v. Simmons-Harris*, No. 00-1751 (2002); see also *Locke v. Davey*, No. 02-1315 (2004).

[49]*Employment Division, Department of Human Resources of Oregon v. Smith*, 494 U.S. 872 (1990)

[50]*Edwards v. Aguillard*, 487 U.S. 578 (1987).

[51]*Tammy Kitzmiller et al. v. Dover Area School District et al.*, 400 F. Supp. 2d 707, Docket No. 4cv2688 (2005).

[52]*District of Columbia v. Heller*, 554 U.S. 570 (2008).

[53]*McDonald v. Chicago*, 561 U.S. 3025 (2010).

[54]*Griswold v. Connecticut*, 381 U.S. 479 (1965); for an assessment of the Ninth Amendment, see Daniel A. Farber, *Retained by the People: The "Silent" Ninth Amendment and the Constitutional Rights Americans Don't Know They Have* (New York: Basic Books, 2007).

[55]*Roe v. Wade*, 401 U.S. 113 (1973).

[56]*Gregg v. United States*, No. 00-939 (2001).

[57]*Webster v. Reproductive Health Services*, 492 U.S. 490 (1989); see also *Rust v. Sullivan*, No. 89-1391 (1991).

[58]*Planned Parenthood v. Casey*, No. 91-744 (1992).

[59]*Ayotte v. Planned Parenthood of Northern New England*, No. 04-1144 (2006).

[60]*Stenberg v. Carhart*, No. 99-830 (2000).

[61]*Gonzalez v. Carhart*, No. 05-380 (2007).

[62]*Bowers v. Hardwick*, 478 U.S. 186 (1986).

[63]*Lawrence v. Texas*, 539 U.S. 558 (2003).

[64]*McNabb v. United States*, 318 U.S. 332 (1943).

[65]The structure and content of the discussion that follows on arrest, search, interrogation, formal charge, trial, appeal, and punishment is informed by Walter F. Murphy and Michael N. Danielson, *Robert K. Carr and Marver H. Bernstein's American Democracy* (Hinsdale, Ill.: Dryden Press, 1977), 465–74.

[66]David Fellman, *Defendants Rights Today* (Madison: University of Wisconsin Press, 1979), 256.

[67]*United States v. Jones*, No. 10-1250 (2012).

[68]*Whren v. United States*, 517 U.S. 806 (1996).

[69]*Horton v. California*, 496 U.S. 128 (1990)

[70]*Michigan v. Sitz*, No. 88-1897 (1990).

[71]*Indianapolis v. Edmund*, No. 99-1030 (2001).

[72]*Kyllo v. United States*, No. 99-8508 (2001). [533 U.S. 27?]

[73]*Ferguson v. Charleston*, No. 99-936 (2001).

[74]*Board of Education of Independent School District No. 92 of Pottawatomie County v. Earls*, No. 01-332 (2002).

[75]*Florence v. Board of Chosen Freeholders*, 10-946 (2012).

[76]*Dickerson v. United States*, No. 99-5525 (2000), reaffirming *Miranda v. Arizona*, 384 U.S. 436 (1966).

[77]*Missouri v. Siebert*, 542 U.S. 600 (2004).

[78]*Maryland v. Shatzer*, No. 08-680 (2010).

[79]*Berghuis v. Thompkins*, No. 08-1470 (2010).

[80]*Johnson v. Zerbst*, 304 U.S. 458 (1938).

[81]*Gideon v. Wainwright*, 372 U.S. 335 (1963).

[82]*Batson v. Kentucky*, 476 U.S. 79 (1986).

[83]*Witherspoon v. Illinois*, 391 U.S. 510 (1968).

[84]*Weeks v. United States*, 232 U.S. 383 (1914).

[85]*United States v. Leon*, 468 U.S. 897 (1984).

[86]*Herring v. United States*, No. 07-513 (2008).

[87]*Nix v. Williams*, 467 U.S. 431 (1984).

[88]*Harmelin v. Michigan*, No. 89-7272 (1991).

[89]*Lockyer v. Andrade*, No. 01-1127 (2003); see also *Ewing v. California*, No. 01-6978 (2003).

[90]*Atkins v. Virginia*, No. 01-8452 (2002); *Panetti v. Quarterman*, No. 06-6407 (2007).

[91]*Roper v. Simmons*, No. 03-633 (2005); *Kennedy v. Louisiana*, No. 07-343 (2008).

[92]*Graham v. Florida*, No. 08-7412 (2010).

[93]*Wilson v. Seiter*, No. 89-7376 (1991).

[94]*Brown v. Plata*, No. 09-1233 (2011).

[95]*Townsend v. Sain*, 372 U.S. 293 (1963).

[96]*Keeney v. Tamaya-Reyes*, No. 90-1859 (1992); see also *Coleman v. Thompson*, No. 89-7662 (1991).

[97]*Bowles v. Russell*, No. 06-5306 (2007).

[98]*Maples v. Thomas*, No. 10-63 (2012).

[99]*Felker v. Turpin*, No. 95-8836 (1996); but see *Stewart v. Martinez-Villareal*, No. 97-300 (1998).

[100]*Williams v. Taylor,* No. 99-6615 (2000).

[101]Alejandro Del Carmen, *Racial Profiling in America* (Upper Saddle River, N.J.: Prentice-Hall, 2007).

[102]ACLU study, 1999. A 1999 report by the New Jersey Attorney General's Office revealed a similar pattern in that state.

[103]See Heather MacDonald, "Fighting Crime Where the Criminals Are," *New York Times,* June 25, 2010.

[104]"Justices: Judges Can Slash Crack Sentences," CNN.com, December 10, 2007.

[105]*Kimbrough v. United States,* No. 06-6330 (2007).

[106]*Korematsu v. United States,* 323 U.S. 214 (1944).

[107]Case cited in Charles Lane, "In Terror War, 2nd Track for Suspects," *Washington Post,* December 1, 2001, A1.

[108]*Rasul v. Bush,* No. 03-334 (2004); *al-Odah v. United States,* No. 03-343 (2004).

[109]*Hamdi v. Rumsfeld,* No. 03-6696 (2004); see also *Rumsfeld v. Padilla,* No. 03-1027 (2004).

[110]*Hamdan v. Rumsfeld,* No. 05-184 (2006).

[111]*Boumediene et al. v. Bush,* No. 06-1195 (2008).

[112]See Alpheus T. Mason, *The Supreme Court: Palladium of Freedom* (Ann Arbor: University of Michigan Press, 1962); see also Jeffrey Rosen, *The Most Democratic Branch: How the Courts Serve America* (New York: Oxford University Press, 2006).

Chapter 5

[1]Abraham Lincoln, "Speech on the Dred Scott Decision," Springfield, Illinois, June 26, 1857.

[2]*Washington Post* wire story, May 14, 1991.

[3]Robert Nisbet, "Public Opinion versus Popular Opinion," *Public Interest* 41 (1975): 171.

[4]See, for example, Gloria J. Browne-Marshall, *Race, Law, and American Society: 1607 to Present* (New York: Routledge, 2007).

[5]*Plessy v. Ferguson,* 163 U.S. 537 (1896).

[6]Ada Lois Sipuel Fisher, Danney Gable, and Robert Henry, *A Matter of Black and White: The Autobiography of Ada Lois Sipuel Fisher* (Norman: University of Oklahoma Press, 1996).

[7]*Brown v. Board of Education of Topeka,* 347 U.S. 483 (1954).

[8]*Swann v. Charlotte-Mecklenburg County Board of Education,* 402 U.S. 1 (1971).

[9]Christopher Jencks and Meredith Phillips, eds., *The Black-White Test Score Gap* (Washington, D.C.: Brookings Institution, 1998).

[10]*Milliken v. Bradley,* 418 U.S. 717 (1974).

[11]*Board of Education of Oklahoma City v. Dowell,* 498 U.S. 237 (1991).

[12]*Parents Involved in Community Schools v. Seattle,* No. 05-908551 U.S. 701 (2007); *Meredith, Custodial Parent and Next Friend of McDonald v. Jefferson County Board of Education,* No. 05-915548 U.S. 938 (2007).

[13]U.S. Department of Education statistics, 2010.

[14]*Loving v. Virginia,* 388 U.S. 1 (1967).

[15]*Craig v. Boren,* 429 U.S. 190 (1976).

[16]*Rostker v. Goldberg,* 453 U.S. 57 (1980).

[17]*United States v. Virginia,* 518 U.S. 515 (1996)No. 94-1941 (1996).

[18]Blackmon, *Slavery by Another Name.*

[19]Eric J. Sundquist, *King's Dream: The Legacy of Martin Luther King's "I Have a Dream" Speech* (New Haven, Conn.: Yale University Press, 2009).

[20]See Kathleen S. Sullivan, *Women and Rights Discourse in Nineteenth-Century America* (Baltimore, Md.: Johns Hopkins University Press, 2007).

[21]*Tinker v. Colwell,* 193 U.S. 473 (1904).

[22]See Jane Mansbridge, *Why We Lost the ERA* (Chicago: University of Chicago Press, 1986).

[23]Marshall, Gazn, *Why David Sometimes Wins: Leadership, Organization and Strategy in the California Farm Worker Movement* (New York: Oxford University Press, 2009).

[24]*Lau v. Nichols,* 414 U.S. 563 (1974).

[25]Michael J. Klarman, *From Jim Crow to Civil Rights: The Supreme Court and the Struggle for Racial Equality* (New York: Oxford University Press, 2004), 236.

[26]*Smith v. Allwright,* 321 U.S. 649 (1944).

[27]*League of United Latin American Voters v. Perry,* 548U. S. 399 (2006), No. 05-204 (2006).

[28]*Miuller v. Johnson,* No. 94-631515 U.S. 900 (1995); *Bush v. Verag,* No. 94-805517 U.S. 952 (1996); *Shaw v. Hunt,* No. 94-923517 U.S. 899 (1996).

[29]See Manny Fernandez, "Study Finds Disparities in Mortgages by Race," *New York Times,* October 15, 2007; see also U.S. Conference of Mayors report, 1998; Survey by Federal Financial Institutions Examination Council, 1998.

[30]"Public Backs Affirmative Action, But Not Minority Preferences," Pew Research Center report, June 2, 2009, Web release.

[31]*University of California Regents v. Bakke,* 438 U.S. 265 (1978).

[32]*Fullilove v. Klutnick,* 448 U.S. 448 (1980).

[33]*Adarand v. Pena,* 515 U.S. 200 (1995).

[34]*Ricci v. DeStefano,* 557 U.S. 687 (2009).

[35]*Gratz v. Bollinger,* 539 U.S. 244 (2003).

[36]*Grutter v. Bollinger,* 539 U.S. 306 (2003).

[37]See, for example, Alejandro Del Carmen, *Racial Profiling in America* (Upper Saddle River, N.J.: Prentice-Hall, 2007).

[38]Data from U.S. Census Bureau and Centers for Disease Control and Prevention, 2010.

[39]Data from National Office of Drug Control Policy, 1997.

[40]Data from U.S. Department of Justice, 2010.

[41]See Keith Reeves, *Voting Hopes or Fears?* (New York: Oxford University Press, 1997); Tali Mendelberg, *The Race Card* (Princeton, N.J.: Princeton University Press, 2001).

[42]Jennifer L. Lawless and Richard L. Fox, *It Takes a Candidate: Why Women Don't Run for Office* (New York: Cambridge University Press, 2005).

[43]U.S. Department of Education, 2006.

[44]See Sara M. Evans and Barbara Nelson, *Wage Justice* (Chicago: University of Chicago Press, 1989).

[45]*Wal-Mart v. Dukes,* No. 10-277 (2011).

[46]*Pennsylvania State Police v. Suders,* No. 03-95542 U.S. 129 (2004).

[47]*Burlington Northern and Santa Fe Railroad Company v. White,* No. 05-259548 U.S. 53 (2006).

[48]Eric C. Henson et al., *The State of the Native Nations: Conditions under U.S. Policies of Self-Determination* (New York: Oxford University Press, 2007).

[49]See David E. Wilkins, *American Indian Politics and the American Political System* (Lanham, Md.: Rowman & Littlefield, 2006).

[50]William Evans and Julie Topoleski, "The Social and Economic Impact of Native American Casinos," National Bureau of Economic Research, Working Paper No. 9198, September 2002, Cambridge, Massachusetts.

[51]W. Dale Mason, "Tribes and States: A New Era in Intergovernmental Affairs," *Publius* 28 (1998): 129.

[52]Data from U.S. Census Bureau, 2008; see also Daniel McCool, Susan M. Olson, and Jennifer L. Robinson, *Native Vote: American Indians, the Voting Rights Act, and the Right to Vote* (New York: Cambridge University Press, 2007).

[53]See Timothy P. Fong, *Contemporary Asian American Experience: Beyond the Model Minority* (Upper Saddle River, N.J.: Prentice-Hall, 2009).

[54]See Gordon Chang, ed., *Asian Americans and Politics* (Stanford, Calif.: Stanford University Press, 2001).

[55]See William N. Eskridge Jr., *Dishonorable Passions: Sodomy Laws in America, 1861–2003* (New York: Viking, 2008);

Nancy D. Polikoff, *Beyond (Straight and Gay) Marriage: Valuing All Families under the Law* (Boston: Beacon Press, 2009); Craig A. Rimmerman and Clyde Wilcox, *The Politics of Same-Sex Marriage* (Chicago: University of Chicago Press, 2007).

[56]*Romer v. Evans,* 517 U.S. 620 (1996).

[57]*Lawrence v. Texas,* 539 U.S. 558 (2003).

[58]The estimate was compiled by author in 2012 from multiple sources.

[59]*White House Blog,* May 10, 2012. http:// www.whitehouse.gov/blog/2012/ 05/10/obama-supports-same-sex-marriage.

[60]Justin Sink, "Romney Opposes Gay Marriage, Says Obama 'Changed His View'," *The Hill,* May 9, 2012.

[61]*Kimel v. Florida Board of Regents,* No. 98-791528 U.S. 62 (2000); but see *CBOCS West, Inc. v. Humphries,* No. 06-1431553 U.S. 442 (2008).

[62]*Board of Trustees of the University of Alabama v. Garrett,* No. 99-1240 (2002); *Tennessee v. Lane,* No. 02-1667541 U.S. 509 (2004).

[63]Gunnar Myrdal, *An American Dilemma: The Negro Problem and Modern Democracy* (New York: Harper, 1944).

[64]See Joe R. Feagin, *The White Racial Frame: Centuries of Racial Framing and Counter-Framing* (New York: Routledge, 2009).

Chapter 6

[1]James Bryce, *The American Commonwealth,* vol. 2 (Indianapolis, Ind.: Liberty Fund, 1995), 225. First published in 1888.

[2]Quinnipiac University survey, Quinnipiac University Polling Institute, November 18, 2009.

[3]Ibid.

[4]See Brandice Canes-Wrone, *Who Leads Whom? Presidents, Policy, and the Public* (Chicago: University of Chicago Press, 2005).

[5]Elisabeth Noelle-Neumann, *The Spiral of Silence,* 2d ed. (Chicago: University of Chicago Press, 1993), ch. 1.

[6]Herbert Hyman, *Political Socialization* (Glencoe, Ill.: Free Press, 1959), 51.

[7]M. Kent Jennings and Richard G. Niemi, *Generations and Politics* (Princeton, N.J.: Princeton University Press, 1981).

[8]See Orit Ichilov, *Political Socialization, Citizenship Education, and Democracy* (New York: Teachers College Press, 1990).

[9]See, however, Dietram A. Scheufele, Matthew C. Nisbet, and Dominique Brossard, "Pathways to Political Participation: Religion, Communication Contexts, and Mass Media,"

International Journal of Public Opinion Research 15 (Autumn 2003): 300–324.

[10]Noelle-Neumann, *Spiral of Silence.*

[11]Walter Lippmann, *Public Opinion* (New York: Free Press, 1965), ch. 1.

[12]Thomas E. Patterson, *The Vanishing Voter* (New York: Knopf, 2003), 89–90.

[13]Jon Western, *Selling Intervention and War: The Presidency, the Media, and the American Public* (Baltimore, Md.: Johns Hopkins University Press, 2005); see also Wojtek Mackiewicz Wolfe, *Winning the War of Words: Selling the War on Terror from Afghanistan to Iraq* (Westport, Conn.: Praeger, 2008).

[14]See Angus Campbell, Philip Converse, Warren Miller, and Donald Stokes, *The American Voter* (New York: Wiley, 1960), chs. 3 and 4.

[15]Martin P. Wattenberg, *Where Have All the Voters Gone?* (Cambridge, Mass.: Harvard University Press, 2002).

[16]See, Sidney Kraus *Televised Presidential Debates and Public Policy* (New York: Routledge, 2000).

[17]Rasmussen poll, October 10, 2009.

[18]Donald Green, Bradley Palmquist, and Eric Schickler, *Partisan Hearts and Minds* (New Haven, Conn.: Yale University Press, 2002).

[19]Daniel Bell, *The End of Ideology* (New York: Collier, 1961), 67.

[20]Daniel Boorstin, *The Genius of American Politics* (Chicago: University of Chicago Press, 1953).

[21]Mariya Karimjee, "Ron Paul Dominates Youth Vote During Iowa Caucuses," *Global Post,* January 4, 2012.

[22]Kenneth D. Wald, *Religion and Politics in the United States* (Lanham, Md.: Rowman & Littlefield, 2003).

[23]CNN/USA Today poll conducted by the Gallup Organization, 1997.

[24]Lois Duke Whitaker, ed., *Voting the Gender Gap* (Urbana: University of Illinois Press, 2008).

[25]Los Angeles Times poll, November 2011.

[26]Cass Sunstein, *Republic.com 2.0* (Princeton, N.J.: Princeton University Press, 2007).

[27]See, for example, Dean R. Hoge and Teresa L. Ankney, "Occupations and Attitudes of Student Activists Ten Years Later," *Journal of Youth and Adolescence* 11 (1982): 365.

[28]See Herbert Asher, *Polling and the Public,* 7th ed. (Washington, D.C.: CQ Press, 2007).

[29]Political Arithmetic, May 31, 2007; see at http://politicalarithmetik.blogspot.com/2007/05/support-for-death-penalty-and-question.html.

[30]Robert J. Samuelson, "What If We're to Blame? Public Opinion and Muddled

Policies," *Washington Post,* November 1, 2006.

[31]"Study Finds Widespread Misperceptions on Iraq Highly Related to Support for War," Program on International Policy Attitudes, School of Public Affairs, University of Maryland, October 2, 2003; see at http://www.pipa.org/ OnlineReports/Iraq/IraqMedia_Oct03/ IraqMedia_Oct03_pr.pdf.

[32]Joshua Buntin III, "Start with Civics 101," *Miami Herald,* January 21, 2008, 25A.

[33]Survey of students of the eight Ivy League schools by Luntz & Weber Research and Strategic Services, for the University of Pennsylvania's Ivy League Study, November 13–December 1, 1992.

[34]See R. Michael Alvarez and John Brehm, *Hard Choices, Easy Answers* (Princeton, N.J.: Princeton University Press, 2002); see also Samuel L. Popkin, *The Reasoning Voter* (Chicago: University of Chicago Press, 1991).

[35]Robert S. Erikson, Michael B. MacKuen, and James A. Stimson, *The Macro Polity* (New York: Cambridge University Press, 2008), xxi.

[36]V. O. Key Jr., *Public Opinion and American Democracy* (New York: Alfred A. Knopf, 1964).

[37]Benjamin I. Page and Robert Y. Shapiro, "Effects of Public Opinion on Policy," *American Political Science Review* 77 (March 1983): 178; see also Richard Sobel, *The Impact of Public Opinion on U.S. Foreign Policy* (New York: Oxford University Press, 2001); James Stimson, *Tides of Consent: How Public Opinion Shapes American Politics* (New York: Cambridge University Press, 2004).

[38]John W. Kingdon, *Agendas, Alternatives, and Public Policies,* 2d ed. (New York: Longman, 2003), 148–49.

[39]Jeff Manza and Fay Lomax Cook, "A Democratic Polity: Three Views of Policy Responsiveness to Public Opinion in the United States" *American Politics Research* 30 (2002): 630–67.

[40]Vincent Hutchings, *Public Opinion and Democratic Accountability: How Citizens Learn about Politics* (Princeton, N.J.: Princeton University Press, 2005).

[41]See, for example, Sidney Verba and Norman H. Nie, *Participation in America: Political Democracy and Social Equality* (New York: Harper & Row, 1972), 332.

[42]Robert D. Benford and David A. Snow, "Framing Processes and Social Movements," *Annual Review of Sociology* 40 (2000): 611–39.

[43]Scott McClellan, *What Happened: Inside the Bush White House and Washington's Culture of Deception* (New York: Public Affairs, 2008).

[44]See William Domhoff, *Who Rules America?* 5th ed. (New York: McGraw-Hill, 2005).

[45]Noam Chomsky and Edward S. Herman, *Manufacturing Consent: The Political Economy of the Mass Media* (New York: Pantheon, 2002).

[46]Page and Shapiro, "Effects of Public Opinion on Policy," 189.

[47]Erikson et al., *The Macro Polity,* 314; James A. Stimson and Robert S. Erickson, "Dynamic Representation," *The American Political Science Review* 89 (1995): 543–65.

Chapter 7

[1]Walter Lippmann, *Public Opinion* (New York: Free Press, 1965), 36.

[2]Quoted in Ralph Volney Harlow, *The Growth of the United States* (New York: Henry Holt, 1943), 312.

[3]Mark N. Franklin, *Voter Turnout and the Dynamics of Electoral Competition in Established Democracies since 1945* (New York: Cambridge University Press, 2004).

[4]Thomas E. Patterson, *The Vanishing Voter* (New York: Knopf, 2002), 134.

[5]Ibid.

[6]Russell Dalton, "The Myth of the Disengaged American," Web publication of the Comparative Study of Electoral Systems, October 2005, 2.

[7]Patterson, *Vanishing Voter,* 179–80.

[8]*Crawford et al. v. Marion County Election Board et al.,* No. 07-21 (2008).

[9]Ivor Crewe, "Electoral Participation," in David Butler, Howard R. Penniman, and Austin Ranney, eds., *Democracy at the Polls* (Washington, D.C.: American Enterprise Institute, 1981), 251–53.

[10]Richard Boyd, "Decline of U.S. Voter Turnout," *American Politics Quarterly* 9 (April 1981): 142.

[11]Larry Bartels, *Unequal Democracy: The Political Economy of the Gilded Age* (Princeton, N.J.: Princeton University Press, 2008).

[12]Patterson, *Vanishing Voter,* 135.

[13]David C. Leege, Kenneth D. Wald, Brian S. Krueger, and Paul D. Mueller, *The Politics of Cultural Differences* (Princeton, N.J.: Princeton University Press, 2002).

[14]Jose Antonio Vargas, "Obama Raised Half a Billion Online," washingtonpost.com, November 20, 2008, p. 1.

[15]See Bruce Bimber and Richard Davis, *Campaigning Online* (New York: Oxford University Press, 2003); Bruce Bimber, *Information and American Democracy* (New York: Cambridge University Press, 2003); Joe Trippi, *The Revolution Will Not Be Televised* (New York: HarperCollins, 2004).

[16]Dalton, "Myth of the Disengaged American," 2.

[17]Robert Putnam, *Bowling Alone* (New York: Simon & Schuster, 2000); but see Cliff Zukin et al., *A New Engagement: Political Participation, Civic Life, and the Changing American Citizen* (New York: Oxford University Press, 2006).

[18]Russell J. Dalton, *The Good Citizen: How a Younger Generation Is Reshaping American Politics,* rev. ed. (Washington, D.C.: CQ Press, 2008).

[19]Mark Hugo Lopez, "Volunteering among Young People," Web-released report of The Center for Information & Research on Civic Learning and Engagement," School of Public Affairs, University of Maryland, College Park, Maryland. February 2004.

[20]See Benjamin Ginsberg, *The Consequences of Consent* (New York: Random House, 1982), ch. 2.

[21]See, for example, Charles J. Stewart, Craig Allen Smith, and Robert E. Denton Jr., *Persuasion and Social Movements,* 5th ed. (Long Grove, Ill.: Waveland Press, 2007).

[22]Dalton, *Citizen Politics,* 38.

[23]Pew Research Center poll, November 29, 2011.

[24]CBS News/New York Times poll, October 25, 2011.

[25]Public Policy Polling, November 16, 2011.

[26]William Watts and Lloyd A. Free, eds., *The State of the Nation* (New York: University Books, Potomac Associates, 1967), 97.

[27]Sidney Verba and Norman Nie, *Participation in America* (New York: Harper & Row, 1972), 131.

[28]Bartels, *Unequal Democracy.*

Chapter 8

[1]E. E. Schattschneider, *Party Government* (New York: Rinehart, 1942), 1.

[2]See John Aldrich, *Why Parties? The Origin and Transformation of Political Parties in America* (Chicago: University of Chicago Press, 1995); L. Sandy Maisel, *American Political Parties and Elections* (New York: Oxford University Press, 2007).

[3]E. E. Schattschneider, *The Semisovereign People: A Realist's View of Democracy in America* (New York: Holt, Rinehart & Winston, 1961), 140.

[4]Thomas E. Patterson, *The Vanishing Voter* (New York: Knopf, 2002), ch. 2.

[5]See Richard P. McCormick, *The Second American Party System: Party Formation in the Jacksonian Era* (Chapel Hill: University of North Carolina Press, 1966).

[6]Alexis de Tocqueville, *Democracy in America (1835–1840),* eds. J. P. Mayer and A. P. Kerr (Garden City, N.Y.: Doubleday/Anchor, 1969), 60.

[7]Aldrich, *Why Parties?* 151.

[8]Kristi Andersen, *The Creation of a Democratic Majority, 1928–1936* (Chicago: University of Chicago Press, 1979).

[9]See Kevin Phillips, *The Emerging Republican Majority* (New Rochelle, N.Y.: Arlington House, 1969).

[10]See Arthur C. Paulson, *Electoral Realignment and the Outlook for American Democracy* (Boston: Northeastern University Press, 2006).

[11]Lewis L. Gould, *Grand Old Party* (New York: Random House, 2003); but also see Jacob S. Hacker and Paul Pierson, *Off Center: The Republican Revolution and the Erosion of American Democracy* (New Haven, Conn.: Yale University Press, 2006).

[12]See John B. Judis and Ruy Teixeira, *The Emerging Democratic Majority* (New York: Scribner, 2002).

[13]See Duncan Black, "On the Rationale of Group Decision-Making," *Journal of Political Economy* 56 (1948): 23–24; Anthony Downs, *An Economic Theory of Democracy* (New York: HarperCollins, 1957).

[14]Mark Brewer, *Party Images in the Electorate* (New York: Routledge, 2008).

[15]Jeffrey M. Stonecash, *Political Parties Matter: Realignment and the Return of Partisan Voting* (Boulder, Colo.: Lynne Rienner Publishers, 2005).

[16]See Lois Duke Whitaker, ed., *Voting the Gender Gap* (Urbana: University of Illinois Press, 2008); Karen M. Kaufmann, "The Gender Gap," *PS: Political Science & Politics,* July 2006, pp. 447–53.

[17]John Green, Mark Rozell, and William Clyde Wilcox, eds., *The Christian Right in American Politics* (Washington, D.C.: Georgetown University Press, 2003).

[18]James G. Gimpel, "Latinos and the 2002 Election: Republicans Do Well When Latinos Stay Home," Center for Immigration Studies, University of Maryland, January 2003, Web download; see also Jorge Ramos, *The Latino Wave: How Hispanics Are Transforming Politics in America* (New York: Harper Paperbacks, 2005); F. Chris Garcia and Gabriel Sanchez, *Hispanics and the U.S. Political System: Moving into the Mainstream*

(Upper Saddle River, N.J.: Prentice-Hall, 2007).

[19]Micah L. Sifrey, *Spoiling for a Fight: Third-Party Politics in America* (New York: Routledge, 2003).

[20]Daniel A. Mazmanian, *Third Parties in Presidential Elections* (Washington, D.C.: Brookings Institution, 1984), 143–44.

[21]Lewis L. Gould, *Four Hats in the Ring: The 1912 Election and the Birth of Modern American Politics* (Lawrence: University Press of Kansas, 2008).

[22]See Lawrence Goodwyn, *The Populist Movement* (New York: Oxford University Press, 1978).

[23]See Anthony King, *Running Scared* (New York: Free Press, 1997); but see James E. Campbell, *The American Campaign: U.S. Presidential Campaigns and the National Vote* (College Station: Texas A&M Press, 2008).

[24]See Paul S. Herrnson and John C. Green, eds., *Responsible Partisanship* (Lawrence: University Press of Kansas, 2003).

[25]See Marjorie Randon Hershey, Party Politics in America, 13th ed. (New York: Longman, 2009).

[26]Joseph Napolitan, *The Election Game and How to Win It* (New York: Doubleday, 1972); for a contemporary look at the campaigning process, see D. Sunshine Hillygus and Todd G. Shields, *The Persuadable Voter: Wedge Issues in Presidential Campaigns* (Princeton, N.J.: Princeton University Press, 2008).

[27]Center for Responsive Politics data, 2012.

[28]David B. Magleby, J. Quin Monson, and Kelly D. Patterson, eds., *Dancing Without Partners: How Candidates, Parties and Interest Groups Interact in the New Campaign Finance Environment* (Provo, Utah: Brigham Young University Press, 2005).

[29]*Citizens United v. Federal Election Commission*, 558 U.S. 50 (2010).

[30]David Chagall, *The New King-Makers* (New York: Harcourt Brace Jovanovich, 1981).

[31]Lawrence R. Jacobs and Robert Y. Shapiro, *Politicians Don't Pander: Political Manipulation and the Loss of Democratic Responsiveness* (Chicago: University of Chicago Press, 2000).

[32]Emmett H. Buell Jr. and Lee Sigelman, *Attack Politics: Negativity in Presidential Campaigns since 1960* (Lawrence: University Press of Kansas, 2008). For opposing views on the effect of negative advertising, see Stephen Ansolabehere and Shanto Iyengar, *Going Negative* (New York: Free Press, 1995), and John Geer, *In Defense of Negativity* (Chicago: University of Chicago Press, 2006).

[33]Darrell M. West, *Air Wars: Television Advertising in Election Campaigns, 1952–2004*, 4th ed. (Washington, D.C.: CQ Press, 2005), 140–46.

[34]See, for example, http://factcheck.org/2012/06/romneys-solar-flareout/.

[35]Ibid., 12.

[36]Brad Lockerbie, *Do Voters Look to the Future?* (Albany: State University of New York Press, 2009).

Chapter 9

[1]E. E. Schattschneider, *The Semisovereign People: A Realist's View of Democracy in America* (New York: Holt, Rinehart & Winston, 1960), 35.

[2]Ceci Connolly, "New Bill Would Raise Rates, Says Insurance Group: Report Issued Before Key Committee Vote," *Washington Post,* October 12, 2009; see at http://www.washingtonpost.com/wp-dyn/content/article/2009/10/11/AR2009101102207.html.

[3]Center for Responsive Politics data, 2010.

[4]Anthony J. Nownes, *Total Lobbying: What Lobbyists Want (and How They Try to Get It)* (New York: Cambridge University Press, 2006).

[5]See Matthew J. Burbank, Ronald J. Hrebenar, and Robert C. Benedict, *Parties, Interest Groups, and Political Campaigns* (Boulder, Colo.: Paradigm Publishers, 2008).

[6]Alexis de Tocqueville, *Democracy in America (1835–1840)*, eds. J. P. Mayer and A. P. Kerr (Garden City, N.Y.: Doubleday/Anchor, 1969), bk. 2, ch. 4.

[7]Kay Lehman Schlozman and John T. Tierney, *Organized Interests and American Democracy* (New York: Harper & Row, 1986), 54; see also Jeffrey M. Berry and Clyde Wilcox, *The Interest Group Society*, 5th ed. (New York: Longman, 2008).

[8]E. Pendleton Herring, *Group Representation before Congress* (Washington, D.C.: Brookings Institution, 1929), 78.

[9]U.S. Bureau of Labor, statistics, 2011.

[10]See Jack L. Walker, *Mobilizing Interest Groups in America* (Ann Arbor: University of Michigan Press, 1991).

[11]Christopher J. Bosso, "The Color of Money: Environmental Groups and the Pathologies of Fund Raising," in Allan J. Cigler and Burdett Loomis, eds., *Interest Group Politics*, 4th ed. (Washington, D.C.: CQ Press, 1995), 101–3.

[12]See Nownes, *Total Lobbying*. The author is indebted to Professor Anthony Nownes of the University of Tennessee for the observations contained in this paragraph.

[13]Mancur Olson, *The Logic of Collective Action*, rev. ed. (Cambridge, Mass.: Harvard University Press, 1971), 64.

[14]Theda Skocpol, *Diminished Democracy* (Norman: University of Oklahoma Press, 2003).

[15]Olson, *Logic of Collective Action*, 147.

[16]Ibid.

[17]Jeffrey N. Birnbaum, "Washington's Power 25: Which Pressure Groups Are Best at Manipulating the Laws We Live By?" *Fortune*, December 8, 1997, Web copy.

[18]Center for Responsive Politics, 2010.

[19]Frank R. Baumgartner, Jeffrey M. Berry, Marie Hojnacki, David C. Kimball, and Beth L. Leech, *Lobbying and Policy Change: Who Wins, Who Loses, and Why* (Chicago: University of Chicago Press, 2009).

[20]Norman J. Ornstein and Shirley Elder, *Interest Groups, Lobbying, and Policymaking* (Washington, D.C.: CQ Press, 1978), 82–86.

[21]See Paul S. Herrnson, Ronald G. Shaiko, and Clyde Wilcox, *The Interest Group Connection: Electioneering, Lobbying, and Policymaking in Washington*, 2d ed. (Washington, D.C.: CQ Press, 2004).

[22]Quoted in a *National Journal* excerpt in Thomas E. Patterson, *The American Democracy,* 9th ed. (New York: McGraw-Hill, 2009), 245b.

[23]See John Mark Hansen, *Gaining Access* (Chicago: Chicago University Press, 1991); Bruce Wolpe and Bertram Levine, *Lobbying Congress* (Washington, D.C.: CQ Press, 1996).

[24]Bara Vaida, "K-Street Paradox: $1.3 Million Per Hour," *The National Journal*, March 13, 2010.

[25]Quoted in Ornstein and Elder, *Interest Groups, Lobbying, and Policymaking*, 77.

[26]Steve Reinberg, "Debate Builds over Drug Companies' Fees to FDA," *Washington Post,* April 13, 2007; see at http://www.washingtonpost.com/wp-dyn/content/article/2007/04/13/AR2007041301449.html.

[27]Paul J. Quirk, *Industry Influence in Federal Regulatory Agencies* (Princeton, N.J.: Princeton University Press, 1981); John E. Chubb, *Interest Groups and the Bureaucracy: The Politics of Energy* (Stanford, Calif.: Stanford University Press, 1983), 200–201.

[28]Lee Epstein and C. K. Rowland, "Interest Groups in the Courts," *American Political Science Review* 85 (1991): 205–17.

[29]Richard Davis, *Electing Justice: Fixing the Supreme Court Nomination Process* (New York: Oxford University Press, 2005).

[30] Hugh Heclo, "Issue Networks and the Executive Establishment," in Anthony King, ed., *The New American Political System* (Washington, D.C.: American Enterprise Institute, 1978), 87–124.

[31] Ornstein and Elder, *Interest Groups, Lobbying, and Policymaking,* 88–93.

[32] "Why the Lobbying Disclosure Act Needs to Be Broadened to Include Grass-Roots Lobbying," Posting on Congress Watch, a website of Public Citizen; see at http://www.cleanupwashington.org/policy/page.cfm?id=7861&SectionID=108&SubSecID=1009&SecID=1407.

[33] Quoted in Mark Green, "Political PAC-Man," *The New Republic,* December 13, 1982, 20; see also Richard Skinner, *More Than Money: Interest Group Action in Congressional Elections* (Lanham, Md.: Rowman & Littlefield, 2006): Mark J. Rozell, Clyde Wilcox, and David Madland, *Interest Groups in American Campaigns,* 2d ed. (Washington, D.C.: CQ Press, 2005).

[34] Quoted in Larry Sabato, *PAC Power: Inside the World of Political Action Committees* (New York: Norton, 1984), 72.

[35] See, for example, Ezra Klein, "Wall Street Giving More to GOP for the First Time Since 2004," *Washington Post,* April 28, 2010; see at http://voices.washingtonpost.com/ezra-klein/2010/04/wall_street_giving_more_to_gop.html.

[36] *Citizens United v. Federal Election Commission,* 558 U.S. 50 (2010).

[37] Matea Gold and Tom Hamburger, "Democrats Following Republicans Into Field of Undisclosed Donors," *Los Angeles Times,* April 7, 2011.

[38] Walker, *Mobilizing Interest Groups in America,* 112.

[39] Theodore J. Lowi, *The End of Liberalism: The Second Republic of the United States* (New York: Norton, 1979).

[40] Larry Bartels, *Unequal Democracy: The Political Economy of the New Gilded Age* (Princeton, N.J.: Princeton University Press, 2008).

[41] Olson, *Logic of Collective Action.* See also Jonathan Rauch, *Demosclerosis: The Silent Killer of American Government* (New York: Times Books, 1994); and Peter J. Peterson, *Running on Empty: How the Democratic and Republican Parties Are Bankrupting Our Future and What Americans Can Do About It* (New York: Farrar, Strauss, and Giroux, 2005).

Chapter 10

[1] Theodore H. White, *The Making of the President, 1972* (New York: Bantam Books, 1973), 327.

[2] See Bill Kovach and Tom Rosenstiel, *The Elements of Journalism* (New York: Three Rivers Press, 2001).

[3] See Rodger Streitmatter, *Mightier Than the Sword: How the News Media Have Shaped American History* (Westport, Conn.: Praeger Publishers, 2008).

[4] Frank Luther Mott, *American Journalism, a History: 1690–1960* (New York: Macmillan, 1962), 114–15; see also Si Sheppard, *The Partisan Press: A History of Media Bias in the United States* (Jefferson, N.C.: McFarland, 2007).

[5] Edwin Emery, *The Press and America: An Interpretive History of the Mass Media* (Englewood Cliffs, N.J.: Prentice-Hall, 1977), 350.

[6] Quoted in Mott, *American Journalism,* 529.

[7] Quoted in David Halberstam, *The Powers That Be* (New York: Knopf, 1979), 208–9.

[8] Kathleen Hall Jamieson and Karlyn Kohrs Campbell, *The Interplay of Influence,* rev. ed. (Boston: Wadsworth, 2005), 4.

[9] Michael Schudson, "What Time Means in a News Story," Occasional Paper No. 4 (New York: Gannett Center for Media Studies, 1986), 8.

[10] Thomas E. Patterson, "Of Polls, Mountains: U.S. Journalists and Their Use of Election Surveys," *Public Opinion Quarterly* 69 (Special Issue 2005): 716–24.

[11] Donald Shaw and Maxwell McCombs, *The Emergence of American Political Issues: The Agenda-Setting Function of the Press* (St. Paul, Minn.: West Publishing, 1977).

[12] Bernard C. Cohen, *The Press and Foreign Policy* (Princeton, N.J.: Princeton University Press, 1963), 13.

[13] Thomas E. Patterson, *The American Democracy,* 5th ed. (New York: McGraw-Hill, 2001), 309–10.

[14] See Kathleen Hall Jamieson, *Eloquence in an Electronic Age* (New York: Oxford University Press, 1988), 42.

[15] Stephen J. Farnsworth and S. Robert Lichter, *The Mediated Presidency: Television News and Presidential Governance* (Lanham, Md.: Rowman & Littlefield, 2006).

[16] Kiku Adatto, "Sound Bite Democracy," Joan Shorenstein Center on the Press, Politics, and Public Policy, Research Paper R-2, Harvard University, June 1990.

[17] Center for Media and Public Affairs studies, available at: http://www.cmpa.com/studies.htm.

[18] Robert Entman, "Framing: Towards Clarification of a Fractured Paradigm," in Denis McQuail, ed., *McQuail's Reader in Mass Communication Theory* (London: Sage Publications, 2002), 391–92.

[19] Michael Levy, "Disdaining the News," *Journal of Communication* (1981): 24–31.

[20] Thomas Patterson, *Out of Order* (New York: Knopf, 1993), ch. 2.

[21] Thomas E. Patterson, *The Vanishing Voter* (New York: Knopf, 2002), 59.

[22] W. Lance Bennett, Regina G. Lawrence, and Steven Livingston, *When the Press Fails: Political Power and the News Media from Iraq to Katrina* (Chicago: University of Chicago Press, 2008).

[23] Walter Lippmann, *Public Opinion* (New York: Free Press, 1965), 214. First published in 1922.

[24] See Mark Harmon, "Non-Presidential U.S. Newspaper Endorsements, 2002, 2004, 2006," paper presented at the annual meeting of the Midwest Political Science Association, Chicago, April 12, 2007.

[25] Bernard Goldberg, *Bias: A CBS Insider Exposes How the Media Distort News* (New York: Harper Paperbacks, 2003).

[26] David H. Weaver, Randal A. Beam, Bonnie J. Brownlee, Paul S. Voakes, G. Cleveland Wilhoit, *The American Journalist in the 21st Century* (Mahwah, N.J.: LEA, 2006).

[27] David D'Alessio and Mike Allen, "Media Bias in Presidential Elections: A Meta-Analysis," *Journal of Communication* 50 (2000): 133–56.

[28] Center for Media and Public Affairs, Media Monitor, various dates.

[29] Michael Robinson, "Public Affairs Television and the Growth of Political Malaise," *American Political Science Review* 70 (1976): 409–32.

[30] Center for Media and Public Affairs, Media Monitor, various dates.

[31] Mark Rozell, "Press Coverage of Congress," in Thomas Mann and Norman Ornstein, eds., *Congress, the Press, and the Public* (Washington, D.C.: American Enterprise Institute and Brookings Institution, 1994), 109.

[32] Joseph N. Cappella and Kathleen Hall Jamieson, *Spiral of Cynicism* (New York: Oxford University Press, 1997), 159.

[33] Robinson, "Public Affairs Television and the Growth of Political Malaise."

[34] The press's negativity and sensationalism have had another effect as well; they have damaged the press's credibility. According to a 2007 survey conducted by the Center for Public Leadership at Harvard University's John F. Kennedy School of Government, the press has the lowest public confidence rating of any major U.S. institution.

[35] William Cole, ed., *The Most of A. J. Liebling* (New York: Simon, 1963), 7.

[36]See Kerbel, *Netroots;* Eric Boehlert, *Bloggers on the Bus* (New York: Free Press, 2010).

[37]Natalie Jomini Stroud, "Media Use and Political Predispositions: Revisiting the Concept of Selective Exposure," *Political Behavior* 30 (2008): 341–66.

[38]Jonathan S. Morris, "Slanted Objectivity? Perceived Media Bias, Cable News Exposure, and Political Attitudes," *Social Science Quarterly* 88 (2007): 725.

[39]Kathleen Hall Jamieson and Joseph N. Cappella, *Echo Chamber* (New York: Oxford University Press, 2008), 232.

[40]Richard Davis, *Politics Online* (New York: Routledge, 2005), 43.

[41]Cited in Ken Auletta, "Non-Stop News," *The New Yorker,* January 25, 2010, p. 38.

[42]Marcus Prior, *Post-Broadcast Democracy* (New York: Cambridge University Press, 2007).

[43]Robinson, "Public Affairs Television and the Growth of Political Malaise."

[44]Donald F. Roberts, Uila G. Foehr, Victoria J. Rideout, and Mollyann Brodie, "Kids and Media at the New Millennium," A Kaiser Family Foundation Report, November 1999, p. 19.

[45]See David T. Z. Mindich, *Tuned Out: Why Americans under 40 Don't Follow the News* (New York: Oxford University Press, 2005).

[46]Martin P. Wattenberg, *Is Voting for Young People?* (New York: Pearson Longman, 2008), 32.

[47]Thomas E. Patterson, "Young People and News," Report of the Joan Shorenstein Center on the Press, Politics, and Public Policy, John F. Kennedy School of Government, Harvard University, June 2007.

[48]Ibid., 75–80.

Chapter 11

[1]Roger H. Davidson and Walter J. Oleszek, *Congress and Its Members,* 10th ed. (Washington, D.C.: CQ Press, 2008), 4.

[2]See Paul S. Herrnson, *Congressional Elections: Campaigning at Home and in Washington,* 5th ed. (Washington, D.C.: CQ Press, 2008).

[3]See Gary C. Jacobson, *The Politics of Congressional Elections,* 5th ed. (New York: Longman, 2001).

[4]David Mayhew, *Congress: The Electoral Connection* (New Haven, Conn.: Yale University Press, 2004), 5.

[5]Bruce Cain, John Ferejohn, and Morris P. Fiorina, *The Personal Vote* (Cambridge, Mass.: Harvard University Press, 1987).

[6]Information provided by Clerk of the House.

[7]"Congressional Staff: Duties and Functions," CRS Report for Congress, April 21, 2003, 1; see at http://www.llsdc.org/attachments/wysiwyg/544/CRS-98-340.pdf.

[8]Edward Sidlow, *Challenging the Incumbent: An Underdog's Undertaking* (Washington, D.C.: CQ Press, 2003); David C. W. Parker, *The Power of Money in Congressional Campaigns, 1880–2006* (Norman: University of Oklahoma Press, 2008). See also Marian Currinder, *Money in the House: Campaign Funds and Congressional Party Politics* (Boulder, Colo.: Westview Press, 2008).

[9]Federal Elections Commission data, 2012.

[10]Quoted in Jennifer Babson and Kelly St. John, "Momentum Helps GOP Collect Record Amounts from PACs," *Congressional Quarterly Weekly Report,* December 3, 1994, 3456.

[11]Quoted in "A Tale of Myths and Measures: Who Is Truly Vulnerable?" *Congressional Quarterly Weekly Report,* December 4, 1993, 7; see also Dennis F. Thompson, *Ethics in Congress* (Washington, D.C.: Brookings Institution, 1995).

[12]James E. Campbell, *The Presidential Pulse of Congressional Elections* (Lexington: University Press of Kentucky, 1993).

[13]Robert Erikson, "The Puzzle of Midterm Losses," *Journal of Politics* 50 (November 1988): 1011–29.

[14]See Eric D. Lawrence, Forrest Maltzman, and Steven S. Smith, "Who Wins? Party Effects in Legislative Voting," *Legislative Studies Quarterly* 31 (2006): 33–69.

[15]Linda L. Fowler and Robert D. McClure, *Political Ambition* (New Haven, Conn.: Yale University Press, 1989).

[16]*Congressional Quarterly Weekly Report,* various dates.

[17]Linda Witt, Karen M. Paget, and Glenna Matthews, *Running as a Woman: Gender and Power in American Politics* (New York: Free Press, 1993); Sue Thomas, *How Women Legislate* (New York: Oxford University Press, 1994); Tali Mendelberg, *The Race Card* (Princeton, N.J.: Princeton University Press, 2001).

[18]Beth Reingold, ed., *Legislative Women: Getting Elected, Getting Ahead* (Boulder, Colo.: Lynne Reinner Publishers, 2008).

[19]Cited in Ryan Lizza, "The Obama Memos," *The New Yorker,* January 30, 2012, 36.

[20]Steven Smith, *Party Influence in Congress* (New York: Cambridge University Press, 2007); Barbara Sinclair, *Party Wars: Polarization and the Politics of National Policy Making* (Norman: University of Oklahoma Press, 2006).

[21]Quoted in Stephen E. Frantzich and Claude Berube, *Congress: Games and Strategies* (Lanham, MD: Rowman and Littlefield, 2009), 159.

[22]Randall Strahan, *Leading Representatives: The Agency of Leaders in the Politics of the U.S. House* (Baltimore, Md.: Johns Hopkins University Press, 2007); David King, *Turf Wars* (Chicago: University of Chicago Press, 1997).

[23]See Stephen E. Frantzich and Steven E. Schier, *Congress: Games and Strategies* (Dubuque, Iowa: Brown & Benchmark, 1995), 127.

[24]See Gerald S. Strom, *The Logic of Lawmaking* (Baltimore, Md.: Johns Hopkins University Press, 1990).

[25]See Barbara Sinclair, *Unorthodox Lawmaking: New Legislative Processes in the U.S. Congress,* 3d ed. (Washington, D.C.: CQ Press, 2007).

[26]See Jon R. Bond and Richard Fleisher, eds., *Polarized Politics: Congress and the President in a Partisan Era* (Washington, D.C.: CQ Press, 2000).

[27]See Gary Orfield, *Congressional Power: Congress and Social Change* (New York: Harcourt Brace Jovanovich, 1975).

[28]James L. Sundquist, "Congress and the President: Enemies or Partners?" in Lawrence C. Dodd and Bruce I. Oppenheimer, eds., *Congress Reconsidered* (New York: Praeger, 1977), 240.

[29]Barry C. Burden, *Personal Roots of Representation* (Princeton, N.J.: Princeton University Press, 2007).

[30]Keith Krehbiel, "Are Congressional Committees Composed of Preference Outliers?" *American Political Science Review* 84 (1990): 149–64; Richard L. Hall and Bernard Grofman, "The Committee Assignment Process and the Conditional Nature of Committee Bias," *American Political Science Review* 84 (1990): 1149–66.

[31]Fareed Zakaria, "Why Political Polarization Has Gone Wild in America (and What To Do About It)," *CNN World,* July 24, 2011.

[32]Frances E. Lee, *Beyond Ideology: Politics, Principles, and Partisanship in the U.S. Senate* (Chicago: University of Chicago Press, 2009).

[33]Joel A. Aberbach and Mark A. Peterson, eds., *The Executive Branch* (New York: Oxford University Press, 2005), 534–535.

[34]Joel Aberback, *Keeping a Watchful Eye* (Washington, D.C.: Brookings Institution, 1990); David Rosenbloom, *Building a Congress Centered Public Administration* (Tuscaloosa: University of Alabama Press, 2001).

Chapter 12

[1]Woodrow Wilson, *Constitutional Government in the United States* (New York: Columbia University Press, 1908), 67.

[2]George Packer, "Obama's Lost Year," *The New Yorker,* March 15, 2010, 41.

[3]James W. Davis, *The American Presidency* (New York: Harper & Row, 1987), 13; Sidney Milkis and Michael Nelson, *The American Presidency: Origins and Development, 1790–2007,* 5th ed. (Washington, D.C.: CQ Press, 2007); see also Bruce Ackerman, *The Failure of the Founding Fathers* (Cambridge, Mass.: Belknap Press of Harvard University Press, 2005)

[4]See Barry M. Blechman and Stephen S. Kaplan, *Force without War* (Washington, D.C.: Brookings Institution, 1978); Arthur M. Schlesinger Jr., *War and the American Presidency* (New York: W. W. Norton, 2004).

[5]*United States v. Belmont,* 57 U.S. 758 (1937).

[6]Robert DiClerico, *The American President,* 5th ed. (Englewood Cliffs, N.J.: Prentice-Hall, 1999), 47.

[7]James Bryce, *The American Commonwealth* (New York: Commonwealth Edition, 1908), 230.

[8]Quoted in Wilfred E. Binkley, *President and Congress,* 3d ed. (New York: Vintage, 1962), 142.

[9]Peri E. Arnold, *Remaking the Presidency* (Lawrence: University Press of Kansas, 2009).

[10]Theodore Roosevelt, *An Autobiography* (New York: Scribner's, 1931), 383.

[11]See Richard M. Pious, *The American Presidency* (New York: Basic Books, 1979), 83.

[12]Harry S Truman, *Years of Trial and Hope* (New York: Signet, 1956), 535.

[13]Erwin C. Hargrove, *The Effective Presidency: Lessons on Leadership from John F. Kennedy to George W. Bush* (Boulder, Colo.: Paradigm, 2007).

[14]See Thomas S. Langston, *The Cold War Presidency: A Documentary History* (Washington, D.C.: CQ Press, 2006).

[15]See Garry Willis, *Bomb Power: The Modern Presidency and the National Security State* (New York: Penguin Press, 2010).

[16]James W. Ceaser, *Presidential Selection: Theory and Development* (Princeton, N.J.: Princeton University Press, 1979).

[17]John S. Jackson and William J. Crotty, *The Politics of Presidential Selection* (New York: Longman, 2001).

[18]William Mayer, *The Front-Loading Problem in Presidential Nominations* (Washington, D.C.: Brookings Institution Press, 2004).

[19]See Thomas E. Patterson, *The Vanishing Voter* (New York: Knopf, 2003), 120.

[20]See Roderick P. Hart, *Seducing America: How Television Charms the Modern Voter* (Thousand Oaks, Calif.: Sage, 1998).

[21]Quoted in Stephen J. Wayne, *Road to the White House, 1992* (New York: St. Martin's Press, 1992), 143; but see Jody C. Baumgartner, *The American Vice Presidency Reconsidered* (Westport, Conn.: Praeger, 2006).

[22]Shirley Anne Warshaw, *The Co-Presidency of Bush and Cheney* (Stanford, Calif.: Stanford Politics and Policy, 2009); see Barton Gellman and Jo Becker, "Angler: The Cheney Vice Presidency," *Washington Post,* June 24–27, 2007.

[23]John P. Burke, *The Institutionalized Presidency* (Baltimore, Md.: Johns Hopkins University Press, 1992); Charles E. Walcott and Karen M. Hult, *Governing the White House* (Lawrence: University Press of Kansas, 1995).

[24]See Jeffrey E. Cohen, *The Politics of the United States Cabinet* (Pittsburgh: University of Pittsburgh Press, 1988); Shirley Anne Warshaw, *Powersharing: White House–Cabinet Relations in the Modern Presidency* (Albany: State University of New York Press, 1995).

[25]James Pfiffner, *The Modern Presidency* (New York: St. Martin's Press, 1994), 123; James Pfiffner, "Recruiting Executive Branch Leaders: The Office of Presidential Personnel," Brookings Institution, Spring 2001; see at http://www.brookings.edu/research/articles/2001/03/spring-governance-pfiffner Web article.

[26]Quoted in James MacGregor Burns, "Our Super-Government—Can We Control It?" *New York Times,* April 24, 1949, 32.

[27]See Paul C. Light, *Thickening Government: Federal Hierarchy and the Diffusion of Accountability* (Washington, D.C.: Brookings Institution, 1995).

[28]David Goetsch, *Effective Leadership* (Upper Saddle River, N.J.: Prentice-Hall, 2004).

[29]Stephen Skowronek, *Presidential Leadership in Political Time* (Lawrence: University of Kansas Press, 2008).

[30]Quoted in Emmet John Hughes, *The Ordeal of Power: A Political Memoir of the Eisenhower Years* (New York: Athenaeum 1963), 124.

[31]Erwin Hargrove, *The Power of the Modern Presidency* (New York: Knopf, 1974); see also John H. Kessel, *Presidents, the Presidency, and the Political Environment* (Washington, D.C.: CQ Press, 2001); Stephen Skowronek, *Presidential Leadership in Political Time: Reprise and Reappraisal* (Lawrence: University Press of Kansas, 2008).

[32]Quoted in Ryan Lizza, "The Obama Memos," *The New Yorker,* January 30, 2012, 49.

[33]James P. Pfiffner, *The Strategic Presidency: Hitting the Ground Running,* 2d ed. (Chicago: Dorsey Press, 1996).

[34]Aaron Wildavsky, "The Two Presidencies," *Trans-Action,* December 1966, 7.

[35]Pfiffner, *Modern Presidency,* ch. 6.

[36]Thomas P. (Tip) O'Neill, with William Novak, *Man of the House: The Life and Political Memoirs of Speaker Tip O'Neill* (New York: Random House, 1987), 297.

[37]Charles O. Jones, *The Presidency in a Separated System* (Washington, D.C.: Brookings Institution, 2005).

[38]Quoted in Lizza, "The Obama Memos," 44.

[39]Richard E. Neustadt, *Presidential Power and the Modern Presidents* (New York: Free Press, 1990), 71–72.

[40]Ibid., 33.

[41]Quoted in Lizza, "The Obama Memos," 49.

[42]Charlie Savage, "Senator Considers Suit over Bush Law Challenge," *Boston Globe,* June 28, 2006; see at http://www.boston.com/news/nation/washington/articles/2006/06/28/senator_considers_suit_over_bush_law_challenge/.

[43]Charles O. Jones, *The President in a Separated System* (Washington, D.C.: Brookings Institution, 2005), 173.

[44]John E. Mueller, "Presidential Popularity from Truman to Johnson," *American Political Science Review* 64 (March 1970): 18–34; Kathleen Frankovic, "Public Opinion in the 1992 Campaign," in Gerald M. Pomper, ed., *The Election of 1992* (Chatham, N.J.: Chatham House, 1993); Chris J. Dolan, *The Presidency and Economic Policy* (Lanham, Md.: Rowman & Littlefield, 2007).

[45]Samuel Kernell, *Going Public: New Strategies of Presidential Leadership,* 3d ed. (Washington, D.C.: CQ Press, 1997), 1; see also Robert M. Eisinger, *The Evolution of Presidential Polling* (New York: Cambridge University Press, 2003); Stephen J. Farnsworth and S. Robert Lichter, *Mediated Presidency: Television News & Presidential Governance* (Lanham, Md.: Rowman & Littlefield, 2005).

[46]Jeffrey E. Cohen, *The Presidency in the Era of 24-Hour News* (Princeton, N.J.: Princeton University Press, 2008).

[47]Hugh Heclo, "Introduction: The Presidential Illusion," in Hugh Heclo and Lester M. Salamon, eds., *The Illusion of Presidential Government* (Boulder, Colo.: Westview Press, 1981), 2.

[48]Theodore J. Lowi, *The "Personal" Presidency: Power Invested, Promise Unfulfilled* (Ithaca, N.Y.: Cornell University Press, 1985).

Chapter 13

[1]Max Weber, *Economy and Society* (New York: Bedminster Press, 1968), 223. Translated and edited by Guenther Roth and Claus Wittich. Originally published in 1921.

[2]Ibid., 23.

[3]Office of Personnel Management data, 2010.

[4]Gregory A. Huber, *The Craft of Bureaucratic Neutrality: Interests and Influence in Governmental Regulation of Occupational Safety* (New York: Cambridge University Press, 2007); Herbert Kaufman, "Emerging Conflicts in the Doctrine of Public Administration," *American Political Science Review* 50 (December 1956): 1060.

[5]See Allen Schick, *The Federal Budget: Politics, Policy, Process*, 3rd ed. (Washington, D.C.: Brookings Institution, 2007).

[6]Michael Lipsky, *Street-Level Bureaucracy* (New York: Russell Sage Foundation, 1980).

[7]See Cornelius M. Kerwin, *Rulemaking*, 3d ed. (Washington, D.C.: CQ Press, 2003); Daniel E. Hall, *Administrative Law: Bureaucracy in a Democracy* (Upper Saddle River, N.J.: Prentice-Hall, 2005).

[8]Steven Kelman, "Occupational Safety and Health Administration," in James Q. Wilson, ed., *The Politics of Regulation* (New York: Basic Books, 1980), 239–40.

[9]See Hugh Heclo, *A Government of Strangers* (Washington, D.C.: Brookings Institution, 1977), 117–18.

[10]Quoted in Aaron Wildavsky, *The Politics of the Budgetary Process*, 4th ed. (Boston: Little, Brown, 1984), 19; see also Dennis D. Riley, *Bureaucracy and the Policy Process: Keeping the Promises* (Lanham, Md.: Rowman & Littlefield, 2005).

[11]Joel D. Aberbach and Bert A. Rockman, "Clashing Beliefs within the Executive Branch," *American Political Science Review* 70 (June 1976): 461.

[12]Norton E. Long, "Power and Administration," *Public Administration Review* 10 (Autumn 1949): 269; Joel D. Aberbach and Bert A. Rockman, *In the Web of Politics* (Washington, D.C.: Brookings Institution, 2000).

[13]See B. Guy Peters, *The Politics of Bureaucracy*, 5th ed. (New York: Routledge, 2001).

[14]See B. Dan Wood and Richard W. Waterman, *Bureaucratic Dynamics* (Boulder, Colo.: Westview Press, 1994); Edward C. Page and Bill Jenkins, *Policy Bureaucracy: Government with a Cast of Thousands* (New York: Oxford University Press, 2005).

[15]Long, "Power and Administration," 269; see also John Mark Hansen, *Gaining Access* (Chicago: University of Chicago Press, 1991).

[16]Charles T. Goodsell, *The Case for Bureaucracy*, 2d ed. (Chatham, N.J.: Chatham House, 1985), 55–60.

[17]William T. Gormley Jr. and Steven J. Balla, *Bureaucracy and Democracy* (Washington, D.C.: CQ Press, 2003); Kevin B. Smith, *Public Administration: Power and Politics in the Fourth Branch of Government* (New York: Oxford University Press, 2006).

[18]James P. Pfiffner, "The National Performance Review in Perspective," working paper 94–4, Institute of Public Policy, George Mason University, 1994, 2.

[19]Ibid., 12.

[20]Kaufman, "Emerging Conflicts," 1062.

[21]See Paul Light, *Thickening Government* (Washington, D.C.: Brookings Institution, 1995); James G. March and Johan P. Olson, "Organizing Political Life: What Administrative Reorganization Tells Us about Government," *American Political Science Review* 77 (June 1983): 281–96.

[22]David E. Lewis, *The Politics of Presidential Appointments: Political Control and Bureaucratic Performance* (Princeton, N.J.: Princeton University Press, 2008).

[23]Heclo, *Government of Strangers*, 104.

[24]Ibid., 225.

[25]See Joel D. Aberbach, *Keeping a Watchful Eye* (Washington, D.C.: Brookings Institution, 1990).

[26]Douglas A. Van Belle and Kenneth M. Mash, *A Novel Approach to Politics* (Washington, D.C.: CQ Press, 2006).

[27]See Donald Kettl, *Deficit Politics* (New York: Macmillan, 1992).

[28]David Rosenbloom, "The Evolution of the Administrative State, and Transformations of Administrative Law," in David Rosenbloom and Richard Schwartz, eds., *Handbook of Regulation and Administrative Law* (New York: Marcel Dekker, 1994), 3–36.

[29]*Pigeford v. Veneman*, U.S. District Court for the District of Columbia, Civil Action No. 97-1978 (1999).

[30]See *Vermont Yankee Nuclear Power Corp. v. National Resources Defense Council, Inc.*, 435 U.S. 519 (1978); *Chevron v. National Resources Defense Council*, 467 U.S. 837 (1984); *Heckler v. Chaney*, 470 U.S. 821 (1985); but see *FDA v. Brown & Williamson Tobacco Co.*, 529 U.S. 120 (2000).

[31]See Mark W. Huddleston, "The Carter Civil Service Reforms," *Political Science Quarterly* (Winter 1981–82): 607–22.

[32]Ed O'Keefe, "Senior Executive Service Needs Overhaul, Outside Study Finds," *Washington Post*, August 20, 2009.

[33]Joe Davidson, "Whistleblower 'Bunny' Davidson Wins Settlement Near $1 Million," *Washington Post*, July, 26, 2011, Web release. http://www.washingtonpost.com/blogs/federaleye/post/whistleblower-bunny-greenhouse-wins-settlement-near-1-million/2011/04/15/gIQANfFAbI_blog.html.

[34]See Brian J. Cook, *Bureaucracy and Self-Government* (Baltimore, Md.: Johns Hopkins University Press, 1996).

Chapter 14

[1]*Marbury v. Madison*, 5 U.S. 137 (1803).

[2]*Citizens United v. Federal Election Commission*, 558 U.S. 50 (2010).

[3]Org. 138, *South Carolina v. North Carolina* (2010).

[4]Linda Camp Keith, "The United States Supreme Court and Judicial Review of Congress, 1803–2001," *Judicature* 9 (2007): 166.

[5]Rebecca Mae Salokar, *The Solicitor General: The Politics of Law* (Philadelphia: Temple University Press, 1992); see also Cornell W. Clayton, *The Politics of Justice: The Attorney General and the Making of Legal Policy* (Armonk, N.Y.: Sharpe, 1992).

[6]Henry Glick, *Courts, Politics, and Justice*, 3d ed. (New York: McGraw-Hill, 1993), 120.

[7]Timothy R. Johnson, Paul Wahlbeck, and James Spriggs, "The Influence of Oral Arguments on the U.S. Supreme Court," *American Political Science Review*, 100 (2006): 99–113.

[8]Lawrence Baum, *The Supreme Court*, 8th ed. (Washington, D.C.: CQ Press, 2003), 120.

[9]*Lee v. Weisman*, 505 U.S. 577 (1992); See also, Forest Maltzman, Paul Wahlbeck, and James Spriggs, *The Collegial Game: Crafting Law on the U.S. Supreme Court* (New York: Cambridge University Press, 2000).

[10]From a letter to the author by Frank Schwartz of Beaver College; this section reflects substantially Professor Schwartz's recommendations to the author, as does the later section that addresses the federal court myth.

[11]*Hutto v. Davis*, 370 U.S. 256 (1982).

[12]*Lawrence v. Texas,* No. 02-102 (2003).

[13]*Bowers v. Hardwick,* 478 U.S. 186 (1986).

[14]See Richard Davis, *Electing Justices* (New York: Oxford University Press, 2005).

[15]Robert Scigliano, *The Supreme Court and the Presidency* (New York: Free Press, 1971), 146; see also Lee Epstein and Jack Knight, *The Choices Justices Make* (Washington, D.C.: CQ Press, 1998); Stefanie A. Lundquist, David A. Yalof, and John A. Clark, "The Impact of Presidential Appointments to the Supreme Court: Cohesive and Divisive Voting within Presidential Blocs," *Political Research Quarterly* 53 (2000): 795–814.

[16]Quoted in Baum, *Supreme Court,* 37.

[17]See Lee Epstein and Jeffrey Segal, *Advice and Consent: The Politics of Judicial Appointments* (New York: Oxford University Press, 2005).

[18]See Virginia A. Hettinger et al., *Judging on a Collegial Court: Influences on Federal Appellate Decision Making* (Charlottesville: University of Virginia Press, 2006).

[19]John Gottschall, "Reagan's Appointments to the U.S. Courts of Appeals," *Judicature* 48 (1986): 54.

[20]See Robert A. Carp and Ronald Stidham, *The Federal Courts,* 4th ed. (Washington, D.C.: CQ Press, 2001).

[21]Joseph B. Harris, *The Advice and Consent of the Senate* (Berkeley: University of California Press, 1953), 313.

[22]Jesse J. Holland, "Obama Increases Number of Female, Minority Judges," Associated Press wire story, September 14, 2011.

[23]Quoted in Louis Fisher, *American Constitutional Law* (New York: McGraw-Hill, 1990), 5.

[24]Quoted in Charles P. Curtis, *Law and Large as Life* (New York: Simon & Schuster, 1959), 156–57.

[25]See Lee Epstein and Jack Knight, *The Choices Justices Make* (New York: Longman, 1995); Thomas G. Hansford and James F. Spriggs II, *The Politics of Precedent on the Supreme Court* (Princeton, N.J.: Princeton University Press, 2006).

[26]*Faragher v. City of Boca Raton,* No. 97-282 (1998).

[27]John Schmidhauser, *The Supreme Court* (New York: Holt, Rinehart & Winston, 1964), 6.

[28]Linda Greenhouse, "In Steps Big and Small, Supreme Court Moved Right," *New York Times,* July 1, 2007, Web copy.

[29]Jeffrey A. Segal and Harold J. Spaeth, *The Supreme Court and the Attitudinal Model Revisited* (New York: Cambridge University Press, 2002), 404.

[30]*Bush v. Gore,* 531 U.S. 98 (2000).

[31]See, however, James L. Gibson, Gregory A. Caldeira, and Lester Kenyatta Spence, "The Supreme Court and the U.S. Presidential Election of 2000," *British Journal of Political Science* 33 (2003): 535–56.

[32]Stephen L. Wasby, *The Supreme Court in the Federal Judicial System,* 4th ed. (Chicago: Nelson-Hall, 1993), 53.

[33]Lawrence M. Freidman, *American Law in the Twentieth Century* (New Haven, Conn.: Yale University Press, 2002), 96.

[34]Ross Sandler and David Schoenbrod, *Democracy by Decree* (New Haven, Conn.: Yale University Press, 2003).

[35]See Antonin Scalia, *A Matter of Interpretation: Federal Courts and the Law* (Princeton, N.J.: Princeton University Press, 1997).

[36]Remarks by Antonin Scalia at the University of Delaware, April 30, 2007. Reported on the Web by *University of Delaware Daily.*

[37]Stephen Breyer, "Our Democratic Constitution," James Madison Lecture, New York University Law School, New York, October 22, 2001.

[38]Henry J. Abraham, "The Judicial Function under the Constitution," *News for Teachers of Political Science* 41 (Spring 1984): 14.

[39]Alexander M. Bickel, *The Supreme Court and the Idea of Progress* (New Haven, Conn.: Yale University Press, 1978), 173–81.

[40]Frederic R. Kellogg and Oliver Wendell Holmes Jr., *Legal Theory and Judicial Restraint* (New York: Cambridge University Press, 2006).

[41]*Schenck v. United States,* 249 U.S. 47 (1919).

[42]Frank H. Easterbrook, "Do Liberals and Conservatives Differ in Judicial Activism?" *University of Colorado Law Review* 73 (2002): 1401.

Chapter 15

[1]Marc Allen Eisner, Jeffrey Worsham, and Evan J. Rinquist, *Contemporary Regulatory Policy* (Boulder, Colo.: Lynne Rienner, 2006).

[2]The section titled "Efficiency through Government Intervention" relies substantially on Alan Stone, *Regulation and Its Alternatives* (Washington, D.C.: CQ Press, 1982).

[3]See Marc Allen Eisner, *Regulatory Politics in Transition,* 2d ed. (Baltimore, Md.: Johns Hopkins University Press, 1999).

[4]See Richard A. Harris and Sidney M. Milkis, *The Politics of Regulatory Change* (New York: Oxford University Press, 1996).

[5]Lawrence E. Mitchell, *Corporate Irresponsibility* (New Haven, Conn.: Yale University Press, 2003).

[6]H. Peyton Young, *Equity: In Theory and Practice* (Princeton, N.J.: Princeton University Press, 1995).

[7]American Academy of Pediatrics, "Blood Lead Levels Declining, but Children Still at Risk for Lead Poisoning," March 2, 2009; see at http://www.aap.org/en-us/about-the-aap/aap-press-room/pages/Blood-lead-levels-declining.

[8]Board on Population Health and Public Health Practice, *The Future of Drug Safety: Promoting and Protecting the Health of the Public* (Washington, D.C.: National Academies Press, 2007).

[9]See Thomas Streeter, *Selling the Air* (Chicago: University of Chicago Press, 1996); Robert McChesney, *The Problem of the Media* (New York: Monthly Review Press, 2004); Christopher J. Bosso, *Environment, Inc.: From Grassroots to Beltway* (Lawrence: University Press of Kansas, 2005).

[10]Rachel Carson, *Silent Spring* (Boston: Houghton Mifflin, 1962); see also Lester R. Brown, *Plan B2.0: Rescuing a Planet under Stress and a Civilization in Trouble* (New York: W. W. Norton, 2006).

[11]Robert B. Keiter, *Keeping Faith with Nature* (New Haven, Conn.: Yale University Press, 2003).

[12]*U.S. News & World Report,* June 30, 1975, 25.

[13]*Whitman v. American Trucking Association,* No. 99-1257 (2001).

[14]See Walter A. Rosenbaum, *Environmental Politics and Policy,* 6th ed. (Washington, D.C.: CQ Press, 2004); Norman J. Vig and Michael E. Kraft, eds., *Environmental Policy: New Directions for the Twenty-First Century* (Washington, D.C.: CQ Press, 2003).

[15]Elliot A. Rosen, *Roosevelt, the Great Depression, and the Economics of Recovery* (Charlottesville: University of Virginia Press, 2007).

[16]See Robert Lekachman, *The Age of Keynes* (New York: Random House, 1966); see also Richard Kopke, Geoffrey M. B. Tootell, and Robert K. Trist, eds., *The Macroeconomics of Fiscal Policy* (Cambridge, Mass.: MIT Press, 2006).

[17]See Bruce Bartlett, *Reaganomics: Supply-Side Economics* (Westport, Conn.: Arlington House, 1981).

[18]Paul Krugman, "Hey, Lucky Duckies," *New York Times,* December 3, 2002, A31.

[19]For opposing views on the success of the tax-cutting strategy, see Gene W. Heck, *Building Prosperity: Why Ronald Reagan and the Founding Fathers Were*

Right on the Economy (Lanham, Md.: Rowman & Littlefield, 2007), and Bryan D. Jones and Walter Williams, *The Politics of Bad Ideas: The Great Tax-Cut Delusion and the Decline of Good Government in America* (New York: Longman, 2008).

[20] See Richard Duncan, *The Dollar Crisis: Causes, Consequences, Cures,* rev. ed. (New York: Wiley, 2005).

[21] "Tax Cuts Approved by Congress," *About.com,* May 27, 2001; see at http://usgovinfo.about.com/library/weekly/aa052701a.htm.

[22] Alan O. Ebenstein, *Milton Friedman: A Biography* (New York: Palgrave Macmillan, 2007).

[23] Edward Hadas and Hugh Dixon, "Quantitative Easing: A Therapy of Last Resort," *The New York Times,* January 1, 2009; see at http://www.nytimes.com/2009/01/11/business/worldbusiness/11ihtviews12.1.19248009.html.

[24] Martin Mayer, FED: The Inside Story of How the World's Most Powerful Financial Institution Drives the Markets (New York: Free Press, 2001).

Chapter 16

[1] See Felicia Ann Kornbluh, *The Battle for Welfare Rights: Politics and Poverty in Modern America* (Philadelphia: University of Pennsylvania Press, 2007).

[2] Michael Harrington, *The Other America: Poverty in the United States* (New York: Macmillan, 1962); see also James T. Patterson, *America's Struggle against Poverty in the Twentieth Century* (Cambridge, Mass.: Harvard University Press, 2000).

[3] Charles Murray, *Losing Ground: American Social Policy, 1950–1980* (New York: Basic Books, 1984).

[4] Signe-Mary McKernan and Caroline Ratcliffe, "Events That Trigger Poverty Entries and Exits," *Social Science Quarterly* 86 (2005): 1146–69.

[5] V. O. Key Jr., *The Responsible Electorate* (Cambridge, Mass.: Belknap Press of Harvard University, 1966), 43.

[6] Everett Carll Ladd, *American Political Parties* (New York: Norton, 1970), 205.

[7] Institute on Taxation and Economic Policy poll, 2002.

[8] For a general overview of 1950s and 1960s policy disputes, see James Sundquist, *Politics and Policy* (Washington, D.C.: Brookings Institution, 1968).

[9] See Jason DeParle, *American Dream: Three Women, Ten Kids, and a Nation's Drive to End Welfare* (New York: Penguin, 2005).

[10] See Katherine S. Newman, *No Shame in My Game* (New York: Alfred A. Knopf and Russell Sage Foundation, 1999), 41.

[11] Quoted in Malcolm Gladwell, "The Medicaid Muddle," *Washington Post National Weekly Edition,* January 16–22, 1995, 31.

[12] See Christopher Howard, *The Welfare State Nobody Knows* (Princeton, N.J.: Princeton University Press, 2006).

[13] Alberto Alesina and Edward Glaeser, *Fighting Poverty in the U.S. and Europe* (New York: Oxford University Press, 2006).

[14] Said of George H. W. Bush at the 1988 Democratic Convention. The quote is variously attributed to Ann Richards or Jim Hightower.

[15] For a history of public education, see Joel H. Spring, *The American School 1642–2004* (New York: McGraw-Hill, 2008).

[16] Based on Organization for Economic Cooperation and Development (OECD) data, 2006; see Douglas S. Reed, *On Equal Terms: The Constitutional Politics of Educational Opportunity* (Princeton, N.J.: Princeton University Press, 2003).

[17] Kaiser Family Foundation/*Washington Post*/Kennedy School of Government poll, September 1999.

[18] See, for example, Eugene E. Garcia, "API Test Is an Injustice to Students with Limited English," *San Francisco Chronicle,* January 31, 2000; see at http://www.sfgate.com/cgi-bin/article.cgi?f=/c/a/2000/01/31/ED32348.DTL.

[19] Daniel Koretz, *Measuring Up: What Educational Testing Really Tells Us* (Cambridge, Mass.: Harvard University Press, 2009).

[20] See John E. Chubb and Terry M. Moe, *Politics, Markets, and America's Schools* (Washington, D.C.: Brookings Institution, 1990); Tony Wagner and Thomas Vander Ark, *Making the Grade* (New York: Routledge, 2001).

[21] See Jeffrey R. Henig, *Rethinking School Choice* (Princeton, N.J.: Princeton University Press, 1995).

[22] "34th Annual PDK/Gallup Poll," *Phi Delta Kappan,* 84 (September 2002): 47–50.

[23] See, for example, David Hursh, *High Stakes Testing and the Decline of Teaching and Learning* (Lanham, Md.: Rowman & Littlefield, 2008.)

[24] Press release, Representative John Boehner, January 4, 2003.

[25] "37th Annual PDK/Gallup Poll," *Phi Delta Kappan,* 87 (September 2005): 41–57.

[26] Rick Perry, "Texas Knows Best How to Educate Our Students: Texas Will Not

Apply for Federal Race to the Top Funding," Office of the Governor press release, 2010.

[27] Stanley Feldman and John Zaller, "The Political Culture of Ambivalence: Ideological Responses to the Welfare State," *American Journal of Political Science* 36 (1992): 268–307.

[28] Robert E. Lane, "Market Justice, Political Justice," *American Political Science Review* 80 (June 1986): 383–402.

Chapter 17

[1] See Douglas T. Stuart, *Creating the National Security State* (Princeton, N.J.: Princeton University Press, 2008).

[2] See Mr. X. (George Kennan), "The Sources of Soviet Conduct," *Foreign Affairs* 25 (July 1947): 566–82.

[3] See Wilson Miscamble, *From Roosevelt to Truman: Potsdam, Hiroshima, and the Cold War* (New York: Cambridge University Press, 2008).

[4] David M. Barrett, *Uncertain Warriors: Lyndon Johnson and His Vietnam Advisors* (Lawrence: University Press of Kansas, 1993); see also Stanley Karnow, *Vietnam: A History* (New York: Penguin, 1983).

[5] See Dag Henriksen, *NATO's Gamble* (Annapolis, Md.: Naval Institute Press, 2007).

[6] See Mark Sauter and James Carafano, *Homeland Security* (New York: McGraw-Hill, 2005).

[7] See Ron Susskind, *The One-Percent Solution* (New York: Simon & Schuster, 2007).

[8] West Point speech, June 1, 2002; for an opposing view, see Gary Hart, *The Shield and the Cloak: The Security of the Commons* (New York: Oxford University Press, 2006).

[9] Nick Ritchie, *The Political Road to War with Iraq: Bush, 9/11 and the Drive to Overthrow Saddam* (New York: Routledge, 2007).

[10] Pew Research Center for the People and the Press, "Public Attitudes Toward the War in Iraq: 2003–2008," March 19, 2008; see at http://pewresearch.org/pubs/770/iraq-war-five-year-anniversary.

[11] Remarks of Nicholas Burns, World Affairs Council, Washington, D.C., June 23, 2011.

[12] Statement of the U.S. Secretary of Defense Leon Panetta, January 26, 2012.

[13] Thomas Rid and Thomas A. Keaney, eds., *Understanding Counterinsurgency Warfare* (New York: Routledge, 2010).

[14] See Richard Pearlstein, *Fatal Torture? Transnational Terrorism and the New Global Disorder* (Austin: University of Texas Press, 2004), 15–23.

[15]See Ofira Seliktar, *The Politics of Intelligence and American Wars with Iraq* (New York: Palgrave Macmillan, 2008).

[16]John Mueller, "Trends in Popular Support for the Wars in Korea and Vietnam," *American Political Science Review* 65 (June 1971): 358–75; see also John Mueller, "The Iraq Syndrome," *Foreign Affairs* (November/December 2005).

[17]Pew Research Center for the People and the Press, "Support for U.S. Troop Presence Hits New Low," April 18, 2012; see at http://pewresearch.org/pubs/2247/afghanistan-swing-voters-barack-obama-mitt-romney-troops-withdrawal.

[18]George C. Wilson, *This War Really Matters: Inside the Fight for Defense Dollars* (Washington, D.C.: CQ Press, 2000).

[19]*The World Competitiveness Yearbook* (Lausanne, Switzerland: International Institute for Management Development, 2008).

[20]U.S. government data, various agencies, 2008.

[21]American Assembly Report (cosponsored by the Council on Foreign Relations), *Rethinking America's Security* (New York: Harriman, 1991), 9.

[22]Robert Z. Lawrence, *The United States and the WTO Dispute Settlement System* (New York: Council on Foreign Relations, 2007).

[23]Ted C. Fishman, *China, Inc.: How the Rise of the Next Superpower Challenges America and the World* (New York: Scribner, 2005).

[24]Michael T. Klare, *Rising Powers, Shrinking Plant: The New Geopolitics of Energy* (New York: Holt, 2009).

[25]Hobart Rowen, "The Budget: Fact and Fiction," *Washington Post National Weekly Edition*, January 16–22, 1995, p. 5.

[26]Paola Subacchi and Stephen Pickford, "Legitimacy vs. Effectiveness for the G20: A Dynamic Approach to Global Economic Governance," Chatham House Briefing Paper, Royal Institute of International Affairs, London, England, October 2011, p. 2.

[27]Ibid., p. 7.

Chapter 18

[1]Patricia Kilday Hart, "Texas Dream Act a Dream for Perry's GOP Rivals," *Houston Chronicle*, September 27, 2011; see at http://www.chron.com/news/houston-texas/article/Texas-Dream-Act-a-dream-for-Perry-s-GOP-rivals-2191816.php.

[2]Patrik Jonsson, "Alabama Life Already Changing under Tough Immigration Law," *Christian Science Monitor*, September 29, 2011; see at http://www.csmonitor.com/USA/2011/0929/Alabama-life-already-changing-under-tough-immigration-law.

[3]Peggy Gargis, "Alamaba Sets Nation's Toughest Immigration Law"; see at http://www.reuters.com/article/2011/06/09/us-immigration-alabama-idUSTRE7584C920110609.

[4]Pew Hispanic Center, "Mapping the Latino Electorate"; see at http://pewhispanic.org/docs/?DocID=26.

[5]See, for example, James E. Crisp, "¡Mucho Cuidado! Silencing, Selectivity, and Sensibility in the Utilization of Tejano Voices by Texas Historians" in Monica Perales and Raúl A. Ramos (Eds.), *Recovering the Hispanic History of Texas* (Houston: Arte Público Press, 2010).

[6]From John Steinbeck, *Travels with Charley: In Search of America* (1962), in *The Columbia World of Quotations* (New York: Columbia University Press, 1996), n. 55679.

[7]Terry G. Jordan, *German Seed in Texas Soil: Immigrant Farmers in Nineteenth Century Texas* (Austin: University of Texas Press, 1966).

[8]Robert A. Calvert and Arnold DeLeon, *The History of Texas* (Arlington Heights, IL: Harland Davidson, 1990), 99–100.

[9]U.S. Census Bureau, Population Estimate—2009; www.census.gov.popest/states/tables.

[10]Raul Gonzales was appointed by Governor Mark White to the Texas Supreme Court in 1984. He has subsequently been elected and reelected to the court.

[11]Daniel J. Elazar, *American Federalism: A View from the States* (New York: HarperCollins, 1984).

[12]Ibid., 90.

[13]Ibid.

[14]Ibid., 86.

[15]Platforms of Beauford Jester, 1946 and 1948; Allan Shivers, 1950, 1952, and 1954; Price Daniel, 1956, 1958, and 1960. See James R. Soukup, Clifton McCleskey, and Harry Holloway, *Party and Factional Division in Texas* (Austin: University of Texas Press, 1964).

[16]Roy Morris, *Sheridan: The Life and Wars of General Phil Sheridan* (New York: Crown, 1992).

[17]T. R. Fehrenbach, *Lone Star: A History of Texas and the Texans* (New York: Collier, 1980), 276–77.

[18]Texas Department of Agriculture website; see at http://www.agr.state.tx.us/gt/channel/render/items/0,1218,1670_1693_0_0,00.html.

[19]Mine K. Yücel and Jackson Thies, "Oil and Gas Rises Again in a Diversified Texas," *Southwest Economy*, Federal Reserve Bank of Dallas, First Quarter 2011; see at https://www.dallasfed.org/research/swe/2011/swe1101g.pdf.

[20]D'Ann Petersen, "Texas Transitions to Service Economy," *Southwest Economy*, Issue 3, May/June 2007; Federal Reserve Bank of Dallas; see at www.dallasfed.org/research/swe/2007/swe0703b.cfm.

[21]California: Exports, Jobs, and Foreign Investment March 2010, Export.gov; see at www.trade.gov/td/industry/otea/state_reports/california.html.

[22]"Texas: Crossroads to the World," Texas Ahead, 2010, Issue 3; see at www.texasahead.org/economic_developer/downloads/1313-3TexasAhead_Global.pdf.

[23]Vivek Wadhwa, Ben Rissing, Aneesh Chopra, Ramakrishnan Balasubramanian, and Alyse Freilich, "U.S.-Based Global Intellectual Property Creation," Kauffman Foundation; www.kauffman.org/pdf/WIPO_103107.pdf.

[24]Mine K. Yücel and Jackson Thies, "Oil and Gas Rises Again in a Diversified Texas," *Southwest Economy*, Federal Reserve Bank of Dallas, First Quarter 2011; see at https://www.dallasfed.org/research/swe/2011/swe1101g.

[25]Keith R. Phillips and Emily Kerr, "Texas Economy to Ride Higher in the Saddle in 2011," *Southwest Economy*, Federal Reserve Bank, First Quarter 2011; see at https://www.dallasfed.org/research/swe/2011/swe1101b.pdf.

[26]Julia Preston, "Texas Hospitals Reflect Debate on Immigration," *New York Times*, July 18, 2006; see at www.nytimes.com/2006/07/18/us/18immig.

Chapter 19

[1]Council of State Governments, Book of the States 2011; see at http://knowledgecenter.csg.org/drupal/system/files/1.1_2011.pdf.

[2]Voter turnout data can be accessed at the website of the Texas Secretary of State; http://www.sos.state.tx.us/elections/historical/70-92.shtml.

[3]Vermont Office of the Secretary of State makes voter turnout data available at http://vermont-elections.org/elections1/2010OfficialGEVoterRegandTurnout11.09.pdf.

[4]T. R. Fehrenbach, *Lone Star*, 146–47 (see chap. 19, n. 17).

[5]Ibid., 206.

[6]Ibid., 222–23.

[7]Ibid., 411–14.

[8]Ibid., 436.

[9]Ibid.

[10]Andy Uhler, "Prop 4 Would Let Counties Issue Bonds for Projects," The Texas Tribune, October 27, 2011; see at http://www.texastribune.org/texas-newspaper/texas-news/prop-4-would-let-counties-issue-bonds-for-projects/.

[11]Website of the Texas Office of the Secretary of State, Elections Division; see at http://www.sos.state.tx.us/elections/index.shtml.

[12]Donald S. Lutz, "Toward a Theory of Constitutional Amendment," American Political Science Review 88 (June 1994): 355–70.

[13]Texas Constitution, Art. I, Sec. 3a.

[14]The Book of the States 2003, vol. 35 (Lexington, Ky.: Council of State Governments, 2003), 10, table 1.1.

[15]Lutz, "Toward a Theory of Constitutional Amendment."

[16]Texas Constitution, Art. XVII, Sec. 2.

[17]Lutz, "Toward a Theory of Constitutional Amendment," 359.

[18]Ibid., 360.

[19]Ibid.

[20]Anna Waugh, "Proposition 9 grants pardon to those with deferred adjudication," Your Houston News, October 23, 2011; see at http://www.yourhoustonnews.com/courier/news/proposition-grants-pardon-to-those-with-deferred-adjudication/article_a11d1688-225e-5f59-8ef9-a967b6d023ab.html.

[21]Proposition 2 FAQs, Texas Water Development Board website; http://www.twdb.state.tx.us/newsmedia/constitutional/faqs.asp.

[22]Dave Montgomery, "Texas' Gay Marriage Ban May Have Banned All Marriages," Fort Worth Star-Telegram, November 18, 2009; see at www.mcclatchydc.com/2009/11/18/79112/texas-gay-marriage-ban-may-have.html.

[23]The Book of the States 2005, vol. 37, 10, table 1.1.

Chapter 20

[1]Texans for Public Justice, "Loan-Shark-Financed Campaigns Threaten Payday-Loan Reform" (March 2011); see at http://info.tpj.org/reports/pdf/PaydayReport.mar2011.pdf.

[2]Melissa del Bosque, "The Perils of Payday," Texas Observer, April 30, 2009.

[3]Texans for Public Justice, 4.

[4]Clive S. Thomas, Ronald J. Hrebenar and Anthony J. Nownes, "Interest Group Politics in the States: Four Decades of Developments—The 1960s to the Present," in The Book of States (Lexington, KY: Council of State Governments), 330.

[5]National Conference of State Legislatures; see at http://www.ncsl.org/Portals/1/documents/legismgt/Limits_to_Candidates_2011-2012.pdf.

[6]Thomas et al., 330.

[7]Thanh Tan, "Texas Senate OKs Bills Regulating Payday Lenders," The Texas Tribune, (May 23, 2011); see at http://www.texastribune.org/texas-legislature/82nd-legislative-session/texas-senate-oks-bills-regulating-payday-lenders.

[8]Texans for Public Justice,. 4.

[9]Calvert and DeLeon, The History of Texas, 212 (see chap. 19, n. 3).

[10]Ibid., 387.

[11]U.S. v. Texas, 384 U.S. 155 (1966).

[12]Texas Almanac and State Industrial Guide, 1970–1971 (Dallas: A. H. Belo, 1969), 529.

[13]Texas Almanac and State Industrial Guide, 1974–1975 (Dallas: A. H. Belo, 1973), 529 (see chap. 20, n. 10).

[14]The Book of the States, vol. 30, 23, table 5.6 (see chap. 20, n. 10).

[15]Nixon v. Herndon et al., 273 U.S. 536 (1927); Nixon v. Condon et al., 286 U.S. 73 (1932).

[16]Grovey v. Townsend, 295 U.S. 45 (1935).

[17]Smith v. Allwright, 321 U.S. 649 (1944). Also, in U.S. v. Classic, 313 U.S. 299 (1941), the U.S. Supreme Court ruled that a primary in a one-party state (Louisiana) was an election within the meaning of the U.S. Constitution.

[18]George McKenna, The Drama of Democracy: American Government and Politics, 2nd ed. (Guilford, CT: Dushkin, 1994), 129.

[19]Wilbourn E. Benton, Texas Politics: Constraints and Opportunities, 5th ed. (Chicago: Nelson-Hall, 1984), 65.

[20]C. Richard Hoffstedder, "Inter-Party Competition and Electoral Turnout: The Case of Indiana," American Journal of Political Science 17 (May 1973): 351–66.

[21]Norman R. Luttbeg, "Differential Voting Turnout Decline in the American States," Social Science Quarterly 65 (March 1984): 60–73.

[22]Ibid.

[23]Dara Kam, "Gov. Scott signs contentious election law that limits early voting days, voter registration groups," Palm Beach Post, May 19, 2011; see at http://www.palmbeachpost.com/news/state/gov-scott-signs-contentious-election-law-that-limits-1486093.html?printArticle=y.

[24]Early Voting in Texas, Report #5, Austin Community College, Center for Public Policy and Political Studies; see at http://www.austincc.edu/cppps/earlyvotingfull/report=.pdf.

[25]Mike McIntire and Michael Luo, " A Usually Legal Practice That Wears Black Eyes," The New York Times, May 13, 2008; see at www.nytimes.com/2008/05/13/us/politics/13streetcash.html?_r=2&adxnnl=1&oref=slogin&adxnnlx=1216307215-uoiW43ldORQ/TWOhgysBHg.

[26]Ewen MacAskill, "The High Price of 'Street Money' in Philadelphia Campaigns," The Guardian, April 21, 2008; see at www.guardian.co.uk/world/2008/apr/21/uselections2008.barackobama.

[27]Wayne Slater, "Texas AG Fails to Unravel Large-Scale Voter-Fraud Schemes in His Two-Year Campaign," Dallas Morning News, May 18, 2008; see at www.txcn.com/sharedcontent/dws/news/localnews/tv/stories/DN-votefraud_18tex.ART.State.Edition2.46e18c2.html.

[28]"Texas State Union," Unions.org; see at www.unions.org/home/umap43-.htm.

[29]Robert Lineberry, Equity and Urban Policy: The Distribution of Urban Services (Newbury Park, CA: Sage, 1977).

[30]David Knowles, "Texas Yanks Thomas Jefferson from Teaching Standard," AOL News, March 12, 2010; see at www.aolnews.com/nation/article/texas-removes-thomas-jefferson-from-teaching-standard/19397481.

[31]Keith E. Hamm and Charles W. Wiggins, "The Transformation from Personnel to Information Lobbying," in Interest Group Politics in the Southern States, ed. Ronald J. Hrebenar and Clive S. Thomas (Tuscaloosa: University of Alabama Press, 1992), 152.

[32]Ibid., 157.

[33]The Texas Research League recently changed its name to the Texas Taxpayers and Research Association. It is headquartered in Austin.

[34]Ibid.

[35]Thomas R. Dye, Politics in States and Communities, 7th ed. (Englewood Cliffs, NJ: Prentice Hall, 1991), 112–13.

[36]David F. Prindel, Petroleum Politics and the Texas Railroad Commission (Austin: University of Texas Press, 1981).

Chapter 21

[1] Data for Figure 21.1, for 1952–1985, from James A. Dyer, Arnold Vedlitz, and David B. Hill, "New Voters, Switchers, and Political Party Realignment in Texas," *Western Political Quarterly* 41 (March 1988): 156; for 1994, from "The Texas Poll," 1994, Harte-Hanks Communications; for 1996, 1998, 2002, and 2005, from Texas Poll data, Scripps Howard, University of Texas at Austin.

[2] V. O. Key Jr., *Southern Politics in State and Nation* (New York: Knopf, 1949), 7.

[3] Calvert and DeLeon, *History of Texas,* 201–7 (see chap. 19, n. 3).

[4] James R. Soukup, Clifton McCleskey, and Harry Holloway, *Party and Factional Division in Texas* (Austin: University of Texas Press, 1964), 8.

[5] Ibid., 11.

[6] Douglas O. Weeks, *Texas Presidential Politics in 1952* (Austin: University of Texas, Institute of Public Affairs, 1953), 3–4.

[7] The budget actually increased during this period.

[8] David A. Stockman, *The Triumph of Politics: How the Reagan Revolution Failed* (New York: Harper & Row, 1986).

[9] Dyer, Vedlitz, and Hill, "New Voters, Switchers, and Political Party Realignment in Texas," 164.

[10] John Williams, "Yellow Dogs Lose Bite in East Texas, *Houston Chronicle* (November 18, 2002): 17A, 24A.

[11] Allan Turner, "Snapping Back: GOP Nipping on Heels of Yellow Dog Democrats," *Houston Chronicle,* March 5, 1995, p. 1D.

[12] Ibid.

[13] James A. Dyer, Jan E. Leighley, and Arnold Vedlitz, "Party Identification and Public Opinion: Establishing a Competitive Two Party System," in *Texas Reader,* ed. Tony Champagne and Ted Harpham (New York: Norton, 1997), 113–28.

[14] Walter D. Burnham, *The Current Crisis in American Politics* (Oxford: Oxford University Press, 1982).

[15] Texas Secretary of State, www.sos.state.tx.us.

[16] James A. Anderson, Richard W. Murray, and Edward L. Farley, *Texas Politics: An Introduction,* 6th ed. (New York: HarperCollins, 1992), 34.

[17] The Raza Unida party did not receive enough votes to qualify as a minor party but challenged this in court. The federal court sustained the challenge, and they were allowed to operate as a minor party.

[18] The Libertarian Party of Texas, www.tx.lp.org.

[19] Wayne Slater and Gromer Jeffers Jr., "Many Obama Voters Ignored Other Texas Primary Races," *Dallas Morning News,* March 9, 2008; see at www.dallasnews.com/sharedcontent/dws/dn/latestnews/stories/030908dnpoldemvoters.3a5249f.html.

[20] Associated Press, "Clinton Campaign Wants Texas to Postpone Party Conventions," *Dallas Morning News,* March 16, 2008; see at www.dallasnews.com/shared content/dws/dn/latestnews/stories/031708dnpoltxconventions.c4169f.html.

[21] Interview with Neeley Lewis, Democratic Party chair for Brazos County, Texas, May 30, 1996.

[22] Benton, *Texas Politics,* 80–81 (see chap. 21, n. 11).

[23] Ann O. Bowman and Richard C. Kearney, *State and Local Government* (Boston: Houghton Mifflin, 1990), 158–59. Also see Charles S. Bullock III and Loch K. Johnson, *Runoff Elections in the United States* (Chapel Hill: University of North Carolina Press, 1992).

[24] Jaime Powell, "High Duval Turnout Attracts State's Notice," *Caller-Times,* March 16, 2006; see at www.caller.com/ccct/local_news/article/0,1641,CCCT_811_4546107,00.html.

[25] Norman D. Brown, *Hood, Bonnet and Little Brown Jug: Texas Politics, 1921–1928* (College Station: Texas A&M University Press, 1984).

[26] Bowman and Kearney, *State and Local Government,* 166. The "feel good" and "sainthood" classifications were adopted from this source.

[27] Texans for Public Justice, "Tony Sanchez's War Chest: Who Gives to a $600 Million Man?"; see at www.tpj.org/docs/2002/10/reports/sanchez/page3.html.

[28] Texans for Public Justice, "Governor Perry's War Chest: Who Said Yes to Governor No?"; see at www.tpj.org/docs/2002/10/reports/perry/page3.html.

[29] Lobby Watch, "Texas Loan Stars Incurred $48 Million in Political Debts,"; see at www.tpj.org/lobby_Watch/latetrain.html.

Chapter 22

[1] Samuel C. Patterson, "Legislators and Legislatures in the American States," in *Politics in the American States* (6th ed.), ed. Virginia Gray and Herbert Jacob (Washington, DC: CQ Press, 1996), 164.

[2] Texas Constitution, Art. III, Sec. 26.

[3] Leroy Hardy, Alan Heslop, and Stuart Anderson, *Reapportionment Politics* (Beverly Hills, CA: Sage, 1981), 18.

[4] Gordon E. Baker, *The Reapportionment Revolution: Representation, Political Power and the Supreme Court* (New York: Random House, 1966).

[5] Texas Constitution, Art. III, Sec. 28.

[6] *Bush, Governor of Texas et al. v. Vera et al.,* No. 94-805. Case decided on June 13, 1996.

[7] *Hunt v. Cromartie,* No. 562, U.S. 541 (2001).

[8] Thomas R. Dye, *Politics in States and Communities,* 7th ed. (Englewood Cliffs, NJ: Prentice Hall, 1991), 157 (see chap. 21, n. 23).

[9] Harvey Tucker and Gary Halter, *Texas Legislative Almanac 2001* (College Station: Texas A&M University Press, 2001).

[10] Gary C. Jacobson, *The Politics of Congressional Elections,* 3rd ed. (New York: HarperCollins, 1992).

[11] Kevin A. Hill, "Does the Creation of Majority Black Districts Aid Republicans? An Analysis of the 1992 Congressional Election in Eight Southern States," *Journal of Politics* 57 (May 1995): 348–401.

[12] Samuel C. Patterson, "Legislative Politics in the States," in *Politics in the American States,* 6th ed., 179–86.

[13] Lawrence W. Miller, "Legislative Turnover and Political Careers: A Study of Texas Legislators, 1969–75," PhD dissertation, Texas Tech University, 1977, 43–45.

[14] *The Book of the States 1994–1995,* 29, table A (see chap. 20, n. 10). Also see the National Conference of State Legislatures, www.ncsl.org.

[15] *Presiding Officers of the Texas Legislature, 1846–2002* (Austin: Texas Legislative Council, 2002).

[16] Interview with William P. Hobby, 1993, Texas A&M University, College Station.

[17] *The Book of the States 1998–1999,* 48, table 2.13.

[18] J. William Davis, *There Shall Also Be a Lieutenant Governor* (Austin: University of Texas, Institute of Public Affairs, 1967).

[19] Harvey Tucker, "Legislative Calendars and Workload Management in Texas," *Journal of Politics* 51 (August 1989): 632.

[20] Ibid., 633.

[21] Ibid., 643.

[22] Harvey J. Tucker, "Legislative Workload Congestion in Texas," *Journal of Politics* 49 (1987): 557.

[23] Ibid., 569.

[24] E. Lee Bernick and Charles W. Wiggins, "Legislative Norms in Eleven States,"

Legislative Studies Quarterly 7 (May 1983): 194–95.

[25]Ibid.

[26]National Conference of State Legislatures, *State Legislature* 20 (November 1994): 5.

[27]Ronald K. Snell, "State Experiences with Annual and Biennial Budgeting," National Conference of State Legislatures, April 2011; see at http://www.ncsl.org/documents/fiscal/BiennialBudgeting_May2011.pdf.

[28]Rich Jones, "State Legislatures," in *The Book of the States 1994–1995*, 99.

[29]*The Book of the States 1998–1999*, 64–67, table 7.2.

[30]Dye, *Politics in States and Communities*, 192.

Chapter 23

[1]Thad L. Beyle, "Governors: The Middlemen and Women in Our Political System," in *Politics in the American States*, 6th ed., 197 (see chap. 23, n. 1).

[2]Ibid.

[3]*The Book of the States 2005*, 218, table 4.3 (see chap. 20, n. 10).

[4]*The Book of the States 1994–1995*, 66.

[5]Ibid.

[6]Ann O. Bowman and Richard C. Kearney, *State and Local Government* (Boston: Houghton Mifflin, 1990), 206 (see chap. 22, n. 23).

[7]Wilbourn E. Benton, *Texas: Its Government and Politics*, 2nd ed. (Englewood Cliffs, NJ: Prentice Hall, 1966), 222–24.

[8]Victor E. Harlow, *Harlow's History of Oklahoma*, 5th ed. (Norman, OK: Author, 1967), 294–315.

[9]Daniel R. Grant and Lloyd B. Omdahl, *State and Local Government in America* (Madison, WI: Brown & Benchmark, 1987), 260.

[10]S. M. Morehouse, *State Politics, Parties and Policy* (New York: Holt, Rinehart & Winston, 1981), 206.

[11]Beyle, "Governors," 230.

[12]Ibid., 231.

[13]Gromer Jeffers Jr., "Hutchison Proposes Term Limit for Governor, Other Changes," *Dallas Morning News*, January 19, 2010; see at www.dallasnews.com/sharedcontent/dws/news/localnews/stories/DN-hutchison_20pol.ART.State.Edition1.4ba632f.html; Jason Embry and Corrie MacLaggan, "Newspapers' Poll: Perry Has Comfortable Lead as Voting Starts," *The Statesman*, February 13, 2010; see at www.statesman.com/news/texas-politics/newspapers-poll-perry-has-comfortable-lead-as-voting-237070.html.

[14]Beyle, "Governors," 221.

[15]Until 1996, the voters also elected a state treasurer. In 1996, the voters approved a constitutional amendment abolishing that office. These functions have been transferred to other state agencies.

[16]*Guide to Texas State Agencies* (Austin: University of Texas, Lyndon B. Johnson School of Public Affairs, 1994).

[17]Ibid.

[18]Beyle, "Governors," 231.

[19]*The Book of the States 1998–1999*, 22, table 2.4.

[20]Beyle, "Governors," 234–35.

[21]*The Book of the States 1998–1999*, 20, table 2.3.

[22]James A. Anderson, Richard W. Murray, and Edward L. Farley, *Texas Politics: An Introduction*, 6th ed. (New York: HarperCollins, 1992), 122 (see chap. 22, n. 16).

[23]Deborah K. Wheeler, "Two Men, Two Governors, Two Pardons: A Study of Pardon Policy of Governor Miriam Ferguson." Unpublished copyrighted paper, presented at State Historical Society Meeting, March 1998, Austin.

[24]Bill Hobby, "Speaking of Pardons, Texas Has Had Its Share," *Houston Chronicle* (February 18, 2001): 4C.

[25]*The Book of the States 1996–1997*, 33–34.

[26]Legislative Budget Board, "Fiscal Size-up 2002–2003," 242.

[27]Texas Sunset Advisory Commission, Guide to the Texas Sunset Process (Austin, 1997), 1.

[28]Ibid.

Chapter 24

[1]Herbert Jacob, "Courts: The Least Visible Branch," in *Politics in the American States*, ed. Virginia Gray and Herbert Jacob, 6th ed. (Washington, DC: CQ Press, 1996), 253.

[2]Ibid., 256–58.

[3]Office of Court Administration, Texas Judicial Council, Texas Judicial System Annual Report (Austin: Author, 1994), 31–33.

[4]*The Book of the States 1998–1999*, 131–32, table 4.2 (see chap. 20, n. 10).

[5]Delaware, Maine, Massachusetts, New Hampshire, New Jersey, New York, and Vermont have some judges who are appointed by the governor and can be removed only for cause. Connecticut, Rhode Island, South Carolina, and Virginia have legislative elections. In the other three legislatures using elections, judges serve for life with good behavior. See Jacob, "Courts," 268,

table 7.2. Also see *The Book of the States 1994–1995*, 190–93, table 4.4. There are some slight variations between the Jacob table and the table in *The Book of the States*. This is probably due to interpretations by the writers. Owing to minor variations among states, classification differences are possible.

[6]Richard H. Kraemer and Charldean Newell, *Essentials of Texas Politics* (St. Paul, MN: West, 1980), 281.

[7]James A. Anderson, Richard W. Murray, and Edward L. Farley, *Texas Politics: An Introduction*, 6th ed. (New York: HarperCollins, 1992), 246–47 (see chap. 22, n. 16).

[8]"A Closer Look at Harris County's Vote," *Houston Chronicle*, November 14, 2002, p. 32A.

[9]Anthony Champagne, "Campaign Contributions in Texas Supreme Court Races," *Crime, Law and Social Change* 17 (1992): 91–106.

[10]Gibson and Robison, *Government and Politics in the Lone Star State*, 6th ed. (New York: Prentice Hall, 2008), 281.

[11]Herbert Jacob, "The Effect of Institutional Differences in the Recruitment Process: The Case of State Judges," *Journal of Public Law* 33, no. 113 (1964): 104–19.

[12]Bradley Canon, "The Impact of Formal Selection Processes on Characteristics of Judges—Reconsidered," *Law and Society Review* 13 (May 1972): 570–93.

[13]Richard Watson and Rondal G. Downing, *The Politics of the Bench and Bar: Judicial Selection Under the Missouri Nonpartisan Court Plan* (New York: John Wiley, 1969).

[14]Thomas R. Dye, *Politics in States and Communities*, 7th ed. (Englewood Cliffs, NJ: Prentice Hall, 1991), 236.

[15]William K. Hall and Larry T. Aspin, "What Twenty Years of Judicial Retention and Elections Have Told Us," *Judicature* 70 (1987): 340–47.

[16]Craig F. Emmert and Henry R. Glick, "The Selection of Supreme Court Judges," *American Politics Quarterly* 19 (October 1988): 444–65.

[17]*The Book of the States 1998–1999*, 138–48, table 4.5.

[18]Commission on Judicial Conduct, Annual Report (Austin: Author, 1994).

[19]Office of Court Administration, Texas Judicial Council, Texas Judicial System Annual Report (1994), 173, 179.

[20]Interview with District Court Judge John Delaney, Brazos County courthouse, November 1995.

[21]Texas Code of Criminal Procedure, arts. 19.01–20.22.

[22]"Murder Case Testing Grand Jury Selection," *Houston Chronicle*, March 2, 2002, p. 1A, 16A.

23There were 880,759 Anglos as opposed to 301,981 African Americans according to the Texas Crime Report for 2008, Texas Department of Public Safety; see at www.txdps.state.tx.us/administration/crime_records/pages/crimestatistics.htm#2006.

24Texas Criminal Justice Policy Council, Biennial Report to the Governor and the 78th Texas Legislature, January 2001.

25Texas Criminal Justice Policy Council, *Testing the Case for More Incarceration in Texas: The Record So Far* (Austin: State of Texas, 1995), 43.

26"Death in Decline '09: Los Angeles Holds California Back as Nation Shifts to Permanent Imprisonment," ACLU of Northern California, http://aclunc.org/docs/criminal_justice/death_penalty/death_in_decline_09.pdf.

27See, for example, Sami Hartsfield, "Harris County District Judge Kevin Fine: Ruled Death Penalty Unconstitutional—Is It? Take the Poll!" *Houston Legal Issues Examiner*, March 7, 2010; see at www.examiner.com/x-12971-Houston-Legal-Issues-Examiner~y2010m3d7-Harris-County-District -Judge-Kevin-Fine-Ruled-death-penalty-unconstitutional-is-it-Take-the-poll, and Brian Rogers, "Judge Declares Death Penalty Unconstitutional," *Houston Chronicle*, March 5, 2010; see at www.chron.com/disp/story.mpl/metropolitan/6897252.html.

28Annual Statistical Reports 2007, OCA & Texas Judicial Council, Texas Courts Online; see at www.courts.state.tx.us/pubs/AR2007/toc.htm.

29"Prop. 12 Proponents Gave $5.3 Million to Perry, Dewhurst and Lawmakers in 2002," Texans for Public Justice, August 29, 2003; see at www.tpj.org/press_releases/prop12 _interests.html.

30American Tort Reform Association; see at www.atra.org/wrap/files.cgi/7964_howworks.html.

31Ralph Blumenthal, "More Doctors in Texas After Malpractice Caps," *New York Times*, October 5, 2007; see at www.nytimes.com/2007/10/05/us/0=doctors.html?pagewanted=1&ref=health.

Chapter 25

1*Statistical Abstract of the United States,* 2003, table 421.

2Institute on Taxation and Economic Policy, "Texas Taxes Hit Poor & Middle Class Far Harder Than the Wealthy," January 7, 2003; see at www.itepnet.org/wp2000/tx%20pr.pdf.

3Ibid.

4Texas Coordinating Board, www.thecb.state.tx.us/.

5Permanent University Fund, "Overview," 2007; see at www.utimco.org/funds/allfunds/2007annual/puf_overview.asp.

6Some at TAMU have suggested this is the source of the hook'm horns and the gigum Aggies hand gestures.

7Texas Constitution, Art. VII, Sec. 18.

8Texas Coordinating Board, www.thecb.state.tx.

9*Hopwood v. Texas,* 78 F.3d 932 (5th Cir. 1996), cert. denied, *Texas v. Hopwood,* No. 95-1773 (July 1, 1996).

10*Houston Chronicle,* "81% of U.T.'s Admissions Offers Go to Top 10% Graduates," March 20, 2008, p. 1.

11"Just Say Don't Know: Sexuality Education in Texas Public Schools," The Texas Freedom Network; see at www.tfn.org/site/DocServer/SexEdRort09_web.pdf?docID 5981.

12Pamela K. Kohler R.N., M.P.H., Lisa E. Manhart Ph.D., William E. Lafferty M.D., "Abstinence-Only and Comprehensive Sex Education and the Initiation of Sexual Activity and Teen Pregnancy," *Journal of Adolescent Health*, 42, no. 4 (April 2008): 344–51.

13John Santelli M.D., M.P.H., Mary A. Ott M.D., Maureen Lyon Ph.D., Jennifer Rogers M.P.H., Daniel Summers M.D., Rebecca Schleifer J.D., M.P.H., "Abstinence and abstinence-only education: A review of U.S. policies and programs," *Journal of Adolescent Health,* 38, no. 1 (January 2006): 72–81.

14"U.S. Teenage Pregnancies, Births and Abortions: National and State Trends and Trends by Race and Ethnicity," Guttmacher Institute, January 2010; see at www.guttmacher.org/pubs/USTPtrends.pdf; State Profiles—Texas," the National Campaign to Prevent Teen and Unplanned Pregnancy; see at www.thenationalcampaign.org/state-data/state-profile.aspx?state=texas; Robert T. Garrett, "Texas Has Restrictive Birth Control Policy for Minors," *Dallas Morning News*; see at www.dallasnews.com/sharedcontent/dws/dn/latestnews/stories/090709dntexteenbirths.3eaae55.html.

15"One in Four Girls: Shocking Study on Sexually Transmitted Infections Must Be a Wake-Up Call for Teen Health," *Houston Chronicle*, March 15, 2008, p. B8.

16CNN, "Supreme Court Strikes Down Texas Sodomy Law," November 18, 2003; see at www.cnn.com/2003/LAW/06/26/scotus.sodomy/.

17Robert T. Garrett and Wayne Slater, "Gay Marriage Foes Tackle Divorce Next," *Dallas Morning News*, November 10, 2005; see at www.dallasnews.com/sharedcontent/dws/news/texassouthwest/stories/111005dntexprop2.7a85398.html.

18American Association of University Women, "Public Perceptions of the Pay Gap, 2005;" see at www.aauw.org/research/statedata/upload/table_data.pdf.

19Environmental Science and Technology Online, "One in Five U.S. Women Has High Mercury Levels," March 8, 2006; see at http://pubs.acs.org/subscribe/journals/esthag-w/2006/mar/science/pp_mercury.html.

20Ramon Alvarez, Mary Sanger, Colin Rowan, and Lisa Moore, "Fair Warning: Global Warming and the Lone Star State," Environment Defense Fund, May 2006; see at www.edf.org/documents/5254_Fair Warning.pdf.

21Texas Municipal Water Conservation, Issue Paper 1, 2009, Texas Water Matters; see at www.texaswatermatters.org/pdfs/issue _no1_conservation.pdf, and Forrest Wilder, "Water Conservation in Texas: Good, Bad And Ugly," *The Texas Observer*, March 10, 2010; see at www.texasobserver.org/forrestforthetrees/water-conservation-in-texas-good-bad-and-ugly.

22Michael Milstein, "Beyond Wind Plan, Pickens Eyes Pipelines in Drought-Ridden U.S.," *Popular Mechanics,* October 1, 2009; see at www.popularmechanics.com/science/environment/4275059.

23Clifford Bryan, "Texas is Undisputed Wind Power Leader—It's Not All About Oil Anymore," *Energy Policy Examiner,*April 17, 2010; see at http://www.examiner.com/article/texas-is-undisputed-wind-power-leader-it-s-not-all-about-oil-anymore

24Virginia Gray, "The Socioeconomic and Political Context of States," in *Politics in the American States.*

Chapter 26

1Federal Advisory Commission on Intergovernmental Relations, *State and Local Roles in the Federal System: A–88* (Washington, D.C.: U.S. Government Printing Office, 1982), 59.

2Ibid.

3Terrell Blodgett, *Texas Home-rule Charters* (Austin: Texas Municipal League, 1994).

⁴There are three types (A, B, and C) of cities provided for in Texas state law. However, there are seven variations on the number of council members and their methods of election. See *Vernon's Texas Statutes and Codes Annotated,* vol. 1, 5.001–5.003.

⁵Texas Municipal League, *Handbook for Mayors and Councilmembers in General-law Cities* (Austin: Texas Municipal League, 1994).

⁶*Vernon's Texas Statutes and Codes Annotated,* "Local Government," vol. 1, 9.001–9.008.

⁷Ibid., 7.005.

⁸David L. Martin, *Running City Hall: Municipal Administration in the United States* (Tuscaloosa: University of Alabama Press, 1990), 21–22.

⁹*Vernon's Texas Statutes and Codes Annotated,* "Local Government," vol. 1, 42.021.

¹⁰James A. Svara, *Official Leadership in the City: Patterns of Conflict and Cooperation* (New York: Oxford University Press, 1990), chaps. 2 and 3.

¹¹Blodgett, *Texas Home-rule Charters,* 30–31.

¹²Bradley Robert Rice, *Progressive Cities: The Commission Government Movement in America, 1901–1920* (Austin: University of Texas Press, 1977), 85.

¹³Blodgett, *Texas Home-rule Charters,* 39.

¹⁴Svara, *Official Leadership in the City.*

¹⁵Richard Stillman, *The Rise of the City Manager: A Public Professional in Local Government* (Albuquerque: University of New Mexico Press, 1974), 15.

¹⁶Blodgett, *Texas Home-rule Charters,* 46–47.

¹⁷Svara, *Official Leadership in the City,* 136. Also see Lyndon B. Johnson School of

Public Affairs, *Local Government Election Systems,* Policy Research Report No. 62 (Austin: University of Texas Press, 1984), 46–55, 145–46.

¹⁸International City Management Association, *Municipal Year Book* (Washington, D.C.: Author, 1988), 17.

¹⁹*Vernon's Texas Statutes and Codes Annotated,* "Elections," 41.003.

²⁰For a discussion of San Antonio, see David R. Johnson, John A. Booth, and Richard J. Harris, *The Politics of San Antonio: Community Progress and Power* (Lincoln: University of Nebraska Press, 1983). Also see Richard A. Smith, "How Business Failed Dallas," in *Governing Texas: Documents and Readings,* 2nd ed., ed. Fred Gantt Jr. et al. (New York: Thomas Y. Crowell, 1970), 122–29.

²¹U.S. Department of Commerce, Bureau of the Census, 1997 *Census of Governments: Government Organization,* vol. 1, no. 1 (Washington, DC: U.S. Government Printing Office, 1997), 18, table 13.

²²U.S. Census of Population 2000, www. census.gov.

²³Gary M. Halter and Gerald L. Dauthery, "The County Commissioners Court in Texas," in *Governing Texas,* 3rd ed., ed. Fred Gantt Jr. et al. (New York: Thomas Y. Crowell, 1974), 340–50.

²⁴Robert E. Norwood and Sabrina Strawn, *Texas County Government: Let the People Choose,* 2nd ed. (Austin: Texas Research League, 1984).

²⁵Ibid., 24. Also see John A. Gilmartin and Joe M. Rothe, *County Government in Texas: A Summary of the Major Offices and Officials,* Issue 2 (College

Station: Texas Agricultural Extension Service).

²⁶Norwood and Strawn, *Texas County Government,* 27.

²⁷For an extensive explanation of the county home-rule efforts in Texas, see Wilbourn E. Benton, *Texas: Its Government and Politics,* 2nd ed. (Englewood Cliffs, NJ: Prentice Hall, 1966), 317–81.

²⁸For a discussion of the benefits and problems of special districts, see Virginia Pernod, *Special District, Special Purposes: Fringe Governments and Urban Problems in the Houston Area* (College Station: Texas A&M University Press, 1984).

²⁹2002 *Census of Governments,* 2:17, table 3.

30. Texas Legislative Budget Board home page, www.lbb.state.tx.us.

³¹Nancy Frank, *Charter Schools: Experiments in Reform, an Update* (Austin: Texas Legislative Budget Board, Public Education Team, 1995).

³²2002 *Census of Governments,* 2:17, table 15.

³³Texas Legislative Budget Board home page, www.lbb.state.tx.us.

³⁴Secretary of State, State of Texas, *Votes on Proposed Amendments to the Texas Constitution, 1875–November 1993* (Austin: Author, 1994), 73.

³⁵*Dallas Morning News* (January 12, 1994): 1A.

³⁶Terrence Stutz, "Wimberley School District Challenging Texas' 'Robin Hood' Finance Law," *Dallas Morning News,* January 28, 2008; see at www. dallasnews.com/shared content/ dws/news/texassouthwest/stories/ 012808dntexwimberley.2c73fcc.html.

Credits

Index